D0038561

# PACIFIC NORTHWEST CAMPING

## TOM STIENSTRA

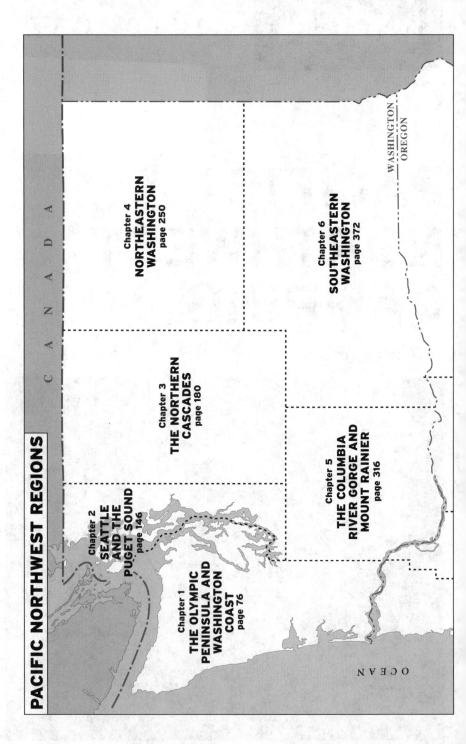

PACIFIC NORTHWEST REGIONS

CANADA

OCEAN

WASHINGTON
OREGON

Chapter 1
THE OLYMPIC
PENINSULA AND
WASHINGTON
COAST
page 76

Chapter 2
SEATTLE
AND THE
PUGET SOUND
page 146

Chapter 3
THE NORTHERN
CASCADES
page 180

Chapter 4
NORTHEASTERN
WASHINGTON
page 250

Chapter 5
THE COLUMBIA
RIVER GORGE AND
MOUNT RAINIER
page 316

Chapter 6
SOUTHEASTERN
WASHINGTON
page 372

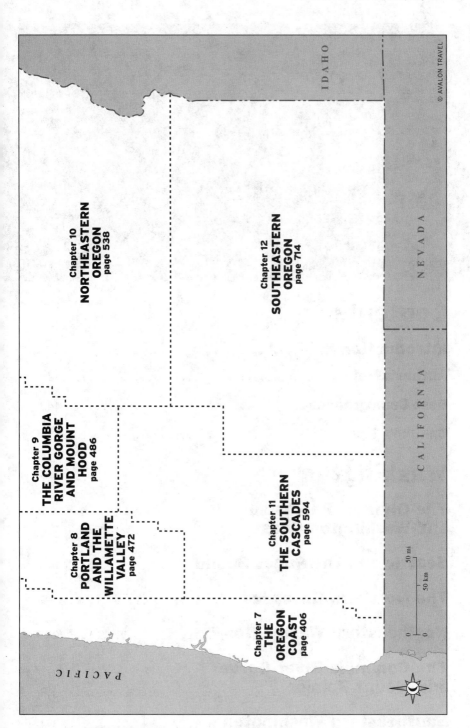

IDAHO

© AVALON TRAVEL

Chapter 10
**NORTHEASTERN OREGON**
page 538

Chapter 12
**SOUTHEASTERN OREGON**
page 714

NEVADA

Chapter 9
**THE COLUMBIA RIVER GORGE AND MOUNT HOOD**
page 486

CALIFORNIA

Chapter 8
**PORTLAND AND THE WILLAMETTE VALLEY**
page 472

Chapter 11
**THE SOUTHERN CASCADES**
page 594

Chapter 7
**THE OREGON COAST**
page 406

PACIFIC

50 mi

50 km

0

0

# Contents

# Oregon

# How to Use This Book
## ABOUT THE CAMPGROUND PROFILES

The campgrounds are listed in a consistent, easy-to-read format to help you choose the ideal camping spot. If you already know the name of the specific campground you want to visit, or the name of the surrounding geological area or nearby feature (town, national or state park, forest, mountain, lake, river, etc.), look it up in the index and turn to the corresponding page. Here is a sample profile:

Campground name and number →

Icons noting activities and facilities at or nearby the campground

**1** SOMEWHERE USA CAMPGROUND

🏃🚴🛶🎣🐕🧗♿🚐⛺

General location of the campground in relation to the nearest major town or landmark →

**Scenic rating: 10**

south of Somewhere USA Lake

Rating of scenic beauty on a scale of 1-10 with 10 the highest rating

Map the campground can be found on and page number the map can be found on

**Map 1.2, page 4**          **BEST (**

Symbol indicating that the campground is listed among the author's top picks

Each campground in this book begins with a brief overview of its setting. The description typically covers ambience, information about the attractions, and activities popular at the campground.

**Campsites, facilities:** This section notes the number of campsites for tents and RVs and indicates whether hookups are available. Facilities such as restrooms, picnic areas, recreation areas, laundry, and dump stations will be addressed, as well as the availability of piped water, showers, playgrounds, stores, and other amenities. The campground's pet policy and wheelchair accessibility is also mentioned here.

**Reservations, fees:** This section notes whether reservations are accepted, and provides rates for tent sites and RV sites. If there are additional fees for parking or pets, or discounted weekly or seasonal rates, they will also be noted here.

**Directions:** This section provides mile-by-mile driving directions to the campground from the nearest major town or highway.

**Contact:** This section provides an address, phone number, and website, if available, for the campground.

## ABOUT THE ICONS

The icons in this book are designed to provide at-a-glance information on activities, facilities, and services available on-site or within walking distance of each campground.

- 🏃 Hiking trails
- 🚴 Biking trails
- 🏊 Swimming
- 🎣 Fishing
- 🚤 Boating
- 🛶 Canoeing and/or kayaking
- ❄ Winter sports
- ♨ Hot springs

- 🐾 Pets permitted
- 🛝 Playground
- ♿ Wheelchair accessible
- 5️⃣ 5 Percent Club
- 🚐 RV sites
- ⛺ Tent sites

## ABOUT THE SCENIC RATING

Each campground profile employs a scenic rating on a scale of 1 to 10, with 1 being the least scenic and 10 being the most scenic. A scenic rating measures only the overall beauty of the campground and environs; it does not take into account noise level, facilities, maintenance, recreation options, or campground management. The setting of a campground with a lower scenic rating may simply not be as picturesque that of as a higher rated campground, however other factors that can influence a trip, such as noise or recreation access, can still affect or enhance your camping trip. Consider both the scenic rating and the profile description before deciding which campground is perfect for you.

## MAP SYMBOLS

| | | |
|---|---|---|
| ═══════ Expressway | 🛡80 Interstate Freeway | ✈ Airfield |
| ─────── Primary Road | 🛡101 U.S. Highway | ✈ Airport |
| ─────── Secondary Road | 21 State Highway | ○ City/Town |
| ▫▫▫▫▫▫ Unpaved Road | 66 County Highway | ▲ Mountain |
| ·············· Ferry | Lake | ⬧ Park |
| ▬▬ · ▬▬ · National Border | Dry Lake | Pass |
| ─── ·· ─── State Border | Seasonal Lake | ◉ State Capital |

## ABOUT THE MAPS

This book is divided into chapters based on major regions in the state; an overview map of these regions precedes the table of contents. Each chapter begins with a map of the region, which is further broken down into detail maps. Campgrounds are noted on the detail maps by number.

Reference to adjacent region

Detail map number and page number

Grid line divides region into detail maps

Region border

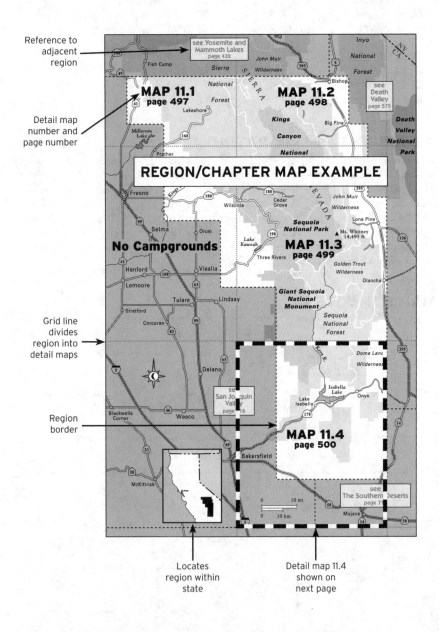

REGION/CHAPTER MAP EXAMPLE

No Campgrounds

Locates region within state

Detail map 11.4 shown on next page

Indicates adjacent detail maps within region

Locates detail map within region

Map number → **Map 11.4**

Sites shown on detail map and the page range where those sites are listed → **Sites 105-117**
**Pages 564-570**

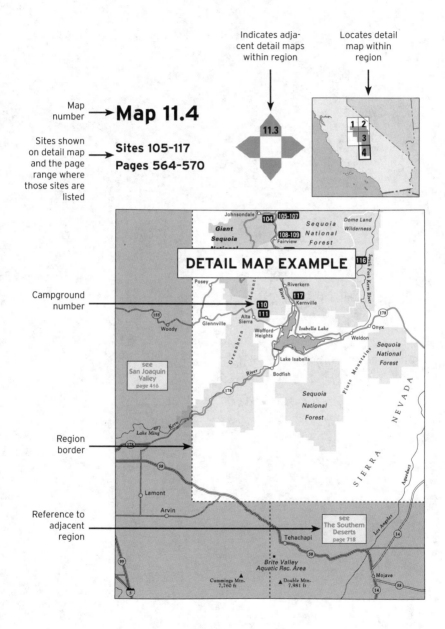

DETAIL MAP EXAMPLE

Campground number

Region border

Reference to adjacent region

# INTRODUCTION

# Author's Note

When my family and friends throughout the Pacific Northwest heard I was writing this book, they all instantly hated me! They figured their favorite spots would be revealed to all. But after reading the book, they don't hate me anymore (except for this one cousin). That is because they have discovered, as I have, that this region is filled with beautiful, little-used campgrounds that are perfect jump-off points for adventure—and there are hundreds of outstanding destinations, in addition to their sprinkling of personal favorites.

Looking for *mystery?* There are hundreds of hidden, rarely used campgrounds listed and mapped in this book that most people have never dreamed of. *Excitement?* At many of them, you'll find the sizzle with the steak: the hike to a great lookout or the big fish at the end of your line. *Fun?* The Camping Tips section of this book can help you take the futility out of your trips and put the fun back in. Add it up, put it in your cash register, and you can turn a camping trip into the satisfying adventure it's meant to be, whether it's just an overnight quickie or a month-long expedition.

Going on a camping trip can be like trying to put hiking boots on an octopus. You've tried it too, eh? Instead of a relaxing and fun trip full of adventure, it turns into a scenario called "You Against the World." You might as well try to fight a volcano. But it doesn't have to be that way, and that's what this book is all about. If you give it a chance, the information herein can remove the snarls, confusion, and occasional, volcanic temper explosions that keep people at home, locked away from the action.

It's estimated that 95 percent of American vacationers use only 5 percent of the country's available recreation areas. With this book, you can leave the herd, wander, and be free. You can join the inner circle, the Five Percenters who know the great hidden areas used by so few people. To join the Five Percent Club, take a hard look at the maps for the areas you wish to visit and the corresponding campground listings. As you study the camps, you'll start to feel a sense of excitement building, a feeling that you are about to unlock a door and venture into a world that is rarely viewed. When you feel that excitement, act on it. Parlay that energy into a great trip.

The campground maps and listings can serve in two ways: 1) If you're on the road late in the day and you're stuck for a spot for the night, you can likely find one nearby; or 2) if you are planning a trip, you can tailor a vacation to fit exactly into your plans rather than heading off and hoping—maybe praying—it turns out all right.

For the latter, you may wish to obtain additional maps, particularly if you are venturing into areas governed by the U.S. Forest Service or Bureau of Land Management. Both are federal agencies that offer low-cost maps detailing all hiking trails, lakes, streams, and backcountry camps reached via logging roads. The Resource Guide at the back of this book details how to obtain these and other maps.

Backcountry camps listed in this book are often in primitive and rugged settings but provide the sense of isolation that you may want from a trip. They also provide good jump-off points for backpacking trips, if that's your calling. These camps are often free, and I have listed hundreds of them.

At the other end of the spectrum are the developed parks for RVs. They offer a home away from home, with everything from full hookups to a grocery store and laundry room. Instead of isolation, an RV park provides a place to shower and get outfitted for food and clean clothes. For RV cruisers, it's a place to stay in high style while touring

## KEEP IT WILD

"Enjoy America's country and leave no trace." That's the motto of the Leave No Trace program, and I strongly support it. Promoting responsible outdoor recreation through education, research, and partnerships is its mission. Look for the Keep It Wild Tips, developed from the policies of Leave No Trace, throughout the Camping Tips portion of this book. This copyrighted information has been reprinted with permission from the Leave No Trace Center for Outdoor Ethics. For more information or materials, please visit www.LNT.org or call 303/442-8222 or 800/332-4100.

the area. RV parks range in price, depending on location, and an advance deposit may be necessary in summer.

Somewhere between the two extremes are hundreds and hundreds of campgrounds that provide a compromise: beautiful settings and some facilities, with a small overnight fee. Piped water, vault toilets, and picnic tables tend to come with the territory. Fees for these sites are usually in the $10-35 range, with the higher-priced sites located near population centers. Because they offer a bit of both worlds, they are in high demand. Reservations are usually advised, and at state parks, particularly during the summer season, you can expect company. This doesn't mean you need to forgo them in hopes of a less confined environment. For one thing, most state parks have set up quotas so that visitors don't feel as if they've been squeezed in with a shoehorn. For another, the same parks are often uncrowded during the off-season and on weekdays.

Before your trip, you'll want to get organized, and that's when you must start putting boots on that giant octopus. The trick to organization for any task is breaking it down to its key components and then solving each element independent of the others. Remember the octopus. Grab a moving leg, jam on a boot, and make sure it's on tight before reaching for another leg. Do one thing at a time, in order, and all will get done quickly and efficiently.

Now you can become completely organized for your trip in just one week, spending just a little time each evening on a given component. Getting organized is an unnatural act for many. By splitting up the tasks, you take the pressure out of planning and put the fun back in.

As you might figure, this is not a hobby for me, as it is for some part-time writers who publish books. This is my full-time job. Because I spend up to 200 days a year in the field, I understand how seriously people take their fun, what they need to know to make their trips work, as well as their underlying fears that they might get stuck for the night without a spot. I get tons of emails and letters, and I read each one carefully. These have been of great benefit. In the process, I have incorporated dozen of suggestions from readers to make this the book they want it to be. Your comments and questions are always welcome and appreciated. As a full-tome outdoors writer, the question I am asked more than any other is: "Where are you going this week?"

All of the answers are in this book.

# Best Campgrounds

Can't decide where to stay? Here are my picks for the best campgrounds in seven different categories.

## BEST◖ Most Scenic

**Fort Flagler State Park,** The Olympic Peninsula and Washington Coast, page 95.
**Kalaloch,** The Olympic Peninsula and Washington Coast, page 101.
**Pacific Beach State Park,** The Olympic Peninsula and Washington Coast,
    page 102.
**Fay Bainbridge Park,** The Olympic Peninsula and Washington Coast, page 121.
**Moran State Park Ferry-In,** Seattle and the Puget Sound, page 157.
**Turn Island State Park Boat-In,** Seattle and the Puget Sound, page 159.
**Camano Island State Park,** Seattle and the Puget Sound, page 169.
**Panorama Point,** The Northern Cascades, page 188.
**Harts Pass Walk-In,** The Northern Cascades, page 202.
**Kamloops Island,** Northeastern Washington, page 277.
**Honey Bear Campground & RV Resort,** The Oregon Coast, page 462.
**Long Bow Group,** Portland and the Willamette Valley, page 483.
**Piety Island Boat-In,** The Columbia River Gorge and Mount Hood, page 525.
**Cove Creek,** The Columbia River Gorge and Mount Hood, page 526.
**Paul Dennis,** The Columbia River Gorge and Mount Hood, page 529.
**Anthony Lakes,** Northeastern Oregon, page 575.
**Scott Lake Walk-In,** The Southern Cascades, page 620.
**North Waldo,** The Southern Cascades, page 634.
**Lava Lake,** The Southern Cascades, page 656.
**Squaw Lake Hike-In,** The Southern Cascades, page 708.

## BEST◖ Families

**Lena Lake Hike-In,** The Olympic Peninsula and Washington Coast, page 108.
**Kitsap Memorial State Park,** The Olympic Peninsula and Washington Coast,
    page 118.
**KOA Lynden/Bellingham,** Seattle and the Puget Sound, page 153.
**Bay View State Park,** Seattle and the Puget Sound, page 164.
**Leavenworth/Pine Village KOA,** The Northern Cascades, page 240.
**Ellensburg KOA,** The Northern Cascades, page 247.
**Curlew Lake State Park,** Northeastern Washington, page 273.
**Shore Acres Resort,** Northeastern Washington, page 299.
**Henley's Silver Lake Resort,** The Columbia River Gorge and Mount Rainier,
    page 323.
**Yakima Sportsman State Park,** Southeastern Washington, page 387.
**Fort Stevens State Park,** The Oregon Coast, page 412.
**Honey Bear Campground & RV Resort,** The Oregon Coast, page 462.
**Cascade Locks Marine Park,** The Columbia River Gorge and Mount Hood,
    page 500.
**Hoover Group Camp,** The Columbia River Gorge and Mount Hood, page 527.
**Twin Lakes Resort,** The Southern Cascades, page 662.

**Indian Mary Park,** The Southern Cascades, page 680.
**Abbott Creek,** The Southern Cascades, page 689.
**Lake of the Woods Resort,** The Southern Cascades, page 698.
**Drews Creek,** Southeastern Oregon, page 736.

## BEST( Fishing

**Coppermine Bottom,** The Olympic Peninsula and Washington Coast, page 101.
**West Beach Resort Ferry-In,** Seattle and the Puget Sound, page 156.
**Doe Island State Park Boat-In,** Seattle and the Puget Sound, page 158.
**Pearrygin Lake State Park,** The Northern Cascades, page 208.
**Chopaka Lake,** Northeastern Washington, page 257.
**Conconully State Park,** Northeastern Washington, page 265.
**Rock Lakes,** Northeastern Washington, page 267.
**Long Lake,** Northeastern Washington, page 279.
**Mallard Bay Resort,** Northeastern Washington, page 311.
**Offut Lake Resort,** The Columbia River Gorge and Mount Rainier, page 322.
**Mossyrock Park,** The Columbia River Gorge and Mount Rainier, page 328.
**Silver Lake Motel and Resort,** The Columbia River Gorge and Mount Rainier,
    page 331.
**Potholes State Park,** Southeastern Washington, page 389.
**Waldport/Newport KOA,** The Oregon Coast, page 431.
**Port of Siuslaw RV Park and Marina,** The Oregon Coast, page 437.
**Carter Lake,** The Oregon Coast, page 439.
**Trillium Lake,** The Columbia River Gorge and Mount Hood, page 510.
**Gone Creek,** The Columbia River Gorge and Mount Hood, page 516.
**Pelton,** The Columbia River Gorge and Mount Hood, page 534.
**Belknap Hot Springs Resort,** The Southern Cascades, page 608.
**Mallard Marsh,** The Southern Cascades, page 656.
**Trapper Creek,** The Southern Cascades, page 671.
**Drews Creek,** Southeastern Oregon, page 736.

## BEST( Hiking

**Campbell Tree Grove,** The Olympic Peninsula and Washington Coast, page 111.
**Moran State Park Ferry-In,** Seattle and the Puget Sound, page 157.
**Silver Fir,** The Northern Cascades, page 185.
**Beaver Plant Lake Hike-In,** The Northern Cascades, page 201.
**Harts Pass Walk-In,** The Northern Cascades, page 202.
**Mount Spokane State Park,** Northeastern Washington, page 309.
**Lower Falls,** The Columbia River Gorge and Mount Rainier, page 355.
**Beacon Rock State Park,** The Columbia River Gorge and Mount Rainier, page 362.
**Nehalem Falls,** The Oregon Coast, page 415.
**Cape Lookout State Park,** The Oregon Coast, page 420.
**Cape Blanco State Park,** The Oregon Coast, page 454.
**Eagle Creek,** The Columbia River Gorge and Mount Hood, page 499.
**Toll Gate,** The Columbia River Gorge and Mount Hood, page 507.
**Belknap Hot Springs Resort,** The Southern Cascades, page 608.
**Boulder Flat,** The Southern Cascades, page 643.

**Campbell Lake,** Southeastern Oregon, page 732.
**Dog Lake,** Southeastern Oregon, page 735.

## BEST( Wildlife-Viewing

**Bear Creek,** The Olympic Peninsula and Washington Coast, page 86.
**Ocean City State Park,** The Olympic Peninsula and Washington Coast, page 104.
**Birch Bay State Park,** Seattle and the Puget Sound, page 152.
**Larrabee State Park,** Seattle and the Puget Sound, page 163.
**Pearrygin Lake State Park,** The Northern Cascades, page 208.
**Napeequa Crossing,** The Northern Cascades, page 228.
**Lake Wenatchee State Park,** The Northern Cascades, page 234.
**Palmer Lake,** Northeastern Washington, page 259.
**Haag Cove,** Northeastern Washington, page 281.
**Big Meadow Lake,** Northeastern Washington, page 285.
**Cape Lookout State Park,** The Oregon Coast, page 420.
**Seal Rocks RV Cove,** The Oregon Coast, page 429.
**Port of Siuslaw RV Park and Marina,** The Oregon Coast, page 437.
**Harris Beach State Park,** The Oregon Coast, page 467.
**Pelton,** The Columbia River Gorge and Mount Hood, page 534.
**Penland Lake,** Northeastern Oregon, page 550.
**Crooked River Ranch RV Park,** The Southern Cascades, page 618.
**Bolan Lake,** The Southern Cascades, page 687.
**Mount Ashland,** The Southern Cascades, page 709.
**Jackson Creek,** Southeastern Oregon, page 728.

# Camping Tips

## SLEEPING GEAR

On an eve long ago in the mountain pines, my dad, brother, and I had rolled out our sleeping bags and were bedded down for the night. After the pre-trip excitement, a long drive, an evening of trout fishing and a barbecue, we were like three tired doggies who had played too much.

But as I looked up at the stars, I was suddenly wide awake. I was still wired. A half hour later? No change. Wide awake.

And as little kids can do, I had to wake up ol' Dad to tell him about it. "Hey, Dad, I can't sleep."

After the initial grimace, he said: "This is what you do. Watch the sky for a shooting star and tell yourself that you cannot go to sleep until you see at least one shooting star. As you wait and watch, you will start getting tired, and it will be difficult to keep your eyes open. But tell yourself, you must keep watching. Then you'll start to really feel tired. When you finally see a shooting star, you'll go to sleep so fast you won't know what hit you."

Well, I tried it that night and I don't even remember seeing a shooting star, I went to sleep so fast.

It's a good trick, and along with having a good sleeping bag, ground insulation, maybe a tent, or a few tricks for bedding down in a pickup truck or RV, you can get a great night's sleep on every camping trip.

More than 20 years after that camping episode with my dad and brother, we made a trip to the planetarium at the Academy of Sciences in San Francisco to see a show. The lights dimmed, and the ceiling turned into a night sky, filled with stars and a setting moon. A scientist began explaining the phenomena of the heavens.

After a few minutes, I began to feel drowsy. Just then, a shooting star zipped across the planetarium ceiling. I went into such a deep sleep, it was like I was in a coma. I didn't wake up until the show was over, the lights were turned back on, and the people were leaving.

Feeling drowsy, I turned to see if Dad had liked the show. Oh yeah? Not only had he gone to sleep too, but he apparently had no intention of waking up, no matter what. Just like a camping trip.

## Sleeping Bags

The first rule of a good nights' sleep is that you must be dry, warm and safe. A good sleeping bag can help plenty. A sleeping bag is a shell filled with heat-retaining insulation. By itself, it is not warm. Your body provides the heat, and the sleeping bag's ability to retain that heat is what makes it warm or cold.

The cheap cotton bags are heavy, bulky, cold, and, when wet, useless. With other options available, their function is limited. Anybody who sleeps outdoors or backpacks should choose otherwise. Use a sleeping bag filled with down or one of the quality poly-fills. Down is light, warm, and aesthetically pleasing to those who don't think camping and technology mix. If you choose a down bag, be sure to keep it double wrapped in plastic garbage bags on your trips to keep it dry. Once it's wet, you'll spend your nights howling at the moon.

The polyfiber-filled bags are not necessarily better than those filled with down, but they can be. Their one key advantage is that even when wet, some poly-fills can retain up to 85 percent of your body heat. This allows you to sleep and get valuable rest even in miserable conditions. In my camping experience, no matter how lucky you may be, there will come a time when you will get caught in an unexpected, violent storm and everything you've got will get wet, including your sleeping bag. That's when a poly-fill bag becomes priceless. You have one and can sleep. Or you don't have one and suffer. It is that simple. Of the synthetic fills, Quallofil made by DuPont is the industry leader.

---

## KEEP IT WILD TIP 1: CAMP WITH CARE

1. Choose an existing, legal site. Restrict activities to areas where vegetation is compacted or absent.
2. Camp at least 75 steps (200 feet) from lakes, streams, and trails.
3. Always choose sites that won't be damaged by your stay.
4. Preserve the feeling of solitude by selecting camps that are out of view when possible.
5. Don't dig trenches or build structures or furniture.

---

But just because a sleeping bag uses a high-tech poly-fill doesn't necessarily make it a better bag. There are other factors.

The most important are a bag's temperature rating and weight. The temperature rating of a sleeping bag refers to how cold it can get outside before you start actually feeling cold. Many campers make the mistake of thinking, "I only camp in the summer, so a bag rated at 30 or 40°F should be fine." Later, they find out it isn't so fine, and all it takes is one cold night to convince them of that. When selecting the right temperature rating, visualize the coldest weather you might ever confront, and then get a bag rated for even colder weather.

For instance, if you are a summer camper, you may rarely experience a night in the low 30s or high 20s. A sleeping bag rated at 20°F would be appropriate, keeping you snug, warm, and asleep. For most campers, I advise bags rated at 0 or 10°F.

But guess how the companies come up with their temperature ratings? Usually it's a guy like me field-testing a bag before it is commercially released, and then saying, "Well, it got down to 40°F and I was pretty warm." So they rate it at 30 degrees. Obviously, testers can have different threshold levels for cold, while others base their ratings on how much fill is used.

If you buy a poly-filled sleeping bag, try not to leave it squished in your stuff sack between camping trips. Instead, keep it on a hanger in a closet or use it as a blanket. One thing that can reduce a poly-filled bag's heat-retaining qualities is if the tiny hollow fibers that make up the fill lose their loft. You can avoid this with proper storage.

The weight of a sleeping bag can also be a key factor, especially for backpackers. When you have to carry your gear on your back, every ounce becomes important. Sleeping bags that weigh just 2-3 pounds are available, although they are expensive. But if you hike much, it's worth the price to keep your weight to a minimum. For an overnighter, you can get away with a 4- or 4.5-pound bag without much stress. However, bags weighing five pounds and up should be left back at the car.

I have several sleeping bags; they range from a seven-pounder that feels like a giant sponge to a three-pounder. The heavy-duty model is for pickup-truck camping in cold weather and doubles as a blanket at home. The lightweight bag is for expeditions.

## Insulation Pads

Even with the warmest sleeping bag in the world, if you just lay it down on the ground and try to sleep, you will likely get as cold as a winter cucumber. That is because the cold ground will suck the warmth right out of your body. The solution is to have a layer of insulation between you and the ground. For this, you can use a thin Insulite pad, a lightweight Therm-a-Rest inflatable pad, a foam pad or mattress, an airbed, or a cot. Here is a capsule summary of each:

**Insulite pads:** They are light, inexpensive, roll up quickly for transport, and can double as a seat pad at your camp. The negative side is that in one night, they will compress, making you feel like you are sleeping on granite. But they are light and they help keep you warm in the wilderness.

**Therm-a-Rest pads:** These are a real luxury for wilderness travel because they do everything an Insulite pad does, but they also provide a cushion. The negative side is that they are expensive by comparison, and if they get a hole in them, they become worthless without a patch kit. Most wilderness campers carry one "bonus item"—and a full-length Therm-A-Rest is often what they choose.

**Foam mattresses, air beds, and cots:** These are excellent for car campers. The new line of air beds, especially the thicker ones, are outstanding and inflate quickly with an electric motor inflator that plugs into a power plug or cigarette lighter in your vehicle. Foam mattresses are also excellent; I think they are the most comfortable of all, but their size precludes many from considering them. I've found that cots work great, too. I've always had one and they're great for drive-in tent sites. For camping in the back of a pickup truck with a camper shell, the cots with three-inch legs are best, of course. Here's the trick: Put a blanket over the sleeping surface, then add a Therm-A-Rest pad; you need insulation to keep the cold air beneath you from sucking out the warmth.

## A Few Tricks

When surveying a camp area, the most important consideration should be to select a good spot for sleeping. Everything else is secondary. Ideally, you want a flat area that is wind-sheltered and on ground soft enough to drive stakes into. Yeah, and I want to win the lottery, too.

Sometimes, the ground will have a slight slope to it. In that case, always sleep with your head on the uphill side. If you sleep parallel to the slope, every time you roll over, you'll find yourself rolling down the hill. If you sleep with your head on the downhill side, you'll get a headache that feels as if an ax is embedded in your brain.

When you've found a good spot, clear it of all branches, twigs, and rocks, of course. A good tip is to dig a slight indentation in the ground where your hip will fit. Since your body is not flat, but has curves and edges, it will not feel comfortable on flat ground. Some people even get severely bruised on the sides of their hips when sleeping on flat, hard ground. For that reason alone, they learn to hate camping. What a shame, especially when the problem is solved easily with a Therm-a-Rest pad, foam insulation, an air bed, or a cot.

After the ground is prepared, throw a ground cloth over the spot, which will keep much of the morning dew off you. In some areas, particularly where fog is a problem, morning dew can be heavy and get the outside of your sleeping bag quite wet. In that case, you need overhead protection, such as a tent or some kind of roof, like a poncho or tarp with its ends tied to trees.

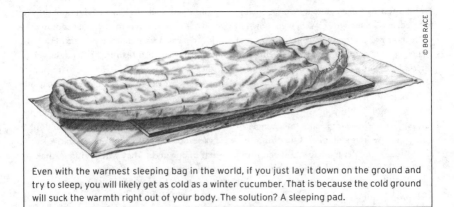

© BOB RACE

Even with the warmest sleeping bag in the world, if you just lay it down on the ground and try to sleep, you will likely get as cold as a winter cucumber. That is because the cold ground will suck the warmth right out of your body. The solution? A sleeping pad.

© SABRINA YOUNG

Tents vary in complexity, size, and price. Be sure to buy the one that's right for you.

## A Great Nights' Sleep

Some people sleep seven, eight hours at camp, but it comes in 10 installments. They keep waking up. They wake up and half their body is paralyzed. Heh, heh, heh. They can't get comfortable. To solve this, practice camp-style sleeping at home until you get it perfect. At home, you have flexibility and complete control over your sleeping surface. Get it right. Get it just how you like it.

For wilderness travel, my bonus item is an extra inflatable pillow; that's right, I carry two, not one. I inflate them about half full. It puts my head at a perfect comfort zone for deep sleep. Whatever it takes, know how to get a great night's sleep and your entire trip has the chance to feel epic, no matter what you do.

## Tents and Weather Protection

All it takes is to get caught in the rain once without a tent and you will never go anywhere without one again. A tent provides protection from rain, wind, and mosquito attacks. In exchange, you can lose a starry night's view, though some tents now even provide moon roofs.

A tent can be as complex as a four-season, tubular-jointed dome with a rain fly or as simple as a tarp roped up to a tree. They can be as cheap as a $10 tube tent, which is nothing more than a hollow piece of plastic, or as expensive as a $500 five-person deluxe expedition, multi-room dome. They vary greatly in size, price, and assembly time. For those who camp infrequently and want to buy a tent without paying much, off-brand models are available at considerable price discounts. My experience in field-testing outdoor gear, though, is that cheap tents often rip at the seams if subjected to regular use. If you plan on getting a good one, plan on doing plenty of shopping and asking lots of questions. With a little bit of homework, you can get the right answers to these questions:

### WILL IT KEEP ME DRY?

On many one-person and two-person tents, the rain fly does not extend far enough to keep water off the bottom sidewalls of the tent. In a driving rain, water can also drip from the rain fly and onto those sections of the tent. Eventually, the water can leak through to the inside, particularly through the seams.

You must be able to stake out your rain fly so it completely covers all of the tent. If you are tent shopping and this does not appear possible, then don't buy the tent. To prevent potential leaks, use a seam water-proofer, such as Seam Lock, a glue-like substance that can close potential leak areas on tent seams. For large umbrella tents, keep a patch kit handy. Coleman tents, by the way, are guaranteed to keep campers dry.

Another way to keep water out of your tent is to store all wet garments outside the tent, under a poncho. Moisture from wet clothes stashed in the tent will condense on the interior tent walls. If you bring enough wet clothes into the tent, by the next morning you'll feel as if you're camping in a duck blind.

## How Hard Is It to Put Up?

If a tent is difficult to erect in full sunlight, you can just about forget it at night, especially the first night out if you arrive late to camp. Some tents can go up in just a few minutes, without requiring help from another camper. This might be the kind of tent you want.

The way to compare put-up times when shopping for tents is to count the number of connecting points from the tent poles to the tent and the number of stakes required. The fewer, the better. Think simple. My two-person-plus-a-dog tent has seven connecting points and, minus the rain fly, requires no stakes. It goes up in a few minutes.

My bigger family tent, which has three rooms with walls (so we can keep our two kids isolated on each side if necessary), takes about a half hour to put up. That's without anybody's help. With their help, add about 15 minutes. Heh, heh.

Another factor is the tent poles themselves. Always make sure the poles are connected by an interior bungee cord. It takes only an instant to convert them to a complete pole.

Some outdoor shops have tents on display on their showroom floors. Before buying the tent, have the salesperson take the tent down and put it back up. If it takes him more than five minutes, or he says he doesn't have time, then keep looking.

## Is It Roomy Enough?

Don't judge the size of a tent on floor space alone. Some tents that are small on floor space can give the illusion of roominess with a high ceiling. You can be quite comfortable and snug in them.

But remember that a one-person or two-person tent is just that. A two-person tent has room for two people plus gear. That's it. Don't buy a tent expecting it to hold more than it is intended to.

## How Much Does It Weigh?

If you're a hiker, this becomes the preeminent question. If it's much more than six or seven pounds, forget it. A 12-pound tent is bad enough, but get it wet and it's like carrying a piano on your back. On the other hand, weight is scarcely a factor if you camp only where you can take your car. My dad, for instance, used to have this giant canvas umbrella tent that folded down to a neat little pack that weighed about 500 pounds.

## Family Tents

It is always worth spending the time and money to buy a tent you and your family will be happy with.

Many excellent family tents are available for $125-175, particularly from Cabela's, Coleman, Eureka!, North Face, Remington, and Sierra Designs. Guide-approved expedition tents for groups cost more, generally $350-600. Here is a synopsis of some of best tents available:

### Cabela's Two- or Three-Room Cabin
800/237-4444
www.cabelas.com
This beautiful tent features two to three rooms, a 10- by 16-foot floor available in different configurations with removable interior walls. Three doors mean everybody doesn't tromp through the center room for access to

the side rooms. It will stand up to wind, rain, and frequent use.

## COLEMAN MODIFIED DOME

800/835-3278
www.coleman.com
Coleman Modified Dome tents are available in six different single- and multi-room designs. The pole structure is unique, with all four upright poles and one ridgepole shock-corded together for an integrated system that makes setup extremely fast and easy. Yet, because of the ridgepole's engineering, the tent has passed tests in high winds. Mesh panels in the ceiling are a tremendous plus for ventilation.

## COLEMAN WEATHERMASTER

800/835-3278
www.coleman.com
The Weathermaster series features tents with multiple rooms, walls, and ample headroom, and they are guaranteed to keep rain out. The 17- by 9-foot model sleeps six to eight, has a 76-inch ceiling, and has zippered dividers. Since the dividers are removable, you can configure the tent in multiple layouts. The frame is designed with poles adjustable to three different heights to accommodate uneven ground.

## KELTY

800/423-2320
www.kelty.com
Kelty offers top-of-the-line tents based on a sleek dome profile. This is a great package, with mesh sides, tops, and doors, along with a full awning fly and coverage for weather protection. Clip sleeves and rubber-tipped poles for easy slide during setup are nice bonuses.

## REI

800/423-2320
www.rei.com
REI has 94 backpacking tents and 27 tents available for car camping, including their own designs as well as those from other manufacturers. A great backpacking tent for two is the REI Half Dome 2 Plus. The Eureka Copper Canyon 6 is one of the better family values.

## Bivouac Bags

If you like going light or solo, and choose not to own a tent at all, a bivy bag or tarp can be the way to go. Bivy is short for bivouac bag and pronounced "bivvy" as in dizzy, not "bivy" as in ivy, and can provide the extremely lightweight weather protection you require. A bivy bag is a water-repellent shell in which your sleeping bag fits. It is light and tough, and for some is the perfect alternative to a heavy tent. My own bivy weighs 31 ounces and cost around $250; it's made by OR (Outdoor Research), and I just plain love the thing on expeditions. On the downside, however, some say it can be a bit difficult getting settled just right in it, and others say they feel claustrophobic in such close quarters. Once you get used to a bivy, spend a night in a tent; the tent will feel like a room at the Mirage. For me, not a problem.

The idea of riding out a storm in a bivy can be quite worrisome for some. You can hear the rain hitting you, and sometimes even feel the pounding of the drops through the bivy bag. For some, it can be unsettling to try to sleep under such circumstances. On the other hand, I've always looked forward to it. In cold weather, a bivy also helps keep you warm. I've had just one miserable night in mine. That was when my sleeping bag was a bit wet when I started the night. By the middle of the night, the water was condensing from the sleeping bag on the interior walls of the bivy, and then soaking the bag, like a storm cycle. The night hit only about 45°F but I just about froze to death anyway. Otherwise, I've used it on more than 100 expeditions with great results: warm, dry quarters and deep, restful sleeps by night, and a pack lightened without carrying a tent by day.

Many long-distance hikers are switching to light tarps in the continuing mission to minimize weight. They work great in rain and the spacious feel beneath them is fantastic. You just need a tree to tie to and soft enough ground for stakes, so they don't work above tree line. Tarps are great, except when there are bug problems; then you need some kind of mosquito netting. A bivy or tent solves that, of course.

## Pickup Truck Campers

If you own a pickup truck with a camper shell, you can turn it into a self-contained campground with a little work. This can be an ideal way to go: It's fast, portable, and you are guaranteed a dry environment.

But that does not necessarily mean it is a warm environment. In fact, without insulation from the metal truck bed, it can be like trying to sleep on an iceberg. The metal truck bed will get as cold as the air temperature, which is often much colder than the ground temperature. Without insulation, it can be much colder in your camper shell than it would be on the open ground.

When I camp in my rig, I use a large piece of foam for a mattress and insulation. The foam measures four inches thick, 48 inches wide, and 76 inches long. It makes for a bed as comfortable as anything one might ask for. In fact, during the winter, if I don't go camping for a few weeks because of writing obligations, I sometimes will throw the foam on the floor, lay down the old sleeping bag, light a fire, and camp right in my living room. It's in my blood, I tell you. Airbeds and cots are also extremely comfortable and I've used both many times. Whatever you choose, just make sure you have a comfortable sleeping unit. Good sleep makes for great camping trips.

## RVs

The problems RVers encounter come from two primary sources: lack of privacy and light intrusion.

The lack of privacy stems from the natural restrictions of where a land yacht can go. Without careful use of the guide section of this book, owners of RVs can find themselves in parking-lot settings, jammed in with plenty of neighbors. Because RVs often have large picture windows, you lose your privacy, causing some late nights; then, come daybreak, light intrusion forces an early wake up. As a result, you get shorted on your sleep.

The answer is to carry inserts to fit over the inside of your windows. These close off the outside and retain your privacy. And if you don't want to wake up with the sun at daybreak, you don't have to. It will still be dark.

Many campgrounds and RV parks enforce a quiet time. If that is important to you, make sure you don't end up somewhere where a quiet time is optional.

## HIKING AND FOOT CARE

We had set up a nice little camp in the woods, and my buddy, Foonsky, was strapping on his hiking boots, sitting against a big Douglas fir.

"New boots," he said with a grin. "But they seem pretty stiff."

We decided to hoof it down the trail for a few hours, exploring the mountain wildlands that are said to hide Bigfoot and other strange creatures. After just a short while on the trail, a sense of peace and calm seemed to settle in. The forest provides the chance to be purified with clean air and the smell of trees, freeing you from all troubles.

But it wasn't long before a look of trouble was on Foonsky's face. And no, it wasn't from seeing Bigfoot.

"Got a hot spot on my toe," he said.

Immediately, we stopped. He pulled off his right boot, then his sock, and inspected the left side of his big toe. Sure enough, a blister had bubbled up, filled with fluid, but hadn't popped. From his medical kit, Foonsky cut a small piece of moleskin to fit over the blister and taped it to hold it in place. In a few minutes we were back on the trail.

A half hour later, there was still no sign of Bigfoot. But Foonsky stopped again and pulled off his other boot. "Another hot spot." On the little toe of his left foot was another small blister, over which he taped a Band-Aid to keep it from further chafing against the inside of his new boot.

## KEEP IT WILD TIP 2:
## KEEP THE WILDERNESS WILD

1. Let nature's sound prevail. Avoid loud voices and noises.
2. Leave radios and tape players at home. At drive-in camping sites, never open car doors with music playing.
3. Careful guidance is necessary when choosing any games to bring for children. Most toys, especially any kind of gun toys with which children simulate shooting at each other, shouldn't be allowed on a camping trip.
4. Control pets at all times or leave them with a sitter at home.
5. Treat natural heritage with respect. Leave plants, rocks, and historical artifacts where you find them.

In just a few days, ol' Foonsky, a strong, 6-foot-5, 200-plus-pound guy, was walking around like a sore-hoofed horse that had been loaded with a month's worth of supplies and ridden over sharp rocks. Well, it wasn't the distance that had done Foonsky in; it was those blisters. He had them on eight of his 10 toes and was going through Band-Aids, moleskin, and tape like a walking emergency ward. If he'd used any more tape, he would've looked like a mummy from an Egyptian tomb.

If you've ever been in a similar predicament, you know the frustration of wanting to have a good time, wanting to hike and explore the area where you have set up a secluded camp, only to be held up by several blisters. No one is immune—all are created equal before the blister god. You can be forced to bow to it unless you get your act together.

What causes blisters? In almost all cases, it is the simple rubbing of a foot against the rugged interior of a boot. That can be worsened by several factors:

1. A very stiff boot or one in which your foot moves inside as you walk, instead of a boot that flexes as if it were another layer of skin.

2. Thin, ragged, or dirty socks. This is the fastest route to blisters. Thin socks will allow your feet to move inside your boots, ragged socks will allow your skin to chafe directly against the boot's interior, and dirty socks will wrinkle and fold, also rubbing against your feet instead of cushioning them.

3. Soft feet. By themselves, soft feet will not cause blisters, but in combination with a stiff boot or thin socks, they can cause terrible problems. The best way to toughen up your feet is to go barefoot. In fact, some of the biggest, toughest-looking guys you'll ever see, from Hells Angels to pro football players, have feet that are as soft as a baby's butt. Why? Because they never go barefoot and don't hike much.

## The Perfect Boot

Every hiker eventually conducts a search for the perfect boot in the mission for ideal foot comfort and freedom from blisters. While there are many entries in this search—in fact, so many that it can be confusing—there is a way to find that perfect boot for you.

To stay blister-free, the most important factors are socks and boot flexibility. If there is any foot slippage from a thin sock or a stiff boot, you can rub up a blister in minutes. For instance, I never wear stiff boots and I sometimes wear two fresh sets of SmartWools.

My search for the perfect boot included discussions with the nation's preeminent long-distance hikers, Brian Robinson of Mountain View (7,200 miles in 2001) and Ray Jardine of Oregon (2,700 miles of Pacific Crest Trail in three months). Both believe that the weight of a shoe is the defining factor when selecting hiking footwear. They both go as light as possible, believing that heavy boots will eventually wear you out by forcing you to pick up several pounds on your feet over and over again.

It is absolutely critical to stay away from very stiff boots and thin socks. Always wear the right style boots for what you have in mind and then protect your feet with carefully selected socks. If you are still so unfortunate as to get a blister or two, it means knowing how to treat them fast so they don't turn your walk into a sore-footed endurance test.

## Selecting the Right Boots

The first time we did the John Muir Trail, I hiked 400 miles in three months; that is, 150 miles in a two-month general-training program, then 250 miles in three weeks from Mount Whitney to Yosemite Valley. In that span, I got just one blister, suffered on the fourth day of the 250-miler. I treated it immediately and suffered no more. One key is wearing the right boot, and for me, that means a boot that acts as a thick layer of skin that is flexible and pliable to my foot. I want my feet to fit snugly in them, with no interior movement.

There are four kinds of hiking footwear, most commonly known as: 1. Hiking boots; 2. Hunting boots; 3. Mountaineering boots; 4. Athletic shoes. Select the right one for you or pay the consequences.

One great trick when on a hiking vacation is to bring all four, and then for each hike, wear different footwear. This has many benefits. By changing boots, you change the points of stress for your feet and legs, greatly reducing soreness and the chance of creating a hot spot on a foot. It also allows you to go light on flat trails and heavy on steep trails, where additional boot weight can help with traction in downhill stretches.

### HIKING BOOTS

Lightweight hiking boots are basically Gore-Tex walking shoes. They are designed for day walks or short backpacking trips and look like rugged, lightweight athletic shoes, designed with a Gore-Tex top for lightness and a Vibram sole for traction. These are perfect for people who like to walk but rarely carry a heavy backpack. Because they are flexible, they are easy to break in, and with fresh socks, they rarely cause blister problems. Because they are light, general hiking fatigue is greatly reduced. Like many, I've converted over 100 percent to them.

On the negative side, because hiking boots are light, traction can be far from great on steep, gravelly surfaces. In addition, they provide less than ideal ankle support, which can be a problem in rocky areas, such as along a stream where you might want to go trout fishing.

Regardless of the distance you anticipate, they are the footwear of choice. My personal preference is Merrell's, but New Balance, Salomon, Asolo, Zamberlan, Vasque, and others make great hiking boots. Many of the greatest long-distance hikers in America wear trail running shoes.

### HUNTING BOOTS

Hunting boots are also called backpacking boots, super boots, or wilderness boots. They feature high ankle support, deep Vibram lug sole, built-in orthotics and arch support, and waterproof exterior.

They have fallen out of favor among campers and backpackers. On the negative side, hunting boots can be quite hot, weigh a ton, and if they get wet, take days to dry. Because they are heavy, they can wear you out. Often, the extra weight can add days to long-distance expeditions, cutting into the number of miles a hiker is capable of on a daily basis.

They are still popular among mountaineers who hunt. Their weight and traction make them good for trekking off-trail or for carrying heavy packs because they provide additional support. They also can stand up to hundreds of miles of wilderness use, constantly being banged against rocks and walked through streams while supporting 200 pounds.

My favorite hunting boot is made by Mendl, out of Germany. I have also used Danner, Cabela's and RedWing.

## Mountaineering Boots

Mountaineering boots are identified by mid-range tops, laces that extend almost as far as the toe area, and ankle areas that are as stiff as a board. The lack of "give" is what endears them to mountaineers. Their stiffness is preferred when rock-climbing, walking off-trail on craggy surfaces, or hiking along the edge of streambeds where walking across small rocks can cause you to turn your ankle. Because these boots don't give on rugged, craggy terrain, they reduce ankle injuries and provide better traction.

The drawback to stiff boots is that if you don't have the proper socks and your foot starts slipping around in the boot, blisters will inevitably follow. If you just want to go for a walk or a good tromp with a backpack, then hiking shoes or hunting boots will serve you better.

Vasque makes my favorite mountaineering boots for rock climbing.

### At the Store

There are many styles, brands, and price ranges to choose from. If you wander about comparing all their many features, you will get as confused as a kid in a toy store.

Instead, go into the store with your mind clear about what you want, find it, and buy it. If you want the best, expect to spend $85-200 for hiking boots, $100-250 for hunting boots, $250-300 for mountaineering boots. If you go much cheaper, well, then you are getting cheap footwear.

This is one area where you don't want to scrimp, so try not to yelp about the high cost. Instead, walk into the store believing you deserve the best, and that's exactly what you'll pay for.

You don't always get what you pay for, though. Once, I spent $200-plus on some hunting boots that turned out to be miserable blister-makers and I had to throw them out. Even after a year of trying to get my money's worth, I never felt they worked right on the trail. Adios. Move on to what works.

If you plan to use the advice of a shoe salesperson, first look at what kind of boots he or she is wearing. If the salesperson isn't even wearing boots, then their advice may not be worth much. Most people I know who own quality boots, including salespeople, wear them almost daily if their jobs allow, since boots are the best footwear available. However, even these well-meaning folks can offer sketchy advice. Plenty of hikers claim to wear the world's greatest boot! Instead of asking how great the boot is, ask, "How many blisters did you get when you hiked 12 miles a day for a week?"

Enter the store with a precise use and style in mind. Rather than fish for suggestions, tell the salesperson exactly what you want, try two or three brands of the same style, and always try on both boots in a pair simultaneously so you know exactly how they'll feel. If possible, walk up and down stairs with them. Are they too stiff? Are your feet snug yet comfortable, or do they slip? Do they have that "right" kind of feel when you walk?

If you get the appropriate answers to those questions, then you're on your way to blister-free, pleasure-filled days of walking.

## Socks

People can spend so much energy selecting the right kind of boots that they virtually overlook wearing the right kind of socks. One goes with the other.

Your socks should be thick enough to cushion your feet as well as fit snugly. Without good socks, you might tie your bootlaces too tight—and that's like putting a tourniquet on your feet. You should have plenty of clean socks on hand, or plan on washing what you have on your trip. As socks are worn, they become compressed, dirty, and damp. If they fold over, you'll rub up a blister in minutes.

My companions believe I go overboard when it comes to socks, that I bring too many and wear too many. But it works, so that's where the complaints stop. So how many do I wear? Well, it varies. On day hikes, I have found a sock called a SmartWool that makes my size 13s feel as if they're walking on pillows. I often wear two of them; that is, two on each foot. Several manufacturers now produce socks that are the equivalent of SmartWools, but are a lot less expensive. SmartWool socks and other similar socks are a synthetic composite. They can partially wick moisture away from the skin.

Some hikers wear multiple socks and it works for them—a comfortable cotton-poly blend sock on the interior and wool sock on the exterior. This will cushion your foot, provide that just-right snug fit in your boot, and give you some additional warmth and insulation in cold weather. It is critical to keep the interior sock clean. If you wear a sock over and over again, it will compact, lose its cushion, and start wrinkling or folding over while you hike and a blister will be born.

Do not wear thin cotton socks. Your foot can get damp and mix with dirt, which can cause a hot spot to start on your foot. Eventually, you get blisters, lots of them.

## Inner Sole

If you are like most folks, the bottoms of your feet are rarely exposed and can be quite soft. You can take additional steps in their care. The best tip is keeping a fresh inner sole footpad in your boot. I prefer Dr. Scholl's gel pad or the equivalent. Some new inner soles can be slippery for a few days, which, if your foot slides around while you're hiking, can cause blisters. Just like new boots and new socks, they need to be broken in before an expedition.

Another cure for soft feet is to get out and walk or jog on a regular basis before your camping trip. On one trip on the Pacific Coast Trail, I ran into the long-distance master Jardine. He swore that going barefoot regularly is the best way to build up foot strength and arch support, while toughening up the bottom of your feet.

If you plan to use a foot pad and wear two heavy socks, you will need to use these items when sizing boots. Do not buy shoes if you're wearing thin cotton socks; wear the socks you're planning to wear when hiking, insert the inner sole, and then see how they feel. That's the only right way to size a hiking boot.

## Treating Blisters

The key to treating blisters is fast work at the first sign of a hot spot. If you feel a hot spot, never keep walking, figuring that the problem will go away or that you will work through it. Wrong! Stop immediately and go to work.

Before you remove your socks, check to see if the sock has a wrinkle in it, a likely cause of the problem. If so, either change socks or pull them tight, removing the tiny folds, after taking care of the blister.

To take care of the blister, forget Moleskin. (They changed how they manufacture it and I've found it will slide off the blister while hiking.) Instead, use "Second Skin," which adheres over the top of the blister and does not dislodge. For small blisters, Band-Aids can do the job, but these have to be replaced daily, and sometimes with even more frequency. At night, clean your feet and sleep without socks. That will allow your feet to dry and heal.

## Tips in the Field

Three other items that can help your walking are an Ace bandage, a pair of gaiters, and hiking poles.

For sprained ankles and twisted knees, an Ace bandage can be like an insurance policy to get you back on the trail and out of trouble. In many cases, a hiker with a twisted ankle or sprained knee has relied on a good wrap with a four-inch bandage for the added support to get home. Always buy the Ace bandages that come with the clips permanently attached, so you don't have to worry about losing them.

Gaiters are leggings made of Gore-Tex that fit from just below your knees, over your calves, and attach under your boots. They are of particular help when walking in damp areas or in places where rain is common. As your legs brush against ferns or low-lying plants, gaiters deflect the moisture. Without them, pants can get soaked wet in short order.

Many hikers would never hit the trail without hiking poles. Personally, they are not for me; I like to hike in rhythm and keeping my arms swinging effortlessly. I don't like to have to watch where I'm putting my poles all the time. But for those who have trouble with footing, a cranky knee or ankle, or want the upper body workout, poles can be a good fit. If it floats your boat, bring 'em.

Another tip: Should your boots become wet, never try to force-dry them. Some well-meaning folks will try to dry them quickly at the edge of a campfire, or at home, actually put the boots in an oven. While this may dry the boots, it can also loosen the glue that holds them together, ultimately weakening them until one day they fall apart in a heap.

A better bet is to treat the leather so the boots become water-repellent. Silicone-based liquids are the easiest to use and least greasy of the treatments available.

A final tip is to have another pair of light-weight shoes or moccasins that you can wear around camp and, in the process, give your feet the rest they deserve.

## CLOTHING AND WEATHER PROTECTION

What started as an innocent pursuit of the perfect campground evolved into one heck of a predicament for Foonsky and me.

We had parked at the end of a logging road and then bushwhacked our way down a canyon to a pristine trout stream. On my first cast—a little flip into the plunge pool of a waterfall—I caught a 16-inch rainbow trout, a real beauty that jumped three times. Magic stuff.

Then, just across the stream, we saw it: The Perfect Camping Spot. On a sandbar on the edge of the forest, there lay a flat spot, high and dry above the river. Nearby was plenty of downed wood collected by past winter storms that we could use for firewood. And, of course, this beautiful trout stream was bubbling along just 40 yards from the site.

But nothing is perfect, right? To reach it, we had to wade across the river, although it didn't appear to be too difficult. The cold water tingled a bit, and the river came up surprisingly high, just above the belt. But it would be worth it to camp at The Perfect Spot.

Once across the river, we put on some dry clothes, set up camp, explored the woods, and fished the stream, catching several nice trout for dinner. But late that afternoon, it started raining. What? Rain in the summertime? Nature makes its own rules. By the next morning, it was still raining, pouring like a Yosemite waterfall from a solid gray sky.

That's when we noticed The Perfect Spot wasn't so perfect. The rain had raised the river level too high for us to wade back across. We were marooned, wet, and hungry.

"Now we're in a heck of a predicament," said Foonsky, the water streaming off him.

Getting cold and wet on a camping trip with no way to warm up is not only unnecessary and uncomfortable, it can be a fast ticket to hypothermia, the number one killer of campers in the woods. By definition, hypothermia is a condition in which body temperature is lowered to the point that it causes illness. It is particularly dangerous because the afflicted are usually unaware it is setting in. The first sign is a sense of apathy, then a state of confusion, which can lead eventually to collapse (or what appears to be sleep), then death.

You must always have a way to get warm and dry in short order, regardless of any conditions you may face. If you have no way of getting dry, then you must take emergency steps to prevent hypothermia. (See the steps detailed in *First Aid and Insect Protection* in this chapter.)

But you should never reach that point. For starters, always have spare sets of clothing tucked away so no matter how cold and wet you might get, you have something dry to put on. On hiking trips, I always carry a second set of clothes, sealed to stay dry, in a plastic garbage bag. I keep a third set waiting back at the truck.

If you are car camping, your vehicle can cause an illusory sense of security. But with

## KEEP IT WILD TIP 3: TRAVEL LIGHTLY

1. Visit the backcountry in small groups.
2. Below tree line, always stay on designated trails.
3. Don't cut across switchbacks.
4. When traveling cross-country where no trails are available, follow animal trails or spread out with your group so no new routes are created.
5. Read your map and orient yourself with landmarks, a compass, and an altimeter. Avoid marking trails with rock cairns, tree scars, or ribbons.

an extra set of dry clothes stashed safely away, there is no illusion. The security is real. And remember, no matter how hot the weather is when you start your trip, always be prepared for the worst. Foonsky and I learned the hard way.

So both of us were soaking wet on that sandbar. With no other choice, we tried holing up in the tent for the night. A sleeping bag with Quallofil or another polyester fiberfill can retain warmth even when wet, because the fill is hollow and retains its loft. So as miserable as it was, the night passed without incident.

The rain stopped the next day and the river dropped a bit, but it was still rolling big and angry. Using a stick as a wading staff, Foonsky crossed about 80 percent of the stream before he was dumped, but he made a jump for it and managed to scramble to the riverbank. He waved for me to follow. "No problem," I thought.

It took me 20 minutes to reach nearly the same spot where Foonsky had been dumped. The heavy river current was above my belt and pushing hard. Then, in the flash of an instant, my wading staff slipped on a rock. I teetered in the river current and was knocked over like a bowling pin. I became completely submerged. I went tumbling down the river, heading right toward the waterfall. While underwater, I looked up at the surface, and I can remember how close it seemed yet how out of control I was. Right then, this giant hand appeared, and I grabbed it. It was Foonsky. If it weren't for that hand, I would have sailed right over the waterfall.

My momentum drew Foonsky right into the river, and we scrambled in the current, but I suddenly sensed the river bottom under my knees. On all fours, the two of us clambered ashore. We were safe.

"Thanks, ol' buddy," I said.

"Man, we're wet," he responded. "Let's get to the rig and get some dry clothes on."

## The Art of Layering

The most important element for enjoying the outdoor experience in any condition is to stay dry and warm. There is no substitute. You must stay dry and you must stay warm.

Thus comes the theory behind layering, which suggests that as your body temperature fluctuates or the weather shifts, you simply peel off or add available layers as needed—and have a waterproof shell available in case of rain.

The introduction of a new era of outdoor clothing has made it possible for campers to turn choosing clothes into an art form. Like art, it's much more expensive than throwing on a pair of blue jeans, a T-shirt, and some flannel, but, for many, it is worth the price.

In putting together your ideal layering system, there are some general considerations. What you need to do is create a system that effectively combines elements of breathability, durability, insulation, rapid drying, water repellence, wicking, and wind resistance, while still being lightweight and offering the necessary freedom of movement, all with just a few garments.

The basic intent of a base layer is to manage moisture. Your base layer will be the first article of clothing you put on and the last to come off. Since your own skin will be churning out the perspiration, the goal of this second skin is to manage the moisture and move it away from you. The best base layers are made of bicomponent knits, that is, blends of polyester and cotton, which provide wicking and insulating properties in one layer.

The way it works is that the side facing your skin is water-hating, while the side away from your skin is water-loving; thus, it pulls or "wicks" moisture through the material. You'll stay dry and happy, even with only one layer on, something not possible with old single-function weaves. The best include Capilene, Driclime, Lifa, Polartec 100, and Thermax. The only time that cotton should become a part of your base layer is if you wish to keep cool, not warm, such as in a hot desert climate where evaporative cooling becomes your friend, not your enemy.

Stretch fleece and microdenier pile also provide a good base layer, though they can be used as a second layer as well. Microdenier pile can be worn alone or layered under or over other pieces; it has excellent wicking capability as well as more windproof potential.

The next layer should be a light cotton shirt or a long-sleeved cotton/wool shirt, or both, depending on the coolness of the day. For pants, many just wear blue jeans when camping, but blue jeans can be hot and tight, and once wet, they tend to stay that way. Putting on wet blue jeans on a cold morning is a torturous way to start the day. A better choice is pants made from nylon with detachable leggings; these are light, have a lot of give, and dry quickly. If the weather is quite warm, nylon shorts that have some room to them can be the best choice. My preference is for The North Face dark-green expedition hiking shorts.

Finally, you should top the entire ensemble off with a thin, windproof, water-resistant layer. You want this layer to breathe, yet not be so porous that rain runs through it. Patagonia's Velocity shell is one of the best; its outer fabric is treated with DWR (Durable Water Repellent finish) and the coating is by Gore-tex. Patagonia, Marmot, and The North Face and others all offer their own versions. Though condensation will still build up inside, it manages to get rid of enough moisture.

Note: It is critical to know the difference between "water-resistant" and "waterproof." (This is covered under the *Rain Gear* section in this chapter.)

But hey, why does anybody need all this fancy stuff just to go camping? Fair question. You don't have to opt for this aerobic-function fashion statement. It is unnecessary on many camping trips. The fact is that you must be ready for anything when you venture into the outdoors. The new era of outdoor clothing works, and it works better than anything that has come before. Regardless of what you choose, weather should never be a nuisance or cause discomfort. There is no such thing as bad weather, so the saying goes, only bad gear.

## Hats

Another word of advice: Always pack along a warm hat for those times when you need to seal in warmth. You lose a large percentage of heat through your head. At night in cold weather, I wear a skullcap. During the day, I almost always wear a wide-brimmed hat, something like those that the legendary outlaws wore 150 years ago. There's actually logic behind it: My hat is made of waterproof canvas, is rigged with a lariat (it can be cinched down when it's windy), and has a wide brim that keeps the tops of my ears from being sunburned. If you're outside a lot, do not wear baseball hats—the tops of your ears will burn to a red crisp. Years ago, that's how an old friend of mine lost his ears to skin cancer.

### HEAD LIGHT

I've tried many head lights and the Trail Torch Hat Light is my favorite by a mile (www.halibut.net). It comes with five white and green LED lights in a horizontal row that clips under the bill of your hat. For the best option, order the set with three green lights (for night vision) and two white lights. (At night you'll look like a jet coming in for a landing.)

## Vests and Parkas

In cold weather, you should take the layer system one step further with a warm vest and a parka jacket. Vests are especially useful because they provide warmth without the bulkiness of a parka. The warmest vests and parkas are either filled with down or Quallofil, or they are made with a cotton/wool mix. Each has its respective merits and problems. Down fill provides the most warmth for the amount of weight, but becomes useless when wet, closely resembling a wet dishrag. Quallofil keeps much of its heat-retaining quality even when wet, but it is expensive. Vests made of cotton/wool mixes are the most attractive and also are quite warm, but they can be as heavy as a ship's anchor when wet.

Sometimes, the answer is combining a parka with a vest. One of my best camping companions wears a good-looking cotton/wool vest and a parka filled with Quallofil. The vest never gets wet, so weight is not a factor.

## Rain Gear

One of the most miserable nights of my life was on a camping trip for which I hadn't brought my rain gear or a tent. Hey, it was early August, the temperature had been in the 90s for weeks, and if anybody had said it was going to rain, I would have told him to consult a brain doctor. But rain it did. And as I got wetter and wetter, I kept saying to myself, "Hey, it's summer, it's not supposed to rain." Then I remembered one of the 10 commandments of camping: Forget your rain gear and you can guarantee it will rain.

To stay dry, you need some form of water-repellent shell. It can be as simple as a $5 poncho made out of plastic or as elaborate as a $300 Gore-Tex jacket-and-pants set. What counts is not how much you spend, but how dry you stay.

The most important thing to realize is that waterproof and water-resistant are completely different things. In addition, there is no such thing as rain gear that is both waterproof and breathable. The more waterproof a jacket is, the less it breathes. Conversely, the more breathable a jacket is, the less waterproof it becomes.

If you wear water-resistant rain gear in an sustained downpour, you'll get soaked. Water-resistant rain gear is appealing because it breathes and will keep you dry in the light stuff, such as mist, fog, even a little splash from a canoe paddle. But in rain? Forget it.

So what is the solution?

I've decided that the best approach is a set of fairly light but 100 percent-waterproof rain gear. I recently bought a hooded jacket and pants from Coleman, and my assessment is that it is the most cost-efficient rain gear I've ever had. All I can say is, hey, it works: I stay dry, it doesn't weigh much, and it didn't cost a fortune.

The absolute best foul weather gear made is by Simms, both jacket and bib. While it is expensive, you will stay dry and warm in any condition but that in which you need a survival suit.

You can also stay dry with any of the waterproof plastics and even heavy-duty rubber-coated outfits made for commercial fishermen. But these are uncomfortable during anything but a heavy rain. Because they are heavy and don't breathe, you'll likely get soaked anyway (that is, from your own sweat), even if it isn't raining hard.

On backpacking trips, I still stash a super-lightweight, water-repellent slicker for day hikes and a poncho, which I throw over my pack at night to keep it dry. But, otherwise, I never go anywhere—*anywhere*—without my rain gear.

Some do just fine with a cheap poncho, and note that ponchos can serve other uses in addition to a raincoat. Ponchos can be used as a ground tarp, as a rain cover for supplies or a backpack, or can be snapped together and roped up to trees in a pinch to provide a quick storm ceiling if you don't have a tent. The problem with ponchos is that in a hard rain, you just don't stay dry. First your legs get wet, then they get soaked. Then your arms follow the same pattern. If you're wearing cotton, you'll find that once part of the garment gets wet, the water spreads until, alas, you are dripping wet, poncho and all. Before long, you start to feel like a walking refrigerator.

One high-cost option is to buy a Gore-Tex rain jacket and pants. Gore-Tex is actually not a fabric, as is commonly believed, but a laminated film that coats a breathable fabric. The result is lightweight, water-repellent, breathable jackets and pants. They are perfect for campers, but they cost a fortune.

Some hiking buddies of mine have complained that the older Gore-Tex rain gear loses its water-repellent quality over time. However, manufacturers insist that this is the result of water seeping through seams, not leaks in the jacket. At each seam, tiny needles have pierced the fabric, and as tiny as the holes are, water will find a way through. An application of Seam Lock, especially at major seams around the shoulders of a jacket, can usually fix the problem.

If you don't want to spend the big bucks for Gore-Tex rain gear but want more rain protection than a poncho affords, a coated nylon jacket is the compromise that many choose. They are inexpensive, have the highest water-repellency of any rain gear, and are warm, providing a good outer shell for your layers of clothing. But they are not without fault. These jackets don't breathe at all, and if you zip them up tight, you can sweat a river.

My brother Rambob gave me a nylon jacket before a mountain-climbing expedition. I wore that cheap special all the way to the top with no complaints; it's warm and 100 percent waterproof. The one problem with nylon comes when temperatures drop below freezing. It gets so stiff that it feels as if you are wearing a straitjacket.

There's one more jacket-construction term to know: DWR, or Durable Water-Repellent finish. All of the top-quality jackets these days are DWR-treated. The DWR causes water to bead up on the shell. When the DWR wears off, even a once-waterproof jacket will feel like a wet dishrag.

Also note that ventilation is the key to coolness. The only ventilation on most shells is often the zipper. But waterproof jackets need additional openings. Look for mesh-backed pockets and underarm zippers, as well as cuffs, waists, and hems that can be adjusted to open wide. Storm flaps (the baffle over the zipper) that close with hook-and-loop material or snaps let you leave the zipper open for airflow into the jacket.

## Other Gear

What are the three items most commonly forgotten on a camping trip? A hat, sunglasses, and lip balm.

A hat is crucial, especially when you are visiting high elevations. Without one you are constantly exposed to everything nature can give you. The sun will dehydrate you, sap your energy, sunburn your head, and in worst cases, cause sunstroke. Start with a comfortable hat. Then finish with sunglasses, lip balm, and sunscreen for additional protection. They will help protect you from extreme heat.

To guard against extreme cold, it's a good idea to keep a pair of thin ski gloves stashed away with your emergency clothes, along with a wool ski cap, or a skull cap. The gloves should be thick enough to keep your fingers from stiffening up, but pliable enough to allow full movement so you don't have to take them off to complete simple tasks, like lighting a stove. An alternative to gloves is glovelets, which look like gloves with no fingers. In any case, just because the weather turns cold doesn't mean that your hands have to.

## FOOD AND COOKING GEAR

It was a warm, crystal clear day, a perfect day for skydiving. That was exactly the case for my old pal Foonsky, who had never before tried the sport. But a funny thing happened after he jumped out of the plane and pulled on the rip cord: His parachute didn't open.

In total free fall, Foonsky watched the earth below getting closer and closer. Not one to panic, he calmly pulled the ripcord on the emergency parachute. Again, nothing happened. No parachute, no nothing.

The ground was getting ever closer, and as he tried to search for a soft place to land, Foonsky detected a small object shooting up toward him, growing larger as it approached. It looked like a camper.

Figuring this was his last chance, Foonsky shouted as they passed in midair, "Hey, do you know anything about parachutes?"

The other fellow just yelled back as he headed off into space, "Do you know anything about lighting camping stoves?"

Well, Foonsky got lucky and his parachute opened. As for the other guy, well, he's probably in orbit like a NASA weather satellite. If you've ever had a mishap while lighting a camping stove, you know exactly what I'm talking about.

When it comes to camping, all gear is not created equal. Nothing is more important than lighting your stove easily and having it reach full heat without feeling as if you're playing with a short fuse to a miniature bomb. If your stove does not work right, your trip can turn into a disaster, regardless of how well you have planned the other elements. In addition, a bad stove will add an underlying sense of foreboding to your day. You will constantly have the inner suspicion that your darn stove is going to foul up again.

## Camping Stoves

If you are buying a camping stove, remember this one critical rule: Do not leave the store with a new stove unless you have been shown exactly how to use it.

Know what you are getting. Many stores that specialize in outdoor recreation equipment now staff experienced campers/employees who will demonstrate the use of every stove they sell. While they're at it, they'll also describe the stoves' respective strengths and weaknesses.

An innovation by Peak 1 is a two-burner butane-powered backpacking stove that allows you to boil water and heat a pot of food simultaneously. While that has long been standard for car campers using Coleman's legendary camp stove, it was previously unheard of for wilderness campers in high-elevation areas. It's a fantastic stove.

The standard Coleman car camping stove, the green one with the two burners, is a legend around the world. Electronic ignition has solved all the old lighting problems.

A stove that has developed a cult-like following is the little Sierra, which burns small twigs and pinecones, then uses a tiny battery-driven fan to develop increased heat and cooking ability. It's an excellent alternative for long-distance backpacking trips, as it solves the problem of carrying a fuel bottle, especially on expeditions for which large quantities of fuel would otherwise be needed. Some tinkering with the flame (a very hot one) is required, and they are legal and functional only in the alpine zone where dry wood is available. Also note that in years with high fire danger, the U.S. Forest Service enacts rules prohibiting open flames, and fires are also often prohibited above an elevation of 10,000 feet.

The MSR Whisperlite is an icon among backpackers. I've gone through several of them. It uses white gas in a separate fuel container so you can easily monitor fuel consumption. The one flaw is the connector links from the fuel line. After a few years of heavy use, they can develop leaks; ignite and you've got meltdown.

For heavy, long-term use, ease of cleaning the burner is the most important. If you camp often, especially with a smaller stove, the burner holes will eventually become clogged. Some stoves have a built-in cleaning needle: a quick twist of the knob and you're in business. Others require disassembly and a protracted cleaning session using special tools. If a stove is difficult to clean, you will tend to put off the tiresome chore, and your stove will sputter and pant while you watch that pot of water sitting there, staying cold.

Before making a purchase, have the

© SABRINA YOUNG

**Stoves are available in many sizes and burn a variety of fuels.**

salesperson show you how to clean the burner head. Except in the case of large, multi-burner family-style camping stoves, which rarely require cleaning, this run-through can do more to determine the long-term value of a stove than any other factor.

## Fuels for Camping Stoves

White gas and butane have long been the most popular camp fuels, but a newly developed fuel could dramatically change that.

LPG (liquid petroleum gas) comes in cartridges for easy attachment to a stove or lantern. At room temperature, LPG is delivered in a combustible gaseous form. When you shake the cartridge, the contents sound liquid; that is because the gas liquefies under pressure, which is why it is so easy to use. Large amounts of fuel can be compressed into small canisters.

The following summaries detail the benefits and drawbacks of other available fuels:

**Butane:** You don't have to worry about explosions when using stoves that burn bottled butane fuel. Butane requires no pouring, pumping, or priming, and butane stoves are the easiest to light. Just turn a knob and light—that's it. On the minus side, because it comes in bottles, you never know precisely how much fuel you have left. And when a bottle is empty, you have a potential piece of litter. (Never litter. Ever.)

The other problem with butane is that it just plain does not work well in cold weather or when there is little fuel left in the cartridge. Since you cannot predict mountain weather in spring or fall, you might wind up using more fuel than originally projected. That can be frustrating, particularly if your stove starts wheezing when there are still several days left to go. In addition, with most butane cartridges, if there is any chance of the temperature falling below freezing, you often have to sleep with the cartridge to keep it warm. Otherwise, forget about using it come morning.

**Butane/Propane:** This blend offers higher octane performance than butane alone, solving the cold temperature doldrums somewhat. However, propane burns off before butane, so there's a performance drop as the fuel level in the cartridge lowers.

**Coleman Max Performance Fuel:** This fuel offers a unique approach to solving the consistent burn challenge facing all pressurized gas cartridges: operating at temperatures at or below 0°F. Using a standard propane/butane blend for high-octane performance, Coleman gets around the drop-off in performance other cartridges experience by using a version of fuel injection. A hose inside the cartridge pulls liquid fuel into the stove, where it vaporizes—a switch from the standard approach of pulling only a gaseous form of the fuel into a stove. By drawing liquid out of the cartridge, Coleman gets around the tendency of propane to burn off first and allows each cartridge to deliver a consistent mix of propane and butane to the stove's burners throughout the cartridge's life.

**Denatured alcohol:** Though this fuel burns cleanly and quietly and is virtually explosion-proof, it generates much less heat than pressurized or liquid gas fuels.

**Kerosene:** Never buy a stove that uses kerosene for fuel. Kerosene is smelly and messy, generates low heat, needs priming, and is virtually obsolete as a camp fuel in the United States. As a test, I once tried using a kerosene stove. I could scarcely boil a pot of water. In addition, some kerosene leaked out when the stove was packed, ruining everything it touched. The smell of kerosene never did go away. Kerosene remains popular in Europe only because most campers there haven't yet heard much about white gas. When they do, they will demand it.

**Primus Tri-Blend:** This blend is made up of 20 percent propane, 70 percent butane, and 10 percent isobutane and is designed to burn with more consistent heat and efficiency than standard propane/butane mixes.

**Propane:** Now available for single-burner stoves using larger, heavier cartridges to accommodate higher pressures, propane offers the very best performance of any of the pressurized gas canister fuels.

**White gas:** White gas is the most popular camp fuel in the United States because it is inexpensive and effective—not to mention, sold at most outdoor recreation stores and many supermarkets. It burns hot, has virtually no smell, and evaporates quickly when spilled. If you are caught in wet, miserable weather and can't get a fire going, you can use white gas as an emergency fire starter; however, if you do so, use it sparingly and never on an open flame.

White gas is a popular fuel both for car campers who use the large, two-burner stoves equipped with a fuel tank and a pump and for hikers who carry a lightweight backpacking stove. On the latter, lighting can require priming with a gel called priming paste, which some people dislike. Another problem with white gas is that it can be extremely explosive.

As an example, I once almost burned my beard completely off in a mini-explosion while lighting one of the larger stoves designed for car camping. I was in the middle of cooking dinner when the flame suddenly shut down. Sure enough, the fuel tank was empty, and after refilling it, I pumped the tank 50 or 60 times to regain pressure. When I lit a match, the sucker ignited from three feet away. The resulting explosion was like a stick of dynamite going off, and immediately the smell of burning beard was in the air. In a flash, my once thick, dark beard had been reduced to a mass of little, yellow, burned curlicues.

My error? After filling the tank, I forgot to shut the fuel cock off while pumping up the pressure in the tank. As a result, the stove burners were slowly emitting the gas/air mixture as I pumped the tank, filling the air above the stove. Then, strike a match from even a few feet away and ka-boom!

## Building Fires

One summer expedition took me to the Canadian wilderness in British Columbia for a 75-mile canoe trip on the Bowron Lake Circuit, a chain of 13 lakes, six rivers, and seven portages. It is one of the greatest canoe trips in the world, a loop that ends just a few hundred feet from its starting point. But at the first camp at Kibbee Lake, my stove developed a fuel leak

---

# KEEP IT WILD TIP 4: CAMPFIRES

1. Fire use can scar the backcountry. If a fire ring is not available, use a lightweight stove for cooking.
2. Where fires are permitted, use existing fire rings away from large rocks or overhangs.
3. Don't char rocks by building new rings.
4. Gather sticks from the ground that are no larger than the diameter of your wrist.
5. Don't snap branches of live, dead, or downed trees, which can cause personal injury and also scar the natural setting.
6. Put the fire "dead out" and make sure it's cold before departing. Remove all trash from the fire ring and sprinkle dirt over the site.
7. Remember that some forest fires can be started by a campfire that appears to be out. Hot embers burning deep in the pit can cause tree roots to catch fire and burn underground. If you ever see smoke rising from the ground, seemingly from nowhere, dig down and put the fire out.

---

at the base of the burner, and the nuclear-like blast that followed just about turned Canada into a giant crater.

As a result, we had to complete the final 70 miles of the trip without a stove, cooking instead on open fires each night. The problem was compounded by the weather. It rained eight of the 10 days. Rain? In Canada, raindrops the size of silver dollars fall so hard they actually bounce on the lake surface. We had to stop paddling a few times to empty the rainwater out of the canoe. At the end of the day, we'd make camp and then face the critical decision: either make a fire or go to bed cold and hungry.

Equipped with an ax, at least we had a chance for success. Although the downed wood was soaked, I was able to make my own fire-starting tinder from the chips of split logs; no matter how hard it rains, the inside of a log is always dry.

In miserable weather, matches don't stay lit long enough to get tinder started. Instead, we used either a candle or the little waxlike fire-starter cubes that remain lit for several minutes. From those, we could get the tinder going. Then we added small, slender strips of wood that had been axed from the interior of the logs. When the flame reached a foot high, we added the logs, their dry interior facing in. By the time the inside of the logs had caught

fire, the outside was drying from the heat. It wasn't long before a royal blaze was brightening the rainy night.

That's a worst-case scenario, and I hope you will never face anything like it. Nevertheless, being able to build a good fire and cook on it can be one of the more satisfying elements of a camping trip. At times, just looking into the flames can provide a special satisfaction at the end of a good day.

However, never expect to build a fire for every meal or, in some cases, even to build one at all. Many state and federal campgrounds have been picked clean of downed wood. During the fire season, the danger of forest fires can force rangers to prohibit fires altogether. In either case, you must use your camp stove or go hungry.

But when you can build a fire and the resources for doing so are available, it will enhance the quality of your camping experience. Of the campgrounds listed in this book, those where you are permitted to build fires will usually have fire rings. In primitive areas where you can make your own fire, you should dig a ring eight inches deep, line the edges with rock, and clear all the needles and twigs in a five-foot radius. The next day, when the fire is dead, you can scatter the rocks, fill over the black charcoal with dirt, and then spread pine needles and twigs over it. Nobody will even know you camped there. That's the best way I know to keep a secret spot a real secret.

When you start to build a campfire, the first thing you will notice is that no matter how good your intentions, your fellow campers will not be able to resist moving the wood around. Watch. You'll be getting ready to add a key piece of wood at just the right spot, and your companion will stick his mitts in, confidently believing he has a better idea. He'll shift the fire around and undermine your best-thought-out plans.

So I enforce a rule on camping trips: One person makes the fire while everybody else stands clear or is involved with other camp tasks, such as gathering wood, getting water, putting up tents, or planning dinner. Once the fire is going strong, then it's fair game; anyone adds logs at his or her discretion. But in the early, delicate stages of the campfire, it's best to leave the work to one person.

Before a match is ever struck, you should gather a complete pile of firewood. Then, start small, with the tiniest twigs you can find, and slowly add larger twigs as you go, crisscrossing them like a miniature tepee. Eventually, you will get to the big chunks that produce high heat. The key is to get one piece of wood burning into another, which then burns into another, setting off what I call the chain of flame. Conversely, single pieces of wood set apart from each other will not burn.

On a dry summer evening at a campsite where plenty of wood is available, about the only way you can blow the deal is to get impatient and try to add the big pieces too quickly. Do that and you'll get smoke, not flames, and it won't be long before every one of your fellow campers is poking at your fire. It will drive you crazy, but they just won't be able to help it.

## Cooking Gear

I like traveling light, and I've found that all I need for cooking is a pot, small frying pan, metal pot grabber, fork, knife, cup, and matches. If you want to keep the price of food low and also cook customized dinners each night,

a small pressure cooker can be just the ticket. (See *Keeping the Price Down* in this chapter.) I store all my gear in one small bag that fits into my pack. If I'm camping out of my four-wheel-drive rig, I can easily keep track of the little bag of cooking gear. Going simple, not complicated, is the key to keeping a camping trip on the right track.

You can get more elaborate by buying complete kits with plates, a coffeepot, large pots, and other cookware, but what really counts is having a single pot that makes you happy. It needs to be just the right size, not too big or small, and stable enough so it won't tip over, even if it is at a slight angle on a fire, filled with water at a full boil. Mine is just six inches wide and 4.5 inches deep. It holds better than a quart of water and has served me well for several hundred camp dinners.

The rest of your cook kit is easy to complete. The frying pan should be small, light-gauge aluminum, and Teflon-coated, with a fold-in handle so it's no hassle to store. A pot grabber is a great addition. This little aluminum gadget clamps to the edge of pots and allows you to lift them and pour water with total control and without burning your fingers. For cleanup, take along a plastic scrubber and a small bottle filled with dish soap, and you're in business.

A sierra cup, a wide aluminum cup with a wire handle, is an ideal item to carry because you can eat out of it as well as use it for drinking. This means no plates to scrub after dinner, so washing up is quick and easy. In addition, if you go for a hike, you can clip its handle to your belt. Some people bring a giant cup called a "Fair Share." In expeditions where food has to be rationed, they manage to get a lot more than their "fair share" because a cup of food looks so small in these giant vessels.

If you opt for a more formal setup, complete with plates, glasses, silverware, and the like, you can end up spending more time preparing and cleaning up after meals than enjoying the country you are exploring. In addition, the more equipment you bring, the more loose ends you will have to deal with, and loose ends can cause plenty of frustration. If you have a choice, go simple.

Remember what Thoreau said: "A man is rich in proportion to what he can do without."

## Food and Cooking Tricks

On a trip to the Bob Marshall Wilderness in western Montana, I woke up one morning, yawned, and said, "What've we got for breakfast?"

The silence was ominous. "Well," finally came the response, "we don't have any food left."

"What!?"

"Well, I figured we'd catch trout for meals every other night."

On the return trip, we ended up eating wild berries, buds, and, yes, even roots (not too tasty). When we finally landed the next day at a suburban pizza parlor, we nearly ate the wooden tables.

Running out of food on a camping trip can do more to turn reasonable people into violent grumps than any other event. There's no excuse for it, not when figuring meals can be done precisely and with little effort. You should not go out and buy a bunch of food, throw it in your rig, and head off for yonder. That leaves too much to chance. And if you've ever been really hungry in the woods, you know it's worth a little effort to guard against a day or two of starvation. Here's a three-step solution:

1. Draw up a general meal-by-meal plan and make sure your companions like what's on it.

2. Tell your companions to buy any specialty items (such as a special brand of coffee) on their own and not to expect you to take care of everything.

3. Put all the food on your living room floor and literally plan out every day of your trip, meal by meal, putting the food in plastic bags as you go. That way, you will know exact food quotas and you won't go hungry.

Fish for your dinner? There's one guarantee as far as that goes: If you expect to catch fish for meals, you will most certainly get skunked. If you don't expect to catch fish for meals, you will probably catch so many they'll be coming out of your ears. I've seen it a hundred times.

## Keeping the Price Down

"There must be some mistake," I said with a laugh. "Whoever paid $750 for camp food?"

But the amount was as clear as the digital numbers on the cash register: $753.27.

"How is this possible?" I asked the clerk.

"Just add it up," she responded, irritated.

Then I started figuring. The freeze-dried backpack dinners cost $6 apiece. A small pack of beef jerky went for $2, the beef sticks for $0.75, granola bars for $0.50. Multiply it all by four hungry men, including Foonsky.

The dinners alone cost close to $500. Add in the usual goodies—candy, coffee, dried fruit, granola bars, jerky, oatmeal, soup, and Tang—and I felt as if an earthquake had struck when I saw the tab.

A lot of campers have received similar shocks. In preparation for their trips, campers shop with enthusiasm. Then they pay the bill in horror.

Well, there are solutions, lots of them. You can eat gourmet-style in the outback without having your wallet cleaned out. But it requires do-it-yourself cooking, more planning, and careful shopping. It also means transcending the push-button, I-want-it-now attitude that so many people can't leave behind when they go to the mountains.

Now when Foonsky, Mr. Furnai, Rambob, and I sit down to eat such a meal, we don't call it "eating." We call it "hodgepacking" or "time to pack your hodge." After a particularly long day on the trail, you can do some serious hodgepacking.

If your trip is a shorter one, say for a weekend, consider bringing more fresh food to add some sizzle to the hodge. You can design a hot soup/stew mix that is good enough to eat at home.

Start by bringing a pot of water to a full boil, and then add pasta, ramen noodles, or macaroni. While it simmers, cut in a potato, carrot, onion, and garlic clove, and

## HOW TO MAKE BEEF JERKY IN YOUR OWN KITCHEN

Start with a couple of pieces of meat: lean top round, sirloin, or tri-tip. Cut them into 3/16-inch strips across the grain, trimming out the membrane, gristle, and fat. Marinate the strips for 24 hours in a glass dish. The fun begins in picking a marinade. Try two-thirds teriyaki sauce, one-third Worcester-shire sauce. You can customize the recipe by adding pepper, ground mustard, bay leaf, red wine vinegar, garlic, and, for the brave, Tabasco sauce.

After a day or so, squeeze out each strip of meat with a rolling pin, lay them in rows on a cooling rack over a cookie sheet, and dry them in the oven at 125°F for 12 hours. Thicker pieces can take as long as 18-24 hours.

That's it. The hardest part is cleaning the cookie sheet when you're done. The easiest part is eating your own homemade jerky while sitting at a lookout on a mountain ridge. The do-it-yourself method for jerky may take a day or so, but it is cheaper and can taste better than any store-bought jerky.

*—my thanks to Jeff Patty for this recipe*

cook for about 10 minutes. When the vegetables have softened, add in a soup mix or two, maybe some cheese, and you are just about in business. But you can still ruin it and turn your hodge into slodge. Make sure you read the directions on the soup mix to determine cooking time. It can vary widely. In addition, make sure you stir the whole thing up; otherwise, you will get those hidden dry clumps of soup mix that taste like garlic sawdust.

How do I know? Well, it was up near Kearsarge Pass in the Sierra Nevada, where, feeling half-starved, I dug into our nightly hodge. I will never forget that first bite—I damn near gagged to death. Foonsky laughed at me, until he took his first bite (a nice big one) and then turned green.

Another way to trim food costs is to make your own beef jerky, the trademark staple of campers for more than 200 years. A tiny packet of beef jerky costs $2, and for that 250-mile expedition, I spent $150 on jerky alone. Never again. Now we make our own and get big strips of jerky that taste better than anything you can buy.

For a crew of four, you can get by with two freeze-dried dinners that you cook right in the container pouch. Liam Furniss discovered that by adding a separate bonus pack of garlic-seasoned mashed potatoes, which cook in 90 seconds; everybody has plenty of food. That goes even for his dad Mo, with his gigantic, crater-of-the-moon "Fair Share" cup.

You can supplement your eats with sweets, nuts, freeze-dried fruits, and drink mixes. In any case, make sure you keep the dinner menu varied. If you and your buddies look into your dinner cups and groan, "Ugh, not this again," you will soon start dreaming of cheeseburgers and french fries instead of hiking, fishing, and finding beautiful campsites.

If you are car camping and have a big ice chest, you can bring virtually anything to eat and drink. If you are on the trail and don't mind paying the price, the newest freeze-dried dinners provide another option.

Some of the biggest advances in the outdoors industry have come in the form of freeze-dried dinners. Some of them are almost good enough to serve in restaurants. Sweet-and-sour pork over rice, tostadas, Burgundy chicken—it sure beats the poopy goop we used to eat, like the old soupy chili-mac dinners that tasted bad and looked so unlike food that consumption was nearly impossible, even for my dog, Rebel. Foonsky usually managed to get it down, but just barely.

To provide an idea of how to plan a menu, consider what my companions and I ate while hiking 250 miles on California's John Muir Trail:

**Breakfast:** instant soup, oatmeal (never get plain), one beef or jerky stick, coffee or hot chocolate.

**Lunch:** one beef stick, two jerky sticks, one granola bar, dried fruit, half cup of pistachio nuts, Tang, one small bag of M&Ms.

**Dinner:** instant soup, one freeze-dried dinner (split between two people), one milk bar, rainbow trout.

What was that last item? Rainbow trout? Right! Unless you plan on it, you can catch them every night.

## Trout Dinner

If all this still doesn't sound like your idea of a gourmet but low-cost camping meal, well, you are forgetting the main course: rainbow trout. Remember: If you don't plan on catching them for dinner, you'll probably land more than you can finish in one night's hodgepacking.

Some campers go to great difficulties to cook their trout, bringing along frying pans, butter, grills, tinfoil, and more, but all you need is some seasoned salt and a campfire.

Rinse the gutted trout, and while it's still wet, sprinkle on a good dose of seasoned salt, both inside and out. Clear any burning logs to the side of the campfire, then lay the trout right on the coals, turning it once so both sides are cooked. Sound ridiculous? Sound like you are throwing the fish away? Sound like the fish will burn up? Sound like you will have to eat the campfire ash? Wrong on all counts. The fish cooks perfectly, the ash doesn't stick, and after cooking trout this way, you may never fry again.

If you can't convince your buddies, who may insist that trout should be fried, then make sure you have butter to fry it in, not oil. Also make sure you cook them all the way through, so the meat strips off the backbone in two nice, clean fillets. The fish should end up looking like one that Sylvester the Cat just drew out of his mouth—only the head, tail, and a perfect skeleton.

# FIRST AID AND INSECT PROTECTION

Mountain nights don't get any more perfect, I thought as I lay in my sleeping bag.

The sky looked like a mass of jewels and the air tasted sweet and smelled of pines. A shooting star fireballed across the sky, and I remember thinking, "It just doesn't get any better."

Just then, as I was drifting into sleep, a mysterious buzz appeared from nowhere and deposited itself inside my left ear. Suddenly awake, I whacked my ear with the palm of my hand, hard enough to cause a minor concussion. The buzz disappeared. I pulled out my flashlight and shined it on my palm, and there, lit in the blackness of night, lay the squished intruder: a mosquito, dead amid a stain of blood.

Satisfied, I turned off the light, closed my eyes, and thought of the fishing trip planned for the next day. Then I heard them. It was a squadron of mosquitoes making landing patterns around my head. I tried to grab them with an open hand, but they dodged the assault and flew off. Just 30 seconds later, another landed in my left ear. I promptly dispatched the invader with a rip of the palm.

Now I was completely awake, so I got out of my sleeping bag to retrieve some mosquito repellent. But en route, several of the buggers swarmed and nailed me in the back and arms. After I applied the repellent and settled snugly again in my sleeping bag, the mosquitoes would buzz a few inches from my ear. After getting a whiff of the poison, they would fly off. It was like sleeping in a sawmill.

The next day, drowsy from little sleep, I set out to fish. I'd walked but 15 minutes when I brushed against a bush and felt a stinging sensation on the inside of my arm, just above the wrist. I looked down: A tick had his clamps in me. I ripped it out before he could embed his head into my skin.

After catching a few fish, I sat down against a tree to eat lunch and just watch the water go by. My dog, Rebel, sat down next to me and stared at the beef jerky I was munching as if it were a T-bone steak. I finished eating, gave him a small piece, patted him on the head, and said, "Good dog." Right then, I noticed an itch on my arm where a mosquito had drilled me. I unconsciously scratched it. Two days later, in that exact spot, some nasty red splotches started popping up. Poison oak. By petting my dog and then scratching my arm, I had transferred the oil residue of the poison oak leaves from Rebel's fur to my arm.

When I returned home, Foonsky asked me about the trip.

"Great," I said. "Mosquitoes, ticks, poison oak. Can hardly wait to go back."

"Sorry I missed out," he answered.

## Mosquitoes, No-See-Ums, and Horseflies

On a trip to Canada, Foonsky and I were fishing a small lake from the shore when suddenly a black horde of mosquitoes could be seen moving across the lake toward us. It was like when the French army looked across the Rhine and saw the Wehrmacht coming. There was a buzz in the air. We fought them off for a few minutes, then made a fast retreat to the truck and jumped in, content the buggers had been foiled. But in some way still unknown to us, the mosquitoes gained entry to the truck. In 10 minutes, we squished 15 of them as they attempted to plant their oil drills into our skins. Just outside the truck, the black horde waited for us to make a tactical error, such as rolling down a window. It finally took a miraculous hailstorm to squelch the attack.

When it comes to mosquitoes, no-see-ums, gnats, and horseflies, there are times when there is nothing you can do. However, in most situations, you can muster a defense to repel the attack.

When under heavy attack by mosquitoes, the first key is to wear clothing too heavy for them to drill through. Expose a minimum of skin, wear a hat, and tie a bandanna around your neck, preferably one that has been sprayed with repellent. If you try to get by with just

a thin cotton T-shirt and nylon shorts, you will be declared a federal mosquito sanctuary.

So, first, your skin must be well covered, with only your hands and face exposed. Second, you should have your companion spray your clothes with repellent. (I prefer Deep Woods Off!) Third, you should dab liquid repellent directly on your skin.

At night, the easiest way to get a good sleep without mosquitoes buzzing in your ear is to sleep in a bug-proof tent. If the nights are warm and you want to see the stars, new tent models are available that have a skylight covered with mosquito netting. If you don't like tents on summer evenings, mosquito netting rigged with an air space at your head can solve the problem. Otherwise, prepare to get bitten, even with the use of mosquito repellent.

A newer option is a battery-powered, clip-on mosquito repellent made by Off! that is also portable. It includes a canister that lasts 12 hours and a small fan, so you can set right next to you. That's right, you don't spray it on.

If your problems are with no-see-ums or biting horseflies, then you need a slightly different approach. No-see-ums are tiny black insects that look like nothing more than a sliver of dirt on your skin. Then you notice something stinging, and when you rub the area, you scratch up a little no-see-um. The results are similar to mosquito bites, making your skin itch, splotch, and, when you get them bad, swell. In addition to using the techniques described to repel mosquitoes, you should go one step further.

The problem is that no-see-ums are tricky little devils. Somehow, they can actually get under your socks and around your ankles, where they will bite to their hearts' content all night long while you sleep, itch, sleep, and itch some more. The best solution is to apply a liquid repellent to your ankles, then wear clean socks.

Horseflies are another story. They are rarely a problem, but when they get their dander up, they can cause trouble you'll never forget.

## KEEP IT WILD TIP 5: SANITATION

If no refuse facility is available:

1. Deposit human waste in "cat holes" dug 6-8 inches deep. Cover and disguise the cat hole when finished.
2. Deposit human waste at least 75 paces (200 feet) from any water source or camp.
3. Use toilet paper sparingly. When finished, carefully burn it in the cat hole, then bury it.
4. If no appropriate burial locations are available, such as in popular wilderness camps above tree line in granite settings, then all human refuse should be double-bagged and packed out.
5. At boat-in campsites, chemical toilets are required. Chemical toilets can also solve the problem of larger groups camping for long stays at one location where no facilities are available.
6. To wash dishes or your body, carry water away from the source and use small amounts of biodegradable soap. Scatter dishwater after all food particles have been removed.
7. Scour your campsites for even the tiniest piece of trash and any other evidence of your stay. Pack out all the trash you can, even if it's not yours. Finding cigarette butts, for instance, provides special irritation for most campers. Pick them up and discard them properly.
8. Never litter. Never. Or you become the enemy of all others.

Always wear sunglasses when you hike. If you enter an area with flies, the moisture from your eyes will attract them. The sunglasses will keep them from getting in your eyes.

On one trip, Foonsky and I were paddling a canoe along the shoreline of a Lake Quesnel in British Columbia. This giant horsefly, about the size of a fingertip, started dive-bombing the canoe. After 20 minutes, it landed on Foonsky's thigh. He immediately slammed it with an open hand, then let out a blood-curdling "Yeeeee-ow!" that practically sent ripples across the lake. When Foonsky whacked it, the horsefly had somehow turned around and bit him on the hand, leaving a huge red welt.

In the next 10 minutes, that big fly strafed the canoe on more dive-bomb runs. I finally got my canoe paddle, swung it as if it were a baseball bat, and nailed that horsefly as if I'd hit a home run. It landed about 15 feet from the boat, still alive and buzzing in the water. While I was trying to figure what it would take to kill this bugger, a large rainbow trout surfaced and snatched it out of the water, finally avenging the assault.

If you have horsefly or yellow jacket problems, you'd best just leave the area. One, two,

or a few can be dealt with. More than that and your fun camping trip will be about as fun as being roped to a tree and stung by an electric shock rod.

On most trips, you will spend time doing everything possible to keep from getting bitten by mosquitoes or no-see-ums. When your attempts fail, you must know what to do next, and fast, especially if you are among those ill-fated campers who get big, red lumps from a bite inflicted from even a microscopic mosquito.

A fluid called After Bite or a dab of ammonia should be applied immediately to the bite. To start the healing process, apply a first-aid gel (not a liquid), such as the one made by Campho-Phenique.

### DEET

What is DEET? You're not likely to find the word DEET on any repellent label. That's because DEET stands for N,N diethyl-m-toluamide. If the label contains this scientific name, the repellent contains DEET. Despite fears of DEET-associated health risks and the increased attention given natural alternatives, DEET-based repellents are still acknowledged as by far the best option when serious insect protection is required.

On one trip, I had a small bottle of mosquito repellent in the same pocket as a Swiss army knife. Guess what happened? The mosquito repellent leaked a bit and literally melted the insignia right off the knife. DEET will also melt synthetic clothes. That is why, in bad mosquito country, I'll expose a minimum of skin, just hands and face (with full beard), apply the repellent only to my cheeks and the back of my hands, and perhaps wear a bandanna sprinkled with a few drops as well. That does the trick, with a minimum of exposure to the repellent.

### "Natural" Repellents

Are natural alternatives a safer choice than DEET? Some are potentially hazardous if ingested, and most are downright painful if they find their way into the eyes or onto mucus membranes. For example, pennyroyal is perhaps the most toxic of the essential oils used to repel insects and can be deadly if taken internally. Other oils used include cedarwood, citronella, and perhaps the most common, eucalyptus and peppermint.

How effective are natural repellents? The average effective repelling time of a citronella product appears to range from 1.5-2 hours, so it must be reapplied to be effective.

What other chemical alternatives are there? Another line of defense against insects is the chemical permethrin, used on clothing, not on skin. Permethrin-based products are designed to repel and kill arthropods or crawling insects, making them a preferred repellent for ticks. The currently available products remain effective—repelling and killing chiggers, mosquitoes, and ticks—for two weeks and through two launderings.

## Ticks

Ticks are nasty little vermin that will wait in ambush, jump on unsuspecting prey, and then crawl to a prime location before filling their bodies with their victim's blood.

I call them Dracula bugs, but by any name they can be a terrible camp pest. Ticks rest on grass and low plants and attach themselves to those who brush against the vegetation (dogs are particularly vulnerable). Typically, they can be found no more than 18 inches above ground, and if you stay on the trails, you can usually avoid them.

There are two common species of ticks. The common coastal tick is larger, brownish in color, and prefers to crawl around before putting its clamps on you. The feel of any bug crawling on your skin can be creepy, but consider it a forewarning of assault; you can just pick the tick off and dispatch it. The coastal tick's preferred destination is usually the back of your neck, just where the hairline starts. The other species, the wood tick, is small and black, and when he puts his clamps in, it's immediately painful. When a wood tick gets into a dog for a few days, it can cause a large red welt. In either case, ticks should be removed as soon as possible.

If you have hiked in areas infested with ticks, it is advisable to shower as soon as possible, washing your clothes immediately. If you just leave your clothes in a heap, a tick can crawl out and invade your home. They like warmth, and one way or another, they can end up in your bed. Waking up in the middle of the night with a tick crawling across your chest can be unsettling, to put it mildly.

Once a tick has its clampers in your skin, you must determine how long it has been there. If it has been a short time, the most painless and effective method for removal is to take a pair of sharp tweezers and grasp the little devil, making certain to isolate the mouth area, then pull him out. Reader Johvin Perry sent in the suggestion to coat the tick with Vaseline, which will cut off its oxygen supply, after which it may voluntarily give up the hunt.

If the tick has been in longer, you may wish to have a doctor extract it. Some people will burn a tick with a cigarette or poison it with lighter fluid, but neither is advisable. No matter how you do it, you must take care to remove all of the tick, especially its clawlike mouth.

The wound, however small, should then be cleansed and dressed. First, apply liquid peroxide, which cleans and sterilizes, and then apply a dressing coated with a first-aid gel, such as First-Aid Cream, Campho-Phenique, or Neosporin.

Lyme disease, which can be transmitted by the bite of a deer tick, is rare but common enough to warrant some attention. To prevent tick bites, some people tuck their pant legs into their hiking socks and spray tick repellent, called Permamone, on their pants.

The first symptom of Lyme disease is a bright red, splotchy rash that develops around the bite area. Other possible early symptoms include headache, nausea, fever, and/or a stiff neck. If any of these happen, or if you have any doubts, you should see your doctor immediately. If you do get Lyme disease, don't panic. Doctors say it is easily treated in the early stages with simple antibiotics. If you are nervous about getting Lyme disease, carry a small plastic bag with you when you hike. If a tick manages to get his clampers into you, put the tick in the plastic bag after you pull it out. Then give it to your doctor for analysis to see if the tick is a carrier of the disease.

During the course of my hiking and camping career, I have removed ticks from my skin hundreds of times without any problems. However, if you are worried about ticks, you can buy a tick removal kit from any outdoors store. These kits allow you to remove ticks in such a way that their toxins are guaranteed not to enter your bloodstream.

If you are particularly wary of ticks or perhaps even have nightmares of them, wear long pants that are tucked into your socks, as well as a long-sleeved shirt tucked securely into your pants and held with a belt. Clothing should be light in color, making it easier to see ticks, and tightly woven so ticks have trouble hanging on. On one hike with my mom, Eleanor, I brushed more than 100 ticks off my blue jeans in less than an hour, while she did not pick up a single one on her polyester pants.

Perform tick checks regularly, especially on the back of the neck. The combination of DEET insect repellents applied to the skin and permethrin repellents applied directly to clothing is considered to be the most effective line of defense against ticks.

## Poison Oak

After a nice afternoon hike, about a five-miler, I was concerned about possible exposure to poison oak, so I immediately showered and put on clean clothes. Then I settled into a chair with my favorite foamy elixir to watch the end of a baseball game. But the game went on for hours, 18 innings; meanwhile, my dog, tired from the hike, went to sleep on my bare ankles.

A few days later, I had a case of poison oak. My feet looked as though they had been on fire and put out with an ice pick. The lesson? Don't always trust your dog, give him a bath as well, and beware of extra-inning ball games.

You can get poison oak only from direct contact with the oil residue from the plant's leaves. It can be passed in a variety of ways, as direct as skin-to-leaf contact or as indirect as leaf to dog, dog to sofa, sofa to skin. Once you have it, there is little you can do but feel horribly itchy. Applying Caladryl lotion or its equivalent can help because it contains antihistamines, which attack and dry the itch.

My pal Furniss offers a tip that may sound crazy but seems to work. You should expose the afflicted area to the hottest water you can stand, then suddenly immerse it in cold water. The hot water opens the skin pores and gets the "itch" out, and the cold water then quickly seals the pores.

In any case, you're a lot better off if you don't get poison oak to begin with. Remember that poison oak can disguise itself. In the spring, it is green; then it gradually turns reddish in the summer. By fall, it becomes a bloody, ugly-looking red. In the winter, it loses its leaves altogether and appears to be nothing more than the barren, brown sticks of a small plant. However, at any time and in any form, its contact with skin can quickly lead to infection.

Some people are more easily afflicted than others, but if you are one of the lucky few who aren't, don't cheer too loudly. While some people can be exposed to the oil residue of poison oak with little or no effect, the body's resistance can gradually be worn down with repeated exposure. At one time, I could practically play in the stuff and the only symptom would be a few little bumps on the inside of my wrist. Now, more than 15 years later, my resistance has broken down. If I merely brush against poison oak now, in a few days the exposed area can look as if it were used for a track meet.

So regardless of whether you consider yourself vulnerable or not, you should take heed to reduce your exposure. That can be done by staying on trails when you hike and making sure your dog does the same. Remember, the worst stands of poison oak are usually brush-infested areas just off the trail. Also protect yourself by dressing so your skin is completely covered, wearing long-sleeved shirts, long pants, and boots. If you suspect you've been exposed, immediately wash your clothes and then wash yourself with aloe vera, rinsing with a cool shower.

And don't forget to give your dog a bath as well.

## Sunburn

The most common injury suffered on camping trips is sunburn, yet some people wear it as a badge of honor, believing that it somehow enhances their virility. Well, it doesn't. Neither do suntans. Too much sun can lead to serious burns or sunstroke.

Both are easy enough to avoid. Use a high-level sunscreen on your skin, apply lip balm, and wear sunglasses and a hat. If any area gets burned, apply first-aid cream, which will soothe and provide moisture to the parched skin.

The best advice is not to get even a suntan. Those who tan are involved in a practice that can eventually ruin their skin and possibly lead to cancer.

## Giardia and Cryptosporidium

You have just hiked in to your backwoods spot, you're thirsty and a bit tired, but you smile as you consider the prospects. Everything seems perfect—there's not a stranger in sight, and you have nothing to do but relax with your pals.

You toss down your gear, grab your cup, dip it into the stream, and take a long drink of that ice-cold mountain water. It seems crystal pure and sweeter than anything you've ever tasted. It's not till later that you find out it can be just like drinking a cup of poison.

Whether you camp in the wilderness or not, if you hike, you're going to get thirsty. And if your canteen runs dry, you'll start eyeing any water source. Stop! Do not pass Go. Do not drink.

By drinking what appears to be pure mountain water without first treating it, you can ingest a microscopic protozoan called *Giardia lamblia*. The ensuing abdominal cramps can make you feel like your stomach and intestinal tract are in a knot, ready to explode. With that comes long-term diarrhea that is worse than even a bear could imagine.

Doctors call the disease giardiasis, or giardia for short, but it is difficult to diagnose. One friend of mine who contracted giardia was told he might have stomach cancer before the proper diagnosis was made.

Drinking directly from a stream or lake does not mean you will get giardia, but you are taking a giant chance. There is no reason to assume such a risk, potentially ruining your trip and enduring weeks of misery.

A lot of people are taking that risk. I made a personal survey of campers in the Yosemite National Park wilderness, and found that roughly only one in 10 was equipped with some kind of water-purification system. The result, according to the Public Health Service, is that an average of 4 percent of all backpackers and campers suffer giardiasis. According to the Parasitic Diseases Division of the Center for Infectious Diseases, the rates range from 1 percent to 20 percent across the country.

But if you get giardia, you are not going to care about the statistics. "When I got giardia, I just about wanted to die," said Henry McCarthy, a California camper. "For about 10 days, it was the most terrible thing I have ever experienced. And through the whole thing, I kept thinking? I shouldn't have drunk that water, but it seemed all right at the time.'"

That is the mistake most campers make. The stream might be running free, gurgling over boulders in the high country, tumbling into deep, oxygenated pools. It looks pure. Then in a few days, the problems suddenly start. Drinking untreated water from mountain streams is a lot like playing Russian roulette. Sooner or later the gun goes off.

## SteriPEN

We would never do another wilderness trip without one and I keep mine with me all the time. By using UV light, the SteriPEN destroy viruses, bacteria and protozoa (like Giardia) that can make you sick. Dip your water bottle in a cold stream, purify the water with the UV light in under two minutes, and drink all the cold, clean mountain water you can. It's like having a cooler full of ice-cold water with you all the time. On expeditions of more than four days, make sure you bring extra batteries.

### FILTERS

Handheld filters are getting more compact, lighter, easier to use, and often less expensive. Having to boil water or endure chemicals that leave a bad taste in the mouth has been all but eliminated.

With a filter, you just pump and drink. Filtering strains out microscopic contaminants, rendering the water clear and somewhat pure. How pure? That depends on the size of the filter's pores—what manufacturers call pore-size efficiency. A filter with a pore-size efficiency

of one micron or smaller will remove protozoa, such as *Giardia lamblia* and cryptosporidium, as well as parasitic eggs and larva, but it takes a pore-size efficiency of less than 0.4 micron to remove bacteria. All but one of the filters recommended here do that.

A good backcountry water filter weighs less than 20 ounces, is easy to grasp, simple to use, and a snap to clean and maintain. At the very least, buy one that will remove protozoa and bacteria. (A number of cheap, pocket-sized filters remove only *Giardia lamblia* and cryptosporidium. That, in my book, is risking your health to save money.) Consider the flow rate, too: A liter per minute is good.

All filters will eventually clog—it's a sign that they've been doing their job. If you force water through a filter that's becoming difficult to pump, you risk injecting a load of microbial nasties into your bottle. Some models can be back-washed, brushed, or, as with ceramic elements, scrubbed to extend their useful lives. And if the filter has a pre-filter to screen out the big stuff, use it: It will give your filter a boost in mileage, which can then top out at about 100 gallons per disposable element. Any of the filters reviewed here will serve well on an outing into the wilds, providing you always play by the manufacturer's rules.

**First Need Deluxe:** The filter pumps smoothly and puts out more than a liter per minute. The 15-ounce First Need Deluxe from General Ecology does something no other handheld filter will do: It removes protozoa, bacteria, and viruses without using chemicals. Such effectiveness is the result of a fancy three-stage matrix system. The First Need has been around since 1982. Additional cartridges mean you just replace the cartridge, not the entire unit. If you drop the filter and unknowingly crack the cartridge, all the little nasties can get through. A small point worth noting.

**Basic Designs Ceramic:** It clogs quickly and therefore is not a good choice for long trips. The Basic Designs Ceramic Filter Pump weighs eight ounces and is as stripped-down a filter as you'll find. The pump is simple, easy to use, and quite reliable. The ceramic filter effectively removes protozoa and bacteria, making it ideal and cost effective for backpacking—but it won't protect against viruses. Also, the filter element is too bulbous to work directly from a shallow water source; as with the PentaPure, you'll have to decontaminate a pot, cup, or bottle to transfer your unfiltered water.

**Katadyn Hiker Pro:** The Katadyn effectively removes protozoa and bacteria. I found it challenging to put any kind of power behind the pump's tiny handle, and the filtered water comes through at a paltry half-liter per minute. It also requires more cleaning than most filters—though the good news is that the element is made of long-lasting ceramic.

**MSR MiniWorks:** The 14-ounce MiniWorks looks similar to the more expensive WaterWorks, and, like the WaterWorks, is fully field-maintainable, while guarding against protozoa, bacteria, and chemicals. It attaches directly to a standard one-quart Nalgene water bottle. Takes about 90 seconds to filter that quart.

**MSR WaterWorks II Ceramic:** At 17.4 ounces, the WaterWorks II isn't light. You get a better flow rate (90 seconds per liter), an easy pumping action, and—like the original Mini Filter—a long-lasting ceramic cartridge. This filter is a good match for the person who encounters a lot of dirty water—its three-stage filter weeds out protozoa, bacteria, and chemicals. The MSR can be completely disassembled in the field for troubleshooting and cleaning.

**SweetWater WalkAbout:** The WalkAbout is perfect for the day hiker or backpacker who obsesses on lightening the load. The filter weighs just 8.5 ounces, is easily cleaned in the field, and removes both protozoa and bacteria: a genuine bargain. There are some trade-offs, however, for its diminutiveness. Water delivery is a tad slow at just under a liter per minute, but filter cartridges are now good for up to 100 gallons.

The big drawback with filters is that if you pump water from a mucky lake, the filter can clog in a few days. Therein lies the weakness.

Once plugged up, it is useless, and you have to replace it or take your chances. One trick to extend the filter life is to fill your cook pot with water, let the sediment settle, then pump from there. As an insurance policy, always have a spare filter canister on hand.

## BOILING WATER

Except for water filtration, this is the only treatment that you can use with complete confidence. According to the federal Parasitic Diseases Division, it takes a few minutes at a rolling boil to be certain you've killed *Giardia lamblia*. At high elevations, boil for 3-5 minutes. A side benefit is that you'll also kill other dangerous bacteria that live undetected in natural waters.

But to be honest, boiling water is a thorn for most people on backcountry trips. For one thing, if you boil water on an open fire, what should taste like crystal-pure mountain water tastes instead like a mouthful of warm ashes. If you don't have a campfire, it wastes stove fuel. And if you are thirsty *now,* forget it. The water takes hours to cool.

The only time boiling always makes sense, however, is when you are preparing dinner. The ash taste will disappear in whatever freeze-dried dinner, soup, or hot drink you make.

## WATER-PURIFICATION PILLS

I bring water-purification pills for back-up use only. They are cheap and, in addition, they kill most of the bacteria, regardless of whether you use iodine crystals or potable aqua iodine tablets. The problem is they just don't always kill *Giardia lamblia,* and that is the one critter worth worrying about on your trip. That makes water-treatment pills unreliable and dangerous.

Another key element is the time factor. Depending on the water's temperature, organic content, and pH level, these pills can take a long time to do the job. A minimum wait of 20 minutes is advised. Most people don't like waiting that long, especially when they're hot and thirsty after a hike and thinking, "What the heck, the water looks fine."

And then there is the taste. On one trip, my water filter clogged and we had to use the iodine pills instead. It doesn't take long to get tired of iodine-tinged water. Mountain water should be one of the greatest tasting beverages of the world, but the iodine kills that.

### No Treatment

This is your last resort and, using extreme care, can be executed with success. Michael Furniss, the renowned hydrologist, has shown me the difference between safe and dangerous water sources.

When I was in the Boy Scouts, I remember a scoutmaster actually telling me if you could find water running over a rock for at least five feet, it was a guarantee of its purity. Imagine that. What we've learned is that the safe water sources are almost always small springs in high, craggy mountain areas. The key is making sure no one has been upstream from where you drink. We drink untreated water only when we can see the source, such as a spring.

Furniss mentioned that another potential problem in bypassing water treatment is that even in settings free of *Giardia lamblia,* you can still ingest other bacteria that cause stomach problems.

## Hypothermia

No matter how well planned your trip might be, a sudden change in weather can turn it into a puzzle for which there are few answers. Bad weather or an accident can set in motion a dangerous chain of events.

Such a chain of episodes occurred for my brother Rambob and me on a fishing trip one fall day just below the snow line. The weather had suddenly turned very cold, and ice was forming along the shore of the lake. Suddenly, the canoe became terribly imbalanced, and, just that quickly, it flipped. The little life vest seat cushions were useless, and using the canoe as a paddleboard, we tried to kick our way back to shore where my dad was going crazy at the thought of his two sons drowning before his eyes. It took 17 minutes in that 38-degree water,

but we finally made it to shore. When they pulled me out of the water, my legs were dead, not strong enough even to hold up my weight. In fact, I didn't feel so much cold as tired, and I just wanted to lie down and go to sleep.

I closed my eyes, and my brother-in-law, Lloyd Angal, slapped me in the face several times, then got me on my feet and pushed and pulled me about.

In the celebration over our making it to shore, only Lloyd had realized that hypothermia was setting in. Hypothermia is the condition in which the temperature of the body is lowered to the point that it causes poor reasoning, apathy, and collapse. It can look like the afflicted person is just tired and needs to sleep, but that sleep can be the first step toward a coma.

Ultimately, my brother and I shared what little dry clothing remained. Then we began hiking around to get muscle movement, creating internal warmth. We ate whatever munchies were available because the body produces heat by digestion. But most important, we got our heads as dry as possible. More body heat is lost through wet hair than any other single factor.

A few hours later, we were in a pizza parlor replaying the incident, talking about how only a life vest can do the job of a life vest. We decided never again to rely on those little flotation seat cushions that disappear when the boat flips.

We had done everything right to prevent hypothermia: Don't go to sleep, start a physical activity, induce shivering, put dry clothes on, dry your head, and eat something. That's how you fight hypothermia. In a dangerous situation, whether you fall in a lake or a stream or get caught unprepared in a storm, that's how you can stay alive.

After being in that ice-bordered lake for almost 20 minutes and then finally pulling ourselves to the shoreline, we discovered a strange thing. My canoe was flipped right-side up and almost all of its contents were lost: tackle box, flotation cushions, and cooler. But remaining were one paddle and one fishing rod, the trout rod my grandfather had given me for my 12th birthday.

Lloyd gave me a smile. "This means that you are meant to paddle and fish again," he said with a laugh.

## Getting Unlost

I could not have been more lost. There I was, a guy who is supposed to know about these things, transfixed by confusion, snow, and hoofprints from a big deer.

I discovered that it is actually quite easy to get lost. If you don't get your bearings, getting found is the difficult part. This occurred on a wilderness trip where I'd hiked in to a remote lake and then set up a base camp for a deer hunt.

"There are some giant bucks up on that rim," confided Mr. Furnai, who lives near the area. "But it takes a mountain man to even get close to them."

That was a challenge I answered. After four-wheeling it to the trailhead, I tromped off with pack and rifle, gut-thumped it up 100 switchbacks over the rim, then followed a creek drainage up to a small but beautiful lake. The area was stark and nearly treeless, with bald granite broken only by large boulders. To keep from getting lost, I marked my route with piles of small rocks to act as directional signs for the return trip.

But at daybreak the next day, I stuck my head out of my tent and found eight inches of snow on the ground. I looked up into a gray sky filled by huge, cascading snowflakes. Visibility was about 50 yards, with fog on the mountain rim. "I better get out of here and get back to my truck," I said to myself. "If my truck gets buried at the trailhead, I'll never get out."

After packing quickly, I started down the mountain. But after 20 minutes, I began to get disoriented. You see, all the little piles of rocks I'd stacked to mark the way were now buried in snow, and I had only a smooth white blanket of snow to guide me. Everything looked the same, and it was snowing even harder now.

Five minutes later, I started chewing on some jerky to keep warm, then suddenly stopped. Where was I? Where was the creek

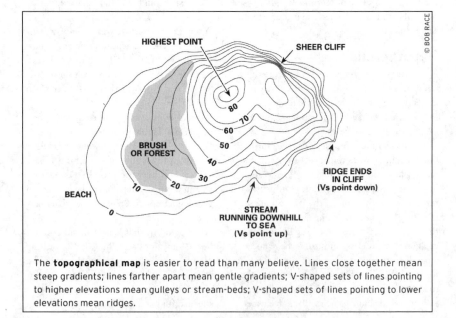

© BOB RACE

The **topographical map** is easier to read than many believe. Lines close together mean steep gradients; lines farther apart mean gentle gradients; V-shaped sets of lines pointing to higher elevations mean gulleys or stream-beds; V-shaped sets of lines pointing to lower elevations mean ridges.

Rock cairns (small piles of rocks) can act as directional signs to keep you from getting lost.

it to north. Because of the fog, there was no way to spot landmarks, such as prominent mountaintops, to verify my position. Then I checked the altimeter, which read 4,900 feet. Well, the elevation at my lake was 5,320 feet. That was critical information.

I scanned the elevation lines on the map and was able to trace the approximate area of my position, somewhere downstream from the lake, yet close to a 4,900-foot elevation. "Right here," I said, pointing to a spot on the map with my finger. "I should pick up the switchback trail down the mountain somewhere off to the left, maybe just 40 or 50 yards away."

Slowly and deliberately, I pushed through the light, powdered snow. In five minutes, I suddenly stopped. To the left, across a 10-foot depression in the snow, appeared a flat spot that veered off to the right. "That's it! That's the crossing."

In minutes, I was working down the switchbacks, on my way, no longer lost. I thought of the hoofprints I had seen, and now that I knew my position, I wanted to head back and spend the day hunting. Then I looked up at the sky, saw it filled with falling snowflakes, and envisioned my truck buried deep in snow. Alas, this time logic won out over dreams.

In a few hours, now trudging through more than a foot of snow, I was at my truck at a spot called Doe Flat, and next to it was a giant, all-terrain U.S. Forest Service vehicle and two rangers.

"Need any help?" I asked them.

They just laughed. "We're here to help you," one answered. "It's a good thing you filed a trip plan with our district office in Gasquet. We wouldn't have known you were out here."

"Winter has arrived," said the other. "If we don't get your truck out now, it will be stuck here until next spring. If we hadn't found you, you might have been here until the end of time."

They connected a chain from the rear axle of their giant rig to the front axle of my truck and started towing me out, back to civilization. On the way to pavement, I figured I had

drainage? Isn't this where I was supposed to cross over a creek and start the switchbacks down the mountain?

Right then, I looked down and saw the tracks of a huge deer, the kind Mr. Furnai had talked about. What a predicament: I was lost and snowed in and seeing big hoofprints in the snow. Part of me wanted to abandon all safety and go after that deer, but a little voice in the back of my head won out. "Treat this as an emergency," it said.

The first step in any predicament is to secure your present situation, that is, to make sure it does not get any worse. I unloaded my rifle (too easy to slip, fall, and have a misfire), took stock of my food (three days' worth), camp fuel (plenty), and clothes (rain gear keeping me dry). Then I wondered, "Where the hell am I?"

I took out my map, compass, and altimeter, then opened the map and laid it on the snow. It immediately began collecting snowflakes. I set the compass atop the map and oriented gotten some of the more important lessons of my life. Always file a trip plan and have plenty of food, fuel, and a camp stove you can rely on. Make sure your clothes, weather gear, sleeping bag, and tent will keep you dry and warm. Always carry a compass, altimeter, and map with elevation lines, and know how to use them, practicing in good weather to get the feel of it.

And if you get lost and see the hoofprints of a giant deer, well, there are times when it is best to pass them by.

# CATCHING FISH, AVOIDING BEARS, AND HAVING FUN

Feet tired and hot, stomachs growling, we stopped our hike for lunch beside a beautiful little river pool that was catching the flows from a long but gentle waterfall. My brother Rambob passed me a piece of jerky. I took my boots off, then slowly dunked my feet into the cool, foaming water.

I was gazing at a towering peak across a canyon when suddenly, Wham! There was a quick jolt at the heel of my right foot. I pulled my foot out of the water to find that, incredibly, a trout had bitten it.

My brother looked at me as if I had antlers growing out of my head. "Wow!" he exclaimed. "That trout almost caught himself an outdoors writer!"

It's true that in remote areas trout sometimes bite on almost anything, even feet. On one high-country trip, I caught limits of trout using nothing but a bare hook. The only problem is that the fish will often hit the splitshot sinker instead of the hook. Of course, fishing isn't usually that easy. But it gives you an idea of what is possible.

America's wildlands are home to a remarkable abundance of fish and wildlife. Deer browse with little fear of man, bears keep an eye out for your food, and little critters, such as squirrels and chipmunks, are daily companions. Add in the fishing, and you've got yourself a camping trip.

Your camping adventures will evolve into premium outdoor experiences if you can work in a few good fishing trips, avoid bear problems, and occasionally add a little offbeat fun with some camp games.

## Trout and Bass

He creeps up on the stream as quietly as an Indian scout, keeping his shadow off the water. With his little spinning rod he'll zip his lure within an inch or two of its desired mark, probing along rocks, the edges of riffles, pocket water, or wherever he can find a change in river habitat. Rambob is trout fishing, and he's a master at it.

In most cases, he'll catch a trout on his first or second cast. After that, it's time to move up the river, giving no spot much more than five minutes' due. Stick and move, stick and move, stalking the stream like a bobcat zeroing in on an unsuspecting rabbit. He might keep a few trout for dinner, but mostly he releases what he catches. Rambob doesn't necessarily fish for food. It's the feeling that comes with it.

You don't need a million dollars' worth of fancy gear to catch fish. What you need is the right outlook, and that can be learned. That goes regardless of whether you are fishing for trout or bass, the two most popular fisheries in the United States. Your fishing tackle selection should be as simple and clutter-free as possible.

At home, I've got every piece of fishing tackle you might imagine, more than 30 rods and many tackle boxes, racks and cabinets filled with all kinds of stuff. I've got one lure that looks like a chipmunk and another that resembles a miniature can of beer with hooks. If I hear of something new, I want to try it and usually do. It's a result of my lifelong fascination with the sport.

But if you just want to catch fish, there's an easier way to go. And when I go fishing, I take that path. I don't try to bring everything. It would be impossible. Instead, I bring a relatively small amount of gear. At home, I scan my tackle boxes for equipment and lures, make my selections, and bring just the essentials.

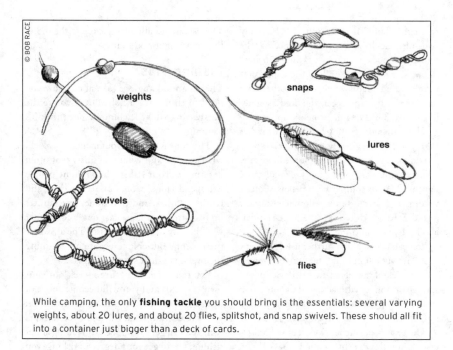

© BOB RACE

weights

snaps

lures

swivels

flies

While camping, the only **fishing tackle** you should bring is the essentials: several varying weights, about 20 lures, and about 20 flies, splitshot, and snap swivels. These should all fit into a container just bigger than a deck of cards.

Rod, reel, and tackle will fit into a side pocket of my backpack or a small carrying bag.

So what kind of rod should be used on an outdoor trip? For most camper/anglers, I suggest the use of a light, multi-piece spinning rod that will break down to a small size. The lowest-priced, quality six-piece rod on the market is the Daiwa 6.5-foot pack rod, number 6752, which is made of a graphite/glass composite that gives it the quality of a much more expensive model. And it comes in a hard plastic carrying tube for protection. Other major rod manufacturers, such as Fenwick, offer similar premium rods. It's tough to miss with any of them.

The use of graphite/glass composites in fishing rods has made them lighter and more sensitive, yet stronger. The only downside to graphite as a rod material is that it can be brittle. If you rap your rod against something, it can crack or cause a weak spot. That weak spot can eventually snap under even light pressure, like setting a hook or casting. Of course, a bit of care will prevent that from ever occurring.

If you haven't bought a fishing reel in some time, you will be surprised at the quality and price of micro spinning reels on the market. The reels come tiny and strong, with rear-control drag systems. Among others, Abu, Cardinal, Shimano, Sigma all make premium reels. They're worth it. With your purchase, you've just bought a reel that will last for years and years.

The one downside to spinning reels is that after long-term use, the bail spring will weaken. As a result, after casting and beginning to reel, the bail will sometimes not flip over and allow the reel to retrieve the line. Then you have to do it by hand. This can be incredibly frustrating, particularly when stream fishing, where instant line pickup is essential. The solution is to have a new bail spring installed every few years. This is a cheap, quick operation for a tackle expert.

You might own a giant tackle box filled with lures but, on your fishing trip, you are better off to fit just the essentials into a small container. One of the best ways to do that is to use the Plano Micro-Magnum 3414, a tiny two-sided tackle box for trout anglers that fits into a shirt pocket. In mine, I can fit 20 lures in one side of the box and 20 flies, split-shot weights, and snap swivels in the other. For bass lures, which are bigger, you need a slightly larger box, but the same principle applies.

There are more fishing lures on the market than you can imagine, but a few special ones can do the job. I make sure these are in my box on every trip. For trout, I carry a small black Panther Martin spinner with yellow spots, a small gold Kastmaster, a yellow Roostertail, a gold Z-Ray with red spots, a Super Duper, and a Mepps Lightning spinner.

You can take it a step further using insider's wisdom. My old pal Ed "the Dunk" showed me his trick of taking a tiny Dardevle spoon, spray painting it flat black, and dabbing five tiny red dots on it. It's a real killer, particularly in tiny streams where the trout are spooky.

The best trout catcher I've ever used on rivers is a small metal lure called a Met-L Fly. On days when nothing else works, it can be like going to a shooting gallery. The problem is that the lure is nearly impossible to find. Rambob and I consider the few we have remaining so valuable that if the lure is snagged on a rock, a cold swim is deemed mandatory for its retrieval. I've been able snag about five of these and they only get pulled out when fishing turns into Mission Impossible.

For bass, you can also fit all you need into a small plastic tackle box. I have fished with many bass pros, and all of them actually use just a few lures: twist-tail grubs, Senkos, Brush Hog, a white spinner bait, a surface plug called a Zara Spook, and AC plug. At times, like when the bass move into shoreline areas during the spring, shad minnow imitations like those made by Rebel or Rapala can be dynamite. My favorite is the one-inch, blue-silver Rapala. Every spring as the lakes begin to warm and the fish snap out of their winter doldrums, I like to float and paddle around in my small raft. I'll cast that little Rapala along the shoreline and catch and release hundreds of bass, bluegill, and sunfish.

The fish are usually sitting close to the shoreline, awaiting my offering.

## Fishing Tips

There's an old angler's joke about how you need to think like a fish. But if you're the one getting zilched, you may not think it's so funny.

The irony is that it is your mental approach, what you see and what you miss, that often determines your fishing luck. Some people will spend a lot of money on tackle, lures, and fishing clothes, and that done, just saunter up to a stream or lake, cast out, and wonder why they are not catching fish. The answer is their mental outlook. They are not attuning themselves to their surroundings.

You must live on nature's level, not your own. Try this and you will become aware of things you never believed even existed. Soon you will see things that will allow you to catch fish. You can get a head start by reading about fishing, but to get your degree in fishing, you must attend the University of Nature.

On every fishing trip, regardless of what you fish for, try to follow three hard-and-fast rules:

1. Always approach the fishing spot so you will be undetected.

2. Present your lure, fly, or bait in a manner so it appears completely natural, as if no line was attached.

3. Stick and move, hitting one spot, working it the best you can, then moving to the next.

### APPROACH

No one can just walk up to a stream or lake, cast out, and start catching fish as if someone had waved a magic wand. Instead, give the fish credit for being smart. After all, they live there.

Your approach must be completely undetected by the fish. Fish can sense your presence through sight and sound, though these factors are misinterpreted by most people. By sight, fish rarely actually see you; more often, they see your shadow on the water or the movement of your arm or rod while casting. By sound, they don't necessarily hear you

© BOB RACE

The rule of the wild is that wildlife will congregate wherever there is a distinct change in habitat. To find where fish are hiding, look where a riffle pours into a small pond, where a rapid plunges into a deep hole and flattens, and around submerged trees, rock piles, and boulders in the middle of a long riffle.

talking, but they do detect the vibrations of your footsteps along the shore, a rock being kicked, or the unnatural plunking sound of a heavy cast hitting the water. Any of these elements can spook them off the bite. In order to fish undetected, you must walk softly, keep your shadow off the water, and keep your casting motion low. All of these key elements become easier at sunrise or sunset, when shadows are on the water. At midday, the sun is at its peak, causing a high level of light penetration in the water. This can make the fish skittish to any foreign presence.

Like a hunter, you must stalk the spots. When my brother Rambob sneaks up on a fishing spot, he is like a burglar sneaking through an unlocked window.

## PRESENTATION

Your lure, fly, or bait must appear in the water as if no line were attached, so it looks as natural as possible. My pal Mo Furniss has skin-dived in rivers to watch what the fish see when somebody is fishing.

"You wouldn't believe it," he said. "When the lure hits the water, every trout within 40 feet, like 15, 20 trout, will do a little zigzag. They all see the lure and are aware something is going on. Meanwhile, onshore the guy casting doesn't get a bite and thinks there aren't any fish in the river."

If your offering is aimed at fooling a fish into striking, it must appear as part of the natural habitat, like an insect just hatching or a small fish looking for a spot to hide. That's where you come in.

After you have sneaked up on a fishing spot, you should zip your cast upstream and start your retrieval as soon as it hits the water. If you let the lure sink to the bottom and then start the retrieval, you have no chance. A minnow, for instance, does not sink to the bottom, then start swimming. On rivers, the retrieval should be more of a drift, as if the "minnow" is in trouble and the current is sweeping it downstream.

When fishing on trout streams, always hike and cast upriver and retrieve as the offering drifts downstream in the current. This is effective because trout will sit almost motionless, pointed upstream, finning against the current. This way, they can see anything coming their direction, and if a potential food morsel arrives, all they need to do is move over a few inches, open their mouths, and they've got an easy lunch. Thus, you must cast upstream.

Conversely, if you cast downstream, your retrieval will bring the lure from behind the fish, where he cannot see it approaching. And I've never seen a trout that had eyes in its tail. In addition, when retrieving a downstream lure, the river current will tend to sweep your lure inshore to the rocks.

## FINDING SPOTS

A lot of anglers don't catch fish, and a lot of hikers never see any wildlife. The key is where they are looking.

The rule of the wild is that fish and wildlife will congregate wherever there is a distinct change in the habitat. This is where you should begin your search. To find deer, for instance, forget probing a thick forest, but look for where it breaks into a meadow or a clear-cut has splayed a stand of trees. That's where the deer will be.

In a river, it can be where a riffle pours into a small pool, a rapid plunges into a deep hole and flattens, a big boulder in the middle of a long riffle, a shoreline point, a rock pile, a submerged tree. Look for the changes. Conversely, long, straight stretches of shoreline will not hold fish—the habitat is lousy.

On rivers, the most productive areas are often where short riffles tumble into small oxygenated pools. After sneaking up from the downstream side and staying low, you should zip your cast so the lure plops gently into the white water just above the pool. Start your retrieval instantly; the lure will drift downstream and plunk into the pool. Bang! That's where the trout will hit. Take a few more casts and then head upstream to the next spot.

With a careful approach and lure

presentation and by fishing in the right spots, you have the ticket to many exciting days on the water.

## Of Bears and Food

The first time you come nose-to-nose with a bear can make your skin quiver.

Even the sight of mild-mannered black bears, the most common bear in America, can send shock waves through your body. They weigh 250-400 pounds and have large claws and teeth that are made to scare campers. When they bound, the muscles on their shoulders roll like ocean breakers. But in California, you don't have to be scared of them. They aren't interested in you, just your food.

Bears in camping areas are accustomed to sharing the mountains with hikers and campers. They have become specialists in the food-raiding business. As a result, you must be able to bear-proof your camp or be able to scare the fellow off. Many campgrounds provide bear- and raccoon-proof food lockers. In most wilderness areas, bear-proof food canisters are required. Never leave your food or trash in your car!

Bear-proof food canisters are so effective in wilderness areas at Yosemite, Kings Canyon-Sequoia, and Mount Whitney that I never see bears on trips there anymore—they've given up on backpackers. Instead, they head to the drive-in campgrounds where they can walk right in and often find food sitting out on top of picnic tables.

No problem. Use the bear-proof food lockers. The bear will just move on to the next site on his daily mooching round.

## Food Hangs

If you are staying at one of the backpack sites listed in this book, it is unlikely that there will be food lockers available. Your car will not be there, either. The solution is to make a bear-proof food hang, suspending all of your food wrapped in a plastic garbage bag from a rope in midair, 10 feet from the trunk of a tree and 20 feet off the ground. (Counterbalancing

two bags with a rope thrown over a tree limb is very effective, but finding an appropriate limb can be difficult.)

The food hang is accomplished by tying a rock to a rope, then throwing it over a high but sturdy tree limb. Next, tie your food bag to the rope and hoist it in the air. When you are satisfied with the position of the food bag, tie off the end of the rope to another tree. In an area frequented by bears, a good food bag is a necessity—nothing else will do.

I've been there. On one trip, my pal Foonsky and my brother Rambob left to fish. I was stoking up an evening campfire when I felt the eyes of an intruder on my back. I turned around and saw a big bear heading straight for our camp. In the next half hour, I scared the bear off twice, but then he got a whiff of something sweet in my brother's pack.

The bear rolled into camp like a truck, grabbed the pack, ripped it open, and plucked out the Tang and the Swiss Miss. The 350-pounder then sat astride a nearby log and lapped at the goodies like a thirsty dog drinking water.

Once a bear gets his mitts on your gear, he considers it his. I took two steps toward the pack, and that bear jumped off the log and galloped across the camp right at me. Scientists say a man can't outrun a bear, but they've never seen how fast I can go up a granite block with a bear on my tail.

Shortly thereafter, Foonsky returned to find me perched on top of the rock and demanded to know how I could let a bear get our Tang. It took all three of us, Foonsky, Rambob, and me, charging at once and shouting like madmen, to clear the bear out of camp and send him off over the ridge. We learned never to let food sit unattended.

## The Grizzly

When it comes to grizzlies, well, my friends, you need what we call an attitude adjustment. Or that big ol' bear may just decide to adjust your attitude for you, making your stay at the park a short one.

## GRIZZLY BEAR TERRITORY

If you are hiking in a wilderness area in Canada or Alaska that may have grizzlies, it is necessary to wear bells on your pack. That way the bear will hear you coming and likely get out of your way. Keep talking, singing, or maybe even debating the country's foreign policy, but do not fall into a silent hiking vigil. And if a breeze is blowing in your face, you must make even more noise (a good excuse to rant and rave about the government's domestic affairs). Noise is important because your smell will not be carried in the direction you are hiking. As a result, the bear will not smell you coming.

If a bear can hear you and smell you, it will tend to get out of the way and let you pass without your knowing it was even close by. The exceptions are if you are carrying fish or lots of sweets in your pack or if you are wearing heavy, sweet deodorants or makeup. All of these are bear attractants.

Grizzlies are nothing like black bears. They are bigger, stronger, have little fear, and take what they want. Some people believe there are many different species of this critter, such as Alaskan brown, silvertip, cinnamon, and Kodiak, but the truth is they are all grizzlies. Any difference in appearance has to do with diet, habitat, and life habits, not speciation. By any name, they all come big.

The first thing you must do is determine if there are grizzlies in the area where you are camping. That can usually be done by asking local rangers. If you are heading into Yellowstone or Glacier National Park, or the Bob Marshall Wilderness of Montana, well, you don't have to ask. They're out there, and they're the biggest and potentially most dangerous critters you could run into.

One general way to figure the size of a bear is from his footprint. Take the width of the footprint in inches, add one to it, and you'll have an estimated length of the bear in feet. For instance, a nine-inch footprint equals a 10-foot bear. Any bear that big is a grizzly. In fact, most grizzly footprints average about 9-10 inches across, and black bears (though they may be brown in color) tend to have footprints only 4.5-6 inches across.

Most encounters with grizzlies occur when hikers fall into a silent march in the wilderness with the wind in their faces, and they walk around a corner and right into a big, unsuspecting grizzly. If you do this and see a big

hump just behind its neck, don't think twice. It's a grizzly.

And then what should you do? Get up a tree, that's what. Grizzlies are so big that their claws cannot support their immense weight, and thus they cannot climb trees. And although young grizzlies can climb, they rarely want to get their mitts on you.

If you do get grabbed, every instinct in your body will tell you to fight back. Don't believe it. Play dead. Go limp. Let the bear throw you around a little. After awhile, you'll become unexciting play material and the bear will get bored. My grandmother was grabbed by a grizzly in Glacier National Park and, after a few tosses and hugs, was finally left alone to escape.

Some say it's a good idea to tuck your head under his chin, since that way the bear will be unable to bite your head. I'll take a pass on that one. If you are taking action, any action, it's a signal that you are a force to be reckoned with, and he'll likely respond with more aggression. And bears don't lose many wrestling matches.

What grizzlies really like to do, believe it or not, is to pile a lot of sticks and leaves on you. Just let them, and keep perfectly still. Don't fight them; don't run. And when you have a 100 percent chance (not 98 or 99) to dash up a nearby tree, that's when you let fly. Once safely in a tree, you can hurl down insults and let your aggression out.

In a wilderness camp, there are special precautions you should take. Always hang your food at least 100 yards downwind of camp and get it high; 30 feet is reasonable. In addition, circle your camp with rope and hang the bells from your pack on it. Thus, if a bear walks into your camp, he'll run into the rope, the bells will ring, and everybody will have a chance to get up a tree before ol' griz figures out what's going on. Often, the unexpected ringing of bells is enough to send him off in search of a quieter environment.

You see, more often than not, grizzlies tend to clear the way for campers and hikers. So be smart, don't act like bear bait, and always have a plan if you are confronted by one.

My pal Foonsky had such a plan during a wilderness expedition in Montana's northern Rockies. On our second day of hiking, we started seeing scratch marks on the trees 13-14 feet off the ground.

"Mr. Griz made those," Foonsky said. "With spring here, the grizzlies are coming out of hibernation and using the trees like a cat uses a scratch board to stretch the muscles."

The next day, I noticed Foonsky had a pair of track shoes tied to the back of his pack. I just laughed.

"You're not going to outrun a griz," I said. "In fact, there's hardly any animal out here in the wilderness that man can outrun."

Foonsky just smiled.

"I don't have to outrun a griz," he said. "I just have to outrun you!"

## Fun and Games

"Now what are we supposed to do?" the young boy asked his dad.

"Yeah, Dad, think of something," said another son.

Well, Dad thought hard. This was one of the first camping trips he'd taken with his sons and one of the first lessons he received was that kids don't appreciate the philosophical release of mountain quiet. They want action and lots of it. With a glint in his eye, Dad searched around the camp and picked up 15 twigs, breaking them so each was four inches long. He laid them in three separate rows, three twigs in

one row, five twigs in another, and seven in the other.

"OK, this game is called 3-5-7," said Dad. "You each take turns picking up sticks. You are allowed to remove all or as few as one twig from a row, but here's the catch: You can pick only from one row per turn. Whoever picks up the last stick left is the loser."

I remember this episode well because those two little boys were my brother Bobby, as in Rambobby, and I. And to this day, we still play 3-5-7 on campouts, with the winner getting to watch the loser clean the dishes. What I have learned in the span of time since that original episode is that it does not matter what your age is: Campers need options for camp fun.

Some evenings, after a long hike or ride, you feel too worn out to take on a serious romp downstream to fish or a climb up to a ridge for a view. That is especially true if you have been in the outback for a week or more. At that point, a lot of campers will spend their time resting and gazing at a map of the area, dreaming of the next day's adventure, or just take a seat against a rock, watching the colors of the sky and mountain panorama change minute by minute. But kids in the push-button video era, and a lot of adults too, want more. After all, "I'm on vacation. I want some fun."

There are several options, such as the 3-5-7 twig game, and they should be just as much a part of your trip planning as arranging your gear.

For kids, plan on games, the more physically challenging the competition, the better. One of the best games is to throw a chunk of wood into a lake and challenge the kids to hit it by throwing rocks. It wreaks havoc on the fishing, but it can keep kids totally absorbed for some time. Target practice with a wrist-rocket slingshot—firing rocks at small targets, like pinecones set on a log—is also all-consuming for kids.

You can also set kids off on little missions near camp, such as looking for the footprints of wildlife, searching out good places to have a "snipe hunt," picking up twigs to get the evening fire started, or having them take the water purifier to a stream to pump some drinking water into a canteen. The latter is an easy, fun, yet important task that will allow kids to feel a sense of equality they often don't get at home.

For adults, the appeal should be more to the intellect. A good example is star and planet identification, and while you are staring into space, you're bound to spot a few asteroids or shooting stars. A star chart can make it easy to find and identify many distinctive stars and constellations, such as Pleiades (the Seven Sisters), Orion, and others from the zodiac, depending on the time of year. With a little research, this can add a unique perspective to your trip. You could point to Polaris, one of the most easily identified of all stars, and note that navigators in the 1400s used it to find their way. Polaris, of course, is the North Star and is at the end of the handle of the Little Dipper. Pinpointing Polaris is quite easy. First find the Big Dipper and then find the outside stars of the ladle of the Big Dipper. They are called the "pointer stars" because they point right at Polaris.

A tree identification book can teach you a few things about your surroundings. It is also a good idea for one member of the party to research the history of the area you have chosen and another to research the geology. With shared knowledge, you end up with a deeper love of wild places.

Another way to add some recreation into your trip is to bring a board game, a number of which have been miniaturized for campers. The most popular are chess, checkers, and cribbage. The latter comes with an equally miniature set of playing cards. And if you bring those little cards, that opens a vast set of other possibilities. With kids along, for instance, just take three queens out of the deck and you can play Old Maid.

But there are more serious card games, and they come with high stakes. Such occurred on one high-country trip where Foonsky, Rambob, and I sat down for a late-afternoon game of poker. In a game of seven-card stud, I caught a straight on the sixth card and felt like a dog licking on a T-bone. Already, I had bet several Skittles and peanut M&Ms on this promising hand.

Then I examined the cards Foonsky had face up. He was showing three sevens, and acting as happy as a grizzly with a pork chop—or a full house. He matched my bet of two peanut M&Ms, then raised me three SweetTarts, one Starburst, and one sour apple Jolly Rancher. Rambob folded, but I matched Foonsky's bet and hoped for the best as the seventh and final card was dealt.

Just after Foonsky glanced at that last card, I saw him sneak a look at my grape stick and beef jerky stash.

"I raise you a grape stick," he said.

Rambob and I both gasped. It was the highest bet ever made, equivalent to a million dollars laid down in Las Vegas. Cannons were going off in my chest. I looked hard at my cards. They looked good, but were they good enough?

Even with a great hand like I had, a grape stick was too much to gamble, my last one with 10 days of trail ahead of us. I shook my head and folded my cards. Foonsky smiled at his victory.

But I still had my grape stick.

## Old Tricks Don't Always Work

Most people are born honest, but after a few camping trips, they usually get over it.

I remember some advice I got from Rambob, normally an honest soul, on one camping trip. A giant mosquito had landed on my arm and he alerted me to an expert bit of wisdom.

"Flex your arm muscles," he commanded, watching the mosquito fill with my blood. "He'll get stuck in your arm, then he'll explode."

For some reason, I believed him. We both proceeded to watch the mosquito drill countless holes in my arm.

Alas, the unknowing face sabotage from their most trusted companions on camping

## KEEP IT WILD TIP 6:
## PLAN AHEAD AND PREPARE

1. Learn about the regulations and issues that apply to the area you're visiting.
2. Avoid heavy-use areas.
3. Obtain all maps and permits.
4. Bring extra garbage bags to pack out any refuse you come across.

trips. It can arise at any time, usually in the form of advice from a friendly, honest-looking face, as if to say, "What? How can you doubt me?" After that mosquito episode, I was a little more skeptical of my dear old brother. Then the next day, when another mosquito was nailing me in the back of the neck, out came this gem:

"Hold your breath," he commanded. I instinctively obeyed. "That will freeze the mosquito," he said, "then you can squish him."

But in the time I wasted holding my breath, the little bugger was able to fly off without my having the satisfaction of squishing him. When he got home, he probably told his family, "What a dummy I got to drill today!"

Over the years, I have been duped numerous times with dubious advice:

On a grizzly bear attack: "If he grabs you, tuck your head under the grizzly's chin; then he won't be able to bite you in the head." This made sense to me until the first time I saw a nine-foot grizzly 40 yards away. In seconds, I was at the top of a tree, which suddenly seemed to make the most sense.

On coping with animal bites: "If a bear bites you in the arm, don't try to jerk it away. That will just rip up your arm. Instead, force your arm deeper into his mouth. He'll lose his grip and will have to open it to get a firmer hold, and right then you can get away." I was told this in the Boy Scouts. When I was 14, I had a chance to try it out when a friend's dog bit me as I tried to pet it. What happened? When I shoved my arm deeper into his mouth, he bit me three more times.

On cooking breakfast: "The bacon will curl up every time in a camp frying pan. So make

sure you have a bacon stretcher to keep it flat." As a 12-year-old Tenderfoot, I spent two hours looking for the bacon stretcher until I figured out the camp leader had forgotten it. It wasn't for several years that I learned that there is no such thing.

On preventing sore muscles: "If you haven't hiked for a long time and you are facing a rough climb, you can keep from getting sore muscles in your legs, back, and shoulders by practicing the 'Dead Man's Walk.' Simply let your entire body go slack, and then take slow, wobbling steps. This will clear your muscles of lactic acid, which causes them to be so sore after a rough hike." Foonsky pulled this one on me. Rambob and I both bought it and tried it while we were hiking up Mount Whitney, which requires a 6,000-foot elevation gain in six miles. In one 45-minute period, about 30 other hikers passed us and looked at us as if we were suffering from some rare form of mental aberration.

Fish won't bite? No problem: "If the fish are not feeding or will not bite, persistent anglers can still catch dinner with little problem. Keep casting across the current, and eventually, as they hover in the stream, the line will feed across their open mouths. Keep reeling and you will hook the fish right in the side of the mouth. This technique is called 'lining.' Never worry if the fish will not bite, because you can always line 'em." Of course, heh, heh, heh, that explains why so many fish get hooked in the side of the mouth.

On keeping bears away: "To keep bears away, urinate around the borders of your campground. If there are a lot of bears in the area, it is advisable to go right on your sleeping bag." Yeah, surrrrrre.

On disposing of trash: "Don't worry about packing out trash. Just bury it. It will regenerate into the earth and add valuable minerals." Bears, raccoons, skunks, and other critters will dig up your trash as soon as you depart, leaving one huge mess for the next camper. Always pack out everything.

Often the advice comes without warning. That was the case after a fishing trip with a female companion, when she outcaught me two to one, the third such trip in a row. I explained this to a shopkeeper, and he nodded, then explained why.

"The male fish are able to detect the female scent on the lure, and thus become aroused into striking."

Of course! That explains everything!

## Getting Revenge

I was just a lad when Foonsky pulled the old snipe-hunt trick on me. It took nearly 30 years to get revenge.

You probably know about snipe hunting. The victim is led out at night in the woods by a group, and then is left holding a bag.

"Stay perfectly still and quiet," Foonsky explained. "You don't want to scare the snipe. The rest of us will go back to camp and let the woods settle down. Then when the snipe are least expecting it, we'll form a line and charge through the forest with sticks, beating bushes and trees, and we'll flush the snipe out right to you. Be ready with the bag. When we flush the snipe out, bag it. But until we start our charge, make sure you don't move or make a sound or you will spook the snipe and ruin everything."

I sat out there in the woods with my bag for hours, waiting for the charge. I waited, waited, and waited. Nothing happened. No charge, no snipe. It wasn't until well past midnight that I figured something was wrong. When I finally returned to camp, everybody was sleeping.

Well, I tell ya, don't get mad at your pals for the tricks they pull on you. Get revenge. About 25 years later, on the last day of a camping trip, the time finally came.

"Let's break camp early," Foonsky suggested to Mr. Furnai and me. "Get up before dawn, eat breakfast, pack up, and be on the ridge to watch the sun come up. It will be a fantastic way to end the trip."

"Sounds great to me," I replied. But when Foonsky wasn't looking, I turned his alarm clock ahead three hours. So when the alarm sounded at the appointed 4:30am wake-up time, Mr. Furnai and I knew it was actually only 1:30am.

Foonsky clambered out of his sleeping bag and whistled with a grin. "Time to break camp."

"You go ahead," I answered. "I'll skip breakfast so I can get a little more sleep. At the first sign of dawn, wake me up, and I'll break camp."

"Me, too," said Mr. Furnai.

Foonsky then proceeded to make some coffee, cook a breakfast, and eat it, sitting on a log in the black darkness of the forest, waiting for the sun to come up. An hour later, with still no sign of dawn, he checked his clock. It now read 5:30am. "Any minute now we should start seeing some light," he said.

He made another cup of coffee, packed his gear, and sat there in the middle of the night, looking up at the stars, waiting for dawn. "Anytime now," he said. He ended up sitting there all night long.

Revenge is sweet. Before a fishing trip at a lake, I took Foonsky aside and explained that the third member of the party, Jimbobo, was hard of hearing and very sensitive about it. "Don't mention it to him," I advised. "Just talk real loud."

Meanwhile, I had already told Jimbobo the same thing. "Foonsky just can't hear very good."

We had fished less than 20 minutes when Foonsky got a nibble.

"GET A BITE?" shouted Jimbobo.

"YEAH!" yelled back Foonsky, smiling. "BUT I DIDN'T HOOK HIM!"

"MAYBE NEXT TIME!" shouted Jimbobo with a friendly grin.

Well, they spent the entire day yelling at each other from the distance of a few feet. They never did figure it out. Heh, heh, heh.

That is, I thought so, until we made a trip salmon fishing. I got a strike that almost knocked my fishing rod out of the boat. When I grabbed the rod, it felt as if Moby Dick were on the other end. "At least a 25-pounder," I said. "Maybe bigger."

The fish dove, ripped off line, and then bulldogged. "It's acting like a 40-pounder," I announced, "Huge, just huge. It's going deep. That's how the big ones fight."

Some 15 minutes later, I finally got the "salmon" to the surface. It turned out to be a coffee can that Foonsky had clipped on the line with a snap swivel. By maneuvering the boat, he made the coffee can fight like a big fish.

This all started with a little old snipe hunt years ago. You never know what your pals will try next. Don't get mad. Get revenge.

# CAMPING OPTIONS
## Boat-In Seclusion

Most campers would never think of trading in their cars, pickup trucks, or RVs for a boat, but people who go by boat on a camping trip enjoy virtually guaranteed seclusion and top-quality outdoor experiences.

Camping with a boat is a do-it-yourself venture in living under primitive circumstances. Yet at the same time, you can bring along any luxury item you wish, from giant coolers, stoves, and lanterns to portable gasoline generators. Weight is almost never an issue.

Many outstanding boat-in campgrounds in beautiful surroundings are available. The best are on the shores of lakes accessible by canoe or skiff, and at offshore islands reached by saltwater cruisers. Several boat-in camps are detailed in this book.

If you want to take the adventure a step further and create your own boat-in camp, perhaps near a special fishing spot, this is a go-for-it deal that provides the best way possible to establish your own secret campsite. But most people who set out freelance style forget three critical items for boat-in camping: a shovel, a sunshade, and an ax. Here is why these items can make a key difference in your trip:

**Shovel:** Many lakes and virtually all reservoirs have steep, sloping banks. At reservoirs subject to drawdowns, what was lake bottom in the spring can be a campsite in late summer. If you want a flat area for a tent site, the only answer is to dig one out yourself. A shovel gives you that option.

**Sunshade:** The flattest spots to camp along lakes often have a tendency to support only sparse tree growth. As a result, a natural shield from sun and rain is rarely available. What? Rain in the summer? Oh yeah, don't get me started. A light tarp, set up with poles and staked ropes, solves the problem.

**Ax:** Unless you bring your own firewood, which is necessary at some sparsely wooded reservoirs, there is no substitute for a good, sharp ax. With an ax, you can almost always find dry firewood, since the interior of an otherwise wet log will be dry. When the weather turns bad is precisely when you will most want a fire. You may need an ax to get one going.

In the search to create your own personal boat-in campsite, you will find that the flattest areas are usually the tips of peninsulas and points, while the protected back ends of coves are often steeply sloped. At reservoirs, the flattest areas are usually near the mouths of the feeder streams and the points are quite steep. On rivers, there are usually sandbars on the inside of tight bends that make for ideal campsites.

Almost all boat-in campsites developed by government agencies are free of charge, but you are on your own. Only in extremely rare cases is piped water available.

Any way you go, by canoe, skiff, or power cruiser, you end up with a one-in-a-million campsite you can call your own.

## Desert Outings

It was a cold, snowy day in Missouri when 10-year-old Rusty Ballinger started dreaming about the vast deserts of the West.

"My dad was reading aloud from a Zane Grey book called *Riders of the Purple Sage*," Ballinger said. "He would get animated when he got to the passages about the desert. It wasn't long before I started to have the same feelings."

That was in 1947. Since then Ballinger has spent a good part of his life exploring the West, camping along the way. "The deserts are the best part. There's something about the uniqueness of each little area you see," Ballinger said. "You're constantly surprised. Just the time of day and the way the sun casts a different color. It's like the lady you care about. One time she smiles, the next time she's pensive. The desert is like that. If you love nature, you can love the desert. After a while, you can't help but love it."

A desert adventure is not just an antidote for a case of cabin fever in the winter. Whether you go by RV, pickup truck, car, or on foot, it provides its own special qualities.

If you go camping in the desert, your approach has to be as unique as the setting. For starters, don't plan on any campfires, but bring a camp stove instead. And unlike in the mountains, do not camp near a water hole. That's because an animal, such as a badger, coyote, or desert bighorn, might be desperate for water, and if you set up camp in the animal's way, you may be forcing a confrontation.

In some areas, there is a danger of flash floods. An intense rain can fall in one area, collect in a pool, then suddenly burst through a narrow canyon. If you are in its path, you could be injured or drowned. The lesson? Never camp in a gully.

"Some people might wonder 'What good is this place?'" Ballinger said. "The answer is that it is good for looking at. It is one of the world's unique places."

## CAMP ETHICS AND POLITICS

The perfect place to set up a base camp turned out to be not so perfect. In fact, according to Doug Williams of California, it did not even exist.

Williams and his son, James, had driven deep into Angeles National Forest, prepared to set up camp and then explore the surrounding area on foot. But when they reached their destination, no campground existed.

"I wanted a primitive camp in a national forest where I could teach my son some basics," said the senior Williams. "But when we got there, there wasn't much left of the camp, and it had been closed. It was obvious that the area had been vandalized."

It turned out not to be an isolated incident. A lack of outdoor ethics practiced by a few people using the unsupervised campgrounds available on national forestland has caused the U.S. Forest Service to close a few of them and make extensive repairs to others.

"There have been sites closed, especially in Angeles and San Bernardino National Forests in Southern California," said David Flohr, regional campground coordinator for the U.S. Forest Service. "It's an urban type of thing, affecting forests near urban areas, and not just Los Angeles. They get a lot of urban users and they bring with them a lot of the same ethics they have in the city. They get drinking and they're not afraid to do things. They vandalize and run. Of course, it is a public facility, so they think nobody is getting hurt."

But somebody is getting hurt, starting with the next person who wants to use the campground. And if the ranger district budget doesn't have enough money to pay for repairs, the campground is then closed for the next arrivals. Just ask Doug and James Williams.

In an era of considerable fiscal restraint for the U.S. Forest Service, vandalized campgrounds could face closure instead of repair. Williams had just a taste of it, but Flohr, as camping coordinator, gets a steady diet.

"It starts with behavior," Flohr said. "General rowdiness, drinking, partying, and then vandalism. It goes all the way from the felt-tip pen things (graffiti) to total destruction, blowing up toilet buildings with dynamite. I have seen toilets destroyed totally with shotguns. They burn up tables, burn barriers. They'll burn up signs for firewood, even the shingles right off the roofs of the bathrooms. They'll shoot anything, garbage cans, signs. It can get a little hairy. A favorite is to remove the stool out of a toilet building. We've had people fall in the open hole."

The National Park Service had similar problems some years back, especially with rampant littering. Park Director Bill Mott responded by creating an interpretive program that attempts to teach visitors the wise use of natural areas, and to have all park workers set examples by picking up litter and reminding others to do the same.

The U.S. Forest Service has responded with a similar program, making brochures available that detail the wise use of national forests. The four most popular brochures are titled: "Rules for Visitors to the National Forest," "Recreation in the National Forests," "Is the Water Safe?" and "Backcountry Safety Tips." These include details on campfires, drinking water from lakes or streams, hypothermia, safety, and outdoor ethics.

Flohr said even experienced campers sometimes cross over the ethics line unintentionally. The most common example, he said, is when campers toss garbage into the outhouse toilet, rather than packing it out in a plastic garbage bag.

"They throw it in the vault toilet bowls, which just fills them up," Flohr said. "That creates an extremely high cost to pump it. You know why? Because some poor guy has to pick that stuff out piece by piece. It can't be pumped."

At most backcountry sites, the U.S. Forest Service has implemented a program called "Pack it in, pack it out," even posting signs that remind all visitors to do so. But a lot of people don't do it, and others may even uproot the signs and burn them for firewood.

On a trip to a secluded lake near Carson Pass in the Sierra Nevada, I arrived at a small, little-known camp where the picnic table had been spray painted and garbage had been strewn about. A pristine place, the true temple of God, had been defiled.

## Getting Along with Fellow Campers

The most important thing about a camping, fishing, or hunting trip is not where you go, how many fish you catch, or how many shots you fire. It often has little to do with how beautiful the view is, how easily the campfire lights, or how sunny the days are.

Oh yeah? Then what is the most important factor? The answer: The people you are with. It is that simple.

Who would you rather camp with? Your enemy at work or your dream mate in a good mood? Heh, heh. You get the idea. A camping trip is a fairly close-knit experience, and you can make lifetime friends or lifelong enemies in the process. That is why your choice of companions is so important. Your own behavior is equally consequential.

Yet most people spend more time putting together their camping gear than considering why they enjoy or hate the company of their chosen companions. Here are 10 rules of behavior for good camping mates:

1. **No whining:** Nothing is more irritating than being around a whiner. It goes right to the heart of adventure, since often the only difference between a hardship and an escapade is simply whether or not an individual has the spirit for it. The people who do can turn a rugged day in the outdoors into a cherished memory. Those who don't can ruin it with their incessant sniveling.

2. **Activities must be agreed upon:** Always have a meeting of the minds with your companions over the general game plan. Then everybody will possess an equal stake in the outcome of the trip. This is absolutely critical. Otherwise they will feel like merely an addendum to your trip, not an equal participant, and a whiner will be born (see number one).

3. **Nobody's in charge:** It is impossible to be genuine friends if one person is always telling another what to do, especially if the orders involve simple camp tasks. You need to share the space on the same emotional plane, and the only way to do that is to have a semblance

## KEEP IT WILD TIP 7: RESPECT OTHER USERS

1. Horseback riders have priority over hikers. Step to the downhill side of the trail and talk softly when encountering horseback riders.
2. Hikers and horseback riders have priority over mountain bikers. When mountain bikers encounter other users even on wide trails, they should pass at an extremely slow speed. On very narrow trails, they should dismount and get off to the side so hikers or horseback riders can pass without having their trip disrupted.
3. Mountain bikes aren't permitted on most single-track trails and are expressly prohibited in designated wilderness areas and all sections of the Pacific Crest Trail. Mountain bikers breaking these rules should be confronted and told to dismount and walk their bikes until they reach a legal area.
4. It's illegal for horseback riders to break off branches that may be in the path of wilderness trails.
5. Horseback riders on overnight trips are prohibited from camping in many areas and are usually required to keep stock animals in specific areas where they can do no damage to the landscape.

of equality, regardless of differences in experience. Just try ordering your mate around at home for a few days. You'll quickly see the results, and they aren't pretty.

4. **Equal chances at the fun stuff:** It's fun to build the fire, fun to get the first cast at the best fishing spot, and fun to hoist the bagged food for a bear-proof food hang. It is not fun to clean the dishes, collect firewood, or cook every night. So obviously, there must be an equal distribution of the fun stuff and the not-fun stuff, and everybody on the trip must get a shot at the good and the bad.

5. **No heroes:** No awards are bestowed for achievement in the outdoors, yet some guys treat mountain peaks, big fish, and big game as if they are prizes in a trophy competition. Actually, nobody cares how wonderful you are, which is always a surprise to trophy chasers. What people care about is the heart of the adventure, the gut-level stuff.

6. **Agree on a wake-up time:** It is a good idea to agree on a general wake-up time before closing your eyes for the night, and that goes regardless of whether you want to sleep in late or get up at dawn. Then you can proceed on course regardless of what time you crawl out of your sleeping bag in the morning, without the risk of whining (see number one).

7. **Think of the other guy:** Be self-aware instead of self-absorbed. A good test is to count the number of times you say, "What do you think?" A lot of potential problems can be solved quickly by actually listening to the answer.

8. **Solo responsibilities:** There are a number of essential camp duties on all trips, and while they should be shared equally, most should be completed solo. That means that when it is time for you to cook, you don't have to worry about me changing the recipe on you. It means that when it is my turn to make the fire, you keep your mitts out of it.

9. **Don't let money get in the way:** Of course everybody should share equally in trip expenses, such as the cost of food, and it should be split up before you head out yonder. Don't let somebody pay extra, because that person will likely try to control the trip. Conversely, don't let somebody weasel out of paying a fair share.

10. **Accordance on the food plan:** Always have complete agreement on what you plan to eat each day. Don't figure that just because you like Steamboat's Sludge, everybody else will, too, especially youngsters. Always, always, always check for food allergies, such as nuts, onions, or cheese, and make sure each person brings his or her own personal coffee brand. Some people drink only decaffeinated; others might gag on anything but Burma monkey beans.

Obviously, it is difficult to find companions who will agree on all of these elements. This is why many campers say that the best camping buddies they'll ever have are their mates, who know all about them and like them anyway.

## OUTDOORS WITH KIDS

How do you get a youngster excited about the outdoors? How do you compete with the television and remote control? How do you prove to a kid that success comes from persistence, spirit, and logic, which the outdoors teaches, and not from pushing buttons?

The answer is in the Ten Camping Commandments for Kids. These are lessons that will get youngsters excited about the outdoors and that will make sure adults help the process along, not kill it. I've put this list together with the help of my own kids, Jeremy and Kris, and their mother, Stephani. Some of the commandments are obvious, some are not, but all are important:

1. Take children to places where there is a guarantee of action. A good example is camping in a park where large numbers of wildlife can be viewed, such as squirrels, chipmunks, deer, and even bears. Other good choices include fishing at a small pond loaded with bluegill or hunting in a spot where a kid can shoot a .22 at pinecones all day. Boys and girls want action, not solitude.

2. Enthusiasm is contagious. If you aren't excited about an adventure, you can't expect a child to be. Show a genuine zest for life in the outdoors, and point out everything as if it is the first time you have ever seen it.

3. Always, always, always be seated when talking to someone small. This allows the adult and child to be on the same level. That is why fishing in a small boat is perfect for adults and kids. Nothing is worse for youngsters than having a big person look down at them and give them orders. What fun is that?

4. Always *show* how to do something, whether it is gathering sticks for a campfire, cleaning a trout, or tying a knot. Never tell—always show. A button usually clicks to "off"

when a kid is lectured. But kids can learn behavior patterns and outdoor skills by watching adults, even when the adults are not aware they are being watched.

5. Let kids be kids. Let the adventure happen, rather than trying to force it within some preconceived plan. If they get sidetracked watching pollywogs, chasing butterflies, or sneaking up on chipmunks, let them be. A youngster can have more fun turning over rocks and looking at different kinds of bugs than sitting in one spot, waiting for a fish to bite.

6. Expect short attention spans. Instead of getting frustrated about it, use it to your advantage. How? By bringing along a bag of candy and snacks. Where there is a lull in the camp activity, out comes the bag. Don't let them know what goodies await, so each one becomes a surprise.

7. Make absolutely certain the child's sleeping bag is clean, dry, and warm. Nothing is worse than discomfort when trying to sleep, but a refreshing sleep makes for a positive attitude the next day. In addition, kids can become quite scared of animals at night. A parent should not wait for any signs of this, but always play the part of the outdoor guardian, the one who will take care of everything.

8. Kids quickly relate to outdoor ethics. They will enjoy eating everything they kill, building a safe campfire, and picking up all their litter, and they will develop a sense of pride that goes with it. A good idea is to bring extra plastic garbage bags to pick up any trash you come across. Kids long remember when they do something right that somebody else has done wrong.

9. If you want youngsters hooked on the outdoors for life, take a close-up photograph of them holding up fish they have caught, blowing on the campfire, or completing other camp tasks. Young children can forget how much fun they had, but they never forget if they have a picture of it.

10. The least important word you can ever say to a kid is "I." Keep track of how often you

are saying "Thank you" and "What do you think?" If you don't say them very often, you'll lose out. Finally, the most important words of all are: "I am proud of you."

## PREDICTING WEATHER

Foonsky climbed out of his sleeping bag, glanced at the nearby meadow, and scowled hard.

"It doesn't look good," he said. "Doesn't look good at all."

I looked at my adventure companion of 20 years, noting his discontent. Then I looked at the meadow and immediately understood why: *"When the grass is dry at morning light, look for rain before the night."*

"How bad you figure?" I asked him.

"We'll know soon enough, I reckon," Foonsky answered. *"Short notice, soon to pass. Long notice, long it will last."*

When you are out in the wild, spending your days fishing and your nights camping, you learn to rely on yourself to predict the weather. It can make or break you. If a storm hits the unprepared, it can quash the trip and possibly endanger the participants. But if you are ready, a potential hardship can be an adventure.

You can't rely on TV weather forecasters, people who don't even know that when all the cows on a hill are facing north, it will rain that night for sure. God forbid if the cows are all sitting. But what do you expect from TV?

Foonsky made a campfire, started boiling some water for coffee and soup, and we started to plan the day. In the process, I noticed the smoke of the campfire: It was sluggish, drifting and hovering.

"You notice the smoke?" I asked, chewing on a piece of homemade jerky.

"Not good," Foonsky said. "Not good." He knew that sluggish, hovering smoke indicates rain.

"You'd think we'd have been smart enough to know last night that this was coming," Foonsky said. "Did you take a look at the moon or the clouds?"

"I didn't look at either," I answered. "Too busy eating the trout we caught." You see, if the moon is clear and white, the weather will be good the next day. But if there is a ring around the moon, the number of stars you can count inside the ring equals the number of days until the next rain. As for clouds, the high, thin ones—called cirrus—indicate a change in the weather.

We were quiet for a while, planning our strategy, but as we did so, some terrible things happened: A chipmunk scampered past with his tail high, a small flock of geese flew by very low, and a little sparrow perched on a tree limb quite close to the trunk.

"We're in for trouble," I told Foonsky.

"I know, I know," he answered. "I saw 'em, too. And come to think of it, no crickets were chirping last night either."

"Damn, that's right!"

These are all signs of an approaching storm. Foonsky pointed at the smoke of the campfire and shook his head as if he had just been condemned. Sure enough, now the smoke was blowing toward the north, a sign of a south wind. *"When the wind is from the south, the rain is in its mouth."*

"We'd best stay hunkered down until it passes," Foonsky said.

I nodded. "Let's gather as much firewood now as we can, get our gear covered up, then plan our meals."

"Then we'll get a poker game going."

As we accomplished these camp tasks, the sky clouded up, then darkened. Within an hour, we had gathered enough firewood to make a large pile, enough wood to keep a fire going no matter how hard it rained. The day's meals had been separated out of the food bag so it wouldn't have to be retrieved during the storm. We buttoned two ponchos together, staked two of the corners with ropes to the ground, and tied the other two with ropes to different tree limbs to create a slanted roof/shelter.

As the first raindrop fell with that magic sound on our poncho roof, Foonsky was just starting to shuffle the cards.

"Cut for deal," he said.

Just as I did so, it started to rain a bit harder. I pulled out another piece of beef jerky and started chewing on it. It was just another day in paradise.

Weather lore can be valuable. Here is the list I have compiled over the years:

*When the grass is dry at morning light,*
*Look for rain before the night.*

*Short notice, soon to pass.*
*Long notice, long it will last.*

*When the wind is from the east,*
*'Tis fit for neither man nor beast.*

*When the wind is from the south,*
*The rain is in its mouth.*

*When the wind is from the west,*
*Then it is the very best.*

*Red sky at night, sailors' delight.*
*Red sky in the morning, sailors take warning.*

*When all the cows are pointed north,*
*Within a day rain will come forth.*

*Onion skins very thin, mild winter coming in.*
*Onion skins very tough, winter's going to be very rough.*

*When your boots make the squeak of snow,*
*Then very cold temperatures will surely show.*

*If a goose flies high, fair weather ahead.*
*If a goose flies low, foul weather will come instead.*

Small signs provided by nature and wildlife can also be translated to provide a variety of weather information:

A thick coat on a woolly caterpillar means a big, early snow is coming.

Chipmunks will run with their tails up before a rain.

Bees always stay near their hives before a rainstorm.

When the birds are perched on large limbs near tree trunks, an intense but short storm will arrive.

On the coast, if groups of seabirds are flying a mile inland, look for major winds.

If crickets are chirping very loudly during the evening, the next day will be clear and warm.

If the smoke of a campfire at night rises in a thin spiral, good weather is assured for the next day.

If the smoke of a campfire at night is sluggish, drifting and hovering, it will rain the next day.

If there is a ring around the moon, count the number of stars inside the ring, and that is how many days until the next rain.

If the moon is clear and white, the weather will be good the next day.

High, thin clouds, or cirrus, indicate a change in the weather.

Oval-shaped lenticular clouds indicate high winds.

Two levels of clouds moving in different directions indicate changing weather soon.

Huge, dark, billowing clouds, called cumulonimbus, suddenly forming on warm afternoons in the mountains mean that a short but intense thunderstorm with lightning can be expected.

When squirrels are busy gathering food for extended periods, it means good weather is ahead in the short term, but a hard winter is ahead in the long term.

And God forbid if all the cows are sitting down....

# CAMPING GEAR CHECKLIST

## COOKING GEAR

- Camp stove and fuel
- Dish soap and scrubber
- Fire-starter cubes
- Heavy-duty paper plates
- Ice chest and drinks
- Itemized food, separated by groups
- Knife, fork, cup
- Large, heavy-duty garbage bags
- Matches stored in resealable (such as Ziploc) bags
- One lighter for each camper
- Paper towels
- Plastic spatula and stir spoon
- Pot grabber or pot holder
- Salt, pepper, spices
- Two pots and no-stick pan
- Water jug or lightweight plastic "cube"

### Optional Cooking Gear

- Aluminum foil
- Ax or hatchet
- Barbecue tongs
- Can opener
- Candles
- Dustpan
- Grill or hibachi
- Plastic clothespins
- Tablecloth
- Whisk broom
- Wood or charcoal for barbecue

## CLOTHING

- Cotton/canvas pants
- Gore-Tex parka or jacket
- Gore-Tex rain pants
- Lightweight, breathable shirt
- Lightweight fleece jacket
- Medium-weight fleece vest
- Polypropylene underwear
- Rain jacket and pants, or poncho
- Sunglasses
- Waterproofed, oilskin wide-brimmed hat

### Optional Clothing

- Gloves
- Shorts
- Ski cap

## HIKING GEAR

- Backpack or daypack
- Hiking boots
- Fresh bootlaces
- Innersole or foot cushion (for expeditions)
- Moleskin and medical tape
- SmartWool (or equivalent) socks
- Water-purification system

### Optional Hiking Gear

- Backup lightweight shoes or moccasins
- Gaiters
- Water-repellent boot treatment

## Sleeping Gear

- Ground tarp
- Sleeping bag
- Tent or bivy bag
- Therm-a-Rest pad

### Optional Sleeping Gear

- Air bed
- Cot
- Catalytic heater
- Foam pad for truck bed

- Mosquito netting
- Mr. Heater and propane tank (for use in pickup truck camper shell)
- Pillow (even in wilderness)
- RV windshield light screen
- Seam Lock for tent stitching

## FIRST AID

- Ace bandage
- After-Bite for mosquito bites (before you scratch them)
- Aspirin
- Biodegradable soap
- Caladryl for poison oak
- Campho-Phenique gel for bites (after you scratch them)
- Mosquito repellent
- Lip balm
- Medical tape to affix pads
- Neosporin for cuts
- Roller gauze
- Sterile gauze pads
- Sunscreen
- Tweezers

### Optional First Aid

- Athletic tape for sprained ankle
- Cell phone or coins for phone calls
- Extra set of matches
- Mirror for signaling
- Thermometer

## RECREATION GEAR

- All required permits and licenses
- Fishing reel with fresh line
- Fishing rod
- Knife

- Leatherman tool or needle-nose pliers
- Small tackle box with flies, floats, hooks, lures, snap swivels, and splitshot

### Optional Recreation Gear

- Backpacking cribbage board
- Deck of cards
- Folding chairs
- Guidebooks
- Hammock
- Mountain bike
- Reading material

## OTHER NECESSITIES

- Duct tape
- Extra plastic garbage bags
- Flashlight and batteries
- Lantern and fuel
- Maps
- Nylon rope for food hang
- Spade for cat hole
- Toilet paper
- Toothbrush and toothpaste
- Towelettes
- Wristwatch

## OTHER OPTIONAL ITEMS

- Altimeter
- Assorted bungee cords
- Binoculars
- Camera with fresh battery and digital card or film
- Compass
- Feminine hygiene products
- GPS unit
- Handkerchief
- Notebook and pen

# Washington

# WASHINGTON REGIONS

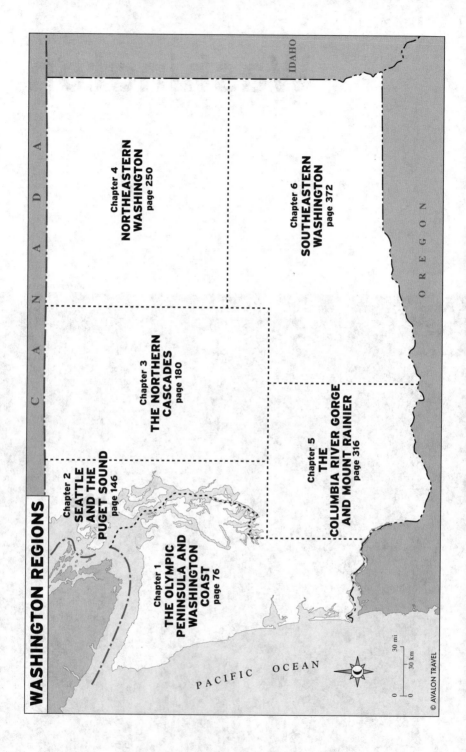

Chapter 2
**SEATTLE AND THE PUGET SOUND**
page 146

Chapter 1
**THE OLYMPIC PENINSULA AND WASHINGTON COAST**
page 76

Chapter 3
**THE NORTHERN CASCADES**
page 180

Chapter 4
**NORTHEASTERN WASHINGTON**
page 250

Chapter 5
**THE COLUMBIA RIVER GORGE AND MOUNT RAINIER**
page 316

Chapter 6
**SOUTHEASTERN WASHINGTON**
page 372

CANADA

IDAHO

OREGON

PACIFIC OCEAN

0 — 30 mi
0 — 30 km

© AVALON TRAVEL

# THE OLYMPIC PENINSULA AND WASHINGTON COAST

© NATALIA BRATSLAVSKY/123RF

Vast, diverse, and beautiful, the Olympic Peninsula is like no other landscape. Water borders the region on three sides: the Pacific Ocean to the west, the Strait of Juan de Fuca to the north, and the inlets of Hood Canal to the east. At its center are Olympic National Park and Mount Olympus, with rainforests on its slopes feeding rivers and lakes that make up the most dynamic river complex in America. Almost every one of these rivers provides campsites, often within walking distance of prime steelhead fishing spots. A series of stellar campgrounds ring the perimeter foothills of Mount Olympus, both in Olympic National Park and at the state parks and areas managed by the Department of Natural Resources. Your campsite can be your launch pad for adventure—just be sure to bring your rain gear.

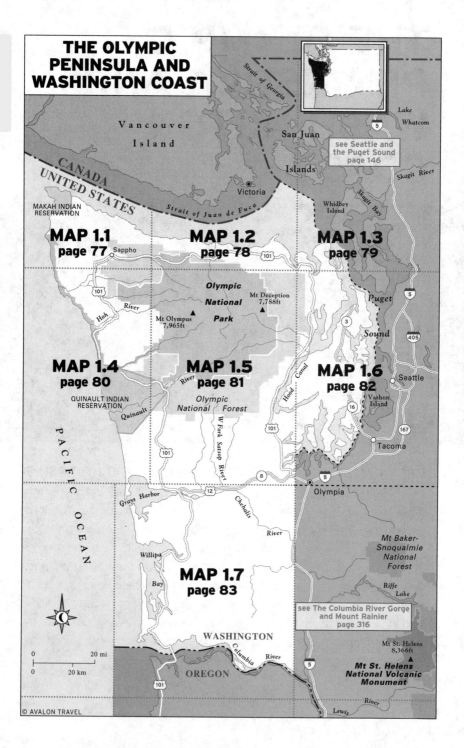

# THE OLYMPIC PENINSULA AND WASHINGTON COAST

Strait of Georgia

Vancouver Island

San Juan Islands

see Seattle and the Puget Sound page 146

Lake Whatcom

Skagit River

CANADA

UNITED STATES

Victoria

Strait of Juan de Fuca

Whidbey Island

Skagit Bay

MAKAH INDIAN RESERVATION

**MAP 1.1**
**page 77**

Sappho

**MAP 1.2**
**page 78**

101

**MAP 1.3**
**page 79**

101

Puget

5

Hoh River

Olympic

National

Mt Deception 7,788ft ▲

Park

Mt Olympus 7,965ft ▲

3

Sound

405

**MAP 1.4**
**page 80**

QUINAULT INDIAN RESERVATION

Quinault

River

**MAP 1.5**
**page 81**

Olympic National Forest

W Fork Satsop River

Hood Canal

**MAP 1.6**
**page 82**

Vashon Island

16

Seattle

167

P A C I F I C   O C E A N

101

101

8

12

Grays Harbor

Chehalis

Tacoma

5

Olympia

Willipa

Bay

River

Mt Baker-Snoqualmie National Forest

Riffe Lake

**MAP 1.7**
**page 83**

see The Columbia River Gorge and Mount Rainier page 316

WASHINGTON

0    20 mi
0    20 km

Columbia     River

OREGON

101

5

Mt St. Helens 8,366ft ▲

**Mt St. Helens National Volcanic Monument**

Lewis     River

© AVALON TRAVEL

# Map 1.1

**Sites 1-8**
**Pages 84-87**

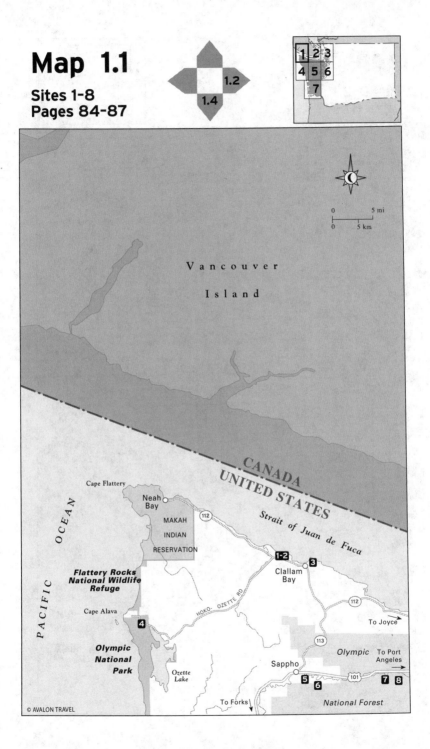

# Map 1.2

**Sites 9-23
Pages 87-93**

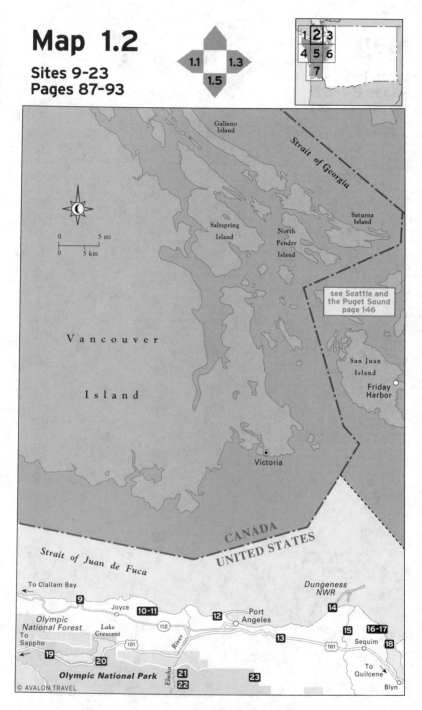

Galiano Island

Strait of Georgia

Saltspring Island

North Pender Island

Saturna Island

see Seattle and the Puget Sound page 146

Vancouver

Island

San Juan Island

Friday Harbor

Victoria

CANADA

UNITED STATES

Strait of Juan de Fuca

To Clallam Bay

**9**

Joyce

**10-11**

Dungeness NWR

**14**

Olympic National Forest

Lake Crescent

**12**

Port Angeles

To Sappho

112

River

101

**13**

**15**

**16-17**

Sequim

**18**

**19**

**20**

101

To Quilcene

**Olympic National Park**

Elwha

**21**
**22**

**23**

Blyn

© AVALON TRAVEL

0   5 mi
0   5 km

# Map 1.3

### Sites 24-28
### Pages 94-96

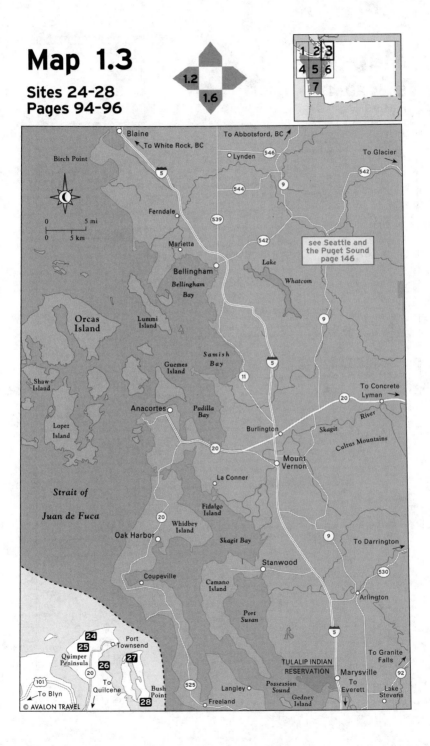

# Map 1.4
**Sites 29-47**
**Pages 96-104**

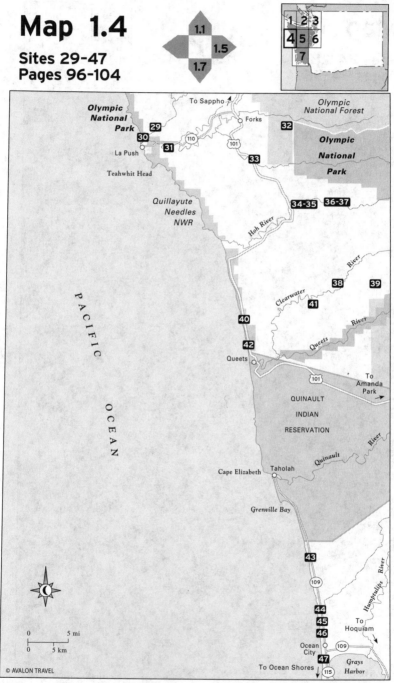

© AVALON TRAVEL

# Map 1.5

**Sites 48-76**
**Pages 104-117**

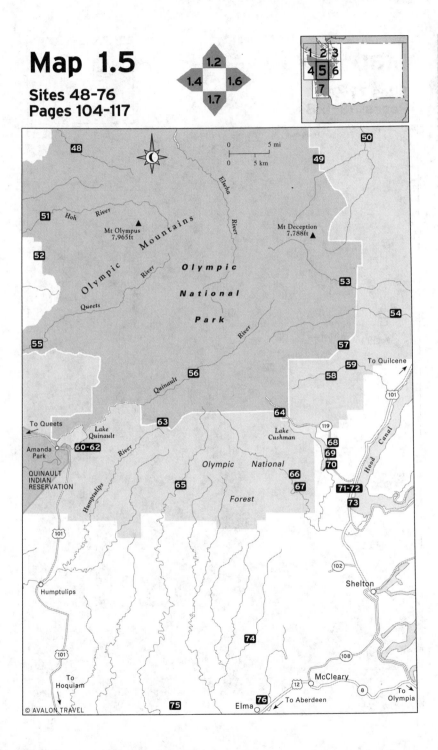

# Map 1.6

## Sites 77-95
## Pages 118-128

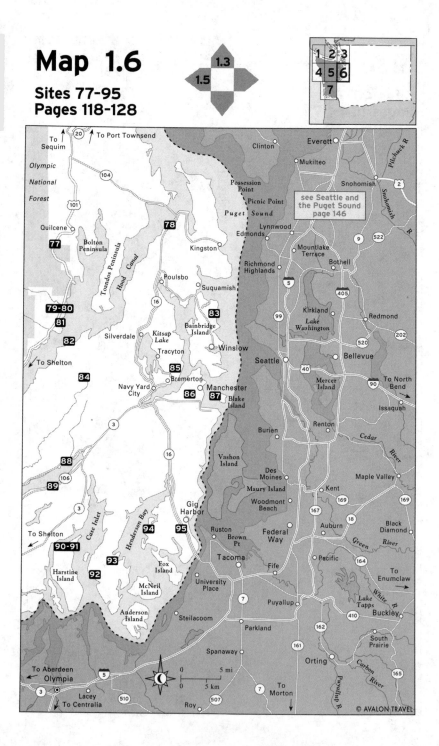

1.3
1.5

1 2 3
4 5 6
7

To Sequim
To ↑ 20 ↑ To Port Townsend
Olympic
National
Forest
104
101
Quilcene
77
Bolton Peninsula
Toandos Peninsula
Hood Canal
78
Kingston
Poulsbo
16
Suquamish
79-80
81
82
Silverdale
Kitsap Lake
Tracyton
84
85
Navy Yard City
Bremerton
86
3
16
88
106
89
3
Case Inlet
Henderson Bay
90-91
92
93
94
95
Gig Harbor
Ruston
Brown Pt
Harstine Island
Fox Island
McNeil Island
Anderson Island
University Place
Steilacoom
To Aberdeen
Olympia
5
3
Lacey
To Centralia
510
Roy
507

Clinton
Everett
Mukilteo
Pilchuck R
Possession Point
Picnic Point
Snohomish
2
Puget Sound
Lynnwood
Edmonds
see Seattle and the Puget Sound page 146
9
522
Snohomish R
Mountlake Terrace
Bothell
Richmond Highlands
5
405
99
Kirkland
Lake Washington
Redmond
202
Bainbridge Island
83
Winslow
520
Seattle
Bellevue
40
Mercer Island
90
To North Bend
Manchester
87
Blake Island
Issaquah
Burien
Renton
Cedar River
Vashon Island
Des Moines
Maury Island
Woodmont Beach
Kent
167
169
Maple Valley
169
Auburn
18
Black Diamond
Green River
164
To Enumclaw
Federal Way
Pacific
Tacoma
Fife
White R
Lake Tapps
Buckley
410
Puyallup
Parkland
162
South Prairie
Spanaway
161
Orting
Carbon River
165
Puyallup R
To Morton
7
7

0      5 mi
0      5 km

© AVALON TRAVEL

# Map 1.7

**Sites 96-127
Pages 128-143**

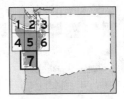

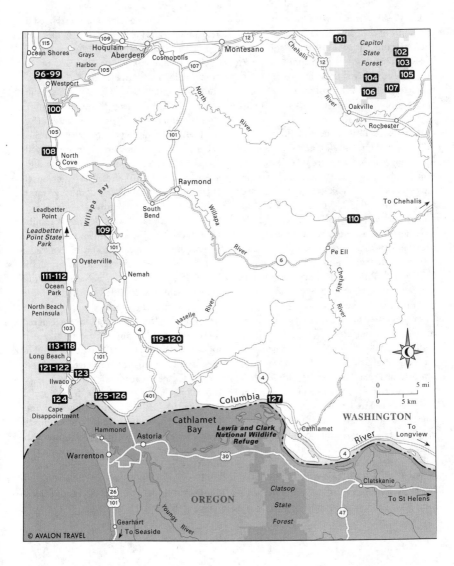

## 1 VAN RIPER'S RESORT

[icons]

Scenic rating: 7

on Clallam Bay in Sekiu

**Map 1.1, page 77**

Part of this campground hugs the waterfront and the other part sits on a hill overlooking the Strait of Juan de Fuca. Most sites are graveled, many with views of the strait. Other sites are grassy, without views. Note that some of the campsites are rented for the entire summer season. Hiking, fishing, and boating are among the options here, with salmon fishing being the principal draw. The beaches in the area, a mixture of sand and gravel, provide diligent rock hounds with agates and fossils.

**Campsites, facilities:** There are 100 sites with full or partial hookups (30 amps) for tents or RVs of any length. Some sites are pull-through. A mobile home, a house, and 12 motel rooms are also available. Picnic tables are provided; fire rings and cable TV are available at some sites. Restrooms with flush toilets and showers, drinking water, a dump station, firewood, and ice are available. A store, café, and coin laundry are located within one mile. Boat docks, launching facilities, and rentals are available. Leashed pets are permitted; no pets are allowed in cabins or other buildings.

**Reservations, fees:** Reservations are not accepted for campsites. Sites are $18-30 per night. Open April-September. Some credit cards are accepted.

**Directions:** From Port Angeles, take U.S. 101 west and drive 41 miles to Sappho Junction and Highway 113. Continue north on Highway 113 for nine miles to a fork with Highway 112. Take Highway 112 for two miles to Sekiu and Front Street. Turn right and drive 0.25 mile to the resort on the right.

**Contact:** Van Riper's Resort, 280 Front Street, Sekiu, 360/963-2334, www.vanripersresort.com.

## 2 OLSON'S RESORT

[icons]

Scenic rating: 5

in Sekiu

**Map 1.1, page 77**

Olson's Resort is large with full services, and the nearby marina is salmon-fishing headquarters. In fact, the resort caters to anglers, offering all-day salmon-fishing trips and boat moorage. Chartered trips can be arranged by reservation. A tackle shop, cabins, houses, and a motel are also available. Other recreation options include hiking, boating, and beach-combing for agates and fossils.

**Campsites, facilities:** There are 55 sites for tents or RVs of any length (no hookups), 45 sites with for tents or RVs of any length (full hookups), 10 camping cabins, four furnished cabins, 14 motel rooms, and four houses available. Picnic tables are provided, and fire rings are available at most sites. Restrooms with flush toilets and showers, drinking water, a dump station, coin laundry, convenience store, bait and tackle, and ice are available. Boat docks, launching facilities, boat rentals, bait, tackle, fish-cleaning station, and gear storage are also available on-site. A restaurant is within walking distance. Some facilities are wheelchair accessible. Leashed pets are allowed, with certain restrictions.

**Reservations, fees:** Reservations are required for the motel and cabins, but are not accepted for campsites. RV sites are $30 per night, tent sites are $22 per night. Some credit cards are accepted. Open year-round.

**Directions:** From Port Angeles, drive 41 miles west on U.S. 101 to Sappho Junction and Highway 113. Continue north on Highway 113 for nine miles to a fork with Highway 112. Take Highway 112 for two miles to Sekiu and Front Street. Turn right and drive one block to the resort on the right.

**Contact:** Olson's Resort, 444 Front Street, Sekiu, 360/963-2311.

## 3 SAM'S MOBILE HOME AND RV PARK

### Scenic rating: 5

on Clallam Bay

**Map 1.1, page 77**

Sam's is an alternative to other resorts on Clallam Bay. It's a family-oriented park with grassy sites and many recreation options nearby. A mobile home park is adjacent to the RV park. Beaches are within walking distance. Those wanting to visit Cape Flattery, Hoh Rain Forest, or Port Angeles will find this a good central location.

**Campsites, facilities:** There are 21 sites, including some pull-through sites, with full hookups for RVs of any length and four sites for tents. Picnic tables are provided at some sites. Restrooms with flush toilets and showers, a dump station, Wi-Fi, and coin laundry are available. Propane gas, gasoline, a store, café, and ice are located within one mile. Boat docks, launching facilities, and boat rentals are located within two miles. Some facilities are wheelchair accessible. Leashed pets are permitted.

**Reservations, fees:** Reservations are accepted. RV sites are $24 per night, tent sites are $15 per night, $2 per person per night for more than two people. Credit cards are not accepted. Open year-round.

**Directions:** From Aberdeen, drive north on U.S. 101 for 119 miles to Sappho and Highway 113. Turn north on Highway 113 and drive nine miles to Clallam Bay and Highway 112. Continue straight on Highway 112 and drive into Clallam Bay. Just as you come into town, the park is on the right at 17053 Highway 112.

**Contact:** Sam's Mobile Home and RV Park, 17053 Hwy. 112, Clallam Bay, 360/963-2402.

## 4 OZETTE

### Scenic rating: 6

on Lake Ozette in Olympic National Park

**Map 1.1, page 77**

Many people visit this site located on the shore of Lake Ozette just a few miles from the Pacific Ocean. Set close to a trailhead road and ranger station, with multiple trailheads nearby, this camp is a favorite for both hikers and boaters and is one of the first to fill in the park.

**Campsites, facilities:** There are 15 sites for tents or RVs up to 21 feet long. Picnic tables and fire grills are provided. Pit toilets are available. There is no drinking water and garbage must be packed out. Leashed pets are permitted.

**Reservations, fees:** Reservations are not accepted. Sites are $12 per night, plus a $15 national park entrance fee per vehicle. Open year-round, weather permitting.

**Directions:** From Port Angeles, drive west on U.S. 101 to the junction with Highway 112. Bear right on Highway 112 and drive to Hoko-Ozette Road. Turn left and drive 21 miles to the ranger station. The camp parking lot is across from the ranger station on the northwest corner of Lake Ozette.

**Contact:** Olympic National Park, 360/565-3130, www.nps.gov/olym.

## 5 BEAR CREEK MOTEL AND RV PARK

### Scenic rating: 7

on Bear Creek

**Map 1.1, page 77**

This quiet little spot is set where Bear Creek empties into the Sol Duc River. It's private and developed, with a choice of sunny or shaded sites in a wooded setting. There are many recreation options in the area, including fishing, hunting, and nature and hiking trails leading to the ocean. Sol Duc Hot Springs is 25 miles north and well worth the trip. A restaurant next to the camp serves family-style meals.

**Campsites, facilities:** There are 12 sites for RVs of any length (full hookups); all sites are pull-through. There is also an area for tent camping and a motel on the premises. Picnic tables and fire rings are provided. Restrooms with flush toilets and showers, drinking water, a dump station, a café, and firewood are available. Boat-launching facilities are located within 0.5 mile. Some facilities are wheelchair accessible. Leashed pets are permitted.

**Reservations, fees:** Reservations are not accepted. RV sites are $25 per night, tent sites are $15 per night. Some credit cards are accepted. Open year-round.

**Directions:** From Aberdeen, drive north on U.S. 101 to Forks. Continue past Forks for 15 miles to Milepost 205 (just past Sappho) to the park on the right at 205860 Highway 101 West.

**Contact:** Bear Creek Motel and RV Park, Milepost 206, Beaver, 360/327-3660, www.hungrybearcafemotel.com.

## 6 BEAR CREEK

### Scenic rating: 8

on the Sol Duc River

**Map 1.1, page 77**   BEST (

Fishing for salmon and hiking along the Sol Duc River make this a good launch point for recreation. There are also good opportunities for wildlife-viewing and photography, including a wheelchair-accessible viewing platform overlooking the Sol Duc River. This camp is also popular in the fall with hunters.

**Campsites, facilities:** There are 14 sites for tents. Vault toilets and fire pits are available. There is no drinking water and garbage must be packed out. Some facilities are wheelchair accessible. Leashed pets are permitted.

**Reservations, fees:** Reservations are not accepted. There is no fee for camping, but a Discover Pass is required. Open year-round.

**Directions:** From Olympia on I-5, take Exit 104 and drive north on U.S. 101 to the Aberdeen/Highway 8 exit. Turn west on Highway 8 and drive 36 miles to Aberdeen. Continue through Aberdeen four miles to U.S. 101 and turn north and drive to Forks. Continue past Forks for 15 miles to Milepost 206 (two miles past Sappho) to the campground on the right.

**Contact:** Department of Natural Resources, Olympic Region, 360/374-6131, www.dnr.wa.gov.

## 7 KLAHOWYA

### Scenic rating: 9

on the Sol Duc River in Olympic National Forest

**Map 1.1, page 77**

Klahowya features great views of Lake Crescent and Mount Olympus. It's a good choice if you don't want to venture far from U.S. 101 yet want to retain the feel of being in Olympic National Forest. Set along the Sol Duc River, this 32-acre camp is pretty and wooded, with hiking trails in the area. A favorite, Kloshe Nanitch Trail, is across the river and leads up to a lookout on Snider Ridge overlooking Sol Duc Valley. Pioneer's Path Trail, an easy, wheelchair-accessible, 0.3-mile loop with interpretive signs starts in the camp. Fishing for salmon and steelhead, in season, can be good about 0.25 mile downstream from camp; always check regulations. This camp gets medium use, but can fill up on weekends.

**Campsites, facilities:** There are 55 sites for tents or RVs up to 30 feet long and two hike-in tent sites requiring a 500-foot walk. Picnic tables and fire grills are provided. Drinking water, garbage bins, and vault and flush toilets are available. An amphitheater with summer interpretive programs is also available. A boat ramp is nearby. Some facilities are wheelchair accessible. Leashed pets are permitted.

**Reservations, fees:** Reservations are not accepted. Sites are $17 per night, $5 per night per additional vehicle. Open May-late October, weather permitting.

**Directions:** From U.S. 101 in Port Angeles, drive west for about 33 miles (10 miles west of Lake Crescent) to the campground on the right side of the road, close to Milepost 212. (Coming from the other direction on U.S. 101, drive eight miles east of Sappho to the campground.)

**Contact:** Olympic National Forest, Pacific Ranger District, 360/374-6522, www.fs.usda. us.

# 8 LITTLETON HORSE CAMP

### Scenic rating: 8

on Littleton Creek near Mount Muller Trailhead in Olympic National Forest

**Map 1.1, page 77**

This new campground allows equestrian campers to explore more than 25 miles of trails including Mount Muller, Olympic Discovery trails, and Snider Ridge. The trail from camp heads through some lush vine maple tunnel trails and continues along panoramic ridge tops. Some sites are adjacent to stock corrals.

**Campsites, facilities:** There are six sites for tents or RVs and stock trailers, and five walk-in tent sites. Picnic tables and fire grills are provided. Vault toilets and garbage bins are available. There is no drinking water, but stock water is available May-October. Some facilities are wheelchair accessible. Leashed pets are permitted.

**Reservations, fees:** Reservations are not accepted. Sites are $10 per night, $5 per night per additional vehicle. Open year-round, weather permitting.

**Directions:** Littleton Horse Camp is located approximately 24 miles east of Forks and 31 miles west of Port Angeles. From U.S. 101, follow Forest Service Road 3071 (near Milepost 216) to the campground.

**Contact:** Olympic National Forest, Pacific Ranger District, 360/374-6522, www.fs.usda.gov.

# 9 LYRE RIVER

### Scenic rating: 7

on the Lyre River

**Map 1.2, page 78**

This prime spot is one of the rare free campgrounds on the Olympic Peninsula. Although quite primitive, it does offer drinking water and an even more precious commodity in these parts: privacy. The camp is set along the Lyre River, about 0.5 mile from where it enters the Strait of Juan de Fuca. A popular camp for anglers, Lyre River offers good salmon fishing during fish migrations; always check fishing regulations. A wheelchair-accessible fishing pier is available.

**Campsites, facilities:** There are 11 primitive sites for tents only. Picnic tables, fire grills, and tent pads are provided. Vault toilets and drinking water are available. Garbage must be packed out. A roofed group shelter is available. Some facilities are wheelchair accessible. Leashed pets are permitted.

**Reservations, fees:** Reservations are not accepted. There is no fee for camping, but a Discover Pass is required. Open year-round, with limited services in winter.

**Directions:** From U.S. 101 in Port Angeles, drive north five miles to a fork with Highway 112. Turn right (west) on Highway 112 and drive about 15 miles to Milepost 46. Look to the right for a paved road between Mileposts 46 and 47, then turn right (north) and drive 0.4 mile to the camp entrance road on the left.

**Contact:** Department of Natural Resources, Olympic Region, 360/374-6131, www.dnr. wa.gov.

# 10 CRESCENT BEACH RV PARK

### Scenic rating: 6

in Port Angeles on the Strait of Juan de Fuca

**Map 1.2, page 78**

Set on a half-mile stretch of sandy beach, this

campground makes a perfect weekend spot. Popular activities include swimming, fishing, surfing, sea kayaking, and beachcombing. It borders Salt Creek Recreation Area, with direct access available. Numerous attractions and recreation options are available in Port Angeles.

**Campsites, facilities:** There are 41 sites with full or partial hookups (30 and 50 amps) for tents or RVs of any length and a grassy area for tent camping. Picnic tables and fire rings are provided. Restrooms with flush toilets and coin showers, coin laundry, firewood, Wi-Fi, recreation field, and horseshoe pits are available. Some facilities are wheelchair accessible, including a boardwalk that allows beach access. Leashed pets are permitted.

**Reservations, fees:** Reservations are accepted. Sites are $37-42 per night, $6 per person per night for more than two people, $5 per extra vehicle (one-time fee per stay) unless towed, and $6 per night per pet. Weekly and monthly rates are available. Credit cards are accepted. Open year-round.

**Directions:** From U.S. 101 in Port Angeles, drive north five miles to a fork with Highway 112. Turn right (west) on Highway 112 and drive 10 miles to Camp Hayden Road (between Mileposts 53 and 54). Turn right on Camp Hayden Road and drive four miles to the park on the left, on the beach.

**Contact:** Crescent Beach RV Park, 2860 Crescent Beach Road, Port Angeles, 360/928-3344, www.olypen.com/crescent.

## 11 SALT CREEK RECREATION AREA

🏃 🏊 🚣 🎣 🐕 🚵 ♿ 🚐 ⛺

**Scenic rating: 8**

west of Port Angeles near the Strait of Juan de Fuca

**Map 1.2, page 78**

The former site of Camp Hayden, a World War II-era facility, Salt Creek Recreation Area is a great spot for gorgeous ocean views, fishing, and hiking near Striped Peak, which overlooks the campground. Only a small beach area is available because of the rugged coastline, but there is an exceptionally good spot for tidepool viewing on the park's west side. The park covers 196 acres and overlooks the Strait of Juan de Fuca. It is known for its Tongue Point Marine Life Sanctuary. Recreation options include nearby hiking trails, swimming, fishing, horseshoes, and field sports. It's a good layover spot if you're planning to take the ferry out of Port Angeles to Victoria, British Columbia. The camp fills up quickly most summer weekends.

**Campsites, facilities:** There are 92 sites, some with partial hookups (30 and 50 amps), for tents or RVs of any length. Some sites are pull-through. Picnic tables and fire rings are provided. Restroom with flush toilets and coin showers, dump station, firewood, a playground, and a reservable covered picnic shelter are available. A camp host is onsite. Some facilities are wheelchair accessible. Leashed pets are permitted.

**Reservations, fees:** Reservations are accepted only by mail or in person ($7 reservation fee). RV sites are $24-27 per night, tent sites are $19-22 per night, $5 per extra vehicle per night. Credit cards are not accepted. Open year-round.

**Directions:** From U.S. 101 in Port Angeles, drive north five miles to a fork with Highway 112. Turn right (west) on Highway 112 and drive 13 miles to Camp Hayden Road. Turn right (north) near Mile Marker 54 and drive 3.5 miles to the park entrance on the left. Note that the gate closes at 10pm.

**Contact:** Salt Creek Recreation Area, Clallam County, 3506 Camp Hayden Road, Port Angeles, 360/928-3441, www.clallam.net/Parks.

## 12 AL'S RV PARK

🏃 🚴 🚣 🏊 🎣 🐕 ♿ 🚐 ⛺

**Scenic rating: 8**

near Port Angeles

**Map 1.2, page 78**

This campground is a good choice for RV

owners. The campground is set in the country at about 1,000 feet elevation yet is centrally located and not far from the Strait of Juan de Fuca. Nearby recreation options include an 18-hole golf course and a full-service marina. Olympic National Park and the Victoria ferry are a short drive away.

**Campsites, facilities:** There are 33 sites with full hookups (20, 30, and 50 amps) for RVs up to 40 feet long and a grassy area for tents. Picnic tables are provided. No open fires are allowed. Restrooms with flush toilets and showers, drinking water, cable TV, modem access, and a coin laundry are available. A store, café, propane gas, and ice are located within 0.5 mile. Boat docks and launching facilities are located within two miles. Some facilities are wheelchair accessible. Leashed pets are permitted.

**Reservations, fees:** Reservations are not accepted. RV sites are $28 per night, tent sites are $18 per night, $3 per person per night for more than two people. Weekly and monthly rates available. Credit cards are not accepted. Open year-round.

**Directions:** From Port Angeles, take U.S. 101 east for two miles to North Brook Avenue. Turn left (north) on North Brook Avenue, then left (almost immediately) on Lees Creek Road, and drive 0.5 mile to the park on the right.

**Contact:** Al's RV Park, 3506 Camp Hayden Road, 360/457-9844.

## 13 KOA PORT ANGELES-SEQUIM

🧍 🚲 🏊 🏕 🚶 ♿ 🚐 ⛺

**Scenic rating: 5**

near Port Angeles

**Map 1.2, page 78**

This is a private, developed camp covering 13 acres in a country setting. A pleasant park, it features the typical KOA offerings, including a pool, recreation hall, and playground. Horseshoe pits and a sports field are also available. Hayrides are available in summer. Nearby recreation

options include miniature golf, an 18-hole golf course, marked hiking trails, and tennis courts, and nearby side trips include Victoria, Butchart Gardens, and whale-watching tours.

**Campsites, facilities:** There are 82 sites with full and partial hookups (20, 30, and 50 amps) for tents or RVs of any length, 19 sites for tents, 12 cabins, and one lodge. Some sites are pull-through. Picnic tables and fire pits are provided. Restrooms with flush toilets and showers, drinking water, cable TV, Wi-Fi, propane gas, firewood, dump station, convenience store, coin laundry, ice, a playground, miniature golf, organized activities, bicycle rentals, a game room, and a seasonal heated swimming pool and spa are available. A café is located within two miles. Some facilities are wheelchair accessible. Leashed pets are permitted.

**Reservations, fees:** Reservations are accepted at 800/562-7558. Sites are $20-80 per night, $5-6.50 per person per night for more than two people (ages six and older), and $5.50 per extra vehicle per night. Some credit cards are accepted. Open March-October.

**Directions:** In Port Angeles, go east on Highway 101 for seven miles to O'Brien Road. Turn right on O'Brien Road and drive half a block to the campground on the right.

**Contact:** KOA Port Angeles-Sequim, 360/457-5916, www.koa.com.

## 14 DUNGENESS RECREATION AREA

🧍 🚣 🏕 🚶 ♿ 🚐 ⛺

**Scenic rating: 5**

between Port Angeles and Sequim near the Strait of Juan de Fuca

**Map 1.2, page 78**

This 216-acre park overlooks the Strait of Juan de Fuca and is set near the Dungeness National Wildlife Refuge. Quite popular, it fills up on summer weekends. A highlight, the refuge sits on a seven-mile spit with a historic lighthouse at its end. Bird-watchers often spot bald eagles in the wildlife refuge. There is a one-mile bluff trail, and equestrian trails are available. A 100-acre upland hunting area is open during season. Nearby recreation options include marked hiking trails, fishing, and golfing. The toll ferry at Port Angeles can take you to Victoria, British Columbia.

**Campsites, facilities:** There are 66 sites, including five pull-through sites, for tents or RVs of any length (no hookups) and eight hike-in/bike-in sites. Picnic tables and fire grills are provided. Restrooms with flush toilets and coin showers, drinking water, firewood, dump station, a playground, and a picnic area are available. A camp host is on-site. Some facilities are wheelchair accessible. Leashed pets are permitted.

**Reservations, fees:** Reservations are accepted only by downloading a reservation form at www.clallam.net/CountyParks. Sites are $22 per night, $5 per extra vehicle per night. Discount for Clallam County residents. Open year-round; entrance gates close at dusk.

**Directions:** From Sequim, drive north on U.S. 101 for four miles to Kitchen-Dick Road. Turn right (north) on Kitchen-Dick Road and drive three miles to the park on the left.

**Contact:** Dungeness Recreation Area, Clallam County, 554 Voice of America West, Sequim, 360/683-5847, www.clallam.net/Parks.

## 15 SEQUIM WEST INN & RV PARK

### Scenic rating: 5
in Sequim near the Dungeness River

Map 1.2, page 78

This two-acre camp is near the Dungeness River and within 10 miles of Dungeness National Wildlife Refuge. It's located in town and is a pleasant spot with full facilities and an urban setting. An 18-hole golf course and a full-service marina at Sequim Bay are close by.

**Campsites, facilities:** There are 27 pull-through sites for tents or RVs of any length (30 and 50 amp full hookups), 17 cabins, and 21 motel rooms. Picnic tables are provided. No open fires are allowed. Restrooms with flush toilets and showers, drinking water, cable TV, coin laundry, a pay phone, and ice are available. Propane gas, gasoline, a store, and a café are located within one mile. Some facilities are wheelchair accessible. Leashed pets are permitted.

**Reservations, fees:** Reservations are accepted. Sites are $29-34 per night, $2 per person per night for more than two adults. Some credit cards are accepted. Open year-round.

**Directions:** From Sequim and U.S. 101, take the Washington Street exit and drive west on Washington Street for 2.7 miles to the park on the left.

**Contact:** Sequim West Inn & RV Park, 740 W. Washington, Sequim, 360/683-4144 or 800/528-4527, http://sequimwestinn.com.

## 16 RAINBOW'S END RV PARK

### Scenic rating: 6
near Sequim

Map 1.2, page 78

This park, located just west of Sequim, is pretty and clean. It features a pond (no fishing), a creek running through the campground, and beautiful views of the Olympic Mountains. There is a special landscaped area available for reunions, weddings, and other gatherings. Nearby recreation opportunities include an 18-hole golf course, marked bike trails, a full-service marina, and tennis courts.

**Campsites, facilities:** There are 10 sites for tents and 39 sites with full hookups (30 and 50 amps), including some pull-through sites, for RVs of any length. Picnic tables are provided at all sites; fire pits are provided at tent sites. Restrooms with flush toilets and showers, drinking water, dump station, cable TV, Wi-Fi, propane gas, firewood, coin laundry, a dog park, and a clubhouse are available. A store, café, and ice are located within one mile. Leashed pets are permitted.

**Reservations, fees:** Reservations are accepted. RV sites are $27-36 per night, tent sites are $30 per night, $2 per person per night for more than two people, $2 per extra vehicle per night. Weekly and monthly rates are available. Some credit cards are accepted. Open year-round.

**Directions:** From Sequim, drive west on U.S. 101 for one mile past the River Road exit to the park on the right (along the highway).

**Contact:** Rainbow's End RV Park, 261831 Hwy. 101, Sequim, 360/683-3863, www.rainbowsendrvpark.com.

## 17 JOHN WAYNE'S WATERFRONT RESORT

### Scenic rating: 5

on Sequim Bay

**Map 1.2, page 78**

This is Sequim Bay headquarters for salmon anglers. The camp is set in a wooded, hilly area, close to many activity centers and with an 18-hole golf course nearby.

**Campsites, facilities:** There are 42 sites with full hookups (30 amps) for tents or RVs of any length (30 sites are pull-through) and eight cabins. Picnic tables are provided. Restrooms with flush toilets and showers, drinking water, cable TV, community fire rings, Wi-Fi, store, firewood, clubhouse, volleyball, badminton, horseshoe pits, tetherball, walking trails, and coin laundry are available. Boat docks and launching facilities are located across the street from the resort. Leashed pets are permitted.

**Reservations, fees:** Reservations are accepted. Sites are $28-42 per night, $3 per pet per night. Some credit cards are accepted. Open year-round.

**Directions:** In Sequim, drive north 2.5 miles on U.S. 101 to Whitefeather Way (located between Mileposts 267 and 268). Turn right (north) on Whitefeather Way and drive 0.5 mile to West Sequim Bay Road. Turn left (west) and drive one block to the resort on the left.

**Contact:** John Wayne's Waterfront Resort, 2634 West Sequim Bay Road, Sequim, 360/681-3853, www.johnwaynewaterfrontresort.com.

## 18 SEQUIM BAY STATE PARK

### Scenic rating: 8

on Sequim Bay

**Map 1.2, page 78**

Sequim translates to "quiet waters," which is an appropriate description of this area. Set in the heart of Washington's rain shadow, a region with far less rainfall than the surrounding areas, Sequim averages only 17 inches of rainfall a year. The 92-acre park features 4,909 feet of saltwater shoreline; two sandbars shield the park from the Strait of Juan de Fuca's rough waters. There is one mile of hiking trails.

**Campsites, facilities:** There are 49 sites for tents or RVs (no hookups), 16 sites with full hookups (30 amps) for RVs up to 40 feet long, three primitive tent sites near the water, and one tent-only group site for up to 40 people (available mid-May-mid-September). Picnic tables and fire grills are provided. Restrooms with flush toilets and coin showers, drinking water, a dump station, a picnic area with kitchen shelters, an amphitheater, athletic fields, a basketball court, tennis courts, horseshoe pits, playground, and interpretive center are available. Boat docks, launching facilities, and boat mooring are also available. Some facilities are wheelchair accessible. Leashed pets are permitted.

**Reservations, fees:** Reservations are accepted at 888/CAMP-OUT (888/226-7688) or www.goingtocamp.com ($6.50-8.50 reservation fee). Sites are $23-37 per night, $12 per night for hike-in/bike-in sites, $10 per extra vehicle per night, and the group site is $81.69 per night. Boat moorage is $0.60 per foot with a $12 minimum. Some credit cards are accepted. Open year-round.

**Directions:** From Olympia on I-5, turn north

on U.S. 101 and drive 100 miles (near Sequim) to the park entrance on the right (along the highway). The park is located 3.5 miles southeast of the town of Sequim.

**Contact:** Sequim Bay State Park, 360/683-4235; state park information, 360/902-8844, www.parks.wa.gov.

# 19 FAIRHOLME

### Scenic rating: 9
on Lake Crescent in Olympic National Park

**Map 1.2, page 78**

This camp is set on the shore of Lake Crescent, a pretty lake situated within the boundary of Olympic National Park, at an elevation of 580 feet. The campsites lie along the western end of the lake, in a cove with a boat ramp. Located less than one mile off U.S. 101, Fairholme gets heavy use during tourist months; some highway noise is audible at some sites. A naturalist program is often available in the summer. Waterskiing is permitted at Lake Crescent, but personal watercraft are prohibited.

**Campsites, facilities:** There are 88 sites for tents or RVs up to 21 feet long. Picnic tables and fire grills are provided. A dump station, restrooms with flush toilets (summer season), and drinking water are available. A store and café are located within one mile. Boat-launching facilities and rentals are nearby on Lake Crescent. Some facilities are wheelchair accessible. Leashed pets are permitted.

**Reservations, fees:** Reservations are not accepted. Sites are $12 per night, plus a $15 per vehicle national park entrance fee. Open May-October, weather permitting.

**Directions:** From Port Angeles, drive west on U.S. 101 for about 26 miles and continue along Lake Crescent to North Shore Road. Turn right and drive 0.5 mile to the camp on North Shore Road on the right.

**Contact:** Olympic National Park, 360/565-3130, www.nps.gov/olym.

# 20 LOG CABIN RESORT

### Scenic rating: 10
on Lake Crescent in Olympic National Park

**Map 1.2, page 78**

Log Cabin Resort is one of my wife's favorite spots. This pretty camp along the shore of Lake Crescent is a good spot for boaters, as it features many sites near the water with excellent views. Fishing and swimming are two options at this family-oriented resort. It is home to a strain of Beardslee trout. Note the fishing is catch-and-release. Waterskiing is permitted, but no personal watercraft are allowed. A marked hiking trail traces the lake's 22-mile shoreline. This camp is extremely popular in the summer months; you may need to make reservations 3-12 months in advance.

**Campsites, facilities:** There are 38 sites with full hookups (20 and 30 amps) for RVs of any length, four sites for tents, and 28 cabins. Picnic tables and fire barrels are provided. A dump station, restrooms with flush toilets and coin showers, a store, café, gift shop, coin laundry, firewood, ice, and a recreation field are available. Boat docks, launching facilities, and boat rentals are available. Some facilities are wheelchair accessible. Leashed pets are permitted.

**Reservations, fees:** Reservations are accepted. RV sites are $45 per night, tent sites are $23-33 per night, $5 per person per night for more than two people, $2 per extra vehicle per night, $15 per pet per night. Some credit cards are accepted. Open Memorial Day weekend-mid-September.

**Directions:** In Port Angeles, drive 18 miles north on U.S. 101 to East Beach Road. Turn right and drive three miles (along Lake Crescent) to the camp on the left.

**Contact:** Log Cabin Resort, 360/928-3325, www.olympicnationalparks.com.

## 21 ELWHA

### Scenic rating: 7

on the Elwha River in Olympic National Park

**Map 1.2, page 78**

The Elwha River is the backdrop for this popular camp with excellent hiking trails close by in Olympic National Park. The elevation is 390 feet. Fishing is good in season at nearby Lake Mills; check regulations. Check at one of the visitors centers for maps and backcountry information.

**Campsites, facilities:** There are 40 sites for tents or RVs up to 35 feet long. Picnic tables and fire grills are provided. Pit toilets are available. There is no drinking water and garbage must be packed out. Some facilities are wheelchair accessible. Leashed pets are permitted.

**Reservations, fees:** Reservations are not accepted. Sites are $12 per night, plus a $15 national park entrance fee per vehicle. Open year-round.

**Directions:** From Port Angeles, drive west on U.S. 101 for about nine miles (just past Lake Aldwell) to the signed entrance road on the left. Turn left at the entrance road and drive three miles south along the Elwha River to the campground on the left.

**Contact:** Olympic National Park, 360/565-3130, www.nps.gov/olym.

## 22 ALTAIRE

### Scenic rating: 8

on the Elwha River in Olympic National Park

**Map 1.2, page 78**

A pretty and well-treed camp with easy highway access, Altaire is set on the Elwha River about one mile from Lake Mills. Boating is prohibited on the river between Upper Lake Mills Trail and the campground. Fishing is good in season; check regulations. The elevation is 450 feet. Altaire also makes for a nice layover spot before taking the ferry at Port Angeles to Victoria, British Columbia.

**Campsites, facilities:** There are 30 sites for tents or RVs up to 35 feet long. Picnic tables and fire grills are provided. Restrooms with flush toilets, drinking water, and garbage bins are available. Some facilities are wheelchair accessible. Leashed pets are permitted.

**Reservations, fees:** Reservations are not accepted. Sites are $12 per night, plus a $15 national park entrance fee per vehicle. Open late May-October.

**Directions:** From Port Angeles, drive west on U.S. 101 for about nine miles (just past Lake Aldwell) to the signed entrance road on the left. Turn left at the signed entrance road and drive four miles south along the Elwha River.

**Contact:** Olympic National Park, 360/565-3130, www.nps.gov/olym.

## 23 HEART O' THE HILLS

### Scenic rating: 9

in Olympic National Park

**Map 1.2, page 78**

Heart O' the Hills is nestled on the northern edge of Olympic National Park at an elevation of 1,807 feet. You can drive into the park on Hurricane Ridge Road and take one of numerous hiking trails. Little Lake Dawn is less than 0.5 mile to the west, but note that most of the property around this lake is privately owned. Naturalist programs are available in summer months.

**Campsites, facilities:** There are 105 sites for tents or RVs up to 21 feet long. Picnic tables and fire pits are provided. Restrooms with flush toilets, drinking water, and garbage bins are available. Some facilities are wheelchair accessible. Leashed pets are permitted.

**Reservations, fees:** Reservations are not accepted. Sites are $12 per night, plus a $15 national park entrance fee per vehicle. Open year-round, weather permitting.

**Directions:** From U.S. 101 in Port Angeles at

Hurricane Ridge Road, turn left and drive five miles to the camp on the left. (Access roads can be impassable in severe weather.)
**Contact:** Olympic National Park, 360/565-3130, www.nps.gov/olym.

## 24 FORT WORDEN STATE PARK

🚶 🚴 🚗 🐕 ♿ 🚙 ⛺

in Port Townsend

**Scenic rating: 9**

**Map 1.3, page 79**

This park is set on the northeastern tip of the Olympic Peninsula, at the northern end of Port Townsend, on a high bluff with views of Puget Sound. Highlights here include great lookouts and two miles of beach trails over the Strait of Juan de Fuca as it feeds into Puget Sound. The park covers 433 acres at historic Fort Worden (on which construction was begun in 1897 and decommissioned in 1953) and includes buildings from the turn of the 20th century. It has 11,020 feet of saltwater shoreline. Recreation options include 12 miles of marked hiking and biking trails, including five miles of wheelchair-accessible trails. The Coast Artillery Museum, Rothschild House, Commanding Officers Quarters, and the Marine Science Center and Natural History Museum are open during the summer season. A ferry at Port Townsend will take you across the strait to Whidbey Island. Special note on reservations: This is an extremely popular park and campground and reservations are required online up to five months in advance or in person up to 11 months in advance.

**Campsites, facilities:** There are 80 sites with full or partial hookups (30 and 50 amps) for tents or RVs up to 75 feet long, including some pull-through sites, five hike-in/bike-in sites, one non-motorized boat-in site, and one group camp for up to 200 people. Other lodging includes 36 Victoria-era houses and two dormitories. Picnic tables and fire grills are provided. Restrooms with flush toilets and coin showers,

drinking water, coin laundry, a store, dump station, and firewood are available. A seasonal restaurant, conference facilities, a sheltered amphitheater, athletic fields, and interpretive activities are available nearby. Boat docks, buoys, floats, and launching facilities are also nearby, as are several golf courses. Some facilities are wheelchair accessible. Leashed pets are permitted.

**Reservations, fees:** Reservations are accepted at 360/344-4431 or www.parks.wa.gov ($8.50 reservation fee). Sites are $36-42 per night, hike-in/bike-in and boat-in sites are $13-22 per night, $10 per extra vehicle per night, the group camp is $2 per person per night ($25 reservation fee), and the dorms and houses are $210-700 per night. Boat moorage is $0.60 per foot with a $12 minimum. Open year-round.

**Directions:** From Port Townsend, take Highway 20 north through town to Kearney Street. Turn left on Kearney Street and drive to the first stop sign, at Blaine Street. Turn right on Blaine Street and drive to the next stop sign, on Cherry Street. Turn left at Cherry Street and drive 1.75 miles to the park entrance at the end of the road.

**Contact:** Fort Worden State Park, 360/344-4400; state park information, 360/902-8844, www.parks.wa.gov.

## 25 POINT HUDSON MARINA & RV PARK

🎣 🚗 🐕 ♿ 🚙

in Port Townsend

**Scenic rating: 5**

**Map 1.3, page 79**

Point Hudson RV Park is located on the site of an old Coast Guard station near the beach in Port Townsend. This public facility is owned by the Port of Port Townsend. The park features ocean views and 2,000 feet of beach frontage. Known for its Victorian architecture, Port Townsend is called Washington's Victorian seaport. Fishing and boating are popular here, and nearby recreation opportunities include an 18-hole municipal golf course, a full-service marina, Old Fort Townsend State Park, Fort Flagler State Park, and Fort Worden State Park.

**Campsites, facilities:** There are 60 sites with full hookups (30 amps) for RVs of any length. Some sites are pull-through. Picnic tables are provided at some sites. No fires are allowed. Restrooms with flush toilets and coin showers, drinking water, cable TV, Wi-Fi, three restaurants, and coin laundry are available. A 100-plus-slip marina is on-site. Some facilities are wheelchair accessible. Leashed pets are permitted.

**Reservations, fees:** Reservations are accepted. Sites are $27-42 per night, $5 per extra vehicle per night. Some credit cards are accepted. Open year-round.

**Directions:** From Port Townsend on State Route 20, take the Water Street exit. Turn left (north) and continue (the road becomes Sims Way and then Water Street) to the end of Water Street at the marina. Turn left for registration.

**Contact:** Point Hudson Marina & RV Park, 360/385-2828, www.portofpt.com.

## 26 FORT TOWNSEND STATE PARK

### Scenic rating: 10

near Quilcene

Map 1.3, page 79

This 367-acre park features a thickly wooded landscape, nearly 4,000 feet of saltwater shoreline on Port Townsend Bay, and 6.5 miles of hiking trails. Built in 1856, the historic fort is one of the oldest remaining in the state. The scenic campground has access to a good clamming beach (check regulations), and visitors can take two different short, self-guided walking tours. Note that the nearest boat ramps are at Port Townsend, Fort Flagler, and Hadlock. Mooring buoys are located just offshore of the park on the west side of Port Townsend Bay.

**Campsites, facilities:** There are 40 sites for tents or RVs up to 40 feet long, one hike-in/bike-in site, and one group site for up to 80 people. Picnic tables and fire grills are provided. Restrooms with flush toilets and coin showers, drinking water, a playground, ballfields, boat buoys, firewood, a dump station, and a picnic area with a kitchen shelter are available. Some facilities are wheelchair accessible. Leashed pets are permitted.

**Reservations, fees:** Reservations are accepted at www.goingtocamp.com ($6.50-8.50 reservation fee). Sites are $22-37 per night, $10 per extra vehicle per night, hike-in/bike-in sites are $12 per night. Call 360/385-3595 to reserve the group camp ($25 reservation fee); rates vary seasonally and according to group size. Open mid-April-mid-October, weather permitting.

**Directions:** From Port Townsend and State Route 20, drive south on State Route 20 for two miles to Old Fort Townsend Road. Turn left and drive 0.5 mile to the park entrance road.

**Contact:** Fort Townsend State Park, 360/344-4431 or 360/385-3595; state park information, 360/902-8844, www.parks.wa.gov.

## 27 FORT FLAGLER STATE PARK

### Scenic rating: 10

near Port Townsend

Map 1.3, page 79          BEST (

Historic Fort Flagler is a pretty and unique state park, set on Marrowstone Island east of Port Townsend. The camp overlooks Puget Sound and offers 19,100 feet of gorgeous saltwater shore. The park's 784 acres include five miles of trails for hiking and biking, an interpretive trail, and a military museum featuring gun batteries that are open in the summer. The RV sites are situated right on the beach, with views of the Olympic and Cascade Mountains. Anglers like this spot for year-round rockfish and salmon fishing, and crabbing and clamming are good in season (check regulations). Fort Flagler, under construction on some level from 1897 until its closure in 1953, offers summer tours. There is a youth hostel in the park.

**Campsites, facilities:** There are 57 sites for tents, 57 sites with full hookups (30 amps) for RVs up to 50 feet long, two hike-in/bike-in sites, four vacation homes, a group tent site for up to 40 people, and a group site for tents or RVs of any length for up to 100 people. Picnic tables and fire grills are provided. Restrooms with flush toilets and coin showers, drinking water, interpretive activities, a dump station, playground, picnic shelters that can be reserved, a camp store, boat buoys, moorage dock, and a launch are available. Some facilities are wheelchair accessible. Leashed pets are permitted.

**Reservations, fees:** Reservations are accepted May-September at 888/CAMP-OUT (888/226-7688) or www.goingtocamp.com ($6.50-8.50 reservation fee). Sites are $23-27 per night, $10 per extra vehicle per night, $12 per night for hike-in/bike-in sites. The group sites are $137.64-280.83 per night with a minimum of 26 people. The vacation homes are $88-191 per night for 4-8 people and are available year-round. Some credit cards are accepted. Open year-round, weather permitting.

**Directions:** From Port Townsend at Highway 20, drive to Highway 19 (Airport cutoff) and make a slight left turn on Highway 19. Drive 3.5 miles to the traffic light at Ness Corner Road and turn left. Drive about one mile on Ness Corner Road to Oak Bay Road/Highway 116. Continue one mile on Highway 116 and turn left at Flagler Road to stay on Highway 116. Remain on Flagler Road and drive about 6.5 miles to the end of the road and the park and campground.

**Contact:** Fort Flagler State Park, 360/385-1259; state park information, 360/902-8844, www.parks.wa.gov.

## 28 KINNEY POINT STATE PARK

**Scenic rating: 10**

on Marrowstone Island

**Map 1.3, page 79**

Kinney Point is located on the south end of Marrowstone Island, part of Washington's Cascade Marine Trail. You'll need a nonmotorized boat to reach the campsites at this 76-acre park; once you do, 683 feet of shoreline await.

**Campsites, facilities:** There are three primitive sites for tents. A vault toilet and kayak rack are available. There is no drinking water and all garbage must be packed out. Leashed pets are permitted.

**Reservations, fees:** Reservations are not accepted. Sites are $12 per night. Open year-round.

**Directions:** From Fort Flagler or Mystery Bay State Parks, head south down Marrowstone Island to Kinney Point.

**Contact:** Kinney Point State Park, 360/385-1259; state park information, 360/902-8844, www.parks.wa.gov.

## 29 MORA

**Scenic rating: 8**

in Olympic National Park

**Map 1.4, page 80**

At an elevation of 50 feet, this is a good out-of-the-way choice near the Pacific Ocean and the Olympic Coast Marine Sanctuary. The Quillayute River feeds into the ocean near the camp, and upstream lies the Bogachiel, a prime steelhead river in winter months. A naturalist program is available during the summer. This camp includes eight sites that require short walks, and several of them are stellar.

**Campsites, facilities:** There are 94 sites for tents or RVs up to 35 feet long and one walk-in tent site. Picnic tables and fire pits are provided. Restrooms with flush toilets, drinking water, garbage bins, and a dump station are available. Some facilities are wheelchair accessible. Leashed pets are permitted.

**Reservations, fees:** Reservations are not accepted. Sites are $12 per night, plus a $15 national park entrance fee per vehicle. Open year-round.

**Directions:** From Aberdeen, drive north on U.S. 101 for 108 miles to Forks. Continue past Forks for two miles to La Push Road/Highway 110. Turn left (west) and drive 12 miles to the campground on the left (well marked along the route).

**Contact:** Olympic National Park, 360/565-3130, www.nps.gov/olym.

## 30 QUILEUTE OCEANSIDE RESORT

### Scenic rating: 8

near Forks

**Map 1.4, page 80**

This park is set along the Pacific Ocean and the coastal Dungeness National Wildlife Refuge. Operated by the Quileute Nation, it has some of the few ocean sites available in the area and offers such recreation options as fishing, surfing, beachcombing, boating, whale-watching, and sunbathing.

**Campsites, facilities:** There are 66 sites for RVs of any length (30 and 50 amp full hookups), six sites for tents, and 20 beach campsites. Picnic tables and fire rings are provided. Restrooms with flush toilets and coin showers, and a coin laundry are available. Gasoline, propane gas, and a convenience store with a deli and ice are nearby. Boat docks, a marina, and launching facilities are located within one mile. Some facilities are wheelchair accessible. Leashed pets are permitted.

**Reservations, fees:** Reservations are accepted. Tent sites are $20 per night, RV sites are $40 per night, $5 additional vehicle per night, $10 per pet per night. Some credit cards are accepted. Open year-round.

**Directions:** From the town of Forks, drive north on U.S. 101 for 2.5 miles to La Push Road/Highway 110. Turn left (west) and drive 13 miles on La Push Road, which becomes Ocean Front Drive. Turn left onto Ocean Drive. The campground will be on the right.

**Contact:** Quileute Oceanside Resort, 330 Ocean Drive, La Push, 360/374-5267 or 800/487-1267, www.quileuteoceanside.com.

## 31 THREE RIVERS RESORT

### Scenic rating: 8

near Forks on the Quillayute River

**Map 1.4, page 80**

Three Rivers Resort is a small, private camp set at the junction of the Quillayute, Sol Duc, and Bogachiel Rivers. Situated above this confluence, about six miles upstream from the ocean, this pretty spot features wooded, spacious sites. Hiking and fishing are popular here, and there is a fishing guide service. Salmon and steelhead migrate upstream, best on the Sol Duc and Bogachiel Rivers; anglers should check regulations. The coastal Dungeness National Wildlife Refuge and Pacific Ocean, which often offer good whale-watching in the spring, are a short drive to the west. Hoh Rain Forest, a worthwhile side trip, is about 45 minutes away.

**Campsites, facilities:** There are 11 sites for tents, nine sites with partial hookups for RVs, two sites with full hookups (30 and 50 amps) for tents or RVs of any length, and six rental cabins. Picnic tables and fire pits are provided. Restrooms with flush toilets and coin showers, a convenience store, gas station, a café, coin laundry, firewood, and ice are available. Leashed pets are permitted.

**Reservations, fees:** Reservations are accepted. Tent sites are $14 per night, $7 per second tent per night, RV sites are $16-18 per night, $5 per pet per night. Some credit cards are accepted. Open year-round.

**Directions:** From Aberdeen, drive north on U.S. 101 for 108 miles to Forks. Continue past

Forks for two miles to La Push Road/Highway 110. Turn left (west) and drive eight miles to the resort on the right.

**Contact:** Three Rivers Resort, 7765 LaPush Road, Forks, 360/374-5300, www.threeriversresortandguideservice.com.

## 32 KLAHANIE

### Scenic rating: 8
on the North Fork Klahanie River

**Map 1.4, page 80**

This camp is likely off the radar of many travelers, so it is worth checking out. Sites nestle amid large, old-growth spruce and lots of ferns. It is quite pretty, set along a riparian zone on the South Fork Calawah River, and features a hiking trail that hugs the river for 0.25 mile and a second trail that follows the river for about one mile, starting at the east end of the campground.

**Campsites, facilities:** There are 15 sites for tents or RVs up to 21 feet. Picnic tables and fire grills are provided. Vault toilets are available. There is no drinking water and garbage must be packed out. Leashed pets are permitted.

**Reservations, fees:** Reservations are not accepted. Sites are $10 per night. Open May-Labor Day.

**Directions:** From Aberdeen, drive north on U.S. 101 to Forks. Continue past Forks for one mile to Forest Road 29. Turn right (east) and drive five miles to the campground on the right.

**Contact:** Olympic National Forest, Pacific Ranger District, 360/374-6522, www.fs.usda.gov.

## 33 BOGACHIEL STATE PARK

### Scenic rating: 6
on the Bogachiel River

**Map 1.4, page 80**

A good base camp for salmon or steelhead fishing trips, this 123-acre park is set on the Bogachiel River, with marked hiking trails in the area. It can be noisy at times because a logging mill is located directly across the river from the campground. Also note that there is highway noise, and you can see the highway from some campsites. A one-mile hiking trail is nearby, and opportunities for wildlife-viewing are outstanding in the park. Hunting is popular in the adjacent national forest. This region is heavily forested, with lush vegetation fed by an average of 140-160 inches of rain each year. This park was established in 1931.

**Campsites, facilities:** There are 26 sites for tents or RVs (no hookups), six sites with partial hookups (30 amps) for RVs up to 40 feet long, two hike-in/bike-in sites, and one group tent camp with a covered shelter for up to 20 people. Picnic tables and fire grills are provided. Restrooms with flush toilets and coin showers, drinking water, dump station, and a picnic area are available. A primitive boat ramp is nearby. Some facilities are wheelchair accessible. Leashed pets are permitted.

**Reservations, fees:** Reservations are not accepted for individual sites but are required for the group camp at 360/374-6356. Sites are $22-35 per night, the hike-in/bike-in site is $12 per night, $10 per extra vehicle per night. The group site is $60 per night. Open year-round, with some sites closed in winter.

**Directions:** From Olympia on I-5, take Exit 104 and drive north on U.S. 101 to the Aberdeen/Highway 8 exit. Turn west on Highway 8 and drive 36 miles to Aberdeen. Continue through Aberdeen four miles to U.S. 101. Turn north on U.S. 101 and drive 102 miles to the park (six miles south of Forks) on the left side of the road.

**Contact:** Bogachiel State Park, Northwest Region, 360/374-6356; state park information, 360/902-8844, www.parks.wa.gov.

## 34 COTTONWOOD

**Scenic rating: 8**

on the Hoh River

**Map 1.4, page 80**

This primitive camp is set along the Hoh River, providing an alternative to Hoh Oxbow, Willoughby Creek, and Minnie Peterson campgrounds. Like Hoh Oxbow, Cottonwood offers the bonus of a boat launch. Its distance from the highway makes it quieter here. The camp is popular for anglers and hunters (in season).

**Campsites, facilities:** There are nine sites for tents or RVs up to 30 feet long, including a group site for up to 10 people. Picnic tables, fire grills, and tent pads are provided. Vault toilets and a boat launch are available. There is no drinking water and garbage must be packed out. Some facilities are wheelchair accessible. Leashed pets are permitted.

**Reservations, fees:** Reservations are not accepted. There is no fee for camping, but a Discover Pass is required. Open year-round.

**Directions:** From Olympia on I-5, take Exit 104 and drive north on U.S. 101 to the Aberdeen/ Highway 8 exit. Turn west on Highway 8 and drive 36 miles to Aberdeen. Continue through Aberdeen four miles to U.S. 101. Turn north on U.S. 101 and drive 92 miles to Oil City Road between Mileposts 177 and 178. Turn left (west) on Oil City Road and drive 2.3 miles. Turn left on Road H4060 (gravel) and drive one mile to the camp at the end of the road.

**Contact:** Department of Natural Resources, Olympic Region, 360/374-6131, www.dnr. wa.gov.

## 35 HOH OXBOW

**Scenic rating: 7**

on the Hoh River

**Map 1.4, page 80**

This is the most popular of the five camps on the Hoh River. It's primitive and close to the highway, and the price is right. The adjacent boat launch makes this the camp of choice for anglers, best in fall and winter for salmon and steelhead; check regulations. It is also a popular hunters' camp in the fall. One downer: There is some highway noise within range of the campsites. You can't see the traffic, but you can hear it, which can be irritating for those who want perfect quiet.

**Campsites, facilities:** There are eight sites for tents or RVs up to 25 feet. Picnic tables, fire grills, and tent pads are provided. Vault toilets and a hand boat launch are available. There is no drinking water, and garbage must be packed out. Some facilities are wheelchair accessible. Leashed pets are permitted.

**Reservations, fees:** Reservations are not accepted. There is no fee for camping, but a Discover Pass is required. Open year-round.

**Directions:** From Aberdeen, drive north on U.S. 101 for 90 miles to the campground (15 miles south of Forks). Exit between Mileposts 176 and 177 and look for the campground on the right, next to the river. Note: The road in is narrow and not advised for RVs or trailers.

**Contact:** Department of Natural Resources, Olympic Region, 360/374-6131, www.dnr. wa.gov.

## 36 WILLOUGHBY CREEK

**Scenic rating: 9**

in Hoh Clearwater State Forest

**Map 1.4, page 80**

This little-known camp along Willoughby Creek and the Hoh River is tiny and rustic, with good fishing nearby for steelhead and salmon during peak migrations in season. The area gets heavy rainfall. Other campground options in the vicinity include Hoh Oxbow, Cottonwood, and Minnie Peterson.

**Campsites, facilities:** There are three sites for self-contained RVs up to 16 feet long. Picnic tables and fire grills are provided. There are no toilets and drinking water is not available.

Garbage must be packed out. Leashed pets are permitted.

**Reservations, fees:** Reservations are not accepted. There is no fee for camping, but a Discover Pass is required. Open year-round.

**Directions:** From Olympia on I-5, take Exit 104 and drive north on U.S. 101 to the Aberdeen/Highway 8 exit. Turn west on Highway 8 and drive 36 miles to Aberdeen. Continue through Aberdeen four miles to U.S. 101. Turn north on U.S. 101 and drive about 90 miles. Exit between Mileposts 178 and 179. At Hoh Rain Forest Road/Upper Hoh Valley Road, turn east and drive 3.5 miles to the campground on the right.

**Contact:** Department of Natural Resources, Olympic Region, 360/374-6131, www.dnr. wa.gov.

## 37 MINNIE PETERSON
🏕️ 🛶 🐴 ♿ 🚐 ⛰️

**Scenic rating: 9**

on the Hoh River

**Map 1.4, page 80**

If location is everything, then it's why this campground has become popular. Minnie Peterson is set on the Hoh River on the edge of the Hoh Rain Forest. It's quite pretty, forested with Sitka spruce and western hemlock, and offers nice riverside sites. Bring your rain gear.

**Campsites, facilities:** There are nine sites for tents or RVs up to 30 feet long. Picnic tables, fire grills, and tent pads are provided. Vault toilets are available. There is no drinking water and garbage must be packed out. Some facilities are wheelchair accessible. Leashed pets are permitted.

**Reservations, fees:** Reservations are not accepted. There is no fee for camping, but a Discover Pass is required. Open year-round.

**Directions:** From Olympia on I-5, take Exit 104 and drive north on U.S. 101 to the Aberdeen/Highway 8 exit. Turn west on Highway 8 and drive 36 miles to Aberdeen. Continue through Aberdeen four miles to U.S. 101. Turn

north on U.S. 101 and drive about 90 miles. Exit between Mileposts 178 and 179. At Hoh Rain Forest Road/Upper Hoh Valley Road, turn east and drive 4.5 miles to the campground on the left.

**Contact:** Department of Natural Resources, Olympic Region, 360/374-6131, www.dnr. wa.gov.

## 38 UPPER CLEARWATER
🏕️ 🛶 🚐 🎣 🐴 ⛰️

**Scenic rating: 8**

on the Clearwater River

**Map 1.4, page 80**

This is one of the three primitive camps set along the Clearwater River. Upper Clearwater is a great camp: It's very pretty, is unused by most tourists, and has a boat ramp. Campsites sit amid a forest of western hemlock, red alder, and big leaf maple.

**Campsites, facilities:** There are seven sites for tents only. Picnic tables, fire grills, and tent pads are provided. Vault toilets and a covered shelter are available. There is no drinking water and garbage must be packed out. There are unimproved boat-launching facilities for small crafts, such as river dories, rafts, canoes, and kayaks. Leashed pets are permitted.

**Reservations, fees:** Reservations are not accepted. There is no fee for camping. Open year-round.

**Directions:** From Olympia on I-5, take Exit 104 and drive north on U.S. 101 to the Aberdeen/Highway 8 exit. Turn west on Highway 8 and drive 36 miles to Aberdeen. Continue through Aberdeen four miles to U.S. 101. Turn north on U.S. 101 and drive about 60 miles to Milepost 147. Turn north on Clearwater Mainline Road and drive about 13 miles to C-3000 Road (a gravel one-lane road). Turn right and drive 3.3 miles to the camp entrance on the right.

**Contact:** Department of Natural Resources, Olympic Region, 360/374-6131, www.dnr. wa.gov.

## 39 YAHOO LAKE

🚶 �]] 📷 ⛺

**Scenic rating: 10**

on Yahoo Lake in Hoh Clearwater State Forest

**Map 1.4, page 80**

Yahoo Lake is the most primitive and remote campground in the Olympic Region. The lakeside campground is set at an elevation of 2,400 feet and is a lovely secret known only to a rugged few.

**Campsites, facilities:** There are three walk-in sites for tents only. Picnic tables, fire grills, and tent pads are provided. There are toilets, no drinking water, and garbage must be packed out. Leashed pets are permitted.

**Reservations, fees:** Reservations are not accepted. There is no fee for camping, but a Discover Pass is required. Open year-round.

**Directions:** From Olympia on I-5, take Exit 104 and drive north on U.S. 101 to the Aberdeen/Highway 8 exit. Turn west on Highway 8 and drive 36 miles to Aberdeen. Continue through Aberdeen four miles to U.S. 101. Turn north on U.S. 101 and drive about 60 miles to Milepost 147. Turn north on Clearwater Mainline Road and drive about 13 miles to C-3000 Road (a gravel one-lane road). Turn right and drive 0.8 mile to C-3100 Road. Turn right on C-3100 Road (paved one-lane, then gravel one-lane). Continue 6.1 miles to trailhead. This road is not recommended for motor-home travel.

**Contact:** Department of Natural Resources, Olympic Region, Jefferson County, 360/374-6131, www.dnr.wa.gov.

## 40 KALALOCH

🚶 🚣 📷 ♿ � ⛺

**Scenic rating: 10**

in Olympic National Park

**Map 1.4, page 80**      **BEST (**

This camp, located on a bluff above the beach, offers some wonderful oceanview sites—which explains its popularity. It can fill quickly. Like other camps set on the coast of the Olympic Peninsula, heavy rain in winter and spring is common, and it's often foggy in the summer. A naturalist program is offered in the summer months. There are several good hiking trails in the area; check out the visitors center for maps and information.

**Campsites, facilities:** There are 170 sites for tents or RVs up to 35 feet long. A group tent site can accommodate up to 30 people (drinking water and pit toilets are provided). Picnic tables and fire grills are provided. Restrooms with flush toilets, drinking water, garbage bins, food lockers, fish cleaning stations, and a dump station are available. A store and a restaurant are located within one mile. Some facilities are wheelchair accessible. Leashed pets are permitted in the campground.

**Reservations, fees:** Reservations are accepted June 20-September 3 at 877/444-6777 or www.recreation.gov ($9-10 reservation fee). Sites are $14-18 per night, plus a $15 national park entrance fee per vehicle. The group site is $2 per person per night, plus a $20 reservation fee. Open year-round.

**Directions:** From Aberdeen, drive north on U.S. 101 for 83 miles to the campground on the left. It is located near the mouth of the Kalaloch River five miles north of the U.S. 101 bridge over the Queets River.

**Contact:** Olympic National Park, 360/565-3130, www.nps.gov/olym.

## 41 COPPERMINE BOTTOM

🚶 🚣 🚲 📷 � ⛺

**Scenic rating: 9**

on the Clearwater River

**Map 1.4, page 80**      **BEST (**

Few tourists ever visit this primitive, hidden campground set on the Clearwater River, a tributary of the Queets River, which runs to the ocean. The river dory-launching facility is a bonus and makes this a perfect camp for anglers and river runners who want to avoid the usual U.S. 101 crowds. Salmon fishing is popular here during the migratory journey of the anadromous fish.

**Campsites, facilities:** There are 10 sites for tents or RVs up to 30 feet long and one group site for up to 10 people. Picnic tables, fire grills, and tent pads are provided. Vault toilets, a group shelter, and a hand boat launch are available. There is no drinking water and garbage must be packed out. Leashed pets are permitted.

**Reservations, fees:** Reservations are not accepted. There is no fee for camping, but a Discover Pass is required. Open year-round.

**Directions:** From Olympia on I-5, take Exit 104 and drive north on U.S. 101 to the Aberdeen/Highway 8 exit. Turn west on Highway 8 and drive 36 miles to Aberdeen. Continue through Aberdeen four miles to U.S. 101. Turn north on U.S. 101 and drive about 60 miles to Milepost 147. Turn north on Clearwater Mainline Road and drive about 14 miles to C-3000 Road. Turn right (east) on C-3000 Road (a gravel one-lane road) and drive two miles to C-1010 Road. Turn right on C-1010 Road and drive one mile. The camp is on the left.

**Contact:** Department of Natural Resources, Olympic Region, 360/374-6131, www.dnr.wa.gov.

## 42 SOUTH BEACH

### Scenic rating: 6

in Olympic National Park

**Map 1.4, page 80**

Little South Beach campground is located in an open field with little shade or privacy, but the payoff is that it is just a stone's throw from the ocean.

**Campsites, facilities:** There are 50 sites for tents or RVs up to 21 feet long. Picnic tables and fire grills are provided. Drinking water and non-accessible restrooms with flush toilets are available during summer. In winter, only pit toilets are available, and there is no drinking water. Leashed pets are permitted in the campground.

**Reservations, fees:** Reservations are not accepted. Sites are $10 per night, plus a $15 national park entrance fee per vehicle. Open late May-mid-September.

**Directions:** From Aberdeen, drive north on U.S. 101 for 65 miles to the campground.

**Contact:** Olympic National Park, 360/565-3130, www.nps.gov/olym.

## 43 PACIFIC BEACH STATE PARK

### Scenic rating: 10

near Pacific Beach

**Map 1.4, page 80**          **BEST (**

This is the only state park campground in Washington where you can see the ocean from your campsite. Set on just nine acres, within the town of Pacific Beach, it boasts 2,300 feet of beachfront. This spot is great for long beach walks, although it can be windy, especially in the spring and early summer. Because of those winds, this is a great place for kite-flying. Clamming (for razor clams) is permitted only in season. Note that rangers advise against swimming or body surfing because of strong riptides. Vehicle traffic is allowed seasonally on the uppermost portions of the beach, but ATVs are not allowed in the park, on the beach, or on sand dunes. This camp is popular and often fills up quickly.

**Campsites, facilities:** There are 22 sites for tents, 42 sites with partial hookups (30 amps) for RVs up to 60 feet long, and two yurts. Picnic tables are provided. No fires are permitted, except on the beach; charcoal and propane barbecues are allowed in campsites. Restrooms with flush toilets and coin showers, drinking water, a dump station, and a picnic area are available. Some facilities are wheelchair accessible. Leashed pets are permitted.

**Reservations, fees:** Reservations are accepted at 888/CAMP-OUT (888/226-7688) or www.goingtocamp.com ($6.50-8.50 reservation fee). Sites are $20-39 per night, hike-in/bike-in sites are $12 per night, $10 per extra vehicle per night, and yurts are $50.13-86.74 per night. Some credit cards are accepted. Open year-round.

**Directions:** From Hoquiam, drive north on State Route 109 for 37 miles to Pacific Beach and Main Street. Turn left on Main Street and drive 0.5 mile to 2nd Street. Turn left on 2nd Street and continue to the park entrance.

**Contact:** Pacific Beach State Park, 360/276-4297; state park information, 360/902-8844, www.parks.wa.gov.

## 44 RIVERSIDE RV RESORT

### Scenic rating: 8
near Copalis Beach

**Map 1.4, page 80**

River access is a bonus at this nice and clean six-acre resort. Most sites have a river view. Salmon fishing can be good in the Copalis River, and a boat ramp is available nearby for anglers. Other options include swimming and beachcombing.

**Campsites, facilities:** There are 56 sites with full hookups (30 amps) for RVs of any length and 15 sites for tents. Some sites are pull-through. Picnic tables and fire grills are provided. Restrooms with flush toilets and coin showers, drinking water, a dump station, Wi-Fi, firewood, and a recreation hall are available. A boat dock, launching facilities, and boat rentals are nearby. Some facilities are wheelchair accessible. Leashed pets are permitted.

**Reservations, fees:** Reservations are accepted. Tent sites are $18 per night, RV sites are $23 per night, $2 per person per night for more than two people. Some credit cards are accepted. Open year-round.

**Directions:** From Hoquiam, drive west on State Route 109 for 22 miles to Copalis Beach. The park is off the highway on the left.

**Contact:** Riverside RV Resort, 6 Condra Road, 360/289-2111 or 800/500-2111, www.riversidervresort.net.

## 45 TIDELANDS RESORT

### Scenic rating: 7
near Copalis Beach

**Map 1.4, page 80**

This flat, wooded resort covers 47 acres and provides beach access and a great ocean view. It's primarily an RV park, and the sites are pleasant. Ten sites are set on sand dunes, while the rest are in a wooded area. In the spring, azaleas and wildflowers abound. Horseshoe pits and a sports field offer recreation possibilities. Though it's more remote than at the other area campgrounds, clamming is an option in season. Various festivals are held in the area from spring through fall.

**Campsites, facilities:** There are 25 sites for tents or RVs (no hookups), 35 sites with full or partial hookups (20 and 30 amps) for tents or RVs of any length, one rental trailer, and three cottages. Some sites are pull-through. Picnic tables and fire pits are provided. Restrooms with flush toilets and coin showers, drinking water, firewood, cable TV, and a play area are available. A casino and horseback riding are within five miles. A golf course is within six miles. Leashed pets are permitted.

**Reservations, fees:** Reservations are accepted. RV sites are $26-30 per night, tent sites are $20 per night. Some credit cards are accepted. Open year-round.

**Directions:** From Hoquiam, drive west on State Route 109 for about 20 miles to the resort on the left. It is located between Mileposts 20 and 21, about one mile south of Copalis Beach.

**Contact:** Tidelands Resort, 2991 State Route 109 North, 360/289-8963, www.tidelandsresort.com.

## 46 OCEAN MIST RESORT

### Scenic rating: 9
on Conners Creek near Ocean City

**Map 1.4, page 80**

Always call to determine whether space is

available before planning a stay here. This is a membership resort RV campground, and members always come first. If space is available, they will rent sites to the public. Surf fishing is popular in the nearby Pacific Ocean, while the Copalis River offers salmon fishing and canoeing opportunities. It's about a one-block walk to the beach. There's a golf course within five miles.

**Campsites, facilities:** There are 110 sites with full hookups (50 amps) for RVs up to 45 feet long, a grassy area for tents, two trailers, and two cabins. Picnic tables are provided. Restrooms with flush toilets and showers, drinking water, cable TV, Wi-Fi, dump station, two community fire pits, a spa, clubhouse, two playgrounds, ball courts, horseshoe pits, and coin laundry are available. A grocery store is within one mile in Ocean City. Some facilities are wheelchair accessible. Leashed pets are permitted.

**Reservations, fees:** Reservations are accepted in the summer. Tent sites are $10 per night, and RV sites are $40-42 per night. Some credit cards are accepted. Open year-round.

**Directions:** From Hoquiam, drive west on State Route 109 for 19 miles to the resort on the left (one mile north of Ocean City).

**Contact:** Ocean Mist Resort, 2781 State Route 109, Ocean City, 360/289-3656, www. kmresorts.com.

# 47 OCEAN CITY STATE PARK

**Scenic rating: 9**

near Hoquiam

**Map 1.4, page 80**     **BEST (**

This 170-acre oceanfront camp, an excellent example of coastal wetlands and dune succession, features ocean beach, dunes, and dense thickets of pine surrounding freshwater marshes. The Ocean Shores Interpretive Center is located on the south end of Ocean Shores near the marina (open summer season only). This area is part of the Pacific Flyway, and the migratory route for gray whales and

other marine mammals lies just offshore. Spring wildflowers are excellent and include lupine, buttercups, and wild strawberry. This is also a good area for surfing and kite-flying, with springs typically windy. Beachcombing, clamming, and fishing are possibilities at this park. An 18-hole golf course is nearby.

**Campsites, facilities:** There are 149 sites for tents or self-contained RVs (no hookups), 29 sites with full hookups (30 amps) for RVs up to 50 feet long; some sites are pull-through. There are also three hike-in/bike-in sites and one group camp for tents only that can accommodate 20-30 people. A second group camp for 20-40 people and two RVs (with hookups) is also available. Picnic tables and fire rings are provided. Restrooms with flush toilets and coin showers, drinking water, dump station, sheltered picnic area, and firewood are available. A ballfield and amphitheater are available nearby. A camp host is on-site. Some facilities are wheelchair accessible. Leashed pets are permitted.

**Reservations, fees:** Reservations are accepted at 888/226-7688 (CAMP-OUT) or www.goingtocamp.com ($6.50-8.50 reservation fee). Sites are $24-42 per night, hike-in/bike-in sites are $14 per night, $10 per extra vehicle per night, and group sites are $110.29-113.63 per night. Some credit cards are accepted. Open year-round.

**Directions:** From Hoquiam, drive northwest on State Route 109 for 16 miles to State Route 115. Turn left and drive 1.2 miles south to the park on the right (1.5 miles north of Ocean Shores).

**Contact:** Ocean City State Park, 360/289-3553; state park information, 360/902-8844, www.parks.wa.gov.

# 48 SOL DUC

**Scenic rating: 10**

on the Sol Duc River in Olympic National Park

**Map 1.5, page 81**

This site is a nice hideaway, with nearby Sol

Duc Hot Springs a highlight. The problem is that this camp is very popular. It fills up quickly on weekends, and a fee is charged to use the hot springs, which have been fully developed since the early 1900s. The camp is set at 1,680 feet along the Sol Duc River.

**Campsites, facilities:** There are 82 sites for tents or RVs up to 35 feet long. There is also one group site for 9-24 people and up to eight head of stock (there are pit toilets, but no drinking water). Picnic tables and fire pits are provided. Restrooms with flush toilets and drinking water are available in the summer season; there is no water in the winter season, but pit toilets are available. A dump station is available nearby, and a store and café are within one mile. Some facilities are wheelchair accessible. Leashed pets are permitted.

**Reservations, fees:** Reservations are accepted for the group site only at 360/565-2955 (March 1-April 15) and at 360/327-3534 (April 16-October 31). Sites are $14 per night, plus a $15 national park entrance fee per vehicle. Call for group rates. Open May-late October, with limited facilities in winter.

**Directions:** From Port Angeles, continue on U.S. 101 for 27 miles, just past Lake Crescent. Turn left at the Sol Duc turnoff and drive 12 miles to the camp.

**Contact:** Olympic National Park, 360/565-3130, www.nps.gov/olym.

## 49 DEER PARK 🏃 🐕 ⛺

### Scenic rating: 9
near Blue Mountain in Olympic National Park

**Map 1.5, page 81**

This camp is set in the Olympic Peninsula's high country at an elevation of 5,400 feet, just below 6,000-foot Blue Mountain. There are numerous trails in the area, including a major trailhead into the backcountry of Olympic National Park and the Buckhorn Wilderness.

**Campsites, facilities:** There are 14 sites for tents only. Picnic tables and fire grills are provided. Pit toilets are available. There is no drinking water. At times, garbage must be packed out. Leashed pets are permitted.

**Reservations, fees:** Reservations are not accepted. Sites are $10 per night, plus a $15 per vehicle park entrance fee. Open mid-June-late September.

**Directions:** From Port Angeles, drive east on U.S. 101 for about five miles to Deer Park Road. Turn right (south) and drive 18 miles to the campground at the end of the road. Note that the last six miles are gravel, steep and narrow, closed to RVs and trailers, and often closed to all vehicles in winter.

**Contact:** Olympic National Park, 360/565-3132, ww.nps.gov/olym.

## 50 DUNGENESS FORKS 🏃 🚲 🐕 ⛺

### Scenic rating: 7
on the Dungeness and Gray Wolf Rivers in Olympic National Forest

**Map 1.5, page 81**

This pretty, wooded spot is nestled at the confluence of the Dungeness and Gray Wolf Rivers at an elevation of 1,000 feet. It offers seclusion, yet easy access from the highway. The campsites are set in the forest. If you want quiet, you'll often find it here. The Upper Dungeness Trailhead, located about seven miles south of camp, provides access to Buckhorn Wilderness and Olympic National Park. The trailhead for Gray Wolf Trail is four miles from camp, but note that portions of this trail are sometimes closed due to slides; check with rangers before embarking on a long trip. The Gray Wolf River is closed to fishing year-round to protect salmon. Fishing is permitted on the Dungeness River. Check regulations.

**Campsites, facilities:** There are 10 sites for tents only. Picnic tables and fire rings are provided. Vault toilets are available. There is no drinking water, and garbage must be packed out. Leashed pets are permitted.

**Reservations, fees:** Reservations are not

accepted. Sites are $14 per night, $5 per extra vehicle per night. Open May-September, weather permitting.

**Directions:** From Olympia on I-5, turn north on U.S. 101 and drive approximately 100 miles to Palo Alto Road, located 1.5 miles north of Sequim Bay State Park and 3 miles southeast of Sequim. Turn left (south) on Palo Alto Road and drive about seven miles to Forest Road 2880. Turn right (west) and drive one mile (after crossing Dungeness River Bridge) to the campground on the right. Obtaining a U.S. Forest Service map is advised. Trailers and RVs are not recommended because of the steep, narrow, and unpaved access road.

**Contact:** Olympic National Forest, Hood Canal Ranger District, Quilcene Office, 360/765-2200, www.fs.fed.us.

## 51 HOH

♿🚴🏕♿🚐⛺

### Scenic rating: 10

in Olympic National Park

**Map 1.5, page 81**

This camp at a trailhead leading into the interior of Olympic National Park is located in the beautiful heart of a temperate, old-growth rainforest. Hoh Oxbow, Cottonwood, Willoughby Creek, and Minnie Peterson campgrounds are nearby, set downstream on the Hoh River, outside national park boundaries. In the summer, there are naturalist programs, and a visitors center is nearby. This is one of the most popular camps in the park. The elevation is 578 feet.

**Campsites, facilities:** There are 88 sites for tents or RVs up to 21 feet long. Picnic tables and fire grills are provided. Restrooms with flush toilets and drinking water are available. A dump station is nearby. Some facilities are wheelchair accessible. Leashed pets are permitted.

**Reservations, fees:** Reservations are not accepted. Sites are $12 per night, plus a $15 national park entrance fee per vehicle. Open year-round.

**Directions:** From Aberdeen, drive north on U.S. 101 for about 90 miles to Milepost 176. Turn east on Hoh River Road and drive 19 miles to the campground on the right (near the end of the road).

**Contact:** Olympic National Park, 360/565-3130, www.nps.gov/olym.

## 52 SOUTH FORK HOH

♿🚴🏕♿🚐⛺

### Scenic rating: 10

in Hoh Clearwater State Forest

**Map 1.5, page 81**

This rarely used, beautiful camp set along the cascading South Fork of the Hoh River is way out there. It's tiny and primitive but offers a guarantee of peace and quiet, something many U.S. 101 cruisers would cheerfully give a limb for after a few days of fighting crowds. The South Fork Trailhead in Olympic National Park is two miles away. When conditions are right, fishing for steelhead can be excellent (check regulations).

**Campsites, facilities:** There are seven sites for tents or RVs up to 30 feet long. Picnic tables, fire grills, and tent pads are provided. Vault toilets are available. There is no drinking water and garbage must be packed out. Some facilities are wheelchair accessible. Leashed pets are permitted.

**Reservations, fees:** Reservations are not accepted. There is no fee for camping, but a Discover Pass is required. Open year-round.

**Directions:** From Olympia on I-5, take Exit 104 and drive north on U.S. 101 to the Aberdeen/Highway 8 exit. Turn west on Highway 8 and drive 36 miles to Aberdeen. Continue through Aberdeen four miles to U.S. 101. Turn north on U.S. 101 and drive about 94 miles. Exit at Milepost 176. At Hoh Mainline Road turn east and drive 6.5 miles. Turn left on Road H1000 and drive 7.5 miles to the campground on the right. Obtaining a Department of Natural Resources (DNR) map is advised.

**Contact:** Department of Natural Resources,

Olympic Region, 360/374-6131, www.dnr.wa.gov.

## 53 DOSEWALLIPS WALK-IN
🚶 🚵 🐴 ⛺

### Scenic rating: 7
on the Dosewallips River in Olympic National Park

Map 1.5, page 81

This road is closed to vehicles due to a road washout at Milepost 10. You can still get to the campground on foot or mountain bike, but it requires a 5.5-mile hike or bike ride. Set on the Dosewallips River at an elevation of 1,500 feet, the camp provides a major trailhead into the backcountry of Olympic National Park. The trail follows the Dosewallips River over Anderson Pass, proceeds along the Quinault River, and ultimately reaches Quinault Lake. Other hiking trails are available nearby. Dosewallips is a more remote option to Collins.

**Campsites, facilities:** There are 30 sites for tents only. Picnic tables and fire grills are provided. Pit toilets are available. There is no drinking water. Leashed pets are permitted.

**Reservations, fees:** Reservations are not accepted. There is no entrance fee and no fee for camping. Open mid-May-late September, weather permitting.

**Directions:** From Olympia on I-5, drive north on U.S. 101 for 60 miles to a signed turnoff near Brinnon (located about 1 mile north of Dosewallips State Park) for Forest Road 2610 (County Road 2500). Turn left (west) and drive 15 miles along the Dosewallips River to the washout. Note that the access road is not paved and is not recommended for RVs or trailers.

**Contact:** Olympic National Park, 360/565-3132, www.nps.gov/olym.

## 54 COLLINS

### Scenic rating: 7
on the Duckabush River in Olympic National Forest

Map 1.5, page 81

Most vacationers cruising U.S. 101 don't have a clue about this quiet spot set on a great launch point for adventure, yet it's only five or six miles from the highway. This four-acre camp is located on the Duckabush River at 200 feet elevation. It has small, shaded sites, river access nearby, and plenty of fishing and hiking; check fishing regulations. Just one mile from camp is Duckabush Trail, which connects to trails in Olympic National Park. Murhut Falls Trail starts about three miles from the campground, providing access to a 0.8-mile trail to the falls. It's a 1.5-mile drive to Dosewallips State Park and a 30- to 35-minute drive to Olympic National Park.

**Campsites, facilities:** There are six sites for tents and 10 sites for RVs up to 21 feet long. Picnic tables and fire rings are provided. Vault toilets are available. There is no drinking water and garbage must be packed out. Leashed pets are permitted.

**Reservations, fees:** Reservations are not accepted. Sites are $14 per night, $5 per each additional vehicle. Open May-September, weather permitting.

**Directions:** From Olympia on I-5, drive north on U.S. 101 for 59 miles to Forest Road 2510 (near Duckabush). Turn left on Forest Road 2510 and drive six miles west to the camp on the left.

**Contact:** Olympic National Forest, Hood Canal Ranger District, Quilcene Office, 360/765-2200, www.fs.fed.us.

## 55 QUEETS WALK-IN

### Scenic rating: 9

on the Queets River in Olympic National Park

**Map 1.5, page 81**

This primitive camp on the shore of the Queets River is a gem if you don't mind bringing your own water (or purifying river water). A trailhead leads into the interior of Olympic National Park. The elevation is 290 feet.

Note: The Queets Road reroute is now open, but trailers are not recommended. Check the road status in winter.

**Campsites, facilities:** There are 20 primitive sites for tents only. Picnic tables and fire pits are provided. Pit toilets are available. There is no drinking water and garbage must be packed out. Leashed pets are permitted.

**Reservations, fees:** Reservations are not accepted. Sites are $10 per night, plus a $15 national park entrance fee. Open year-round.

**Directions:** From Aberdeen, drive north on U.S. 101 for 38 miles to Lake Quinault, and continue for 19 miles to a signed turnoff for the campground at Forest Road 21. Turn right (northeast) on Forest Road 21 (an unpaved road) and drive 14 miles (along the Queets River) to the campground at the end of the road; not recommended for RVs or trailers.

**Contact:** Olympic National Park, 360/565-3130, www.nps.gov/olym.

## 56 GRAVES CREEK

### Scenic rating: 6

near the Quinault River in Olympic National Park

**Map 1.5, page 81**

A road washout now requires a hike of 4.5 miles to reach this spot. This camp is located at an elevation of 540 feet and is a short distance from a trailhead leading into the backcountry of Olympic National Park. The East Fork Quinault River is nearby, and there are lakes in the area.

**Campsites, facilities:** There are 30 sites for tents or RVs up to 21 feet long. Picnic tables and fire pits are provided. Pit toilets are available, but there is no drinking water. Leashed pets are permitted.

**Reservations, fees:** Reservations are not accepted. Sites are $12 per night, plus a $15 national park entrance fee per vehicle. Open year-round.

**Directions:** From Aberdeen, drive north on U.S. 101 for 38 miles to the Lake Quinault turnoff and South Shore Road. Turn east on South Shore Road and drive 15 miles to the road washout. Park and hike 4.5 miles to the campground. The Graves Creek Ranger Station is located nearby.

**Contact:** Olympic National Park, 360/565-3130, www.nps.gov/olym.

## 57 LENA LAKE HIKE-IN

### Scenic rating: 8

near the Hamma Hamma River in Olympic National Forest

**Map 1.5, page 81**      **BEST (**

Lena Lake is one of the most popular lakes on the Olympic Peninsula. Though it is comparatively crowded in the summer, you can usually get a site. The 55-acre lake is nestled along the Hamma Hamma drainage, between rugged peaks and adjacent to the Brothers Wilderness. It takes a three-mile hike-in from the trailhead at Lena Creek to reach this camp. This adventure is suitable for the entire family—an outstanding way to turn youngsters on to backpacking. It's a lovely setting, too, with a pleasantly mild climate in summer. The lake is good for swimming and fishing for rainbow trout. The elevation is 1,800 feet.

**Campsites, facilities:** There are 29 primitive, hike-in sites for tents only. A compost toilet and fire rings are available. There is no drinking water and garbage must be packed out. Leashed pets are permitted.

**Reservations, fees:** Reservations are not

accepted. There is no fee for camping, but there is a $5 fee per day to park at the trailhead. Open May-September, weather permitting.

**Directions:** From Olympia on I-5, turn north on U.S. 101 and drive about 37 miles to Hoodsport. Continue north on U.S. 101 for 14 miles to Forest Road 25. Turn left (west) on Forest Road 25 and drive eight miles to the Lena Creek Camp and the trailhead. Hike 3.2 miles north to Lena Lake. Campsites are scattered around the lake.

**Contact:** Olympic National Forest, Hood Canal Ranger District, 360/877-5254, www.fs.fed.us.

# 58 LENA CREEK

### Scenic rating: 7
on the Hamma Hamma River in Olympic National Forest

**Map 1.5, page 81**

This seven-acre camp, set amid both conifers and hardwoods, is located where Lena Creek empties into the Hamma Hamma River. A popular trailhead camp, Lena Creek features a three-mile trail from camp to Lena Lake, with four additional miles to Upper Lena Lake. A map of Olympic National Forest details the trail and road system. The camp is rustic with some improvements.

**Campsites, facilities:** There are 13 sites for tents or RVs to 21 feet. Picnic tables and fire rings are provided. Vault toilets and drinking water are available. Garbage must be packed out. Leashed pets are permitted.

**Reservations, fees:** Reservations are not accepted. Sites are $14 per night, $5 per extra vehicle per night. Open mid-May-September.

**Directions:** From Olympia on I-5, turn north on U.S. 101 and drive about 37 miles to Hoodsport. Continue north on U.S. 101 for 14 miles to Forest Road 25. Turn left (west) on Forest Road 25 and drive eight miles to the camp on the left.

**Contact:** Olympic National Forest, Hood Canal Ranger District, Quilcene Office, 360/765-2200, www.fs.fed.us.

# 59 HAMMA HAMMA

### Scenic rating: 7
on the Hamma Hamma River in Olympic National Forest

**Map 1.5, page 81**

This camp is set on the Hamma Hamma River at an elevation of 600 feet. It's small and primitive, but it can be preferable to some of the developed camps on the U.S. 101 circuit. The Civilian Conservation Corps is memorialized in a wheelchair-accessible interpretive trail that begins in the campground and leads 0.25 mile along the river. The sites are set among conifers and hardwoods.

**Campsites, facilities:** There are 15 sites for tents or RVs up to 21 feet long. Picnic tables and fire rings are provided. Vault toilets are available. There is no drinking water, and garbage must be packed out. (In season, drinking water is available two miles away at Lena Creek Campground.) Some facilities are wheelchair accessible. Leashed pets are permitted.

**Reservations, fees:** Reservations are not accepted. Sites are $14 per night, $5 per night per additional vehicle. Open May-September, weather permitting.

**Directions:** From Olympia on I-5, turn north on U.S. 101 and drive 37 miles to Hoodsport. Continue on U.S. 101 for 14 miles north to Forest Road 25. Turn left on Forest Road 25 and drive seven miles to the camp on the left side of the road.

**Contact:** Olympic National Forest, Hood Canal Ranger District, Quilcene Office, 360/765-2200, www.fs.fed.us.

# 60 WILLABY

### Scenic rating: 8
on Lake Quinault in Olympic National Forest

**Map 1.5, page 81**

This pretty, 14-acre wooded camp is set on the shore of Lake Quinault, which covers about six square miles. Part of the Quinault Reservation, the camp is adjacent to where Willaby Creek empties into the lake. The campsites vary—some are open with lake views, while others are more private with no view. The forest floor is covered with wall-to-wall greenery, with exceptional moss growth, and the tree cover consists of Douglas fir, western red cedar, western hemlock, and big-leaf maple. Quinault Rain Forest Nature Trail and the Quinault National Recreation Trail System are nearby. The elevation is 200 feet.

Note: As of September 2013, the Quinault Reservation has suspended all lake activities, such as fishing and boating, until further notice due to an ongoing water quality study. Swimming is "at your own risk."

**Campsites, facilities:** There are 32 sites for tents or RVs up to 16 feet long and two walk-in sites for tents only. Picnic tables and fire pits are provided. Drinking water, garbage bins, and restrooms with flush toilets are available. Launching facilities and rentals are available at nearby Lake Quinault. Some facilities are wheelchair accessible. Leashed pets are permitted.

**Reservations, fees:** Reservations are not accepted. Sites are $15-20 per night, $8 per extra vehicle per night. Open year-round, weather permitting

**Directions:** From Aberdeen, drive north on U.S. 101 for 42 miles to the Lake Quinault-South Shore turnoff. Turn right (northeast) on South Shore Road and drive 1.5 miles to the camp on the southern shore of the lake.

**Contact:** Olympic National Forest, Pacific Ranger District, Quinault Office, 360/288-2525, www.fs.fed.us; Quinault Reservation, 360/276-8215 x305.

where Falls Creek empties into Quinault Lake. A canopy of lush big-leaf maple hangs over the campground, which features both drive-in and walk-in sites; the latter require about a 125-yard walk. Quinault Rain Forest Nature Trail and the Quinault National Recreation Trail System are nearby. The camp is located adjacent to the Quinault Ranger Station and historic Lake Quinault Lodge at an elevation of 200 feet.

Note: As of September 2013, the Quinault Reservation has suspended all lake activities, such as fishing and boating, until further notice due to an ongoing water quality study. Swimming is "at your own risk."

**Campsites, facilities:** There are 10 walk-in sites for tents only and 21 sites for tents or RVs up to 16 feet long. Picnic tables and fire pits are provided. Drinking water and restrooms with flush toilets are available. A camp host has firewood for sale nearby. A picnic area, boat launching facilities, and boat rentals are available at Lake Quinault. Some facilities are wheelchair accessible. Leashed pets are permitted.

**Reservations, fees:** Reservations are not accepted. Sites are $15-20 per night, $8 per extra vehicle per night. Open Memorial Day weekend-Labor Day weekend.

**Directions:** From Aberdeen, drive north on U.S. 101 for 42 miles to the Lake Quinault-South Shore turnoff. Turn right (northeast) on South Shore Road and drive 2.5 miles to the camp on the southeast shore of Lake Quinault. Make a very sharp left turn into the campground.

**Contact:** Olympic National Forest, Pacific Ranger District, Quinault Office, 360/288-2525, www.fs.fed.us; Quinault Reservation, 360/276-8215 x305.

## 61 FALLS CREEK

**Scenic rating: 8**

on Lake Quinault in Olympic National Forest

**Map 1.5, page 81**

This scenic, wooded three-acre camp is set

## 62 GATTON CREEK WALK-IN

**Scenic rating: 9**

on Lake Quinault in Olympic National Forest

**Map 1.5, page 81**

This five-acre wooded camp is set on the shore

of Lake Quinault (elevation 200 feet), where Gatton Creek empties into it. Lake Quinault covers about six square miles and is part of the Quinault Indian Nation, which has jurisdiction here. The camp features great views across the lake to the forested slopes of Olympic National Park. Reaching the campsites requires about a 100-yard walk from the parking area. About nine miles of loop trails are accessible here; Quinault Rain Forest Nature Trail and the Quinault National Recreation Trail System are nearby.

Note: As of September 2013, the Quinault Reservation has suspended all lake activities, such as fishing and boating, until further notice due to an ongoing water quality study. Swimming is "at your own risk."

**Campsites, facilities:** There are 15 walk-in sites for tents and 10 overflow sites for RVs up to 24 feet long. Picnic tables and fire pits are provided at the tent sites. Vault toilets, firewood, and a picnic area are available. Some facilities are wheelchair accessible. Leashed pets are permitted.

**Reservations, fees:** Reservations are not accepted. Sites are $12 per night. Open late May-early October, weather permitting.

**Directions:** From Aberdeen, drive north on U.S. 101 for 42 miles to the Lake Quinault-South Shore turnoff. Turn right (northeast) on South Shore Road and drive three miles to the camp on the southeast shore of Lake Quinault.

**Contact:** Olympic National Forest, Pacific Ranger District, Quinault Office, 360/288-2525, www.fs.fed.us; Quinault Reservation, 360/276-8215 x305.

## 63 CAMPBELL TREE GROVE
🚶 🛶 🎣 ♿ 🚐 ⛺

### Scenic rating: 8
on the Humptulips River in Olympic National Forest

Map 1.5, page 81                    BEST (

This 14-acre camp is set amid dense, old-growth forest featuring stands of both conifers and hardwoods, with licorice ferns growing on the trunks and branches of the big leaf maples. The camp is a favorite for hikers, with trailheads nearby that provide access to the Colonel Bob Wilderness. One of the best, the 3,400-foot climb to the Colonel Bob Summit provides an 8.5-mile round-trip accessible from the Pete's Creek Trailhead, which is located a couple of miles south of camp on Forest Road 2204. Note that much of this summit hike is a great butt-kicker. The West Fork of the Humptulips River runs near the camp, and Humptulips Trail provides access. Fishing is an option here as well; check state regulations.

**Campsites, facilities:** There are eight tent sites and three sites for RVs up to 16 feet long. Picnic tables and fire grills are provided. Vault toilets and garbage bins are available. There is no drinking water. Some facilities are wheelchair accessible. Leashed pets are permitted.

**Reservations, fees:** Reservations are not accepted. There is no fee for camping. Open May-October, weather permitting.

**Directions:** From Aberdeen, drive north on U.S. 101 for 22 miles to Humptulips and continue for another five miles to Forest Road 22 (Donkey Creek Road). Turn right and drive eight miles to Forest Road 2204. Turn left (north) and drive nine miles to the campground.

**Contact:** Olympic National Forest, Pacific Ranger District, Quinault Office, 360/288-2525, www.fs.fed.us.

## 64 STAIRCASE
🚶 🛶 🎣 🐕 ♿ 🚐 ⛺

### Scenic rating: 9
on the North Fork of the Skokomish River in Olympic National Park

Map 1.5, page 81

This camp is located near the Staircase Rapids of the North Fork of the Skokomish River, about one mile from where it empties into Lake Cushman. The elevation is 765 feet. A major trailhead at the camp leads to the backcountry of Olympic National Park, and other trails are nearby. Hiking trails along the river can be accessed nearby. Stock facilities are also available nearby. Note that Staircase Road is closed in winter.

**Campsites, facilities:** There are 47 sites for tents or RVs up to 35 feet long. Picnic tables and fire pits are provided. Restrooms with flush toilets and drinking water are available during the summer season. In winter, only pit toilets are available. Some facilities are wheelchair accessible. Leashed pets are permitted in camp.

**Reservations, fees:** Reservations are not accepted. Sites are $12 per night, plus a $15 national park entrance fee per vehicle. Open year-round, with limited winter services.

**Directions:** From Olympia on I-5, take U.S. 101 and drive north about 37 miles to the town of Hoodsport and Lake Cushman Road (County Road 119). Turn left (west) and drive 17 miles to the camp at the end of the road (set about one mile above the inlet of Lake Cushman). The last several miles of the road are unpaved.

**Contact:** Olympic National Park, 360/565-3130, www.nps.gov/olym.

## 65 COHO

**Scenic rating: 10**

on Wynoochee Lake in Olympic National Forest

| Map 1.5, page 81 | BEST ( |
| --- | --- |

This eight-acre camp sits on the shore of Wynoochee Lake, which is 4.4 miles long and covers 1,140 acres. The camp is set at an elevation of 900 feet. The fishing season opens June 1 and closes October 31. Powerboats, waterskiing, and personal watercraft are permitted. Points of interest include Working Forest Nature Trail, Wynoochee Dam Viewpoint and exhibits, and 16-mile Wynoochee Lake Shore Trail, which circles the lake. This is one of the most idyllic drive-to settings you could hope to find.

**Campsites, facilities:** There are 46 sites for tents or RVs up to 36 feet long, 10 walk-in sites for tents only, and three yurts. Picnic tables are provided. Drinking water and flush toilets are available. A dump station is nearby. Boat docks and launching facilities are available at Wynoochee Lake. Leashed pets are permitted.

**Reservations, fees:** Reservations are accepted at 877/444-6777 ($10 reservation fee) or www.recreation.gov ($9 reservation fee). Sites are $16-20 per night, $5 per extra vehicle per night, the group site is $40 per night, and yurts are $65 per night. Open May-November, weather permitting.

**Directions:** From Olympia on I-5, take Exit 104 and drive north on U.S. 101 to the Aberdeen/Highway 8 exit. Turn west on Highway 8 and drive 36 miles (it becomes Highway 12 at Elma) to Montesano. Continue two miles on Highway 12 to Wynoochee Valley Road. Turn right (north) on Wynoochee Valley Road and drive 12 miles to Forest Road 22. Continue north on Forest Road 22 (a gravel road) for 23 miles to Wynoochee Lake. Just south of the lake, bear left and drive on Forest Road 2294 (which runs along the lake's northwest shore) for one mile to the camp on the west shore of Wynoochee Lake. Obtaining a U.S. Forest Service map is helpful.

**Contact:** Olympic National Forest, Hood Canal Ranger District, Quilcene Office, 360/765-2200, www.fs.fed.us.

## 66 BROWN CREEK

**Scenic rating: 9**

on Brown Creek in Olympic National Forest

| Map 1.5, page 81 |
| --- |

Brown Creek is little known among out-of-town visitors. While this camp is accessible to two-wheel-drive vehicles, the access road connects to a network of primitive, backcountry forest roads. It is situated within the vast Olympic National Forest, which offers many opportunities for outdoor recreation.

Wheelchair-accessible Brown Creek Nature Trail begins at the hand pump and makes a one-mile loop around the camp, featuring views of an active beaver pond. Obtain a U.S. Forest Service map to expand your trip.

**Campsites, facilities:** There are 12 sites for tents or RVs up to 20 feet long and eight sites for tents only. Picnic tables and fire rings are provided. Drinking water (summer only) and vault toilets are available. Garbage must be packed out. Some facilities are wheelchair accessible. Leashed pets are permitted.

**Reservations, fees:** Reservations are not accepted. Sites are $14 per night, $5 per extra vehicle per night. Open year-round, weather permitting.

**Directions:** From Olympia on I-5, take Exit 104 for U.S. 101/Highway 8. Drive north on U.S. 101 for 31 miles (about six miles past Shelton) to Skokomish Valley Road. Turn left (west) and drive 5.3 miles to Forest Road 23. Turn right on Forest Road 23 and drive nine miles to Forest Road 2353. Turn right on Forest Road 2353 and drive one mile to the South Fork Skokomish River Bridge. Cross the bridge, turn right sharply onto Forest Road 2340 and drive 0.25 mile to the camp. Obtaining a U.S. Forest Service map is advisable.

**Contact:** Olympic National Forest, Hood Canal Ranger District, Quilcene Office, 360/765-2200, www.fs.fed.us.

## 67 LEBAR HORSE CAMP
🏇 🛶 🐕 🚐 ⛰️

**Scenic rating: 9**

in Olympic National Forest

**Map 1.5, page 81**

This camp is exclusively for people with horses or pack animals, such as mules, mollies, llamas, and goats. The camp provides access to Lower South Fork Skokomish Trail, a 10.9-mile trip, one-way. The camp features beautiful old-growth forest, with western hemlock and Douglas fir.

**Campsites, facilities:** There are 13 sites for

tents or RVs up to 28 feet long for the exclusive use of campers with pack animals. Picnic tables, fire grills, hitching posts, and high lines are provided. Vault toilets are available. There is no drinking water, and garbage must be packed out. A day-use area with a picnic shelter is available nearby. Leashed pets are permitted.

**Reservations, fees:** Reservations are not accepted. Sites are $10 per night, $5 per extra vehicle per night. Open May-September, weather permitting.

**Directions:** From Olympia on I-5, take Exit 104 for U.S. 101/Highway 8. Drive north on U.S. 101 for 31 miles (about six miles past Shelton) to Skokomish Valley Road. Turn left (west) and drive 5.3 miles to Forest Road 23. Turn right on Forest Road 23 and drive nine miles to Forest Road 2353. Turn right on Forest Road 2353 and drive one mile to the South Fork Skokomish River Bridge. Cross the bridge, turn left sharply to remain on Forest Road 2353, and drive 0.5 mile to the camp. Obtaining a U.S. Forest Service map is advisable.

**Contact:** Olympic National Forest, Hood Canal Ranger District, 360/765-2200, www. fs.fed.us.

## 68 BIG CREEK
🏇 🛶 🚐 🐕 🚗 ⛰️

**Scenic rating: 7**

near Lake Cushman in Olympic National Forest

**Map 1.5, page 81**

Big Creek is an alternative to Staircase camp on the North Fork of Skokomish River and Camp Cushman and Recreation Park, both of which get heavier use. The sites here are large and well spaced for privacy over 30 acres, primarily of second-growth forest. Big Creek runs adjacent to the campground. A four-mile loop trail extends from camp and connects to Mount Eleanor Trail. A bonus: Two walk-in sites are located along the creek.

**Campsites, facilities:** There are 23 sites for

tents or RVs up to 30 feet long. Picnic tables and fire grills are provided. Drinking water, vault toilets, and a sheltered picnic area are available. A boat dock and ramp are located at nearby Lake Cushman. Garbage must be packed out. Leashed pets are permitted.

**Reservations, fees:** Reservations are not accepted. Sites are $14 per night, $5 per extra vehicle per night. Open May-September, weather permitting.

**Directions:** From Olympia on I-5, take Exit 104 for U.S. 101/Highway 8. Drive north on U.S. 101 for 37 miles to Hoodsport and Lake Cushman Road (Highway 119). Turn left on Lake Cushman Road and drive nine miles (two miles north of Camp Cushman) to the T intersection with Forest Road 24. Turn left and the campground is on the right.

**Contact:** Olympic National Forest, Hood Canal Ranger District, Quilcene Office, 360/765-2200, www.fs.fed.us; visitors center, 360/877-2021.

## 69 SKOKOMISH PARK AT LAKE CUSHMAN

### Scenic rating: 10

on Lake Cushman near Hoodsport

**Map 1.5, page 81**    **BEST (**

Set in the foothills of the Olympic Mountains on the shore of Lake Cushman, this 500-acre park features a 10-mile-long blue-water mountain lake, eight miles of park shoreline, forested hillsides, and awesome views of snowcapped peaks. Beach access and good trout fishing are other highlights. The park has eight miles of hiking trails. Windsurfing, waterskiing, and swimming are all popular here. A nine-hole golf course is nearby.

**Campsites, facilities:** There are 50 sites for tents or RVs up to 30 feet long (no hookups), 29 sites with full hookups (20 and 30 amps) for RVs up to 30 feet long, two hike-in/bike-in sites, and one group camp for up to 80 people. Picnic tables and fire grills are provided.

Restrooms with flush toilets and coin showers, drinking water, a camp store, picnic area, amphitheater, horseshoe pits, badminton, volleyball court, ice, and firewood are available. A restaurant is within five miles. Boat docks and launching facilities are also available. Some facilities are wheelchair accessible. Leashed pets are permitted.

**Reservations, fees:** Reservations are recommended ($7 reservation fee). RV sites are $32 per night, tent sites are $25 per night, hike-in/bike-in sites are $20 per night, $10 per extra vehicle per night. The group camp is a minimum of $90 per night. Some credit cards are accepted. Open year-round, weather permitting.

**Directions:** From Olympia on I-5, take the U.S. 101 exit and drive north 37 miles to Hoodsport and Highway 119 (Lake Cushman Road). Turn left (west) on Lake Cushman Road and drive 7.5 miles to the park on the left.

**Contact:** Skokomish Park at Lake Cushman, 7211 N Lake Cushman Rd., Hoodsport, 360/877-5760, www.skokomishpark.com.

## 70 LAKE CUSHMAN RESORT

### Scenic rating: 10

on Lake Cushman near Hoodsport

**Map 1.5, page 81**

This campground on Lake Cushman has full facilities for water sports, including boat launching and rentals. Waterskiing and fishing are popular. Lake Cushman Dam makes a good side trip. Trails in the Olympic National Forest and Staircase in the Olympic National Park and a nine-hole golf course are nearby.

**Campsites, facilities:** There are 50 sites for tents or RVs up to 22 feet long (no hookups), 21 sites with partial hookups (20 amps) for RVs up to 40 feet long, and 11 cabins. Double and triple tent sites are also available. Picnic tables and fire rings are provided. Drinking water, flush and portable toilets, firewood, a convenience store, boat docks and launching facilities, mooring, and boat rentals are available. Groups can be accommodated. Some facilities are wheelchair accessible. Leashed pets are permitted.

**Reservations, fees:** Reservations are recommended. RV sites are $28-35 per night, tent sites are $22-30 per night, $5 per each additional person per night, $6 per each additional vehicle, $10 per pet per stay, and mooring is $10-15 per day. Off-season rates available October 1-April 30. Some credit cards are accepted. Open mid-April-mid-October; cabins are open year-round.

**Directions:** From Olympia on I-5, take the U.S. 101 exit and drive north 37 miles to Hoodsport and Highway 119/Lake Cushman Road. Turn left (west) on Lake Cushman Road and drive 4.5 miles to the resort on the left.

**Contact:** Lake Cushman Resort, 4621 N. Lake Cushman Rd., Hoodsport, 360/877-9630 or 800/588-9630, www.lakecushman.com.

## 71 REST-A-WHILE RV PARK

🏊 🚣 ➡ ⛵ 🐕 🚐 ⛺

### Scenic rating: 5

on Hood Canal north of Hoodsport

**Map 1.5, page 81**

This seven-acre park, located at sea level on Hood Canal, offers waterfront sites and a private beach for clamming and oyster gathering, not to mention plenty of opportunities to fish, boat, and scuba dive. It's an alternative to Potlatch State Park and Glen-Ayr RV Park.

**Campsites, facilities:** There are 95 sites for tents or RVs of any length (30 and 50 amps), two tent sites, and one rental trailer. Some sites are pull-through. Picnic tables are provided and fire rings are provided at some sites. Restrooms with flush toilets and showers, drinking water, cable TV, Wi-Fi, propane gas, firewood, a clubhouse, restaurant, coin laundry, and ice are available. A café is within walking distance. Boat and kayak rentals and a private beach for clamming and oyster gathering (in season) are

also available. Some facilities are wheelchair accessible. Leashed pets are permitted.

**Reservations, fees:** Reservations are accepted. RV sites are $33-38 per night, tent sites are $30 per night, and $7 per person per night for more than two people. Some credit cards are accepted. Open year-round.

**Directions:** From Olympia on I-5, take Exit 104 for U.S. 101/Highway 8. Drive north on U.S. 101 for 37 miles to Hoodsport. Continue 2.5 miles north on U.S. 101 to the park located at Milepost 329.

**Contact:** Rest-A-While RV Park, 27001 N. US Hwy. 101, Hoodsport, 360/877-9474 or 866/637-9474, www.restawhile.com.

## 72 GLEN-AYR RV PARK & MOTEL

🏊 🚣 ➡ 🐕 🚐

### Scenic rating: 5

on Hood Canal near Hoodsport

**Map 1.5, page 81**

This fully developed, nine-acre park is located at sea level on Hood Canal, where there are opportunities to fish and scuba dive. Salmon fishing is especially excellent. Swimming and boating round out the options. The park also has a spa, moorage, horseshoe pits, recreation field, and a motel.

**Campsites, facilities:** There are 36 sites with full hookups (30 and 50 amps) for RVs of any length, 14 motel rooms, a townhouse, and two suites with kitchens. Some sites are pull-through. Picnic tables are provided. No open fires are allowed. Restrooms with flush toilets and showers, drinking water, cable TV, Wi-Fi, propane gas, ice, a spa, recreation hall, barbecue, gazebo (with interior dining), seasonal organized activities, and coin laundry are available. A store and café are within one mile. A boat dock is located across the street from the park, with moorage for guests. Leashed pets are permitted.

**Reservations, fees:** Reservations are accepted. Sites are $33-43 per night, $5 per person per night for more than two people, $5 per extra vehicle per night. Some credit cards are accepted. Open year-round.

**Directions:** From Olympia on I-5, take Exit 104 for U.S. 101/Highway 8. Drive north on U.S. 101 for 37 miles to Hoodsport. Continue one mile north on U.S. 101 to the park on the left.

**Contact:** Glen-Ayr RV Park & Motel, 25381 N. US Highway 101, Hoodsport, 360/877-9522 or 866/877-9522, www.glenayr.com.

## 73 POTLATCH STATE PARK

🚶 🚴 ⛵ 🎣 🛥 🛶 🎣 🐕 ♿ 🚐 ⛺

**Scenic rating: 8**

on Hood Canal

**Map 1.5, page 81**

This state park features good shellfish harvesting in season. The park has 9,570 feet of shoreline on Hood Canal. There are 1.5 miles of trails for hiking and biking, but the shoreline and water bring people here for the good kayaking, windsurfing, scuba diving, clamming, and fishing. The park is named for the potlatch, a Skyhomish gift-giving ceremony. There are four major rivers, the Skokomish, Hamma Hamma, Duckabush, and Dosewallips, within a 30-mile radius of the park. The park receives an annual rainfall of 64 inches.

**Campsites, facilities:** There are 35 sites with full or partial hookups (30 and 50 amps) for RVs up to 60 feet long, 38 sites for tents, and two hike-in/bike-in sites. Picnic tables and fire grills are provided. Restrooms with flush toilets and coin showers, drinking water, a dump station, firewood, an amphitheater, a picnic area, and seasonal interpretive programs are available. Five mooring buoys are located at the park, and a boat launch and dock are available nearby. Groceries, gas, and propane are available three miles away. Some facilities are wheelchair accessible. Leashed pets are permitted.

**Reservations, fees:** Reservations are accepted in summer at 888/226-7688 or www.goingto-camp.com. Sites are $17-42 per night, $12 per

night for hike-in/bike-in sites, $10 per extra vehicle per night, $12 buoy fee per night. Open year-round.

**Directions:** From Olympia on I-5, take Exit 104 for U.S. 101/Highway 8. Drive north on U.S. 101 for 22 miles to Shelton. Continue north on U.S. 101 for 12 miles to the park on the right (located along the shoreline of Annas Bay on Hood Canal).

**Contact:** Potlatch State Park, 360/877-5361; state park information, 360/902-8844, www.parks.wa.gov.

## 74 SCHAFER STATE PARK

🚶 ⛵ 🎣 🛥 🛶 🐕 ♿ 🚐 ⛺

**Scenic rating: 8**

on the Satsop River

**Map 1.5, page 81**

This unique destination boasts many interesting features, including buildings constructed from native stone. A heavily wooded, rural camp, Schafer State Park covers 119 acres along the East Fork of the Satsop River. The river is well known for fishing and rafting. Fish for sea-run cutthroat in summer, salmon in fall, and steelhead in late winter. There are good canoeing and kayaking spots, some with Class II and III rapids, along the Middle and West Forks of the Satsop. Three miles of hiking trails are also available. At one time, this park was the Schafer Logging Company Park and was used by employees and their families.

**Campsites, facilities:** There are 32 sites for tents, 10 sites with partial hookups (30 amps) for RVs up to 40 feet long, two hike-in/bike-in sites, and two group sites for up to 50 and 100 people respectively. Picnic tables and fire grills are provided. Restrooms with flush toilets and coin showers, drinking water, picnic shelters that can be reserved, a dump station, and horseshoe pits are available. Some facilities are wheelchair accessible. Leashed pets are permitted.

**Reservations, fees:** Reservations are accepted for summer at 888/226-7688 www.goingto-camp.com. Sites are $20-42 per night, $10 per extra vehicle per night, hike-in/bike-in sites are $12 per night, and the group sites are $69.89-209.67 per night. Open late April-early October, weather permitting.

**Directions:** From Olympia on I-5, take Exit 104 to U.S. 101. Drive west on U.S. 101 for six miles to Highway 8. Turn west on Highway 8 and drive to Elma (Highway 8 becomes Highway 12). Continue west on Highway 12 for five miles to the Brady exit/West Satsop Road (four miles east of Montesano). Turn right (north) on West Satsop Road and drive eight miles to Schafer Park Road. Turn right and drive two miles to the park.

**Contact:** Schafer State Park, 360/482-3852; state park information, 360/902-8844, www. parks.wa.gov.

## 75 LAKE SYLVIA STATE PARK

**Scenic rating: 8**

on Lake Sylvia

**Map 1.5, page 81**                    **BEST (**

This 234-acre state park on the shore of Lake Sylvia features nearly three miles of freshwater shoreline. The park is located in a former logging camp in a wooded area set midway between Olympia and the Pacific Ocean. Expect plenty of rustic charm, with displays of old logging gear, a giant ball carved out of wood from a single log, and some monstrous stumps. The lake is good for fishing and ideal for canoes, prams, or small boats with oars or electric motors; no gas motors are permitted. Five miles of hiking trails and a 0.5-mile wheelchair-accessible trail meander through the park. Additional recreation options include trout fishing and swimming.

**Campsites, facilities:** There are 35 sites with no hookups and four sites with partial hookups for tents or RVs up to 30 feet long, two hike-in/bike-in sites, and one group site for up to 60 people and 10 vehicles. Picnic tables and fire grills are provided. Restrooms with flush toilets and coin showers, drinking water,

a dump station, boat launch, picnic area, a kitchen shelter that can be reserved, firewood, and a playground are available. A coin laundry and grocery store are located within two miles. Some facilities are wheelchair accessible. Leashed pets are permitted.

**Reservations, fees:** Reservations are accepted for individual sites and are required for the group site at 888/CAMP-OUT (888/226-7688) or www.goingtocamp.com ($6.50-8.50 reservation fee). Sites are $17-39 per night, $10 per extra vehicle per night, hike-in/bike-in sites are $12 per night, and the group site is $70.46-140.92 per night (20-person minimum). Open early April-mid-October, weather permitting.

**Directions:** From Olympia on I-5, take Exit 104 to U.S. 101. Drive west on U.S. 101 six miles to Highway 8. Turn west on Highway 8 (becomes Highway 12) and drive 26 miles to Montesano and West Pioneer Street (the only stoplight in town). Turn left on West Pioneer Street and drive three blocks to 3rd Street. Turn right and drive two miles to the park entrance (route is well signed).

**Contact:** Lake Sylvia State Park, 360/249-3621; state park information, 360/902-8844, www.parks.wa.gov.

## 76 TRAVEL INN RESORT

**Scenic rating: 7**

on Lake Sylvia near Elma

**Map 1.5, page 81**

This is a membership campground, which means sites for RV travelers are available only if there is extra space. It can be difficult to get a spot May-September, but the park opens up significantly in the off-season. There are five major rivers or lakes within 15 minutes of this camp (Satsop, Chehalis, Wynoochee, Black River, and Lake Sylvia). Nearby Lake Sylvia State Park provides multiple marked hiking trails. Additional recreation options include trout fishing, swimming, and golf (three miles away).

**Campsites, facilities:** There are 200 sites with full or partial hookups (30 and 50 amps) for RVs of any length and three tent sites. Picnic tables are provided. Restrooms with flush toilets and showers, drinking water, coin laundry, two community fire pits, a gazebo, a seasonal heated swimming pool, playground, basketball, volleyball, badminton, shuffleboard, game room, cable TV, Wi-Fi and modem access, seasonal organized activities, and a clubhouse are available. A grocery store, gas station, propane, and restaurant are available within one mile. Some facilities are wheelchair accessible. Leashed pets are permitted.

**Reservations, fees:** Reservations are accepted May-September. Sites are $40-42 per night. No credit cards are accepted. Open year-round.

**Directions:** From Olympia on I-5, take Exit 104 to U.S. 101. Drive west on U.S. 101 for six miles to Highway 8. Turn west on Highway 8 and drive to Elma (Highway 8 becomes Highway 12). Take the first Elma exit and drive to the stop sign and Highway 12/East Main Street. Turn right and drive about 200 yards to the end of the highway and a stop sign. Turn right and drive another 200 yards to the resort on the right.

**Contact:** Travel Inn Resort, 801 East Main, Elma, 360/482-3877 or 800/871-2888, www.kmresorts.com.

## 77 FALLS VIEW

### Scenic rating: 8
on the Big Quilcene River in Olympic National Forest

**Map 1.6, page 82**      BEST (

A viewing area to a pretty waterfall on the Big Quilcene River, where you see a narrow, 100-foot cascade, is only a 150-foot walk from the campground. That explains why, despite the rustic setting, this spot on the edge of the Olympic National Forest has a host of facilities and is popular. Enjoy the setting of mixed conifers and rhododendrons along a one-mile scenic loop trail, which overlooks the river and provides views of the waterfall. A picnic area is also located near the waterfall.

**Campsites, facilities:** There are 30 sites for tents or RVs up to 21 feet long. Picnic tables and fire pits are provided. Vault toilets are available. There is no drinking water. Leashed pets are permitted.

**Reservations, fees:** Reservations are not accepted. Sites are $10 per night, $5 per extra vehicle per night. Open May-September, weather permitting.

**Directions:** From Olympia on I-5, turn north on U.S. 101 and drive approximately 70 miles to the campground entrance on the left (located about four miles south of Quilcene).

**Contact:** Olympic National Forest, Hood Canal Ranger District, Quilcene Office, 360/765-2200, www.fs.fed.us.

## 78 KITSAP MEMORIAL STATE PARK

### Scenic rating: 10
on Hood Canal

**Map 1.6, page 82**      BEST (

Kitsap Memorial State Park is a beautiful spot for campers along Hood Canal. The park covers only 58 acres but features sweeping views of Puget Sound and 1,797 feet of shoreline. The park has 1.5 miles of hiking trails and two open grassy fields for family play. Note that the nearest boat launch is four miles away, north on State Route 3 at Salisbury County Park. An 18-hole golf course and swimming, fishing, and hiking at nearby Anderson Lake Recreation Area are among the activities available. A short drive north will take you to historic Old Fort Townsend, which makes an excellent day trip.

**Campsites, facilities:** There are 21 sites for tents or RVs up to 30 feet long, 18 sites with partial hookups (30 amps) for RVs, three hike-in/bike-in sites, a group camp for 20-56 people, four cabins, and a vacation house. Picnic tables and fire grills are provided. Restrooms with flush toilets and showers, drinking water, a dump station, sheltered picnic area, firewood, a playground, ballfields, and a community meeting hall are available. Two gas stations with mini-marts are located just outside the park. Two boat buoys are available. Some facilities are wheelchair accessible. Leashed pets are permitted.

**Reservations, fees:** Reservations are not accepted for individual campsites, but are required for the group camp at 888/CAMP-OUT (888/226-7688) or www.goingtocamp.com ($6.50-8.50 reservation fee). Sites are $17-39 per night, hike-in/bike-in sites are $12 per night, $10 per extra vehicle per night. The group camp is $150.42 per night, cabins are $59-69 per night, and the vacation house is $132-176 per night. Open year-round.

**Directions:** From Tacoma on I-5, turn north on Highway 16 and drive 44 miles (Highway 16 turns into Highway 3). Continue north on Highway 3 and drive six miles to Park Street. Turn left and drive 200 yards to the park entrance on the right (well marked). The park is located four miles south of the Hood Canal Bridge.

**Contact:** Kitsap Memorial State Park, 360/779-3205; state park information, 360/902-8844, www.parks.wa.gov.

## 79 COVE RV PARK
🏊 🛶 🚐 🐴 🚑 ⛺

### Scenic rating: 5
near Dabob Bay near Brinnon

**Map 1.6, page 82**

This five-acre private camp enjoys a rural setting close to the shore of Dabob Bay (said to be home of the world's largest clam pile), yet it is fully developed. Campsites are graveled and grassy with a few trees. A walking trail skirts Marple Creek and scuba diving is popular in this area. Dosewallips State Park is a short drive away and a possible side trip.

**Campsites, facilities:** There are 24 sites with full hookups (30 and 50 amps) for RVs up to 40 feet long and six sites for tents. Picnic tables and fire rings are provided. Restrooms with flush toilets and coin showers, drinking water, cable TV, Wi-Fi, propane gas, a convenience store, bait and tackle, loaner bikes, coin laundry, community barbecue area, basketball hoop, horseshoe pits, and ice are available. Boat docks and launching facilities are on Hood Canal 2.2 miles from the park. Leashed pets are permitted.

**Reservations, fees:** Reservations are accepted. RV sites are $30 per night, tent sites are $20 per night. Some credit cards are accepted. Open April 1-October 31.

**Directions:** From Olympia on I-5, drive north on U.S. 101 for 60 miles to Brinnon (located about one mile north of Dosewallips State Park). Continue three miles north on U.S. 101 to the park on the right (before Milepost 303).

**Contact:** Cove RV Park, 303075 N. Highway 101, Brinnon, 360/796-4723 or 866/796-4723, www.coverv.com.

## 80 SEAL ROCK
🏃 🛶 🛶 🚐 🏊 🐴 ♿ 🚑 ⛺

### Scenic rating: 9
on Dabob Bay in Olympic National Forest

**Map 1.6, page 82**

Seal Rock is a 30-acre camp set along the shore near the mouth of Dabob Bay. This is one of the few national forest campgrounds anywhere located on saltwater. It brings with it the opportunity to harvest oysters and clams in season, and it is an outstanding jumping-off point for scuba diving. Most campsites are set along the waterfront, spaced among trees. Carry-in boats, such as kayaks and canoes, can be launched from the north landing. Native American Nature Trail and Marine Biology Nature Trail begin at the day-use area. These are short walks, each less than 0.5 mile. This camp is extremely popular in the summer, often filling up quickly.

**Campsites, facilities:** There are 41 sites for tents or RVs up to 21 feet long. Picnic tables and fire rings are provided. Restrooms with flush toilets, drinking water, garbage bins, and a picnic area are available. A camp host is on-site in summer. Boat docks and launching facilities are nearby on Hood Canal and in Dabob Bay. Some facilities, including viewing areas and trails, are wheelchair accessible. Leashed pets are permitted.

**Reservations, fees:** Reservations are not accepted. Sites are $18 per night, $5 per each additional vehicle. Open May-September, weather permitting.

**Directions:** From Olympia on I-5, drive north on U.S. 101 for 62 miles to Brinnon (located about one mile north of Dosewallips State Park). Continue two miles north on U.S. 101 to Seal Rock and the camp on the right.

**Contact:** Olympic National Forest, Hood Canal Ranger District, Quilcene Office, 360/765-2200, www.fs.fed.us.

## 81 DOSEWALLIPS STATE PARK

### Scenic rating: 8

on Dosewallips Creek

**Map 1.6, page 82**

This 425-acre park is set on the shore of Hood Canal at the mouth of Dosewallips River. Most sites are grassy and are located in scenic and rustic settings. The campsite is popular because it's set right off a major highway; reservations or early arrival are advised. The park features 5,500 feet of saltwater shoreline on Hood Canal and 5,400 feet of shoreline on both sides of the Dosewallips River. Check regulations for fishing and clamming, which fluctuate according to time, season, and supply. There is no formal swimming area on the river, though it is a popular park activity. Please note that the river can be swift and may not be a suitable for younger children. Mushrooming is available in season and the park hosts an annual "Shrimp Fest," often in April. Access is not affected by the nearby slide area.

**Campsites, facilities:** There are 140 sites for tents or RVs up to 60 feet long (no hookups), 40 sites with full hookups (30 amps) for RVs up to 60 feet long, two hike-in/bike-in sites, three platform tent rentals, two group sites for up to 50 and 80 people, and three cabins. Picnic tables and fire rings are provided. Restrooms with flush toilets and coin showers, drinking water, a sheltered picnic area, interpretive activities, and a summer Junior Ranger Program are available. A wildlife-viewing platform, horseshoe pits, saltwater boat-launching facilities, and overnight mooring sites are available within the park. A store and café are available nearby. Some facilities are wheelchair accessible. Leashed pets are permitted.

**Reservations, fees:** Reservations are accepted at 888/CAMP-OUT (888/226-7688) or www.goingtocamp.com ($6.50-8.50 reservation fee). Sites are $21-27 per night, $10 per extra vehicle per night; hike-in/bike-in sites are $14 per night, platform tent rentals are $49.73 per night, group sites are $154.70 per night, cabins are $65.20 per night, and mooring is $0.60 per foot ($12 minimum). Some credit cards are accepted. Open year-round.

**Directions:** From Olympia on I-5, drive north on U.S. 101 for 61 miles (one mile south of Brinnon) to the state park entrance on the left.

**Contact:** Dosewallips State Park, 360/796-4415; state park information, 360/902-8844, www.parks.wa.gov.

## 82 SCENIC BEACH STATE PARK

### Scenic rating: 10

on Hood Canal

**Map 1.6, page 82**

Scenic Beach is an exceptionally beautiful state park with beach access and superb views of the Olympic Mountains. It features 1,500 feet of saltwater beachfront on Hood Canal. The park is also known for its wild rhododendrons in spring. Wheelchair-accessible paths lead to a country garden, gazebo, rustic bridge, and large trees. Many species of birds and wildlife can often be seen here. This camp is also close to Green Mountain Forest, where there is extensive hiking. A boat ramp is 0.5 mile east of the park. A nice touch here is that park staff will check out volleyballs and horseshoes during the summer.

**Campsites, facilities:** There are 52 sites for tents or RVs up to 60 feet long (some pull-through), two hike-in/bike-in sites, and a group camp for 20-50 people. Picnic tables and fire grills are provided. Restrooms with flush toilets and coin showers, drinking water, and a dump station are available. A sheltered picnic area, playground, horseshoe pits, and volleyball fields are nearby. A boat ramp, dock, and moorage are available within one mile. Some facilities are wheelchair accessible. Leashed pets are permitted.

**Reservations, fees:** Reservations are accepted at 888/CAMP-OUT (888/226-7688) or www.goingtocamp.com ($6.50-8.50 reservation fee). Sites are $23-31 per night, $10 per extra vehicle per night, hike-in/bike-in sites are $12 per night, and the group site is $140.46 per night. Open year-round, weather permitting.

**Directions:** From the junction at Highway 16 and Highway 3 in Bremerton, turn north on Highway 3 and drive about nine miles and take the first Silverdale exit (Newberry Hill Road). Turn left and drive approximately three miles to the end of the road. Turn right on Seabeck Highway and drive six miles to Scenic Beach Road. Turn right and drive one mile to the park.

**Contact:** Scenic Beach State Park, 360/830-5079; state park information, 360/902-8844, www.parks.wa.gov.

## 83 FAY BAINBRIDGE PARK

**Scenic rating: 10**

on Bainbridge Island

**Map 1.6, page 82**   BEST (

This former state park is now run by the local parks and recreation district. Set on the edge of Puget Sound, it still offers beauty and great recreation. The park covers just 17 acres but features 1,420 feet of saltwater shoreline on the northeast corner of the island. You can hike several miles along the beach at low tide; the water temperature is typically about 55°F in summer. The primitive walk-in sites are heavily wooded, and the developed sites have great views of the sound. On clear days, campers can enjoy views of Mount Rainier and Mount Baker to the east, and at night the park provides beautiful vistas of the lights of Seattle. Clamming, diving, picnicking, beachcombing, and kite-flying are popular here. In the winter months, there is excellent salmon fishing just offshore of the park.

**Campsites, facilities:** There are 26 sites for tents or RVs up to 40 feet long (water only), 10 sites for tents only, and four hike-in/bike-in sites. Picnic tables and fire grills are provided. Restrooms with flush toilets and coin showers, drinking water, sheltered picnic areas, firewood, horseshoes, and playground are available. Mooring buoys are available nearby. A store and café are located within three miles. Some facilities are wheelchair accessible. Leashed pets are permitted.

**Reservations, fees:** Reservations are not accepted. Sites are $15-23 per night, $10 per extra vehicle per night, hike-in/bike-in sites are $5 per person per night. Open year-round, weather permitting.

**Directions:** From Tacoma at I-5, turn north on Highway 16 and drive 30 miles to Bremerton to the junction with Highway 3. Turn north on Highway 3 and drive 18 miles to Highway 305. Turn south on Highway 305 and drive over the bridge to Bainbridge Island and continue three miles to Day Road. Turn left and drive 1.5 miles to Sunrise Drive. Turn left and drive two miles to the park on the right.

Note: From Seattle, this camp can be more easily accessed by taking the Bainbridge Island ferry and then Highway 305 north to Day Road at the northeast end of the island. From there, follow the directions above.

**Contact:** Bi Park District office, 206/842-2306 ext.118, www.biparks.org/parksandfacilities/pkfaybainbridge.

## 84 GREEN MOUNTAIN HIKE-IN

**Scenic rating: 7**

in Green Mountain State Forest

**Map 1.6, page 82**

This is a prime spot. Operated by the Department of Natural Resources, the campground is located in Green Mountain State Forest. The Backcountry Horsemen of Washington hosts the camp, which features facilities for horses. Hand-pumped stock water is available, a plus for such a primitive site. Note that if the gate is closed, a four-mile hike is required to reach the sites.

**Campsites, facilities:** There are 12 hike-in sites for tents only. Picnic tables and fire grills are provided. Vault toilets, a group shelter, and facilities for horses, including horse corrals, are available. There is no drinking water, and garbage must be packed out. Some facilities are wheelchair accessible. Leashed pets are permitted.

**Reservations, fees:** Reservations are not accepted. There is no fee for camping, but a Discover Pass is required. Open year-round, but a gate limits vehicular access to the camp 9am-6pm weekdays April-September; walk-in access is available when the gate is closed. A free map and brochure are available.

**Directions:** From Tacoma on I-5, turn north on Highway 16 and drive 30 miles to Bremerton and the junction with Highway 3. Turn north on Highway 3 and drive to Newberry Hill Road. Turn left onto Seabeck Highway and drive two miles to Holly Road. Turn right on Holly Road and drive 2.2 miles to Tahuya Lake Road. Turn left and drive one mile to Green Mountain Road and the Department of Natural Resources (DNR) parking lot and trailhead. If the gate is closed, hike four miles to the campground.

**Contact:** Department of Natural Resources, South Puget Sound Region, 360/825-1631, www.dnr.wa.gov.

## 85 ILLAHEE STATE PARK

**Scenic rating: 9**

near Bremerton

**Map 1.6, page 82**

This 75-acre park, named for a Native American word for earth or country, features the last stand of old-growth forest in Kitsap County, including one of the largest yew trees in America. The park also features 1,785 feet of saltwater frontage. The campsites are located in a pretty, forested area, and some are grassy. The shoreline is fairly rocky, set on the shore of Port Orchard Bay, although there is a small sandy area for sunbathers. Clamming is popular here. A fishing pier is available for anglers. Note that large vessels can be difficult to launch at the ramp here.

**Campsites, facilities:** There are 23 sites for tents or RVs up to 40 feet long (no hookups), two sites for tents or RVs up to 35 feet long (50 amp full hookups), and two hike-in/bike-in sites. Picnic tables and fire grills are provided. Restrooms with flush toilets and coin showers, drinking water, firewood, dump station, and a pier are available. Boat docks, launching facilities, five mooring buoys, and 356 feet of moorage float space are also available. A sheltered picnic area, horseshoes, volleyball, a field, and a playground are nearby. A coin laundry and ice are located within one mile. Some facilities are wheelchair accessible. Leashed pets are permitted.

**Reservations, fees:** Reservations are not accepted. Sites are $17-42 per night, hike-in/bike-in sites are $12 per night, $10 per extra vehicle per night. Moorage is a $0.60 per foot ($12 per night minimum). Open year-round.

**Directions:** On Highway 3, drive to Bremerton and the East Bremerton exit. Drive east for 7.5 miles to Sylvan Way. Turn left and drive 1.5 miles to the park entrance road.

**Contact:** Illahee State Park, 360/478-6460; state park information, 360/902-8844, www.parks.wa.gov.

## 86 MANCHESTER STATE PARK

Scenic rating: 9

near Port Orchard

Map 1.6, page 82

Manchester State Park is set on the edge of Port Orchard, providing excellent lookouts across Puget Sound. The park covers 111 acres, with 3,400 feet of saltwater shoreline on Rich Passage in Puget Sound. The landscape is filled with fir maple, hemlock, cedar, alder, and ash, which are very pretty in the fall. There are approximately 2.5 miles of hiking trails, including an interpretive trail. Group and day-use reservations are available. Note that the beach is closed to shellfish harvesting. In the early 1900s, this park site was used as a U.S. Coast Guard defense installation. A gun battery remains from the park's early days, along with two other buildings that are on the register of National Historical Monuments.

**Campsites, facilities:** There are 35 sites for tents, 15 sites with partial hookups (30 amps) for tents or RVs up to 60 feet long, three hike-in/bike-in sites, and one group site with hookups (30 amps) for tents or RVs that can accommodate up to 130 people. Picnic tables and fire grills are provided. Restrooms with flush toilets and coin showers, drinking water, dump station, firewood, sheltered picnic area, volleyball field, and horseshoe pit are available. Some facilities are wheelchair accessible. Leashed pets are permitted.

**Reservations, fees:** Reservations are accepted for individual sites (mid-May-mid-September) and the group site at 888/CAMP-OUT (888/226-7688) or www.goingtocamp.com ($6.50-8.50 reservation fee). Sites are $20-39 per night, hike-in/bike-in sites are $12 per night, $10 per extra vehicle per night. The group site is $139.91 per night. Some credit cards are accepted. Open year-round, with limited winter facilities.

**Directions:** From Tacoma on I-5, turn north on Highway 16 and drive to the Port Orford/ Sedgwick Road exit and Highway 160. Turn right (east) and drive one mile to Long Lake Road. Turn left and drive six miles to Milehill. Turn right on Milehill and drive about one mile to Colchester Road. Turn left on Colchester Road and drive through Manchester, continuing for two miles to the park.

Note: Directions to this park are flawed on most website maps and in other books. Use the directions above, and when nearing the camp, you will note the route is signed.

**Contact:** Manchester State Park, 360/871-4065; state park information, 360/902-8844, www.parks.wa.gov.

## 87 BLAKE ISLAND BOAT-IN STATE PARK

Scenic rating: 10

near Seattle

Map 1.6, page 82

Blake Island offers a boat-in camp on a small island in the middle of the massive Seattle metropolitan area. At night, it can seem almost surreal. The park covers 475 acres and features magnificent views of the Seattle skyline and Olympic Mountains. It boasts five miles of saltwater shoreline, a 0.75-mile nature trail, and 15.5 miles of hiking and biking trails. Good bottom fishing is available off the reef. The tidelands make up an underwater park. Blake Island was an ancestral camping ground of the Suquamish tribe, and according to legend, the renowned Chief Seattle was born here. Native American-style dinners and dancing are available at Tillicum Village, a concession on the island. A bonus: primitive sites on the west side of the island available only by canoe or kayak.

**Campsites, facilities:** There are 48 boat-in sites, four boat-in sites for non-motorized craft, and one group camp for up to 100 people. Picnic tables and fire grills are provided (only charcoal and gas grills are permitted). Drinking water, restrooms with flush toilets and coin showers, firewood, 1,500 feet of mooring with 24 mooring buoys, and two picnic shelters with a fire pit are available. There are also interpretive activities, horseshoe pits, volleyball, and a field. Garbage must be packed out. A store and snack bar are available nearby. Some facilities are wheelchair accessible. Leashed pets are permitted.

**Reservations, fees:** Reservations are not accepted for individual sites, but are required for the group camp at 888/CAMP-OUT (888/226-7688) or www.goingtocamp.com. Sites are $12-19 per night, and the group camp is $69.96-279.82 per night (20-person minimum). Buoys are $12 per night. Open year-round.

**Directions:** Blake Island is located eight miles west of Seattle, between Vashon and Bainbridge Islands. It is best reached by launching from Bremerton, Port Orchard, or Manchester. From Manchester it is a two-mile cruise east to the island. Then trace the shore around to the buoy floats. There are four main camping areas located between Vashon Island and Bainbridge Island. The park can also be reached by tour boat through Argosy Cruises, 206/623-1445 or 206/622-8687.

**Contact:** Blake Island Boat-In State Park, 360/731-8330; state park information, 360/902-8844, www.parks.wa.gov.

# 88 BELFAIR STATE PARK
🚶 🚲 ⛵ 🏊 🦌 👨‍👩‍👧 ♿ 🚐 ⛺

**Scenic rating: 8**

on Hood Canal

**Map 1.6, page 82**

Belfair State Park is situated along the southern edge of Hood Canal, spanning 65 acres with 3,720 feet of saltwater shoreline. This park is known for its saltwater tidal flats, wetlands, and wind-blown beach grasses. Beach walking and swimming are good. The camp is set primarily amid conifer forest and marshlands on Hood Canal with nearby streams, tideland, and wetlands. A gravel-rimmed pool that is separate from Hood Canal creates a unique swimming area; water level is determined by the tides. Note that the DNR Tahuya Multiple-Use Area is nearby with trails for motorcycles, mountain biking, hiking, horseback riding, and off-road vehicles. Big Mission Creek and Little Mission Creek, both located in the park, are habitat for chum salmon during spawning season in fall.

**Campsites, facilities:** There are 120 sites for tents, 47 sites with full hookups (30 amps) for RVs up to 60 feet long, three hike-in/bike-in sites, and one water trail site. Picnic tables and fire grills are provided. Restrooms with flush toilets and coin showers, drinking water, firewood, a bathhouse, dump station, swimming lagoon, playground, badminton, volleyball court, and horseshoe pits are available. A store and restaurant are located nearby. Some facilities are wheelchair accessible. Leashed pets are permitted.

**Reservations, fees:** Reservations are accepted at 888/CAMP-OUT (888/226-7688) or www.goingtocamp.com ($6.50-8.50 reservation fee). Sites are $20-35 per night, $10 per extra vehicle per night, hike-in/bike-in sites are $12 per night, and the water trail site is $12 per night. Some credit cards are accepted. Open year-round.

**Directions:** From Tacoma on I-5, drive to the Highway 16 west exit. Take Highway 16 northwest and drive about 27 miles toward Bremerton and Belfair (after the Port Orchard exits, note that the highway merges into three lanes). Get in the left lane for the Belfair/State Route 3 south exit. Take that exit and turn left at the traffic signal. Take State Route 3 eight miles south to Belfair to State Route 300 (at the signal just after the Safeway). Turn right and drive three miles to the park entrance.

**Contact:** Belfair State Park, 360/275-0668; state park information, 360/902-8844, www. parks.wa.gov.

## 89 TWANOH STATE PARK

near Union

**Scenic rating: 8**

**Map 1.6, page 82**

This state park is set on the shore of Hood Canal at one of the warmest saltwater bodies in Puget Sound—and likely the warmest saltwater beach in the state. Twanoh, from a Native American word meaning gathering place, covers 182 acres, with 3,167 feet of saltwater shoreline. Swimming and oyster, clam, and crab harvesting are popular here. Winter smelting is also popular; check regulations. In late fall, the chum salmon can be seen heading up the small creek; fishing for them is prohibited. Most of the park buildings are made of brick, stone, and round logs, built by the Civilian Conservation Corps in the 1930s. You'll also see extensive evidence of logging from the 1890s. Amenities include a tennis court, horseshoe pits, and a concession stand.

**Campsites, facilities:** There are 25 sites for tents or RVs (no hookups), 22 sites with full hookups (30 and 50 amps) for RVs up to 35 feet long, and a group tent camp for up to 70 people. Picnic tables and fire grills are provided. Restrooms with flush toilets and coin showers and drinking water are available. A seasonal snack bar, sheltered picnic area, firewood, boat ramp, boat dock, moorage buoys, marine pump-out station, wading pool, horseshoes, badminton, and volleyball are available nearby. Some facilities are wheelchair accessible. Leashed pets are permitted.

**Reservations, fees:** Reservations are accepted only for the group site at 888/226-7688 or www.goingtocamp.com. Sites are $20-35 per night, $10 per extra vehicle per night. The group camp is $196.69 per night with (20-person minimum), plus a $25 reservation fee. Open April-October, weather permitting.

**Directions:** From Bremerton, take Highway 3 southwest to Belfair and Highway 106. Turn right (west) and drive eight miles to the park.

If driving from U.S. 101, turn east on Highway 106 and drive 12 miles to the park.

**Contact:** Twanoh State Park, 360/275-2222; state park information, 360/902-8844, www.parks.wa.gov.

## 90 JARRELL COVE STATE PARK

on Harstine Island

**Scenic rating: 8**

**Map 1.6, page 82**

Most visitors to this park arrive by boat. Campsites are near the docks, set on a rolling, grassy area. The park covers just 43 acres but boasts 3,500 feet of saltwater shoreline on the northeast end of Harstine Island in South Puget Sound. The park's dense forest presses nearly to the water's edge at high tides—a beautiful setting. At low tides, tideland mud flats are unveiled. The beach is rocky and muddy—not exactly Hawaii. Hiking and biking are limited to just one mile of trail.

**Campsites, facilities:** There are 22 sites for tents or RVs up to 34 feet long, one boat-in site (non-motorized boats only), and a group camp with a kitchen shelter that accommodates up to 45 people. Picnic tables and fire grills are provided. Restrooms with flush toilets and coin showers and drinking water are available. Boat docks, a marine pump-out station, and 14 mooring buoys are available. A picnic area and a horseshoe pit are nearby. Some facilities are wheelchair accessible. Leashed pets are permitted.

**Reservations, fees:** Reservations are accepted and are required for the group camp at 888/CAMP-OUT (888/226-7688) or www.goingtocamp.com ($6.50-8.50 reservation fee). Sites are $12-31 per night, $10 per extra vehicle per night, and the group site is $69.89-139.78 per night (20-person minimum). Buoys are $12 per night, docking fees are $0.60 per foot ($12 minimum). Open year-round.

**Directions:** From Olympia on I-5, turn north

on U.S. 101 and drive 22 miles to Shelton and Highway 3. Turn north on Highway 3 and drive about eight miles to Pickering Road. Turn right and drive to the Harstine Bridge. Cross the bridge and continue to North Island Drive. Turn left and drive four miles to Wingert Road. Turn left and drive 0.25 mile to the park on the left.

**Contact:** Jarrell Cove State Park, 360/426-9226; state park information, 360/902-8844, www.parks.wa.gov.

# 91 JARRELL'S COVE MARINA
🚶🚴🛶🎣🛶🐕♿🚐

### Scenic rating: 6
near Shelton

**Map 1.6, page 82**

The marina and nearby Puget Sound are the big draws here. This small camp features 1,000 feet of shoreline and 0.5 mile of public beach. Clamming is available in season.

**Campsites, facilities:** There are three sites with partial hookups for RVs up to 40 feet long. Picnic tables and barbecues are provided. Restrooms with flush toilets and coin showers, drinking water, propane gas, a dump station, a seasonal convenience store, bait and tackle, coin laundry, gasoline, marine fuel, boat docks, and moorage are available. Some facilities are wheelchair accessible. Leashed pets are permitted.

**Reservations, fees:** Reservations are accepted. Sites are $30 per night. Some credit cards are accepted. Open year-round, with limited winter facilities.

**Directions:** From Olympia on I-5, turn north on U.S. 101 and drive 22 miles to Shelton and Highway 3. Turn north on Highway 3 and drive about eight miles to Pickering Road. Turn right and drive to the Harstine Bridge. Cross the bridge and continue to North Island Drive. Turn left on North Island Drive and drive 2.8 miles to Haskell Hill Road. Turn left (west) on Haskell Hill Road and drive one mile to the marina.

**Contact:** Jarrell's Cove Marina, 220 E. Wilson Rd., Shelton, 360/426-8823 or 800/362-8823.

# 92 JOEMMA BEACH STATE PARK
🚶🛶🛏️🐕♿🚐🏕️

### Scenic rating: 8
on Puget Sound

**Map 1.6, page 82**

This beautiful camp set along the shore of the peninsula provides an alternative to nearby Penrose Point State Park. It covers 122 acres and features 3,000 feet of saltwater frontage on the southeast Kitsap Peninsula. This area is often excellent for boating, fishing, and crabbing. It is a forested park with the bonus of boat-in campsites. Hiking is limited to a trail less than a mile long.

**Campsites, facilities:** There are 19 sites for tents or RVs up to 40 feet long, four primitive tent sites, two hike-in/bike-in sites, and two boat-in sites (non-motorized boats only). Picnic tables and fire grills are provided. Vault toilets, drinking water, boat-launching facilities, a dock and mooring buoys, and a picnic shelter that can be reserved are available. A grocery store is approximately five miles away. Some facilities are wheelchair accessible. Leashed pets are permitted.

**Reservations, fees:** Reservations are not accepted. Sites are $17-31 per night, hike-in/bike-in and boat-in sites are $12 per night, $10 per extra vehicle per night. Moorage is $0.60 per foot with a $12 per night minimum. Open year-round.

**Directions:** From Tacoma, drive north on Highway 16 for about 10 miles to Highway 302/Purdy exit. At the light turn left onto Highway 302, which changes into Key Peninsula Highway. Stay on Key Peninsula Highway and drive about 15 miles to Whiteman Road. Turn right on Whiteman Road and drive four miles to Bay Road. Turn right and drive one mile to the park entrance (stay on the asphalt road when entering the park).

**Contact:** Joemma Beach State Park, 253/884-1944; state park information, 360/902-8844, www.parks.wa.gov.

## 93 PENROSE POINT STATE PARK

🧍 🚲 🛶 🚤 🐎 ♿ 🚐 ⛺

**Scenic rating: 8**

on Puget Sound

**Map 1.6, page 82**

This park on Carr Inlet on Puget Sound, overlooking Lake Bay, has a remote feel, but it's actually not far from Tacoma. The park covers 162 acres, with two miles of saltwater frontage on Mayo Cove and Carr Inlet. The camp has impressive stands of fir and cedars nearby, along with ferns and rhododendrons. The park has 2.5 miles of trails for biking and hiking. Bay Lake is a popular fishing lake for trout and is located one mile away; a boat launch is available there. Penrose is known for its excellent fishing, crabbing, clamming, and oysters. The nearest boat launch to Puget Sound is located three miles away in the town of Home.

**Campsites, facilities:** There are 82 sites for tents or RVs up to 35 feet (no hookups), one water trail boat-in site, and a group camp for tents or RVs for 20-50 people. Picnic tables and fire grills are provided. Restrooms with flush toilets and coin showers, drinking water, a dump station, firewood, horseshoe pits, sheltered picnic areas, an interpretive trail, and a beach are available. Boat docks, a marine pump-out station, and mooring buoys are nearby. Some facilities are wheelchair accessible. Leashed pets are permitted.

**Reservations, fees:** Reservations are accepted and are required for the group camp at 888/CAMP-OUT (888/226-7688) or www.goingtocamp.com ($6.50-8.50 reservation fee). Sites are $20-37 per night, $10 per extra vehicle per night, primitive sites and boat-in sites are $12 per night, and the group site is $2.25 per person per night, with a minimum of 20 people per night. Boat mooring is $0.60 per foot with a $12 minimum. Some credit cards are accepted. Open year-round.

**Directions:** From Tacoma, drive north on Highway 16 for about 10 miles to Highway 302/Purdy exit. At the light turn left onto Highway 302, which changes into Key Peninsula Highway. Stay on Key Peninsula Highway and drive south nine miles through the towns of Key Center and Home to Cornwall Road KPS (second road after crossing the Home Bridge). Drive 1.25 miles more to 158 Avenue KPS. Turn left and continue on 158 Avenue KPS to the park entrance.

**Contact:** Penrose Point State Park, 253/884-2514; state park information, 360/902-8844, www.parks.wa.gov.

## 94 KOPACHUCK STATE PARK

🧍 🛶 🚤 🐎 ♿ 🚐 ⛺

**Scenic rating: 8**

on Puget Sound

**Map 1.6, page 82**

Note: As of late 2013, the campground was open for day-use only until some hazardous trees could be removed.

Located on Henderson Bay on Puget Sound near Tacoma, this park covers 109 acres, with 5,600 feet of saltwater shoreline. Sandy beaches are located about 250 yards down the hill from the campground. Noteworthy are the scenic views and dramatic sunsets across Puget Sound and the Olympic Mountains. A unique element is Cutts Island (also called Deadman's Island), which is located 0.5-mile from shore and is accessible only by boat. (There is no camping on the island.) Two miles of hiking trails are available. Fishing access is by boat only; a boat launch is located not far from camp.

**Campsites, facilities:** There are 41 sites for tents or RVs up to 35 feet (no hookups), five primitive sites, one primitive boat-in site (no motorized boats permitted), and two group sites for up to 20 and 35 people respectively. Picnic tables and fire grills are provided.

Restrooms with flush toilets and coin showers, drinking water, a dump station, covered picnic areas, a Junior Ranger Program (seasonal), interpretive activities, and boat buoys are available. A small store is approximately one mile away. Some facilities are wheelchair accessible. Leashed pets are permitted.

**Reservations, fees:** Reservations are not accepted for individual sites, but are required for the group site at 253/265-3606. Sites are $21 per night, $10 per extra vehicle per night, and the boat-in site is $14 per night. The group site is $2.25 per person per night with a 20-person minimum. Open year-round.

**Directions:** From Tacoma on I-5, turn north on Highway 16. Drive seven miles north to the third Gig Harbor exit (Wollochet Drive NW). Take that exit and follow the signs for about seven miles to Kopachuck State Park. Note: The road changes names several times, but the route is well signed.

**Contact:** Kopachuck State Park, 253/265-3606; state park information, 360/902-8844, www.parks.wa.gov.

## 95 GIG HARBOR RV RESORT

### Scenic rating: 7

near Tacoma

**Map 1.6, page 82**

This is a popular layover spot for folks heading up to Bremerton. Just a short jaunt off the highway, it's pleasant, clean, and friendly. An 18-hole golf course, full-service marina, and tennis courts are located nearby. Look for the great view of Mount Rainier from the end of the harbor.

**Campsites, facilities:** There are 93 sites, most with full or partial hookups (20, 30 and 50 amps), including some long-term rentals, for tents or RVs of any length and one cabin. Some sites are pull-through. Restrooms with flush toilets and showers, drinking water, cable TV, Wi-Fi, propane gas, a dump station, a clubroom, coin laundry, playground,

horseshoe pits, sports field, and a seasonal heated swimming pool are available. Some facilities are wheelchair accessible. Leashed pets are permitted.

**Reservations, fees:** Reservations are accepted. Tent sites are $22 per night, RV sites are $36 per night, $3 per each additional person per night, $4 per each additional vehicle per night. Some credit cards are accepted. Open year-round.

**Directions:** From Tacoma, drive northwest on Highway 16 for 12 miles to the Burnham Drive NW exit. Take that exit and enter the roundabout to the first right and Burnham Drive NW. Turn right on Burnham Drive NW and drive 1.25 miles to the resort on the left.

**Contact:** Gig Harbor RV Resort, 9515 Burnham Dr. NW, Gig Harbor, 253/858-8138 or 800/526-8311, www.gigharborrvresort.com.

## 96 AMERICAN SUNSET RV AND TENT RESORT

### Scenic rating: 8

near Westport Harbor

**Map 1.7, page 83**

If location is everything, then this RV camp, set on a peninsula, is a big winner. It covers 32 acres and is 10 blocks from the ocean; hiking and biking trails are nearby. The park is divided into two areas: one for campers, another for long-term rentals. Nearby are Westhaven and Westport Light State Parks, popular with hikers, rockhounds, scuba divers, and surf anglers. Fishing and crabbing off the docks are also options; you can also swim, but not off the docks. Monthly rentals are available in summer.

**Campsites, facilities:** There are 120 sites with full hookups (20, 30, and 50 amps) for RVs up to 45 feet long, 50 sites for tents or RVs up to 30 feet (no hookups), one lighthouse unit, one beach house, one cabana, and one rental mobile home. Some sites are pull-through. Picnic tables and fire rings are provided. Restrooms with flush toilets and showers, drinking water, satellite TV, Wi-Fi, coin laundry, a convenience store, propane, a seasonal heated swimming pool, horseshoe pits, a playground, and a fish-cleaning station are available. A marina is located three blocks away. Leashed pets are permitted.

**Reservations, fees:** RV Sites are $37 per night, tent sites are $22. Some discounts are available. Some credit cards are accepted. Open year-round.

**Directions:** From Aberdeen, drive south on State Route 105 for 22 miles to Westport and Montesano Street (the first exit in Westport). Turn right (northeast) on Montesano Street and drive three miles to the resort on the left.

**Contact:** American Sunset RV and Tent Resort, 360/268-0207 or 800/569-2267, www.americansunsetrv.com.

## 97 TOTEM RV PARK

### Scenic rating: 8

in Westport

**Map 1.7, page 83**

This 3.2-acre park is set 300 yards from the ocean and features an expanse of sand dunes between the park and the ocean. It has large, grassy sites close to Westhaven State Park, which offers day-use facilities. The owner is a fishing guide and can provide detailed fishing information. The salmon fishing within 10 miles of this park is often excellent in summer. Marked biking trails and a full-service marina are within five miles of the park.

**Campsites, facilities:** There are 80 sites with full or partial hookups (30 and 50 amps) for tents or RVs of any length. Some sites are pull-through. Restrooms with flush toilets and coin showers, drinking water, cable TV, Wi-Fi, a dump station, coin laundry, and ice are available. A pavilion, barbecue facilities with kitchen, and a fish-cleaning station are also available. Boat docks, launching facilities, and fishing charters are nearby. Propane gas, a store, and café are within 0.5 mile. Some

facilities are wheelchair accessible. Leashed pets are permitted.

**Reservations, fees:** Reservations are accepted. Sites are $24-27 per night. Some credit cards are accepted. Open year-round.

**Directions:** From Aberdeen, drive south on State Route 105 for 20 miles to the turnoff for Westport. Turn right (north) on the State Route 105 spur and drive 4.3 miles to the docks and Nyhus Street. Turn left on Nyhus Street and drive two blocks to the park on the left.

**Contact:** Totem RV Park, 360/268-0025 or 888/TOTEM-RV (888/868-3678).

## 98 HOLAND CENTER

### Scenic rating: 6

in Westport

**Map 1.7, page 83**

This pleasant, 18-acre RV park is one of several in the immediate area. The sites are graveled or grassy, with ample space and pine trees in between. There is no beach access from the park, but full recreational facilities are available nearby. About half of the sites are long-term rentals.

**Campsites, facilities:** There are 85 sites with full hookups for RVs up to 35 feet long. Some picnic tables are provided. No open fires are allowed. Restrooms with flush toilets and coin showers, cable TV, coin laundry, and storage sheds are available. Propane gas, a store, café, and ice are located within one mile. Boat docks and launching facilities are nearby. Leashed pets are permitted.

**Reservations, fees:** Reservations are accepted. Sites are $30 per night. Credit cards are not accepted. Open year-round.

**Directions:** From Aberdeen, drive south on State Route 105 for 22 miles to Westport. Continue on State Route 105 to a Y intersection. Bear right on Montesano Street and drive approximately two miles to Wilson Street. The park is on the left.

**Contact:** Holand Center, State Route 105 and Wilson Street, 360/268-9582.

## 99 PACIFIC MOTEL AND RV PARK

**Scenic rating: 5**

near Twin Harbors

Map 1.7, page 83

This five-acre park has shaded sites in a wooded setting. It's near Twin Harbors and Westport Light State Park, a day-use park nearby. Both parks have beach access. A full-service marina is located within two miles. About 25 percent of the sites are occupied with long-term rentals.

**Campsites, facilities:** There are 80 sites with full hookups (20, 30, and 50 amps) for RVs of any length, including 25 pull-through sites, and 12 sites for tents. Picnic tables and fire pits are provided. Restrooms with flush toilets and coin showers, drinking water, propane gas, a dump station, fish-cleaning station, recreation hall with a kitchen, cable TV, Wi-Fi, coin laundry, and a seasonal heated swimming pool are available. A store, café, and ice are located within one mile. Boat-launching and boat docks are nearby in a full-service marina. Leashed pets are permitted.

**Reservations, fees:** Reservations are accepted. RV sites are $32 per night, tent sites are $20 per night, $2 per person per night for more than two people. Some credit cards are accepted. Open year-round.

**Directions:** From Aberdeen, drive south on State Route 105 for approximately 21 miles to Westport. Go past the first Westport exit to a stop sign. Turn right onto the State Route 105 spur (becomes Forrest Street in Westport) and drive 1.8 miles to the park on the right.

**Contact:** Pacific Motel and RV Park, 360/268-9325, www.pacificmotelandrv.com.

## 100 TWIN HARBORS STATE PARK

**Scenic rating: 8**

near Westport

Map 1.7, page 83

The park covers 172 acres and is located four miles south of Westhaven. It was a military training ground in the 1930s. The campsites are close together and often crammed to capacity in the summer. Highlights include beach access and marked hiking trails, including Shifting Sands Nature Trail. The most popular recreation activities are surf fishing, surfing, beachcombing, and kite-flying. Fishing boats can be chartered nearby in Westport.

**Campsites, facilities:** There are 219 tent sites, 42 sites with for tents or RVs up to 35 feet long (30 amp full hookups), four hike-in/bike-in sites, and one group site for up to 60 people (no electricity). Picnic tables and fire grills are provided. Restrooms with flush toilets and coin showers, drinking water, a dump station, a picnic area with a kitchen shelter, and horseshoe pits are available. A store, café, and ice are available within one mile. Some facilities are wheelchair accessible. Leashed pets are permitted.

**Reservations, fees:** Reservations are accepted for individual sites and are required for the group site at 888/CAMP-OUT (888/226-7688) or www.goingtocamp.com ($6.50-8.50 reservation fee). Sites are $20-42 per night, $10 per extra vehicle per night, and hike-in/bike-in sites are $12 per night. Group rates vary according to size (20-person minimum, 60-person maximum, 10 vehicle limit). Some credit cards are accepted. Open year-round.

**Directions:** From Aberdeen, drive south on State Route 105 for 17 miles to the park entrance on the left (three miles south of Westport).

**Contact:** Twin Harbors State Park, 360/268-9717; state park information, 360/902-8844, www.parks.wa.gov.

## 101 PORTER CREEK

### Scenic rating: 7

on Porter Creek in Capitol Forest

**Map 1.7, page 83**

This primitive, rustic campground is located about 30 miles from Olympia. It is set in the Capitol Forest along the shore of Porter Creek and is managed by the Department of Natural Resources. It offers trails for hiking, horseback riding, or motorbikes. The camp serves as a launch point for a variety of trips. Most campers take the 0.5-mile trail to Porter Falls, departing from the trailhead just across the road. Within three miles, you can also access trails that lead to a network of 87 miles of off-road vehicle trails and 84 miles of trails for non-motorized use—mountain biking is popular here. With corrals and hitching posts available, this camp is popular among horseback riders.

**Campsites, facilities:** There are 16 sites for tents or RVs up to 16 feet (no hookups). Picnic tables and fire grills are provided. There is no drinking water, and garbage must be packed out. Vault toilets, corrals, hitching posts, and horse-loading ramps are available. All-terrain vehicles are permitted. Some facilities are wheelchair accessible. Leashed pets are permitted.

**Reservations, fees:** Reservations are not accepted. There is no fee for camping, but a Discover Pass is required. Open May-November, weather permitting.

**Directions:** On I-5, drive to Exit 88 (10 miles north of Chehalis) and U.S. 12. Turn west on U.S. 12 and drive 21 miles to Porter and Porter Creek Road. Turn right (northeast) on Porter Creek Road and drive 3.4 miles (last half mile is gravel) to a junction. Continue straight on B-Line Road for 0.6 mile to the campground on the left.

**Contact:** Department of Natural Resources, Pacific Cascade Region North, 360/577-2025, www.dnr.wa.gov.

## 102 MIDDLE WADDELL

### Scenic rating: 7

on Waddell Creek in Capitol Forest

**Map 1.7, page 83**

This wooded campground is nestled along Waddell Creek in Capitol Forest. The trails in the immediate vicinity are used primarily for all-terrain vehicles (ATVs), making for some noise. There is an extensive network of ATV trails in the area. Mountain bikers tend to prefer Fall Creek camp.

**Campsites, facilities:** There are 24 sites for tents or RVs of any length. Picnic tables and fire grills are provided. Vault toilets are available. There is no drinking water, and garbage must be packed out. A camp host is on-site. Some facilities are wheelchair accessible. Leashed pets are permitted.

**Reservations, fees:** Reservations are not accepted. There is no fee for camping, but a Discover Pass is required. Open May-November, weather permitting.

**Directions:** From Olympia on I-5, drive south for about 10 miles to Exit 95 and Highway 121. Turn west on Highway 121 and drive four miles to Littlerock. Continue west for one mile to Waddell Creek Road. Turn right and drive three miles and look for the campground entrance road on the left.

**Contact:** Department of Natural Resources, Pacific Cascade Region North, 360/577-2025, www.dnr.wa.gov.

## 103 FALL CREEK

### Scenic rating: 7

on Fall Creek in Capitol Forest

**Map 1.7, page 83**

With good access to an 84-mile network of trails for non-motorized use, this camp is something of a mountain-biking headquarters. Although ATVs are allowed in the campground, they are not allowed on the adjacent trails. This wooded camp on Fall Creek in Capitol Forest also provides horse facilities.

**Campsites, facilities:** There are eight sites for tents or RVs up to 45 feet (no hookups). Picnic tables and fire grills are provided. There is no drinking water, and garbage must be packed out. Vault toilets, corrals, a hitching post, a watering trough, and a horse-loading ramp are available. A day-use staging area is also available. Some facilities are wheelchair accessible. Leashed pets are permitted.

**Reservations, fees:** Reservations are not accepted. There is no fee for camping, but a Discover Pass is required. Open May-November, weather permitting.

**Directions:** From Olympia, take I-5 to exit 95 onto Maytown Road SW and turn west. (If coming from I-5 South, you will cross under I-5.) Drive west on Maytown Road SW to Littlerock, where the road becomes 128th Avenue SW. Continue on 128th Avenue SW until it ends at Waddell Creek Road SW. Turn right (northwest) on Waddell Creek Road SW and drive two miles to the Triangle. Turn left. The road will become Sherman Valley Road SW. Drive one mile on Sherman Valley Road SW; the pavement ends and it becomes the "C-Line" road and enters the Capitol Forest. Drive four miles and turn left at the second turnoff to the left, Road C-6000, signed Fall Creek Campground. Drive three miles to the campground on the right, just beyond a small bridge.

**Contact:** Department of Natural Resources, Pacific Cascade Region North, 360/577-2025, www.dnr.wa.gov.

## 104 SHERMAN VALLEY/ NORTH CREEK
🚶 🚲 🐕 ⛰️

### Scenic rating: 8
on Cedar Creek in Capitol Forest

**Map 1.7, page 83**

One of several secluded camps located in the Capitol Forest, Sherman Valley is managed by the Department of Natural Resources. Its

pleasant, shady campsites are set along the shore of Porter Creek. The forest here is primarily alder and fir trees. Hiking trails can be found at nearby North Creek camp. As with North Creek, this camp is used by hunters in season.

**Campsites, facilities:** There are four primitive sites for tents or RVs up to 25 feet long and three walk-in sites. Picnic tables and fire grills are provided. Vault toilets are available. There is no drinking water, and garbage must be packed out. Mountain bikes are permitted on the roads only; trails are reserved for hikers. Leashed pets are permitted.

**Reservations, fees:** Reservations are not accepted. There is no fee for camping, but a Discover Pass is required. Open May-November, weather permitting.

**Directions:** From Olympia, take I-5 south to Exit 95 onto Maytown Road SW. Take that exit and turn southwest on Maytown Road. Follow Maytown Road west past Littlerock Road (the road becomes 128th Ave. SW). Continue west on 128th to where it ends at Waddell Creek Road SW. Turn right on Waddell Creek Road SW and drive two miles to the Triangle. Turn left (the road will become Sherman Valley Road SW) and drive one mile (the pavement ends and the road becomes C-Line Road and enters Capitol Forest), and continue four miles to Road C-6000. Turn left (signed Falls Creek Campground) and drive three miles (just beyond a small bridge) to the campground on the right.

**Contact:** Department of Natural Resources, Pacific Cascade Region North, 360/577-2025, www.dnr.wa.gov.

## 105 MARGARET MCKENNY
🚶 🚲 🐕 ♿ ⛰️

### Scenic rating: 7
in Capitol Forest

**Map 1.7, page 83**

With trails linked to an extensive network of trails for non-motorized use only, this camp is used primarily as a trailhead for horseback riders and mountain bikers. Most of the campsites are well away from the stream, but seven walk-in sites are available, where a 300- to 400-foot walk down a stairway takes you to pretty streamside campsites.

**Campsites, facilities:** There are 21 primitive sites for tents or RVs up to 45 feet long and four walk-in sites. Picnic tables, fire pits, and grills are provided. There is no drinking water, and garbage must be packed out. Vault toilets, a campfire circle, and a horse-loading ramp are available. A campground host is on-site during the summer season. Some facilities are wheelchair accessible. Leashed pets are permitted.

**Reservations, fees:** Reservations are not accepted. There is no fee for camping, but a Discover Pass is required. Open May-November, weather permitting.

**Directions:** From Olympia on I-5, drive south for about 10 miles to Exit 95 and Highway 121. Turn west on Highway 121 and drive four miles to Littlerock. Continue west for one mile to Waddell Creek Road. Turn right and drive 2.5 miles and look for the campground entrance road on the left.

**Contact:** Department of Natural Resources, Pacific Cascade Region North, 360/577-2025, www.dnr.wa.gov.

## 106 NORTH CREEK/ SHERMAN VALLEY
🚶 🚴 🛶 🐕 ♿ 🚐 ⛺

Scenic rating: 8

on Cedar Creek

Map 1.7, page 83

This little-known, wooded campground managed by the Department of Natural Resources is set along Cedar Creek, which offers fishing. There are trails for hikers only (no horses or mountain bikes are allowed). A four-mile loop trail leads to Sherman Valley (a bridge has been out on this trail, with a longer alternative route available; call before planning a hike). Hunters use this camp in the fall. For a side trip, visit

the Chehalis River, a five-mile drive to the west. A canoe launch off U.S. 12 is available north of Oakville.

**Campsites, facilities:** There are five primitive sites for tents or RVs up to 25 feet long. Picnic tables and fire grills are provided. Vault toilets are available. There is no drinking water, and garbage must be packed out. Mountain bikes are permitted on the roads only; trails are reserved for hikers. Some facilities are wheelchair accessible. Leashed pets are permitted.

**Reservations, fees:** Reservations are not accepted. There is no fee for camping, but a Discover Pass is required. Open May-November, weather permitting.

**Directions:** From Olympia, take I-5 to Exit 95 onto Maytown Road SW. Take that exit and turn southwest on Maytown Road drive to Littlerock (where the road becomes 128th Ave. SW) and continue on 128th to where it ends at Waddell Creek Road SW. Turn right on Waddell Creek Road SW and drive two miles to the Triangle. Turn left (the road will become Sherman Valley Road SW) and drive one mile (the pavement ends and the road becomes C-Line Road and enters Capitol Forest), and continue four miles to Road C-6000. Turn left (signed Falls Creek Campground) and drive three miles (just beyond a small bridge) to the campgrounds.

**Contact:** Department of Natural Resources, Pacific Cascade Region North, 360/577-2025, www.dnr.wa.gov.

## 107 MIMA FALLS TRAILHEAD
🚶 🐕 ♿ 🚐 ⛺

Scenic rating: 10

near Mima Falls

Map 1.7, page 83

The highlight here is the five-mile loop trail for hikers and horseback riders that leads to beautiful 90-foot Mima Falls. The campground is quiet and pretty. This spot can be a first-rate choice. One of the unique qualities of this campground is that it provides facilities for both wheelchair users and horseback riders. The trail is not wheelchair accessible, but wheelchair users on horses can access the trip to Mima Falls. The trail runs across the brink of the falls.

**Campsites, facilities:** There is a primitive, dispersed camping area for about five tents or RVs up to 25 feet long. Picnic tables and fire grills are provided. Vault toilets and a horse-loading ramp are available. There is no drinking water, and garbage must be packed out. Some facilities are wheelchair accessible. Leashed pets are permitted.

**Reservations, fees:** Reservations are not accepted. There is no fee for camping, but a Discover Pass is required. Open May-November, weather permitting.

**Directions:** From Olympia, drive south on I-5 for 10 miles to Highway 121. Turn west on Highway 121 and drive four miles west to Littlerock. Continue west for one mile to Mima Road. Turn left on Mima Road and drive 1.5 miles to Bordeaux Road. Turn right on Bordeaux Road and drive 0.5 mile to Marksman Road. Turn right and drive about 0.6 mile to the campground access road on the left. Turn left and drive 200 yards to the campground.

**Contact:** Department of Natural Resources, Pacific Cascade Region North, 360/577-2025, www.dnr.wa.gov.

## 108 GRAYLAND BEACH STATE PARK
🏃 🚣 🛏 🐕 ♿ 🚐 ⛺

### Scenic rating: 8
near Grayland

**Map 1.7, page 83**

This state park features 412 acres and almost 7,500 feet of beach frontage. All the campsites are within easy walking distance of the ocean. The campsites are relatively spacious for a state park, but they are not especially private. This park is popular with out-of-towners, especially during summer. Recreation options include fishing, beachcombing, and kite-flying. The best spot for surfing is five miles north at Westhaven State Park.

**Campsites, facilities:** There are 100 sites, including 58 with full hookups (30 and 50 amps), for tents and RVs up to 60 feet long, four hike-in/bike-in sites, and 16 yurts. Picnic tables and fire grills are provided. Drinking water and restrooms with flush toilets and coin showers, an amphitheater, and a dump station are available. Some facilities are wheelchair accessible. Leashed pets are permitted.

**Reservations, fees:** Reservations are accepted at 888/CAMP-OUT (888/226-7688) or www.goingtocamp.com ($6.50-8.50 reservation fee). Sites are $12-42 per night, $10 per extra vehicle per night, hike-in/bike-in sites are $12 per night, and yurts are $49-97.72 per night. Some credit cards are accepted. Open year-round.

**Directions:** From Aberdeen, drive south on State Route 105 for 22 miles to the park entrance. The park is just south of the town of Grayland on the right (west).

**Contact:** Grayland Beach State Park, 360/267-4301; state park information, 360/902-8844, www.parks.wa.gov.

## 109 BAY CENTER/ WILLAPA BAY KOA
🏃 🚴 🚣 🛏 🐕 ♿ 🚐 ⛺

### Scenic rating: 7
on Willapa Bay

**Map 1.7, page 83**

This KOA is 200 yards from Willapa Bay, within walking distance of a beach that seems to stretch to infinity. A trail leads to the beach and from here you can walk for miles in either direction. The beach sand is mixed with agates, driftwood, and seaweed. Dungeness crabs, clams, and oysters all live near shore. Another bonus is that herds of Roosevelt elk roam the nearby woods. Believe it or not, there are also black bears, although they are seldom seen here. The park covers five acres, and the campsites are graveled and shaded.

**Campsites, facilities:** There are 42 sites

with full or partial hookups (20, 30, and 50 amps) for RVs of any length, 23 sites for tents, four cabins, and two yurts. Some sites are pull-through. Picnic tables and fire rings are provided. Restrooms with flush toilets and showers, drinking water, propane gas, dump station, cable TV, Wi-Fi, a recreation hall, camp store, firewood, coin laundry, and ice are available. A café, boat docks, and launching facilities are nearby. Some facilities are wheelchair accessible. Leashed pets are permitted, with certain restrictions.

**Reservations, fees:** Reservations are accepted at 800/562-7810. Sites are $30-37 per night, $5 per person per night for more than two people, $4 per extra vehicle per night. Some credit cards are accepted. Open mid-March-December 1.

**Directions:** From Nemah on U.S. 101, drive north for five miles to Bay Center/Dike exit (located between Mileposts 42 and 43, 16 miles south of Raymond). Turn left (west) and drive three miles to the campground.

**Contact:** Bay Center/Willapa Bay KOA, 360/875-6344, www.koa.com.

## 110 RAINBOW FALLS STATE PARK

🚶 🚵 🏊 🎣 🐴 👨‍👩‍👧 ♿ 🚐 🏕️

**Scenic rating: 8**

on the Chehalis River Bay

**Map 1.7, page 83**

This 139-acre park is set on the Chehalis River and boasts 3,400 feet of freshwater shoreline. The camp features stands of old-growth cedar and fir and is named after a few small cascades with drops of about 10 feet. The park has 10 miles of hiking trails, including an interpretive trail, seven miles of bike trails, and seven miles of horse trails. A pool at the base of Rainbow Falls is excellent for swimming. Another attraction, a small fuchsia garden, has more than 40 varieties. There are also several log structures built by the Civilian Conservation Corps in 1935.

**Campsites, facilities:** There are 45 sites for tents or RVs up to 32 feet (no hookups), eight sites with partial hookups (30 and 50 amps) for tents or RVs up to 60 feet long, three hike-in/bike-in sites, three equestrian sites with hitching points and stock water, and one group site for up to 60 people. Picnic tables and fire rings are provided. Restrooms with flush toilets and coin showers, drinking water, a dump station, firewood, a picnic area, interpretive activities, a playground, horseshoe pits, and a softball field are available. Some facilities are wheelchair accessible. Leashed pets are permitted.

**Reservations, fees:** Reservations are accepted only for the group site at 360/291-3767. Sites are $20-27 per night, $10 per extra vehicle per night, and hike-in/bike-in sites are $12 per night. Open year-round.

**Directions:** From Chehalis on I-5, take Exit 77 to drive west 11.7 miles on Highway 6 to milepost 40. Drive 0.4 mile past the marker to River Road. Turn right (west) on River Road and drive 2.7 miles to the Bailey Bridge. Turn right to cross the bridge and immediately turn left onto Leudinghaus Road. Drive 2.2 miles west on Leudinghaus Road to the park entrance on the left. Once inside the park, the campground is on the right.

**Contact:** Rainbow Falls State Park, 360/291-3767 or 360/902-8844, www.parks.wa.gov.

## 111 OCEAN PARK RESORT

🏊 🎣 🚐 🐴 👨‍👩‍👧 ♿ 🚐 🏕️

**Scenic rating: 5**

on Willapa Bay

**Map 1.7, page 83**

This wooded, 10-acre campground is located 0.5 mile from Willapa Bay. With grassy, shaded sites, it caters primarily to RVs. Fishing, crabbing, and clamming are popular in season. Ocean Park has several festivals during the summer season. During these festivals, this resort fills up. To the north, Leadbetter Point State Park provides a side-trip option.

**Campsites, facilities:** There are 70 sites with

full hookups for RVs of any length, 13 sites for tents, and a two-bedroom mobile home. Some sites are pull-through. Picnic tables are provided. Fire pits are provided at tent sites. Restrooms with flush toilets and coin showers, drinking water, propane gas, a recreation hall, coin laundry, playground, firewood, and a basketball hoop are available. A store and café are available within one mile. Boat docks and launching facilities are located nearby on Willapa Bay. Some facilities are wheelchair accessible. Leashed pets are permitted, with certain restrictions.

**Reservations, fees:** Sites are $26-32 per night, plus $3 per person per night for more than two people. Some credit cards are accepted. Open year-round.

**Directions:** From Kelso/Longview on I-5, turn west on Highway 4 and drive 63 miles to U.S. 101. Turn south on U.S. 101 and drive 13 miles to the junction with Highway 103. Turn right (north) on Highway 103 and drive 11 miles to the town of Ocean Park and 259th Street. Turn right (east) on 259th Street and drive two blocks to the resort at the end of the road.

**Contact:** Ocean Park Resort, 360/665-4585 or 800/835-4634, www.opresort.com.

## 112 WESTGATE CABINS & RV PARK

### Scenic rating: 9

near Long Beach

**Map 1.7, page 83**

Highlights at this pretty and clean four-acre camp include beach access, oceanfront sites (about one-fourth have ocean views), and all the amenities. There are 28 miles of beach that can be driven on. Additional facilities within five miles of the park include an 18-hole golf course.

**Campsites, facilities:** There are 39 sites with full hookups (30 amps) for RVs up to 50 feet long and six cabins. Some sites are pull-through. Picnic tables are provided. Restrooms

with flush toilets and showers, drinking water, cable TV, Wi-Fi, coin laundry, gas station, a recreation hall with kitchen, a fish-cleaning station, and ice are available. A store and café are available about four miles away. Boat docks and launching facilities are located nearby on Willapa Bay. Leashed pets are permitted, but not in cabins.

**Reservations, fees:** Reservations are accepted. Sites are $38 per night, plus $2 per person per night for more than two people. Some credit cards are accepted. Open year-round.

**Directions:** From Kelso/Longview on I-5, turn west on Highway 4 and drive 63 miles to U.S. 101. Turn left (south) on U.S. 101 and drive 13 miles to the junction with Highway 103. Turn right (north) on Highway 103 and drive nine miles to the park on the left (located at the south edge of the town of Ocean Park).

**Contact:** Westgate Cabins & RV Park, 360/665-4211, www.vacationwestgate.com.

## 113 ANDERSEN'S RV PARK ON THE OCEAN

### Scenic rating: 7

near Long Beach

**Map 1.7, page 83**

Timing is everything here. When the dates are announced for the local festivals, reservations start pouring in and the sites at this park can be booked a year in advance. Located near the city limits of Long Beach, this five-acre camp features a path through the dunes that will get you to the beach in a flash. It is set in a flat, sandy area with gravel sites. Recreation options include beach bonfires, beachcombing, surf fishing, and clamming (seasonal). Additional facilities found within five miles of the park include marked dune trails, a nine-hole golf course, a riding stable, and tennis courts. The park is big-rig friendly.

**Campsites, facilities:** There are 60 sites for tents or RVs of any length (20, 30, and 50 amp full hookups). Picnic tables and fire pits are provided.

Restrooms with flush toilets and showers, drinking water, cable TV, Wi-Fi, a dump station, coin laundry, ice, propane, fax machine, group facilities, a horseshoe pit, and a playground are available. A store and café are available within two miles. Some facilities are wheelchair accessible. Leashed pets are permitted.

**Reservations, fees:** Reservations are recommended. Sites are $30-50 per night, plus $2 per person per night for more than two people. Some credit cards are accepted. Open year-round.

**Directions:** From Kelso/Longview on I-5, turn west on Highway 4 and drive 63 miles to U.S. 101. Turn left (south) on U.S. 101 and drive 13 miles to the junction with Highway 103. Turn right (north) on Highway 103 and drive five miles to the park on the left.

**Contact:** Andersen's RV Park on the Ocean, 360/642-2231 or 800/645-6795, www.andersensrv.com.

## 114 OCEANIC RV PARK

### Scenic rating: 3

in Long Beach

**Map 1.7, page 83**

This two-acre park is located in the heart of downtown, within walking distance of restaurants and stores. It is also within five miles of an 18-hole golf course, marked bike trails, and a full-service marina.

**Campsites, facilities:** There are 18 pull-through sites with full hookups (30 and 50 amps) for RVs of any length. No open fires are allowed. Restrooms with flush toilets and showers, Wi-Fi, coin laundry, a restaurant, and propane gas are available. A store and ice are located within one mile. Boat docks, launching facilities, and boat rentals are nearby. Leashed pets are permitted.

**Reservations, fees:** Reservations are accepted. Sites are $35 per night, plus $5 per person per night for more than two people. Open year-round.

**Directions:** From Kelso/Longview on I-5, turn west on Highway 4 and drive 63 miles to U.S. 101. Turn left (south) on U.S. 101 and drive 13 miles to the junction with Highway 103. Turn right (north) on Highway 103 and drive two miles to Long Beach. Continue to the park at the south junction of Pacific Highway (Highway 103) and 5th Avenue on the right.

**Contact:** Oceanic RV Park, 360/642-3836.

## 115 MERMAID INN AND RV PARK

### Scenic rating: 3

near Long Beach

**Map 1.7, page 83**

Situated along the highway, this three-acre park is within four blocks of the beach. It is also within five miles of several nine-hole golf courses, a full-service marina, and a riding stable.

**Campsites, facilities:** There are 11 sites with full hookups (20 and 30 amps) for RVs up to 40 feet and 10 motel rooms. Picnic tables are provided. Restrooms with flush toilets and showers, drinking water, cable TV, Wi-Fi, a picnic area with barbecue, a fish-cleaning station, and coin laundry are available. Propane gas, a gas station, store, restaurant, and ice are located within one mile. Leashed pets are permitted, with certain restrictions.

**Reservations, fees:** Reservations are accepted. Sites are $25-35, $1.50 per person per night for more than two people. Some credit cards are accepted. Open year-round.

**Directions:** From Kelso/Longview on I-5, turn west on Highway 4 and drive 63 miles to U.S. 101. Turn left (south) on U.S. 101 and drive 13 miles to the junction with Highway 103. Turn right (north) on Highway 103 and drive three miles to the park on the right.

**Contact:** Mermaid Inn and RV Park, 360/642-2600, www.mermaidinnatlongbeachwa.com.

## 116 DRIFTWOOD RV PARK

### Scenic rating: 2

near Long Beach

**Map 1.7, page 83**

This two-acre park features grassy, shaded sites and beach access close by. A fenced pet area is a bonus. Additional facilities within five miles of the park include a nine-hole golf course and a full-service marina.

**Campsites, facilities:** There are 56 sites with full hookups (30 amps) for RVs of any length. Many sites are pull-through. Picnic tables are provided and portable fire pits can be rented. Restrooms with flush toilets and showers, drinking water, coin laundry, cable TV, Wi-Fi, group facilities, and a fenced pet area are available. Propane gas, a gas station, store, and restaurant are available within one mile. Some facilities are wheelchair accessible. Leashed pets are permitted, with certain restrictions.

**Reservations, fees:** Reservations are accepted. Sites are $25-33 per night, plus $3 per person per night for more than two people. Some credit cards are accepted. Open year-round.

**Directions:** From Kelso/Longview on I-5, turn west on Highway 4 and drive 63 miles to U.S. 101. Turn left (south) on U.S. 101 and drive 13 miles to the junction with Highway 103. Turn right (north) on Highway 103 and drive 2.25 miles to the park on the right, at 14th Street North and Pacific Avenue.

**Contact:** Driftwood RV Park, 360/642-2711 or 888/567-1902, www.driftwoodrvpark.net.

## 117 SAND CASTLE RV PARK

### Scenic rating: 3

in Long Beach

**Map 1.7, page 83**

This park is set across the highway from the ocean. Although not particularly scenic, it is clean and does provide nearby beach access. The park covers two acres, has grassy areas, and is one of several in the immediate area. Additional facilities found within five miles of the park include a nine-hole golf course, marked bike trails, a full-service marina, and two riding stables.

**Campsites, facilities:** There are 38 sites with full hookups (30 and 50 amps) for RVs of any length and an area for tent camping. Some sites are pull-through. Picnic tables are provided. Restrooms with flush toilets and coin showers, drinking water, cable TV, Wi-Fi, a snack bar, ice, coin laundry, and a fish-cleaning station are available. Propane gas, a gas station, a store, and a café are available within one mile. Boat docks, launching facilities, and rentals are within five miles. Leashed pets are permitted.

**Reservations, fees:** Reservations are accepted. RV sites are $28.50-36.50 per night, tent sites are $25 per night, $2 per person per night for more than two people, $5 per extra vehicle per night. Some credit cards are accepted. Open year-round.

**Directions:** From Kelso/Longview on I-5, turn west on Highway 4 and drive 63 miles to U.S. 101. Turn left (south) on U.S. 101 and drive 13 miles to the junction with Highway 103. Turn right (north) on Highway 103 and drive two miles to the park on the right.

**Contact:** Sand Castle RV Park, 360/642-2174, www.sandcastlerv.com.

## 118 PACIFIC HOLIDAY RESORT

### Scenic rating: 5

near Long Beach

**Map 1.7, page 83**

This is a membership-only resort RV campground, and members always come first. If space is available, they will rent sites to the public. One of the finest razor clam and surf fishing beaches in the world is just outside your door on the beautiful Long Beach Peninsula. Excellent deep-sea fishing at Ilwaco is just eight miles away. Oysters and Dungeness crabs abound at Willapa Bay, just five miles away, and lake and stream fishing are just minutes from this campground. There's also a golf course a long drive (and a short putt) away.

**Campsites, facilities:** There are 119 sites with full hookups for RVs of any length and 10 sites for tents. Picnic tables are provided. Restrooms with flush toilets and showers, drinking water, cable TV, swimming pool, game room, playground, and a coin laundry are available. Some facilities are wheelchair accessible. Leashed pets are permitted.

**Reservations, fees:** Reservations are required. Sites are $25-45 per night, $1 per night per additional vehicle. Some credit cards are accepted. Open year-round.

**Directions:** From Kelso/Longview on I-5, turn west on Highway 4 and drive 63 miles to U.S. 101. Turn left (south) on U.S. 101 and drive 13 miles to the junction with Highway 103. Turn right (north) on Highway 103. The resort will be on the left.

**Contact:** Pacific Holiday Resort, 12109 Pacific Way, Long Beach, 360/642-2770, www. sunriseresorts.com.

## 119 WESTERN LAKES

### Scenic rating: 9

near Naselle

**Map 1.7, page 83**

You want quiet and solitude? You found it. This tiny, primitive jewel of a campground sits near two lakes—Snag Lake and Western Lake (the lower lake)—in a wooded area near Western Lakes, just outside of Naselle. Snag Lake, the area's feature, provides fishing for rainbow trout, brook trout, and cutthroat trout. No gas motors are permitted, so it is ideal for float tubes, prams, rowboats, or canoes (with electric motors permitted). There are some good hiking trails nearby, including a route that connects the two lakes. The lake and campground offer good views of Radar Ridge. It's a prime camp for travelers heading

to the coast who want a day or two of privacy before they hit the crowds.

**Campsites, facilities:** There are four walk-in sites for tents. Picnic tables and fire grills are provided. Vault toilets are available. There is no drinking water, and garbage must be packed out. Some facilities are wheelchair accessible. Leashed pets are permitted.

**Reservations, fees:** Reservations are not accepted. There is no fee for camping, but a Discover Pass is required. Open year-round.

**Directions:** From Kelso/Longview on I-5, turn west on Highway 4 and drive 60 miles (near Naselle) to Milepost 3 and C-Line Road. Turn right (north) and head uphill on C-Line Road (two-lane gravel road), take the left fork at Naselle Youth Camp entrance, and drive 2.9 miles to C-2600 (gravel one-lane road). Turn left on Road C-2600 and drive 0.9 mile (after 0.4 mile it becomes C-Line Road) to C-2650. Turn right and drive 0.3 miles to the campground on the right at Western Lake.

**Contact:** Department of Natural Resources, Pacific Cascade Region North, 360/577-2025, www.dnr.wa.gov.

## 120 SNAG LAKE

### Scenic rating: 9

near Naselle

**Map 1.7, page 83**

This is a classic little DNR camp on small Snag Lake—the kind of place time forgot. Any other clichés? No, seriously, time did forget this place. Very few people know about this spot and it can get you away from the crowds. Tiny Snag Lake is perfect for canoeing, fishing, wildlife-watching, or just kicking back. Gold Lake is nearby, as are several other small lakes.

**Campsites, facilities:** There are five walk-in sites for tents only. Picnic tables and fire grills are provided. Vault toilets are available. There is no drinking water and garbage must be packed out. Leashed pets are permitted.

**Reservations, fees:** Reservations are not accepted. There is no fee for camping. Open year-round.

**Directions:** From Kelso/Longview on I-5, turn west on Highway 4 and drive 60 miles (near Naselle) to Milepost 3 and C-Line Road. Turn right (north) and head uphill on C-Line Road (two-lane gravel road). Take the left fork at Naselle Youth Camp entrance, and drive 2.9 miles to C-2600 (gravel one-lane road). Turn left on Road C-2600 and drive 0.6 mile to C-2650. Turn right and drive 0.2 mile to the campground.

**Contact:** Department of Natural Resources, Pacific Cascade Region North, 360/577-2025, www.dnr.wa.gov.

## 121 SOU'WESTER LODGE
🧍🚵 ⛵ 🛶 🐕 🚐 ⛺

### Scenic rating: 7
in Seaview on the Long Beach Peninsula

**Map 1.7, page 83**

This one-of-a-kind place features a lodge that dates back to 1892, vintage trailers available for rent, and cottages. Various cultural events are held at the park throughout the year, including fireside evenings with theater and chamber music. The park covers three acres, provides beach access, and is one of the few sites in the immediate area that provides spots for tent camping. This park often attracts creative people such as musicians and artists, and some arrive for vacations in organized groups. It is definitely not for Howie and Ethel from Iowa. Fishing is a recreation option. The area features the Lewis and Clark Interpretive Center, a lighthouse, museums, fine dining, bicycle and boat rentals, bicycle and hiking trails, and bird sanctuaries. Additional facilities found within five miles of the park include an 18-hole golf course, a full-service marina, and a riding stable. The lodge was originally built for U.S. Senator Henry Winslow Corbett.

A side note: Tch-Tch stands for "trailers, classic, hodge-podge." Like I said, the place is

unique—and management has a great sense of humor.

**Campsites, facilities:** There are 28 sites with full hookups (20 and 30 amps) for RVs of any length, 13 sites for tents, a historic lodge, four cottages, and 12 1950s-style trailers in vintage condition. Some RV sites are pull-through. Picnic tables are provided at some sites. Restrooms with flush toilets and showers, drinking water, Wi-Fi, a classic VHS library, picnic area with pavilion, and community fire pits and grills are available. Propane gas, dump station, a store, gas station, café, and ice are located within one mile. Boat-launching facilities are nearby. Some facilities are wheelchair accessible. Leashed pets are permitted.

**Reservations, fees:** Reservations are accepted. Sites are $20-30 per night. Some credit cards are accepted. Open year-round.

**Directions:** From Kelso/Longview on I-5, turn west on Highway 4 and drive 63 miles to U.S. 101. Turn left (south) on U.S. 101 and drive 13 miles to the junction with Highway 103 (flashing light). Turn left to stay on U.S. 101 and drive one block to Seaview Beach Access Road (38th Place). Turn right and drive toward the ocean. Look for the campground on the left.

**Contact:** Sou'Wester Lodge, 360/642-2542, www.souwesterlodge.com.

## 122 CAUFFMAN WILDWOOD CAMPGROUND & RV PARK
🛶 🐕 🚐 ⛺

### Scenic rating: 5
in Long Beach

**Map 1.7, page 83**

Cauffman Wildwood is situated on Washington's tradition-steeped southwestern coast—the Long Beach Peninsula. Surrounded by the Pacific Ocean, the Columbia River, and Willapa Bay, this is a favorite vacation destination and a refuge for migrating birds and those seeking solitude by the ocean.

**Campsites, facilities:** There are 28 grassy

sites with full hookups (20 and 30 amps) for RVs up to 60 feet, 26 wooded sites for tents, and seven group sites for up to 10 tents. Picnic tables and fire pits are provided. Restrooms with flush toilets and coin showers, drinking water, Wi-Fi, a small lake with fish, children's activities, and firewood are available. Leashed pets are permitted.

**Reservations, fees:** Reservations are accepted. RV sites are $30-35 per night, tent sites are $20 per night, $5 per each additional person per night. Some credit cards are accepted. Open April-October.

**Directions:** From Kelso on I-5, turn west on Highway 4 and drive 60 miles to Highway 401. Turn left (south) on Highway 101 South and drive 15 miles to Peninsula Road/Sandridge Road. The campground will be on the left.

**Contact:** Wildwood Campground & RV Park, 5411 Sandridge Road, Long Beach, 360/642-2131, www.wildwoodcampsites.com.

## 123 ILWACO KOA

**Scenic rating: 5**

near Fort Canby State Park

**Map 1.7, page 83**

This 17-acre camp is about nine miles from the beach and includes a secluded area for tents. You'll find a boardwalk nearby, as well as the Lewis and Clark Museum, lighthouses, an amusement park, and fishing from a jetty or charter boats. The Washington State International Kite Festival is held in Long Beach the third week of August. The World Kite Museum and Hall of Fame, also in Long Beach, is open year-round. Additional facilities found within five miles of the campground include a maritime museum, hiking trails, and a nine-hole golf course. In my experience, attempts to phone this park were thwarted by a busy signal for weeks.

**Campsites, facilities:** There are 17 sites with full hookups and 20 sites with partial hookups for RVs of any length, a tent area for up to 40 tents, three group sites for up to 24 people each, and five cabins. All RV sites are pull-through. Picnic tables and fire rings are provided. Restrooms with flush toilets and showers, drinking water, cable TV, propane gas, a dump station, recreation hall, a camp store, coin laundry, ice, horseshoe pits, volleyball net, and a playground are available. Some facilities are wheelchair accessible. Leashed pets are permitted.

**Reservations, fees:** Reservations are accepted at 800/562-3258. Sites are $21-62 per night, $5 per person per night for more than two people. Some credit cards are accepted. Open mid-May-mid-September.

**Directions:** From Kelso/Longview on I-5, turn west on Highway 4 and drive 63 miles to U.S. 101. Turn left (south) on U.S. 101 and drive 13 miles to the junction with Highway 103. The campground is located at the junction.

**Contact:** Ilwaco KOA, 360/642-3292, www.koa.com.

## 124 CAPE DISAPPOINTMENT STATE PARK

**Scenic rating: 10**

near Ilwaco

**Map 1.7, page 83**

This park covers 1,882 acres on the Long Beach Peninsula and is fronted by the Pacific Ocean. There is access to 27 miles of ocean beach and two lighthouses. The park contains old-growth forest, lakes, both freshwater and saltwater marshes, streams, and tidelands. It is the choice spot in the area for tent campers. There are two places to camp: a general camping area and the Lake O'Neil area, which offers sites right on the water. Highlights at the park include hiking trails and opportunities for surf, jetty, and ocean fishing. An interpretive center highlights the Lewis and Clark expedition as well as maritime and military history. North Head Lighthouse is open for touring. Colbert House Museum is open during the summer.

**Campsites, facilities:** There are 83 sites with full or partial hookups (20 and 30 amps) for tents or RVs of any length, 152 sites for tents or RVs of any length (no hookups), five primitive tent sites, three cabins, 14 yurts, and three vacation homes. Picnic tables and fire grills are provided. Restrooms with flush toilets and coin showers, drinking water, a dump station, boat ramp, dock (135 feet), a picnic area, interpretive activities, a horseshoe pit, athletic fields, a small store, and firewood are available. Some facilities are wheelchair accessible. Leashed pets are permitted.

**Reservations, fees:** Reservations are accepted at 888/CAMP-OUT (888/226-7688) or www.goingtocamp.com ($6.50-8.50 reservation fee). Sites are $20-40 per night, primitive tent sites are $12 per night, cabins and yurts are $49-75 per night, and vacation homes are $253-479 per night. Some credit cards are accepted. Open year-round.

**Directions:** From the junction of Highway 4 and Highway 103 (a flashing light, south of Nemah), turn west on Highway 103 (toward Ilwaco) and drive two miles to Ilwaco and Highway 100. Turn right and drive three miles to the park entrance on the right.

**Contact:** Cape Disappointment State Park, 360/642-3078; state park information, 360/902-8844, www.parks.wa.gov.

## 125 RIVER'S END RV PARK

### Scenic rating: 6
near Fort Columbia State Park

Map 1.7, page 83

This wooded park spreads over five acres and has riverside access. Salmon fishing is available here. Additional facilities found within five miles of the campground include marked bike trails and a full-service marina. Also nearby is Fort Columbia State Park.

**Campsites, facilities:** There are 75 sites with full or partial hookups (30 amps) for tents or RVs of any length. Some sites are pull-through.

Picnic tables are provided, and fire pits are available at some sites. Restrooms with flush toilets and coin showers, drinking water, cable TV, a dump station, a recreation hall, coin laundry, firewood, a fish-cleaning station, and ice are available. A gas station, store, and café are located within one mile. Boat docks and launching facilities are nearby on the Columbia River. Some facilities are wheelchair accessible. Leashed pets are permitted.

**Reservations, fees:** Reservations are accepted. Sites are $28 per night, $5 per person per night for more than two people. Credit cards are not accepted. Open April-late October.

**Directions:** From Kelso/Longview on I-5, turn west on Highway 4 and drive 60 miles to Highway 401. Turn left (south) on Highway 401 and drive 14 miles to the park entrance (just north of Chinook) on the left.

**Contact:** River's End Campground and RV Park, 360/777-8317.

## 126 MAUCH'S SUNDOWN RV PARK

### Scenic rating: 5
near Fort Columbia State Park

Map 1.7, page 83

The park covers four acres, has riverside access, and is in a wooded, hilly setting with grassy sites. About 50 percent of the sites are rented monthly, usually throughout the summer. Nearby fishing from shore is available.

**Campsites, facilities:** There are 44 sites with full or partial hookups (30 amps) for tents or RVs of any length. Some sites are pull-through. Picnic tables are provided. No open fires are allowed. Restrooms with flush toilets and coin showers, drinking water, a dump station, and a coin laundry are available. A café is located within three miles. Boat docks and launching facilities are nearby on the Columbia River. Small pets are permitted.

**Reservations, fees:** Reservations are accepted. Sites are $15-30 per night, $2 per person per night for more than two people. Some credit cards are accepted. Open year-round.

**Directions:** From Kelso/Longview on I-5, turn west on Highway 4 and drive 60 miles to Highway 401. Turn left (south) on Highway 401 and drive to U.S. 101. Take U.S. 101 to the right and continue for 0.5 mile (do not go over the bridge) to the park on the right.

**Contact:** Mauch's Sundown RV Park, 360/777-8713.

## 127 SKAMOKAWA VISTA PARK

**Scenic rating: 7**

near the Columbia River

Map 1.7, page 83

This public camp covers 70 acres and features a half mile of sandy beach and a Lewis and Clark interpretive site. A short hiking trail is nearby. The camp also has nearby access to the Columbia River, where recreational options include fishing, swimming, and boating. Additional facilities found within five miles of the park include a full-service marina and tennis courts. In Skamokawa, River Life Interpretive Center stays open year-round.

**Campsites, facilities:** There are 14 sites with full hookups and 24 sites with partial hookups for RVs of any length, 16 sites for tents or RVs of any length (no hookups), and five yurts. Group camping is also available. Picnic tables and fire pits are provided. Restrooms with flush toilets and coin showers, drinking water, a dump station, ice, firewood, tennis courts, basketball courts, a group picnic shelter, geocaching, and two playgrounds are available. A café is located within walking distance. Boat docks, launching facilities, and kayak rentals are nearby. Some facilities are wheelchair accessible. Leashed pets are permitted, with some restrictions.

**Reservations, fees:** Reservations are accepted. RV sites are $21-28 per night, tent sites are $18 per night, and yurts are $40-48 per night. Some credit cards are accepted. Open year-round.

**Directions:** From Kelso/Longview on I-5, turn west on Highway 4 and drive 35 miles to Skamokawa. Continue west on Highway 4 for 0.5 mile to the park on the left.

**Contact:** Skamokawa Vista Park, Port of Wahkiakum No. 2, 360/795-8605, www.vistapark. wordpress.com.

# SEATTLE AND THE PUGET SOUND

Seattle offers a wide array of recreation, with a pre-eminent scope of parks and campgrounds: many state parks are home to gorgeous water-view campsites; well-furnished RV parks offer a layover respite; and hidden lakes, such as Cascade Lake on Orcas Island, will surprise you with their beauty. But—you need a boat to do it right. A powerboat, sailboat, or kayak offers near-unlimited access to Puget Sound and the linked inlets, bays, and canals—not to mention boat-in campsites. And with some 25 boat-in campsites available, often along calm, sheltered waters, there is no better place to sea kayak.

One of my favorite views anywhere is from the top of Mount Constitution on Orcas Island. On a clear day, you can look out over an infinity of sun-swept charm—and you'll know this is why you came.

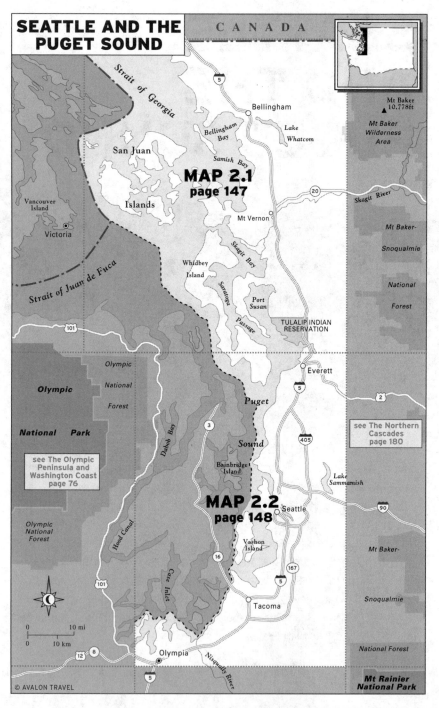

# SEATTLE AND THE PUGET SOUND

CANADA

Mt Baker
▲ 10,778ft

Mt Baker
Wilderness
Area

Strait of Georgia

5

Bellingham

Lake
Whatcom

Bellingham
Bay

San Juan

Samish Bay

**MAP 2.1**
**page 147**

20

Skagit River

Mt Vernon

Mt Baker-

Vancouver
Island

Islands

Snoqualmie

Victoria

Whidbey
Island

Skagit Bay

National

Strait of Juan de Fuca

Saratoga

Port
Susan

Forest

Passage

TULALIP INDIAN
RESERVATION

101

Olympic

National

Everett

5

Forest

Puget

2

**Olympic**

3

see The Northern
Cascades
page 180

405

**National    Park**

Sound

see The Olympic
Peninsula and
Washington Coast
page 76

Dabob Bay

Bainbridge
Island

Lake
Sammamish

**MAP 2.2**
**page 148**

Seattle

90

Olympic
National
Forest

Hood Canal

Vashon
Island

167

Mt Baker-

16

5

101

Case Inlet

Snoqualmie

0        10 mi
0        10 km

Tacoma

National Forest

12    8

Olympia

Nisqually River

**Mt Rainier**
**National Park**

5

© AVALON TRAVEL

# Map 2.1

## Sites 1-48
## Pages 149-171

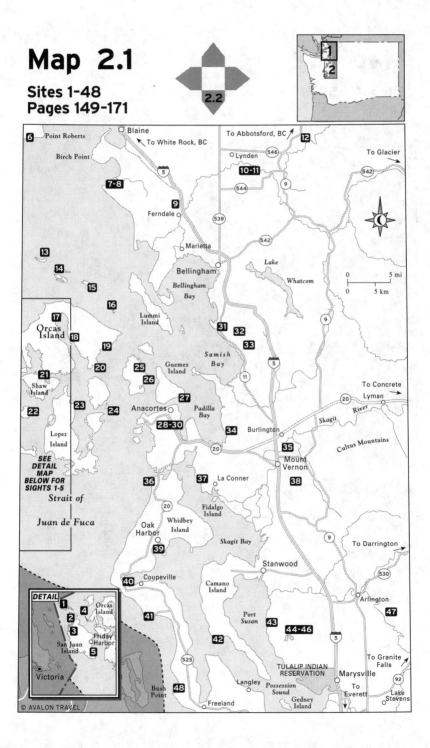

2.2

# Map 2.2

## Sites 49-59
## Pages 172-177

2.1

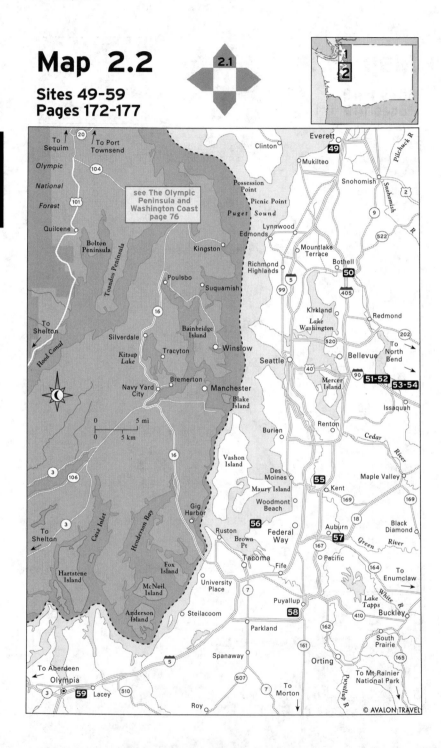

To Sequim · To Port Townsend
20

Olympic
104
National
101
Forest
Quilcene

Bolton Peninsula

Toandos Peninsula

see The Olympic Peninsula and Washington Coast page 76

Kingston

Poulsbo
Suquamish

To Shelton

16

Silverdale
Kitsap Lake
Tracyton

Bainbridge Island

Winslow

Navy Yard City
Bremerton
Manchester
Blake Island

Hood Canal

0   5 mi
0   5 km

16

3   106

Case Inlet

Henderson Bay

Gig Harbor

3
To Shelton

Hartstene Island

McNeil Island

Fox Island

Anderson Island

5

To Aberdeen
Olympia
3   510   Lacey
59

Roy

507

7
To Morton

Everett
49

Clinton
Mukilteo
Snohomish
Pilchuck R

Possession Point
Picnic Point
Puget Sound

Lynnwood
Edmonds
Richmond Highlands

Mountlake Terrace
Bothell

2
9
522

R

99
5

I-5
520

Kirkland
Lake Washington

Redmond
202

To North Bend

50
405

Seattle
40

Mercer Island

Bellevue

90
51-52
53-54

Issaquah

Cedar River

Burien
Renton

Vashon Island

Des Moines
55   Kent
Maple Valley
169
169

Maury Island
Woodmont Beach

18
Auburn
57

Black Diamond

Green River
164
To Enumclaw

56
Federal Way

167
Pacific

Ruston
Brown Pt
Tacoma   Fife

University Place
7

Steilacoom

Puyallup
58

Lake Tapps
410
Buckley

White R

162
Parkland

161
Orting

South Prairie
165

Puyallup R

To Mt. Rainier National Park

Spanaway

© AVALON TRAVEL

# 1 STUART ISLAND MARINE STATE PARK BOAT-IN

🚶 🚣 ⛴ 🛶 🐕 ⛺

### Scenic rating: 9

northwest of San Juan Island

**Map 2.1, page 147**

For most campers, this is really stalking the unknown. Stuart Island is a remote little spot on the edge of Canadian waters that covers 153 acres and has excellent harbors for mooring. It's the westernmost of the marine parks, making it a jumping-off point for Sucia Island, Orcas Island, and San Juan Island parks. There is good fishing at nearby Reid and Provost Harbors. On holiday weekends, it usually fills up; on summer weekends, it is typically about 70 percent filled; and on weekdays, it is about half filled. That makes it the second busiest park in the area, receiving about 70,000 visitors per year.

**Campsites, facilities:** There are 18 primitive boat-in campsites, including four reserved for non-motorized boaters only. Picnic tables and fire rings are provided. Drinking water (summer season only) and pit and composting toilets are available. There are also 20 buoys, and floats are available for overnight moorage for boats up to 45 feet. Garbage must be packed out. Leashed pets are permitted.

**Reservations, fees:** Reservations are not accepted. Sites are $12 per night, moorage is $0.60 per foot per boat with a $12 minimum, and buoys are $12 per night. Open year-round, with limited facilities in winter.

**Directions:** The park is on the north side of Stuart Island and is accessible only by boat. Stuart Island is located northwest of San Juan Island.

**Contact:** San Juan Marine Area, South, 360/378-2044; state park information, 360/902-8844, www.parks.wa.gov.

# 2 POSEY ISLAND STATE PARK BOAT-IN

⛴ 🚣 ⛺

### Scenic rating: 9

near Roche Harbor

**Map 2.1, page 147**

This is a beautiful little spot you'll want all to yourself. It's difficult to get here, however, as you must arrive by non-motorized boat—kayak, canoe, or pelican sailboat. The best way to reach the camp is by sea kayak, paddling in from San Juan Island out of Roche Harbor. There are no docks or mooring buoys. Situated on a one-acre island, this is not only one of the smallest designated campgrounds in Washington, but also one of the most idyllic and beautiful to reach by small boat, with lots of wildflowers in spring, including chocolate lilies. In an attempt to keep it from being loved to death, no more than 16 people are permitted on the island at one time. There's not much here, and that's exactly why it is so well loved. Everything becomes simplified, so it feels as if you have the entire world to yourself. And on Posey Island, you do.

**Campsites, facilities:** There are two primitive boat-in campsites. A maximum of 16 people are allowed at any time. Picnic tables and fire rings are provided. A composting toilet is available. There is no drinking water. Garbage must be packed out.

**Reservations, fees:** Reservations are accepted mid-May-September at 360/378-2044 or www.goingtocamp.com ($6.50-8.50 reservation fee). Sites are $12 per night. Open year-round.

**Directions:** This little island is located just north of Roche Harbor (on San Juan Island) and is accessible only by small boat. From Roche Harbor, you head northwest and cruise about one mile from the outlet to reach Posey Island.

**Contact:** San Juan Marine Area, South, 360/378-2044; state park information, 360/902-8844, www.parks.wa.gov.

## 3 LAKEDALE RESORT FERRY-IN

🚴 🏊 ⛵ 🚐 🦌 🚗 ⛺

### Scenic rating: 7

on San Juan Island

**Map 2.1, page 147**

This is a nice spot on 82 acres for visitors who want the solitude of an island camp, yet all the amenities of a privately run campground. Fishing, swimming, and boating are available at the three Lakedale lakes. A sand volleyball court, a half-court basketball area, and a grassy sports field are also on-site. Roche Harbor and Wescott Bay are nearby to the north, and Friday Harbor and its restaurants are nearby to the south.

**Campsites, facilities:** There are 64 sites for tents and seven sites with partial hookups for tents or RVs up to 40 feet long. There are also six group tent sites for up to 20-40 people each, six log cabins, one longhouse, and 10 luxury lodge rooms. Picnic tables and fire rings are provided. Restrooms with flush toilets and coin showers, drinking water, and firewood are available. A convenience store and ice are available. Boat docks, a swimming beach, and boat and fishing gear rentals are available on-site. Leashed pets are permitted in campgrounds and log cabins.

**Reservations, fees:** Reservations are accepted. Tent sites are $45-57 per night, RV sites are $64 per night, hike-in/bike-in sites are $35 per night, group sites are $200 per night, cabins are $179-279 per night with a fee of $35 per pet. Discounts are offered off-season. Some credit cards are accepted. Open Memorial Day-September for camping; cabins and lodge rooms are available year-round.

**Directions:** From Burlington and Highway 20, turn west on Highway 20 and drive 12 miles to the Highway 20 North spur, following signs to the San Juan Islands Ferry Terminal in Anacortes. Take the ferry to Friday Harbor on San Juan Island. From the ferry landing at Friday Harbor, drive two blocks on Spring Street to 2nd Street. Turn right (northwest) on 2nd Street and drive 0.5 mile to Tucker Avenue

(it becomes Roche Harbor Road). Continue 4.5 miles to the resort on the left.

**Contact:** Lakedale Resort, 360/378-2350 or 800/617-CAMP (800/617-2267), www. lakedale.com; Washington State Ferries information, 206/464-6400 or 888/808-7977 (Washington state only).

## 4 JONES ISLAND MARINE STATE PARK BOAT-IN

🚶 ⛵ 🚐 🚣 🦌 ⛺

### Scenic rating: 9

near Orcas Island

**Map 2.1, page 147**

This small island may seem like a hidden spot, but it is an easy boat ride out of Doe Harbor at Orcas Island. It gets about the second heaviest use of all the island campgrounds in the region. The campground is near the beach, so you don't have to carry your gear very far. The area offers good fishing and scuba diving. A note of caution: Raccoons have become pests, and campers are advised to keep food well contained. Rangers here make a special request that campers not feed the raccoons, deer, or other wildlife. Sunsets often provide breathtaking beauty from this island. In addition, it is set amid a national wildlife and migratory bird refuge. Another plus is that two big lawn areas are ideal for family and group camping. Note that the docks are in place April-mid-October.

**Campsites, facilities:** There are 24 primitive boat-in campsites (two sites are for non-motorized boaters only) and a group site for up to 65 people. There is also an eight-person Adirondack shelter. Picnic tables and fire rings are provided. Drinking water (summer season only) and composting toilets are available. Boat buoys and floats are available for overnight moorage for boats up to 45 feet. Leashed pets are permitted.

**Reservations, fees:** Reservations are not accepted for single sites, but are required for the group site ($25 nonrefundable reservation fee). Sites are $12 per night; moorage is $0.60 per foot per boat with a $12 minimum and buoys are $12 per night. The group site is $38.24 per night for a minimum of 16 people; $2.39 per person for up to 60 people (maximum). The Adirondack is $23 per night ($7 reservation fee). Open year-round, with limited facilities in winter; docks are removed October-March.

**Directions:** The campground is on tiny Jones Island, located between Orcas Island and San Juan Island. This camp is accessible only by boat. Look for the boat buoys just offshore from the campsites.

**Contact:** San Juan Marine Area, South, 360/378-2044; state park information, 360/902-8844, www.parks.wa.gov.

## 5 GRIFFIN BAY BOAT-IN

### Scenic rating: 9

on San Juan Island

**Map 2.1, page 147**

This tiny, remote camp is ideal for kayakers who want the place to themselves. It receives little use, yet it's located on one of the prettiest islands in the area and is a favorite among in-the-know kayakers. Only non-motorized boats are permitted to land. The island covers just 12 acres, with two campsites and two mooring buoys.

**Campsites, facilities:** There are two primitive boat-in campsites. Picnic tables and fire pits are provided. Pit toilets and three picnic sites are available. There is no drinking water, and garbage must be packed out.

**Reservations, fees:** Reservations are not accepted. Sites are $12 per night, buoys are $12 per night. Open year-round, with limited facilities in winter.

**Directions:** Griffin Bay is on the southeast side of San Juan Island (south of Friday Harbor). The campground is accessible only by non-motorized boat.

**Contact:** San Juan Marine Area North, 360/376-2073; state park information, 360/902-8844, www.parks.wa.gov.

## 6 LIGHTHOUSE MARINE PARK

### Scenic rating: 6

on Point Roberts

**Map 2.1, page 147**

This park is located on Point Roberts—so remote you must drive through Canada and then return south into the United States to reach it. The park features a boardwalk, a boat launch, and a sandy beach. Wildlife-watching and hiking are favorite activities here because of the beautiful views.

**Campsites, facilities:** There are 30 sites for tents and RVs. Group camping is also available. Picnic tables and fire pits are provided. Drinking water and restrooms with flush toilets and coin showers are available. A kitchen shelter is available for rent. A grocery store, a cafe, and a coin laundry are located within one mile. Leashed pets are permitted.

**Reservations, fees:** Reservations are accepted ($8 reservation fee) and are recommended. Sites are $18-22 per night, group sites are $80-120 per night. Some credit cards accepted. Open May-September.

**Directions:** From Bellingham, take I-5 north through Blaine and the border customs into Canada to Highway 99 North. Continue northwest on Highway BC 99N for 18 miles to BC 17. Turn left (west) and drive six miles to the town of Tsawwassen and 56th Street. Turn left on 56th Street and drive to the Point Roberts border crossing. Drive straight on Tyee Drive, past the marina, to Lighthouse Marine Park on the left.

**Contact:** Lighthouse Marine Park, Whatcom County Parks and Recreation, 360/945-4911, www.co.whatcom.wa.us/parks.

## 7 BIRCH BAY STATE PARK

### Scenic rating: 8

on Birch Bay

**Map 2.1, page 147**                    **BEST (**

Birch Bay State Park covers 194 acres and features nearly two miles of beach as well as great views of the Canadian coast range and some of the San Juan Islands. For water lovers, it has the best of both worlds, with 8,255 feet of saltwater shoreline and 14,923 feet of freshwater shoreline on Terrell Creek. More than 100 different species of birds, many of which migrate on the Pacific Flyway, can be seen here. Terrell Creek Marsh Interpretive Trail extends 0.5 mile through a forest of black birch trees, Douglas fir, and western hemlock and one of the few remaining saltwater/freshwater estuaries in northern Puget Sound. Bald eagles and great blue herons feed along the banks of Terrell Creek. Several 18-hole golf courses are located nearby. The campground is divided into two loops; hookups for RVs are in the North Loop.

**Campsites, facilities:** There are 147 sites for tents or self-contained RVs, 20 sites with full or partial hookups (30 amps) for RVs up to 60 feet long, one primitive group site for tents and RVs that can accommodate up to 40 people, and two group camps with five sites each. Picnic tables and fire grills are provided. Restrooms with flush toilets and coin showers and a dump station are available. A boat ramp (for boats less than 16 feet only), a picnic area with a sheltered kitchen and electricity, an amphitheater, basketball court, interpretive activities, and a camp host are available. A store, restaurant, coin laundry, and ice are located within one mile. Some facilities are wheelchair accessible. Leashed pets are permitted.

**Reservations, fees:** Reservations are accepted and are required for groups at 888/CAMP-OUT (888/226-7688) or www.goingtocamp. com ($6.50-8.50 reservation fee). Sites are $22-28 per night, $10 per extra vehicle per night. The group sites are $109.40-$112.71 per person per night. Some credit cards are accepted. Open year-round.

**Directions:** From Bellingham, drive north on I-5 to Exit 266. At Exit 266 take Grandview west and continue seven miles to Jackson Road. Turn right on Jackson Road and drive one mile to Helweg Road. Turn left and drive 0.25 mile to the reservation office.

**Contact:** Birch Bay State Park, 360/371-2800; state park information, 360/902-8844, www.parks.wa.gov.

## 8 BEACHSIDE RV PARK

### Scenic rating: 8

on Birch Bay

**Map 2.1, page 147**

This pretty park is surrounded by evergreens and bay views. Hiking, fishing, mountain biking, and nearby golf are also options. Note that most sites are filled with monthly renters.

**Campsites, facilities:** There are 72 pull-through sites with full hookups (30 and 50 amps) for RVs and five tent sites. Picnic tables are provided. Restrooms with flush toilets and showers, drinking water, a group fire pit, Wi-Fi, a library, lounge, DVD/video exchange, horseshoe pit, barbecue area, and coin laundry are available. A boat launch, grocery store, and restaurant are located within one mile. Leashed pets are permitted with certain restrictions.

**Reservations, fees:** Reservations are recommended at 800/596-9586. Sites are $25-33 per night. Weekly and monthly rates available. Some credit cards are accepted. Open year-round.

**Directions:** From Bellingham, drive north on I-5 to Exit 270. Turn west on Birch Bay-Lynden Road and drive five miles to Birch Bay Drive. Turn left and drive one mile to the park on the left.

**Contact:** Beachside RV Park, 360/371-5962, www.beachsidervpark.com.

## 9 THE CEDARS RV RESORT

### Scenic rating: 5

in Ferndale

Map 2.1, page 147

This resort provides more direct access from I-5 than nearby Windmill Inn or KOA Lynden, and you can usually get a site here. It's a nice, clean park covering 22 acres with spacious sites and trees. Horseshoe pits, a game room, and a recreation field provide possible activities for campers. Several golf courses are nearby.

**Campsites, facilities:** There are 167 sites with full or partial hookups (20, 30, and 50 amps), including pull-through sites, for tents or RVs of any length and a grassy area for dispersed tent camping. Picnic tables and fire pits are provided. Restrooms with flush toilets and showers, drinking water, cable TV, Wi-Fi, two dump stations, coin laundry, a playground, horseshoe pits, badminton, volleyball, recreation room, a seasonal heated pool, convenience store, and ice are available. Leashed pets are permitted.

**Reservations, fees:** Reservations are accepted. Tent sites are $30 per night, RV sites are $39.50-42.50 per night, $3 per pet per night. Some credit cards accepted. Open year-round.

**Directions:** From Bellingham on I-5, drive north to Ferndale and Exit 263. Take Exit 263 and turn right (north) on Portal Way. Drive less than one mile to the resort on the left.

**Contact:** The Cedars RV Resort, 360/384-2622, www.holidaytrailsresorts.com/thecedars.

## 10 WINDMILL INN

### Scenic rating: 7

near the Nooksack River

Map 2.1, page 147

This nice little spot, only 15 minutes from Puget Sound, is set near the Nooksack River and Wiser Lake. As the last stop before the U.S./Canada border, the camp serves primarily as a layover for people heading north. The quiet and pretty setting abounds with trees and flowers. Area attractions include Mount Baker, the quaint little shops of Lynden, and the nearby Birch Bay area, which offers many recreation options.

**Campsites, facilities:** There are eight sites for tents or RVs of any length and 15 motel rooms. Picnic tables are provided. Restrooms with flush toilets and coin showers, drinking water, cable TV, and a park are available. A store, propane gas, a café, coin laundry, and ice are available within one mile. Boat-launching facilities are located within 1.5 miles.

**Reservations, fees:** Reservations are not accepted. Sites are $18-25 per night, plus $1 per person per night for more than two people. Some credit cards are accepted. Open year-round.

**Directions:** In Bellingham on I-5, take Exit 256 for Highway 539 (called Meridian Street in Bellingham). Turn north on Highway 539 and drive 10 miles to Lynden. The RV park is on the right side of the road as you enter Lynden.

**Contact:** Windmill Inn, 360/354-3424.

## 11 KOA LYNDEN/ BELLINGHAM

### Scenic rating: 9

in Lynden

Map 2.1, page 147     BEST (

Lynden is a quaint Dutch town with a windmill and the Pioneer Museum. The park features green lawns, flowers, and trees surrounding a miniature golf course and three fishing ponds, where you can fish for trout. This KOA stars as a unique layover spot for vacationers heading north to Canada via Highway 539 and Highway 546. Nearby recreational options include several golf courses. Bellingham, a historic waterfront town with good restaurants and Victorian mansions, is also close by.

**Campsites, facilities:** There are 30 sites for tents or RVs (no hookups), 107 sites with full or partial hookups (30 and 50 amps) for RVs up to 60 feet, and 15 cabins. Some sites are pull-through. Picnic tables are provided and most sites have fire pits. Restrooms with flush toilets and showers, drinking water, Wi-Fi, propane gas, a dump station, firewood, a recreation hall, convenience store, café (summer season only), espresso bar, ice cream parlor, coin laundry, ice, a playground, miniature golf, horseshoe pits, volleyball, and a seasonal heated swimming pool are available. Fishing tackle and boat rentals are available. Leashed pets are permitted.

**Reservations, fees:** Reservations are not accepted. Sites are $30-75 per night, $4-5 per person per night for more than two people. Some credit cards are accepted. Open year-round.

**Directions:** From I-5 at Bellingham, take Exit 256 to Highway 539. Turn north and drive 12 miles to Highway 546. Turn east on Badger Road and drive three miles to Line Road. Turn right on Line Road and drive 0.5 mile to the campground on the right.

**Contact:** KOA Lynden/Bellingham, 360/354-4772, www.koa.com.

## 12 SUMAS RV PARK
🎣 🚐 ▲

**Scenic rating: 5**

in Sumas

**Map 2.1, page 147**

Located near the U.S./Canada border, this campground is a layover spot to spend American dollars before heading into British Columbia and making the conversion. The camp is set in the grassy flatlands; it has graveled sites and a few trees. Nearby recreation options include an 18-hole golf course.

**Campsites, facilities:** There is a grassy area for tents and 50 sites with full or partial hookups (20, 30, and 50 amps) for tents or RVs of any length. Some are pull-through.

Picnic tables are provided at some sites; fire rings are provided at most sites. Restrooms with flush toilets and coin showers, drinking water, modem access, a dump station, and coin laundry are available. A store, ice, café, rodeo grounds, and a ballpark are located within one mile. Leashed pets are permitted.

**Reservations, fees:** Reservations are accepted. Tent sites are $10 per night, RV sites are $25 per night, $4 per person per night for more than two people. Some credit cards accepted. Open year-round.

**Directions:** From I-5 at Bellingham, take Exit 256 to Highway 539. Turn north on Highway 539 and drive 12 miles to Highway 546. Turn right (east) on Highway 546 (Badger Road) and drive 14 miles (the road becomes Highway 9) to Sumas and look for Cherry Street. Turn right (south) at Cherry Street (the road becomes Easterbrook Road) and drive two blocks to the park on the left.

**Contact:** Sumas RV Park, 9600 Easterbrook Rd., 360/988-8875 or 866/213-5180, http://sumasrvpark.com.

## 13 PATOS ISLAND STATE PARK BOAT-IN
🏃 🛶 🚣 🐕 ▲

**Scenic rating: 9**

near Sucia Island

**Map 2.1, page 147**

If you're going to get stranded on an island, this is not a bad choice, provided you like your companion. There are good hiking trails and excellent fishing and clam-digging opportunities here. Covering approximately 200 acres, it's primitive and used by few. Patos Lighthouse is a favorite attraction on this island. It also features great views of the Canadian islands, and sunsets are often drop-dead beautiful.

**Campsites, facilities:** There are seven primitive boat-in campsites. Picnic tables and fire rings are provided. Vault and pit toilets are available. There is no drinking water and garbage must be packed out. Two boat buoys are available for overnight moorage. Leashed pets are permitted.

**Reservations, fees:** Reservations are not accepted. Sites are $12 per night, buoys are $12 per night. Open year-round, with limited facilities in winter.

**Directions:** The park is located on the west side of Patos Island, which is 2.5 miles northwest of Sucia Island and five miles northwest of Orcas Island. It's accessible only by boat and is the northernmost of the coastal islands.

**Contact:** San Juan Marine Area, North, 360/376-2073; state park information, 360/902-8844, www.parks.wa.gov.

## 14 SUCIA ISLAND MARINE STATE PARK BOAT-IN

🚶 🎣 🏊 ⚓ 🐕 ♿ ⛺

### Scenic rating: 9

near Orcas Island

**Map 2.1, page 147**

Here's a classic spot with rocky outcrops for lookout points and good beach and fishing areas. Sucia Island covers 562 acres and provides opportunities for hiking, clamming, crabbing, kayaking, and scuba diving. Although primitive, the campground is beautiful and well worth the trip, making it the busiest park in the chain of San Juan Islands. It also has the most moorage. This camp is full during summer, often even on weekdays.

**Campsites, facilities:** There are 60 primitive boat-in campsites and three group sites for up to 50 people each. There is also an eight-person Adirondack shelter. Picnic tables and fire rings are provided. Drinking water (summer season only), vault and composting toilets, three picnic shelters, and two docks are also available. Garbage must be packed out. Boat buoys and floats are available for overnight moorage, and you can anchor without a fee in all bays and coves. Some facilities are wheelchair accessible. Leashed pets are permitted.

**Reservations, fees:** Reservations are not accepted for individual sites, but are required

for the group sites at 360/376-2073. Sites are $12 per night, buoys are $12 per night. The group site is $38.24 per night for a minimum of 16 people; $2.39 per person up to 50 people (maximum). The Adirondack is $23 per night ($7 reservation fee). Open year-round, with limited facilities in winter.

**Directions:** The park located is on the north side of Sucia Island (2.5 miles north of Orcas Island). It's accessible only by boat.

**Contact:** San Juan Marine Area North, 360/376-2073; state park information, 360/902-8844, www.parks.wa.gov.

## 15 MATIA ISLAND STATE PARK BOAT-IN

🚶 🎣 🏊 ⚓ 🐕 ⛺

### Scenic rating: 9

near Orcas Island

**Map 2.1, page 147**

Campsites here are located just a short walk from the docking facilities (available April-October), a big plus since many of the other island campgrounds don't have docks. Otherwise the camp is primitive, so it gets lighter use than the other campgrounds set on islands in the area. A one-mile loop trail from the campground leads through an old-growth cedar forest. Other highlights include good fishing and beachcombing. Scuba diving is also popular. This island is a U.S. Fish and Wildlife refuge.

**Campsites, facilities:** There are six primitive boat-in campsites. Fire grills are provided; open fires outside of grills are not permitted. Composting toilets are available. There is no drinking water, and garbage must be packed out. There is a boat dock, and buoys and floats are available for overnight moorage. Note that docks are in place April-October, weather permitting. Leashed pets are permitted only in campground and moorage areas.

**Reservations, fees:** Reservations are not accepted. Sites are $12 per night, moorage is $0.60 per foot per boat ($12 minimum), and buoys are $12 per night. Open year-round, with limited facilities in winter.

**Directions:** The campground is located on the northeast side of Matia Island, which is 2.5 miles northeast of Orcas Island (between Clark Island to the southeast, Sucia Island to the northwest, and Orcas Island to the south). It's accessible only by boat.

**Contact:** San Juan Marine Area, North, 360/376-2073; state park information, 360/902-8844, www.parks.wa.gov.

## 16 CLARK ISLAND STATE PARK BOAT-IN

### Scenic rating: 9

northeast of Orcas Island

**Map 2.1, page 147**

Clark Island State Park offers beautiful beaches with opportunities for scuba diving, beach-combing, and sunbathing. It is a short boat trip from nearby Orcas Island. You can pretend you're on a deserted Caribbean island. Well, almost. From the campground there are excellent views of the other nearby islands.

**Campsites, facilities:** There are nine primitive boat-in campsites, with a maximum of four people per site, and a group site for up to 12 people. Picnic tables and fire rings are provided. Vault toilets are available. There is no drinking water and garbage must be packed out. Boat buoys for overnight moorage are available for boats up to 45 feet long. Leashed pets are permitted.

**Reservations, fees:** Reservations are accepted for the group site at 360/376-2073 ($25 reservation fee). Sites are $12 per night, buoys are $12 per night. Open year-round, with limited facilities in winter.

**Directions:** The campground is on tiny Clark Island, located northeast of Orcas Island. It's accessible only by boat. Look for the moorage floats set just offshore from the campsites.

**Contact:** San Juan Marine Area, South, 360/378-2044; state park information, 360/902-8844, www.parks.wa.gov.

## 17 WEST BEACH RESORT FERRY-IN

### Scenic rating: 9

on Orcas Island

**Map 2.1, page 147**    **BEST (**

Right on the beach, this resort offers salmon fishing, boating, swimming, and an apple orchard. Some sites have ocean views and rent by the week in July and August. An excellent alternative to Moran State Park, which is often full, it offers the same recreation opportunities. There is excellent fishing, crabbing, and scuba diving at the resort, and fishing charters and guided kayak tours are available. The beaches at Orcas Island are prime spots for whale-watching and beautiful views, especially at sunrise and sunset.

**Campsites, facilities:** There are 12 sites with tents or RVs of any length (20 and 30 amp full hookups), 15 sites for tents, and one overflow area for tents. There are also five tent cabins. Picnic tables and fire pits are provided. Restrooms with flush toilets and coin showers (March-October only), a convenience store, café, playground, coin laundry, ice, Wi-Fi, fish-cleaning station, and firewood are available. A spa is available for a fee. Also on-site are a boat ramp, dock, full-service marina, rentals, moorage, and dry storage. A dump station is nearby. Leashed pets are permitted.

**Reservations, fees:** Reservations are accepted. Sites are $28-49 per night for up to three people, $7 per person per night for each additional person (maximum of six), $7 per extra vehicle per night, and $7 per pet per night. Some credit cards are accepted. Open year-round.

**Directions:** From Burlington and I-5, take exit 230 (San Juan Islands) for Highway 20. Turn west on Highway 20 and drive 12 miles to the Highway 20 North spur, following signs to the San Juan Islands Ferry Terminal in Anacortes. Take the ferry to Orcas Island. From the ferry landing, turn left and drive nine miles on Horseshoe Highway/Orcas Road to the entrance of Eastsound. Continue 0.25 mile to Enchanted Forest Road. Turn left and drive 2.4 miles to the end of Enchanted Forest Road and the resort.

**Contact:** West Beach Resort, 360/376-2240 or 877/WEST-BCH (877/937-8224), www. westbeachresort.com; Washington State Ferries, 206/464-6400 or 888/808-7977 (Washington only).

## 18 MORAN STATE PARK FERRY-IN

🥾 🚲 🛶 🚤 🐴 ♿ 🚐 ⛺

**Scenic rating: 10**

on Orcas Island

**Map 2.1, page 147**       **BEST (**

This state park is drop-dead beautiful. It covers 5,252 acres, with surprise lakes, hiking trails, and the best mountaintop views anywhere in the chain of islands. There are actually four separate campgrounds plus a primitive area. You can drive to the summit of Mount Constitution, which tops out at 2,409 feet, then climb up the steps to a stone observation tower (built in 1936 by the Civilian Conservation Corps). The tower provides sensational 360-degree views of Vancouver, Mount Baker, the San Juan Islands, the Cascade Mountains, and several cities on the distant shores of mainland America and Canada. No RVs are allowed on the winding road to the top. There are five freshwater lakes (no gas-motor boats permitted) with fishing for rainbow trout, cutthroat trout, and kokanee salmon, 33 miles of hiking trails, 11 miles of biking trails, and six miles of horse trails. The landscape features old-growth forest, primarily lodgepole pine, and several small waterfalls. Nearby recreation options include a nine-hole golf course.

**Campsites, facilities:** There are 136 sites for tents or RVs up to 45 feet (no hookups), including some pull-through sites, 15 primitive hike-in/bike-in tent sites, and one vacation house for up to 10 people. Picnic tables and fire grills are provided. Restrooms with flush toilets and coin showers, drinking water, a dump station, a picnic area with log kitchen shelter, firewood, and a snack bar are available. Boat docks, limited fishing supplies, launching facilities, and boat rentals are located at the concession stand in the park. Some facilities are wheelchair accessible. Leashed pets are permitted.

**Reservations, fees:** Reservations are accepted at 888/CAMP-OUT (888/226-7688) or www. goingtocamp.com ($6.50-8.50 reservation fee). Sites are $17-31 per night, bike-in/hike-in sites are $12 per night, and $10 per extra vehicle per night. Reservations for the vacation house are accepted at 800/360-4240 for $98-131 per night. Note that some campers consider the ferry-crossing fee for RVs very high; call ahead for prices. Some credit cards are accepted. Open year-round.

**Directions:** From Seattle on I-5, drive north to Burlington and Highway 20. Turn west on Highway 20 and drive 12 miles to the Highway 20 North spur, following signs to the San Juan Islands Ferry Terminal in Anacortes. Take the ferry to Orcas Island. From the ferry landing, turn left on Horseshoe Highway/Orcas Road and drive 13 miles to Moran State Park (well marked). Stop at the campground registration booth for directions to your site.

**Contact:** Moran State Park Ferry-In, 360/376-2326; state park information, 360/902-8844, www.parks.wa.gov; Washington State Ferries, 206/464-6400 or 888/808-7977 (Washington state only).

## 19 OBSTRUCTION PASS STATE PARK HIKE-IN

🥾 🏊 🚤 🐴 ⛺

**Scenic rating: 8**

on Orcas Island

**Map 2.1, page 147**

It takes a ferryboat ride, a tricky drive, and a 0.5-mile walk to reach this campground, but that helps set it apart from others. Your journey will take you to a unique, primitive spot set in a forested area with good hiking near the shore of Orcas Island. The irony is that Obstruction Pass is so unusual that it is often heavily used. Moran State Park, also on this island, is a more developed alternative with many recreation options.

**Campsites, facilities:** There are 11 primitive hike-in sites for tents only. Picnic tables and fire grills are provided. Vault toilets are available. There is no drinking water, and garbage must be packed out. Three mooring buoys are available. Open year-round, with limited facilities in winter. Leashed pets are permitted.

**Reservations, fees:** Reservations are not accepted. Sites are $12 per night, buoys are $12 per night. Open year-round.

**Directions:** From Seattle on I-5, drive north to Burlington and Highway 20. Turn west on Highway 20 and drive 12 miles to the Highway 20 North spur, following signs to the San Juan Islands Ferry Terminal in Anacortes. Take the ferry to Orcas Island, then drive on the Horseshoe Highway past Moran State Park and continue to the town of Olga and Doe Bay Road. Drive east on Doe Bay Road for 0.5 mile to Obstruction Pass Road. Turn right and drive 0.7 mile to Trailhead Road. Bear right and drive straight for less than a mile to the parking area. Hike 0.5 mile to the campground.

**Contact:** Obstruction Pass State Park and Moran State Park, 360/376-2326; San Juan Marine Area North, 360/376-2073; state park information, 360/902-8844, www.parks. wa.gov; Washington State Ferries, 206/464-6400 or 888/808-7977 (Washington state only).

## 20 DOE ISLAND STATE PARK BOAT-IN

🏃 🏊 🚣 ⛴ 🐕 ⛺

### Scenic rating: 9

near Orcas Island

**Map 2.1, page 147**          **BEST (**

Note: Doe island was not open for camping as of early 2014; the Coast Guard is working on improving the reef marker buoys. Call to check availability.

Doe Island State Park is a tiny, primitive park that receives little use. It has a rocky shoreline, which makes an ideal fish habitat, and the scuba diving and fishing are exceptional. Docking is available April-mid-October; please note that the mooring buoys located just offshore are privately owned.

**Campsites, facilities:** There are five primitive boat-in campsites. Fire rings are provided. Vault toilets are available. There is no drinking water, and garbage must be packed out. Docking is available April-mid-October, weather permitting. Leashed pets are permitted.

**Reservations, fees:** Reservations are not accepted. Sites are $12 per night, moorage is $0.60 per foot per boat ($12 minimum), and buoys are $12 per night. Open year-round, with limited facilities in winter.

**Directions:** This small, secluded island is just off the southeastern shore of Orcas Island off Doe Bay. It's accessible only by boat.

**Contact:** San Juan Marine Area, North, 360/376-2073; state park information, 360/902-8844, www.parks.wa.gov.

## 21 BLIND ISLAND STATE PARK BOAT-IN

🚣 🏊 🚣 🐕 ⛺

### Scenic rating: 9

near Shaw Island

**Map 2.1, page 147**

This island has few trees and is known for its rocky shoreline. It's dangerous and ill-advised to try beaching cruiser-style boats. Only non-motorized boats are permitted, and skilled kayakers will not have difficulty landing unless the water is rough. Blind Island State Park is a designated natural area and is committed to conserving a natural environment in a minimally developed state. This is not a place for large groups to throw big barbecues, but rather a quiet place for campers to enjoy the natural environment.

**Campsites, facilities:** There are four primitive boat-in campsites. Picnic tables and fire rings are provided. Composting toilets are available. There is no drinking water and garbage must be packed out. Boat buoys are available for overnight moorage. Leashed pets are permitted.

**Reservations, fees:** Reservations are not accepted. Sites are $12 per night, buoys are $12 per night. Open year-round, with limited facilities in winter.

**Directions:** The campground is located just west of the Shaw Island ferry landing on little Blind Island in Blind Bay. The nearest boat ramps are at Obstruction Pass on Orcas Island or Odlin County Park on Lopez Island.

**Contact:** San Juan Marine Area, South, 360/378-2044; state park information, 360/902-8844, www.parks.wa.gov.

## 22 TURN ISLAND STATE PARK BOAT-IN

### Scenic rating: 10

near Friday Harbor

Map 2.1, page 147                    BEST (

This spot is gorgeous, and while this is one of about 30 campgrounds in the area that can be reached only by boat, note that Turn Island State Park has no docks, only mooring buoys. This tiny island is just off San Juan Island's eastern side. Quiet, primitive, and beautiful, this spot offers good trails for tromping around and year-round angling for rockfish. There are pretty beaches for shell collectors. The island is within the San Juan Islands National Wildlife Refuge.

**Campsites, facilities:** There are 12 primitive boat-in campsites. Picnic tables and fire rings are provided. Composting toilets are available. There is no drinking water and garbage must be packed out. Boat buoys are available for overnight moorage. Leashed pets are permitted.

**Reservations, fees:** Reservations are not accepted. Sites are $12 per night, buoys are

$12 per night. Open year-round, with limited facilities in winter.

**Directions:** Turn Island is located off the northeast tip of San Juan Island (in the San Juan Channel). It is accessible only by boat.

**Contact:** San Juan Marine Area South, 360/378-2044; state park information, 360/902-8844, www.parks.wa.gov.

## 23 SPENCER SPIT STATE PARK FERRY-IN

### Scenic rating: 9

on Lopez Island

Map 2.1, page 147

Spencer Spit State Park offers one of the few island campgrounds accessible to cars via ferry. It also features walk-in sites for privacy, which require anywhere from a 50-foot to a 200-yard walk to the tent sites. A sand spit extends far into the water and provides a lagoon and good access to prime clamming areas. The park covers 138 acres. Picnicking, beachcombing, and sunbathing are some pleasant activities for campers looking for relaxation.

**Campsites, facilities:** There are 37 sites for tents or self-contained RVs up to 20 feet long (no hookups), seven primitive walk-in sites for tents only, seven hike-in/bike-in sites, three marine trail sites, one Adirondack for up to eight people, and three group sites for up to 50 people each. Picnic tables and fire grills are provided. Restrooms with flush toilets, drinking water, a picnic area, two kitchen shelters, and a dump station are available; 12 mooring buoys are available on the Cascadia Marine Trail. Boat docks and a launch are within two miles, and showers are approximately three miles away. Some facilities are wheelchair accessible. Leashed pets are permitted.

**Reservations, fees:** Reservations are accepted at 888/CAMP-OUT (888/226-7688) or www.goingtocamp.com ($6.50-8.50 reservation fee, $25 for groups). Sites are $17-31 per night, primitive and marine trail sites are $12 per night, the Adirondack is $25-30 per night, $10 per extra vehicle per night, and $12 per night for mooring buoys. Group site fees vary with size of group. Open year-round, with limited winter facilities.

**Directions:** From Seattle on I-5, drive north to Burlington and Highway 20. Turn west on Highway 20 and drive 12 miles to the Highway 20 North spur, following signs to the San Juan Islands Ferry Terminal in Anacortes. Take the ferry to Lopez Island. The park is within four miles of the ferry terminal.

**Contact:** Spencer Spit State Park, 360/468-2251; state park information, 360/902-8844, www.parks.wa.gov; Washington State Ferries, 206/464-6400 or 888/808-7977 (Washington state only).

## 24 JAMES ISLAND STATE PARK BOAT-IN

**Scenic rating: 9**

near Decatur Island

Map 2.1, page 147

Small, hidden James Island provides good opportunities for hiking, fishing, and scuba diving. The 200-acre island is quiet and primitive, with lots of trees and a pretty beach for walking or sunbathing.

**Campsites, facilities:** There are 13 primitive boat-in campsites and two designated sites for non-motorized boaters. Picnic tables and fire rings are provided. Composting and pit toilets are available. There is no drinking water, and garbage must be packed out. Boat floats and four buoys are available for moorage off the east side of the island. A moorage dock on the west side of the island is open April-mid-October. Leashed pets are permitted.

**Reservations, fees:** Reservations are not accepted. Sites are $12 per night, moorage is $0.60 per foot per boat for boats up to 45 feet ($12 minimum), and buoys are $12 per night. Open year-round, with limited facilities in winter.

**Directions:** This island is east of Decatur Island in Rosario Strait and is only accessible by boat. The campground is on the east side of the island.

**Contact:** San Juan Marine Area, South, 360/378-2044; state park information, 360/902-8844, www.parks.wa.gov.

## 25 PELICAN BEACH BOAT-IN

**Scenic rating: 9**

on Cypress Island

Map 2.1, page 147

This forested island campground offers a group shelter, beach access, and hiking trails. It is located in the Cypress Island Natural Resource Conservation Area. The 1.2-mile trail to Eagle Cliff is a must, although it is closed February-mid-July to protect endangered species. Like Cypress Head, this scenic camp is set on the oceanfront in a well-treed area. Pelican Beach has become even more popular than Cypress Head, not only with individual kayakers, but also with commercial operations that work as outfitters who organize trips for small groups of kayakers. The rangers ask that you practice low-impact camping here.

**Campsites, facilities:** There are several primitive boat-in campsites. Pit toilets and a group picnic shelter are available. There is no drinking water, and garbage must be packed out. Six mooring buoys are available nearby. Leashed pets are permitted but are not allowed at the lake or on the Eagle Cliff trails.

**Reservations, fees:** Reservations are not accepted. There is no fee for camping, but a Discover Pass is required. Open year-round.

**Directions:** This camp is set on the east shore of Cypress Island and is accessible only by boat. Cypress Island can be accessed by boat from Anacortes. Cruise west through Guemes Channel to Bellingham Channel (located between Cypress Island and Guemes Island). Turn north in Bellingham Channel and cruise

to the campground on the southeast side of Cypress Island, just north of Cypress Head.
**Contact:** Department of Natural Resources, Northwest Region, 360/856-3500, www.dnr.wa.gov.

## 26 CYPRESS HEAD BOAT-IN
🏕 🏊 🚤 🦮 ⛺

**Scenic rating: 9**

on Cypress Island

Map 2.1, page 147

An alternative to Pelican Beach, this primitive but pretty camp is situated right on Puget Sound in a forested setting of primarily Douglas fir and madrone. This camp is popular and often gets heavy use from kayakers. A trail provides access to Cypress Island Natural Resource Conservation area. The rangers ask that you practice low-impact camping.

**Campsites, facilities:** There are seven primitive boat-in campsites. Picnic tables and fire grills are provided. Vault toilets are available. There is no drinking water, and garbage must be packed out. Four mooring buoys are available nearby. Leashed pets are permitted.

**Reservations, fees:** Reservations are not accepted. There is no fee for camping, but a Discover Pass is required. Open year-round.

**Directions:** This camp is set on the east shore of Cypress Island and is accessible only by boat. Cypress Island can be accessed by boat from Anacortes. Cruise west through Guemes Channel to Bellingham Channel (located between Cypress Island and Guemes Island). Turn north in Bellingham Channel and cruise to the campground on the southeast side of Cypress Island (just north of Deepwater Bay, just south of Pelican Beach Campground).

**Contact:** Department of Natural Resources, Northwest Region, 360/856-3500, www.dnr.wa.gov.

## 27 SADDLEBAG ISLAND STATE PARK BOAT-IN
🏕 🏊 🚤 🚐 🦮 ⛺

**Scenic rating: 9**

near Guemes Island

Map 2.1, page 147

Saddlebag Island State Park is a good cruise from Anacortes. The island is quiet and primitive, with a nice beach near the campground for beachcombing and fine crabbing in the bay. Wildflowers are in bloom April-June. This island receives moderate use.

**Campsites, facilities:** There are five primitive boat-in campsites and one site for non-motorized boaters only. Picnic tables and fire rings are provided. Vault toilets are available. There is no drinking water or mooring buoys, and garbage must be packed out. Leashed pets are permitted.

**Reservations, fees:** Reservations are not accepted. Sites are $12 per night. Open year-round, with limited facilities in winter.

**Directions:** From Seattle on I-5, drive north to Burlington and Highway 20. Turn west on Highway 20 and drive 12 miles to the Highway 20 North spur, following signs to the San Juan Islands Ferry Terminal in Anacortes. Launch your boat and cruise northeast around the southeast tip of Guemes Island. As you approach, Hat Island will be to your right, Huckleberry Island to your left, and Saddlebag Island straight ahead in Padilla Bay. Continue to Saddlebag Island. The camp is accessible only by boat.

**Contact:** Saddlebag Island State Park, 360/757-0227; state park information, 360/902-8844, www.parks.wa.gov.

## 28 PIONEER TRAILS RV RESORT & CAMPGROUND
🏕 🏊 🏖 🏠 🦮 🚐

**Scenic rating: 9**

near Anacortes on Fidalgo Island

Map 2.1, page 147

This site offers resort camping in the beautiful

San Juan Islands. Tall trees, breathtaking views, cascading waterfalls, and country hospitality can all be found here. Side trips include nearby Deception Pass State Park (eight minutes away) and ferries to Victoria (British Columbia), Friday Harbor, Orcas Island, and other nearby islands (it is imperative to arrive early at the ferry terminal). Nearby recreation activities include horseshoes, an 18-hole golf course, relaxing spas, and lake fishing. Those familiar with this park may remember the group of old covered wagons that were here; they're gone now.

**Campsites, facilities:** There are 150 sites with full hookups (30, 50, and 100 amps), including some pull-through sites, for RVs of any length and five cabins. Picnic tables and fire rings are provided. Restrooms with flush toilets and showers, drinking water, a dump station, cable TV, Wi-Fi, a pay phone, and coin laundry are available. A recreation hall, playground, horseshoe pits, and a basketball court are available nearby. Leashed pets are permitted with certain restrictions.

**Reservations, fees:** Reservations are recommended. Sites are $34 per night, $5 per extra vehicle per night, $3 per night per each additional person. A three-night minimum is required on holidays. Some credit cards are accepted. Open year-round.

**Directions:** From Burlington and I-5, take Exit 230 for Highway 20 West. Drive west and cross over the Padilla Bridge onto Fidalgo Island. Watch for the Highway 20 sign and turn left at Mile Post 48. Go up the hill and take the first road on the right (Miller Road). Drive 0.25 mile, and look for the park on the right side of the road.

**Contact:** Pioneer Trails RV Resort & Campground, 360/293-5355 or 888/777-5355, www.pioneertrails.com.

## 29 WASHINGTON PARK

🚶 🚴 🚐 🎣 🛶 ♿ 🚙 ⛰

**Scenic rating: 6**

in Anacortes

**Map 2.1, page 147**

This 220-acre city park is set in the woods on a peninsula at the west end of Fidalgo Island. It features many hiking trails. A 2.2-mile paved loop route for vehicles, hikers, and bicyclists stretches around the perimeter of the park. The Washington State Ferry terminals are located 0.5 mile away, providing access to the San Juan Islands. This is a popular camp, and it's a good idea to arrive early to claim your spot.

**Campsites, facilities:** There are 68 sites, including 46 with partial hookups, for tents or RVs up to 35 feet, a dispersed area for hike-in/bike-in camping, and one group tent site for up to 30 people. Some sites are pull-through. Restrooms with flush toilets and coin showers, drinking water, a playground, recreation field, dump station, a picnic area that can be reserved, and a boat launch are available. Some facilities are wheelchair accessible. Leashed pets are permitted.

**Reservations, fees:** Reservations are accepted online at www.cityofanacortes.org. Sites are $20-25 per night; the group site is $90 per night. Open year-round.

**Directions:** From Burlington and I-5, turn west on Highway 20 and drive to Anacortes and Commercial Avenue. Turn right on Commercial Avenue and drive approximately 0.5 mile to 12th Street. Turn left and drive about three miles (west of the ferry landing the road changes names several times) to Sunset Avenue. Turn left on Sunset Avenue. The park entrance and campground will be on the left.

**Contact:** Washington Park, City of Anacortes, 360/293-1927; Parks and Recreation, 360/293-1918, www.cityofanacortes.org.

## 30 FIDALGO BAY RESORT

### Scenic rating: 4

near Anacortes on Fidalgo Bay

**Map 2.1, page 147**

This 40-acre park is five minutes from Anacortes and right on Fidalgo Bay, providing easy access to boating, fishing, and swimming. More than one mile of beach is available. A golf course is available two miles away. A number of sites are filled with monthly renters. This resort is owned by the Samish Indian Nation.

**Campsites, facilities:** There are 141 sites with full hookups (20, 30, and 50 amps), including many pull-through sites, for RVs of any length. Picnic tables and fire pits are provided at most sites. Restrooms with flush toilets and showers, drinking water, cable TV, Wi-Fi access, a clubhouse, a large fire pit, a small boat launch, a convenience store, video rentals, propane, and a coin laundry are available. Leashed pets are permitted.

**Reservations, fees:** Reservations recommended at 800/727-5478. Sites are $34-62 per night, $2 per person per night for more than two people, $4.50 per night per extra vehicle, $2 per night per pet. Winter rates available. Some credit cards accepted. Open year-round.

**Directions:** From Burlington and Highway 20, turn west on Highway 20 and drive about 14 miles to Fidalgo Bay Road. Turn right on Fidalgo Bay Road and drive one mile to the resort on the right.

**Contact:** Fidalgo Bay Resort, 360/293-5353 or 800/727-5478, www.fidalgobay.com.

## 31 LARRABEE STATE PARK

### Scenic rating: 9

on Samish Bay

**Map 2.1, page 147**         **BEST (**

Larrabee State Park—the first state park established in Washington—sits on Samish Bay in Puget Sound and boasts 8,100 feet of saltwater shoreline. The park's 2,683-acres include two freshwater lakes, coves, and tidelands, as well as 13.7 miles of hiking trails and 11.7 miles of mountain-biking trails. A setting of conifers and thick forests mixes with waterways, streams, and marsh before concluding at a beautiful stretch of coastline, a prime spot for sunsets and wildlife-viewing. Fishing is available on Fragrance Lake and Lost Lake, which are hike-in lakes. Chuckanut Mountain is nearby. A relatively short drive south will take you to Anacortes, where you can catch a ferry to islands in the San Juan chain.

**Campsites, facilities:** There are 51 sites for tents, 26 sites for tents or RVs up to 60 feet long (30 amp full hookups), eight primitive tent sites, and a group site for up to 40 people. Picnic tables and fire grills are provided. Restrooms with flush toilets and coin showers, drinking water, a dump station, a picnic area with electricity and a covered shelter, amphitheater, and firewood are available. Boat-launching facilities are available nearby. Some facilities are wheelchair accessible. Leashed pets are permitted.

**Reservations, fees:** Reservations are accepted at 888/CAMP-OUT (888/226-7688) or www.goingtocamp.com ($6.50-8.50 reservation fee). Tent sites are $17-31 per night, primitive tent sites are $12 per night, sites with hookups are $27-42 per night, $10 per extra vehicle per night, group site is $69.89-279.56 per night. Some credit cards are accepted. Open year-round with limited winter facilities.

**Directions:** From Bellingham on I-5, take Exit 250 to Fairhaven Parkway. Turn right on Fairhaven Parkway. Drive less than a mile to State Route 11/Chuckanut Drive (second stoplight). Turn left (stay left at the next stoplight) and drive six miles to the park entrance on the right.

**Contact:** Larrabee State Park, 360/676-2093; state park information, 360/902-8844, www.parks.wa.gov.

## 32 LIZARD LAKE HIKE-IN

### Scenic rating: 6

near Bellingham

**Map 2.1, page 147**

Lizard Lake is located just 0.2 mile north by trail from Lily Lake, but this hike-in/equestrian camp is even smaller and more isolated. It's set in a pretty, forested area. This is a prime area for hiking, and hikers and horse packers alike use the nearby trails. Fishing is an option at Lily Lake.

**Campsites, facilities:** There are three primitive hike-in sites for tents only. Tent pads and fire grills are provided. There are no toilets or drinking water; practice backcountry sanitation methods. Garbage must be packed out. Leashed pets are permitted.

**Reservations, fees:** Reservations are not accepted. There is no fee for camping, but a Discover Pass is required. Open year-round.

**Directions:** From Bellingham on I-5, drive south to Exit 240 to Samish Lake Road and drive 0.5 mile north to Barrel Springs Road. Turn left and drive one mile to Road B-1000. Turn right and drive 1.5 miles to the Blanchard Hill Trailhead. Hike 3.2 miles, bear left, and continue 0.75 mile (just past Lily Lake) to the campground. A map is advisable and available at www.dnr.wa.gov.

**Contact:** Department of Natural Resources, Northwest Region, 360/856-3500, www.dnr. wa.gov.

## 33 LILY LAKE HIKE-IN

### Scenic rating: 6

near Bellingham

**Map 2.1, page 147**

This tiny, remote hike-in campground is one of those camps that few people ever go to or even know about. Set on little Lily Lake, it's completely secluded and primitive; you'll have to pack in everything you need and pack out everything that's left. Recreation options include fishing and hiking; hikers and horse packers alike use the nearby trails. Nearby Lizard Lake provides an even smaller camp.

**Campsites, facilities:** There are six primitive hike-in sites for tents only. Tent pads and fire rings are provided. There are no toilets or drinking water. Garbage must be packed out. Leashed pets are permitted.

**Reservations, fees:** Reservations are not accepted. There is no fee for camping, but a Discover Pass is required. Open year-round.

**Directions:** From Bellingham on I-5, drive south to Exit 240. On Samish Lake Road drive 0.5 mile north to Barrel Springs Road. Turn left and drive one mile to Road B-1000. Turn right and drive 1.5 miles to the Blanchard Hill Trailhead. Hike 3.2 miles, bear left, and continue 0.5 mile to the campground. A map is advisable and available at www.dnr.wa.gov.

**Contact:** Department of Natural Resources, Northwest Region, 360/856-3500, www.dnr. wa.gov.

## 34 BAY VIEW STATE PARK

### Scenic rating: 10

on Padilla Bay

**Map 2.1, page 147**     **BEST (**

This campground set on Padilla Bay has a large, grassy area for kids, making it a good choice for families. Bordering 11,000 acres of Padilla Bay and the National Estuarine Sanctuary, this 25-acre park boasts 1,285 feet of saltwater shoreline. From the park, you can enjoy views of the San Juan Islands fronting Padilla Bay. On a clear day, you can see the Olympic Mountains to the west and Mount Rainier to the south. Kayakers should note that Padilla Bay becomes a large mud flat during low tides. Windsurfing is becoming popular, but tracking tides and wind is required. The Breazeale Padilla Bay Interpretive Center is located 0.5 mile north of the park. For a nice day trip, take the ferry at Anacortes to Lopez

Island (there are several campgrounds there as well).

**Campsites, facilities:** There are 46 sites for tents or self-contained RVs, 29 sites with full hookups for RVs up to 60 feet long, one group tent site for up to 20-64 people, and four cabins. Picnic tables and fire rings are provided. Restrooms with flush toilets and coin showers, drinking water, firewood, a dump station, and a picnic area with a beach shelter are available. Horseshoes, volleyball, interpretive activities, windsurfing, waterskiing, swimming, and boating are available. A store and coin laundry are eight miles away in Burlington. Some facilities are wheelchair accessible. Leashed pets are permitted.

**Reservations, fees:** Reservations are accepted for individual sites and are required for groups at 888/226-7688 (CAMP-OUT) or www.goingtocamp.com ($6.50-8.50 reservation fee). Sites are $17-42 per night, $10 per extra vehicle per night. Cabins are $69-79 per night with a $15 pet fee. Call for group site fees. Some credit cards are accepted. Open year-round, but some campsites are closed in winter.

**Directions:** From Seattle on I-5, drive north to Burlington and Exit 230 for Highway 20. Turn west on Highway 20 and drive seven miles west (toward Anacortes) to Bay View-Edison Road. Turn right (north) on Bay View-Edison Road and drive four miles to the park on the right.

**Contact:** Bay View State Park, 360/757-0227; state park information, 360/902-8844, www.parks.wa.gov.

## 35 BURLINGTON/ ANACORTES KOA

**Scenic rating: 5**

in Burlington

Map 2.1, page 147

This is a fine KOA campground, complete with all the amenities. The sites are spacious and comfortable. Possible side trips include tours of the Boeing plant in Everett, about 30 miles away, Victoria, Vancouver Island, and the San Juan Islands.

**Campsites, facilities:** There are 120 sites, most with full or partial hookups, for tents or RVs of any length and 11 cabins. Some sites are pull-through. Restrooms with flush toilets and showers, drinking water, a dump station, cable TV, Wi-Fi, a coin laundry, limited groceries, ice, propane gas, firewood, and a barbecue area are available. There is also an indoor heated pool, spa, recreation hall, game room, playground, nine-hole miniature golf, bicycle rentals, horseshoe pits, and a sports field. Leashed pets are permitted.

**Reservations, fees:** Reservations are recommended in the summer at 800/562-9154. Sites are $43-47 per night, plus $2.50-4 per person per night for more than two people. Some credit cards are accepted. Open year-round.

**Directions:** From Burlington and I-5, take Exit 232/Cook Road. Turn right on Cook Road and drive 100 feet to Old Highway 99. Turn left and drive 3.5 miles to the campground on the right.

**Contact:** Burlington/Anacortes KOA, 360/724-5511, www.koa.com.

## 36 DECEPTION PASS STATE PARK

**Scenic rating: 10**

on Whidbey Island

Map 2.1, page 147

This state park is located at beautiful Deception Pass on the west side of Whidbey Island. It features 4,134 acres with almost 15 miles of saltwater shoreline and six miles of freshwater shoreline on three lakes. The landscape ranges from old-growth forest to sand dunes. This diverse habitat has attracted 174 species of birds. An observation deck overlooks the Cranberry Lake wetlands. The park also features spectacular views of shoreline, mountains, and islands, often with dramatic sunsets. At one spot, rugged cliffs drop to the turbulent waters of Deception Pass. Recreation options include fishing at Pass Lake, a freshwater lake within the park. Fly-fishing for trout is a unique bonus for anglers. Note that each lake has different regulations for boating. Scuba diving is also popular. The park provides 38 miles of hiking trails, 1.2 miles of wheelchair-accessible trails, and six miles of biking trails. There are several historic Civilian Conservation Corps buildings throughout the park. One thing to consider: You may occasionally see (and hear) U.S. Navy jets from nearby Whidbey Island Air Station flying near the campground for several hours at a time.

**Campsites, facilities:** There are 167 sites for tents or self-contained RVs up to 50 feet (no hookups), 143 sites with partial hookups (30 amps) for RVs up to 50 feet long, five hiker/biker tent sites, and three group sites for up to 50 people each. Some sites are pull-through. Picnic tables and fire rings are provided. Restrooms with flush toilets and coin showers, drinking water, and a dump station are available. A concession stand, park store, firewood, horseshoe pit, an amphitheater, interpretive activities, a sheltered picnic area with electricity and a kitchen, a boat launch, boat rentals, and mooring buoys are available nearby. Some facilities are wheelchair accessible. Leashed pets are permitted.

**Reservations, fees:** Reservations are accepted at 888/CAMP-OUT (888/226-7688) or www.parks.wa.gov/reservations ($6.50-8.50 reservation fee). Sites without hookups are $23 per night, sites with hookups are $31-35 per night, hiker/biker sites are $12 per night, $10 per extra vehicle per night, and the group site is $140.59 per night. Some credit cards are accepted. Open year-round, with limited winter services.

**Directions:** From Seattle on I-5, drive north to Burlington and Exit 230/Highway 20. Take that exit and drive west on Highway 20 for 12 miles to Highway 20 South. Turn south on Highway 20 South and drive six miles (across the bridge at Deception Pass) and continue to the park entrance (three miles south of the bridge) on the right.

**Contact:** Deception Pass State Park, 360/675-2417; state park information, 360/902-8844, www.parks.wa.gov.

## 37 HOPE ISLAND STATE PARK BOAT-IN

🏕️ 🚣 ⛰️

**Scenic rating: 8**

in Skagit Bay

Map 2.1, page 147

Here's your chance to have an island all to yourself. This camp on the north side of Hope Island is lightly used and is a primitive alternative to the more developed drive-to sites nearby. Located between Squaxin Island and Steamboat Island, it features a 106-acre county park in Puget Sound and a landscape of old-growth forests and saltwater marshes. The park has a 1.5-mile beach, the top spot. The catch? You must have a boat to reach it. Solitude is your reward. A little-known option, a single campsite for kayakers is on the northeast tip of Skagit Island. It's largely a secret, and with no mooring buoy, likely to remain that way. Note that there are two Hope Islands in this region; this island was named by Commander Charles Wilkes, who was charting Puget Sound.

**Campsites, facilities:** There are five primitive boat-in campsites. Fire rings are provided. Vault toilets and five mooring buoys are available. There is no drinking water, and garbage must be packed out.

**Reservations, fees:** Reservations are not accepted. Sites are $12 per night, buoys are $12 per night. Open year-round, with limited facilities in winter.

**Directions:** Hope Island is in Skagit Bay, directly between the Swinomish Reservation on Fidalgo Island to the east and Whidbey Island to the west. After launching from the harbor at Cornet on Whidbey Island, cruise east out of Cornet Bay and turn south (Skagit Island will be on your left). Continue one mile to Hope Island. The boating access is on the north side of the island. It's accessible only by private boat.

**Contact:** Hope Island (Mason) State Park, 360/426-9226; state park information (and mooring permit), 360/902-8844, www.parks. wa.gov.

## 38 RIVERBEND RV PARK

**Scenic rating: 5**

on the Skagit River

**Map 2.1, page 147**

Riverbend RV Park is a pleasant layover spot for I-5 travelers. While not particularly scenic, it is clean and spacious. Access to the Skagit River here is a high point, with fishing for salmon, trout, and Dolly Varden in season; check regulations. Nearby recreational options include a casino and an 18-hole golf course. Note that about half of the sites are filled with monthly renters.

**Campsites, facilities:** There are 90 sites with full hookups (30 and 50 amps) for RVs of any length and 25 sites for tents. Most sites are pull-through. Picnic tables are provided at RV sites and fire pits are at some tent sites. Restrooms with flush toilets and coin showers, drinking water, a dump station, coin laundry, a playground, and horseshoe pits are available. A store, café, and ice are located within 0.25 mile. Leashed pets are permitted with certain restrictions.

**Reservations, fees:** Reservations are accepted. RV sites are $30 per night, tent sites are $16 per night. Some credit cards are accepted. Open year-round.

**Directions:** From Seattle on I-5, drive north to Mount Vernon and the College Way exit. Take the College Way exit and drive one block west to Freeway Drive. Turn right (north) and drive 0.25 mile to Stewart Road. Turn left and drive a short distance to the park entrance on the right.

**Contact:** Riverbend RV Park, 360/428-4044.

## 39 STAYSAIL RV

**Scenic rating: 4**

in Oak Harbor on Whidbey Island

**Map 2.1, page 147**

This popular city park fills quickly on summer weekends. With graveled sites, it is geared toward RVers but is also suitable for tent campers. Fishing, swimming, boating, and sunbathing are all options in the vicinity. Several miles of paved trails run along the waterfront. A full-service marina is nearby. Within a few miles are an 18-hole golf course and tennis courts. Fort Ebey and Fort Casey State Parks are both a short drive away and make excellent side trips.

**Campsites, facilities:** There are 56 sites with full hookups for RVs of any length and 30 sites for tents. Picnic tables are provided. No campfires are allowed. Restrooms with flush toilets and coin showers, drinking water, and a dump station are available. A playground, picnic shelter, ballfields, volleyball, basketball, and tennis courts, and horseshoe pits are also available. Propane gas, a store, café, coin laundry, and ice are available within one mile. Boat-launching facilities, swimming, a lagoon, wading pools, a day-use area, and walking trails are at Oak Harbor. Some facilities are wheelchair accessible. Leashed pets are permitted.

**Reservations, fees:** Reservations are not accepted. Sites are $12-20 per night. Open year-round.

**Directions:** From Burlington and I-5, turn west on Highway 20 and drive 28 miles to the intersection of Highway 20 and Pioneer Way in the town of Oak Harbor on Whidbey Island. Drive straight through the intersection onto Beeksma Drive and continue about one block to the park on the left.

**Contact:** Staysail RV Park, City of Oak Harbor, 360/279-4530, www.oakharbor.org.

## 40 FORT EBEY STATE PARK

🏃 🚴 🏊 🛶 🐕 ♿ 🚐 ⛺

### Scenic rating: 9

on Whidbey Island

**Map 2.1, page 147**

This park is situated on the west side of Whidbey Island at Point Partridge. It covers 645 acres and has access to a rocky beach that is good for exploring. There are also 28 miles of trails for hiking and biking. Fort Ebey is the site of a historic World War II bunker, where concrete platforms mark the locations of the historic gun batteries. Other options here include fishing and wildlife viewing. There is limited fishing available for smallmouth bass at Lake Pondilla, which is only about 100 yards away from the campground and a good place to see bald eagles. The saltwater shore access provides a good spot for surfing and paragliding.

**Campsites, facilities:** There are 50 sites, including 10 sites with electricity, for tents or self-contained RVs up to 70 feet long, one boat-in site, and four hike-in/bike-in sites. Picnic tables and fire grills are provided. Restrooms with flush toilets and coin showers, drinking water, firewood, amphitheater, and picnic area are available. Some facilities are wheelchair accessible. Leashed pets are permitted.

**Reservations, fees:** Reservations are accepted at 888/CAMP-OUT (888/226-7688) or www.goingtocamp.com ($6.50-8.50 reservation fee). Sites are $26-39 per night, hike-in/bike-in sites are $12 per night, $10 per extra vehicle per night. Some credit cards are accepted. Open year-round.

**Directions:** From Burlington and I-5, turn west on Highway 20 and drive 23 miles (Whidbey Island) to Libbey Road (eight miles past Oak Harbor). Turn right and drive 1.5 miles to Hill Valley Drive. Turn left and enter the park.

**Contact:** Fort Ebey State Park, 360/678-4636; state park information, 360/902-8844, www.parks.wa.gov.

## 41 FORT CASEY STATE PARK

🏃 🏊 🛶 🚐 🐕 ♿ 🚐 ⛺

### Scenic rating: 10

on Whidbey Island

**Map 2.1, page 147**

Fort Casey State Park offers more than 10,000 feet of shoreline on Puget Sound at Admiralty Inlet; fishing is often good in this area, in season. The park's 467 acres include a lighthouse, Keystone Spit, and 1.8 miles of hiking trails. As part of Ebey's Landing National Historic Reserve, there is a coast artillery post featuring two historic guns on display. The lighthouse and interpretive center are open seasonally. Remote-control glider flying is allowed in a designated area, and there is a parade field perfect for kite-flying. The underwater park, another highlight, attracts divers. You can also take a ferry from here to Port Townsend on the Olympic Peninsula.

**Campsites, facilities:** There are 21 sites for tents and 14 sites with partial hookups for tents or self-contained RVs up to 40 feet long. Picnic tables and fire grills are provided. Restrooms with flush toilets and coin showers, drinking water, a seasonal interpretive center, a picnic area, firewood, and an amphitheater are available. Boat-launching facilities are located in the park. Some facilities are wheelchair accessible. Leashed pets are permitted.

**Reservations, fees:** Reservations are not accepted. Sites are $17-39 per night, $10 per extra vehicle per night. Open year-round.

**Directions:** From Burlington and I-5, turn west on Highway 20 and drive 35 miles to Coupeville. Continue south on Highway 20 (adjacent to Whidbey Island Naval Air Station) and then turn right (still Highway 20, passing Crockett Lake and the Camp Casey barracks) to the park entrance.

**Contact:** Fort Casey State Park, 360/678-4519; state park information, 360/902-8844, www.parks.wa.gov.

## 42 CAMANO ISLAND STATE PARK

🚶 🚲 🏊 ⛵ 🎣 🏕 🐎 ♿ 🚐 ⛺

**Scenic rating: 10**

on Camano Island

**Map 2.1, page 147**          **BEST (**

This park features panoramic views of Puget Sound, the Olympic Mountains, and Mount Rainier. Set on the southwest point of Camano Island, near Lowell Point and Elger Bay along the Saratoga Passage, this wooded camp offers quiet and private campsites. The park covers 134 acres and features 6,700 feet of rocky shoreline and beach, three miles of hiking trails, and just one mile of bike trails. Good inshore angling for rockfish is available year-round, and salmon fishing is also good in season. A diving area with kelp is available. There is also a self-guided nature trail.

**Campsites, facilities:** There are 88 sites for tents or self-contained RVs up to 40 feet long, two hiker/biker sites, one group site for up to 100 people, and five cabins. Picnic tables and fire grills are provided. Restrooms with flush toilets and coin showers, drinking water, a dump station, firewood, a playground, a sheltered picnic area with a kitchen, summer interpretive programs, an amphitheater, and a large grassy play area in the day-use area are available. Boat-launching facilities are located in the park. An 18-hole golf course is nearby. Some facilities are wheelchair accessible. Leashed pets are permitted.

**Reservations, fees:** Reservations are not accepted for individual sites, but are required for the cabins and the group site at 360/387-1550. Sites are $20-35 per night, $10 per extra vehicle per night. Cabins are $65.31-78.60 per night. The group site is $70.02 per night for 1-25 people, $140.04 per night for 26-50 people, $210.05 per night for 51-75 people, and $280.07 per night for 76-100 people. Open year-round.

**Directions:** From Seattle on I-5, drive north (17 miles north of Everett) to Exit 212. Take Exit 212 to Highway 532. Drive west on Highway 532 to Stanwood and continue three miles (to Camano Island) to a fork. Bear left at the fork and continue south for six miles on East Camano Drive, bearing to the right where the road becomes Elger Bay Road, to Mountain View Road. Turn right and drive two miles (climbs a steep hill) and continue to Lowell Point Road. Turn left and continue to the park entrance road. (The park is 14 miles southwest of Stanwood).

**Contact:** Camano Island State Park, 360/387-3031; state park information, 360/902-8844, www.parks.wa.gov.

## 43 KAYAK POINT COUNTY PARK

🚶 ⛵ 🎣 🚤 🏕 🐎 ♿ 🚐 ⛺

**Scenic rating: 5**

near Tulalip Indian Reservation on Puget Sound

**Map 2.1, page 147**

This camp usually fills on summer weekends. Set on the shore of Puget Sound, this large, wooded county park covers 428 acres on Port Susan. It provides good windsurfing and whale-watching as well as hiking; there's an 18-hole golf course nearby. Good for crabbing and fishing, a pier is also available.

**Campsites, facilities:** There are 32 sites with partial hookups, including some pull-through sites, for tents or RVs up to 32 feet and 10 yurts with heat and electricity for up to five people. Picnic tables and fire rings are provided. Restrooms with flush toilets and showers, drinking water, firewood, a picnic area with covered shelter, and a 300-foot fishing pier are available. Launching facilities are located in the park. Some facilities are wheelchair accessible. Leashed pets are permitted.

**Reservations, fees:** Reservations are accepted at 425/388-6600 or www.reserveamerica.com ($2 reservation fee). Sites are $28-32 per night, $10 per each additional vehicle per night, and yurts are $45-75 per night. Some credit cards are accepted. Open year-round.

**Directions:** From Everett and I-5, drive 5

miles north to Exit 199 (Tulalip) at Marysville. Take Exit 199, bear left on Tulalip Road, and drive west for 13 miles (road name changes to Marine Drive) through the Tulalip Indian Reservation to the park entrance road on the left (marked for Kayak Point).

**Contact:** Kayak Point County Park, Snohomish County, 425/388-6600 or 360/652-7992, www.reserveamerica.com.

## 44 WENBERG COUNTY PARK

### Scenic rating: 8

on Lake Goodwin

Map 2.1, page 147

Wenberg County Park is set along the east shore of Lake Goodwin, where the trout fishing can be great. The park covers 46 acres with 1,140 feet of shoreline frontage on the lake. Powerboats are allowed, and a seasonal concession stand provides food. Hiking is limited to a 0.5-mile trail. This is a popular weekend spot for Seattle-area residents.

Management of Wenberg Park was transferred from the state to Snohomish County, and with that came several significant changes. The reservation protocol is different, of course, and no alcohol is permitted.

**Campsites, facilities:** There are 21 sites for tents and 50 sites with partial hookups (30 amps) for RVs up to 40 feet long. Some sites are pull-through. Picnic tables and fire grills are provided. Restrooms with flush toilets and coin showers, drinking water, a dump station, two sheltered picnic areas, concession stand, firewood, swimming beach with bathhouse, and a playground are available. Boat-launching facilities and docks are located on Lake Goodwin. Some facilities are wheelchair accessible. Leashed pets are permitted.

**Reservations, fees:** Reservations are accepted at www.reserveamerica.com. Sites are $21-30 per night, $10 per extra vehicle per night. Some credit cards are accepted. Open year-round.

**Directions:** From Everett on I-5, drive north to Exit 206. Take Exit 206/Smokey Point, turn

west, and drive 2.4 miles to Highway 531. Bear right on Highway 531 and drive 2.7 miles to East Lake Goodwin Road. Turn left and drive 1.6 miles to the park entrance on the right.

**Contact:** Wenberg County Park, 360/652-7417, www1.co.snohomish.wa.us.

## 45 CEDAR GROVE SHORES RV PARK

### Scenic rating: 5

on Lake Goodwin

Map 2.1, page 147

This wooded resort is set on the shore of Lake Goodwin near Wenberg County Park. The camp is a busy place in summer, with highlights including trout fishing, waterskiing, and swimming. A security gate is closed at night. Tent campers should try Lake Goodwin Resort. An 18-hole golf course is nearby.

**Campsites, facilities:** There are 48 sites with full hookups (30 and 50 amps) for RVs of any length. Some sites are pull-through. Restrooms with flush toilets and coin showers, drinking water, coin laundry, a dump station, modem access, propane gas, ice, a clubhouse, a recreation room, horseshoe pits, and firewood are available. A store and café are located within one mile. Boat docks and launching facilities are nearby on Lake Goodwin. Some facilities are wheelchair accessible. Leashed pets are permitted.

**Reservations, fees:** Reservations are accepted. Sites are $27-42 per night, $5 per adult per night for more than two people. Some credit cards are accepted. Open year-round.

**Directions:** From Everett on I-5, drive north for 10 miles to Exit 206. Take Exit 206/Smokey Point and drive west for 2.2 miles to Lakewood Road. Turn right and drive 3.2 miles to Westlake Goodwin Road. Turn left (the park is marked) and drive 0.75 mile to the resort on the left.

**Contact:** Cedar Grove Shores RV Park, 360/652-7083 or 866/342-4981, www.cg-srvpark.com.

## 46 LAKE GOODWIN RESORT

### Scenic rating: 5

on Lake Goodwin

Map 2.1, page 147

This private campground is set on Lake Goodwin, which is known for good trout fishing. Motorboats are permitted on the lake, and an 18-hole golf course is located nearby. Other activities include swimming in the lake, horseshoe pits, shuffleboard, and a recreation field.

**Campsites, facilities:** There are 85 sites with full or partial hookups (30 and 50 amps) for RVs of any length, 11 sites for tents, and four cabins. Some sites are pull-through. Picnic tables and fire grills are provided. Restrooms with flush toilets and coin showers, drinking water, propane gas, a convenience store with recreation equipment, coin laundry, ice, Wi-Fi, a playground, and firewood are available. Boat moorage and a fishing pier are located nearby on Lake Goodwin.

**Reservations, fees:** Reservations are accepted at 800/242-8169. RV sites are $40-55 per night, tent sites are $26 per night. Some credit cards are accepted. Open year-round.

**Directions:** From Everett on I-5, drive north for 10 miles to Exit 206. Take Exit 206/Smokey Point, turn west, and drive two miles to Highway 531/Lakewood Road. Bear right on Highway 531 and drive 3.5 miles to the resort on the left.

**Contact:** Lake Goodwin Resort, 360/652-8169 or 800/242-8169, www.lakegoodwin-resort.com.

## 47 RIVER MEADOWS COUNTY PARK WALK-IN

### Scenic rating: 6

on the Stillaguamish River

Map 2.1, page 147

This Snohomish County park has 150 acres of open meadows and forests along the banks of the Stillaguamish River. The campground gets light to average use. This area of the river is popular for non-motorized boating such as canoeing, kayaking, and inner tubing. Hiking trails meander through the park, and other activities include cycling, bird-watching, and fishing for steelhead in season. The Festival of the River is held in August. Native Americans once occupied the property, and ancient Olcott artifacts have been found here.

**Campsites, facilities:** There are 12 walk-in sites for tents only and six yurts. Picnic tables and fire pits are provided at the tent sites. Flush toilets, drinking water, reservable picnic shelters, and a swimming beach are available. Some facilities are wheelchair accessible. Leashed pets are permitted.

**Reservations, fees:** Reservations are accepted at www.reserveamerica.com ($2 reservation fee). Sites are $22 per night, yurts are $45-80 per night. Some credit cards are accepted. Open year-round.

**Directions:** From Seattle, drive north on I-5 to Exit 203 and the junction with Highway 530. Turn east on Highway 530 and drive approximately 3.5 miles to the town of Arlington and Highway 9. Turn left (north) and drive a short distance to Highway 530. Turn right (east) on Highway 530 and drive approximately one mile to Arlington Heights Road. Turn right (south) and drive two miles to Jordan Road. Bear right and drive approximately three miles to the park entrance on the right.

**Contact:** River Meadows County Park, 360/435-3441; Snohomish County Parks, 425/388-6600, www1.co.snohomish.wa.us; www.reserveamerica.com.

## 48 SOUTH WHIDBEY STATE PARK

### Scenic rating: 10

on Whidbey Island

Map 2.1, page 147

This park is located on the southwest end of

Whidbey Island. It covers 347 acres and provides opportunities for hiking, picnicking, and beachcombing along a sandy beach. There are spectacular views of Puget Sound and the Olympic Mountains. The park features old-growth forest, tidelands for clamming and crabbing (check current regulations), and campsites set in the seclusion of lush forest undergrowth. The park has 4,500 feet of saltwater shoreline on Admiralty Inlet and 3.5 miles of hiking trails.

**Campsites, facilities:** There are 46 sites for tents or RVs up to 45 feet (no hookups), eight sites with partial hookups (30 amps) for tents or RVs up to 45 feet long, three hike-in/bike-in sites, and one group site for tents and RVs up to 28 feet long that can accommodate up to 60 people. Picnic tables and fire grills are provided. Restrooms with flush toilets and coin showers, drinking water, a dump station, convenience store, a picnic area with a log kitchen shelter, an amphitheater, interpretive activities, a seasonal Junior Ranger program, and firewood are available. Some facilities are wheelchair accessible. Leashed pets are permitted.

**Reservations, fees:** Reservations are accepted at 888/CAMP-OUT (888/226-7688) or www.goingtocamp.com ($6.50-8.50 reservation fee). Sites are $23-35 per night, hike-in/bike-in sites are $12 per night, $10 per extra vehicle per night, and the group site is $70.02-210.05 per night. Some credit cards are accepted. Open February-November.

**Directions:** From Seattle on I-5, drive north to Burlington and the Highway 20 exit. Take Highway 20 west and drive 28 miles (past Coupeville on Whidbey Island) until it becomes Highway 525. Continue south on Highway 525 to Smugglers Cove Road (the park access road, well marked). Turn right and drive six miles to the park entrance. The park can also be reached easily with a ferry ride from Mukilteo (located southwest of Everett) to Clinton (this also makes a great bike trip to the state park).

**Contact:** South Whidbey State Park, 360/331-4559; state park information, 360/902-8844, www.parks.wa.gov.

## 49 LAKESIDE RV PARK

**Scenic rating: 6**

in Everett

**Map 2.2, page 148**

With 75-100 of the 150 RV spaces dedicated to permanent rentals, this camp can be a crapshoot for vacationers in summer; the remaining spaces get filled nightly with vacationers all summer. The park is landscaped with annuals, roses, other perennials, and shrubs, which provide privacy and gardens for each site. There's a pond stocked with trout year-round, providing fishing for a fee.

**Campsites, facilities:** There are 150 sites, some pull-through, with full hookups (20, 30, and 50 amps) for RVs of any length and nine sites for tents. Restrooms with flush toilets and showers, drinking water, cable TV, coin laundry, propane gas, a playground, off-leash dog area, horseshoe pits, modem access, and pay phones are available. Some facilities are wheelchair accessible. Leashed pets are permitted.

**Reservations, fees:** Reservations are recommended at 800/468-7275. Tent sites are $13.83-15.37 per night, and RV sites are $34.73-38.59 per night. Some credit cards are accepted. Open year-round.

**Directions:** From Everett on I-5, drive north to Exit 186. Take Exit 186 and turn west on 128th Street. Drive about two miles to Old Highway 99. Turn left and drive 0.25 mile to the park on the left.

**Contact:** Lakeside RV Park, 425/347-2970 or 800/468-7275.

## 50 LAKE PLEASANT RV PARK

**Scenic rating: 6**

on Lake Pleasant

**Map 2.2, page 148**

A large, developed camp geared primarily toward RVers, this park is set on Lake Pleasant.

The setting is pretty, with lakeside sites and plenty of trees. Just off the highway, it's a popular camp, so expect lots of company, especially in summer. This is a good spot for a little trout fishing. The lake is not suitable for swimming. Note that half of the 196 sites are monthly rentals. All sites are paved.

**Campsites, facilities:** There are 196 sites with full hookups (30 and 50 amps) for RVs up to 45 feet long; half of these sites are available for overnight use. Some sites are pull-through. Picnic tables are provided. No campfires are allowed. Restrooms with flush toilets and showers, drinking water, cable TV, modem and Wi-Fi access, a dump station, coin laundry, a playground, and propane gas are available. Some facilities are wheelchair accessible. Leashed pets are permitted with certain restrictions.

**Reservations, fees:** Reservations are recommended. Sites are $44 per night. Some credit cards are accepted. Open year-round.

**Directions:** From the junction of I-5 and I-405 (just south of Seattle), take I-405 and drive to Exit 26. Take that exit to the Bothell/Everett Highway over the freeway and drive south for about one mile; look for the park on the left side.

**Contact:** Lake Pleasant RV Park, 425/487-1785 or 800/742-0386.

## 51 TRAILER INNS RV PARK/BELLEVUE

### Scenic rating: 5

near Lake Sammamish State Park

**Map 2.2, page 148**

This park features all the amenities for RV travelers. Lake Sammamish State Park is about two miles away. Nearby recreation options include an 18-hole golf course, hiking trails, marked bike trails, and tennis courts.

**Campsites, facilities:** There are 103 sites with full hookups (30 and 50 amps) for RVs up to 45 feet long. Some sites are pull-through and

about half of the sites are permanently rented. Picnic tables are provided. Restrooms with flush toilets and showers, drinking water, propane gas, cable TV, modem and Wi-Fi access, a recreation hall, an indoor swimming pool, spa, sauna, a coin laundry, ice, picnic area, and a playground are available. A store and a cafe are available within one mile. Leashed pets are permitted.

**Reservations, fees:** Reservations are accepted at 800/659-4684. Sites are $22-48 per night, $5 per person per night for more than two people. Weekly rates available. Some credit cards accepted. Open year-round.

**Directions:** At the junction of I-405 and I-90 south of Seattle, turn east on I-90 and drive 1.5 miles to Exit 11A. Take Exit 11A (a two-avenue exit) and stay in the right lane for 150th Avenue SE. After the lanes split, stay in the left lane and drive to the intersection of 150th Avenue SE and 37th. Continue straight through the light and look for the park entrance at the fifth driveway on the right (about one mile from I-90).

**Contact:** Trailer Inns RV Park and Recreation Center, 425/747-9181 or 800/659-4684, www.trailerinnsrv.com.

## 52 VASA PARK RESORT

### Scenic rating: 5

on Lake Sammamish

**Map 2.2, page 148**

I was giving a seminar in Bellevue one evening when a distraught-looking couple walked in and pleaded, "Where can we camp tonight?" I answered, "Just look in the book," and they ended up staying at this camp. It was the easiest sale I ever made. This is the most rustic of the parks in the immediate Seattle area. The resort is on the western shore of Lake Sammamish, and the state park is at the south end of the lake. Lake activities include fishing for smallmouth bass, waterskiing, and personal watercraft riding. There is a two-week maximum stay during the summer. An 18-hole golf course, hiking trails, and marked bike trails are close by. The park is within easy driving distance of Seattle.

**Campsites, facilities:** There are 16 sites for tents or RVs of any length (partial hookups) and six sites with full hookups for RVs of any length. Picnic tables are provided. Restrooms with flush toilets and coin showers, drinking water, a dump station, coin laundry, a playground, and a boat-launching facility are available. Propane gas, firewood, a store, and a café are located within one mile. Leashed pets are permitted.

**Reservations, fees:** Reservations are accepted. Sites are $28-35 per night, $2-4 per adult per night for more than two people, $1.50 per child. Some credit cards are accepted. Open mid-May-mid-October.

**Directions:** From Bellevue, drive east on I-90 to Exit 13. Take Exit 13 to West Lake Sammamish Parkway SE and drive north for one mile; the resort is on the right. Note: Larger rigs should pull into the parking lot on the left.

**Contact:** Vasa Park Resort, 425/746-3260, www.vasaparkresort.com.

## 53 ISSAQUAH VILLAGE RV PARK
🏍 🐕 ♿ 🚐

**Scenic rating: 7**

in Issaquah

**Map 2.2, page 148**

Although Issaquah Village RV Park doesn't allow tents, it's set in a beautiful environment ringed by the Cascade Mountains, making it a scenic choice in the area. Lake Sammamish State Park is just a few miles north. Most of the sites are asphalt, and 20 percent are long-term rentals.

**Campsites, facilities:** There are 56 sites, including two pull-through sites, with full hookups (30 and 50 amps) for RVs of any length. Picnic tables are provided. Restrooms with flush toilets and showers, drinking water, cable TV, Wi-Fi, a dump station, pay phone, coin laundry, picnic areas, playground, and propane gas are available. Some facilities are wheelchair accessible. Leashed pets are permitted.

**Reservations, fees:** Reservations are recommended. Sites are $44-49.50 per night. Some credit cards are accepted. Open year-round.

**Directions:** From Seattle on I-405 (preferred) or I-5, drive to the junction of I-90. Take I-90 east and drive 17 miles to Exit 17 (Front Street). Drive under the freeway and turn right at 229th Avenue SE. Turn right on SE 66th Street (about 50 feet from the first right turn). Proceed on 66th, as it turns into 1st Avenue and brings you to the park entrance.

**Contact:** Issaquah Village RV Park, 425/392-9233 or 800/258-9233, www.ivrvpark.com.

## 54 BLUE SKY RV PARK
🏍 🛶 🐕 ♿ 🚐

**Scenic rating: 5**

near Lake Sammamish State Park in Issaquah

**Map 2.2, page 148**

Blue Sky RV Park is situated in an urban setting just outside of Seattle. It provides a good off-the-beaten-path alternative to the more crowded metro area, yet it is still only a short drive from the main attractions in the city. Nearby Lake Sammamish State Park provides more rustic recreation opportunities, including hiking and fishing. All sites are paved and level, and about half of the sites are filled with monthly renters.

**Campsites, facilities:** There are 51 sites with full hookups for RVs of any length. Some sites are pull-through. Picnic tables are provided at some sites. Restrooms with flush toilets and showers, drinking water, cable TV, coin laundry, and a covered picnic pavilion with barbecue are available. Some facilities are wheelchair accessible. Leashed pets are permitted.

**Reservations, fees:** Reservations are accepted. Sites are $40 per night, $5 per person per night for more than two people. Open year-round.

**Directions:** From I-5 in Seattle, drive east on I-90 for 22 miles to Exit 22 (Preston/Fall City exit). Turn right at the stop sign, then turn left onto 302nd Avenue SE. Proceed 0.5 mile to the campground entrance at the end of the road.
**Contact:** Blue Sky RV Park, 9002 302nd Ave. SE, Issaquah, 425/222-7910, www.bluesky-preston.com.

## 55 SEATTLE/TACOMA KOA

**Scenic rating: 5**

in Kent on the Green River

**Map 2.2, page 148**

This is a popular urban campground, not far from the highway yet in a pleasant setting. The sites are spacious, and many are pull-throughs that accommodate large RVs. A public golf course is located nearby. During the summer, take a tour of Seattle from the campground. The tour highlights include the Space Needle, Pike Place Market, Pioneer Square, Woodland Park Zoo, Seattle Aquarium, Boeing Museum of Flight, Safeco Field, and Puget Sound.

**Campsites, facilities:** There are 147 sites with full or partial hookups (30 and 50 amps) for RVs up to 55 feet long and 14 sites for tents. Restrooms with flush toilets and showers, drinking water, a dump station, coin laundry, Wi-Fi, limited groceries, firewood, propane gas, ice, RV supplies, free movies, and a seasonal pancake breakfast are available. A large playground, a seasonal heated swimming pool, three-wheel fun-cycle rentals, and a recreation room are also available. Cable TV is provided at some sites. Some facilities are wheelchair accessible. Leashed pets are permitted with certain restrictions.

**Reservations, fees:** Reservations are recommended at 800/562-1892. Sites are $31.95-52.95 per night, $4-5 per person per night for more than two people, $1.50 per pet per night. Some credit cards are accepted. Open year-round.

**Directions:** From Seattle, drive south on I-5 for 10 miles to Exit 152 for 188th Street/Orillia Road. Drive east on Orillia Road for three miles (the road becomes 212th Street) to the campground on the right.
**Contact:** Seattle/Tacoma KOA, 253/872-8652, www.koa.com.

## 56 DASH POINT STATE PARK

**Scenic rating: 8**

near Federal Way

**Map 2.2, page 148**

This urban state park set on Puget Sound features unobstructed water views. The park covers 388 acres, with 3,300 feet of saltwater shoreline and 12 miles of trails for hiking and biking. Fishing, windsurfing, swimming, boating, and mountain biking are all popular. Tacoma offers a variety of activities and attractions, including the Tacoma Art Museum (with a children's gallery); the Washington State Historical Society Museum; the Seymour Botanical Conservatory at Wrights Park; Point Defiance Park, Zoo, and Aquarium; the Western Washington Forest Industries Museum; and the Fort Lewis Military Museum.

**Campsites, facilities:** There are 114 tent sites, 27 sites with partial hookups for RVs up to 40 feet long, and a group site for up to 80 people. Picnic tables and fire grills are provided. Restrooms with flush toilets and coin showers, drinking water, an amphitheater, two sheltered picnic areas, and firewood are available. Some facilities are wheelchair accessible. Leashed pets are permitted.

**Reservations, fees:** Reservations are accepted for individual sites and required for the group site at 888/CAMP-OUT (888/226-7688) or www.goingtocamp.com ($6.50-8.50 reservation fee). Sites are $20-39 per night, $10 per extra vehicle per night; group site fees vary by occupancy (20-person minimum). Open year-round.

**Directions:** On I-5 in Tacoma, drive to Exit 143/320th Street. Take that exit and turn west on 320th Street and drive four miles to 47th Street (a T intersection). Turn right on 47th Street and drive to Highway 509 (another T intersection). Turn left on Highway 509/Dash Point Road and drive one mile to the park. Note: The camping area is on the south side of the road; the day-use area is on the north side of the road.

**Contact:** Dash Point State Park, 253/661-4955; state park information, 360/902-8844, www.parks.wa.gov.

## 57 GAME FARM WILDERNESS PARK CAMP
🏃 🛶 🎣 ♿ � 🏕

### Scenic rating: 6
on the Stuck River in Auburn

**Map 2.2, page 148**

The Game Farm Wilderness Park is just minutes from downtown Auburn and centrally located to Mount Rainier, Seattle, and the Cascade Mountains. The campground is located along the scenic Stuck River and is adjacent to an 18-hole disc golf course.

**Campsites, facilities:** There are 18 sites with partial hookups for tents or RVs of any length, with a maximum of eight people per site. Picnic tables and fire grills are provided. Restrooms with flush toilets, drinking water (available March-November), a picnic shelter, and a dump station are available. Some facilities are wheelchair accessible. Leashed pets are permitted.

**Reservations, fees:** Reservations are accepted at 253/931-3043. Sites are $25 per night, with a discount for Auburn residents. Some credit cards are accepted. Open April-mid-October, with a one-week maximum stay limit.

**Directions:** On I-5 (north of Tacoma), drive to Exit 142 and Highway 18. Turn east on Highway 18 and drive to the Auburn/Enumclaw exit. Take that exit and drive to the light at Auburn Way. Turn left on Auburn Way South and drive one mile to Howard Road. Exit to the right on Howard Road and drive 0.2 mile

to the stop sign at R Street. Turn right on R Street and drive 1.5 miles to Stuck River Drive SE (just over the river). Turn left and drive 0.25 mile upriver to the park on the left at 2401 Stuck River Drive.

**Contact:** City of Auburn Parks and Recreation Department, 253/931-3043, www.auburnwa.gov.

## 58 MAJESTIC MOBILE MANOR RV PARK
🏃 🚲 🏊 🛶 � 🦌 🚙

### Scenic rating: 7
on the Puyallup River near Tacoma

**Map 2.2, page 148**

This clean, pretty park along the Puyallup River and with views of Mount Rainier caters to RVers. (Note that at least half of the sites are filled with monthly renters.) Recreation options within 10 miles include an 18-hole golf course, a full-service marina, and tennis courts. Tacoma offers a variety of activities and attractions, including the Tacoma Art Museum (with a children's gallery); the Washington State Historical Society Museum; the Seymour Botanical Conservatory at Wrights Park; Point Defiance Park, Zoo, and Aquarium; the Western Washington Forest Industries Museum; and the Fort Lewis Military Museum.

**Campsites, facilities:** There are 88 sites with full hookups for RVs up to 75 feet. Restrooms with flush toilets and showers, drinking water, cable TV, Wi-Fi access, propane gas, a dump station, a recreation hall, a convenience store, coin laundry, ice, and a seasonal heated swimming pool are available. Leashed pets are permitted.

**Reservations, fees:** Reservations are accepted. Sites $34 per night, $2 per person per night for more than two people. Open year-round.

**Directions:** From the north end of Tacoma on I-5, take Exit 135 to Highway 167. Drive east on Highway 167 (River Road) for four miles to the park on the right.

**Contact:** Majestic Mobile Manor RV Park, 253/845-3144 or 800/348-3144, www.majesticrvpark.com.

# 59 OLYMPIA CAMPGROUND

🧍‍♂️ 🚲 ♒ 🏠 🐕 🚙 ⛰️

**Scenic rating: 7**

near Olympia

**Map 2.2, page 148**

This campground in a natural, wooded setting has all the comforts. Nearby recreation options include an 18-hole golf course, hiking trails, marked bike trails, and tennis courts.

**Campsites, facilities:** There are 95 sites with full or partial hookups (20 and 30 amps) for tents or RVs of any length and two cabins. Some sites are pull-through. Picnic tables are provided and fire rings are at some sites. Restrooms with flush toilets and showers, drinking water, modem and Wi-Fi access, propane gas, a dump station, recreation hall, convenience store, coin laundry, ice, a playground, seasonal heated swimming pool, gas station, and firewood are available. A café is located within two miles. Leashed pets are permitted.

**Reservations, fees:** Reservations are accepted. Sites are $21-33 per night, $10 per person per night for more than two people. Some credit cards are accepted. Open year-round.

**Directions:** From Olympia on I-5, take Exit 101 to Tumwater Boulevard. Turn left and drive 0.25 mile to Center Street. Turn right and drive one mile to 83rd Avenue (Center ends at 83rd). Turn right and drive an eighth of a mile to the park on the left. Turn in at the Texaco station entrance (the campground is behind the store).

**Contact:** Olympia Campground, 360/352-2551, www.olympiacampground.com.

# THE NORTHERN CASCADES

Mount Baker is the centerpiece in a forested landscape with hundreds of lakes, rivers, and hidden campgrounds. The only limit here is weather. The Northern Cascades are deluged with snowfall in winter and Mount Baker often receives a foot per day for weeks. Although that shortens the recreation season to just a few months in summer, it also has another effect. With so many destinations available for such a short time, many remain largely undiscovered. First-time campers should start with the state parks, which offer beautiful, easy-to-reach settings. Many roadside camps provide choice layover spots for vacationing travelers. Seasoned campers can search for lesser-known camps in the national forests. Many beautiful spots are set alongside lakes and streams, often with trailheads into nearby wilderness that feature abundant wildlife, good fishing, and great hiking.

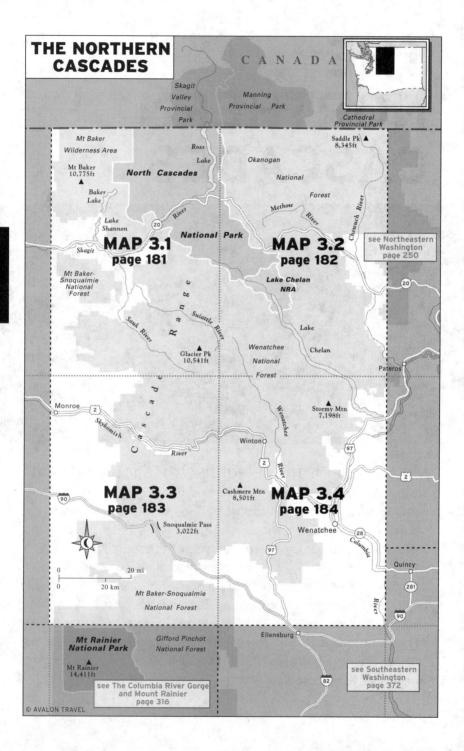

# THE NORTHERN CASCADES

C A N A D A

Skagit Valley Provincial Park

Manning Provincial Park

Cathedral Provincial Park

Mt Baker Wilderness Area

Ross Lake

Saddle Pk ▲ 8,345ft

Okanogan

Mt Baker 10,775ft ▲

**North Cascades**

National

Baker Lake

Methow River

Forest

Chewuch River

Lake Shannon

River

20

**National Park**

**MAP 3.1**
page 181

**MAP 3.2**
page 182

see Northeastern Washington page 250

Skagit

Mt Baker-Snoqualmie National Forest

20

Lake Chelan NRA

Sauk River

Suiattle River

C a s c a d e   R a n g e

Glacier Pk 10,541ft ▲

Wenatchee

National

Lake

Chelan

Pateros

Forest

Monroe

2

Skykomish

River

Winton ○

Wenatchee River

Stormy Mtn 7,198ft ▲

97

2

90

**MAP 3.3**
page 183

Cashmere Mtn 8,501ft ▲

**MAP 3.4**
page 184

Wenatchee

28

Columbia

Snoqualmie Pass 3,022ft

0        20 mi
0     20 km

97

Quincy

281

River

90

Mt Baker-Snoqualmie

National   Forest

Ellensburg

**Mt Rainier National Park**

Gifford Pinchot National Forest

see Southeastern Washington page 372

Mt Rainier ▲ 14,411ft

see The Columbia River Gorge and Mount Rainier page 316

82

© AVALON TRAVEL

# Map 3.1

### Sites 1-40
### Pages 185-202

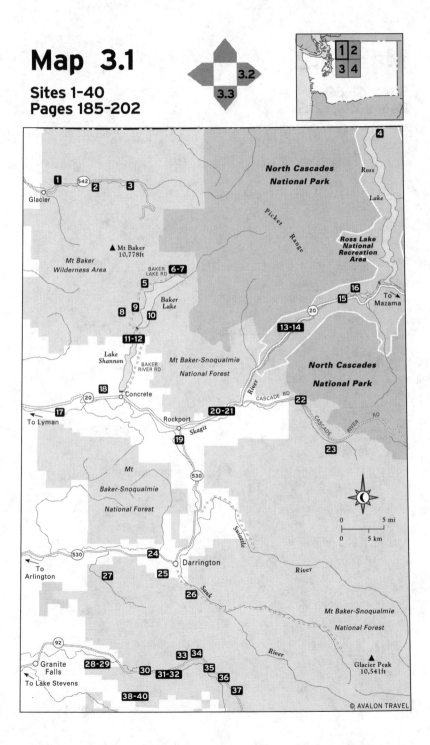

# Map 3.2

**Sites 41-69**
**Pages 202-216**

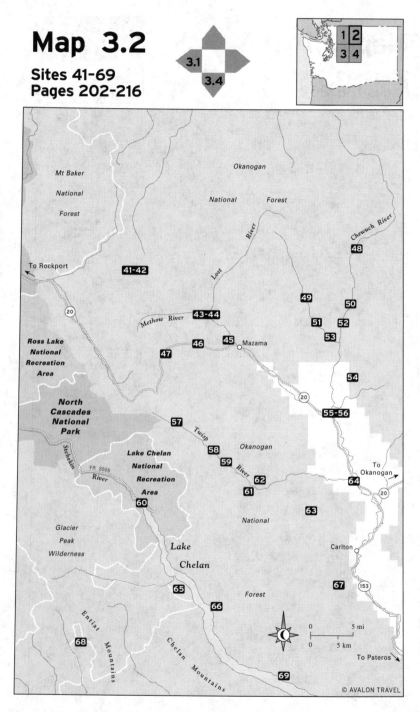

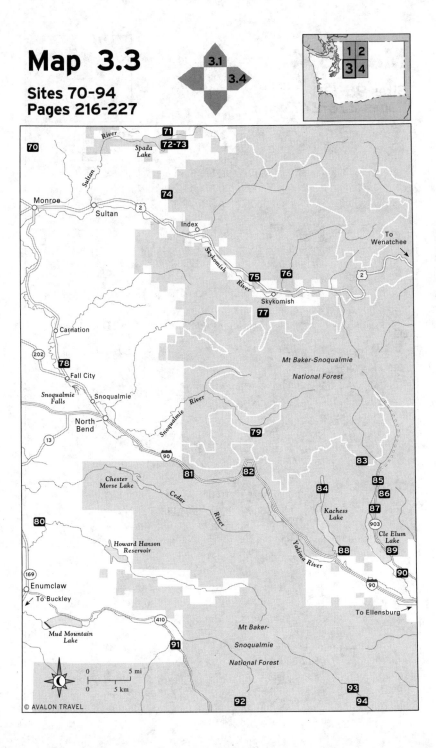

# Map **3.3**

**Sites 70-94**
**Pages 216-227**

3.1

3.4

1 2
3 4

River

Sultan

70

71

72-73

Spada Lake

74

Monroe

Sultan

2

Index

To Wenatchee

Skykomish River

75

76

2

Skykomish

77

Carnation

Mt Baker-Snoqualmie

National Forest

202

78

Fall City

Snoqualmie Falls

Snoqualmie

North Bend

Snoqualmie River

13

79

83

90

Chester Morse Lake

81

82

84

85

86

Cedar River

Kachess Lake

87

903

Cle Elum Lake

80

Howard Hanson Reservoir

Yakima River

88

89

169

90

Enumclaw

To Buckley

90

To Ellensburg

Mud Mountain Lake

410

Mt Baker-

91

Snoqualmie

0    5 mi

0    5 km

National Forest

93

94

© AVALON TRAVEL

92

# Map 3.4

## Sites 95-138
## Pages 228-247

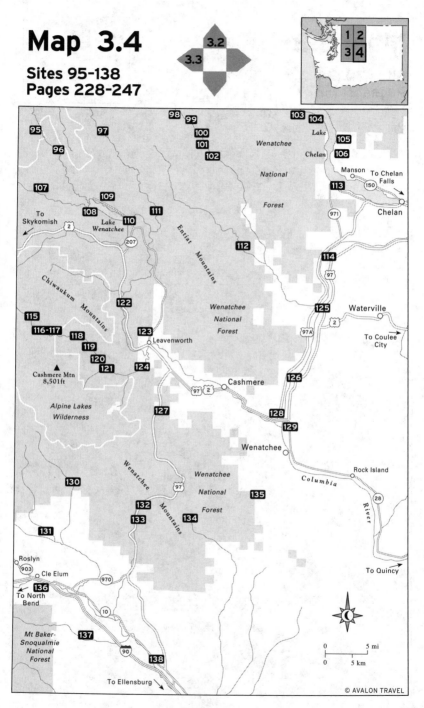

# ① DOUGLAS FIR

## Scenic rating: 10

on the Nooksack River in Mount
Baker-Snoqualmie National Forest

Map 3.1, page 181

Set along the Nooksack River, this camp features river views from some campsites. It is a beautiful camp, surrounded by old-growth Douglas fir, silver fir, and western hemlock. Trout fishing is available on the river, and there are hiking trails in the area.

**Campsites, facilities:** There are 30 sites for tents or RVs up to 55 feet long. Picnic tables and fire grills are provided. Drinking water, vault toilets, and a picnic shelter are available. A store, café, coin laundry, and ice are located within five miles at Glacier. Some facilities are wheelchair accessible. Leashed pets are permitted.

**Reservations, fees:** Reservations are accepted at 877/444-6777 ($10 reservation fee) or www.recreation.gov ($9 reservation fee). Sites are $18-20 per night, $9 per night per additional vehicle. Open May-September, weather permitting.

**Directions:** From Bellingham on I-5, take the Highway 542 exit and drive 33 miles to Glacier. Continue two miles northeast on Highway 542 to the campground on the left.

**Contact:** Mount Baker-Snoqualmie National Forest, Mount Baker Ranger District, 360/856-5700, www.fs.usda.gov or www.hoodoo.com.

# ② EXCELSIOR GROUP CAMP

## Scenic rating: 6

near the Nooksack River in Mount
Baker-Snoqualmie National Forest

Map 3.1, page 181

This campground is set near the Nooksack River less than one mile from Nooksack Falls and 1.5 miles from the site of the Excelsior Mine. The Excelsior Pass Trailhead is about five minutes away. There are numerous hiking trails available within a 30-minute drive in the Mount Baker Wilderness.

**Campsites, facilities:** There are two group tent sites for up to 50 and 75 people each. Picnic tables and fire grills are provided. Vault toilets, garbage bins, and drinking water are available. Leashed pets are permitted.

**Reservations, fees:** Reservations are accepted at 877/444-6777 ($10 reservation fee) or www.recreation.gov ($9 reservation fee). Sites are $75-100 per night. Open May-late September, weather permitting.

**Directions:** From Bellingham on I-5, take the Highway 542 exit and drive 37.5 miles (6.5 miles east of Glacier) to the camp on the right. Note: RVs and trailers are not recommended for this road.

**Contact:** Mount Baker-Snoqualmie National Forest, Mount Baker Ranger District, 360/856-5700, www.fs.usda.gov.

# ③ SILVER FIR

## Scenic rating: 9

on the North Fork of the Nooksack River in
Mount Baker-Snoqualmie National Forest

Map 3.1, page 181       BEST (

This campground is set on the North Fork of the Nooksack River. It is within 30 minutes of the Heather Meadows area, which provides some of the best hiking trails in the entire region. In addition, a one-mile round-trip to Artist Ridge promises views of Mount Baker and Mount Shuksan. The first part of the trail to the first viewpoint is wheelchair accessible. Fishing is available nearby, and in the winter the area offers cross-country skiing. You're strongly advised to obtain a U.S. Forest Service map in order to take maximum advantage of the recreational opportunities in the area.

**Campsites, facilities:** There are 20 sites for tents or RVs of any length including a few double sites. Picnic tables and barbecue grills are provided. Drinking water, vault toilets, garbage bins, and a group picnic shelter are available. Some facilities are wheelchair accessible. Leashed pets are permitted.

**Reservations, fees:** Reservations are accepted at 877/444-6777 ($10 reservation fee) or www.recreation.gov ($9 reservation fee). Sites are $16-30 per night, $8 per night per additional vehicle. Open May-early September, weather permitting.

**Directions:** From I-5 at Bellingham, turn east on Highway 542 and drive 33 miles to Glacier. Continue east on Highway 542 for 12.5 miles to the campground on the right.

**Contact:** Mount Baker-Snoqualmie National Forest, Mount Baker Ranger District, 360/856-5700, www.fs.usda.gov or www.hoodoo.com.

## 4 HOZOMEEN

### Scenic rating: 9

on Ross Lake in Ross Lake National Recreation Area

**Map 3.1, page 181**

Hozomeen campground, at 1,600 feet elevation, is just inside the U.S./Canada border at the northeast end of Ross Lake. It takes quite an effort to get here, which tends to weed out all but the most stalwart campers. This is good news for those few, for they will find a quiet, uncrowded camp in a beautiful setting. No firewood gathering is permitted here.

**Campsites, facilities:** There are 75 sites for tents or RVs of any length (but getting there requires traveling over 39 miles of rough road). Picnic tables and fire grills are provided. Pit toilets and drinking water are available. Garbage must be packed out. A boat launch on nearby Ross Lake is available. Some facilities are wheelchair accessible. Leashed pets are permitted.

**Reservations, fees:** There is no entrance fee for North Cascades National Park. Reservations are not accepted. There is no fee for camping. Open mid-June-September.

**Directions:** This campground is accessible only through Canada. From the town of Hope, British Columbia, turn south on Silver-Skagit Road; it is a narrow dirt/gravel road, which is often rough. Drive south for 39 miles to the campground at the north end of Ross Lake.

**Contact:** North Cascades National Park, 360/856-5700, www.nps.gov/noca.

## 5 PARK CREEK

### Scenic rating: 6

near Baker Lake in Mount Baker-Snoqualmie National Forest

**Map 3.1, page 181**

This pretty camp is set at an elevation of 800 feet on Park Creek amid a heavily wooded area comprising old-growth Douglas fir and western hemlock. Park Creek is a feeder stream to nearby Baker Lake. The camp is primitive and small but gets its fair share of use.

**Campsites, facilities:** There are 12 sites for tents or RVs up to 36 feet long. Picnic tables and fire grills are provided. Vault toilets are available, but there is no drinking water. Boat docks, launching facilities, and rentals are nearby on Baker Lake. Leashed pets are permitted.

**Reservations, fees:** Reservations are accepted at 877/444-6777 ($10 reservation fee) or www.recreation.gov ($9 reservation fee). Sites are $12 per night, $6 per night per additional vehicle. Open mid-May-early September, weather permitting.

**Directions:** From I-5 at Burlington, turn east on Highway 20 and drive approximately 24 miles to Milepost 82 and Baker Lake Highway (Forest Road 11). Turn north on Baker Lake Highway and drive about 19.5 miles to Forest Road 1144. Turn left (northwest) and drive about 200 yards to the campground on the left. Obtaining a U.S. Forest Service map is helpful.

**Contact:** Mount Baker-Snoqualmie National Forest, Mount Baker Ranger District, 360/856-5700, www.fs.usda.gov.

# 6 SHANNON CREEK

**Scenic rating: 9**

near Baker Lake in Mount Baker-Snoqualmie
National Forest

**Map 3.1, page 181**

This pretty camp is set at an elevation of 909 feet at the north end of Baker Lake.

**Campsites, facilities:** There are 19 sites, including two double sites, for tents or RVs up to 36 feet long. Picnic tables and fire grills are provided. Drinking water, garbage bins, firewood, a picnic shelter, and vault toilets are available. A boat launch is available, and docks and rentals are nearby on Baker Lake. Some facilities are wheelchair accessible. Leashed pets are permitted.

**Reservations, fees:** Reservations are accepted at 877/444-6777 ($10 reservation fee) or www. recreation.gov ($9 reservation fee). Sites are $14-16 per night, $25 per night for the double sites, and $7 per night per additional vehicle. Open mid-May-mid-September, weather permitting.

**Directions:** From I-5 at Burlington, turn east on Highway 20 and drive approximately 24 miles to Milepost 82 and Baker Lake Highway (Forest Road 11). Turn north on Baker Lake Highway and drive. Obtaining a U.S. Forest Service map is helpful.

**Contact:** Mount Baker-Snoqualmie National Forest, Mount Baker Ranger District, 360/856-5700, www.fs.usda.gov.

# 7 SWIFT CREEK CAMPGROUND

**Scenic rating: 9**

near Baker Lake in Mount Baker-Snoqualmie
National Forest

**Map 3.1, page 181**

Formerly the private Baker Lake Resort, newly christened Swift Creek Campground resides in mixed-conifer forest on the edge of picturesque Baker Lake. The camp is in a prime location for hiking, boating, and fishing, as well as skiing and snowshoeing in winter months. There is a small beach on-site and an impressive view of Mount Baker's 10,781-foot snowcapped peaks.

**Campsites, facilities:** There are 20 single sites, two double sites, and two group sites for tents or RVs up to 40 feet long. Picnic tables and fire grills are provided. Drinking water, garbage bins, firewood, and vault toilets are available. A paved boat ramp (suitable for large boats) and a 20-slip dock are on-site. Boat rentals are available nearby. Some facilities are wheelchair accessible. Leashed pets are permitted.

**Reservations, fees:** Reservations are accepted at 877/444-6777 ($10 reservation fee) or www. recreation.gov ($9 reservation fee). Single sites are $18 per night, double sites are $34 per night, the group site is $75 per night, $9 per night per additional vehicle. Open mid-May-mid-September, weather permitting.

**Directions:** Swift Creek Campground is three miles south of Shannon Creek (see listing in this chapter) on same road. From I-5 at Mount Vernon, take Exit 230 and head east on Highway 20/North Cascades Highway for 18 miles. Pass Sedro-Woolley and take Baker Lake Road to Baker Lake. Swift Creek Campground is about halfway up the lake on the right side, just past Milepost 20. Obtaining a U.S. Forest Service map is helpful.
GPS Coordinates: 48.72889, -121.65722

**Contact:** Mount Baker-Snoqualmie National Forest, Mount Baker Ranger District, 360/856-5700, www.fs.usda.gov or www. hoodoo.com.

# 8 BOULDER CREEK

**Scenic rating: 8**

near Baker Lake in Mount Baker-Snoqualmie
National Forest

**Map 3.1, page 181**

This camp provides an alternative to Horseshoe Cove. It is set on Boulder Creek about one mile from the shore of Baker Lake. Fishing is fair here for rainbow trout, but typically far better at Baker Lake. A boat launch is located at Panorama Point, about 15 minutes away. Wild berries can be found in the area in season. The campground offers prime views of Mount Baker.

**Campsites, facilities:** There are eight sites for tents or RVs up to 22 feet long and one group site for up to 25 people. Picnic tables and fire grills are provided. Vault toilets are available, but there is no drinking water. Boat docks and launching facilities are nearby on Baker Lake. Leashed pets are permitted.

**Reservations, fees:** Reservations are required for the group site and are available for some family sites at 877/444-6777 ($10 reservation fee) or www.recreation.gov ($9 reservation fee). Family sites are $14 per night, $7 per night per additional vehicle; the group site is $40 per night. Open mid-May-early September, weather permitting.

**Directions:** From I-5 at Burlington, turn east on Highway 20 and drive approximately 24 miles to Milepost 82 and Baker Lake Highway (Forest Road 11). Turn north on Baker Lake Highway and drive 17.4 miles to the campground on the right.

**Contact:** Mount Baker-Snoqualmie National Forest, Mount Baker Ranger District, 360/856-5700, www.fs.usda.gov or www.hoodoo.com.

## 9 PANORAMA POINT

### Scenic rating: 10

on Baker Lake in Mount Baker-Snoqualmie National Forest

**Map 3.1, page 181**    BEST (

With incredible scenic views of Mount Baker, Mount Shuk, Baker Lake, and Anderson Mountain, this camp is true to its name. Panorama Point is a well-maintained campground on the northwest shore of Baker Lake. The reservoir is one of the better fishing lakes in the area, often with good prospects for rainbow

trout. Powerboating and waterskiing are permitted. Hiking trails are nearby.

**Campsites, facilities:** There are 16 sites for tents or RVs up to 45 feet long and a few multi-sites. Picnic tables are provided. Drinking water, vault toilets, firewood, and garbage bins are available. A convenience store and ice are located within one mile. A boat ramp is adjacent to the camp. Boat docks and rentals are nearby. Some facilities are wheelchair accessible. Leashed pets are permitted.

**Reservations, fees:** Reservations are accepted at 877/444-6777 ($10 reservation fee) or www.recreation.gov ($9 reservation fee). Sites are $16-30 per night, $7 per night per additional vehicle. Open mid-May-mid-September, weather permitting.

**Directions:** From I-5 at Burlington, turn east on Highway 20 and drive approximately 24 miles to Milepost 82 and Baker Lake Highway (Forest Road 11). Turn north on Baker Lake Highway and drive 18.7 miles to the campground entrance on the right on the shore of Baker Lake.

**Contact:** Mount Baker-Snoqualmie National Forest, Mount Baker Ranger District, 360/856-5700, www.fs.usda.gov or www.hoodoo.com.

## 10 MAPLE GROVE

### Scenic rating: 9

on Baker Lake in Mount Baker-Snoqualmie National Forest

**Map 3.1, page 181**    BEST (

Looking for a quiet spot on the edge of a popular lake? Here it is. This rustic campground on the shore of Baker Lake is hike-in or boat-in only. Many camps on this lake fill on summer weekends, and boating activity, including fishing, powerboating, and waterskiing, is high. Privacy and great mountain views are your reward for the extra effort, and it's all free.

**Campsites, facilities:** There are five primitive tent sites that are accessible only by boat or on foot. Picnic tables and fire grills are provided. Vault toilets are available. There is no drinking water. Boat-launching facilities and a dock are located nearby on Baker Lake. Leashed pets are permitted.

**Reservations, fees:** Reservations are not accepted. A Northwest Forest Pass ($5 daily fee or $30 annual fee per parked vehicle) is required when parking at the trailhead. Open year-round.

**Directions:** From I-5 at Burlington, turn east on Highway 20 and drive approximately 24 miles to Milepost 82 and Baker Lake Highway (Forest Road 11). Turn left (north) on Baker Lake Highway and drive 13.3 miles to Forest Road 1106. Turn right (east) on Forest Road 1106 and drive across Baker Dam to Forest Road 1107. Turn left and drive 0.5 mile to the parking area and the trailhead on the left. To reach the camp by boat, launch at one of the campgrounds on the west side of the lake (Horseshoe Cove is the closest). Or take Trail 610/Baker Lake Trail (located on the east side of the lake, 0.5 mile north of the dam) and walk in four miles to the camp. Obtaining a U.S. Forest Service map is recommended.

**Contact:** Mount Baker-Snoqualmie National Forest, Mount Baker Ranger District, 360/856-5700, www.fs.usda.gov.

## 11 HORSESHOE COVE/GROUP

🚶 🏊 🚣 🚤 🎣 🐎 ♿ 🚐 ⛺

**Scenic rating: 9**

on Baker Lake in Mount Baker-Snoqualmie National Forest

**Map 3.1, page 181**

This camp is set along 5,000-acre Baker Lake. Anglers will often find good fishing for rainbow trout and kokanee salmon. Other highlights include swimming access from the campground and a boat ramp. Some hiking trails can be found nearby. The Baker Lake Basin has many trails, and the Mount Baker National Recreation area is located within 30 minutes.

**Campsites, facilities:** There are 35 single and two multi-sites for tents or RVs up to 40 feet long and three group sites for up to 25 people each. Picnic tables and fire grills are provided. Drinking water, flush toilets, garbage bins, and firewood are available. A boat ramp and swimming beach are adjacent to camp. Canoes, kayaks, and paddleboats are available for rent; check with the camp host. Some facilities are wheelchair accessible. Leashed pets are permitted.

**Reservations, fees:** Reservations are accepted at 877/444-6777 ($10 reservation fee) or www.recreation.gov ($9 reservation fee). Single sites are $18 per night, $30 for multi and group sites are $75 per night. Open May-September, weather permitting.

**Directions:** From I-5 at Burlington, turn east on Highway 20 and drive approximately 24 miles to Milepost 82 and the Baker Lake Highway (Forest Road 11). Turn north on Baker Lake Highway and drive about 14.8 miles to Forest Road 1118. Turn right (east) on Forest Road 1118 and drive two miles to the campground. A U.S. Forest Service map is recommended.

**Contact:** Mount Baker-Snoqualmie National Forest, Mount Baker Ranger District, 360/856-5700, www.fs.usda.gov or www.hoodoo.com.

## 12 BAY VIEW NORTH/ SOUTH GROUP

🚶 🏊 🚣 🚤 🐎 🚐 ⛺

**Scenic rating: 9**

on Baker Lake in Mount Baker-Snoqualmie National Forest

**Map 3.1, page 181**

These are two group camps set along Baker Lake, which covers 5,000 acres and offers fishing for rainbow trout and kokanee salmon. The camps are located in a forest, though not a dense one, and there is an open feel to the area. Many sites are close to the water. This campground is primarily for organizations (like church groups or scouts) who want several sites in one location as well as separation of individual sites.

**Campsites, facilities:** There are two group sites for tents or RVs up to 30 feet long for up to 100 people each. Picnic tables and fire grills are provided. Vault toilets, garbage bins, and firewood are available. There is no drinking water. A boat ramp is located nearby near Horseshoe Cove Camp. Leashed pets are permitted.

**Reservations, fees:** Reservations are accepted at 877/444-6777 ($10 reservation fee) or www.recreation.gov ($9 reservation fee). Sites are $75 per night. Some credit cards are accepted. Open mid-May-mid-September, weather permitting.

**Directions:** From I-5 at Burlington, turn east on Highway 20 and drive approximately 24 miles to Milepost 82 and the Baker Lake Highway (Forest Road 11). Turn north on Baker Lake Highway and drive about 14.8 miles to Forest Road 1118. Turn right (east) on Forest Road 1118 and drive 1.75 miles to Forest Road 1118.011. Turn left and drive 0.75 mile to the campground. A U.S. Forest Service map is recommended.

**Contact:** Mount Baker-Snoqualmie National Forest, Mount Baker Ranger District, 360/856-5700 www.fs.usda.gov or www.hoodoo.com.

## 13 GOODELL CREEK

**Scenic rating: 7**
on Goodell Creek and the Skagit River in Ross Lake National Recreation Area

**Map 3.1, page 181**

Goodell Creek Campground is an alternative to nearby, larger Newhalem Creek campground. This one is set at 500 feet elevation, where Goodell Creek pours into the Skagit River in the Ross Lake National Recreation Area. It's a popular put-in camp for raft trips downriver; that makes the group sites popular here. No firewood gathering is permitted.

**Campsites, facilities:** There are 21 sites for tents or RVs up to 22 feet long and three group sites (one at Upper Goodell and two at Lower Goodell) for up to 50 people each for tents or RVs up to 30 feet long. Picnic tables and fire rings are provided. Drinking water is available in the family sites, but not in the group sites. Pit toilets, garbage bins, and a picnic shelter are available. A dump station is across the road at Newhalem Creek campground. Some facilities are wheelchair accessible. Leashed pets are permitted.

**Reservations, fees:** Reservations are required for group sites only at 877/444-6777 or www.recreation.gov ($9 reservation fee). Sites are $10 per night, and group sites are $25 per night. There is no entrance fee for North Cascades National Park. Family sites are open year-round, but there are no services (and no fees) in the winter; group sites are open Memorial Day weekend-September.

**Directions:** On I-5, drive to Exit 230/Highway 20 at Burlington. Turn east on Highway 20, and drive 46 miles to Marblemount. Continue east on Highway 20 for 13 miles to the campground entrance. RVs and buses are not allowed on the road to Upper Goodell campground.

**Contact:** North Cascades National Park, 360/856-5700, www.nps.gov/noca/.

## 14 NEWHALEM CREEK

**Scenic rating: 7**
near the Skagit River in Ross Lake National Recreation Area

**Map 3.1, page 181**

This spot is set along the Skagit River west of Newhalem at 500 feet elevation. Good hiking possibilities abound in the immediate area, and naturalist programs are available. Be sure to visit the North Cascades Visitor Center at the top of the hill from the campground. No firewood gathering is permitted here. If this camp is full, try Goodell Creek Campground, located just one mile west on Highway 20.

**Campsites, facilities:** There are 111 sites for tents or RVs of any length, and two group sites for tents or RVs up to 45 feet long for up to 30 people each. Picnic tables and fire grills are provided. Restrooms with flush toilets, drinking water, and a dump station are available. The group camp has a covered pavilion. Some facilities are wheelchair accessible. Leashed pets are permitted.

**Reservations, fees:** Reservations are accepted for family sites and are required for group camps at 877/444-6777 or www.recreation.gov ($9 reservation fee). Family sites are $12 per night; group sites are $32 per night. There is no entrance fee for North Cascades National Park. Open mid-May-mid-September.

**Directions:** On I-5, drive to Exit 230/Highway 20 at Burlington. Turn east on Highway 20, and drive 46 miles to Marblemount. Continue 14 miles east on Highway 20 to the camp.

**Contact:** North Cascades National Park, 360/856-5700, www.nps.gov/noca/.

## 15 GORGE LAKE

### Scenic rating: 9
on Gorge Lake on the Skagit River in Ross Lake National Recreation Area

**Map 3.1, page 181**

This small camp is set near the north shore of Gorge Lake, with lake views from many sites, and close to Colonial Creek and Goodell Creek. There is some tree cover. Gorge Lake is very narrow and has trout fishing (check regulations). The camp is not well known and gets low use. One problem here is that the lake level can fluctuate (but not as much as Ross Lake), leaving the camps high and dry. No firewood gathering is permitted. There are two other lakes nearby on the Skagit River—Diablo Lake and Ross Lake. The elevation is 900 feet.

**Campsites, facilities:** There are six sites for tents or RVs up to 22 feet long. Picnic tables

and fire grills are provided. Vault toilets are available. There is no drinking water, and garbage must be packed out. A boat ramp is nearby. Leashed pets are permitted.

**Reservations, fees:** Reservations are not accepted. There is no fee for camping. There is no entrance fee for North Cascades National Park. Open year-round.

**Directions:** From I-5 near Burlington, take exit 230 for Highway 20. Turn east on Highway 20 and drive 46 miles to Marblemount. Continue east on Highway 20 for another 20 miles to the junction with Diablo Road. Bear left and drive 0.6 mile to the campground on the right.

**Contact:** North Cascades National Park, 360/856-5700, www.nps.gov/noca/.

## 16 COLONIAL CREEK

### Scenic rating: 7
on Diablo Lake in Ross Lake National Recreation Area

**Map 3.1, page 181**

Colonial Creek Campground sits at an elevation of 1,200 feet along the shore of Diablo Lake in the Ross Lake National Recreation Area. The five-mile-long lake offers many hiking and fishing opportunities. A naturalist program and guided walks are available during the summer months. No firewood gathering is permitted at this campsite.

**Campsites, facilities:** There are 142 campsites for tents or RVs up to 45 feet long, including a few walk-in tent sites. Picnic tables and fire grills are provided. Restrooms with flush toilets, drinking water, garbage bins, a dump station, three boat docks, and a boat ramp are available. Some facilities are wheelchair accessible, including a fishing pier. Leashed pets are permitted.

**Reservations, fees:** Reservations are not accepted. Sites are $12 per night. There is no entrance fee for North Cascades National Park. Open mid-May-mid-October; 18 lakefront sites are open through the winter (no services provided).

**Directions:** From I-5 at Burlington, take Exit 230 and drive east to Highway 20. Turn east on Highway 20 and drive 46 miles to Marblemount. Continue east on Highway 20 for 24 miles to the campground entrance.

**Contact:** North Cascades National Park, 360/856-5700, www.nps.gov.noca/.

## 17 RASAR STATE PARK
🚶 🚴 🛶 🏊 🐕 🏕 ♿ 🚐 ⛺

### Scenic rating: 8

on the Skagit River

**Map 3.1, page 181**

This park borders North Cascade National Park and is also near 10,778-foot Mount Baker and the Baker River watershed. Fishing the 4,000 feet of shoreline and hiking are the attractions here, as is bird-watching.

**Campsites, facilities:** There are 20 sites with partial hookups (30 amps) for tents or RVs up to 40 feet long, three primitive hike-in/bike-in sites, eight walk-in sites, two four-person Adirondack shelters, three cabins, and three group sites for 20-80 people. Picnic tables and fire grills are provided. Restrooms with flush toilets and coin showers, drinking water, dump station, a kitchen shelter, an amphitheater, playground, and park store are available. Firewood gathering is prohibited, but firewood is available for sale. Some facilities are wheelchair accessible. Leashed pets are permitted.

**Reservations, fees:** Reservations are required for the group site and are accepted for the sites at 888/CAMP-OUT (888/226-7688) or www.parks.wa.gov/reservations ($6.50-8.50 reservation fee). Sites are $12-39 per night, $10 per extra vehicle per night; group sites are $148.77-325.09 per night; cabins are $84.85-$102.49 per night; and shelters are $22-23 per night. Open year-round.

**Directions:** From I-5 at Burlington, take Exit 232 (Cook Road) and drive six miles (to a traffic light) to Highway 20 in Sedro-Woolley.

Turn left (east) on Highway 20 and drive 15 miles to Lusk Road. Turn right on Lusk Road and drive 0.75 mile to Cape Horn Road. Turn left on Cape Horn Road and drive one mile to the park entrance.

**Contact:** Rasar State Park, 360/826-3942; state park information, 360/902-8844, www.parks.wa.gov.

## 18 CREEKSIDE CAMPING
🚴 🛶 🏕 🚐 ⛺

### Scenic rating: 6

near the Skagit River

**Map 3.1, page 181**

This pretty, wooded campground is centrally located to nearby recreational opportunities at Baker Lake and the Skagit River. Trout fishing is good here, and tackle is available nearby. Horseshoe pits and a recreation hall are also available. About half of the sites are filled with monthly renters.

**Campsites, facilities:** There are 29 sites with full or partial hookups (20 and 30 amp) for tents, trailers, or RVs up to 40 feet long. Picnic tables and fire rings are provided. Restrooms with flush toilets and showers, drinking water, a dump station, coin laundry, games and videos, and horseshoe pits are available. A café is located within one mile. Leashed pets are permitted.

**Reservations, fees:** Reservations are recommended. RV sites are $30 per night; tent sites are $20 per night. Open year-round.

**Directions:** From Seattle, drive north on I-5 to Exit 232 (Cook Road). Take the exit up and over the highway to the flashing light and Highway 20. Turn left on Cook Road/Highway 20 and drive four miles to the light at Highway 20. Turn left at Highway 20 and drive 17 miles to Baker Lake Road, between Mileposts 182 and 183. Turn left on Baker Lake Road and drive 0.25 mile to the camp on the right.

**Contact:** Creekside Camping, 39602 Baker Lake Road, Concrete, 360/826-3566.

## 19 HOWARD MILLER STEELHEAD PARK

**Scenic rating: 5**

on the Skagit River

**Map 3.1, page 181**

This Skagit County Park provides grassy sites and access to the Skagit River. The river is designated a Wild and Scenic River. The steelhead fishing is often good in season. Campsites at this spot are sunny and spacious. Groups can be accommodated. A bald eagle sanctuary is located at the east end of the park. November-January is the best time to see bald eagles here. This camp is most popular in July, August, and September, when the weather is best, but also attracts visitors in early winter who arrive primarily for bald eagle-watching.

**Campsites, facilities:** There are 56 sites with full or partial hookups for tents or RVs of any length, 10 walk-in tent sites, and two cabins. Picnic tables and fire pits are provided. Restrooms with flush toilets and coin showers, drinking water, a dump station, a clubhouse, picnic shelter, playground, interpretive center, and horseshoe pits are available. A store and ice are located within one mile. Boat-launching facilities are located in the park. Some facilities are wheelchair accessible. Leashed pets are permitted.

**Reservations, fees:** Reservations are recommended ($7 reservation fee). RV sites are $25-30 per night, tent sites are $16 per night, cabins are $65 per night, and it's $5 per extra vehicle per night. Winter rates available. Some credit cards are accepted. Open year-round.

**Directions:** On I-5, drive to Exit 230/Highway 20 at Burlington. Turn east on Highway 20, and drive 44 miles to Rockport and Rockport-Darrington Road (Highway 530). Turn right (south) and drive three blocks to the camp on the right.

**Contact:** Howard Miller Steelhead Park, 360/853-8808; Skagit County Parks, 360/336-9414, www.skagitcounty.net/parksandrecreation.

## 20 WILDERNESS VILLAGE AND RV PARK

**Scenic rating: 6**

near the Skagit River

**Map 3.1, page 181**

This RV park is located near the Skagit River. Cool and wooded, it offers nice, grassy sites and nearby access to the river and fishing. Horseshoe pits and a sports field provide recreation alternatives. Rockport State Park and hiking trails are nearby. Bald eagles can often be viewed on the Skagit River in December and January. A one-mile trail (round-trip) can be accessed along the river.

**Campsites, facilities:** There are 32 pull-through sites with full hookups for RVs of any length and 20 tent sites. Picnic tables and fire rings are provided. Restrooms with flush toilets and coin showers, and coin laundry are available. A café and ice are located within two miles. Leashed pets are permitted.

**Reservations, fees:** Reservations are accepted. Sites are $13-22 per night. Open year-round.

**Directions:** From Burlington, drive east on Highway 20 for 44 miles to Rockport. Continue east on Highway 20 for five miles to the park. The park is between Mileposts 102 and 103 on the right.

**Contact:** Wilderness Village and RV Park, 5550 Highway 20, Rockport, 360/873-2571 or 360/421-2976, http://wildernessvillagervpark.com.

## 21 SKAGIT RIVER RESORT

**Scenic rating: 9**

on the Skagit River

**Map 3.1, page 181**

This beautiful camp is nestled in the trees along the Skagit River. The resort covers 125 acres, including 1.5 miles of river frontage. A restaurant called The Eatery has received awards for its pecan pie and is also known for its home-style meals. Fishing, river walks, and nearby hiking trails among the glaciers and waterfalls can be accessed close to the campground. There are also three hydroelectric plants nearby that offer tours. Recreational facilities include horseshoes and a sports field for volleyball, croquet, and badminton. This resort is popular July-September, when reservations are often required to get a spot.

**Campsites, facilities:** There are 48 sites for tents or RVs of any length (full hookups), 40 cabins, seven theme cabins, five chalets, and six mobile homes. Some sites are pull-through. Restrooms with flush toilets and coin showers, drinking water, Wi-Fi, a pay phone, coin laundry, horseshoe pits, a restaurant, bunny-hole golf, and a sports field for volleyball, croquet, and badminton are available. Some facilities are wheelchair accessible. Leashed pets are permitted.

**Reservations, fees:** Reservations are recommended. RV sites are $30-35 per night, tent sites are $20, $15 per pet per night (in cabins). Some credit cards are accepted. Open year-round.

**Directions:** From Burlington, drive east on Highway 20 for 44 miles to Rockport. Continue east on Highway 20 for six miles to the resort on the left (between Mileposts 103 and 104).

**Contact:** Skagit River Resort, 360/873-2250 or 800/273-2606, www.northcascades.com.

## 22 MARBLE CREEK

**Scenic rating: 7**
on Marble Creek in Mount Baker-Snoqualmie National Forest

**Map 3.1, page 181**

This primitive campground is set on Marble Creek amid old-growth Douglas fir and western hemlock. Fishing for rainbow trout is possible here. A trailhead to Hidden Lake just inside the boundary of North Cascades National Park can be found about five miles from camp at the end of Forest Road 1540.

**Campsites, facilities:** There are 23 sites for tents or RVs up to 40 feet long, including a few multi-sites. Picnic tables and fire grills are provided. Vault toilets, garbage bins, and firewood are available. There is no drinking water. Some facilities are wheelchair accessible. Leashed pets are permitted.

**Reservations, fees:** Reservations are accepted at 877/444-6777 ($10 reservation fee) or www.recreation.gov ($9 reservation fee). Sites are $14 per night, $20 for multi-site, and $7 per night per additional vehicle. Open mid-May-mid-September, weather permitting.

**Directions:** From I-5 in Burlington, take Exit 230/Highway 20. Turn east on Highway 20 and drive 46 miles to Marblemount and Forest Road 15 (Cascade River Road). Cross the bridge, turn east on Cascade River Road, and drive eight miles to Forest Road 1530. Turn right (south) on Forest Road 1530 and drive to the campground. Obtaining a U.S. Forest Service map is advised.

**Contact:** Mount Baker-Snoqualmie National Forest, Mount Baker Ranger District, 360/856-5700, www.fs.usda.gov or www.hoodoo.com.

## 23 MINERAL PARK: EAST AND WEST

**Scenic rating: 7**
in Mount Baker-Snoqualmie National Forest

**Map 3.1, page 181**

This campground is just six miles from Cascade Pass along a narrow, bumpy gravel road and is best suited for tent and small trailers. Campsites are near the Cascade River at the convergence of the North and South Forks.

**Campsites, facilities:** There are 24 sites, including two double sites, for tents or RVs up to 32 feet long. Picnic tables and fire grills are provided. Vault toilets, firewood, and garbage bins are available, but there is no drinking water. Leashed pets are permitted.

**Reservations, fees:** Reservations are accepted

at 877/444-6777 ($10 reservation fee) or www. recreation.gov ($9 reservation fee). Sites are $12 per night, $6 per night per additional vehicle, and double sites are $20 per night. Open mid-May-mid-September, weather permitting.

**Directions:** From I-5 in Burlington, take Exit 230/Highway 20. Turn east on Highway 20 and drive 46 miles to Marblemount and Forest Road 15 (Cascade River Road). Cross the bridge over the Skagit River, turn east on Cascade River Road, and drive 16 miles to the campground. Obtaining a U.S. Forest Service map is advised.

**Contact:** Mount Baker-Snoqualmie National Forest, Mount Baker Ranger District, 360/856-5700, www.fs.usda.gov or www. hoodoo.com.

## **24** SQUIRE CREEK COUNTY PARK
🚶 🏕 ♿ 🚐 ⛺

**Scenic rating: 7**
on Squire Creek

Map 3.1, page 181

This pretty park is set amid old-growth forest, primarily Douglas fir and cedar, along Squire Creek. A family-oriented park, it often fills on summer weekends. The park covers 53 acres and features several nearby trailheads. A trail from the park provides a 4.5-mile loop that heads toward White Horse Mountain. Other trailheads are located within five miles in nearby Mount Baker-Snoqualmie National Forest, about three miles from the boundaries of the Boulder River Wilderness. No alcohol is permitted in this park.

**Campsites, facilities:** There are 33 sites for tents or RVs up to 40 feet long (no hookups). Picnic tables and fire rings are provided. Restrooms with flush toilets, coin showers, drinking water, firewood, and picnic shelters that can be reserved are available. A store is located three miles east in Darrington. Some facilities are wheelchair accessible. Leashed pets are permitted.

**Reservations, fees:** Reservations are accepted at 877/444-6777 or www.ReserveAmerica. com ($7.75 reservation fee). Sites are $22 per night, $10 per night per additional vehicle. Open year-round, with limited winter services.

**Directions:** From Seattle, drive north on I-5 to Exit 208 and the junction with Highway 530. Turn east on Highway 530 and drive 26 miles to the park on the left. The park is at Milepost 45.2, approximately three miles west of the town of Darrington.

**Contact:** Squire Creek County Park, 360/435-3441, www.snocoparks.org.

## **25** CASCADE KAMLOOPS TROUT FARM AND RV PARK
🚶 🚴 🛶 ❄ 🐎 ♿ 🚐 ⛺

**Scenic rating: 5**
in Darrington

Map 3.1, page 181

Campers will find a little bit of both worlds at this campground—a rustic quietness and a family atmosphere with all facilities available. A bonus is the trout pond, which is stocked year-round. No boats are allowed. Nearby recreation options include marked hiking trails, snowmobiling, cross-country skiing, river rafting, and tennis.

**Campsites, facilities:** There are 30 sites with full hookups for RVs up to 40 feet long and 12 tent sites. Picnic tables and fire rings are provided. Restrooms with flush toilets and showers, drinking water, a dump station, firewood, coin laundry, Wi-Fi access, a community fire pit, trout pond, and recreation hall are available. Propane gas, a store, café, and ice are located within one mile. Some facilities are wheelchair accessible. Leashed pets are permitted.

**Reservations, fees:** Reservations are accepted. RV sites are $28 per night, tent sites are $17 per night, $2 per extra vehicle per night, $2 per person per night for more than two people, and $1 per pet per night. Weekly and monthly rates available. Some credit cards are accepted. Open year-round.

**Directions:** From Seattle, drive north on I-5 to Exit 208 and the junction with Highway 530. Turn east on Highway 530 and drive 32 miles to the Darrington/Madison Avenue exit. Turn right on Madison Avenue and drive about four blocks to Darrington Street. Turn right and drive two blocks to the park on the right.

**Contact:** Cascade Kamloops Trout Farm and RV Park, 360/436-1003, www.glacierview.net/kamloops/rv.

# 26 CLEAR CREEK

## Scenic rating: 8

on Clear Creek and the Sauk River in Mount Baker-Snoqualmie National Forest

**Map 3.1, page 181**

This nice, secluded spot is set in old-growth fir on the water, but it doesn't get heavy use. It's located at the confluence of Clear Creek and the Sauk River, a designated Wild and Scenic River. Fishing is available for rainbow trout, Dolly Varden trout, whitefish, and steelhead in season. A trail from camp leads about one mile up to Frog Pond.

**Campsites, facilities:** There are 13 sites for tents or RVs up to 40 feet long. Picnic tables and fire grills are provided. Vault toilets, garbage bins, and firewood are available. There is no drinking water. A store, café, coin laundry, and ice are located within four miles. Some facilities are wheelchair accessible. Leashed pets are permitted.

**Reservations, fees:** Reservations are accepted at 877/444-6777 ($10 reservation fee) or www.recreation.gov ($9 reservation fee). Sites are $14 per night, $7 per extra vehicle per night. Open late May-mid-September, weather permitting.

**Directions:** From Seattle, drive north on I-5 to Exit 208 and the junction with Highway 530. Turn east on Highway 530 and drive 32 miles to Darrington and Forest Road 20 (Mountain Loop Highway). Turn right (south)

on Forest Road 20 and drive 3.3 miles to the campground entrance on the left.

**Contact:** Mount Baker-Snoqualmie National Forest, Darrington Ranger District, 360/436-1155, www.fs.usda.gov or www.hoodoo.com.

# 27 RIVER MEADOWS COUNTY PARK

## Scenic rating: 5

on the Stillaguamish River near Arlington

**Map 3.1, page 181**

This 150-acre camp on the shore of the Stillaguamish River offers a wide variety of activities. There are miles of trails for hiking, a mile of river for fishing or swimming, open meadows for seasonal activities ranging from kite-flying and kickball to snowshoeing and cross-country skiing. There's even geocaching.

**Campsites, facilities:** There are 14 sites for tents or RVs of any length (no hookups), three of which are walk-in sites for tents only. Six yurts are also available. Picnic tables and fire rings are provided. Restrooms with flush toilets, drinking water, firewood, and three reservable picnic shelters are available. A store is located five miles away in Arlington. Some facilities are wheelchair accessible. Leashed pets are permitted.

**Reservations, fees:** Reservations are accepted at 877/444-6777 or www.ReserveAmerica.com ($7.75 reservation fee). Sites are $22 per night, $10 per night per additional vehicle, and yurts are $55-80 per night. Open year-round, with limited winter services.

**Directions:** From Seattle, drive north on I-5 for 42 miles to Exit 208 and the junction with Highway 530. Turn east on Highway 530 and drive five miles to Arlington Heights Road. Turn right on Arlington Heights Road and drive 1.5 miles to Jordan Road. Take a sharp right onto Jordan Road and drive about two miles to park on right.

**Contact:** River Meadows County Park, 20416 Jordan Road, Arlington, 360/435-3441, http://www1.co.snohomish.wa.us.

## 28 TURLO

### Scenic rating: 8

on the South Fork of the Stillaguamish River in Mount Baker-Snoqualmie National Forest

**Map 3.1, page 181**

The westernmost camp on this stretch of Highway 92, Turlo is set at 900 feet elevation along the South Fork of the Stillaguamish River. A U.S. Forest Service Public Information Center is nearby. Riverside campsites are available, and the fishing can be good here. A few hiking trails can be found in the area.

**Campsites, facilities:** There are 18 sites for tents or RVs up to 40 feet long. Picnic tables and fire rings are provided. Vault toilets, drinking water, garbage bins, and firewood are available. A camp host is on-site. A store, café, and ice are located one mile away. Some facilities are wheelchair accessible. Leashed pets are permitted.

**Reservations, fees:** Reservations are accepted at 877/444-6777 ($10 reservation fee) or www.recreation.gov ($9 reservation fee). Sites are $16 per night, $8 per extra vehicle per night. Open year-round, weather permitting.

**Directions:** From I-5 and Everett, turn east on U.S. 2 and drive five miles to Highway 9. Turn north and drive four miles to Highway 92. Turn east on Highway 92 and drive approximately 15 miles to the town of Granite Falls. Continue another 11 miles east on Highway 92 to the campground entrance on the right.

**Contact:** Mount Baker-Snoqualmie National Forest, Darrington Ranger District, 360/436-1155 www.fs.usda.gov or www.hoodoo.com.

## 29 VERLOT

### Scenic rating: 9

on the South Fork of the Stillaguamish River in Mount Baker-Snoqualmie National Forest

**Map 3.1, page 181**

This pretty campground is set along the South Fork of the Stillaguamish River. Some campsites provide river views. The camp is a short distance from the Lake Twenty-Two Research Natural Area and Maid of the Woods Trail. Fishing is another recreation option.

**Campsites, facilities:** There are 24 single and two multi-sites for tents or RVs up to 40 feet long. Picnic tables and fire rings are provided. Restrooms with flush toilets, drinking water, garbage bins, firewood, and a visitors center are available. A store, café, and ice are located within one mile. Some facilities are wheelchair accessible. Leashed pets are permitted.

**Reservations, fees:** Reservations are accepted at 877/444-6777 ($10 reservation fee) or www.recreation.gov ($9 reservation fee). Sites are $18 per night, $24-30 for multi-sites, and $9 per extra vehicle per night. Open year-round, weather permitting.

**Directions:** From I-5 and Everett, turn east on U.S. 2 and drive five miles to Highway 9. Turn north and drive four miles to Highway 92. Turn east on Highway 92 and drive approximately 15 miles to the town of Granite Falls, and continue another 11.6 miles east on Highway 92 to the campground entrance on the right.

**Contact:** Mount Baker-Snoqualmie National Forest, Darrington Ranger District, 360/436-1155, www.fs.usda.gov or www.hoodoo.com.

## 30 GOLD BASIN

### Scenic rating: 9

on the South Fork of the Stillaguamish River in Mount Baker-Snoqualmie National Forest

**Map 3.1, page 181**

This is the largest campground in Mount Baker-Snoqualmie National Forest; since it's loaded with facilities, it's a favorite with RVers. Set at an elevation of 1,100 feet along the South Fork of the Stillaguamish River, the campground features riverside sites, easy access, and a wheelchair-accessible interpretive trail. This area once provided good fishing, but a slide upstream put clay silt into the water, and it has hurt the fishing. Rafting and hiking are options.

**Campsites, facilities:** There are 80 sites without hook-ups for tents or RVs up to 45 feet long, 10 tent-only sites, and one group site for up to 75 people. Picnic tables and fire rings are provided. Drinking water, restrooms with flush toilets and coin showers, firewood, and garbage bins are available. A camp host is on-site. A store, café, and ice are located within 2.5 miles. Some facilities are wheelchair accessible. Leashed pets are permitted.

**Reservations, fees:** Reservations are accepted at 877/444-6777 ($10 reservation fee) or www.recreation.gov ($9 reservation fee). Sites are $22-35 per night, $10 per extra vehicle per night. The group site is $100-125 per night. Open mid-May-September, weather permitting.

**Directions:** From I-5 and Everett, turn east on Highway 92 and drive about 15 miles to the town of Granite Falls and Mountain Loop Highway. Continue east on Mountain Loop Highway for 13.5 miles to the campground entrance on the left.

**Contact:** Mount Baker-Snoqualmie National Forest, Darrington Ranger District, 360/436-1155, www.fs.usda.gov or www.hoodoo.com.

## 31 MARTEN CREEK GROUP CAMP
🥾 🚴 ⛲ 🛶 🐕 ♿ 🚐 ⛺

### Scenic rating: 7
in Mount Baker-Snoqualmie National Forest

**Map 3.1, page 181**

This campground is about 10 miles east of the Verlot Visitors Center, on the South Fork of the Stillaguamish River where it converges with Marten Creek. Sites are wooded and situated close to the river's bank, which is quite steep. The elevation is 1,420 feet.

**Campsites, facilities:** There is one group site for up to 25 people. Picnic tables and fire rings are provided. Vault toilets and garbage bins

are available, but there is no drinking water. Leashed pets are permitted.

**Reservations, fees:** Reservations are accepted at 877/444-6777 ($10 reservation fee) or www.recreation.gov ($9 reservation fee). The site is $65 per night. Open mid-May-mid-September, weather permitting.

**Directions:** From I-5 and Everett, turn east on Highway 92 and drive about 15 miles to the town of Granite Falls and Mountain Loop Highway. Continue east on Mountain Loop Highway for 20 miles to the campground.

**Contact:** Mount Baker-Snoqualmie National Forest, Darrington Ranger District, 360/436-1155, www.fs.usda.gov or www.hoodoo.com.

## 32 ESSWINE GROUP CAMP
🥾 🚴 🛶 🐕 🚐 ⛺

### Scenic rating: 6
in Mount Baker-Snoqualmie National Forest

**Map 3.1, page 181**

This small, quiet camp is a great place for a restful group getaway. Even though the elevation is only 1,600 feet, it still has a beautiful view. The only drawback? No drinking water. Fishing access is available nearby. The Boulder River Wilderness is located to the north; see a U.S. Forest Service map for trailhead locations.

**Campsites, facilities:** There is one group site for tents or RVs up to 35 feet long for up to 25 people. Picnic tables and fire pits are provided. Vault toilets, garbage bins, and firewood are available, but there is no drinking water. A store, café, and ice are located within seven miles. Leashed pets are permitted.

**Reservations, fees:** Reservations are accepted at 877/444-6777 ($10 reservation fee) or www.recreation.gov ($9 reservation fee). The site is $75 per night. Open mid-May-September, weather permitting.

**Directions:** From I-5 and Everett, turn east on Highway 92 and drive about 15 miles to the town of Granite Falls and Mountain Loop Highway. Continue northeast on Mountain

Loop Highway for 16 miles to the campground entrance on the left.

**Contact:** Mount Baker-Snoqualmie National Forest, Darrington Ranger District, 360/436-1155, www.fs.usda.gov or www.hoodoo.com.

## 33 BOARDMAN CREEK GROUP CAMP
🏃 🚣 🎣 🐾 ♿ 🚐 ⛺

### Scenic rating: 7
on the South Fork of the Stillaguamish River in Mount Baker-Snoqualmie National Forest

**Map 3.1, page 181**

Boardman is located at the far end of the Mountain Loop Road, about eight miles east of the Verlot Public Service Center on the Stillaguamish River. River access highlights this pretty camp, converted from a single-site into a group campground. The fishing near here can be excellent for rainbow trout, Dolly Varden, whitefish, and steelhead in season. The camp road parallels the Loop Road. Forest roads in the area will take you to several backcountry lakes, including Boardman Lake, Lake Evan, and Ashland Lakes. Get a U.S. Forest Service map, set up your camp, and go for it.

Insider's tip: When not reserved by groups, Boardman is available for individuals on a first-come, first-served basis; check with the Gold Basin host.

**Campsites, facilities:** There is one group camp for up to 35 people and RVs of any length. Picnic tables and fire pits are provided. Vault toilets, garbage bins, and firewood are available. There is no drinking water. A camp host is available Memorial Day-Labor Day. Some facilities are wheelchair accessible. Leashed pets are permitted.

**Reservations, fees:** Reservations are accepted at 877/444-6777 ($10 reservation fee) or recreation.gov ($9 reservation fee). The site is $60 per night. Open late May-early September, weather permitting.

**Directions:** From I-5 and Everett, turn east

on Highway 92 and drive about 15 miles to the town of Granite Falls and Mountain Loop Highway. Continue northeast on Mountain Loop Highway for 16.5 miles to the campground entrance on the left.

**Contact:** Mount Baker-Snoqualmie National Forest, Darrington Ranger District, 360/436-1155, www.fs.usda.gov or www.hoodoo.com.

## 34 BEDAL
🏃 🚣 🎣 ♿ 🚐 ⛺

### Scenic rating: 9
on the Sauk River in Mount Baker-Snoqualmie National Forest

**Map 3.1, page 181**

A bit primitive, this campground is set at the confluence of the North and South Forks of the Sauk River. It offers shaded sites, river views, and good fishing. North Fork Falls is about one mile up the North Fork from camp and worth the trip.

**Campsites, facilities:** There are 21 single and one double sites for tents or RVs up to 21 feet long. Picnic tables and fire grills are provided. Vault toilets, garbage bins, firewood, and a picnic shelter are available. There is no drinking water. A U.S. Forest Service district office is located 19 miles from the campground, in Darrington. Some facilities are wheelchair accessible. Leashed pets are permitted.

**Reservations, fees:** Reservations are accepted at 877/444-6777 ($10 reservation fee) or www.recreation.gov ($9 reservation fee). Single sites are $14 per night, the double is $25 per night, $7 per extra vehicle per night. Open May-early September, weather permitting.

**Directions:** From Seattle, drive north on I-5 to Exit 208 and the junction with Highway 530. Turn east on Highway 530 and drive 32 miles to Darrington and Forest Road 20 (Mountain Loop Highway). Turn right (south) on Forest Road 20 and drive 19 miles to the campground on the right. Obtaining a U.S. Forest Service map is advised.

**Contact:** Mount Baker-Snoqualmie National

Forest, Darrington Ranger District, 360/436-1155, www.fs.usda.gov or www.hoodoo.com.

## 35 RED BRIDGE
🚶🚴🛶🏕🛖♿🚙⛺

### Scenic rating: 9
on the South Fork of Stillaguamish River in Mount Baker-Snoqualmie National Forest

**Map 3.1, page 181**

Red Bridge is a classic spot, one of several in the vicinity, and a good base camp for a backpacking expedition. The campground is set at 1,300 feet elevation on the South Fork of the Stillaguamish River near Mallardy Creek. It has pretty, riverside sites with old-growth fir. Swimming, tubing, and canoeing are not recommended in this particular part of the river; the water surface can be deceptive and there are powerful undercurrents, so please use extreme caution. A trailhead two miles east of camp leads to Granite Pass in the Boulder River Wilderness.

**Campsites, facilities:** There are 15 sites for tents or RVs up to 40 feet long including a few multi-sites. Picnic tables and fire grills are provided. There is no drinking water, but vault toilets, garbage bins, and firewood are available. Some facilities are wheelchair accessible. Leashed pets are permitted.

**Reservations, fees:** Reservations are accepted at 877/444-6777 ($10 reservation fee) or www.recreation.gov ($9 reservation fee). Single sites are $14 per night, multi-sites are $25 per night, $7 per extra vehicle per night. Open mid-May–mid-September, weather permitting.

**Directions:** From I-5 and Everett, turn east on Highway 92 and drive about 15 miles to the town of Granite Falls and Mountain Loop Highway. Continue northeast on Mountain Loop Highway for 18 miles to the campground entrance on the right.

**Contact:** Mount Baker-Snoqualmie National Forest, Darrington Ranger District, 360/436-1155, www.fs.usda.gov or www.hoodoo.com.

## 36 TULALIP MILL GROUP CAMP
🚶🛶🏕♿🚙⛺

### Scenic rating: 7
on the South Fork of the Stillaguamish River in Mount Baker-Snoqualmie National Forest

**Map 3.1, page 181**

This campground is set along the South Fork of the Stillaguamish River, close to several other camps: Turlo, Verlot, Gold Basin, Esswine, Boardman Creek, Coal Creek Bar, and Red Bridge. A trailhead about one mile east of camp leads north into the Boulder River Wilderness. Numerous creeks and streams crisscross this area, providing good fishing prospects.

**Campsites, facilities:** There is one group camp for tents or RVs up to 22 feet long for up to 60 people. Picnic tables and fire grills are provided. Vault toilets and garbage bins are available. There is no drinking water. Some facilities are wheelchair accessible. Leashed pets are permitted.

**Reservations, fees:** Reservations are accepted at 877/444-6777 ($10 reservation fee) or www.recreation.gov ($9 reservation fee). Note that for online reservations, this camp is mistakenly called Tulalip and not Tulalip Mill. The site is $85 per night. Open mid-May–September, weather permitting.

**Directions:** From I-5 and Everett, turn east on Highway 92 and drive about 15 miles to the town of Granite Falls and Mountain Loop Highway. Continue east on Mountain Loop Highway for 18.5 miles to the campground entrance on the right.

**Contact:** Mount Baker-Snoqualmie National Forest, Darrington Ranger District, 360/436-1155, www.fs.usda.gov or www.hoodoo.com.

## 37 COAL CREEK GROUP CAMP

🏃 🚴 🐕 🚙 ⛺

### Scenic rating: 8

on the South Fork of the Stillaguamish River in Mount Baker-Snoqualmie National Forest

**Map 3.1, page 181**

A U.S. Forest Service map will unlock the beautiful country around this campground set along the South Fork of the Stillaguamish River. Fishing access is available for rainbow trout, Dolly Varden, whitefish, and steelhead in season. Nearby forest roads lead to Coal Lake and a trailhead that takes you to other backcountry lakes.

**Campsites, facilities:** There is one group site for tents or RVs up to 30 feet long for up to 25 people. Picnic tables and fire grills are provided. Vault toilets, garbage bins, and firewood are available. There is no drinking water. Leashed pets are permitted.

**Reservations, fees:** Reservations are accepted at 877/444-6777 ($10 reservation fee) or www. recreation.gov ($9 reservation fee). The site is $75 per night. Open mid-May-late September, weather permitting.

**Directions:** From I-5 and Everett, turn east on Highway 92 and drive about 15 miles to the town of Granite Falls and Mountain Loop Highway. Continue northeast on Mountain Loop Highway for 23.5 miles to the campground entrance on the left.

**Contact:** Mount Baker-Snoqualmie National Forest, Darrington Ranger District, 360/436-1155, www.fs.usda.gov or www.hoodoo.com.

## 38 BEAVER PLANT LAKE HIKE-IN

🏃 🏊 🐕 ⛺

### Scenic rating: 8

on Beaver Plant Lake

**Map 3.1, page 181**          **BEST (**

This campground is on Beaver Plant Lake, one of four campgrounds detailed in the area

(the others are Upper Ashland Lake, Lower Ashland Lake, and Twin Falls Lake camps). Excellent hiking trails are a highlight of the region. This trail system is within the Morningstar Natural Resource Conservation Area, and much of the trails are on raised boardwalk. One hiking trail connects to all four lakes. From this trail, you can also access Bald Mountain Trail, which then leads to Cutthroat Trail. It's a nine-mile hike from Beaver Plant Lake to Cutthroat Lake. Department of Natural Resources (DNR) pleads: "Please stay on the trails."

**Campsites, facilities:** There are five tent sites. Fire grills are provided. There is no drinking water and garbage must be packed out. Leashed pets are permitted.

**Reservations, fees:** Reservations are not accepted. There is no fee for camping, but a Discover Pass is required. Open year-round, weather permitting.

**Directions:** From I-5 and Everett, turn east on Highway 92 and drive about 15 miles to the town of Granite Falls and Mountain Loop Highway. Continue east on Mountain Loop Highway for 15 miles to Forest Road 4020. Turn right (south) on Forest Road 4020 and drive 2.5 miles to Forest Road 4021. Turn right on Forest Road 4021 and drive two miles to the Ashland Lakes Trailhead. From the trailhead, hike 2.1 miles to the campground.

**Contact:** Department of Natural Resources, Northwest Region, 360/856-3500, www.dnr.wa.gov.

## 39 UPPER ASHLAND LAKE HIKE-IN

🏃 🏊 🐕 ⛺

### Scenic rating: 9

near Upper Ashland Lake

**Map 3.1, page 181**

Reaching this primitive and beautiful camp requires a 2.5-mile hike that's well worth the effort. The site is little known, so you can expect quiet and privacy. Several good hiking trails can be found near camp; the rangers ask that you stay on the trails. A map available from the Department of Natural Resources is helpful.

**Campsites, facilities:** There are four tent sites. Fire grills are provided. There is no drinking water and garbage must be packed out. Leashed pets are permitted.

**Reservations, fees:** Reservations are not accepted. There is no fee for camping, but a Discover Pass is required. Open mid-June-October, weather permitting.

**Directions:** From I-5 and Everett, turn east on Highway 92 and drive about 15 miles to the town of Granite Falls and Mountain Loop Highway. Turn north on Mountain Loop Highway and drive 15 miles to Forest Road 4020. Turn right (south) on Forest Road 4020 and drive 2.5 miles to Forest Road 4021. Turn right on Forest Road 4021 and drive 2.6 miles to the Ashland Lakes Trailhead. From the trailhead, hike 2.5 miles to the campground.

**Contact:** Department of Natural Resources, Northwest Region, 360/856-3500, www.dnr.wa.gov.

## 40 LOWER ASHLAND LAKE HIKE-IN
🚶 🏊 🏕 ⛰

### Scenic rating: 8
on Lower Ashland Lake

**Map 3.1, page 181**

This campground on Lower Ashland Lake, set adjacent to Upper Ashland Lake, can be reached by hiking in three miles. The camp is within the Morningstar Basin Natural Resource Conservation Area, and there is a trail system that connects the four campgrounds and lakes in the area. DNR pleads: "Please stay on the trails."

**Campsites, facilities:** There are five tent sites. Fire rings are provided. There is no drinking water and garbage must be packed out. Leashed pets are permitted.

**Reservations, fees:** Reservations are not

accepted. There is no fee for camping, but a Discover Pass is required. Open mid-June-October, weather permitting.

**Directions:** From I-5 and Everett, turn east on Highway 92 and drive about 15 miles to the town of Granite Falls and Mountain Loop Highway. Turn north on Mountain Loop Highway and drive 15 miles to Forest Road 4020. Turn right (south) on Forest Road 4020 and drive 2.5 miles to Forest Road 4021. Turn right on Forest Road 4021 and drive two miles to the Ashland Lakes Trailhead. From the trailhead, hike three miles to the campground.

**Contact:** Department of Natural Resources, Northwest Region, 360/856-3500, www.dnr.wa.gov.

## 41 HARTS PASS WALK-IN
🚶 🏕 ♿ ⛰

### Scenic rating: 10
near the Pasayten Wilderness in Okanogan and Wenatchee National Forests

**Map 3.2, page 182**      **BEST (**

At 6,198 feet elevation, Harts Pass is one of the highest drive-through mountain passes in Washington. It features great panoramic views of Mount Gardner, Silver Star, Tower, Golden Horn, Mount Azurite, Ballard, Crater Mountain, Mount Baker (on a clear day), Jack Mountain, the Pickets Range, Pasayten Peak, and Mount Robinson. This pretty little campground is near the Pasayten Wilderness, which offers 500 miles of trails leading to alpine meadows and glacier-fed lakes and streams, and along ridges to spectacular mountain heights. The Pacific Crest Trail passes near the camp and offers a great view of the northern Cascade Range. No trailers are permitted on the access road.

**Campsites, facilities:** There are five walk-in tent sites requiring a 50-foot walk. No RVs or trailers are allowed. Picnic tables and fire grills are provided. Vault toilets are available, but there is no drinking water. Garbage must be packed out. Some facilities are wheelchair accessible. Leashed pets are permitted.

**Reservations, fees:** Reservations are not accepted. Sites are $8 per night for one vehicle, $5 per each additional vehicle. Open mid-July-late September, weather permitting.

**Directions:** From Burlington, drive east on Highway 20 for 120 miles to Mazama Road. Turn left on Mazama Road and drive 0.25 mile to County Road 9140. Turn left and drive northwest for seven miles to Lost River, where the pavement ends and the road soon becomes Forest Road 5400. Continue on Forest Road 5400 for 12.5 miles northwest to the campground (across from a guard station). Note: Forest Road 5400 is a narrow, curving road with steep slide cliffs that is closed to trailers. Drive slowly and yield to trucks.

**Contact:** Okanogan and Wenatchee National Forests, Methow Valley Ranger District, 509/996-4003, www.fs.usda.gov; Methow Valley Visitor Center, 509/996-4000.

## 42 MEADOWS

### Scenic rating: 9

near the Pacific Crest Trail in Okanogan and Wenatchee National Forests

**Map 3.2, page 182**

Set adjacent to the Pacific Crest Trail, this campground is about one mile from Harts Pass and offers the same opportunities. With its plentiful spruce and subalpine fir, the camp is beautiful in summer; springtime brings an array of wildflowers. No trailers are permitted on the access road.

**Campsites, facilities:** There are 14 tent sites. Picnic tables and fire grills are provided. Vault toilets are available. There is no drinking water, and garbage must be packed out. Some facilities are wheelchair accessible. Leashed pets are permitted.

**Reservations, fees:** Reservations are not accepted. Sites are $8 per night for one vehicle, $5 per each additional vehicle. Open mid-July-September, weather permitting.

**Directions:** From Burlington, drive east on Highway 20 for 120 miles to Mazama Road. Turn left on Mazama Road and drive 0.25 mile to County Road 9140. Turn left and drive northwest for seven miles to Lost River, where the pavement ends and the road soon becomes Forest Road 5400. Continue on Forest Road 5400 for 12.5 miles to Forest Road 5400-500. Turn left (south) and drive one mile to the campground. Note: Forest Road 5400 is a narrow, curving road with steep slide cliffs that is closed to trailers. Drive slowly and yield to trucks.

**Contact:** Okanogan and Wenatchee National Forests, Methow Valley Ranger District, 509/996-4003, www.fs.usda.gov; Methow Valley Visitor Center, 509/996-4000.

## 43 BALLARD

### Scenic rating: 6

near the Methow River in Okanogan and Wenatchee National Forests

**Map 3.2, page 182**

Ballard is set at an elevation of 2,521 feet, about 0.5 mile from River Bend. Numerous hiking trails can be found in the area, as well as access to West Fork Methow and Lost River Monument Creek Trails. It is also possible to hike west and eventually hook up with the Pacific Crest Trail. Possible side trips include Winthrop to the south, which boasts a historical museum, a state fish hatchery, and Pearrygin Lake State Park. Livestock are not permitted in the campground, but a hitching rail and stock truck dock are available at the Robinson Creek Trailhead near the campground, where there are several primitive sites.

**Campsites, facilities:** There are seven sites for tents or RVs up to 28 feet long. Picnic tables and fire grills are provided. Vault toilets are available, but there is no drinking water. Garbage must be packed out. Some facilities are wheelchair accessible. Leashed pets are permitted. No livestock are permitted in camp.

**Reservations, fees:** Reservations are not

accepted. Sites are $8 per night for one vehicle, $5 per each additional vehicle. Open late May-October, weather permitting.

**Directions:** From Burlington, drive east on Highway 20 for 120 miles to Mazama Road. Turn left on Mazama Road and drive 0.25 mile to County Road 9140. Turn left and drive northwest for seven miles to Lost River, where the pavement ends and the road soon becomes Forest Road 5400. Continue northwest on Forest Road 5400 for two miles to the campground on the left.

**Contact:** Okanogan and Wenatchee National Forests, Methow Valley Ranger District, 509/996-4003, www.fs.usda.gov; Methow Valley Visitor Center, 509/996-4000.

## 44 RIVER BEND

**Scenic rating: 6**

on the Methow River in Okanogan and Wenatchee National Forests

**Map 3.2, page 182**

This campground is located along the Methow River at 2,600 feet elevation, about two miles from the boundary of the Pasayten Wilderness. Several trails near the camp provide access to the wilderness, and another trail follows the Methow River west for about eight miles before hooking up with the Pacific Crest Trail near Azurite Peak.

**Campsites, facilities:** There are five sites for tents, trailers, or RVs up to 30 feet long. Picnic tables and fire grills are provided. Vault toilets are available. There is no drinking water, and garbage must be packed out. Leashed pets are permitted.

**Reservations, fees:** Reservations are not accepted. Sites are $8 per night for one vehicle, $5 per each additional vehicle. Open late May-late October, weather permitting.

**Directions:** From Burlington, drive east on Highway 20 for 120 miles to Mazama Road. Turn left on Mazama Road and drive 0.25 mile to County Road 9140. Turn left and drive

northwest for seven miles to Lost River, where the pavement ends and the road soon becomes Forest Road 5400. Continue northwest on Forest Road 5400 for two miles to Forest Road 5400-600. Continue straight on Forest Road 5400-600 and drive 0.5 mile to the campground on the left.

**Contact:** Okanogan and Wenatchee National Forests, Methow Valley Ranger District, 509/996-4003, www.fs.usda.gov; Methow Valley Visitor Center, 509/996-4000.

## 45 EARLY WINTERS

**Scenic rating: 6**

on Early Winters Creek in Okanogan and Wenatchee National Forests

**Map 3.2, page 182**

Located on each side of the highway, this campground has an unusual configuration. The confluence of Early Winters Creek and the Methow River mark the site of this campground. The elevation is 2,160 feet. You'll find great views of Goat Wall here. Campsites are flat, and the open landscape, set in a sparse lodgepole pine and fir forest, provides an arid feel to the area. Several hiking trails can be found within five miles, including one that leads south to Cedar Creek Falls. Other possible side trips include Goat Wall to the north and the town of Winthrop to the south, which boasts a historical museum, a state fish hatchery, and Pearrygin Lake State Park.

**Campsites, facilities:** There are 12 sites for tents or RVs up to 24 feet long. Picnic tables and fire grills are provided. Drinking water, vault toilets, and garbage bins are available. There is a small store and snack bar in Mazama, about two miles away. Some facilities are wheelchair accessible. Leashed pets are permitted.

**Reservations, fees:** Reservations are not accepted. Sites are $8 per night for one vehicle, $5 per each additional vehicle. Open mid-May-October, weather permitting.

**Directions:** From Burlington, drive east on

Highway 20 for 116 miles to the campground (if you reach County Road 1163 near Mazama, you have gone two miles too far).

**Contact:** Okanogan and Wenatchee National Forests, Methow Valley Ranger District, 509/996-4003, www.fs.usda.gov; Methow Valley Visitor Center, 509/996-4000.

## 46 KLIPCHUCK

### Scenic rating: 7

on Early Winters Creek in Okanogan and Wenatchee National Forests

**Map 3.2, page 182**

This camp is located at an elevation of 3,000 feet along Early Winters Creek. The camp area is set amid majestic trees, primarily Douglas fir and subalpine firs. Klipchuck provides hiking aplenty, but note that rattlesnakes are occasionally seen in this area. A short loop trail from the camp leads about five miles up and over Delancy Ridge to Driveway Butte and down to the creek, although the trail is somewhat overgrown. Another trail starts nearby on Forest Road 200 (Sandy Butte-Cedar Creek Road) and goes two miles up Cedar Creek to lovely Cedar Creek Falls. Still another option from the campground is a four-mile trail along Early Winters Creek. This region is best visited in the spring and fall, with summer hot and dry.

**Campsites, facilities:** There are 46 sites for tents or RVs up to 34 feet long. Sites can be combined to accommodate groups. Picnic tables and fire grills are provided. Drinking water, vault toilets, and garbage bins are available. Some facilities are wheelchair accessible. Leashed pets are permitted.

**Reservations, fees:** Reservations are not accepted. Sites are $12 per night for one vehicle, $5 per each additional vehicle. Open late May-late September, weather permitting.

**Directions:** From Burlington, drive east on Highway 20 for 115 miles to Forest Road 300. (If you reach the Methow River Valley, you have gone four miles past the turnoff.) Turn

left (marked) and drive northwest one mile to the camp at the end of the road. Camp is 19 miles northwest of Winthrop.

**Contact:** Okanogan and Wenatchee National Forests, Methow Valley Ranger District, 509/996-4003, www.fs.usda.gov; Methow Valley Visitor Center, 509/996-4000.

## 47 LONE FIR

### Scenic rating: 9

on Early Winters Creek in Okanogan and Wenatchee National Forests

**Map 3.2, page 182**

Lone Fir is set at 3,640 feet elevation along the banks of Early Winters Creek. A loop trail through the campground woods is wheelchair accessible for 0.4 mile. The area has had some timber operations in the past, but there are no nearby clear-cuts. To the west, Washington Pass Overlook offers a spectacular view. Anglers can fish in the creek, and many hiking and biking trails crisscross the area, including the trailhead for Cutthroat Lake. Other possible side trips include Goat Wall to the north and the town of Winthrop to the south, which boasts a historical museum, a state fish hatchery, and Pearrygin Lake State Park.

**Campsites, facilities:** There are 27 sites for tents or RVs up to 36 feet long. Picnic tables and fire grills are provided. Drinking water, vault toilets, and garbage bins are available. Some facilities are wheelchair accessible. Leashed pets are permitted.

**Reservations, fees:** Reservations are not accepted. Sites are $12 per night for one vehicle, $5 per each additional vehicle. Open late June-September, weather permitting.

**Directions:** From Burlington, drive east on Highway 20 for 107 miles to the campground (11 miles west of Mazama) on the right.

**Contact:** Okanogan and Wenatchee National Forests, Methow Valley Ranger District, 509/996-4003, www.fs.usda.gov; Methow Valley Visitor Center, 509/996-4000.

## 48 CAMP FOUR

### Scenic rating: 6

on the Chewuch River in Okanogan and
Wenatchee National Forests

**Map 3.2, page 182**

Camp Four is the smallest and most primitive
of the three camps along the Chewuch River
(the others are Chewuch and Falls Creek). It
is set at an elevation of 2,400 feet. Trailers are
not recommended. There are three trailheads
five miles north of camp: two at Lake Creek
and another at Andrews Creek. They all have
corrals, hitching rails, truck docks, and water
for stock at the trailheads, but no livestock
are permitted in the campground itself. Trails
leading into the Pasayten Wilderness leave
from both locations.

**Campsites, facilities:** There are three tent
sites and two sites for tents or RVs up to 16
feet long. Fire grills and picnic tables are provided. Vault toilets are available, but there is
no drinking water. Garbage must be packed
out. Some facilities are wheelchair accessible.
Leashed pets are permitted, but no livestock
are permitted in camp.

**Reservations, fees:** Reservations are not accepted. Sites are $8 per night for one vehicle,
$5 per each additional vehicle. Open late May-
October, weather permitting.

**Directions:** From Burlington, drive east on
Highway 20 for 134 miles to Winthrop and
County Road 1213/West Chewuch Road.
Turn north on County Road 1213/West
Chewuch Road and drive 6.5 miles (where it
merges with Forest Road 51). Continue north
on Forest Road 51 for 11 miles to the camp-
ground on the right.

**Contact:** Okanogan and Wenatchee National Forests, Methow Valley Ranger District,
509/996-4003, www.fs.usda.gov; Methow
Valley Visitor Center, 509/996-4000.

## 49 HONEYMOON

### Scenic rating: 8

on Eightmile Creek in Okanogan and
Wenatchee National Forests

**Map 3.2, page 182**

This small camp is set along Eightmile Creek at
an elevation of 3,280 feet. If you continue north
seven miles to the end of Forest Road 5130,
you'll reach a trailhead that provides access
to the Pasayten Wilderness. Why is it named
Honeymoon? Well, it seems that a forest ranger
and his bride chose this quiet and secluded spot
along the creek to spend their wedding night.

**Campsites, facilities:** There are five sites for
tents or small RVs up to 18 feet long. Picnic tables
and fire grills are provided. Vault toilets are available, but there is no drinking water. Garbage
must be packed out. Some facilities are wheelchair accessible. Leashed pets are permitted.

**Reservations, fees:** Reservations are not
accepted. Sites are $8 per night, $5 per each
additional vehicle. Open late May-September,
weather permitting.

**Directions:** From Burlington, drive east on
Highway 20 for 134 miles to Winthrop and
County Road 1213/West Chewuch Road.
Turn north on County Road 1213/West
Chewuch Road and drive 6.5 miles (where
it merges with Forest Road 5130). Continue
north on Forest Road 5130 for 10 miles to the
campground on the right.

**Contact:** Okanogan and Wenatchee National Forests, Methow Valley Ranger District,
509/996-4003, www.fs.usda.gov; Methow
Valley Visitor Center, 509/996-4000.

## 50 CHEWUCH

### Scenic rating: 6

on the Chewuch River in Okanogan and
Wenatchee National Forests

**Map 3.2, page 182**

Chewuch Camp is set along the Chewuch

River at an elevation of 2,278 feet and is surrounded by ponderosa pines. It is a small camp where catch-and-release fishing is a highlight. There are also hiking and biking trails in the area. By traveling north, you can access trailheads that lead into the Pasayten Wilderness. This camp provides an alternative to the more developed nearby Falls Creek campground.

**Campsites, facilities:** There are 16 sites for tents or RVs up to 35 feet long. Picnic tables and fire grills are provided. Drinking water, vault toilets, and garbage bins are available. Some facilities are wheelchair accessible. Leashed pets are permitted.

**Reservations, fees:** Reservations are not accepted. Sites are $12 per night for one vehicle, $5 per each additional vehicle. Open late May-November, weather permitting.

**Directions:** From Burlington, drive east on Highway 20 for 134 miles to Winthrop and County Road 1213/West Chewuch Road. Turn north on County Road 1213/West Chewuch Road and drive 6.5 miles (where it merges with Forest Road 51). Continue north on Forest Road 51 for seven miles to the campground on the right.

**Contact:** Okanogan and Wenatchee National Forests, Methow Valley Ranger District, 509/996-4003, www.fs.usda.gov; Methow Valley Visitor Center, 509/996-4000.

## 51 FLAT

### Scenic rating: 6

on Eightmile Creek in Okanogan and Wenatchee National Forests

**Map 3.2, page 182**

This campground is set along Eightmile Creek, two miles from where it empties into the Chewuch River. The elevation is 2,858 feet. Buck Lake is about three miles away. This is the closest of six camps to County Road 1213. Other options include Honeymoon, Nice, and Falls Creek.

**Campsites, facilities:** There are 12 sites for tents or RVs up to 36 feet long. Picnic tables and fire grills are provided. Vault toilets and drinking water are available. Garbage must be packed out. Some facilities are wheelchair accessible. Leashed pets are permitted.

**Reservations, fees:** Reservations are not accepted. Sites are $8 per night, $5 per each additional vehicle. Open early May-November, weather permitting.

**Directions:** From Burlington, drive east on Highway 20 for 134 miles to Winthrop and County Road 1213 (West Chewuch Road). Turn north on West Chewuch Road and drive 6.5 miles (the road becomes Forest Road 51). Continue on Forest Road 51 and drive three miles to Forest Road 5130 (Eightmile Creek Road). Turn left (northwest) and drive two miles to the campground on the left.

**Contact:** Okanogan and Wenatchee National Forests, Methow Valley Ranger District, 509/996-4003, www.fs.usda.gov; Methow Valley Visitor Center, 509/996-4000.

## 52 FALLS CREEK

### Scenic rating: 7

on the Chewuch River in Okanogan and Wenatchee National Forests

**Map 3.2, page 182**

About a 20-minute drive out of Winthrop, Falls Creek is a quiet and pretty campground located at the confluence of its namesake, Falls Creek, and the Chewuch River. The elevation is 2,100 feet. Highlights include fishing access and a 0.25-mile trail (wheelchair accessible) to a waterfall located across the road from the campground.

**Campsites, facilities:** There are seven sites for tents or RVs up to 18 feet long. Picnic tables and fire grills are provided. Vault toilets and drinking water are available. Garbage must be packed out. Some facilities are wheelchair accessible. Leashed pets are permitted.

**Reservations, fees:** Reservations are not

accepted. Sites are $8 per night for one vehicle, $5 per each additional vehicle. Open May-late September, weather permitting.

**Directions:** From Burlington, drive east on Highway 20 for 134 miles to Winthrop and County Road 1213 (West Chewuch Road). Turn north on West Chewuch Road and drive 6.5 miles (becomes Forest Road 51). Continue on Forest Road 51 and drive 5.2 miles to the campground on the right. Obtaining a U.S. Forest Service map is advised.

**Contact:** Okanogan and Wenatchee National Forests, Methow Valley Ranger District, 509/996-4003, www.fs.usda.gov; Methow Valley Visitor Center, 509/996-4000.

## 53 NICE

### Scenic rating: 6
on Eightmile Creek in Okanogan and Wenatchee National Forests

**Map 3.2, page 182**

Nice is situated along Eightmile Creek, about four miles from Buck Lake. Youngsters will enjoy exploring a nearby beaver pond. A trail leading into the Pasayten Wilderness can be found at the end of Forest Road 5130. Pearrygin Lake State Park is just a few miles to the south, near Winthrop. Note: There is no turnaround area for RVs.

**Campsites, facilities:** There are three sites for tents or RVs up to 35 feet. Picnic tables and fire grills are provided. Vault toilets are available, but there is no drinking water. Garbage must be packed out. Some facilities are wheelchair accessible. Leashed pets are permitted.

**Reservations, fees:** Reservations are not accepted. Sites are $8 per night for one vehicle, $5 per each additional vehicle. Open late May-late September, weather permitting.

**Directions:** From Burlington, drive east on Highway 20 for 134 miles to Winthrop and County Road 1213 (West Chewuch Road). Turn north on West Chewuch Road and drive 6.5 miles (the road becomes Forest Road 51).

Continue on Forest Road 51 and drive three miles to Forest Road 5130 (Eightmile Creek Road). Turn left (northwest) and drive four miles to the campground on the left.

**Contact:** Okanogan and Wenatchee National Forests, Methow Valley Ranger District, 509/996-4003, www.fs.usda.gov; Methow Valley Visitor Center, 509/996-4000.

## 54 PEARRYGIN LAKE STATE PARK

### Scenic rating: 8
on Pearrygin Lake

**Map 3.2, page 182**                    **BEST (**

Pearrygin Lake is fed from underground springs and Pearrygin Creek, the lifeblood for this setting and the adjacent 696-acre state park. Located in the beautiful Methow Valley, it's ringed by the Northern Cascade Mountains. The park is known for its expansive green lawns, which lead to 8,200 feet of waterfront and sandy beaches. The camp is frequented by red-winged and yellow-headed blackbirds, as well as by marmots. Wildflower- and wildlife-viewing are excellent in the spring. The campground has access to a sandy beach and facilities for swimming, boating, waterskiing, fishing, and hiking. The sites are set close together and don't offer much privacy, but they are spacious and shaded, and a variety of recreation options make it worth the crunch.

**Campsites, facilities:** There are 67 tent sites, 50 sites with full hookups (15 and 30 amp), and 27 sites with partial hookups for tents or RVs up to 60 feet long. There are also two hike-in/bike-in sites, two cabins, a vacation house, and two group sites for up to 48 and 80 people each. Picnic tables and fire grills are provided. Restrooms with flush toilets and coin showers, drinking water, a dump station, firewood, Junior Ranger program, horseshoe pits, swimming beach, and volleyball court are available. A store, deli, and ice are located within one mile. Boat launching and dock facilities and boat rentals are available. Some facilities are wheelchair accessible. Leashed pets are permitted.

**Reservations, fees:** Reservations are accepted for family sites and are required for group camps, cabins, and the vacation house at 888/ CAMP-OUT (888/226-7688) or www.parks. wa.gov/reservations ($6.50-8.50 reservation fee). Tent sites are $17-31 per night, RV sites with partial hookups are $27-39 per night, RV sites with full hookups are $27-42 per night, $10 per extra vehicle per night, hike-in/bike-in sites are $12 per night, and group sites are $2.25 per person per night. Cabins are $75.69 per night and the vacation house is $167.84 per night with a two-night minimum. Some credit cards are accepted. Open April-early November.

**Directions:** From Winthrop and Highway 20, drive north through town (road changes to East Chewuch Road). Continue 1.5 miles north from town to Bear Creek Road. Turn right and drive 1.5 miles to the end of the pavement and the park entrance on the right. Turn right, drive over the cattle guard, and continue 0.75 miles to the West Campground or 1.5 miles to the East Campground.

**Contact:** Pearrygin Lake State Park, 509/996-2370; state park information, 360/902-8844, www.parks.wa.gov.

## 55 KOA WINTHROP

**Scenic rating: 7**

on the Methow River

**Map 3.2, page 182**

Here's another campground set along the Methow River, which offers opportunities for fishing, boating, swimming, and rafting. The park has a free shuttle into Winthrop, an interesting town with many restored, early-1900s buildings lining the main street. One such building, the Shafer Museum, displays an array of period items. If you would like to observe wildlife, take a short, two-mile drive southeast out of Winthrop on County Road 9129 on

the east side of the Methow River. Turn east on County Road 1631 into Davis Lake and follow the signs to the Methow River Habitat Management Area Headquarters. Depending on the time of year, you may see mule deer, porcupines, bobcats, mountain lions, snowshoe hares, black bears, red squirrels, and many species of birds. If you're looking for something tamer, other nearby recreation options include an 18-hole golf course and tennis courts.

**Campsites, facilities:** There are 60 sites with full or partial hookups for RVs of any length, 15 sites with no hookups for RVs of any length, and 35 tent sites. There are also 20 one- and two-room cabins. Some sites are pull-through. Picnic tables and fire grills are provided. Restrooms with flush toilets and showers, drinking water, firewood, a dump station, recreation hall, high-speed modem and Wi-Fi access, bike and video rentals, a convenience store, coin laundry, ice, a playground, and a seasonal heated swimming pool are available. Propane gas and a café are located within one mile. There is a courtesy shuttle to and from Winthrop. Some facilities are wheelchair accessible. Leashed pets are permitted.

**Reservations, fees:** Reservations are accepted at 800/562-2158. Sites are $32-43 per night, $3-7 per person per night for more than two people. Some credit cards are accepted. Open mid-April-October.

**Directions:** From Winthrop, drive east on Highway 20 for one mile to the camp on the left. The camp is between Mileposts 194 and 195.

**Contact:** KOA Winthrop, 509/996-2258, www.koa.com.

## 56 BIG TWIN LAKE CAMPGROUND

**Scenic rating: 5**

on Big Twin Lake

**Map 3.2, page 182**

As you might figure from the name, this campground is set along the shore of Big Twin Lake. With its sweeping lawn and shade trees, the camp features views of the lake from all campsites. No gas motors are permitted on the lake. Fly-fishing is good for rainbow trout, with special regulations in effect: one-fish limit, single barbless hook, artificial lures only. This is an ideal lake for a float tube, rowboat with a casting platform, or a pram. A short drive out of Winthrop (County Road 9129) leads to the Methow River Habitat Management Area Headquarters. Depending on the time of year, you may see mule deer, porcupines, bobcats, mountain lions, snowshoe hares, black bears, red squirrels, and many species of birds. Other recreation options include an 18-hole golf course and tennis courts.

**Campsites, facilities:** There are 50 sites with full or partial hookups for RVs of any length, and 35 tent sites. Some sites are pull-through. Picnic tables and fire grills are provided. Restrooms with flush toilets and coin showers, drinking water, a dump station, firewood, ice, Wi-Fi, and a playground are available. Boat docks, launching facilities, and boat rentals are on Big Twin Lake. Some facilities are wheelchair accessible. Leashed pets are permitted.

**Reservations, fees:** Reservations are accepted. RV sites are $30 per night tent sites are $24 per night, $7 per person per night for more than two people, $7 per extra vehicle per night. Monthly rates are available. Open mid-April-October.

**Directions:** From Winthrop, drive east on Highway 20 for three miles to Twin Lakes Road. Turn right (west) on Twin Lakes Road and drive two miles to the campground on the right.

**Contact:** Big Twin Lake Campground, 509/996-2650, www.methownet.com/bigtwin.

## 57 ROADS END

### Scenic rating: 8

on the Twisp River in Okanogan and Wenatchee National Forests

**Map 3.2, page 182**

This quiet trailhead camp is located at the end of Twisp River Road. Set at an elevation of 3,600 feet along the Twisp River, it features a major trailhead that provides fishing access and a chance to hike for mountain views and explore the Lake Chelan-Sawtooth Wilderness. The trail intersects with Copper Creek Trail and the Pacific Crest Trail about nine miles from the camp. A U.S. Forest Service map is essential. Note that this camp is closed in the off-season to protect bull trout, an endangered species.

**Campsites, facilities:** There are four sites for tents or small RVs up to 16 feet long. Picnic tables and fire grills are provided. Vault toilets are available. There is no drinking water, and garbage must be packed out. Some facilities are wheelchair accessible. Leashed pets are permitted.

**Reservations, fees:** Reservations are not accepted. Sites are $8 per night for one vehicle, $5 per each additional vehicle. Open late May-early September, weather permitting.

**Directions:** From Burlington, drive east on Highway 20 for 145 miles to Twisp and County Road 9114 (Twisp River Road). Turn west on County Road 9114 and drive 11 miles (becomes Forest Road 44, then eventually Forest Road 4440). Continue west for 13.5 miles to the campground. Obtaining a U.S. Forest Service map is advisable.

**Contact:** Okanogan and Wenatchee National Forests, Methow Valley Ranger District, 509/996-4003, www.fs.usda.gov; Methow Valley Visitor Center, 509/996-4000.

## 58 SOUTH CREEK

### Scenic rating: 6

on the Twisp River in Okanogan and Wenatchee National Forests

**Map 3.2, page 182**

Although small, quiet, and little known, South Creek Campground packs a wallop with good recreation options. It's set at the confluence of the Twisp River and South Creek at a major trailhead that accesses the Lake Chelan-Sawtooth Wilderness. The South Creek Trailhead provides a hike to Louis Lake. The elevation at the camp is 3,100 feet.

**Campsites, facilities:** There are four sites for tents or RVs up to 24 feet long. Picnic tables and fire grills are provided. A vault toilet is available. There is no drinking water, and garbage must be packed out. Some facilities are wheelchair accessible. Leashed pets are permitted.

**Reservations, fees:** Reservations are not accepted. Sites are $8 per night, $5 extra vehicle fee. Open late May-September, weather permitting.

**Directions:** From Burlington, drive east on Highway 20 for 145 miles to Twisp and County Road 9114 (Twisp River Road). Turn right on County Road 9114 and drive 17.5 miles (becomes Forest Road 44). Continue west (becomes Forest Road 4440 and a dirt road) for 4.5 miles to the campground on the left.

**Contact:** Okanogan and Wenatchee National Forests, Methow Valley Ranger District, 509/996-4003, www.fs.usda.gov; Methow Valley Visitor Center, 509/996-4000.

## 59 POPLAR FLAT
🏃 🏕 ♿ 🚐 ⛺

### Scenic rating: 7
on the Twisp River in Okanogan and Wenatchee National Forests

**Map 3.2, page 182**

This campground is set at 2,900 feet elevation along the Twisp River. This area provides many wildlife-viewing opportunities for deer, black bears, and many species of birds. Several trails in the area, including Twisp River Trail, follow streams and some provide access to the Lake Chelan-Sawtooth Wilderness.

**Campsites, facilities:** There are 16 sites for tents or RVs up to 22 feet long including a group site for up to 12 people. Picnic tables and fire grills are provided. Drinking water, vault toilets, and garbage bins are available. A day-use picnic area with a shelter is nearby. Some facilities are wheelchair accessible. Leashed pets are permitted.

**Reservations, fees:** Reservations are not accepted. Sites are $12 per night for one vehicle, $5 per each additional vehicle. Open mid-May-September, weather permitting.

**Directions:** From Burlington, drive east on Highway 20 for 145 miles to Twisp and County Road 9114 (Twisp River Road). Turn west on County Road 9114 and drive 11 miles (becomes Forest Road 44 and then Forest Road 4440). Continue west for 9.5 miles to the campground on the left.

**Contact:** Okanogan and Wenatchee National Forests, Methow Valley Ranger District, 509/996-4003, www.fs.usda.gov; Methow Valley Visitor Center, 509/996-4000.

## 60 WEAVER POINT BOAT-IN
🏃 ♨ 🛶 ⛵ ⛺

### Scenic rating: 7
on Lake Chelan in North Cascades National Park

**Map 3.2, page 182**

The largest campground in the Stehekin area, this boat-in campground on Lake Chelan gets high use on summer weekends. The only direct access to Stehekin is by boat or an 8.5-mile hike to Stehekin Landing from the campground; a shuttle is also available for the first four miles. It's a fairly easy tromp, with no steep grades.

**Campsites, facilities:** There are 22 sites accessible only by boat, ferry, or floatplane. Picnic tables and fire grills are provided. Drinking water and vault toilets are available. Garbage must be packed out. Food storage lockers are available and must be used. One dock is available for boats.

**Reservations, fees:** Reservations are not accepted. There is no fee for camping. There is no entrance fee for North Cascades National Park. There is a $5 per day docking fee (or $40 annual pass). Open year-round, with limited facilities in winter.

**Directions:** From Wenatchee, drive on U.S. 97 for approximately 40 miles to Chelan and the ferry. Take the ferry and proceed to Weaver

Point. The campground is also directly accessible by floatplane. (Call Chelan Seaplanes at 509/682-5555 for more information.)

**Contact:** North Cascades National Park, 360/856-5700, www.nps.gov/noca; Lake Chelan Boat Company, 509/682-4584, www.ladyofthelake.com.

## 61 TWISP RIVER HORSE CAMP

**Scenic rating: 7**

on the Twisp River in Okanogan and Wenatchee National Forests

**Map 3.2, page 182**

This camp is only for horses and their owners. It is set on the Twisp River at an elevation of 3,000 feet. The camp features nearby access to trails, including North Fork Twisp River Trail, which leads to Copper Pass, and South Fork Twisp River Trail, which leads to Lake Chelan National Recreation Area and Twisp Pass. South Creek Trail is also available and leads from the camp to Lake Chelan National Recreation Area.

**Campsites, facilities:** There are 12 sites for tents or RVs up to 30 feet long. Picnic tables and fire grills are provided. Vault toilets are available. There is no drinking water, and garbage must be packed out. For horses, a loading ramp, hitching rails, and feed stations are available. Some facilities are wheelchair accessible. Leashed pets are permitted.

**Reservations, fees:** Reservations are not accepted. Northwest Forest Pass ($5 daily fee or $30 annual fee per parked vehicle) is required. Open May-September, weather permitting.

**Directions:** From Burlington, drive east on Highway 20 for 145 miles to Twisp and County Road 9114 (Twisp River Road). Turn west on County Road 9114 and drive 11 miles (becomes Forest Road 44). Continue west on Forest Road 44 for 3.5 miles to War Creek Campground on the left. Continue 250 yards to Forest Road 4430. Turn left (drive over the

bridge) and drive approximately nine miles (the road becomes Forest Road 4435) to the campground on the right.

**Contact:** Okanogan and Wenatchee National Forests, Methow Valley Ranger District, 509/996-4003, www.fs.usda.gov; Methow Valley Visitor Center, 509/996-4000.

## 62 WAR CREEK

**Scenic rating: 6**

on the Twisp River in Okanogan and Wenatchee National Forests

**Map 3.2, page 182**

This trailhead camp is set at 2,400 feet elevation and provides several routes into the Lake Chelan-Sawtooth Wilderness. War Creek Trail, Eagle Creek Trail, and Oval Creek Trail all offer wilderness access and trout fishing. Backpackers can extend this trip into Lake Chelan National Recreation Area, for a 15-mile trek that finishes at the shore of Lake Chelan and the National Park Service outpost. Rattlesnakes are occasionally spotted in this region in the summer.

**Campsites, facilities:** There are 10 sites for tents or RVs up to 22 feet long. Picnic tables and fire grills are provided. Vault toilets, drinking water, and firewood are available. Garbage must be packed out. Some facilities are wheelchair accessible. Leashed pets are permitted.

**Reservations, fees:** Reservations are not accepted. Sites are $8 per night for one vehicle, $5 per each additional vehicle. Open May-October, weather permitting.

**Directions:** From Burlington, drive east on Highway 20 for 145 miles to Twisp and County Road 9114 (Twisp River Road). Turn west on County Road 9114 and drive 11 miles (becomes Forest Road 44). Continue west on Forest Road 44 for 3.5 miles to the campground on the left.

**Contact:** Okanogan and Wenatchee National Forests, Methow Valley Ranger District,

509/996-4003, www.fs.usda.gov; Methow Valley Visitor Center, 509/996-4000.

# 63 BLACKPINE LAKE

### Scenic rating: 7
on Blackpine Lake in Okanogan and Wenatchee National Forests

**Map 3.2, page 182**

This campground features great views of some local peaks. About one-third of the campsites have views; the rest are set in a forest of Douglas fir and ponderosa pine. This popular spot often fills up on summer weekends and occasionally even during the week. Fishing is available for stocked rainbow trout. Note that boating is permitted, but no gas motors are allowed, only electric motors. Less than 0.25 mile long, an interpretive trail leads around the north end of the lake.

**Campsites, facilities:** There are 23 sites for tents or RVs up to 30 feet long. Picnic tables and fire grills are provided. Drinking water, vault toilets, and garbage bins are available. A boat launch and two floating docks are available nearby. Some facilities are wheelchair accessible. Leashed pets are permitted.

**Reservations, fees:** Reservations are not accepted. Sites are $12 per night, $5 per each additional vehicle. Open May-September, weather permitting.

**Directions:** From Burlington, drive east on Highway 20 for 145 miles to Twisp and County Road 9114 (Twisp River Road). Turn west on County Road 9114 and drive 10 miles to County Road 1090. Turn left and drive over a bridge (becomes Forest Road 43) and continue eight miles to the campground on the right.

**Contact:** Okanogan and Wenatchee National Forests, Methow Valley Ranger District, 509/996-4003, www.fs.usda.gov; Methow Valley Visitor Center, 509/996-4000.

# 64 RIVERBEND RV PARK

### Scenic rating: 6
on the Methow River

**Map 3.2, page 182**

The shore of the Methow River skirts this campground, and there is a nice separate area for tent campers set right along the river. Some of the RV sites are also riverfront. Trout fishing, river rafting, and swimming are popular here. The nearby Methow River Habitat Management Area Headquarters offers wildlife-viewing for mule deer, porcupines, bobcats, mountain lions, snowshoe hares, black bears, red squirrels, and many species of birds. Other recreation options include an 18-hole golf course and tennis courts.

**Campsites, facilities:** There are 69 sites with full hookups (20, 30, and 50 amps) for RVs of any length and 35 sites for tents. Some sites are pull-through. Picnic tables and fire pits are provided. Restrooms with flush toilets and coin showers, an RV dump station, firewood, a convenience store, coin laundry, ice, a playground, horseshoe pits, propane gas, Wi-Fi access, group picnic shelter, and RV storage are available. Groups can be accommodated. Leashed pets are permitted.

**Reservations, fees:** Reservations are recommended at 800/686-4498. RV sites are $33-38 per night, tent sites are $25-35 per night, $5-7 per person per night for more than two people, $5 per night per extra vehicle, and $5 per pet. Weekly and monthly rates available. Some credit cards are accepted. Open year-round.

**Directions:** From Twisp, drive west on Highway 20 for two miles to the park on the right, between Mileposts 199 and 200.

**Contact:** Riverbend RV Park, 509/997-3500 or 800/686-4498, www.riverbendrv.com.

## 65 DOMKE LAKE FERRY-IN, HIKE-IN

🏃 🚣 🚤 🐕 ⛺

### Scenic rating: 9

near the Glacier Peak Wilderness in Wenatchee National Forest

**Map 3.2, page 182**

Little known and little used, this spot is a perfect jumping-off point for a wilderness backpacking trip. Domke Lake is about one mile long and 0.5 mile wide and offers good fishing by boat. Trails continue past the lake into the Glacier Peak Wilderness. The camp is set at 2,210 feet elevation and is one of three national forest campgrounds near Domke Lake.

**Campsites, facilities:** There are four tent sites accessible only by boat, ferry, or floatplane. Picnic tables and fire rings are provided. Pit toilets are available, but there is no drinking water. Garbage must be packed out. Boat rentals are available nearby at Domke Lake Resort. Be prepared to protect food from bears; bear-proof food hangs or canisters are required. Leashed pets are permitted.

**Reservations, fees:** Reservations are not accepted; there is no camping fee. A $5 per-day (or $40 Season Pass) dock-site fee is required at Lucerne or Refrigerator Harbor campgrounds if you bring a private boat. For ferry rates, which vary according to boat and age of passenger, phone 509/682-4584; typically rates are in the $35-60 range round-trip. Open May-late October, weather permitting.

**Directions:** From Wenatchee, drive north on U.S. 97-A for 40 miles to Chelan and the ferry. Take the ferry and proceed 41 miles to Lucerne. From Lucerne, hike, bike, or motorbike on Trail 1280 for 2.5 miles to Domke Lake and the campground. The campground is also directly accessible by floatplane. (Call Chelan Seaplanes at 509/682-5555 for more information.)

**Contact:** Okanogan and Wenatchee National Forests, Chelan Ranger District, 509/682-4900, www.fs.usda.gov; Lake Chelan Boat Company, 509/682-4584, www.ladyofthelake.com.

## 66 PRINCE CREEK

🏃 🚣 🚤 ⛺

### Scenic rating: 10

on Lake Chelan in Wenatchee National Forest

**Map 3.2, page 182**

This camp is set along the east shore of Lake Chelan at the mouth of Prince Creek, 18 miles south of Stehekin on Trail 1247. It's a busy camp on summer weekends. A trail from camp follows Prince Creek into the Lake Chelan-Sawtooth Wilderness and then connects to a network of other trails, all of which lead to various lakes and streams. Be prepared to protect food from bears; use bear-proof food hangs or the on-site bear box provided. The elevation is 1,100 feet.

**Campsites, facilities:** There are six tent sites accessible only by boat, ferry, or floatplane. Picnic tables and fire rings are provided. Vault toilets are available, but there is no drinking water. Garbage must be packed out. A floating dock can accommodate about three boats.

**Reservations, fees:** Reservations are not accepted. There is no fee for camping. There is a $5 per day docking fee (or $40 Season Pass) when bringing a private boat. Open May-mid-November, weather permitting.

**Directions:** From Wenatchee, drive on U.S. 97-A about 40 miles to Chelan and the ferry. Take the ferry and proceed to Prince Creek, 35 miles from Chelan. Note that the ferry will not stop here if water level does not allow for safe landing, which sometimes occurs in the early spring. The campground is also directly accessible by floatplane. (Call Chelan Seaplanes at 509/682-5555 for more information.)

**Contact:** Okanogan and Wenatchee National Forest, Chelan Ranger District, 509/682-4900, www.fs.usda.gov; Lake Chelan Boat Company, 509/682-4584, www.ladyofthelake.com.

## 67 FOGGY DEW

🚶 🚴 🏕 ♿ 🚐 ⛺

### Scenic rating: 6

on Foggy Dew Creek in Okanogan and
Wenatchee National Forests

**Map 3.2, page 182**

This private, remote campground is set at the
confluence of Foggy Dew Creek and the North
Fork of Old Creek. The elevation is 2,400 feet.
Several trails for hiking and horseback riding
nearby provide access to various backcountry
lakes and streams. To get to the trailheads,
follow the forest roads near camp. Bicycles are
allowed on Trails 417, 429, and 431. There is
also access to a motorcycle-use area.

**Campsites, facilities:** There are 12 sites for
tents or RVs up to 25 feet long. Picnic tables
and fire grills are provided. Vault toilets are
available. There is no drinking water, and
garbage must be packed out. Some facilities
are wheelchair accessible. Leashed pets are
permitted.

**Reservations, fees:** Reservations are not accepted. Sites are $8 per night for one vehicle,
$5 per each additional vehicle. Open late May-
September, weather permitting.

**Directions:** From Burlington, drive east on
Highway 20 for 145 miles to Twisp. Continue
east on Highway 20 for three miles to Highway
153. Turn south on Highway 153 and drive
12 miles to County Road 1029 (Gold Creek
Road). Turn right (south) and drive one mile
to Forest Road 4340. Turn right (west) and
drive four miles to the campground on the left.

**Contact:** Okanogan and Wenatchee National Forests, Methow Valley Ranger District,
509/996-4003, www.fs.usda.gov; Methow
Valley Visitor Center, 509/996-4000.

## 68 PHELPS CREEK AND EQUESTRIAN

🚶 🚴 🏊 🛶 🏕 🚐 ⛺

### Scenic rating: 7

on the Chiwawa River in Wenatchee National
Forest

**Map 3.2, page 182**

These camps are set at an elevation of 2,800
feet at the confluence of Phelps Creek and the
Chiwawa River. There's a key trailhead for
backpackers and horseback riders nearby that
provides access to the Glacier Peak Wilderness
and Spider Meadows. Phelps Creek Trail is
routed out to Spider Meadows, a five-mile hike
one-way, and Buck Creek Trail extends into
the Glacier Peak Wilderness. The Chiwawa
River is closed to fishing to protect endangered
species. A U.S. Forest Service map is advisable.

**Campsites, facilities:** There are seven sites
for tents or RVs up to 30 feet long at Phelps
Creek and six sites for tents or RVs up to 30
feet long at Phelps Creek Equestrian. Picnic
tables and fire grills are provided. Vault toilets
are available. There is no drinking water, but
stock water is available at Trinity Trailhead.
Garbage must be packed out. Horse facilities,
including loading ramps and high lines, are
nearby. Leashed pets are permitted.

**Reservations, fees:** Reservations are not
accepted. Sites are $12 per night for one ve-
hicle, $8 per each additional vehicle. Open
mid-June-October, weather permitting.

**Directions:** From I-5 and Everett, turn east
on U.S. 2 and drive 87 miles to State Route
207. Turn north on State Route 207 and drive
four miles to Chiwawa Loop Road. Turn right
(east) on Chiwawa Loop Road and drive 1.4
miles to Chiwawa River Road (Forest Road
6200). Bear left (north) and continue for 23.6
miles to the campground (the last 12 miles of
road are gravel).

**Contact:** Okanogan and Wenatchee National
Forests, Wenatchee River Ranger District,
Lake Wenatchee Ranger Station, 509/548-
2550, www.fs.usda.gov.

## 69 DEER POINT BOAT-IN
🏃 🚣 🚤 ⛺

### Scenic rating: 9

on Lake Chelan in Wenatchee National Forest

Map 3.2, page 182

Here's another little-known spot set along the remote east shore of Lake Chelan. It provides good protection from down-lake winds but is exposed to up-lake winds. Anglers at Lake Chelan often use this spot as their boat-in camp headquarters. Be prepared to protect food from bears; use bear-proof food hangs or use the bear box that is on-site.

**Campsites, facilities:** There are five tent sites accessible only by boat, ferry, or floatplane. Picnic tables and fire rings are provided. Vault toilets are available. There is no drinking water, and garbage must be packed out. A floating dock can accommodate about eight boats.

**Reservations, fees:** Reservations are not accepted. There is no fee for camping. There is a $5 per day dock-site fee (or $40 annual pass) when bringing a private boat. For ferry rates, which vary according to boat and age of passenger, phone 509/682-4584; typically rates are in the $35-60 range round-trip. Open May-October, weather permitting.

**Directions:** From Wenatchee, drive north on U.S. 97 approximately 40 miles to Chelan and the ferry. Take the ferry and proceed to Deer Point (the ferry does not schedule a stop at this campground but will usually stop here if you request it in advance). The campground is also directly accessible by floatplane. (Call Chelan Seaplanes at 509/682-5555 for more information.)

**Contact:** Okanogan and Wenatchee National Forests, Chelan Ranger District, 509/682-4900, www.fs.usda.gov; Lake Chelan Boat Company, 509/682-4584, www.ladyofthelake.com.

## 70 FLOWING LAKE COUNTY PARK
🏊 🚣 🚐 🦌 🎿 ♿ 🏖 ⛺

### Scenic rating: 6

near Snohomish

Map 3.3, page 183

This campground has a little something for everyone, including swimming, powerboating, waterskiing, and good fishing on Flowing Lake. The campsites are in a wooded setting (that is, no lake view), and it is a 0.25-mile walk to the beach. A one-mile nature trail is nearby. Note the private homes on the lake; all visitors are asked to respect the privacy of the owners.

**Campsites, facilities:** There are 36 sites, most with partial hookups, for tents or RVs up to 40 feet long; some sites are pull-through. Four cabins are also available. Picnic tables and fire grills are provided. Restrooms with flush toilets and coin showers, drinking water, and firewood are available. A picnic shelter, a fishing dock, launching facilities, swimming beach, playground, and amphitheater are available nearby. Some facilities are wheelchair accessible. Leashed pets are permitted.

**Reservations, fees:** Reservations are accepted at 425/388-6600 or www.snocoparks.org ($7.75 reservation fee). Tent sites are $22 per night, RV sites are 28-32 per night, $10 per night for a second vehicle, cabins are $45-50 per night. Open year-round with limited winter facilities.

**Directions:** From I-5 and Everett, take the Snohomish-Wenatchee exit and turn east on U.S. 2; drive to Milepost 10, and look for 100th Street SE (Westwick Road). Turn left and drive two miles (becomes 171st Avenue SE) to 48th Street SE. Turn right and drive about 0.5 mile into the park at the end of the road.

**Contact:** Flowing Lake County Park, 360/568-2274; Snohomish County Parks, 425/388-6600, www.snocoparks.org.

## 71 CUTTHROAT LAKES HIKE-IN

**Scenic rating: 9**

on Bald Mountain

**Map 3.3, page 183**

Reaching this spot is worth the effort. After hiking in 4.5 miles, you'll find beautiful lakeside camps, trout fishing, and hiking. The "lakes" are actually small ponds, but they're very pretty. No campfires are allowed; backpacking stoves are required for cooking. DNR pleads: "Please stay on the trails."

**Campsites, facilities:** There are five tent sites at this primitive, hike-in campground. Campfires are not allowed. There is no drinking water and garbage must be packed out. Leashed pets are permitted.

**Reservations, fees:** Reservations are not accepted. There is no fee for camping. Open mid-June-October, weather permitting.

**Directions:** From I-5 and Everett, turn east on Highway 92 and drive about 15 miles to the town of Granite Falls and Mountain Loop Highway. Continue northeast on Mountain Loop for 18 miles to Forest Road 4030 (at the bridge). Turn right (south) and drive for three miles to Forest Road 4032 (follow the Mallardy Ridge signs). Bear right and take Forest Road 4032 for one mile to the end, where the Bailey trailhead begins. Hike 4.5 miles to Cutthroat Lakes.

**Contact:** Department of Natural Resources, Northwest Region, 360/856-3500, www.dnr. wa.gov.

## 72 LITTLE GREIDER LAKE HIKE-IN

**Scenic rating: 10**

on Little Greider Lake

**Map 3.3, page 183**

This is prime country for hiking, backpacking, and trout fishing, and the rangers ask that you stay on trails and avoid walking through meadows and wetlands. The primitive, wooded campground is on Little Greider Lake. Similar to the Big Greider camp, pretty Little Greider gets more use. But hey, the truth is that in this area, Boulder Lake is the most desirable spot of all.

**Campsites, facilities:** There are six tent sites at this primitive, hike-in campground. Fire grills are provided. There is no drinking water and garbage must be packed out. Leashed pets are permitted.

**Reservations, fees:** Reservations are not accepted. There is no fee for camping. Open mid-June-October, weather permitting.

**Directions:** From I-5 and Everett, turn east on U.S. 2 and drive 24 miles to Sultan. Continue 0.5 mile east to Sultan Basin Road. Turn left (north) on Sultan Basin Road and drive 13.6 miles to Olney Pass, where all vehicles must register. Continue to a fork in the road and Road SLS 4000. Bear right on Road SLS 4000 and drive 6.5 miles. Note that the road to the Greider Lake Trailhead has been decommissioned. From the trailhead, the hike is now 4.5 miles to the campground.

**Contact:** Department of Natural Resources, Northwest Region, 360/856-3500, www.dnr. wa.gov.

## 73 BIG GREIDER LAKE HIKE-IN

**Scenic rating: 10**

on Big Greider Lake

**Map 3.3, page 183**

This primitive campground on Big Greider Lake is a hideaway in a gorgeous setting, set at the base of a large rock basin. Although campers are few, a lot of day hikers do make the three-mile tromp to the lake. DNR pleads: "Please stay on the trails." The landscape features subalpine terrain. Fishing is an option. This camp provides an alternative to Little Greider Lake campground, adjacent to Little Greider Lake.

**Campsites, facilities:** There are three tent sites at this primitive, hike-in campground. Fire grills are provided. There is no drinking water and garbage must be packed out. Leashed pets are permitted.

**Reservations, fees:** Reservations are not accepted. There is no fee for camping. Open mid-June-October, weather permitting.

**Directions:** From I-5 and Everett, turn east on U.S. 2 and drive 24 miles to Sultan. Continue 0.5 mile east to Sultan Basin Road. Turn left (north) on Sultan Basin Road and drive 13.6 miles to Olney Pass, where all vehicles must register. Continue to a fork in the road and Road SLS 4000. Bear right on Road SLS 4000 and drive 6.5 miles. Note that the road to the Greider Lake Trailhead has been decommissioned. From the trailhead, the hike is now five miles to the campground.

**Contact:** Department of Natural Resources, Northwest Region, 360/856-3500, www.dnr.wa.gov.

## 74 WALLACE FALLS STATE PARK WALK-IN

🚶 🚴 🏊 🛶 🚣 🐾 ♿ ⛺

**Scenic rating: 8**

near Gold Bar

**Map 3.3, page 183**                    **BEST (**

This 4,735-acre park is extremely busy on summer days. The centerpiece is its namesake 265-foot waterfall, but there is also plenty of shoreline along the Wallace and Skykomish Rivers, as well as Wallace, Jay, and Shaw Lakes. (Note that cougars have been spotted near Wallace Falls.) The campground is located in a heavily treed area at the trailhead to the falls. The trail leads along the Wallace River and is a lovely hike. The park has 12 miles of hiking trails, including a 0.25-mile interpretive trail, and five miles of biking trails. Nearby recreation options include fishing for trout and steelhead (in season), swimming, rafting, kayaking, and canoeing at Big Eddy Park, five miles east. Rock climbing is possible at Index Town Wall, 12 miles east.

**Campsites, facilities:** There are two walk-in tent sites and five cabins. Picnic tables and fire grills are provided. Restrooms with flush toilets, drinking water, firewood, and interpretive activities are available. A picnic area with kitchen shelters is available nearby. Some facilities are wheelchair accessible. Leashed pets are permitted.

**Reservations, fees:** Reservations are not accepted for campsites but are required for cabins ($8.50-10.50 reservations fee) at 888/226-7688 or www.parks.wa.gov/reservations. Sites are $22-23 per night, $10 per extra vehicle per night, cabins are $65.25-76.31 per night. Open year-round.

**Directions:** From I-5 and Everett, turn east on U.S. 2 and drive 28 miles to the town of Gold Bar, and look for the sign for Wallace Falls State Park. Turn left (northeast) at the sign and drive two miles to the park.

**Contact:** Wallace Falls State Park, 360/793-0420; state park information, 360/902-8844, www.parks.wa.gov.

## 75 MONEY CREEK CAMPGROUND

🚶 🏕 ♿ 🚐 ⛺

**Scenic rating: 5**

on the Skykomish River in Mount Baker-Snoqualmie National Forest

**Map 3.3, page 183**

You have a little surprise waiting for you here. Trains go by regularly day and night, and the first time it happens while you're in deep sleep, you might just launch a hole right through the top of your tent. The Burlington Northern rail runs along the western boundary of the campground. By now you've got the picture: This can be a noisy camp. Money Creek Campground is on the Skykomish River, with hiking trails a few miles away. The best of these is Dorothy Lake Trail.

**Campsites, facilities:** There are 24 sites, including two double sites, for tents or RVs up to 40 feet long. Picnic tables and fire grills are provided. Vault toilets, drinking water, garbage bins, and firewood are available. A store, café, and ice are located 3.5 miles to the east. Some facilities are wheelchair accessible. Leashed pets are permitted.

**Reservations, fees:** Reservations are accepted at 877/444-6777 ($10 reservation fee) or www.recreation.gov ($9 reservation fee). Single sites are $18-20 per night, double sites are $32-40 per night, $9 per extra vehicle per night. Open mid-May-mid-September, weather permitting.

**Directions:** From I-5 and Everett, turn east on U.S. 2 and drive 46 miles to Old Cascade Highway, 11 miles east of Index. Turn right (south) on Old Cascade Highway and drive across the bridge to the campground.

**Contact:** Mount Baker-Snoqualmie National Forest, Skykomish Ranger District, 360/677-2414, www.fs.usda.gov or www.hoodoo.com.

## 76 BECKLER RIVER

### Scenic rating: 7

on the Beckler River in Mount Baker-Snoqualmie National Forest

**Map 3.3, page 183**

Located on the Beckler River at an elevation of 900 feet, this camp has scenic riverside sites in second-growth timber, primarily Douglas fir, cedar, and big leaf maple. Fishing at the campground is poor; it's better well up the river. The Skykomish Ranger Station, which sells maps, is just a couple of miles away.

**Campsites, facilities:** There are 27 sites, including two double sites, for tents or RVs up to 40 feet long. Picnic tables and fire grills are provided. Vault toilets, drinking water, and firewood are available. A camp host is on-site. A store, café, and ice are located within two miles. Some facilities are wheelchair accessible. Leashed pets are permitted.

**Reservations, fees:** Reservations are accepted at 877/444-6777 ($10 reservation fee) or www.recreation.gov ($9 reservation fee). Single sites are $16 per night, double sites are $30 per night, $8 per extra vehicle per night. Open late May-early September, weather permitting.

**Directions:** From I-5 and Everett, turn east on U.S. 2 and drive 49 miles to Skykomish. Continue east on U.S. 2 for 0.5 mile to Forest Road 65. Turn left (north) on Forest Road 65 and drive 1.6 miles to the camp on the left.

**Contact:** Mount Baker-Snoqualmie National Forest, Skykomish Ranger District, 360/677-2414, www.fs.usda.gov or hoodoo.com.

## 77 MILLER RIVER GROUP

### Scenic rating: 8

near the Alpine Lakes Wilderness in Mount Baker-Snoqualmie National Forest

**Map 3.3, page 183**

This campground is located along the Miller River, a short distance from the boundary of the Alpine Lakes Wilderness. If you continue another seven miles on Forest Road 6410, you'll get to a trailhead leading to Dorothy Lake, a 1.5-mile hike. This pretty lake is two miles long. The trail continues past the lake to many other backcountry lakes. Backpackers must limit their party to no more than 12 people per group. A U.S. Forest Service map is essential. The camp host at nearby Money Creek oversees this campground.

**Campsites, facilities:** There is one reservable group camp for up to 100 people, plus 18 single sites, for tents or RVs up to 30 feet long. Picnic tables and fire grills are provided. Vault toilets, drinking water, and a group picnic area are available. A store, café, and ice are within five miles. Some facilities are wheelchair accessible. Leashed pets are permitted.

**Reservations, fees:** Reservations are accepted at 877/444-6777 ($10 reservation fee) or www.recreation.gov ($9 reservation fee). Single sites are $14 per night plus $7 extra vehicle fee. Group sites are $75 per night for up to 30 people, $125 per night for 31-75 people, and $150 per night for 76-100 people. Open mid-May-mid-September, weather permitting.

**Directions:** From I-5 and Everett, turn east on U.S. 2 and drive 46 miles to Old Cascade Highway, 11 miles east of Index. Turn right (south) on Old Cascade Highway (across the bridge) and drive one mile to Forest Road 6410. Turn right (south) and drive two miles to the campground on the left.

**Contact:** Mount Baker-Snoqualmie National Forest, Skykomish Ranger District, 360/677-2414, www.fs.usda.gov or hoodoo.com.

## 78 SNOQUALMIE RIVER RV PARK & CAMPGROUND

**Scenic rating: 7**

on the Snoqualmie River

**Map 3.3, page 183**

If you're in the Seattle area and stuck for a place for the night, this pretty 10-acre park set along the Snoqualmie River might be a welcome option. Approximately one-third of the sites are filled with monthly renters. Activities include fishing, swimming, road biking, and rafting. Nearby recreation options include several nine-hole golf courses. A worthwhile side trip is beautiful Snoqualmie Falls, 3.5 miles away.

**Campsites, facilities:** There are 92 sites with full or partial hookups for RVs of any length and 29 sites for tents. Picnic tables and fire rings are provided. Restrooms with flush toilets and showers, drinking water, firewood, and a playground are available. Propane gas, a store, café, coin laundry, and ice are located within 3.5 miles. Boat-launching facilities are located within 0.5 mile. Leashed pets are permitted, with certain restrictions.

**Reservations, fees:** Reservations are accepted. Sites are $28-41 per night, plus $6 per person per night for more than two people. Some credit cards are accepted. Open year-round with limited winter facilities.

**Directions:** From the junction of I-5 and I-90 south of Seattle, turn east on I-90. Drive east for 26 miles to Exit 22 (Preston-Fall City). Take that exit and turn north on Preston-Fall

City Road and drive 4.5 miles to SE 44th Place. Turn right (east) and drive one mile to the park at the end of the road.

**Contact:** Snoqualmie River RV Park & Campground, 425/222-5545, www.srcghsg.com.

## 79 MIDDLE FORK

**Scenic rating: 8**

on the North Fork of the Snoqualmie River in Mount Baker-Snoqualmie National Forest

**Map 3.3, page 183**

Set at an elevation of 1,600 feet, this is one of the newest and most remote campgrounds in the Mount Baker-Snoqualmie National Forest. Getting there is a challenge, but this spot is popular with locals who tough out the graveled, potholed road to swim and fish here.

**Campsites, facilities:** There are 39 sites for tents or RVs up to 45 feet long including a few doubles and two group sites for up to 25 people. Picnic tables and fire grills are provided. Drinking water, pit toilets, a camp host, picnic shelter, and firewood are available. Some facilities are wheelchair accessible. Leashed pets are permitted.

**Reservations, fees:** Reservations are accepted at 877/444-6777 ($10 reservation fee) or www.recreation.gov ($9 reservation fee). Single sites are $14 per night, double sites are $25 per night, $7 extra vehicle fee. The group site is $40 per night. Open mid-May-early October, weather permitting.

**Directions:** In Seattle on I-5, turn east on I-90 and drive to North Bend and Exit 34. Take that exit and drive north on 468th Street for 0.6 mile to SE Middle Fork Road (Forest Service Road 56). Turn right and drive 12 miles to the campground (0.5 mile past the Middle Fork Trail trailhead). Obtaining a U.S. Forest Service map is advisable.

**Contact:** Mount Baker-Snoqualmie National Forest, Snoqualmie Ranger District, North Bend office, 425/888-1421, www.fs.usda.gov or hoodoo.com.

## 80 KANASKAT-PALMER STATE PARK

### Scenic rating: 8

on the Green River

**Map 3.3, page 183**

This wooded campground offers private campsites near the Green River. The park covers 320 acres with two miles of river frontage; the river can be accessed from the day-use area but not from the campground. It is set on a small, low, forested plateau. In summer, the river is ideal for expert-level rafting and kayaking, and the park is used as a put-in spot for the rafting run down the Green River Gorge. This area has much mining history, and coal mining continues, as does cinnabar mining (the base ore for mercury). Nearby Flaming Geyser gets its name from a coal seam. In winter, the river attracts a run of steelhead and salmon. The park has three miles of hiking trails.

**Campsites, facilities:** There are 31 sites for tents, 19 pull-through sites with partial hookups (30 amps) for RVs up to 50 feet long, three yurts, and one group camp for up to 80 people, which includes two Adirondack shelters, a picnic shelter, and a community fire ring. Picnic tables are provided. Restrooms with flush toilets and showers, drinking water, a sheltered picnic area, horseshoe pits, and a dump station are available. A convenience store and deli are within two miles. Some facilities are wheelchair accessible. Leashed pets are permitted.

**Reservations, fees:** Reservations are accepted for individual sites in summer and are required for the group camp at 888/CAMP-OUT (888/226-7688) or www.parks.wa.gov/reservations ($6.50-8.50 reservation fee). Sites are $17-35 per night, $10 per extra vehicle per night, and yurts are $53.21-64.07 per night. Group camp fees vary according to size; rates average $2.25 per person per night. Some credit cards are accepted. Open year-round, weather permitting.

**Directions:** From Puyallup at the junction of Highway 167 and Highway 410, turn southeast on Highway 410 and drive 25 miles to Enumclaw and Porter Street/Highway 169. Turn right and drive three miles to SE 400th Street. Turn right on SE 400th Street and drive one mile to SE 392nd Street. Veer right on SE 392nd Street and drive one mile to SE Vezie Cumberland Road. Turn left and drive three miles to Cumberland Kanasket Road SE and continue 2.5 miles to the park.

**Contact:** Kanaskat-Palmer State Park, 360/886-0148; state park information, 360/902-8844, www.parks.wa.gov.

## 81 TINKHAM

### Scenic rating: 9

on the Snoqualmie River in Mount Baker-Snoqualmie National Forest

**Map 3.3, page 183**

This camp is often used as an overflow for Denny Creek. About half of the sites face the Snoqualmie River, making this a pretty spot. Fishing can be good (check regulations) and the creek provides hiking options. Wilderness trails for the Alpines Lakes Wilderness are located 5-10 miles away. The elevation is 1,600 feet.

**Campsites, facilities:** There are 47 sites for tents or RVs up to 40 feet long. Picnic tables and fire pits are provided. Drinking water, vault toilets, garbage bins, and firewood are available. A camp host is on-site. Some facilities are wheelchair accessible. Leashed pets are permitted.

**Reservations, fees:** Reservations are accepted at 877/444-6777 ($10 reservation fee) or www.recreation.gov ($9 reservation fee). Sites are $16-18 per night, $7 per extra vehicle per night. Open mid-May-mid-September, weather permitting.

**Directions:** In Seattle on I-5, turn east on I-90. Drive east on I-90 to Exit 42. Take that exit and turn right on Tinkham Road (Forest Road 55), and drive southeast 1.5 miles to the campground on the left. Obtaining a U.S. Forest Service map is advisable.

**Contact:** Mount Baker-Snoqualmie National Forest, Snoqualmie Ranger District, North Bend office, 425/888-1421, www.fs.usda.gov or hoodoo.com.

## 82 DENNY CREEK

### Scenic rating: 9
in Mount Baker-Snoqualmie National Forest

**Map 3.3, page 183**              BEST (

This camp is set at 1,900 feet elevation along Denny Creek, which is pretty and offers nearby recreation access. The campground is secluded in an area of Douglas fir, hemlock, and cedar, with hiking trails available in addition to swimming opportunities. Denny Creek Trail starts from the campground and provides a 4.5-mile round-trip hike that features Keckwulee Falls and Denny Creek Waterslide. You can climb to Hemlock Pass and Melakwa Lake. There is access for backpackers into the Alpine Lakes Wilderness.

**Campsites, facilities:** There are 29 single sites, some with partial hookups (30 amps), and four double sites for tents or RVs up to 40 feet long; there is also one group site with partial hookups for up to 35 people. Picnic tables and fire grills are provided. Drinking water, flush toilets, and firewood are available. Some facilities are wheelchair accessible. Leashed pets are permitted.

**Reservations, fees:** Reservations are accepted at 877/444-6777 ($10 reservation fee) or www.recreation.gov ($9 reservation fee). Sites are $20-24 per night, double sites are $32 per night, $10 per extra vehicle per night. The group site is $85 per night. Open mid-May-mid-September, weather permitting.

**Directions:** In Seattle on I-5, turn east on I-90. Drive east on I-90 to Exit 47. Take that exit, cross the freeway, and at the T intersection turn right and drive 0.25 mile to Denny Creek Road (Forest Road 58). Turn left on

Denny Creek Road and drive two miles to the campground on the left.

**Contact:** Mount Baker-Snoqualmie National Forest, Snoqualmie Ranger District, North Bend office, 425/888-1421, www.fs.usda.gov or hoodoo.com.

## 83 OWHI WALK-IN

### Scenic rating: 9
on Cooper Lake in Wenatchee National Forest

**Map 3.3, page 183**

This spot has everything you need for a drive-to wilderness experience. Well, everything but drinking water. It's located on the shore of Cooper Lake, near the boundary of the Alpine Lakes Wilderness. The campsites require a walk of 100-300 feet. Some sites have lake views, whereas others have lots of vegetation and provide privacy. The old-growth Douglas fir and western hemlock are highlights. A nearby trailhead provides access to several lakes in the wilderness and extends to the Pacific Crest Trail. Fishing, swimming, and canoeing are all popular at Cooper Lake. No motors, including electric motors, are permitted at the lake, making it ideal for canoes, float tubes, and prams. The campground is minimally developed. The elevation is 2,800 feet.

**Campsites, facilities:** There are 22 walk-in sites for tents only. Picnic tables and fire grills are provided. Vault toilets and garbage bins are available, but there is no drinking water. Primitive boat-launching facilities are nearby. Leashed pets are permitted.

**Reservations, fees:** Reservations are not accepted. Sites are $14 per night, $6 per night for an extra vehicle with a two-vehicle maximum. Open late May-early October, weather permitting.

**Directions:** In Seattle on I-5, turn east on I-90. Drive east on I-90 for 78 miles to Exit 80 (2 miles before Cle Elum). Turn north on Bullfrog Road and drive four miles to Highway 903. Turn left (north) on Highway 903

and drive 16 miles to Forest Road 46. Turn left (west) on Forest Road 46 and drive five miles to Forest Road 4616 (pavement ends). Turn right and drive less than 0.5 mile to the campground. Campsites are located 100-300 feet from the parking lot; camping is not allowed in the parking lot.

**Contact:** Okanogan and Wenatchee National Forests, Cle Elum Ranger District, 509/852-1100, www.fs.usda.gov.

## 84 KACHESS & KACHESS GROUP

🥾 🚵 🏊 🛶 🐎 ♿ 🚐 ⛺

### Scenic rating: 8
on Kachess Lake in Wenatchee National Forest

**Map 3.3, page 183**

This is the only campground on the shore of Kachess Lake, but note that the water level can drop significantly in summer during low-rain years. It is the most popular campground in the local area, often filling in July and August, especially on weekends. Recreation opportunities include waterskiing, fishing, hiking, and bicycling. A trail from camp heads north into the Alpine Lakes Wilderness. The elevation is 2,300 feet.

**Campsites, facilities:** There are 122 single sites and 30 double sites for tents or RVs up to 32 feet long. A group site for 20-50 people is also available. Picnic tables and fire grills are provided. Drinking water, flush and vault toilets, firewood, and a camp host are available. Some facilities are wheelchair accessible. Leashed pets are permitted, but are not allowed in swimming areas.

**Reservations, fees:** Reservations are accepted for family sites and required for the group site at 877/444-6777 ($10 reservation fee) or www.recreation.gov ($9 reservation fee). Sites are $20-40 per night, $8 per extra vehicle per night. The group site is $110 per night. Open late May-mid-September, weather permitting.

**Directions:** In Seattle on I-5, turn east on I-90. Drive east on I-90 for 59 miles to Exit 62. Take that exit to Forest Road 49 and turn northeast; drive 5.5 miles to the campground on the right at the end of the paved road.

**Contact:** Okanogan and Wenatchee National Forests, Cle Elum Ranger District, 509/852-1100, www.fs.usda.gov.

## 85 SALMON LA SAC

🥾 🚵 🏊 🛶 🐎 ♿ 🚐 ⛺

### Scenic rating: 6
on the Cle Elum River in Wenatchee National Forest

**Map 3.3, page 183**

This is a base camp for backpackers and day hikers and is also popular with kayakers. It's located along the Cle Elum River at 2,400 feet elevation, about 0.25 mile from a major trailhead, the Salmon La Sac Trailhead. Hikers can follow creeks heading off in several directions, including into the Alpine Lakes Wilderness. A campground host is available for information.

**Campsites, facilities:** There are 69 sites, including 12 double sites, for tents or RVs up to 21 feet long. Picnic tables and fire grills are provided. Drinking water and vault toilets are available. Some facilities are wheelchair accessible. Leashed pets are permitted.

**Reservations, fees:** Reservations are accepted at 877/444-6777 ($10 reservation fee) or www.recreation.gov ($9 reservation fee). Sites are $20-40 per night, $8 per extra vehicle per night (applies to the second vehicle at single sites; third and fourth vehicles at double sites). Open late May-mid-September, weather permitting.

**Directions:** In Seattle on I-5, turn east on I-90. Drive east on I-90 for 78 miles to Exit 80 (2 miles before Cle Elum). Take that exit, turn north on Bullfrog Road, and drive four miles to Highway 903. Continue north on Highway 903 for 17 miles to the campground on the left.

**Contact:** Okanogan and Wenatchee National Forests, Cle Elum Ranger District, 509/852-1100, www.fs.usda.gov.

## 86 RED MOUNTAIN

### Scenic rating: 6

on the Cle Elum River in Wenatchee National Forest

**Map 3.3, page 183**

This alternative to nearby Wish Poosh has two big differences: There is no drinking water, and it's not on Cle Elum Lake. The camp sits along the Cle Elum River one mile from the lake, just above where the river feeds into it. The elevation is 2,200 feet.

**Campsites, facilities:** There are 10 sites for tents and small RVs up to 20 feet long. Picnic tables and fire grills are provided. Vault toilets and garbage bins are available, but there is no drinking water. Leashed pets are permitted.

**Reservations, fees:** Reservations are not accepted. Sites are $14 per night, $6 per night for a second vehicle with a two-vehicle maximum. Open mid-May-late November, weather permitting.

**Directions:** In Seattle on I-5, turn east on I-90. Drive east on I-90 for 78 miles to Exit 80 (2 miles before Cle Elum). Take that exit and turn north on Bullfrog Road; drive four miles to Highway 903. Continue north on Highway 903 for 14 miles to the campground on the left.

**Contact:** Okanogan and Wenatchee National Forests, Cle Elum Ranger District, 509/852-1100, www.fs.usda.gov.

## 87 CLE ELUM RIVER & CLE ELUM GROUP

### Scenic rating: 6

on the Cle Elum River in Wenatchee National Forest

**Map 3.3, page 183**

The gravel roads in the campground make this setting a bit more rustic than nearby Salmon La Sac. It serves as a valuable overflow campground for Salmon La Sac and is similar in setting and opportunities. The group site fills on most summer weekends. A nearby trailhead provides access into the Alpine Lakes Wilderness.

**Campsites, facilities:** There are 23 sites, including some pull-through, for tents or RVs up to 30 feet long and a group site for up to 100 people. Picnic tables and fire grills are provided. Drinking water, firewood, and vault toilets are available. Leashed pets are permitted.

**Reservations, fees:** Reservations are not accepted for family sites but are required for the group site at 877/444-6777 ($10 reservation fee) or www.recreation.gov ($9 reservation fee). Sites are $16-32 per night, $7 per extra vehicle per night (applies to a second vehicle at single sites; third and fourth vehicles for double sites). The group site is $110 per night. Open late May-mid-September, weather permitting.

**Directions:** In Seattle on I-5, turn east on I-90. Drive east on I-90 for 78 miles to Exit 80 (2 miles before Cle Elum). Take that exit, turn north on Bullfrog Road, and drive four miles to Highway 903. Continue north on Highway 903 for 13 miles to the campground on the left.

**Contact:** Okanogan and Wenatchee National Forests, Cle Elum Ranger District, 509/852-1100, www.fs.usda.gov.

## 88 LAKE EASTON STATE PARK

### Scenic rating: 8

on Lake Easton

**Map 3.3, page 183**

This campground offers many recreational opportunities. For starters, it's set along the shore of Lake Easton on the Yakima River in the Cascade foothills. The landscape features old-growth forest, dense vegetation, and freshwater marshes, and the park covers 516 acres of the best of it. Two miles of trails for hiking and biking are available. The park provides opportunities for both summer and winter recreation, including swimming, fishing, boating, cross-country skiing, and snowmobiling. Note that high-speed boating is not recommended because Lake Easton is a shallow reservoir with stumps often hidden just below the water surface; the boat speed limit is 10 mph (10-horsepower motor limit). Nearby recreation options include an 18-hole golf course and hiking trails. Kachess Lake and Keechelus Lake are just a short drive away.

**Campsites, facilities:** There are 137 sites, including 45 sites with hookups (30 amps), for RVs up to 60 feet long, as well as two primitive walk-in tent sites and one group site for up to 50 people. Picnic tables and fire grills are provided. Restrooms with flush toilets and showers, drinking water, a dump station, an amphitheater, a playground, basketball, horseshoe pits, Junior Ranger program, movie nights, and a swimming beach are available. A store, café, and ice are located within one mile. Boat-launching facilities, dock, and floats are located on Lake Easton. Some facilities are wheelchair accessible. Leashed pets are permitted.

**Reservations, fees:** Reservations are accepted for all sites and are required for the group site at 888/CAMP-OUT (888/226-7688) or www.parks.wa.gov/reservations ($6.50-8.50 reservation fee). RV sites are $29-28 per night, walk-in tent sites are $12 per night, $10 per extra vehicle per night, and the group site is $2.25 per person per night (plus $25 reservation fee). Some credit cards are accepted. Open May-mid-October, with limited winter facilities.

**Directions:** From Seattle, drive east on I-90 for 68 miles to Exit 70. Take that exit to Lake Easton Road. Turn right and drive 1.5 miles to Lake Easton State Park Road. Turn right and enter park.

**Contact:** Lake Easton State Park, 509/656-2586; state park information, 360/902-8844, www.parks.wa.gov.

## 89 WISH POOSH

### Scenic rating: 7
on Cle Elum Lake in Wenatchee National Forest

**Map 3.3, page 183**

This popular camp is set on the shore of Cle Elum Lake. It fills up on summer weekends and holidays. It is great midweek, when many sites are usually available. While the lake is near the camp, note that because it is an irrigation reservoir, the lake level falls rapidly each year. Waterskiing, sailing, fishing, and swimming are among recreation possibilities. The camp sits at an elevation of 2,400 feet.

**Campsites, facilities:** There are 34 sites, including four double sites, for tents or RVs up to 30 feet long. Picnic tables and fire grills are provided. Restrooms with flush toilets, drinking water, a camp host, and firewood are available. Boat-launching facilities are located on Cle Elum Lake. A restaurant and ice are available nearby. Leashed pets are permitted.

**Reservations, fees:** Reservations are accepted at 877/444-6777 ($10 reservation fee) or www.recreation.gov ($9 reservation fee). Sites are $20-40 per night, $8 per extra vehicle per night (applies to second vehicle at single sites; third and fourth vehicles at double sites). Open mid-May-mid-September, weather permitting.

**Directions:** In Seattle on I-5, turn east on I-90. Drive east on I-90 for 78 miles to Exit 80 (2 miles before Cle Elum). Take that exit, turn north on Bullfrog Road, and drive four miles to Highway 903. Continue north on Highway 903 for eight miles to the campground on the left.

**Contact:** Okanogan and Wenatchee National Forests, Cle Elum Ranger District, 509/852-1100, www.fs.usda.gov.

## 90 CAYUSE HORSE CAMP

🚶 🚵 🛶 🐴 🚐 ⛺

### Scenic rating: 6

on the Cle Elum River in Wenatchee National Forest

Map 3.3, page 183

Cayuse is for horse campers only. It's located along the Cle Elum River at major trailheads for horses and hikers and marked trails for bikers. Hikers can follow creeks heading off in several directions, including into the Alpine Lakes Wilderness. The elevation is 2,400 feet.

**Campsites, facilities:** There are 11 single sites and three double sites for tents or RVs up to 35 feet long. Picnic tables and fire pits are provided. Drinking water, vault toilets, and a camp host are available. Stock facilities include corrals, troughs, and hitching posts. Bring your own stock feed. Leashed pets are permitted.

**Reservations, fees:** Reservations are accepted at 877/444-6777 ($10 reservation fee) or www. recreation.gov ($9 reservation fee). Sites are $20-40 per night, $8 per night for each additional vehicle (applies to second vehicle at single sites; third or fourth vehicle at double sites). Open mid-May-mid-September, weather permitting.

**Directions:** In Seattle on I-5, turn east on I-90. Drive east on I-90 for 78 miles to Exit 80 (2 miles before Cle Elum). Take that exit and turn north on Bullfrog Road; drive four miles to Highway 903. Continue north on Highway 903 for 17 miles to the campground on the right.

**Contact:** Okanogan and Wenatchee National Forests, Cle Elum Ranger District, 509/852-1100, www.fs.usda.gov.

## 91 DALLES

🚶 🛶 🐴 ♿ 🚐 ⛺

### Scenic rating: 10

in Mount Baker-Snoqualmie National Forest

Map 3.3, page 183

This campground is set at the confluence of Minnehaha Creek and the White River. Aptly, its name means "rapids." A nature trail is nearby, and the White River entrance to Mount Rainier National Park is about 14 miles south on Highway 410. The camp sits amid a grove of old-growth trees; a particular point of interest is a huge old Douglas fir that is 9.5 feet in diameter and more than 235 feet tall. This is one of the prettiest camps in the area. It gets moderate use in summer.

**Campsites, facilities:** There are 46 sites for tents or RVs up to 40 feet long. Picnic tables and fire grills are provided. Vault toilets, drinking water, and firewood are available. A camp host is on-site. There is a large shaded picnic area for day use. Some facilities are wheelchair accessible. Leashed pets are permitted.

**Reservations, fees:** Reservations are accepted at 877/444-6777 ($10 reservation fee) or www. recreation.gov ($9 reservation fee). Sites are $18-20 per night, $9 per extra vehicle per night. Open mid-May-late September, weather permitting.

**Directions:** From Enumclaw, drive east on Highway 410 for 25.5 miles to the campground (3 miles inside the forest boundary) on the right.

**Contact:** Mount Baker-Snoqualmie National Forest, White River Ranger District, 360/825-6585, www.fs.usda.gov or hoodoo.com.

## 92 CORRAL PASS

🚶 🛶 🐴 ⛺

### Scenic rating: 10

in Mount Baker-Snoqualmie National Forest

Map 3.3, page 183

This is the most remote of the campgrounds in the area. Set at an elevation of 5,600 feet, it's primitive, quiet, and an ideal base camp for a hiking trip. Groups of horse-packers heading into the adjacent Norse Peak Wilderness frequent the camp. The best trip is the two-mile backpack up to Hidden Lake and then along a river canyon for four miles to Echo Lake. Several trails nearby lead to backcountry fishing lakes and streams. In late summer and fall, visitors can find wild berries in the area.

**Campsites, facilities:** There are 20 tent sites. Picnic tables and fire grills are provided. Vault toilets, garbage bins, hitch rails, and a horse-loading ramp are available. There is no drinking water. Downed firewood can be gathered. Leashed pets are permitted.

**Reservations, fees:** Reservations are not accepted. There is no fee for camping, but a Northwest Forest Pass ($5 daily fee or $30 annual pass per parked vehicle) is required. Open June-late September, weather permitting.

**Directions:** From Enumclaw, drive east on Highway 410 for 31.6 miles to Forest Road 7174 (near Silver Springs Camp). Turn left (east) and drive seven miles to the camp on the right. This curvy dirt road is not suitable for RVs or trailers.

**Contact:** Mount Baker-Snoqualmie National Forest, White River Ranger District, 360/825-0660, www.fs.usda.gov.

## 93 CROW CREEK

### Scenic rating: 5

on the Little Naches River in Wenatchee National Forest

**Map 3.3, page 183**

Set at an elevation of 2,900 feet, this campground on the Little Naches River is popular with off-road bikers and four-wheel-drive enthusiasts and is similar to Kaner Flat, except that there is no drinking water. A trail heading out from the camp leads into the backcountry and then forks in several directions. One route leads to the American River, another follows West Quartz Creek, and another goes along Fife's Ridge into the Norse Peak Wilderness (where no motorized vehicles are permitted). There is good seasonal hunting and fishing in this area.

**Campsites, facilities:** There are 15 sites for tents or RVs up to 30 feet long. Picnic tables and fire grills are provided. Vault toilets and garbage bins are available. There is no drinking

water. Downed firewood may be gathered. Leashed pets are permitted.

**Reservations, fees:** Reservations are not accepted. Sites are $10 per night, $5 per extra vehicle per night. Open May-October, weather permitting.

**Directions:** From Yakima, drive northwest on U.S. 12 for 18 miles to Highway 410. Bear northwest on Highway 410 and drive 24.5 miles to Little Naches Road/Forest Road 1900. Turn northeast and drive 2.5 miles to Forest Road 1902. Turn left (west) and drive 0.5 mile to the campground on the right.

**Contact:** Okanogan and Wenatchee National Forests, Naches Ranger District, 509/653-1400, www.fs.usda.gov.

## 94 KANER FLAT

### Scenic rating: 7

near the Little Naches River in Wenatchee National Forest

**Map 3.3, page 183**

This campground is set near the Little Naches River, at an elevation of 2,678 feet. It is located at the site of a wagon-train camp on the Old Naches Trail, a route used in the 1800s by wagon trains, Native Americans, and the U.S. Cavalry on their way to westside markets. The narrow-clearance Naches Trail is now used by motorcyclists and four-wheel-drive enthusiasts. Kaner Flat is popular among that crowd, and it is larger and more group-friendly than nearby Crow Creek campground.

**Campsites, facilities:** There are 43 single sites and six double sites for tents or RVs up to 30 feet long. Picnic tables and fire grills are provided. Restrooms with flush toilets, drinking water, and vault toilets are available. Some facilities are wheelchair accessible. Leashed pets are permitted.

**Reservations, fees:** Reservations are not accepted. Sites are $12-24 per night, $5 per night for each additional vehicle. Open mid-May-late November, weather permitting.

**Directions:** From Yakima, drive northwest on U.S. 12 for 18 miles to Highway 410. Bear northwest on Highway 410 and drive 24.5 miles to Little Naches Road/Forest Road 1900. Turn northeast and drive 2.5 miles to the campground on the right.

**Contact:** Okanogan and Wenatchee National Forests, Naches Ranger District, 509/653-1400, www.fs.usda.gov.

## 95 WHITE RIVER FALLS

### Scenic rating: 9

on the White River in Wenatchee National Forest

**Map 3.4, page 184**

Although very primitive, this quiet and beautiful campground is a perfect spot for those seeking solitude near the wilderness. It's next to White River Falls on the White River and close to a major trailhead that connects to a network of hiking trails into the Glacier Peak Wilderness. There is no viewing platform or fence at White River Falls, and viewing can be dangerous. People have slipped here and fallen to their deaths. There is no RV turnaround at the camp. The elevation is 2,100 feet.

**Campsites, facilities:** There are five sites for tents only. Picnic tables and fire grills are provided. Vault toilets are available, but there is no drinking water. Garbage must be packed out. Leashed pets are permitted.

**Reservations, fees:** Reservations are not accepted. There is no fee for camping. Open June-mid-October, weather permitting.

**Directions:** From Leavenworth, drive west on U.S. 2 for 15 miles to Coles Corner and State Route 207. Turn north and drive 10 miles to Forest Road 6400 (White River Road). Turn right and drive 9.9 miles to the campground on the left. Note: Due to road damage, trailers are not recommended.

**Contact:** Okanogan and Wenatchee National Forests, Wenatchee River Ranger District,

Lake Wenatchee Ranger Station, 509/548-2550, www.fs.usda.gov.

## 96 NAPEEQUA CROSSING

### Scenic rating: 8

on the White and Napeequa Rivers in Wenatchee National Forest

**Map 3.4, page 184**                    **BEST (**

A trail across the road from this camp on the White River heads east for about 3.5 miles to Twin Lakes in the Glacier Peak Wilderness. It's definitely worth the hike, with scenic views and wildlife observation as your reward. But note that Twin Lakes is closed to fishing. Sightings of ospreys, bald eagles, and golden eagles can brighten the trip. This is also an excellent spot for fall colors.

**Campsites, facilities:** There are five sites for tents or RVs up to 30 feet long. Picnic tables and fire grills are provided. Vault toilets are available, but you are advised to bring your own toilet paper. There is no drinking water, and garbage must be packed out. Leashed pets are permitted.

**Reservations, fees:** Reservations are not accepted. There is no fee for camping. Open year-round, weather and snow level permitting.

**Directions:** From Leavenworth, drive west on U.S. 2 for 14 miles to Coles Corner and State Route 207. Turn north and drive 10 miles to Forest Road 6400 (White River Road). Turn right and drive 5.9 miles to the campground on the left.

**Contact:** Okanogan and Wenatchee National Forests, Wenatchee River Ranger District, 509/548-2550, www.fs.usda.gov.

## 97 CHIWAWA HORSE CAMP

### Scenic rating: 8

in Wenatchee National Forest

**Map 3.4, page 184**

This camp is not designated solely for horse

campers, as many horse camps are. Rather, it's for all users, but it features many facilities for horseback riding. It is seldom full but is popular among equestrians. Two short trails specifically designed for physically challenged visitors lead around the campground, covering about a mile. A trailhead at the camp also provides access to a network of backcountry trails. The elevation is 2,500 feet.

**Campsites, facilities:** There are 21 sites for tents or RVs up to 45 feet long. Some sites are pull-through. Picnic tables and fire grills are provided. Drinking water and vault toilets are available. Garbage must be packed out. Horse facilities include mounting ramps, high lines, water troughs, and a loading ramp. Some facilities are wheelchair accessible. Leashed pets are permitted.

**Reservations, fees:** Reservations are not accepted. Sites are $12 per vehicle per night. Open May-October, weather permitting.

**Directions:** From I-5 and Everett, turn east on U.S. 2 and drive 87 miles to State Route 207. Turn right on State Route 207 and drive 4.3 miles to Chiwawa Loop Road. Turn right and drive 1.2 miles to Chiwawa River Road/Forest Road 6200. Turn left and drive 14.8 miles to the campground on the right. Note: The last five miles are gravel.

**Contact:** Okanogan and Wenatchee National Forests, Wenatchee River Ranger District, 509/548-2550, www.fs.usda.gov.

## 98 COTTONWOOD

🏃 🚲 🛶 🐴 ♿ 🚐 ⛺

### Scenic rating: 8

on the Entiat River in Wenatchee National Forest

**Map 3.4, page 184**

Cottonwood Camp is set along the Entiat River, adjacent to a major trailhead leading into the Glacier Peak Wilderness. Note that dirt bikes are allowed on four miles of trail, Entiat River Trail to Myrtle Lake, but no motorcycles or mountain bikes are allowed inside

the boundary of the Glacier Peak Wilderness; violators will be prosecuted by backcountry rangers. In other words, cool your jets. Let backpackers have some peace and quiet. A bonus near the camp is good berry picking in season. Trout fishing is another alternative. The camp is set at an elevation of 3,100 feet.

**Campsites, facilities:** There are 25 sites for tents or RVs up to 20 feet long. Picnic tables and fire grills are provided. Drinking water, vault toilets, and garbage bins are available. Some facilities are wheelchair accessible. Leashed pets are permitted.

**Reservations, fees:** Reservations are not accepted. Sites are $10 per night, $8 extra vehicle fee. Open June-mid-October, weather permitting.

**Directions:** From I-5 and Everett, turn east on U.S. 2 and drive 120 miles to U.S. 2/U.S. 97. Bear right on U.S. 2/U.S. 97 and drive one mile to Euclid Avenue/U.S. 97. Take that ramp and drive 18 miles on U.S. 97/U.S. 97-A to Entiat River Road. Turn left (northwest) and drive 37 miles to the campground.

**Contact:** Okanogan and Wenatchee National Forests, Entiat Ranger District, 509/784-4700, www.fs.usda.gov.

## 99 NORTH FORK

🏃 🚲 🛶 🐴 🚐 ⛺

### Scenic rating: 8

on the Entiat River in Wenatchee National Forest

**Map 3.4, page 184**

One of eight campgrounds nestled along the Entiat River, North Fork is located near the confluence of the Entiat and the North Fork of the Entiat River. Highlights of this pretty, shaded camp include access to river fishing and Entiat Falls, which are located about 0.5 mile downstream. Note: No fishing is permitted in the vicinity of Entiat Falls to protect the bull trout; check regulations. The elevation is 2,500 feet.

**Campsites, facilities:** There are eight sites for tents, including one site for small RVs up to 20 feet long. Picnic tables and fire grills are provided. Drinking water, pit toilets, and garbage bins are available. Leashed pets are permitted.

**Reservations, fees:** Reservations are not accepted. Sites are $10 per vehicle per night, $8 per night per additional vehicle. Open June-mid-October, weather permitting.

**Directions:** From I-5 and Everett, turn east on U.S. 2 and drive 120 miles to U.S. 2/U.S. 97. Bear right on U.S. 2/U.S. 97 and drive one mile to Euclid Avenue/U.S. 97. Take that ramp and drive 18 miles on U.S. 97/U.S. 97-A to Entiat River Road. Turn left (northwest) and drive 32 miles to the campground on the left.

**Contact:** Okanogan and Wenatchee National Forests, Entiat Ranger District, 509/784-4700, www.fs.usda.gov.

## 100 SILVER FALLS

### Scenic rating: 10
on the Entiat River in Wenatchee National Forest

**Map 3.4, page 184**          **BEST (**

This campground is set in an enchanted spot at the confluence of Silver Creek and the Entiat River. A trail from camp leads 0.5 mile to the base of beautiful Silver Falls. This trail continues in a loop for another mile past the falls, parallel to the river. Fishing is available above Entiat Falls, located two to three miles upriver from Silver Falls. The elevation at the camp is 2,400 feet.

**Campsites, facilities:** There are 30 sites for tents or RVs up to 30 feet long, plus one group site for up to 40 people. Picnic tables and fire grills are provided. Drinking water, vault toilets, and garbage bins are available. A camp host is available in summer. Some facilities are wheelchair accessible. Leashed pets are permitted.

**Reservations, fees:** Reservations are accepted for the group site at 877/444-6777 ($10 reservation fee) or www.recreation.gov ($9 reservation fee). Sites are $12 per night, $10 per night per additional vehicle; the group site is $60 per night. Open mid-May-mid-October, weather permitting.

**Directions:** From I-5 and Everett, turn east on U.S. 2 and drive 120 miles to U.S. 2/U.S. 97. Bear right on U.S. 2/U.S. 97 and drive one mile to Euclid Avenue/U.S. 97. Take that ramp and drive 18 miles on U.S. 97/U.S. 97-A to Entiat River Road. Turn left (northwest) and drive 29 miles to the campground on the left.

**Contact:** Okanogan and Wenatchee National Forests, Entiat Ranger District, 509/784-4700, www.fs.usda.gov.

## 101 LAKE CREEK/ENTIAT

### Scenic rating: 7
on the Entiat River in Wenatchee National Forest

**Map 3.4, page 184**

This camp is located at the confluence of Lake Creek and the Entiat River, at a trail crossroads. It ties in to the Mad Lake trail system, where all-purpose trails are available for hiking, horseback riding, and mountain biking. Another trail ties in to a loop system that features the Devils Backbone to Ramona Park. These also link to a network of trails in the Lake Creek Basin in the Chelan Mountains, and several others head south and west into the Entiat Mountains. Fishing is available on the Entiat River, but not in the vicinity of Entiat Falls. Check fishing regulations. Note that there is another Lake Creek Camp in the Lake Wenatchee and Leavenworth Ranger District.

**Campsites, facilities:** There are 18 single sites and one double site for tents or RVs up to 30 feet long. Picnic tables and fire grills are provided. Drinking water and vault toilets are available. Some facilities are wheelchair accessible. Leashed pets are permitted.

**Reservations, fees:** Reservations are not accepted. Sites are $10 per night, $8 per night per additional vehicle. Open May-mid-October, weather permitting.

**Directions:** From I-5 and Everett, turn east on U.S. 2 and drive 120 miles to U.S. 2/U.S. 97. Bear right on U.S. 2/U.S. 97 and drive one mile to Euclid Avenue/U.S. 97. Take that ramp and drive 18 miles on U.S. 97/U.S. 97-A to Entiat River Road. Turn left (northwest) and drive 27 miles to the campground on the left.

**Contact:** Okanogan and Wenatchee National Forests, Entiat Ranger District, 509/784-4700, www.fs.usda.gov.

## 102 FOX CREEK

### Scenic rating: 7

on the Entiat River in Wenatchee National Forest

**Map 3.4, page 184**

This camp is located along the Entiat River near Fox Creek. Fishing is prohibited in the vicinity of Entiat Falls, so make sure you understand the regulations. This camp features several campsites that are closer to the river than those at nearby Lake Creek, making it the more popular campground of the two. The elevation is 2,100 feet.

**Campsites, facilities:** There are 16 sites for tents or RVs up to 32 feet long. Picnic tables and fire grills are provided. Drinking water, vault toilets, and garbage bins are available. Some facilities are wheelchair accessible. Leashed pets are permitted.

**Reservations, fees:** Reservations are not accepted. Sites are $10 per night, $8 per night per additional vehicle. Open May-mid-October, weather permitting.

**Directions:** From I-5 and Everett, turn east on U.S. 2 and drive 120 miles to U.S. 2/U.S. 97. Bear right on U.S. 2/U.S. 97 and drive one mile to Euclid Avenue/U.S. 97. Take that ramp and drive 18 miles on U.S. 97/U.S. 97-A to Entiat River Road. Turn left (northwest) and drive 26 miles to the campground.

**Contact:** Okanogan and Wenatchee National Forests, Entiat Ranger District, 509/784-4700, www.fs.usda.gov.

## 103 SNOWBERRY BOWL

### Scenic rating: 7

near Lake Chelan in Wenatchee National Forest

**Map 3.4, page 184**

Snowberry Bowl is set less than four miles from Twenty-Five Mile Creek State Park and Lake Chelan. Sites are nestled amid a forest of Douglas fir and ponderosa pine, which provide privacy screening. The elevation is 2,000 feet.

**Campsites, facilities:** There are seven sites for tents or RVs up to 40 feet long and two double sites for up to 15 people each. Picnic tables, fire rings, and tent pads on sand are provided. Drinking water, vault toilets, and garbage bins are available. Some facilities are wheelchair accessible. Leashed pets are permitted.

**Reservations, fees:** Reservations are not accepted. Single sites are $10 per night, double sites are $20 per night, $8 per night per additional vehicle. Open year-round, with limited winter facilities.

**Directions:** From Chelan, drive south on U.S. 97-A for three miles to South Lakeshore Road. Turn right and drive 13.5 miles (passing the state park) to Shady Pass Road. Turn left and drive 2.5 miles to a Y intersection with Slide Ridge Road. Bear left and drive 0.5 mile to the campground on the right.

**Contact:** Okanogan and Wenatchee National Forests, Chelan Ranger District, 509/682-4900, www.fs.usda.gov.

## 104 TWENTY-FIVE MILE CREEK STATE PARK

### Scenic rating: 8

near Lake Chelan

**Map 3.4, page 184**                    **BEST (**

This campground is located on Twenty-Five Mile Creek near where it empties into Lake Chelan. A 235-acre marine camping park, it sits on the forested south shore of Lake

Chelan between the mountains and the lake, surrounded by spectacular scenery, featuring a rocky terrain with forested areas. Known for its boat access, this park can serve as your launching point for exploring the uplake wilderness portions of Lake Chelan. Fishing access for trout and salmon is close by, and fishing supplies, a dock, a modern marina, and boat moorage are available. There is also a small wading area for kids. Forest Road 5900, which heads west from the park, accesses several trailheads leading into the U.S. Forest Service lands of the Chelan Mountains.

**Campsites, facilities:** There are 46 sites for tents, 21 sites with full or partial hookups (30 amps) for RVs up to 30 feet long, and a group site for 20-50 people. Picnic tables and fire grills are provided. Restrooms with flush toilets, coin showers, and drinking water are available. A dump station, firewood, a boat dock, fishing pier, marina, boat ramp, boat moorage, a picnic area, gasoline, and a seasonal camp store are available at the park. Some facilities are wheelchair accessible. Leashed pets are permitted.

**Reservations, fees:** Reservations are accepted at 888/CAMP-OUT (888/226-7688) or www. parks.wa.gov/reservations ($6.50-8.50 reservation fee). Sites are $17-42 per night, $10 per night per extra vehicle. The group site is $2.25 per person per night. Some credit cards are accepted. Open late March-October, weather permitting.

**Directions:** From Chelan, drive south on U.S. 97-A for three miles to South Lakeshore Road. Turn right and drive 15 miles to the park on the right.

**Contact:** Twenty-Five Mile Creek State Park, 509/687-3610; state park information, 360/902-8844, www.parks.wa.gov; Lake Chelan Boat Company, 509/682-4584, www. ladyofthelake.com.

## 105 MITCHELL CREEK BOAT-IN

### Scenic rating: 8

on Lake Chelan in Wenatchee National Forest

**Map 3.4, page 184**

This is one of 13 national forest campgrounds set on Lake Chelan. It can be reached by private boat, floatplane, or ferry. Though the ferry does not make a scheduled stop, it's possible to arrange a drop-off at the campsite with advance notice.

**Campsites, facilities:** There are seven tent sites accessible only by boat, ferry, or floatplane. Picnic tables and fire rings are provided. Vault toilets and a group shelter are available, but there is no drinking water. Garbage must be packed out. An on-site floating dock has a 17-boat capacity.

**Reservations, fees:** Reservations are not accepted. There is no fee for camping. There is a $5 per day dock-site fee if bringing a private boat. Open May-late October, weather permitting.

**Directions:** From Wenatchee, drive north on U.S. 97-A for 40 miles to the town of Chelan. Take your boat to the campground, 15 miles from Chelan. The campground is also directly accessible by floatplane. (Call Chelan Seaplanes at 509/682-5555 for more information.)

**Contact:** Okanogan and Wenatchee National Forests, Chelan Ranger District, 509/682-4900, www.fs.usda.gov.

## 106 KAMEI RESORT

### Scenic rating: 6

on Lake Wapato

**Map 3.4, page 184**

This resort is on Lake Wapato, about two miles from Lake Chelan. Note that this is a seasonal lake that closes in early September. No open fires are allowed. If you have an extra day, take the ferry ride on Lake Chelan.

**Campsites, facilities:** There are 55 sites with partial hookups (30 amp) for tents or RVs of any length. A rental trailer is also available. Picnic tables are provided. Restrooms with flush toilets and showers, drinking water, and ice are available. Boat docks, launching facilities, and rentals are nearby. Some facilities are wheelchair accessible. Leashed pets are permitted.

**Reservations, fees:** Reservations are accepted beginning in January each year. Sites are $25 per night. Open late April–late August.

**Directions:** From Chelan, drive west on Highway 150 for seven miles to Wapato Lake Road. Turn right (north) on Wapato Lake Road and drive four miles to the resort on the right.

**Contact:** Kamei Resort, 509/687-3690, www.golakechelan.net.

## 107 SODA SPRINGS-LITTLE WENATCHEE RIVER

**Scenic rating: 7**

on the Little Wenatchee River in Wenatchee National Forest

**Map 3.4, page 184**

Set along Little Wenatchee River Road, this campground is a small, quiet, closer-to-civilization alternative to Tumwater. But note that it lacks both drinking water and a trailer turnaround. It's off the beaten path in a pleasant wooded area, at an elevation of 2,000 feet. A small, cold soda spring is located next to the campground. There are some excellent hiking trails nearby.

**Campsites, facilities:** There are five sites for tents only. Picnic tables and fire grills are provided. Vault toilets are available, but there is no drinking water. Garbage must be packed out. Leashed pets are permitted.

**Reservations, fees:** Reservations are not accepted. There is no fee for camping. Open May-late October, weather permitting.

**Directions:** From I-5 and Everett, turn east on U.S. 2 and drive 87 miles to State Route 207. Turn north on State Route 207 and drive 11 miles to Forest Road 6500. Turn left (west) on Forest Road 6500 and drive seven miles to the campground on the left.

**Contact:** Okanogan and Wenatchee National Forests, Wenatchee River Ranger District, Wenatchee River Ranger Station, 509/548-2550, www.fs.usda.gov.

## 108 GLACIER VIEW

**Scenic rating: 9**

on Lake Wenatchee in Wenatchee National Forest

**Map 3.4, page 184**

This popular campground is set on the southwestern shore of Lake Wenatchee, near the head of the lake. It's a happening spot for boating, swimming, fishing, and windsurfing, and it fills up on summer weekends. Fishing is average. There are also some good hiking trails in the area and a golf course within a 10-minute drive. The camp sits at an elevation of 1,900 feet. Insider's note: The walk-in sites are set on the lake's shore, requiring a walk of about 100 feet.

**Campsites, facilities:** There are 23 sites for tents or small RVs 15 feet or less. Picnic tables and fire grills are provided. Drinking water, vault toilets, and garbage bins are available. A primitive boat launch for small boats is available. Some facilities are wheelchair accessible. Leashed pets are permitted.

**Reservations, fees:** Reservations are not accepted. Sites are $15 per night, $9 per night per extra vehicle, $5 boat launch fee. Open May-mid-October, weather permitting.

**Directions:** From Leavenworth, drive west on U.S. 2 for 14 miles to State Route 207. Turn right on State Route 207 North and drive 3.5 miles to Cedar Brae Road. Turn left (west) on Cedar Brae Road and drive 0.3 mile to campground sign. Turn left at sign and drive 3.4 miles to Forest Road 6607, a gravel road. Continue on Forest Road 6607 to the campground at the end of the road.

**Contact:** Okanogan and Wenatchee National Forests, Wenatchee River Ranger District, Lake Wenatchee Ranger Station, 509/548-2550, www.fs.usda.gov.

## 109 LAKE WENATCHEE STATE PARK

🚶 🚴 🏊 🎣 🛶 🎿 🐎 👤 ♿ 🚐 ⛺

### Scenic rating: 8

on Lake Wenatchee

**Map 3.4, page 184**          **BEST (**

Lake Wenatchee is the centerpiece for a 489-acre park with two miles of waterfront. Glaciers and the Wenatchee River feed Lake Wenatchee, and the river, which bisects the park, helps make it a natural wildlife area. Thanks to a nice location and pull-through sites that are spaced just right, you can expect plenty of company at this campground. The secluded campsites are set at the southeast end of Lake Wenatchee, which offers plenty of recreation opportunities, with a boat ramp nearby. A swimming beach is available at the north shore. There are eight miles of hiking trails, seven miles of bike trails, five miles of horse trails in and around the park, and a 1.1-mile interpretive snowshoe trail in winter. Note that no horse facilities are available right in the park, but horse rentals are nearby. In winter, there are 11 miles of multi-use trails and 23 miles of groomed cross-country skiing trails. Note: Bears are active in the park, so all food must be stored in bear-proof facilities.

**Campsites, facilities:** In the South Camp there are 100 sites for tents or RVs up to 40 feet (no hookups) and one group tent site for 20-50 people. In the North Camp there are 55 sites for tents or RVs of any length (no hookups), 42 sites with partial hookups (30 and 50 amps) for RVs of any length, and one group site for up to 80 people. Picnic tables and fire grills are provided. Restrooms with flush toilets and showers, drinking water, a dump station, a store, ice, firewood, two picnic shelters, amphitheater, volleyball, a restaurant, a playground, and guided horseback rides are available. Boat docks, launching facilities, rentals, and golf are nearby. Some facilities are wheelchair accessible. Leashed pets are permitted.

**Reservations, fees:** Reservations are accepted and required for the group camp at 888/CAMP-OUT (888/226-7688) or www.parks.wa.gov/reservations ($6.50-8.50 reservation fee). Sites are $17-39 per night, $10 per extra vehicle per night. The group site is $69.70-278.81 per night with a 20-person minimum. Open year-round, with limited winter facilities.

**Directions:** From Leavenworth, drive west on U.S. 2 for 15 miles to State Route 207 at Coles Corner. Turn right (north) and drive 3.5 miles to Cedar Brae Road. Turn left on Cedar Brae Road and drive 2.5 miles to the south park entrance. For the north park entrance, continue past Cedar Brae Road for one mile.

**Contact:** Lake Wenatchee State Park, 509/763-3101; state park information, 360/902-8844, www.parks.wa.gov.

## 110 NASON CREEK

🏊 🚐 ♿ 🚐 ⛺

### Scenic rating: 7

near Lake Wenatchee in Wenatchee National Forest

**Map 3.4, page 184**

This campground is located on Nason Creek near Lake Wenatchee, bordering Lake Wenatchee State Park. Recreation activities include swimming and waterskiing. Boat rentals, horseback riding, and golfing are available nearby.

**Campsites, facilities:** There are 73 sites, including a few double sites, for tents or RVs of any length. Some sites are pull-through. Picnic tables and fire grills are provided. Drinking water, restrooms with flush toilets and showers, and garbage bins are available. Boat-launching facilities are nearby. Some facilities are wheelchair accessible.

**Reservations, fees:** Reservations are not accepted. Sites are $20 per night, $11 per night per extra vehicle. Open mid-May-mid-October, weather permitting.

**Directions:** From I-5 and Everett, turn east on U.S. 2 and drive 87 miles to State Route 207, 1 mile west of Winton. Turn right on State Route 207 and drive 3.5 miles to Cedar Brae Road. Turn left (west) and drive 100 yards to the campground.

**Contact:** Okanogan and Wenatchee National Forests, Wenatchee River Ranger District, Lake Wenatchee Ranger Station, 509/548-2550, www.fs.usda.gov.

## 111 GOOSE CREEK

### Scenic rating: 7

on Goose Creek in Wenatchee National Forest

**Map 3.4, page 184**

With trails for dirt bikes available directly from the camp, Goose Creek is used primarily by motorcycle riders. A main trail links to the Entiat off-road vehicle trail system, so this camp gets high use during the summer. The camp is set near a small creek.

**Campsites, facilities:** There are 26 single sites and three double sites for tents or RVs of any length. Picnic tables and fire rings are provided. Drinking water, vault toilets, and garbage bins are available. Some facilities are wheelchair accessible. Leashed pets are permitted.

**Reservations, fees:** Reservations are not accepted. Sites are $12-24 per vehicle per night. Open mid-May-late October, weather permitting.

**Directions:** From I-5 and Everett, turn east on U.S. 2 and drive 87 miles to State Route 207, 1 mile west of Winton. Turn north on State Route 207 and drive 4.3 miles to Chiwawa Loop Road. Turn right and drive 1.5 miles to Chiwawa River Road/Forest Road 6200. Turn left and drive three miles to Forest Road

6100. Turn right and drive 0.6 mile to the camp on the right.

**Contact:** Okanogan and Wenatchee National Forests, Wenatchee River Ranger District, Lake Wenatchee Ranger Station, 509/548-2550, www.fs.usda.gov.

## 112 PINE FLATS

### Scenic rating: 5

near Entiat River, in Wenatchee National Forest

**Map 3.4, page 184**

This camp has ready access to the Mad River off-road vehicle (ORV) area and is popular with bikers and ORV enthusiasts. The area boasts more than 100 miles of trails, which are ideal for quads and dirt bikes. It ties into many loop trails. The elevation is 1,600 feet.

**Campsites, facilities:** There are six sites for tents only and one group site for tents only that accommodates 20-50 people. Picnic tables and fire grills are provided. Drinking water and pit and flush toilets are available. Garbage must be packed out.

**Reservations, fees:** Reservations are not accepted for individual sites but are required for the group site at 877/444-6777 ($10 reservation fee) or www.recreation.gov ($10 reservation fee). Sites are $8 per night per vehicle, $6 per night per additional vehicle; the group site is $60 per night. Open late May-October, weather permitting.

**Directions:** From Wenatchee, drive north on U.S. 2/U.S. 97 for 1.5 miles to U.S. 97/U.S. 97-A. Drive north 14 miles on U.S. 97/U.S. 97-A to Entiat River Road. Turn left (northwest) at Entiat River Road and drive 10 miles to Mad River Road/Forest Service Road 5700. Turn left at Mad River Road/Forest Service Road 5700 and drive just over one mile to the campground.

**Contact:** Okanogan and Wenatchee National Forest, Entiat Ranger District, 509/784-4700, www.fs.usda.gov.

## 113 LAKE CHELAN STATE PARK

### Scenic rating: 10

on Lake Chelan

**Map 3.4, page 184**      **BEST (**

This park is the recreation headquarters for Lake Chelan. It provides boat docks and concession stands on the shore of the 55-mile lake. The park covers 127 acres, featuring 6,000 feet of shoreline on the forested south shore. Water sports include fishing, swimming, scuba diving, and waterskiing. Summers tend to be hot and dry, but expansive lawns looking out on the lake provide a fresh feel, especially in the early evenings. A daily ferry service provides access to the roadless community at the head of the lake. The word "chelan" is a Chelan Indian word and translates to both "lake" and "blue water." Nearby attractions include the Holden Mine site and Holden Village and hiking in Glacier Peak Wilderness.

**Campsites, facilities:** There are 109 sites for tents, 35 sites with full or partial hookups (30 and 50 amps) for RVs up to 30 feet long, and five hike-in/bike-in tent sites. Picnic tables and fire grills are provided. Restrooms with flush toilets and coin showers, drinking water, firewood, a picnic area with a kitchen shelter, a dump station, store, restaurant, ice, playground, horseshoe pits, ball field, beach area, boat dock, and launching facilities and moorage are available. Some facilities are wheelchair accessible. Leashed pets are permitted.

**Reservations, fees:** Reservations are accepted at 888/CAMP-OUT (888/226-7688) or www.parks.wa.gov/reservations ($6.50-8.50 reservation fee). RV sites with hookups are $26-42 per night, tent sites are $17-31 per night, primitive sites are $12 per night, $10 per extra vehicle per night. Some credit cards are accepted. Open year-round, weather permitting.

**Directions:** From Wenatchee, drive north on U.S. 97-A for nine miles to State Route 971 (Navarre Coulee Road). Turn left (north) and drive seven miles to the end of the highway at South Lakeshore Road. Turn right, then immediately look for the park entrance to the left.

**Contact:** Lake Chelan State Park, 509/687-3710; state park information, 360/902-8844, www.parks.wa.gov.

## 114 DAROGA STATE PARK

### Scenic rating: 5

on the Columbia River

**Map 3.4, page 184**

This 90-acre state park is set along 1.5 miles of shoreline on the Columbia River. It sits on the elevated edge of the desert scablands. This camp fills up quickly on summer weekends. Desert Canyon Golf Course is two miles away. Fishing, along with walking and biking trails, are available out of the camp.

**Campsites, facilities:** There are 28 sites with partial hookups (30 amps) for tents or RVs up to 32 feet long, 17 walk-in or boat-in sites (requiring a 0.25-mile trip), and two group sites for 50-150 people each. Some sites are pull-through. Picnic tables and fire pits are provided. Restrooms with flush (near RV sites) and vault (near walk-in sites) toilets, coin showers, drinking water, a dump station, firewood, a swimming beach, boat-launching facilities and docks, a playground, baseball field, basketball courts, softball and soccer fields, and a picnic area with a kitchen shelter are available. Some facilities are wheelchair accessible. Leashed pets are permitted.

**Reservations, fees:** Reservations are accepted at 888/CAMP-OUT (888/226-7688) or www.parks.wa.gov/reservations ($6.50-8.50 reservation fee). Sites are $12-39 per night, $10 per extra vehicle per night; group sites are $136.87-410.62 per night. Open mid-March-mid-October, weather permitting.

**Directions:** From East Wenatchee, drive north on U.S. 97 (east side of the Columbia River) for 18 miles to the camp. For boat-in camps, launch boats from the ramp at the park and drive 0.25 mile.

**Contact:** Daroga State Park, 509/664-6380; state park information, 360/902-8844, www. parks.wa.gov.

## 115 BLACKPINE HORSE CAMP

### Scenic rating: 8

near the Alpine Lakes Wilderness in Wenatchee National Forest

**Map 3.4, page 184**

Blackpine Creek Horse Camp is used primarily by horse campers for horse pack trips. It is set on Black Pine Creek near Icicle Creek at a major trailhead leading into the Alpine Lakes Wilderness. It's one of seven rustic camps on the creek, with the distinction of being the only one with facilities for horses. The elevation is 3,000 feet.

**Campsites, facilities:** There are 10 sites for tents or RVs up to 60 feet long. Picnic tables and fire grills are provided. Solar pumped drinking water, vault toilets, and garbage bins are available. Horse facilities, including a hitching rail and loading ramp, are also available. Leashed pets are permitted.

**Reservations, fees:** Reservations are not accepted. Sites are $15 per night, $8 per night per extra vehicle. Open mid-May-late October, weather permitting.

**Directions:** From I-5 and Everett, turn east on U.S. 2 and drive 103 miles to Leavenworth and County Road 76 (Icicle River Road). Turn south and drive 19.2 miles to the campground on the left. Note: Because of road washout, access may change in future.

**Contact:** Okanogan and Wenatchee National Forests, Wenatchee River Ranger District, 509/548-2550, www.fs.usda.gov.

## 116 ROCK ISLAND

### Scenic rating: 8

near the Alpine Lakes Wilderness in Wenatchee National Forest

**Map 3.4, page 184**

Rock Island is one of several campgrounds in the immediate area along Icicle Creek and is located about one mile from the trailhead that takes hikers into the Alpine Lakes Wilderness. This is a pretty spot with good fishing access. The elevation is 2,900 feet.

**Campsites, facilities:** There are 20 single sites and two double sites for tents or RVs up to 22 feet long. Picnic tables and fire grills are provided. Drinking water, vault toilets, and garbage bins are available. Some facilities are wheelchair accessible. Leashed pets are permitted.

**Reservations, fees:** Reservations are not accepted. Sites are $14 per vehicle per night, $9 per night per extra vehicle. Open May-late October, weather permitting.

**Directions:** From I-5 and Everett, turn east on U.S. 2 and drive 103 miles to Leavenworth and County Road 7600/Icicle Creek Road. Turn right (south) and drive 17.7 miles to the campground.

**Contact:** Okanogan and Wenatchee National Forests, Wenatchee River Ranger District, 509/548-2550, www.fs.usda.gov.

## 117 CHATTER CREEK

### Scenic rating: 8

near the Alpine Lakes Wilderness in Wenatchee National Forest

**Map 3.4, page 184**

Icicle and Chatter Creeks are the backdrop for this creekside campground. The elevation is 2,800 feet. Trails lead out in several directions from the camp into the Alpine Lakes Wilderness.

**Campsites, facilities:** There are 12 sites for

tents or RVs up to 22 feet long and one group site for up to 45 people and 12 vehicles. Picnic tables and fire grills are provided. Drinking water, vault toilets, garbage bins, firewood, and a picnic shelter with fireplace are available. Some facilities are wheelchair accessible. Leashed pets are permitted.

**Reservations, fees:** Reservations are required for the group site at 877/444-6777 ($10 reservation fee) or www.recreation.gov ($9 reservation fee). Sites are $15 per night, $9 per night per extra vehicle; the group site is $85 per night with no extra vehicle charge. Some credit cards are accepted. Open April-late October, weather permitting.

**Directions:** From I-5 and Everett, turn east on U.S. 2 and drive 103 miles to Leavenworth and County Road 7600/Icicle River Road. Turn right (south) and drive 16.1 miles to the campground on the right.

**Contact:** Okanogan and Wenatchee National Forests, Wenatchee River Ranger District, 509/548-2550, www.fs.usda.gov.

## 118 IDA CREEK
🏃 🎣 🐕 ♿ 🚐 ⛺

### Scenic rating: 8
on Icicle Creek in Wenatchee National Forest

**Map 3.4, page 184**

This campground is one of several small, quiet camps along Icicle and Ida Creeks. Recreation options are similar to Chatter Creek and Rock Island campgrounds, hiking and fishing among them.

**Campsites, facilities:** There are 10 sites for tents or RVs up to 30 feet long. Picnic tables and fire grills are provided. Drinking water, vault toilets, and garbage bins are available. Some facilities are wheelchair accessible. Leashed pets are permitted.

**Reservations, fees:** Reservations are not accepted. Sites are $14 per night, $9 per night per extra vehicle. Open May-late October, weather permitting.

**Directions:** From I-5 and Everett, turn east on

U.S. 2 and drive 103 miles to Leavenworth and County Road 7600/Icicle River Road. Turn right (south) and drive 14.2 miles to the campground on the left.

**Contact:** Okanogan and Wenatchee National Forests, Wenatchee River Ranger District, 509/548-2550, www.fs.usda.gov.

## 119 JOHNNY CREEK
🏃 🎣 🐕 ♿ 🚐 ⛺

### Scenic rating: 8
on Icicle Creek in Wenatchee National Forest

**Map 3.4, page 184**

Johnny Creek campground is split into two parts, which sit on both sides of the road along Icicle and Johnny Creeks. It is fairly popular. Upper Johnny has a forest setting, whereas Lower Johnny is set alongside the creek, with adjacent forest. Nearby recreation opportunities include trail access into the Alpine Lakes Wilderness, horseback riding, and a golf course. The elevation is 2,300 feet.

**Campsites, facilities:** There are 56 single sites and nine double sites for tents or RVs up to 50 feet long. Picnic tables and fire grills are provided. Drinking water, vault toilets, and garbage bins are available. Some facilities are wheelchair accessible. Leashed pets are permitted.

**Reservations, fees:** Reservations are not accepted. Single sites are $16-19 per night, double sites are $28-32 per night, $9-10 per night per extra vehicle fee. Open May-late October, weather permitting.

**Directions:** From I-5 and Everett, turn east on U.S. 2 and drive 103 miles to Leavenworth and County Road 7600/Icicle River Road. Turn right (south) and drive 12.4 miles to the campground (with camps on each side of the road).

**Contact:** Okanogan and Wenatchee National Forests, Wenatchee River Ranger District, 509/548-2550, www.fs.usda.gov.

## 120 BRIDGE CREEK

### Scenic rating: 8

on Icicle Creek in Wenatchee National Forest

**Map 3.4, page 184**

This camp is a small, quiet spot along Icicle and Bridge Creeks. The elevation is 1,800 feet. About two miles south of the camp at Eightmile Creek, a trail accesses the Alpine Lakes Wilderness. Horseback-riding opportunities are within four miles, and golf is within five miles.

**Campsites, facilities:** There are six sites for tents or small RVs up to 19 feet long and one group site for up to 70 people. Picnic tables and fire grills are provided. Drinking water, vault toilets, garbage bins, and firewood are available. The group site does not have drinking water. Leashed pets are permitted.

**Reservations, fees:** Reservations are required for the group site at 877/444-6777 ($10 reservation fee) or www.recreation.gov ($9 reservation fee). Sites are $16 per night, $9 per night per extra vehicle. The group site is $85 per night. Open mid-April-late October, weather permitting.

**Directions:** From I-5 and Everett, turn east on U.S. 2 and drive 103 miles to Leavenworth and County Road 7600/Icicle River Road. Turn right (south) and drive 9.4 miles to the campground on the left.

**Contact:** Okanogan and Wenatchee National Forests, Wenatchee River Ranger District, 509/548-2550, www.fs.usda.gov.

## 121 EIGHTMILE

### Scenic rating: 8

near the Alpine Lakes Wilderness in Wenatchee National Forest

**Map 3.4, page 184**

Trailheads are located within two miles of this campground along Icicle and Eightmile Creeks, providing access to fishing, as well as a backpacking route into the Alpine Lakes Wilderness. Horseback-riding opportunities are within four miles, and golf is within five miles. The elevation is 1,800 feet.

**Campsites, facilities:** There are 41 single sites and four double sites for tents or RVs up to 50 feet long. There is also one group site for up to 70 people and 25 vehicles. Picnic tables and fire grills are provided. Drinking water, vault toilets, and garbage bins are available. Some facilities are wheelchair accessible. Leashed pets are permitted.

**Reservations, fees:** Reservations are required for the group site at 877/444-6777 ($10 reservation fee) or www.recreation.gov ($9 reservation fee). Single sites are $19 per night, double sites are $32 per night, $10 per night per extra vehicle; the group site is $85 per night. Open mid-April-late October.

**Directions:** From I-5 and Everett, turn east on U.S. 2 and drive 103 miles to Leavenworth and County Road 7600/Icicle River Road. Turn right (south) and drive eight miles to the campground on the left.

**Contact:** Okanogan and Wenatchee National Forests, Wenatchee River Ranger District, 509/548-2550, www.fs.usda.gov.

## 122 TUMWATER

### Scenic rating: 7

near the Alpine Lakes Wilderness in Wenatchee National Forest

**Map 3.4, page 184**

This large, popular camp provides a little bit of both worlds. It provides a good layover spot for campers cruising U.S. 2, but it also features two nearby forest roads, each less than a mile long, which end at trailheads that provide access to the Alpine Lakes Wilderness. The camp is on the Wenatchee River in Tumwater Canyon. This section of river is closed to fishing. The elevation is 2,050 feet.

**Campsites, facilities:** There are 84 single sites and two double sites for tents or RVs up to 50 feet long; there is also one electric group site for tents or RVs up to 25 feet long that can accommodate up to 70 people and 40 vehicles. Picnic tables and fire grills are provided. Drinking water, restrooms with flush toilets, firewood, picnic shelter with fireplace, playground, horseshoes, and basketball court are available. Some facilities are wheelchair accessible. Leashed pets are permitted.

**Reservations, fees:** Reservations are required for the group site at 877/444-6777 ($10 reservation fee) or www.recreation.gov ($9 reservation fee). Single sites are $20 per night, double sites are $34 per night, $11 per night per extra vehicle; the group site is $95 per night. Open May-mid-October, weather permitting.

**Directions:** From I-5 and Everett, turn east on U.S. 2 and drive 99 miles to the campground (10 miles west of Leavenworth).

**Contact:** Okanogan and Wenatchee National Forests, Wenatchee River Ranger District, 509/548-2550, www.fs.usda.gov.

## 123 LEAVENWORTH/ PINE VILLAGE KOA

🏕🏊🛶🐕🥾♿🚐⛰

**Scenic rating: 8**

near the Wenatchee River

**Map 3.4, page 184**      **BEST (**

This lovely resort on 30 acres is near the Bavarian-themed village of Leavenworth, to which the park provides a free shuttle in the summer. The spectacularly scenic area is surrounded by the Cascade Mountains and set among ponderosa pines. The camp has access to the Wenatchee River, not to mention many luxurious extras, including a spa and a heated pool. The park allows campfires and has firewood available. Nearby recreation options include an 18-hole golf course, horseback riding, white-water rafting, and hiking trails. Make a point to spend a day in Leavenworth if possible; it offers authentic German food and architecture, along with music and art shows in the summer.

**Campsites, facilities:** There are 60 sites with full hookups and 60 sites with partial hookups (30 and 50 amps) for RVs up to 65 feet long, 40 tent sites, 20 cabins, two cottages, and 15 lodges. Some sites are pull-through. Picnic tables are provided, and fire grills are available at some sites. Restrooms with flush toilets and showers, drinking water, dump stations, Wi-Fi access, bicycle rentals, firewood, a recreation hall, cable TV, a convenience store, propane, coin laundry, ice, a playground, horseshoe pits, volleyball, a spa and sauna, a seasonal heated swimming pool, snack bar and espresso stand, doggie run, and a beach area are available. A café is located within one mile. Some facilities are wheelchair accessible. Leashed pets are permitted.

**Reservations, fees:** Reservations are accepted at 800/562-5709. RV sites are $26-84 per night, tent sites are $22-54 per night, $5 per extra vehicle per night, and $5 per person per night for more than two people. Some credit cards are accepted. Open year round.

**Directions:** From I-5 and Everett, turn east on U.S. 2 and drive 103 miles to Leavenworth. Continue east on U.S. 2 for 0.25 mile to River Bend Drive. Turn left (north) and drive 0.5 mile to the campground on the right.

**Contact:** Leavenworth/Pine Village KOA, 509/548-7709, www.koa.com.

## 124 ICICLE RIVER RV RESORT

🏕🏊🛶🐕🚐

**Scenic rating: 9**

on Icicle River

**Map 3.4, page 184**

This pretty, wooded spot is set along the Icicle River, where fishing and swimming are available. The 50-acre resort is clean and scenic. An 18-hole golf course and hiking trails are nearby. Note that tent camping is not permitted here, but eight cabins are available for rent.

**Campsites, facilities:** There are 108 sites with full or partial (30 and 50 amps) hookups for

RVs of any length, six rustic cabins, and two full-service cabins. Picnic tables and fire pits (at most sites) are provided. Restrooms with flush toilets and showers, drinking water, coin laundry, cable TV, Wi-Fi access, a spa, firewood, and propane gas are available. Horseshoe pits and two pavilions are available nearby. Leashed pets are permitted only in the campground.

**Reservations, fees:** Reservations are accepted. Sites are $35-44 per night, $5 per extra vehicle per night, $5 per person per night for more than two adults, $3 for each child. Some credit cards are accepted. Open April-mid-October, weather permitting.

**Directions:** From I-5 and Everett, turn east on U.S. 2 and drive 103 miles to Leavenworth and County Road 7600/Icicle Road. Turn right (south) and drive three miles to the resort on the left.

**Contact:** Icicle River RV Resort, 509/548-5420, www.icicleriverrv.com.

## 125 ENTIAT CITY PARK

### Scenic rating: 8

on the Columbia River

Map 3.4, page 184

Note: As this book went to press, Entiat will be closed all through 2014 for improvements, but is scheduled to reopen in 2015.

If you're hurting for a spot for the night, you can usually find a campsite here. The campground is on Lake Entiat, which is a dammed portion of the Columbia River. Access to nearby launching facilities makes this a good camping spot for boaters. Waterskiing and personal watercraft are allowed. A dirt trail leads from the lake to the town of Entiat.

**Campsites, facilities:** There are 25 tent sites and 31 sites with partial hookups for RVs of any length. Picnic tables and barbecue stands are provided. Restrooms with flush toilets and coin showers, drinking water, a dump station, and a playground are available. Boat

docks and launching facilities are nearby. A store, café, propane, and coin laundry are available within 1.5 miles. Some facilities are wheelchair accessible. No open fires, dogs, or alcohol are permitted.

**Reservations, fees:** Reservations are available at 800/736-8428 ($5 reservation fee). Sites are $22-28 per night, $2 per extra adult per night, $2 per extra vehicle per night. Group rates are available. Open year-round.

**Directions:** From Wenatchee, drive north on U.S. 97-A for 16 miles to Entiat; the park entrance is on the right (Shearson Street is adjacent on the left). Turn right and drive a short distance to the park along the shore of Lake Entiat.

**Contact:** Entiat City Park, 800/736-8428; City Hall, 509/784-1500, www.entiat.org.

## 126 LINCOLN ROCK STATE PARK

### Scenic rating: 5

on Lake Entiat

Map 3.4, page 184

Lincoln Rock State Park is an 80-acre park set along the shore of Lake Entiat, created by the Rocky Reach Dam on the Columbia River. The park features lawns and shade trees amid an arid landscape. There are two miles of paved, flat trails suitable for both hiking and biking. Water sports include swimming, boating, and waterskiing. Beavers are occasionally visible in the Columbia River. Oh, yeah, and the name? Look for a basalt outcropping in the shape of the former president's famous profile and you'll see why.

**Campsites, facilities:** There are 67 sites with partial or full hookups (30 amps) for RVs up to 65 feet long, 27 sites for tents or self-contained RVs up to 60 feet long, and four cabins. Picnic tables and fire grills are provided. Restrooms with flush toilets and coin showers, drinking water, dump station, playground, athletic fields, horseshoe pits, swimming beach, amphitheater, interpretive center, three picnic shelters, and firewood are available. Boat docks, moorage, and launching facilities are located on Lake Entiat. Some facilities are wheelchair accessible. Leashed pets are permitted.

**Reservations, fees:** Reservations are accepted at 888/CAMP-OUT (888/226-7688) or www.parks.wa.gov/reservations ($6.50-8.50 reservation fee). Sites are $17-42 per night, $10 per extra vehicle per night; cabins are $63.84-85.48 per night. Some credit cards are accepted. Open March-mid-October, weather permitting.

**Directions:** From East Wenatchee, drive northeast on U.S. 2 for seven miles to the park on the left.

**Contact:** Lincoln Rock State Park, 509/884-8702; state park information, 360/902-8844, www.parks.wa.gov.

## 127 BLU-SHASTIN RV RESORT

🧗 🚵 ⛵ 🏊 ❄️ 🐕 ♿ 🐎 🚐 ⛺

**Scenic rating: 6**

near Peshastin Creek

Map 3.4, page 184

This 13-acre park is set in a mountainous area near Peshastin Creek. Gold panning in the river is a popular activity here; during the gold rush, the Peshastin was the best-producing river in the state—and it still is. The camp has sites on the riverbank and plenty of shade trees. A heated pool, recreation field, and horseshoe pits provide possible activities in the park. Hiking trails and marked bike trails are nearby. Rafting, tubing, and golfing are nearby and are popular in the summer. Snowmobiling is an option during the winter.

**Campsites, facilities:** There are 86 sites for tents or RVs of any length (20 and 30 amp full hookups); four sites are pull-through. Picnic tables and fire rings are provided. Restrooms with flush toilets and showers, drinking water, Wi-Fi, cable TV, a recreation hall, firewood,

coin laundry, ice, a playground, horseshoes, badminton, volleyball, and a seasonal heated swimming pool are available. Propane gas, a store, and a café are located within seven miles. Leashed pets are permitted.

**Reservations, fees:** Reservations are recommended at 888/548-4184. Sites are $26-30 per night. Some credit cards are accepted. Open year-round, weather permitting.

**Directions:** From Leavenworth, drive east on U.S. 2 for five miles to U.S. 97. Turn right (south) on U.S. 97 and drive seven miles to the park on the right.

**Contact:** Blu-Shastin RV Park, 509/548-4184 or 888/548-4184, www.blushastin.com.

## 128 WENATCHEE RIVER COUNTY PARK

🚐 🐕 ♿ 🚐

**Scenic rating: 5**

on the Wenatchee River

Map 3.4, page 184

This camp is set along the Wenatchee River, situated between the highway and the river. Though not the greatest setting, with some highway noise, it is convenient for RV campers. You can usually get a tree-covered site in the campground, despite it being a small park. The adjacent river is fast moving and provides white-water rafting in season, with a put-in spot at the park.

**Campsites, facilities:** There are 43 sites with full hookups, four sites with partial hookups, and two sites with no hookups for RVs of any length. Several sites are pull-through. Picnic tables and fire pits are provided. Drinking water, restrooms with flush toilets and coin showers, a recreation room, propane, coin laundry, dump station, sand volleyball court, playground, ping-pong table, horseshoe pit, golfing cage, basketball hoop, media and bicycle lending library, and Wi-Fi are available. A convenience store and a restaurant are within 0.5 mile. Some facilities are wheelchair accessible. Leashed pets are permitted.

**Reservations, fees:** Reservations are available at 509/667-7503. Sites are $25-30 per night, $5 per night per person for more than four people, and $5 per extra vehicle per night. Some credit cards are accepted. Open April 1-October 31.

**Directions:** From Wenatchee and U.S. 2, take the State Route 285/N. Wenatchee exit, keeping left to merge onto State Route 285/N. Wenatchee Avenue. Drive 2.5 miles to N. Miller. Turn south and drive a short distance to Washington Street. Turn left and drive 0.5 mile to Orondo Avenue. Turn left and drive a short distance to the park entrance on the left.

**Contact:** Wenatchee River County Park, 509/667-7503, www.wenatcheeriverpark.org.

## 129 WENATCHEE CONFLUENCE STATE PARK

🚶 🚲 🏊 🛶 ⛵ 🏕 🐎 🎣 ♿ 🚐 ⛺

**Scenic rating: 10**

on the Columbia River

**Map 3.4, page 184**

This 197-acre state park is set at the confluence of the Wenatchee and Columbia Rivers. The park features expansive lawns shaded by deciduous trees and fronted by the two rivers. Wenatchee Confluence has something of a dual personality: The north portion of the park is urban and recreational, while the southern section is a designated natural wetland area. There are 10.5 miles of paved trail for hiking, biking, and in-line skating. A pedestrian bridge crosses the Wenatchee River. An interpretive hiking trail is available in the Horan Natural Area. Other recreation possibilities include fishing, swimming, boating, and waterskiing. Sports enthusiasts will find playing fields as well as tennis and basketball courts. Daroga State Park and Lake Chelan to the north offer side-trip possibilities.

**Campsites, facilities:** There are 51 sites with full hookups (30 amps) for RVs up to 65 feet long, eight tent sites, and a group tent site for 50-300 people. Picnic tables and fire grills are provided. Restrooms with flush toilets and coin showers, drinking water, a boat launch, dump station, swimming beach, playground, horseshoe pits, a picnic shelter that can be reserved, and athletic fields are available. Some facilities are wheelchair accessible. Leashed pets are permitted.

**Reservations, fees:** Reservations are accepted at 888/CAMP-OUT (888/226-7688) or www. parks.wa.gov/reservations ($6.50-8.50 reservation fee). Sites are $12-42 per night, $10 per extra vehicle per night. The group site is $203.32-677.73 per night, no extra vehicle fee. Some credit cards are accepted. Open year-round.

**Directions:** From Wenatchee and U.S. 2, take the Easy Street exit and drive south to Penny Road. Turn left and drive a short distance to Chester Kimm Street. Turn right and drive to a T intersection and Old Station Road. Turn left on Old Station Road and drive past the railroad tracks to the park on the right. The park is 1.3 miles from U.S. 2.

**Contact:** Wenatchee Confluence State Park, 509/664-6373; state park information, 360/902-8844, www.parks.wa.gov.

## 130 BEVERLY

🚶 🚲 🛶 🏕 🚐 ⛺

**Scenic rating: 8**

on the North Fork of the Teanaway River in Wenatchee National Forest

**Map 3.4, page 184**

This primitive campground is set on the North Fork of the Teanaway River, a scenic area of the river. It is primarily a hiker's camp, with several trails leading up nearby creeks and into the Alpine Lakes Wilderness. Self-issued permits (available at the trailhead) are required for wilderness hiking. The elevation is 3,100 feet.

**Campsites, facilities:** There are four single sites and six double sites for tents or RVs up to 21 feet long. Picnic tables and fire grills are provided. Vault toilets are available, but there is no drinking water. Garbage must be packed out. Leashed pets are permitted.

**Reservations, fees:** Reservations are not accepted. Sites are $8 per night per vehicle. Open June-mid-November, weather permitting.

**Directions:** In Seattle on I-5, turn east on I-90. Drive east on I-90 for 78 miles to Cle Elum and Exit 85. Take Exit 85 to Highway 970. Turn east on Highway 970 and drive seven miles to Teanaway Road (Highway 970). Turn left (north) on Teanaway Road and drive 13 miles to the end of the paved road. Bear right (north) on Forest Road 9737 and drive four miles to the campground on the left.

**Contact:** Okanogan and Wenatchee National Forests, Cle Elum Ranger District, 509/852-1100, www.fs.usda.gov.

## 131 INDIAN CAMP

### Scenic rating: 6
on the Middle Fork of the Teanaway River

**Map 3.4, page 184**

This campground along the Middle Fork of the Teanaway River is located in a primitive setting with sunny, open sites along the water. Fishing for brook trout is best here when the season first opens in June. Quiet and solitude are highlights of this little-used camp. It's an easy drive from here to trailheads accessing the Mount Stuart Range. Be sure to bring your own drinking water. This is a popular snowmobile area in winter.

**Campsites, facilities:** There are 11 sites for tents or RVs up to 35 feet long. Picnic tables and fire grills are provided. Pit toilets are available, but there is no drinking water. Garbage must be packed out. Some saddle-stock facilities are available, including hitching posts. Some facilities are wheelchair accessible. Leashed pets are permitted.

**Reservations, fees:** Reservations are not accepted. There is no fee for camping, but a Discover Pass is required. Open year-round, weather and snow level permitting.

**Directions:** From Seattle, drive east on I-90 for 80 miles to Cle Elum and Exit 85 and Highway 970. Turn east on Highway 970 and drive 6.9 miles to Teanaway Road. Turn left on Teanaway Road and drive 7.3 miles to West Fork Teanaway Road. Turn left and drive 0.6 mile to Middle Fork Teanaway Road. Turn right and drive 3.9 miles to the campground on the left.

**Contact:** Department of Natural Resources, Southeast Region, 509/925-8510, www.dnr.wa.gov.

## 132 SWAUK

### Scenic rating: 6
on Swauk Creek in Wenatchee National Forest

**Map 3.4, page 184**

Some decent hiking trails can be found at this campground along Swauk Creek. A short loop trail, about one mile round-trip, is the most popular. Fishing is marginal, and there is some highway noise from U.S. 97. The elevation is 3,200 feet. Three miles east of the camp on Forest Road 9716 is Swauk Forest Discovery Trail. This three-mile interpretive trail explains some of the effects of logging and U.S. Forest Service management of the forest habitat.

**Campsites, facilities:** There are 21 sites, including two double sites, for tents or RVs up to 25 feet long. Fire grills and picnic tables are provided. Flush and vault toilets and firewood are available. There is no drinking water. Leashed pets are permitted.

**Reservations, fees:** Reservations are not accepted. Sites are $16 per night, double sites are $32 per night, $7 per extra vehicle per night (applies to third and fourth vehicle at double sites). Open late May-early September, weather permitting.

**Directions:** In Seattle on I-5, turn east on I-90. Drive east on I-90 for 80 miles to Cle Elum and Exit 85. Take Exit 85 to Highway 970. Turn east on Highway 970 and drive 20

miles north on Highway 970/U.S. 97 to the campground on the right (near Swauk Pass).
**Contact:** Okanogan and Wenatchee National Forests, Cle Elum Ranger District, 509/852-1100, www.fs.usda.gov.

## 133 MINERAL SPRINGS

### Scenic rating: 6
on Swauk Creek in Wenatchee National Forest

**Map 3.4, page 184**

This campground is at the confluence of Medicine and Swauk Creeks. Note that this camp is set along a highway, so there is some highway noise. Fishing, berry picking, and hunting are good in season in this area. It is at an elevation of 2,800 feet. Most use the camp as a one-night layover spot.

**Campsites, facilities:** There are six sites for tents or RVs up to 21 feet long and one group site for 20-50 people. Picnic tables and fire rings are provided. Drinking water, vault toilets, and a camp host are available. Leashed pets are permitted. A restaurant is nearby.

**Reservations, fees:** Reservations are required for the group site at 877/444-6777 ($10 reservation fee) or www.recreation.gov ($9 reservation fee). Sites are $16 per night, $7 per extra vehicle per night. The group site is $80 per night. Open mid-May-mid-September, weather permitting.

**Directions:** From Seattle, drive east on I-90 for 80 miles to Cle Elum and Exit 85 and Highway 970. Turn northeast on Highway 970 and drive 17 miles to the campground on the left.

**Contact:** Okanogan and Wenatchee National Forests, Cle Elum Ranger District, 509/852-1100, www.fs.usda.gov.

## 134 KEN WILCOX HORSE CAMP

### Scenic rating: 8
near Swauk Creek at Haney Meadows in Wenatchee National Forest

**Map 3.4, page 184**

Note: The Table Rock Fire in 2012 burned many of the trees sheltering the sites along the back side of this campground. The campground closed for the 2013 season to remove some of the hazard trees, but is expected to reopen in 2014. Call to confirm availability before planning a trip here.

This scenic camp near Haney Meadows has been adopted by a local equestrian association that helps maintain the horse trails; it is also the launch point for an extensive trail system. The last couple miles of road are pretty rough though, suitable only for high-clearance vehicles or pickups. The elevation is 5,500 feet.

**Campsites, facilities:** There are 25 sites for tents or RVs up to 30 feet long. Picnic tables and fire pits are provided. Vault toilets are available. There is no drinking water, although stock water is available. Garbage must be packed out. Stock facilities include hitching equipment, such as rails and rings for suspending a high line.

**Reservations, fees:** Reservations are not accepted. There is no fee for camping, but a Northwest Forest Pass ($5 daily fee or $30 annual fee per parked vehicle) is required. Open early July-mid-October, weather permitting (the access road is not plowed).

**Directions:** In Seattle on I-5, turn east on I-90. Drive east on I-90 for 80 miles to Cle Elum and Exit 85. Take Exit 85 to Highway 970. Turn east on Highway 970 and drive 24 miles to the summit of Blewett (Swauk) Pass and Forest Road 9716. Turn right on Forest Road 9716 (gravel) and drive about four miles to Forest Road 9712. Turn left on Forest Road 9712 and drive about five miles to the camp on the left.

**Contact:** Okanogan and Wenatchee National Forests, Cle Elum Ranger District, 509/852-1100, www.fs.usda.gov.

## 135 SQUILCHUCK STATE PARK

🚶 🚴 ❄️ 🐕 ♿ � ⛺

**Scenic rating: 7**

southwest of Wenatchee

**Map 3.4, page 184**

This 288-acre park (Squilchuc is Chinook for "muddy water") sits at an elevation of 4,000 feet in a fir and pine forest. Recreation opportunities include 10 miles of hiking and biking trails; in winter, this park sees sledding, snowshoeing, and cross-country skiing.

**Campsites, facilities:** There is one group site for tents or RVs up to 30 feet long (no hookups) that can accommodate 20-150 people. Picnic tables and fire rings are provided. A restroom with flush toilets and coin showers, drinking water, and a lodge with kitchen are available. Some facilities are wheelchair accessible. Leashed pets are permitted.

**Reservations, fees:** Reservations are required at 509/664-6373 ($25 reservation fee). The group site is $135.55-$406.64 per night. Open May-mid-September, with limited winter facilities.

**Directions:** From U.S. 2 in Wenatchee, drive south on Wenatchee Avenue to Squilchuck Road and follow the signs for about eight miles to the park.

**Contact:** Wenatchee Confluence State Park, 509/664-6373; state park information, 360/902-8844, www.parks.wa.gov.

## 136 TRAILER CORRAL RV PARK

🚶 🏊 � 🐕 � ⛺

**Scenic rating: 7**

near the Yakima River

**Map 3.4, page 184**

This wooded campground about one mile from the Yakima River offers a choice of grassy or graveled sites. Nearby recreation options include an 18-hole golf course, marked hiking trails, and tennis courts.

**Campsites, facilities:** There are 23 sites with full or partial hookups for RVs of any length, three tent sites, and six cabins. Picnic tables and cable TV are provided, and fire rings are available on request. Restrooms with flush toilets and showers, firewood, and coin laundry are available. A store is located within one mile. Boat-launching facilities are nearby. Leashed pets are permitted.

**Reservations, fees:** Reservations are accepted. Sites are $17-22 per night, $2 per person per night for more than two people. Open year-round.

**Directions:** From Seattle, drive east on I-90 for 80 miles to Cle Elum and Exit 85 and Highway 970. Turn east on Highway 970 and drive 1.5 mile to the park on the left.

**Contact:** Trailer Corral, 509/674-2433.

## 137 ICEWATER CREEK

🚶 🚴 🏊 🐕 � ⛺

**Scenic rating: 7**

on Taneum Creek in Wenatchee National Forest

**Map 3.4, page 184**

Icewater Creek camp is most popular with off-road motorcyclists because there are two ORV trails leading from the camp, both of which network with an extensive system of off-road riding trails. The best route extends along the South Fork Taneum River area. The campground sports small trees and open sites. Fishing is fair, primarily for six- to eight-inch cutthroat trout.

**Campsites, facilities:** There are 14 sites for tents or RVs up to 26 feet long, including three double sites. Picnic tables and fire rings are provided. Firewood is available. There is no drinking water. Leashed pets are permitted.

**Reservations, fees:** Reservations are not accepted. Single sites are $16 per night, double sites are $32 per night, $7 per night for each additional vehicle. Open May-late September, weather permitting.

**Directions:** From Seattle, take I-5 east to I-90.

Drive east on I-90 for 80 miles to Cle Elum. Continue east for 9.3 miles to Exit 93/Elks Height Road. Take that exit and drive to the stop sign at Elks Height Road. Turn left and drive 0.3 mile to Taneum Road. Turn right on Taneum Road and drive 3.4 miles to East Taneum Road. Turn right on East Taneum Road and drive 0.1 miles to West Taneum Road. Turn right on West Taneum Road and drive 8.4 miles to the campground on the left.

**Contact:** Okanogan and Wenatchee National Forests, Cle Elum Ranger District, 509/852-1100, www.fs.usda.gov.

## 138 ELLENSBURG KOA

🏊 🛶 🏠 🚶 ♿ 🚐 ⛺

### Scenic rating: 8

in Ellensburg on the Yakima River

**Map 3.4, page 184**    **BEST (**

This KOA is one of the few campgrounds in a 25-mile radius. Exceptionally clean and scenic, it offers well-maintained, shaded campsites along the Yakima River. Rafting and fly-fishing on the nearby Yakima River are popular. Other nearby recreation options includes a nine-hole golf course and tennis courts. The Kittitas County Historical Museum is in town at 3rd and Pine Streets.

**Campsites, facilities:** There are 95 sites with full or partial hookups (30 and 50 amps) for RVs of any length, 37 sites for tents, and four cabins. Some sites are pull-through. Picnic tables and fire rings are provided. Restrooms with flush toilets and showers, cable TV, a dump station, propane, Wi-Fi, firewood, bicycle rentals, convenience store, coin laundry, ice, a playground, video rentals, a horseshoe pit, volleyball, a seasonal wading pool, and a seasonal heated swimming pool are available. A café is located within one mile. Extra parking is available for horse trailers, vans, and boats. Some facilities are wheelchair accessible. Leashed pets are permitted.

**Reservations, fees:** Reservations are accepted at 800/562-7616. RV sites are $34-41 per night, tent sites are $19-28 per night, $3-4 per person per night for more than two people, and $3 per extra vehicle per night. Some credit cards are accepted. Open mid-February-mid-November.

**Directions:** From Seattle, drive east on I-90 for 106 miles to Exit 106 (near Ellensburg). Take that exit and continue less than a mile to Thorp Highway. Turn right at Thorp Highway and drive a short distance to the KOA entrance (well marked).

**Contact:** Ellensburg KOA, 32 S. Thorp Hwy., Ellensburg, 509/925-9319, www.koa.com.

# NORTHEASTERN WASHINGTON

A lot of people call this area "God's country," and once you've camped here you'll understand why. The vast number of lakes, streams, and forests provide unlimited adventure. National forests like Colville, Kaniksu, and Wenatchee are ideal for mountain hideaways. You'll find remote ridges and valleys with conifers, along with many small streams and lakes. The Pacific Northwest's largest river system—including the Columbia River, Franklin D. Roosevelt Lake, and the Spokane River—carves waterways and features campsites with boating and facilities. You could spend a lifetime here—days hiking and fishing, and nights camping out under the stars. And that's exactly what some people do, like my friend Rich Landers, the outdoors writer for the *Spokane Spokesman-Review*. My favorite destinations are the dozens of lesser-known camps, often along small lakeshores, that provide good fishing and hiking. This is a wilderness to enjoy.

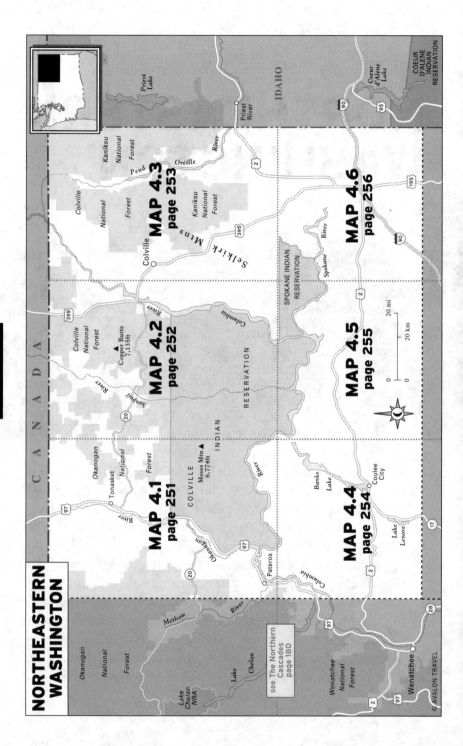

NORTHEASTERN WASHINGTON

CANADA

IDAHO

Okanogan National Forest

Lake Chelan NRA

Lake Chelan

Methow River

Wenatchee National Forest

Wenatchee

see The Northern Cascades page 180

Okanogan River

Tonasket

MAP 4.1 page 251

Moses Mtn 6,774ft

COLVILLE INDIAN RESERVATION

Pateros

Columbia

Colville National Forest

Copper Butte 7,135ft

Sanpoil River

MAP 4.2 page 252

Columbia River

Colville National Forest

Kaniksu National Forest

Pend Oreille

Colville

Selkirk Mtns

Kaniksu National Forest

Priest Lake

Priest River

MAP 4.3 page 253

MAP 4.6 page 256

Spokane River

SPOKANE INDIAN RESERVATION

COEUR D'ALENE INDIAN RESERVATION

Coeur d'Alene Lake

MAP 4.4 page 254

Banks Lake

Coulee City

Lake Lenore

MAP 4.5 page 255

0        20 mi
0        20 km

© AVALON TRAVEL

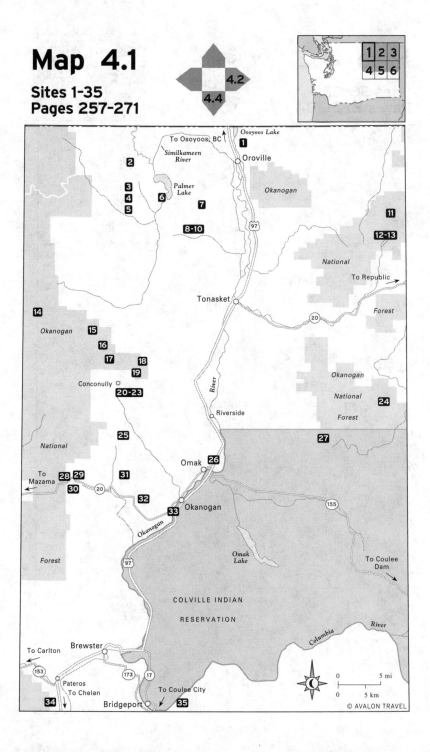

# Map 4.1

**Sites 1-35**
**Pages 257-271**

4.2
4.4

| 1 | 2 | 3 |
| 4 | 5 | 6 |

To Osoyoos, BC
Osoyoos Lake
1
Oroville

Similkameen River

2

3
4
6
5

Palmer Lake

7

Okanogan

8-10

97

11

12-13

National

To Republic

Tonasket

Forest

14

20

Okanogan

15

16

17
18

19

Conconully

20-23

River

Okanogan

Riverside

National

24

25

Forest

National

27

Omak

26

To Mazama

28  29

30

31

20

32

155

33  Okanogan

Okanogan

Omak Lake

To Coulee Dam

Forest

97

COLVILLE INDIAN

RESERVATION

Columbia River

Brewster

To Carlton

153

Pateros
To Chelan

173  17

34

Bridgeport

To Coulee City

35

0      5 mi
0      5 km

© AVALON TRAVEL

# Map 4.2

### Sites 36-63
### Pages 272-284

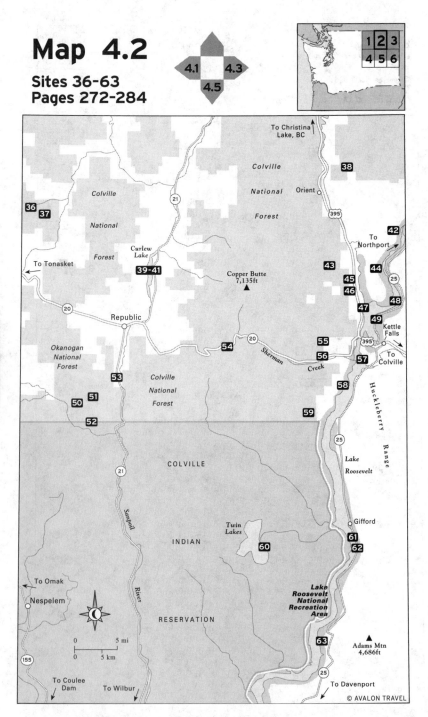

# Map 4.3

## Sites 64-97
## Pages 284-300

4.2
4.6

1 2 3
4 5 6

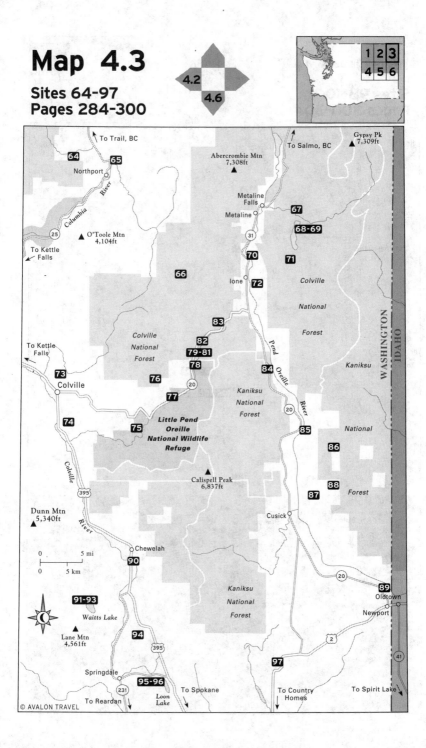

To Trail, BC

64

65
Northport

To Salmo, BC

Abercrombie Mtn
7,308ft ▲

Gypsy Pk
7,309ft ▲

Columbia River

25

To Kettle
Falls

▲ O'Toole Mtn
4,104ft

Metaline
Falls

Metaline

67

68-69

31

66

70

71

Ione

72

Colville

National

Forest

83

To Kettle
Falls

73
Colville

Colville
National
Forest

82

79-81

78

76

20

84

Pend Oreille River

Kaniksu

National

Forest

WASHINGTON    IDAHO

74

77

Kaniksu
National
Forest

20

85

National

86

75

**Little Pend
Oreille
National Wildlife
Refuge**

88

Colville River

395

▲ Calispell Peak
6,837ft

87

Forest

Dunn Mtn
5,340ft ▲

Cusick

River

0        5 mi
0        5 km

Chewelah

90

Kaniksu

National

Forest

20

89
Oldtown

Newport

91-93

Waitts Lake

▲
Lane Mtn
4,561ft

94

395

2

Springdale

231

95-96

Loon
Lake

To Spokane

97

To Country
Homes

41

To Spirit Lake

To Reardan

© AVALON TRAVEL

# Map 4.4

## Sites 98-106
## Pages 300-304

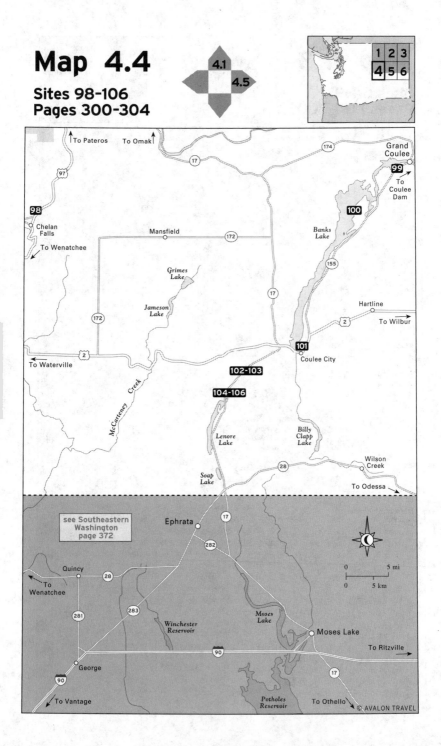

# Map 4.5

## Sites 107-114
## Pages 304-308

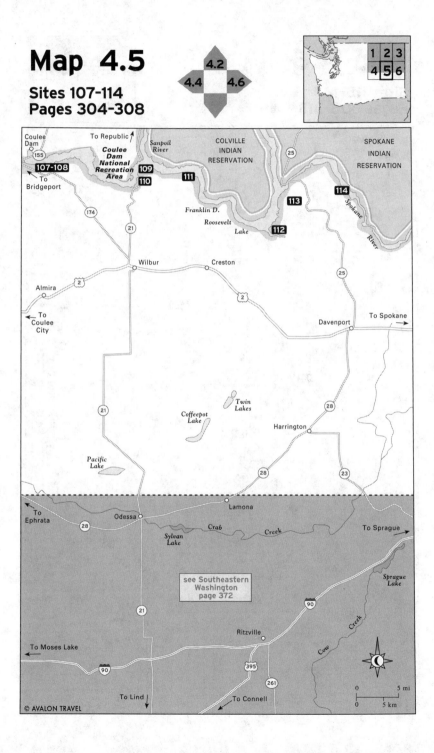

4.2
4.4    4.6

1 2 3
4 5 6

Coulee Dam
155
107-108
To Bridgeport

To Republic
Coulee Dam National Recreation Area

Sanpoil River

109
110
111

COLVILLE INDIAN RESERVATION

25

SPOKANE INDIAN RESERVATION

113
114

Franklin D. Roosevelt Lake

112

Spokane River

174

21

Wilbur
Creston

2

Almira
2
To Coulee City

25

Davenport
To Spokane

21

Twin Lakes
Coffeepot Lake

28
Harrington

Pacific Lake

28
23

To Ephrata
28
Odessa
Lamona

Crab Creek
Sylvan Lake

To Sprague

21

see Southeastern Washington page 372

90
Sprague Lake

Cow Creek

To Moses Lake
90

Ritzville

395
261

To Lind
To Connell

0        5 mi
0        5 km

© AVALON TRAVEL

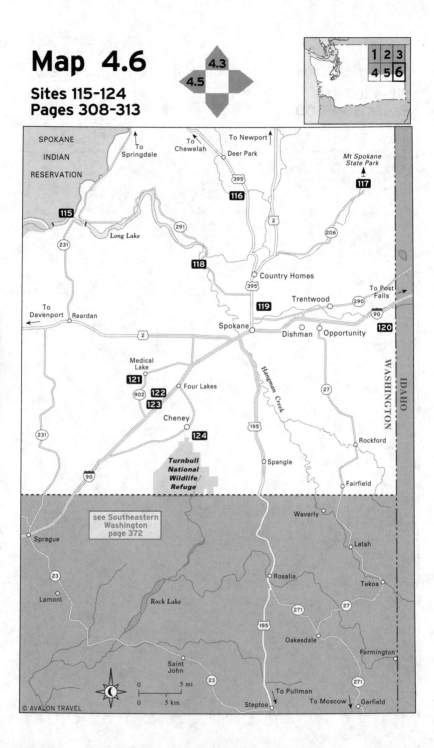

# Map 4.6
**Sites 115-124**
**Pages 308-313**

# 1 OSOYOOS LAKE VETERANS MEMORIAL PARK

🏊 🛶 🚤 ❄ 🐕 � 🏕

**Scenic rating: 9**

on Osoyoos Lake

**Map 4.1, page 251**

The park is set along the shore of Osoyoos Lake, a 14-mile-long lake created from the Okanogan River, located south of the Canadian Rockies. The park covers 47 acres and provides a base of operations for a fishing vacation. The lake has rainbow trout, kokanee salmon, smallmouth bass, crappie, and perch. Fishing gear and concessions are available. Water sports are also popular in the summer, and in winter, this is an ideal location for ice-skating, ice fishing, and snow play. Expansive lawns lead down to the sandy shore of the lake, which is a winter nesting area for geese. A nine-hole golf course is nearby. A historical note: Many years ago, the area was the site of the annual *okanogan* (rendezvous) of the Salish Indians from what are now Washington and British Columbia. They would gather and share supplies of fish and game for the year.

**Campsites, facilities:** There are 86 sites for tents or RVs up to 32 feet long (no hookups); 18 sites should have full hookups in 2014. There are also six primitive tent sites. Picnic tables and fire grills are provided. Restrooms with flush toilets and coin showers, dump station, a store, café, firewood, horseshoes, and volleyball are available. A coin laundry and ice machine are located within one mile. Boat-launching and dock facilities are nearby. Leashed pets are permitted.

**Reservations, fees:** Reservations are accepted online. Sites are $16-35 per night, $10 per extra vehicle per night. Some credit cards are accepted. Open April-October, weather permitting.

**Directions:** From Oroville, just south of the Canadian border, drive north on U.S. 97 for one mile to the park entrance on the right.

**Contact:** Osoyoos Lake Veterans Memorial Park, 509/476-3321, https://orovillepark.goingtocamp.com.

# 2 CHOPAKA LAKE

🏊 🛶 🚤 🐕 ♿ 🚐 🏕

**Scenic rating: 8**

on Chopaka Lake

**Map 4.1, page 251**          **BEST (**

This campground provides a classic setting for the expert angler. It's nestled along the western shore of Chopaka Lake, which is extremely popular with trout anglers. No motorboats are permitted on the lake. That makes it a winner for fly fishers (barbless hooks required) using float tubes.

**Campsites, facilities:** There are 16 sites for tents or RVs up to 20 feet long. Picnic tables and fire grills are provided. Vault toilets, drinking water, a fishing platform, and primitive boat-launching facilities are available. Garbage must be packed out. Some facilities are wheelchair accessible. Leashed pets are permitted.

**Reservations, fees:** Reservations are not accepted. There is no fee for camping, but a Discover Pass is required. Open year-round, weather permitting; drive-in access is usually passable mid-April-mid-November.

**Directions:** From Wenatchee, drive north on U.S. 97 for 120 miles to Tonasket and Forest Street. Turn left and drive 0.2 mile (crossing the Okanogan River) to Highway 7. Turn right (north) on Highway 7 (Loomis-Oroville Highway) and drive five miles. At the fork, continue on Loomis-Oroville Highway for about 12 miles to Toats Coulee Road, 2.1 miles north of Loomis. Turn left and drive 5.5 miles to Toats Coulee campground. Continue 2.1 miles to Nine Mile Road. Turn right and drive approximately 3.5 miles to Chopaka Road. Turn right and drive 3.5 miles to Chopaka Lake Road. Turn left and drive one mile to the camp on the left.

**Contact:** Department of Natural Resources, Northeast Region, 509/684-7474, www.dnr.wa.gov.

## 3 COLD SPRINGS

### Scenic rating: 8

near Cold Creek

Map 4.1, page 251

It's quite a drive to get here, but you'll be happy you made the effort to reach this pretty forested camp. Campsites are located near a small stream amid a forest of lodgepole pine, western larch, and several species of fir, including Douglas fir. Trails for horseback riding, hiking, and snowmobiling run through the area. Because the camp is little known and remote, it's advisable to obtain a map of the area from the Department of Natural Resources.

**Campsites, facilities:** There are nine campsites for tents or RVs up to 20 feet long. Picnic tables, fire grills, and tent pads are provided. Vault toilets and drinking water are available. Garbage must be packed out. Some facilities are wheelchair accessible. Leashed pets are permitted.

**Reservations, fees:** Reservations are not accepted. There is no fee for camping, but a Discover Pass is required. Open year-round.

**Directions:** From Wenatchee, drive north on U.S. 97 for 120 miles to Tonasket and Forest Street. Turn left and drive 0.2 mile (crossing the Okanogan River) to Highway 7. Turn right (north) on Highway 7 (Loomis-Oroville Highway) and drive five miles. At the fork, continue on Loomis-Oroville Highway for about 12 miles to Toats Coulee Road, 2.1 miles north of Loomis. Turn left and drive 5.5 miles to the Toats Coulee camp. Continue on the main road for 2.1 miles to Nine Mile Road. Turn right and drive approximately 5.5 miles to the camp on the left.

**Contact:** Department of Natural Resources, Northeast Region, 509/684-7474, www.dnr. wa.gov.

## 4 NORTH FORK NINE MILE

### Scenic rating: 6

on the North Fork of Toats Coulee Creek

Map 4.1, page 251

Deer and black bears frequent this campground situated in the forest along the North Fork of Toats Coulee Creek and Nine Mile Creek. This camp is popular in the fall with hunters. Trout fishing is fair at Toats Coulee Creek; check regulations. It's advisable to obtain a map from the Department of Natural Resources that details the area.

**Campsites, facilities:** There are 11 sites for tents or RVs up to 20 feet long. Picnic tables and fire grills are provided. Vault toilets and drinking water are available. Garbage must be packed out. Some facilities are wheelchair accessible. Leashed pets are permitted.

**Reservations, fees:** Reservations are not accepted. There is no fee for camping, but a Discover Pass is required. Open year-round, weather permitting.

**Directions:** From Wenatchee, drive north on U.S. 97 for 120 miles to Tonasket and Forest Street. Turn left and drive 0.2 mile (crossing the Okanogan River) to Highway 7. Turn right (north) on Highway 7 (Loomis-Oroville Highway) and drive five miles. At the fork, continue on Loomis-Oroville Highway for about 12 miles to Toats Coulee Road, 2.1 miles north of Loomis. Turn left and drive 5.5 miles to the Toats Coulee camp. Continue 2.3 miles to the campground, 0.2 mile past Nine Mile Road.

**Contact:** Department of Natural Resources, Northeast Region, 509/684-7474, www.dnr. wa.gov.

## 5 TOATS COULEE

### Scenic rating: 6

on Toats Coulee Creek

Map 4.1, page 251

Toats Coulee consists of two primitive

campsites set a short distance apart. The camp is set in a wooded spot along Toats Coulee Creek. Trout fishing is available; check regulations. The best hiking is located 10 miles northwest in the Pasayten Wilderness (to reach this trailhead, continue driving up the campground road). These camps are popular in the fall with hunters. In the winter, a road for snowmobile use follows the South Fork of Toats Coulee Creek, swinging south and then heading east along Cecil Creek.

**Campsites, facilities:** There are nine single sites and two double sites for tents or RVs up to 20 feet long. Picnic tables and fire grills are provided. Vault toilets are available. There is no drinking water and garbage must be packed out. Some facilities are wheelchair accessible. Leashed pets are permitted.

**Reservations, fees:** Reservations are not accepted. There is no fee for camping, but a Discover Pass is required. Open year-round.

**Directions:** From Wenatchee, drive north on U.S. 97 for 120 miles to Tonasket and Forest Street. Turn left and drive 0.2 mile (crossing the Okanogan River) to Highway 7. Turn right (north) on Highway 7 (Loomis-Oroville Highway) and drive five miles. At the fork, continue on Loomis-Oroville Highway for about 12 miles to Toats Coulee Road, 2.1 miles north of Loomis. Turn left and drive 5.5 miles to the camp on the left.

**Contact:** Department of Natural Resources, Northeast Region, 509/684-7474, www.dnr.wa.gov.

## 6 PALMER LAKE

**Scenic rating: 9**

on Palmer Lake

Map 4.1, page 251 — BEST

This shorefront camp is the only one at Palmer Lake. The campsites are set close to the lake's very scenic shore. It fills up during the summer, even on weekdays, frequently with visitors from Canada. Fishing is often

good for kokanee salmon and rainbow trout. Powerboating and waterskiing are permitted. There are numerous migration routes in the region; the Sinlahekin Valley to the south of Palmer Lake is part of the winter range for deer. Endangered bighorn sheep, cougars, bald and golden eagles, black bears, and grouse are among the wildlife that can be spotted.

**Campsites, facilities:** There are eight sites for tents or RVs up to 20 feet long. Picnic tables and fire grills are provided. Vault toilets are available. There is no drinking water and garbage must be packed out. Some facilities are wheelchair accessible. A primitive boat launch is located at the opposite end of the lake; four-wheel drive is required. Leashed pets are permitted.

**Reservations, fees:** Reservations are not accepted. There is no fee for camping, but a Discover Pass is required. Open year-round, weather permitting.

**Directions:** From Wenatchee, drive north on U.S. 97 for 120 miles to Tonasket and Forest Street. Turn left and drive 0.2 mile, crossing the Okanogan River, to Highway 7. Turn right (north) on Highway 7 (Loomis-Oroville Highway) and drive 18.5 miles, 8.5 miles past Loomis. Stay to the right and drive to the camp at the north end of the lake.

**Contact:** Department of Natural Resources, Northeast Region, 509/684-7474, www.dnr.wa.gov.

## 7 SUN COVE RESORT

**Scenic rating: 9**

on Wannacut Lake near Oroville

Map 4.1, page 251

This beautiful resort is surrounded by trees and hills and set along the shore of Wannacut Lake, a spring-fed lake that doesn't get much traffic. The lake is approximately three miles long and 2.5 miles wide. An 8-mph speed limit is enforced for boats. Fishing, swimming, boating, and hiking are all summertime options.

The park provides full facilities, including a heated pool, playground, and recreation hall. **Campsites, facilities:** There are 27 sites for RVs of any length, including 19 sites with full hookups, 10 sites for tents, two cottages, and 10 motel units with kitchens. Picnic tables are provided. No wood fires are allowed. Restrooms with flush toilets and coin showers, a dump station, recreation hall, general store, restaurant, coin laundry, ice, fishing supplies and fishing licenses, a playground, horseshoe pits, and a seasonal heated swimming pool are available. Boat docks, launching facilities, and rentals are also available. Some facilities are wheelchair accessible. Leashed pets are permitted in the campground.

**Reservations, fees:** Reservations are accepted. Sites are $30 per night. Some credit cards are accepted. Open late April-mid-October.

**Directions:** From Oroville, just south of the Canadian border, drive west on Ellemehan Mountain Road for about six miles to Wannacut Lake Road. Turn left (south) and drive five miles to the resort at the end of the road.

**Contact:** Sun Cove Resort, 93 E. Wannacut Lane, Oroville, 509/476-2223, www.thesuncoveresort.com.

# 8 SPECTACLE LAKE RESORT

### Scenic rating: 7

on Spectacle Lake

**Map 4.1, page 251**

This pleasant resort on the shore of long, narrow Spectacle Lake has grassy, shaded sites. Space is usually available here, although reservations are accepted. Recreation options include boating, fishing, swimming, waterskiing, watercraft, and hunting (in season).

**Campsites, facilities:** There are 34 sites for tents or RVs of any length (20 and 30 amp full hookups) and 16 motel rooms with kitchenettes. Picnic tables and fire pits are provided. Restrooms with flush toilets and showers, propane gas, a dump station, a convenience store,

coin laundry, ice, a playground, volleyball, horseshoes, recreation hall, exercise room, and seasonal heated swimming pool are available. Boat docks, launching facilities, and rentals are also nearby. Some facilities are wheelchair accessible. Leashed pets are permitted.

**Reservations, fees:** Reservations are accepted. Sites are $30 per night. Some credit cards are accepted. Open mid-April-late October.

**Directions:** In Tonasket on U.S. 97, turn west (left if arriving from the south), cross the bridge, and continue to Highway 7. Turn right on Highway 7 and drive about 12 miles to Holmes Road. Turn left (south) on Holmes Road and drive 0.5 mile to McCammon Road. Turn right (west) and drive one block to the resort at the end of the road.

**Contact:** Spectacle Lake Resort, 10 McCammon Rd., Tonasket, 509/223-3433, www.spectaclelakeresort.com.

# 9 SONORA POINT RESORT

### Scenic rating: 7

on Spectacle Lake

**Map 4.1, page 251**

This resort on Spectacle Lake is an alternative to Spectacle Lake Resort. The camp features pretty lake views and full facilities. Nearby activities include swimming, fishing, hunting, and horseback riding, including overnight trail rides.

**Campsites, facilities:** There are 34 sites with full hookups (30 amps) for RVs of any length and 12 sites with partial hookups for tents or RVs to 30 feet. Some sites are pull-through. Picnic tables are provided, and fire pits are available on request. Restrooms with flush toilets and showers, ice, firewood, convenience store, fish cleaning station, a recreation room, horseshoe pits, volleyball, boat docks, and launching facilities are available. Some facilities are wheelchair accessible. Leashed pets are permitted.

**Reservations, fees:** Reservations are recommended. Sites are $29-36 per night. Winter discounts available. Weekly discounts available. Some credit cards are accepted. Open late March-November, weather permitting.

**Directions:** From Ellisford, turn west on Ellisford Bridge Road. Drive 0.5 mile to Highway 7. Turn left (south) and drive one mile to Loomis Highway. Turn right and drive 6.5 miles to the resort on the left.

**Contact:** Sonora Point Resort, 761 Loomis Oroville Highway, Tonasket, 509/223-3700, www.sonorapointresort.com.

## 10 SPECTACLE FALLS RESORT

### Scenic rating: 8
on Spectacle Lake

**Map 4.1, page 251**

Spectacle Falls Resort is set on the shore of Spectacle Lake. It is open only as long as fishing is available, which means a closing in late July. Be sure to phone ahead of time to verify that the resort is open. Nearby recreation options include hiking, swimming, fishing, tennis, and horseback riding, including guided trails and overnight rides. Rainbow Resort provides an alternative.

**Campsites, facilities:** There are 10 pull-through sites with full hookups for RVs of any length and four mobile homes. Picnic tables are provided. Restrooms with flush toilets and showers, ice, boat docks, launching facilities, and boat rentals are available. Leashed pets are permitted.

**Reservations, fees:** Reservations are required. Sites are $21 per night, $2 per person per night for more than two people, $5 per extra vehicle per night. Open April 1-July 31 and August 1-September 30.

**Directions:** From Tonasket on U.S. 97, turn northwest on Loomis Highway and drive 15 miles to the resort on the left.

**Contact:** Spectacle Falls Resort, 879 Loomis Oroville Rd., Tonasket, 509/223-4141.

## 11 LOST LAKE

### Scenic rating: 7
on Lost Lake in Okanogan National Forest

**Map 4.1, page 251**

This camp is set on the shore of Lost Lake at an elevation of 3,800 feet. As a launch point for fishing, swimming, hiking, hunting, and horseback riding, it keeps visitors happy. No gas motors are permitted on the lake. The lake is similar to Beth and Beaver Lakes, but rounder. The Big Tree Botanical Area is about one mile away. Note that the group site is often booked one year in advance.

**Campsites, facilities:** There are 19 sites for tents or RVs up to 31 feet long, including six double sites. There is also one group site for up to 100 people. Picnic tables and fire rings are provided. Drinking water, vault toilets, and garbage bins are available. Boat-launching facilities and swimming platforms, a ball field, and horseshoe pits are nearby. Some facilities are wheelchair accessible. Leashed pets are permitted.

**Reservations, fees:** Reservations are not available for single and double sites but are required for the group site at 877/444-6777 ($10 reservation fee) or www.recreation.gov ($9 reservation fee). Sites are $12 per night, $5 per night per additional vehicle; group sites are $40 per night for 1-25 people, $60 per night for 26-50 people, and $80 per night for 51-100 people. Open May-mid-October, weather permitting.

**Directions:** From East Wenatchee, drive north on U.S. 97 for 120 miles to Tonasket and Highway 20. Turn east on Highway 20 and drive 20 miles to Bonaparte Lake Road (County Road 4953). Turn left (north) and drive six miles to Forest Road 32. Turn right (north) and drive four miles to Forest Road 33. Bear left (northwest) and drive five miles to a four-way intersection. Turn left on Forest Road 33-050 and drive 0.3 mile to the campground on the right.

**Contact:** Okanogan and Wenatchee National

Forests, Tonasket Ranger District, 509/486-2186, www.fs.usda.gov.

## 12 BONAPARTE LAKE

### Scenic rating: 7
on Bonaparte Lake in Okanogan National Forest

**Map 4.1, page 251**

This campground is located on the southern shore of Bonaparte Lake at an elevation of 3,600 feet. The lake is stocked with rainbow trout, brook trout, and mackinaw trout. A 10-mph speed limit keeps the lake quiet, ideal for fishing. Several trails nearby provide access to Mount Bonaparte Lookout.

**Campsites, facilities:** There are 25 single sites and three double sites for tents or RVs of any length and one bike-in/hike-in site (requiring a walk of less than 100 feet). Picnic tables and fire grills are provided. Drinking water, vault toilets, and garbage bins are available. A store, café, gas, and ice are available within one mile. Boat docks and launching facilities are also available. Some facilities are wheelchair accessible. Leashed pets are permitted.

**Reservations, fees:** Reservations are not accepted. Sites are $12 per night per vehicle, $5 per night per additional vehicle, and $8 for bike-in/hike-in sites. Open mid-May-mid-October, weather permitting.

**Directions:** From East Wenatchee, drive north on U.S. 97 for 120 miles to Tonasket and Highway 20. Turn east on Highway 20 and drive 20 miles to Bonaparte Lake Road (County Road 4953). Turn left (north) and drive six miles to Bonaparte Lake and Forest Road 32 and the campground on the left.

**Contact:** Okanogan and Wenatchee National Forests, Tonasket Ranger District, 509/486-2186, www.fs.usda.gov.

## 13 BONAPARTE LAKE RESORT

### Scenic rating: 6
on Bonaparte Lake

**Map 4.1, page 251**

Fishing is popular at this resort, set on the southeast shore of Bonaparte Lake. A 10-mph speed limit keeps the lake quiet, ideal for fishing. Other recreational activities include hiking and hunting in the nearby U.S. Forest Service lands and snowmobiling, cross-country skiing, and ice fishing in the winter. Poker tournaments are held occasionally.

**Campsites, facilities:** There are 30 sites with full hookups (20 and 30 amps) for RVs of any length, 15 sites for tents, and 10 cabins. Some sites are pull-through. Picnic tables and fire rings are provided. Restrooms with flush toilets and showers, propane, a dump station, firewood, a recreation hall, convenience store, restaurant, coin laundry, ice, boat docks, launching facilities, and boat rentals are available. Some facilities are wheelchair accessible. Leashed pets are permitted.

**Reservations, fees:** Reservations are accepted. Sites are $15-22 per night. Some credit cards are accepted. Open year-round, with limited winter facilities.

**Directions:** From East Wenatchee, drive north on U.S. 97 for 20 miles to Tonasket and Highway 20. Turn east on Highway 20 and drive 20 miles to Bonaparte Lake Road (County Road 4953). Turn left (north) and drive six miles to Bonaparte Lake and the resort on the left.

**Contact:** Bonaparte Lake Resort, 615 Bonaparte Lake Rd., Tonasket, 509/486-2828, www.bonapartelakeresort.com.

## 14 TIFFANY SPRINGS

### Scenic rating: 7
near Tiffany Lake in Okanogan National Forest

**Map 4.1, page 251**

Set at an elevation of 6,800 feet, this camp

is less than a mile hike from Tiffany Lake. Tiffany Mountain rises 8,200 feet in the distance. The lake provides fishing for rainbow trout and brook trout. There are also some good hiking trails in the area. The Tiffany Mountain area provides a network of 26 miles of hiking trails, accessed from either here at Tiffany Springs or at Tiffany Lake.

**Campsites, facilities:** There are six sites for tents or small RVs up to 16 feet long. Picnic tables and fire grills are provided. Vault toilets are available. There is no drinking water, and garbage must be packed out. Some facilities are wheelchair accessible. Leashed pets are permitted.

**Reservations, fees:** Reservations are not accepted. There is no fee for camping. Open June-mid-October, weather permitting.

**Directions:** From East Wenatchee, drive north on U.S. 97 for 88 miles to Okanogan and County Road 9229. Turn north and drive 17.5 miles northwest to Conconully and County Road 2017. Turn left on County Road 2017 and drive two miles (road becomes Forest Road 42) to Forest Road 37. Turn right (northwest) on Forest Road 37 and drive 21 miles to Forest Road 39. Turn right (northeast) on Forest Road 39 and proceed eight miles to the campground on the left.

**Contact:** Okanogan and Wenatchee National Forests, Tonasket Ranger District, 509/486-2186, www.fs.usda.gov.

## 15 SALMON MEADOWS

### Scenic rating: 6
on Salmon Creek in Okanogan National Forest

Map 4.1, page 251

This camp is located along Salmon Creek at an elevation of 4,500 feet. Come in the spring for a spectacular wildflower display in an adjacent meadow. The camp features a forest setting, mainly Douglas fir, spruce, and some western larch. Trails from the campground are routed out to Angel Pass, two miles one-way, for views of the Tiffany area.

**Campsites, facilities:** There are seven single sites and one double site for tents or small RVs up to 16 feet long. Picnic tables and fire grills are provided. Drinking water, vault toilets, and a horse corral are available. A gazebo is available at the day-use area. Garbage must be packed out. Leashed pets are permitted.

**Reservations, fees:** Reservations are not accepted. Sites are $8 per night, $5 per night per additional vehicle. Open mid-May-mid-October, weather permitting.

**Directions:** From East Wenatchee, drive north on U.S. 97 for 88 miles to Okanogan and County Road 9229. Turn left (north) on County Road 9229 and drive 17.5 miles to Conconully and County Road 2361. Continue northwest on County Road 2361 and drive five miles (becomes Forest Road 38) to Kerr Campground. Continue past Kerr for 4.5 miles to the campground on the right.

**Contact:** Okanogan and Wenatchee National Forests, Tonasket Ranger District, 509/486-2186, www.fs.usda.gov.

## 16 KERR

### Scenic rating: 6
on Salmon Creek in Okanogan National Forest

Map 4.1, page 251

This camp sits at an elevation of 3,100 feet along Salmon Creek, about four miles north of Conconully Reservoir, and is one of many campgrounds near the lake. Fishing prospects are marginal for trout here. There are numerous recreation options available at Conconully Reservoir, including far better fishing.

**Campsites, facilities:** There are 12 sites for tents or RVs up to 30 feet long. Picnic tables and fire grills are provided. Drinking water and vault toilets are available. Garbage must be packed out. Some facilities are wheelchair accessible. Leashed pets are permitted.

**Reservations, fees:** Reservations are not accepted. Sites are $8-16 per night, $5 per night

per additional vehicle. Open mid-May-mid-October, weather permitting.
**Directions:** From East Wenatchee, drive north on U.S. 97 for 88 miles to Okanogan and County Road 9229. Turn left (north) on County Road 9229 and drive 17.5 miles to Conconully and County Road 2361. Continue northwest on County Road 2361 and drive four miles (becomes Forest Road 38) to the campground on the left.
**Contact:** Okanogan and Wenatchee National Forests, Tonasket Ranger District, 509/486-2186, www.fs.usda.gov.

## 17 ORIOLE

### Scenic rating: 6
on Salmon Creek in Okanogan National Forest

**Map 4.1, page 251**

This camp is located at 2,900 feet elevation along Salmon Creek and offers a creek view from some of the campsites. This forest setting features well-spaced campsites among western larch and lodgepole pine. This is a primitive camp, similar to Kerr and Salmon Meadows, which are also set on Salmon Creek.
**Campsites, facilities:** There are eight single sites and two double sites for tents or small trailers. Picnic tables and fire grills are provided. Drinking water, vault toilets, and garbage bins are available. Some facilities are wheelchair accessible. Leashed pets are permitted.
**Reservations, fees:** Reservations are not accepted. Sites are $8 per night, $5 per night per additional vehicle. Open mid-May-October, weather permitting.
**Directions:** From East Wenatchee, drive north on U.S. 97 for 88 miles to Okanogan and County Road 9229. Turn left (north) on County Road 9229 and drive 17.5 miles to Conconully and County Road 2361. Continue northwest on County Road 2361 and drive 2.5 miles to Forest Road 025. Turn left and drive 0.5 mile (crossing the creek) to the campground on the left.

**Contact:** Okanogan and Wenatchee National Forests, Tonasket Ranger District, 509/486-2186, www.fs.usda.gov.

## 18 SUGARLOAF

### Scenic rating: 6
on Sugarloaf Lake in Okanogan National Forest

**Map 4.1, page 251**

Sugarloaf Lake is a small lake, about 20 acres, and this small camp is set near its shore. It provides fishing for rainbow trout, but the lake level often drops substantially during summer, so this camp gets little use in late summer and early fall. Conconully State Park and Information Center are nearby.
**Campsites, facilities:** There are four tent sites. Picnic tables and fire rings are provided. Hand-pumped drinking water and vault toilets are available. Garbage must be packed out. Boat-launching facilities are available nearby. No boats with gas motors are permitted. Leashed pets are permitted.
**Reservations, fees:** Reservations are not accepted. Sites are $8 per night, $5 per night per additional vehicle. Open mid-May-mid-October, weather permitting.
**Directions:** From East Wenatchee, drive north on U.S. 97 for 88 miles to Okanogan and County Road 9229. Turn north and drive about 17.5 miles northwest to Conconully and County Road 4015. Turn right (northwest) on County Road 4015 and drive 4.5 miles to the campground on the left.
**Contact:** Okanogan and Wenatchee National Forests, Tonasket Ranger District, 509/486-2186, www.fs.usda.gov.

## 19 KOZY KABINS AND RV PARK

### Scenic rating: 7

near Conconully Reservoir

**Map 4.1, page 251**

This quiet and private park in Conconully has a small creek running through it and plenty of greenery. A full-service marina is located close by. There is hunting in season, and snowmobiling is an option in the winter. If you continue northeast of town on County Road 4015, the road will get a bit narrow for a while but will widen again when you enter the Sinlahekin Habitat Management Area, which is managed by the Department of Fish and Wildlife. There are some primitive campsites in this valley, especially along the shores of the lakes in the area.

**Campsites, facilities:** There are 15 sites with full hookups (30 amps) for RVs up to 40 feet long, six tent sites, and seven cabins. Picnic tables are provided. Restrooms with flush toilets and coin showers, a community fire pit, and firewood are available. Propane gas, general store, café, coin laundry, and ice are located within one block. Boat docks, launching facilities, and boat rentals are nearby. Leashed pets are permitted.

**Reservations, fees:** Reservations are accepted at 888/502-2246. RV sites are $26 per night, tent sites are $12 per night. Some credit cards are accepted. Open year-round.

**Directions:** From U.S. 97 in Okanogan, turn north (left if arriving from the south) on Pine Street/Conconully Highway and drive 17.5 miles northwest to Conconully and Broadway Street. Turn right (east) and drive one block to A Avenue. The park is at the junction of A Avenue and Broadway Street.

**Contact:** Kozy Kabins and RV Park, 509/826-6780.

## 20 CONCONULLY STATE PARK

### Scenic rating: 9

on Conconully Reservoir

**Map 4.1, page 251**   **BEST (**

Conconully State Park, which dates to 1910, is set along Conconully Reservoir and covers 81 acres, with 5,400 feet of shoreline. Anglers will be happy here, with opportunities for trout, bass, and kokanee salmon. A boat launch, beach access, swimming, and fishing provide all sorts of water sports possibilities. A 0.5-mile nature trail is available. A side-trip option is Sinlahekin Habitat Management Area, which is accessible via County Road 4015. This route heads northeast along the shore of Conconully Reservoir on the other side of U.S. 97. The road is narrow at first, but it becomes wider as it enters the Habitat Management Area.

**Campsites, facilities:** There are 51 sites with no hookups and 15 sites with partial hookups for tents or RVs up to 60 feet long. There are also five cabins. Picnic tables and fire grills are provided. Restrooms with flush toilets and coin showers, a dump station, firewood, and a playground are available. A store, café, coin laundry, and ice are located within one mile. Boat-launching and dock facilities are nearby. A sheltered picnic area, horseshoe pits, baseball field, and interpretive activities are available nearby. Some facilities are wheelchair accessible. Leashed pets are permitted.

**Reservations, fees:** Reservations are accepted at 888/226-7588 or www.goingtocamp.com ($6.50 reservation fee). Sites are $17-39 per night, $10 per extra vehicle per night. The cabins are $59.24-75.69 per night. Open year-round.

**Directions:** On U.S. 97 at Omak, take the North Omak exit. At the base of the hill, turn right and drive two miles until you reach Conconully Road. Turn right and drive 15 miles north to the park entrance.

**Contact:** Conconully State Park, 509/826-7408; state park information, 360/902-8844, www.parks.wa.gov.

## 21 CONCONULLY LAKE RESORT

### Scenic rating: 6

on Upper Conconully Lake

Map 4.1, page 251

This is the only resort along the shore of Conconully Lake, which is 3.5 miles long. Tents are permitted, but this is a prime vacation destination for RVers. Trout fishing, swimming, boating, waterskiing, and riding personal watercraft are all options here. There are ATV trails in the area and snowmobile rentals are available.

**Campsites, facilities:** There are 11 sites for RVs of any length (30 amp full hookups), four cabins, and one apartment. Picnic tables and fire pits are provided. Restrooms with flush toilets and coin showers and ice are available. Propane, gasoline, a dump station, limited groceries, a gift shop, and bait and tackle are available. A café and a coin laundry are located within one mile. Boat docks, launching facilities, moorage, and a variety of boat rentals are available. Some facilities are wheelchair accessible. Leashed pets are permitted.

**Reservations, fees:** Reservations are accepted. RV sites are $30 per night, tent sites are $17 per night, plus $2 per person per night for more than two people. Some credit cards are accepted. Open late April-October.

**Directions:** From U.S. 97 in Okanogan, turn north (left if arriving from the south) on Pine Street/Conconully Highway and drive 17.5 miles northwest to Conconully and Lake Street. Turn right on Lake Street and drive one mile to the resort on the right.

**Contact:** Conconully Lake Resort, 509/826-0813 or 800/850-0813, www.upperconconullylakeresort.com.

## 22 LIAR'S COVE RESORT

### Scenic rating: 6

on Conconully Reservoir

Map 4.1, page 251

Roomy sites for RVs can be found at this camp on the shore of Conconully Reservoir. Tents are allowed, too. Fishing, swimming, boating, and hiking opportunities are located nearby.

**Campsites, facilities:** There are 35 sites for tents or RVs of any length (30 and 50 amp full hookups), two cabins, one mobile home, and three motel rooms. Picnic tables and fire pits are provided. Restrooms with flush toilets and coin showers, cable TV, Wi-Fi, ice, swimming beach, boat docks, launching facilities, and boat and water toy rentals are available. Propane gas, a dump station, store, and café are within one mile. Some facilities are wheelchair accessible. Leashed pets are permitted.

**Reservations, fees:** Reservations are accepted. RV sites are $30-33 per night, tent sites are $20 per night. Some credit cards are accepted. Open April-October.

**Directions:** From U.S. 97 in Okanogan, turn north (left if arriving from the south) on Pine Street/Conconully Highway and drive 16.5 miles northwest to Conconully and look for the park on the left. It's located 0.25 mile south of Conconully.

**Contact:** Liar's Cove Resort, 509/826-1288 or 800/830-1288, www.liarscoveresort.com.

## 23 SHADY PINES RESORT

### Scenic rating: 6

on Conconully Reservoir

Map 4.1, page 251

This camp is set on the western shore of Conconully Reservoir. It is near Conconully State Park and provides an option if the state park campground is full—a common occurrence in summer. But note that on summer weekends, this camp often fills as well. The nearby

Sinlahekin Habitat Management Area, which is managed by the Department of Fish and Wildlife, offers a possible side trip.

**Campsites, facilities:** There are 21 sites with full hookups (20, 30, and 50 amps) for RVs up to 40 feet, two tent sites, and six cabins. Some sites are pull-through. Picnic tables and fire rings are provided. Restrooms with flush toilets and coin showers, ice, firewood, gift and tackle shop, fish-cleaning station, coin laundry, boat-launching facilities, and boat rentals are available. Propane gas, a dump station, store, café, and coin laundry are located within one mile. Some facilities are wheelchair accessible. Leashed pets are permitted.

**Reservations, fees:** Reservations are accepted at 800/552-2287. RV sites are $28-30 per night, tent sites are $21 per night, $7 per night per extra vehicle. Weekly rates available. Some credit cards are accepted. Open mid-April-late October.

**Directions:** From U.S. 97 in Okanogan, turn north (left if arriving from the south) on Pine Street/Conconully Highway and drive 16.5 miles northwest to Conconully and Broadway Street. Turn left (west) and drive one mile. The park is on the west shore of the lake.

**Contact:** Shady Pines Resort, 509/826-2287, www.shadypinesresort.com.

## 24 LYMAN LAKE

### Scenic rating: 5

on Lyman Lake in Okanogan National Forest

**Map 4.1, page 251**

Little known and little used, this campground along the shore of Lyman Lake is an idyllic spot for those wanting solitude and quiet. The lake is quite small, just five acres at most, but fishing for stocked rainbow trout is an option.

**Campsites, facilities:** There are four sites for tents or RVs up to 30 feet long. Picnic tables and fire grills are provided. Vault toilets are available. There is no drinking water, and garbage must be packed out. Leashed pets are permitted.

**Reservations, fees:** Reservations are not accepted. There is no fee for camping. Open mid-May-mid-October, weather permitting.

**Directions:** From East Wenatchee, drive north on U.S. 97 for 120 miles to Tonasket and Highway 20. Turn east on Highway 20 and drive 12.5 miles to County Road 9455. Turn right (southeast) on County Road 9455 and drive 13 miles to County Road 3785. Turn right (south) on County Road 3785 and drive 2.5 miles to the campground entrance on the right.

**Contact:** Okanogan and Wenatchee National Forests, Tonasket Ranger District, 509/486-2186, www.fs.usda.gov.

## 25 ROCK LAKES

### Scenic rating: 8

on Rock Lake

**Map 4.1, page 251**          **BEST (**

This camp is set in a forested area along the shore of Rock Lake. Fishing for rainbow trout and brook trout is a plus at Rock Lake. A downer is that access for launching even car-top boats is difficult, requiring a 0.25-mile hike. That makes it a better bet for float tubes. Note that the best fishing is early in the season and that the lake level often drops because of irrigation use. Some roads in the area are used by hikers and bikers. A good bet is to combine a trip here with nearby Leader Lake. Highway 20 east of I-5 is a designated scenic route.

**Campsites, facilities:** There are eight sites for tents or RVs up to 20 feet long. Picnic tables and fire pits are provided. Vault toilets are available. There is no drinking water, and garbage must be packed out. Leashed pets are permitted.

**Reservations, fees:** Reservations are not accepted. There is no fee for camping, but a Discover Pass is required. Open year-round.

**Directions:** From East Wenatchee, drive north on U.S. 97 for 88 miles to Okanogan and Highway 20. Turn west and drive 10 miles to Loup

Loup Canyon Road. Turn left on Loup Loup Canyon Road and drive 4.8 miles to Rock Lakes Road. Turn left on Rock Lakes Road and drive 5.8 miles to the campground entrance. Turn left and drive 0.25 mile to the campground.
**Contact:** Department of Natural Resources, Northeast Region, 509/684-7474, www.dnr. wa.gov.

## 26 CARL PRECHT MEMORIAL RV PARK

**Scenic rating: 6**
in Omak on the Okanogan River

**Map 4.1, page 251**
East Side Park is in the town of Omak, along the shore of the Okanogan River. Home to the Omak Stampede and World Famous Suicide Race, it covers about 76 acres and features the Carl Precht RV Park, with campsites positioned on concrete pads surrounded by grass. Trout fishing is often good here, and there is a boat ramp near the campground. Nearby recreation options include an 18-hole golf course, a swimming pool, and a sports field.
**Campsites, facilities:** There are 68 sites with full hookups (20 and 30 amps) for RVs of any length and five tent sites. Some sites are pull-through. Picnic tables are provided. Restrooms with flush toilets and coin showers (seasonal), a dump station, a picnic area, Wi-Fi, a seasonal heated swimming pool, a playground, tennis and basketball courts, baseball and soccer fields, horseshoe pits, a skateboarding park, and a fitness trail are available. A store, café, gasoline, and ice are located within one mile. Some facilities are wheelchair accessible. Leashed pets are permitted.
**Reservations, fees:** Reservations are not accepted. RV sites are $30-35 per night, tent sites are $15 per night. Winter rates available. Open year-round, weather permitting.
**Directions:** From U.S. 97 in Omak, turn west (left, if coming from the south) on Highway 155 and drive 0.3 mile to the campground on the left.

**Contact:** City of Omak, 509/826-1170, www. omakcity.com.

## 27 CRAWFISH LAKE

**Scenic rating: 8**
on Crawfish Lake in Okanogan National Forest

**Map 4.1, page 251**
This pretty, remote, and primitive camp is set at 4,500 feet elevation along the shore of Crawfish Lake. Crawdads were once abundant here, but overfishing has depleted their numbers. Swimming and fishing for trout are more popular.
**Campsites, facilities:** There are 15 single sites and four double sites for tents or RVs up to 30 feet long. Picnic tables and fire grills are provided. Vault toilets are available. There is no drinking water, and garbage must be packed out. Boat-launching facilities are located on the lake. Some facilities are wheelchair accessible. Leashed pets are permitted.
**Reservations, fees:** Reservations are not accepted. There is no fee for camping. Open mid-May-mid-October, weather permitting.
**Directions:** From East Wenatchee, drive north on U.S. 97 for 102 miles to Riverside and County Road 9320. Turn right (east) on County Road 9320 and drive 20 miles (becomes Forest Road 30) to Forest Road 30-100. Turn right and drive 0.5 mile to the campground on the right.
**Contact:** Okanogan and Wenatchee National Forests, Tonasket Ranger District, 509/486-2186, www.fs.usda.gov.

## 28 LOUP LOUP

**Scenic rating: 6**
near Loup Loup Ski Area in Okanogan National Forest

**Map 4.1, page 251**
This camp provides a good setup for large groups of up to 100 people. It is located next

to the Loup Loup Ski Area at 4,200 feet elevation. The camp features a setting of western larch trees, along with good access to biking and hiking trails as well as the ski area.

**Campsites, facilities:** There are 25 sites for tents or RVs up to 36 feet long. Picnic tables and fire rings are provided. Drinking water, vault toilets, and garbage bins are available. Some facilities are wheelchair accessible. Leashed pets are permitted.

**Reservations, fees:** Reservations are not accepted. Sites are $12 per night, $5 extra vehicle fee with two-vehicle maximum. Open May-mid-October, weather permitting.

**Directions:** From East Wenatchee, drive north on U.S. 97 for 88 miles to Okanogan and Highway 20. Turn west and drive 21 miles to Forest Road 42. Turn right (north) on Forest Road 42 and drive one mile to the campground on the left.

**Contact:** Okanogan and Wenatchee National Forests, Methow Valley Ranger District, 509/996-4003, www.fs.usda.gov; Methow Valley Visitor Center, 509/996-4000.

## 29 SPORTSMAN CAMP
🚶 🚴 🐴 ♿ 🚐 ⛺

### Scenic rating: 6
on Sweat Creek, in Lower Loomis State Forest

Map 4.1, page 251

In season, this is a popular camp with hunters, who may bring horses; although there are no livestock facilities, horses are allowed in the camp. The landscape is shady and grassy with a small stream. Some roads in the area can be used by hikers and bikers. Highway 20 east of I-5 is a designated scenic route.

**Campsites, facilities:** There are four sites for tents or RVs up to 20 feet long and a small, dispersed area for tents. Picnic tables and fire pits are provided. Vault toilets are available, but there is no drinking water. Garbage must be packed out. A gazebo shelter with a fire pit is also available. Some facilities are wheelchair accessible. Leashed pets are permitted.

**Reservations, fees:** Reservations are not accepted. There is no fee for camping, but a Discover Pass is required. Open year-round, weather permitting.

**Directions:** From East Wenatchee, drive north on U.S. 97 for 88 miles to Okanogan and Highway 20. Turn west and drive 15 miles to Sweat Creek Road. Turn right on Sweat Creek Road and drive one mile to the campground on the right.

**Contact:** Department of Natural Resources, Northeast Region, 509/684-7474, www.dnr.wa.gov.

## 30 JR
🚶 🚴 🛶 ❄ 🐴 ♿ 🚐 ⛺

### Scenic rating: 7
on Frazier Creek in Okanogan National Forest

Map 4.1, page 251

This camp is located along Frazier Creek near the Loup Loup summit and ski area at an elevation of 3,900 feet. Recreation possibilities in the surrounding area include fishing, hunting, cross-country skiing, snowmobiling, hiking, and bicycling. This is a small layover for travelers looking for a spot on Highway 20.

**Campsites, facilities:** There are six sites for tents or RVs up to 16 feet long. Picnic tables and fire rings are provided. Vault toilets are available. There is no drinking water, and garbage must be packed out. Leashed pets are permitted.

**Reservations, fees:** Reservations are not accepted. Sites are $8 per night, $5 extra vehicle fee. Open late May-mid-October, weather permitting.

**Directions:** From East Wenatchee, drive north on U.S. 97 for 88 miles to Okanogan and Highway 20. Turn west and drive 22 miles to the campground on the right.

**Contact:** Okanogan and Wenatchee National Forests, Methow Valley Ranger District, 509/996-4003, www.fs.usda.gov; Methow Valley Visitor Center, 509/996-4000.

# 31 ROCK CREEK

### Scenic rating: 6

on Rock Creek and Loup Loup Creek

**Map 4.1, page 251**

This wooded campground is situated at the confluence of Rock and Loup Loup Creeks. A group picnic shelter with a barbecue is available. The camp is used primarily in the fall as a base camp for hunters and occasionally during the summer, mostly on weekends. It's advisable to obtain a map detailing the area from the Department of Natural Resources.

**Campsites, facilities:** There are five sites for tents or RVs up to 20 feet long. Picnic tables and fire pits are provided. Vault toilets, drinking water, and a picnic area are available. Some facilities are wheelchair accessible. Leashed pets are permitted.

**Reservations, fees:** Reservations are not accepted. There is no fee for camping, but a Discover Pass is required. Open year-round.

**Directions:** From East Wenatchee, drive north on U.S. 97 for 88 miles to Okanogan and Highway 20. Turn west and drive 10 miles to Loup Loup Canyon Road. Turn left on Loup Loup Canyon Road and drive 3.9 miles to the camp on the left.

**Contact:** Department of Natural Resources, Northeast Region, 509/684-7474, www.dnr. wa.gov.

# 32 LEADER LAKE

### Scenic rating: 7

on Leader Lake

**Map 4.1, page 251**

This primitive but pretty camp is set along the shore of Leader Lake. It is just far enough off the beaten path to get missed by many travelers. The camp has forest cover. The boat ramp is a bonus, and trout fishing can be good in season. Note that the water level often drops in summer because of irrigation use.

**Campsites, facilities:** There are 16 sites for tents or RVs up to 30 feet long. Picnic tables and fire pits are provided. Vault toilets are available. There is no drinking water, and garbage must be packed out. Boat-launching facilities are nearby. Some facilities are wheelchair accessible. Leashed pets are permitted.

**Reservations, fees:** Reservations are not accepted. There is no fee for camping, but a Discover Pass is required. Open year-round.

**Directions:** From East Wenatchee, drive north on U.S. 97 for 88 miles to Okanogan and Highway 20. Turn west and drive eight miles to Leader Lake Road. Turn left and drive 0.4 mile to the campground.

**Contact:** Department of Natural Resources, Northeast Region, 509/684-7474, www.dnr. wa.gov.

# 33 AMERICAN LEGION PARK

### Scenic rating: 6

on the Okanogan River

**Map 4.1, page 251**

This city park is located along the shore of the Okanogan River in an urban setting. The sites are graveled and sunny. Anglers may want to try their hand at the excellent bass fishing here. There is a historical museum at the park. A local farmers market is held on summer weekends.

**Campsites, facilities:** There are 35 sites for tents or RVs of any length (no hookups); all sites are pull-through. Picnic tables are provided. Restrooms with flush toilets, coin showers, and drinking water are available. A boat ramp is nearby. A store, café, coin laundry, gasoline, and ice are located within one mile. Some facilities are wheelchair accessible. Leashed pets are permitted.

**Reservations, fees:** Reservations are not accepted. Sites are $4 per night, $6 per vehicle per night. Open April-October, weather permitting.

**Directions:** From East Wenatchee, drive north

on U.S. 97 for 88 miles to Okanogan and Highway 215. Turn left (north) on Highway 215/2nd Avenue and drive about three miles to the campground on the right.

**Contact:** Okanogan City Hall, 509/422-3600, www.okanagoncity.com.

## 34 ALTA LAKE STATE PARK

**Scenic rating: 8**

on Alta Lake

**Map 4.1, page 251**

This state park is nestled among the pines along the shore of Alta Lake. The park covers 186 acres, and the lake is two miles long and 0.25 mile wide. Alta Lake brightens a region where the mountains and pines meet the desert and features good trout fishing in summer, along with a boat launch and a 0.5-mile-long swimming beach. Windsurfing is often excellent on windy afternoons. Because of many hidden rocks just under the lake surface, waterskiing can be dangerous. An 18-hole golf course and a riding stable are close by, and a nice one-mile hiking trail leads up to a scenic lookout. Lake Chelan is about 30 minutes away.

**Campsites, facilities:** There are 91 developed tent sites, 32 sites with partial hookups for RVs up to 38 feet long, and two group sites for 20-85 people. Picnic tables and fire grills (campfires are not allowed after July 1) are provided. Restrooms with flush toilets and coin showers, firewood, a dump station, a small camp store, and ice are available. A sheltered picnic area is available nearby. Some facilities are wheelchair accessible. Boat-launching facilities are nearby. Leashed pets are permitted.

**Reservations, fees:** Reservations are accepted at 888/226-7688 or www.goingtocamp.com ($6.50 reservation fee). Sites are $17-39 per night, $10 per extra vehicle per night. The group site is $96.54 per night with a minimum of 15 people. Open April-October, weather permitting.

**Directions:** From East Wenatchee, drive north on U.S. 97 for 64 miles to Highway 153 (just south of Pateros). Turn left (northwest) on Highway 153 and drive two miles to Alta Lake Road. Turn left (southwest) and drive two miles to the park.

**Contact:** Alta Lake State Park, 509/923-2473; state park information, 360/902-8844, www.parks.wa.gov.

## 35 BRIDGEPORT STATE PARK

**Scenic rating: 8**

on Rufus Woods Lake

**Map 4.1, page 251**

Bridgeport State Park is located along the shore of Rufus Woods Lake, a reservoir on the Columbia River above Chief Joseph Dam. It's a big place, covering 748 acres, including 7,500 feet of shoreline and 18 acres of lawn, with some shade amid the desert landscape. Highlights include beach access, a boat launch, and the aptly named "haystacks," unusual volcanic formations. Fishing is best by boat because shore fishing requires a Colville Tribe fishing license (for sale at the Bridgeport Hardware Store), in addition to a state fishing license. The lake has plenty of rainbow trout and walleye. Windsurfing in the afternoon wind and waterskiing are popular at the lake. Nearby recreation options include a nine-hole golf course.

**Campsites, facilities:** There are 14 sites for tents or RVs (no hookups), 20 sites with partial hookups for RVs up to 45 feet long, and one group site for 20-75 people. Picnic tables and fire grills are provided. Restrooms with flush toilets and coin showers, a picnic area, and a dump station are available. A store, café, and ice are located within two miles. Boat docks and launching facilities are nearby on both the upper and lower portions of the reservoir. Interpretive programs are available in summer. Some facilities are wheelchair accessible. Leashed pets are permitted.

**Reservations, fees:** Reservations are accepted at 888/226-7688 or www.goingtocamp.com ($6.50 reservation fee). Sites are $17-39 per night, $10 per night per additional vehicle. Group sites are $68.01-208.16 per night. Open mid-March-October.

**Directions:** From East Wenatchee, drive north on U.S. 97 for 71 miles to Highway 17. Turn south on Highway 17 and drive eight miles southeast to the park entrance on the left.

**Contact:** Bridgeport State Park, 509/686-7231; state park information, 360/902-8844, www.parks.wa.gov.

## 36 BETH LAKE

### Scenic rating: 7

on Beth Lake in Okanogan National Forest

Map 4.2, page 252

This campground is set between Beth Lake and Beaver Lake, both small, narrow lakes stocked with rainbow trout and brook trout. A 1.9-mile-long hiking trail (one-way) connects the two lakes. Other side trips in the area include Lost Lake, Bonaparte Lake, and several hiking trails, one of which leads up to the Mount Bonaparte Lookout. The elevation is 2,800 feet.

**Campsites, facilities:** There are 13 sites for tents or RVs up to 35 feet long, plus one double site. Picnic tables and fire rings are provided. Drinking water, vault toilets, and garbage bins are available. Boat-launching facilities are available nearby. Some facilities are wheelchair accessible. Leashed pets are permitted.

**Reservations, fees:** Reservations are not accepted. Single sites are $8 per night, double sites are $10 per night, $5 per night per additional vehicle. Open mid-May-mid-October, weather permitting.

**Directions:** From East Wenatchee, drive north on U.S. 97 for 120 miles to Tonasket and Highway 20. Turn east on Highway 20 and drive 20 miles to Bonaparte Lake Road (County Road 4953). Turn left (north) and

drive six miles to Bonaparte Lake and Forest Road 32. Continue (north) on Forest Road 32 and drive six miles to County Road 9480. Turn left (northwest) and drive one mile to the campground on the left.

**Contact:** Okanogan and Wenatchee National Forests, Tonasket Ranger District, 509/486-2186, www.fs.usda.gov.

## 37 BEAVER LAKE

### Scenic rating: 7

on Beaver Lake in Okanogan National Forest

Map 4.2, page 252

This camp calls the southeastern shore of long, narrow Beaver Lake home. Situated at 2,700 feet elevation, it is one of several lakes in this area. Beth Lake is nearby and accessible with an hour-long hike. Both Beaver and Beth Lakes are stocked with trout. (The Department of Fish and Wildlife has proposed treating the lake to remove certain species of fish that are negatively impacting the trout population.) In addition to fishing, swimming, hunting, and hiking are all possibilities here.

**Campsites, facilities:** There are nine single and two multiple sites for tents or RVs up to 21 feet long. Picnic tables are provided. Drinking water, vault toilets, and garbage bins are available. Boat-launching facilities are located within 100 yards of the campground. No boats with gas engines are permitted; electric motors are allowed. Leashed pets are permitted.

**Reservations, fees:** Reservations are not accepted. Sites are $8-16 per night, plus $5 per additional vehicle per night. Open mid-May-mid-October, weather permitting.

**Directions:** From East Wenatchee, drive north on U.S. 97 for 120 miles to Tonasket and Highway 20. Turn east on Highway 20 and drive 24 miles to Bonaparte Lake Road (County Road 4953). Turn left (north) and drive six miles to Bonaparte Lake and Forest Road 32. Continue (north) on Forest Road

32 and drive six miles to the campground on the left.

**Contact:** Okanogan and Wenatchee National Forests, Tonasket Ranger District, 509/486-2186, www.fs.usda.gov.

## 38 PIERRE LAKE

**Scenic rating: 8**
on Pierre Lake in Colville National Forest

**Map 4.2, page 252**

At just 105 acres, Pierre Lake is a quiet jewel of a camp near the Canadian border and only a short drive from U.S. 395. It is popular and usually fills on summer weekends. The camp is set on the west shore of the lake where there is fishing for rainbow trout, cutthroat trout, brook trout, crappie, bass, and catfish. While there is no speed limit, the lake is too small for big, fast boats.

**Campsites, facilities:** There are 15 sites for tents or RVs up to 24 feet long. Picnic tables and fire grills are provided. Drinking water and vault toilets are available. Garbage must be packed out. Boat docks and launching facilities are available on-site. A convenience store and ice are located within seven miles. Some facilities are wheelchair accessible. Leashed pets are permitted.

**Reservations, fees:** Reservations are not accepted. Sites are $6 per night. Open mid-April-mid-October, weather permitting.

**Directions:** From Spokane, drive north on U.S. 395 for 74 miles to Colville. Continue north on U.S. 395 for about 25 miles to Barstow and Pierre Lake Road (County Road 4013). Turn right (north) on Pierre Lake Road and drive nine miles to the campground on the west side of Pierre Lake.

**Contact:** Colville National Forest, Three Rivers Ranger District, 509/738-7700, www.fs.usda.gov.

## 39 CURLEW LAKE STATE PARK

**Scenic rating: 8**
on Curlew Lake

**Map 4.2, page 252**   BEST (

Boredom is banned at this park, set on the eastern shore of Curlew Lake. The park covers 123 acres, and the lake is 5.5 miles long. Fishing is often good for trout and largemouth bass at the lake, and there are additional lakes and streams in the region. There is also beach access, swimming, waterskiing, and hiking, with two miles of hiking and biking trails in the park. The park is also used as a base for bicycle touring, with mountain biking available on a fairly steep trail that provides a view of the valley. There is an active osprey nest, and nearby recreation options include a nine-hole golf course. The park borders an airfield and is located in the heart of a historic gold-mining district.

**Campsites, facilities:** There are 25 sites with full hookups (30 amps) for RVs up to 45 feet long, 57 developed tent sites, and two primitive tent sites. Picnic tables and fire rings are provided. Restrooms with flush toilets and coin showers, a dump station, drinking water, firewood, ice, and boat-launching and dock facilities are available. Boat fuel is available at the marina on the north side of the lake. Some facilities are wheelchair accessible. Leashed pets are permitted.

**Reservations, fees:** Reservations are accepted for some sites at 888/226-7688 or www.goingtocamp.com ($6.50 reservation fee). Sites are $12-42 per night, $10 per extra vehicle per night. Open April-October, weather permitting.

**Directions:** From Spokane on I-90, turn north on U.S. 395 and drive 87 miles to Kettle Falls and Highway 20. Turn west on Highway 20 and continue 34 miles to Highway 21 (2 miles east of Republic). Turn right (north) and drive six miles to the park entrance on the left.

**Contact:** Curlew Lake State Park, 509/775-3592; state park information, 360/902-8844, www.parks.wa.gov.

## 40 TIFFANYS RESORT

🏊 🎣 🚤 🐕 🏕 🚐 ⛺

### Scenic rating: 7

on Curlew Lake

**Map 4.2, page 252**

Tiffanys Resort is located in a pretty, wooded setting along the western shore of Curlew Lake. This 6.5-mile-long lake is good for waterskiing. Fishing can be good for rainbow trout and largemouth bass. Most of the sites are fairly spacious. This is a smaller, more private alternative to Black Beach Resort.

**Campsites, facilities:** There are 15 sites for tents or RVs up to 40 feet (30 and 50 amp full hookups), four sites for tents, and 19 cabins. Picnic tables are provided, and fire pits are available on request. Restrooms with flush toilets and showers, firewood, a convenience store, coin laundry, ice, Wi-Fi, basketball hoop, volleyball, horseshoes, a playground, and a swimming beach are available. Boat docks, launching facilities, fish-cleaning stations, and rentals are available. Leashed pets are permitted.

**Reservations, fees:** Reservations are accepted. Sites are $25-33 per night, $3-5 per night per additional person. Some credit cards are accepted. Open April-late October.

**Directions:** From Colville, drive west on Highway 20 for 36 miles into the town of Republic and Klondike Road. Turn right on Klondike Road and drive 10.2 miles (Klondike Road will turn into West Curlew Lake Road) to Tiffany Road. Turn right and drive 0.5 mile to the resort at the end of the road.

**Contact:** Tiffanys Resort, 509/775-3152, www.tiffanysresort.com.

## 41 BLACK BEACH RESORT

🏊 🎣 🚤 🐴 ♿ 🛶 🚐 ⛺

### Scenic rating: 7

on Curlew Lake

**Map 4.2, page 252**

Here's another resort along Curlew Lake. This one is much larger than Tiffanys Resort, with beautiful waterfront sites and full facilities. Waterskiing, personal watercraft, swimming, and fishing are all options. Fossil digging near the town of Republic is also popular.

**Campsites, facilities:** There are 86 sites for tents or RVs of any length (20 and 30 amp full hookups), nine sites for tents or RVs of any length (no hookups), and 12 lodging units. Some sites are pull-through. Picnic tables are provided, and fire pits are available at some sites. Restrooms with flush toilets and coin showers, dump station, convenience store, coin laundry, Wi-Fi, firewood, ice, volleyball, basketball hoop, horseshoes, and a playground are available. Boat docks, launching facilities, a fish cleaning station, and boat rentals are located at the resort. Some facilities are wheelchair accessible. Leashed pets are permitted.

**Reservations, fees:** Reservations are accepted. RV sites are $29-31 per night, tent sites are $27 per night, $4 per person per night for more than four people, $5 pet fee. Weekly and monthly rates available. Some credit cards are accepted. Campground open April-October; four cabins are available in winter.

**Directions:** From Colville, drive west on Highway 20 for approximately 36 miles to the town of Republic and Klondike Road. Turn right on Klondike Road (will become West Curlew Lake Road) and drive 7.5 miles to Black Beach Road. Turn right and drive 0.75 mile to the resort.

**Contact:** Black Beach Resort, 509/775-3989, www.blackbeachresort.com.

## 42 NORTH GORGE

🏊 🎣 🚤 🐴 🐕 🚐 ⛺

### Scenic rating: 7

on Franklin Roosevelt Lake in Lake Roosevelt National Recreation Area

**Map 4.2, page 252**

This is the first and northernmost of many campgrounds I discovered along the west shore of 130-mile-long Franklin Roosevelt Lake, which was formed by damming the Columbia

River at Coulee. Recreation options include waterskiing and swimming, plus fishing for walleye, trout, bass, and sunfish. During the winter, the lake level lowers; for a unique trip, walk along the lake's barren edge. Note that this campground provides full facilities May 1-September 30, then limited facilities in the off-season. Lake Roosevelt National Recreation Area offers recreation options such as free ranger programs, guided canoe trips, historical tours, campfire talks, and guided hikes. Watch for bald eagles in winter. Side-trip options include visiting the Colville Tribal Museum and touring the Grand Coulee Dam Visitor Center.

**Campsites, facilities:** There are 12 sites for tents or RVs up to 26 feet long. Picnic tables and fire grills are provided. Drinking water, vault toilets, boat docks, and launching facilities are available. Note that if the lake level drops below an elevation of 1,272 feet, there is no drinking water. Leashed pets are permitted.

**Reservations, fees:** Reservations are not accepted. Sites are $10 per night ($5 per night in off-season), $6 boat-launch fee (good for seven days). Open year-round, with limited winter access.

**Directions:** From Spokane on I-90, drive north on U.S. 395 for 84 miles to the town of Kettle Falls and Highway 25. Turn right (north) on Highway 25 and drive 20 miles to the campground entrance.

**Contact:** Lake Roosevelt National Recreation Area, 509/754-7800, www.nps.gov/laro.

## 43 DAVIS LAKE

### Scenic rating: 8
on Davis Lake in Colville National Forest

Map 4.2, page 252

This tiny campground is set at 4,600 feet elevation at Little Davis Lake. It is a scenic spot, and the fishing for cutthroat trout is often good. Only small boats are permitted on the small, shallow lake, which covers just 17 acres. No gas motors are permitted, but the lake can be ideal for float tubes, canoes, and prams with electric motors or oars. A one-mile trail loops the lake.

**Campsites, facilities:** There are four sites for tents or RVs up to 16 feet long. Picnic tables and fire grills are provided. Vault toilets are available. There is no drinking water, and garbage must be packed out. A primitive boat ramp is available nearby. Leashed pets are permitted.

**Reservations, fees:** Reservations are not accepted. There is no fee for camping. Open mid-May-October, weather permitting.

**Directions:** From Spokane, drive north on U.S. 395 for 84 miles to Kettle Falls. Continue north on U.S. 395 for nine miles to Deadman Creek Road. Turn west on Deadman Creek Road and drive about three miles to County Road 465 (Jack Knife cutoff). Turn right and drive 2.5 miles. Bear right and drive about 0.5 mile to County Road 480. Turn left and drive about three miles to County Road 080. Turn right and drive about three miles to Davis Lake. Note: The access road is very rough; high-clearance vehicles are recommended.

**Contact:** Colville National Forest, Three Rivers Ranger District, 509/738-7700, www. fs.usda.gov.

## 44 SNAG COVE

### Scenic rating: 8
on Franklin Roosevelt Lake in Lake Roosevelt National Recreation Area

Map 4.2, page 252

Snag Cove has a setting similar to North Gorge campground. It is set amid ponderosa pines along the west shore of Franklin Roosevelt Lake. This small camp has just nine sites, but the nearby boat launch makes it a find.

**Campsites, facilities:** There are nine sites for tents or RVs up to 35 feet long. Picnic tables and fire grills are provided. Vault toilets are available. When the lake level drops (to elevation 1,265 feet), there is no drinking water. Boat-launching facilities and docks are nearby. Some facilities are wheelchair accessible. Leashed pets are permitted.

**Reservations, fees:** Reservations are not accepted. Sites are $5-10 per night, $6 boat-launch fee (good for seven days). Open year-round, weather permitting.

**Directions:** From Spokane, turn north on U.S. 395 and drive 84 miles to the town of Kettle Falls. Continue north on U.S. 395 (crossing the Columbia River) for seven miles to the Hedlund Bridge turnoff. Turn right, cross Hedlund Bridge, and drive 7.5 miles to the campground on the right.

**Contact:** Lake Roosevelt National Recreation Area, 509/754-7800, www.nps.gov/laro.

## 45 NORTH LAKE RV PARK AND CAMPGROUND
🚶 🚴 🏊 🛶 ⛴ 🐕 ♿ 🚐 ⛺

### Scenic rating: 7
on Franklin Roosevelt Lake

**Map 4.2, page 252**

This campground is set along the long, narrow Kettle River Arm of Franklin Roosevelt Lake. A country resort, it is usually quiet and peaceful. A highlight is easy access to the lake, with no steep walk like at so many other campgrounds. A one-mile loop nature trail is available along the lakeshore, where wild turkeys and deer are often spotted. It's close to marked bike trails, a full-service marina, and tennis courts. Riding stables are available 20 miles away, and a golf course is within 15 miles. Colville National Forest East Portal Interpretive Area, 10 miles away, is a good side trip. (Drive south to the junction of Highway 20 and continue southwest for about six miles.) Highlights include a nature trail and the Bangs Mountain auto tour, a five-mile drive that takes you through old-growth forest to Bangs Mountain Vista overlooking the Roosevelt Lake-Kettle Falls area.

**Campsites, facilities:** There are 17 sites for tents or RVs of any length (30 and 50 amp

full hookups), five cabins, and two apartments with kitchens. Some sites are pull-through. An overflow camping area is also available. Picnic tables and fire grills are provided. Restrooms with flush toilets and coin showers, drinking water, coin laundry, playground, horseshoe pits, volleyball, Wi-Fi, a convenience store, and firewood are available. Lake swimming and fishing are on-site. A restaurant is available within five miles. Some facilities are wheelchair accessible. Leashed pets are permitted.

**Reservations, fees:** Reservations are recommended. Sites are $15-28 per night. Weekly and monthly rates are available. Open year-round.

**Directions:** From Spokane, turn north on U.S. 395 and drive 84 miles to the town of Kettle Falls. Continue north on U.S. 395 for 6.5 miles (toward Canada) to Roosevelt Road. Turn right (east) and drive 300 yards to the resort on the right.

**Contact:** North Lake RV Park and Campground, 509/738-2593, www.northlakervparkandcampground.com.

## 46 KETTLE RIVER
🏊 🛶 ⛴ 🐕 ♿ 🚐 ⛺

### Scenic rating: 7
on Franklin Roosevelt Lake in Lake Roosevelt National Recreation Area

**Map 4.2, page 252**

Kettle River campground is set along the long, narrow Kettle River Arm of Franklin Roosevelt Lake; it features campsites amid ponderosa pines. The nearest boat launch is located at Napoleon Bridge.

**Campsites, facilities:** There are 13 sites for tents or RVs up to 40 feet long. Picnic tables and fire grills are provided. Vault toilets are available. When the lake level drops below an elevation of 1,272 feet, there is no drinking water. Boat docks are nearby. Some facilities are wheelchair accessible. Leashed pets are permitted.

**Reservations, fees:** Reservations are not

accepted. Sites are $5-10 per night. Open year-round, weather permitting.

**Directions:** From Spokane, turn north on U.S. 395 and drive 84 miles to the town of Kettle Falls. Continue north on U.S. 395 (crossing the Columbia River) for seven miles to the campground on the right.

**Contact:** Lake Roosevelt National Recreation Area, 509/754-7800, www.nps.gov/laro.

## 47 KAMLOOPS ISLAND

### Scenic rating: 10
on Franklin Roosevelt Lake in Lake Roosevelt National Recreation Area

**Map 4.2, page 252**     BEST (

This is one of the more primitive campgrounds located along Franklin Roosevelt Lake. Located at Kamloops Island, an optimum area for waterskiing and fishing, it features unbelievably beautiful views of water and mountains. It is located near the mouth of the Kettle River Arm of the lake. While the scenic beauty merits a 10, note that the nearest boat launch is way across the lake at Kettle Falls and that if the lake level drops below an elevation of 1,272 feet, there is no drinking water.

**Campsites, facilities:** There are 17 sites for tents or RVs to 40 feet long. Picnic tables and fire grills are provided. Vault toilets are available. When the lake level drops, there is no drinking water. Boat docks are nearby. Leashed pets are permitted.

**Reservations, fees:** Reservations are not accepted. Sites are $5-10 per night. Open year-round, weather permitting.

**Directions:** From Spokane, turn north on U.S. 395 and drive 84 miles to the town of Kettle Falls. Continue north on U.S. 395 (crossing the Columbia River) for seven miles to the Hedlund Bridge turnoff. Turn right, cross Hedlund Bridge, and drive to the campground on the left.

**Contact:** Lake Roosevelt National Recreation Area, 509/754-7800, www.nps.gov/laro.

## 48 EVANS

### Scenic rating: 9
on Franklin Roosevelt Lake in Lake Roosevelt National Recreation Area

**Map 4.2, page 252**

This campground is another in a series set along the shore of Franklin Roosevelt Lake. This one sits along the eastern shoreline, just south of the town of Evans. Fishing, swimming, and waterskiing are among the activities here. Lake Roosevelt National Recreation Area offers recreation options such as free ranger programs, guided canoe trips, historical tours, campfire talks, and guided hikes. Watch for bald eagles in winter. Side-trip options include visiting the Colville Tribal Museum and touring the Grand Coulee Dam Visitor Center.

**Campsites, facilities:** There are 43 sites for tents or RVs up to 55 feet long and one group site for tents or RVs up to 55 feet long for up to 25 people. Picnic tables and fire pits are provided. Drinking water (seasonal) and flush toilets are available. A boat dock, launch facilities, a dump station, playground, swimming beach, camp host, and a picnic area are available nearby. Some facilities are wheelchair accessible. Leashed pets are permitted.

**Reservations, fees:** Reservations are not accepted for individual sites but are required for the group site at 877/444-6777 or www.recreation.gov ($9 reservation fee). Sites are $5-10 per night, the group site is $53 per night (plus $25 reservation fee), $6 boat-launch fee (good for seven days). Open year-round, with limited facilities in the winter.

**Directions:** From Spokane on I-90, drive north on U.S. 395 for 84 miles to the town of Kettle Falls and Highway 25. Turn right (north) on Highway 25 and drive eight miles to the campground entrance on the left.

**Contact:** Lake Roosevelt National Recreation Area, 509/754-7800 or 509/754-7889, www.nps.gov/laro.

## 49 MARCUS ISLAND

### Scenic rating: 8

on Franklin Roosevelt Lake in Lake Roosevelt National Recreation Area

**Map 4.2, page 252**

Located south of Evans camp on the eastern shore of Franklin Roosevelt Lake, this campground is quite similar to that camp. Waterskiing, fishing, and swimming are the primary recreation options. Lake Roosevelt National Recreation Area offers numerous recreation options, such as free programs conducted by rangers that include guided canoe trips, historical tours, campfire talks, and guided hikes. This lake is known as a prime location to view bald eagles, especially in winter. Side-trip options include visiting the Colville Tribal Museum in the town of Coulee Dam and touring the Grand Coulee Dam Visitor Center. Almost one mile long and twice as high as Niagara Falls, the dam is one of the largest concrete structures ever built; it is open for self-guided tours.

**Campsites, facilities:** There are 25 sites for tents or RVs up to 40 feet long. Picnic tables and fire grills are provided. Drinking water, vault toilets, and a picnic area are available. A boat launch and dock are available nearby. Note that if the lake level drops below an elevation of 1,265 feet, there is no drinking water. Leashed pets are permitted.

**Reservations, fees:** Reservations are not accepted. Sites are $5-10 per night, $6 boat-launch fee (good for seven days). Open year-round, weather permitting.

**Directions:** From Spokane on I-90, drive north on U.S. 395 for 84 miles to the town of Kettle Falls and Highway 25. Turn right (north) on Highway 25 and drive four miles to the campground entrance on the left.

**Contact:** Lake Roosevelt National Recreation Area, 509/754-7800, www.nps.gov/laro.

## 50 SWAN LAKE

### Scenic rating: 8

on Swan Lake in Colville National Forest

**Map 4.2, page 252**

Scenic views greet visitors on the drive to Swan Lake and at the campground as well. The camp is set on the shore of Swan Lake, at an elevation of 3,700 feet. Swan Lake Trail, a beautiful hiking trail, circles the lake. Fishing for rainbow trout is an option. Swimming, boating (gas motors prohibited), mountain biking, and hiking are some of the possibilities here. This is a good out-of-the-way spot for RV cruisers seeking a rustic setting. It commonly fills on summer weekends.

**Campsites, facilities:** There are 21 sites, including six double sites, for tents or RVs of any length, four walk-in sites for tents only, and a group site for 20-50 people. Picnic tables and fire grills are provided. Drinking water, vault toilets, and garbage bins are available. A picnic shelter with barbecue, a boat dock, and launching facilities are available nearby. Gas motors are prohibited on the lake. Some facilities are wheelchair accessible. Leashed pets are permitted.

**Reservations, fees:** Reservations are not accepted for individual sites, but are required for the group site at 877/444-6777 ($10 reservation fee) or www.recreation.gov ($9 reservation fee). Single sites are $8 per night, double sites are $10 per night, $2 per additional vehicle. The group site is $35 per night. Open May-November, weather permitting.

**Directions:** From Spokane on I-90, turn north on U.S. 395 and drive 87 miles to Highway 20. Turn west on Highway 20 and drive 36 miles to the town of Republic and Highway 21. Turn south on Highway 21 and drive seven miles to Forest Road 53 (Scatter Creek Road). Turn right (southwest) on Forest Road 53 and drive eight miles to the campground at the end of the road.

**Contact:** Colville National Forest, Republic Ranger District, 509/775-3305, www.fs.usda.gov.

## 51 FERRY LAKE

### Scenic rating: 7

on Ferry Lake in Colville National Forest

**Map 4.2, page 252**

Ferry Lake is one of three fishing lakes within a four-square-mile area; the others are Swan Lake and Long Lake. Swimming, boating (gas motors prohibited), mountain biking, and hiking are some of the possibilities here.

**Campsites, facilities:** There are nine sites for tents or RVs up to 20 feet long. Fire grills and picnic tables are provided. Vault toilets and garbage bins are available. No drinking water is available. Launching facilities are nearby. Leashed pets are permitted.

**Reservations, fees:** Reservations are not accepted. Sites are $6 per night, $2 per extra vehicle per night. Open May-October, weather permitting.

**Directions:** From Spokane on I-90, turn north on U.S. 395 and drive 87 miles to Highway 20. Turn west on Highway 20 and drive 36 miles to the town of Republic and Highway 21. Turn south on Highway 21 and drive seven miles to Forest Road 53 (Scatter Creek Road). Turn right (southwest) on Forest Road 53 and drive about seven miles to Forest Road 5330. Turn right (north) on Forest Road 5330 and drive one mile to Forest Road 100. Turn right and drive one mile to the campground on the left.

**Contact:** Colville National Forest, Republic Ranger District, 509/775-3305, www.fs.usda.gov.

## 52 LONG LAKE

### Scenic rating: 9

on Long Lake in Colville National Forest

**Map 4.2, page 252**                **BEST (**

Long Lake is the third and smallest of the three lakes in this area; the others are Swan Lake and Ferry Lake. Expert anglers can have a quality experience here fly-fishing for cutthroat trout.

No gas motors are allowed on the lake, and fishing is restricted (fly-fishing only), but it's ideal for a float tube or a pram. The lake is set adjacent to little Fish Lake, and a 0.5-mile trail runs between the two. The drive on Highway 21 south of Republic is particularly beautiful, with views of the Sanpoil River.

**Campsites, facilities:** There are 12 sites for tents or RVs up to 30 feet long. Picnic tables and fire grills are provided. Drinking water, vault toilets, and garbage bins are available. Primitive launching facilities are nearby. Leashed pets are permitted.

**Reservations, fees:** Reservations are not accepted. Sites are $8 per night, $2 per extra vehicle per night. Open May-October, weather permitting.

**Directions:** From Spokane on I-90, turn north on U.S. 395 and drive 87 miles to Highway 20. Turn west on Highway 20 and drive 36 miles to the town of Republic and Highway 21. Turn south on Highway 21 and drive seven miles to Forest Road 53 (Scatter Creek Road). Turn right (southwest) on Forest Road 53 and drive seven miles to Forest Road 400. Turn left (south) and drive 1.5 miles to the camp on the right.

**Contact:** Colville National Forest, Republic Ranger District, 509/775-3305, www.fs.usda.gov.

## 53 TEN MILE

### Scenic rating: 7

on the Sanpoil River in Colville National Forest

**Map 4.2, page 252**

This spot is secluded and primitive. Located about nine miles from Swan Lake, Ferry Lake, and Long Lake, this campground along the Sanpoil River is a good choice for a multi-day trip visiting each of the lakes. The Sanpoil River provides fishing for rainbow trout, and a hiking trail leads west from camp for about 2.5 miles.

**Campsites, facilities:** There are eight sites for

tents or RVs up to 21 feet long. Picnic tables and fire rings are provided. Vault toilets and garbage bins are available. There is no drinking water. Leashed pets are permitted.

**Reservations, fees:** Reservations are not accepted. Sites are $6 per night, $2 per extra vehicle per night; fees are charged Memorial Day weekend-Labor Day weekend. Open mid-May-mid-October, weather permitting.

**Directions:** From Spokane on I-90, turn north on U.S. 395 and drive 87 miles to Highway 20. Turn west on Highway 20 and drive 36 miles to Republic and Highway 21. Turn south on Highway 21 and drive 10 miles to the campground entrance on the left.

**Contact:** Colville National Forest, Republic Ranger District, 509/775-3305, www.fs.usda. gov.

## 54 SHERMAN OVERLOOK

### Scenic rating: 6

at Sherman Pass in Colville National Forest

**Map 4.2, page 252**

Sherman Pass Scenic Byway (Highway 20) runs through here, so the camp has some road noise. This roadside campground is located near Sherman Pass (5,575 feet elevation), one of the few high-elevation mountain passes open year-round in Washington. Several nearby trails provide access to various peaks and vistas in the area. One of the best is the Kettle Crest National Recreation Trail, with the trailhead located one mile from camp. This trail extends for 45 miles, generally running north to south, and provides spectacular views of the Cascades on clear days. No other campgrounds are in the immediate vicinity.

**Campsites, facilities:** There are 10 sites for tents or RVs up to 24 feet long. Picnic tables and fire grills are provided. Drinking water and vault toilets are available. Garbage must be packed out. Some facilities are wheelchair accessible. Leashed pets are permitted.

**Reservations, fees:** Reservations are not

accepted. Sites are $6 per night. Open June-mid-September, weather permitting.

**Directions:** From Spokane on I-90, turn north on U.S. 395 and drive 87 miles to Highway 20. Turn west on Highway 20 and drive 19.5 miles to the campground on the right.

**Contact:** Colville National Forest, Three Rivers Ranger District, 509/738-7700, www. fs.usda.gov.

## 55 TROUT LAKE

### Scenic rating: 8

on Trout Lake in Colville National Forest

**Map 4.2, page 252**

Trout Lake is a little lake, just eight acres, at an elevation of 3,100 feet. It provides fishing for rainbow trout, with prospects similar to that of Davis Lake. No gas motors are permitted, but electric motors are allowed on small boats. Nearby, five-mile-long Hoodoo Canyon Trail, accessible for hiking or biking, offers spectacular views; stock animals are prohibited.

**Campsites, facilities:** There are five sites for tents only. Picnic tables and fire pits are provided. Vault toilets are available. There is no drinking water, and garbage must be packed out. A very small boat ramp is available nearby. Some facilities are wheelchair accessible. Leashed pets are permitted.

**Reservations, fees:** Reservations are not accepted. There is no fee for camping. Open late May-September, weather permitting.

**Directions:** From Spokane, turn north on U.S. 395 and drive 87 miles to Colville and Highway 20. Turn west on Highway 20 and drive 15 miles (crossing the Columbia River) to Trout Lake Road (Forest Road 020). Turn right on Trout Lake Road and drive five miles to the campground at the end of the road.

**Contact:** Colville National Forest, Three Rivers Ranger District, 509/738-7700, www. fs.usda.gov.

## 56 CANYON CREEK

🏃 ☄ 🐕 ♿ 🚐 ⛺

### Scenic rating: 7

near the East Portal Historical Site in Colville National Forest

**Map 4.2, page 252**

This campground is located 0.4 mile from the highway, just far enough to keep it from road noise. It's a popular spot among campers looking for a layover, with the bonus of trout fishing in the nearby creek. Canyon Creek lies within hiking distance of the East Portal Historical Site. The camp is set in a pretty area not far from the Columbia River, which offers a myriad of recreation options. The Bangs Mountain Auto Tour, a scenic route with mountain vistas, is a good side trip.

**Campsites, facilities:** There are 12 sites for tents or RVs up to 30 feet long. Picnic tables and fire grills are provided. Vault toilets are available. There is no drinking water, and garbage must be packed out. Some facilities are wheelchair accessible. Leashed pets are permitted.

**Reservations, fees:** Reservations are not accepted. Sites are $6 per night. Open late April-early October, weather permitting.

**Directions:** From Spokane, drive north on U.S. 395 for 87 miles to Highway 20. Turn west on Highway 20 and drive 18 miles (crossing the Columbia River) to Forest Road 136. Turn left (south) and drive for 0.3 mile to the campground on the left.

**Contact:** Colville National Forest, Three Rivers, Ranger District, 509/738-7700, www.fs.usda.gov.

## 57 KETTLE FALLS

🏊 ☄ 🚤 🐕 🏃 ♿ 🚐 ⛺

### Scenic rating: 8

on Franklin Roosevelt Lake in Lake Roosevelt National Recreation Area

**Map 4.2, page 252**

Kettle Falls campground is located along the eastern shore of Roosevelt Lake, about two miles south of the highway bridge near West Kettle Falls. The camp only fills occasionally. In the summer, rangers offer evening campfire programs. Waterskiing, swimming, and fishing are all options. Local side trips include St. Paul's Mission in Kettle Falls, which was built in 1846 and is one of the oldest churches in Washington.

**Campsites, facilities:** There are 76 sites for tents or RVs of any length; some sites are pull-through. Picnic tables and fire grills are provided. Restrooms with flush toilets, drinking water, a dump station, firewood, a small marina (late May-early September) with a store, swimming beach, softball fields, amphitheater, picnic shelter, camp host, and a playground are available. A store is located within one mile. Boat docks, fuel, fish-cleaning stations, and launching facilities are available. Some facilities are wheelchair accessible. Leashed pets are permitted.

**Reservations, fees:** Reservations are accepted for individual sites and required for group sites at 877/444-6777 or www.recreation.gov ($9 reservation fee). Sites are $5-10 per night, the group site is $53 per night ($25 reservation fee), $6 boat-launch fee (good for seven days). Some credit cards are accepted. Open year-round, with limited winter facilities.

**Directions:** From Spokane, drive north on U.S. 395 for 84 miles to the town of Kettle Falls. Continue on U.S. 395 for three miles to Kettle Park Road. Turn left and drive two miles to the campground on the right.

**Contact:** Lake Roosevelt National Recreation Area, 509/754-7800 or 509/754-7889, www.nps.gov/laro.

## 58 HAAG COVE

🏊 ☄ 🐕 ♿ 🚐 ⛺

### Scenic rating: 8

on Franklin Roosevelt Lake in Lake Roosevelt National Recreation Area

**Map 4.2, page 252**     **BEST (**

This campground is tucked away in a cove along the western shore of Franklin Roosevelt Lake (Columbia River), about two miles south of Highway 20. A good side trip is to the Sherman Creek Habitat Management Area, located just north of camp. It's rugged and steep, but a good place to see and photograph wildlife, including bald eagles, golden eagles, and 200 other species of birds, along with the occasional black bear, cougar, and moose. Note that no boat launch is available at this camp, but boat ramps are available at Kettle Falls and French Rock. Also note that no drinking water is available if the lake level drops below an elevation of 1,275 feet.

**Campsites, facilities:** There are 16 sites for tents or RVs up to 35 feet long. Picnic tables and fire grills are provided. Drinking water and vault toilets are available. Boat docks are available nearby. Some facilities are wheelchair accessible. Leashed pets are permitted.

**Reservations, fees:** Reservations are not accepted. Sites are $5-10 per night. Open year-round, weather permitting, with limited winter access.

**Directions:** From Spokane, drive north on U.S. 395 for 84 miles to the town of Kettle Falls and Highway 20. Continue on Highway 20 and drive 7.5 miles to Kettle Falls Road. Turn left (south) and drive two miles to the campground on the right.

**Contact:** Lake Roosevelt National Recreation Area, 509/754-7800, www.nps.gov/laro.

## 59 LAKE ELLEN EAST & LAKE ELLEN WEST

### Scenic rating: 7
on Lake Ellen in Colville National Forest

**Map 4.2, page 252**

This 82-acre lake is a favorite for power boating (with no speed limit) and fishing for rainbow trout, which are a good size and plentiful early in the season. There are two small camps available here. The boat launch is located at the west end of the lake. It is located about three miles west of the Columbia River and the Lake Roosevelt National Recreation Area.

**Campsites, facilities:** There are 11 sites at Lake Ellen East and five sites at Lake Ellen West for tents or RVs up to 18 feet long. Picnic tables and fire grills are provided. Vault toilets and are available. There is no drinking water, and garbage must be packed out. Boat docks are available nearby. Some facilities are wheelchair accessible. Leashed pets are permitted.

**Reservations, fees:** Reservations are not accepted. Sites are $6 per night. Open mid-April-October, weather permitting.

**Directions:** From Spokane, drive north on U.S. 395 for 87 miles to Colville and Highway 20. Turn west on Highway 20 and drive 14 miles (crossing the Columbia River) to County Road 3. Turn left and drive south for 4.5 miles to County Road 412. Turn right on County Road 412 and drive five miles to the Lake Ellen Campground or continue another 0.7 mile to Lake Ellen West Campground.

**Contact:** Colville National Forest, Three Rivers Ranger District, 509/738-7700, www.fs.usda.gov.

## 60 RAINBOW BEACH RESORT

### Scenic rating: 8
on Twin Lakes Reservoir

**Map 4.2, page 252**

This quality resort is set along the shore of Twin Lakes Reservoir in the Colville Indian Reservation. Busy in summer, the camp fills up virtually every day in July and August. Nearby recreation options include hiking trails, marked bike trails, a full-service marina, and tennis courts.

**Campsites, facilities:** There are nine sites with full hookups for RVs of any length, including five pull-through sites, seven sites for tents, and 26 cabins. Picnic tables and fire pits are provided (in tent sites). Restrooms with flush toilets and coin showers, drinking water, propane gas, gasoline, firewood, a recreation hall, a convenience store, coin laundry, ice, a roped swimming area, boat rentals, docks and launching facilities, a playground, volleyball, and horseshoe pits are available. Leashed pets are permitted.

**Reservations, fees:** Reservations are accepted. Sites are $20-25 per night, $15 per pet per stay. Some credit cards are accepted. Campsites are available April-October; cabins are available year-round.

**Directions:** From Spokane, drive north on U.S. 395 for 84 miles to the town of Kettle Falls and Highway 20. Turn east on Highway 20 and drive five miles to the turnoff for Inchelium Highway. Turn left (south) and drive about 20 miles to Inchelium and Bridge Creek-Twin Lakes County Road. Turn right (west) and drive two miles to Stranger Creek Road. Turn left and drive 0.25 mile to the resort on the right.

**Contact:** Rainbow Beach Resort, 509/722-5901.

## 61 CLOVERLEAF

### Scenic rating: 8

on Franklin Roosevelt Lake in Lake Roosevelt National Recreation Area

**Map 4.2, page 252**

Cloverleaf is a small and primitive camp located on the east shore of Roosevelt Lake, just south of the town of Gifford. In this particular area of Roosevelt Lake, waterskiing and other high-speed boating are not advised because of submerged hazards, but fishing is fine. The tree cover in the area consists primarily of ponderosa pine. Lake Roosevelt National Recreation Area offers recreation options such as free ranger programs, guided canoe trips, historical tours, campfire talks, and guided hikes. Watch for bald eagles in winter. Side-trip options include visiting the Colville Tribal Museum and touring the Grand Coulee Dam Visitor Center. Note that no drinking water is available if the lake level drops below 1,282 feet elevation. Gifford campground to the south provides an alternative when this camp is full.

**Campsites, facilities:** There are nine sites

for tents only. Picnic tables and fire grills are provided. Drinking water and vault toilets are available. A dock and a picnic area are nearby. Leashed pets are permitted.

**Reservations, fees:** Reservations are not accepted. Sites are $5-10 per night, $6 boat-launch fee (good for seven days). Open April-October.

**Directions:** From Spokane on I-90, drive west for four miles to U.S. 2. Turn west on U.S. 2 and drive 34 miles to Highway 25. Turn right (north) on Highway 25 and drive 61 miles to Davenport and the campground (located about two miles south of Gifford).

**Contact:** Lake Roosevelt National Recreation Area, 509/754-7800, www.nps.gov/laro.

## 62 GIFFORD

### Scenic rating: 7

on Franklin Roosevelt Lake in Lake Roosevelt National Recreation Area

**Map 4.2, page 252**

Fishing and waterskiing are two of the draws at this camp on the eastern shore of Franklin Roosevelt Lake (Columbia River). The nearby boat ramp is a big plus.

**Campsites, facilities:** There are 42 sites for tents or RVs up to 55 feet long and one group site for tents or RVs up to 20 feet long that can accommodate up to 50 people and 15 vehicles. Picnic tables and fire grills are provided. Drinking water (seasonal) and flush and vault toilets are available. A camp host is on-site. Boat docks and launching facilities, a dump station, playground, and a picnic area are nearby. Some facilities are wheelchair accessible. Leashed pets are permitted.

**Reservations, fees:** Reservations are not accepted for individual sites but are required for the group site at 877/444-6777 or www.recreation.gov ($25 reservation fee). Sites are $5-10 per night, the group site is $53 per night, $6 boat-launch fee (good for seven days). Open year-round, with limited winter facilities.

**Directions:** From Spokane on I-90, drive west for four miles to U.S. 2. Turn west on U.S. 2 and drive 34 miles to Davenport and Highway 25. Turn right (north) on Highway 25 and drive 60 miles to the campground (located about three miles south of Gifford) on the left.

**Contact:** Lake Roosevelt National Recreation Area, 509/754-7800, 509/754-7889, or 509/738-2300, www.nps.gov/laro.

## 63 HUNTERS
🏊 🚣 🚐 🦌 🥾 🚙 ⛺

### Scenic rating: 8

on Franklin Roosevelt Lake in Lake Roosevelt National Recreation Area

**Map 4.2, page 252**

This campground, on a shoreline point along Franklin Roosevelt Lake (Columbia River), offers good swimming, fishing, and waterskiing. It is located on the east shore of the lake, adjacent to the mouth of Hunters Creek and near the town of Hunters. Note: No drinking water is available if the lake level drops below an elevation of 1,245 feet.

**Campsites, facilities:** There are 37 sites for tents or RVs up to 55 feet long and three group sites for tents or RVs up to 26 feet long that can accommodate up to 25 people each. Picnic tables and fire grills are provided. Drinking water, restrooms with flush toilets, vault toilets, a dump station, playground, and a picnic area are available. A camp host is on-site. A store and ice are available within one mile. Boat docks and launching facilities are nearby. Leashed pets are permitted.

**Reservations, fees:** Reservations are not accepted for individual sites but are required for group sites at 877/444-6777 or www.recreation.gov ($9 reservation fee). Sites are $5-10 per night, $6 boat-launch fee (good for seven days), and the group site is $53 per night ($25 reservation fee). Open year-round, with limited winter facilities.

**Directions:** From Spokane on I-90, drive west for four miles to U.S. 2. Turn west on U.S. 2 and drive 34 miles to Davenport and Highway 25. Turn north on Highway 25 and drive 47 miles to Hunters and the campground access road on the left (west) side of the road (well marked). Turn left at the access road and drive two miles to the campground at the end of the road.

**Contact:** Lake Roosevelt National Recreation Area, 509/754-7800 or 509/754-7889, www.nps.gov/laro.

## 64 SHEEP CREEK
🚶 🚵 🚣 🎣 🐕 ♿ 🚙 ⛺

### Scenic rating: 8

near the Columbia River and the Canadian border

**Map 4.3, page 253**

This campground is in a forested area along Sheep Creek, about four miles from the Columbia River and close to the Canadian border. Although a primitive camp, it has drinking water and is a "locals' spot" on the Fourth of July weekend. A wheelchair-accessible fishing platform and trail are available. Sheep Creek provides opportunities for trout fishing. Huckleberry picking is good in August.

**Campsites, facilities:** There are 11 sites for tents or RVs up to 30 feet long. Picnic tables and fire grills are provided. Vault toilets, drinking water, and a group picnic shelter with barbecues are available. Garbage must be packed out. Restaurants and stores are located within five miles. Some facilities are wheelchair accessible. Leashed pets are permitted.

**Reservations, fees:** Reservations are not accepted. There is no fee for camping, but a Discover Pass is required. Open mid-April-November, weather permitting.

**Directions:** From Spokane, drive north on U.S. 395 for 87 miles to Kettle Falls and Highway 25. Turn north on Highway 25 and drive 33 miles to Northport. Continue north on Highway 25 for 0.75 mile to Sheep Creek Road (across the Columbia River Bridge). Turn left on Sheep Creek Road and drive 4.3 miles (on a gravel road) to the campground entrance on the right.

**Contact:** Department of Natural Resources, Northeast Region, 509/684-7474, www.dnr.wa.gov.

## 65 UPPER COLUMBIA RV PARK AND CAMPGROUND

### Scenic rating: 5

near Colville on the Columbia River

Map 4.3, page 253

This rustic resort is set on a peaceful stretch of the upper Columbia River amid forests and wildflowers. Campsites are grassy, and the natural greenery provides privacy. Summertime recreation options include berry picking, bird- and wildlife-watching, fishing, hiking, and gold panning.

**Campsites, facilities:** There are 22 sites for tents or RVs up to 60 feet, all with full hookups (20, 30, or 50 amps), and two cabins. Some sites are pull-through. Picnic tables and fire pits are provided. Restrooms with flush toilets and coin showers, a dump station, convenience store, and a playground are available. Gasoline and a boat launch are within five miles. Leashed pets are permitted in the campground.

**Reservations, fees:** Reservations are accepted. Tent sites are $20 per night, RV sites are $25 per night, $2 per night per extra person, and cabins are $59-69 per night. Weekly and monthly rates are available. Some credit cards are accepted. Open year-round, with higher rates November-March.

**Directions:** From Spokane, drive north on Highway 395 for about 70 miles to Colville. Take the Williams Lake exit and drive 18 miles to Highway 25. Turn right and drive to the Waneta customs sign. Turn right on Northport Waneta Road and drive five miles to the campground entrance.

**Contact:** Upper Columbia RV Park and Campground, 4706 Northport Waneta Rd., Colville, 509/732-4367, www.campingfriend.com/UpperColumbiaRVParkandCampground.

## 66 BIG MEADOW LAKE

### Scenic rating: 8

on Big Meadow Lake in Colville National Forest

Map 4.3, page 253            BEST

Big Meadow Lake is set at 3,400 feet elevation and has 71 surface acres. The camp, located in a scenic area, is quiet, remote, and relatively unknown, and the lake provides trout fishing. The U.S. Forest Service has built a wildlife-viewing platform, where ospreys, ducks, geese, and occasionally even moose, elk, and cougars may be spotted.

**Campsites, facilities:** There are 17 sites for tents or RVs up to 32 feet long and a historic cabin nearby. Fire grills and picnic tables are provided. Vault toilets are available. There is no drinking water, and garbage must be packed out. A boat launch, restrooms, and a wheelchair-accessible nature trail and fishing pier are available nearby. Some facilities are wheelchair accessible. Leashed pets are permitted.

**Reservations, fees:** Reservations are not accepted. There is no fee for camping. Open May-November, weather permitting.

**Directions:** From Spokane, drive north on U.S. 395 for 87 miles to Colville and Highway 20. Turn east on Highway 20 and drive one mile to Colville-Aladdin Northpoint Road (County Road 9435). Turn north and drive 20 miles to Meadow Creek Road. Turn right (east) and drive six miles to the campground on the right. Note: The surface of the access road changes dramatically depending on the season.

**Contact:** Colville National Forest, Three Rivers Ranger District, Colville Office, 509/684-7000, www.fs.usda.gov.

## 67 MILL POND
🏃 🏊 🚣 🐕 ♿ 🚐 ⛺

### Scenic rating: 6
near Sullivan Lake in Colville National Forest

Map 4.3, page 253

Mill Pond campground, located along the shore of a small reservoir just north of Sullivan Lake, offers a good base camp for backpackers. Note that boat size is limited to crafts that can be carried and hand launched; about a 50-foot walk from the parking area to the lake is necessary. A 1.5-mile hiking trail (no bikes) circles Mill Pond and ties into a historical and wheelchair-accessible interpretive trail (located at the opposite end of the lake). For more ambitious hikes, nearby Hall Mountain Trail and Elk Creek Trail provide beautiful valley and mountain views. Nearby Sullivan Lake is well known for giant, but elusive, brown trout; it produced the state record. There are also rainbow trout in the lake.

**Campsites, facilities:** There are 10 sites for tents or RVs up to 25 feet long. Picnic tables and fire grills are provided. Drinking water, vault toilets, and garbage service are available. Boats can be hand launched after a 50-foot walk; no gas motors are permitted. Supplies are available in Metaline Falls. Some facilities are wheelchair accessible. Leashed pets are permitted.

**Reservations, fees:** Reservations are not accepted. Sites are $16 per night, $8 per night extra vehicle fee. Open late May-early September, weather permitting.

**Directions:** From Spokane, drive north on U.S. 395 for six miles to U.S. 2. Turn northeast on U.S. 2 and drive 30 miles to the Metaline turnoff and Highway 211 North. Turn northwest on Highway 211 and drive 15 miles to Usk and Highway 20. Turn left (northwest) and drive 31 miles to Tiger and Highway 31. Continue (north) on Highway 31 and drive three miles to the sign marking the Sullivan Lake Ranger Station. Turn right on Sullivan Lake Road/County Road 9345 and drive a short distance, cross the bridge over the Pend Oreille River, and continue 13 miles to the campground on the left.

**Contact:** Colville National Forest, Sullivan Lake Ranger District, 509/446-7500, www.fs.usda.gov.

## 68 EAST SULLIVAN
🏃 🏊 🚣 🚤 🐕 ♿ 🚐 ⛺

### Scenic rating: 7
on Sullivan Lake in Colville National Forest

Map 4.3, page 253

East Sullivan campground is the largest on Sullivan Lake and by far the most popular. It fills up in summer. The camp is located on the lake's north shore. Some come here to try to catch giant brown trout or smaller, more plentiful rainbow trout. The boating and hiking are also good. The beautiful Salmo-Priest Wilderness is located just three miles to the east. It gets light use, which means quiet, private trails. This is a prime place to view wildlife, so carry binoculars while hiking for a chance to spot the rare woodland caribou and Rocky Mountain bighorn sheep. A nearby grass airstrip provides an opportunity for fly-in camping, but pilots should note that there are chuckholes present and holes from lots of ground squirrels. Only planes suited for primitive landing conditions should be flown in; check Federal Aviation Administration (FAA) guide to airports.

**Campsites, facilities:** There are 38 sites, including six double sites, for tents or RVs up to 55 feet long and one group site for up to 40 people; some sites are pull-through. Picnic tables and fire grills are provided. Drinking water and vault toilets are available. A boat dock, launching facilities, a picnic area, swimming area and floating platform, camp host, and dump station are nearby. Some facilities are wheelchair accessible. Leashed pets are permitted.

**Reservations, fees:** Reservations are accepted for individual sites and are required for the group site at 877/444-6777 ($10 reservation fee) or www.recreation.gov ($9 reservation fee). Sites are $16-32 per night, $8 per night extra vehicle fee, and the group site is $60 per night. Open mid-May-September, weather permitting.

**Directions:** From Spokane, drive north on U.S. 395 for six miles to U.S. 2. Turn northeast on U.S. 2 and drive 30 miles to the Metaline turnoff and Highway 211 North. Turn northwest on Highway 211 and drive 15 miles to Usk and Highway 20. Turn left (northwest) and drive 31 miles to Tiger and Highway 31. Continue (north) on Highway 31 and drive three miles to the sign marking the Sullivan Lake Ranger Station. Turn right on Sullivan Lake Road/County Road 9345 and drive a short distance, cross the bridge over the Pend Oreille River, and continue 12 miles to the campground on the left.

**Contact:** Colville National Forest, Sullivan Lake Ranger District, 509/446-7500 or 801/226-3564, www.fs.usda.gov.

## 69 WEST SULLIVAN

🏃 🚣 🐟 🚐 🐕 ♿ 🚙 ⛺

### Scenic rating: 7

on Sullivan Lake in Colville National Forest

**Map 4.3, page 253**

If East Sullivan is full, this small campground set along the northwestern shore of Sullivan Lake can fit the bill. This is a popular destination for boating, fishing for trout, swimming, sailing, waterskiing, and hiking. Beautiful Salmo-Priest Wilderness, three miles to the east, provides quiet, private trails. Wildlife-viewing is prime here; carry binoculars to spot caribou and bighorn sheep.

**Campsites, facilities:** There are 10 sites for tents or RVs up to 30 feet long. Picnic tables and fire grills are provided. Drinking water and vault toilets, a picnic shelter, a developed swimming beach, and a floating swim platform are available. A camp host is on-site. A dump station is within one mile. Some facilities are wheelchair accessible. Leashed pets are permitted.

**Reservations, fees:** Reservations are accepted at 877/444-6777 ($10 reservation fee) or www.recreation.gov ($9 reservation fee). Sites are $16 per night through mid-September, $8 extra vehicle fee; mid-September through October, sites are $8 per night with limited services until winter closure. Open mid-May-October 31, weather permitting.

**Directions:** From Spokane, drive north on U.S. 395 for six miles to U.S. 2. Turn northeast on U.S. 2 and drive 30 miles to the Metaline turnoff and Highway 211 North. Turn northwest on Highway 211 and drive 15 miles to Usk and Highway 20. Turn left (northwest) and drive 31 miles to Tiger and Highway 31. Continue (north) on Highway 31 and drive three miles to the sign marking the Sullivan Lake Ranger Station. Turn right on Sullivan Lake Road/County Road 9345 and drive a short distance, cross the bridge over the Pend Oreille River, and continue 12 miles to the campground on the left (set at the foot of Sullivan Lake, just across the road from the Sullivan Lake Ranger Station).

**Contact:** Colville National Forest, Sullivan Lake Ranger District, 509/446-7500, www.fs.usda.gov.

## 70 EDGEWATER

🚣 🚐 🐕 ♿ 🚙 ⛺

### Scenic rating: 6

on the Pend Oreille River in Colville National Forest

**Map 4.3, page 253**

Edgewater Camp is set on the shore of the Pend Oreille River about two miles downstream from the Box Canyon Dam. Although not far out of Ione, the camp has a primitive feel to it. Fishing for largemouth bass, rainbow trout, and brown trout is popular here, though suckers and squawfish present somewhat of a problem.

**Campsites, facilities:** There are 19 single sites and one double site for tents or RVs up to 72 feet long. Picnic tables and fire grills are provided. Drinking water is available until Labor Day. Vault toilets, garbage bins, and firewood are available. A boat launch and a picnic area are available nearby. Leashed pets are permitted.

**Reservations, fees:** Reservations are accepted at 877/444-6777 ($10 reservation fee) or www.recreation.gov ($9 reservation fee). Sites are $16-32 per night, $8 per extra vehicle per night. Open mid-May-early September, weather permitting.

**Directions:** From Spokane, drive north on U.S. 395 for six miles to U.S. 2. Turn northeast on U.S. 2 and drive 30 miles to the Metaline turnoff and Highway 211 North. Turn northwest on Highway 211 and drive 15 miles to Usk and Highway 20. Turn left (northwest) and drive 34 miles to Tiger and Highway 31. Continue on Highway 31 and drive 15 miles to the town of Metaline Falls (Highway 31 is known as Lehigh Avenue in town); continue 2.5 miles to Sullivan Lake Road (County Road 9345). Turn right (east) on Sullivan Lake Road and drive 0.25 mile to County Road 3669. Turn left (north) on County Road 3669 and drive two miles to the campground entrance road on the left. Turn left and drive 0.25 mile to the campground.

**Contact:** Colville National Forest, Sullivan Lake Ranger District, 509/446-7500, www.fs.usda.gov.

## 71 NOISY CREEK & NOISY CREEK GROUP

**Scenic rating: 7**

on Sullivan Lake in Colville National Forest

**Map 4.3, page 253**

This campground is situated on the southeast end of Sullivan Lake, adjacent to where Noisy Creek pours into Sullivan Lake. Note that the lake level can be drawn down for irrigation, leaving this camp well above the lake. Noisy Creek Trail near camp heads east along Noisy Creek and then north up to Hall Mountain

(elevation 6,323 feet), a distance of 5.3 miles; this is bighorn sheep country. The Lakeshore Trailhead is located at the nearby day-use area. Waterskiing is allowed on the 3.5-mile-long lake, and the boat ramp near the camp provides a good launch point.

**Campsites, facilities:** There are 19 sites for tents or RVs up to 45 feet long and one group camp for up to 50 people. If the group camp is not reserved, it is available as an overflow area. Picnic tables and fire grills are provided. Drinking water and flush toilets are available. A camp host is on-site. Boat-launching facilities and a picnic area are nearby. Some facilities are wheelchair accessible. Leashed pets are permitted.

**Reservations, fees:** Reservations are accepted for individual sites and required for the group camp at 877/444-6777 ($10 reservation fee) or www.recreation.gov ($9 reservation fee). Sites are $16 per night, $8 per night extra vehicle fee, and the group site is $60 per night. Open May-September, weather permitting.

**Directions:** From Spokane, drive north on U.S. 395 for six miles to U.S. 2. Turn northeast on U.S. 2 and drive 30 miles to the Metaline turnoff and Highway 211 North. Turn northwest on Highway 211 and drive 15 miles to Usk and Highway 20. Turn left (northwest) and drive 31 miles to Tiger and Highway 31. Continue (north) on Highway 31 and drive three miles to the sign marking the Sullivan Lake Ranger Station. Turn right on Sullivan Lake Road/County Road 9345 and drive a short distance, cross the bridge over the Pend Oreille River, and continue nine miles to the campground on the right (on the south end of Sullivan Lake).

**Contact:** Colville National Forest, Sullivan Lake Ranger District, 509/446-7500, www.fs.usda.gov.

## 72 IONE RV PARK AND MOTEL

### Scenic rating: 8

on the Pend Oreille River

**Map 4.3, page 253**

This camp is a good layover spot for campers with RVs or trailers who want to stay in town. The park sits on the shore of the Pend Oreille River, which offers fishing, swimming, several bike trails, and boating. The city park is adjacent to this property. In the winter, bighorn sheep may be spotted north of town.

**Campsites, facilities:** There are 19 sites for tents or RVs of any length (15, 20, and 30 amp full hookups), seven tent sites, and 11 motel rooms. Picnic tables are provided. Restrooms with flush toilets and showers, drinking water, dump station, and coin laundry are available. A store, café, and ice are located within one mile. Boat docks, launching facilities, and a park with a playground are nearby. Leashed pets are permitted.

**Reservations, fees:** Reservations are accepted. RV sites are $20 per night, tent sites are $5 per night. Some credit cards are accepted. Open year-round.

**Directions:** From Spokane, drive north on U.S. 2 for 48 miles to the junction with Highway 211 at the Washington/Idaho border. Turn west on Highway 211 and drive 48 miles northwest to Tiger and Highway 31. Turn right (north) on Highway 31 and drive four miles to Ione. Cross a spillway (it looks like a bridge) on Highway 31 and continue a short distance to the park on the right.

**Contact:** Ione RV Park and Motel, 509/442-3213.

## 73 DOUGLAS FALLS

### Scenic rating: 8

on Mill Creek

**Map 4.3, page 253**     **BEST (**

This campground is just outside of Colville in a wooded area along Mill Creek. A 0.2-mile walk from the campground takes you to a beautiful overlook of Douglas Falls. Another unique highlight is a cabled free-span bridge. And best of all, this camp is free!

**Campsites, facilities:** There are 12 sites for tents or RVs up to 30 feet long. Picnic tables and fire grills are provided. Vault toilets, drinking water, and a group picnic shelter are available. Garbage must be packed out. A camp host is on-site. A baseball field is nearby. Some facilities are wheelchair accessible. Leashed pets are permitted.

**Reservations, fees:** Reservations are not accepted. There is no fee for camping, but a Discover Pass is required. Open Memorial Day weekend-November, weather permitting.

**Directions:** From Spokane, drive north on U.S. 395 for 87 miles to Colville and Highway 20. Turn east on Highway 20 and drive 1.1 miles to Aladdin Road. Turn left (north) and drive two miles to Douglas Falls Road. Turn left and drive three miles to the campground on the left.

**Contact:** Department of Natural Resources, Northeast Region, 509/684-7474, www.dnr.wa.gov.

## 74 ROCKY LAKE

### Scenic rating: 6

near Colville

**Map 4.3, page 253**

The campground is set on Rocky Lake, a shallow, weedy pond lined with a lot of rocks. This camp is good for overnight camping, but nearby Douglas Falls is better for a long-term stay. Fishing for rainbow trout is an option. If you backtrack about 10 miles on Rocky Lake Road, you'll see the entrance signs for the Little Pend Oreille Wildlife Refuge, a premium area for hiking, fishing, hunting, and wildlife photography.

**Campsites, facilities:** There are seven sites for tents or RVs up to 20 feet long. Picnic tables and fire grills are provided. Vault toilets, drinking water, and a boat launch are available. Garbage must be packed out. Some facilities are wheelchair accessible. Leashed pets are permitted.

**Reservations, fees:** Reservations are not accepted. There is no fee for camping, but a Discover Pass is required. Sites are available from the Opening Day of fishing season to June 1; other times, the camp is open only for day-use. Call ahead to confirm.

**Directions:** From Spokane, drive north on U.S. 395 for 87 miles to Colville and Highway 20. Turn east on Highway 20 and drive six miles to Artman-Gibson Road. Turn right on Artman-Gibson Road and drive 3.2 miles to a one-lane gravel road. Turn right on the gravel road (unnamed) and drive about 0.5 mile. Bear left and continue another two miles to the campground.

**Contact:** Department of Natural Resources, Northeast Region, 509/684-7474, www.dnr. wa.gov.

## 75 STARVATION LAKE

🏊 🚐 🐕 ♿ 🚗 🏕

### Scenic rating: 8

near Colville

**Map 4.3, page 253**

Starvation Lake is only 15 feet deep and has a weed problem, so it's OK for trout fishing but not for swimming. It is possible to drown here if you get your feet tangled in the weeds. Ospreys and bald eagles frequent the area. It's advisable to obtain a detailed map of the area. The camp is used extensively by locals during the early fishing season (end of April-early June) but is not crowded thereafter, when the fishing becomes catch-and-release; check regulations. Boats must not exceed 16 feet.

**Campsites, facilities:** There are eight sites for tents or RVs up to 30 feet long. Some sites are pull-through. Picnic tables and fire grills are provided. Vault toilets, drinking water, primitive boat launch, and a fishing dock are

available. A camp host is on-site. Garbage must be packed out. Some facilities are wheelchair accessible. Leashed pets are permitted.

**Reservations, fees:** Reservations are not accepted. There is no fee for camping, but a Discover Pass is required. Open mid-April-November, weather permitting.

**Directions:** From Spokane, drive north on U.S. 395 for 74 miles to Colville and Highway 20. Turn east on Highway 20 and drive 10.5 miles to a gravel road (sign says Starvation Lake). Turn right on the gravel road and drive 0.3 mile to the intersection. Turn left and drive 0.5 mile to the campground on the right.

**Contact:** Department of Natural Resources, Northeast Region, 509/684-7474, www.dnr. wa.gov.

## 76 LITTLE TWIN LAKES

🏊 🚐 🐕 🚗 🏕

### Scenic rating: 6

on Little Twin Lakes in Colville National Forest

**Map 4.3, page 253**

Sites at this pretty, wooded campground on the shore of Little Twin Lakes have lake views and are free. Fishing is best here for cutthroat trout. Nearby Lake Roosevelt National Recreation Area offers recreation options, and side-trip ideas include Colville Tribal Museum and Grand Coulee Dam Visitor Center.

**Campsites, facilities:** There are seven sites for tents or RVs up to 16 feet long. Fire grills and picnic tables are provided. There is no drinking water. Vault toilets and firewood are available. Garbage must be packed out. Boat docks and launching facilities are located nearby. Leashed pets are permitted.

**Reservations, fees:** Reservations are not accepted. There is no fee for camping. Open May-early September, weather permitting.

**Directions:** From Spokane, drive north on U.S. 395 for 87 miles to Colville and Highway 20. Turn east on Highway 20 and drive 12.5 miles to County Road 4915. Turn left (northeast) and drive 1.5 miles to Forest Road 4939.

Turn right (north) and drive 4.5 miles to the campground on the right.

**Contact:** Colville National Forest, Three Rivers Ranger District, Colville Office, 509/684-7000, www.fs.usda.gov.

## 77 FLODELLE CREEK

### Scenic rating: 8

near Colville

**Map 4.3, page 253**

This campground is set where hiking, hunting, and fishing are quite good. It's advisable to obtain a detailed map of the area. Off-road vehicle trails are available at this camp and at nearby Sherry Creek camp, and they are often in use, so don't count on a particularly quiet camping experience. This spot can provide good fishing, best for brook trout. Wildlife includes black bears, moose, mosquitoes, and black gnats, the latter occasionally so prevalent that they are considered wildlife. Be prepared.

**Campsites, facilities:** There are eight sites for tents or RVs up to 30 feet long. Picnic tables and fire grills are provided. Vault toilets and drinking water are available. Garbage must be packed out. Some facilities are wheelchair accessible. Leashed pets are permitted.

**Reservations, fees:** Reservations are not accepted. There is no fee for camping, but a Discover Pass is required. Open May-November, weather permitting.

**Directions:** From Spokane, drive north on U.S. 395 for 87 miles to Colville and Highway 20. Turn east on Highway 20 and drive 19.4 miles to an unnamed two-lane gravel road on the right. Turn right on that road and drive 0.25 mile to the campground entrance road on the left.

**Contact:** Department of Natural Resources, Northeast Region, 509/684-7474, www.dnr.wa.gov.

## 78 SHERRY CREEK

### Scenic rating: 6

near Sherry Lake

**Map 4.3, page 253**

This old fire camp is set near the off-road vehicle (ORV) trail network of the Pend Oreille Lake system. It is located on Sherry Creek, about three miles from Sherry Lake and is basically a fishing camp, with lots of brook trout and a few rainbow trout. It's advisable to obtain a detailed map of the area. Biking and hiking on the ORV trails is an option. The 78-mile network of ORV trails can be accessed from this campground. This area has good numbers of black bears and even some moose, and because it is set next to a wetland, there can be tons of mosquitoes in summer. Snowmobiling and cross-country skiing are popular in the winter.

**Campsites, facilities:** There are 10 sites for tents or RVs up to 50 feet long, including three group sites for 12-16 people each. Some sites are pull-through. Picnic tables and fire pits are provided. Vault toilets, drinking water, and a ramp for unloading OHVs are available. Garbage must be packed out. Leashed pets are permitted.

**Reservations, fees:** Reservations are not accepted. There is no fee for camping, but a Discover Pass is required. Open May-November, weather permitting.

**Directions:** From Spokane, drive north on U.S. 395 for 74 miles to Colville and Highway 20. Turn east on Highway 20 and drive 23.8 miles to a gravel road. Turn right and drive approximately 0.5 mile to the campground.

**Contact:** Department of Natural Resources, Northeast Region, 509/684-7474, www.dnr.wa.gov.

## 79 LAKE GILLETTE

### Scenic rating: 8
on Lake Gillette in Colville National Forest

**Map 4.3, page 253**

This pretty and popular camp is situated right on the shore of Lake Gillette. Like neighboring East Gillette Campground, it fills up quickly in the summer. The camp is popular with off-road vehicle (OHV) users, primarily motorcyclists. An OHV system can't be accessed directly from the campground, but is close. Note that OHV riding in and out of camp is prohibited. Fishing at Lake Gillette is best for cutthroat trout.

**Campsites, facilities:** There are eight single sites and six double sites for tents or RVs up to 50 feet long. Fire grills and picnic tables are provided. Drinking water, vault toilets, bear-proof garbage bins, firewood, and an amphitheater are available. A camp host is on-site. A store, ice, gas, and a café are located within one mile. Boat docks, launching facilities, and rentals are nearby. Some facilities are wheelchair accessible. Leashed pets are permitted.

**Reservations, fees:** Reservations are not accepted. Single sites are $14 per night, double sites are $16 per night, $6 per extra vehicle per night. Open mid-May-early September, weather permitting.

**Directions:** From Spokane, drive north on U.S. 395 for 74 miles to Colville and Highway 20. Turn east on Highway 20 and drive 20 miles to County Road 4987 (Lake Gillette Road). Turn right (east) on Lake Gillette Road and drive 0.5 mile to the campground on the left.

**Contact:** Colville National Forest, Three Rivers Ranger District, Colville Office, 509/684-7000, www.fs.usda.gov.

## 80 GILLETTE

### Scenic rating: 7
near Lake Gillette in Colville National Forest

**Map 4.3, page 253**

This beautiful and extremely popular campground, located just south of Beaver Lodge Resort and Lake Thomas, is near Lake Gillette, one in a chain of four lakes. There are a few hiking and biking trails in the area. In winter, downhill and cross-country skiing is available.

**Campsites, facilities:** There are 30 sites for tents or RVs up to 55 feet long. Picnic tables and fire grills are provided. Drinking water, vault toilets, restrooms with flush toilets, and bear-proof garbage bins are available. A camp host is on-site. A store and ice are located within one mile. Boat docks, launching facilities, and rentals are nearby. Some facilities are wheelchair accessible. Leashed pets are permitted.

**Reservations, fees:** Reservations are not accepted. Sites are $14 per night, $6 per extra vehicle per night. Open late May-early September, weather permitting.

**Directions:** From Spokane, drive north on U.S. 395 for 74 miles to Colville and Highway 20. Turn east on Highway 20 and drive 20 miles to County Road 4987 (Lake Gillette Road). Turn right (east) on Lake Gillette Road and drive 0.5 mile to the campground on the right.

**Contact:** Colville National Forest, Three Rivers Ranger District, Colville Office, 509/684-7000, www.fs.usda.gov.

## 81 BEAVER LODGE RESORT

### Scenic rating: 9
on Lake Thomas

**Map 4.3, page 253**

This developed camp is set along the shore of Lake Gillette, one in a chain of four lakes. A highlight in this area: the numerous opportunities for off-road vehicles (OHVs) provided by a network of OHV trails. In addition, hiking trails and marked bike trails are close to the camp. In winter, downhill and cross-country skiing are available.

**Campsites, facilities:** There are 14 sites with full or partial hookups (30 amps) for tents or RVs up to 34 feet long, 24 sites for tents or RVs up to 40 feet (no hookups), and 10 cabins. Picnic tables and fire pits are provided. Restrooms with flush toilets and coin showers, drinking water, gasoline, propane gas, firewood, a convenience store, café, ice, boat rentals, and a playground are available. A dump station is located within one mile. Boat docks and launching facilities are nearby. Some facilities are wheelchair accessible. Leashed pets are permitted.

**Reservations, fees:** Reservations are accepted. Sites are $13-30 per night, cabins are $60-99, $5 per extra vehicle per night. Some credit cards are accepted. Open year-round.

**Directions:** From Spokane, drive north on U.S. 395/Division Street for 74 miles to Colville and Highway 20. Turn east on Highway 20 and drive 25 miles to the resort on the right.

**Contact:** Beaver Lodge Resort, 509/684-5657, www.beaverlodgeresort.org.

## 82 LAKE THOMAS

### Scenic rating: 6

on Lake Thomas in Colville National Forest

**Map 4.3, page 253**

This camp on the shore of Lake Thomas offers a less crowded alternative to the campgrounds at Lake Gillette. The lake provides fishing for cutthroat trout. Other nearby options include Lake Gillette and Beaver Lodge Resort, with trails, boating, and winter sports.

**Campsites, facilities:** There are 16 sites for tents or RVs up to 16 feet long. Picnic tables and fire grills are provided. Drinking water, vault toilets, and bear-proof garbage bins are available. A camp host is on-site. Boat docks,

launching facilities, and rentals are nearby. Some facilities are wheelchair accessible. Leashed pets are permitted.

**Reservations, fees:** Reservations are not accepted. Sites are $14 per night, $6 per extra vehicle per night. Open late May-early September, weather permitting; the boat ramp remains open until snow closure.

**Directions:** From Spokane, drive north on U.S. 395 for 74 miles to Colville and Highway 20. Turn east on Highway 20 and drive 20 miles to County Road 4987 (Lake Gillette Road). Turn right (east) on Lake Gillette Road and drive one mile to the campground on the left.

**Contact:** Colville National Forest, Three Rivers Ranger District, 509/684-7000, www.fs.usda.gov.

## 83 LAKE LEO

### Scenic rating: 6

on Lake Leo in Colville National Forest

**Map 4.3, page 253**

Lake Leo is the northernmost and quietest camp on the chain of lakes in the immediate vicinity. This lake provides fishing for cutthroat trout. Frater and Nile Lakes, both fairly small, are located one mile north. In winter, a Nordic ski trail starts adjacent to the camp. Fishing and boating are two recreation options here.

**Campsites, facilities:** There are eight sites for tents or RVs up to 30 feet long. Picnic tables and fire grills are provided. Drinking water, vault toilets, and bear-proof garbage bins are available. A boat ramp and launching facilities are nearby. Some facilities are wheelchair accessible. Leashed pets are permitted.

**Reservations, fees:** Reservations are not accepted. Sites are $12 per night, $6 per extra vehicle per night. Open mid-April-September, with reduced services and fees after Labor Day weekend; the boat ramp remains open until snow closure.

**Directions:** From Spokane on I-90, drive north on U.S. 395 for 74 miles to Colville and Highway 20. Turn east on Highway 20 and drive 23 miles to the campground entrance on the right.

**Contact:** Colville National Forest, Three Rivers Ranger District, 509/684-7000, www.fs.usda.gov.

## 84 BLUESLIDE RESORT

### Scenic rating: 7

on the Pend Oreille River

**Map 4.3, page 253**

This resort is situated along the western shore of the Pend Oreille River. It offers a headquarters for anglers and vacationers. Four or five bass tournaments are held each spring during May and June, and the river is stocked with both rainbow trout and bass. The resort offers full facilities for anglers, including tackle and a marina. The park is lovely, with grassy, shaded sites, and is located along the waterfowl migratory path. Lots of groups camp here in the summer. Recreation options include bicycling nearby. All-terrain vehicle (ATV) trails here can take you all the way to Canada.

**Campsites, facilities:** There are 49 sites with full or partial hookups (20, 30, and 50 amps), including four pull-through sites, for tents or RVs of any length, three tent sites, and five cabins. Picnic tables and fire pits are provided. Restrooms with flush toilets and showers, drinking water, a meeting hall, a community fire pit, several sports fields, a convenience store, propane, coin laundry, ice, firewood, a playground, basketball, tetherball, volleyball, horseshoe pits, a seasonal heated swimming pool, boat docks, and launching facilities are available. Leashed pets are permitted.

**Reservations, fees:** Reservations are accepted. Sites are $25-50 per night. Some credit cards are accepted. Open mid-May-mid-October.

**Directions:** From Spokane, drive north on Division Street for six miles to U.S. 2. Turn

north on U.S. 2 and drive 26 miles northeast to Highway 211. Turn left and drive 18 miles to Highway 20. Turn left and drive 22 miles to the park (located on the right at Milepost 400).

**Contact:** Blueslide Resort, 509/445-1327, www.blueslideresort.com.

## 85 PANHANDLE

### Scenic rating: 9

on the Pend Oreille River in Colville National Forest

**Map 4.3, page 253**

Among tall trees and with views of the river, this is a scenic spot to set up camp along the eastern shore of the Pend Oreille River. This camp is located in an area of mature trees and makes a good base for a fishing or waterskiing trip. Fishing for largemouth and smallmouth bass is popular, with an annual bass tournament held every summer in the area. A network of hiking trails can be accessed by taking forest roads to the east.

**Campsites, facilities:** There are 13 sites for tents or RVs up to 33 feet long. Picnic tables and fire grills are provided. Drinking water, vault toilets, bear-proof garbage bins, and firewood are available. A camp host is on-site. A small boat launch is nearby. Some facilities are wheelchair accessible. Leashed pets are permitted.

**Reservations, fees:** Reservations are accepted at 877/444-6777 ($10 reservation fee) or www.recreation.gov ($9 reservation fee). Sites are $16 per night, $8 extra vehicle fee. Open late May-early September, weather permitting; the boat ramp remains open until snow closure.

**Directions:** From Spokane, drive north on U.S. 395/Division Street for six miles to U.S. 2. Turn north on U.S. 2 and drive 30 miles to the Metaline turnoff and Highway 211 North. Take Highway 211 North and drive 15 miles to the junction of Highway 20. Cross Highway 20, driving through the town of Usk. Continue across the Pend Oreille River to Le Clerc Road.

Turn left and drive 15 miles north on Le Clerc Road to the campground on the left.
**Contact:** Colville National Forest, Newport Ranger District, 509/447-7300, www.fs.usda.gov.

## 86 BROWNS LAKE
🚶 🏊 🚣 🎣 🛶 🏕 ♿ 🚐 ⛰

**Scenic rating: 8**
on Browns Lake in Colville National Forest

**Map 4.3, page 253**

This campground is set along the shore of Browns Lake, with lakeside sites bordering old-growth hemlock and cedar. No motorized boats are permitted on the lake, and only fly-fishing is allowed, so it can be ideal for float tubes, canoes, and prams. A 1.25-mile hiking trail leaves the campground and ties into a wheelchair-accessible interpretive trail with beautiful views along the way. At the end of the trail sits a fishing-viewing platform in Browns Creek, which feeds into the lake. South Skookum Lake is about five miles away.

**Campsites, facilities:** There are 18 sites for tents or RVs up to 28 feet long. Picnic tables and fire grills are provided. Vault toilets are available. There is no drinking water. A primitive boat launch is available for small boats, such as canoes, rowboats, and inflatables. Some facilities are wheelchair accessible. Leashed pets are permitted.

**Reservations, fees:** Reservations are not accepted. Sites are $14 per night until early September, then $8 per night until October 31; $8 per extra vehicle per night. Open May-end October, weather permitting.

**Directions:** From Spokane, drive north on U.S. 395/Division Street for six miles to U.S. 2. Turn north on U.S. 2 and drive 30 miles to the Metaline turnoff and Highway 211 North. Turn northwest on Highway 211 and drive 15 miles to Usk and Highway 20. Drive north on Highway 20 a short distance to County Road 3389. Turn right (east) on Kings Lake-Boswell Road (County Road 3389) and drive

(over the Pend Oreille River) five miles to a fork with Forest Road 5030. Turn left and drive three miles to the campground at the end of the road.
**Contact:** Colville National Forest, Newport Ranger District, 509/447-7300, www.fs.usda.gov.

## 87 SKOOKUM CREEK
🚶 🚴 🏊 🎣 🛶 🏕 🏊 🐕 ♿ 🚐 ⛰

**Scenic rating: 5**
near the Pend Oreille River

**Map 4.3, page 253**

Skookum Creek campground is set in a wooded area along Skookum Creek, about 1.5 miles from where it empties into the Pend Oreille River. It's a good canoeing spot, has drinking water, and gets little attention. And you can't beat the price of admission—free.

**Campsites, facilities:** There are 10 sites for tents or RVs up to 30 feet long. Picnic tables and fire grills are provided. Drinking water and vault toilets are available. Garbage must be packed out. A group picnic shelter with a barbecue is available nearby. Some facilities are wheelchair accessible. Leashed pets are permitted.

**Reservations, fees:** Reservations are not accepted. There is no fee for camping, but a Discover Pass is required. Open mid-April-October, weather permitting.

**Directions:** From Spokane, drive north on U.S. 395 for six miles to U.S. 2. Turn north on U.S. 2 and drive 41 miles to Newport and Highway 20. Turn west on Highway 20 and drive 16 miles northwest to the town of Usk. Continue east across the bridge for 0.9 mile to Le Clerc Road. Turn right on Le Clerc Road and drive 2.2 miles to a one-lane gravel road. Turn left and drive a short distance to another gravel road. Turn left and drive 0.25 mile to the campground.
**Contact:** Department of Natural Resources, Northeast Region, 509/684-7474, www.dnr.wa.gov.

## 88 SOUTH SKOOKUM LAKE

### Scenic rating: 7

on South Skookum Lake in Colville National Forest

**Map 4.3, page 253**

This camp is situated on the western shore of South Skookum Lake, at the foot of Kings Mountain (elevation 4,383 feet). This is a good fishing lake, stocked with cutthroat trout, and is popular with families. A 1.3-mile hiking trail circles the water. South Baldy, a staffed fire lookout, is nearby and is a nice day-hike destination.

**Campsites, facilities:** There are 25 sites for tents or RVs up to 30 feet long. Picnic tables and fire rings are provided. Drinking water, garbage bins, and vault toilets are available. A camp host is on-site. A boat ramp for small boats and several docks, including a wheelchair-accessible fishing dock, are available nearby. Some facilities are wheelchair accessible. Leashed pets are permitted.

**Reservations, fees:** Reservations are not accepted. Sites are $16 per night, $8 per extra vehicle per night. Open late May-September, weather permitting.

**Directions:** From Spokane, drive north on U.S. 395/Division Street for six miles to U.S. 2. Turn north on U.S. 2 and drive 30 miles to the Metaline turnoff and Highway 211. Turn northwest on Highway 211 and drive 15 miles to Usk and Highway 20. Drive north on Highway 20 a short distance to Kings Lake-Boswell Road (County Road 3389). Turn right (east) on Kings Lake-Boswell Road and drive eight miles (over the Pend Oreille River) to the campground entrance road on the right. Turn right and drive 0.25 mile to the campground.

**Contact:** Colville National Forest, Newport Ranger District, 509/447-7300, www.fs.usda.gov.

## 89 PIONEER PARK

### Scenic rating: 8

on the Pend Oreille River in Colville National Forest

**Map 4.3, page 253**

Pioneer Park Campground is set along the shore of Box Canyon Reservoir on the Pend Oreille River near Newport. The launch and adjoining parking area are suitable for larger boats. Waterskiing and water sports are popular here. There is a wheelchair-accessible interpretive trail with a boardwalk and beautiful views of the river. Signs along the way explain the history of the Kalispel tribe.

**Campsites, facilities:** There are 17 sites for tents or RVs up to 33 feet long. Picnic tables and fire rings are provided. Drinking water, vault toilets, bear-proof garbage bins, firewood, and a sheltered picnic area are available. A camp host is on-site. Boat docks, launching facilities, and rentals are nearby. Some facilities are wheelchair accessible. Leashed pets are permitted.

**Reservations, fees:** Reservations are accepted at 877/444-6777 ($10 reservation fee) or www.recreation.gov ($9 reservation fee). Sites are $16 per night, $8 extra vehicle fee. Open early May-early September, weather permitting.

**Directions:** From Spokane, drive north on U.S. 395 for six miles to U.S. 2. Turn north on U.S. 2 and drive 41 miles to Newport. Continue across the Pend Oreille River to Le Clerc Road (County Road 9305). Turn left on Le Clerc Road and drive two miles to the campground on the left.

**Contact:** Colville National Forest, Newport Ranger District, 509/447-7300, www.fs.usda.gov.

## 90 THE 49ER MOTEL & RV PARK

🚶 🚲 🏊 ❄️ 🐕 🚐 ⛺

### Scenic rating: 6

near Chewelah

**Map 4.3, page 253**

This region is the heart of mining country. The park has grassy sites and is located next to a motel in a mountainous setting. Nearby recreation options include a 27-hole golf course, hiking trails, and marked bike trails. This park is a good deal for RV cruisers—a rustic setting right in town. In winter, note that the 49 Degrees North Ski & Snowboard Park is located 12 miles to the east.

**Campsites, facilities:** There are 26 sites for tents or RVs up to 40 feet long (20 and 30 amp full hookups) and 13 motel rooms. Most sites are pull-through. Picnic tables are provided. Restrooms with flush toilets and showers, drinking water, a dump station, cable TV, and phone hookups are available. Propane gas, gasoline, a store, café, ice, and coin laundry are within one mile. Leashed pets are permitted.

**Reservations, fees:** Reservations are accepted. RV sites are $22 per night, tent sites are $10 per person per night, $5 pet fee per stay. Weekly and monthly rates available. Some credit cards are accepted. Open year-round.

**Directions:** From Spokane, drive north on U.S. 395 for 44 miles to Chewelah; the park is on the right (on U.S. 395 at the south edge of town, well marked).

**Contact:** The 49er Motel & RV Park, 509/935-8613 or 888/412-1994, www.49er-motel.com.

## 91 WINONA BEACH RESORT

🏊 🎣 🚣 🚐 🐕 ♿ 🚐 ⛺

### Scenic rating: 9

on Waitts Lake

**Map 4.3, page 253**

This beautiful and comfortable resort on the shore of Waitts Lake has spacious sites and friendly folks. The park fills up in July and August, and during this time cabins are available for rent (by the week, not the night). In the spring, fishing for brown trout and rainbow trout can be quite good. The trout head to deeper water in the summer, and bluegill and perch are easier to catch then. Waterskiing is also popular.

**Campsites, facilities:** There are 54 sites with full hookups (30 amps), including 20 lakeside sites, and three sites with partial hookups (electricity and water) for tents or RVs up to 40 feet long, seven sites for tents, and eight cabins. Picnic tables and fire rings are provided. Restrooms with flush toilets and coin showers, drinking water, a dump station, firewood, a snack bar, general store, playground, volleyball, horseshoe pits, basketball, a swimming beach, an antique store, and ice are available. Boat docks, launching facilities, and boat rentals are on-site. Some facilities are wheelchair accessible. Leashed pets are permitted.

**Reservations, fees:** Reservations are accepted. RV sites are $29 per night, tent sites are $20 per night, $2 per extra vehicle per night, $3.50 per night per extra person over four, and $3.50 per pet per night. Weekly and monthly rates available. Some credit cards are accepted. Open April-September.

**Directions:** From Spokane, drive north on U.S. 395 for 42 miles to the Valley-Waitts Lake exit. Turn left (west) at that exit and drive one mile to Highway 231. Turn right (north) on Highway 231 and drive 1.5 miles to the town of Valley and Valley-Waitts Lake Road. Turn left and drive three miles to Winona Beach Road. Turn left and drive 0.25 mile to the resort at the end of the road.

**Contact:** Winona Beach Resort, 509/937-2231, www.winonabeach.com.

## 92 SILVER BEACH RESORT

🚶 🏊 🎣 🚐 🐕 ♿ 🚣 🚐

### Scenic rating: 6

on Waitts Lake

**Map 4.3, page 253**

Silver Beach Resort offers grassy sites on the

shore of Waitts Lake, where fishing and waterskiing are popular. In the spring, fishing for brown trout and rainbow trout can be quite good.

**Campsites, facilities:** There are 51 sites for RVs up to 36 feet long (30 amp full hookups), including two pull-through sites, and six cabins. Picnic tables are provided and fire pits can be rented. Restrooms with flush toilets and coin showers, drinking water, Wi-Fi, propane gas, a dump station, convenience store, restaurant, coin laundry, ice, firewood, a playground, boat docks, launching facilities, and boat rentals are available. Some facilities are wheelchair accessible. Leashed pets are permitted.

**Reservations, fees:** Reservations are accepted. Sites are $35 per night, $4 per person per night for more than two people, and $3.50 per pet per night. Cabins are $95-130 per night. Weekly rates are available. Some credit cards are accepted. Open mid-April-mid-September.

**Directions:** From Spokane, drive north on U.S. 395 for 42 miles to the Valley-Waitts Lake exit. Turn left (west) at that exit and drive six miles to Waitts Lake and the resort on the left-hand side near the shore of the lake.

**Contact:** Silver Beach Resort, 509/937-2811, www.silverbeachresort.net.

## 93 TEALS WAITTS LAKE RESORT

**Scenic rating: 7**

on Waitts Lake

**Map 4.3, page 253**

The shore of Waitts Lake is home to this clean, comfortable resort, where lake views are available and ice fishing is popular in the winter. Hunting is possible in the fall. Waterskiing is also popular.

**Campsites, facilities:** There are 21 sites for tents or RVs up to 40 feet long (30 amp full hookups). Picnic tables and fire rings are provided. Restrooms with flush toilets and showers, drinking water, a camp store, restaurant,

firewood, boat docks, boat rentals, launching facilities, and ice are available. Leashed pets are permitted.

**Reservations, fees:** Reservations are accepted. Sites are $28-38 per night, $7 per extra person per night, $7 per pet per night. Some credit cards are accepted. Open year-round.

**Directions:** From Spokane, drive north on U.S. 395 for 42 miles to the Valley-Waitts Lake exit. Turn left (west) at that exit and drive one mile to Highway 231. Turn right (north) on Highway 231 and drive 1.5 miles to the town of Valley and Valley-Waitts Lake Road. Turn left and drive three miles to the resort on the left.

**Contact:** Teals Waitts Lake Resort, 509/937-2400.

## 94 JUMP OFF JOE LAKE RESORT

**Scenic rating: 7**

on Jump Off Joe Lake

**Map 4.3, page 253**

Located on the edge of Jump Off Joe Lake, this wooded campground offers lake views and easy boating access. Recreational activities include boating, fishing, and swimming. Spokane and Grand Coulee Dam are both within a short drive and provide excellent side-trip options. Within 10 miles to the north are an 18-hole golf course and casino.

**Campsites, facilities:** There are 20 sites for tents, 20 sites for tents or RVs of any length (30 amp full hookups), and five cabins. Picnic tables and fire rings are provided. Restrooms with flush toilets and coin showers, drinking water, horseshoe pits, recreation field, a swimming beach, a convenience store, and a picnic area are available. The resort also rents boats and has a boat ramp and dock. Some facilities are wheelchair accessible. Leashed pets are permitted.

**Reservations, fees:** Reservations are accepted. Sites are $24-26 per night, $5 per night

per extra person, $5 per pet per night. Some credit cards are accepted. Open April-October.
**Directions:** From Spokane, drive north on U.S. 395 for about 40 miles (three miles south of the town of Valley) to the Jump Off Joe Road exit (Milepost 198). Take that exit, turn west, and drive 1.2 miles to the resort on the right.
**Contact:** Jump Off Joe Lake Resort, 509/937-2133.

## 95 SHORE ACRES RESORT

**Scenic rating: 8**

on Loon Lake

**Map 4.3, page 253**      **BEST (**

Located along the shore of Loon Lake at 2,400 feet elevation, this family-oriented campground has a long expanse of beach and offers an alternative to Granite Point Park across the lake. Some sites have lake views. Loon Lake is approximately four miles long, and waterskiing, wakeboarding, and personal watercraft are allowed. Fishing is best for mackinaw trout in spring (downriggers suggested) as well as kokanee salmon and rainbow trout. Warm weather brings perch, sunfish, and bass out of their hiding places.

**Campsites, facilities:** There are 25 sites for RVs up to 40 feet long (full hookups) and 11 cabins. Picnic tables are provided. Restrooms with flush toilets and showers, drinking water, a dump station, cable TV, a general store, restaurant, tackle, firewood, ice, community fire pits, a playground, a swimming area, boat docks, personal watercraft and boat rentals, moorage, and launching facilities are available. Some facilities are wheelchair accessible. Leashed pets are permitted with certain restrictions.

**Reservations, fees:** Reservations are accepted. Sites are $35-40 per night, $6.50 per night per extra person, $4 per night per extra vehicle, and $5 per pet per night. Cabins are $115-140 per night. Weekly and monthly rates available. Some credit cards are accepted. Open mid-April-September.

**Directions:** From Spokane, drive north on U.S. 395 for 30 miles to Highway 292. Turn left (west) on Highway 292 and drive two miles to Shore Acres Road. Turn left and drive another two miles to the resort.
**Contact:** Shore Acres Resort, 509/233-2474, www.shoreacresresort.com.

## 96 GRANITE POINT PARK

**Scenic rating: 8**

on Loon Lake

**Map 4.3, page 253**

This camp is located on the shore of Loon Lake, a clear, clean, spring-fed lake that covers 1,200 acres and features a sandy beach and swimming area. The RV park features grass sites—no concrete. In the spring, mackinaw trout range 4-30 pounds and can be taken by deepwater trolling (downriggers suggested). Easier to catch are kokanee salmon and rainbow trout in the 12- to 14-inch class. A sprinkling of perch, sunfish, and bass come out of their hiding places when the weather heats up. Waterskiing and windsurfing are popular in summer months, and personal watercraft are allowed.

**Campsites, facilities:** There are 80 sites with full hookups (30 amps) for RVs up to 40 feet long and 27 cottages with kitchens. Note that some spots are filled with long-term renters. Picnic tables are provided. Restrooms with flush toilets and showers, drinking water, a recreation hall, convenience store, café, coin laundry, ice, a playground, basketball and volleyball courts, horseshoe pits, three swimming areas with a 0.75-mile beach, two swimming docks, boat docks, boat rentals, and launching facilities are available. Propane gas is located within one mile.

**Reservations, fees:** Reservations are accepted. Sites are $32-35 per night. Weekly and monthly rates available. Open May-September.
**Directions:** From Spokane, drive north on U.S. 395/Division Street for 26 miles (8 miles

past the town of Deer Park) to the park on the left.

**Contact:** Granite Point Park, 509/233-2100, www.granitepointpark.com.

## 97 PEND OREILLE COUNTY PARK

**Scenic rating: 6**

near Newport

**Map 4.3, page 253**

This 440-acre park is wooded and features eight miles of trails throughout for hikers, bicyclists, and equestrians. There is some road noise from U.S. 2, but it's not intolerable. Pend Oreille is the only campground around, and it's not a bad choice if you're looking for a layover spot. It's a good alternative to the often-crowded Mount Spokane State Park. Nearby activities include fishing and hunting.

**Campsites, facilities:** There are 17 sites for tents only. Picnic tables and fire pits are provided. Restrooms with flush toilets, drinking water, firewood, and a picnic area are available. A camp host is on-site. Some facilities are wheelchair accessible. Leashed pets are permitted.

**Reservations, fees:** Reservations are not accepted. Sites are $10 per night. Open late May-early September, weather permitting.

**Directions:** From Spokane, drive north on U.S. 395/Division Street for six miles to U.S. 2. Turn north on U.S. 2 and drive 31 miles to the county park entrance on the left (west side). Or from Newport: Drive east on U.S 2 for 15 miles (past County Road 211) to the park entrance on the right.

**Contact:** Pend Oreille County, Department of Public Works, 509/447-4821, www.pendoreilleco.org.

## 98 LAKESHORE RV PARK AND MARINA

**Scenic rating: 7**

on Lake Chelan

**Map 4.4, page 254**

This municipal park and marina on Lake Chelan is a popular family camp, with fishing, swimming, boating, waterskiing, personal watercraft, and hiking among the available activities. City amenities are within walking distance. The camp fills up in the summer, including on weekdays in July and August. This RV park covers 22 acres, featuring a large marina and a 15-acre day-use area. An 18-hole championship golf course and putting green, lighted tennis courts, a water-slide park, bowling alley, and a visitors center are nearby. A casino is six miles west of Chelan. A trip worth taking, the ferry ride goes to several landings on the lake; the ferry terminal is 0.5 mile from the park.

**Campsites, facilities:** There are 165 sites for tents or RVs up to 40 feet long (30 and 50 amp full hookups). Some sites are pull-through. Picnic tables are provided. Restrooms with flush toilets and coin showers, Wi-Fi, cable TV, a dump station, a covered picnic area, playground, putting course, Rally Alley, snack bar, swimming beaches, tennis courts, volleyball, and basketball are available. A store, café, coin laundry, ice, and propane gas are available within one mile. A marina with boat docks, paddleboard and watercraft rentals, and launching facilities are on-site. Some facilities are wheelchair accessible. Leashed pets are permitted, except during some holiday periods.

**Reservations, fees:** Reservations are accepted at 509/682-8023 ($5 reservation fee). RV sites are $28-55 per night, $5 per person per night for more than four people, $6 per night per additional vehicle; tent sites are $22-35 per night. Monthly rates available November 1-April 30. Some credit cards are accepted. Open year-round.

**Directions:** From Wenatchee, drive north on

U.S. 97-A for 38 miles to Chelan (after crossing the Dan Gordon Bridge, the road name changes to Saunders Street). Continue for 0.1 mile to Johnson Street. Turn left and drive 0.2 mile (becomes Highway 150/Manson Highway) to the campground on the left.

**Contact:** City of Chelan, Lakeshore RV Park and Marina, 509/682-8023, www.chelancityparks.com.

## 99 COULEE PLAYLAND RESORT

**Scenic rating: 7**

near the Grand Coulee Dam

**Map 4.4, page 254**

This park on North Banks Lake, south of the Grand Coulee Dam, is pretty and well treed, with spacious sites for both tents and RVs. The Grand Coulee Laser Light Show (seasonal) is just three miles away and is well worth a visit. Boating, fishing for many species, waterskiing, and personal watercraft are all popular. In addition, hiking trails, marked bike trails, a full-service marina, and tennis courts are close by.

**Campsites, facilities:** There are 65 sites with full or partial hookups (20, 30, and 50 amps) for tents or RVs of any length, seven tent sites, and one yurt. Some sites are pull-through. Picnic tables and fire grills are provided. Restrooms with flush toilets and coin showers, a dump station, Wi-Fi, a general store, coin laundry, firewood, ice, a playground, boat docks, launching facilities, boat rentals, gas, and a bait and tackle shop are available. Propane gas and a café are located within one mile. Some facilities are wheelchair accessible. Leashed pets are permitted.

**Reservations, fees:** Reservations are accepted. Sites are $37-44 per night, $6 per extra person per night. The yurt is $99 per night. Some credit cards are accepted. Open year-round, with limited winter facilities.

**Directions:** From the junction of Highway 17 and U.S. 2 (north of Ephrata), drive east on U.S. 2 for five miles to Highway 155. Turn left (north) and drive 26 miles to Grand Coulee and Electric City. The resort is just off the highway on the left.

**Contact:** Coulee Playland Resort, 509/633-2671 or 888/633-2671, www.couleeplayland.com.

## 100 STEAMBOAT ROCK STATE PARK

**Scenic rating: 10**

on Banks Lake

**Map 4.4, page 254**

Steamboat Rock State Park is surrounded by desert. The park covers 3,522 acres and features nine miles of shoreline along Banks Lake, a reservoir created by the Grand Coulee Dam. A column of basaltic rock, with a surface area of 600 acres, rises 800 feet above the lake. Two campground areas and a large day-use area are set on green lawns sheltered by tall poplars. The park has 13 miles of hiking and biking trails, as well as 10 miles of horse trails. There is also a swimming beach. Fishing and waterskiing are popular; so is rock climbing. A hiking trail leads to Northrup Lake. Horse trails are also available in nearby Northrup Canyon. The one downer is mosquitoes, which are very prevalent in early summer. During the winter, the park is used by snowmobilers, cross-country skiers, and ice anglers.

**Campsites, facilities:** There are 100 sites with full hookups (50 amps) for RVs up to 50 feet long, 26 sites for tents or RVs up to 30 feet long (no hookups), 80 primitive sites (including five equestrian sites), 12 hike-in/boat-in sites, and a group site for 20-50 people. Picnic tables and fire grills are provided. Restrooms with flush toilets and coin showers, a dump station, firewood, a café, a playground, and volleyball are available. Boat-launching facilities, docks, moorage, and a marine dump station are nearby. Some facilities are wheelchair accessible. Leashed pets are permitted.

**Reservations, fees:** Reservations are accepted (except for primitive sites) at 888/CAMP-OUT (888/226-7688) or www.parks.wa.gov/reservations ($6.50-8.50 reservation fee). Sites are $17-42 per night, primitive sites are $12 per night, $10 per extra vehicle per night. Some credit cards are accepted. Open year-round, with limited winter facilities.

**Directions:** From East Wenatchee, drive north on U.S. 2 for 70 miles to Highway 155 (5 miles east of Coulee City). Turn north and drive 16 miles to the park on the left.

**Contact:** Steamboat Rock State Park, 509/633-1304; state park information, 360/902-8844, www.parks.wa.gov.

## 101 COULEE CITY PARK

### Scenic rating: 6

on Banks Lake

Map 4.4, page 254

Coulee City Park is a well-maintained park located in shade trees on the southern shore of 30-mile-long Banks Lake. You can see the highway from the park, and there is some highway noise. Campsites are usually available. The busiest time of the year is Memorial Day weekend because of the local rodeo. Boating, fishing, waterskiing, and riding personal watercraft are popular. A one-mile walking trail leads from the campground and meanders along the eastern shore of the lake. An 18-hole golf course is close by.

**Campsites, facilities:** There is a large grassy area for tents and 55 sites for tents or RVs of any length (30 and 50 amp full hookups). Some sites are pull-through. Picnic tables and fire rings are provided. Restrooms with flush toilets and showers, group fire pits, a dump station, swimming beach, and a playground are available. Propane gas, gasoline, firewood, a store, restaurant, coin laundry, and ice are located within one mile. Boat docks and launching facilities are on-site. Some facilities are wheelchair accessible. Leashed pets are permitted.

**Reservations, fees:** Reservations are not accepted. Sites are $25-30 per night, $5 per extra vehicle per night. Open April-late October, weather permitting.

**Directions:** From Coulee City, drive east on U.S. 2 for 0.5 mile to the park on the left. The park is within the city limits.

**Contact:** Coulee City Park, 509/632-5331, www.couleecity.com.

## 102 SUN LAKES STATE PARK

### Scenic rating: 10

on Park Lake

Map 4.4, page 254    BEST (

Sun Lakes State Park is situated on the shore of Park Lake, which is used primarily by anglers, boaters, and water-skiers. This 4,027-acre park features 12 miles of shoreline and nine lakes. A trail at the north end of Lake Lenore (a 15-minute car drive) leads to the Lake Lenore Caves. Dry Falls, a former waterfall, lies near the foot of the park. The cascades are history, however, and now only a barren 3.5-mile-wide, 400-foot climb awaits. An interpretive center at Dry Falls is open May-September. Nearby recreation possibilities include a nine-hole golf course and miniature golf.

**Campsites, facilities:** There are 152 sites for tents or RVs (no hookups), 39 sites for RVs up to 65 feet long (30 and 50 amp full hookups), and one group camp for 20-100 people. Picnic tables and fire pits are provided. Restrooms with flush toilets and coin showers, a dump station, snack bar, coin laundry, ice, horseshoe pits, playground, drinking water, and firewood are available. A store is located within one mile. Boat docks, launching facilities, moorage, and boat rentals are nearby. Some facilities are wheelchair accessible. Leashed pets are permitted.

**Reservations, fees:** Reservations are accepted at 888/CAMP-OUT (888/226-7688) or www.goingtocamp.com ($6.50 reservation fee). Sites are $23-37 per night, the group site is $69.50-278.05 per night. Some credit cards are accepted. Open year-round.

**Directions:** From Ephrata, drive northeast on Highway 28 to Soap Lake and Highway 17. Turn left (north) on Highway 17 and drive 17 miles to the park on the right.

**Contact:** Sun Lakes State Park, 509/632-5583; state park information, 360/902-8844, www. parks.wa.gov.

## 103 SUN LAKES PARK RESORT

**Scenic rating: 6**

in Sun Lakes State Park

**Map 4.4, page 254**

Run by the concessionaire that operates within Sun Lakes State Park, this camp offers full facilities and is a slightly more developed alternative to the state park's campground.

**Campsites, facilities:** There are 119 sites for tents or RVs of any length (20, 30, and 50 amp full hookups) and 61 cabins. Some sites are pull-through. Picnic tables are provided. Campers may use their own barbecue; all fires must be off the ground and self-contained. Restrooms with flush toilets and coin showers, propane gas, dump station, convenience store and gift shop, firewood, snack bar, coin laundry, ice, a playground, boat rentals, a seasonal heated swimming pool, miniature golf, and a nine-hole golf course are available. Boat docks and launching facilities are nearby. Some facilities are wheelchair accessible. Leashed pets are permitted.

**Reservations, fees:** Reservations are accepted. Sites are $36-42 per night, $5 per extra vehicle per night. Open mid-April-mid-October, weather permitting.

**Directions:** From Ephrata, drive northeast on Highway 28 to Soap Lake and Highway 17. Turn left (north) on Highway 17 and drive 17 miles to the Sun Lakes Park on the right. Enter the park and drive to the resort (well marked).

**Contact:** Sun Lakes Park Resort, 509/632-5291, www.sunlakesparkresort.com.

## 104 BLUE LAKE RESORT

**Scenic rating: 6**

on Blue Lake

**Map 4.4, page 254**

Blue Lake Resort is set in a desertlike area along the shore of Blue Lake between Sun Lakes State Park and Lake Lenore Caves State Park. Both parks make excellent side trips. Activities at Blue Lake include trout fishing, swimming, boating, waterskiing, and riding personal watercraft. Tackle and boat rentals are available at the resort. Blue Lake is one of the most popular Opening Day lakes in Washington and is regularly planted with rainbow, brown, and tiger trout fingerlings.

**Campsites, facilities:** There are 80 sites with full or partial hookups, including six pull-through sites, for RVs of any length, 30 tent sites, and 10 cabins. Picnic tables and fire pits are provided. Restrooms with flush toilets and showers, a dump station, firewood, Wi-Fi, a store, propane, ice, tackle, RV and boat storage, a roped swimming area, volleyball, a playground, horseshoe pits, badminton, and a marina with boat docks, launching facilities, fish-cleaning station, boat fuel, and boat rentals are available. Some facilities are wheelchair accessible. Leashed pets are permitted.

**Reservations, fees:** Reservations are accepted at 509/632-5364 or www.bluelakeresortwashington.com. Sites are $22 per night, plus $5 per person per night for more than four people, $5 per night for additional vehicle. Some credit cards are accepted. Open April-September.

**Directions:** From the junction of I-90 and Highway 17 (just south of Moses Lake), drive north on Highway 17 for 36 miles to the resort on the right. The resort is 15 miles south of Coulee City.

**Contact:** Blue Lake Resort, 509/632-5364 or 509/632-5388, www.bluelakeresortwashington.com.

## 105 LAURENT'S SUN VILLAGE RESORT

🚶‍♂️🚲🏊🛶🚤🎣🐕🚙🏕️

**Scenic rating: 6**

on Blue Lake

**Map 4.4, page 254**

Like Blue Lake Resort, this campground is situated along the shore of Blue Lake. The hot desert setting is perfect for swimming and fishing. Late July and early August are the busiest times of the year here. Nearby recreation possibilities include a nine-hole golf course and miniature golf.

**Campsites, facilities:** There are 95 sites, most with full hookups, for RVs of any length and four tent sites. Some sites are pull-through. Picnic tables are provided. Restrooms with flush toilets and coin showers, group fire pits, propane gas, dump station, coin laundry, a store, café, bait and tackle, ice, firewood, a playground, boat docks, launching facilities, and boat rentals are available. Leashed pets are permitted.

**Reservations, fees:** Reservations are accepted. Sites are $28 per night, $3 per person per night for more than four people, $4 per night for each additional vehicle, $5 per night per pet. Weekly rates available. Some credit cards are accepted. Open late April-late September.

**Directions:** From the junction of I-90 and Highway 17 (just south of Moses Lake), drive north on Highway 17 for 36 miles to Blue Lake and Park Lake Road. Turn right (east) on Park Lake Road (the south entrance) and drive 0.5 mile to the resort on the right.

**Contact:** Laurent's Sun Village Resort, 509/632-5664 or 509/632-5360, www.laurentsresort.com.

## 106 COULEE LODGE RESORT

🚶‍♂️🏊🛶🚤🐕🚙🏕️

**Scenic rating: 8**

on Blue Lake

**Map 4.4, page 254**

This camp is set at Blue Lake, which often provides outstanding fishing for a mix of stocked rainbow trout and brown trout in early spring. Blue Lake offers plenty of summertime recreation options, including a swimming beach. Nearby recreation possibilities include a nine-hole golf course and miniature golf.

**Campsites, facilities:** There are 18 sites for tents or RVs up to 35 feet long (30 amp full hookups), 14 sites for tents only. Six cabins and eight mobile homes are also available. Some sites are pull-through. Picnic tables and fire pits are provided. Restrooms with flush toilets and coin showers, propane gas, convenience store, firewood, coin laundry, boat docks, boat and personal watercraft rentals, launching facilities, and ice are available. A café is located within five miles. Leashed pets are permitted.

**Reservations, fees:** Reservations are accepted. Sites are $28-30 per night, $5 per each additional person per night, $5 per extra vehicle per night, and $5 per pet per night. Cabin rates are $75-125 per night and mobile home rates are $95-125 per night. Some credit cards are accepted. Open mid-April-September.

**Directions:** From the junction of I-90 and Highway 17 (just south of Moses Lake), drive north on Highway 17 for 39 miles to the north end of Blue Lake.

**Contact:** Coulee Lodge Resort, 509/632-5565, www.couleelodgeresort.com.

## 107 SPRING CANYON

🚶‍♂️🏊🚤🐕🎣♿🚙🏕️

**Scenic rating: 6**

on Franklin Roosevelt Lake in Lake Roosevelt National Recreation Area

**Map 4.5, page 255** **BEST (**

This large, developed campground is a popular vacation destination. Fishing for bass, walleye, trout, and sunfish is popular at Franklin Roosevelt Lake, as is waterskiing. The campground is not far from Grand Coulee Dam. Lake Roosevelt National Recreation Area offers numerous activity options, such as free programs conducted by rangers that include guided canoe trips, historical tours, campfire talks, and guided hikes. This lake is known as a prime location to view bald eagles, especially in winter. Side-trip options include visiting the Colville Tribal Museum in the town of Coulee Dam and touring the Grand Coulee Dam Visitor Center. Almost one mile long and twice as high as Niagara Falls, the dam is one of the largest concrete structures ever built. It is open for self-guided tours.

**Campsites, facilities:** There are 87 sites for tents or RVs up to 55 feet long and two group sites for tents or RVs up to 26 feet long that accommodate up to 25 people each. Picnic tables and fire grills are provided. Drinking water (seasonal), restrooms with flush toilets, a dump station, picnic area, swimming beach, playground, and amphitheater are available. A camp host is on-site. Boat docks, launching facilities, marine dump station, and fish-cleaning station are nearby. Some facilities are wheelchair accessible. Leashed pets are permitted.

**Reservations, fees:** Reservations are accepted for family sites and required for the group site sites at 877/444-6777 or www.recreation.gov ($9 reservation fee). Sites are $5-10 per night, $6 boat-launch fee (good for seven days), and the group sites are $53 per night ($25 reservation fee). Open year-round, weather permitting.

**Directions:** From the junction of I-90 and Highway 17 (just south of Moses Lake), drive north on Highway 17 for 45 miles to U.S. 2. Turn east on U.S. 2 and drive five miles to Highway 155. Turn left (north) and drive 26 miles to Grand Coulee and Highway 174. Turn right (east) on Highway 174 and drive three miles to the campground entrance on the left.

**Contact:** Lake Roosevelt National Recreation Area, 509/754-7800, www.nps.gov/laro.

## 108 LAKEVIEW TERRACE MOBILE AND RV PARK

### Scenic rating: 6

near Franklin Roosevelt Lake

**Map 4.5, page 255**

This pleasant resort is situated near Franklin Roosevelt Lake, which was created by Grand Coulee Dam. It provides a slightly less crowded alternative to the national park camps in the vicinity. A mobile home park is also on the property. Nearby Spring Canyon offers a full-service marina and various recreation options on the water.

**Campsites, facilities:** There are 20 pull-through sites with full hookups (30 and 50 amps) for RVs of any length and three sites for tents only. Restrooms with flush toilets and showers, a coin laundry, and a playground are available. Boat docks, launching facilities, and rentals are nearby. Some facilities are wheelchair accessible. Leashed pets are permitted.

**Reservations, fees:** Reservations are recommended. Sites are $20-35 per night. Credit cards are not accepted. Open year-round.

**Directions:** From Grand Coulee, drive east on Highway 174 for 3.5 miles to the park entrance on the left.

**Contact:** Lakeview Terrace Mobile and RV Park, 509/633-2169.

## 109 KELLER FERRY

### Scenic rating: 7

on Franklin Roosevelt Lake in Lake Roosevelt National Recreation Area

**Map 4.5, page 255**

This camp is set along the shore of Franklin Roosevelt Lake, a large reservoir created by Grand Coulee Dam, which sits about 15 miles west of camp. Franklin Roosevelt Lake is known for its walleye fishing; although more than 30 species live in this lake, 90 percent of the fish caught are walleye. They average 1-4 pounds and always travel in schools. Trout and salmon often swim below the bluffs near Keller Ferry. Waterskiing, fishing, and swimming are all recreation options here.

**Campsites, facilities:** There are 55 sites for tents or RVs up to 25 feet long and two group sites for tents or RVs up to 16 feet long for up to 25 people each. Picnic tables and fire grills are provided. Drinking water (seasonal) and restrooms with flush toilets are available. A dump station, ice, a picnic area, a swimming beach, and a playground are available nearby. Boat docks, launching facilities, fuel, and fish-cleaning stations are also nearby. Some facilities are wheelchair accessible. Leashed pets are permitted.

**Reservations, fees:** Reservations are accepted for individual sites and required for group sites at 877/444-6777 or www.recreation.gov ($9 reservation fee). Sites are $5-10 per night, $6 boat-launch fee (good for seven days), and the group site is $53 per night ($25 reservation fee). Open year-round, weather permitting.

**Directions:** From Spokane on U.S. 90, turn west on U.S. 2 and drive 71 miles to Wilbur and Highway 21. Turn north and drive 14 miles to the campground on the left.

**Contact:** Lake Roosevelt National Recreation Area, 509/754-7800 or 509/654-7889, www.nps.gov/laro.

## 110 RIVER RUE RV PARK

**Scenic rating: 7**

near the Columbia River

**Map 4.5, page 255**

This camp is located in high desert terrain yet is surrounded by lots of trees. You can fish, swim, water ski, or rent a houseboat at Lake Roosevelt, one mile away. Personal watercraft are allowed. Another nearby side trip is to the Grand Coulee Dam. A nine-hole golf course is available in Wilbur.

**Campsites, facilities:** There are 24 sites with full or partial hookups (20, 30, and 50 amps)

for tents or RVs of any length and eight sites for tents or RVs of any length (no hookups). Some sites are pull-through. Picnic tables and fire rings are provided. Restrooms with flush toilets and showers, limited groceries, ice, a snack bar, RV supplies, fishing tackle, and propane gas are available. Recreational facilities include a playground and horseshoe pits. Some facilities are wheelchair accessible. Leashed pets are permitted.

**Reservations, fees:** Reservations are accepted. Sites are $31.50 per night, plus $3 per person per night for more than two people. Winter rates available. Some credit cards are accepted. Open year-round with limited winter services.

**Directions:** On U.S. 2 at Wilbur, drive west on U.S. 2 for one mile to Highway 174. Turn right (north) on Highway 174 and drive 0.25 mile to Highway 21. Turn right (north) on Highway 21 and drive 13 miles to the park on the right.

**Contact:** River Rue RV Park, 509/647-2647, www.riverrue.com.

## 111 JONES BAY

**Scenic rating: 6**

on Franklin Roosevelt Lake in Lake Roosevelt National Recreation Area

**Map 4.5, page 255**

This small and primitive campground is set on Jones Bay on Franklin Roosevelt Lake. Well known by locals, it gets high use on summer weekends but is quiet most weekdays. The camp is located at the bottom of a canyon in a cove with ponderosa pines. Fishing for bass, walleye, trout, and sunfish is popular at Franklin Roosevelt Lake.

**Campsites, facilities:** There are nine sites for tents or RVs up to 30 feet long. Picnic tables and fire grills are provided. Vault toilets are available. There is no drinking water. A boat launch and dock are nearby. Leashed pets are permitted.

**Reservations, fees:** Reservations are not accepted. Sites are $5-10 per night; $6 boat-launch fee (good for seven days). Open year-round, weather permitting, with limited winter access.

**Directions:** From Spokane on U.S. 90, turn west on U.S. 2 and drive 71 miles to Wilbur and Highway 21. Turn right (north) on Highway 21 and drive seven miles to Jones Bay Road (a dirt road, marked). Turn right and drive eight miles to the campground entrance road on the right. A high-clearance vehicle is recommended.

**Contact:** Lake Roosevelt National Recreation Area, 509/754-7800, www.nps.gov/laro.

## 112 HAWK CREEK

### Scenic rating: 8
on Franklin Roosevelt Lake in Lake Roosevelt National Recreation Area

**Map 4.5, page 255**

This pleasant camping spot is located along the shore of Roosevelt Lake (Columbia River), adjacent to the mouth of Hawk Creek. This is often a good fishing spot for walleye, trout, and bass. Note that there is no drinking water if the lake level drops below an elevation of 1,265 feet.

**Campsites, facilities:** There are 21 sites for tents or RVs up to 45 feet long. Picnic tables and fire grills are provided. Drinking water and vault toilets are available. Boat docks and launching facilities are nearby. Leashed pets are permitted.

**Reservations, fees:** Reservations are not accepted. Sites are $5-10 per night; there is a $6 boat-launch fee (good for seven days). Open year-round, with limited winter facilities.

**Directions:** From Spokane on I-90, drive west for four miles to U.S. 2. Turn west on U.S. 2 and drive 34 miles to Davenport and Highway 25. Turn right (north) on Highway 25 and drive 23 miles to Miles-Creston Road. Turn left (northwest) and drive 10 miles to

the campground at the mouth of Hawk Creek on the left.

**Contact:** Lake Roosevelt National Recreation Area, 509/754-7800, www.nps.gov/laro.

## 113 FORT SPOKANE

### Scenic rating: 8
on Franklin Roosevelt Lake in Lake Roosevelt National Recreation Area

**Map 4.5, page 255**

Rangers offer evening campfire programs and guided daytime activities at this modern campground on the shore of Roosevelt Lake. This park also hosts living-history demonstrations. Fort Spokane is one of more than two dozen campgrounds on the 130-mile-long lake. A 190-mile scenic vehicle route encircles most of the lake.

**Campsites, facilities:** There are 67 sites for tents or RVs of any length, four sites for tents only, and two group sites for tents or RVs up to 26 feet long that can accommodate up to 45 people each. Picnic tables and fire grills are provided. Restrooms with flush toilets, drinking water (seasonal), a dump station, and a playground are available. A camp host is on-site. A picnic area, swimming beach, and visitors center are nearby. A store, gas station, and ice are located within one mile. Boat docks, launching facilities, and a marine dump station are nearby. Some facilities are wheelchair accessible. Leashed pets are permitted.

**Reservations, fees:** Reservations are not accepted for individual sites but are required for group sites at 877/444-6777 or www.recreation.gov ($9 reservation fee). Sites are $5-10 per night, $6 boat-launch fee (good for seven days), group sites are $78 per night ($25 reservation fee). Open year-round, with limited winter facilities.

**Directions:** From Spokane on I-90, drive west for four miles to U.S. 2. Turn west on U.S. 2 and drive 34 miles to Davenport and Highway 25. Turn right (north) on Highway 25 and drive 22 miles to the campground entrance on the right.

**Contact:** Lake Roosevelt National Recreation Area, 509/754-7800, 509/754-7889, or 509/633-3830, www.nps.gov/laro.

## 114 PORCUPINE BAY

### Scenic rating: 8

on Franklin Roosevelt Lake in Lake Roosevelt National Recreation Area

**Map 4.5, page 255**

This camp is extremely popular, and the sites are filled most of the summer. Its proximity to a nearby dock and launch makes it an especially good spot for campers with boats. A swimming beach is located adjacent to the campground.

**Campsites, facilities:** There are 31 sites for tents or RVs up to 50 feet long. Picnic tables and fire grills are provided. Drinking water, vault toilets, restrooms with flush toilets, dump station, picnic area, and playground are available. Boat docks and launching facilities are nearby. Some facilities are wheelchair accessible. Leashed pets are permitted.

**Reservations, fees:** Reservations are not accepted. Sites are $5-10 per night; $6 boat-launch fee (good for seven days). Open year-round, weather permitting, with limited winter access.

**Directions:** From Spokane on I-90, drive west for four miles to U.S. 2. Turn west on U.S. 2 and drive 34 miles to Davenport and Highway 25. Turn right (north) on Highway 25 and drive 19 miles to Porcupine Bay Road. Turn right (east) and drive 4.3 miles to the campground at the end of the road.

**Contact:** Lake Roosevelt National Recreation Area, 509/754-7800, www.nps.gov/laro.

## 115 LAKE SPOKANE CAMPGROUND

### Scenic rating: 8

on the Spokane River

**Map 4.6, page 256**

This campground is located about 45 minutes from Spokane. The camp is set on a terrace above Lake Spokane (Spokane River), where fishing can be good for rainbow trout and the occasional brown trout. This area is also popular for power boating, waterskiing, and personal watercraft. Crowded in summer, it gets a lot of use from residents of the Spokane area. Note that this campground and lake were previously known as Long Lake.

**Campsites, facilities:** There are 11 sites for tents or RVs up to 30 feet long. Picnic tables and fire grills are provided. Drinking water, vault toilets, and garbage bins are available. A camp host is on-site. A boat launch, dock, swimming beach, and a day-use area are nearby. Some facilities are wheelchair accessible. Leashed pets are permitted.

**Reservations, fees:** Reservations are not accepted. There is no fee for camping, but a Discover Pass is required. Open May-September, weather permitting.

**Directions:** From Spokane on I-90, drive west for four miles to U.S. 2. Turn west on U.S. 2 and drive 21 miles to Reardan and Highway 231. Turn right (north) on Highway 231 and drive 14.2 miles to Highway 291. Turn right and drive 4.7 miles to the campground entrance on the right.

**Contact:** Department of Natural Resources, Northeast Region, 509/684-7474, www.dnr.wa.gov.

## 116 DRAGOON CREEK

### Scenic rating: 5

near the Little Spokane River

**Map 4.6, page 256**

This spot is frequented by locals but is often

missed by out-of-town vacationers. The camp is set along Dragoon Creek, a tributary to the Little Spokane River. Its campsites are situated in a forest of ponderosa pine and Douglas fir. Although fairly close to U.S. 395, it remains quiet and rustic.

**Campsites, facilities:** There are 22 sites for tents or RVs up to 30 feet long. Picnic tables and fire grills are provided. Vault toilets and drinking water are available. Garbage must be packed out. Some facilities are wheelchair accessible. Leashed pets are permitted.

**Reservations, fees:** Reservations are not accepted. There is no fee for camping, but a Discover Pass is required. Open May-September, weather permitting, with a camp host available.

**Directions:** From Spokane, drive north on U.S. 395 for 10.2 miles to North Dragoon Creek Road. Turn left on North Dragoon Creek Road and drive 0.4 mile to the campground entrance at the end of the road.

**Contact:** Department of Natural Resources, Northeast Region, 509/684-7474, www.dnr.wa.gov.

## 117 MOUNT SPOKANE STATE PARK

### Scenic rating: 8

on Mount Spokane

**Map 4.6, page 256**      **BEST (**

This state park provides one of the better short trips available out of Spokane. It is set on the slopes of Mount Spokane (5,883 feet), and little brother Mount Kit Carson (5,180 feet) sits alongside it. The park covers 13,643 acres in the Selkirk Mountains and features a stunning view from the top of Mount Spokane. The lookout takes in Washington, Idaho, Montana, and Canada. The park has 86 miles of hiking trails, occasionally routed into old-growth forest and amid granite outcroppings. The Mount Spokane Ski and Snowboard Park operates here in winter. The park receives an average of 300 inches of snow annually.

**Campsites, facilities:** There are eight sites for tents and a group camp for up to 50 people. Picnic tables and fire grills are provided. Restrooms with flush toilets and drinking water are available. A picnic area with a kitchen shelter is available. Leashed pets are permitted.

**Reservations, fees:** Reservations are not accepted. Sites are $20-31 per night, $10 per extra vehicle per night; call for group rates. Open late May-September, weather permitting.

**Directions:** From Spokane, drive north on U.S. 395 for six miles to U.S. 2. Turn north on U.S. 2 and drive six miles to Highway 206. Turn right (northeast) on Highway 206 and drive 15 miles to the park.

**Contact:** Mount Spokane State Park, 509/238-4258; state park information, 360/902-8844, www.parks.wa.gov.

## 118 RIVERSIDE STATE PARK

### Scenic rating: 8

near Spokane

**Map 4.6, page 256**

This 10,000-acre park is set along the Spokane and Little Spokane Rivers and features freshwater marshes in a beautiful setting. There are many recreation options, including fishing for bass, crappie, and perch, 55 miles of hiking and biking trails, and 25 miles of trails for horseback riding, as well as riding stables in the park. The 37-mile Centennial Trail can be accessed from the park. The park also has a 600-acre riding area for dirt bikes in summer and snowmobiles in winter. An 18-hole golf course is located nearby. A local point of interest is the unique Bowl and Pitcher rock formation in the Spokane River.

**Campsites, facilities:** There are four different camping areas with a total of 30 sites for tents, 37 sites with partial hookups (30 and 50 amps) for tents or RVs up to 45 feet long, 10 equestrian sites with corrals, and two group tent sites for 40 and 60 people respectively (20-person minimum). Picnic tables and fire grills are provided. Restrooms with flush toilets and showers, drinking water, a picnic area with a kitchen shelter, dump station, interpretive center, camp store, firewood, and horse stable are available. A restaurant, gasoline, groceries, and ice are located within three miles. Boat-launching facilities, a dock, and boat rentals are located on-site. Some facilities are wheelchair accessible. Leashed pets are permitted.

**Reservations, fees:** Reservations are accepted for individual sites and required for group sites at 888/CAMP-OUT (888/226-7688) or www.goingtocamp.com ($6.50 reservation fee). Sites are $12-39 per night, $10 per extra vehicle per night. The group sites are $70.84-212.52 per night. Open year-round, with limited number of sites available in winter.

**Directions:** In Spokane on I-90, take Exit 280/Maple Street North (cross the Maple Street Bridge), and drive north 1.1 miles to Maxwell Street. Turn left (west) and drive 1.9 miles, bearing left along the Spokane River to the park entrance. From the park entrance, continue for 1.5 miles on Aubrey L. White Parkway to the campground.

Alternate route for long RVs: In Spokane on I-90, take Exit 280/Maple Street North (cross the Maple Street Bridge), and drive north 4.5 miles to Francis Avenue. Turn left and drive three miles to Rifle Club Road. Turn left and drive to Aubrey L. White Parkway and the park entrance. From the entrance, continue 1.5 miles to the campground.

**Contact:** Riverside State Park, 509/465-5064, www.riversidestatepark.org; state park information, 360/902-8844, www.parks.wa.gov.

## 119 TRAILER INNS RV PARK/SPOKANE

### Scenic rating: 5

in Spokane

**Map 4.6, page 256**

This large RV park makes a good layover spot on the way to Idaho. It's as close to a hotel as an RV park can get. The pull-through sites are shaded. Nearby recreation options include an 18-hole golf course, a racquet club, and tennis courts. Note that when busy, many of the sites are taken by monthly campers.

**Campsites, facilities:** There are 93 sites for tents or RVs of any length (15, 30, and 50 amp full hookups); in summer, only about 10 sites are available for overnight campers. Some sites are pull-through. Picnic tables are provided. Restrooms with flush toilets and showers, drinking water, propane gas, cable TV, phone hookups, Wi-Fi and modem access, TV room, coin laundry, ice, a picnic area, and a playground are available. A dump station, store, and café are within one mile. Leashed pets are permitted.

**Reservations, fees:** Reservations are accepted at 800/659-4864. RV sites are $26-34 per night, tent sites are $20 per night, plus $5 per person per night for more than two people. Weekly rates available. Some credit cards are accepted. Open year-round.

**Directions:** Note that your route will depend on the direction you're heading: In Spokane eastbound on I-90, take Exit 285 (Sprague Avenue/Eastern Road) to Eastern Road. Drive 0.1 mile on Eastern Road to 4th Avenue. Turn right (west) on 4th Avenue and drive two blocks to the park. In Spokane westbound on I-90, take Exit 284 (Havana Street). Drive one block south on Havana Street to 4th Avenue. Turn left (east) on 4th Avenue and drive one mile to the park.

**Contact:** Trailer Inns RV Park/Spokane, 509/535-1811, www.trailerinnsrv.com.

## 120 KOA SPOKANE

### Scenic rating: 5

on the Spokane River

**Map 4.6, page 256**

This KOA campground is located close to the shore of the Spokane River. Nearby you'll find the 37-mile Centennial Trail along the river, as well as an 18-hole golf course and tennis courts. Other options include touring the gardens of Manito Park or visiting Riverfront Park, which has an IMAX theater and aerial gondola rides over the Spokane River.

**Campsites, facilities:** There are 150 sites with full hookups (30 and 50 amps) for RVs of any length, 50 sites for tents, and seven cabins (four deluxe). Some sites are pull-through. Picnic tables are provided. No wood fires are allowed, but portable fire rings are available. Restrooms with flush toilets and showers, drinking water, cable TV, a dump station, playground, convenience store, coin laundry, ice, Wi-Fi, pet walk, volleyball, horseshoe pits, basketball, and a seasonal heated swimming pool are available. A café and gasoline are located within two miles. Some facilities are wheelchair accessible. Leashed pets are permitted.

**Reservations, fees:** Reservations are accepted at 800/562-3309. Sites are $33-42 per night, plus $3-4 per night per person for more than two people. Some credit cards are accepted. Open year-round.

**Directions:** From Spokane, drive east on I-90 for 13 miles to Barker/Exit 293. Take that exit to Barker Road. Turn north on Barker Road and drive 1.5 miles to the campground on the left.

**Contact:** KOA Spokane, 509/924-4722, www.koa.com.

## 121 WEST MEDICAL LAKE RESORT

### Scenic rating: 7

on West Medical Lake

**Map 4.6, page 256**

This resort functions primarily as a fish camp for anglers. There are actually two lakes: West Medical is the larger of the two and has better fishing, with boat rentals available; Medical Lake is just 0.25-mile wide and 0.5-mile long, and boating is restricted to rowboats,

canoes, kayaks, and sailboats. The lakes got their names from the wondrous medicinal powers once attributed to their waters. This family-operated shorefront resort, one of several campgrounds on these lakes, is a popular spot for Spokane locals.

**Campsites, facilities:** There are 20 tent sites and 20 sites for tents or RVs up to 40 feet long (full hookups). Picnic tables are provided at all sites and fire pits are provided at tent sites. Restrooms with flush toilets and showers, drinking water, a café, bait, tackle, and ice are available. Boat and fishing docks, launching facilities, a fish-cleaning station, and boat and barge rentals are nearby. Some facilities are wheelchair accessible. Leashed pets are permitted.

**Reservations, fees:** Reservations are accepted. RV sites are $25 per night, tent sites are $18 per night. Some credit cards are accepted. Open late April-September.

**Directions:** In Spokane on I-90, drive west to Exit 264 and Salnave Road. Take that exit and turn north on Salnave Road; drive six miles to Fancher Road. Turn right (west) and drive 200 yards. Bear left on Fancher Road and drive 200 yards to the resort.

**Contact:** West Medical Lake Resort, 509/299-3921.

## 122 MALLARD BAY RESORT

### Scenic rating: 8

on Clear Lake

**Map 4.6, page 256**    **BEST (**

This popular fishing resort is on the shore of Clear Lake, which is two miles long, 0.5-mile wide, and used for waterskiing, personal watercraft, windsurfing, and sailing. Most of the campsites are lakeshore sites on a 20-acre peninsula. Marked bike trails are nearby.

**Campsites, facilities:** There are 40 sites with partial hookups (20 and 30 amps) for tents or RVs of any length. Picnic tables and fire pits are provided. Restrooms with flush toilets and showers, drinking water, propane gas, a dump station, camp store, bait and tackle, ice, swimming facilities with a diving board, a playground, basketball court, boat docks, launching facilities, fishing pier, fish-cleaning stations, and boat rentals are available. Some facilities are wheelchair accessible. Leashed pets are permitted.

**Reservations, fees:** Reservations are accepted. Sites are $23.95 per night. Open late April-Labor Day weekend.

**Directions:** In Spokane on I-90, drive west to Exit 264 and Salnave Road. Take that exit and turn north on Salnave Road; drive 1.5 miles to a junction and Mallard Bay Lane. Turn right on Mallard Bay Lane and drive 0.5 mile (bearing right at the intersection) on a dirt road to the resort at the end of the road.

**Contact:** Mallard Bay Resort, 509/299-3830.

## 123 SUN COVE RESORT

**Scenic rating: 7**

on Clear Lake

**Map 4.6, page 256**

This resort at Clear Lake features a 300-foot dock with benches that can be used for fishing. If you figured that most people here are anglers, well, that is correct. Fishing can be good for rainbow trout, brown trout, largemouth bass, crappie, bullhead, and catfish. Most of the campsites are at least partially shaded. Summer weekends are often busy.

**Campsites, facilities:** There are 17 sites with full or partial hookups (30 and 50 amps) for RVs up to 40 feet long and 10 sites for tents only. Picnic tables and fire pits are provided. Restrooms with flush toilets and coin showers, drinking water, a café, ice, bait and tackle, boat docks and launch, boat rentals, and moorage are available. Some facilities are wheelchair accessible. Leashed pets are permitted.

**Reservations, fees:** Reservations are accepted. RV sites with full hookups are $35 per night, RV sites with partial hookups are $30 per night, tent sites are $25 per night, plus $5 per person per night for more than four people. Some credit cards are accepted. Open mid-April-mid-October.

**Directions:** In Spokane on I-90, drive west to Exit 264 and Salnave Road. Take that exit and turn right (north) on Salnave Road; drive a short distance to Clear Lake Road. Turn right (north) on Clear Lake Road and drive three miles to the resort on the left (well signed).

**Contact:** Sun Cove Resort, 509/299-3717.

## 124 PONDEROSA FALLS

**Scenic rating: 6**

west of Spokane

**Map 4.6, page 256**

Formerly Yogi Bear's Camp Resort, Ponderosa Falls is now a member of the KM Resorts family. The resort is located 10 minutes from downtown Spokane, yet provides a wooded, rural setting with towering ponderosa pines. Highlights include an 18-hole golf course nearby and several other courses within 20 minutes of the resort.

**Campsites, facilities:** There are 165 sites for tents or RVs up to 40 feet long (30 and 50 amp full hookups), five cabins, and six bungalows. Some sites are pull-through. Picnic tables are provided. No open fires are allowed. Restrooms with flush toilets and showers, drinking water, cable TV, Wi-Fi, a dump station, propane, coin laundry, an RV wash station, and three playgrounds are available. Other facilities include a camp store, activity center with an indoor pool, spa, exercise room, game room, snack shack, dog walk, and various sports facilities (volleyball, basketball, badminton, miniature golf, and daily, organized recreational activities). Some facilities are wheelchair accessible. Leashed pets are permitted.

**Reservations, fees:** Reservations are accepted. RV sites are $40-42 per night, tent sites are $25 per night. Some credit cards are accepted. Open year-round.

**Directions:** In Spokane on I-90, drive to Exit 272. Take that exit, turn east on Hayford Road (becomes Aero Road), and drive approximately two miles to Thomas Mallen Road. Turn right (south) on Thomas Mallen Road and drive 0.25 mile to the resort on the right.

**Contact:** Ponderosa Falls, 509/747-9415 or 800/494-7275 (800/494-PARK), www.km-resorts.com.

# THE COLUMBIA RIVER GORGE AND MOUNT RAINIER

© NATALIA BRATSLAVSKY/123RF

Standing at the rim of Mount St. Helens volcano is like looking inside the bowels of the earth. Half-moon crater walls drop almost 2,100 feet down to a lava plug dome, one mile across and still building, where a wisp of smoke emerges from the center. At its edges, plumes of dust rise from continuous rock falls. The plug dome gives way to the blast zone where the mountain completely blew out its side, spreading across 230 square miles of devastation. It's largely a moonscape but for Spirit Lake on the northeast flank, where thousands of trees still float, log-jammed from the eruption in May 1980. Beyond this scene, the most famous spots are Mounts St. Helens, Rainier, and Adams; the latter are two of most beautiful mountains in the Cascade Range. St. Helens provides the most eye-popping views and most developed visitors centers, Rainier the most pristine wilderness, and Adams some of the best lakeside camps. All offer outstanding hiking and excellent campgrounds.

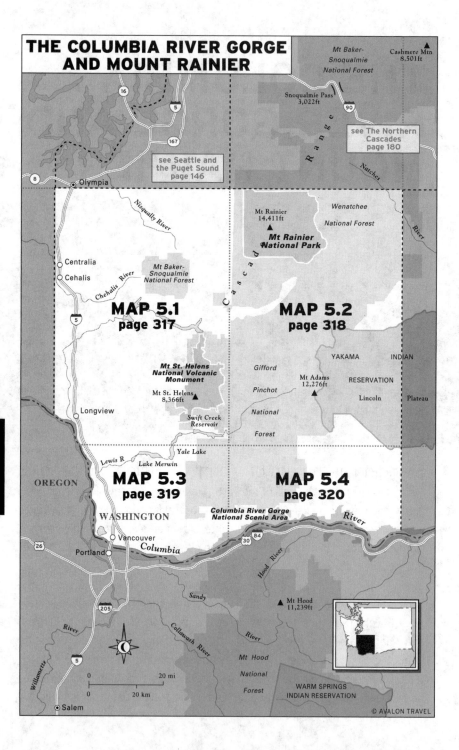

# THE COLUMBIA RIVER GORGE AND MOUNT RAINIER

Mt Baker-Snoqualmie National Forest

Cashmere Mtn 8,501ft

Snoqualmie Pass 3,022ft

see The Northern Cascades page 180

see Seattle and the Puget Sound page 146

Olympia

Nisqually River

Mt Rainier 14,411ft

Mt Rainier National Park

Wenatchee National Forest

River

Centralia

Cehalis

Chehalis River

Mt Baker-Snoqualmie National Forest

**MAP 5.1**
page 317

Cascade

Range

**MAP 5.2**
page 318

YAKAMA          INDIAN

Gifford

Mt Adams 12,276ft

RESERVATION

Mt St. Helens National Volcanic Monument

Mt St. Helens 8,366ft

Pinchot

Lincoln

Plateau

Longview

Swift Creek Reservoir

National

Forest

Yale Lake

Lewis R

Lake Merwin

**MAP 5.3**
page 319

**MAP 5.4**
page 320

OREGON

WASHINGTON

Columbia River Gorge National Scenic Area

River

Vancouver

Columbia

Portland

Hood River

Sandy

Mt Hood 11,239ft

River

Collawash River

River

Mt Hood

National

Forest

Willamette

20 mi

20 km

WARM SPRINGS INDIAN RESERVATION

Salem

© AVALON TRAVEL

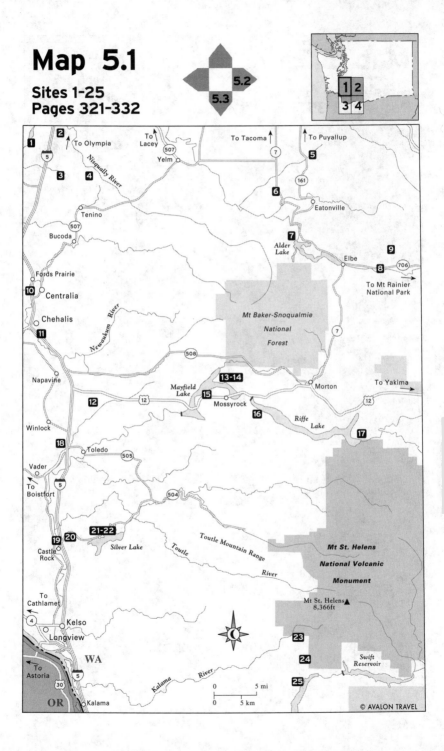

# Map 5.1

## Sites 1-25
## Pages 321-332

5.2

5.3

To Olympia
To Lacey
To Tacoma
To Puyallup
Yelm
507
7
5
Nisqually River
161
6
Eatonville
Tenino
507
Bucoda
7
Alder Lake
Elbe
9
706
8
Fords Prairie
To Mt Rainier National Park
Centralia
10
Newaukum River
Mt Baker-Snoqualmie
Chehalis
National
11
Forest
7
Napavine
508
To Yakima
13-14
Mayfield Lake
15
Morton
12
12
12
Mossyrock
Winlock
16
Riffe Lake
18
Toledo
505
17
Vader
To Boistfort
5
504
21-22
Toutle Mountain Range
Mt St. Helens
19 20
Silver Lake
Toutle
National Volcanic
Castle Rock
River
Monument
To Cathlamet
Mt St. Helens
8,366ft
Kelso
Longview
23
WA
24
Swift Reservoir
To Astoria
30
25
OR
Kalama
Kalama River
0      5 mi
0      5 km
© AVALON TRAVEL

# Map 5.2

## Sites 26-79
## Pages 333-357

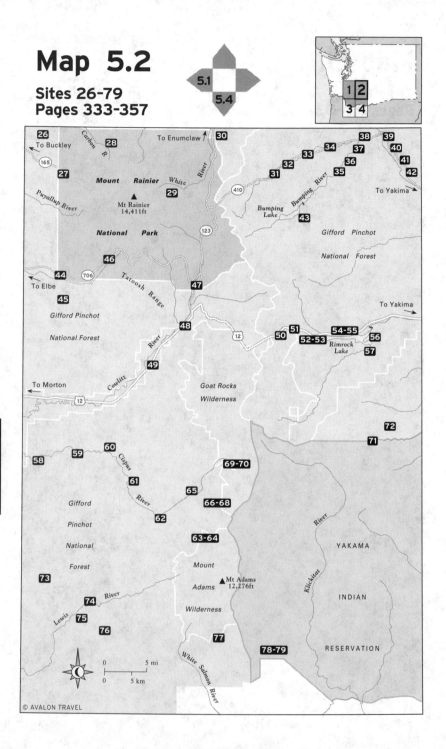

5.1

5.4

1 2
3 4

26
To Buckley

Carbon R.

28

To Enumclaw

30

165

27

Puyallup River

Mount   Rainier   White

Mt Rainier
14,411ft

29

River

410

31

32

33

34

38

39

40

37

36

35

41

42

To Yakima

National   Park

Bumping
Lake

Bumping River

43

Gifford   Pinchot

National   Forest

123

46

44

706

To Elbe

45

Tatoosh Range

47

Gifford Pinchot

National Forest

River

48

12

50

51

54-55

52-53

Rimrock
Lake

56

57

To Yakima

49

Cowlitz

To Morton

12

Goat Rocks

Wilderness

72

71

58

59

60

Cispus

61

River

65

69-70

66-68

62

Gifford

Pinchot

National

Forest

63-64

Mount

Adams

Mt Adams
12,276ft

River

YAKAMA

INDIAN

73

74

River

Lewis

75

76

Wilderness

77

White Salmon River

78-79

Klickitat

RESERVATION

0        5 mi

0        5 km

© AVALON TRAVEL

# Map **5.3**

## Sites 80-90
## Pages 358-362

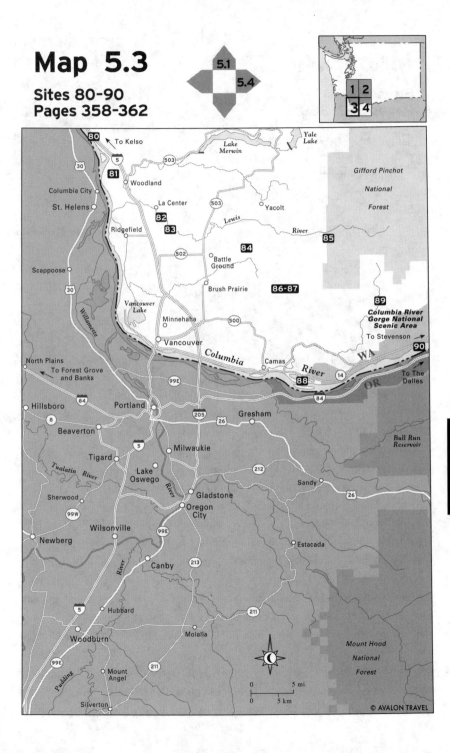

# Map 5.4

**Sites 91-104**
**Pages 363-369**

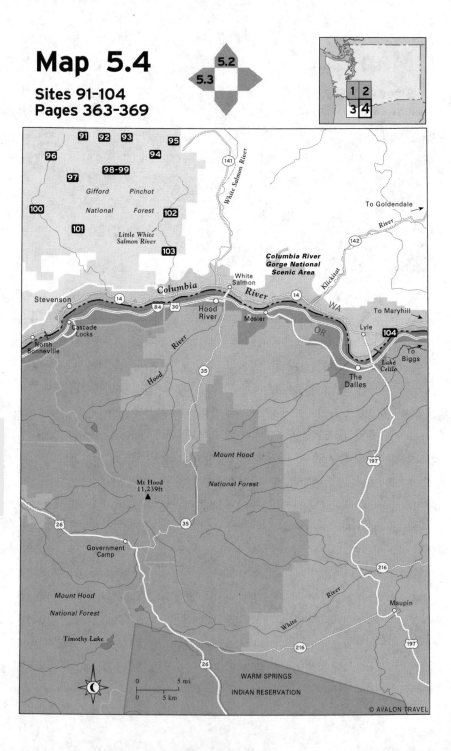

© AVALON TRAVEL

# **1** COLUMBUS PARK

### Scenic rating: 8

on Black Lake

**Map 5.1, page 317**

This spot along the shore of Black Lake is pretty enough for special events, such as weddings and reunions. The campsites are wooded, and a stream (no fishing) runs through the campground. Black Lake is good for fishing, however. An 18-hole golf course is nearby.

**Campsites, facilities:** There are 29 sites for tents or RVs up to 40 feet long (30 amp partial hookups) and one tent site. There are also 46 sites with full hookups that are usually rented by the month. Picnic tables are provided. Restrooms with flush toilets and showers, drinking water, a dump station, coin laundry, ice, firewood, propane, a playground, volleyball, horseshoe pits, boat docks, and launching facilities are available. A picnic area for special events is nearby. Propane gas and a store are located within one mile; there is a restaurant within three miles. Some facilities are wheelchair accessible. Leashed pets are permitted, but not on the swimming beach.

**Reservations, fees:** Reservations are accepted and are recommended during summer. Sites are $25 per night. Open year-round.

**Directions:** From I-5 in Olympia, take Exit 104, which merges onto U.S. 101. Drive northwest on U.S. 101 for 1.7 miles to Black Lake Boulevard. Turn left (south) on Black Lake Boulevard and drive 3.5 miles to the park on the left.

**Contact:** Columbus Park, 360/786-9460 or 866/848-9460, www.columbuspark.net.

# **2** AMERICAN HERITAGE CAMPGROUND

### Scenic rating: 6

near Olympia

**Map 5.1, page 317**

This spacious, wooded campground situated just 0.5 mile off the highway is close to many activities, including an 18-hole golf course, hiking trails, marked bike trails, and tennis courts. The park features novelty cycle rentals, free wagon rides, and free nightly movies during the summer season. It's pretty and exceptionally clean, making for a pleasant layover on your way up or down I-5. The park has a 5,000-square-foot pavilion for special events or groups.

**Campsites, facilities:** There are 72 sites with full or partial hookups (30 amps) for tents or RVs of any length, 23 sites for tents, and one cabin. Picnic tables and fire rings are provided. Restrooms with flush toilets and showers, drinking water, propane gas, dump station, group pavilion, seasonal recreation programs, a convenience store, coin laundry, ice, a playground, a seasonal heated swimming pool, and firewood are available. Leashed pets are permitted.

**Reservations, fees:** Reservations are accepted. RV sites are $30-35 per night, tent sites are $22 per night, $4-10 per person per night for more than two people. Some credit cards are accepted. Open year-round, with limited winter facilities.

**Directions:** From Olympia, drive five miles south on I-5 to Exit 99. Take that exit and drive 0.25 mile east to Kimmie Street. Turn right (south) on Kimmie Street and drive 0.25 mile to the end of the road to the campground on the left.

**Contact:** American Heritage Campground, 360/943-8778, www.americanheritagecampground.com.

# **3** MILLERSYLVANIA STATE PARK

### Scenic rating: 8

on Deep Lake

**Map 5.1, page 317**

Millersylvania State Park is set on the shore of Deep Lake and features 3,300 feet of waterfront. The park has 8.6 miles of hiking trails amid an abundance of old-growth cedar and fir trees, of which 7.6 miles are open to bikes. Boating at Deep Lake is restricted to hand-launched boats, with a 5-mph speed limit. A fishing dock is available at the boat-launch area. Another highlight: a one-mile fitness trail. Look for the remains of a former railroad and skid trails dating from the 1800s, still present in the park.

**Campsites, facilities:** There are 120 developed tent sites, 48 sites with partial hookups (30 and 50 amps) for RVs up to 45 feet long, and a group site for 20-40 people. There is also a two-story Lakeside Cottage and an Environmental Learning Center with 16 heated cabins that can accommodate 40-150 people. Picnic tables and fire grills are provided. Restrooms with flush toilets and coin showers, drinking water, a dump station, firewood boat docks and launching facilities, exercise trail, and amphitheater are available. A picnic area, boat rentals, summer interpretive activities, and horseshoe pits are nearby. A store, restaurant, and ice are located within one mile. Some facilities are wheelchair accessible. Leashed pets are permitted.

**Reservations, fees:** Reservations are accepted at 888/CAMP-OUT (888/226-7688) or www.goingtocamp.com ($6.50-8.50 reservation fee). Sites are $20-39 per night, $10 per extra vehicle per night. Group camp fees vary according to group size and season. The cottage is $189-252 per night; the Environmental Learning Center is $10.77 per person plus a $25 non-refundable reservation fee. Some credit cards are accepted. Open year-round, with limited facilities mid-November-March.

**Directions:** From Olympia, drive south on I-5 for 10 miles to Exit 95 and Highway 121. Turn east on Maytown Road (Highway 121) and drive 2.7 miles to Tilley Road. Turn left (north) and drive 1.3 miles to the park.

**Contact:** Millersylvania State Park, 360/753-1519; state park information, 360/902-8844, www.parks.wa.gov.

# 4 OFFUT LAKE RESORT

**Scenic rating: 8**

on Offut Lake

**Map 5.1, page 317**　　　　BEST (

This wooded campground is set on Offut Lake, just enough off the beaten track to provide a bit of seclusion. Fishing, swimming, and boating are favorite activities here. Anglers will find everything they need, including tackle and boat rentals, at the resort. Boating is restricted to a 5-mph speed limit, and no gas motors are permitted on the lake. Several fishing derbies are held here every year.

**Campsites, facilities:** There are 31 sites with full or partial hookups (30 and 50 amps) for RVs up to 40 feet long, 25 sites for tents, and nine cabins. Picnic tables, fire rings, and cable TV are provided. Restrooms with flush toilets and coin showers, drinking water, Wi-Fi, a picnic shelter, dump station, firewood, a convenience store, bait and tackle, coin laundry, ice, a playground, basketball, and horseshoe pits are available. Boat rentals and docks are available; no gas motors are permitted. Some facilities are wheelchair accessible. Leashed pets are permitted.

**Reservations, fees:** Reservations are accepted. RV sites are $30-37 per night, tent sites are $20 per night, $8 per person per night for more than two adults and two children, $5 per extra vehicle per night, $5 moorage fee per night, and $3 per pet per night. Some credit cards are accepted. Open year-round.

**Directions:** From Olympia, drive south on I-5 for seven miles to Exit 99. Take that exit and turn east on 93rd Avenue; drive four miles to Old Highway 99. Turn right (south) and drive four miles to Offut Lake Road. Turn left (east) and drive 1.5 miles to the resort.

**Contact:** Offut Lake Resort, 360/264-2438, www.offutlakeresort.com.

## 5 RAINBOW RV RESORT

🛶🚤🏕🐕♿🚐⛺

**Scenic rating: 8**

on Tanwax Lake

**Map 5.1, page 317**

This wooded park along the shore of Tanwax Lake has spacious sites with views of mountains, forest, and lake. Highlights include good fishing for trout, perch, crappie, bass, bluegill, catfish, and bullhead. Powerboating and waterskiing are popular on hot summer weekends.

**Campsites, facilities:** There are about 60 sites with full hookups for tents or RVs up to 40 feet long. Picnic tables are provided at most sites, and portable fire pits are available. Restrooms with flush toilets and coin showers, drinking water, propane gas, firewood, recreation hall, convenience store, coin laundry, a café, ice, cable TV, boat docks and launch, boat rentals, and boat moorage are available. Some facilities are wheelchair accessible. Leashed pets are permitted.

**Reservations, fees:** Reservations are accepted. RV sites are $28-30 per night, tent sites are $15 per night. Some credit cards are accepted. Open year-round.

**Directions:** From Tacoma, drive south on I-5 to Exit 127 and Highway 512. Turn east on Highway 512 and drive to Highway 161. Turn right (south) on Highway 161 and drive to Tanwax Drive. Turn left (east) on Tanwax Drive and continue 200 yards to the resort.

**Contact:** Rainbow RV Resort, 360/879-5115, www.rainbowrvresort.com.

## 6 HENLEY'S SILVER LAKE RESORT

🛶🚐🏕🐕♿🚐⛺

**Scenic rating: 8**

on Silver Lake

**Map 5.1, page 317**    **BEST (**

Silver Lake is a 150-acre, spring-fed lake that can provide good trout fishing. This full-facility resort is set up as a family vacation destination. A rarity, this private campground caters both to tent campers and RVers. Silver Lake is beautiful and stocked with trout. Highlights include a 250-foot fishing dock and rental rowboats.

**Campsites, facilities:** There are 20 sites with full or partial hookups for RVs, a large area for dispersed tent camping, and six cabins. Picnic tables are provided and fire pits are available at most sites. Restrooms with flush toilets, drinking water, showers, snacks, bait and tackle, boat rentals, a boat ramp, and a dock are available. A grocery store, gasoline, and supplies are available within 3.5 miles. Some facilities are wheelchair accessible. Leashed pets are permitted except in the cabins.

**Reservations, fees:** Reservations are accepted. RV sites are $32 per night, tent sites are $24 per night, $8 per extra person per night, $5 per extra vehicle per night. Cabins are $85 per night. Open year-round, weather permitting.

**Directions:** From Tacoma, drive south on I-5 for five miles to Exit 127 and Highway 512. Turn east on Highway 512 and drive two miles to Highway 7. Turn right (south) on Highway 7 and drive 19 miles (2 miles straight beyond the blinking light) to Silver Lake Road on the right (well marked). Turn right and drive 0.25 mile to the resort entrance on the left.

**Contact:** Henley's Silver Lake Resort, 360/832-3580, www.henleysilverlake.com.

## 7 ALDER LAKE PARK

🛶🚤🚐🏕🛶♿🚐⛺

**Scenic rating: 6**

on Alder Lake

**Map 5.1, page 317**

The 161-acre recreation area at Alder Lake features four camping areas and a group camp; one of the camps is located four miles east of the main park entrance. Alder Lake is a 3,065-acre lake (7.5 miles long) often with good fishing for kokanee salmon, rainbow trout, and cutthroat trout. Rocky Point features a sunny beach and is set near the mouth of feeder streams, often the best fishing spots on the lake. At the west end of the lake, anglers can catch catfish, perch, and crappie. The campsites have lots of trees and shrubbery. On clear, warm summer weekends, these camps can get crowded. The camps are always booked full for summer holiday weekends as soon as reservations are available in January. Another potential downer, the water level fluctuates here. Powerboating, waterskiing, and personal watercraft are allowed at this lake. Mount Rainier Scenic Railroad leaves from Elbe regularly and makes its way through the forests to Mineral Lake. It features open deck cars, live music, and restored passenger cars.

**Campsites, facilities:** There are four camping areas with approximately 161 sites with full or partial hookups (30 and 50 amps) for tents or RVs up to 40 feet, 45 sites for tents, and one group area with 35 sites for tents or RVs (full hookups). Picnic tables and fire rings are provided. Restrooms with flush toilets and coin showers, drinking water, vault toilets, and a dump station are available. Boat docks and launching facilities are available nearby. A swimming beach, picnic area, playground, and fishing dock are also available nearby. Some facilities are wheelchair accessible. Leashed pets are permitted.

**Reservations, fees:** Reservations are accepted at 888/CAMP-OUT (888/226-7688) or www.tacomapower.com ($6.50-8.50 reservation fee). For group reservations, phone 360/569-2778 ($15 group reservation fee). Sites are $22-31 per night, $10 per extra vehicle per night. The group camp is $31 per site per night, with a five-site minimum. Some credit cards are accepted. Open year-round, excluding December 20-January 1.

**Directions:** From Chehalis, drive south on I-5 for six miles to U.S. 12. Turn east and drive 31 miles to Morton and Highway 7. Turn north on Highway 7 and drive 17 miles to Elbe. Bear left on Highway 7 and drive to the park entrance road on the left (on the east shore of

Alder Lake). Turn left and drive 0.2 mile to the park entrance gate.

**Contact:** Alder Lake Park, Tacoma Power, 360/569-2778, www.tacomapower.com.

## 8 SAHARA CREEK HORSE CAMP

**Scenic rating: 6**

near Elbe

**Map 5.1, page 317**

While this camp is called a "horse camp," it is actually a multiple-use camp open to campers without horses. This pretty camp is set near the foot of Mount Rainier and features multiple trailheads and a camp host on-site. Note that no motorized vehicles or mountain bikes are allowed on trails. In winter, miles of groomed cross-country ski trails are available in the area.

**Campsites, facilities:** There are 18 sites for tents or RVs up to 25 feet long. Picnic tables and fire pits are provided. Drinking water, stock water, a covered pavilion, vault toilets, high lines, a horse mounting ramp, and hitching posts are available. Garbage must be packed out. Some facilities are wheelchair accessible. Leashed pets are permitted.

**Reservations, fees:** Reservations are not accepted. There is no fee for camping, but a Discover Pass is required. Open year-round.

**Directions:** From Chehalis, drive south on I-5 for six miles to U.S. 12. Turn east and drive 31 miles to Morton and Highway 7. Turn north on Highway 7 and drive 17 miles to Elbe and Highway 706. Turn right (east) and drive five miles to the campground on the left.

**Contact:** Department of Natural Resources, South Puget Sound Region, 360/825-1631, www.dnr.wa.gov.

## 9 ELBE HILLS

**Scenic rating: 6**

near Elbe

Map 5.1, page 317

Elbe Hills is not an official, designated campground, but rather a trailhead with room for three campsites for four-wheelers, equestrians, or hikers. The Department of Natural Resources manages this wooded campground and provides eight miles of trails for short-wheelbase four-wheel-drive vehicles. The area features a technical obstacle course. In some places, you must have a winch to make it through the course. In winter, groomed cross-country ski trails are available in the area. Note: The area is always gated, and arrangements for access must be made in advance.

**Campsites, facilities:** There are three primitive sites for tents or RVs up to 25 feet long. Picnic tables and fire grills are provided. Vault toilets and a group shelter are available. There is no drinking water and garbage must be packed out. Leashed pets are permitted.

**Reservations, fees:** Reservations are not accepted. There is no fee for camping, but a Discover Pass is required. Open year-round, weather permitting.

**Directions:** From Chehalis, drive south on I-5 for six miles to U.S. 12. Turn east and drive 31 miles to Morton and Highway 7. Turn north on Highway 7 and drive 17 miles to Elbe and Highway 706. Turn right (east) and drive six miles to Stoner Road (a Department of Natural Resources access road). Turn left and drive 2.5 miles to The 9 Road. Bear right on The 9 Road and drive one mile; look for a spur road on the left. Turn left and drive about 100 yards to the four-wheel-drive trailhead.

**Contact:** Department of Natural Resources, South Puget Sound Region, 360/825-1631, www.dnr.wa.gov.

## 10 PEPPERTREE WEST MOTOR INN & RV PARK

**Scenic rating: 5**

in Centralia

Map 5.1, page 317

If you're driving I-5 and looking for a stopover, this spot is a good choice for tent campers and RVers. Surrounded by Chehalis Valley farmland, it's near an 18-hole golf course, hiking trails, and tennis courts.

**Campsites, facilities:** There are 42 sites with full or partial hookups (30 amps) for RVs up to 40 feet, a grassy area for tents, and 25 motel rooms. Most sites are pull-through. Restrooms with flush toilets and coin showers, drinking water, cable TV, a dump station, coin laundry, and ice are available. Boat-launching facilities are nearby. A store, propane, and a café are also nearby. Some facilities are wheelchair accessible. Leashed pets are permitted.

**Reservations, fees:** Reservations are accepted. RV sites are $25 per night, tent sites are $7 per night. Some credit cards are accepted. Open year-round.

**Directions:** From Centralia on I-5, take Exit 81 to Melon Street. Turn west and then take the first right (Alder Street) to the park (located in the southeast corner of Centralia).

**Contact:** Peppertree West Motor Inn & RV Park, 360/736-1124.

## 11 STAN HEDWALL PARK

**Scenic rating: 5**

on the Newaukum River

Map 5.1, page 317

This park is set along the Newaukum River, and its proximity to I-5 makes it a good layover spot for vacation travelers. Recreational opportunities include fishing, hiking, and golf; an 18-hole course and hiking trails are nearby.

**Campsites, facilities:** There are 29 sites with partial hookups (30 and 50 amps) for tents or

RVs of any length. Picnic tables are provided. Restrooms with flush toilets and coin showers, drinking water, a dump station, cable TV, horseshoe pits, and a playground are available. Propane gas, a store, café, and coin laundry are located within one mile. Leashed pets are permitted.

**Reservations, fees:** Reservations are accepted. Sites are $15 per night. Open April-November, weather permitting.

**Directions:** From Chehalis on I-5, take Exit 76 to Rice Road. Turn south and drive 0.13 mile to the park.

**Contact:** Stan Hedwall Park, City of Chehalis, 360/748-0271, www.ci.chehalis.wa.us.

## 12 LEWIS AND CLARK STATE PARK

### Scenic rating: 8

near Chehalis

**Map 5.1, page 317**

The highlight of this state park is an immense old-growth forest that contains some good hiking trails and a 0.5-mile nature trail. This famous grove lost half of its old-growth trees along the highway when they were blown down in the legendary 1962 Columbus Day storm. This was a cataclysmic event for one of the last major stands of old-growth forest in the state. The park covers 621 acres and features primarily Douglas fir and red cedar, wetlands, and dense vegetation. There are eight miles of trails, including five miles of horse trails. June is Youth Fishing Month, when youngsters age 14 and younger can fish the creek. Jackson House tours, in which visitors can see a pioneer home built in 1845 north of the Columbia River, are available year-round by appointment.

**Campsites, facilities:** There are 25 sites for tents or self-contained RVs (no hookups), nine sites with full hookups (30 amps) for RVs up to 35 feet long, five primitive equestrian sites, one hiker-biker site, and two group camps for up to 50 people each. A bunkhouse for up to 24 people is also available. Picnic tables and fire grills are provided. Restrooms with flush toilets and coin showers, drinking water, a small store, firewood, a picnic area, an amphitheater, day-use area that can be reserved, playground, horseshoe pits, volleyball, badminton, and interpretive activities are available. Leashed pets are permitted.

**Reservations, fees:** Reservations are not accepted for family sites but are required for the bunkhouse at 360/902-8600 or 800/360-4240. Sites are $21 per night, equestrian sites are $14 per night, $10 per extra vehicle per night. The bunkhouse is $10.77 per person with a 15-person minimum. Call for group site rates. Open April-late September.

**Directions:** From Chehalis, drive south on I-5 six miles to Exit 68 and U.S. 12. Turn east on U.S. 12 for three miles to Jackson Highway. Turn right and drive three miles to the park entrance on the right.

**Contact:** Lewis and Clark State Park, 360/864-2643; state park information, 360/902-8844, www.parks.wa.gov.

## 13 IKE KINSWA STATE PARK

### Scenic rating: 8

on Mayfield Lake

**Map 5.1, page 317**

This state park is set alongside the north shore of Mayfield Lake. The park features 8.5 miles of shore, forested campsites, 2.5 miles of hiking trails, and two miles of bike trails. Mayfield Lake is a treasure trove of recreational possibilities. Fishing is a year-round affair here, with trout and tiger muskie often good. Boating, waterskiing, swimming, and driftwood collecting are all popular. The park is named after a prominent member of the Cowlitz tribe. Two fish hatcheries are located nearby. A spectacular view of Mount St. Helens can be found at a vista point 11 miles east. This popular campground often fills on summer weekends. Be sure to reserve well in advance.

**Campsites, facilities:** There are 31 developed tent sites, 72 sites with full or partial hookups (30 amps) for RVs up to 36 feet long, two primitive tent sites, and five cabins. Picnic tables and fire grills are provided. Restrooms with flush toilets and coin showers, drinking water, a dump station, store, playground, picnic area, horseshoe pits, and firewood are available. Boat docks and launching facilities are nearby. Some facilities are wheelchair accessible. Leashed pets are permitted.

**Reservations, fees:** Reservations are accepted at 888/CAMP-OUT (888/226-7688) or www.goingtocamp.com ($6.50-8.50 reservation fee). RV sites are $28-42 per night, tent sites are $21-22 per night, primitive sites are $12 per night, $10 per extra vehicle per night, and cabins are $65-77 per night. Some credit cards are accepted. Some camping sections are open year-round.

**Directions:** From Chehalis, drive south on I-5 six miles to Exit 68 and U.S. 12. Turn east on U.S. 12 and drive 14 miles to Silver Creek Road (State Route 122). Turn left (north) and drive 1.9 miles to a Y intersection. Bear right on State Route 122/Harmony Road and drive 1.6 miles to the park entrance.

**Contact:** Ike Kinswa State Park, 360/983-3402; state park information, 360/902-8844, www.parks.wa.gov.

## 14 HARMONY LAKESIDE RV PARK

### Scenic rating: 6

on Mayfield Lake

Map 5.1, page 317

This park fills up on weekends in July, August, and September. It is set on Mayfield Lake, a 10-mile-long lake with numerous recreational activities, including fishing, boating, riding personal watercraft, and waterskiing. Some sites feature lake views. Nearby Ike Kinswa State Park is a side-trip option.

**Campsites, facilities:** There are 80 sites with

full or partial hookups (30 and 50 amps) for RVs of any length; some sites are pull-through. Cabins are also available. Picnic tables and fire grills are provided. Restrooms with coin showers, drinking water, a dump station, ice, firewood, Wi-Fi, cable TV, coin laundry, boat docks, and launching facilities are available. Group facilities, including a banquet and meeting room, are also available. Leashed pets are permitted.

**Reservations, fees:** Reservations are recommended. Sites are $37.25-52.25 per night, cabins are $79-175 per night, $5 per night for each additional person, $11 per night for each additional vehicle. Winter and monthly rates are available. Some credit cards are accepted. Open year-round.

**Directions:** From Chehalis, drive south on I-5 for six miles to Exit 68 and U.S. 12. Turn east on U.S. 12 and drive 21 miles to Mossyrock (Highway 122). Turn left (north) and drive 3.5 miles to the park on the left.

**Contact:** Harmony Lakeside RV Park, 360/983-3804, www.mayfieldlake.com.

## 15 MAYFIELD LAKE PARK

### Scenic rating: 7

on Mayfield Lake

Map 5.1, page 317

Mayfield Lake is the centerpiece of this 50-acre park. Insider's tip: Campsites 42-54 are set along the lake's shoreline. The camp has a relaxing atmosphere and comfortable, wooded sites. Fishing is primarily for trout, bass, and silver salmon. Other recreational activities include waterskiing, swimming, and boating. For a great side trip, tour nearby Mount St. Helens.

**Campsites, facilities:** There are 55 sites with partial hookups for tents or RVs up to 45 feet and a group camp with 12 sites for tents or RVs up to 45 feet long. Picnic tables and fire rings are provided. Restrooms with flush toilets and coin showers, drinking water, boat launch, dump station, a day-use area with a picnic shelter that can be reserved, playground, horseshoe pits, and a volleyball court are available. Some facilities are wheelchair accessible. Leashed pets are permitted.

**Reservations, fees:** Reservations are accepted at 888/CAMP-OUT (888/226-7688) or www.tacomapower.com ($6.50-8.50 reservation fee). Sites are $29-32 per night, $10 per extra vehicle per night. The group camp is $180 per night ($15 reservation fee). Open mid-April-mid-October; the group camp is open Memorial Day weekend-mid-October.

**Directions:** From Longview, drive north on I-5 to Exit 68 and U.S. 12. Turn east on U.S. 12 and drive approximately 17 miles to Beach Road. Turn left and drive 0.25 mile to the park entrance.

**Contact:** Mayfield Lake Park, Tacoma Power, 360/985-2364, www.tacomapower.com.

# 16 MOSSYROCK PARK

🚶 🚴 ⛵ 🏊 🛶 🐴 🎣 ♿ 🚐 ⛺

### Scenic rating: 8

on Riffe Lake

**Map 5.1, page 317**      **BEST (**

This park is located along the southwest shore of Riffe Lake. It is an extremely popular campground. For anglers, it provides the best of both worlds: a boat launch on Riffe Lake, which offers coho salmon, rainbow trout, and bass, and nearby Swofford Pond, a 240-acre pond stocked with rainbow trout, brown trout, bass, catfish, and bluegill. Swofford Pond is located south of Mossyrock on Swofford Road; no gas motors are permitted. This campground provides access to a 0.5-mile loop nature trail. Bald eagles and ospreys nest on the north side of the lake in the 14,000-acre Cowlitz Wildlife Area.

**Campsites, facilities:** There are 101 sites with partial hookups for tents or RVs of any length, 12 walk-in sites, three group camps (60 sites) with partial hookups for tents or RVs of any length, and a primitive group camp (10 sites) for tents or RVs of any length. Picnic tables

and fire rings are provided. Restrooms with flush toilets and coin showers, drinking water, a dump station, seasonal convenience store, seasonal snack bar, coin laundry, fish-cleaning stations, two boat launches, playground, picnic area that can be reserved, a swimming area, horseshoe pit, volleyball net, BMX track, camp host, and interpretive displays are available. Some facilities are wheelchair accessible. Leashed pets are permitted.

**Reservations, fees:** Reservations are accepted at 888/CAMP-OUT (888/226-7688) or www.tacomapower.com ($6.50-8.50 reservation fee, $15 group reservation fee). Sites are $16-29 per night, $10 per extra vehicle per night. The primitive group camp is $180 per night and the other group camps are $22-26 per site per night with a minimum of five sites. Some credit cards are accepted in summer. Open year-round, excluding December 20-January 1.

**Directions:** From Chehalis, drive south on I-5 six miles to Exit 68 and Highway 12 East. Take Highway 12 East and drive 21 miles to Williams Street (flashing yellow light). Turn right and drive several blocks in the town of Mossyrock to a T intersection with State Street. Turn left and drive 3.5 miles (becomes Mossyrock Road East, then Ajlune Road) to the park. Ajlune Road leads right into the park.

**Contact:** Mossyrock Park, Tacoma Power, 360/983-3900, www.tacomapower.com.

# 17 TAIDNAPAM PARK

🏊 🛶 🚐 🏕 🐴 ♿ 🚐 ⛺

### Scenic rating: 8

on Riffe Lake

**Map 5.1, page 317**

This 50-acre park is located at the east end of Riffe Lake. Nestled in a cover of Douglas fir and maple, it is surrounded by thousands of acres of undeveloped greenbelt. Fishing is permitted year-round at the lake, with coho salmon, rainbow trout, and bass available. This camp was named after the Upper Cowlitz Indians, also known as Taidnapam.

**Campsites, facilities:** There are 139 sites with full or partial hookups for tents or RVs of any length, 24 walk-in tent sites, and a group camp (22 sites) with full or partial hookups for tents or RVs of any length. There is also a primitive group camp with 12 sites. Picnic tables and fire rings are provided. Restrooms with flush toilets and coin showers, drinking water, dump station, a fishing bridge, fish-cleaning stations, two boat launches, picnic shelter, playground, swimming beach, horseshoe pit, volleyball net, and interpretive displays are available. Some facilities are wheelchair accessible. Leashed pets are permitted.

**Reservations, fees:** Reservations for individual sites are accepted at 888/CAMP-OUT (888/226-7688) or www.tacomapower.com ($6.50-8.50 reservation fee). Group reservations are accepted at 360/497-7707 ($15 group reservation fee). Sites are $29-31 per night, $10 per extra vehicle per night, and walk-in sites are $16 per night. The group camp is $29-31 per site per night with a minimum of 10 sites; the primitive group camp is $180 per night for all 12 sites. Some credit cards are accepted in summer season. Open year-round, excluding December 20-January 1.

**Directions:** From Chehalis, drive south on I-5 to Exit 68 and Highway 12 East. Take Highway 12 East and drive 37 miles (5 miles past Morton) to Kosmos Road. Turn right and drive 200 yards to No. 100 Champion Haul Road. Turn left and drive four miles to the park entrance on the right.

**Contact:** Taidnapam Park, Tacoma Power, 360/497-7707, www.tacomapower.com.

## 18 RIVER OAKS RV PARK & CAMPGROUND

**Scenic rating: 8**

on the Cowlitz River

Map 5.1, page 317

This camp is set right on the Cowlitz River, with opportunities for boating and fishing for sturgeon, steelhead, and salmon in season. Swimming is not recommended because of the cold water. The park provides nearby access to Mount St. Helens. Note that some sites are filled with monthly renters.

**Campsites, facilities:** There are 30 sites with no hookups and 30 sites with full hookups (30 and 50 amps) for RVs of any length; some sites are pull-through. Picnic tables and fire rings are provided. Restrooms with flush toilets and showers, drinking water, firewood are available. A store with propane gas, bait and tackle, and a café are located within 0.3 mile. A boat-launch and mooring buoys are available nearby. Some facilities are wheelchair accessible. Leashed pets are permitted.

**Reservations, fees:** Reservations are accepted. Sites are $15-25 per night, $5 per person per night for more than two people. Weekly and monthly rates available. Open year-round.

**Directions:** From Castle Rock on I-5, take Exit 59 for Highway 506. Turn west on Highway 506 and drive 0.3 mile to the park on the left.

**Contact:** River Oaks RV Park & Campground, 360/864-2895, www.riveroaksrvpark.com.

## 19 PARADISE COVE RESORT & RV PARK

**Scenic rating: 7**

near the Toutle River

Map 5.1, page 317

This wooded park is situated about 400 yards from the Toutle River and 0.5 mile from the Cowlitz River. Take your pick: Seaquest State Park and Silver Lake to the east provide two excellent, activity-filled side-trip options. This is a major stopover for visits to Mount St. Helens.

**Campsites, facilities:** There are 50 sites for tents or RVs of any length (20, 30, and 50 amp full hookups) and a large dispersed tent camping area. Some sites are pull-through.

Picnic tables are provided. Restrooms with flush toilets and showers, drinking water, and coin laundry are available. Some facilities are wheelchair accessible. Leashed pets are permitted.

**Reservations, fees:** Reservations are accepted. Sites are $12-30 per night. Some credit cards are accepted. Open year-round.

**Directions:** From Longview, drive 10 miles north on I-5 to Castle Rock and Exit 52. Take Exit 52 and turn right on the frontage road and drive a short distance to Burma Road. Turn left and drive a short distance to the resort, just off the freeway (within view of the freeway).

**Contact:** Paradise Cove Resort & RV Park, 112 Burma Rd., 360/274-6785, http://paradisecove.faithweb.com.

## 20 LONGVIEW NORTH/ MOUNT ST. HELENS KOA

### Scenic rating: 6

near Silver Lake

Map 5.1, page 317

This RV park is located just outside Castle Rock, only three miles from the Mount St. Helens Visitor Center. It is close to the highway. Fishing and boating are available nearby on Silver Lake. Note that some sites are filled with monthly renters.

**Campsites, facilities:** There are 90 sites with full or partial hookups (20 and 30 amps) for tents or RVs up to 45 feet long and 10 sites for tents. Picnic tables are provided. Restrooms with flush toilets and coin showers, drinking water, cable TV, modem access, coin laundry, propane gas, horseshoe pits, a meeting room, and dump station are available. A convenience store and gasoline are nearby. Some facilities are wheelchair accessible. Leashed pets are permitted.

**Reservations, fees:** Reservations are recommended in the summer. RV sites are $33.50-39.50 per night, tent sites are $25.50 per night, $3-5 per person per night for more than two

people. Some credit cards are accepted. Open year-round.

**Directions:** From Longview, drive 10 miles north on I-5 to Castle Rock and Exit 49 and Highway 504. Take Exit 49 and drive east on Highway 504 for two miles to Tower Road. Turn left (well signed) and drive a short distance to a Y intersection and Schaffran Road. Bear right and drive approximately 300 yards to the park on the right

**Contact:** Longview North/Mount St. Helens KOA, 360/274-8522, www.koa.com.

## 21 SEAQUEST STATE PARK

### Scenic rating: 6

near Silver Lake

Map 5.1, page 317

This camp fills nightly because it is set along the paved road to the awesome Johnston Ridge Observatory, the premier lookout of Mount St. Helens. This state park is adjacent to Silver Lake, one of Western Washington's finest fishing lakes for bass and trout. But that's not all: The Mount St. Helens Visitor Center is located across the road from the park entrance. This heavily forested, 475-acre park features more than one mile of lake shoreline and 5.5 miles of trails for hiking and biking. The park is popular for day use as well as camping. No hunting or fishing is allowed.

The irony of the place is that some out-of-towners on vacation think that this park is located on the ocean because of its name, Seaquest. The park has nothing to do with the ocean, of course; it is named after Alfred L. Seaquest, who donated the property to the state for parkland. One interesting fact: He stipulated in his will that if liquor were ever sold on the property that the land would be transferred to Willamette University.

**Campsites, facilities:** There are 92 sites, including 33 sites with partial hookups (30 amps), for tents or RVs. There are also four hike-in/bike-in sites and five yurts. Picnic tables and fire grills are provided. Restrooms with flush toilets and coin showers, drinking water, a picnic area, playground, horseshoe pits, dump station, firewood, and a volleyball court are available. A store is within three miles. Some facilities are wheelchair accessible. Leashed pets are permitted.

**Reservations, fees:** Reservations are accepted at 888/CAMP-OUT (888/226-7688) or www.goingtocamp.com ($6.50-8.50 reservation fee). Sites are $27-42 per night, hike-in/bike-in sites are $12 per night, $10 per extra vehicle per night, and yurts are $59-69 per night. Some credit cards are accepted. Open year-round.

**Directions:** From Longview, drive 10 miles north on I-5 to Castle Rock and Exit 49 and Highway 504. Take Exit 49 and drive east on Highway 504 for 5.5 miles to the park.

**Contact:** Seaquest State Park, 360/274-8633; state park information, 360/902-8844, www.parks.wa.gov.

## 22 SILVER LAKE MOTEL AND RESORT
🏊 🚣 🛥 🐕 🎣 ♿ 🚐 ⛺

**Scenic rating: 8**

on Silver Lake

**Map 5.1, page 317**          **BEST (**

This park is set near the shore of Silver Lake and features a view of Mount St. Helens. One of Washington's better lakes for largemouth bass and trout, Silver Lake also has perch, crappie, and bluegill. Powerboating, personal watercraft riding, and waterskiing are popular. This spot is considered a great anglers' camp. The sites are set along a horseshoe-shaped driveway on grassy sites. Access is quick to Mount St. Helens, nearby to the east.

**Campsites, facilities:** There are 19 sites with full or partial hookups (30 amps) for RVs of any length, eight sites for tents, five cabins, and six motel rooms. Picnic tables are provided. Restrooms with flush toilets and coin showers, drinking water, Wi-Fi, meeting room, a convenience store, bait and tackle, fish-cleaning

station, ice, boat docks, boat rentals, launching facilities, and a playground are available. A dump station is within one mile, and a café is within four miles. Some facilities are wheelchair accessible. Leashed pets are permitted in the campground.

**Reservations, fees:** Reservations are accepted. RV sites are $29 per night, tent sites are $25 per night, $5 per extra vehicle per night. Some credit cards are accepted. Open mid-March-mid-November.

**Directions:** From Longview, drive 10 miles north on I-5 to Castle Rock and Exit 49 and Highway 504. Take Exit 49 and drive east on Highway 504 for six miles to the resort on the right.

**Contact:** Silver Lake Motel and Resort, 360/274-6141, www.silverlake-resort.com.

## 23 KALAMA HORSE CAMP
🥾 🐎 🐕 ♿ 🚐 ⛺

**Scenic rating: 8**

near Mount St. Helens

**Map 5.1, page 317**

The most popular horse camp in the area, Kalama Horse Camp receives the enthusiastic volunteer support of local equestrians. The camp fills on weekends partly because of a network of 53 miles of horse trails accessible from camp. It is located very near Mount St. Helens.

**Campsites, facilities:** There are 17 sites for tents or RVs up to 25 feet long and two double sites. Picnic tables and fire grills are provided. Vault toilets are available. There is no drinking water and garbage must be packed out. Horse facilities include 10- by 10-foot corrals, a staging and mounting assist area, stock water, a stock-loading ramp, hitching rails, and manure disposal bins. A 24- by 36-foot log cabin shelter with a picnic area with horseshoe pits is also available. Boat-launching facilities are located on Lake Merrill. Some facilities are wheelchair accessible. Leashed pets are permitted.

**Reservations, fees:** Reservations are not

accepted. Sites are $8-12 per night, $16 per night for double sites, $5 per night per extra vehicle. Open April-mid-December, weather permitting.

**Directions:** From Woodland on I-5, take Exit 21 for Highway 503. Drive east on Highway 503 for 23 miles to the Highway 503 spur. Continue northeast on the Highway 503 spur to Forest Road 81 (at Yale Lake, one mile south of Cougar). Turn left on Forest Road 81 and drive about eight miles to the camp on the right.

**Contact:** Gifford Pinchot National Forest, Mount St. Helens National Volcanic Monument, 360/449-7800, www.fs.usda.gov.

## 24 MERRILL LAKE

### Scenic rating: 7
near Mount St. Helens

**Map 5.1, page 317**

Campers seeking a quiet setting will enjoy this site, which has a reputation as the top fly-fishing area of Western Washington. Due to its popularity, there is a three-day stay limit. The campground is nestled in old-growth Douglas fir on the shore of Lake Merrill, very near Mount St. Helens. It's free and provides an alternative to the more developed parks in the area, especially those along the main access roads to viewing areas of the volcano. The lake provides fishing for brown trout and cutthroat trout but is restricted to fly-fishing only, with no gas motors permitted. These restrictions make it ideal for fly fishers with prams or float tubes.

**Campsites, facilities:** There are eight sites for tents only. Picnic tables, fire grills, and tent pads are provided. Vault toilets are available. There is no drinking water and garbage must be packed out. A campground host is on-site. Boat-launching facilities are located on Lake Merrill. Some facilities are wheelchair accessible. Leashed pets are permitted.

**Reservations, fees:** Reservations are not accepted. There is no fee for camping, but a

Discover Pass is required. Open April 15-November, weather permitting.

**Directions:** From Woodland on I-5, take Exit 21 for Highway 503. Drive east on Highway 503 for 23 miles to the Highway 503 spur. Continue northeast on the Highway 503 spur to Forest Road 81 (at Yale Lake, one mile south of Cougar). Turn left on Forest Road 81 and drive 4.5 miles to the campground access road on the left.

**Contact:** Department of Natural Resources, Pacific Cascade Region, South, 360/577-2025 or 360/274-4196, www.dnr.wa.gov; Pacific Cascade Region information, 360/274-2055.

## 25 LONE FIR RESORT

### Scenic rating: 4
near Yale Lake

**Map 5.1, page 317**

This private campground is located near Yale Lake (the smallest of four lakes in the area) and, with grassy sites and plenty of shade trees, is designed primarily for RV use. Mount St. Helens provides a side-trip option. The trailhead for the summit climb is located nearby at Climber's Bivouac on the south flank of the volcano; a primitive campground with dispersed sites for hikers only is available there. Note: This trailhead is the only one available for the summit climb. Though infrequent, the trail to the summit can be closed because of volcanic activity at the plug dome.

**Campsites, facilities:** There are 36 sites with full hookups (30 and 50 amps) for RVs of any length, a grassy area for tents, four cabins, and 12 motel rooms. Some sites are pull-through. Picnic tables are provided, and fire pits are available at some sites. Restrooms with flush toilets and coin showers, satellite TV, drinking water, coin laundry, clubhouse, playground, Wi-Fi, community fire pit, horseshoe pits, ice, a snack bar, snowshoe rentals, restaurant, and a seasonal heated swimming pool are available. Propane gas, a store, boat docks, and launching facilities are nearby. Some facilities are wheelchair accessible. Leashed pets are permitted.

**Reservations, fees:** Reservations are accepted. RV sites are $30 per night, tent sites are $20 per night for up to four people, $5 per night for each extra person. Some credit cards are accepted. Open year-round.

**Directions:** In Woodland on I-5, take Exit 21 for Highway 503. Drive east on Highway 503 for 29 miles to Cougar and the resort turnoff (marked, in town, with the park visible from the road) on the left.

**Contact:** Lone Fir Resort, 360/238-5210, www.lonefirresort.com.

## 26 EVANS CREEK
🏃 🚴 🐴 ⛰️

### Scenic rating: 7
on Evans Creek in Mount Baker-Snoqualmie National Forest

Map 5.2, page 318

This primitive campground is located close to Evans Creek in an off-road-vehicle area near the northwestern corner of Mount Rainier National Park. If you're looking for a quiet, secluded spot, this isn't it. The two nearby roads that lead into the park are secondary or gravel roads and provide access to several other primitive campgrounds and backcountry trails in the park. A national forest map details the back roads and hiking trails.

**Campsites, facilities:** There are 23 sites for tents or small trailers. Picnic tables and fire grills are provided. Drinking water and vault toilets are available. Garbage must be packed out. Downed wood can be gathered for campfires. Leashed pets are permitted.

**Reservations, fees:** Reservations are not accepted. There is no fee for camping, but a Northwest Forest Pass ($5 daily fee, $30 annual fee per vehicle) is required to park at the trailhead. Open year-round, weather permitting.

**Directions:** From Tacoma on I-5, turn east on Highway 167 and drive nine miles to Highway 410. Continue 11 miles east on Highway 410

to the town of Buckley and Highway 165. Turn south on Highway 165 and drive 11 miles to Forest Road 7920. Turn left and drive 1.5 miles to the campground on the right.

**Contact:** Mount Baker-Snoqualmie National Forest, White River Ranger District, 360/825-6585, www.fs.usda.gov.

## 27 MOWICH LAKE WALK-IN
🏃 🛶 🐴 ⛰️

### Scenic rating: 8
near the Carbon River in Mount Rainier National Park

Map 5.2, page 318

This walk-in camp features campsites set adjacent to and above Mowich Lake, with a lake view from some of the sites. A 200-yard walk is required to reach the campsites. Some backpackers use the camp as a launch point for trips into the Mount Rainier Wilderness. The Wonderland Trail can be accessed at this campground. Fishing is poor for trout at Mowich Lake because it is not stocked and lacks a habitat for natural spawning.

**Campsites, facilities:** There are 10 walk-in sites for tents only. Picnic tables are provided at some sites. Vault toilets are available. There is no drinking water and garbage must be packed out. Campfires are not permitted; use a backpacking stove. Leashed pets are permitted in camp, but not on trails.

**Reservations, fees:** Reservations are not accepted. There is a $15 per vehicle park entrance fee. Open June-October, weather permitting.

**Directions:** From Tacoma on I-5, turn east on Highway 167 and drive nine miles to Highway 410. Continue 11 miles east on Highway 410 to the town of Buckley and Highway 165. Turn right (south) on Highway 165 and drive to a fork with Carbon River Park Road. Bear right and stay on Highway 165 for eight miles to the campground at the end of the road. Only high-clearance vehicles are recommended on this access road.

**Contact:** Mount Rainier National Park, 360/569-2211, www.nps.gov/mora.

## 28 IPSUT CREEK

**Scenic rating: 8**

near the Carbon River in Mount Rainier National Park

**Map 5.2, page 318**

This camp is only open to hikers with a backcountry camping permit; access requires a five-mile hike in and a Wilderness Permit from Mount Rainier National Park. From the campground, the seven-mile (round-trip) Carbon Glacier Trail follows the Carbon River through the forest to the snout of the glacier; watch for falling rocks. In addition, the Carbon River Rain Forest Nature Trail begins at the Carbon River entrance to the park. This 0.3-mile loop trail explores the only inland rainforest at Mount Rainier National Park. Note that fishing is prohibited on Ipsut Creek above the campground at the water supply intake. The elevation is 2,300 feet.

**Campsites, facilities:** There are 29 sites for tents and two group camps for up to 25 and 30 people respectively. Picnic tables and fire rings are provided. Drinking water, vault toilets, and a small amphitheater are available. Leashed pets are permitted in camp, but not on trails.

**Reservations, fees:** Reservations are not accepted. Sites are $9 per night, plus $15 per vehicle park entrance fee. Group sites are $20-25 per night. Open mid-summer to early fall, weather permitting.

**Directions:** From Puyallup, drive east on Highway 167 to Highway 410. Turn east on Highway 410 and drive 11 miles to the town of Buckley and Highway 165. Turn right (south) on Highway 165 and drive to a fork with Carbon River Park Road. Bear left and drive five miles to the campground on the left.

Note: Since a flood in 2006, the road has been closed to vehicles but campers are permitted on bicycles.

**Contact:** Mount Rainier National Park, 360/569-2211, www.nps.gov/mora.

## 29 WHITE RIVER

**Scenic rating: 7**

on the White River in Mount Rainier National Park

**Map 5.2, page 318**

This campground is set on the White River at 4,400 feet elevation. The Glacier Basin Trail, a seven-mile round-trip, starts at the campground and leads along the Emmons Moraine for a short distance before ascending above it. A view of the Emmons Glacier, the largest glacier in the continental United States, is possible by hiking the spur trail, the Emmons Moraine Trail. It is sometimes possible to spot mountain goats, as well as mountain climbers, on the surrounding mountain slopes. Note that another trail near camp leads a short distance (but vertically, for a rise of 2,200 feet) to the Sunrise Visitor Center. Local rangers recommend that trailers be left at the White River Campground and the 11-mile road trip to Sunrise be made by car. From there, you can take several trails that lead to backcountry lakes and glaciers. Also note that this campground is located in what is considered a geo-hazard zone, where there is risk of a mudflow, although it hasn't happened in recent years.

**Campsites, facilities:** There are 112 sites for tents or RVs up to 27 feet. Picnic tables and fire grills are provided. Flush toilets and drinking water are available. A small amphitheater is nearby. Some facilities are wheelchair accessible. Leashed pets are permitted in camp, but not on trails or in the wilderness.

**Reservations, fees:** Reservations are not accepted. Sites are $12 per night, plus $15 per vehicle park entrance fee. Some credit cards are accepted. Open July-mid-September.

**Directions:** From Enumclaw, drive southeast on Highway 410 to the entrance of Mount Rainier National Park and White River Road. Turn right and drive seven miles to the campground on the left.

**Contact:** Mount Rainier National Park, 360/569-2211, www.nps.gov/mora.

## 30 SILVER SPRINGS

### Scenic rating: 9
in Mount Baker-Snoqualmie National Forest

**Map 5.2, page 318**

Silver Springs campground along the White River on the northeastern border of Mount Rainier National Park offers a good alternative to the more crowded camps in the park. It's located in a beautiful section of large old-growth forest, primarily with Douglas fir, cedar, and hemlock which tower over the White River. Salmon can be seen heading upriver at certain times of year. Recreational options include kayaking, fishing, and hiking. A U.S. Forest Service information center is located one mile away from the campground entrance on Highway 410.

**Campsites, facilities:** There are 55 sites for tents or RVs up to 40 feet long and two double sites. Picnic tables and fire grills are provided. Flush toilets, drinking water, and downed firewood for gathering are available. The group site has a picnic shelter. Some facilities are wheelchair accessible. Leashed pets are permitted.

**Reservations, fees:** Reservations are accepted at 877/444-6777 ($10 recreation fee) or www.recreation.gov ($9 reservation fee). Single sites are $20 per night, double sites are $32 per night, $10 per night extra vehicle fee. Open mid-May-late September, weather permitting.

**Directions:** From Enumclaw, drive east on Highway 410 for 31 miles (1 mile south of the turnoff for Corral Pass) to the campground entrance on the right.

**Contact:** Mount Baker-Snoqualmie National Forest, White River Ranger District, 360/825-6585, www.fs.fed.us or www.hoodoo.com.

## 31 LODGEPOLE

### Scenic rating: 6
on the American River in Wenatchee National Forest

**Map 5.2, page 318**

This campground is set at an elevation of 3,500 feet along the American River, just eight miles east of the boundary of Mount Rainier National Park. Winter activities in the park include cross-country skiing, snowshoeing, and inner-tube sledding down slopes. Fishing access is available nearby.

**Campsites, facilities:** There are 34 sites for tents or RVs up to 42 feet long. Call to confirm site availability for large RVs. Picnic tables and fire grills are provided. Drinking water, vault toilets, garbage service, and firewood are available. A camp host is on-site. Some facilities are wheelchair accessible. Leashed pets are permitted.

**Reservations, fees:** Reservations are accepted at 877/444-6777 ($10 reservation fee) or www.recreation.gov ($9 reservation fee). Sites are $18 per night, $9 per night for each additional vehicle. Open mid-May-mid-September, weather permitting.

**Directions:** From Yakima, drive northwest on U.S. 12 for 18 miles to Highway 410. Bear northwest on Highway 410 and drive 40.5 miles (8 miles east of the national park boundary) to the campground on the right.

**Contact:** Okanogan and Wenatchee National Forests, Naches Ranger District, 509/653-1401, www.fs.usda.gov or www.hoodoo.com.

## 32 PLEASANT VALLEY

### Scenic rating: 7
on the American River in Wenatchee National Forest

**Map 5.2, page 318**

It's always strange how campgrounds get their names. Pleasant Valley? More like

Camp Thatcher, as in Thatcher ants, which have infested the campground and can inflict painful bites on you and your pet. Even the Forest Service advises, "Camp at your own risk. No refunds." If you're still set on camping here, plan to stay off the ground and away from the anthills, or bring an RV. That said, the campground (elevation of 3,300 feet) does provide a good base camp for a hiking or fishing trip. A trail from the camp follows Kettle Creek up to the American Ridge and Kettle Lake in the William O. Douglas Wilderness. It joins another trail that follows the ridge and then drops down to Bumping Lake (a U.S. Forest Service map is essential). You can fish here for whitefish, steelhead, trout, and salmon in season; check regulations. In the winter, the area is popular with cross-country skiers.

**Campsites, facilities:** There are 17 sites for tents or RVs up to 32 feet long. Picnic tables and fire grills are provided. Drinking water, garbage service, vault toilets, and a picnic shelter are available. Downed firewood may be gathered. A camp host is on-site. Some facilities are wheelchair accessible. Leashed pets are permitted.

**Reservations, fees:** Reservations are accepted at 877/444-6777 ($10 reservation fee) or www.recreation.gov ($9 reservation fee). Sites are $16 per night, $8 per night for each additional vehicle. Open mid-May-mid-September, weather permitting.

**Directions:** From Yakima, drive northwest on U.S. 12 for 18 miles to Highway 410. Bear northwest on Highway 410 and drive 37 miles to the campground on the left.

**Contact:** Okanogan and Wenatchee National Forests, Naches Ranger District, 509/653-1401, www.fs.usda.gov or www.hoodoo.com.

## 33 HELLS CROSSING

### Scenic rating: 7
on the American River in Wenatchee National Forest

**Map 5.2, page 318**

Hells Crossing campground lies along the American River at an elevation of 3,250 feet. A steep trail from the camp leads up to Goat Peak and follows the American Ridge in the William O. Douglas Wilderness. Other trails join the ridgeline trail and connect with lakes and streams. Fishing here is for trout, steelhead, salmon, and whitefish in season; check regulations.

**Campsites, facilities:** There are 12 sites, including two multi-family sites, for tents or RVs up to 20 feet long and six sites for tents only. Picnic tables and fire grills are provided. Drinking water (at the west end of camp) and vault toilets are available. Downed firewood may be gathered. Leashed pets are permitted.

**Reservations, fees:** Reservations are accepted at 877/444-6777 ($10 reservation fee) or www. recreation.gov ($9 reservation fee). Sites are $17-19 per night for single sites, $34 per night for double sites, and $5 per night for each additional vehicle. Open mid-May-mid-September, weather permitting.

**Directions:** From Yakima, drive northwest on U.S. 12 for 18 miles to Highway 410. Bear northwest on Highway 410 and drive 33.5 miles to the campground on the right.

**Contact:** Okanogan and Wenatchee National Forests, Naches Ranger District, 509/653-1401, www.fs.usda.gov or www.hoodoo.com.

## 34 PINE NEEDLE GROUP CAMP

### Scenic rating: 7
on the American River in Wenatchee National Forest

**Map 5.2, page 318**

This reservations-only group campground sits

on the edge of the William O. Douglas Wilderness along the American River at an elevation of 3,000 feet. There are trails leading south into the backcountry at nearby camps; consult a U.S. Forest Service map. The camp is easy to reach, rustic, and beautiful. Fishing is available for whitefish, trout, steelhead, and salmon in season. For a side trip, visit Bumping Lake to the south, where recreation options include boating, fishing, and swimming.

**Campsites, facilities:** There is one group site for tents or RVs up to 30 feet long that can accommodate up to 60 people. Picnic tables and fire grills are provided. Vault toilets are available. There is no drinking water here, but it is available 2.5 miles west at Hells Crossing campground. Garbage must be packed out. Downed firewood may be gathered. Leashed pets are permitted.

**Reservations, fees:** Reservations are accepted at 877/444-6777 ($10 reservation fee) or www. recreation.gov ($9 reservation fee). The camp is $50 per night. Open mid-May-mid-November, weather permitting.

**Directions:** From Yakima, drive northwest on U.S. 12 for 18 miles to Highway 410. Bear northwest on Highway 410 and drive 30.5 miles to the campground on the left.

**Contact:** Okanogan and Wenatchee National Forests, Naches Ranger District, 509/653-1401, www.fs.usda.gov.

## 35 COUGAR FLAT
🏃 🛶 🐕 ♿ 🚐 ⛺

### Scenic rating: 5
on the Bumping River in Wenatchee National Forest

**Map 5.2, page 318**

Cougar Flat suffered heavy storm damage in 2013. At time of publication, it remained closed until repairs could be completed. Call to confirm availability.

One of several camps in the immediate vicinity, this spot along the Bumping River is close to good fishing; a trail from the camp

follows the river and then heads up the tributaries. The elevation is 3,100 feet.

**Campsites, facilities:** There are eight sites for tents or RVs up to 40 feet long and four walk-in sites for tents only. Picnic tables and fire grills are provided. Drinking water, vault toilets, and garbage bins are available. Some facilities are wheelchair accessible. Leashed pets are permitted.

**Reservations, fees:** Reservations are accepted at 877/444-6777 ($10 reservation fee) or www. recreation.gov ($9 reservation fee). Sites are $15-17 per night, $5 per night for each additional vehicle. Open mid-May-mid-September, weather permitting.

**Directions:** From Yakima, drive northwest on U.S. 12 for 18 miles to Highway 410. Turn left (northwest) on Highway 410 and drive 28.5 miles to Forest Road 1800. Turn left (southwest) and drive six miles (along the Bumping River) to the campground on the left.

**Contact:** Okanogan and Wenatchee National Forests, Naches Ranger District, 509/653-1401, www.fs.usda.gov or www.hoodoo.com.

## 36 SODA SPRINGS
🏃 🚲 🛶 〰️ 🐕 ♿ 🚐 ⛺

### Scenic rating: 6
on the Bumping River in Wenatchee National Forest

**Map 5.2, page 318**

Highlights at this camp along Bumping River include natural mineral springs and a nature trail. The mineral spring is located next to a trail across the river from the campground, where the water bubbles up out of the ground. This cold-water spring is popular with some campers for soaking and drinking. Many campers use this camp for access to nearby Bumping Lake. Fishing access is available. A sheltered picnic area is provided.

**Campsites, facilities:** There are 26 sites for tents or RVs up to 30 feet long. Picnic tables and fire grills are provided. Drinking water, vault toilets, firewood, a picnic shelter with a fireplace, and garbage service are available. A camp host is on-site. Some facilities are wheelchair accessible. Leashed pets are permitted.

**Reservations, fees:** Reservations are accepted at 877/444-6777 ($10 reservation fee) or www.recreation.gov ($9 reservation fee). Sites are $18 per night, $9 per night for each additional vehicle. Open mid-May-mid-September, weather permitting.

**Directions:** From Yakima, drive northwest on U.S. 12 for 18 miles to Highway 410. Turn left (northwest) on Highway 410 and drive 28.5 miles to Forest Road 1800. Turn left (southwest) and drive five miles (along the Bumping River) to the campground on the left.

**Contact:** Okanogan and Wenatchee National Forests, Naches Ranger District, 509/653-1401, www.fs.usda.gov or www.hoodoo.com.

## 37 CEDAR SPRINGS

### Scenic rating: 6

on the Bumping River in Wenatchee National Forest

**Map 5.2, page 318**

The Bumping River runs alongside this camp, set at an elevation of 2,800 feet. Fishing here follows the seasons for trout, steelhead, and whitefish; check regulations. If you continue driving southwest for 11 miles on Forest Road 1800/Bumping River Road, you'll reach Bumping Lake, where recreation options abound.

**Campsites, facilities:** There are 15 sites for tents or RVs up to 22 feet long, including two double sites. Picnic tables and fire grills are provided. Drinking water and vault toilets are available. Leashed pets are permitted.

**Reservations, fees:** Reservations are accepted at 877/444-6777 ($10 reservation fee) or www.recreation.gov ($9 reservation fee). Single sites are $16 per night, and $8 per night for each additional vehicle. Open mid-May-mid-September, weather permitting.

**Directions:** From Yakima, drive northwest

on U.S. 12 for 18 miles to Highway 410. Bear northwest on Highway 410 and drive 28.5 miles to the campground access road (Forest Road 1800/Bumping River Road). Turn left (southwest) and drive 0.5 mile to the campground on the left.

**Contact:** Okanogan and Wenatchee National Forests, Naches Ranger District, 509/653-1401, www.fs.usda.gov or www.hoodoo.com.

## 38 INDIAN FLAT GROUP CAMP

### Scenic rating: 7

on the American River in Wenatchee National Forest

**Map 5.2, page 318**

This reservations-only group campground is set along the American River at an elevation of 2,600 feet. Fishing access is available for trout, steelhead, and whitefish in season; check regulations. A trail starts just across the road from camp and leads into the backcountry, west along Fife's Ridge, and farther north to the West Quartz Creek drainage.

**Campsites, facilities:** There is one group site for tents or RVs up to 30 feet long, with a maximum capacity of 66 campers and 22 vehicles. Picnic tables and fire grills are provided. Drinking water, vault toilets, and firewood are available. Garbage must be packed out. Leashed pets are permitted.

**Reservations, fees:** Reservations are accepted at 877/444-6777 ($10 reservation fee) or www.recreation.gov ($9 reservation fee). The camp is $70 per night on weekdays and $100 per night on weekends. Open late May-mid-November, weather permitting.

**Directions:** From Yakima, drive northwest on U.S. 12 for 18 miles to Highway 410. Bear northwest on Highway 410 and drive 27 miles to the campground on the left.

**Contact:** Okanogan and Wenatchee National Forests, Naches Ranger District, 509/653-1401, www.fs.usda.gov.

## 39 LITTLE NACHES

**Scenic rating: 5**

on the Little Naches River in Wenatchee
National Forest

**Map 5.2, page 318**

This campground on the Little Naches River
near the American River is just 0.1 mile off the
road and 24 miles from Mount Rainier. The
easy access is a major attraction for highway
cruisers, but the location also means you can
sometimes hear highway noise, and at four
sites, you can see highway vehicles. Trees act
as a buffer between the highway and the campground at other sites. Fishing access is available
from camp. The elevation is 2,562 feet.

**Campsites, facilities:** There are 17 sites for
tents or RVs up to 49 feet long and one double
site. Picnic tables and fire grills are provided.
Drinking water, vault toilets, firewood, and
garbage service are available. A camp host is
on-site. Leashed pets are permitted.

**Reservations, fees:** Reservations are accepted
at 877/444-6777 ($10 reservation fee) or www.
recreation.gov ($9 reservation fee). Sites are
$14-26 per night, $7 per night for each additional vehicle. Open mid-May-mid-September,
weather permitting.

**Directions:** From Yakima, drive northwest
on U.S. 12 for 18 miles to Highway 410. Bear
northwest on Highway 410 and drive 25 miles
to the campground access road (Forest Road
1900). Turn left and drive 100 yards to the
campground on the left.

**Contact:** Okanogan and Wenatchee National
Forests, Naches Ranger District, 509/653-
1401, www.fs.usda.gov or www.hoodoo.com.

## 40 HALFWAY FLAT

**Scenic rating: 7**

on the Naches River in Wenatchee National Forest

**Map 5.2, page 318**

Fishing, hiking, and off-road vehicle (OHV)
opportunities abound at this campground along
the Naches River. A motorcycle trail leads from
the campground into the backcountry adjacent to
the William O. Douglas Wilderness; no motorized vehicles are permitted in the wilderness itself,
however. Do not expect peace and quiet. This
campground is something of a chameleon—
sometimes primarily a family campground, but
at other times dominated by OHV users.

**Campsites, facilities:** There are eight single
sites and three double sites for tents or RVs up
to 27 feet long and an area for dispersed tent
or RV camping. Picnic tables and fire grills
are provided. Drinking water, vault toilets,
and garbage service are available. Some facilities are wheelchair accessible. Leashed pets
are permitted.

**Reservations, fees:** Reservations are not
accepted. Sites are $10 per night, dispersed
campsites are $8 per night, $5 per night per
additional vehicle. Open mid-May-mid-September, weather permitting.

**Directions:** From Yakima, drive northwest
on U.S. 12 for 18 miles to Highway 410. Turn
left (northwest) on Highway 410 and drive 17
miles to Forest Road 1704. Turn left and drive
one mile to the campground.

**Contact:** Okanogan and Wenatchee National
Forests, Naches Ranger District, 509/653-
1401, www.fs.usda.gov.

## 41 SAWMILL FLAT

**Scenic rating: 6**

on the Naches River in Wenatchee National Forest

**Map 5.2, page 318**

This campground on the Naches River near
Halfway Flat is used by motorcyclists more
than any other types of campers. It offers fishing access and a hiking trail that leads west
from Halfway Flat campground for several
miles into the backcountry. Fishing is primarily for trout in summer, whitefish in winter—
check regulations. Another trailhead is located
at Boulder Cave to the south.

**Campsites, facilities:** There are 24 sites for tents or RVs 38 feet long. Picnic tables and fire grills are provided. Drinking water, vault toilets, garbage bins, firewood, and an Adirondack group shelter are available. A camp host is on-site in summer. Downed firewood may be gathered. Some facilities are wheelchair accessible. Leashed pets are permitted.

**Reservations, fees:** Reservations are accepted at 877/444-6777 ($10 reservation fee) or www.recreation.gov ($9 reservation fee). Sites are $18 per night, $9 per night for each additional vehicle. Open mid-May-mid-September, weather permitting.

**Directions:** From Yakima, drive northwest on U.S. 12 for 18 miles to Highway 410. Bear northwest on Highway 410 and drive 23.5 miles to the campground on the left.

**Contact:** Okanogan and Wenatchee National Forests, Naches Ranger District, 509/653-1401, www.fs.usda.gov or www.hoodoo.com.

## 42 COTTONWOOD

**Scenic rating: 7**

on the Naches River in Wenatchee National Forest

**Map 5.2, page 318**

Pretty, shaded sites and river views are the main draw at this camp along the Naches River. The fishing is similar to that of the other camps in the area—primarily for trout in summer and whitefish in winter. The elevation here is 2,300 feet.

**Campsites, facilities:** There are 13 sites for tents or RVs up to 22 feet long and three sites for tents only. Picnic tables and fire grills are provided. Drinking water, vault toilets, and garbage service are available. A store, café, and ice are available nearby. Leashed pets are permitted.

**Reservations, fees:** Reservations are accepted at 877/444-6777 ($10 reservation fee) or www.recreation.gov ($9 reservation fee). Sites are $16 per night, $8 per night for each additional vehicle. Open mid-May-mid-September, weather permitting.

**Directions:** From Yakima, drive northwest on U.S. 12 for 18 miles to Highway 410. Turn left (northwest) on Highway 410 and drive 17.5 miles to the campground on the left.

**Contact:** Okanogan and Wenatchee National Forests, Naches Ranger District, 509/653-1401, www.fs.usda.gov or www.hoodoo.com.

## 43 BUMPING LAKE CAMPGROUND

**Scenic rating: 7**

on Bumping Lake in Wenatchee National Forest

**Map 5.2, page 318**

This popular campground is set at an elevation of 3,200 feet near Bumping Lake amid a forest of primarily lodgepole pine. One of the more developed camps in the area, Bumping comprises two campgrounds—an upper and a lower section—and both fill quickly on summer weekends. A variety of water activities are allowed on Bumping Lake, including waterskiing, fishing (for salmon and trout), and swimming; the nearby boat launch makes it a winner for campers with boats. A picnic area is adjacent to the boat facilities and several hiking trails lead into the William O. Douglas Wilderness surrounding the lake. Woods and water—this spot has them both.

**Campsites, facilities:** There are 56 sites for tents or RVs up to 40 feet long and one site for tents only. Picnic tables and fire grills are provided. Drinking water, vault toilets, a boat launch, and a dump station ($10 fee) are available. Some facilities are wheelchair accessible. Leashed pets are permitted.

**Reservations, fees:** Reservations are accepted at 877/444-6777 ($10 reservation fee) or www.recreation.gov ($9 reservation fee). RV sites are $18-34 per night, tent sites are $18-20 per night, $9 per night for each additional vehicle. Open June-mid-September, weather permitting.

**Directions:** From Yakima, drive northwest on U.S. 12 for 18 miles to Highway 410. Turn left (northwest) on Highway 410 and drive 28.5 miles to Forest Road 1800. Turn left (southwest) and drive 11 miles (along the Bumping River); look for the campground entrance road on the right.

**Contact:** Wenatchee National Forest, Naches Ranger District, 509/653-1401, www.fs.usda.gov or www.hoodoo.com.

# 44 MOUNTHAVEN RESORT

**Scenic rating: 6**

near Mount Rainier National Park

**Map 5.2, page 318**

This campground is located within 0.5 mile of the Nisqually (southwestern) entrance to Mount Rainier National Park. In turn, it can provide a launching point for your vacation. One option: Enter the park at the Nisqually entrance, then drive on Nisqually Paradise Road for about five miles to Longmire Museum; general park information and exhibits about the plants and geology of the area are available. If you then continue into the park for 10 more miles, you'll arrive at the Jackson Visitor Center in Paradise, which has more exhibits and an observation deck. This road is the only one into the park that's open year-round. Winter activities in the park include cross-country skiing, snowshoeing, and inner-tube sledding down slopes. A creek runs through this wooded camp.

**Campsites, facilities:** There are 16 sites with full hookups (20 and 30 amps) for RVs of any length, one site for tents only, and nine furnished cabins. Picnic tables and fire grills are provided. A restroom with a toilet and shower, drinking water, coin laundry, pay phone, firewood, and a playground are available. A restaurant and a store are within one mile. Leashed pets are permitted.

**Reservations, fees:** Reservations are accepted at 800/456-9380. RV sites are $38 per night for up to four people, tent sites are $25-38 per night, $3 per night for each additional person, $3 per pet per night. Some credit cards are accepted. Open year-round.

**Directions:** From Chehalis, drive south on I-5 for 10 miles to U.S. 12. Turn east and drive 31 miles to Morton and Highway 7. Turn left (north) on Highway 7 and drive 17 miles to Elbe and Highway 706. Turn right (east) on Highway 706 and drive to Ashford; continue for six miles to the resort on the right.

**Contact:** Mounthaven Resort, 360/569-2594, www.mounthaven.com.

# 45 BIG CREEK

**Scenic rating: 8**

on Big Creek in Gifford Pinchot National Forest

**Map 5.2, page 318**

This camp is useful as an overflow spot for Mount Rainier Sound and for those who want to avoid driving their RV on the windy park roads. It is set along a stream next to a rural residential area in a forest setting made up of Douglas fir, western hemlock, western red cedar, and big leaf and vine maple.

**Campsites, facilities:** There are 24 sites for tents or RVs up to 40 feet long. Picnic tables and fire rings are provided. Drinking water, firewood, and vault toilets are available. A camp host is on-site. Some facilities are wheelchair accessible. Leashed pets are permitted.

**Reservations, fees:** Reservations are accepted at 877/444-6777 ($10 reservation fee) or www.recreation.gov ($9 reservation fee). Single sites are $18 per night, double sites are $34 per night, $9 per night for each additional vehicle. Open May-mid-September.

**Directions:** On I-5, drive to Exit 68 (south of Chehalis) and U.S. 12. Turn east on U.S. 12 and drive 62 miles to Packwood and Forest Road 52/Skate Creek Road. Turn left (northwest) and drive 23 miles to the campground on the left.

**Contact:** Gifford Pinchot National Forest, Cowlitz Valley Ranger District, 360/497-1100, www.fs.usda.gov or www.hoodoo.com.

## 46 COUGAR ROCK

### Scenic rating: 9

in Mount Rainier National Park

**Map 5.2, page 318**

Cougar Rock is a national park campground at 3,180 feet elevation at the foot of awesome Mount Rainier. To the east lies the Nisqually Vista Trail, a beautiful 1.2-mile loop trail. It begins at the visitors center at Paradise and provides stellar views of Mount Rainier and the Nisqually Glacier. Fishing tends to be marginal. As in all national parks, no trout are stocked, and lakes without natural fisheries provide zilch. Nearby Mounthaven Resort offers winter activities in Mount Rainier Park, such as cross-country skiing, snowshoeing, and inner-tube sledding down slopes.

**Campsites, facilities:** There are 173 sites for tents or RVs up to 35 feet long and five group sites for up to 24-40 people each. Picnic tables and fire rings are provided. Restrooms with flush toilets, drinking water, a dump station, and an amphitheater are available. A general store is located two miles away at Longmire. Some facilities are wheelchair accessible. Leashed pets are permitted.

**Reservations, fees:** Reservations are accepted at 877/444-6777 or www.recreation. gov ($9 reservation fee). Sites are $12-15 per night, plus a $15 per vehicle park entrance fee. Group sites are $40-64 per night. Open late May-late September.

**Directions:** From Tacoma, drive south on I-5 for five miles to Highway 512. Turn east on Highway 512 and drive two miles to Highway 7. Turn right (south) on Highway 7 and drive to Elbe and Highway 706. Continue east on Highway 706 and drive 12 miles to the park entrance. Continue 11 miles to the campground entrance on the left (about 2 miles past the Longmire developed area).

**Contact:** Mount Rainier National Park, 360/569-2211, www.nps.gov/mora.

## 47 OHANAPECOSH

### Scenic rating: 8

on the Ohanapecosh River in Mount Rainier National Park

**Map 5.2, page 318**   **BEST (**

This camp is set at an elevation of 1,914 feet at the foot of North America's most beautiful volcano, 14,410-foot Mount Rainier. It is also set along the Ohanapecosh River, adjacent to the Ohanapecosh Visitor Center, which features exhibits on the history of the forest, plus visitor information. A 0.5-mile loop trail leads from the campground, behind the visitors center, to Ohanapecosh Hot Springs. The Silver Falls Trail, a three-mile loop trail, follows the Ohanapecosh River to 75-foot Silver Falls. Warning: Do not climb on the wet rocks near the waterfall; they are wet and slippery. Note that Stevens Canyon Road heading west and Highway 123 heading north are closed by snowfall in winter.

**Campsites, facilities:** There are 188 sites for tents or RVs up to 32 feet and one group site for up to 25 people. Picnic tables and fire rings are provided. Flush and vault toilets, drinking water, and a dump station are available. An amphitheater is nearby. Some facilities are wheelchair accessible. Leashed pets are permitted in camp, but not on trails.

**Reservations, fees:** Reservations are accepted at 877/444-6777 or www.recreation.gov ($9 reservation fee). Sites are $12-15 per night, plus a $15 per vehicle park entrance fee. The group site is $40 per night. Some credit cards are accepted. Open mid-May-September.

**Directions:** On I-5, drive to Exit 68 (south of Chehalis) and U.S. 12. Turn east on U.S. 12 and drive 72 miles (7 miles past Packwood) to Highway 123. Turn left (north) and drive 6.5 miles to the Ohanapecosh entrance to the park. As you enter the park, the camp is on the left, next to the visitors center.

**Contact:** Mount Rainier National Park, 360/569-2211, www.nps.gov/mora.

## 48 LA WIS WIS

### Scenic rating: 9
on the Cowlitz River in Gifford Pinchot National Forest

**Map 5.2, page 318**

This camp is ideally located for day trips to Mount Rainier and Mount St. Helens. It's set at an elevation of 1,400 feet along the Clear Fork of the Cowlitz River, near the confluence with the Ohanapecosh River. Trout fishing is an option. The landscape features an old-growth forest of Douglas fir, western hemlock, western red cedar, and Pacific yew, with undergrowth of big leaf maple. A 200-yard trail provides access to the Blue Hole on the Ohanapecosh River, a deep pool designated by an observation point and interpretive signs. Another trail leads less than 0.25 mile to Purcell Falls. The entrance to Mount Rainier National Park is about seven miles south of the camp.

**Campsites, facilities:** There are 122 sites for tents or RVs up to 40 feet long, including a few double sites, and the Coho Group site. Picnic tables and fire rings are provided. Flush and vault toilets, drinking water, garbage bins, and firewood are available. Some facilities are wheelchair accessible. Leashed pets are permitted.

**Reservations, fees:** Reservations are accepted at 877/444-6777 ($10 reservation fee) or www.recreation.gov ($9 reservation fee). Single sites are $20 per night, double sites are $38 per night, $10 per extra vehicle per night, the group site is $90 per night. Open late May-early September, weather permitting.

**Directions:** On I-5, drive to Exit 68 (south of Chehalis) and U.S. 12. Turn east on U.S. 12 and drive 69 miles (about 6 miles past Packwood) to Forest Road 1272. Turn left and drive 0.5 mile to the campground on the left.

**Contact:** Gifford Pinchot National Forest, Cowlitz Valley Ranger District, 360/497-1100, www.fs.usda.gov or www.hoodoo.com.

## 49 PACKWOOD RV PARK

### Scenic rating: 6
in Packwood

**Map 5.2, page 318**

This is a pleasant campground, especially in the fall when the maples turn color. Groups are welcome. Mount Rainier National Park is located just 25 miles north, and this camp provides a good alternative if the park is full. Nearby recreation options include a riding stable. Note that some sites are filled with monthly renters.

**Campsites, facilities:** There are 100 sites, most with full hookups (30 amps), for RVs up to 60 feet long and many tent sites. Some sites are pull-through. Picnic tables are provided at some sites and portable fire pits are available on request. Restrooms with flush toilets and showers, cable TV, firewood, and coin laundry are available. A café, store, and propane and diesel gas are within walking distance. Leashed pets are permitted.

**Reservations, fees:** Reservations are accepted. RV sites are $30 per night, tent sites are $10-18 per night. Open year-round.

**Directions:** On I-5, drive to Exit 68 (south of Chehalis) and U.S. 12. Turn east on U.S. 12 and drive 65 miles to Packwood. The park is on the left (north) side of the highway in town at 12985 U.S. Highway 12.

**Contact:** Packwood RV Park, 360/494-5145, www.packwoodrv.com.

## 50 WHITE PASS

### Scenic rating: 7
on Leech Lake in Wenatchee National Forest

**Map 5.2, page 318**

This campground on the shore of Leech Lake sits at an elevation of 4,500 feet and boasts nearby trails leading into the Goat Rocks Wilderness to the south and the William O. Douglas Wilderness to the north. A trailhead for the Pacific Crest Trail is also nearby. Beautiful Leech Lake is popular for fly-fishing for rainbow trout. Note that this is the only type of fishing allowed here—check regulations. No gas motors are permitted on Leech Lake. White Pass Ski Area is located across the highway, 0.2 mile away.

**Campsites, facilities:** There are 16 sites for tents or RVs up to 20 feet long. Picnic tables and fire grills are provided. Vault toilets, garbage bins, and firewood are available. There is no drinking water. A store and ice are located within one mile. Boat-launching facilities are nearby. No gas motors on boats are allowed; electric motors are permitted. Leashed pets are permitted.

**Reservations, fees:** Reservations are not accepted. Sites are $8 per night, $5 per night per additional vehicle. Open mid-May-mid-September, weather permitting.

**Directions:** On I-5, drive to Exit 68 (south of Chehalis) and U.S. 12. Turn east on U.S. 12 and drive 81 miles (1 mile past the White Pass Ski Area) to the campground entrance road on the left side. Turn left (north) and drive 200 yards to Leech Lake and the campground.

**Contact:** Okanogan and Wenatchee National Forests, Naches Ranger District, 509/653-1401, www.fs.usda.gov.

## 51 DOG LAKE

### Scenic rating: 5
on Dog Lake in Wenatchee National Forest

Map 5.2, page 318

Set on the shore of Dog Lake at 3,400 feet elevation is little Dog Lake campground. Fishing can be good for native rainbow trout, and the lake is good for hand-launched boats, such as canoes and prams. Nearby trails lead into the William O. Douglas Wilderness.

**Campsites, facilities:** There are eight sites for tents or RVs up to 24 feet long. Picnic tables and fire grills are provided. Vault toilets and garbage bins are available. There is

no drinking water. No horses are allowed in the campground. Leashed pets are permitted.

**Reservations, fees:** Reservations are not accepted. Sites are $8 per night, $5 per extra vehicle per night. Open mid-May-early September, weather permitting.

**Directions:** On I-5, drive to Exit 68 (south of Chehalis) and U.S. 12. Turn east on U.S. 12 and drive 84 miles (3 miles past the White Pass Ski Area) to the campground entrance road on the left side.

**Contact:** Okanogan and Wenatchee National Forests, Naches Ranger District, 509/653-1401, www.fs.usda.gov.

## 52 CLEAR LAKE NORTH

### Scenic rating: 7
on Clear Lake in Wenatchee National Forest

Map 5.2, page 318

This primitive campground is set along the shore of Clear Lake at an elevation of 3,100 feet; it gets relatively little use. A 5-mph speed limit keeps the lake quiet and ideal for fishing, which is often good for rainbow trout. It is stocked regularly in the summer. Clear Lake is the forebay for Rimrock Lake. Swimming is allowed.

**Campsites, facilities:** There are 33 sites for tents or RVs up to 22 feet long and three double sites. Picnic tables and fire grills are provided. Vault toilets and garbage service are available. There is no drinking water at Clear Lake North, but there is drinking water at Clear Lake South campground. Boat docks and launching facilities are nearby. Some facilities are wheelchair accessible. Leashed pets are permitted.

**Reservations, fees:** Reservations are not accepted. Sites are $10 per night, $5 per extra vehicle per night. Open mid-May-mid-November, weather permitting.

**Directions:** From Yakima, drive northwest on U.S. 12 for 17 miles to the junction with Highway 410. Turn west on U.S. 12 and drive 31 miles to Forest Road 1200. Turn left (south) and drive 0.25 mile to Forest Road 1200-740. Continue south for 0.5 mile to the campground.

**Contact:** Okanogan and Wenatchee National Forests, Naches Ranger District, 509/653-1401, www.fs.usda.gov.

## 53 CLEAR LAKE SOUTH

**Scenic rating: 7**

in Wenatchee National Forest

**Map 5.2, page 318**

This campground (elevation 3,100 feet) is located near the east shore of Clear Lake, which is the forebay for Rimrock Lake. Fishing and swimming are recreation options. For winter travelers, several Sno-Parks in the area offer snowmobiling and cross-country skiing. Many hiking trails lie to the north.

**Campsites, facilities:** There are 22 sites for tents or RVs up to 22 feet long. Picnic tables and fire grills are provided. Drinking water, vault toilets, and garbage bins are available. Downed firewood may be gathered. Boat-launching facilities are nearby. Some facilities are wheelchair accessible. Leashed pets are permitted.

**Reservations, fees:** Reservations are not accepted. Sites are $10 per night, $5 per extra vehicle per night. Open mid-May-mid-November, weather permitting.

**Directions:** From Yakima, drive northwest on I-82 for 17 miles to the junction with Highway 410. Turn west on U.S. 12 and drive 31 miles to Forest Road 1200. Turn left (south) and drive one mile to Forest Road 1200-740. Continue south and drive 0.25 mile to the campground.

**Contact:** Okanogan and Wenatchee National Forests, Naches Ranger District, 509/653-1401, www.fs.usda.gov.

## 54 SILVER BEACH RESORT

**Scenic rating: 8**

on Rimrock Lake

**Map 5.2, page 318**

This resort along the shore of Rimrock Lake is one of several camps in the immediate area. It's very scenic, with beautiful lakefront sites. Hiking trails, marked bike trails, a full-service marina, a sandy swimming beach, and a riding stable are close by.

**Campsites, facilities:** There are 46 sites with full or partial hookups and 20 sites with no hookups for tents or RVs up to 40 feet long. Some sites are pull-through. There are also three cabins with kitchens and 16 motel rooms. Picnic tables and fire pits are provided. Restrooms with flush toilets and coin showers, a café, convenience store, dump station, bait and tackle, propane gas, ice, a playground, boat docks, launching facilities, and boat and personal watercraft rentals are available. Some facilities are wheelchair accessible. Leashed pets are permitted.

**Reservations, fees:** Reservations are accepted. Sites are $20-30 per night, $10 per extra vehicle per night. Some credit cards are accepted. Open year-round, with limited winter facilities.

**Directions:** From Yakima, drive northwest on U.S. 12 for 40 miles to the resort on the left.

**Contact:** Silver Beach Resort, 509/672-2500, www.silverbeach.biz.

## 55 INDIAN CREEK

**Scenic rating: 7**

on Rimrock Lake in Wenatchee National Forest

**Map 5.2, page 318**

Fishing, swimming, and waterskiing are among the activities at this shorefront campground on Rimrock Lake (elevation 3,000 feet). The camp is adjacent to Rimrock Lake Marina and Silver Beach Resort. This is a developed lake and an extremely popular campground, often filling on summer weekends. Fishing is often good for rainbow trout. The treasured Indian Creek Trail and many other excellent hiking trails about 5-10 miles north of the campground lead into the William O. Douglas Wilderness.

**Campsites, facilities:** There are 38 sites for tents or RVs up to 45 feet long. Picnic tables and fire grills are provided. Drinking water, vault toilets, and garbage bins are available. Downed firewood may be gathered. A camp host is on-site. A café, store, ice, boat docks, launching facilities, and rentals are nearby. Leashed pets are permitted.

**Reservations, fees:** Reservations are accepted at 877/444-6777 ($10 reservation fee) or www.recreation.gov ($9 reservation fee). Sites are $20 per night, $10 per extra vehicle per night. Open mid-May-mid-September, weather permitting.

**Directions:** From Yakima, drive northwest on I-82 for 17 miles to the junction with Highway 410. Turn west on U.S. 12 and drive 20 miles to Rimrock Lake and the campground entrance at the lake.

**Contact:** Okanogan and Wenatchee National Forests, Naches Ranger District, 509/653-1401, www.fs.usda.gov or www.hoodoo.com.

## 56 PENINSULA

**Scenic rating: 7**
on Rimrock Lake in Wenatchee National Forest

**Map 5.2, page 318**

Fishing for silvers and rainbow trout, swimming, and waterskiing are all allowed at Rimrock Lake (elevation 3,000 feet), where this shorefront recreation area and camp are located. The lake is stocked regularly in summer and is popular, in part because of the nearby boat ramp. This camp is one of several on the lake. A point of interest, the nearby emergency airstrip here features a grass runway. A nearby Sno-Park offers wintertime fun, including cross-country skiing and snowmobiling.

**Campsites, facilities:** There is a dispersed camping area for 60 tents or RVs up to 20 feet long. Picnic tables are provided. Vault toilets and garbage bins are available. There is no drinking water. Boat docks and launching facilities are nearby. Some facilities are wheelchair accessible. Leashed pets are permitted.

**Reservations, fees:** Reservations are not accepted. Sites are $8 per night, $5 per night per additional vehicle. Open May-mid-November, weather permitting.

**Directions:** From Yakima, drive northwest on I-82 for 17 miles to the junction with Highway 410. Turn west on U.S. 12 and drive 22 miles to Forest Road 1200. Turn left (south) and drive three miles (across the cattle guard) to Forest Road 711. Turn right (west) and drive a short distance to the campground.

**Contact:** Okanogan and Wenatchee National Forests, Naches Ranger District, 509/653-1401, www.fs.usda.gov.

## 57 SOUTH FORK GROUP CAMP

**Scenic rating: 8**
on the South Fork of the Tieton River in Wenatchee National Forest

**Map 5.2, page 318**

South Fork Group Camp is set at 3,000 feet elevation along the South Fork of the Tieton River, less than one mile from where it empties into Rimrock Lake. Note that fishing is prohibited to protect the bull trout. By traveling a bit farther south on Tieton River Road, you can see huge Blue Slide, an enormous prehistoric rock and earth slide that has a curious blue tinge to it. Note: In 2009, a fire burned south of this area.

**Campsites, facilities:** There is one group site for tents or RVs up to 40 feet long that accommodates up to 80 people. Picnic tables and fire grills are provided. Vault toilets are available. There is no drinking water and garbage must be packed out. Some facilities are wheelchair accessible. Leashed pets are permitted.

**Reservations, fees:** Reservations are accepted at 877/444-6777 ($10 reservation fee) or www.recreation.gov ($9 reservation fee). The site is $60 per night. Open May-mid-November, weather permitting.

**Directions:** From Yakima, drive northwest on I-82 for 17 miles to the junction with Highway 410. Turn west on U.S. 12 and drive 22 miles to Forest Road 1200. Turn left (south) and drive four miles to Forest Road 1203. Bear left and drive 0.75 mile to Forest Road 1203-517. Turn right and drive 200 feet to the campground.

**Contact:** Okanogan and Wenatchee National Forests, Naches Ranger District, 509/653-1401, www.fs.usda.gov.

## 58 IRON CREEK

**Scenic rating: 7**

on the Cispus River in Gifford Pinchot National Forest

**Map 5.2, page 318**

This popular U.S. Forest Service campground is set along the Cispus River near its confluence with Iron Creek. Trout fishing is available. The landscape features primarily Douglas fir, western red cedar, and old-growth forest on fairly flat terrain. The camp is also located along the access route that leads to the best viewing areas on the eastern flank for Mount St. Helens. Take a 25-mile drive to Windy Ridge Vista Point for a breathtaking view of Spirit Lake and the blast zone of the volcano.

**Campsites, facilities:** There are 80 single sites and 18 double sites for tents or RVs up to 40 feet long. Picnic tables and fire rings are provided. Drinking water, vault toilets, firewood, and an amphitheater are available. A camp host is on-site. Some facilities are wheelchair accessible. Leashed pets are permitted.

**Reservations, fees:** Reservations are accepted at 877/444-6777 ($10 reservation fee) or www.recreation.gov ($9 reservation fee). Sites are $20-38 per night, $10 per extra vehicle

per night. Open mid-May-early September, weather permitting.

**Directions:** From Chehalis, drive south on I-5 for six miles to Exit 68 and U.S. 12. Turn east on U.S. 12 and drive 48 miles to Randle and Highway 131. Turn south on Highway 131 and drive one mile (becomes Forest Road 25). Continue south on Forest Road 25 and drive nine miles to a fork. Bear left at the fork, continue across the bridge, turn left, and drive two miles to the campground entrance on the left (along the south shore of the Cispus River).

**Contact:** Gifford Pinchot National Forest, Cowlitz Valley Ranger District, 360/497-1100, www.fs.usda.gov or www.hoodoo.com.

## 59 TOWER ROCK

**Scenic rating: 5**

on the Cispus River in Gifford Pinchot National Forest

**Map 5.2, page 318**

Tower Rock campground along the Cispus River is an alternative to nearby Iron Creek and North Fork. It has shaded and sunny sites, with lots of trees and plenty of room. The camp is set fairly close to the river; some sites feature river frontage. It is also fairly flat and forested with Douglas fir, western hemlock, red cedar, and big leaf maple. Fishing for trout is popular here.

**Campsites, facilities:** There are 22 sites for tents or RVs up to 40 feet long. Picnic tables and fire grills are provided. Drinking water, vault toilets, and firewood are available. Leashed pets are permitted.

**Reservations, fees:** Reservations are accepted at 877/444-6777 ($10 reservation fee) or www.recreation.gov ($9 reservation fee). Sites are $18 per night, $9 per extra vehicle per night. Open mid-May-mid-September, weather permitting.

**Directions:** From Chehalis, drive south on I-5 for six miles to Exit 68 and U.S. 12. Turn east on U.S. 12 and drive 48 miles to Randle and Highway 131. Turn right (south) on Highway

131 and drive one mile to Forest Road 23. Turn left on Forest Road 23 and drive eight miles to Forest Road 28. Turn right and drive two miles to Forest Road 76. Turn right and drive two miles to the campground entrance road on the right.

**Contact:** Gifford Pinchot National Forest, Cowlitz Valley Ranger District, 360/497-1100, www.fs.usda.gov or www.hoodoo.com.

## 60 NORTH FORK, ELK, BEAVER, AND BEAR GROUP

### Scenic rating: 6

on the Cispus River in Gifford Pinchot National Forest

**Map 5.2, page 318**

This campground offers single sites, double sites, and group camps, with the North Cispus River flowing between the sites for individual and group use. Campsites are set back from the river in a well-forested area, however some trees have weak roots; campsites may be periodically closed to remove diseased trees. A national forest map details the backcountry access to the Valley Trail, which is routed up the Cispus River Valley for 16.7 miles. This trailhead provides access for hikers, bikers, all-terrain vehicles, and horses. Note that if you explore Road 2300-083 15 miles west you will find Layser Cave, a Native American archeological site that is open to the public. The elevation is 1,500 feet.

**Campsites, facilities:** There are 33 sites for tents or RVs up to 31 feet long, including a few multi-sites, and three group camps that accommodate up to 35 people each. Picnic tables and fire grills are provided. Drinking water, vault toilets, garbage bins, and firewood are available. Leashed pets are permitted.

**Reservations, fees:** Reservations are accepted at 877/444-6777 ($10 reservation fee) or www.recreation.gov ($9 reservation fee). Single sites are $18 per night, double sites are

$34 per night, $9 per extra vehicle per night, and group sites are $75-100 per night. Open mid-May-mid-September, weather permitting.

**Directions:** From Chehalis, drive south on I-5 for six miles to Exit 68 and U.S. 12. Turn east on U.S. 12 and drive 48 miles to Randle and Highway 131. Turn right (south) on Highway 131 and drive one mile to Forest Road 23. Bear left and drive 11 miles to the campground on the left.

**Contact:** Gifford Pinchot National Forest, Cowlitz Ranger District, 360/497-1100, www.fs.usda.gov or www.hoodoo.com.

## 61 BLUE LAKE CREEK

### Scenic rating: 7

near Blue Lake in Gifford Pinchot National Forest

**Map 5.2, page 318**

This camp is set at an elevation of 1,900 feet along Blue Lake Creek. With access to a network of all-terrain vehicle (ATV) trails, it is a significant camp for ATV owners. There is nearby access to 16.7-mile Valley Trail. This camp is also near the launch point for the 3.5-mile hike to Blue Lake; the trailhead lies about a half mile from camp.

**Campsites, facilities:** There are 11 sites for tents or RVs up to 30 feet long. Picnic tables and fire rings are provided. Vault toilets and garbage bins are available. Drinking water is not always available, so bring your own. Firewood can be gathered outside of the campground area. A camp host is on-site. Some facilities are wheelchair accessible. Leashed pets are permitted.

**Reservations, fees:** Reservations are accepted at 877/444-6777 ($10 reservation fee) or www.recreation.gov ($9 reservation fee). Sites are $12 per night, $5 per extra vehicle per night. Open mid-May-mid-September, weather permitting.

**Directions:** From Chehalis, drive south on I-5 for six miles to Exit 68 and U.S. 12. Turn east on U.S. 12 and drive 48 miles to Randle and Highway 131. Turn right (south) on Highway 131 and drive one mile to Forest Road 23. Turn south and drive about 10 miles to the campground on the left.

**Contact:** Gifford Pinchot National Forest, Cowlitz Ranger District, 360/497-1100, www.fs.usda.gov or www.hoodoo.com.

## 62 ADAMS FORK

**Scenic rating: 7**

on the Cispus River in Gifford Pinchot National Forest

**Map 5.2, page 318**

Adams Fork campground is set at 2,600 feet elevation along the Upper Cispus River near Adams Creek and is popular with off-road vehicle (ORV) enthusiasts. There are many miles of trails designed for use by ORVs. A trail just 0.5 mile away leads north to Blue Lake, which is about a five-mile hike (one-way) from the camp. Most of the campsites are small, but a few are large enough for comfortable RV use. The area has many towering trees. The Cispus River provides trout fishing.

**Campsites, facilities:** There are 22 single sites and one double site for tents or RVs up to 22 feet long. A group camp accommodates 20-50 people. Picnic tables and fire grills are provided. Drinking water and vault toilets are available. Firewood may be gathered outside the campground area. Leashed pets are permitted.

**Reservations, fees:** Reservations are accepted at 877/444-6777 ($10 reservation fee) or www.recreation.gov ($9 reservation fee). Single sites are $16 per night, the double site is $30, the group site is $35-45 per night, $5 per extra vehicle per night. Open May-mid-September, weather permitting.

**Directions:** On I-5, drive to Exit 68 (south of Chehalis) and U.S. 12. Turn east on U.S. 12 and drive 48 miles to Randle and U.S. 131. Turn right (south) and drive one mile to Forest

Road 23. Turn left (southeast) and drive 18 miles to Forest Road 21. Turn left (southeast) on Forest Road 21 and drive five miles to Forest Road 56. Turn right on Forest Road 56 and drive 200 yards to the campground on the left.

**Contact:** Gifford Pinchot National Forest, Cowlitz Valley Ranger District, 360/497-1100, www.fs.usda.gov or www.hoodoo.com.

## 63 OLALLIE LAKE

**Scenic rating: 9**

on Olallie Lake in Gifford Pinchot National Forest

**Map 5.2, page 318**

Located at an elevation of 4,200 feet, this campground lies on the shore of Olallie Lake, one of several small alpine lakes in the area fed by streams coming off the glaciers on nearby Mount Adams (elevation 12,276 feet). Trout fishing is good here in early summer. The campsites are situated close to the lake and feature gorgeous views of Mount Adams across the lake. Several of the campsites are small, and there is one larger area with room for RVs. A word to the wise: Mosquitoes can be a problem in the spring and early summer.

**Campsites, facilities:** There are eight single sites and one double site for tents or RVs up to 22 feet long. Picnic tables and fire rings are provided. Vault toilets are available, but there is no drinking water. Firewood may be gathered outside the campground area. Boat-launching facilities are nearby, but gasoline motors are prohibited on the lake. Some facilities are wheelchair accessible. Leashed pets are permitted.

**Reservations, fees:** Reservations are not accepted. Sites are $12 per night, $6 per night per additional vehicle. Open June-September, weather permitting.

**Directions:** From Chehalis, drive south on I-5 for 10 miles to Exit 68 and U.S. 12. Turn east on U.S. 12 and drive 48 miles to Randle and U.S. 131. Turn right (south) and drive one mile to Forest Road 23. Turn left (southeast) and drive 29 miles to Forest Road 2329. Turn left (northeast) and drive one mile to a junction with Forest Road 5601. Bear left and drive 0.5 mile to the campground on the right.

**Contact:** Gifford Pinchot National Forest, Cowlitz Valley Ranger District, 360/497-1100, www.fs.usda.gov or www.hoodoo.com.

## 64 TAKHLAKH LAKE

**Scenic rating: 9**

on Takhlakh Lake in Gifford Pinchot National Forest

**Map 5.2, page 318**

This campground is situated along the shore of Takhlakh Lake—one of five lakes in the area, all accessible by car. It's a beautiful place, set at 4,500 feet elevation, but, alas, mosquitoes abound until late July. A viewing area (Mount Adams is visible across the lake) is available for visitors, while the more ambitious can go berry picking, fishing, and hiking. This lake is much better than nearby Horseshoe Lake, and the fishing is much better, especially for trout early in the season. The Takhlakh Meadow Loop Trail, a barrier-free trail, provides a 1.5-mile hike. This is a very remote area, so don't expect cell service.

**Campsites, facilities:** There are 54 sites for tents or RVs up to 40 feet long. Picnic tables are provided. Vault toilets and garbage bins are available. There is no drinking water. Firewood may be gathered outside the campground area. A camp host is on-site. Boat-launching facilities are available in the day-use area, but gasoline motors are prohibited on the lake. Some facilities are wheelchair accessible. Leashed pets are permitted.

**Reservations, fees:** Reservations are accepted at 877/444-6777 ($10 reservation fee) or www.recreation.gov ($9 reservation fee). Single sites are $18 per night, double sites are $34 per night, $9 per night for each additional

vehicle. Open mid-June-late September, weather permitting.

**Directions:** From Chehalis, drive south on I-5 for 10 miles to Exit 68 and U.S. 12. Turn east on U.S. 12 and drive 48 miles to Randle and U.S. 131. Turn right (south) and drive one mile to Forest Road 23. Turn left (southeast) and drive 29 miles to Forest Road 2329. Turn left (northeast) and drive 1.5 miles to the campground entrance road on the right.

**Contact:** Gifford Pinchot National Forest, Cowlitz Valley Ranger District, 360/497-1100, www.fs.usda.gov or www.hoodoo.com.

## 65 CAT CREEK

**Scenic rating: 5**

on Cat Creek and the Cispus River in Gifford Pinchot National Forest

**Map 5.2, page 318**

This small, rustic camp is set along Cat Creek at its confluence with the Cispus River, about 10 miles from the summit of Mount Adams. The camp, which features a forested setting, gets a lot of all-terrain vehicle (ATV) use. A trail starts less than one mile from camp and leads up along Blue Lake Ridge to Blue Lake. The area has many towering trees and the Cispus River provides trout fishing.

**Campsites, facilities:** There are five undefined sites for tents or RVs up to 15 feet long. Picnic tables and fire grills are provided. Vault toilets and firewood are available. There is no drinking water and garbage must be packed out. Firewood may be gathered outside the campground area. Some facilities are wheelchair accessible. Leashed pets are permitted.

**Reservations, fees:** Reservations are not accepted. There is no fee for camping. Open June-mid-September, weather permitting.

**Directions:** On I-5, drive to Exit 68 (south of Chehalis) and U.S. 12. Turn east on U.S. 12 and drive 48 miles to Randle and U.S. 131. Turn right (south) and drive one mile to Forest Road 23. Turn left (southeast) and drive 18

miles to Forest Road 21. Turn left (southeast) on Forest Road 21 and drive six miles to the campground on the right.

**Contact:** Gifford Pinchot National Forest, Cowlitz Valley Ranger District, 360/497-1100, www.fs.usda.gov.

## 66 HORSESHOE LAKE

### Scenic rating: 9

on Horseshoe Lake in Gifford Pinchot National Forest

**Map 5.2, page 318**

This camp is set on the shore of picturesque, 10-acre Horseshoe Lake. The campsites are poorly defined, more like camping areas, though some are close to the lake. A trail runs partway around the lake and is open to mountain bikers and horseback riders (who occasionally come from a nearby camp). Fishing for trout is just fair in the lake, which is stocked infrequently. The water is too cold for swimming. A trail from the camp, about a three-mile round-trip, goes up to nearby Green Mountain (elevation 5,000 feet). This is a multi-use trail that ties into the High Lakes Trail system. Another trail heads up the north flank of Mount Adams. Berry picking is an option in the late summer months.

**Campsites, facilities:** There are 10 sites for tents or RVs up to 16 feet long. Picnic tables and fire rings are provided. Vault toilets are available. There is no drinking water and garbage must be packed out. Firewood may be gathered outside the campground area. Primitive launching facilities are located on the lake, but gasoline motors are prohibited on the water. Leashed pets are permitted.

**Reservations, fees:** Reservations are not accepted. Sites are $12 per night, $6 per each additional vehicle. Open mid-June-late September, weather permitting.

**Directions:** From Chehalis, drive south on I-5 for 10 miles to Exit 68 and U.S. 12. Turn east on U.S. 12 and drive 48 miles to Randle

and U.S. 131. Turn right (south) and drive one mile to Forest Road 23. Turn left (southeast) and drive 29 miles to Forest Road 2329. Turn left (northeast) and drive seven miles (bearing right at the junction with Forest Road 5601) to Forest Road 078. Turn left on Forest Road 078 and drive 1.5 miles to the campground on the left.

**Contact:** Gifford Pinchot National Forest, Cowlitz Valley Ranger District, 360/497-1100, www.fs.usda.gov or www.hoodoo.com.

## 67 KEENE'S HORSE CAMP

### Scenic rating: 7

on the South Fork of Spring Creek in Gifford Pinchot National Forest

**Map 5.2, page 318**

This equestrians-only camp is set at 4,200 feet elevation along the South Fork of Spring Creek on the northwest flank of Mount Adams (elevation 12,276 feet). The Pacific Crest Trail passes within a couple miles of the camp. Several trails lead from here into the backcountry and to several alpine meadows. The meadows are fragile, so walk along their outer edges. Nearby Goat Rocks Wilderness has 50 miles of trails open to horses; other trails meander outside of the wilderness boundary.

**Campsites, facilities:** There are 16 sites in two areas for tents or RVs up to 22 feet long. Picnic tables and fire grills are provided. Vault toilets, water troughs, a mounting ramp, manure bins, hitching facilities (high lines), and stock water are available. There is no drinking water. Firewood may be gathered outside the campground area. Some facilities are wheelchair accessible. Leashed pets are permitted.

**Reservations, fees:** Reservations are accepted at 877/444-6777 ($10 reservation fee) or www.recreation.gov ($9 reservation fee). Sites are $14 per night, $7 extra vehicle fee. Open mid-June-late September.

**Directions:** On I-5, drive to Exit 68 (south of Chehalis) and U.S. 12. Turn east on U.S. 12

and drive 48 miles to Randle and U.S. 131. Turn right (south) and drive one mile to Forest Road 23. Turn left (southeast) and drive 18 miles to Forest Road 21. Turn left (southeast) on Forest Road 21 and drive five miles to Forest Road 56. Turn right on Forest Road 56 and drive five miles to Forest Road 5603. Turn right and drive five miles to Forest Road 2329. Turn right and drive two miles to the camp on the right.

**Contact:** Gifford Pinchot National Forest, Cowlitz Valley Ranger District, 360/497-1100, www.fs.usda.gov or www.hoodoo.com.

## 68 KILLEN CREEK

### Scenic rating: 7

near Mount Adams in Gifford Pinchot National Forest

**Map 5.2, page 318**

This wilderness trailhead camp is ideal as a launch point for backpackers. The campground, set along Killen Creek at the foot of 12,276-foot Mount Adams, marks the start of a three-mile trail that leads up the mountain and connects with the Pacific Crest Trail. It's worth the effort. The Killen Trail goes up to secondary ridges and shoulders of Mount Adams for stunning views. Berry picking is a summertime option.

**Campsites, facilities:** There are nine sites for tents or RVs up to 22 feet long. Picnic tables and fire grills are provided. Vault toilets are available, but there is no drinking water. Garbage must be packed out. Firewood may be gathered outside the campground area. Leashed pets are permitted.

**Reservations, fees:** Reservations are not accepted. Sites are $12 per night, $6 extra vehicle fee. Open June-mid-September, weather permitting.

**Directions:** On I-5, drive to Exit 68 (south of Chehalis) and U.S. 12. Turn east on U.S. 12 and drive 48 miles to Randle and U.S. 131. Turn right (south) and drive one mile

to Forest Road 23. Turn left (southeast) and drive 29 miles to Forest Road 2329. Turn left (northeast) and drive six miles to Forest Road 073. Turn left (west) and drive 200 yards to the campground.

**Contact:** Gifford Pinchot National Forest, Cowlitz Valley Ranger District, 360/497-1100, www.fs.usda.gov or www.hoodoo.com.

## 69 WALUPT LAKE

### Scenic rating: 8

on Walupt Lake in Gifford Pinchot National Forest

**Map 5.2, page 318**

This popular spot, set at 3,900 feet elevation along the shore of Walupt Lake, is a good base camp for a multi-day vacation. The trout fishing is often good here; check regulations. But note that only small boats are advisable here because the launch area at the lake is shallow and it can take a four-wheel-drive vehicle to get a boat in and out. A small swimming beach is nearby. In addition, several nearby trails lead into the backcountry and to other smaller alpine lakes. One trail out of the campground leads to the upper end of the lake, then launches off to the Goat Rocks Wilderness; it's an outstanding hike, and the trail is also excellent for horseback rides.

**Campsites, facilities:** There are 34 sites for tents or RVs up to 22 feet long and 10 walk-in sites. Picnic tables are provided. Drinking water and vault toilets are available. Fire rings are located next to the campground. There is primitive boat access with a 10-mph speed limit; no waterskiing is allowed. Leashed pets are permitted.

**Reservations, fees:** Reservations are accepted at 877/444-6777 ($10 reservation fee) or www.recreation.gov ($9 reservation fee). Sites are $18-34 per night, $9 per night for each additional vehicle. Open mid-June-mid-September.

**Directions:** On I-5, drive to Exit 68 (south of Chehalis) and U.S. 12. Turn east on U.S.

12 and drive 62 miles to Forest Road 21 (2.5 miles southwest of Packwood). Turn right (southeast) and drive 20 miles to Forest Road 2160. Turn left (east) and drive 4.5 miles to the campground.

**Contact:** Gifford Pinchot National Forest, Cowlitz Valley Ranger District, 360/497-1100, www.fs.usda.gov or www.hoodoo.com.

## 70 WALUPT HORSE CAMP

### Scenic rating: 7

near the Goat Rocks Wilderness in Gifford Pinchot National Forest

**Map 5.2, page 318**

This camp is for horse campers only and is set about one mile from Walupt Lake, which is good for trout fishing and has a 10-mph speed limit for boats. Several trails lead from the lake into the backcountry of the southern Goat Rocks Wilderness, which has 50 miles of trails that can be used by horses; other trails meander outside of the wilderness boundary. If you have planned a multi-day horse-packing trip, bring in your own feed for the horses. (Feed must be pellets or processed grain and only certified "weed-seed-free" hay is allowed.)

**Campsites, facilities:** There are nine equestrian sites for tents or RVs up to 22 feet long. Picnic tables and fire grills are provided. Drinking water, vault toilets, and firewood are available. Garbage must be packed out. A horse ramp and high lines are available. Leashed pets are permitted.

**Reservations, fees:** Reservations are not accepted. Single sites are $16 per night, multi-sites are $30 per night, $8 extra vehicle fee. Open June-late September, weather permitting.

**Directions:** On I-5, drive to Exit 68 (south of Chehalis) and U.S. 12. Turn east on U.S. 12 and drive 62 miles to Forest Road 21 (2.5 miles southwest of Packwood). Turn right (southeast) and drive 20 miles to Forest Road 2160. Turn left (east) and drive 3.5 miles to the campground on the right.

**Contact:** Gifford Pinchot National Forest, Cowlitz Valley Ranger District, 360/497-1100, www.fs.usda.gov or www.hoodoo.com.

## 71 CLOVER FLATS

### Scenic rating: 8

near the Goat Rocks Wilderness

**Map 5.2, page 318**

Clover Flats campground is located in the subalpine zone on the slope of Darland Mountain, which peaks at 6,982 feet. Trails connect the area with the Goat Rocks Wilderness, six miles to the west. This is a popular area for winter sports.

**Campsites, facilities:** There are nine sites for tents or RVs up to 24 feet. Picnic tables, fire grills, and tent pads are provided. Vault toilets and drinking water are available. Garbage must be packed out. Some facilities are wheelchair accessible. Leashed pets are permitted.

**Reservations, fees:** Reservations are not accepted. There is no fee for camping, but a Discover Pass is required. Open year-round, weather permitting; snow limits access except from mid-July through October.

**Directions:** From Yakima, drive south on I-82 for two miles to the Union Gap exit. Take that exit and turn right on East Valley Mall Road. Drive one mile to 3rd Avenue. Turn left and drive 0.25 mile to Ahtaman Road. Turn right (west) and drive 20 miles to Tampico and Road A-3000 (North Fork Road). Turn right (west) and drive 9.5 miles to the Ahtaman Camp. Continue to a junction with A-2000 (Middle Fork Road). Bear left and drive nine miles to the camp on the left. Note: The last few miles of Road A-2000 are very steep and unpaved, with a 12 percent grade. Only high-clearance vehicles are recommended.

**Contact:** Department of Natural Resources, Southeast Region, 509/925-8510, www.dnr.wa.gov.

## 72 TREE PHONES

🚶 🚴 🏇 ♿ 🚐 ⛺

**Scenic rating: 7**

on the Middle Fork of Ahtanum Creek

**Map 5.2, page 318**

Forested Tree Phones campground is set along the Middle Fork of Ahtanum Creek at an elevation of 4,800 feet. It is close to hiking, motorbiking, and horseback-riding trails. A shelter with a wood stove is available year-round for picnics. During summer, there are beautiful wildflower displays.

**Campsites, facilities:** There are 12 sites for tents or RVs up to 40 feet. Picnic tables, fire grills, and tent pads are provided. Drinking water and vault toilets are available. A 20- by 40-foot snow shelter and hitching rails are also available. Stock are not permitted to drink from the creek. Some facilities are wheelchair accessible. Leashed pets are permitted.

**Reservations, fees:** Reservations are not accepted. There is no fee for camping, but a Discover Pass is required. Open year-round, weather permitting (heavy snows are expected late November-March).

**Directions:** From Yakima, drive south on I-82 for two miles to the Union Gap exit. Take that exit and turn right on East Valley Mall Road. Drive one mile to 3rd Avenue. Turn left and drive 0.25 mile to Ahtaman Road. Turn right (west) and drive 20 miles to Tampico and Road A-3000 (North Fork Road). Turn right (west) and drive 9.5 miles to the Ahtaman Camp. Continue to a junction with A-2000 (Middle Fork Road). Bear left and drive six miles to the camp. Note: Only high-clearance vehicles are recommended.

**Contact:** Department of Natural Resources, Southeast Region, 509/925-8510, www.dnr.wa.gov.

## 73 GREEN RIVER HORSE CAMP

🚶 🏇 ♿ 🚐 ⛺

**Scenic rating: 8**

near Green River in Gifford Pinchot National Forest

**Map 5.2, page 318**

This premier equestrians-only horse camp is set on the Green River near an area of beautiful, old-growth timber. The campsites, however, are in a reforested clear-cut area with trees about 25-40 feet tall. The camp features access to great trails into the Mount St. Helens blast area. The lookout from Windy Ridge is one of the most drop-dead awesome views in North America, spanning Spirit Lake, the blast zone, and the open crater of Mount St. Helens. The campground features high lines at each site, and the access is designed for easy turning and parking with horse trailers.

**Campsites, facilities:** There are eight sites that can accommodate up to two trailer rigs or three vehicles each. Picnic tables, fire grills, and high lines are provided. Vault toilets are available. No drinking water is provided, but it is available five miles north at Norway Pass Trailhead. Stock water must be hand-carried from the river; however, new facilities are currently under construction. Garbage must be packed out. Some facilities are wheelchair accessible. Leashed pets are permitted.

**Reservations, fees:** Reservations are not accepted. There is no fee for camping. Open mid-May-November, weather permitting.

**Directions:** From Chehalis, drive south on I-5 for six miles to Exit 68 and U.S. 12. Turn east on U.S. 12 and drive 48 miles to Randle and Highway 131. Turn right (south) and drive one mile (becomes Forest Road 25). Continue south and drive 19 miles to Forest Road 99. Turn right (west, toward Windy Ridge) and drive 8.5 miles to Forest Road 26. Turn right (north) and drive five miles to Forest Road 2612 (gravel). Turn left (west) and drive about two miles to the campground entrance on the left.

**Contact:** Gifford Pinchot National Forest, Mount St. Helens National Volcanic Monument, 360/449-7800, www.fs.usda.gov.

## 74 LEWIS RIVER HORSE CAMP

### Scenic rating: 7

near the Lewis River and Quartz Creek in Gifford Pinchot National Forest

**Map 5.2, page 318**

During summer, this camp caters to equestrians only. The camp is not particularly scenic, but the area around it is: There are six waterfalls nearby on the Lewis River. There are also many trails, all of which are open to mountain bikers and some to motorcycles. The spectacular Lewis River Trail is available for hiking, mountain biking, or horseback riding, and there is a wheelchair-accessible loop. Several other hiking trails in the area branch off along backcountry streams.

**Campsites, facilities:** There are nine sites for tents or RVs up to 35 feet long. Picnic tables and fire rings are provided. A composting toilet is available. There is no drinking water and garbage must be packed out. Horse facilities include high lines, mounting ramp, stock water, and three corrals. Some facilities are wheelchair accessible. Leashed pets are permitted.

**Reservations, fees:** Reservations are not accepted. Sites are $5 per night. Open May-November, weather permitting.

**Directions:** From Woodland on I-5, take Exit 21 for Highway 503. Drive east on Highway 503 and drive 23 miles to the Highway 503 spur. Drive northeast on the Highway 503 spur road for seven miles (becomes Forest Road 90). Continue east on Forest Road 90 for 33 miles to Forest Road 93. Turn left and drive a short distance to the campground (along the Lewis River) on the right.

**Contact:** Gifford Pinchot National Forest, Mount St. Helens National Volcanic Monument, 360/449-7800, www.fs.usda.gov.

## 75 LOWER FALLS

### Scenic rating: 10

on the Lewis River in Gifford Pinchot National Forest

**Map 5.2, page 318**     **BEST (**

This camp is set at 1,400 feet elevation in the primary viewing area for six major waterfalls on the Lewis River. The spectacular Lewis River Trail is available for hiking or horseback riding, and it features a wheelchair-accessible loop. Several other hiking trails in the area branch off along backcountry streams. The sites are paved and set among large fir trees on gently sloping ground; access roads were designed for easy RV parking. Note that above the falls, the calm water in the river looks safe, but it is not! Stay out. In addition, the Lewis River Trail goes along cliffs, providing beautiful views but potentially dangerous hiking.

**Campsites, facilities:** There are 42 sites for tents or RVs up to 60 feet long and two group sites for up to 20 people each. Picnic tables and fire grills are provided. Drinking water and composting toilets are available. Some facilities are wheelchair accessible. Leashed pets are permitted.

**Reservations, fees:** Reservations are not accepted. Single sites are $15 per night, double sites are $30 per night, $5 per extra vehicle per night. Group sites are $35 per night. Open May-November, weather permitting.

**Directions:** From Woodland on I-5, take Exit 21 for Highway 503. Drive east on Highway 503 for 23 miles to the Highway 503 spur. Drive northeast on the Highway 503 spur for seven miles (becomes Forest Road 90). Continue east on Forest Road 90 for 30 miles to the campground (along the Lewis River) on the right.

**Contact:** Gifford Pinchot National Forest, Mount St. Helens National Volcanic Monument, 360/449-7800, www.fs.usda.gov.

## 76 TILLICUM

### Scenic rating: 8

near Meadow Lake in Gifford Pinchot National
Forest

**Map 5.2, page 318**

This pretty camp is primitive but well forested, and within walking distance of several
recreation options. A 4.5-mile trail from the
camp leads southwest past little Meadow Lake
to Squaw Butte, then over to Big Creek. It's a
nice hike, as well as an excellent ride for mountain bikers. This is a premium area for picking
huckleberries in August and early September.
The Lone Butte area about five miles to the
south provides a side trip. There are two lakes
nearby, Big and Little Mosquito Lakes, which
are fed by Mosquito Creek. While we're on the
subject, mosquito attacks in late spring and
early summer can be like squadrons of World
War II bombers moving in. The Pacific Crest
Trail passes right by camp.

**Campsites, facilities:** There are 24 sites for
tents or RVs up to 18 feet long. Picnic tables
and fire grills are provided. A vault toilet and
garbage service are available. There is no
drinking water. Some facilities are wheelchair
accessible. Leashed pets are permitted.

**Reservations, fees:** Reservations are not
accepted. Sites are $5 per night, $5 extra vehicle fee. Open June-late September, weather
permitting.

**Directions:** From Vancouver, Washington,
on I-205, take Highway 14 and drive east for
66 miles to Highway 141. Turn left (north) on
Highway 141 and drive 25 miles to Trout Lake
and County Road 141 (Forest Road 24). Turn
left (west) and drive two miles to a fork. Bear
left at the fork and drive 20 miles (becomes
Forest Road 24) to the campground on the left.

**Contact:** Gifford Pinchot National Forest,
Mount St. Helens National Volcanic Monument, 360/449-7800, www.fs.usda.gov.

## 77 MORRISON CREEK

### Scenic rating: 7

on Morrison Creek in Gifford Pinchot National
Forest

**Map 5.2, page 318**

Here's a prime yet little-known spot. This
camp is located along Morrison Creek at an
elevation of 4,600 feet, near the southern
slopes of 12,276-foot Mount Adams. Nearby
trails will take you to the snowfields and alpine
meadows of the Mount Adams Wilderness. In
particular, the Shorthorn Trail is accessible
from this campground.

**Campsites, facilities:** There are 12 sites for
tents. Picnic tables and fire rings are provided
in some sites. Vault toilets are available, but
there is no drinking water. Garbage must be
packed out. Some facilities are wheelchair accessible. Leashed pets are permitted.

**Reservations, fees:** Reservations are not accepted. There is no fee for camping. Open
late June-late September, weather permitting.

**Directions:** From White Salmon, take Grangeview Loop Road to W. Jewett Boulevard/
WA-141. Turn right on WA-141 and drive 21.4
miles to the campground.

Alternately, from Hood River, Oregon,
drive north on Highway 35 (over the Columbia
River) to Highway 14. Turn left and drive two
miles to Highway 141-A. Turn right (north) on
Highway 141-A and drive 20 miles to County
Road 17 (just 200 yards east of the town of
Trout Lake). Turn right (north) and drive two
miles to Forest Road 80. Turn right (north)
and drive 3.5 miles to Forest Road 8040. Bear
left (north) and drive six miles to the campground on the left.

Note: The access road is rough and is not
recommended for RVs, motor homes, or
trailers.

**Contact:** Gifford Pinchot National Forest,
Mount Adams Ranger District, 509/395-3400,
www.fs.usda.gov.

## **78** ISLAND CAMP

### Scenic rating: 8
on Bird Creek

**Map 5.2, page 318**

Island campground sits in a forested area along Bird Creek and is close to lava tubes and blowholes. A strange one-foot-wide slit in the ground (too small to climb into and explore) can be reached by walking about 0.75 mile. Bird Creek provides a chance to fish for brook trout in late spring. In the winter, the roads are used for snowmobiling. A snowmobile shelter with a wood stove is available year-round for picnics.

**Campsites, facilities:** There are six sites for tents or RVs up to 16 feet. Picnic tables, fire grills, and tent pads are provided. Vault toilets are available, but there is no drinking water. Garbage must be packed out. Some facilities are wheelchair accessible. Leashed pets are permitted.

**Reservations, fees:** Reservations are not accepted. There is no fee for camping, but a Discover Pass is required. Open May-October, with limited winter access.

**Directions:** From Yakima, drive south on I-82 for 15 miles to U.S. 97. Turn south and drive 49 miles to Goldendale and Highway 142. Turn right (west) and drive 10 miles to Counts Road. Turn right (northwest) and drive 26 miles to Glenwood; continue for 0.25 mile to Bird Creek Road. Turn right and drive 0.9 mile to K-3000 Road (still Bird Creek Road). Turn left, drive over the cattle guard, and drive 1.2 miles to Road S-4000. Turn right and drive 1.3 miles to Road K-4000. Turn left and drive 3.4 miles to Road K-4200. Turn left and drive 1.1 miles to the campground entrance on the left. Turn left and drive 0.25 mile to the campground.

**Contact:** Department of Natural Resources, Southeast Region, 509/925-8510, www.dnr. wa.gov.

## **79** BIRD CREEK

### Scenic rating: 7
near the Mount Adams Wilderness

**Map 5.2, page 318**

Bird Creek campground is set in a forested area of old-growth Douglas fir and ponderosa pine along Bird Creek. This spot lies just east of the Mount Adams Wilderness and is one of two camps in the immediate area. (The other, Island Camp, is within three miles. It is also a primitive site, but it features snowmobile trails.)

**Campsites, facilities:** There are 12 sites for tents or RVs up to 22 feet and one group camp for tents or RVs up to 35 feet that can accommodate up to 25 people. Picnic tables, fire grills, and tent pads are provided. Pit and vault toilets are available, but there is no drinking water. Garbage must be packed out. Some facilities are wheelchair accessible. Leashed pets are permitted.

**Reservations, fees:** Reservations are not accepted. There is no fee for camping, but a Discover Pass is required. Open May-mid-October, weather permitting.

**Directions:** From Yakima, drive south on I-82 for 15 miles to U.S. 97. Turn south and drive 49 miles to Goldendale and Highway 142. Turn right (west) and drive 10 miles to Counts Road. Turn right (northwest) and drive 26 miles to Glenwood. From the post office in Glenwood, continue 0.25 mile to Bird Creek Road. Turn right and drive 0.9 mile. Turn left (still Bird Creek Road), cross the cattle guard to Road K-3000, and drive 1.2 miles to Road S-4000 (gravel). Turn right and drive 1.3 miles to Road K-4000. Turn left and drive two miles to the campground on the left.

**Contact:** Department of Natural Resources, Southeast Region, 509/925-8510, www.dnr. wa.gov.

## 80 CAMP KALAMA RV PARK AND CAMPGROUND

🏊 ⛵ 🚣 🐎 🚴 ♿ 🚐 ⛺

### Scenic rating: 6

on the Kalama River

Map 5.3, page 319

This campground has a rustic setting, with open and wooded areas and some accommodations for tent campers. It's set along the Kalama River, where salmon and steelhead fishing is popular. A full-service marina is nearby. Note that some sites are filled with monthly renters.

**Campsites, facilities:** There are 118 sites with full or partial hookups (20, 30, and 50 amps) for RVs of any length and 50 sites for tents. Some sites are pull-through. Picnic tables and fire pits are provided. Restrooms with flush toilets and coin showers, drinking water, cable TV, Wi-Fi, propane gas, two dump stations, general store, café, banquet room, firewood, coin laundry, ice, boat-launching facilities, a beach area, and a playground are available. Some facilities are wheelchair accessible. Leashed pets are permitted.

**Reservations, fees:** Reservations are accepted. RV sites are $33 per night, tent sites are $22 per night, $1.50 per person per night for more than two adults, $1.50 per night per extra vehicle, and $1 per pet per night. Weekly and monthly rates are available. Some credit cards are accepted. Open year-round.

**Directions:** From the north end of Kalama (between Kelso and Woodland) on I-5, take Exit 32 and drive south on the frontage road for one block to the campground.

**Contact:** Camp Kalama RV Park and Campground, 360/673-2456 or 800/750-2456, www.kalama.com/~campkalama.

## 81 COLUMBIA RIVERFRONT RV PARK

🚶 ⛵ 🐎 🚴 ♿ 🚐

### Scenic rating: 8

near Portland

Map 5.3, page 319

Columbia Riverfront RV Park is located directly on the Columbia River, north of Portland. That means it is away from freeway noise, airports, and train tracks. Quiet? Oh yeah. The park encompasses 10 acres and boasts 900 feet of sandy beach, perfect for fishing for steelhead or salmon and beachcombing.

**Campsites, facilities:** There are 76 sites with full hookups for RVs up to 78 feet; some sites are pull-through. Picnic tables are provided, but only beach sites have fire rings. Drinking water, restrooms with flush toilets and coin showers, a park store (with groceries, propane, and ice), horseshoe pits, Wi-Fi, cable TV, coin laundry, swimming pool (seasonal), and a playground are available. Some facilities are wheelchair accessible. Leashed pets are permitted, with breed restrictions.

**Reservations, fees:** Reservations are recommended. Sites are $37-50 per night.

**Directions:** From I-5 in Woodland, take Exit 22 and turn south onto Dike Access Road. Drive two miles on Dike Access Road to the T intersection and turn left onto Dike Road. Drive one mile on Dike Road to the campground on the right.

**Contact:** Columbia Riverfront RV Park, 360/225-2227 or 800/845-9842, www.columbiariverfrontrvpark.com.

## 82 PARADISE POINT STATE PARK

🚶 🏊 ⛵ 🚣 🐎 ♿ 🚐 ⛺

### Scenic rating: 8

on the East Fork of the Lewis River

Map 5.3, page 319

Paradise Point is named for the serenity that once blessed this area. Alas, it has lost much of that peacefulness since the freeway went in next to the park. To reduce traffic noise, stay at one of the wooded sites in the small apple orchard; the sites in the grassy areas have little noise buffer. This park covers 88 acres and features 1,680 feet of river frontage. The two-mile hiking trail is good for families and children. Note that the dirt boat ramp is primitive and nonfunctional when the water level drops; it is recommended for car-top boats only. Fishing on the East Fork of the Lewis River is a bonus.

**Campsites, facilities:** There are 58 sites for tents or RVs up to 50 feet long (no hookups), 18 sites with partial hookups (30 and 50 amps) for tents or RVs up to 40 feet long, nine hike-in/bike-in sites, and two yurts. Picnic tables and fire grills are provided. Restrooms with flush toilets and coin showers, drinking water, a dump station, firewood, an amphitheater, and summer interpretive programs are available. A primitive, dirt boat-launching area is located nearby on East Fork Lewis River. Some facilities are wheelchair accessible. Leashed pets are permitted.

**Reservations, fees:** Reservations are accepted at 888/CAMP-OUT (888/226-7688) or goingtocamp.com ($6.50 reservation fee). Sites are $21-28 per night, hike-in/bike-in sites are $12 per night, $10 per extra vehicle per night, and yurts are $64.72 per night. Some credit cards are accepted. Open year-round, with some sites closed October-April.

**Directions:** From Vancouver, Washington, drive north on I-5 for 15 miles to Exit 16 (La Center/Paradise Point State Park exit). Take that exit and turn right, then almost immediately at Paradise Park Road, turn left and drive one mile to the park.

**Contact:** Paradise Point State Park, 360/263-2350; state park information, 360/902-8844, www.parks.wa.gov.

## 83 BIG FIR CAMPGROUND AND RV PARK

### Scenic rating: 6

near Paradise Point State Park

**Map 5.3, page 319**

Big Fir campground is set in a heavily wooded, rural area not far from Paradise Point State Park. It's nestled among hills and features shaded gravel sites and wild berries. Recreation opportunities include hiking and fishing on the East Fork of the Lewis River.

**Campsites, facilities:** There are 37 sites with full hookups (30 and 50 amps) for RVs of any length and 33 sites for tents. Some sites are pull-through. Picnic tables and barbecues are provided; no wood fires are allowed. Restrooms with flush toilets and coin showers, drinking water, volleyball, croquet, a horseshoe pit, board games, Wi-Fi, limited groceries, and ice are available. Boat-launching facilities are located within 1.5 miles. Leashed pets are permitted.

**Reservations, fees:** Reservations are accepted. Sites are $20-30 per night, $2 per night per extra vehicle. Some credit cards are accepted. RV sites are open year-round; tent sites are open Memorial Day-Labor Day.

**Directions:** From Vancouver, Washington, drive north on I-5 to Exit 14 (Ridgefield exit). Take that exit to Highway 269. Drive east on Highway 269 (the road's name changes several times) for two miles to 10th Avenue. Turn right and drive to the first intersection at 259th Street. Turn left and drive two miles to the park on the right (route is well marked).

**Contact:** Big Fir Campground and RV Park, 360/887-8970 or 800/532-4397.

## 84 BATTLE GROUND LAKE STATE PARK

🚶 🚴 🏊 🛶 🛥 🏇 ♿ 🚐 ⛺

**Scenic rating: 8**

on Battle Ground Lake

Map 5.3, page 319

The centerpiece of this state park is Battle Ground Lake, a spring-fed lake that is stocked with trout but popular for bass and catfish fishing as well. Underground lava tubes feed water into the lake, which is similar to Crater Lake in Oregon, though smaller. The park covers 280 acres, primarily forested with conifers, in the foothills of the Cascade Mountains. There are 10 miles of trails for hiking and biking, including a trail around the lake, and an additional five miles of trails open to horses; a primitive equestrian camp is also available. The lake is good for swimming and fishing, and it has a nice beach area; boats with gas motors are not allowed. If you're traveling on I-5 and looking for a layover, this camp, just 15 minutes from the highway, is ideal. In July and August, the area hosts several fairs and celebrations. Like many of the easy-access state parks on I-5, this one fills up quickly on weekends.

**Campsites, facilities:** There are 25 sites for tents or RVs up to 35 feet long (no hookups), six sites with partial hookups (50 amps) for RVs, 15 primitive hike-in sites, one group site for 25-32 people, a horse camp for 10-16 people, and four cabins. Picnic tables and fire grills are provided. Restrooms with flush toilets and coin showers, drinking water, a dump station, a store, firewood, a seasonal snack bar, sheltered picnic area, amphitheater, summer interpretive programs, a playground, horseshoe pits, and an athletic field are available. Boat-launching facilities and rentals are nearby. Carts are provided to tote your gear the 0.25-0.5 mile to the primitive sites. Some facilities are wheelchair accessible. Leashed pets are permitted.

**Reservations, fees:** Reservations are accepted at 888/CAMP-OUT (888/226-7688) or www.goingtocamp.com ($6.50-8.50 reservation fee).

Sites are $17-39 per night, hike-in sites are $12 per night, $10 per night per extra vehicle, cabins are $59-81.18 per night. Some credit cards are accepted. Open year-round.

**Directions:** From I-5 southbound, take Exit 11; from I-5 northbound, take Exit 9. Drive to the city of Battle Ground (well marked); continue to the east end of town to Grace Avenue. Turn left on NE Grace Avenue and drive three miles (a marked route) to the park.

**Contact:** Battle Ground Lake State Park, tel. 360/687-4621; state park information, 360/902-8844, www.parks.wa.gov.

## 85 SUNSET FALLS

🚶 🚴 🛶 🏇 ♿ 🚐 ⛺

**Scenic rating: 9**

on the East Fork of the Lewis River in Gifford Pinchot National Forest

Map 5.3, page 319

This campground is located at an elevation of 1,000 feet along the East Fork of the Lewis River. Fishing, hiking, and huckleberry and mushroom picking are some of the favored pursuits of visitors. Scenic Sunset Falls is located just upstream of the campground. A barrier-free viewing trail leads to an overlook.

**Campsites, facilities:** There are 18 sites for tents or RVs up to 22 feet long. Picnic tables and fire grills are provided. Vault toilets and garbage service are available. There is no drinking water. Some facilities are wheelchair accessible. Leashed pets are permitted.

**Reservations, fees:** Reservations are accepted at 877/444-6777 ($10 reservation fee) or www.recreation.gov ($9 reservation fee). Sites are $12 per night, $5 per extra vehicle per night. Open year-round.

**Directions:** From Vancouver, Washington, drive north on I-5 about seven miles to County Road 502. Turn east on Highway 502 and drive six miles to Highway 503. Turn left and drive north for five miles to Lucia Falls Road. Turn right and drive eight miles to Moulton Falls and Old County Road 12. Turn right on

Old County Road 12 and drive seven miles to the Forest Boundary and the campground entrance on the right.

**Contact:** Gifford Pinchot National Forest, Mount St. Helens National Volcanic Monument, 360/449-7800, www.fs.usda.gov.

## 86 COLD CREEK CAMP

**Scenic rating: 6**

on Cedar Creek

Map 5.3, page 319

The late Waylon Jennings once told me that few things worth remembering come easy, right? Well, sometimes. First, don't expect to find a "cold creek" here. There just is no such thing. And second, the directions are complicated. This campground is set in a forested area with plenty of trails nearby for hiking and horseback riding. The camp gets minimal use. A large shelter is available at the day-use area.

**Campsites, facilities:** There are eight sites for tents or RVs up to 20 feet long, including one group camp for up to six people. Picnic tables, fire grills, and tent pads are provided. Vault toilets are available. There is no drinking water, and garbage must be packed out. A camp host is on-site. Some facilities are wheelchair accessible. Leashed pets are permitted.

**Reservations, fees:** Reservations are accepted at 360/577-2025. There is no fee for camping, but a Discover Pass is required. Open year-round with a seven-day stay limit, weather permitting.

**Directions:** From Vancouver, Washington, drive north on I-5 to Exit 9 and NE 179th Street. Turn east and drive 5.5 miles to Highway 503. Turn right and drive 1.5 miles to NE 159th Street. Turn left on NE 159th Street and drive three miles to 182nd Avenue. Turn right and drive one mile to NE 139th. Turn left and drive eight miles (becomes Rawson, then Road L-1400) to Road L-1000. Turn left and drive four miles to the campground entrance road.

Turn left, past the yellow gate, and drive one mile to the camp.

**Contact:** Department of Natural Resources, Pacific Cascade Region South, 360/577-2025, www.dnr.wa.gov.

## 87 ROCK CREEK CAMPGROUND AND HORSE CAMP

**Scenic rating: 6**

on Rock Creek

Map 5.3, page 319

This camp is located in a wooded area along Rock Creek. It is popular among equestrians and mountain bikers, especially on weekends, because of the Tarbell Trail, a 25-mile loop trail that is accessible from the campground and goes to the top of Larch Mountain (this road becomes Rawson, then L-1400).

**Campsites, facilities:** There are 19 sites for tents or RVs up to 20 feet long. Picnic tables, fire grills, and tent pads are provided. Vault toilets, a horse-loading ramp, stock water, and corrals are available. There is no drinking water, and garbage must be packed out. There is a camp host on-site. Some facilities are wheelchair accessible. Leashed pets are permitted.

**Reservations, fees:** Reservations are not accepted. There is no fee for camping, but a Discover Pass is required. Open year-round with a seven-day limit, weather permitting.

**Directions:** From Vancouver, Washington, drive north on I-5 to Exit 9 and NE 179th Street. Turn east and drive 5.5 miles to Highway 503. Turn right and drive 1.5 miles to NE 159th Street. Turn left on NE 159th Street and drive three miles to 182nd Avenue. Turn right and drive one mile to NE 139th (Road L-1400). Turn left and drive eight miles (road becomes Rawson, then L-1400) to Road L-1000. Turn left and drive 4.5 miles (passing Cold Creek Campground after three miles) to Road L-1200/Dole Valley Road. Turn left and drive 200 yards to the campground on your right.

**Contact:** Department of Natural Resources, Pacific Cascade Region South, 360/577-2025, www.dnr.wa.gov.

## 88 REED ISLAND BOAT-IN

### Scenic rating: 10

east of Washougal on Reed Island

**Map 5.3, page 319**

Where else can you have your own personal island? Only in Washington, that's where. Reachable only by boat, this 510-acre marine park is part of the Columbia River Water Trail. Activities include boating, bird-watching, and picnicking, and there is a heron rookery on the southwest side of the island.

**Campsites, facilities:** There are two primitive sites for tents only. Picnic tables and pedestal stoves are provided. There is no drinking water or toilets. Garbage must be packed out. Leashed pets are permitted.

**Reservations, fees:** Reservations are not accepted. Sites are $12 per night. Open year-round.

**Directions:** From the Port of Camas, head east on the Columbia River for approximately three miles. Signs on the southwest end of the island indicate where the campsites are located.

**Contact:** Reed Island State Park, 360/902-8844, www.parks.wa.gov.

## 89 DOUGAN CREEK

### Scenic rating: 7

near the Washougal River

**Map 5.3, page 319**

Insider's note: Dougan Creek campground is available only when a camp host is on-site. This small, remote campground is located on Dougan Creek, where it empties into the Washougal River. Heavily forested with second-growth Douglas fir, it features pretty sites with river views.

**Campsites, facilities:** There are seven sites for tents or RVs up to 20 feet long. Picnic tables, fire grills, and tent pads are provided. Vault toilets are available. There is no drinking water, and garbage must be packed out. Some facilities are wheelchair accessible. Leashed pets are permitted.

**Reservations, fees:** Reservations are not accepted. There is no fee for camping, but a Discover Pass is required. Open year-round, weather permitting.

**Directions:** From Vancouver, Washington, on I-205, take Highway 14 and drive east for 20 miles to Highway 140. Turn north on Highway 140 and drive five miles to Washougal River Road. Turn right on Washougal River Road and drive about seven miles until you come to the end of the pavement and pass the picnic area on the left. The campground is 0.25 mile beyond the picnic area.

**Contact:** Department of Natural Resources, Pacific Cascade Region South, 360/577-2025, www.dnr.wa.gov.

## 90 BEACON ROCK STATE PARK

### Scenic rating: 8

in Columbia River Gorge National Scenic Area

**Map 5.3, page 319**　　　　　**BEST (**

This state park features Beacon Rock, the second-largest monolith in the world, which overlooks the Columbia River Gorge. Lewis and Clark gave Beacon Rock its name on their expedition to the Pacific Ocean in 1805. The Beacon Rock Summit Trail, a 1.8-mile round-trip hike, provides excellent views of the gorge. Beacon Rock State Park covers nearly 5,000 acres and includes 9,500 feet of shoreline along the Columbia River and more than 22 miles of nearby trails open for hiking, mountain biking, and horseback riding. An eight-mile loop trail to Hamilton Mountain (2,300 feet elevation) is one of the best hikes, featuring even better views than from Beacon Rock. Rock climbing is excellent here, with the climbing season running mid-July-January. Fishing for sturgeon, salmon, steelhead, smallmouth bass (often excellent), and walleye is available in season on the Lower Columbia River below Bonneville Dam; check regulations.

**Campsites, facilities:** There are 26 sites for tents or small RVs (no hookups), five sites with full hookups (30 amps) for RVs, two equestrian sites with high line, and one group site for up to 200 people. Picnic tables and fire grills are provided. Restrooms with flush toilets and coin showers, drinking water, picnic areas, and a playground are available. Boat docks and launching facilities, moorage, and boat pumpout are also available. Some facilities are wheelchair accessible. Leashed pets are permitted.

**Reservations, fees:** Reservations are not accepted for family sites but are required for the group camp at 888/CAMP-OUT (888/226-7688) or www.parks.wa.gov/reservations ($6.50-8.50 reservation fee). Sites are $17-42 per night, equestrian sites are $12 per night, $10 per night per extra vehicle. The group site is $68.20-555.08 with a 20-person minimum. The boat launch fee is $7, with daily mooring $0.60 per foot ($12 minimum). Open April-October, with two sites available year-round.

**Directions:** From Vancouver, Washington, take Highway 14 and drive east for 35 miles. The park straddles the highway; follow the signs to the campground.

**Contact:** Beacon Rock State Park, 509/427-8265; state park information, 360/902-8844, www.parks.wa.gov.

## 91 CULTUS CREEK
🚶 🚴 🐕 ♿ 🚐 ⛺

### Scenic rating: 7

near the Indian Heaven Wilderness in Gifford Pinchot National Forest

**Map 5.4, page 320**

This camp is set at an elevation of 4,000 feet along Cultus Creek on the edge of the Indian Heaven Wilderness. Situated amid gentle terrain, the sites are graveled and level. The camp is popular during the fall huckleberry season, when picking is good, but gets light use the rest of the year. Nearby trails lead into the backcountry, which has numerous small meadows and lakes among old-growth stands of fir and pine. Horse trails are available as well. Access to the Pacific Crest Trail requires a two-mile climb.

**Campsites, facilities:** There are 50 sites for tents or RVs up to 32 feet long. Picnic tables and fire grills are provided. Vault toilets and firewood are available. There is no drinking water, and garbage must be packed out. Some facilities are wheelchair accessible. Leashed pets are permitted.

**Reservations, fees:** Reservations are not accepted. Sites are $10 per night, $5 per night per additional vehicle. Open late June-late September, weather permitting.

**Directions:** From Vancouver, Washington, on I-205, take Highway 14 east and drive 66 miles to State Route 141-A. Turn left (north) on State Route 141-A and drive 28 miles (becomes Forest Road 24); continue two miles to a junction. Turn right (staying on Forest Road 24) and drive 13.5 miles to the campground.

**Contact:** Gifford Pinchot National Forest, Mount Adams Ranger District, 509/395-3400, www.fs.fed.us.

## 92 LITTLE GOOSE HORSE CAMP
🚶 🐕 🚐 ⛺

### Scenic rating: 5

on Little Goose Creek in Gifford Pinchot National Forest

**Map 5.4, page 320**

Located near Little Goose Creek (between Smokey and Cultus campgrounds), this camp has sites ranging from good to poor and is lightly used in fall. Note that the access road is paved but rough and not recommended for

RVs or trailers; campers with horse trailers must drive slowly. (The camp sits close to the road and is sometimes dusty.) Several trails lead out from the campground. Huckleberry picking is quite good in August and early September. The elevation is 4,000 feet.

**Campsites, facilities:** There are eight sites for tents or RVs up to 24 feet long and three sites for campers with stock animals. Picnic tables and fire grills are provided. Vault toilets are available. There is no drinking water and garbage must be packed out. Leashed pets are permitted.

**Reservations, fees:** Reservations are not accepted. There is no fee for camping. Open late June-late September, weather permitting.

**Directions:** From Vancouver, Washington, on I-205, take Highway 14 east and drive 66 miles to State Route 141-A. Turn left (north) on State Route 141-A and drive 28 miles (becomes Forest Road 24); continue two miles to a junction. Turn right (staying on Forest Road 24) and drive eight miles (one mile past Smokey Creek) to the campground.

**Contact:** Gifford Pinchot National Forest, Mount Adams Ranger District, 509/395-3400, www.fs.usda.gov.

## 93 SMOKEY CREEK

### Scenic rating: 7

near the Indian Heaven Wilderness in Gifford Pinchot National Forest

**Map 5.4, page 320**

This primitive, little-used campground is set in an area of old-growth Douglas fir along Smokey Creek. A trail leading into the Indian Heaven Wilderness passes near the camp. Berry picking can be good here in summer and early fall. The elevation is 3,700 feet.

**Campsites, facilities:** There are three sites for tents only. Picnic tables and fire rings are provided. Pit toilets are available. There is no drinking water, and garbage must be packed out. Leashed pets are permitted.

**Reservations, fees:** Reservations are not accepted. There is no fee for camping. Open July-late September, weather permitting.

**Directions:** From Vancouver, Washington, on I-205, take Highway 14 east and drive 66 miles to State Route 141-A. Turn left (north) on State Route 141-A and drive 28 miles (becomes Forest Road 24); continue two miles to a junction. Turn right (staying on Forest Road 24) and drive seven miles to the campground.

**Contact:** Gifford Pinchot National Forest, Mount Adams Ranger District, 509/395-3400, www.fs.usda.gov.

## 94 PETERSON PRAIRIE AND GROUP

### Scenic rating: 8

near the town of Trout Lake in Gifford Pinchot National Forest

**Map 5.4, page 320**

Here's a good base camp if you want a short ride to town as well as access to the nearby wilderness areas. Peterson Prairie is a prime spot for huckleberry picking in the fall. A trail from the camp leads about one mile to nearby ice caves; a stairway into the caves provides access to a variety of ice formations. An area Sno-Park with snowmobiling and cross-country skiing trails is open for winter recreation. The elevation is 2,800 feet.

**Campsites, facilities:** There are 21 single sites and six double sites for tents or RVs up to 32 feet long and two group sites for 20-50 people. Picnic tables and fire grills are provided. Drinking water, vault toilets, and firewood are available. A camp host is available in summer. Leashed pets are permitted.

**Reservations, fees:** Reservations are accepted at 877/444-6777 ($10 reservation fee) or www.recreation.gov ($9 reservation fee). Single sites are $16 per night, double sites are $30 per night, $8 per extra vehicle per night. The group site is $75 per night. Open May-mid-September, weather permitting.

**Directions:** From White Salmon, take Grangeview Loop Road to W. Jewett Boulevard/WA-141. Turn right on WA-141 and drive 26 miles to Carson Guler Road/NF Development Road 24. Follow Carson Guler Road/NF Development Road 24 two miles to the campground.

Alternately, from Hood River, Oregon, drive north on Highway 35 (over the Columbia River) to Highway 14. Turn left and drive two miles to Highway 141-A. Turn right (north) on Highway 141-A and drive 25.5 miles to Forest Road 24 (5.5 miles beyond and southwest of the town of Trout Lake). Bear right (west) and drive 2.5 miles to the campground on the left.

**Contact:** Gifford Pinchot National Forest, Mount Adams Ranger District, 509/395-3400, www.fs.usda.gov or www.hoodoo.com.

## 95 TROUT LAKE CREEK

**Scenic rating: 7**

on Trout Lake Creek in Gifford Pinchot National Forest

### Map 5.4, page 320

This spot makes a popular base camp for folks fishing at Trout Lake (five miles away). Many anglers will spend the day at the lake, where fishing is good for stocked rainbow trout, then return to this camp for the night. Some bonus brook trout are occasionally caught at Trout Lake. The camp is set along a creek in a forest of Douglas fir. In season, berry picking can be good here.

**Campsites, facilities:** There are 17 sites for tents or RVs up to 28 feet long. Picnic tables and fire rings are provided. Vault toilets are available. There is no drinking water, and garbage must be packed out. Leashed pets are permitted.

**Reservations, fees:** Reservations are not accepted. Sites are $10 per night, $5 per night per additional vehicle. Open mid-May–mid-September, weather permitting.

**Directions:** From White Salmon, take Grangeview Loop Road to W. Jewett Boulevard/WA-141. Turn right on WA-141 and drive 22 miles to Trout Creek Road/Trout Lake Creek Road. Turn right on Trout Creek Road/Trout Lake Creek Road and drive four miles to National Forest Development Road 010. Take a slight right and drive about 0.5 mile to the campground on the left.

Alternately, from Hood River, Oregon, drive north on Highway 35 (over the Columbia River) to Highway 14. Turn left and drive two miles to Highway 141-A. Turn right (north) on Highway 141-A and drive 25 miles north to Forest Road 88. Turn right and drive four miles to Forest Road 8810. Turn right and drive 1.5 miles to Forest Road 8810-010. Turn right and drive 0.25 mile to the campground on the right. Note that the access road is rough.

**Contact:** Gifford Pinchot National Forest, Mount Adams Ranger District, 509/395-3400, www.fs.usda.gov.

## 96 PARADISE CREEK

**Scenic rating: 9**

on Paradise Creek and the Wind River in Gifford Pinchot National Forest

### Map 5.4, page 320

This camp is located deep in Gifford Pinchot National Forest at the confluence of Paradise Creek and the Wind River. It gets light use despite easy access and easy RV parking. The well-shaded campsites are set among old-growth woods, primarily Douglas fir, cedar, and western hemlock. Lava Butte, located a short distance from the camp, is accessible by trail; the 1.2-mile round-trip hike from the campground provides a good view of the valley. Fishing is closed here. The elevation is 1,500 feet.

**Campsites, facilities:** There are 42 sites for tents or RVs up to 40 feet long. Picnic tables and fire grills are provided. Drinking water, vault toilets, and firewood are available. A camp host is on-site. Some facilities are wheelchair accessible. Leashed pets are permitted.

**Reservations, fees:** Reservations are accepted at 877/444-6777 ($10 reservation fee) or www.recreation.gov ($9 reservation fee). Sites are $18 per night, double sites are $34 per night, $9 per extra vehicle per night. Open mid-May-mid-September, weather permitting.

**Directions:** From Vancouver, Washington, take Highway 14 east and drive 50 miles to Carson and the Wind River Highway (County Road 30). Turn left (north) on the Wind River Highway and drive 20 miles to the camp on the right.

**Contact:** Gifford Pinchot National Forest, Mount Adams Ranger District, 509/395-3400, www.fs.usda.gov or www.hoodoo.com

## 97 FALLS CREEK HORSE CAMP

### Scenic rating: 5

near the Pacific Crest Trail in Gifford Pinchot National Forest

**Map 5.4, page 320**

Falls Creek sits at the threshold of a great launch point for hiking, horseback riding, and mountain biking. The camp is set along Race Track Trail, adjacent to the western border of Indian Heaven Wilderness. A wilderness trailhead is available right at the camp. There are 90 miles of trail for horses and hiking and 40 miles for mountain bikes. Although this is a multiple-use campground, the sites are small and the turnaround is tight for RVs.

The camp has been intermittently closed due to trees hazards, so call to confirm availability before heading out.

**Campsites, facilities:** There are four sites for tents or RVs up to 15 feet long. Picnic tables and fire grills are provided. Pit toilets and a loading ramp for horses are available. There is no drinking water and garbage must be packed out. Some facilities are wheelchair accessible. Leashed pets are permitted.

**Reservations, fees:** Reservations are not accepted. There is no fee for camping, but a free wilderness permit is required; a self-issued permit is available at the trailhead. Open mid-June-November.

**Directions:** From Vancouver, Washington, on I-205, take Highway 14 and drive east for 50 miles to Carson and the Wind River Highway (County Road 30). Turn left (north) on the Wind River Highway and drive 9.5 miles to Forest Road 6517. Continue 1.5 miles to Forest Road 65. Turn left and drive 15 miles to the campground on the left.

**Contact:** Gifford Pinchot National Forest, Mount Adams Ranger District, 509/395-3400, www.fs.usda.gov.

## 98 CREST HORSE CAMP

### Scenic rating: 6

bordering Big Lava Bed in Gifford Pinchot National Forest

**Map 5.4, page 320**

Crest Horse Camp is a small, primitive, multiple-use camp set near the Pacific Crest Trail, adjacent to the eastern boundary of the Indian Heaven Wilderness. It is an excellent jumping-off spot for wilderness treks with horses or other stock animals. The camp features a forested setting, primarily second-growth Douglas fir. Adjacent to the camp is the Big Lava Bed, a volcanic flow known for its lava tubes and lava tube caves.

**Campsites, facilities:** There are three sites for tents or RVs up to 16 feet long. Only one back-in is allowed at this site; other vehicles must park on the road. Picnic tables and fire pits are provided. A vault toilet and a loading ramp and high lines for horses are available. There is no drinking water and garbage must be packed out. Some facilities are wheelchair accessible. Leashed pets are permitted.

**Reservations, fees:** Reservations are not accepted. There is no fee for camping. Open mid-May-mid-October, weather permitting.

**Directions:** From Vancouver, Washington, take Highway 14 east and drive 50 miles to Carson and the Wind River Highway (County Road 30). Turn left (north) and drive nine miles to Forest Road 6517. Turn right (east) on Forest Road 6517 and drive 1.5 miles to Forest Road 65. Turn left (north) on Forest Road 65 and drive about 10 miles to Forest Road 60. Turn right and drive two miles to the camp on the right.

**Contact:** Gifford Pinchot National Forest, Mount Adams Ranger District, 509/395-3400, www.fs.usda.gov.

## 99 GOOSE LAKE
🏊 🎣 🚐 🐕 🚗 ⛺

**Scenic rating: 8**

on Goose Lake in Gifford Pinchot National Forest

**Map 5.4, page 320**

This campground is set along the shore of beautiful Goose Lake at an elevation of 3,200 feet. Though the lake is quite pretty, the camp itself is set well above the lake and is not as nice; it can also be crowded in summer. Trout fishing and berry picking are available and a 5-mph speed limit is enforced on the lake. Adjacent to the camp is the northern edge of Big Lava Bed, a volcanic flow known for its lava tubes and lava tube caves.

**Campsites, facilities:** There are 18 walk-in sites for tents situated on a hillside, though the sites themselves are level. Roadside parking is available. There is also one site for RVs up to 18 feet long. Picnic tables and fire rings are provided. Vault toilets and firewood are available, but there is no drinking water. A camp host is on-site. A boat ramp is nearby. Leashed pets are permitted.

**Reservations, fees:** Reservations are not accepted. Sites are $10 per night, $5 per extra vehicle per night. Open mid-May–mid-September, weather permitting.

**Directions:** From Vancouver, Washington, on I-205, take Highway 14 east and drive 46 miles

to County Road 30/Wind River Road. Turn left and drive six miles to Panther Creek Road and Forest Road 6517. Turn right on Forest Road 6517 and drive 10 miles to a four-way intersection called Four Corners. Turn right on Forest Road 60 and drive 10 miles to the campground on the left.

**Contact:** Gifford Pinchot National Forest, Mount Adams Ranger District, 509/395-3400, www.fs.usda.gov.

## 100 BEAVER
🏃 🐕 ♿ 🚐 ⛺

**Scenic rating: 7**

on the Wind River in Gifford Pinchot National Forest

**Map 5.4, page 320**

This is the closest campground north of Stevenson in the Columbia Gorge. Set along the Wind River at an elevation of 1,100 feet, it features pretty, shaded sites. The campsites are paved, and a large grassy day-use area is nearby. Hiking highlights include two nearby trailheads. Two miles north is the trailhead for the Trapper Creek Wilderness with 30 miles of trails, including a loop possibility. Three miles north is the Falls Creek Trail. No fishing is permitted.

**Campsites, facilities:** There are 18 sites for tents or RVs up to 25 feet long, five double sites, and one group site for up to 40 people. Picnic tables and fire grills are provided. Drinking water, firewood, and flush and vault toilets are available. A camp host is on-site. Some facilities are wheelchair accessible. Leashed pets are permitted.

**Reservations, fees:** Reservations are accepted at 877/444-6777 ($10 reservation fee) or www.recreation.gov ($9 reservation fee). Sites are $20 per night, double sites are $34 per night, $10 per extra vehicle per night. The group site is $100 per night. Open early May–late September.

**Directions:** From Vancouver, Washington, take Highway 14 east and drive 50 miles to

Carson and the Wind River Highway (County Road 30). Turn left (north) and drive 12 miles to the campground entrance (five miles past Stabler) on the left.

**Contact:** Gifford Pinchot National Forest, Mount Adams Ranger District, 509/395-3400, www.fs.usda.gov or www.hoodoo.com.

## 101 PANTHER CREEK AND HORSE CAMP
🥾🚲🛶🐕♿🚐⛺

**Scenic rating: 8**
on Panther Creek in Gifford Pinchot National Forest

**Map 5.4, page 320**

This campground is set along Panther Creek in a second-growth forest of Douglas fir and western hemlock, adjacent to an old-growth forest. The sites are well defined, but despite a paved road to the campground and easy parking and access, it gets light use. The camp lies 3.5 miles from the Wind River, an option for those who enjoy fishing, hiking, and horseback riding. The Pacific Crest Trail is accessible from the adjacent Panther Creek Horse Camp. The elevation is 1,000 feet.

**Campsites, facilities:** There are 33 sites for tents or RVs up to 25 feet long, including six double sites, and one equestrian site with a stock loading ramp at the adjacent horse camp. Picnic tables and fire rings are provided. Drinking water, pit toilets, garbage bins, and firewood are available. A camp host is on-site. Some facilities are wheelchair accessible. Leashed pets are permitted.

**Reservations, fees:** Reserve at 877/444-6777 or www.recreation.gov ($10 reservation fee). Single sites are $18 per night, double sites are $34 per night, $5 per extra vehicle per night. The horse site is free. Open mid-May-mid-September.

**Directions:** From Vancouver, Washington, take Highway 14 east and drive 50 miles to Carson and the Wind River Highway (County Road 30). Turn north and drive nine miles to

Forest Road 6517 (just past Stabler). Turn right (east) on Forest Road 6517 and drive 1.5 miles to the campground entrance road on the right.
**Contact:** Gifford Pinchot National Forest, Mount Adams Ranger District, 509/395-3400, www.fs.usda.gov or www.hoodoo.com.

## 102 OKLAHOMA
🛶🐕♿🚐⛺

**Scenic rating: 7**
on the Little White Salmon River in Gifford Pinchot National Forest

**Map 5.4, page 320**

Pretty Oklahoma campground is set along the Little White Salmon River at an elevation of 1,700 feet. Located close to the Columbia River Gorge, it features a paved road all the way into the campground and easy RV parking. The camp features some open meadow, but is generally flat and gets light use. Fishing can be excellent in this area and the river is stocked in the spring with rainbow trout.

The camp was named after the large influx of homesteaders that moved into the area around 1893. They were likened to the "Oklahoma Boomers" of the great land rush two years earlier.

**Campsites, facilities:** There are 13 single sites and one double site for tents or RVs up to 40 feet long. Picnic tables and fire rings are provided. Drinking water and vault toilets are available. Some facilities are wheelchair accessible. Leashed pets are permitted.

**Reservations, fees:** Reservations are accepted at 877/444-6777 or www.recreation.gov ($10 reservation fee). Single sites are $16 per night, double sites are $30 per night, $8 per night for each additional vehicle. Open mid-May-mid-September, weather permitting.

**Directions:** From White Salmon: Take N. Main Avenue to E. Jewett Boulevard. Turn left on E. Jewett Boulevard and drive 0.5 mile to SE 6th Avenue/Dock Grade Road. Turn right on SE 6th Avenue/Dock Grade Road and drive 0.8 mile to Lewis and Clark Highway/

WA-14W. Turn right on Lewis and Clark Highway/WA-14W and drive 1.5 miles to Cook Underwood Road. Turn right on Cook Underwood Road and drive 8.3 miles to Willard Road. Turn right on Willard Road and drive two miles to Oklahoma Road. Turn right on Oklahoma Road and drive five miles to National Forest Development Road 18/Oklahoma Road. Turn right on National Forest Development Road 18/Oklahoma Road and drive three miles to the campground on the left.

From Hood River, Oregon: Drive north on Highway 35 for one mile over the Columbia River to Highway 14. Turn left on Highway 14 and drive about five miles to Cook and County Road 1800. Turn right (north) and drive 14 miles (becomes Cook-Underwood Road, then Willard Road, then Oklahoma Road) to the campground entrance at the end of the paved road.

**Contact:** Gifford Pinchot National Forest, Mount Adams Ranger District, 509/395-3400, www.fs.usda.gov or www.hoodoo.com.

## 103 MOSS CREEK

### Scenic rating: 7

on the Little White Salmon River in Gifford Pinchot National Forest

**Map 5.4, page 320**

This campground is set at 1,400 feet elevation, about one mile from the Little White Salmon River. Although it's a short distance from Willard and Big Cedars County Park, the camp gets light use. The river provides good fishing prospects for trout in the spring, usually with few other people around. The sites are generally small but are shaded and still functional for most RVs. The road is paved all the way to the campground.

**Campsites, facilities:** There are 17 sites for tents or RVs up to 40 feet long. Picnic tables and fire grills are provided. Drinking water, vault toilets, and firewood are available. A camp host is available in the summer. Some facilities are wheelchair accessible. Leashed pets are permitted.

**Reservations, fees:** Reservations are accepted at 877/444-6777 ($10 reservation fee) or www.recreation.gov ($9 reservation fee). Sites are $16 per night, and $8 per night for each additional vehicle. Open mid-May-mid-September, weather permitting.

**Directions:** From White Salmon: Take N. Main Avenue to E. Jewett Boulevard. Turn left on E. Jewett Boulevard and drive 0.5 mile to SE 6th Avenue/Dock Grade Road. Turn right on SE 6th Avenue/Dock Grade Road and drive 0.8 mile to Lewis and Clark Highway/WA-14W. Turn right on Lewis and Clark Highway/WA-14W and drive 1.5 miles to Cook Underwood Road. Turn right on Cook Underwood Road and drive 8.3 miles to Willard Road. Watch for the fish hatchery, then turn right on Willard Road and drive two miles to Oklahoma Road. Turn right on Oklahoma Road and drive 1.3 miles to the campground on the left.

From Hood River, Oregon: Drive north on Highway 35 for one mile over the Columbia River to Highway 14. Turn left on Highway 14 and drive about five miles to Cook and County Road 1800. Turn right (north) and drive 10 miles (becomes Cook-Underwood Road, then Willard road, then Oklahoma Road) to the campground entrance on the right.

**Contact:** Gifford Pinchot National Forest, Mount Adams Ranger District, 509/395-3400, www.fs.usda.gov or www.hoodoo.com.

## 104 COLUMBIA HILLS STATE PARK

### Scenic rating: 10

near the Dalles Dam

**Map 5.4, page 320**

You may remember this park by its former name: Horsethief Lake State Park. The 338-acre park boasts 7,500 feet of Columbia River shoreline. It also adjoins the 3,000-acre Dalles

Mountain Ranch State Park. Horsethief Lake, created by the Dalles Dam, covers approximately 100 acres and is part of the Columbia River. Horsethief Butte, adjacent to the lake, dominates the skyline. The bloom of lupine and balsamroot in mid-April creates stunning views. Rock climbing in the park is popular, but the river canyon is often windy, especially in late spring and early summer. Most people find the place as a spot to camp while driving along the Columbia River Highway. There are hiking trails and access to both the lake and the Columbia River. The boat speed limit is 5 mph, and anglers can try for trout and bass. Guided tours on weekends feature pictographs and petroglyphs; reservations are required at 509/767-1159.

**Campsites, facilities:** There are eight sites with partial hookups (15 amps, converters available) for tents or RVs up to 30 feet long, four sites for tents or RVs up to 30 feet long (no hookups), six primitive tent sites, and one hike-in/bike-in site. Picnic tables and fire grills are provided. Drinking water, restrooms with flush toilets and coin showers, firewood, a dump station, a horseshoe pit, and a picnic area are available. A store is within three miles. Boat-launching facilities are located on both the lake and the river. Leashed pets are permitted.

**Reservations, fees:** Reservations are accepted at 888/226-7688 or www.goingtocamp.com. Sites are $17-39 per night, $12 per night for primitive sites and the hike-in/bike-in site, $10 per extra vehicle per night. Open April-late October.

**Directions:** From Dallesport, drive east on 6th Avenue to Dallesport Road. Turn left on Dallesport Road and drive 2.3 miles to Lewis and Clark Highway/WA-14E. Turn right at Lewis and Clark Highway/WA-14E and drive four miles to the campground on the left.

Alternately, from The Dalles in Oregon, turn north on Highway 197, cross over the Columbia River, and drive four miles to Highway 14. Turn right (east) and drive two miles to Milepost 85 and the park entrance on the right.

**Contact:** Columbia Hills State Park, 509/767-1159; state park information, 360/902-8844, www.parks.wa.gov.

# SOUTHEASTERN WASHINGTON

© LARRY LAWHEAD/123RF

The expansive domain of southeastern Washington
is a surprise for many newcomers. Instead of the high mountains of the Cascades, there are rolling hills. Instead of forests, there are miles of wheat fields.
Instead of a multitude of streams, there are giant rivers like the Columbia and
the Snake. Just one pocket of mountains and a somewhat sparse forest sit in
the southeast corner of the state, in a remote sector of Umatilla National Forest. More than 200 years ago, the Lewis and Clark Expedition routed through
this area. Today, major highways like I-82 and U.S. 395 link the region to other
destinations. A network of camps is set along these highways, including RV
parks created to serve the needs of travelers. Of the area parks, the state parks
offer the best campgrounds.

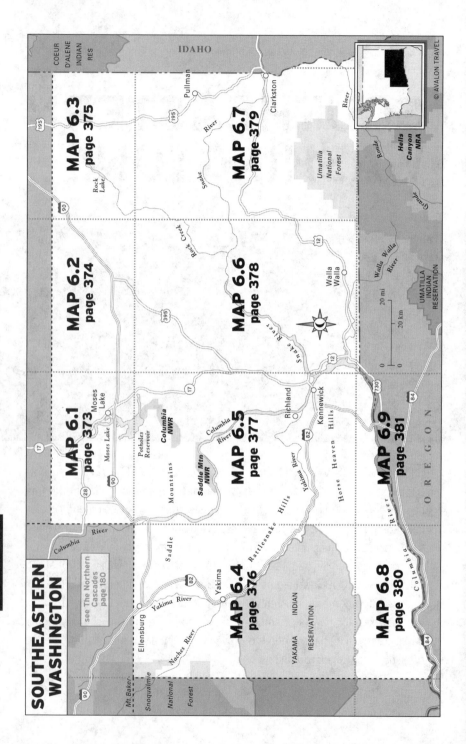

SOUTHEASTERN WASHINGTON

IDAHO

MAP 6.3 page 375

MAP 6.2 page 374

MAP 6.1 page 373

MAP 6.7 page 379

MAP 6.6 page 378

MAP 6.5 page 377

MAP 6.9 page 381

MAP 6.4 page 376

MAP 6.8 page 380

see The Northern Cascades page 180

Hells Canyon NRA

Umatilla National Forest

UMATILLA INDIAN RESERVATION

YAKAMA INDIAN RESERVATION

COEUR D'ALENE INDIAN RES

Pullman

Clarkston

Walla Walla

Richland

Kennewick

Moses Lake

Yakima

Ellensburg

Rock Lake

Columbia NWR

Saddle Mtn NWR

Potholes Reservoir

Mountains

Saddle

Rattlesnake Hills

Horse Heaven Hills

Snake River

Columbia River

Yakima River

Naches River

Rock Creek

Grande Ronde River

Walla Walla River

OREGON

195

90

28

17

90

395

17

82

82

12

12

730

84

84

© AVALON TRAVEL

20 mi

20 km

# Map 6.1

## Sites 1-3
## Page 382

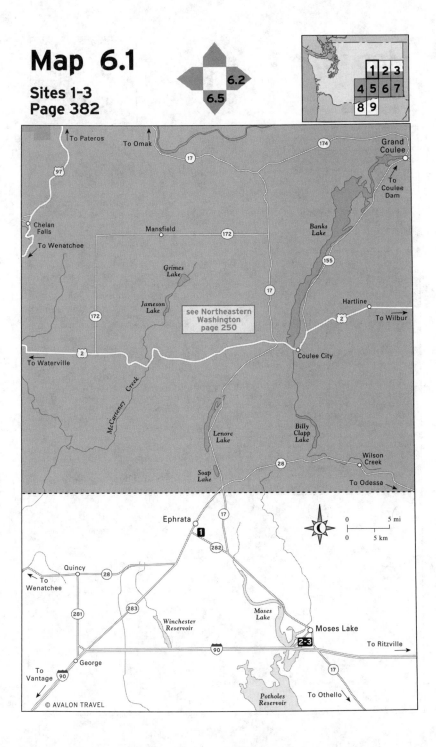

6.2

6.5

1 2 3
4 5 6 7
8 9

To Pateros

To Omak

17

174

Grand Coulee

97

To Coulee Dam

Chelan Falls

Mansfield

172

Banks Lake

To Wenatchee

Grimes Lake

155

Jameson Lake

see Northeastern Washington page 250

Hartline

2

To Wilbur

172

2

To Waterville

McCartaney Creek

Coulee City

Lenore Lake

Billy Clapp Lake

Wilson Creek

28

Soap Lake

To Odessa

Ephrata

17

0        5 mi
0        5 km

1

282

Quincy

28

To Wenatchee

281

283

Winchester Reservoir

Moses Lake

Moses Lake

2·3

To Ritzville

90

George

90

17

To Vantage

Potholes Reservoir

To Othello

© AVALON TRAVEL

# Map 6.2

**Site 4
Page 383**

6.1  6.3
6.6

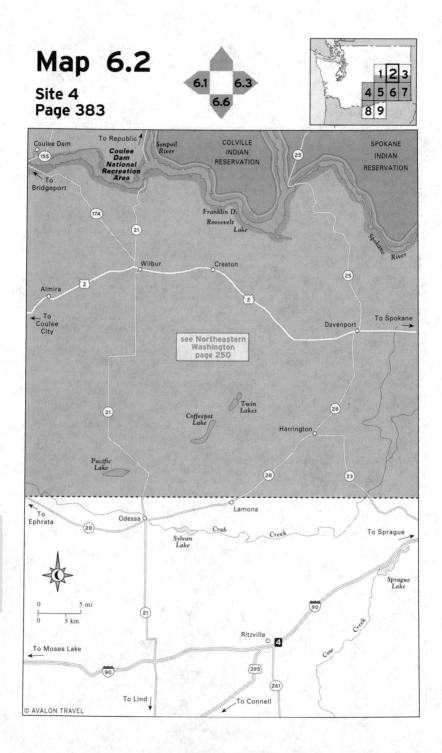

- Coulee Dam
- 155
- To Republic →
- To Bridgeport
- *Coulee Dam National Recreation Area*
- *Sampoil River*
- COLVILLE INDIAN RESERVATION
- SPOKANE INDIAN RESERVATION
- 25
- 174
- 21
- *Franklin D. Roosevelt Lake*
- *Spokane River*
- Wilbur
- Creston
- 2
- Almira
- 2
- 25
- To Coulee City
- Davenport
- To Spokane →
- see Northeastern Washington page 250
- 21
- *Twin Lakes*
- *Coffeepot Lake*
- Harrington
- 28
- *Pacific Lake*
- 28
- 23
- To Ephrata
- 28
- Odessa
- Lamona
- *Crab* *Creek*
- To Sprague →
- *Sylvan Lake*
- *Sprague Lake*
- 0   5 mi
- 0   5 km
- 21
- 90
- Ritzville
- 4
- To Moses Lake ←
- 90
- 395
- *Cow* *Creek*
- To Lind ↓
- 261
- To Connell ↙
- © AVALON TRAVEL

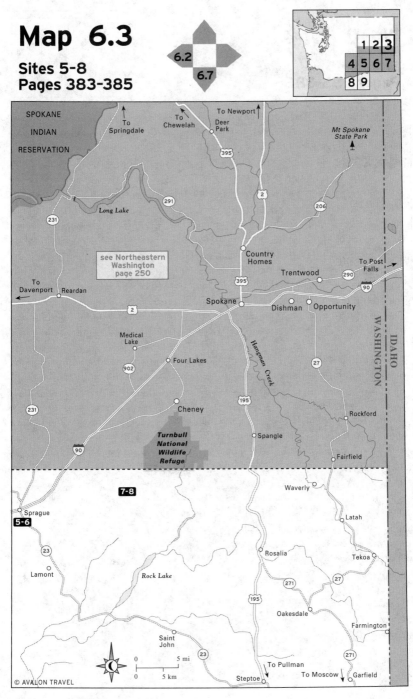

# Map 6.3

**Sites 5-8**
**Pages 383-385**

6.2

6.7

1 2 3
4 5 6 7
8 9

SPOKANE
INDIAN
RESERVATION

To Newport

To
Springdale

To
Chewelah

Deer
Park

Mt Spokane
State Park

395

291

2

206

Long Lake

231

see Northeastern
Washington
page 250

Country
Homes

Trentwood

To Post
Falls

395

290

To
Davenport

Reardan

2

Spokane

Dishman

Opportunity

90

WASHINGTON

IDAHO

Medical
Lake

Hangman Creek

902

Four Lakes

27

231

Cheney

195

Rockford

Turnbull
National
Wildlife
Refuge

Spangle

Fairfield

90

**7-8**

Waverly

Sprague

**5-6**

Latah

23

Rosalia

Tekoa

Lamont

Rock Lake

271

27

195

Oakesdale

Farmington

Saint
John

23

271

To Pullman

Steptoe

To Moscow

Garfield

0          5 mi
0          5 km

© AVALON TRAVEL

# Map 6.4

**Sites 9-15**
**Pages 385-388**

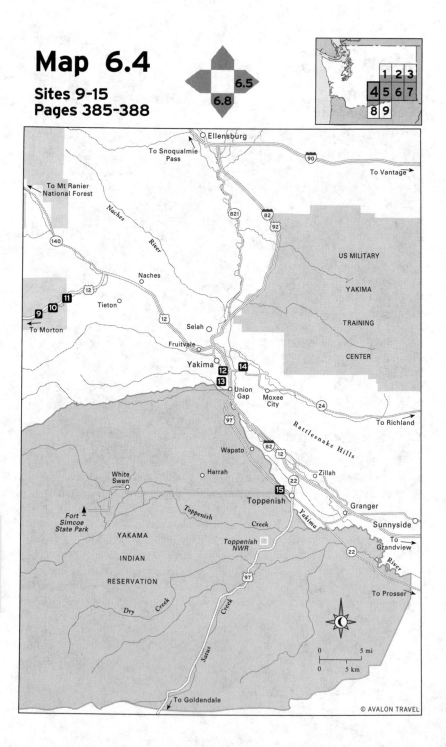

© AVALON TRAVEL

# Map **6.5**

## Sites 16-21
## Pages 388-391

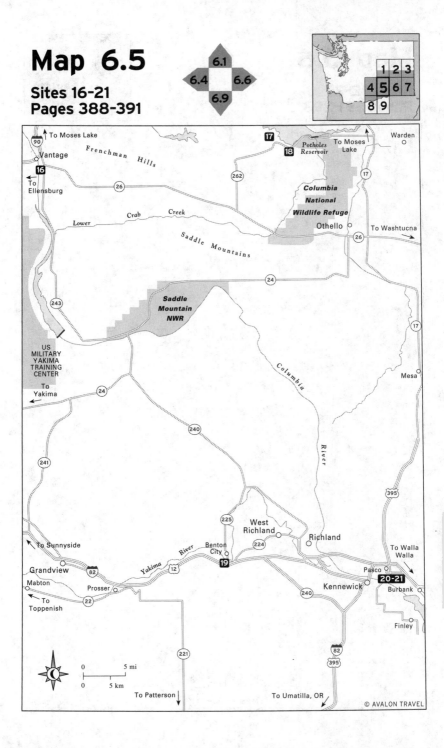

# Map 6.6

## Sites 22-27
## Pages 391-393

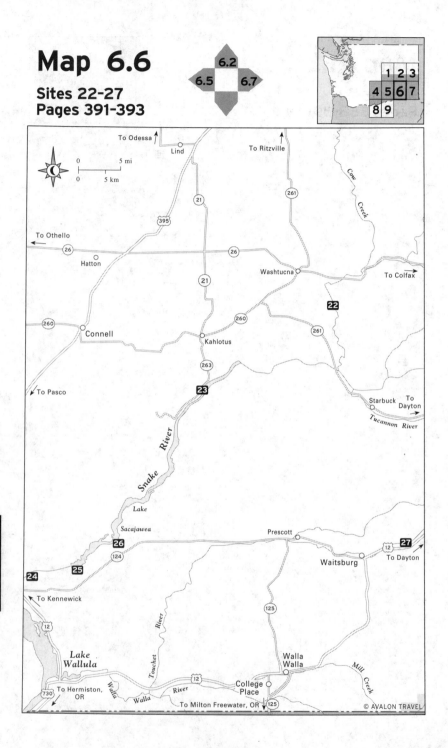

# Map 6.7

**Sites 28-38**
**Pages 394-399**

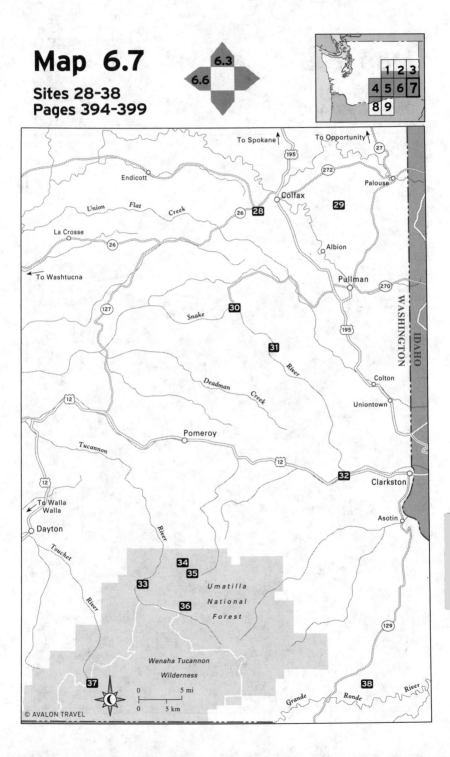

6.3

6.6

| 1 | 2 | 3 |
| 4 | 5 | 6 | 7 |
| 8 | 9 |

To Spokane
To Opportunity

195
27
272

Endicott
Palouse

Union Flat Creek
Colfax
26 **28**
**29**

La Crosse
26
Albion

To Washtucna
Pullman
270

127
Snake
**30**

**31**
River
195

Deadman Creek
Colton

12
Uniontown

Tucannon
Pomeroy
12

**32**
Clarkston

12
To Walla Walla

Dayton
Asotin

Touchet
River

**34**
**35**
Umatilla
**33**
National
**36**
Forest

129

Wenaha Tucannon
Wilderness

**37**

0        5 mi
0        5 km

**38**
Grande    Ronde    River

WASHINGTON    IDAHO

© AVALON TRAVEL

# Map 6.8

**Sites 39-40
Pages 399-400**

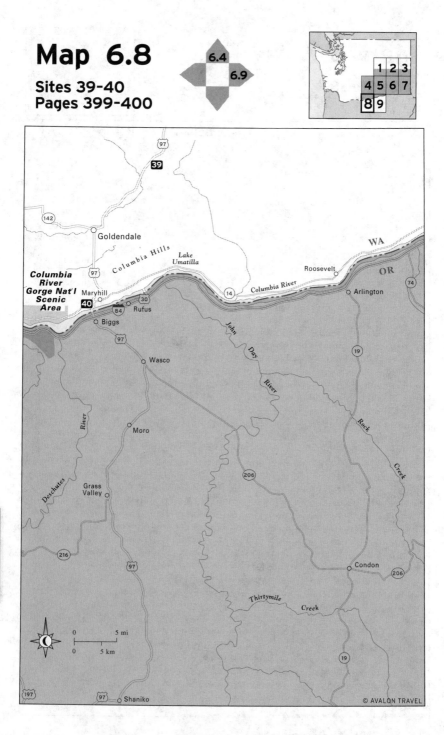

© AVALON TRAVEL

# Map 6.9

**Sites 41-42**
**Pages 400-401**

6.5
6.8

1 2 3
4 5 6 7
8 9

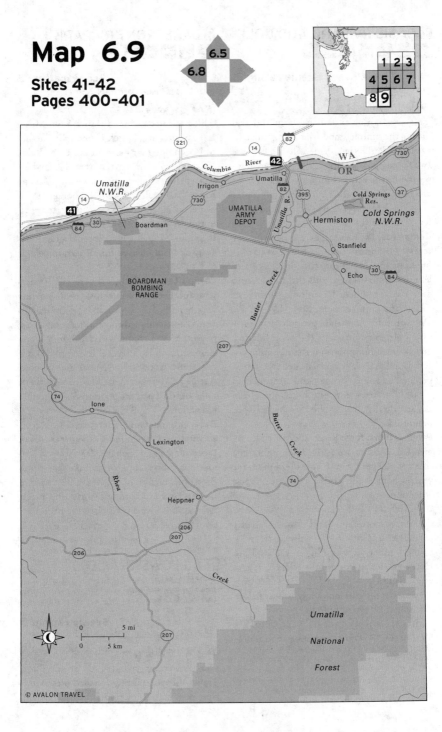

© AVALON TRAVEL

# 1 OASIS RV PARK AND GOLF

**Scenic rating: 5**

near Soap Lake

**Map 6.1, page 373**

This area can be extremely warm and arid during the summer months, but, fortunately, Oasis RV Park offers shaded sites. There are two fishing ponds at the resort: One has crappie, while the other is for kids and has trout and bass. There is also a nine-hole golf course at the park. Mineral baths are located just a few miles north.

**Campsites, facilities:** There are 12 sites for tents only and 69 sites with full or partial hookups (30 amps) for tents or RVs of any length. Some sites are pull-through. Picnic tables are provided. Restrooms with flush toilets and coin showers, cable TV, Wi-Fi, a playground, horseshoe pits, picnic area, a nine-hole golf course, an 18-hole miniature golf course, dump station, a store, propane, coin laundry, ice, a seasonal heated swimming pool, and a youth fishing pond are available. A café is located within one mile. Some facilities are wheelchair accessible. Leashed pets are permitted.

**Reservations, fees:** Reservations are recommended. RV sites are $23-30 per night, tent sites are $20 per night, $5 per night per extra vehicle. Some credit cards are accepted. Open year-round.

**Directions:** From Spokane, take I-90 west to the Moses Lake exit and Highway 17. Turn northeast on Highway 17 and drive 32.7 miles to the Y junction with Highway 282. Take Highway 282 and drive four miles to Highway 281/283 (a stoplight). Turn left and drive 1.9 miles to the park on the right (just before reaching the town of Ephrata).

**Contact:** Oasis RV Park and Golf, 509/754-5102 or 877/754-5102, www.oasisrvandgolfresort.com.

# 2 LAKEFRONT RV PARK

**Scenic rating: 5**

near Moses Lake State Park

**Map 6.1, page 373**

This park sits a short distance from Moses Lake State Park, which is open for day-use only. The primary appeal is Moses Lake, Washington's largest freshwater lake, where you will find shady picnic spots with tables and fire grills, beach access, and moorage floats. Waterskiing and personal watercraft are allowed on the lake. Bird hunting is popular in season. Sand dunes are located a few miles away and can be used for all-terrain-vehicle (ATV) activities.

**Campsites, facilities:** There are 50 sites with full hookups (30 amps) for RVs of any length; half of the sites are long-term rentals. Some sites are pull-through. Picnic tables are provided. A restroom with flush toilets and showers, coin laundry, cable TV, dump station, and boat docks and launch are available. A store and restaurant are located within one mile. Leashed pets are permitted with certain restrictions.

**Reservations, fees:** Reservations are accepted. Sites are $35 per night. Open year-round.

**Directions:** From Spokane, drive west on I-90 to Moses Lake and Exit 176. Take that exit to Broadway, turn right, and drive 0.75 mile to Burress Avenue. Turn left (west) on Burress Avenue and drive one block to the park.

**Contact:** Lakefront RV Park, 509/765-8294.

# 3 WILLOWS TRAILER VILLAGE

**Scenic rating: 5**

near Moses Lake State Park

**Map 6.1, page 373**

One of two campgrounds in the area, Willows Trailer Village has grassy, shaded sites, horseshoe pits, barbecues, and a recreation field.

Most recreation opportunities can be found at Moses Lake, including picnicking, beach access, waterskiing, and moorage floats. Birdwatching and sand dunes for ATV riding are nearby. Note that there are some permanent site rentals at this RV park, but a landscape barrier separates them from the other sites.

**Campsites, facilities:** There are 20 sites for tents and 68 sites for RVs of any length; all RV sites are pull-through and most have full hookups (30 and 50 amps). Picnic tables are provided. A restroom with flush toilets and coin showers, propane, a convenience store, ice, coin laundry, playground, and horseshoe pits are available. There is also a hair salon on-site. Some facilities are wheelchair accessible. Leashed pets are permitted.

**Reservations, fees:** Reservations are accepted. Sites are $28.50-34.50 per night, $3 per person per night for more than two people. Open year-round.

**Directions:** From Spokane, drive west on I-90 to Moses Lake and Exit 179 and Highway 17. Turn south on Highway 17 and drive 2.5 miles to Road M SE. Turn right and drive 0.5 mile to the park on the left.

**Contact:** Willows Trailer Village, 509/765-7531.

## ◢ CEDARS INN/ RITZVILLE RV PARK

🏊 🐕 ⛺ ♿ 🚐 ⛰

**Scenic rating: 7**

in Ritzville

**Map 6.2, page 374**

If you have an RV, well, this might be the only site to stake it on within a radius of 25 miles. Ritzville RV Park is adjacent to Cedars Inn. A nine-hole golf course and tennis courts are just across the street. Burroughs Historical Museum is a possible side trip in town. The nearest fishing is at Sprague Lake, 22 miles north on U.S. 395.

**Campsites, facilities:** There are 39 pull-through sites for tents or RVs of any length

(30 and 50 amp full hookups). Restrooms with flush toilets and showers, cable TV, a dump station, coin laundry, Wi-Fi, ice, a playground, and seasonal heated swimming pool are available. Propane, a store, gift shop, café, and restaurant are located within one mile. Some facilities are wheelchair accessible. Leashed pets are permitted.

**Reservations, fees:** Reservations are accepted for groups only. Sites are $15-30 per night. Some credit cards are accepted. Open year-round, with limited winter facilities.

**Directions:** From Pasco, take U.S. 395 north and drive 85 miles to Ritzville and I-90. Take I-90 east and drive 0.5 mile to Exit 221. Take that exit and drive 0.25 mile to Smitty's Boulevard. Turn right and drive a short distance to the motel/RV check-in on the left.

**Contact:** Cedars Inn/Ritzville RV Park, 1513 S. Smitty's Blvd., Ritzville, 509/659-1007, www.cedarsinnritzville.com.

## ◢ FOUR SEASONS CAMPGROUND & RESORT

🏊 🚣 ⛺ 🐕 🚐 ⛰

**Scenic rating: 7**

on Sprague Lake

**Map 6.3, page 375**

This campground along the shore of Sprague Lake, one of the top fishing waters in the state, has spacious sites with plenty of vegetation. The fishing for rainbow trout is best in May and June, with some bass in spring and fall. Because there is an abundance of natural feed in the lake, the fish reach larger sizes here than in neighboring lakes. Walleye up to 10 pounds are taken here. Crappie and catfish are also abundant, with a sprinkling of perch and bluegill. In late July-August, a fair algae bloom is a turnoff for swimmers and water-skiers.

**Campsites, facilities:** There are 38 sites with full or partial hookups (30 and 50 amps) for RVs of any length; some sites are pull-through. There are also four cabins. Tent camping is allowed when space is available. Picnic tables and fire pits are provided. Restrooms with flush toilets and coin showers, drinking water, a dump station, firewood, ice, a convenience store with fishing tackle, a fish-cleaning station, a small basketball court are available. Boat and fishing docks, launching facilities, slips, and rentals are nearby. Leashed pets are permitted.

**Reservations, fees:** Reservations are accepted. RV sites are $30 per night, tent sites are $23 per night, $5 per night for more than four people, $2 per night for extra vehicle, $1 per night per pet. Open mid-April-mid-October, weather permitting.

**Directions:** From Spokane, drive west on I-90 for 35 miles to Exit 245. Take Exit 245 and drive south to 4th Street. Turn right and drive one block to B Street. Turn left and drive two blocks to 1st Street. Turn right and drive one mile through the town of Sprague to a Y intersection (from here, the resort is six miles away). Continue (over the railroad tracks and then under I-90) to Lake Road. Turn left and drive (parallel to the freeway) until the road bears to the right to Bob Lee Road. Turn left on Bob Lee Road and drive (over I-90) to the resort.

**Contact:** Four Seasons Campground and Resort, 509/257-2332, www.fourseasonscampground.com.

# 6 SPRAGUE LAKE RESORT

🛶 🚤 🎣 🚶 ♿ 🚐 ⛺

### Scenic rating: 5

on Sprague Lake

Map 6.3, page 375

This developed campground is located on the shore of Sprague Lake, about 35 miles from Spokane. It offers a pleasant, grassy setting with about 50 cottonwood and native trees on the property. Sprague Lake is one of the top fishing waters in the state—look for rainbow trout, bass, walleye, crappie, catfish, perch, and bluegill. A late-summer algae bloom tends to leave swimmers and water-skiers landlocked.

**Campsites, facilities:** There are 50 sites for tents and 31 pull-through sites with full or partial hookups for RVs of any length. Picnic tables and fire grills are provided. Restrooms with flush toilets and coin showers, drinking water, a small store, coin laundry, Wi-Fi, ice, firewood, a playground, boat docks, launching facilities, and rentals are available. Some facilities are wheelchair accessible, including a paved area lakeside for fishing. Leashed pets are permitted.

**Reservations, fees:** Reservations are accepted. Sites are $27-37 per night, plus $2 per person per night for more than two people. Weekly and monthly rates available. Open April-November.

**Directions:** From Spokane, drive west on I-90 to the Sprague Business Center exit. Take that exit to Sprague Lake Road and continue two miles to the resort on the left (well signed).

**Contact:** Sprague Lake Resort, 509/257-2864, www.spraguelakeresort.com.

# 7 KLINK'S WILLIAMS LAKE RESORT

🛶 🚤 🚣 🎣 🚶 ♿ 🚐 ⛺

### Scenic rating: 6

on Williams Lake

Map 6.3, page 375

This family-oriented resort is set on the shore of Williams Lake, which is less than three miles long and is popular for swimming and waterskiing. The resort has a swimming area with a floating dock and slide. This lake is also one of the top fishing lakes in the region for rainbow and cutthroat trout. Rocky cliffs border the lake in some areas. Note that about 100 permanent residents live at the resort.

An option for a side trip is Turnbull National Wildlife Refuge, an expanse of marsh and pine that is a significant stopover point for migratory birds on the Pacific Flyway. This is a prime spot and only a 30-minute drive out of Spokane, yet it is relatively unknown.

**Campsites, facilities:** There are 60 sites with full or partial hookups (30 and 50 amps) for

RVs of any length, 15 sites for tents, and seven log cabins. Picnic tables and fire grills are provided. Restrooms with flush toilets and coin showers, drinking water, Wi-Fi, propane, a dump station, firewood, a general store, bait, tackle and fishing licenses, café, restaurant, ice, a playground, covered pavilion for group use, boat docks, launching facilities, and boat rentals are available. Some facilities are wheelchair accessible. Leashed pets are permitted.

**Reservations, fees:** Reservations are recommended. Sites are $30-40 per night. Weekly rates available. Some credit cards are accepted. Open mid-April-October.

**Directions:** From Spokane, drive west on I-90 for 10 miles to Exit 270 and Highway 904. Turn south on Highway 904 and drive four miles to Cheney and Cheney Plaza Road. Turn left (south) on Cheney Plaza Road and drive 12 miles to Williams Lake Road. Turn right (west) and drive two miles to the resort on the left.

**Contact:** Klink's Williams Lake Resort, 18617 W. Williams Lake Rd., Cheney, 509/235-2391, www.klinksresort.com.

# 8 BUNKER'S RESORT

### Scenic rating: 8

on Williams Lake

**Map 6.3, page 375**

Bunker's Resort is set on the shore of Williams Lake. The lake is stocked with rainbow, cutthroat, and triploid trout; fishing season is from the last Saturday in April through September. Waterskiing, wakeboarding, and personal watercraft are allowed; swimming is also popular.

**Campsites, facilities:** There are six sites with full or partial hookups (30 amps) for RVs up to 34 feet long, eight tent sites, and four cabins. Picnic tables and fire pits are provided. Restrooms with flush toilets and coin showers, drinking water, propane, remove dump station, a restaurant, convenience store, bait and tackle, ice, boat and fishing docks, launching facilities, and boat rentals are available. Some facilities are wheelchair accessible. Leashed pets are permitted.

**Reservations, fees:** Reservations are accepted. Sites are $25-35 per night. Some credit cards are accepted. Open mid-April-September.

**Directions:** From Spokane, drive west on I-90 for 10 miles to Exit 270 and Highway 904. Turn south on Highway 904 and drive six miles to Cheney and Mullinex Road. Turn left (south) on Mullinex Road and drive 12 miles to the resort.

**Contact:** Bunker's Resort, 509/235-5212 or 800/404-6674, www.bunkersresort.com.

# 9 HAUSE CREEK

### Scenic rating: 7

on the Tieton River in Wenatchee National Forest

**Map 6.4, page 376**

Several creeks converge at this campground along the Tieton River (elevation 2,500 feet). The Tieton Dam, which creates Rimrock Lake, is located just upstream. Hause Creek is one of the larger, more developed camps in the area. Willows campground provides a primitive alternative.

**Campsites, facilities:** There are 42 sites for tents or RVs up to 30 feet, including a few multi-family sites. Picnic tables and fire grills are provided. Drinking water, flush toilets, firewood, and garbage bins are available. A camp host is on-site. Boat docks, launching facilities, and rentals are located on Rimrock Lake. Some facilities are wheelchair accessible. Leashed pets are permitted.

**Reservations, fees:** Reservations are accepted at 877/444-6777 ($10 reservation fee) or www.recreation.gov ($9 reservation fee). Sites are $18 per night, $35 per night for multi-family sites, and $9 per extra vehicle per night. Open late May-September, weather permitting.

**Directions:** From Yakima, drive northwest

on U.S. 12 for 18 miles to the junction with Highway 410. Turn west on U.S. 12 and drive 22 miles to the campground on the left.

**Contact:** Okanogan and Wenatchee National Forests, Naches Ranger District, 509/653-1400, www.fs.usda.gov.

## 10 WILLOWS

### Scenic rating: 5

on the Tieton River in Wenatchee National Forest

Map 6.4, page 376

This primitive, beautiful, and easily accessible camp can be found on the Tieton River at 2,400 feet elevation. Rimrock Lake to the west provides many recreation options, and hiking trails leading into the William O. Douglas Wilderness are within driving distance.

**Campsites, facilities:** There are 13 sites for tents or RVs up to 35 feet and one site for tents only. Picnic tables and fire grills are provided. Drinking water, pit toilets, firewood, and garbage service are available. Some facilities are wheelchair accessible. Leashed pets are permitted.

**Reservations, fees:** Reservations are accepted at 877/444-6777 ($10 reservation fee) or www.recreation.gov ($9 reservation fee). Sites are $14 per night, $7 per night per extra vehicle. Open mid-May-September, weather permitting.

**Directions:** From Yakima, drive northwest on I-82 for 17 miles to the junction with Highway 410. Turn west on U.S. 12 and drive 16 miles to the campground on the left.

**Contact:** Okanogan and Wenatchee National Forests, Naches Ranger District, 509/653-1400, www.fs.usda.gov.

## 11 WINDY POINT

### Scenic rating: 5

on the Tieton River in Wenatchee National Forest

Map 6.4, page 376

This campground, located along the Tieton River at an elevation of 2,000 feet, is more isolated than the camps set westward toward Rimrock Lake. Drinking water is a bonus. Fishing access is available.

**Campsites, facilities:** There are 10 sites for tents or RVs up to 37 feet. Picnic tables and fire grills are provided. Drinking water and vault toilets are available. Garbage service and firewood are available nearby. Some facilities are wheelchair accessible. Leashed pets are permitted.

**Reservations, fees:** Reservations are not accepted. Sites are $14 per night, $7 per extra vehicle per night. Open mid-May-September, weather permitting.

**Directions:** From Yakima, drive northwest on I-82 for 17 miles to the junction with Highway 410. Turn west on U.S. 12 and drive nine miles to the campground on the left.

**Contact:** Okanogan and Wenatchee National Forests, Naches Ranger District, 509/653-1400, www.fs.usda.gov.

## 12 CIRCLE H RV RANCH

### Scenic rating: 8

in Yakima

Map 6.4, page 376

This pleasant, centrally located, and clean park with a Western flavor has comfortable, spacious sites among ornamental trees and roses. Nearby recreation options include an 18-hole golf course, hiking trails, and marked bike trails.

**Campsites, facilities:** There are 69 sites with full hookups (20, 30 and 50 amps) for RVs of any length, and 12 tent sites. Some sites are pull-through. Picnic tables and barbecues are provided. Restrooms with flush toilets and showers, a recreation hall, coin laundry, Wi-Fi access, clubhouse, playgrounds, horseshoes, a tennis court, tetherball, volleyball, and basketball, an 18-hole miniature golf course, and a seasonal heated swimming pool are available. Propane, a store, casino, and shopping center are located within one mile. Mini storage units are available for a fee. Some facilities are wheelchair accessible. Leashed pets are permitted.

**Reservations, fees:** Reservations are accepted. Sites are $25-29 per night, $4 per person per night for more than two people. Some credit cards are accepted. Open year-round.

**Directions:** In Yakima on I-82, take Exit 34 West and drive one block to South 18th Street. Turn right (north) and drive 0.25 mile to the campground on the right.

**Contact:** Circle H RV Ranch, 1107 S. 18th St., Yakima, 509/457-3683, www.circlehrvranch.com.

## 13 TRAILER INNS RV PARK/YAKIMA

🥾 🚴 🏊 ⛵ 🐕 🛶 ♿ 🚐 ⛺

### Scenic rating: 7

in Yakima

**Map 6.4, page 376**

This spot has many of the luxuries you'd find in a hotel, including a pool, spa, on-site security, and a large-screen TV. An 18-hole golf course, hiking trails, marked bike trails, and tennis courts are close by. Local pond fishing, as well as fishing in the Yakima River, is available. It's especially pretty in the fall when the sycamores turn color. The region has become known for its wineries and breweries. A variety of fresh produce is available in the local area in season.

**Campsites, facilities:** There are 135 sites for tents or RVs of any length (15, 30, and 50 amp full hookups). Some sites are pull-through. Picnic tables are provided and some sites have gas barbecues. Restrooms with flush toilets and showers, cable TV, Wi-Fi, propane, a dump station, a recreation hall, coin laundry, ice, an indoor heated swimming pool, a whirlpool, TV room, dog walk, enclosed barbecue area (no open fires permitted), and a playground are available. A store and café are within one block. Some facilities are wheelchair accessible. Leashed pets are permitted.

**Reservations, fees:** Reservations are accepted at 800/659-4784. RV sites are $28-42 per night, tent sites are $20 per night, $5 per person per night for more than two people, and $5 per extra vehicle per night. Weekly and monthly rates available. Some credit cards are accepted. Open year-round.

**Directions:** In Yakima on I-82, take Exit 31 and drive south for one block on North 1st Street to the park on the right (west side of the road).

**Contact:** Trailer Inns RV Park, 1610 N. 1st St., Yakima, 509/452-9561 or 800/659-4784, www.trailerinnsrv.com.

## 14 YAKIMA SPORTSMAN STATE PARK

🥾 🏊 ⛵ 🐕 🛶 ♿ 🚐 ⛺

### Scenic rating: 8

on the Yakima River

**Map 6.4, page 376**                    **BEST** (

Yakima Sportsman State Park is a popular layover spot for visitors attending events in the Yakima area. Campsites and picnic areas are shaded, thanks to the park's location on the Yakima River floodplain. There is a fishing pond for children (no anglers over age 15 are allowed), access to the river for adult anglers, and an unpaved roadway on the river dike for hikers and horseback riders. A put-in for kayaking and rafting is an approximately 20-minute drive away. No swimming is allowed. Nearby recreation options include bird-watching, an 18-hole golf course, and hiking trails.

**Campsites, facilities:** There are 30 sites for tents and 37 sites with full hookups (50 amps) for RVs up to 60 feet long; some sites are pull-through. Picnic tables and fire grills are provided. Restrooms with flush toilets and coin showers, a dump station, firewood, playground, horseshoe pit, and picnic shelter are available. A store and ice are within one mile. Some facilities are wheelchair accessible. Leashed pets are permitted.

**Reservations, fees:** Reservations are accepted in peak season only at 888/CAMP-OUT (888/226-7688) or www.goingtocamp ($6.50 reservation fee); sites are first-come first-served during winter months. Sites are $22-29 per night, $10 per extra vehicle per night. Some credit cards are accepted. Open year-round.

**Directions:** In Yakima, drive on I-82 to Milepost 34 and the Highway 24 exit. Turn east on Highway 24 and drive one mile to Keys Road. Turn left and drive 0.75 mile to South 33rd Street. Turn left and drive approximately 300 feet to the park entrance on the left.

**Contact:** Yakima Sportsman State Park, 509/575-2774; state park information, 360/902-8844, www.parks.wa.gov.

## 15 YAKAMA NATION RV PARK

Scenic rating: 3

near the Yakima River

Map 6.4, page 376

The park is set within the Yakama Indian Reservation (the tribe spells its name differently from the river and town), close to a casino and movie theater. The Toppenish National Wildlife Refuge, the best side trip, is almost always a good spot to see a large variety of birds. Nearby Toppenish, a historic Old West town with a museum, is also worth a side trip.

**Campsites, facilities:** There are 125 sites with full hookups (20, 30, and 50 amps) for RVs of any length, 10 sites for tents only, and 20 tepees (both permanent and portable) for up to eight people each. Picnic tables are provided; fire pits are provided in the tepee area.

Restrooms with flush toilets and showers, cable TV, Wi-Fi, a dump station, playground, recreation room, exercise room, jogging track, basketball, volleyball, tennis courts, a seasonal heated swimming pool, spa, sauna, and coin laundry are available. A picnic shelter is available in the tent area. A restaurant and grocery store are located within 1.5 miles. Some facilities are wheelchair accessible. Leashed pets are permitted.

**Reservations, fees:** Reservations are accepted at 800/874-3087. RV sites are $40-45 per night, tent sites are $20 per night, $4 per person per night for more than two people. Tepees are $35-55 per night for up to eight campers, plus $5 per night for each additional person. Tepees and tent camping are available spring through fall only. Winter and group rates available. Some credit cards are accepted. Open year-round.

**Directions:** From Yakima, drive south on U.S. 97 for 16 miles to the resort on the right.

**Contact:** Yakama Nation RV Resort, 509/865-2000 or 800/874-3087, www.ynrv. com; Toppenish National Wildlife Refuge, 509/546-8300.

## 16 GINKGO PETRIFIED FOREST/WANAPUM STATE RECREATION AREA

Scenic rating: 7

on the Columbia River and Wanapum Lake

Map 6.5, page 377

The site of an ancient petrified forest, Ginkgo Petrified Forest State Park is a National Natural Landmark. This fossilized forest is set along Wanapum Lake in the course of the Columbia River. Ginkgo is a huge park, covering 7,740 acres and surrounding the 27,000 feet of shoreline of Wanapum Lake. The park features an interpretive center and trail.

Although completely separate, Wanapum State Recreation Area is linked to Ginkgo Petrified Forest State Park. Camping, however, is permitted only at the Wanapum Recreation Area, which is three miles south of I-90. Recreation options include hiking (three miles of trails), swimming, boating, waterskiing, and fishing. There are also several historical Civilian Conservation Corps structures from the 1930s. The Wanapum campground is set up primarily for RVs, with full hookups, restrooms, and showers. Note that the park always fills up during the Gorge concert season.

**Campsites, facilities:** There are 50 sites with full hookups (30 amps) for RVs up to 50 feet long. Picnic tables and fire grills are provided. Restrooms with flush toilets and coin showers and firewood are available. Boat docks, launching facilities, a museum, a swimming beach, and a picnic area are nearby. Some facilities are wheelchair accessible. Leashed pets are permitted.

**Reservations, fees:** Reservations are accepted in season at 888/CAMP-OUT (888/226-7688) or www.parks.wa.gov/reservations ($6.50-8.50 reservation fee). Sites are $32-37 per night, $10 per extra vehicle per night. Open year-round, weather permitting; weekends and holidays only November-March.

**Directions:** From Ellensburg, drive east on I-90 to the Vantage Highway/Huntzinger Road (Exit 136). Take that exit, turn south on Huntzinger Road, and drive three miles to the campground on the left.

**Contact:** Wanapum State Recreation Area, 509/856-2700; state park information, 360/902-8844, www.parks.wa.gov.

## 17 POTHOLES STATE PARK

### Scenic rating: 8

on Potholes Reservoir

**Map 6.5, page 377**                    **BEST (**

This park is set on Potholes Reservoir, also known as O'Sullivan Reservoir (because of the O'Sullivan Dam), where fishing is the highlight. Trout, walleye, bass, crappie, and perch are among the species taken here. Waterskiing

and hiking (on one mile of hiking trails) are other recreation options. A side trip to the Columbia Wildlife Refuge, located two miles southeast of the park, is recommended. Note: Do not confuse Potholes Reservoir with the Potholes Lakes, a 30- to 45-minute drive away.

**Campsites, facilities:** There are 61 sites for tents or RVs up to 50 feet long (no hookups), 55 sites for tents or RVs up to 50 feet long (30 amp full hookups), five cabins, and a group site for up to 50 people. Picnic tables and fire grills are provided. Restrooms with flush toilets and showers, a dump station, a playground, volleyball courts, firewood, and a sheltered picnic area are available. Boat-launching facilities and rentals are nearby. Some facilities are wheelchair accessible. Leashed pets are permitted.

**Reservations, fees:** Reservations are accepted at 888/CAMP-OUT (888/226-7688) or www.goingtocamp.com ($6.50 reservation fee). Tent sites are $12 per night, RV sites are $29-36 per night, $10 per night per extra vehicle, the group site is $135.18 per night, and cabins are $65-$80 per night. Open year-round.

**Directions:** From I-90 at Moses Lake, take Exit 179 and Highway 17. Turn south and drive nine miles to Highway 262. Turn right (west) and drive 11 miles to the resort on the southern shore of Potholes Reservoir (well signed).

**Contact:** Potholes State Park, 509/346-2759; state park information, 360/902-8844, www.parks.wa.gov.

## 18 MAR DON RESORT

### Scenic rating: 7

on Potholes Reservoir

**Map 6.5, page 377**

This resort is located on Potholes Reservoir and provides opportunities for fishing, swimming, and boating. A marina, tackle, and boat rentals are all available. Hiking trails and marked bike trails are close by. Many visitors find the café and cocktail lounge a nice bonus.

The Columbia National Wildlife Refuge is located nearby to the south and provides exceptional bird-watching; pelicans and kingfishers are common, and bald eagles and migratory sandhill cranes are often seen as well.

**Campsites, facilities:** There are 88 sites for tents or RVs of any length (no hookups) and 187 sites with full or partial hookups for tents or RVs of any length; some sites are pull-through. Three rental homes, nine cottages, and 18 motel rooms are also available. Picnic tables and fire rings are provided. A restroom with flush toilets and coin showers, drinking water, propane, a dump station, a small convenience store, a boutique, coin laundry, ice, a playground, fish-cleaning station, boat moorage, boat rentals, and launching facilities are available. Some facilities are wheelchair accessible. Leashed pets are permitted with breed restrictions.

**Reservations, fees:** Reservations are accepted. RV sites are $30-39 per night, tent sites are $34 per night, $10 per extra vehicle per night, $5 per extra person per night, and $3 per pet per night. Winter rates available. Some credit cards are accepted. Open year-round.

**Directions:** From Highway 17 in Moses Lake, drive south nine miles to Highway 262. Turn right (west) and drive 10 miles to the resort on the southern shore of Potholes Reservoir.

**Contact:** Mar Don Resort, 509/346-2651 or 800/416-2736, www.mardonresort.com.

## 19 BEACH RV PARK

### Scenic rating: 8

on the Yakima River

**Map 6.5, page 377**

This park along the shore of the Yakima River is a pleasant spot with spacious RV sites, a large grassy area, and poplar trees and shrubs that provide privacy between many of the sites. Note that Beach RV is the only park in the area that has tent camping available. Fishing for bass and trout is available in season.

Nearby recreation options include an 18-hole golf course and a full-service marina, both within 12 miles.

**Campsites, facilities:** There are 100 sites with full hookups (20, 30 and 50 amps) for RVs of any length, including some pull-through sites, and 25 sites for tents. Picnic tables are provided; fire pits are provided in the tent area only. Restrooms with flush toilets and free showers, cable TV, Wi-Fi, and coin laundry are available. Propane, a dump station, a store, and a café are located within one mile. Boat-launching facilities are nearby. Leashed pets are permitted.

**Reservations, fees:** Reservations are accepted. RV sites are $38 per night, tent sites are $24 per night, $4 per person per night for more than two people, $2 per night per extra vehicle. Weekly and group rates available. Some credit cards are accepted. Open year-round.

**Directions:** From Pasco, drive west on U.S. 12 past Richland and continue eight miles to Exit 96 and the Benton City/West Richland exit. Take that exit and drive one block north to Abby Avenue. Turn left (west) and drive 1.5 blocks to the park.

**Contact:** Beach RV Park, 509/588-5959, www.beachrv.net.

## 20 GREENTREE RV & MOBILE HOME PARK

### Scenic rating: 6

in Pasco

**Map 6.5, page 377**

This shady park in urban Pasco is close to an 18-hole golf course, hiking trails, and a full-service marina. The Franklin County Historical Museum, which is located in town, and the Sacajawea State Park Museum and Interpretive Center, located three miles southeast of town, both offer extensive collections of Native American artifacts. Note that most sites are filled with monthly rentals.

**Campsites, facilities:** There are 40 sites with

full hookups for RVs up to 40 feet. A coin laundry is available, but there are no toilets. A mini storage facility is on-site. Propane, a store, café, and ice are located within one mile. Boat docks, launching facilities, and rentals are nearby. Some facilities are wheelchair accessible. Leashed pets are permitted, with certain restrictions.

**Reservations, fees:** Reservations are accepted. Sites are $20 per night. Weekly and monthly rates available. Open year-round.

**Directions:** In Pasco on I-82, take Exit 13 onto 4th Avenue and continue a short distance to the park entrance driveway on the right.

**Contact:** Greentree RV & Mobile Home Park, 509/547-6220.

## 21 ARROWHEAD RV PARK

**Scenic rating: 5**

near the Columbia River

**Map 6.5, page 377**

Arrowhead provides a decent layover spot in Pasco. The park has both trees and grassy areas. Nearby recreation options include an 18-hole golf course, a full-service marina, and tennis courts. Some sites are filled with monthly renters.

**Campsites, facilities:** There are 80 sites for tents or RVs of any length (20, 30, and 50 amp full hookups) and a large grassy area for tents. Some sites are pull-through. Picnic tables are provided. Restroom with flush toilets and showers, drinking water, Wi-Fi, and coin laundry are available. A store and café are located within walking distance. Some facilities are wheelchair accessible. Leashed pets are permitted, with certain restrictions.

**Reservations, fees:** Reservations are accepted. Sites are $30-40 per night, $7 per person per night for more than two people. Open year-round.

**Directions:** In Pasco on U.S. 395 North, take the Kartchner Street exit, turn east, and drive a short distance to Commercial Avenue. Turn

right (south) and drive 0.25 mile to the park entrance on the right.

**Contact:** Arrowhead RV Park, 509/545-8206.

## 22 PALOUSE FALLS STATE PARK

**Scenic rating: 10**

on the Snake and Palouse Rivers

**Map 6.6, page 378** **BEST (**

This remote state park is well worth the trip. Spectacular 198-foot Palouse Falls is a sight not to miss. A 0.25-mile wheelchair-accessible trail leads to a waterfall overlook. The park is set at the confluence of the Snake and Palouse Rivers, and it does not receive heavy use, even in summer. The park covers 1,282 acres and features a waterfall observation shelter, shaded picnic facilities, historical displays, and an abundance of wildlife.

**Campsites, facilities:** There are 10 sites for tents or RVs up to 40 feet long (no hookups). Picnic tables and fire grills are provided. Drinking water (in summer), pit toilets, and a picnic area are available. Some facilities are wheelchair accessible. Leashed pets are permitted.

**Reservations, fees:** Reservations are not accepted. Sites are $17 per night, $10 per extra vehicle per night. Open year-round, weather permitting, with limited winter facilities.

**Directions:** From Starbuck, drive northwest on Highway 261 for 15 miles (crossing the river) to the park entrance and Palouse Falls Road. Turn right and drive to the park.

**Contact:** Palouse Falls State Park, 360/902-8844, www.parks.wa.gov.

## 23 WINDUST

**Scenic rating: 6**

on Lake Sacajawea

**Map 6.6, page 378**

With no other campgrounds within a 30-mile

radius, Windust is the only game in town. The camp is located along the shore of Lake Sacajawea near the Lower Monumental Dam on the Snake River. The park covers 54 acres. Swimming, waterskiing, and fishing are popular.

**Campsites, facilities:** There are 24 sites for tents or RVs of any length (no hookups). Picnic tables and fire grills are provided. Flush toilets are available May-September, and pit toilets are provided the rest of the year. Drinking water, garbage bins, dump station, a playground, and a swimming beach are available nearby. No alcohol is permitted. Boat docks and launching facilities are nearby. Some facilities are wheelchair accessible. Leashed pets are permitted.

**Reservations, fees:** Reservations are not accepted. There is no fee for camping. Open mid-May-early September.

**Directions:** From Pasco, drive east on U.S. 12 for 2.5 miles to Pasco/Kahlotus Highway. Turn east and drive 28 miles to Burr Canyon Road. Turn right on Burr Canyon Road and drive 5.2 miles to the park (from the north, Burr Canyon Road becomes Highway 263).

**Contact:** U.S. Army Corps of Engineers, Walla Walla District, 509/547-2048, www.nww.usace.army.mil.

## 24 HOOD PARK

### Scenic rating: 6

on Lake Wallula

**Map 6.6, page 378**

This 99-acre developed park on Lake Wallula provides access for swimming and boating. Some sites are situated near the shoreline, and shaded sites are available. No alcohol is permitted. There are hiking trails throughout the park, along with stocked fishing ponds. Other recreation options include basketball and horseshoes. McNary Wildlife Refuge is right next door, and Sacajawea State Park is within four miles.

**Campsites, facilities:** There are 67 sites with

partial hookups (30 and 50 amps) for tents or RVs of any length. Picnic tables and fire grills are provided. Drinking water, restrooms with flush toilets and showers, a dump station, a playground, horseshoe pits, a basketball court, swimming beach, covered picnic area, and an amphitheater are available. A restaurant and convenience store are located within two miles. Boat docks and launching facilities are nearby. Some facilities are wheelchair accessible. Leashed pets are permitted.

**Reservations, fees:** Reservations are accepted at 877/444-6777 or www.recreation.gov ($9 reservation fee). Sites are $22-24 per night on weekends, $11-12 per night during the week, $4 per night per additional vehicle, and $8 per night for boat camping and in the overflow area. Open May-September.

**Directions:** In Pasco, drive southeast on U.S. 12 for five miles to the junction with Highway 124. Turn left (east) on Highway 124 and drive to the park entrance on the left (just before the town of Burbank). Drive 0.5 mile to the gate entrance.

**Contact:** U.S. Army Corps of Engineers, Walla Walla District, 509/547-2048, www.nww.usace.army.mil.

## 25 CHARBONNEAU PARK

### Scenic rating: 6

on the Snake River

**Map 6.6, page 378**

This shorefront campground is the centerpiece of a 244-acre park set along the Snake River, just above Ice Harbor Dam. Named one of America's Top 100 Family Campgrounds, it is a good spot for fishing, boating, swimming, and waterskiing. An overflow camping area provides a backup if the numbered sites are full. No alcohol is permitted. At Lake Sacajawea, the dam's visitors center (open daily April-October) features exhibits and a view of a salmon fish ladder.

**Campsites, facilities:** There are 52 sites with

full or partial hookups for tents or RVs up to 45 feet long. Some sites are pull-through. Picnic tables and fire grills are provided. Restrooms with flush toilets and showers, a dump station, pay telephone, playground, and volleyball court are available. A camp host is on-site. A marina with boat docks, launching facilities, a marine dump station, a swimming beach, fishing tackle, seasonal snack bar, ice, and a day-use area and picnic shelters are nearby. Some facilities are wheelchair accessible. Leashed pets are permitted.

**Reservations, fees:** Reservations are accepted at 877/444-6777 or www.recreation.gov ($9 reservation fee). Sites are $11-28 per night. Overflow camping is $8 per night. Open April-October with full facilities; there are limited facilities and no fee the rest of the year.

**Directions:** From Pasco, drive southeast on U.S. 12 for five miles to Highway 124. Turn left (east) and drive eight miles to Sun Harbor Road. Turn left (north) and drive two miles to the park.

**Contact:** U.S. Army Corps of Engineers, Walla Walla District, 509/547-2048, www.nww.usace.army.mil.

## 26 FISHHOOK PARK

**Scenic rating: 6**

on Lake Sacajawea

Map 6.6, page 378

If you're driving along Highway 124 and you need a spot for the night, check out this wooded camp along the Snake River. It is a nice spot within a 46-acre park set on Lake Sacajawea, which is a dammed portion of the Snake River. The park provides some lawn area, along with places to swim, fish, and water ski. A one-mile walk along railroad tracks will take you to a fishing pond. This park is popular on summer weekends.

**Campsites, facilities:** There are 11 walk-in tent sites, 41 sites with partial hookups for tents or RVs of any length, and two group tent

sites that can accommodate up to 16 people. Some sites are pull-through. Picnic tables and fire grills are provided. Drinking water, restrooms with flush toilets and showers, a dump station, and playground are available. Boat docks, launching facilities, a swimming beach, and group picnic shelters that can be reserved are nearby. Some facilities are wheelchair accessible. Leashed pets are permitted.

**Reservations, fees:** Reservations are accepted at 877/444-6777 or www.recreation.gov ($9 reservation fee). Walk-in tent sites are $8-22 per night, sites with hookups are $28 per night, $4 per night per additional vehicle, the group tent site is $22 per night, and boat camping is $8 per night. Open mid-May-September. Park gates are locked 10pm-6am.

**Directions:** From Pasco, drive southeast on U.S. 12 for five miles to Highway 124. Turn left (east) and drive 18 miles to Fishhook Park Road. Turn left on Fishhook Park Road and drive four miles to the park.

**Contact:** U.S. Army Corps of Engineers, Walla Walla District, 509/547-2048, www.nww.usace.army.mil.

## 27 LEWIS AND CLARK TRAIL STATE PARK

**Scenic rating: 8**

on the Touchet River

Map 6.6, page 378

Lewis and Clark features an unusual mixture of old-growth forest and riparian habitat, with long-leafed ponderosa pine and cottonwood amid the prairie grasslands. The park is set on 37 acres with frontage along the Touchet River. Fishing for rainbow trout and brown trout can be excellent here. An interpretive display explains much of the history of the area. A seasonal Saturday evening living-history program depicts the story of Lewis and Clark and the site's history here on the original Lewis and Clark Trail. In winter, cross-country skiing and snowshoeing are good here. Note: If it's getting late and you need to stop, consider this camp because it's the only one within 20 miles.

**Campsites, facilities:** There are 24 sites for tents or self-contained RVs up to 28 feet long, 17 sites for tents or RVs of any length available (in the day-use area) for winter use only, and two group sites for up to 100 people each. Picnic tables and fire grills are provided. Restrooms with flush toilets and coin showers, firewood, and a dump station are available. Two fire circles, an amphitheater, interpretive programs, a picnic area, badminton, a baseball field, and a volleyball court are available nearby. A store, café, and ice are located within four miles. Leashed pets are permitted.

**Reservations, fees:** Reservations are accepted for the group site at 509/337-6457 ($25 nonrefundable reservation fee). Reservations for single sites can be made at 888/CAMP-OUT (888/226-7688) or www.goingtocamp.com ($6.50 reservation fee). Sites are $17-24 per night, $10 per extra vehicle per night. Group sites are $2.50 per person. Open April-mid-September, with primitive sites open mid-September-March.

**Directions:** From Walla Walla, drive east on U.S. 12 for 22 miles to Waitsburg. Bear right on U.S. 12 and drive east for 4.5 miles to the park entrance on the left.

**Contact:** Lewis and Clark Trail State Park, 509/337-6457; state park information, 360/902-8844, www.parks.wa.gov.

## 28 PALOUSE EMPIRE FAIRGROUNDS & HORSE CAMP

Scenic rating: 6

west of Colfax

**Map 6.7, page 379**

The camp consists primarily of a large lawn area with shade trees. It is set just off the road, but the highway noise, surprisingly, is relatively limited. All sites are on grass. The park covers 47 acres, with paved trails available around the adjacent fairgrounds. This area is agricultural, with rolling hills, and it is considered the "Lentil Capital of the World." With wash racks, corrals, arenas, and water troughs, the camp encourages horse campers to stay here. It fills up for the Whitman County Fair in mid-September. They turn back the clock every Labor Day weekend with the annual Threshing Bee, where there are demonstrations of historical farming practices dating back to the early 1900s, including the use of draft horses.

**Campsites, facilities:** There are 60 sites with partial hookups for tents or RVs of any length. Large groups can be accommodated. Restrooms with flush toilets and showers, drinking water, and a dump station are available. Restaurants, gas, and supplies are available 4.5 miles away in Colfax. Some facilities are wheelchair accessible. Leashed pets are permitted.

**Reservations, fees:** Reservations are accepted for groups only. Sites are $15 per night, horse stalls $10 per night. Open year-round, weather permitting; limited winter facilities.

**Directions:** From Colfax and Highway 26, drive west on Highway 26 for 4.5 miles to the fairgrounds on the right.

**Contact:** Palouse Empire Fairgrounds & Horse Camp, Whitman County, 509/397-6263, www.palouseempirefair.org.

## 29 KAMIAK BUTTE COUNTY PARK

Scenic rating: 8

east of Colfax

**Map 6.7, page 379**

This quiet and peaceful park gets medium use. Kamiak Butte is a National Natural Landmark with more than five miles of wooded hiking trails. The 3.5-mile Pine Ridge Trail is part of the national trails system, and hikers can obtain excellent views of the Palouse region by walking to the highest point at 3,641 feet. The park gate closes at dusk each night and reopens at 7am.

**Campsites, facilities:** There are seven sites for tents or RVs up to 18 feet long (no hookups). Overflow camping for RVs of any length is available in the parking lot. Picnic tables and fire grills are provided. Drinking water (mid-April–mid-October) and vault and pit toilets are available. A playground, picnic area, amphitheater, and group facilities that can be reserved are available. Some facilities are wheelchair accessible. Leashed pets are permitted.

**Reservations, fees:** Reservations are not accepted. Sites are $15 per night, $5 per night per extra vehicle. Open year-round, with limited winter facilities.

**Directions:** From Colfax, drive east on Highway 272 for five miles to Clear Creek Road. Turn right and drive seven miles to Fugate Road. Turn right and drive 0.5 mile to the park entrance on the left.

**Contact:** Whitman County Parks and Recreation, 509/397-6238, www.whitmancounty. org.

## 30 BOYER PARK AND MARINA

🏃 🚴 ⛵ 🛶 🏊 🐴 ♿ 🚐 ⛺

**Scenic rating: 7**

on Lake Bryan on the Snake River

**Map 6.7, page 379**

This 99-acre park on the north shore of Lake Bryan is located two miles from the Lower Granite Dam. It features 3.5 miles of trails for hiking and biking, and the lake is popular for waterskiing and fishing for sturgeon, steelhead, and salmon. Most campsites are shaded, and all are paved and bordered by a grassy day-use area. The landscape is flat and open, and it gets hot here in summer. The camp is well above the water level, typically about 100 feet above the lakeshore. The camp commonly fills on summer weekends.

**Campsites, facilities:** There are 48 sites with full or partial hookups for tents or RVs up to 70 feet long, seven sites for tents, and four motel rooms. Group camping is also available.

Picnic tables and fire grills are provided. Restrooms with flush toilets and coin showers, drinking water, and a dump station are available. A coin laundry, covered shelters, a swimming area, snack bar, restaurant, convenience store, ice, and gas are available. A marina, fuel dock, fishing licenses, boat docks, a boat launch, moorage, and a marine dump station are nearby. Some facilities are wheelchair accessible. Leashed pets are permitted.

**Reservations, fees:** Reservations are accepted at 509/397-3208 ($10 reservation fee). Tent sites are $15.50-17.50 per night, $8 per night per additional tent. RV sites are $30.50-38.50 per night, $2 per night for extra person, $8 per night per extra vehicle; moorage is $11-15 per night. Winter rates are available. Some credit cards are accepted. Open year-round, with limited winter facilities.

**Directions:** From U.S. 195 at Colfax, turn southwest on Almota Road and drive 17 miles to the park and campground.

**Contact:** Boyer Park, 509/397-3208; Port of Whitman County, 509/397-3791, www. portwhitman.com.

## 31 WAWAWAI COUNTY PARK

🛶 🚐 🐴 ♿ 🚐 ⛺

**Scenic rating: 7**

on Lower Granite Lake

**Map 6.7, page 379**

This park covers 49 acres and is set near the inlet to Lower Granite Lake, about 0.25 mile from the lake. The camp itself is situated on a hillside, and all sites are paved. Some sites have views of a bay, but not the entire lake. Tree cover is a plus. So is a 0.5-mile loop trail that leads to a bird-viewing platform, and a diverse mix of wildlife and geology, making interpretive hikes with naturalists popular. One strange note: An underground house built in 1980 has been converted to a ranger's residence. This camp often fills on summer weekends. No campfires are permitted during the summer season.

**Campsites, facilities:** There are nine sites for tents or RVs up to 24 feet long (no hookups). Some sites are pull-through. Picnic tables and fire grills are provided; fires are restricted in Hells Canyon mid-April–mid-October. Drinking water (mid-April–mid-October) and pit toilets are available. A group picnic shelter that can be reserved and a boat launch are nearby. Some facilities are wheelchair accessible. Leashed pets are permitted.

**Reservations, fees:** Reservations are not accepted. Sites are $15 per night, $5 per extra vehicle per night. Open year-round, with limited winter facilities.

**Directions:** From Colfax, drive south on U.S. 195 for 15 miles to Wawawai-Pullman Road (located just west of Pullman). Turn right (west) and drive approximately 9.5 miles to Wawawai Road. Turn right on Wawawai Road (signed) and drive 5.5 miles to the park.

**Contact:** Wawawai County Park, Whitman County Parks and Recreation, 509/397-6238, www.whitmancounty.org.

## 32 CHIEF TIMOTHY PARK

**Scenic rating: 8**

on the Snake River

Map 6.7, page 379

This unusual park is set on an island composed of glacial tills in the Snake River; it is accessible by car over a bridge. The park covers 282 acres with two miles of shoreline and features a desert landscape. There are 2.5 miles of hiking trails, plus docks for boating campers and a beach area. Water sports include fishing, swimming, boating, waterskiing, and sailing. Outfitters in Clarkston will take you sightseeing up Hells Canyon. (Call the Clarkston Chamber of Commerce at 509/758-7712 for details.)

This former state park is now managed by Northwest Land Management.

**Campsites, facilities:** There are 70 sites, including 33 sites with full or partial hookups

(30 amps), for tents or RVs up to 60 feet long. There are also two primitive sites for tents and four camping cabins. Some sites are pull-through. Picnic tables and fire pits are provided. Restrooms with flush toilets and coin showers, dump station, a picnic area, a small store, firewood, ice, a playground, volleyball court, and horseshoe pits are available. A camp host is on-site. Boat docks and launching facilities, a swimming beach, and beach house are available. Some facilities are wheelchair accessible. Leashed pets are permitted.

**Reservations, fees:** Reservations are accepted at 877/444-6777 or www.recreation.gov. Sites are $24-30 per night, $5 per night per extra vehicle, and cabins are $70 per night. Some credit cards are accepted. Open May-October, weather permitting; walk-in camping is permitted in November.

**Directions:** From Clarkston on the Washington/Idaho border, drive west on U.S. 12 for seven miles to the signed park entrance road on the right. Turn right (north) and drive one mile to the park, which is set on a bridged island in the Snake River.

**Contact:** Northwest Land Management, Chief Timothy Park, 509/758-9580.

## 33 TUCANNON

**Scenic rating: 8**

in Umatilla National Forest

Map 6.7, page 379

For people willing to rough it, this backcountry camp in Umatilla National Forest is the place. It has plenty of hiking, fishing, and hunting, all in a rugged setting. The camp is set along the Tucannon River, which offers a myriad of recreation options for vacationers. It is popular from early spring (the best time for fishing) through fall (when it makes a good hunting camp). In summer, several nearby ponds are stocked with trout, making it a good family destination. There is some tree cover. The elevation is 2,600 feet.

**Campsites, facilities:** There are 15 sites for tents or RVs up to 21 feet long and two sites for tents only. Picnic tables and fire grills are provided. Vault toilets are available, but there is no drinking water. Garbage must be packed out. Two covered shelters are available nearby. Some facilities are wheelchair accessible. Leashed pets are permitted.

**Reservations, fees:** Reservations are not accepted. Sites are $8 per night, $5 per night per additional vehicle. Open year-round, weather permitting.

**Directions:** From Clarkston, drive west on U.S. 12 for 37 miles to Pomeroy. Continue west for five miles to Tatman Mountain Road (signed for Camp Wooten). Turn left (south) and drive 19 miles (becomes Forest Road 47). Once inside the national forest boundary, continue southwest on Forest Road 47 for four miles to the campground on the left.

**Contact:** Umatilla National Forest, Pomeroy Ranger District, 509/843-1891, www.fs.usda. gov.

## 34 ALDER THICKET

### Scenic rating: 7
in Umatilla National Forest

**Map 6.7, page 379**

This is probably the first time you've heard of this place. Hardly anybody knows about it, including people who live relatively nearby in Walla Walla. It is set at an elevation of 5,100 feet, making it a prime base camp for a backcountry hiking adventure in summer or a jumping-off point for a hunting trip in the fall. This is a primitive camp, but it's great if you're looking for quiet and solitude.

**Campsites, facilities:** There are five sites for tents or RVs up to 21 feet long. Picnic tables and fire grills are provided. Vault toilets are available, but there is no drinking water. Garbage must be packed out. Some facilities are wheelchair accessible. Leashed pets are permitted.

**Reservations, fees:** Reservations are not

accepted. There is no fee for camping. Open mid-May-mid-November, weather permitting.

**Directions:** From Clarkston, drive west on U.S. 12 for 37 miles to Pomeroy and Highway 128. Turn south and drive seven miles to a fork. At the fork, continue straight to Forest Road 40 (15 miles from Pomeroy to the national forest boundary) and drive 3.5 miles to the campground on the right.

**Contact:** Umatilla National Forest, Pomeroy Ranger District, 509/843-1891, www.fs.usda. gov.

## 35 BIG SPRINGS

### Scenic rating: 8
in Umatilla National Forest

**Map 6.7, page 379**

This camp is set at an elevation of 5,000 feet. In the fall, primarily hunters use Big Springs; come summer, this nice, cool site becomes a possible base camp for backpacking trips. Although quite primitive with little in the way of activity options, this is a perfect spot to get away from it all. It's advisable to obtain a U.S. Forest Service map.

**Campsites, facilities:** There are six sites for tents or self-contained RVs up to 16 feet and two sites for tents only. Picnic tables are provided. Vault toilets are available, but there is no drinking water. Some facilities are wheelchair accessible. Leashed pets are permitted.

**Reservations, fees:** Reservations are not accepted. There is no fee for camping. Open mid-May-mid-November, weather permitting.

**Directions:** From Clarkston, drive west on U.S. 12 for 37 miles to Pomeroy and Highway 128. Turn south and drive 25 miles to Forest Road 42 (to the Clearwater Lookout Tower). Turn left and continue on Forest Road 42 for five miles to the campground entrance road (Forest Road 4225). Turn left and drive to the campground at the end of the road.

**Contact:** Umatilla National Forest, Pomeroy Ranger District, 509/843-1891, www.fs.usda.gov.

## 36 TEAL SPRING

🚶 🐎 ♿ 🚐 ⛺

### Scenic rating: 8

in Umatilla National Forest

**Map 6.7, page 379**

The views of the Tucannon drainage and the Wenaha-Tucannon Wilderness are astonishing from the nearby lookout. Teal Spring Camp is set at 5,600 feet elevation and is one of several small, primitive camps in the area. Trails in the immediate area provide a variety of good day-hiking options. Hunting is popular in the fall.

**Campsites, facilities:** There are three sites for tents or RVs up to 35 feet and four sites for tents only. Vault toilets are available, but there is no drinking water. Picnic tables and fire grills are provided. Garbage must be packed out. Some facilities are wheelchair accessible. Leashed pets are permitted.

**Reservations, fees:** Reservations are not accepted. There is no fee for camping. Open late May-mid-November, weather permitting.

**Directions:** From Clarkston, drive west on U.S. 12 for 37 miles to Pomeroy and Highway 128. Turn left (south) and drive 25 miles to Forest Road 42 (to the Clearwater Lookout Tower). Turn left and continue on Forest Road 42; drive one mile to the campground entrance road. Turn right and drive 200 yards to the campground.

**Contact:** Umatilla National Forest, Pomeroy Ranger District, 509/843-1891, www.fs.usda.gov.

## 37 GODMAN

🚶 🚲 🐎 ♿ 🚐 ⛺

### Scenic rating: 8

near the Wenaha-Tucannon Wilderness in Umatilla National Forest

**Map 6.7, page 379**

This tiny, little-known spot bordering a wilderness area is set at 6,050 feet elevation and features drop-dead gorgeous views at sunset, as well as a wilderness trailhead. It is used primarily as a base camp for backcountry expeditions. A trailhead provides access to the Wenaha-Tucannon Wilderness for both hikers and horseback riders. Horse facilities are available 0.2 mile away. There are also opportunities for mountain biking, but note that bikes are forbidden past the wilderness boundary. A bonus here is a two-story cabin, the Godman Guard Station. The cabin has a propane stove, refrigerator, heater, and electricity, but there is no indoor restroom. It is available year-round, but is accessible only by snowmobile in the winter months.

**Campsites, facilities:** There are eight sites for tents or RVs up to 16 feet long, plus one cabin which can accommodate up to eight people. Picnic tables and fire grills are provided. Vault toilets and a group picnic shelter are available, but there is no drinking water. Garbage must be packed out. Facilities, including hitching rails and a spring, are available nearby for up to six people with horses, with an additional fee for more than six. There is also a barn about 200 yards up the hill. Some facilities are wheelchair accessible, but assistance may be required. Leashed pets are permitted.

**Reservations, fees:** Reservations are not accepted for campsites. The Godman Guard Station can be reserved at 877/444-6777 ($10 reservation fee) or www.recreation.gov. There is no fee for camping. The cabin is $60-75 per night. Open mid-June-late October; cabin is available year-round.

**Directions:** From Walla Walla, drive northeast on U.S. 12 for 32 miles to Dayton and North Fork Touchet River Road. Turn right on North Fork Touchet River Road and drive 14 miles southeast to the national forest boundary; continue to Kendall Skyline Road. Turn left (south) and drive 11 miles to the campground on the left.

**Contact:** Umatilla National Forest, Pomeroy Ranger District, 509/843-1891, www.fs.usda.gov.

## 38 FIELDS SPRING STATE PARK
🏃 🚲 ⛷ 🐕 ⛺ 🚶 ♿ 🚐 ⛰

**Scenic rating: 8**
near Puffer Butte

**Map 6.7, page 379**

Not many people know about this spot, yet it's a good one, tucked away in the southeast corner of the state. This 792-acre state park is located in the Blue Mountains, set in a forested landscape covering Puffer Butte, with views of Oregon, Idaho, and the Grande Ronde. Basalt dominates the landscape. Two hiking trails lead up to Puffer Butte at 4,500 feet elevation, providing a panoramic view of the Snake River Canyon and the Wallowa Mountains. The park is noted for its variety of birdlife and wildflowers, and there are seven miles of mountain-biking trails, along with three miles of hiking trails. In winter, non-motorized recreation opportunities include cross-country skiing (groomed trails), snowmobiling, snowshoeing, and general snow play; warming huts are available. There is also a retreat center with lodges that can be reserved. Two day-use areas with boat launches, managed by the Department of Fish and Wildlife, are within about 25 miles of the park.

**Campsites, facilities:** There are 20 sites for tents or RVs up to 30 feet long (no hookups), two primitive tent sites, a cabin, two tepees, and two lodges for 12-20 and 20-80 people respectively. Picnic tables and fire grills are provided. Drinking water, restrooms with flush toilets and coin showers, firewood, a dump station, two picnic shelters, two sheltered fire circles, a playground, horseshoe pits, a softball field, and volleyball courts are available. Some facilities are wheelchair accessible. Leashed pets are permitted.

**Reservations, fees:** Reservations are not accepted for campsites but are accepted for tepees and are required for lodges and the cabin at 509/256-3332. Sites are $19 per night, primitive sites are $12 per night, tepees are $20 per night, $10 per extra vehicle per night, lodges

are $10.77 per person, and the cabin is $40 per night. Open year-round, with limited winter facilities.

**Directions:** From Clarkston, turn south on Highway 129 and drive 30 miles (just south of Rattlesnake Pass) to the park entrance on the left (east) side of the road.

**Contact:** Fields Spring State Park, 509/256-3332; state park information, 360/902-8844, www.parks.wa.gov.

## 39 BROOKS MEMORIAL STATE PARK
🏃 🚣 🐕 ⛺ 🚐 ⛰

**Scenic rating: 7**
near the Goldendale Observatory

**Map 6.8, page 380**

Brooks Memorial State Park sits near the South Yakima Valley at an elevation of nearly 3,000 feet. The campground is located on the Little Klickitat River amid the pines of the Simcoe Mountains. The park's 700 acres include nine miles of hiking trails, and occasionally excellent fishing for trout. You can extend your trip into the mountains, where you'll find open meadows with a panoramic view of Mount Hood. Nearby side trips include the Goldendale Observatory and a replica of Stonehenge on State Route 14. Note that the Yakama Indian Nation is two miles north.

**Campsites, facilities:** There are 22 sites for tents or RVs (no hookups), 23 sites with partial hookups (50 amps) for RVs up to 30 feet long, and a primitive group site for 20-50 people. There's also a "Learning Center" for rent, which includes a lodge for 40-72 people and seven 10-person cabins. Picnic tables and fire grills are provided. Restrooms with flush toilets and coin showers, a dump station, and a playground with horseshoe pits and volleyball court are available. A sheltered picnic area, ball field, and store are nearby. Leashed pets are permitted.

**Reservations, fees:** Reservations for single sites can be made at 888/CAMP-OUT

(888/226-7688) or www.goingtocamp.com ($6.50 reservation fee). To reserve a primitive group site, call 509/773-4611. To reserve the lodge and cabins, call 800/360-4240. Sites are $22-32 per night, $10 per extra vehicle per night. Primitive group sites are $2.39 per person for 20-50 people; the lodge and cabins are $10.75 per person (40-person minimum peak season, 20-person minimum off-peak). Open year-round, with limited winter facilities.

**Directions:** From Toppenish, drive south on U.S. 97 for 40 miles to the park on the right (well signed).

**Contact:** Brooks Memorial State Park, 509/773-4611; state park information, 360/902-8844, www.parks.wa.gov.

## 40 MARYHILL STATE PARK
🏕️🚣🛶🚤🏕️🐕♿🚐⛺

### Scenic rating: 8
on the Columbia River

**Map 6.8, page 380**

This 99-acre park has 4,700 feet of frontage along the Columbia River. Fishing, waterskiing, and windsurfing are among the recreation possibilities. The climate here is pleasant March-mid-November. Two interesting places can be found near Maryhill: a full-scale replica of Stonehenge, located on a bluff overlooking the Columbia River about one mile from the park, and the historic Mary Hill home, which is open to the public. Mary Hill's husband, Sam Hill, constructed the Stonehenge replica.

**Campsites, facilities:** There are 50 sites with full hookups (30 and 50 amps) for RVs up to 60 feet long, 20 tent sites, two hike-in/bike-in sites, and one group camp for up to 200 people. Picnic tables and fire pits are provided. Restrooms with flush toilets and showers, a dump station, and a picnic area with covered shelters are available. A café and store are within one mile. Boat docks and launching facilities are nearby. Some facilities are wheelchair accessible. Leashed pets are permitted.

**Reservations, fees:** Reservations are accepted

and are required for the group camp at 888/CAMP-OUT (888/226-7688) or www.parks.wa.gov/reservations ($6.50 reservation fee). Sites are $20-42 per night, $10 per night for hike-in/bike-in sites, $10 per extra vehicle per night. The group camp is $66.34-541.42 per night. Some credit cards are accepted. Open year-round.

**Directions:** From Goldendale and U.S. 97, drive 12 miles south to the park on the left.

**Contact:** Maryhill State Park, 509/773-5007; state park information, 360/902-8844, www.parks.wa.gov.

## 41 CROW BUTTE PARK
🏕️🚣🛶🚤🏕️🐕♿🚐⛺

### Scenic rating: 8
on the Columbia River

**Map 6.9, page 381**

How would you like to be stranded on a romantic island? Well, this park offers that possibility. The park is set on an island in the Columbia River and is the only campground in a 25-mile radius. Sometimes referred to as the "Maui of the Columbia," the park covers 1,312 acres and has several miles of shoreline. It is set on the Lewis and Clark Trail, with the camp situated in a partially protected bay. The highlight of 3.5 miles of hiking trails is a mile-long path that leads to the top of a butte, where you can see Mount Hood, Mount Adams, and the Columbia River Valley. Waterskiing, sailboarding, fishing, swimming, and hiking are among the possibilities here. One downer: Keep an eye out for rattlesnakes, which are occasionally spotted. The Umatilla National Wildlife Refuge is adjacent to the park and allows fishing and hunting in specified areas. Note that this former state park is now run by the Port of Benton.

**Campsites, facilities:** There are 50 sites for tents or RVs up to 90 feet long (20, 30, and 50 amp full hookups) and one primitive group camp for tents only that accommodates up to 100 people. Some sites are pull-through.

Fire grills and picnic tables are provided. Restrooms with flush toilets and coin showers, a sheltered picnic area, a swimming beach, and a dump station are available. Boat-launching and moorage facilities are nearby. A concession stand is open on weekends. Some facilities are wheelchair accessible. Leashed pets are permitted.

**Reservations, fees:** Reservations are accepted at 509/875-2644 or www.crowbutte.com. RV sites are $27 per night, tent sites are $15 per night, $5 per extra vehicle per night. The group site is $60 per night. Open mid-March through October.

**Directions:** From the junction of I-82/U.S. 395 and Highway 20 at Plymouth, just north of the Columbia River, turn west on State Route 14. Drive to Paterson and continue west for 13 miles to the park entrance road at Milepost 155 on the right. Turn right and drive one mile (across the bridge) to the park on the island.

**Contact:** Crow Butte Park, Port of Benton, 509/875-2644, www.crowbutte.com.

# 42 PLYMOUTH PARK

### Scenic rating: 7

near Lake Umatilla

Map 6.9, page 381

Plymouth Park is a family- and RV-style campground set near Lake Umatilla on the Columbia River. The 112-acre park is not located on the shore of the lake, rather about a quarter-mile drive from the water. The camp has tree cover, which is a nice plus, and it fills up on most summer weekends. Each campsite has a tent pad.

**Campsites, facilities:** There are 32 sites with full or partial hookups (30 and 50 amps) for tents or RVs up to 40 feet long. Most sites are pull-through. Picnic tables and fire grills are provided. Restrooms with flush toilets and showers, drinking water, a dump station, playground, and coin laundry are available. A boat dock, boat launch, swimming areas, and covered picnic shelters are available nearby. A store and a restaurant are within five miles. Some facilities are wheelchair accessible. Leashed pets are permitted.

**Reservations, fees:** Reservations are accepted at 877/444-6777 or www.recreation.gov. RV sites are $24-27 per night, tent sites are $15 per night, $5 per night per extra vehicle. Some credit cards are accepted. Open April-October.

**Directions:** From Richland and I-82, drive south on I-82 for about 30 miles to State Route 14. Turn west on State Route 14 and drive two miles to the Plymouth exit. Take that exit and drive south 1.5 miles to Christy Road; turn right and continue 200 yards to the campground entrance on the left.

**Contact:** U.S. Army Corps of Engineers, Walla Walla District, 541/506-7818, www. nww.usace.army.mil; gate attendant, 509/783-1270.

# Oregon

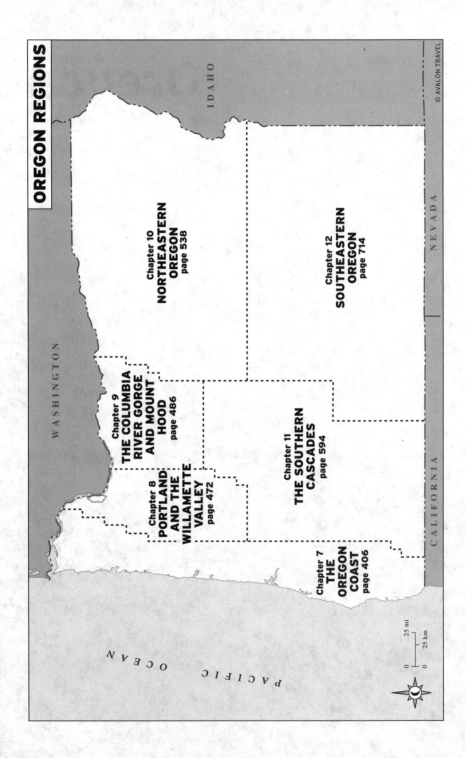

# OREGON REGIONS

WASHINGTON

IDAHO

NEVADA

CALIFORNIA

PACIFIC OCEAN

Chapter 7
THE
OREGON
COAST
page 406

Chapter 8
PORTLAND
AND THE
WILLAMETTE
VALLEY
page 472

Chapter 9
THE COLUMBIA
RIVER GORGE
AND MOUNT
HOOD
page 486

Chapter 10
NORTHEASTERN
OREGON
page 538

Chapter 11
THE SOUTHERN
CASCADES
page 594

Chapter 12
SOUTHEASTERN
OREGON
page 714

0    25 mi

0    25 km

© AVALON TRAVEL

# THE OREGON COAST

Want to treat yourself to a trip you'll treasure forever? Set up camp on one of the most dramatic coasts in North America. The Oregon Coast is home to tidewater rock gardens, cliff-top views that seem to stretch to forever, vast sand dunes, protected bays, beautiful streams with salmon and steelhead, and three major national forests. The most spectacular region may be the Oregon Dunes National Recreation Area, which spans roughly from Coos Bay north past Florence to near the mouth of the Siuslaw River. Whenever I visit, I'm instantly transported to another universe. I have a photo of the dunes in my office. While I'm writing, I often look at the image of a lone raptor soaring past a pyramid of sand—it's my window to this other world.

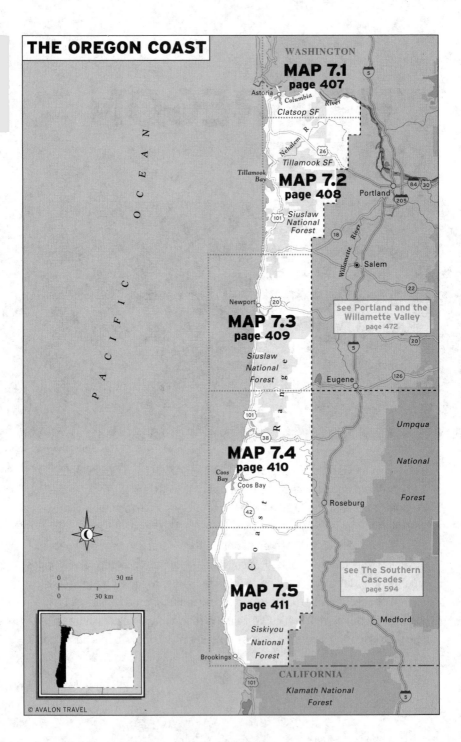

# THE OREGON COAST

WASHINGTON

**MAP 7.1**
page 407

Astoria
Columbia River
Clatsop SF

*Nehalem R*
26
*Tillamook SF*

Tillamook Bay

**MAP 7.2**
page 408

Portland

101
*Siuslaw National Forest*
18

Willamette River
Salem

22

Newport
20

**MAP 7.3**
page 409

see Portland and the
Willamette Valley
page 472

I-5

20

*Siuslaw National Forest*

*Coast Range*

Eugene
126

101
38

**MAP 7.4**
page 410

Umpqua

Coos Bay
Coos Bay
National

42
Roseburg
Forest

see The Southern
Cascades
page 594

**MAP 7.5**
page 411

Medford

*Siskiyou National Forest*

0        30 mi
0        30 km

Brookings

CALIFORNIA

101
*Klamath National Forest*

PACIFIC OCEAN

I-5

© AVALON TRAVEL

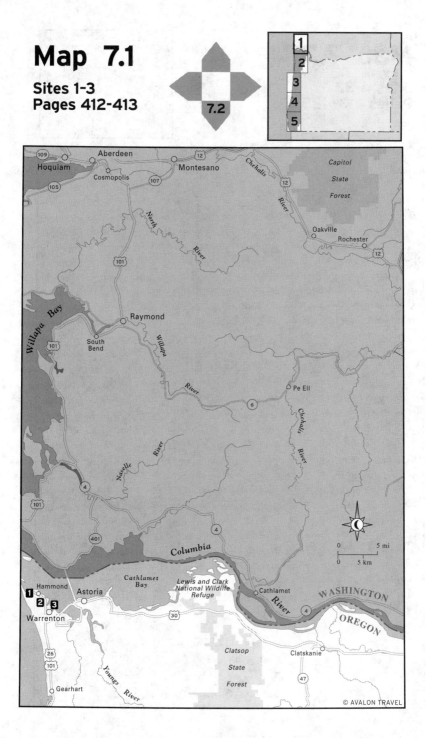

# Map 7.1

**Sites 1-3
Pages 412-413**

7.2

# Map 7.2

**Sites 4-32**
**Pages 413-425**

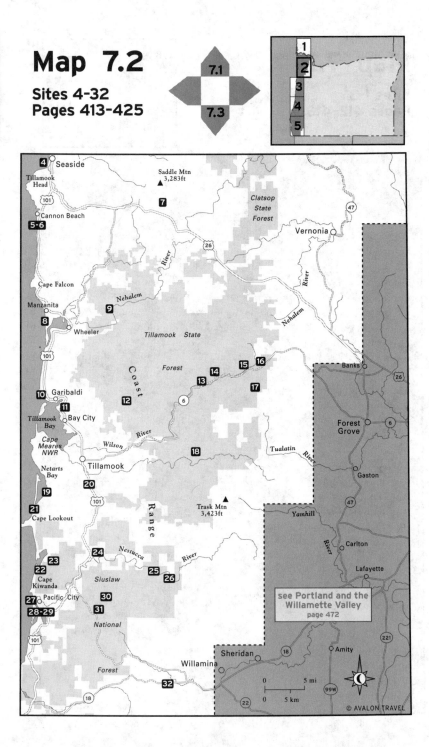

# Map 7.3

## Sites 33-58
## Pages 425-436

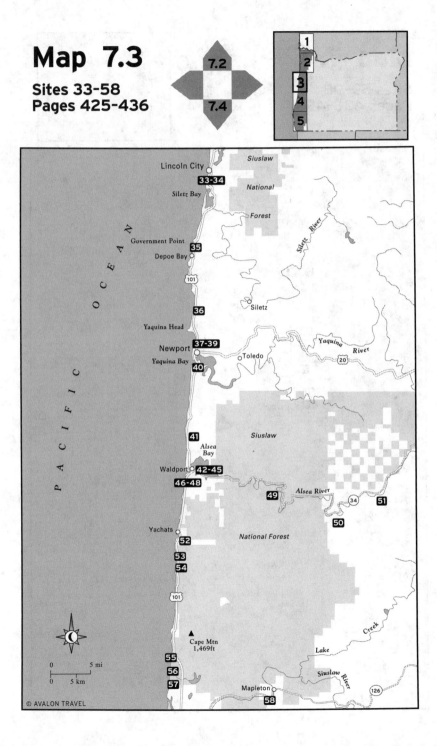

# Map 7.4

**Sites 59-98**
**Pages 436-453**

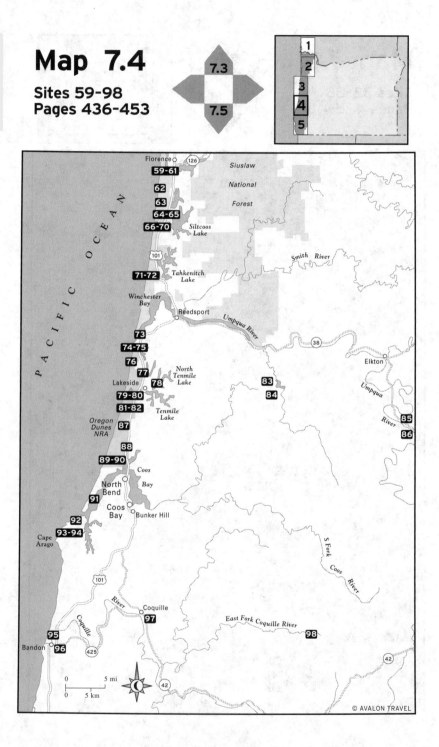

# Map 7.5

**Sites 99-134**
**Pages 454-469**

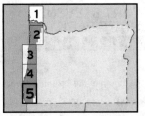

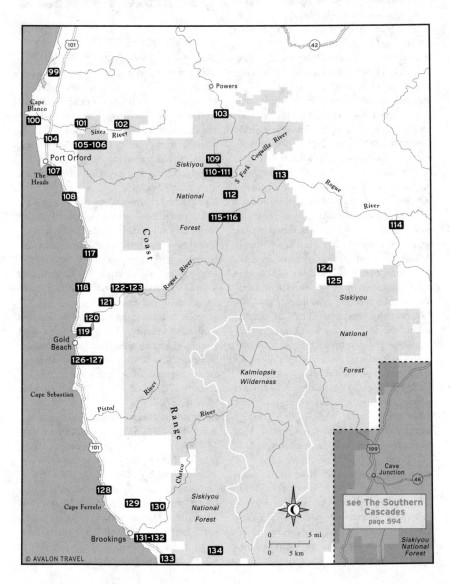

© AVALON TRAVEL

# ■ FORT STEVENS STATE PARK

🚶 🚵 🏊 ⛵ 🎣 🐴 🚣 ♿ 🚐 ⛺

### Scenic rating: 8
at the mouth of the Columbia River

**Map 7.1, page 407**                    **BEST (**

This classic spot is set at the northern tip of Oregon, right where the Columbia River enters the Pacific Ocean. At 3,700 acres, the park offers nine miles of biking trails, six miles of hiking trails, swimming, boating, fishing, and wildlife-viewing in a landscape of forests, wetlands, and dunes. The trailhead for the Oregon Coast Trail is here as well. History buffs will find a museum, tours of the fort and artillery batteries, and the remains of the *Peter Iredale* shipwreck.

**Campsites, facilities:** There are 476 sites with full or partial hookups for tents or RVs up to 60 feet long, 19 sites for tents or small RVs (no hookups), a camping area for hikers and bicyclists, and 15 yurts. Picnic tables and fire grills are provided. Drinking water, restrooms with flush toilets and showers, dump station, a transfer and recycling station, two picnic shelters, firewood, and a playground are available. Boat docks and launching facilities are nearby. Some facilities are wheelchair accessible. Leashed pets are permitted.

**Reservations, fees:** Reservations are accepted at 800/452-5687 or www.oregonstateparks. org ($8 reservation fee). RV sites are $23-27 per night, tent sites are $17-21 per night, $6 per night per person for hikers/bikers, yurts are $41 per night, $5 per night per additional vehicle. Some credit cards are accepted. Open year-round.

**Directions:** From Portland, turn west on U.S. 26 and drive 73 miles to the junction with U.S. 101. Turn right (north) on U.S. 101 and drive about 15 miles (about 0.25 mile past the Camp Rilea Army Base). Turn west on Perkins Road/ Highway 104 at the sign for Fort Stevens State Park and drive about one mile to Ocean View Cemetery Road. Turn left and drive about 2.5 miles (Ocean View Cemetery Road becomes Ridge Road) to the park entrance.

**Contact:** Fort Stevens State Park, 503/861-1671 or 800/551-6949, www.oregonstateparks. org.

# ■ ASTORIA/WARRENTON SEASIDE KOA

🚶 🚵 🏊 ⛵ 🎣 🏊 🐴 🚣 ♿ 🚐 ⛺

### Scenic rating: 3
near Fort Stevens State Park

**Map 7.1, page 407**

This campground is nestled in a wooded area adjacent to Fort Stevens State Park, and tours of that historical military site can be arranged. This camp provides an excellent alternative if the state park campground is full. A host of activities are available in the immediate area, including beachcombing, bicycling, deep-sea fishing, hiking, and kayaking. Horse stables are within 10 miles.

**Campsites, facilities:** There are 311 sites with full or partial hookups for tents or RVs of any length, 54 cabins, and eight deluxe lodges. Some sites are pull-through. Picnic tables and fire pits are provided. Cable TV, 30- and 50-amp service, WiFi, restrooms with flush toilets and showers, coin laundry, meeting room, firewood, limited groceries, ice, snack bar, RV supplies, propane gas, and a picnic area are available. Recreational facilities include a playground, game room, bicycle rentals, miniature golf, horseshoe pits, spa, and a heated indoor swimming pool. Some facilities are wheelchair accessible. Leashed pets are permitted with some restrictions.

**Reservations, fees:** Reservations are accepted at 800/562-8506. Sites are $25-205 per night, $4-5.50 per person per night for more than two people, $2 per pet per night, $5 per night per additional vehicle unless towed. Some credit cards are accepted. Open year-round.

**Directions:** From Portland, turn west on U.S. 26 and drive 73 miles to the junction with U.S. 101. Turn right (north) on U.S. 101 and drive about 15 miles (about 0.25 mile past the Camp Rilea Army Base). Turn west on Perkins Road/

Highway 104 at the sign for Fort Stevens State Park and drive about one mile to Ocean View Cemetery Road. Turn left and drive about 2.5 miles (Ocean View Cemetery Road becomes Ridge Road) to the campground directly across from the state park.

**Contact:** Astoria/Warrenton Seaside KOA, 503/861-2606, www.koa.com.

## 3 KAMPERS WEST RV PARK

### Scenic rating: 7

near Fort Stevens State Park

**Map 7.1, page 407**

Just four miles from Fort Stevens State Park, this privately run camp offers full RV services. Nearby recreation possibilities include an 18-hole golf course, hiking trails, and marked bike trails.

**Campsites, facilities:** There are 160 sites with full or partial (30-amp) hookups for RVs of any length, a small area for tents only, and three park-model cabins. Drinking water and picnic tables are provided, and some sites have fire pits. Restrooms with flush toilets and showers, propane gas, dump station, coin laundry, firewood, cable TV, fish-cleaning and crab-cooking stations, and ice are available. A store and a café are within two miles. Leashed pets are permitted.

**Reservations, fees:** Reservations are accepted. RV sites are $38 per night, tent sites are $28 per night, and cabins are $52 per night. Some credit cards are accepted. Open year-round.

**Directions:** From Portland, turn west on U.S. 30 and drive 105 miles north and west to Astoria and the junction of U.S. 101. Turn south and drive 6.5 miles to the Warrenton/Hammond Junction. Turn right (west) on Warrenton and drive 1.5 miles to the campground on the right.

**Contact:** Kampers West RV Park, 503/861-1814, www.kamperswest.com.

## 4 VENICE RV PARK

### Scenic rating: 3

on the Neawanna River

**Map 7.2, page 408**

This park along the Neawanna River—one of two rivers running through Seaside—is less than a mile from the beach. A great bonus: Crab pot rentals are available. Seaside offers beautiful ocean beaches for fishing and surfing, moped and bike rentals, shops, and a theater. The city provides swings and volleyball nets on the beach. An 18-hole golf course is nearby.

**Campsites, facilities:** There are 14 sites for RVs of any length (full hookups, some pull-through) and six tent sites. Picnic tables are provided. Restrooms with flush toilets and showers, drinking water, WiFi, cable TV, picnic area and a coin laundry are available. A store and a café are within one mile. Some facilities are wheelchair accessible. Leashed pets are permitted.

**Reservations, fees:** Reservations are accepted. RV sites are $31.50 per night, tent sites are $20 per night, $2 per person per night for more than two people, and $2 per pet one time fee. Some credit cards are accepted. Open year-round.

**Directions:** From Portland on I-5, turn west on U.S. 26 and drive 73 miles to the junction with U.S. 101. Turn north on U.S. 101 and drive 5.25 miles to Seaside. Continue to the north end of town and bear left (west) on 24th Avenue. The campground is on the corner (do not cross the bridge) at 1032 24th Avenue.

**Contact:** Venice RV Park, 503/738-8851, www.shopseaside.com/vrv.

## 5 SEA RANCH RV PARK

### Scenic rating: 9

in Cannon Beach

**Map 7.2, page 408**

This park is set in a wooded area with nearby

access to the beach. Activities at the camp include stream fishing, horseback riding, and swimming on the seashore. A golf course is six miles away, and the historic Lewis and Clark Trail is nearby. Elk hunters camp here in season. The beach and the town of Cannon Beach are within walking distance of the park.

**Campsites, facilities:** There are 80 sites with full or partial hookups for tents or RVs up to 40 feet long and seven cabins. Picnic tables and fire rings are provided. Restrooms with flush toilets and showers, horse rentals, firewood, and a dump station are available. Supplies are available within two miles. Leashed pets are permitted.

**Reservations, fees:** Reservations are accepted. RV sites are $38-43 per night, tent sites are $33 per night, cabins are $85-95 per night, $3 per person per night for more than two people, $4 per night per additional vehicle, and $3 per pet per night. Monthly rates are available. Some credit cards are accepted. Open year-round.

**Directions:** From Portland on I-5, turn west on U.S. 26 and drive 73 miles to the junction with U.S. 101. Turn south on U.S. 101 and drive three miles to the Cannon Beach exit. Take that exit and drive on Fir Street for 0.3 mile to the park on the left.

**Contact:** Sea Ranch RV Park, 503/436-2815, www.searanchrv.com.

## 6 RV RESORT AT CANNON BEACH
🏃 🚲 🏊 🐴 🏇 ♿ 🚐

### Scenic rating: 9

near Ecola State Park

Map 7.2, page 408

This private resort is located about seven blocks from one of the nicest beaches in the region and about two miles from Ecola State Park. From the town of Cannon Beach, you can walk for miles in either direction. Nearby recreational facilities include marked bike trails, a riding stable, and tennis courts. The city shuttle service stops here.

**Campsites, facilities:** There are 99 sites with full hookups for RVs of any length; some sites are pull-through. Picnic tables and fire pits are provided. Restrooms with flush toilets and showers, cable TV, propane gas, firewood, recreation hall, playground, horseshoe pits, basketball court, convenience store, spa, coin laundry, ice, gasoline, playground, and a heated swimming pool (year-round) are available. Some facilities are wheelchair accessible. Leashed pets are permitted.

**Reservations, fees:** Reservations are accepted at 800/847-2231. Sites are $32-44 per night, $3 per person per night for more than two people. Weekly and monthly rates available. Some credit cards are accepted. Open year-round.

**Directions:** From Portland on I-5, turn west on U.S. 26 and drive 73 miles to the junction with U.S. 101. Turn south on U.S. 101 and drive four miles to the second Cannon Beach exit at Milepost 29.5. Exit on the left (east) and drive 200 feet to the resort.

**Contact:** RV Resort at Cannon Beach, 503/436-2231, www.cbrvresort.com.

## 7 SADDLE MOUNTAIN STATE NATURAL AREA
🏃 🐴 🏕

### Scenic rating: 7

on Saddle Mountain

Map 7.2, page 408

This inland camp offers a good alternative to the many beachfront parks. A 2.5-mile trail climbs to the top of Saddle Mountain, a great lookout on clear days. The park is a real find for the naturalist interested in rare and unusual varieties of plants, many of which have established themselves along the slopes of this isolated mountain.

**Campsites, facilities:** There are 10 primitive walk-in tent sites and a grassy overflow area for tents. Picnic tables and fire grills are provided. Drinking water (seasonal), garbage bins, flush and vault toilets (seasonal), and a picnic area are available. Leashed pets are permitted.

**Reservations, fees:** Reservations are not accepted. Sites are $5-10 per night, $5 per night per additional vehicle. Open March-October.

**Directions:** From Portland, turn west on U.S. 26 and drive about 63 miles to just before Necanicum Junction and Saddle Mountain Road. Turn right (north) on Saddle Mountain Road and drive seven miles to the park. The road dead-ends at the park.

**Contact:** Ecola State Park, 503/436-2844 or 800/551-6949 (this number reaches Ecola State Park, which manages Saddle Mountain), www.oregonstateparks.org.

## 8 NEHALEM BAY STATE PARK

### Scenic rating: 7

on Nehalem Bay

**Map 7.2, page 408**

This state park on a sandy point separating the Pacific Ocean from Nehalem Bay features six miles of beach frontage. There is no ocean view from the campsites, but the sites are about 150 yards from the ocean. In 2008, beachcombers discovered a pair of historic cannons at low tide, likely dating back to an 1846 shipwreck. Crabbing and fishing on the bay are popular. The Oregon Coast Trail passes through the park. A horse camp with corrals and a 7.5-mile equestrian trail are available. There is also a two-mile bike trail. The neighboring towns of Manzanita and Nehalem offer fine dining and shopping. An airport is adjacent to the park, and there are airstrip fly-in campsites.

**Campsites, facilities:** There are 265 sites with partial hookups for tents or RVs up to 60 feet long, a camping area for hikers and bicyclists, and six primitive fly-in sites next to the airport. There are also 18 yurts and 17 equestrian sites with stock corrals. Drinking water, picnic tables, and fire grills are provided. Restrooms with flush toilets and showers, dump station, playgrounds, firewood, and a meeting hall are available. Boat-launching facilities are nearby on Nehalem Bay, and an airstrip is adjacent to

the park. Some facilities are wheelchair accessible. Leashed pets are permitted.

**Reservations, fees:** Reservations are accepted at 800/452-5687 or www.oregonstateparks.org ($8 reservation fee). Sites are $20-24 per night, $5 per night per additional vehicle, and $5 per person per night for hikers/bikers. Yurts are $36 per night; horse sites are $15-19 per night. Fly-in sites are $6-10 per night, not including tie-down. Some credit cards are accepted. Open year-round.

**Directions:** From Portland, drive west on U.S. 26 for 73 miles to the junction with U.S. 101. Turn south on U.S. 101 and drive 19 miles to Manzanita. Continue south on U.S. 101 for 0.75 mile to Necarney City Road. Turn right and drive 0.2 mile to a stop sign. Turn right and drive 0.75 mile to the park entrance.

**Contact:** Nehalem Bay State Park, 503/368-5154 or 800/551-6949, www.oregonstateparks.org.

## 9 NEHALEM FALLS

### Scenic rating: 10

in Tillamook State Forest

**Map 7.2, page 408**      **BEST (**

This beautiful campground, amid old-growth hemlock and spruce, is located within a two-minute walk of lovely Nehalem Falls. Note that swimming in the pool below the falls is hazardous and not advised. A half-mile loop trail follows the Nehalem River, where fishing and swimming are options.

**Campsites, facilities:** There are 14 sites for tents or RVs up to 40 feet long, six walk-in tent sites, and one group site for up to 20 people. Picnic tables and fire grills are provided. Drinking water, vault toilets, garbage bins, and a recycling center are available. A camp host is on-site. Some facilities are wheelchair accessible. Leashed pets are permitted.

**Reservations, fees:** Reservations are accepted for the group site only online at www.oregon.gov. Sites are $10 per night, $2 per night per additional vehicle, walk-in sites are $5 per night, and the group site is $25 per night. Open May-mid-September.

**Directions:** From Tillamook on U.S. 101 northbound, drive 22 miles to Highway 53. Turn right (east) and drive 1.3 miles to Miami Foley Road. Turn right (south) and drive one mile to Foss Road (narrow and rough). Turn left and drive seven miles to the campground on the left.

**Contact:** Tillamook State Forest, Tillamook District, 503/842-2545, www.oregon.gov.

## 10 BARVIEW JETTY PARK

### Scenic rating: 7

near Garibaldi

**Map 7.2, page 408**

This Tillamook County park covers 160 acres and is located near the beach, in a wooded area adjacent to Tillamook Bay. The sites are set on grassy hills. Nearby recreation options include an 18-hole golf course, surf and scuba fishing, and a full-service marina.

**Campsites, facilities:** There are 242 tent sites, 73 sites with full hookups for tents or RVs of any length, and 20 hiker/biker sites. Some sites are pull-through. Groups can be accommodated. Picnic tables and fire pits are provided. Drinking water, restrooms with flush toilets and showers, a dump station, a fish-cleaning station, WiFi, and a day-use area are available. A camp host is on site. Propane gas, store, café, and ice are within one mile. Some facilities are wheelchair accessible. Leashed pets are permitted.

**Reservations, fees:** Reservations are accepted ($10 reservation fee) at 503/322-3522 or www.co.tillamook.or.us. Sites are $14-34 per night, $5 per night per each additional vehicle, $7 per night per additional tent, $8 per person per night for hiker/biker sites, $5 per pet. Some credit cards are accepted. Open year-round.

**Directions:** From Tillamook, drive north on U.S. 101 for 12 miles to the park on the left (two miles north of the town of Garibaldi).

**Contact:** Barview Jetty Park, Tillamook County, 503/322-3522, www.co.tillamook.or.us/gov/parks.

## 11 BIAK-BY-THE-SEA RV PARK

### Scenic rating: 7

on Tillamook Bay

**Map 7.2, page 408**

This park along the shore of Tillamook Bay is a prime retreat for beachcombing, clamming, crabbing, deep-sea fishing, scuba diving, and surf fishing. The nearby town of Tillamook is home to a cheese factory and a historical museum. Cape Meares State Park, where you can hike through the national wildlife preserve and see how the seabirds nest along the cliffs, makes a good side trip. There is also a golf course nearby. Note that most of the sites are monthly rentals.

**Campsites, facilities:** There are 45 sites with full (50-amp) hookups for RVs of any length and a grassy area for tents. Some sites are pull-through. Picnic tables are provided. Drinking water, restrooms with flush toilets and showers, WiFi, cable TV, convenience store, and a coin laundry are available. Propane gas, café, and ice are within one mile. Boat docks, launching facilities, and rentals are nearby. Some facilities are wheelchair accessible. Leashed pets are permitted.

**Reservations, fees:** Reservations are accepted. RV sites are $29 per night, tent sites are $21 per night. Weekly and monthly rates are available. Some credit cards are accepted. Open year-round.

**Directions:** From Tillamook and U.S. 101, drive north for 10 miles to 7th Street. Turn left on 7th Street and drive to the park on the left (just over the tracks).

**Contact:** Biak-by-the-Sea RV Park, 503/322-2111 or 503/322-3292, www.campingfriend.com/BiakByTheSeaRVPark.

## 12 KILCHIS RIVER PARK

### Scenic rating: 8

on the Kilchis River

**Map 7.2, page 408**

Riverfront campsites are the highlight at this Tillamook County campground. The campground is forested and gets moderate use. Hiking trails are available. Other recreational options include boating, fishing, and swimming.

**Campsites, facilities:** There are 63 sites for tents or RVs of any length (no hookups) and 27 hiker/biker sites. Picnic tables and fire pits are provided. Drinking water, flush toilets, coin showers, playground, garbage bins, boat launch, day-use area, dump station, basketball court, and a volleyball court are available. A camp host is on-site. Some facilities are wheelchair accessible. Leashed pets are permitted.

**Reservations, fees:** Reservations are accepted ($10 reservation fee) at 503/842-6694 or www.co.tillamook.or.us. Sites are $14-24 per night, $5 per night per additional vehicle, $7 per night per additional tent, $8 per person per night for hiker/biker sites, and $5 per pet. Open May-October.

**Directions:** From Tillamook and U.S. 101, take the Alderbrook Loop/Kilches Park exit. Turn onto Alderbrook Loop and drive northeast for approximately one mile to Kilches River Road. Turn right and drive approximately four miles to the park at the end of the road.

**Contact:** Kilchis River Park, Tillamook County, 503/842-6694, www.co.tillamook. or.us/gov/parks.

## 13 JONES CREEK

### Scenic rating: 7

on the Wilson River in Tillamook State Forest

**Map 7.2, page 408**

Set in a forest of alder, fir, hemlock, and spruce, campsites here are spacious and private. The adjacent Wilson River provides opportunities for steelhead and salmon fishing (artificial lures only). A scenic 3.8-mile trail runs along the riverfront. The camp fills up on weekends July-Labor Day.

**Campsites, facilities:** There are 28 sites for tents or RVs of any length, 14 walk-in tent sites, and one group site for up to 20 people. Picnic tables and fire grills are provided. Drinking water, vault toilets, garbage bins, firewood, and a horseshoe pit are available. A camp host is on-site. Some facilities are wheelchair accessible. Leashed pets are permitted.

**Reservations, fees:** Reservations are accepted for the group site only online at www.oregon. gov. Sites are $10 per night, $2 per night per additional vehicle, walk-in sites are $5 per night, and the group site is $25 per night. Open May-mid-September.

**Directions:** From Portland, turn west on U.S. 26 and drive 24 miles to Highway 6. Turn west on Highway 6 and drive 28 miles to Milepost 22.7 and North Fork Road. Turn right and drive 0.25 mile to the campground on the left.

**Contact:** Tillamook State Forest, Tillamook District, 503/842-2545, www.oregon.gov.

## 14 ELK CREEK WALK-IN

### Scenic rating: 7

on Elk Creek in Tillamook State Forest

**Map 7.2, page 408**

This small campground is set among alder, fir, and maple on Elk Creek and borders the Wilson River. The Elk Mountain trailhead is here and a good swimming hole is nearby. Note that Elk Creek is closed to fishing; call ahead for fishing information on the Wilson River, as regulations often change.

**Campsites, facilities:** There are 14 walk-in tent sites. Picnic tables and fire grills are provided. Drinking water and vault toilets are available. Garbage must be packed out. Some facilities are wheelchair accessible. Leashed pets are permitted.

**Reservations, fees:** Reservations are not accepted. Sites are $5 per night, $2 per night per additional vehicle. Open mid-May-October.
**Directions:** From Portland, turn west on U.S. 26 and drive 24 miles to Highway 6. Turn west on Highway 6 and drive 23 miles to Milepost 28 and the campground entrance road on the right. Turn right on Elk Creek Road and drive 0.5 mile to the campground on the left.
**Contact:** Tillamook State Forest, Forest Grove District, 503/357-2191, www.oregon.gov.

## 15 JORDAN CREEK OHV

### Scenic rating: 6
near Jordan Creek in Tillamook State Forest

**Map 7.2, page 408**

This off-highway vehicle (OHV) camp is set at the bottom of a scenic, steep canyon next to Jordan Creek. Wooded campsites are clustered around a central parking area, and the park caters to OHV campers. There are almost 40 miles of OHV trails, varying from moderate to difficult. Note that in order to ride an ATV on roads, you need an ATV sticker, a driver's license, and a spark arrestor. There's no fishing in Jordan Creek.
**Campsites, facilities:** There are six sites for tents or RVs of any length. Overflow RV camping is allowed in the main parking lot. Picnic tables and fire grills are provided. Garbage bins and vault toilets are available. There is no drinking water. Leashed pets are permitted.
**Reservations, fees:** Reservations are not accepted. Sites are $10 per night, $2 per night per additional vehicle. (Motorcycles, ATVs, and 4x4s taken in on trailers do not count as extra vehicles.) Open mid-May-mid-September.
**Directions:** From Tillamook on U.S. 101, turn east on Highway 6 and drive 17.9 miles to Jordan Creek Road. Turn right and drive 2.2 miles to the campground on the right.
**Contact:** Tillamook State Forest, Tillamook District, 503/842-2545, www.oregon.gov.

## 16 GALES CREEK

### Scenic rating: 7
on Gales Creek in Tillamook State Forest

**Map 7.2, page 408**

Gales Creek runs through this heavily forested camp. The Gales Creek Trailhead is accessible from camp, providing access to hiking and mountain biking opportunities. A day-use picnic area is also available.
**Campsites, facilities:** There are 17 sites for tents or RVs up to 35 feet long and four walk-in tent sites. Picnic tables and fire grills are provided. Garbage bins, vault toilets, and drinking water are available. A camp host is on-site. Some facilities are wheelchair accessible. Leashed pets are permitted.
**Reservations, fees:** Reservations are not accepted. RV sites are $10 per night, walk-in tent sites are $5 per night, and an additional vehicle is $2 per night. Open mid-May-October.
**Directions:** From Portland, turn west on U.S. 26 and drive 24 miles to Highway 6. Turn west on Highway 6 and drive 17 miles to the campground entrance road (Rogers Road) on the right at Milepost 35. Turn right on Rogers Road and drive one mile to the campground.
**Contact:** Tillamook State Forest, Forest Grove District, 503/357-2191, www.oregon.gov.

## 17 BROWNS CAMP OHV

### Scenic rating: 6
in Tillamook State Forest

**Map 7.2, page 408**

This camp is located next to the Devil's Lake Fork of the Wilson River and has sites with and without tree cover. Surrounded by miles of OHV trails, it caters to off-highway vehicle campers. Don't expect peace and quiet. No fishing is allowed here.
**Campsites, facilities:** There are 30 sites for tents or RVs up to 45 feet long. Picnic tables and fire grills are provided. Drinking water,

garbage bins, and vault toilets are available. Some facilities are wheelchair accessible. Leashed pets are permitted.

**Reservations, fees:** Reservations are not accepted. Sites are $10 per night, $2 per night per additional vehicle. Open April-October.

**Directions:** From Portland, turn west on U.S. 26 and drive 24 miles to Highway 6. Turn west on Highway 6 and drive 19 miles to Beaver Dam Road. Turn left (south) and drive 2.5 miles to Scoggins Road. Turn left (southeast) and drive 0.5 mile to the campground.

**Contact:** Tillamook State Forest, Forest Grove District, 503/357-2191, www.oregon.gov.

## 18 TRASK RIVER PARK

**Scenic rating: 7**

on the Trask River

**Map 7.2, page 408**

This is a popular campground and park that gets moderate use primarily from the locals in Tillamook County. Some campsites are shaded. Fishing for trout and steelhead is available in season; check current fishing regulations.

**Campsites, facilities:** There are 112 sites for tents or RVs of any length (no hookups), two group camps for up to 48 people, and a hiker/biker area. Picnic tables and fire pits are provided. Drinking water, vault toilets, garbage service, and a day-use area are available. A camp host is on-site. Some facilities are wheelchair accessible. Leashed pets are permitted.

**Reservations, fees:** Reservations are accepted ($10 reservation fee) at 503/842-4559 or www.co.tillamook.or.us. Sites are $14-24 per night, group sites are $90 per night, $5 per night per additional vehicle, $7 per night per additional tent, $8 per person per night for hiker/biker sites, and $5 pet fee. Some credit cards are accepted. Open year-round.

**Directions:** From Tillamook and U.S. 101, turn east on 3rd Street. Drive 2.5 miles to Trask River Road. Turn right and drive 1.5 miles, turning left to stay on Trask River Road. Continue 10 miles to the park.

**Contact:** Trask River Park, Tillamook County, 503/842-4559, www.co.tillamook.or.us/gov/parks.

## 19 NETARTS BAY RV PARK & MARINA

**Scenic rating: 8**

on Netarts Bay

**Map 7.2, page 408**

This camp is one of three on the east shore of Netarts Bay. A golf course is eight miles away. Sunsets and wildlife-viewing are notable here. Some sites are filled with rentals for the summer season.

**Campsites, facilities:** There are 83 sites with full hookups for RVs of any length; some are pull-through sites. Picnic tables are provided, and fire rings are available at some sites. Drinking water, restrooms with flush toilets and showers, propane gas, WiFi, convenience store, in-park office, a meeting room, coin laundry, playground, horseshoe pits, fish-cleaning station, crab-cooking facilities, crab bait, and ice are available. Boat docks, launching facilities, and rentals are available on-site. A store and a café are within one mile. Leashed pets are permitted, with a two-pet maximum.

**Reservations, fees:** Reservations are recommended. Sites are $33-40 per night, $5 per night per extra person, $5 per night per additional vehicle. Winter rates, weekly, and monthly rates are available. Some credit cards are accepted. Open year-round.

**Directions:** From Tillamook and Netarts Highway/Highway 131, drive west on Netarts Highway for six miles to the campground entrance.

**Contact:** Netarts Bay RV Park & Marina, 503/842-7774, www.netartsbay.com.

## 20 PLEASANT VALLEY RV PARK

**Scenic rating: 8**

on the Tillamook River

**Map 7.2, page 408**

Pleasant Valley RV Park sits along the Tillamook River. The park is very clean and provides easy access to many recreation options in the immediate area.

**Campsites, facilities:** There are 10 tent sites and 76 pull-through sites with full or partial hookups for RVs of any length, plus two cabins. Picnic tables and fire rings are provided. Drinking water, restrooms with flush toilets and showers, propane gas, dump station, firewood, a meeting room, cable TV, WiFi, convenience store, coin laundry, ice, and a playground are available. Boat-launching facilities are nearby. Leashed pets are permitted.

**Reservations, fees:** Reservations are accepted. RV sites are $29-32 per night, tent sites are $29 per night, $2 per person per night for more than two people; cabins are $29 per night. Some credit cards are accepted. Open year-round.

**Directions:** From Tillamook and U.S. 101, drive south on U.S. 101 for 7 miles to the campground entrance on the right (west).

**Contact:** Pleasant Valley RV Park, 503/842-4779, www.pleasantvalleyrvpark.com.

## 21 CAPE LOOKOUT STATE PARK

**Scenic rating: 8**

near Netarts Bay

**Map 7.2, page 408**    **BEST (**

This park is set on a sand spit between Netarts Bay and the Pacific. There are more than eight miles of wooded trails, including the Cape Lookout Trail which follows the headland for more than two miles. Another walk will take you out through a variety of estuarine habitats along the five-mile sand spit that extends between the ocean and Netarts Bay. With many species to view, this area is a paradise for bird-watchers. You might also catch the local hang gliders and paragliders that frequent the park. Fishing is another option here.

**Campsites, facilities:** There are 170 sites for tents or RVs (no hookups), 38 sites with full hookups for RVs up to 60 feet long, a tent camping area for hikers and bicyclists, two group tent sites for up to 25 people each, three cabins, and 13 yurts. Picnic tables and fire grills are provided. Restrooms with flush toilets and showers, dump station, garbage bins, meeting hall and picnic shelter, summer interpretive programs, and firewood are available. Some facilities are wheelchair accessible. Leashed pets are permitted.

**Reservations, fees:** Reservations are accepted at 800/452-5687 or www.oregonstateparks.org ($8 reservation fee). RV sites are $15-24 per night, tent sites are $12-19 per night, $5 per person per night for hikers/bikers, $51-71 per night for group sites, $56-76 per night for cabins, and $36 per night for yurts, $5 per night per additional vehicle. Some credit cards are accepted. Open year-round.

**Directions:** From Tillamook and U.S. 101, turn east on 3rd Street (becomes Netarts Highway). Drive approximately five miles to Whiskey Creek Road. Turn left and drive approximately seven miles to the park on the right.

**Contact:** Cape Lookout State Park, 503/842-4981, www.oregonstateparks.org.

## 22 WHALEN ISLAND PARK

**Scenic rating: 6**

in the Sandlake Estuary

**Map 7.2, page 408**

This park is located in the Sandlake Estuary and is close to the beach and Nestucca Bay. The campground is fairly open and has a few trees.

**Campsites, facilities:** There are 34 sites for tents or RVs of any length (no hookups) and 11 hiker/biker sites. Picnic tables and fire pits are provided. Drinking water, flush and chemical toilets, dump station, a day-use area, and a boat launch are available. A camp host is on-site during the summer. Some facilities are wheelchair accessible. Leashed pets are permitted.

**Reservations, fees:** Reservations are accepted ($10 reservation fee). Sites are $14-24 per night, $5 per night per additional vehicle, $7 per night per additional tent, $8 per person per night for hiker/biker sites, and a $5 pet fee. Open year-round.

**Directions:** From Tillamook and U.S. 101, drive south for 11 miles to Sand Lake Road. Turn right (west) and drive approximately 55 miles to a stop sign. Turn left to stay on Sand Lake Road. Continue 4.75 miles south to the park entrance road on the right.

**Contact:** Whalen Island Park, Tillamook County, 503/965-6085, www.co.tillamook. or.us/gov/parks.

## 23 SANDBEACH, EAST DUNES, AND WEST WINDS OHV

### Scenic rating: 5

in Siuslaw National Forest

**Map 7.2, page 408**

Sandbeach campground is set along the shore of Sand Lake, which is actually more like an estuary than a lake since the ocean is just around the bend. This area is known for its beaches with large sand dunes, which are popular with off-road-vehicle enthusiasts. It's noisy and can be windy. East Dunes and West Winds, which used to be the overflow parking area, are nearby. This is the only coastal U.S. Forest Service camping area for many miles, and it's quite popular. If you're planning a trip for midsummer, be sure to reserve far in advance. Holiday permits are required ($10 at the district office) for three-day holiday weekends.

**Campsites, facilities:** There are 82 sites for tents or RVs up to 30 feet long. Picnic tables and fire pits are provided. Drinking water, garbage bins, and flush toilets are available. A camp host is on-site at each campground. Leashed pets are permitted.

**Reservations, fees:** Reservations are accepted during the summer season at 877/444-6777 ($10 reservation fee) or www.recreation. gov ($9 reservation fee). Sites at Sandbeach are $20 per night; sites at East Dunes and West Winds are $15 per night. Additional vehicles cost $8 per night at all campgrounds. Open year-round.

**Directions:** From Tillamook on U.S. 101, drive south for 11 miles to County Road 8. Turn right (west) on County Road 8 and drive approximately 12 miles to the campground.

**Contact:** Siuslaw National Forest, Hebo Ranger District, 503/392-5100, www.fs.usda. gov/siuslaw.

## 24 CAMPER COVE RV PARK AND CAMPGROUND

### Scenic rating: 6

on Beaver Creek

**Map 7.2, page 408**

This small, wooded campground along Beaver Creek is set just far enough off the highway to provide quiet. The park can be used as a base camp for anglers, with seasonal steelhead and salmon fishing in the nearby Nestucca River. It gets crowded here, especially in the summer, so be sure to make a reservation if possible. Ocean beaches are four miles away.

**Campsites, facilities:** There are 25 sites with full or partial hookups for RVs up to 40 feet long, 25 tent sites, and three cabins. Picnic tables and fire pits are provided. Drinking water, restrooms with flush toilets and coin showers, dump station, firewood, recreation hall, coin laundry, and ice are available. Some facilities are wheelchair accessible. Leashed pets are permitted.

**Reservations, fees:** Reservations are accepted. RV sites are $28 per night, tent sites are $20 per night, $3 per person per night for more than two adults, $3 per night per additional vehicle, and $30-40 per night for the cabins. Weekly and monthly rates are available. Open year-round.

**Directions:** From Tillamook and U.S. 101, drive south on U.S. 101 for 12 miles to the park entrance on the right (west), three miles north of Beaver.

**Contact:** Camper Cove RV Park and Campground, 503/398-5334, www.campercovecampground.com.

## 25 ROCKY BEND

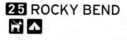

### Scenic rating: 5

on the Nestucca River in Siuslaw National Forest

**Map 7.2, page 408**

This campground along the Nestucca River is a little-known, secluded spot that provides guaranteed peace and quiet. There isn't much in the way of recreational activities out here, but clamming, fishing, hiking, and swimming are available along the coast, a relatively short drive away.

**Campsites, facilities:** There are six tent sites. Picnic tables and fire pits are provided. Vault toilets are available. There is no drinking water and garbage must be packed out. Leashed pets are permitted.

**Reservations, fees:** Reservations are not accepted. There is no fee for camping. Open year-round.

**Directions:** On U.S. 101 southwest of Portland, drive to the tiny town of Beaver and Blaine Road. Turn east on Blaine Road (keep right; Blaine Road turns into Nestucca River Access Road) and drive 15.5 miles to the campground on the right.

**Contact:** Siuslaw National Forest, Hebo Ranger District, 503/392-5100, www.fs.usda.gov/siuslaw.

## 26 DOVRE, FAN CREEK, ALDER GLEN, AND ELK BEND

### Scenic rating: 5

on the Nestucca River

**Map 7.2, page 408**

This is a series of four BLM campgrounds set along the Nestucca River. The camps, separated by alder trees and shrubs, are near the river, and some have river views. Tourists don't know about these spots. The Nestucca is a gentle river, with the water not deep enough for swimming.

**Campsites, facilities:** Dovre has 10 sites, Fan Creek has 11 sites, and Alder Glen has 11 sites; all sites are for tents or small RVs. Elk Bend has five walk-in sites. Picnic tables and fire grills are provided. Drinking water and vault toilets are available. Garbage must be packed out. Some facilities, including a fishing pier at Alder Glen, are wheelchair accessible. Leashed pets are permitted.

**Reservations, fees:** Reservations are not accepted. Sites at Dovre, Fan Creek, and Alder Glen are $10 per night, $5 per night per additional vehicle with a limit of two vehicles per site. There is no fee to camp at Elk Bend. Dovre, Fan Creek, and Alder Glen are open late May-early September; Elk Bend is open year round.

**Directions:** On U.S. 101 southwest of Portland, drive to the tiny town of Beaver and Blaine Road. Turn east on Blaine Road (keep right; Blaine Road turns into Nestucca River Access Road) and drive 17.5 miles to Alder Glen. Continue east for seven more miles to reach Fan Creek and nine more miles to reach Dovre.

**Contact:** Bureau of Land Management, Salem District, 503/815-1134 or 503/375-5646, www.blm.gov/or/districts/salem.

## 27 WOODS COUNTY PARK

🚶 🚴 🛶 🏕️ 🐴 🚐 ⛺

### Scenic rating: 6

on the Kilchis River

**Map 7.2, page 408**

This small Tillamook County park is not well known outside the local area and gets fairly light use. The campground is grassy with few trees. Salmon fishing is a possibility; check current regulations.

**Campsites, facilities:** There are seven tent sites and five sites for RVs up to 45 feet long. Picnic tables and fire pits are provided. Drinking water, flush toilets, garbage containers, and a day-use area are available. A camp host is on-site. Leashed pets are permitted.

**Reservations, fees:** Reservations are accepted ($10 reservation fee) at 503/965-5001 or www.co.tillamook.or.us. Sites are $14-29 per night, $5 per night per additional vehicle, $7 per night per additional tent, and a $5 pet fee. Open May-October, weather permitting.

**Directions:** From Tillamook and U.S. 101, drive approximately 25 miles south to Resort Drive. Turn right (west) and drive three miles (road changes to Brooten Drive) to the park on the right.

**Contact:** Woods County Park, Tillamook County, 503/965-5001, www.co.tillamook.or.us/gov/parks.

## 28 CAPE KIWANDA RV RESORT

🚶 🚴 🛶 🛶 🚤 🏕️ 🚣 ♿ 🚐 ⛺

### Scenic rating: 8

near Cape Kiwanda State Park

**Map 7.2, page 408**

This park is set a short distance from Cape Kiwanda State Park, which is open for day use only. Highlights at the park include a boat launch and hiking trails that lead out to the cape. Four miles south at Nestucca Spit, there is another day-use park, providing additional recreational options. The point extends about three miles and is a good spot for bird-watching. The campsites do not have ocean views, but the ocean is across the road and within walking distance. Surfing is an option.

**Campsites, facilities:** There are 116 sites with full or partial hookups for RVs up to 65 feet long, 10 tent sites, and 14 camping cabins, 8 cottages, and 3 camping cottages. Some sites are pull-through. Picnic tables and fire rings are provided. Drinking water, restrooms with flush toilets and showers, dump station, WiFi, a heated swimming pool (year-round), hot tub, an exercise room, firewood, a recreation hall, coin laundry, propane, a seafood market, deli, gift shop, ATM, sandboard rentals, and a playground are available. Gasoline, a store, and a café are within one mile. Boat docks, launching facilities, and kayak rentals are nearby. Some facilities are wheelchair accessible. Leashed pets are permitted.

**Reservations, fees:** Reservations are recommended. RV sites are $42-48 per night, tent sites are $26 per night, $2-4 per person per night for more than two people, and $4 per night per additional vehicle. Weekly and monthly rates are available. Fall and winter discounts are available. Some credit cards are accepted. Open year-round.

**Directions:** From Tillamook and U.S. 101, drive south on U.S. 101 for 25 miles to the Pacific City exit and Brooten Road. Turn right on Brooten Road and drive three miles toward Pacific City and Three Capes Drive. Turn left, cross the bridge, and bear right on Three Capes Drive. Continue one mile north to the park on the right.

**Contact:** Cape Kiwanda RV Resort, 503/965-6230, www.capekiwandarvresort.com.

## 29 WEBB PARK

🚶 🚴 🛶 🛶 🏕️ ♿ 🚐 ⛺

### Scenic rating: 7

near Cape Kiwanda

**Map 7.2, page 408**

This public campground provides an excellent alternative to the more crowded commercial RV parks off U.S. 101. Although not as developed, it offers a quiet, private setting and access to the ocean. Fishing and swimming are among your options here. The camp is adjacent to Cape Kiwanda and provides convenient access to the beach.

**Campsites, facilities:** There are 30 sites for tents or RVs (no hookups), eight sites with partial hookups for RVs up to 40 feet long, and seven hiker/biker sites. Picnic tables and fire pits are provided. Drinking water, a dump station, fish-cleaning station, and restrooms with flush toilets and showers are available. Beach launching is nearby. Some facilities are wheelchair accessible. Leashed pets are permitted.

**Reservations, fees:** Reservations are accepted ($10 reservation fee) at 503/965-5001 or www.co.tillamook.or.us. Sites are $14-24 per night, $5 per night per additional vehicle, $7 per night per additional tent, $8 per person per night for hiker/biker sites, and a $5 pet fee. Some credit cards are accepted. Open year-round.

**Directions:** From Tillamook and U.S. 101, drive south on U.S. 101 for 25 miles to the Pacific City exit and Highway 30. From Pacific City, turn right (north) and drive to the four-way stop at McPhillips Drive. Turn left on McPhillips Drive and drive 0.5 mile to Cape Kiwanda and the park on the right.

**Contact:** Webb Park, Tillamook County Parks, 503/965-5001, www.co.tillamook.or.us/gov/parks.

## 30 HEBO LAKE

**Scenic rating: 7**
on Hebo Lake in Siuslaw National Forest

**Map 7.2, page 408**

This U.S. Forest Service campground along the shore of Hebo Lake is a secluded spot with sites nestled under trees. The trailhead for the eight-mile-long Pioneer-Indian Trail is located in the campground. The trail around the lake is wheelchair accessible.

**Campsites, facilities:** There are six sites for trailers or RVs up to 18 feet long and six tent

sites. Picnic tables and fire pits are provided. Drinking water, garbage bins, and vault toilets are available. Boats with electric motors are allowed on the lake, but gas motors are not. Some facilities are wheelchair accessible. Leashed pets are permitted.

**Reservations, fees:** Reservations are not accepted. Sites are $12 per night, $5 per night per additional vehicle. Open from mid-April to mid-November, weather permitting.

**Directions:** On U.S. 101 southwest of Portland, drive to the town of Hebo and Highway 22. Turn east on Highway 22 and drive 0.25 mile to Forest Road 14. Turn left (east) and drive five miles to the campground on the right.

**Contact:** Siuslaw National Forest, Hebo Ranger District, 503/392-5100, www.fs.usda.gov/siuslaw.

## 31 CASTLE ROCK

**Scenic rating: 4**
on Three Rivers in Siuslaw National Forest

**Map 7.2, page 408**

This tiny spot along Three Rivers provides tent campers with an inland alternative to the large beachfront RV parks popular on the Oregon coast. Fishing can be good here. Though primitive, this camp is located along the edge of the highway and can fill up quickly.

**Campsites, facilities:** There are four tent sites. Picnic tables, garbage bins, and a vault toilet are provided. There is no drinking water. Leashed pets are permitted.

**Reservations, fees:** Reservations are not accepted. There is no fee for camping. Open year-round, weather permitting.

**Directions:** On U.S. 101 southwest of Portland, drive to the town of Hebo and Highway 22. Turn east on Highway 22 and drive five miles to the campground on the right.

**Contact:** Siuslaw National Forest, Hebo Ranger District, 503/392-5100, www.fs.usda.gov/siuslaw.

## 32 WANDERING SPIRIT RV PARK

Scenic rating: 6

on Rock Creek

**Map 7.2, page 408**

The major draw here is the nearby casino, but there is the added benefit of shaded sites next to Rock Creek, which provides fishing and swimming options. The Yamhill River is 0.5 mile away. Fishing is good for steelhead and salmon in season. Golf courses and wineries are available within 10 miles. There is a combination of monthly rentals and overnighters at this park.

**Campsites, facilities:** There are 129 sites with full hookups (30 and 50 amps) for RVs up to 45 feet long, 11 tent sites, and eight park-model cabins. Some sites are pull-through. Group camping available. Drinking water, cable TV, WiFi, restrooms with showers, dump station, coin laundry, RV storage, RV supplies, and a convenience store are available. Propane, a clubhouse, basketball hoop, an exercise room, and a game room are also available on-site. A 24-hour free bus shuttles campers to and from the Spirit Mountain Casino, restaurants, and shops less than two miles away. Some facilities are wheelchair accessible. Leashed pets are permitted.

**Reservations, fees:** Reservations are accepted at 800/390-6980. RV sites are $35 per night, tent sites are $18 per night, $2 per person per night for more than two people. Weekly and monthly rates are available. Some credit cards are accepted. Open year-round.

**Directions:** From Salem, drive west on Highway 22 about 25 miles to Highway 18. Turn west on Highway 18 and drive seven miles to the park on the left.

**Contact:** Wandering Spirit RV Park, 503/879-5700, www.wanderingspiritrvpark.com.

## 33 DEVIL'S LAKE STATE PARK

Scenic rating: 7

on Devil's Lake

**Map 7.3, page 409**

Oregon's only coastal camp in the midst of a city, Devil's Lake is the center of summertime activity. A take-your-pick deal: You can boat, canoe, fish, kayak, or water ski. A walking path extends from the campground to the boat launch 0.25 mile away. For something different, head west and explore the seven miles of beaches. Lincoln City also has a number of arts and crafts galleries and a weekend farmers market during the summer. East Devil's Lake is two miles east and offers a boat ramp and picnic facilities.

**Campsites, facilities:** There are 54 sites for tents or small RVs (no hookups), 33 sites for tents or RVs up to 55 feet long (full hookups), 10 yurts, and a separate area for hikers and bikers. Picnic tables and fire grills are provided. Drinking water, cable TV, garbage bins, restrooms with flush toilets and showers, an amphitheater, and firewood are available. Boat docks and launching facilities are nearby. Some facilities are wheelchair accessible. Leashed pets are permitted.

**Reservations, fees:** Reservations are accepted at 800/452-5687 or www.oregonstateparks.org ($8 reservation fee). Sites are $17-28 per night, $5 per night per additional vehicle, $6 per person per night for hikers/bikers, and yurts are $40 per night. Boat mooring is $10 per night. Some credit cards are accepted. Open year-round.

**Directions:** From Lincoln City and U.S. 101, take the 6th Street exit. Drive east on 6th Street for one block to the park on the right.

**Contact:** Devil's Lake State Park, 541/994-2002 or 800/551-6949, www.oregonstateparks.org.

## 34 KOA LINCOLN CITY

🚶 🚴 ⛵ 🏊 ⛴ 🐕 ♿ 🚐 ⛺

### Scenic rating: 7

on Devils Lake

**Map 7.3, page 409**

This area offers opportunities for beachcombing, fishing, and tidepool-viewing along a seven-mile stretch of beach. Nearby recreation options include a casino, factory outlets, a golf course, skateboard park, and tennis courts.

**Campsites, facilities:** There are 15 tent sites and 81 sites with full or partial hookups for RVs up to 60 feet long, including some pull-through sites, and 30- and 50-amp service is available. There are also 14 cabins. Picnic tables and some fire pits are provided. Drinking water, cable TV, WiFi, restrooms with flush toilets and showers, dump station, convenience store, snack bar, gift shop, propane gas, ice, RV supplies, video and DVD rentals, coin laundry, firewood, and a playground are available. Some facilities are wheelchair accessible. Leashed pets are permitted, with certain restrictions.

**Reservations, fees:** Reservations are accepted at 800/562-3316. RV sites are $20-40 per night, tent sites are $20-30 per night, $4-5 per person per night for more than two people, $5 per night per additional vehicle. Some credit cards are accepted. Open year-round.

**Directions:** From Portland, drive south on Highway 99 West to Highway 18. Turn west on Highway 18 and drive 47 miles to U.S. 101. Turn south on U.S. 101 and drive 1.5 miles to East Devil's Lake Road. Turn east on East Devil's Lake Road and drive one mile to the park on the left.

**Contact:** KOA Lincoln City, 541/994-2961, www.koa.com.

## 35 SEA AND SAND RV PARK

🐕 🚐

### Scenic rating: 9

near Siletz Bay

**Map 7.3, page 409**

Beachcombing for fossils and agates is popular at this oceanfront park near Gleneden Beach on Siletz Bay. Some sites have ocean views and pleasant terraces. The Siletz River and numerous small creeks are in the area. The park is located 3.5 miles north of Depoe Bay.

**Campsites, facilities:** There are 114 sites with full hookups for RVs up to 40 feet long. Picnic tables are provided and some sites have fire rings. Drinking water, restrooms with flush toilets and showers, cable TV, dump station, firewood, and a coin laundry are available. A store, café, and ice are within one mile. Leashed pets are permitted with breed restrictions.

**Reservations, fees:** Reservations are accepted. Sites are $31-52 per night, $2 per person per night for more than two people, and $10 per night per additional vehicle unless towed. Rates higher on weekends and holidays. Weekly discounts available. Open year-round.

**Directions:** From Lincoln City and U.S. 101, drive south for nine miles on U.S. 101 to the park entrance (on the beach side of the highway).

**Contact:** Sea and Sand RV Park, 541/764-2313 or 877/821-2231, www.seaandsandrvpark.com.

## 36 BEVERLY BEACH STATE PARK

🚶 🚴 🏊 🐕 ♿ 🚐 ⛺

### Scenic rating: 7

near Newport

**Map 7.3, page 409**

This beautiful campground is set in a wooded, grassy area on the east side of U.S. 101. Treed campsites sit along Spencer Creek. A tunnel leads under the roadway to a beach that stretches from Yaguna Head to the Otter Rock headlands. A one-mile hiking trail is available. Just a mile to the north lies a small day-use state park called Devil's Punchbowl, named for an unusual bowl-shaped rock formation with caverns under it where the waves rumble about. For some great ocean views, head north one more mile to the Otter Crest Wayside. The Oregon Coast Aquarium is within a few minutes' drive.

**Campsites, facilities:** There are 128 sites for tents or small RVs, 128 sites with full or partial hookups for tents or RVs up to 65 feet long, a special camping area for hikers and bicyclists, and three group sites for tents or RVs (no hookups) that can accommodate up to 25 people each. There is also a village of 21 yurts. Picnic tables and fire grills are provided. Drinking water, restrooms with flush toilets and showers, cable TV, a playground, a day-use area, garbage bins, and a dump station are available. Some facilities are wheelchair accessible. Leashed pets are permitted.

**Reservations, fees:** Reservations are accepted at 800/452-5687 or www.oregonstateparks.org ($8 reservation fee). Sites are $17-27 per night, $5 per night per additional vehicle, $6 per person per night for hikers/bikers, $40 per night for yurts, and $55-77 for group sites. Some credit cards are accepted. Open year-round.

**Directions:** From Newport and U.S. 101, drive north on U.S. 101 for seven miles to the park entrance on the east side.

**Contact:** Beverly Beach State Park, 541/265-9278 or 800/551-6949, www.oregonstateparks.org.

## 37 AGATE BEACH RV PARK

### Scenic rating: 6

near Newport

**Map 7.3, page 409**

This park is located about half a mile from Agate Beach Wayside, a small state park with beach access. Agate hunting can be good.

Sometimes, a layer of sand covers the agates, and you have to dig a bit. But other times, wave action clears the sand, unveiling the agates at low tides. Beverly Beach State Park is 4.5 miles north. About half of the sites are filled with monthly rentals. There are no ocean views from the campsites.

**Campsites, facilities:** There are 32 sites with full or partial hookups for RVs up to 40 feet long. Picnic tables are provided. Drinking water, cable TV, a restroom with flush toilets and showers, a dump station, and a coin laundry room are available. A store and ice are within one mile. Leashed pets are permitted, with some restrictions.

**Reservations, fees:** Reservations are accepted. Sites are $22-23 per night, $1 per person per night for more than two people, and $1 per night per additional vehicle. Some credit cards are accepted. Open year-round.

**Directions:** From Newport and U.S. 101, drive to the north end of town. The park is on the east side of the road.

**Contact:** Agate Beach RV Park, 6138 N. Coast Highway, Newport, 541/265-7670.

## 38 HARBOR VILLAGE RV PARK

### Scenic rating: 6

on Yaquina Bay

**Map 7.3, page 409**

This wooded and landscaped park is set near the shore of Yaquina Bay. Nearby recreation options include clamming, crabbing, deep-sea fishing, an 18-hole golf course, hiking trails, and a full-service marina.

**Campsites, facilities:** There are 40 sites with full hookups for RVs up to 35 feet long. Note that there are also 100 sites for full-time renters and a mobile-home park for ages 55 and up. Picnic tables are provided. Drinking water, cable TV, WiFi, restrooms with flush toilets and showers and a coin laundry are available. Propane gas, a store, and a café are within one mile. Boat docks, launching facilities, and rentals are nearby. Leashed pets are permitted.

**Reservations, fees:** Reservations are accepted at 888/818-0002. Sites are $30 per night, $5 per person per night for more than two people. Weekly and monthly rates are available. Some credit cards are accepted. Open year-round.

**Directions:** In Newport, drive south on John Moore Road for 0.5 mile to the bay and Bay Boulevard. Bear left and drive a short distance to the park entrance on the left.

**Contact:** Harbor Village RV Park, 541/265-5088, www.harborvillagervpark.com.

## 39 PORT OF NEWPORT MARINA AND RV PARK

**Scenic rating: 7**

on Yaquina Bay

**Map 7.3, page 409**

This public park is set along the shore of Yaquina Bay near Newport, a resort town that offers a variety of attractions. Among them are ocean fishing, a museum and aquarium at the nearby Hatfield Marine Science Center, the Undersea Garden, the Waxworks, Ripley's Believe It or Not, and the Lincoln County Historical Society Museum. Nearby recreation options include an 18-hole golf course, hiking trails, and a full-service marina.

**Campsites, facilities:** There are 143 sites with full hookups for RVs up to 45 feet long. Restrooms with flush toilets and showers, cable TV, Wi-Fi, modem access, dump station, convenience store, coin laundry, fish-cleaning station, and ice are available. A marina with boat docks and launching facilities is available on-site. Some facilities are wheelchair accessible. Leashed pets are permitted.

**Reservations, fees:** Reservations are accepted at 541/867-3321. Sites with hookups are $32-43 per night, sites without hookups are $18 per night, $1 per person per night for more than two people. Discounted rates Nov. 1-May 1.

Weekly rates are available. Some credit cards are accepted. Open year-round.

**Directions:** From Newport and U.S. 101, drive south for 0.5 mile (over the bridge) to Marine Science Drive. Turn right (east) and drive 0.5 mile to the park entrance on the left.

**Contact:** Port of Newport Marina and RV Park, 541/867-3321, www.portofnewport.com.

## 40 SOUTH BEACH STATE PARK

**Scenic rating: 7**

near Newport

**Map 7.3, page 409**

This park along the beach offers opportunities for beachcombing, boating, crabbing, fishing, hiking, and windsurfing. The Oregon Coast Trail passes right through the park. A nature trail circles the campground, and there are hiking and bicycling trails to the beach. A primitive hike-in campground is also available. A naturalist provides campground talks during the summer season. Kayak trips are an option during the summer. The park is within walking distance of Oregon Aquarium. Newport attractions include the Hatfield Marine Science Center, the Undersea Garden, the Waxworks, Ripley's Believe It or Not, and the Lincoln County Historical Society Museum.

**Campsites, facilities:** There are 227 sites with partial hookups for tents or RVs up to 45 feet long, 60 primitive tent sites, a dispersed camping area (without designated sites) for hikers and bicyclists, and an overflow area for RVs. There are also three group sites for up to 25 people each and 27 yurts. Picnic tables and fire grills are provided. Drinking water, restrooms with flush toilets and showers, garbage bins, recycling, a dump station, Wi-Fi, horseshoe pits, playground, a day-use area, meeting hall, and firewood are available. A camp host is on-site. Some facilities are wheelchair accessible. Leashed pets are permitted.

**Reservations, fees:** Reservations are accepted at 800/452-5687 or www.oregonstateparks.org ($8 reservation fee). Sites are $18-27 per night, $5 per night per additional vehicle, $6 per person per night for hikers/bicyclists (three-night limit), $10 for primitive tent sites, $71-77 per night for group sites, and $40 per night for yurts. Some credit cards are accepted. Open year-round.

**Directions:** From Newport and U.S. 101, drive south for three miles to the park entrance on the right.

**Contact:** South Beach State Park, 541/867-4715 or 800/551-6949, www.oregonstateparks.org.

## 41 SEAL ROCKS RV COVE
🚶 🚴 🏊 🎣 🐕 🚐 ⛺

### Scenic rating: 8

near Seal Rock State Park

**Map 7.3, page 409**       **BEST (**

This RV park is situated on the rugged coastline near Seal Rock State Park (open for day use only), where you may find seals, sea lions, and a variety of birds. The ocean views are stunning, and some sites have views.

**Campsites, facilities:** There are 28 sites with full hookups (30 and 50 amps) for RVs of any length and 16 tent sites with 20-amp electricity. Some sites are pull-through. Picnic tables and fire rings are provided. Drinking water, firewood, restrooms with flush toilets and showers, WiFi, and cable TV are available. pets are permitted.

**Reservations, fees:** Reservations are accepted. RV sites are $33-40 per night, tent sites are $22-25 per night, $1-5 per person per night for more than two people, and there's a $5 one-time fee for an additional vehicle unless towed. Winter and weekly rates are available. Open year-round.

**Directions:** From Newport and U.S. 101, drive south for 10 miles to the town of Seal Rock. Continue south on U.S. 101 for 0.25 mile to the park entrance on the left.

**Contact:** Seal Rocks RV Cove, 541/563-3955, www.sealrocksrv.com.

## 42 DRIFT CREEK LANDING
🚶 🚴 🏊 🎣 🚗 🐕 🚐 ⛺

### Scenic rating: 6

on the Alsea River

**Map 7.3, page 409**

Drift Creek Landing is set along the shore of the Alsea River in a heavily treed and mountainous area. The Oregon Coast Aquarium is 15 miles away, and an 18-hole golf course is nearby. There are 10 mobile homes with long-term renters on this property, and more than one-third of the RV sites are taken by monthly renters.

**Campsites, facilities:** There are 50 sites with full hookups for RVs of any length, six sites for tents, and three cabins. Drinking water and picnic tables are provided. Restroom with flush toilets and showers, cable TV, propane gas, recreation hall, convenience store, snack bar, coin laundry, boat docks, boat rentals, moorage, and launching facilities are available. Leashed pets are permitted.

**Reservations, fees:** Reservations are accepted. RV sites are $28-32 per night, and tent sites are $15-17 per night; it's $2 per person per night for more than two people and $5 per night per additional vehicle. Weekly, monthly, and group discounts. Some credit cards are accepted. Open year-round.

**Directions:** From Newport and U.S. 101, drive south for 14 miles to Waldport and Highway 34. Turn east on Highway 34 and drive 3.8 miles to the campground.

**Contact:** Drift Creek Landing, 541/563-3610, www.driftcreeklandingrv.com.

## 43 ALSEA RIVER RV PARK & MARINA

**Scenic rating: 6**

on the Alsea River

### Map 7.3, page 409

This campground is one of several along the shore of the Alsea River. Kayaking and canoeing are popular, as is watching the elk herd across the river. Some of the sites here are filled with monthly rentals.

**Campsites, facilities:** There are 23 sites with full or partial hookups for RVs to 45 feet, five sites for tents, and one cabin. Picnic tables are provided and fire pits are available on request. Drinking water, restrooms with flush toilets and showers, coin laundry, recreation room, bait and tackle, boat docks, boat rentals, and launching facilities are available. Some facilities are wheelchair accessible. Leashed pets are permitted.

**Reservations, fees:** Reservations are accepted at 877/770-6137. RV sites are $21-23 per night, tent sites are $17 per night, $5 per person per night for more than two people, and $5 per night per additional vehicle. Some credit cards are accepted. Open year-round.

**Directions:** From Newport and U.S. 101, drive south for 14 miles to Waldport and Highway 34. Turn east on Highway 34 and drive four miles to the entrance on the left.

**Contact:** Alsea River RV Park & Marina, 541/563-3401, www.alseariverrvpark.com.

## 44 CHINOOK RV PARK

**Scenic rating: 7**

on the Alsea River

### Map 7.3, page 409

This park is set along the shore of the Alsea River, about 3.5 miles from the ocean. The park is filled primarily with monthly rentals, although several RV sites are reserved for short-term campers. Campsites are rented on a space-available basis.

**Campsites, facilities:** There are 34 sites with full or partial hookups for RVs up to 40 feet long and six sites for tents. Picnic tables are provided. Drinking water, cable TV, WiFi, restrooms with flush toilets and showers, a picnic area, ice, off-leash dog run, and a coin laundry are available. A store is within 1.5 miles. Boat docks are nearby. Propane gas and boat launching facilities are available 3.5 miles away. Leashed pets are permitted.

**Reservations, fees:** Reservations are accepted. RV sites are $24-35 per night, tent sites are $18-20 per night, $3 per person per night for more than two people, $5 per night per additional vehicle. Weekly and monthly rates available. Open year-round.

**Directions:** From Newport and U.S. 101, drive south for 14 miles to Waldport and Highway 34. Turn east on Highway 34 and drive 3.3 miles to the park entrance on the left.

**Contact:** Chinook RV Park, 541/563-3485, www.chinookrvpark.com.

## 45 TAYLOR'S LANDING RV PARK

**Scenic rating: 9**

on the Alsea River

### Map 7.3, page 409

This wooded campground is set along the scenic Alsea River. Fall, when the salmon fishing is best, is the prime time here, and the park often fills up. Recreation options include hiking trails, marked bike trails, the Oregon Coast Aquarium, the Sea Lion Caves, and a marina.

**Campsites, facilities:** There are 81 sites for tents or RVs of any length (full hookups). Picnic tables are provided. Drinking water, cable TV, WiFi, and restrooms with flush toilets and showers, propane gas, a café, coin laundry, community fire ring, and boat docks and rentals are available. Boat launching facilities are nearby. Leashed pets are permitted.

**Reservations, fees:** Reservations are accepted. Sites are $27 per night, $1 per person per

night for more than two people. Weekly and monthly rates are available. Open year-round.
**Directions:** From Newport and U.S. 101, drive south for 14 miles to Waldport and Highway 34. Turn east on Highway 34 and drive seven miles to the entrance on the right.
**Contact:** Taylor's Landing RV Park, 541/528-3388, www.taylorslandingrvparkmarina.com.

## 46 WALDPORT/ NEWPORT KOA

### Scenic rating: 8

on Alsea Bay

**Map 7.3, page 409** **BEST (**

This pretty park, set amid some of the oldest pine trees in Oregon, is located within walking distance of the beach, the bay, and downtown Waldport—and to top it off, some of the campsites have beautiful ocean views. Alsea Bay's sandy and rocky shoreline makes this area a favorite with anglers. The crabbing and clamming can also be quite good. Kite flying is popular. South Beach State Park, about five miles north on U.S. 101, offers more fishing and a boat ramp along Beaver Creek. It's open for day use only. Other nearby recreation options include hiking trails, marked bike trails, the Oregon Coast Aquarium, the Sea Lion Caves, and a marina.

**Campsites, facilities:** There are 10 tent sites and 66 sites for RVs up to 60 feet long (full hookups), and 20 cabins. Picnic tables and fire pits are provided. Drinking water, cable TV, restrooms with flush toilets and showers, WiFi, recreation room, propane gas, dump station, store, café, coin laundry, playground, bicycle rentals, and ice are available. Boat docks, launching facilities, and boat rentals are nearby. A café is within one mile. Some facilities are wheelchair accessible. Leashed pets are permitted, with certain restrictions.

**Reservations, fees:** Reservations are accepted at 800/562-3443. RV sites are $31.50-55.50 per night, tent sites are $18.50-26.50 per night, $2-5 per person per night for more than two

people. Some credit cards are accepted. Open year-round.
**Directions:** From Newport and U.S. 101, drive south for approximately 14 miles to Milepost 155 at the north end of the Alsea Bay Bridge. The park is on the west side of the bridge.
**Contact:** Waldport/Newport KOA, 541/563-2250, www.koa.com.

## 47 BEACHSIDE STATE RECREATION SITE

### Scenic rating: 7

near Alsea Bay

**Map 7.3, page 409**

This state park offers about nine miles of beach and is not far from Alsea Bay and the Alsea River. Sites are close to the beach. Nearby attractions include clamming, crabbing, and fishing, as well as hiking and driving tours, tidepools, an aquarium, three lighthouses, science centers, and visitors centers. South Beach State Park, about five miles north on U.S. 101, offers more fishing and a boat ramp along Beaver Creek (day use only).

**Campsites, facilities:** There are 24 sites for tents, 32 sites with partial hookups for RVs up to 40 feet long, two yurts, and a special camping area for hikers and bicyclists. Picnic tables and fire grills are provided. Drinking water, garbage bins, restrooms with flush toilets and showers, recycling, and firewood are available. A horseshoe pit is available nearby. Some facilities are wheelchair accessible. Leashed pets are permitted.

**Reservations, fees:** Reservations are accepted at 800/452-5687 or www.oregonstateparks.org ($8 reservation fee). Sites are $21-26 per night, $5 per night per additional vehicle, $4 per person per night for hikers/bicyclists, and yurts are $40 per night. Some credit cards are accepted. Open mid-March-October, weather permitting.
**Directions:** From Newport and U.S. 101, drive south for 16 miles to Waldport. Continue

south on U.S. 101 for four miles to the park entrance on the west side of the road.
**Contact:** Beachside State Recreation Site, 541/563-3220, www.oregonstateparks.org.

## 48 TILLICUM BEACH

**Scenic rating: 8**
in Siuslaw National Forest

**Map 7.3, page 409**

Oceanview campsites are a big draw at this campground just south of Beachside State Park. Since it's just off the highway and along the water, this camp fills up very quickly in the summer, so expect crowds. Nearby forest roads provide access to streams in the mountains east of the beach area.

**Campsites, facilities:** There are 61 sites for tents or RVs up to 60 feet long; some sites have partial hookups. Picnic tables and fire grills are provided. Flush toilets, garbage bins, firewood, and drinking water are available. Leashed pets are permitted.

**Reservations, fees:** Reservations are required May-September at 877/444-6777 or www. recreation.gov ($9-10 reservation fee). Sites are $24-30 per night, $6 per night per additional vehicle. Open year-round, with reduced capacity in winter.

**Directions:** From Newport and U.S. 101, drive south for 14 miles to Waldport. Continue south on U.S. 101 for 4.5 miles to the campground entrance on the right.

**Contact:** Siuslaw National Forest, Central Coast Ranger District, 541/563-8400, www. fs.usda.gov/siuslaw.

## 49 CANAL CREEK

**Scenic rating: 5**
on Canal Creek in Siuslaw National Forest

**Map 7.3, page 409**

There's one key thing you must know: Vehicles

must be able to cross a small creek to access this site. That accomplished, this pleasant little campground is just off the beaten path in a large, wooded, open area along Canal Creek. It feels remote because of the creek that runs through the campground and the historic homesites nearby, with old fruit trees on the grounds. Yet it has easy access and is close to the coast and all the amenities. The climate here is relatively mild, but, on the other hand, there is the rain in winter—lots of it.

**Campsites, facilities:** There are two groups sites for tents or RVs up to 22 feet. A small group site holds up to 50 people; a larger site holds up to 100 people. Picnic tables and fire grills are provided. Vault toilets are available. There is no drinking water and garbage must be packed out. The group site has a picnic shelter and a play area. Leashed pets are permitted.

**Reservations, fees:** Reservations are required May-September at 877/444-6777 or www.recreation.gov ($9-10 reservation fee). Sites are $125-180 per night. Open mid-May-mid-September.

**Directions:** From Albany, drive west on U.S. 20 for 15 miles to Philomath and Highway 34. Turn south on Highway 34 and drive 52 miles to Forest Road 3462. Turn left (south) and drive four miles to the camp.

**Contact:** Siuslaw National Forest, Central Coast Ranger District, 541/563-3211 or 541/547-8400, www.fs.usda.gov/siuslaw.

## 50 BLACKBERRY

**Scenic rating: 7**
on the Alsea River in Siuslaw National Forest

**Map 7.3, page 409**

Blackberry makes a good base camp for a fishing trip on the Alsea River. The U.S. Forest Service provides boat launches and picnic areas at several spots along this stretch of river. Often, there is a camp host who can give you inside information on nearby recreational opportunities. Large fir trees and lawns separate the sites.

**Campsites, facilities:** There are 32 sites for tents or RVs of any length. Picnic tables and fire grills are provided. Drinking water, garbage bins, and flush toilets are available. There is no firewood. A boat ramp is on-site. Leashed pets are permitted.

**Reservations, fees:** Reservations are required May-September at 877/444-6777 or www.recration.gov ($9-10 reservation fee). Sites are $22 per night, $6 per night per additional vehicle. Open year-round.

**Directions:** From Albany, drive west on U.S. 20 for 15 miles to Philomath and Highway 34. Turn south on Highway 34 and drive 41 miles to the campground entrance on the left.

**Contact:** Siuslaw National Forest, Central Coast Ranger District, 541/563-8400, www.fs.usda.gov/siuslaw.

## 51 ALSEA FALLS

### Scenic rating: 8
adjacent to the south fork of the Alsea River

Map 7.3, page 409                    BEST (

Enjoy the beautiful surroundings of Alsea Falls by exploring the trails that wander through this park and lead to a picnic area by the falls. Trails to McBee Park and Green Peak Falls are accessible from the campground along the south fork of the river. The campsites are situated in a 40-year-old forest of Douglas fir and vine maple. On a warm day, Alsea Falls offers cool relief along the river. The area was named after its original inhabitants, the Alsea people.

**Campsites, facilities:** There are 16 sites for tents or RVs up to 32 feet long. Group camping is also available. Picnic tables and fire pits are provided. Drinking water, vault toilets, and garbage bins are available. A camp host is on site. Some facilities are wheelchair accessible. Leashed pets are permitted.

**Reservations, fees:** Reservations are not accepted. Sites are $12 per night, the group site is $20 per night, $5 per night per additional vehicle. Open mid-May-early September.

**Directions:** From Albany, drive west on U.S. 20 for nine miles to Corvallis. Turn left (south) onto Highway 99 and drive 15 miles to County Road 45120. Turn right (west) and drive five miles to Alpine Junction. Continue along the South Fork Alsea Access Road for nine miles to the campground on the right.

**Contact:** Bureau of Land Management, Salem District Office, 503/375-5646, www.blm.gov/or/districts/salem.

## 52 CAPE PERPETUA

### Scenic rating: 8
on Cape Perpetua in Siuslaw National Forest

Map 7.3, page 409

This U.S. Forest Service campground is set along Cape Creek in the Cape Perpetua Scenic Area. The visitor information center provides hiking and driving maps to guide you through this spectacular region; maps highlight the tidepools and picnic spots. The coastal cliffs are perfect for whale-watching December-March. Neptune State Park is just south and offers additional rugged coastline vistas.

**Campsites, facilities:** There are 38 sites for tents or RVs up to 45 feet long, plus one group site that can accommodate up to 50 people and 102 vehicles. Picnic tables and fire grills are provided. Flush toilets, drinking water, dump station, firewood, and garbage bins are available. A camp host is on-site. Some facilities are wheelchair accessible. Leashed pets are permitted.

**Reservations, fees:** Reservations are accepted at 877/444-6777 or www.recreation.gov ($9-10 reservation fee). Sites are $24 per night, $6 per night per additional vehicle; group sites are $125 per night. Open May-September.

**Directions:** From Newport and U.S. 101, drive south for 23 miles to Yachats. Continue three miles south on U.S. 101 to the entrance on the left.

**Contact:** Siuslaw National Forest, Central Coast Ranger District, 541/563-8400, www.fs.usda.gov/siuslaw; concessionaire 541/547-3676; Cape Perpetua Visitors Center, 541/547-3289.

## 53 SEA PERCH RV PARK

🚶 🛶 🏠 🚐

### Scenic rating: 8

near Cape Perpetua

**Map 7.3, page 409**

Sea Perch sits right in the middle of one of the most scenic areas on the Oregon coast. This private park just south of Cape Perpetua has sites 75 feet from the beach and lawn areas, plus its own shell museum and gift shop. Surf fishing and windsurfing are options here, or head to Cape Perpetua for whale-watching and tidepooling. Big rigs are welcome here.

**Campsites, facilities:** There are 24 sites with full or partial (20, 30, and 50 amp) hookups for RVs of any length, and five ocean villas. Some sites are pull-through. Picnic tables are provided. Drinking water, restrooms with flush toilets and coin showers, dump station, firewood, coin laundry, ice, convenience store, WiFi, picnic area, horseshoe pit, clubroom with recreation hall, exercise room, kitchen, TV, and a beach are available. Leashed pets are permitted.

**Reservations, fees:** Reservations are accepted. Sites are $50-80 per night, $5 per person per night for more than four, $10 per night for an additional vehicle; villa rates are $125-250 per night. Weekly and monthly rates are available. Some credit cards are accepted. Open year-round.

**Directions:** From Newport and U.S. 101, drive south for 23 miles to Yachats. Continue south on U.S. 101 for 6.5 miles to the campground at Milepost 171 on the right.

**Contact:** Sea Perch RV Park, 541/547-3505, www.seaperchrvpark.com.

## 54 ROCK CREEK

🛶 🏠 🚐 🏕

### Scenic rating: 7

on Rock Creek in Siuslaw National Forest

**Map 7.3, page 409**

This little campground is set along Rock Creek just 0.25 mile from the ocean. It's a premium spot for coastal-highway travelers, although it can get packed very quickly. An excellent side trip is to Cape Perpetua, a designated scenic area a few miles up the coast. The cape offers beautiful ocean views and a visitors center that will supply you with information on nature trails, picnic spots, tidepools, and where to find the best viewpoints in the area.

**Campsites, facilities:** There are 15 sites for tents or RVs up to 22 feet long. Fire grills and picnic tables are provided. Flush toilets, garbage bins, and drinking water are available. Leashed pets are permitted.

**Reservations, fees:** Reservations are accepted at 877/444-6777 or www.recreation.gov ($9-10 reservation fee). Sites are $242 per night, $6 per night per additional vehicle. Open mid-May-September.

**Directions:** From Newport and U.S. 101, drive south for 23 miles to Yachats. Continue south on U.S. 101 for 10 miles to the campground entrance on the left.

**Contact:** Siuslaw National Forest, Waldport Central Coast Ranger District, 541/563-3211 8400 or 541/547-3679 (concessionaire), www.fs.usda.gov/siuslaw.

## 55 CARL G. WASHBURNE STATE PARK

🚶 🚴 🏠 🚐 🏕

### Scenic rating: 7

near Florence

**Map 7.3, page 409**

Even though busy Highway 101 lies right next to Washburne State Park, a bank of native plants shields campers from most road noise, so you hear the roar of the ocean instead of traffic. Sites are spacious, with some abutting China Creek, and elk are frequent visitors. Short hikes lead from the campground to a two-mile-long beach, extensive tidepools along the base of the cliffs, and a three-mile trail to Heceta Head Lighthouse. Just three miles south of the park are the Sea Lion Caves, where an elevator takes visitors down into a cavern for an insider's view of the life of a sea lion.

**Campsites, facilities:** There are 56 sites for tents or RVs up to 45 feet long (full hookups), seven primitive walk-in sites, two yurts, and a hiker/biker camping area. Picnic tables, fire pits, drinking water, garbage bins, and a dump station are provided. Firewood and restrooms with flush toilets and showers are available. Leashed pets are permitted.

**Reservations, fees:** Reservations are not accepted, except for yurts. Sites are $16-26 per night, $4-5 per person per night for hikers/bicyclists, and yurts are $39 per night; $5 per night per additional vehicle. Some credit cards are accepted. Open year-round.

**Directions:** From Florence and U.S. 101, drive north for 12.5 miles to the park entrance road (it is well signed, 10 miles south of the town of Yachats). Turn east and drive a short distance to the park.

**Contact:** Carl G. Washburne State Park, 541/547-3416 or 800/551-6949, www.oregonstateparks.org.

# 56 ALDER DUNE
🏃 🏊 🚲 🐾 🚐 ⛺

### Scenic rating: 7
near Alder Lake in Siuslaw National Forest

**Map 7.3, page 409**

This wooded campground is situated near four lakes—Alder Lake, Dune Lake, Mercer Lake (the largest), and Sutton Lake. A boat launch is available at Sutton Lake. An excellent recreation option is to explore the expansive sand dunes in the area by foot (there is no off-road-vehicle access here). Side trips include the Sea Lion Caves, Darlington State Park, Jessie

M. Honeyman Memorial State Park, and the Indian Forest, just four miles north.

**Campsites, facilities:** There are 38 sites for tents or self-contained RVs (no hookups) up to 62 feet long. Picnic tables and fire grills are provided. Flush toilets, garbage bins, and drinking water are available. Leashed pets are permitted.

**Reservations, fees:** Reservations are accepted May-September at 877/444-6777 or www.recreation.gov ($9-10 reservation fee). Sites are $22 per night, $6 per each additional vehicle. Open year-round, weather permitting.

**Directions:** From Florence and U.S. 101, drive north for eight miles to the campground on the left.

**Contact:** Siuslaw National Forest, Central Coast Ranger District, 541/271-6000, www.fs.usda.gov/siuslaw.

# 57 SUTTON
🏃 🏊 🐾 🚐 ⛺

### Scenic rating: 7
near Sutton Lake in Siuslaw National Forest

**Map 7.3, page 409**

This campground is located adjacent to Sutton Creek, not far from Sutton Lake. Vegetation provides some privacy between sites. Holman Vista on Sutton Beach Road offers a beautiful view of the dunes and ocean. Wading and fishing are both popular. A hiking trail system leads from the camp out to the dunes. There is no off-road-vehicle access here. An alternative camp is Alder Dune to the north.

**Campsites, facilities:** There are 66 sites for tents or RVs up to 30 feet; 20 sites have partial hookups. There are also three group sites; one group site accommodates up to 30 people and two group sites accommodate up to 100 people. Picnic tables and fire grills are provided. Flush toilets, garbage bins, and drinking water are available. A boat ramp is nearby. Leashed pets are permitted.

**Reservations, fees:** Reservations are accepted at 877/444-6777 or www.recreation.

gov ($9-10 reservation fee). Sites are $22-26 per night and $85-130 per night for group sites. Open year-round.

**Directions:** From Eugene, drive west on Highway 126 for 61 miles to Florence and U.S. 101. Turn north on U.S. 101 and drive six miles to Sutton Beach Road (Forest Road 794). Turn left (northwest) and drive 1.5 miles to the campground entrance.

**Contact:** Siuslaw National Forest, Central Coast Ranger District, 541/271-6000, www.fs.usda.gov/siuslaw.

## 58 MAPLE LANE RV PARK AND MARINA
🏃 🎣 � 🐕 🚙 🚐 ⛺

### Scenic rating: 5

on the Siuslaw River

**Map 7.3, page 409**

This park along the shore of the Siuslaw River in Mapleton is close to hiking trails. The general area is surrounded by Siuslaw National Forest land. A U.S. Forest Service map details nearby backcountry side-trip options. Fall is the most popular time of the year here, as it's prime time for salmon fishing on the Siuslaw. Most sites are taken by monthly renters.

**Campsites, facilities:** There are 45 sites with full (30 and 50 amp) hookups for RVs up to 40 feet long, 10 tent sites, and two park models. Some sites are pull-through. Drinking water, restrooms with flush toilets and showers, a coin laundry, cable TV, WiFi, and propane gas are available. A bait and tackle shop is open during the fishing season. Boat docks, moorage, and launching facilities are on-site. A store, café, and ice are nearby. Small leashed pets (under 15 pounds) are permitted.

**Reservations, fees:** Reservations are accepted. RV sites are $30-35 per night, tent sites are $20-25 per night, $5 per night for more than two people, and $10 per night per additional vehicle. Weekly and monthly rates are available. Open year-round.

**Directions:** From Eugene, drive west on Highway 126 for 47 miles to Mapleton. Continue on Highway 126 for 0.25 mile past the business district to the park entrance on the left.

**Contact:** Maple Lane RV Park and Marina, 541/268-4822, www.maplelanervparkand-marina.com.

## 59 HARBOR VISTA COUNTY PARK
🏃 🎣 � 🐕 🚴 ♿ 🚐 ⛺

### Scenic rating: 6

near Florence

**Map 7.4, page 410**

This county park out among the dunes near the entrance to the harbor offers a great lookout point from its observation deck. The park is perched above the North Jetty of the Siuslaw River and encompasses 15 acres. Beach access is one mile away. A number of side trips are available, including to the Sea Lion Caves, Darlington State Park, Jessie M. Honeyman Memorial State Park, and the Indian Forest, just four miles north. Florence also has displays of Native American dwellings and crafts.

**Campsites, facilities:** There are 38 sites with partial hookups for tents or RVs up to 60 feet long. Picnic tables, fire rings, and garbage bins are provided. Restrooms with flush toilets and coin showers, dump station, drinking water, and a playground are available. A camp host is on-site. Some facilities are wheelchair accessible. Leashed pets are permitted.

**Reservations, fees:** Reservations are accepted at 541/682-2000 or www.ecomm.lanecounty.org/parks ($10 reservation fee). Sites are $25-27.50 per night, $7 per night per additional vehicle. Some credit cards are accepted. Open year-round.

**Directions:** From Florence and U.S. 101, drive north for four miles to 35th Street. Turn left and drive one mile to where it dead-ends into Rhododendron Drive. Turn right and drive 1.4 miles to North Jetty Road. Turn left and drive half a block to Harbor Vista Road. Turn left and continue to the campground at 87658 Harbor Vista Road.

Note: Follow these exact directions. Previous visitors to this park taking a different route will discover that part of Harbor Vista Road is now gated.

**Contact:** Harbor Vista County Park, 541/902-2114, www.co.lane.or.us.

## 60 B & E WAYSIDE RV PARK

**Scenic rating: 5**

near Florence

**Map 7.4, page 410**

Adjacent to this landscaped RV park is a 28-unit mobile home park for ages 55 and up. Some sites at the RV park are taken by monthly rentals. Nearby recreation options include two golf courses and a riding stable, two miles away.

**Campsites, facilities:** There are 25 sites with full hookups for RVs of any length. Picnic tables are provided. Restrooms with flush toilets and showers, recreation room, storage sheds, WiFi, and a coin laundry are available. Propane gas, a store, ice, a café, and a restaurant are within two miles. Boat-launching facilities are nearby. Some facilities are wheelchair accessible. Small leashed pets are permitted.

**Reservations, fees:** Reservations are accepted. Sites are $31-33 per night, $2 per person per night for more than two people. Weekly and monthly rates are available. Open year-round.

**Directions:** From Florence and U.S. 101, drive north for 1.8 miles to the park on the right.

**Contact:** B & E Wayside RV Park, 3760 Highway 101, Florence, 541/997-6451, www.bandewaysidervpark.com.

## 61 PORT OF SIUSLAW RV PARK AND MARINA

**Scenic rating: 8**

on the Siuslaw River

**Map 7.4, page 410**    **BEST (**

This public resort can be found along the Siuslaw River in a grassy, urban setting. Anglers with boats will find that the U.S. 101 bridge support pilings make good spots for crabbing, as well as fishing for perch and flounder. A new set of docks with drinking water, electricity, gasoline, security, and a fish-cleaning station are available. The Sea Lion Caves and estuary are a bonus for wildlife lovers, and nearby lakes make swimming and waterskiing a possibility. Golf is within driving distance, and horses can be rented about nine miles away.

**Campsites, facilities:** There are 13 tent sites and 92 sites with full or partial hookups for tents or RVs of any length. Picnic tables are provided. Drinking water, restrooms with flush toilets and showers, cable TV, dump station, coin laundry, WiFi, gazebo, fish-cleaning station, and boat docks are available. A camp host is on site. A café, grocery store, and ice are within one mile. Some facilities are wheelchair accessible. Leashed pets are permitted.

**Reservations, fees:** Reservations are accepted at 541/997-3040 or www.portofsiuslaw.com ($10 reservation fee). Sites are $22-32 per night, $2 per night per additional person, $2 per night per additional vehicle. Weekly and monthly rates available. Some credit cards are accepted. Open year-round.

**Directions:** From Florence and U.S. 101, drive south to Nopal Street. Turn left (east) and drive two blocks to 1st Street. Turn left and drive 0.25 mile to the park at the end of the road.

**Contact:** Port of Siuslaw RV Park and Marina 541/997-3040, www.portofsiuslaw.com.

## 62 JESSIE M. HONEYMAN MEMORIAL STATE PARK

**Scenic rating: 7**

near Cleowax Lake

**Map 7.4, page 410**

This popular state park is within walking distance of the shore of Cleawox Lake and adjacent to the dunes of the Oregon Dunes National

Recreation Area. Dunes stretch for two miles between the park and the ocean. The dunes here are quite impressive, with some reaching to 500 feet. In the winter, the area is open to OHV use. For thrill-seekers, sandboard rentals (for sand-boarding on the dunes) are available in nearby Florence. The two lakes in the park offer facilities for boating, fishing, and swimming. A one-mile hiking trail with access to the dunes is available in the park, and off-road-vehicle trails are nearby in the sand dunes.

**Campsites, facilities:** There are 187 sites for tents or RVs (no hookups) up to 60 feet long, 168 sites with full or partial hookups for RVs, a camping area for hikers and bicyclists, six group tent areas for up to 25 people and 10 vehicles each, and 10 yurts. Picnic tables, garbage bins, and fire grills are provided. Drinking water, restrooms with flush toilets and showers, a dump station, seasonal interpretive programs, a playground, an amphitheater, and firewood are available. A meeting hall and picnic shelters can be reserved. Boat docks and launching facilities are nearby. Some facilities are wheelchair accessible. Leashed pets are permitted.

**Reservations, fees:** Reservations are accepted at 800/452-5687 or www.oregonstateparks.org ($8 reservation fee). Sites are $16-26 per night, $5 per night per additional vehicle, $4-5 per person per night for hikers/bicyclists, $39 per night for yurts, and $76 per night for group sites. Some credit cards are accepted. Open year-round.

**Directions:** From Florence and U.S. 101, drive south for three miles to the park entrance on the west side of the road.

**Contact:** Jessie M. Honeyman Memorial State Park, 541/997-3641 or 800/551-6949, www.oregonstateparks.org.

## 63 LAKESHORE RV PARK

### Scenic rating: 5

on Woahink Lake

Map 7.4, page 410

Here's a prime area for vacationers. This park is set along the shore of Woahink Lake, a popular spot to fish for bass, bluegill, catfish, crappie, perch, and trout. It's adjacent to Jessie M. Honeyman Memorial State Park and the Oregon Dunes National Recreation Area. Off-road-vehicle access to the dunes is four miles northeast and three miles south of the park. Hiking trails through the dunes can be found at Honeyman Memorial State Park. Some sites are filled with monthly rentals.

**Campsites, facilities:** There are 20 sites with full 30-amp hookups for RVs of any length; some are pull-through sites. Picnic tables are provided. Drinking water, restrooms with flush toilets and showers, cable TV, recreation hall, WiFi, storage sheds, boat docks, and a coin laundry are available. A café is within three miles. Leashed pets are permitted.

**Reservations, fees:** Reservations are accepted at 866/240-4269. Sites are $29 per night, $2 per person per night for more than two people. Weekly and monthly rates are available. Open year-round.

**Directions:** From Florence and U.S. 101, drive south for four miles to Milepost 195. The park is on the left (east side of road).

**Contact:** Lakeshore RV Park, 541/997-2741, www.lakeshorerv.com.

## 64 MERCER LAKE RESORT

### Scenic rating: 7

on Mercer Lake

Map 7.4, page 410

This resort is in a forested setting situated above the shore of Mercer Lake, one of a number of lakes that have formed among the ancient dunes in this area. The 375-acre lake has 11 miles of shoreline and numerous coves. Fishing for rainbow trout and largemouth bass in the stocked lake is the most popular activity. A sandy swimming beach is also available, and the ocean is four miles away.

**Campsites, facilities:** There are 10 sites with full or partial hookups for RVs up to 40 feet long and 10 cabins. Some sites are pull-through. Picnic tables are provided. No open fires are allowed. Drinking water, restrooms with flush toilets and showers, dump station, coin laundry, cable TV, convenience store, bait, snacks, and ice are available. Boat docks, launching facilities, and fishing boat rentals are on-site. Leashed pets are permitted.

**Reservations, fees:** Reservations are accepted at 800/355-3633. Sites are $30-45 per night, $5 per night per each additional person, $5 per night per additional vehicle, $5 per night per pet. Some credit cards are accepted. Open year-round.

**Directions:** From Florence and U.S. 101, drive north for five miles to Mercer Lake Road. Turn east and drive just under one mile to Bay Berry Lane. Turn left and drive to the resort.

**Contact:** Mercer Lake Resort, 541/997-3633, www.mlroregon.com.

## 65 CARTER LAKE

### Scenic rating: 9
on Carter Lake in Oregon Dunes National Recreation Area

Map 7.4, page 410                    BEST (

This campground sits on the north shore of Carter Lake, and you can fish almost right from your campsite. Boating and fishing are permitted on this long, narrow lake, which is set among dunes overgrown with vegetation. The nearby Taylor Dunes Trail is a half-mile, wheelchair-accessible trail to the dunes past Taylor Lake. Hiking is allowed in the dunes, but there is no off-road-vehicle access here. If you want off-road access, head north one mile to Siltcoos Road, turn west, and drive 1.3 miles to Driftwood II.

**Campsites, facilities:** There are 22 sites for tents or RVs up to 30 feet long. Some sites are pull-through. Picnic tables, garbage service, and fire pits are provided. Drinking water, flush toilets, and firewood are available. A camp host is on-site. Leashed pets are permitted.

**Reservations, fees:** Reservations are accepted at 877/444-6777 ($10 reservation fee) or www.recreation.gov ($9 reservation fee). Sites are $17-20 per night, $5 per night per additional vehicle. Open May-September.

**Directions:** From Florence and U.S. 101, drive south for 8.5 miles to Forest Road 1084. Turn right on Forest Road 1084 and drive west 200 yards to the camp.

**Contact:** Oregon Dunes National Recreation Area, Visitors Center, 541/271-3611, www.fs.usda.gov/siuslaw.

## 66 DRIFTWOOD II

### Scenic rating: 6
near Siltcoos Lake in Oregon Dunes National Recreation Area

Map 7.4, page 410

Primarily a campground for off-road vehicles, Driftwood II is set near the ocean, but without an ocean view, in the Oregon Dunes National Recreation Area. It has off-road-vehicle access. Several small lakes, the Siltcoos River, and Siltcoos Lake are nearby. Note that ATV use is prohibited between 10pm and 6am.

**Campsites, facilities:** There are 62 sites for tents or RVs up to 59 feet long, including nine pull-through sites. Picnic tables, garbage service, and fire grills are provided at back-in sites but not at the pull-through sites. Drinking water and restrooms with flush toilets and showers are available. Boat docks, launching facilities, and rentals can be found about four miles away on Siltcoos Lake. Some facilities are wheelchair accessible. Leashed pets are permitted.

**Reservations, fees:** Reservations are accepted at 877/444-6777 ($10 reservation fee) or www.recreation.gov ($9 reservation fee); search for "Driftwood". Sites are $20 per night. Open year-round.

**Directions:** From Florence and U.S. 101, drive south for seven miles to Siltcoos Beach Road. Turn right and drive 1.5 miles west to the campground.

**Contact:** Oregon Dunes National Recreation Area, Visitors Center 541/271-6000 or 541/271-3611 www.fs.usda.gov/siuslaw.

## 67 LAGOON

### Scenic rating: 9

near Siltcoos Lake in Oregon Dunes National Recreation Area

**Map 7.4, page 410**

One of several campgrounds in the area, this camp is located along the lagoon, about one mile from Siltcoos Lake and set 0.5 mile inland with access to the Siltcoos River. The Lagoon Trail offers prime wildlife-viewing for marine birds and other aquatic species.

**Campsites, facilities:** There are 41 sites for tents or RVs of any length. Picnic tables, garbage service, and fire grills are provided. Drinking water and flush and vault toilets are available. A camp host is on-site. Boat docks, launching facilities, and rentals are nearby on Siltcoos Lake. A dump station is within five miles. Some facilities are wheelchair accessible. Leashed pets are permitted.

**Reservations, fees:** Reservations are accepted at 877/444-6777 ($10 reservation fee) or www.recreation.gov ($9 reservation fee). Sites are $20 per night. Open year-round.

**Directions:** From Florence and U.S. 101, drive south for seven miles to Siltcoos Beach Road. Turn right on Siltcoos Beach Road and drive west for 1.2 miles to the campground.

**Contact:** Oregon Dunes National Recreation Area, Visitors Center 541/271-6000 or 541/271-3611, www.fs.usda.gov/siuslaw.

## 68 DARLINGS RESORT AND MARINA

### Scenic rating: 7

on Siltcoos Lake

**Map 7.4, page 410**

This park, in a rural area along the north shore of Siltcoos Lake, is adjacent to the extensive Oregon Dunes National Recreation Area. Sites are right on the lake; fish from your picnic table. An access point to the dunes for hikers and off-road vehicles is just across the highway. The lake has a full-service marina. About half the sites are taken by monthly rentals.

**Campsites, facilities:** There are 13 sites with partial hookups for RVs up to 38 feet long. Picnic tables and fire pits are provided. Drinking water, restrooms with flush toilets and showers, firewood, convenience store, deli, cable TV, boat docks, boat rentals, launching facilities, and a coin laundry are available. Some facilities are wheelchair accessible. Leashed pets are permitted.

**Reservations, fees:** Reservations are accepted. Sites are $29-32 per night, $7 per night per additional person, $5 per night per additional vehicle. Off-season and monthly rates are available. Some credit cards are accepted. Open May to November 1.

**Directions:** From Florence and U.S. 101, drive south for five miles to North Beach Road. Turn left (east) and drive 0.25 mile to Darlings Loop Road. Turn right and drive 0.25 mile to the resort.

**Contact:** Darlings Resort and Marina, 541/997-2841, www.darlingsresortrv.com.

## 69 TYEE

### Scenic rating: 6

on the Siltcoos River in Oregon Dunes National Recreation Area

**Map 7.4, page 410**

This wooded campground along the shore of the Siltcoos River provides an alternative to Driftwood II and Lagoon. Fishing is permitted at the nearby lake, where there is a canoe portage trail and a boat ramp. Off-road-vehicle access to the dunes is available from Driftwood II, and there are hiking trails in the area.

**Campsites, facilities:** There are 16 sites for tents or RVs up to 30 feet long. Picnic tables, garbage service, and fire grills are provided. Drinking water and vault toilets are available. A camp host is on-site. A store, boat docks, launching facilities, and rentals are nearby. Leashed pets are permitted.

**Reservations, fees:** Reservations are accepted at 877/444-6777 ($10 reservation fee) or www.recreation.gov ($9 reservation fee). Sites are $17-18.35 per night, $5 per night per each additional vehicle. Open May-September.

**Directions:** From Florence and U.S. 101, drive south for six miles to the Westlake turnoff. Take that exit and continue a short distance to the campground.

**Contact:** Oregon Dunes National Recreation Area, Visitors Center 541/271-6000 or 541/271-3611, www.fs.usda.gov/siuslaw.

## 70 WAXMYRTLE

### Scenic rating: 7

near Siltcoos Lake in Oregon Dunes National Recreation Area

**Map 7.4, page 410**

One of three camps in the immediate vicinity, Waxmyrtle is adjacent to Lagoon and less than a mile from Driftwood II. The camp is near the Siltcoos River and a couple of miles from Siltcoos Lake, a good-sized lake with boating facilities where you can fish. A pleasant hiking trail here meanders through the dunes and along the estuary.

**Campsites, facilities:** There are 57 sites for tents or RVs of any length; some sites are pull-through. Picnic tables, garbage service, and fire grills are provided. Drinking water and flush toilets are available. A camp host is on-site. Boat docks, launching facilities, and rentals are nearby on Siltcoos Lake. Leashed pets are permitted.

**Reservations, fees:** Reservations are accepted at 877/444-6777 ($10 reservation fee) or www.recreation.gov ($9 reservation fee). Sites are $20 per night. Open year-round.

**Directions:** From Florence and U.S. 101,

drive south for seven miles to Siltcoos Beach Road. Turn right and drive 1.3 miles west to the campground.

**Contact:** Oregon Dunes National Recreation Area, Visitors Center 541/271-6000 or 541/271-3611, www.fs.usda.gov/siuslaw.

## 71 TAHKENITCH LANDING

### Scenic rating: 6

near Tahkenitch Lake in Oregon Dunes National Recreation Area

**Map 7.4, page 410**

This camp overlooking Tahkenitch Lake (Lake of Many Fingers) has easy access to excellent fishing.

**Campsites, facilities:** There are 28 sites for tents or RVs up to 40 feet long. Picnic tables, fire grills, and garbage service are provided. There is no drinking water. Vault toilets, boat-launching facilities, and a floating dock are available. A camp host is on-site. Some facilities are wheelchair accessible. Leashed pets are permitted.

**Reservations, fees:** Reservations are accepted at 877/444-6777 ($10 reservation fee) or www.recreation.gov ($9 reservation fee). Sites are $17-19 per night, $5 per night per additional vehicle. Open year-round.

**Directions:** From Florence and U.S. 101, drive south for 14 miles to the campground on the east side of the road.

**Contact:** Oregon Dunes National Recreation Area, Visitors Center 541/271-6000 or 541/271-3611, www.fs.usda.gov/siuslaw.

## 72 TAHKENITCH

### Scenic rating: 7

near Tahkenitch Lake in Oregon Dunes National Recreation Area

**Map 7.4, page 410**

This very pretty campground with dense

vegetation is set in a wooded area across the highway from Tahkenitch Lake, which has numerous coves and backwater areas for fishing. A hiking trail close to the camp goes through the dunes out to the beach, as well as to Threemile Lake. If this camp is full, Tahkenitch Landing provides space nearby.

**Campsites, facilities:** There are 26 sites for tents or RVs up to 30 feet long. Some sites are pull-through. Picnic tables, garbage service, and fire grills are provided. Drinking water, firewood, and flush toilets are available. A camp host is on-site. Boat docks and launching facilities are on the lake across the highway. Some facilities are wheelchair accessible. Leashed pets are permitted.

**Reservations, fees:** Reservations are accepted at 877/444-6777 ($10 reservation fee) or www.recreation.gov ($9 reservation fee). Sites are $17-20 per night, $5 per night per additional vehicle. Open mid-May-September.

**Directions:** From Florence and U.S. 101, drive south for 14 miles. The campground entrance is on the right.

**Contact:** Oregon Dunes National Recreation Area, Visitors Center 541/271-6000 or 541/271-3611, www.fs.usda.gov/siuslaw.

## 73 HALF MOON BAY RV PARK

### Scenic rating: 5

adjacent to Oregon Dunes National Recreation Area at Winchester Bay

Map 7.4, page 410

This Douglas County park offers sport fishing and crabbing, lighthouse tours, and beachcombing. If you're looking for tranquility, however, keep in mind that this campground bills itself as *the* campground for the "off-road enthusiast."

**Campsites, facilities:** There are 45 sites for RVs of any length (no hook-ups) and five group sites for 3-5 RVs each. Picnic tables and fire rings are provided. Drinking water

and vault toilets are available. Leashed pets are permitted.

**Reservations, fees:** Reservations are accepted ($10 reservation fee) at 541/957-7001 or www.co.douglas.or.us/parks. Sites are $23 per night, $5 per night per additional vehicle; the group sites are $60-75 per night. Discounts for Douglas County residents. Some credit cards are accepted. Open year-round.

**Directions:** From Reedsport and U.S. 101, drive south for three miles to Salmon Harbor Drive near Winchester Bay. Turn right (west) and drive one mile to the campground.

**Contact:** Half Moon Bay RV Park, 1645 Salmon Harbor Drive, Winchester Bay, 541/957-7001, www.co.douglas.or.us/parks.

## 74 DISCOVERY POINT RESORT & RV PARK

### Scenic rating: 7

on Winchester Bay

Map 7.4, page 410

This resort sits on the shore of Winchester Bay, adjacent to sandy dunes, in a fishing village near the mouth of the Umpqua River. The park was designed around motor sports, and ATVs are available for rent. It is somewhat noisy, but that's what most people come for.

**Campsites, facilities:** There are five tent sites, 70 sites with full hookups for RVs of any length, 13 cabins, and six condos. Some sites are pull-through. Picnic tables and fire pits are provided at most sites. Restrooms with flush toilets and showers, drinking water, cable TV, convenience store, coin laundry, ice are available. A dump station and propane gas are within one mile. Boat docks and launching facilities are nearby. Leashed pets are permitted.

**Reservations, fees:** Reservations are accepted. RV sites are $31-34 per night, tent sites are $16 per night, condos are $260-275 per night, $7 per night per each additional vehicle. Call for cabin rates. Some credit cards are accepted. Open year-round.

**Directions:** From Reedsport and U.S. 101, drive south for two miles to Winchester Bay and Salmon Harbor Drive. Turn right at Salmon Harbor Drive and proceed west for one mile to the resort on the left.

**Contact:** Discovery Point Resort & RV Park, 541/271-3443, www.discoverypointresort.com; ATV rentals, 541/271-9357.

## 75 WINDY COVE COUNTY PARK

### Scenic rating: 7

adjacent to Salmon Harbor at Winchester Bay

Map 7.4, page 410

This Douglas County park actually comprises two campgrounds, Windy Cove A and B. Set near ocean beaches and sand dunes, both offer a variety of additional recreational opportunities, including an 18-hole golf course, hiking trails, and a lighthouse.

**Campsites, facilities:** There are 94 sites for RVs up to 60 feet long and two cabins. Most sites have full or partial hookups. Picnic tables and fire pits are provided. Drinking water, restrooms with flush toilets and showers, a playground, WiFi, and cable TV are available. Propane gas, dump station, a store, café, and ice are within two miles. Boat docks, launching facilities, boat charters, and rentals are nearby. Some facilities are wheelchair accessible. Leashed pets are permitted.

**Reservations, fees:** Reservations are accepted at 541/957-7001 ($10 reservation fee). Sites are $15-23 per night, $3 per night per additional vehicle, cabins are $70 per night. Discounts for Douglas County residents. Some credit cards are accepted. Windy A campsites are closed in winter, but Windy B and the Windy A cabin are open year-round.

**Directions:** From Reedsport and U.S. 101, drive south for three miles to the Windy Cove exit near Winchester Bay. Take that exit and drive west to the park on the left.

**Contact:** Windy Cove County Park, Windy B, 541/271-5634; Windy A, 541/271-4138, www.co.douglas.or.us/parks.

## 76 UMPQUA LIGHTHOUSE STATE PARK

### Scenic rating: 7

on the Umpqua River

Map 7.4, page 410

This park is located near Lake Marie and less than a mile from Salmon Harbor on Winchester Bay. A one-mile trail circles Lake Marie, and swimming and non-motorized boating are allowed. Near the mouth of the Umpqua River, this unusual area features dunes as high as 500 feet. Hiking trails lead out of the park and into the Oregon Dunes National Recreation Area. The park offers more than two miles of beach access on the ocean and 0.5 mile along the Umpqua River. The adjacent lighthouse is still in operation, and tours are available during the summer season.

**Campsites, facilities:** There are 24 sites for tents or RVs up to 45 feet long (no hookups), 9 sites with partial hookups, 10 sites with full hookups for RVs up to 45 feet long, a hiker/bicyclist camp, two cabins, two rustic yurts, and six deluxe yurts. Picnic tables and fire pits are provided. Drinking water, garbage bins, restrooms with flush toilets and showers, and firewood are available. Boat docks and launching facilities are on the Umpqua River. Leashed pets are permitted; one yurt is pet-friendly.

**Reservations, fees:** Reservations are accepted at 800/452-5687 or www.oregonstateparks.org ($8 reservation fee). Sites are $15-24 per night, $5 per night for an additional vehicle, $5 per person per night for hikers/bikers, $39 per night for cabins, $36-76 per night for rustic yurts, and $45-76 for deluxe yurts. Some credit cards are accepted. Open year-round.

**Directions:** From Reedsport and U.S. 101,

drive south for six miles to Umpqua Light-house Road. Turn right (west) and drive one mile to the park.

**Contact:** Umpqua Lighthouse State Park, 541/271-4118 or 800/551-6949, www.oregonstateparks.org.

## 77 WILLIAM M. TUGMAN STATE PARK

### Scenic rating: 7

on Eel Lake

**Map 7.4, page 410**

This campground is set along the shore of Eel Lake, which offers almost five miles of shoreline for boating, fishing, sailing, and swimming. It's perfect for bass fishing. A boat ramp is available, but there is a 10-mph speed limit for boats. Oregon Dunes National Recreation Area is across the highway. Hiking is available just a few miles north at Umpqua Lighthouse State Park. A developed, 2.5-mile trail along the south end of the lake allows hikers to get away from the developed areas of the park and explore the lake's many outlets.

**Campsites, facilities:** There are 94 sites with partial hookups for tents or RVs up to 50 feet long, a camping area for hikers and bicyclists, and 16 yurts. Drinking water, fire rings, and picnic tables are provided. Restrooms with flush toilets and showers, dump station, firewood, and a picnic shelter are available. Boat docks and launching facilities are nearby. Some facilities are wheelchair accessible. Leashed pets are permitted; eight yurts are pet-friendly.

**Reservations, fees:** Reservations are accepted at 800/452-5687 or www.oregonstateparks.org ($8 reservation fee). Sites are $17-20 per night, $5 per night per additional vehicle, $5 per person per night for hikers/bicyclists, and $39 per night for yurts. Some credit cards are accepted. Open year-round.

**Directions:** From Reedsport and U.S. 101, drive south for eight miles to the park entrance on the left (east side of the road).

**Contact:** Sunset Bay State Park, 541/271-4118 or 800/551-6949, www.oregonstateparks.org.

## 78 TENMILE LAKE COUNTY PARK

### Scenic rating: 5

on Tenmile Lake in Lakeside

**Map 7.4, page 410**

Set on the shore of Tenmile Lake, this campground draws anglers eager to fish for rainbow and cutthroat trout, largemouth bass, and catfish. Waterskiing, wakeboarding, and sailing are other recreation options.

**Campsites, facilities:** There are 45 sites for RVs with partial hookups. Picnic tables and fire pits are provided. Drinking water, restrooms with showers and flush toilets, a dump station, fish-cleaning station, fishing dock, boat launch facilities, swimming and wading beach, horseshoe pits, and a reservable picnic shelter are available. Some facilities are wheelchair accessible. Leashed pets are permitted.

**Reservations, fees:** Reservations are accepted at 541/396-7755. Sites are $25-27 per night, $5 per night per additional vehicle. Some credit cards are accepted. Open year-round.

**Directions:** In Coos Bay, take Highway 101 north for 14 miles to Airport Way. Turn right on Airport Way and drive 0.5 mile to N. 8th Street. Turn right on N. 8th Street and drive a short distance to Park Avenue. Turn left on Park Avenue. The park entrance will be on the left.

**Contact:** Tenmile Lake County Park, 170 S. 12th St., Lakeside, 541/396-7759, www.co.coos.or.us.

## 79 NORTH LAKE RESORT AND MARINA

**Scenic rating: 8**

on Tenmile Lake

**Map 7.4, page 410**

This 40-acre resort along the shore of Tenmile Lake is wooded and secluded, has a private beach, and makes the perfect layover spot for U.S. 101 travelers. The lake has a full-service marina, and bass fishing can be good here. About 25 percent of the sites are taken by summer season rentals.

**Campsites, facilities:** There are 24 tent sites and 75 sites with full or partial hookups for RVs of any length. Picnic tables are provided and most sites have fire pits. Restrooms with flush toilets and coin showers, dump station, firewood, convenience store, ice, WiFi, cable TV, drinking water, coin laundry, horseshoe pits, and a volleyball court are available. Boat docks, launching facilities, a fish-cleaning station, and a marina are also available. A café and boat rentals are nearby. Some facilities are wheelchair accessible. Leashed pets are permitted.

**Reservations, fees:** Reservations are accepted. Tent sites are $20 per night; RV sites are $29 per night. Some credit cards are accepted. Open April-October.

**Directions:** From Reedsport and U.S. 101, drive south on U.S. 101 for 11 miles to the Lakeside exit. Take that exit east into town for 0.75 mile (across the railroad tracks) to North Lake Road. Turn left (north) and drive 0.5 mile to the resort on the left.

**Contact:** North Lake Resort and Marina, 541/759-3515, www.northlakeresort.com.

## 80 OSPREY POINT RV RESORT

**Scenic rating: 7**

on Tenmile Lake

**Map 7.4, page 410**

Tenmile is one of Oregon's premier bass fishing lakes and yet is located only three miles from the ocean. The resort is situated in a large, open area adjacent to Tenmile Lake and 0.5 mile from North Lake. A navigable canal connects the lakes. The Oregon Dunes National Recreation Area provides nearby hiking trails, and Elliot State Forest offers wooded trails. With weekend barbecues and occasional live entertainment, Osprey Point is more a destination resort than an overnight stop.

**Campsites, facilities:** There are 132 sites for tents or RVs of any size (full hookups), a grassy area for tents, and five park-model cabins. Picnic tables and fire pits are provided. Drinking water, restrooms with flush toilets and showers, cable TV, WiFi, dump station, coin laundry, restaurant, cocktail lounge, convenience store, full-service marina with boat rentals, boat docks, launch, fishing pier, fish-cleaning station, horseshoe pits, volleyball, tetherball, recreation hall, video arcade, and a pizza parlor are available. Leashed pets are permitted.

**Reservations, fees:** Reservations are accepted. RV sites are $36-47 per night, tent sites are $25 per night, $4 per person per night for more than two people, $3.50 per night per extra vehicle. Monthly and off-season rates are available. Some credit cards are accepted. Open year-round.

**Directions:** From Reedport, drive north on U.S. 101 for 11 miles to the Lakeside exit. Take that exit east into town for 0.75 mile (across the railroad tracks) to North Lake Road. Turn left (north) on North Lake Road and drive 0.5 mile to the resort on the right.

**Contact:** Osprey Point RV Resort, 541/759-2801, www.ospreypoint.net.

## 81 EEL CREEK

**Scenic rating: 8**

near Eel Lake in Oregon Dunes National
Recreation Area

**Map 7.4, page 410**

This campground along Eel Creek is located
near both Eel and Tenmile Lakes. Although
Tenmile Lake allows waterskiing, Eel Lake
does not. Nearby trails offer access to the
Umpqua Dunes Scenic Area, where you'll
find spectacular scenery in an area closed to
off-road vehicles. Off-road access is available
at Spinreel.

**Campsites, facilities:** There are 38 sites, including one double site, for tents or RVs up
to 50 feet long. Some sites are pull-through.
Picnic tables, garbage service, and fire grills are
provided. Drinking water, flush toilets, and
firewood are available. A camp host is on-site.
Boat docks, launching facilities, and rentals are
nearby. Leashed pets are permitted.

**Reservations, fees:** Reservations are accepted at 877/444-6777 ($10 reservation fee)
or www.recreation.gov ($9 reservation fee).
Sites are $20 per night, the double site is $40
per night, $5 per night per additional vehicle.
Open mid-May-September.

**Directions:** From Reedsport and U.S. 101,
drive south for 10.5 miles to the park entrance.

**Contact:** Oregon Dunes National Recreation Area, Visitors Center 541/271-6000 or
541/271-3611, www.fs.usda.gov/siuslaw.

## 82 SPINREEL

**Scenic rating: 6**

on Tenmile Creek in Oregon Dunes National
Recreation Area

**Map 7.4, page 410**

Spinreel campground is set several miles inland
at the outlet of Tenmile Lake in the Oregon
Dunes National Recreation Area. A boat
launch (for drift boats and canoes) is near the
camp. Primarily for off-road-vehicle enthusiasts, Spinreel's other recreational opportunities include hiking trails and off-road-vehicle
access to the dunes. Off-road-vehicle rentals
are available adjacent to the camp.

**Campsites, facilities:** There are 37 sites for
tents or RVs up to 61 feet long. Picnic tables
and fire grills are provided. Drinking water,
garbage service, and flush toilets are available.
Firewood, store, ATV rentals, and a coin laundry are nearby. Boat docks, launching facilities, and rentals are on Tenmile Lake. Some
facilities are wheelchair accessible. Leashed
pets are permitted.

**Reservations, fees:** Reservations are accepted
at 877/444-6777 ($10 reservation fee) or www.
recreation.gov ($9 reservation fee). Sites are
$20 per night. Open year-round.

**Directions:** From Coos Bay, drive north on
U.S. 101 for 10 miles to the campground entrance road (well signed). Turn northwest and
drive one mile to the campground.

**Contact:** Oregon Dunes National Recreation Area, Visitors Center 541/271-6000 or
541/271-3611, www.fs.usda.gov/siuslaw.

## 83 LOON LAKE RECREATION AREA

**Scenic rating: 8**

on Loon Lake

**Map 7.4, page 410**          **BEST (**

Loon Lake was created 1,400 years ago when a
nearby mountain crumbled and slid downhill,
damming a creek with house-sized boulders.
Today, the lake is half a mile wide and nearly
two miles long, covers 260 acres, and is more
than 100 feet deep in places. Its ideal location provides a warm, wind-sheltered summer
climate for various water activities. A nature
trail leads to a waterfall about half a mile away.
Evening interpretive programs are held during
summer weekends.

**Campsites, facilities:** There are 52 sites for
tents or RVs up to 35 feet; some double sites

that can accommodate up to 12 people. Picnic tables and fire pits are provided. Drinking water, restrooms with flush toilets and showers, garbage bins, basketball court, firewood, playground, horseshoe pits, fish-cleaning station, a sand beach, and a boat ramp are available. Some facilities are wheelchair accessible, including the fishing pier. Leashed pets are permitted in the campground, but not on the beach or in the day-use area.

**Reservations, fees:** Reservations are accepted at 877/444-6777 ($10 reservation fee) or www.recreation.gov ($9 reservation fee). Sites are $18 per night, $7 per night per additional vehicle, and $36 per night for group sites. Open late May-September, weather permitting.

**Directions:** From Eugene, drive south on I-5 to Exit 162 and Highway 38. Turn west on Highway 38 and drive 43 miles to Milepost 13.5 and the County Road 3 exit. Turn left (south) and drive 7.5 miles to the campground on the right.

**Contact:** Bureau of Land Management, Coos Bay District Office, 541/756-0100 (winter), 541/599-2254 (summer), www.blm.gov /or/ districts/coosbay.

## 84 LOON LAKE LODGE AND RV

🏃 🚵 ⛵ 🎣 🚤 🚐 ⛺

### Scenic rating: 8

on Loon Lake

Map 7.4, page 410

This resort boasts one mile of lake frontage and nestles among the tall trees on pretty Loon Lake. It's not a long drive from either U.S. 101 or I-5, making it an ideal layover spot for travelers eager to get off the highway. The lake offers good bass fishing, boating, swimming, and waterskiing.

**Campsites, facilities:** There are 24 tent sites, 40 sites with full or partial hookups for tents or RVs up to 40 feet long, four group sites for up to 20-30 people each, 10 cabins, a lake-front house, four yurts, and a six-unit motel. Some RV sites

are pull-through. Picnic tables and fire rings are provided. Pit toilets, flush toilets, showers, and drinking water are available. A general store with deli, WiFi, cable TV, firewood, ice, gasoline and propane, beach access, boat ramp, dock, marina, and boat rentals are also available. Leashed pets are permitted, with certain restrictions.

**Reservations, fees:** Reservations are accepted. Tent sites are $24-38 per night, RV sites are $38-45 per night, $7 per person per night for more than five, $5 per night per additional vehicle. Weekly and monthly rates are available. Some credit cards are accepted. Open April 1 to November 1.

**Directions:** From Eugene, drive south on I-5 to Exit 162 and Highway 38. Turn west on Highway 38 and drive 20 miles through the town of Elkton. Continue on Highway 38 for another 22 miles until you cross a large bridge and reach Loon Lake Road. Turn left at Loon Lake Road and drive nine miles to the resort.

**Contact:** Loon Lake Lodge and RV Resort, 541/599-2244, www.loonlakerv.com.

## 85 EAGLEVIEW GROUP CAMPGROUND

🏊 ⛵ 🐾 🦽 🚐 ⛺

### Scenic rating: 5

on the Umpqua River

Map 7.4, page 410

In a canyon surrounded by deep forest, this lovely spot along the Umpqua River is perfectly suited for weddings, family reunions, and group outings or retreats.

**Campsites, facilities:** There are 10 sites that can accommodate up to 100 people in tents or RVs. Picnic tables and fire grills and are provided. Drinking water, garbage service, vault toilets, a dump station, river access, horseshoe pits, a group area with a large fire pit, and a large covered pavilion are available. A grassy area invites games of croquet, bocce ball, or Frisbee. A camp host is on-site. Some facilities are wheelchair accessible. Leashed pets are permitted.

**Reservations, fees:** Reservations are required at 877/444-6777 ($10 reservation fee) or www. recreation.gov ($9 reservation fee). The site is $130 per night. Open May 10-September 30.

**Directions:** From Roseburg, drive north on I-5 to Exit 136 and Highway 138. Take that exit and drive west on Highway 138 for 12 miles. Cross Bullock Bridge and immediately turn right onto Bullock Road/County Road 57. Drive one mile to Eagleview Campground on the right.

GPS Coordinates: 43.497363, -123.4927

**Contact:** Bureau of Land Management, Roseburg District, 541/440-4930, www.blm.gov/or/districts/roseburg.

## 86 TYEE

### Scenic rating: 7

on the Umpqua River

**Map 7.4, page 410**

Here's a classic spot along the Umpqua River with great salmon, smallmouth bass, and steelhead fishing in season. Boat launches are available a few miles upstream and downstream of the campground. Eagleview Group camp, a BLM campground, is one mile away.

**Campsites, facilities:** There are 15 sites for tents or RVs up to 70 feet long. Picnic tables and fire grills are provided. Drinking water, garbage service, vault toilets, river access, a day-use area with horseshoe pits, and a pavilion are available. A camp host is on-site. A store is within one mile. Some facilities are wheelchair accessible. Leashed pets are permitted.

**Reservations, fees:** Reservations are not accepted. Sites are $10 per night, $4 per night for each additional vehicle. Open late March-mid-November.

**Directions:** From Roseburg, drive north on I-5 to Exit 136 and Highway 138. Take that exit and drive west on Highway 138 for 12 miles. Cross Bullock Bridge and continue to County Road 57. Turn right and drive 0.5 mile to the campground entrance.

**Contact:** Bureau of Land Management, Roseburg District, 541/440-4930, www.blm.gov/or/districts/roseburg.

## 87 RILEY RANCH COUNTY PARK

### Scenic rating: 5

on Butterfield Lake near Oregon Dunes National Recreation Area

**Map 7.4, page 410**

This 135-acre campground, located right next door to Oregon Dunes National Recreation Area, provides access to an Off-Highway Vehicle area. ATVs and equestrian groups are both welcome here and plans are afoot for an ATV learning center. Butterfield Lake offers anglers in non-motorized boats the chance for trout, bass, and crappie.

**Campsites, facilities:** There are 90 sites with partial hookups for RVs and two camping cabins. Picnic tables and fire pits are provided. Drinking water, restrooms with showers and flush toilets, fishing dock, boat launch facilities, swimming and wading beach, horseshoe pits are available. A camp host is on site and a dump station is four miles away. Some facilities are wheelchair accessible. Leashed pets are permitted.

**Reservations, fees:** Reservations are accepted at 541/396-7755. Sites are $30-32 per night, $5 per night per additional vehicle. Some credit cards are accepted. Open year-round.

**Directions:** Riley Ranch County Park is four miles south of Tenmile County Park at Milepost 227 on Highway 101.

**Contact:** Riley Ranch Park, 93507 Riley Ranch Lane, North Bend, 541/396-7759, www.co.coos.or.us.

## 88 OREGON DUNES KOA

### Scenic rating: 5

north of North Bend, next to the Oregon Dunes National Recreation Area

**Map 7.4, page 410**

This ATV-friendly park was winner of KOA Founder's and President's Award for 2013. It has direct access to Oregon Dunes National Recreation Area, which offers miles of ATV trails. The fairly open campground features a landscape of grass, young trees, and a small lake. The ocean is a 15-minute drive away. Mill Casino is about six miles south on U.S. 101. Freshwater and ocean fishing are nearby. A golf course is about five miles away.

**Campsites, facilities:** There are 62 sites for tents or RVs of any size (full hookups), six tent sites, nine camping cabins, and three deluxe cabins. Most sites are pull-through, and 30- and 50-amp service is available. Picnic tables and fire pits are provided for RV sites. Drinking water, restrooms with flush toilets and showers, WiFi, cable TV, coin laundry, convenience store, game room, playground, seasonal organized activities, firewood, propane gas, horseshoe pits, and a picnic shelter are available. ATV rentals are nearby. Some facilities are wheelchair accessible. Leashed pets are permitted, except in cabins.

**Reservations, fees:** Reservations are accepted at 800/562-4236. Tent sites are $20-32 per night, RV sites are $30-65 per night, and it costs $3.50-5 per person per night for more than two people and $4.50 per night per additional vehicle. Some credit cards are accepted. Open year-round.

**Directions:** From Coos Bay, drive north on U.S. 101 past North Bend for nine miles to Milepost 229. The campground entrance road is on the left.

**Contact:** Oregon Dunes KOA, 541/756-4851, www.oregonduneskoa.com.

## 89 WILD MARE HORSE CAMP

### Scenic rating: 7

in Oregon Dunes National Recreation Area

**Map 7.4, page 410**

This horse camp has paved parking, with single and double corrals. No off-road vehicles are allowed within the campground. Horses can be ridden straight out into the dunes and to the ocean; they cannot be ridden on developed trails, such as Bluebill Lake Trail. The heavily treed shoreline gives rise to treed sites with some bushes.

**Campsites, facilities:** There are 11 horse campsites for tents or RVs up to 61 feet long. There is a maximum of two vehicles per site. Picnic tables and fire pits are provided. Drinking water, vault toilets, 12 corrals, and garbage bins are available. Leashed pets are permitted.

**Reservations, fees:** Reservations are accepted at 877/444-6777 ($10 reservation fee) or www.recreation.gov ($9 reservation fee). Sites are $20 per night. Some credit cards are accepted. Open year-round.

**Directions:** From Coos Bay, drive north on U.S. 101 for 1.5 miles to Horsfall Dunes and Beach Access Road. Turn left and drive west for one mile to the campground access road. Turn right and drive 0.75 mile to the campground on the left.

**Contact:** Oregon Dunes National Recreation Area, Visitors Center 541/271-6000 or 541/271-3611, www.fs.usda.gov/siuslaw.

## 90 BLUEBILL

### Scenic rating: 6

on Bluebill Lake in Oregon Dunes National Recreation Area

**Map 7.4, page 410**

This campground gets very little camping pressure, although there are some good hiking trails available. It's located next to little Bluebill Lake, which sometimes dries up during the summer. A one-mile trail goes around the lakebed. The camp is a short distance from Horsfall Lake, which is surrounded by private property. If you continue west on the forest road, you'll come to a picnicking and parking area near the beach. This spot provides off-road-vehicle access to the dunes at the Horsfall day-use area and Horsfall Beach.

**Campsites, facilities:** There are 19 sites for tents or RVs of any length. Picnic tables, garbage service, and fire grills are provided. Vault toilets and drinking water are available. A camp host is on site. Leashed pets are permitted.

**Reservations, fees:** Reservations are accepted at 877/444-6777 ($10 reservation fee) or www. recreation.gov ($9 reservation fee). Sites are $20 per night. Open April-September.

**Directions:** From Coos Bay, drive north on U.S. 101 for 1.5 miles north to Horsfall Dunes and Beach Access Road. Turn west and drive one mile to Horsfall Road. Turn northwest and drive two miles to the campground entrance.

**Contact:** Oregon Dunes National Recreation Area, Visitors Center 541/271-6000 or 541/271-3611, www.fs.usda.gov/siuslaw.

# 91 HORSFALL

## Scenic rating: 4
in Oregon Dunes National Recreation Area

**Map 7.4, page 410**

Horsfall campground is actually a nice, large paved area for parking RVs; it's the staging area for off-road-vehicle access into the southern section of Oregon Dunes National Recreation Area. If Horsfall is full, try nearby Horsfall Beach, an overflow area with 34 tent and RV sites.

**Campsites, facilities:** There are 102 sites for RVs up to 52 feet long. Picnic tables and fire rings are provided. Drinking water, garbage service, restrooms with flush toilets and coin showers are available. Some facilities are wheelchair accessible. Leashed pets are permitted.

**Reservations, fees:** Reservations are accepted at 877/444-6777 ($10 reservation fee) or www. recreation.gov ($9 reservation fee). Sites are $20 per night. Open year-round.

**Directions:** From Coos Bay, drive north on U.S. 101 for 1.5 miles to Horsfall Road. Turn west on Horsfall Road and drive about one mile to the campground access road. Turn on the campground access road (well signed) and drive 0.5 mile to the campground.

**Contact:** Oregon Dunes National Recreation Area, Visitors Center 541/271-6000 541/271-3611, www.fs.usda.gov/siuslaw.

# 92 SUNSET BAY STATE PARK

## Scenic rating: 8
near Sunset Bay

**Map 7.4, page 410**

Scenic Sunset Bay sits on the beautiful Oregon Coast, amid coastal forest and headlands. The sandy beach is secluded, protected by cliffs and conifers, and tidepooling is a popular activity. A series of hiking trails leads to Shore Acres and Cape Arago Parks. Clamming and fishing is available in nearby Charleston. Golfing and swimming are some of the recreation options here.

**Campsites, facilities:** There are 66 sites for tents or self-contained RVs, 63 sites with full or partial hookups for tents or RVs up to 47 feet long, a separate area for hikers and bicyclists, eight yurts, and two group camps for up to 25 and 250 people, respectively. Drinking water, picnic tables, garbage bins, and fire grills are provided. Restrooms with flush toilets and showers, a fish-cleaning station, boat ramp, and firewood are available. A camp host is on-site. A gazebo and meeting hall can be reserved at nearby Shore Acres. A restaurant is within three miles. Some facilities are wheelchair accessible. Leashed pets are permitted, except in yurts; one yurt is pet friendly.

**Reservations, fees:** Reservations are accepted at 800/452-5687 or www.oregonstateparks.

org ($8 reservation fee). Sites are $15-24 per night, $5 per night per additional vehicle, $5 per person per night for hikers/bicyclists, $36 per night for yurts, $71 per night for group camps, and $3 per person per night for more than 25 people. Some credit cards are accepted. Open year-round.

**Directions:** In Coos Bay, take the Charleston/State Parks exit to Empire Coos Bay Highway. Drive west to Newmark Avenue. Bear left and continue to Cape Arago Highway. Turn left and drive about five miles south to Charleston and cross the South Slough Bridge. Continue on Cape Arago Highway about three miles to the park entrance on the left.

**Contact:** Sunset Bay State Park, 541/888-3778 x221 or 800/551-6949, www.oregonstateparks.org.

## 93 BASTENDORFF BEACH PARK

**Scenic rating: 8**

near Cape Arago State Park

**Map 7.4, page 410**

This campground is surrounded by large trees and provides access to the ocean and a small lake. Nearby activities include boating, clamming, crabbing, dune buggy riding, fishing, golfing, swimming, and whale-watching. Swimmers should be aware of undertows and sneaker waves. Horses may be rented near Bandon. A nice side trip is to Shore Acres State Park and Botanical Gardens, about 2.5 miles away.

**Campsites, facilities:** There are 25 tent sites, 74 sites with partial hookups for tents or RVs (of any length), and two cabins. An 18-site group camp is also available. Picnic tables and fire pits are provided. Drinking water, restrooms with flush toilets and coin showers, and two dump stations are available. A fish-cleaning station, horseshoe pits, playground, basketball courts, a softball/volleyball lawn, and a picnic area are also available. Some

facilities are wheelchair accessible. Leashed pets are permitted.

**Reservations, fees:** Reservations are accepted for groups, cabins, and the picnic area at 541/396-7755 ($12 reservation fee) or online; individual campsites can be reserved only online. RV sites are $24-26 per night, tent sites are $16-18 per night, $5 per night per additional vehicle, group camping is $144-184 per night for the first six units and $24-26 per night for each additional unit. Cabins are $35 per night. Winter rates are lower. Some credit cards are accepted. Open year-round.

**Directions:** In Coos Bay, take the Charleston/State Parks exit to Empire Coos Bay Highway. Drive west to Newmark Avenue. Bear left and continue to Cape Arago Highway. Turn left and drive about five miles south to Charleston and cross the South Slough Bridge. Continue on Cape Arago Highway for 1.25 miles to the park entrance.

**Contact:** Bastendorff Beach Park, 541/396-7759, www.co.coos.co.or.us.

## 94 CHARLESTON MARINA RV PARK

**Scenic rating: 7**

on Coos Bay

**Map 7.4, page 410**

This large, developed public park and marina is located near Charleston on the Pacific Ocean. Recreational activities in and near the campground include boating, clamming, crabbing, fishing (halibut, salmon, and tuna), hiking, huckleberry and blackberry picking, and swimming.

**Campsites, facilities:** There are 100 sites for tents or RVs up to 50 feet long (full hookups), six tent sites, and three yurts. Picnic tables are provided. No open fires are allowed. Drinking water, satellite TV, WiFi, restrooms with showers, dump station, coin laundry, playground, fish-cleaning station, crab-cooking facilities, and propane gas are available. A marina with a boarding dock and launch ramp are on-site. Some facilities are wheelchair accessible. Leashed pets are permitted.

**Reservations, fees:** Reservations are accepted at 541/888-9512 or rvpark@charlestonmarina.com. RV sites are $26-29 per night, tent sites are $15 per night, and yurts are $40 per night, $1 per night per additional vehicle. Weekly and monthly rates are available. Some credit cards are accepted. Open year-round.

**Directions:** In Coos Bay, take the Charleston/State Parks exit to Empire Coos Bay Highway. Drive west to Newmark Avenue. Bear left and continue to Cape Arago Highway. Turn left and drive about five miles south to Charleston and cross the South Slough Bridge. Continue to Boat Basin Drive. Turn right and drive 0.2 mile to Kingfisher Drive. Turn right and drive 200 feet to the campground on the left.

**Contact:** Charleston Marina RV Park, 541/888-9512, www.charlestonmarina.com.

## 95 BULLARDS BEACH STATE PARK

### Scenic rating: 7

on the Coquille River

**Map 7.4, page 410**

The Coquille River, which has good fishing in season for both boaters and crabbers, is the centerpiece of this park with four miles of shore access. If fishing is not your thing, the park also has several hiking trails. The Coquille River Lighthouse is at the end of the road that wanders through the park; during the summer, there are tours to the tower. Equestrians can explore the seven-mile horse trail.

**Campsites, facilities:** There are 185 sites with full or partial hookups for tents or RVs up to 64 feet long, a hiker/bicyclist camping area, a primitive horse camp with eight sites and three corrals, and 13 yurts. Drinking water, garbage bins, picnic tables, and fire grills are provided. Restrooms with flush toilets and showers, dump station, playground, firewood,

a yurt meeting hall, and picnic shelters are available. Boat docks and launching facilities are in the park on the Coquille River. Some facilities are wheelchair accessible. Leashed pets are permitted; one yurt is pet friendly.

**Reservations, fees:** Reservations are accepted at 800/452-5687 or www.oregonstateparks.org ($8 reservation fee). Sites are $20-24 per night, $5 per vehicle per night, $5 per person per night for hikers/bicyclists, and yurts are $36 per night. Horse camping is $15-19 per night. Some credit cards are accepted. Open year-round.

**Directions:** In Coos Bay, drive south on U.S. 101 for about 22 miles to the park on the right (west side of road), two miles north of Bandon.

**Contact:** Bullards Beach State Park, 541/347-3501 (May-Sept.) or 800/551-6949 (Oct.-Apr.), www.oregonstateparks.org.

## 96 BANDON RV PARK

### Scenic rating: 6

near Bullards Beach State Park

**Map 7.4, page 410**

This in-town RV park is a good base for many adventures. Some sites are filled with renters, primarily anglers, for the summer season. Rock hounds will enjoy combing for agates and other semiprecious stones hidden along the beaches, while kids can explore the West Coast Game Park Walk-Through Safari petting zoo seven miles south of town. Bandon State Park, four miles south of town, has a nice wading spot in the creek at the north end of the park. Nearby recreation opportunities include two 18-hole golf courses, a riding stable, and tennis courts. Bullards Beach is about 2.5 miles north. Nice folks run this place.

**Campsites, facilities:** There are 45 sites with full hookups for RVs of any length; some are pull-through sites. Picnic tables are provided at most sites. No open fires are allowed. Restrooms with flush toilets and showers, cable TV, WiFi, and a coin laundry are available.

Propane gas and a store are within two blocks. Boat docks and launching facilities are nearby. Some facilities are wheelchair accessible. Leashed pets are permitted.

**Reservations, fees:** Reservations are accepted. Sites are $32 per night, $2 per person per night for more than two people. Monthly rates are available. Some credit cards are accepted. Open year-round.

**Directions:** From Coos Bay, drive south on U.S. 101 for 26 miles to Bandon and the Highway 42S junction. Continue south on U.S. 101 for one block to the park (located on the right at 935 2nd Street Southeast).

**Contact:** Bandon RV Park, 541/347-4122, www.bandonrvpark.com.

## 97 LAVERNE AND WEST LAVERNE GROUP CAMP

**Scenic rating: 9**

in Fairview on the north fork of the Coquille River

**Map 7.4, page 410**

This beautiful, 350-acre park sits on a river with a small waterfall and many trees, including a myrtle grove and old-growth Douglas fir. Mountain bikers can take an old wagon road, and golfers can enjoy any of several courses. There are a few hiking trails and a very popular swimming hole. You can fish for salmon, steelhead, and trout, and the wildlife includes bears, cougars, deer, elk, and raccoons. You can take a side trip to the museums at Myrtle Point and Coos Bay, which display local indigenous items, or an old stagecoach house in Dora.

**Campsites, facilities:** There are 30 tent sites and 46 RV sites with partial hookups for RVs of any length at Laverne. One cabin is also available. There is a large group site at West Laverne B that includes 22 RV sites with partial hookups and an overflow area for dry camping. Picnic tables and fire pits are provided. Drinking water, restrooms with flush toilets and coin showers, garbage bins, dump

station, ice, playground, a picnic area that can be reserved, swimming hole (unsupervised), horseshoe pits, and volleyball and softball areas are available. A restaurant is within 1.5 miles. Propane gas, a store, and gasoline are within five miles. Some facilities are wheelchair accessible. Leashed pets are permitted.

**Reservations, fees:** Reservations are accepted for the group site and cabin ($12 reservation fee) at 541/396-7755 or online; individual campsites can be reserved only online. RV sites are $16-18 per night, tent sites are $11-13 per night, $5 per night per each additional vehicle. The group site is $105-140 per night for the first six camping units, plus $16-18 per night for each additional unit. The cabin is $35 per night. Some credit cards are accepted. Open year-round.

**Directions:** From Coos Bay, drive south on U.S. 101 for six miles to the junction with Highway 42. Turn east and drive 11 miles to Coquille and West Central. Turn left and drive 0.5 mile to Fairview McKinley Road. Turn right and drive eight miles to the Fairview Store. Continue east another five miles (past the store) to the park on the right.

**Contact:** Laverne County Park, Coos County, 541/396-7759, www.co.coos.or.us.

## 98 PARK CREEK

**Scenic rating: 7**

near Coquille

**Map 7.4, page 410**

Want to be by yourself? You came to the right place. This pretty little campground offers peaceful, shady campsites under an old-growth canopy of Douglas fir, myrtle, red cedar, and western hemlock. Relax and enjoy nearby Park Creek and Middle Creek.

**Campsites, facilities:** There are 15 sites for tents or small RVs. Picnic tables and fire grills are provided. Vault toilets are available. There is no drinking water. Leashed pets are permitted.

**Reservations, fees:** Reservations are not accepted. There is no fee for camping. Open mid-May-September 30 with a stay limit of 14 days.

**Directions:** From Coos Bay, drive south on U.S. 101 for six miles to the junction with Highway 42. Turn east and drive 11 miles to Coquille and Coquille Fairview Road. Turn left (east) on Coquille Fairview Road and drive 7.5 miles to Fairview and Coos Bay Wagon Road. Turn right and drive four miles to Middle Creek Access Road. Turn left (east) and drive nine miles to the campground on the right.

**Contact:** Bureau of Land Management, Coos Bay District, 541/756-0100, www.blm.gov/or.

## 99 KOA BANDON/ PORT ORFORD

**Scenic rating: 7**

near the Elk River

Map 7.5, page 411

Winner of the "Best of the Best" award from Trailer Life, this spot is considered just a layover camp, but it offers large, secluded sites nestled among big trees and coastal ferns. A pool and spa are available. During the summer season, a daily pancake breakfast and ice cream social are held. The Elk and Sixes Rivers, where the fishing can be good, are minutes away, and Cape Blanco State Park is just a few miles down the road.

**Campsites, facilities:** There are 46 tent sites and 26 pull-through sites, some with full hookups (20-, 30-, and 50-amp), for RVs of any length. Six cabins are also available. Picnic tables and fire rings are provided. Restrooms with flush toilets and showers, cable TV, WiFi, snack bar, propane gas, dump station, firewood, recreation hall, convenience store, coin laundry, seasonal heated swimming pool, spa, off-leash dog park, horseshoe pits, basketball court, ice, and a playground are available. Leashed pets are permitted.

**Reservations, fees:** Reservations are accepted at 800/562-3298. Sites are $29-40 per night, $3-7 per person per night for more than two people, and $5 per night per additional vehicle. Some credit cards are accepted. Open March-November.

**Directions:** From Bandon, drive south on U.S. 101 for 16 miles to the campground at Milepost 286 near Langlois, on the west side of the highway.

**Contact:** KOA Bandon/Port Orford, 541/348-2358, www.koa.com.

## 100 CAPE BLANCO STATE PARK

**Scenic rating: 8**

between the Sixes and Elk Rivers

Map 7.5, page 411          BEST (

This large park is named for the white (*blanco*) chalk appearance of the sea cliffs here, which rise 200 feet above the ocean. Sea lions inhabit the offshore rocks, and trails and a road lead to the black sand beach below the cliffs. The park offers good fishing access to the Sixes River, which runs for more than two miles through meadows and forests. There are seven miles of trails for horseback riding available and more than eight miles of hiking trails, some with ocean views. Tours of the lighthouse and historic Hughes House are available (Wed.-Mon.).

**Campsites, facilities:** There are 53 sites with partial hookups for tents or RVs up to 65 feet long. Other options include an equestrian camp with eight sites, a hiker/bicyclist camping area, four cabins, and four primitive group sites for tents or RVs for up to 25 people. Garbage bins, picnic tables, drinking water, and fire grills are provided. Firewood and restrooms with flush toilets and showers are available. Some facilities are wheelchair accessible. Leashed pets are permitted; one cabin is pet friendly.

**Reservations, fees:** Reservations are not accepted for single sites, but are accepted for cabins, the group site, and the horse camp at

800/452-5687 or www.oregonstateparks.org ($8 reservation fee). Single sites are $16-20 per night, $5 per night per additional vehicle. The horse camp is $13-17 per night; the hiker/biker sites are $5 per person per night. The group site is $71 per night for the first 25 people, then $3 per each additional person per night. Some credit cards are accepted. Open year-round.

**Directions:** From Coos Bay, turn south on U.S. 101 and drive approximately 46 miles (south of Sixes, five miles north of Port Orford) to Cape Blanco Road. Turn right (northwest) and drive five miles to the campground on the left.

**Contact:** Humbug Mountain State Park, 541/332-6774 or 800/551-6949, www.oregonstateparks.org. (This park is under the same management as Humbug Mountain State Park.)

## 101 EDSON CREEK CAMPGROUND

### Scenic rating: 6

on the Sixes River

Map 7.5, page 411

This is a popular campground along the banks of the Sixes River. Edson is similar to Sixes River Campground, except it has less tree cover and Sixes River has the benefit of a boat ramp.

**Campsites, facilities:** There are 30 sites for tents or RVs up to 30 feet long, and four group sites for 15-50 people each. Picnic tables and fire grills are provided. Drinking water, vault toilets, garbage service, a boat launch, and a camp host are available. Some facilities are wheelchair accessible. Leashed pets are permitted.

**Reservations, fees:** Reservations are not accepted for single sites but are required for group sites at 541/756-0100. Sites are $8 per night and $4 per night for each additional vehicle, with a 14-day stay limit. Open mid-May-September 30, weather permitting.

**Directions:** From Coos Bay, drive south on U.S. 101 for 40 miles to Sixes and Sixes River Road/County Road 184. Turn left (east) on

Sixes River Road and drive four miles to the campground entrance on the left. It's located before the Edson Creek Bridge.

**Contact:** Bureau of Land Management, Coos Bay District, 541/756-0100 or 541/332-8027, www.blm.gov/or.

## 102 SIXES RIVER

### Scenic rating: 6

on the Sixes River

Map 7.5, page 411

Set along the banks of the Sixes River at an elevation of 4,303 feet, this camp is a favorite of anglers, miners, and nature lovers. There are opportunities to pan or sluice for gold year-round or through a special limited permit. Dredging is permitted from July 15 through September. The camp roads are paved.

**Campsites, facilities:** There are 19 sites for tents or small RVs. Picnic tables and fire grills are provided. Vault toilets are available. Some facilities are wheelchair accessible. A camp host is on site. Leashed pets are permitted.

**Reservations, fees:** Reservations are not accepted. Sites are $8 per night, $4 per night for an additional vehicle, with a 14-day stay limit. Open late-May-September 30.

**Directions:** From Coos Bay, drive south on U.S. 101 for 40 miles to Sixes and Sixes River Road/County Road 184. Turn left (east) on Sixes River Road and drive 11 miles to the campground on the right. The last 0.5 mile is an unpaved road.

**Contact:** Bureau of Land Management, Coos Bay District, 541/756-0100, www.blm.gov/or.

## 103 POWERS COUNTY PARK

### Scenic rating: 9

near the south fork of the Coquille River

Map 7.5, page 411

This private and secluded public park in a

wooded, mountainous area is a great stop for travelers going between I-5 and the coast. A 30-acre lake at the park provides a spot for visitors to boat and fish for trout. The lake is stocked with bass, catfish, crappie, and trout. Only electric boat motors are allowed. Swimming is not recommended because of the algae in the lake. A bike trail is available. On display at the park are an old steam donkey and a hand-carved totem pole. The biggest cedar tree in Oregon is reputed to be about 12 miles away.

**Campsites, facilities:** There are 30 sites for tents or RVs up to 54 feet long and 40 sites with partial hookups (20- and 30-amp). Primitive camping for large groups and three cabins are also available. Picnic tables, fire pits, drinking water, restrooms with flush toilets and showers, a dump station, fish-cleaning station, and picnic shelters are provided. Recreational facilities include a boat ramp, horseshoe pits, playground, basketball and volleyball courts, tennis courts, and a softball field. Supplies are available within one mile. Some facilities are wheelchair accessible. Leashed pets are permitted.

**Reservations, fees:** Reservations ($12 reservation fee) are accepted online for the RV sites; cabins can be reserved online or at 541/396-7755. RV sites are $16-18 per night, tent sites are $11-13 per night, and cabins are $35 per night. The group camp is $80 per night for the first six units and $16-18 per night for each additional unit. Some credit cards are accepted. Open year-round.

**Directions:** From Coos Bay, drive south on U.S. 101 for six miles to the junction with Highway 42. Turn east and drive 20 miles to Myrtle Point. Continue on Highway 42 to the Powers Highway (Highway 242) exit. Turn right (southwest) and drive 19 miles to the park on the right.

**Contact:** Powers County Park, Coos County, 541/439-2791, www.co.coos.or.us/ccpark/.

## 104 ELK RIVER CAMPGROUND

**Scenic rating: 7**

near the Elk River

**Map 7.5, page 411**

This quiet and restful camp makes an excellent base for fall and winter fishing on the Elk River, which is known for its premier salmon fishing. A one-mile private access road goes to the river, so guests get their personal fishing holes. About half of the sites are taken by monthly rentals.

**Campsites, facilities:** There are 50 sites with full hookups for RVs up to 40 feet long; some sites are pull-through. Picnic tables are provided. No open fires are allowed. Drinking water, restrooms with showers, dump station, WiFi, cable TV, and a coin laundry are available. Recreational facilities include a sports field, hall, and a boat ramp. Some facilities are wheelchair accessible. Leashed pets are permitted.

**Reservations, fees:** Reservations are recommended. Sites are $25 per night. Weekly and monthly rates are available. Open year-round.

**Directions:** From Port Orford, drive north on U.S. 101 for 1.5 miles to Elk River Road (Milepost 297). Turn right (east) on Elk River Road and drive 1.8 miles to the campground on the left.

**Contact:** Elk River Campground, 541/332-2255.

## 105 LAIRD LAKE

**Scenic rating: 8**

on Laird Lake in Rogue River-Siskiyou National Forest

**Map 7.5, page 411**            **BEST (**

This secluded campground is set at 1,600 feet elevation, along the shore of pretty Laird Lake (six feet at its deepest point). Some old-growth cedar logs are in the lake. Most campers have no idea such a place exists in the area. This very private and scenic spot can be just what you're looking for if you're tired of fighting the crowds at the more developed camps along U.S. 101.

**Campsites, facilities:** There are four sites for tents or RVs up to 25 feet long. There is no drinking water, and garbage must be packed out. Leashed pets are permitted.

**Reservations, fees:** Reservations are not accepted. There is no fee for camping. Open year-round.

**Directions:** From Port Orford, drive north on U.S. 101 for three miles to County Road 208. Turn right and drive 7.5 miles southeast (the road becomes Forest Road 5325). Continue for 15.5 miles (the road bears to the right when you reach the gravel) to the campground. The road is paved for 11 miles and is gravel for the last 4.5 miles to the campground.

**Contact:** Rogue River-Siskiyou National Forest, Powers Ranger District, 541/439-6200, www.fs.usda.gov/rogue-siskiyou.

## 106 BUTLER BAR

### Scenic rating: 6
on the Elk River in Rogue River-Siskiyou National Forest

**Map 7.5, page 411**

This campground, at an elevation of 800 feet, is set back from the shore of the Elk River and surrounded by old-growth and hardwood forest, with some reforested areas nearby. Across the river is the Grassy Knob Wilderness, which has no trails and is generally too rugged to hike. Check fishing regulations before fishing.

**Campsites, facilities:** There are seven sites for tents. Picnic tables and fire grills are provided. Vault toilets are available. There is no drinking water, but river water may be filtered. Garbage must be packed out. Leashed pets are permitted.

**Reservations, fees:** Reservations are not accepted. There is no fee for camping. Open year-round, weather permitting.

**Directions:** From Port Orford, drive north on

U.S. 101 for three miles to County Road 208. Turn right and drive 7.5 miles southeast (the road becomes Forest Road 5325). Continue for 7.5 miles to the campground. The road is paved.

**Contact:** Rogue River-Siskiyou National Forest, Powers Ranger District, 541/439-6200, www.fs.usda.gov/rogue-siskiyou.

## 107 PORT ORFORD RV VILLAGE

### Scenic rating: 5
near the Elk and Sixes Rivers

**Map 7.5, page 411**

Each evening, an informal group campfire and happy hour enliven this campground. Other nice touches include a small gazebo where you can get free coffee each morning and a patio where you can sit. Fishing is good during the fall and winter on the nearby Elk and Sixes Rivers, and the campground has a smokehouse, freezer, and fish-cleaning station. Some sites here are taken by summer season rentals or permanent residents.

**Campsites, facilities:** There are 47 sites with full or partial hookups for RVs of any length and one rental trailer. Some sites are pull-through. Picnic tables are provided. with flush toilets and showers, propane gas, dump station, horseshoe pits, basketball, recreation hall, WiFi, cable TV, book and video library, fish-cleaning station, crab cooker, and a coin laundry are available. Boat docks and launching facilities are nearby. Lake, river, and ocean are all within 1.5 miles. Leashed pets are permitted.

**Reservations, fees:** Reservations are accepted. Sites are $29 per night, $2 per person per night for more than two people, and $5 per night for additional vehicle. Open year-round.

**Directions:** In Port Orford on U.S. 101, drive to Madrona Avenue. Turn east and drive one block to Port Orford Loop. Turn left (north) and drive 0.5 mile to the camp on the left side.

**Contact:** Port Orford RV Village, 541/332-1041, www.portorfordrv.com.

## 108 HUMBUG MOUNTAIN STATE PARK

🚶 🚲 ⛵ 🐕 👨‍🦽 📷 ⛺

### Scenic rating: 7

near Port Orford

**Map 7.5, page 411**

Humbug Mountain, at 1,756 feet elevation, looms over its namesake state park. Fortunately, this natural guardian affords the campground some of the warmest weather on the coast by blocking cold winds from the ocean. Windsurfing and scuba diving are popular, as is hiking the three-mile trail to Humbug Peak. Both ocean and freshwater fishing are accessible nearby.

**Campsites, facilities:** There are 62 sites for tents or RVs (no hookups), 32 sites with partial hookups for RVs up to 55 feet long, and a hiker/ bicyclist camp. Some sites are pull-through. Fire grills, picnic tables, garbage bins, and drinking water are provided. Firewood and restrooms with flush toilets and showers are available. A camp host is on-site. Some facilities are wheelchair accessible. Leashed pets are permitted.

**Reservations, fees:** Reservations are accepted at 541/332-6774. Sites are $13-20 per night, $5 per night per additional vehicle, and $5 per person per night for hikers/bicyclists. The group camp is $71 per night for up to 25 people, plus $2.40 per person per night for additional persons. Some credit cards are accepted. Open year-round.

**Directions:** From Port Orford, drive south on U.S. 101 for six miles to the park entrance on the left.

**Contact:** Humbug Mountain State Park, 541/332-6774 or 800/551-6949, www.oregonstateparks.org.

## 109 MYRTLE GROVE

🚶 🐕 ⛺

### Scenic rating: 6

on the south fork of the Coquille River in Rogue River-Siskiyou National Forest

**Map 7.5, page 411**

This U.S. Forest Service campground is located along the south fork of the Coquille River, a little downstream from Daphne Grove, at an elevation of 500 feet. No fishing is allowed. Campsites are set under a canopy of big leaf maple and Douglas fir in a narrow, steep canyon. The Big Tree Observation Site, home to a huge Port Orford cedar, is a few miles away. The trail that runs adjacent to Elk Creek provides a prime hike. (The road to Big Tree may be closed because of slides, so be sure to check with the ranger district in advance.)

**Campsites, facilities:** There are five tent sites. Picnic tables and fire grills are provided. Vault toilets and garbage bins are available. There is no drinking water. Leashed pets are permitted.

**Reservations, fees:** Reservations are not accepted. There is no fee for camping. Open year-round.

**Directions:** From Coos Bay, drive south on U.S. 101 for six miles to the junction with Highway 42. Turn east and drive 20 miles to Myrtle Point. Continue on Highway 42 to Powers Highway (Highway 242). Turn right (southwest) and drive 18 miles (the road becomes County Road 90) to Powers. Continue for 4.3 miles (the road becomes Forest Road 33). Turn south and drive to the camp. The road is paved all the way to the camp.

**Contact:** Rogue River-Siskiyou National Forest, Powers Ranger District, 541/439-6200 or 541/439-6217, www.fs.usda.gov/rogue-siskiyou.

## 110 DAPHNE GROVE

🐕 👨‍🦽 📷 ⛺

### Scenic rating: 7

on the south fork of the Coquille River in Rogue River-Siskiyou National Forest

**Map 7.5, page 411**

This prime spot is far enough out of the way to attract little attention. At 1,000 feet elevation, it sits along the south fork of the Coquille River and is surrounded by old-growth cedar, Douglas fir, and maple. No fishing is allowed. The road is paved all the way to, and in, the campground, a plus for RVs and "city cars."

**Campsites, facilities:** There are 14 sites for tents or RVs up to 35 feet long. Picnic tables, garbage bins, and fire grills are provided. Vault toilets are available. There is no drinking water, but river water may be filtered. Some facilities are wheelchair accessible. Leashed pets are permitted.

**Reservations, fees:** Reservations are not accepted. Sites are $6 per night, $3 per night per additional vehicle. Open year-round.

**Directions:** From Coos Bay, drive south on U.S. 101 for six miles to the junction with Highway 42. Turn east and drive 20 miles to Myrtle Point. Continue on Highway 42 to Powers Highway (Highway 242). Turn right (southwest) and drive 18 miles (the road becomes County Road 90) to Powers. Continue for 4.3 miles (the road becomes Forest Road 33). Continue for 10.5 miles to the campground entrance.

**Contact:** Rogue River-Siskiyou National Forest, Powers Ranger District, 541/439-6200, www.fs.usda.gov/rogue-siskiyou.

## 111 ISLAND

### Scenic rating: 7

near Coquille River Falls

**Map 7.5, page 411**

Island Camp is an excellent base camp for hikers with many trailheads nearby. It is located along the south fork of the Coquille River at 1,000-foot elevation in Rogue River-Siskiyou National Forest. Nearby hiking opportunities include the Azalea Lake Trail, Panther Ridge Trail, Coquille River Falls Trail, and Sucker Creek Trail. Note: Do not confuse this Island Campground with the Island Campground in Umpqua National Forest.

**Campsites, facilities:** There are five sites for tents or RVs to 16 feet. Picnic tables and fire rings are provided. Vault toilets and garbage

bins are available, but there is no drinking water. Leashed pets are permitted.

**Reservations, fees:** Reservations are not accepted. Sites are $6 per night. Open year-round, with limited winter services.

**Directions:** From Coos Bay, drive south on U.S. 101 for six miles to the junction with Highway 42. Turn east and drive 20 miles to Myrtle Point. Continue on Highway 42 to Powers Highway (Highway 242). Turn right (southwest) and drive 18 miles (the road becomes County Road 90) to Powers. Drive south 17 miles on Forest Service Road 3300 to the campground.

**Contact:** Rogue River-Siskiyou National Forest, Powers Ranger District, 541/439-6200, www.fs.usda.gov/rogue-siskiyou.

## 112 SRU LAKE

### Scenic rating: 8

on Sru Lake in Rogue River-Siskiyou National Forest

**Map 7.5, page 411**

Sru (pronounced "Shrew") campground is set along the shore of one-acre Sru Lake at 2,200 feet elevation in rich, old-growth forest. Sru is more of a pond than a lake, but it is stocked with trout in the spring. Get there early—the fish are generally gone by midsummer. The trailheads for the Panther Ridge Trail and Coquille River Falls Trail are a 10-minute drive from the campground. It's strongly advised that you obtain a U.S. Forest Service map detailing the backcountry roads and trails.

**Campsites, facilities:** There are six sites for tents or RVs up to 21 feet long. Picnic tables and fire rings are provided. Vault toilets are available. There is no drinking water, and garbage must be packed out. Leashed pets are permitted.

**Reservations, fees:** Reservations are not accepted. There is no fee for camping. Open year-round, weather permitting.

**Directions:** From Coos Bay, drive south on

U.S. 101 for six miles to the junction with Highway 42. Turn east and drive 20 miles to Myrtle Point. Continue on Highway 42 to Powers Highway (Highway 242). Turn right (southwest) and drive 18 miles (the road becomes County Road 90) to Powers. Continue for 4.3 miles (the road becomes Forest Road 33). Continue on Forest Road 33 for 15 miles to the South Fork Coquille River Bridge. Continue on Forest Road 33 for 0.5 mile to Forest Road 3347 (paved road). Turn right and drive one mile to the camp.

**Contact:** Rogue River-Siskiyou National Forest, Powers Ranger District, 541/439-6200, www.fs.usda.gov/rogue-siskiyou.

## 113 TUCKER FLAT

**Scenic rating: 7**

on the Rogue River

**Map 7.5, page 411**

Above the clear waters of Mule Creek, this campground borders the Wild Rogue Wilderness. Tucker Flat offers a trailhead into the Wild Rogue Wilderness and lots of evidence of historic mining. Mosquitoes can be a problem, and bears occasionally wander through. The historic Rogue River Ranch is just 0.25 mile away, and the museum and other buildings are open during the summer. The Rogue River Ranch is on the National Register of Historic Places. There are also scenic bridges along Mule Creek. Tucker Flat campground can also be reached by hiking the Rogue River Trail or by floating the Rogue River and hiking up past the Rogue River Ranch. Campers and hikers are advised to stop by the Medford BLM office for maps.

**Campsites, facilities:** There are six primitive tent sites. Picnic tables and fire grills are provided. Vault toilets and bear-proof trash cans are available. There is no drinking water. Some facilities are wheelchair accessible. Leashed pets are permitted.

**Reservations, fees:** Reservations are not accepted. There is no fee for camping. Open May-October, weather permitting.

**Directions:** From Grants Pass, drive one mile north on I-5 to Exit 61. Take that exit and drive west on Merlin-Galice Access Road for 20 miles to the Grave Creek Bridge (the second bridge over the Rogue River). Cross the bridge and drive a short distance to BLM Road 34-8-1. Turn left and drive 16 miles to BLM Road 32-8-31. Turn left and drive seven miles to BLM Road 32-9-14.2. Turn left and drive 15 miles to the campground (around the bend from the Rogue River Ranch). RV travel is discouraged as the roads are curvy, one-lane, and a combination of paved and gravel.

**Contact:** Bureau of Land Management, Medford District, 541/618-2200, www.blm.gov/or/districts/medford.

## 114 ALMEDA PARK

**Scenic rating: 6**

on the Rogue River

**Map 7.5, page 411**

This rustic park, located along the Rogue River and featuring a grassy area, is popular for rafting and swimming. One of the main put-in points for floating the lower section of the river can be found right here. Fishing is also available. The Rogue River Trail is four miles west.

**Campsites, facilities:** There are 31 sites for tents or RVs of any length (no hookups), two group sites for tents or RVs for up to 30 people, and one yurt. Some sites are pull-through. Picnic tables and fire pits are provided. Drinking water, vault toilets, garbage bins, a dump station, and a boat ramp are available. A seasonal camp host is on-site. Some facilities are wheelchair accessible. Leashed pets are permitted.

**Reservations, fees:** Reservations are accepted ($8 reservation fee) at reserveamerica.com. Sites are $19 per night, $5 per night per additional vehicle, and the yurt is $30 per night. The group sites are $32 per night for up to 12 people, and $6 per person per night for more than 12 people. Cash is the only payment method accepted. Open year-round.

**Directions:** From Grants Pass, drive north on I-5 for 3.5 miles to Exit 61 (Merlin-Galice Road). Take that exit and drive on Merlin-Galice Road for 19 miles to the park on the right. The park is approximately 16 miles west of Merlin.

**Contact:** Josephine County Parks, 541/474-5285, www.co.josephine.or.us/parks/index. htm.

## 115 ROCK CREEK

**Scenic rating: 6**

near the south fork of the Coquille River in Rogue River-Siskiyou National Forest

**Map 7.5, page 411**

This little-known camp (elevation 1,400 feet) in a tree-shaded canyon is surrounded by old-growth forest and some reforested areas. It is set near Rock Creek, just upstream from its confluence with the south fork of the Coquille River. No fishing is allowed. For a good side trip, take the one-mile climb to Azalea Lake, a small, shallow lake where there are some hike-in campsites. In July, the azaleas are spectacular.

**Campsites, facilities:** There are seven sites for tents or RVs up to 16 feet long. Picnic tables and fire grills are provided. Vault toilets, garbage bins, and firewood are available. There is no drinking water, but river water may be filtered. Leashed pets are permitted.

**Reservations, fees:** Reservations are not accepted. Sites are $6 per night, $3 per night per additional vehicle. Open year-round, with limited winter facilities.

**Directions:** From Coos Bay, drive south on U.S. 101 for six miles to the junction with Highway 42. Turn east and drive 20 miles to Myrtle Point. Continue on Highway 42 to Powers Highway (Highway 242). Turn right (southwest) and drive 18 miles (the road becomes County Road 90) to Powers. Continue for 4.3 miles (the road becomes Forest Road 33). Continue on Forest Road 33 for 15 miles to the South Fork Coquille River Bridge. Continue on Forest Road 33 for 0.5 mile to Forest Road 3347 (paved road). Turn right and drive 0.5 mile to the camp.

**Contact:** Rogue River-Siskiyou National Forest, Powers Ranger District, 541/439-6200, www.fs.usda.gov/rogue-siskiyou.

## 116 FOSTER BAR

**Scenic rating: 5**

on the Rogue River in Rogue River-Siskiyou National Forest

**Map 7.5, page 411**

This camping area is set near the banks of the Rogue River. There's a take-out point for rafters. Hiking opportunities are good nearby, and you can also fish from the river bar. Agness RV Park provides a nearby camping alternative.

**Campsites, facilities:** There are eight sites for tents. Drinking water, flush toilets, garbage bins, and boat-launching facilities are available. A camp host is on-site. Leashed pets are permitted.

**Reservations, fees:** Reservations are not accepted. Sites are $5 per night, $3 per night per additional vehicle. Open year-round.

**Directions:** From Gold Beach on U.S. 101, turn east on County Road 595 and drive 35 miles (it becomes Forest Road 33) to the junction for Illahe and Foster Bar. Turn right on County Road 375 and drive five miles to the campground.

**Contact:** Rogue River-Siskiyou National Forest, Gold Beach Ranger District, 541/247-3600, www.fs.usda.gov/rogue-siskiyou.

## 117 HONEY BEAR CAMPGROUND & RV RESORT

**Scenic rating: 10**

near Gold Beach

**Map 7.5, page 411**

This campground offers wooded sites with ocean views. The owners have built a huge, authentic chalet, which contains a German deli, recreation area, and a big dance floor. On summer nights, they hold dances with live music. A restaurant is available on-site with authentic German food. A fishing pond is stocked with trout.

**Campsites, facilities:** There are 20 sites for tents or RVs (no hookups) and 65 sites with full hookups for RVs of any length. Thirty are pull-through sites with full hookups and 15 have patios. Picnic tables and fire rings are provided. Restrooms with flush toilets and showers, drinking water, cable TV, WiFi, dump station, firewood, recreation hall, restaurant and kitchen, convenience store, coin laundry, ice, and a playground are available. Some facilities are wheelchair accessible. Leashed pets are permitted.

**Reservations, fees:** Reservations are accepted at 800/822-4444. RV sites are $33-35 per night, tent sites are $19.95 per night, $3 per person per night for more than two people, and $3 per night per additional vehicle. Monthly and winter rates available. Open year-round, weather permitting.

**Directions:** From Gold Beach, drive north on U.S. 101 for eight miles to Ophir Road near Milepost 321. Turn right and drive two miles to the campground on the right side of the road.

**Contact:** Honey Bear Campground & RV Resort, 541/247-2765, www.honeybearrv.com.

## 118 NESIKA BEACH RV PARK

**Scenic rating: 7**

near Gold Beach

**Map 7.5, page 411**

This RV park next to Nesika Beach is a good layover spot for U.S. 101 cruisers. An 18-hole golf course is close by. There are many long-term rentals here.

**Campsites, facilities:** There are six tent sites and 32 sites with full or partial hookups for RVs of any length; some sites are pull-through. Picnic tables are provided, and some tent sites have fire rings. Drinking water, restrooms with flush toilets and showers, a dump station, convenience store, coin laundry, cable TV, propane, and ice are available. Leashed pets are permitted.

**Reservations, fees:** Reservations are accepted. RV sites are $22-25 per night, tent sites are $15 per night, $1 per person per night for more than two people. Weekly and monthly rates are available. Open year-round.

**Directions:** From Gold Beach, drive north on U.S. 101 for six miles to Nesika Road. Turn left and drive 0.75 mile west to the park on the right.

**Contact:** Nesika Beach RV Park, 541/247-6077, www.nbrvp.com.

## 119 INDIAN CREEK RESORT

**Scenic rating: 7**

on the Rogue River

**Map 7.5, page 411**

This campground is set along the Rogue River on the outskirts of the town of Gold Beach. A few sites have river views. Nearby recreation options include boat trips on the Rogue.

**Campsites, facilities:** There are 26 tent sites and 90 sites with full hookups for RVs of any length; some sites are pull-through. Picnic tables are provided, and each seven-site carousel has barbecues and sinks. Drinking water, restrooms with flush toilets and showers, cable

TV, WiFi, firewood, recreation hall, convenience store, sauna, café, coin laundry, ice, horseshoes and croquet, and a playground are available. Propane gas is within two miles. Boat docks, launching facilities, and rentals are nearby. Some facilities are wheelchair accessible. Leashed pets are permitted.

**Reservations, fees:** Reservations are accepted at 541/247-7704. RV sites are $24-32 per night, tent sites are $18 per night, $2 per person per night for more than two people. Weekly, monthly, and winter rates are available. Some credit cards are accepted. Open year-round, with limited winter facilities.

**Directions:** On U.S. 101, drive to the northern end of Gold Beach to Jerry's Flat Road (just south of the Patterson Bridge). Turn left (east) on Jerry's Flat Road and drive 0.5 mile to the resort.

**Contact:** Indian Creek Resort, 541/247-7704, www.indiancreekrv.com.

## 120 LUCKY LODGE RV PARK

### Scenic rating: 6

on the Rogue River

Map 7.5, page 411

Lucky Lodge is a good layover spot for U.S. 101 travelers who want to get off the highway circuit. Set on the shore of the Rogue River, it offers opportunities for boating, fishing, and swimming. Most sites have a view of the river. Nearby recreation options include hiking trails. About two-thirds of the sites are occupied by monthly renters.

**Campsites, facilities:** There are 31 sites with full hookups for RVs of any length, three tent sites, and one cabin. Picnic tables are provided. Drinking water, restrooms with flush toilets and showers, propane gas, a recreation hall, and coin laundry are available. Boat docks and rentals are within eight miles. Some facilities are wheelchair accessible. Leashed pets are permitted.

**Reservations, fees:** Reservations are accepted. RV sites are $33 per night, tent sites

are $22 per night, $4 per person per night for more than two people. Open year-round.

**Directions:** From Gold Beach, drive north on U.S. 101 for four miles (on the north side of the Rogue River) to Rogue River Road. Turn right (east) and drive 3.5 miles to North Bank River Road. Turn right and drive 4.5 miles to the park on the right.

**Contact:** Lucky Lodge RV Park, 541/247-7618.

## 121 KIMBALL CREEK BEND RV RESORT

### Scenic rating: 6

on the Rogue River

Map 7.5, page 411

Kimball Creek campground on the scenic Rogue River is just far enough from the coast to provide quiet and its own distinct character. The resort offers guided fishing trips and sells tickets for jet boat tours. Nearby recreation options include an 18-hole golf course, hiking trails, and boating facilities. Note that about one-third of the sites are monthly rentals.

**Campsites, facilities:** There are 62 sites with full hookups for RVs of any length, 13 tent sites, one park-model cabin, and three motel rooms. Some sites are pull-through. Group camping is available. Picnic tables are provided and there are fire rings at some sites. Drinking water, restrooms with flush toilets and showers, WiFi, cable TV, dump station, recreation hall with library, convenience store with fishing licenses, coin laundry, and ice are available. Boat docks are on-site, and launching facilities are nearby. Leashed pets are permitted.

**Reservations, fees:** Reservations are accepted at 888/814-0633. RV sites are $28.50-40.50 per night, tent sites are $25 per night, $3 per person per night for more than two people. Some credit cards are accepted. Open year-round.

**Directions:** From Gold Beach, drive north

on U.S. 101 for one mile (on the north side of the Rogue River) to Rogue River Road. Turn right (east) and drive about eight miles to the resort on the right.

**Contact:** Kimball Creek Bend RV Resort, 541/247-7580, www.kimballcreek.com.

## 122 QUOSATANA

**Scenic rating: 6**

on the Rogue River in Rogue River-Siskiyou National Forest

**Map 7.5, page 411**

This campground is set along the banks of the Rogue River, upstream from the much smaller Lobster Creek Campground. The campground features a large, grassy area and a barrier-free trail around the campground. Ocean access is just a short drive away, and the quaint town of Gold Beach offers a decent side trip. Nearby Otter Point State Park (day-use only) has further recreation options. The Shrader Old-Growth Trail, Lower Rogue River Trail, and Myrtle Tree Trail provide nearby hiking opportunities. Quosatana makes a good base camp for a hiking or fishing trip.

**Campsites, facilities:** There are 43 sites for tents or RVs up to 32 feet long. Drinking water, fire grills, garbage bins, and picnic tables are provided. Flush toilets, dump station, fish-cleaning station, and a boat ramp are available. A camp host is on-site. Some facilities are wheelchair accessible. Leashed pets are permitted.

**Reservations, fees:** Reservations are not accepted. Sites are $10 per night, $3 per night per additional vehicle. Open year-round.

**Directions:** From Gold Beach on U.S. 101, turn east on County Road 595 and drive 14.5 miles (it becomes Forest Road 33) to the campground on the left.

**Contact:** Rogue River-Siskiyou National Forest, Gold Beach Ranger District, 541/247-3600, www.fs.usda.gov/rogue-siskiyou.

## 123 LOBSTER CREEK

**Scenic rating: 6**

on the Rogue River in Rogue River-Siskiyou National Forest

**Map 7.5, page 411**

This small campground on a river bar along the Rogue River is about a 15-minute drive from Gold Beach, and it makes a good base for a fishing or hiking trip. The area is heavily forested with myrtle and Douglas fir, and the Shrader Old-Growth Trail and Myrtle Tree Trail are nearby.

**Campsites, facilities:** There are seven sites for tents or RVs up to 26 feet long. Fire rings and picnic tables are provided. Drinking water, flush toilets, and garbage bins are available, as is a boat launch. A camp host is on-site. Leashed pets are permitted.

**Reservations, fees:** Reservations are not accepted. Sites are $10 per night, $3 per night per additional vehicle. Camping is also permitted on a gravel bar area for $5 per night. Open year-round, weather permitting.

**Directions:** From Gold Beach on U.S. 101, turn east on County Road 595 and drive 10 miles (it becomes Forest Road 33) to the campground on the left.

**Contact:** Rogue River-Siskiyou National Forest, Gold Beach Ranger District, 541/247-3600, www.fs.usda.gov/rogue-siskiyou.

## 124 BIG PINE

**Scenic rating: 4**

on Myers Creek in Rogue River-Siskiyou National Forest

**Map 7.5, page 411**

This little campground (elevation 2,400 feet) is set near the banks of Myers Creek in a valley of large pine and Douglas fir. Many sites are right on the creek, and all are shaded. One of the world's tallest ponderosa pine trees grows near the campground. A 1.1-mile barrier-free interpretive trail starts at the campground, and a day-use area is available.

**Campsites, facilities:** There are 14 tent sites. Picnic tables and fire grills are provided. Vault toilets, drinking water, and garbage bins are available. Some facilities are wheelchair accessible. Leashed pets are permitted.

**Reservations, fees:** Reservations are not accepted. Sites are $5 per night, $2 per night per additional vehicle. Open late May-mid-October, weather permitting.

**Directions:** From Grants Pass, drive north on I-5 for 3.5 miles to Exit 61 (Merlin-Galice Road). Take that exit and drive northwest for 12.5 miles to Forest Road 25. Turn left on Forest Road 25 and head southwest for 12.8 miles to the campground on the right.

**Contact:** Rogue River-Siskiyou National Forest, Wild Rivers Ranger District, 541/471-6500, www.fs.usda.gov/rogue-siskiyou.

## 125 SAM BROWN

### Scenic rating: 4

near Grants Pass in Rogue River-Siskiyou National Forest

**Map 7.5, page 411**

This campground is located in an isolated area near Grants Pass along Briggs Creek in a valley of pine and Douglas fir. It is set at an elevation of 2,500 feet. Many sites lie in the shade of trees, and a creek runs along one side of the campground. Briggs Creek Trail, Dutchy Creek Trail, and Taylor Creek Trail are nearby and are popular for hiking and horseback riding. An amphitheater is available for small group presentations. Although the campground was spared, the Biscuit Fire of 2002 did burn nearby areas.

**Campsites, facilities:** There are 27 sites for tents or RVs of any length at Sam Brown and seven equestrian tent sites with small corrals across the road at Sam Brown Horse Camp. Picnic tables and fire rings or grills are provided. Drinking water and vault toilets are

available at the horse camp. A picnic shelter, solar shower, and an amphitheater are available. Some facilities are wheelchair accessible. Leashed pets are permitted.

**Reservations, fees:** Reservations are not accepted. Sites are $5 per night, $2 per night per additional vehicle. Open late May-mid-October, weather permitting.

**Directions:** From Grants Pass, drive north on I-5 for 3.5 miles to Exit 61 (Merlin-Galice Road). Take that exit and drive northwest for 12.5 miles to Forest Road 25. Turn left on Forest Road 25 and head southwest for 14 miles to the campground.

**Contact:** Rogue River-Siskiyou National Forest, Wild Rivers Ranger District, 541/471-6500, www.fs.usda.gov/rogue-siskiyou.

## 126 IRELAND'S OCEAN VIEW RV PARK

### Scenic rating: 8

in Gold Beach

**Map 7.5, page 411**

This spot is situated on the beach in the quaint little town of Gold Beach, only one mile from the famous Rogue River. The park is very clean and features blacktop roads and grass beside each site. Recreation options include beachcombing, boating, and fishing. Great ocean views are possible from the observatory/lighthouse.

**Campsites, facilities:** There are 31 sites with full hookups (20-, 30-, and 50-amp) for RVs up to 40 feet long; some sites are pull-through. Picnic tables are provided. No open fires are allowed. Cable TV, restrooms with flush toilets and showers, coin laundry, and WiFi are available. Some facilities are wheelchair accessible. Leashed pets are permitted.

**Reservations, fees:** Reservations are recommended. Sites are $26-36 per night. Weekly and monthly rates are available. Open year-round.

**Directions:** On U.S. 101, drive to the southern

end of Gold Beach (U.S. 101 becomes Ellensburg Avenue). The park is located at 20272 Ellensburg Avenue, across from the U.S. Forest Service office.

**Contact:** Ireland's Ocean View RV Park, 541/247-0148, www.irelandsrvpark.com.

## 127 OCEANSIDE RV PARK

**Scenic rating: 5**

in Gold Beach

**Map 7.5, page 411**

Set 100 yards from the ocean, this park is close to beachcombing terrain, marked bike trails, and boating facilities. The park is also adjacent to the mouth of the Rogue River, in the Port of Gold Beach.

**Campsites, facilities:** There are 80 sites with full or partial hookups for RVs up to 40 feet long and two yurts; some sites are pull-through. Picnic tables and community fire rings are provided. Drinking water, restrooms with flush toilets and showers, coin laundry, WiFi, cable TV, a convenience store, picnic area, and ice are available. Propane gas, a store, and a café are within two miles. Boat docks and launching facilities are nearby. Leashed pets are permitted.

**Reservations, fees:** Reservations are recommended. Sites are $27.27-30.30, $1 per person per night for more than two people; yurts are $35.35 per night. Weekly, monthly, and winter rates are available. Some credit cards are accepted. Open year-round.

**Directions:** On U.S. 101, drive to central Gold Beach and the intersection with Moore Street. Turn west and drive two blocks to Airport Way. Turn right and drive three blocks to South Jetty Road. Turn left and look for the park on the left.

**Contact:** Oceanside RV Park, 541/247-2301, www.oceansiderv1.com.

## 128 WHALESHEAD BEACH RESORT

**Scenic rating: 7**

near Brookings

**Map 7.5, page 411**

This resort, about 0.25 mile from the beach, is set in a forested area with a small stream nearby. Activities at and around the camp include ocean and river fishing, jet boat trips, whale-watching excursions, and a golf course (13 miles away). Each campsite has a deck, and many cabins have an ocean view. One unique feature, a tunnel connects the campground to a trail to the beach.

**Campsites, facilities:** There are 35 sites with full hookups for RVs up to 60 feet long and 50 cabins. Picnic tables are provided at some sites. Cable TV, restrooms with showers, coin laundry, limited groceries, ice, and propane gas are available. WiFi is available at the office. A dump station is six miles away. Leashed pets are permitted.

**Reservations, fees:** Reservations are recommended. Sites are $25 per night, $10 per person per night for more than two people. Some credit cards are accepted. Open year-round.

**Directions:** From Brookings, drive seven miles north on U.S. 101 until you pass Harris Beach. Look for the resort on the right.

**Contact:** Whaleshead Beach Resort, 541/469-7446, www.whalesheadresort.com.

## 129 ALFRED A. LOEB STATE PARK

**Scenic rating: 8**

near the Chetco River

**Map 7.5, page 411**

This park is set in a canyon formed by the Chetco River. The campsites are set in a beautiful old myrtle grove. The 0.75-mile River View Trail follows the Chetco River to a redwood grove. Swimming, fishing, and rafting are popular activities. Nature programs and interpretive tours are available by request.

**Campsites, facilities:** There are 48 sites with partial hookups for tents or RVs up to 50 feet long and three log cabins. Picnic tables, drinking water, garbage bins, and fire grills are provided. Restrooms with flush toilets and showers and firewood are available. A camp host is on-site. Some facilities are wheelchair accessible. Leashed pets are permitted, but not in cabins.

**Reservations, fees:** Reservations are accepted for cabins only at 800/452-5687 or www.oregonstateparks.org ($8 reservation fee). Sites are $16-20 per night, $5 per night per additional vehicle; cabins are $39 per night. Some credit cards are accepted. Open year-round.

**Directions:** On U.S. 101, drive south to Brookings and County Road 784 (North Bank Chetco River Road). Turn northeast and drive eight miles northeast on North Bank Road to the park entrance on the right.

**Contact:** Harris Beach State Park, 541/469-2021 or 800/551-6949, www.oregonstateparks.org.

## 130 HARRIS BEACH STATE PARK

🚶🏻 🚲 ⛰️ 🛶 🚤 🐕 ♿ 🚐 ⛺

**Scenic rating: 8**

near Brookings

Map 7.5, page 411      **BEST (**

This park is prime with wildlife-watching opportunities. Not only is it home to Bird Island, a breeding site for the tufted puffin and other rare birds, but gray whales, harbor seals, and sea lions can be spotted here as well. Tidepooling is also popular. Sites are shaded and well-spaced with plenty of beach and nature trails leading from the campground. In the fall and winter, the nearby Chetco River attracts good runs of salmon and steelhead, respectively.

**Campsites, facilities:** There are 63 sites for tents or RVs up to 50 feet (no hookups), 86 sites with full or partial hookups for RVs up to 60 feet long, a hiker/biker camp, and six yurts. Picnic tables, garbage bins, and fire grills are provided. Drinking water, cable TV, Wi-Fi, restrooms with flush toilets and showers, a dump station, coin laundry, and firewood are available. A camp host is on-site. Some facilities are wheelchair accessible. Leashed pets are permitted in campsites.

**Reservations, fees:** Reservations are accepted at 800/452-5687 or www.oregonstateparks.org ($8 reservation fee). Sites are $16-27 per night, $5 per night per additional vehicle, $5 per night per person for hikers/bikers, $17 per night for group tent sites, and $39 per night for yurts. Some credit cards are accepted. Open year-round.

**Directions:** From Brookings, drive north on U.S. 101 for two miles to the park entrance on the left (west side of road).

**Contact:** Harris Beach State Park, 541/469-2021, www.oregonstateparks.org.

## 131 BEACHFRONT RV PARK

🚶🏻 🚲 ⛰️ 🛶 🚤 🐕 ♿ 🚐 ⛺

**Scenic rating: 8**

near Brookings

Map 7.5, page 411

Beachfront RV, located just this side of the Oregon/California border on the Pacific Ocean, makes a great layover spot. Oceanfront sites are available, and recreational activities include boating, fishing, and swimming. Beach access is available from the park. Plan your trip early, as sites usually book up for the entire summer season. Nearby Harris Beach State Park, with its beach access and hiking trails, makes a good side trip.

**Campsites, facilities:** There are 13 tent sites and 138 sites with full or partial hookups for RVs of any length; some sites are pull-through. Picnic tables and some fire pits are provided. Restrooms with showers, dump station, cable TV, WiFi, public phone, coin laundry, restaurant, ice, and a marina with a boat ramp, boat dock, and snacks are available. Supplies are available nearby. Some facilities are wheelchair accessible. Leashed pets are permitted.

**Reservations, fees:** Reservations are accepted at 800/441-0856. Tent sites are $12-17 per night, RV sites are $22-41 per night, $2 per person per night for more than four people. Weekly rates are available. Some credit cards are accepted. Open year-round.

**Directions:** From Brookings, drive south on U.S. 101 for 2.5 miles to Benham Lane. Turn west on Benham Lane and drive 1.5 miles (it becomes Lower Harbor Road) to Boat Basin Road. Turn left and drive two blocks to the park on the right.

**Contact:** Beachfront RV Park, 541/469-5867 or 800/441-0856, www.beachfrontrvpark. com.

## 132 ATRIVERS EDGE RV RESORT

**Scenic rating: 7**

on the Chetco River

**Map 7.5, page 411**

This resort lies along the banks of the Chetco River, just upstream from Brookings Harbor. A favorite spot for anglers, it features salmon and steelhead trips on the Chetco in the fall and winter. Deep-sea trips for salmon or rockfish are available nearby in the summer. This resort looks like the Rhine Valley in Germany, a pretty canyon between the trees and the river. A golf course is nearby.

**Campsites, facilities:** There are 114 sites with full hookups for RVs of any length; some are pull-through. Group camping is available. Eight cabins are also available. Picnic tables are provided, and fire rings are at some sites. Restrooms with flush toilets and showers, WiFi, cable TV, propane gas, dump station, recreation hall with kitchen, exercise equipment, coin laundry, and recycling station available. Some facilities are wheelchair accessible. Leashed pets are permitted in the campgrounds only.

**Reservations, fees:** Reservations are recommended at 541/469-3356. RV sites are $38-40 per night, $3 per person per night for more than two people. Some credit cards are accepted. Open year-round.

**Directions:** On U.S. 101, drive to the southern end of Brookings (harbor side) and to South Bank Chetco River Road (a cloverleaf exit). Turn east on South Bank Chetco River Road and drive 1.5 miles to the resort entrance on the left (a slanted left turn, through the pillars, well signed).

**Contact:** AtRivers Edge RV Resort, 541/469-3356, www.atriversedge.com.

## 133 SEA BIRD RV PARK

**Scenic rating: 5**

near Brookings

**Map 7.5, page 411**

Sea Bird is one of several parks in the area. Nearby recreation options include marked bike trails, a full-service marina, and tennis courts. A nice, neat park, it features paved roads and gravel/granite sites. There is also a beach for surfing near the park. In summer, most of the sites are reserved for the season. An 18-hole golf course is within 2.5 miles.

**Campsites, facilities:** There are 60 sites with full or partial hookups for RVs of any length; some are pull-through sites. Picnic tables are provided. No open fires are allowed. Restrooms with flush toilets and showers, dump station, cable TV, high-speed modem access, recreation hall, and a coin laundry are available. Boat docks, launching facilities, and rentals are nearby. Some facilities are wheelchair accessible. Leashed pets are permitted.

**Reservations, fees:** Reservations are recommended. Sites are $28 per night, $4 per person per night for more than two people, $20 per night for additional vehicle or boat not fitting in the space. Weekly and monthly rates are available. Open year-round.

**Directions:** In Brookings, drive south on U.S.

101 to the Chetco River Bridge. Continue 0.25 mile south on U.S. 101 to the park entrance on the left.

**Contact:** Sea Bird RV Park, 541/469-3512, www.seabirdrv.com.

# 134 LUDLUM

🏃 ≋ 🛶 🚐 ⛺

### Scenic rating: 5

near Brookings in Rogue River-Siskiyou National Forest

**Map 7.5, page 411**

This small campground is a local favorite, with fine fishing and a great swimming hole in Wheeler Creek. The well-spaced sites offer a nice sense of seclusion. There is an old-fashioned hand pump, and if you put in the work you'll be rewarded with some of the best water you've ever tasted. The Oregon Redwoods hiking trail is located about one mile off U.S. 101 and eight miles south of the campground on Winchuck River Road. The trail has beautiful old-growth redwoods and is worth the trip.

**Campsites, facilities:** There are seven sites for tents or RVs up to 30 feet. Picnic tables and fire rings are provided. Hand-pumped drinking water and vault toilets are available. Garbage must be packed out. Also available for rent is Ludlum House, a renovated 1930's two-story house; there are no beds or electricity, but there is a food prep area, a sink, and a woodstove. Bring your own firewood.

**Reservations, fees:** Reservations are accepted at 877/444-6777 ($10 reservation fee) or www.recreation.gov ($9 reservation fee). Sites are $10 per night, $3 for each additional vehicle. Ludlum House is $60 per night for up to 10 people, $5 for each additional person. Open mid-May-mid-October, weather permitting.

**Directions:** From Brookings, take U.S. 101 south to Winchuck River Road. Drive 11 miles then take the right fork to Forest Service Road 1108 (a gravel road) and continue 1.5 miles to campground.

**Contact:** Rogue River-Siskiyou National Forest, Gold Beach Ranger District, 541/247-3600, www.fs.usda.gov/rogue-siskiyou.

# PORTLAND AND THE WILLAMETTE VALLEY

Portland is an excellent recreation hub, with the Columbia River corridor and Mount Hood to the east, and Eugene and the McKenzie and Willamette Rivers to the south. In between lies Silver Falls State Park, Oregon's largest state park, with a seven-mile hike past 10 awesome waterfalls, some falling more than 100 feet from their brinks. The Willamette Valley stretches from Portland to Cottage Grove and provides a great jumping-off point to adventure. Lakes are plentiful, including Cottage Grove Reservoir, Dorena Lake, Fall Creek Reservoir, and Green Peter Reservoir on the Santiam River. Slow two-lane highways border the streams and provide routes to the coast that can be used to create a loop trip, with many hidden campgrounds to choose from while en route.

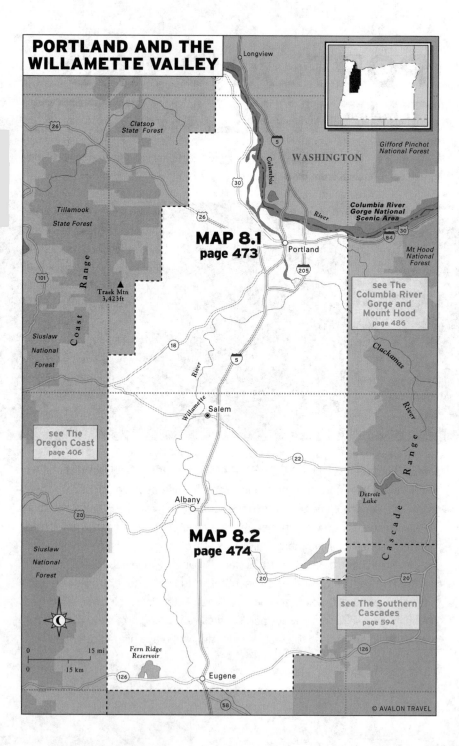

# PORTLAND AND THE WILLAMETTE VALLEY

Longview

WASHINGTON

Clatsop
State Forest

Gifford Pinchot
National Forest

Columbia

River

Columbia River
Gorge National
Scenic Area

Tillamook
State Forest

**MAP 8.1**
**page 473**

Portland

Mt Hood
National
Forest

Coast Range

Trask Mtn
3,423ft

see The
Columbia River
Gorge and
Mount Hood
page 486

Siuslaw

National

Forest

River

Clackamas

River

Willamette

Salem

see The
Oregon Coast
page 406

Cascade Range

Detroit
Lake

Albany

**MAP 8.2**
**page 474**

Siuslaw

National

Forest

see The Southern
Cascades
page 594

0          15 mi

0          15 km

Fern Ridge
Reservoir

Eugene

© AVALON TRAVEL

# Map 8.1

**Sites 1-7
Pages 475-477**

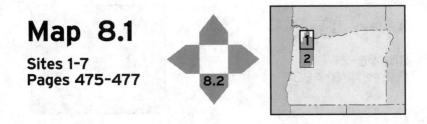

8.2

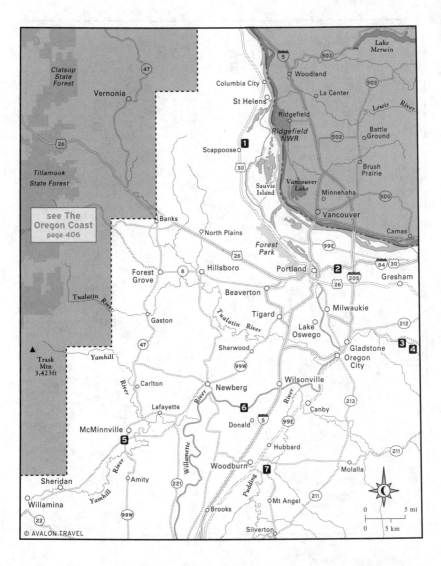

Clatsop State Forest

47

Vernonia

Columbia City

St Helens

Ridgefield

26

Scappoose 1

Tillamook State Forest

30

Sauvie Island

see The Oregon Coast page 406

Banks

North Plains

Forest Park

Forest Grove

8

Hillsboro

26

Tualatin River

Beaverton

Gaston

Tualatin River

Tigard

47

Sherwood

99W

Carlton

Yamhill

River

Newberg

6

Lafayette

McMinnville 5

River

Amity

Sheridan

Willamina

22

Yamhill

99W

221

Willamette

Brooks

Woodburn 7

Padding

Donald

5

99E

Hubbard

Mt Angel

211

Silverton

Lake Oswego

River

Wilsonville

Canby

213

Gladstone
Oregon City

3
4

212

Milwaukie

26

205

Portland 2

84  30

Gresham

99E

Vancouver

Minnehaha

500

Camas

Brush Prairie

Battle Ground

502

Ridgefield NWR

Vancouver Lake

La Center

503

Woodland

5

503

Lewis River

Lake Merwin

Trask Mtn 3,423ft

Molalla

211

0          5 mi

0          5 km

© AVALON TRAVEL

# Map 8.2

**Sites 8-21**
**Pages 478-483**

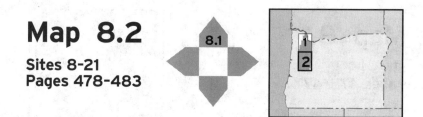

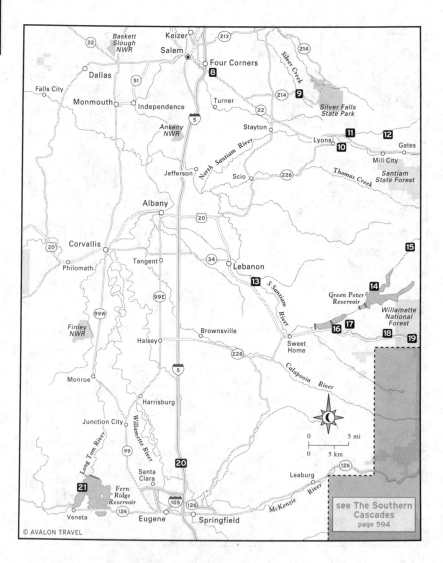

© AVALON TRAVEL

# **1** SCAPPOOSE RV PARK

### Scenic rating: 6

in Scappoose

**Map 8.1, page 473**

This county-operated RV park neighbors the rural Scappoose airport, making it a convenient spot for private pilots. The sites are partially shaded with maple, oak, and spruce trees. Set on the edge of a dike, it is less than a mile from the Columbia River and about a 30-minute drive from Portland.

**Campsites, facilities:** There are four tent sites in dispersed areas and seven sites for RVs up to 41 feet long, six with full (30 amp) hookups. Picnic tables and fire grills are provided. Drinking water, a restroom with flush toilets and showers, a dump station, a playground, and horseshoe pits are available. Some facilities are wheelchair accessible. Leashed pets are permitted.

**Reservations, fees:** Reservations are accepted at 503/366-3984. RV sites are $18-22 per night, tent sites are $7 per night, $7 per night for an additional vehicle. Open year-round.

**Directions:** From Portland, turn west on U.S. 30 and drive to Scappoose. Continue one mile north on U.S. 30 to West Lane Road. Turn right (east) and drive 0.75 mile to Honeyman Road. Turn left and drive one block to the park on the right.

**Contact:** Columbia County, Parks and Recreation, 503/397-2353; Scappoose RV Park, 503/543-3225.

# **2** PORTLAND FAIRVIEW RV PARK

### Scenic rating: 7

east of Portland

**Map 8.1, page 473**

This is a massive yet pretty RV park located eight miles east of downtown Portland. The setting is peaceful, with the entire park landscaped, edged by tall conifers. A small brook runs nearby. Many I-5 ramblers have a chance to unwind for a spell here.

**Campsites, facilities:** There are 407 sites with full hookups (50 amps) for RVs of any length; most sites are pull-through. Picnic tables are provided. Drinking water and restrooms with flush toilets and showers, a barbecue and picnic area, horseshoe pits, seasonal swimming pool, basketball, recreation and fitness centers, Wi-Fi, satellite TV, coin laundry, and parking for boats and tow vehicles are available. Some facilities are wheelchair accessible. Leashed pets are permitted, with some breed restrictions.

**Reservations, fees:** Reservations are accepted online at www.portlandfairviewrv.com. Sites are $38 per night, $3 per night per additional person. Monthly and group rates available. Open year-round.

**Directions:** From I-84/Highway 30 in Portland, take Exit 14 and turn north on NE 207th Avenue. Drive on NE 207th Avenue to NE Sandy Boulevard. Turn right on NE Sandy Boulevard and drive a short distance to the park.

**Contact:** Portland Fairview RV Park, 877/777-1047, www.portlandfairviewrv.com.

# **3** BARTON PARK

### Scenic rating: 6

near the Clackamas River

**Map 8.1, page 473**

Getting here may seem a bit of a maze, but the trip is well worth it. This camp is set on the Clackamas River and is surrounded by woods and tall trees. The river can provide good salmon and steelhead fishing.

**Campsites, facilities:** There are 98 sites for tents or RVs up to 40 feet; sites have partial hookups, and some sites are pull-through. Picnic tables and fire rings are provided. Restrooms with flush toilets and showers, a dump station, picnic area, and firewood are available.

Recreational facilities include horseshoe pits, a playground, volleyball court, softball field, and boat ramp. Supplies are available within one mile. A camp host is on-site. Some facilities are wheelchair accessible. Leashed pets are permitted. Gates are locked 10pm-6am daily.

**Reservations, fees:** Reservations are recommended ($8 reservation fee). Sites are $26 per night, $5 per night per additional vehicle. Some credit cards are accepted. Open May-September; Barton East is open through October 31.

**Directions:** From Portland, drive south on I-5 to I-205. Turn east and drive about 20 miles to Exit 12, the Clackamas/Estacada exit (Highway 212). Turn east on Highway 212/224 and drive 3.2 miles to the Carver exit/Rock Creek junction. Turn right on Highway 224 and drive about 6.5 miles to the town of Barton and Baker's Ferry Road. Turn right and drive 0.2 mile to Barton Park Road. Turn left and drive to the park on the left.

**Contact:** Clackamas County Parks Department, 503/742-4414, www.clackamas.us; Park Ranger, 503/637-3015.

## 4 METZLER PARK

**Scenic rating: 8**

on Clear Creek

**Map 8.1, page 473**

This county campground on a small stream not far from the Clackamas River is a hot spot for fishing, picnicking, and swimming. Be sure to make your reservation early at this very popular park.

**Campsites, facilities:** There are 60 sites with partial hookups and 15 primitive sites for tents or RVs up to 40 feet long. Picnic tables and fire pits are provided. Restrooms with flush toilets and showers, a dump station, playground, picnic areas, firewood, and a recreation field with baseball, basketball, and volleyball are available. Propane and ice are within five miles. Some facilities are wheelchair accessible.

Leashed pets are permitted. Gates are locked 10pm-6am daily.

**Reservations, fees:** Reservations are recommended ($8 reservation fee). Sites are $26 per night, $5 per night per additional vehicle. Some credit cards are accepted. Open May-September.

**Directions:** From Portland, drive south on I-5 to I-205. Turn east and drive about 20 miles to Exit 12, the Clackamas/Estacada exit (Highway 212). Turn east on Highway 212/224 and drive 3.2 miles to the Carver exit/Rock Creek junction. Turn right on Highway 224 and drive approximately 15 miles to Estacada and Highway 211. Turn right, crossing a bridge, and drive four miles to Tucker Road. Turn right and drive 0.5 mile to Metzler Park Road. Turn left and drive 1.6 miles to the park entrance.

**Contact:** Clackamas County Parks Department, 503/742-4414, www.clackamas.us; Park Ranger, 503/630-4743.

## 5 MULKEY RV PARK

**Scenic rating: 7**

near the South Yamhill River

**Map 8.1, page 473**

This wooded park sits near the South Yamhill River. Nearby recreation options include an 18-hole golf course, tennis courts, and the Western Deer Park and Arboretum, which has a playground. Note that most sites are taken by monthly renters.

**Campsites, facilities:** There are 70 sites with full hookups for RVs of any length; some sites are pull-through. Picnic tables are provided. Drinking water, restrooms with flush toilets and showers, a grocery store, propane gas, ice, Wi-Fi, and coin laundry are available. Some facilities are wheelchair accessible. Leashed pets are permitted.

**Reservations, fees:** Reservations are recommended at 877/472-2475. RV sites are $30 per night, $5 per person per night for more than two people. Weekly and monthly rates are available. Some credit cards are accepted. Open year-round.

**Directions:** From Portland, turn south on Highway 99 and drive about 31 miles to McMinnville and Highway 18. Turn southwest on Highway 18 and drive 3.5 miles to the park entrance.

**Contact:** Mulkey RV Park, 503/472-2475, www.mulkeyrv.com.

## 6 CHAMPOEG STATE HERITAGE AREA

🚶 🚲 🛶 🛏 🐕 ♿ 🚐 ⛺

### Scenic rating: 7

on the Willamette River

**Map 8.1, page 473**

Champoeg State Heritage Area lies on the south bank of the Willamette River and features an interpretive center, a botanical garden with native plants, and hiking and bike trails. A junior ranger program is available during the summer. The log cabin museum, the historic Newell House, and the visitors center are also worth a tour. Some of the best sturgeon fishing in North America is on the Willamette River below Oregon City Falls (also called Willamette Falls). I caught my biggest fish here in 2009, a nine-foot sturgeon that weighed 400 pounds. The best fishing guide to the area is Charlie Foster.

**Campsites, facilities:** There are 75 sites with full or partial hookups for tents or RVs up of any length. There are also three group tent areas that accommodate a maximum of 25 people each, six walk-in sites, six cabins, six yurts, a hiker/biker camp, and a 10-site tent and RV group area with electric hookups only. Picnic tables and fire grills are provided. Restrooms with flush toilets and showers, drinking water, garbage bins, a dump station, meeting hall, picnic area, off-leash dog park, disc golf, ice, and firewood are available. Boat docking facilities are nearby. Some facilities are wheelchair accessible. Leashed pets are permitted.

**Reservations, fees:** Reservations are accepted at 800/452-5687 or www.oregonstateparks.org ($8 reservation fee). RV sites are $20-24 per night, tent sites are $15-19 per night, $5 per person per night for hiker/biker sites, the group tent camps are $71 per night, the group RV/tent camp is $101 per night, $10 per RV after the first 10 units; yurts are $36 per night, and cabins are $39 per night, $5 per night per additional vehicle. Some credit cards are accepted. Open year-round.

**Directions:** From Portland, drive south on I-5 to Exit 278, the Donald/Aurora exit. Take that exit and turn right (west) on Ehlen Road and drive three miles to Case Road. Turn right (north) and drive 4.5 miles (the road becomes Champoeg Road) to the park on the right.

**Contact:** Champoeg State Heritage Area, 503/678-1251 or 800/551-6949, www.oregonstateparks.org; Charlie Foster's NW Sturgeon Adventures, 503/820-1189, www.nwsturgeonadventures.com.

## 7 FEYRER PARK

🏊 🛶 🛏 🐕 🥾 ♿ 🚐 ⛺

### Scenic rating: 5

on the Molalla River

**Map 8.1, page 473**

On the scenic Molalla River, this county park offers swimming and excellent salmon fishing. A superb option for weary I-5 cruisers, the park is only 30 minutes off the highway and provides a peaceful, serene environment.

**Campsites, facilities:** There are 20 sites with partial hookups for tents or RVs up to 40 feet long. Picnic tables and fire rings are provided. Drinking water, restrooms with showers, a dump station, and picnic areas are available. There are also a playground, horseshoe pits, volleyball, and softball. A boat ramp is nearby. Supplies are available within three miles. Some facilities are wheelchair accessible. Leashed pets are permitted.

**Reservations, fees:** Reservations are recommended ($8 reservation fee). Sites are $26 per night, $5 per night per additional vehicle. Some credit cards are accepted. Open May-September.

**Directions:** From Portland, drive south on I-5 to Woodburn. Take Exit 271 and drive east on Highway 214; continue (the road changes to Highway 211 at the crossing with Highway 99E) to Molalla and Mathias Road. Turn right and drive 0.25 mile to Feyrer Park Road. Turn right and drive three miles to the park on the left.

**Contact:** Clackamas County Parks Department, 503/742-4414, www.clackamas.us; park ranger, 503/829-6621.

## 8 SALEM CAMPGROUND & RVS
🚶 🚴 🏊 🛶 🐕 🎣 ♿ 🚐 ⛺

**Scenic rating: 5**

in Salem

**Map 8.2, page 474**

This park with shaded sites is located next to I-5 in Salem; expect to hear traffic noise. A picnic area and a lake for swimming are within walking distance, and a nine-hole golf course and hiking trails are nearby. This is a good overnight campground, but not a destination place.

**Campsites, facilities:** There are 170 sites with full hookups (20, 30, and 50 amps) for RVs of any length; some sites are pull-through. There are also 25 tent sites. Picnic tables are provided, and barbecues are available upon request. Group facilities are available. Restrooms with flush toilets and showers, propane, a dump station, a game room, convenience store, coin laundry, ice, a playground, cable TV, Wi-Fi, and drinking water are available. A café is within one mile. Some facilities are wheelchair accessible. Leashed pets are permitted; no pit bulls or rottweilers are allowed.

**Reservations, fees:** Reservations are accepted at 800/826-9605. Sites are $30-36 per night, $5 per person per night for more than two people. Weekly, monthly, and group rates are available. Some credit cards are accepted. Open year-round.

**Directions:** From Salem on I-5, take Exit 253 to Highway 22. Turn east and drive 0.25 mile to Lancaster Drive. Turn right on Lancaster Drive and continue 0.1 mile to Hagers Grove Road. Turn right on Hagers Grove Road and drive a short distance to the campground at the end of the road.

**Contact:** Salem Campground & RVs, 503/581-6736 or 800/826-9605, www.salemrv.com.

## 9 SILVER FALLS STATE PARK
🚶 🚴 🏊 🦌 🎣 ♿ 🚐 ⛺

**Scenic rating: 8**

near Salem

**Map 8.2, page 474**

Oregon's largest state park, Silver Falls covers more than 8,700 acres. Numerous trails crisscross the area, one of which is a seven-mile jaunt that meanders past 10 majestic waterfalls (some more than 100 feet high) in the rainforest of Silver Creek Canyon. Four of these falls have an amphitheater-like surrounding where you can walk behind the falls and feel the misty spray. A horse camp and a 14-mile equestrian trail are available in the park. Fitness-conscious campers can check out the three-mile jogging trail or the four-mile bike trail. There are also a rustic nature lodge and group lodging facilities. Pets are not allowed on the Canyon Trail.

**Campsites, facilities:** There are 45 sites for tents or self-contained RVs (no hookups), 52 sites with partial hookups for tents or RVs up to 60 feet long, three group tent sites for up to 50-75 people each, two group RV areas, five horse sites, a group horse camp, and 14 cabins. Picnic tables and fire grills are provided. Drinking water, garbage bins, restrooms with flush toilets and showers, a dump station, an amphitheater, firewood, ice, and a playground are available. Some facilities are wheelchair accessible. Leashed pets are permitted in the campground.

**Reservations, fees:** Reservations are accepted at 800/452-5687 or www.oregonstateparks.org ($8 reservation fee). Sites are $15-24 per night, $5 per night for an additional vehicle. The group tent site is $51-71 per night; the group RV sites are $60-101 per night for the first 10 units and then $10 per additional unit. Horse campsites are $12-19 per night, the group horse camp is $15-58 per night. Cabins are $35-39 per night. Some credit cards are accepted. RV sites are open year-round, tent sites April-October.
**Directions:** From Salem on I-5, take Exit 253 to Highway 22. Turn east and drive five miles to Highway 214. Turn left (east) and drive 15 miles to the park.
**Contact:** Silver Falls State Park, 503/873-8681, 503/873-4395, or 800/551-6949, 503/873-3890 (trail rides), www.oregonstateparks.org.

## 10 JOHN NEAL MEMORIAL PARK

**Scenic rating: 6**
on the North Santiam River

Map 8.2, page 474

This camp is set on the banks of the North Santiam River, offering good boating and trout fishing possibilities. The park covers about 27 acres, and there are hiking trails. Other recreation options include exploring lakes and trails in the adjacent national forest land or visiting Silver Falls State Park.
**Campsites, facilities:** There are 23 sites for tents or self-contained RVs up to 30 feet long, and a group site for up to 100 people (12 RVs). Picnic tables and fire pits are provided. Restrooms with flush toilets and showers, garbage bins, and drinking water are available. Recreational facilities include a boat ramp, playground, horseshoe pits, picnic areas, and a recreation field. Ice and a grocery store are within one mile. Some facilities are wheelchair accessible. Leashed pets are permitted.

**Reservations, fees:** Reservations are recommended at 541/967-3917 or www.linnparks.com. Sites are $24 per night ($12 reservation fee), $7 per night per additional vehicle, and $200 per night for group sites ($50 reservation fee). Senior discounts available. Some credit cards are accepted for reservations. Open mid-April-mid-September, weather permitting.
**Directions:** From Salem, drive east on Highway 22 for about 20 miles to Highway 226. Turn right and drive south for two miles to Lyons and John Neal Park Road. Turn left (east) and drive a short distance to the campground on the left.
**Contact:** Linn County Parks Department, 541/967-3917, www.linnparks.com.

## 11 FISHERMEN'S BEND

**Scenic rating: 7**
on the North Santiam River

Map 8.2, page 474

Fishermen's Bend is a popular spot for anglers of all ages, and the sites are spacious. The campground was renovated in 2005. A barrier-free fishing and river viewing area and a network of trails provide access to more than a mile of river. There's a one-mile, self-guided nature trail, and the nature center has a variety of displays. The amphitheater has films and activities on weekends. The front gate closes at 10pm.
**Campsites, facilities:** There are 54 sites with full or partial hookups for tents and RVs up to 38 feet long; some sites are pull-through. There are also three group sites (for up to 60 people each) and two cabins. Picnic tables and fire pits are provided. Drinking water, restrooms with flush toilets and showers, a dump station, and garbage containers are available. A boat ramp, fishing pier, day-use area with playgrounds, baseball fields, volleyball and basketball courts, horseshoe pits, firewood, and a picnic shelter are also available. Some facilities are wheelchair accessible. Leashed pets are permitted.

**Reservations, fees:** Reservations are accepted for some campsites, the cabins, and the group sites at 888/444-6777 or www.recreation.gov ($10 reservation fee). Sites are $16-28 per night, $5 per night per each additional vehicle. Group sites are $85-105 per night. Cabins are $40 per night. Open May-October.

**Directions:** From Salem on I-5, take Exit 253 to Highway 22. Turn east and drive 30 miles to the campground on the right.

**Contact:** Bureau of Land Management, Salem District Office, 503/897-2406, www.blm.gov/or/districts/salem.

## 12 ELKHORN VALLEY

### Scenic rating: 7
on the Little North Santiam River

**Map 8.2, page 474**

This pretty campground along the Little North Santiam River, not far from the north fork of the Santiam River, has easy access and on-site hosts and is only a short drive away from a major metropolitan area. Swimming is good here during the summer, and the campground is popular with families. The front gate is locked 10pm-7am daily. This site offers an alternative to Shady Cove, which is about 10 miles to the east.

**Campsites, facilities:** There are 23 sites for tents or RVs up to 24 feet long. Picnic tables and fire grills are provided. Vault toilets, garbage service, and drinking water are available. Some facilities are wheelchair accessible. Leashed pets are permitted.

**Reservations, fees:** Reservations are not accepted. Sites are $14 per night, $5 per night per additional vehicle. There is a 14-day stay limit. Open late May-early September.

**Directions:** From Salem on I-5, take Exit 253 to Highway 22. Turn east and drive 25 miles to Elkhorn Road (Little North Fork Road). Turn left (northeast) and drive nine miles to the campground on the left.

**Contact:** Bureau of Land Management, Salem District Office, 503/897-2406, www.blm.gov/or/districts/salem.

## 13 WATERLOO COUNTY PARK

### Scenic rating: 8
on the South Santiam River

**Map 8.2, page 474**

This campground features more than a mile of South Santiam River frontage. Field sports, fishing, picnicking, and swimming are options here. Small boats with trolling motors are the only boats allowed here. A golf course is within five miles.

**Campsites, facilities:** There are 120 sites for tents or RVs of any length; most have partial hookups. Fire pits and picnic tables are provided. Drinking water, restrooms with flush toilets and showers, a dump station, boat ramps, two playgrounds, day-use area, off-leash dog park, and picnic shelters are available. Some facilities are wheelchair accessible. Leashed pets are permitted.

**Reservations, fees:** Reservations are accepted at 541/967-3917 or www.linnparks.com ($12 reservation fee). Sites are $24-28 per night, $7 per night for an additional vehicle. Senior discounts available. Some credit cards are accepted for reservations. Open year-round.

**Directions:** From Albany, drive east on U.S. 20 for about 20 miles through Lebanon to the Waterloo exit. Turn left (north) at the Waterloo exit and drive approximately two miles to the camp on the right. The camp is on the south side of the South Santiam River, five miles east of Lebanon.

**Contact:** Linn County Parks Department, 541/967-3917, www.linnparks.com.

## 14 WHITCOMB CREEK COUNTY PARK

### Scenic rating: 8

on Green Peter Reservoir

**Map 8.2, page 474**

This camp, located on the north shore of Green Peter Reservoir, is in a wooded area with lots of ferns, which gives it a rainforest feel. Anglers appreciate that Oregon Department of Fish and Wildlife stocks trout here. Other recreation options include hiking, picnicking, sailing, swimming, and waterskiing. Two boat ramps are on the reservoir about a mile from camp.

**Campsites, facilities:** There are 39 sites for tents or RVs up to 30 feet long (no hookups) and one group tent and RV area for up to 100 people. Picnic tables and fire pits are provided. Drinking water is available to haul; vault toilets, garbage bins, and a boat ramp are also available. Supplies are within 15 miles. Some facilities are wheelchair accessible. Leashed pets are permitted.

**Reservations, fees:** Reservations are accepted at 541/967-3917 or www.linnparks.com ($12 reservation fee). Sites are $24 per night, $7 per night per additional vehicle; the group site is $200 per night, plus a $50 reservation fee. Senior discounts available. Some credit cards are accepted. Open mid-April-mid-September.

**Directions:** From Albany, drive east on U.S. 20 for about 35 miles (through Lebanon and Sweet Home) to the Quartzville Road exit (near Foster Reservoir). Turn left (north) on Quartzville Road and drive 15 miles to the park.

**Contact:** Linn County Parks Department, 541/967-3917, www.linnparks.com.

## 15 YELLOWBOTTOM

### Scenic rating: 7

on Quartzville Creek

**Map 8.2, page 474**

Out-of-town visitors always miss this campground across the road from Quartzville Creek. It's nestled under a canopy of old-growth forest. The Rhododendron Trail, which is just under a mile, provides a challenging hike through forest and patches of rhododendrons. Some folks pan for gold here, and swimming is popular in the creek. Though primitive, the camp is ideal for a quiet getaway weekend.

**Campsites, facilities:** There are 22 sites for tents or RVs up to 28 feet long, including some pull-through sites. Picnic tables, garbage bins, and fire grills are provided. Drinking water, vault toilets, and firewood are available. A camp host is on-site seasonally. Some facilities are wheelchair accessible. Leashed pets are permitted.

**Reservations, fees:** Reservations are not accepted. Sites are $12 per night, with a 14-day stay limit, and $5 per night for an additional vehicle. Open mid-June-early September.

**Directions:** From Albany, drive east on U.S. 20 for about 35 miles (through Sweet Home) to Quartzville Road. Turn left (northeast) on Quartzville Road and drive 24 miles to the campground on the left.

**Contact:** Bureau of Land Management, Salem District, 503/897-2406, 503/375-5646, www. blm.gov/or/districts/salem.

## 16 RIVER BEND COUNTY PARK

### Scenic rating: 8

on the South Santiam River

**Map 8.2, page 474**

When River Bend opened in 2005, it was an instant hit. The park has plenty of hiking trails, the river current is calm in summer, and there are swimming beaches. The campground is in a woodsy setting of firs and ferns. Additional water activities include fishing and inner tubing, a favorite. A golf course is within 15 miles.

**Campsites, facilities:** There are 10 sites for tents and self-contained RVs (no hookups),

74 sites with partial hookups for tents and RVs of any length, a group camp for up to 50 people, and three cabins. Picnic tables and fire rings are provided. Drinking water, restrooms with flush toilets and showers, a dump station, picnic area, athletic field, interpretive display, fishing area, and swimming and tubing area are available. An enclosed group shelter is also available. Some facilities are wheelchair accessible. Leashed pets are permitted.

**Reservations, fees:** Reservations are accepted at 541/967-3917 or www.linnparks.com ($12 reservation fee). Sites are $24-28 per night, $7 per night per additional vehicle, $65 per cabin per night. Senior discounts available. Some credit cards are accepted for reservations. Open year-round, with limited winter services.

**Directions:** From Albany, drive east on U.S. 20 to Sweet Home. Continue east on U.S. 20 for five miles to the park on the left.

**Contact:** Linn County Parks Department, 541/967-3917, www.linnparks.com.

## 17 SUNNYSIDE COUNTY PARK

**Scenic rating: 8**

on Foster Reservoir

Map 8.2, page 474

Sunnyside is Linn County's most popular park. Recreation options at this 98-acre park include boating, fishing, swimming, and waterskiing. A golf course is within 15 miles.

**Campsites, facilities:** There are 165 sites for tents or RVs of any length; most sites have partial hookups. There are also three group sites for up to 80 people each. Picnic tables and fire rings are provided; there is also a community fire ring. Drinking water, restrooms with flush toilets and showers, a dump station, playground, dog park, stocked fishing ponds, fish-cleaning station, picnic shelter (available by reservation), volleyball courts, firewood, a boat ramp, and moorage are available. Supplies are available within

three miles. Some facilities are wheelchair accessible. Leashed pets are permitted.

**Reservations, fees:** Reservations are accepted at 541/967-3917 or www.linnparks.com ($12 reservation fee, $50 reservation fee for group site). Individual sites are $24-28 per night, $7 per night for an additional vehicle; group sites are $208 per night. Senior discounts available. Open mid-March-early November.

**Directions:** From Albany, drive east on U.S. 20 for about 35 miles (through Lebanon and Sweet Home) to the Quartzville Road exit (near Foster Reservoir). Turn left (north) on Quartzville Road and drive one mile to the campground on the right. The camp is on the south side of Foster Reservoir.

**Contact:** Linn County Parks Department, 541/967-3917, www.linnparks.com.

## 18 CASCADIA STATE PARK

**Scenic rating: 7**

on the Santiam River

Map 8.2, page 474

Cascadia State Park is set along the banks of the Santiam River. The highlight of this 258-acre park is Soda Creek Falls, with a fun 0.75-mile hike to reach it. Another riverside trail leads through groves of Douglas fir and provides good fishing access. This is a choice spot for a less crowded getaway, and also for reunions and meetings for families, Boy Scouts, and other groups.

**Campsites, facilities:** There are 25 primitive sites for tents or self-contained RVs up to 35 feet long, and two group tent areas for up to 100 people each. Picnic tables, garbage bins, and fire grills are provided. Drinking water, flush and vault toilets, and firewood are available. A camp host is on-site. Some facilities are wheelchair accessible. Leashed pets are permitted.

**Reservations, fees:** Reservations are accepted for group tent areas only at 800/452-5687. Tent sites are $13-17 per night, $5 per night for an additional vehicle. Group tent sites are $17-71 per night for up to 25 people and $3 per night for each additional person. Some credit cards are accepted. Open May-September, weather permitting.

**Directions:** From Albany, drive east on U.S. 20 for 40 miles to the park on the left (14 miles east of the town of Sweet Home).

**Contact:** Cascadia State Park, 541/367-6021 or 800/551-6949, www.oregonstateparks.org.

## 19 LONG BOW GROUP

### Scenic rating: 10
on the South Santiam River

**Map 8.2, page 474**    BEST (

Long Bow campground is located at 1,200 feet in elevation on the South Santiam River. It's a pretty spot with fishing, hiking, and swimming options and a natural amphitheater on-site.

Note: No tents or trailers are allowed at the campground. Instead, your group will camp at one of six shelters that can hold a combined total of 48 people. The reservation fee covers all six shelters.

**Campsites, facilities:** There are six sites with shelters for up to 48 people. Picnic tables and fire grills are provided. Drinking water, vault toilets, and a sheltered cooking and dining area are available. Leashed pets are permitted.

**Reservations, fees:** Reservations are accepted at 877/444-6777 or www.recreation.gov ($9-10 reservation fee). Sites are $125 per night. Open May-September, weather permitting.

**Directions:** From Albany, drive east on U.S. 20 for 43 miles (17 miles past Sweet Home) to Forest Road 2032. Turn right and drive 0.5 mile to the camp on the left.

**Contact:** Willamette National Forest, Sweet Home Ranger District, 541/367-5168, www. fs.usda.gov/willamette.

## 20 ARMITAGE PARK

### Scenic rating: 7
north of Eugene

**Map 8.2, page 474**

This 57-acre county park sits along on the banks of the McKenzie River outside Eugene. Hiking opportunities include the 0.5-mile Crilly Nature Trail through deciduous forest common around this river. Over the years, my brother Rambob, cousins Andy and Neil, and I have caught a lot of trout on the McKenzie in this area. Hopefully you will too.

**Campsites, facilities:** There are 32 sites for tents or RVs and two group sites for up to 16-20 people each. Some sites are pull-through. Picnic tables and fire rings are provided. Drinking water and restrooms with flush toilets are available. A boat ramp, volleyball courts, horseshoe pits, Wi-Fi, and a two-acre dog park are available. Some facilities are wheelchair accessible. Leashed pets are permitted.

**Reservations, fees:** Reservations are accepted ($10 reservation fee) at 541/682-2000 or http:// reservations.lanecounty.org. Single sites are $30-33 per night, group sites are $75 per night, $7 for each additional vehicle. Open year-round.

**Directions:** From Portland, take I-5 to the Eugene area. Take Exit 195A-B and drive 0.7 mile toward Florence/Junction City. Merge onto Belt Line Highway and drive one mile to the Coburg exit. Take that exit and drive 0.2 mile to N. Coburg Road. Turn right on N. Coburg Road and drive 1.8 miles to the campground at 90064 Coburg Road.

**Contact:** Lane County Parks, 541/682-2000, www.lanecounty.org.

## 21 RICHARDSON PARK

### Scenic rating: 7
on Fern Ridge Reservoir

**Map 8.2, page 474**

This pretty Lane County park is a favorite for

sailing and sailboarding, as the wind is consistent. Boating and waterskiing are also popular. There is a walking trail that doubles as a bike trail. A kiosk display in the park features the historic Applegate Trail. Additional activities include fishing, swimming (unsupervised), and wildlife-viewing. The Corps of Engineers has wildlife areas nearby.

**Campsites, facilities:** There are 88 sites with partial hookups for tents or RVs of any length; some sites are pull-through. Picnic tables, and fire pits are provided. Drinking water, restrooms with flush toilets and coin showers, a dump station, picnic areas, sand volleyball area, swimming area, three picnic shelters, playground, amphitheater, and garbage bins are available. A seasonally attended marina offers minimal supplies including ice, a boat launch, and transient boat docks. There is a small town within five miles. Some facilities are wheelchair accessible. Leashed pets are permitted.

**Reservations, fees:** Reservations are recommended at 541/682-2000 or www.lanecounty.org/parks ($10 reservation fee). Sites are $25-27.50 per night, plus $7 per night per additional vehicle. Maximum stay is 14 days within a 30-day period. Some credit cards are accepted. Open April-mid-October.

**Directions:** In Eugene on I-5, drive to Exit 195B and Belt Line Road. Turn west on Belt Line Road and drive 6.5 miles to the Junction City Airport exit and Highway 99. Take that exit, turn left on Highway 99, and drive north for 0.5 mile to Clear Lake Road (the first stoplight). Turn left and drive 8.25 miles to the campground on the left.

**Contact:** Richardson Park, 541/935-2005 or 541/682-2000, www.lanecounty.org/parks; marina, 541/935-2005.

# THE COLUMBIA RIVER GORGE AND MOUNT HOOD

The Columbia River area is a living history lesson, a geological wonder, and a recreation paradise. This waterway carves a deep gorge through the Cascade Range that divides Oregon. The transformation of the Gorge area from forest to grasslands to high desert is quick and striking. Driving west to east from the Portland area, you will pass along the wooded foothills of the Cascade Range to the south. When you pass Hood River, the world suddenly changes: The trees disappear and in their place are rolling grasslands that seem to extend forever. It is often hot and dry here, with strong winds blowing straight down the river. However, the entire time you are within the realm of Mount Hood, an 11,239-foot, diamond-shaped mountain whose flanks support stellar destinations with campsites and small, forested lakes. Mount Hood and its surrounding national forest provide numerous opportunities for camping, fishing, and hiking.

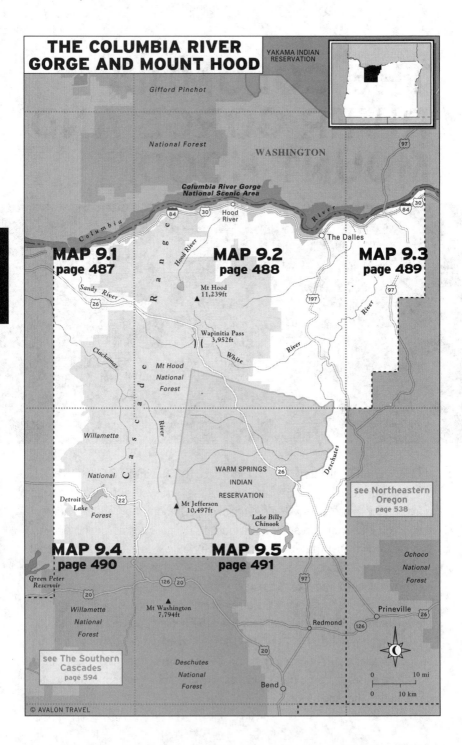

# THE COLUMBIA RIVER GORGE AND MOUNT HOOD

YAKAMA INDIAN RESERVATION

Gifford Pinchot

National Forest

**WASHINGTON**

97

Columbia River Gorge
National Scenic Area

Columbia

84    30

Hood River

River

30

84

The Dalles

## MAP 9.1
### page 487

Sandy River

26

Range

Hood River

Mt Hood
11,239ft

197

## MAP 9.2
### page 488

97

River

## MAP 9.3
### page 489

Clackamas

Mt Hood
National
Forest

Wapinitia Pass
3,952ft

White

River

River

Cascade

Willamette

National

River

26

WARM SPRINGS

INDIAN

RESERVATION

Deschutes

see Northeastern
Oregon
page 538

Detroit
Lake

22

Forest

Mt Jefferson
10,497ft

Lake Billy
Chinook

## MAP 9.4
### page 490

Green Peter
Reservoir

20

126    20

Willamette

National

Forest

Mt Washington
7,794ft

## MAP 9.5
### page 491

97

Ochoco

National

Forest

Prineville

26

Redmond

126

see The Southern
Cascades
page 594

20

Deschutes

National

Forest

Bend

0        10 mi

0        10 km

© AVALON TRAVEL

# Map 9.1

**Sites 1-18**
**Pages 492-499**

9.2

9.4

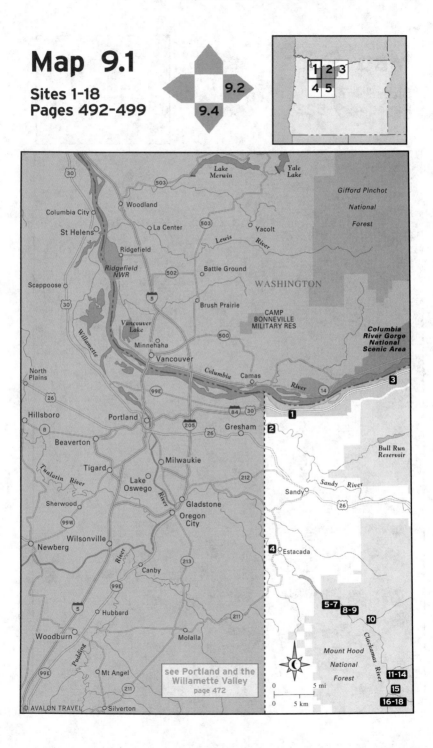

# Map 9.2

**Sites 19-71**
**Pages 499-522**

9.1 9.3
9.5

1 2 3
4 5

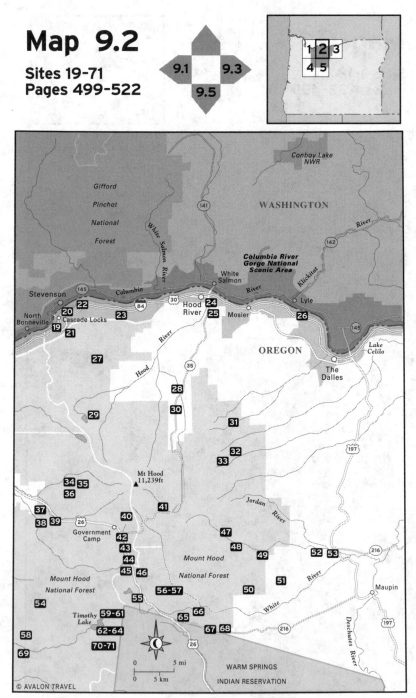

Conboy Lake
NWR

Gifford

Pinchot

National

Forest

WASHINGTON

141

142

White Salmon River

Columbia River
Gorge National
Scenic Area

Klickitat River

Stevenson
145
Columbia
84
30

White
Salmon
River

Lyle

145

22
23

19
20
21
Cascade Locks

North
Bonneville

Hood
River
24
25
Mosier
26

OREGON

Lake
Celilo

The
Dalles

27

Hood
River

35

28

30

31

197

29

32
33

Mt Hood
11,239ft
34 35
36

Jordan River

37
38 39
26
Government
Camp

40

41

47

48

49

52 53

216

42
43
44
45 46

Mount Hood

National Forest

51

River

Maupin

Mount Hood

National Forest

54

55

56-57

50

White

58

59-61

Timothy
Lake
62-64
70-71

65

66

67 68

216

197

Deschutes River

69

0          5 mi
0       5 km

26

WARM SPRINGS

INDIAN RESERVATION

© AVALON TRAVEL

# Map 9.3

## Sites 72-74
## Pages 522-523

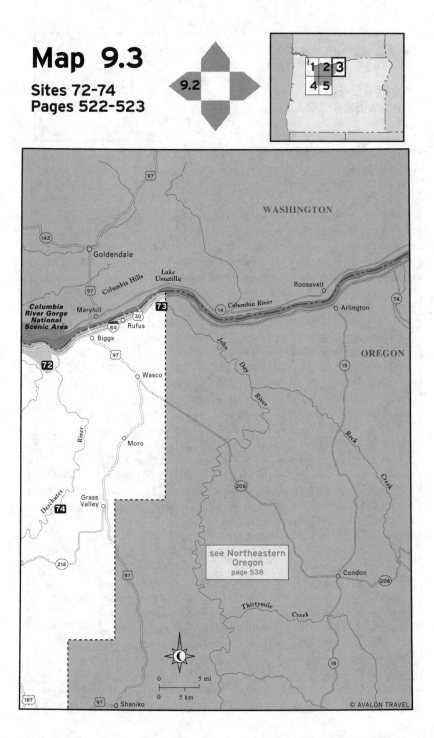

# Map 9.4

**Sites 75-83
Pages 524-527**

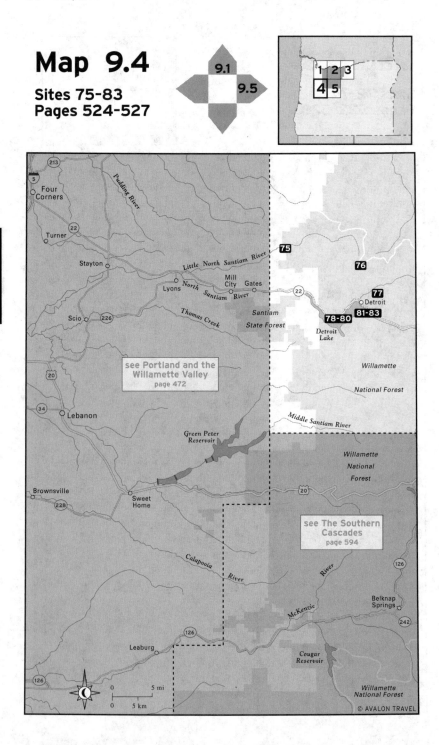

9.1
9.5

1 2 3
4 5

213
5
Four Corners
Pudding River
22
Turner
Stayton
Little North Santiam River
75
76
Lyons
Mill City
Gates
77
North Santiam River
22
Detroit
226
Scio
Thomas Creek
Santiam State Forest
78-80
81-83
Detroit Lake
20
see Portland and the Willamette Valley
page 472
Willamette
34
Lebanon
National Forest
Green Peter Reservoir
Middle Santiam River
Willamette
National
Forest
Brownsville
228
Sweet Home
20
see The Southern Cascades
page 594
Calapooia River
River
126
McKenzie
Belknap Springs
242
Leaburg
126
Cougar Reservoir
126
0        5 mi
0        5 km
Willamette National Forest
© AVALON TRAVEL

# Map 9.5

**Sites 84-103
Pages 527-536**

9.2

9.4

1 2 3
4 5

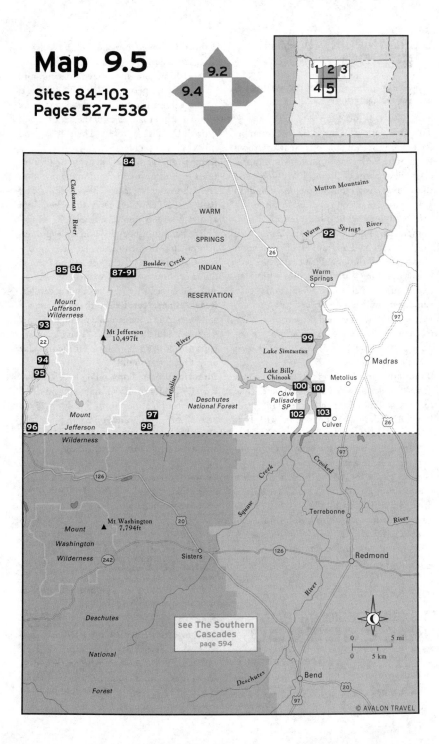

84

Mutton Mountains

*Clackamas River*

WARM

Warm Springs River

SPRINGS

92

26

85 86

87-91

*Boulder Creek*

INDIAN

Warm Springs

RESERVATION

97

Mount
Jefferson
Wilderness

93

22

▲ Mt Jefferson
10,497ft

*River*

99

*Lake Simtustus*

Madras

94

95

*Metolius*

*Lake Billy Chinook*

Metolius

100 101

Cove
Palisades
SP

96

Mount
Jefferson

97

98

Deschutes
National Forest

102

103

Culver

26

Wilderness

126

*Crooked*

97

*Squaw Creek*

Terrebonne

*River*

Mount

▲ Mt Washington
7,794ft

20

Washington

126

Wilderness

242

Sisters

Redmond

Deschutes

*River*

see The Southern
Cascades
page 594

National

0          5 mi

0        5 km

Forest

*Deschutes*

Bend

20

97

© AVALON TRAVEL

# ❶ CROWN POINT RV PARK

🚶 🚴 🛶 🐕 🚐

**Scenic rating: 6**

near the Columbia River

Map 9.1, page 487

This little park is located near the Columbia River along scenic U.S. 30. Nearby Crown Point State Park is open during the day and offers views of the Columbia River Gorge and the historic Vista House, a memorial built in 1918 to honor Oregon's pioneers. Multnomah Falls offers another possible side trip.

**Campsites, facilities:** There are 22 sites with full or partial hookups for RVs of any length. One site is pull-through. Picnic tables are provided. Drinking water, restrooms with flush toilets and coin showers, Wi-Fi, and a coin laundry are available. A store and ice are within walking distance. Leashed pets are permitted.

**Reservations, fees:** Reservations are accepted. Sites are $30-35 per night. Open year-round.

**Directions:** From Portland on I-84 eastbound, drive 16 miles to Exit 22 and Corbett. Take that exit and turn right on Corbett Hill Road. Drive 1.5 miles to a Y intersection with East Historic Columbia River Highway. Bear left and drive 0.25 mile to the park on the right.

Note: The recommended route has a 10 percent grade for 1.5 miles. An alternate route: From Portland on I-84 eastbound, drive to Exit 18/Lewis and Clark State Park. Take that exit and drive to East Historic Columbia River Highway and continue seven miles to the park on the right.

**Contact:** Crown Point RV Park, 503/695-5207.

# ❷ OXBOW REGIONAL PARK

🚶 🚴 🛶 ⛵ 🚐 🎣 ♿ 🚐 ⛺

**Scenic rating: 7**

on the Sandy River

Map 9.1, page 487

This 1,200-acre park along the Sandy River, a short distance from the Columbia River Gorge, is a designated national scenic waterway. Fishing, non-motorized boating, and swimming are permitted here. The water is usually calm, and canoes, kayaks, and rafts are allowed. About 200 acres of the park are old-growth Douglas fir forest. There are several miles of hiking trails.

**Campsites, facilities:** There are 67 sites for tents or RVs up to 35 feet long; some sites are pull-through. Picnic tables, fire pits, and barbecues are provided. Drinking water, flush and vault toilets, showers, firewood, an amphitheater, horseshoe pits, and a playground are available. Boat-launching facilities are on-site. Gates lock at official sunset and open at 6:30am. Services are approximately 10 miles away. Some facilities are wheelchair accessible.

**Reservations, fees:** Reservations are accepted at 800/452 5687. Sites are $22 per night, $5 per night per additional vehicle. There is a park entrance fee of $5 per vehicle for the first day only. Open year-round.

**Directions:** From Portland on I-84, drive to Exit 17/Troutdale. Take that exit and drive on the frontage road for 0.5 mile to 257th Street. Turn right (south) on 257th Street and drive three miles to Division Street. Turn left and drive seven miles to the park entrance on the left.

**Contact:** Metro Regional Parks and Greenspaces, Oxbow Regional Park, 503/663-4708, www.oregonmetro.gov.

# ❸ AINSWORTH STATE PARK

🚶 🐕 🎣 ♿ 🚐 ⛺

**Scenic rating: 8**

along the Columbia River Gorge

Map 9.1, page 487          BEST (

Set along the scenic Columbia River Gorge, Ainsworth State Park is waterfall central, with famous Multnomah Falls a highlight. A 1.3-mile trail leads from the campground to Horsetail Falls and the Nesmith Point Trail shares a great view of St. Peter's Dome. Anglers should check out the Bonneville Fish Hatchery about five miles away.

**Campsites, facilities:** There are 43 sites with full hookups for RVs up to 60 feet long, six walk-in tent sites, and a designated bike-in camping area. Picnic tables and fire grills are provided. Drinking water, restrooms with flush toilets and showers, garbage bins, a dump station, playground, camp host, amphitheater with occasional interpretive programs, and firewood are available. Some facilities are wheelchair accessible. Leashed pets are permitted.

**Reservations, fees:** Reservations are not accepted. Sites are $16-20 per night, $13-17 per night for walk-in tent sites, and $5 per night per additional vehicle. Some credit cards are accepted. Open mid-March-late October, weather permitting.

**Directions:** From Portland on I-84 eastbound, drive 35 miles to Exit 35. Turn southwest on the Columbia River Scenic Highway and continue a short distance to the park; the park is 17 miles east of Troutdale. An alternate route is to take the historic Columbia River Highway, a designated scenic highway, all the way from Portland (37 miles).

**Contact:** Ainsworth State Park, 503/695-2301 or 800/551-6949, www.oregonstateparks.org.

# ▲ MILO MCIVER STATE PARK
🏃🚣🛶⛵🐎♿🚐🏕️

### Scenic rating: 7
on the Clackamas River

**Map 9.1, page 487**

Though only 45 minutes from Portland, this park is far enough off the beaten track to provide a feeling of separation from the metropolitan area. It sits along the banks of the Clackamas River and has a boat ramp. There is fishing for salmon and steelhead in season; check current regulations. Trails for hiking are available, and a 4.5-mile equestrian trail is also accessible; bicycles are not allowed on trails. A fish hatchery is a nearby point of interest.

Every September, actors participate in a Civil War reenactment here.

**Campsites, facilities:** There are 44 sites with partial hookups for RVs up to 50 feet long, nine primitive tent sites, one hiker/bicyclist site, and three group tent areas for up to 50 people each. Picnic tables and fire grills are provided. Drinking water, garbage bins, restrooms with flush toilets and showers, a dump station, picnic shelters, and firewood are available. Boat-launching facilities (canoes, inflatables, and kayaks), a model airplane field, and a 27-hole disc golf course are nearby. Group facilities are available. Some facilities are wheelchair accessible. Leashed pets are permitted, and there is a designated area for off-leash dog runs.

**Reservations, fees:** Reservations are accepted at 800/452-5687 or www.oregonstateparks.org ($8 reservation fee). Tent sites are $14-18 per night, RV sites are $17-21 per night, $5 per night per each additional vehicle. Hiker/biker sites are $4 per person per night and group sites are $54-75 per night for up to 25 people, $3 per each additional person. Some credit cards are accepted. Open mid-March-October.

**Directions:** From Portland, drive east on U.S. 26 to Gresham. Continue 11 miles to Sandy and Highway 211. Turn right (south) and drive six miles to a junction. Turn south (still Highway 211) and drive one mile to Hayden Road. Turn right and drive one mile to Springwater Road. Turn right and drive one mile to the park on the right.

**Contact:** Milo McIver State Park, 503/630-6147, 503/630-7150, or 800/551-6949, www. oregonstateparks.org.

# ▲ PROMONTORY
🏃🚣🐎🏊♿🚐🏕️

### Scenic rating: 7
on North Fork Reservoir

**Map 9.1, page 487**

This Portland General Electric camp on North Fork Reservoir is part of a large recreation area and park. The reservoir, actually a dammed-up overflow of the Clackamas River, encompasses 350 acres. The water is calm and ideal for boating, and the trout fishing is excellent. A trail connects the campground to the marina. A one-acre lake is available for children's fishing.

**Campsites, facilities:** There are 69 sites for tents or self-contained RVs up to 35 feet long (no hookups) and 11 yomes (canvas cabins). There is also a group area for up to 35 people for tents or small self-contained RVs. Picnic tables and fire rings are provided. Restrooms with flush toilets and showers, garbage bins, a playground, horseshoes, a children's fishing pond, and covered picnic shelters are available. The convenience store, marina and fishing pier, and all boating facilities will be closed until 2016 for construction of a salmon passage facility. Some facilities are wheelchair accessible. Leashed pets are permitted.

**Reservations, fees:** Reservations are accepted at 503/630-7229 or www.portlandgeneral. com/parks. Sites are $18 per night, $30 per night for a yome. Some credit cards are accepted. Open mid-May-mid-September.

**Directions:** From Portland, drive east on U.S. 26 to Gresham. Continue 11 miles to Sandy and Highway 211. Turn right (south) and drive six miles to a junction. Turn south (still Highway 211) and drive six miles to Estacada. Continue south on Highway 224 and drive seven miles to the campground on the right. The route is well signed.

**Contact:** Portland General Electric, 503/464-8515, www.portlandgeneral.com/parks; store and marina, 503/630-5152; campground, 503/630-7229.

## 6 LAZY BEND

### Scenic rating: 8

on the Clackamas River in Mount Hood National Forest

**Map 9.1, page 487**

This campground is situated at 800 feet elevation along the banks of the Clackamas River

near the large North Fork Reservoir. It's far enough off the highway to provide a secluded, primitive feeling, though it fills quickly on weekends and holidays. There's only catch-and-release fishing in the Clackamas.

**Campsites, facilities:** There are five sites for tents or RVs up to 23 feet long and 13 sites for tents only. Picnic tables, garbage service, and fireplaces are provided. Drinking water and flush toilets are available. Leashed pets are permitted.

**Reservations, fees:** Reservations are accepted at 877/444-6777 ($10 reservation fee) or www. recreation.gov ($9 reservation fee). Sites are $20-22 per night, $8 per night per additional vehicle. Open early May-late September, weather permitting.

**Directions:** From Portland, drive south on U.S. 205 to the junction with Highway 24. Take the Highway 224/Estacada exit and turn left (south) onto Highway 224. Drive approximately 13 miles to Estacada. Continue south on Highway 224 for 10.5 miles to the campground on the right.

**Contact:** Mount Hood National Forest, Clackamas River Ranger District, 503/630-6861, www.fs.usda.gov/mthood.

## 7 ARMSTRONG

### Scenic rating: 5

on the Clackamas River in Mount Hood National Forest

**Map 9.1, page 487**

Armstrong campground is set at an elevation of 900 feet along the banks of the Clackamas River and offers good fishing access. Fishing is catch-and-release only.

**Campsites, facilities:** There are four sites for tents or RVs up to 40 feet long and seven sites for tents only. Picnic tables and fire rings are provided. Vault toilets and drinking water are available. Garbage service is available in the summer only. Some facilities are wheelchair accessible. Leashed pets are permitted.

**Reservations, fees:** Reservations are accepted

at 877/444-6777 ($10 reservation fee) or www.
recreation.gov ($9 reservation fee). Sites are $17-
19 per night, $8 per night per additional vehicle.
Open year-round, with limited winter services.
**Directions:** From Portland, drive south on
U.S. 205 to the junction with Highway 24.
Take the Highway 224/Estacada exit and turn
left (south) onto Highway 224. Drive approximately 13 miles to Estacada. Continue south
on Highway 224 for 15 miles to the campground on the right.
**Contact:** Mount Hood National Forest,
Clackamas River Ranger District, 503/630-
6861, www.fs.usda.gov/mthood.

## 8 CARTER BRIDGE

### Scenic rating: 5

on the Clackamas River in Mount Hood
National Forest

**Map 9.1, page 487**

This small, flat campground is popular with
anglers. The Clackamas River flows along one
end, and the other end borders the highway,
with peripheral traffic noise.
**Campsites, facilities:** There are 15 sites for
tents or RVs up to 28 feet long. Picnic tables
and fire pits are provided. Vault toilets and
garbage bins are available. There is no drinking
water. Some facilities are wheelchair accessible.
Leashed pets are permitted.
**Reservations, fees:** Reservations are not accepted. Sites are $16 per night, $8 per night
per additional vehicle. Open late May-early
September, weather permitting.
**Directions:** From Portland, drive south on
U.S. 205 to the junction with Highway 24.
Take the Highway 224/Estacada exit and turn
left (south) onto Highway 224. Drive approximately 13 miles to Estacada. Continue south
on Highway 224 for 15.2 miles to the camp-
ground on the left.
**Contact:** Mount Hood National Forest,
Clackamas River Ranger District, 503/630-
6861, www.fs.usda.gov/mthood.

## 9 LOCKABY

### Scenic rating: 6

on the Clackamas River in Mount Hood
National Forest

**Map 9.1, page 487**

This campground sits at an elevation of 900
feet along the banks of the Clackamas River,
next to Armstrong. Fishing in the Clackamas
River is catch-and-release only.
**Campsites, facilities:** There are 30 sites
for tents or RVs up to 15 feet long. Picnic
tables, fireplaces, drinking water, garbage
service, vault toilets, and firewood are available. A camp host is on-site. Leashed pets are
permitted.
**Reservations, fees:** Reservations are accepted
at 877/444-6777 ($10 reservation fee) or www.
recreation.gov ($9 reservation fee). Sites are
$20 per night, $8 per night per additional vehicle. Open late May-early September.
**Directions:** From Portland, drive south on
U.S. 205 to the junction with Highway 24.
Take the Highway 224/Estacada exit and turn
left (south) onto Highway 224. Drive approximately 13 miles to Estacada. Continue south
on Highway 224 for 15.3 miles to the campground on the left.
**Contact:** Mount Hood National Forest,
Clackamas River Ranger District, Estacada
Ranger Station, 503/630-6861, www.fs.usda.
gov/mthood.

## 10 ROARING RIVER

### Scenic rating: 8

on the Roaring River in Mount Hood
National Forest

**Map 9.1, page 487**

Set among old-growth cedars at the confluence
of the Roaring and Clackamas Rivers at an
elevation of 1,000 feet, this campground has
access to the Dry Ridge Trail. The trail starts
in camp, and it's a butt-kicker of an uphill

climb. Several other trails into the adjacent roadless area are accessible from camp.

**Campsites, facilities:** There are 14 sites for tents or RVs up to 16 feet long. Picnic tables and fireplaces are provided. Garbage service, drinking water, and vault toilets are available. Leashed pets are permitted.

**Reservations, fees:** Reservations are accepted at 877/444-6777 ($10 reservation fee) or www.recreation.gov ($9 reservation fee). Sites are $18 per night, $8 per night per additional vehicle. Open mid-May-mid-September, weather permitting.

**Directions:** From Portland, drive south on U.S. 205 to the junction with Highway 24. Take the Highway 224/Estacada exit and turn left (south) onto Highway 224. Drive approximately 13 miles to Estacada. Continue south on Highway 224 for 18 miles to the campground on the left.

**Contact:** Mount Hood National Forest, Clackamas River Ranger District, 503/630-6861, www.fs.usda.gov/mthood.

## 11 SUNSTRIP

### Scenic rating: 3
on the Clackamas River in Mount Hood National Forest

**Map 9.1, page 487**

This campground on the banks of the Clackamas River offers fishing and rafting access. One of several camps along the Highway 224 corridor, Sunstrip is a favorite with rafting and kayaking enthusiasts and can fill up quickly on weekends. The elevation is 1,000 feet. Note: This campground, squeezed between the river and the highway and traversed by power lines, may be a turnoff for those wanting another kind of experience.

**Campsites, facilities:** There are nine sites for tents or RVs up to 60 feet long. Picnic tables and fireplaces are provided. Garbage service, firewood, and vault toilets are available. There is no drinking water. A camp host is on-site. Leashed pets are permitted.

**Reservations, fees:** Reservations are accepted at 877/444-6777 ($10 reservation fee) or www.recreation.gov ($9 reservation fee). Sites are $19-21 per night, $8 per night per additional vehicle. Open year-round, with limited winter services.

**Directions:** From Portland, drive south on U.S. 205 to the junction with Highway 24. Take the Highway 224/Estacada exit and turn left (south) onto Highway 224. Drive approximately 13 miles to Estacada. Continue south on Highway 224 for 19 miles to the campground.

**Contact:** Mount Hood National Forest, Clackamas River Ranger District, 503/630-6861, www.fs.usda.gov/mthood.

## 12 RAINBOW

### Scenic rating: 6
on the Oak Grove Fork of the Clackamas River in Mount Hood National Forest

**Map 9.1, page 487**

Rainbow campground sits at an elevation of 1,400 feet along the banks of the Oak Grove Fork of the Clackamas River, not far from where it empties into the Clackamas River. The camp is less than a quarter mile from Ripplebrook Campground.

**Campsites, facilities:** There are 17 sites for tents only. Picnic tables and fire grills are provided. Drinking water and vault toilets are available. Garbage service is available during the summer. Leashed pets are permitted.

**Reservations, fees:** Reservations are accepted at 877/444-6777 ($10 reservation fee) or www.recreation.gov ($9 reservation fee). Sites are $17-19 per night, $8 per night per additional vehicle. Open year-round, with limited winter services.

**Directions:** From Portland, drive south on U.S. 205 to the junction with Highway 24. Take the Highway 224/Estacada exit and turn left (south) onto Highway 224. Drive approximately 13 miles to Estacada. Continue south on Highway 224 and drive 27 miles in national forest (the road becomes Forest Road 46). Continue south and drive about 100 yards to the campground on the right.

**Contact:** Mount Hood National Forest, Clackamas River Ranger District, 595 N.W. Industrial Way, Estacada, OR 97023, 503/630-6861, www.fs.usda.gov/mthood.

## 13 INDIAN HENRY

### Scenic rating: 8

on the Clackamas River in Mount Hood National Forest

**Map 9.1, page 487**

One of the most popular campgrounds in the Clackamas River Ranger District, Indian Henry hugs the banks of the Clackamas River at an elevation of 1,250 feet and has a wheelchair-accessible trail. Group campsites and an amphitheater are available. The nearby Clackamas River Trail has fishing access.

**Campsites, facilities:** There are 36 sites for tents or RVs up to 40 feet long, 46 sites for tents only, eight group tent sites for up to 30 people, and three yurts. Picnic tables, garbage service, and fire grills are provided. Flush toilets, firewood, and drinking water are available. A camp host is on-site. Some facilities are wheelchair accessible. Leashed pets are permitted.

**Reservations, fees:** Reservations are accepted at 877/444-6777 ($10 reservation fee) or www.recreation.gov ($9 reservation fee). Sites are $18-21 per night, $8 per night per additional vehicle; group sites are $52 per night; yurts are $38-40 per night. Open late May-early September, weather permitting.

**Directions:** From Portland, drive south on U.S. 205 to the junction with Highway 24. Take the Highway 224/Estacada exit and turn left (south) onto Highway 224. Drive approximately 13 miles to Estacada. Continue south on Highway 224 for 23 miles to Forest Road 4620. Turn right and drive 0.5 mile southeast to the campground on the left.

**Contact:** Mount Hood National Forest, Clackamas River Ranger District, 503/630-6861, www.fs.usda.gov/mthood.

## 14 RIPPLEBROOK

### Scenic rating: 7

on the Oak Grove Fork of the Clackamas River in Mount Hood National Forest

**Map 9.1, page 487**

Shaded sites with river views are a highlight at this campground along the banks of the Oak Grove Fork of the Clackamas River, where anglers are limited to artificial lures and catch-and-release only. Note: The road to this camp experiences slides and washouts; check current status before making a trip.

**Campsites, facilities:** There are five sites for RVs up to 19 feet long and nine sites for tents only. Picnic tables, garbage service, and fire grills are provided. Vault toilets are available, but there is no drinking water. Leashed pets are permitted.

**Reservations, fees:** Reservations are accepted at 877/444-6777 ($10 reservation fee) or www.recreation.gov ($9 reservation fee). Sites are $17-19 per night, $8 per night per additional vehicle. Open late April-late September, weather permitting.

**Directions:** From Portland, drive south on U.S. 205 to the junction with Highway 24. Take the Highway 224/Estacada exit and turn left (south) onto Highway 224. Drive approximately 13 miles to Estacada. Continue south on Highway 224 for 26.5 miles to the campground entrance on the left.

**Contact:** Mount Hood National Forest, Clackamas River Ranger District, 503/630-6861, www.fs.usda.gov/mthood.

## 15 RIVERSIDE

🏃 🚴 🏊 🐕 ♿ 🚐 ⛺

### Scenic rating: 8

on the Clackamas River in Mount Hood
National Forest

**Map 9.1, page 487**

The banks of the Clackamas River are home
to this campground (elevation 1,400 feet). A
worthwhile trail leaves the camp and follows
the river for four miles north. Fishing is another
option here, and several old forest roads in the
vicinity make excellent mountain-biking trails.

**Campsites, facilities:** There are 13 sites for
tents only and three sites for tents or RVs up
to 24 feet long. Picnic tables, garbage service,
and fire grills are provided. Vault toilets and
drinking water are available. Some facilities are
wheelchair accessible. Leashed pets are permitted; no horses are allowed in the campground.

**Reservations, fees:** Reservations are accepted at
877/444-6777 ($10 reservation fee) or www.recreation.gov ($9 reservation fee). Sites are $17-19 per
night, $8 per night per additional vehicle. Open
mid-May-late September, weather permitting.

**Directions:** From Portland, drive south on
U.S. 205 to the junction with Highway 24.
Take the Highway 224/Estacada exit and turn
left (south) onto Highway 224. Drive approximately 13 miles to Estacada. Continue south
on Highway 224 for 27 miles and into national
forest (Highway 224 becomes Forest Road 46).
Continue 2.5 miles south on Forest Road 46
to the campground on the right.

**Contact:** Mount Hood National Forest,
Clackamas River Ranger District, 503/630-
6861, www.fs.usda.gov/mthood.

## 16 RIVERFORD

🏊 🐕 🚐 ⛺

### Scenic rating: 4

on the Clackamas and Collawash Rivers in
Mount Hood National Forest

**Map 9.1, page 487**

This campground, just a two-minute walk

from the confluence of the Clackamas and
Collawash Rivers, offers access to good fishing.
Otherwise, it's small, and the sites provide little
privacy. It is set at an elevation of 1,500 feet.
Although there is no drinking water at this
camp, drinking water is available 0.75 mile
away at Riverside Campground.

**Campsites, facilities:** There are eight sites
for tents and two sites for RVs up to 16 feet
long. Picnic tables and fire grills are provided.
A vault toilet is available. Garbage service is
provided in the summer. There is no drinking
water. Leashed pets are permitted.

**Reservations, fees:** Reservations are not accepted. Sites are $16 per night, $7 per night
per additional vehicle. Open year-round, with
limited winter services.

**Directions:** From Portland, drive south on
U.S. 205 to the junction with Highway 24.
Take the Highway 224/Estacada exit and turn
left (south) onto Highway 224. Drive approximately 13 miles to Estacada. Continue south
on Highway 224 for 27 miles in national forest
(the road becomes Forest Road 46). Continue
south on Forest Road 46 for 3.5 miles to the
campground on the right.

**Contact:** Mount Hood National Forest,
Clackamas River Ranger District, 503/630-
6861, www.fs.usda.gov/mthood.

## 17 RAAB GROUP

🏊 🐕 🚐 ⛺

### Scenic rating: 7

on the Collawash River in Mount Hood
National Forest

**Map 9.1, page 487**

Raab Group camp (1,500 feet elevation) is
located along the banks of the Collawash
River, about a mile from its confluence with
the Clackamas River. Raab gets moderate use,
but it's usually quiet and has a nice, secluded
atmosphere with lots of privacy among the
sites.

**Campsites, facilities:** There are 26 sites for
tents or RVs up to 16 feet long and one group

site for 20-50 people. Picnic tables, garbage service, and fire grills are provided. Vault toilets are available. There is no drinking water in the campground; water is available one mile away at Two Rivers Picnic Area. Leashed pets are permitted.

**Reservations, fees:** Reservations are accepted at 877/444-6777 ($10 reservation fee) or www. recreation.gov ($9 reservation fee). Sites are $14 per night, $7 each additional vehicle; the group site is $35-42 per night. Open late May-early September, weather permitting.

**Directions:** From Portland, drive south on U.S. 205 to the junction with Highway 24. Take the Highway 224/Estacada exit and turn left (south) onto Highway 224. Drive approximately 13 miles to Estacada. Continue south on Highway 224 for 27 miles in national forest (the road becomes Forest Road 46). Continue south on Forest Road 46 for 2.5 miles to Forest Road 63. Turn right and drive 1.5 miles to the campground on the right.

**Contact:** Mount Hood National Forest, Clackamas River Ranger District, 503/630-6861, www.fs.usda.gov/mthood.

## 18 KINGFISHER

### Scenic rating: 7

on the Hot Springs Fork of the Collawash River in Mount Hood National Forest

**Map 9.1, page 487**

This pretty campground, surrounded by old-growth forest, sits on the banks of the Hot Springs Fork of the Collawash River and provides fishing access. Catch-and-release is allowed on the main fork of the Collawash but the streams are closed to fishing. It's about three miles from Bagby Hot Springs, a U.S. Forest Service day-use area. The hot springs are an easy 1.5-mile hike from the day-use area. The camp sits at 1,250 feet elevation.

**Campsites, facilities:** There are 16 sites for tents only, seven sites for tents or RVs up to 66 feet long, and a few double sites. Picnic tables

and fireplaces are provided. Garbage service is provided during the summer. Vault toilets and drinking water are available. Leashed pets are permitted.

**Reservations, fees:** Reservations are accepted at 877/444-6777 ($10 reservation fee) or www. recreation.gov ($9 reservation fee). Sites are $19-40 per night, $8 per night per additional vehicle. Open year-round, weather permitting, with limited winter facilities.

**Directions:** From Portland, drive south on U.S. 205 to the junction with Highway 24. Take the Highway 224/Estacada exit and turn left (south) onto Highway 224. Drive approximately 13 miles to Estacada. Continue south on Highway 224 for 27 miles in national forest (the road becomes Forest Road 46). Continue south on Forest Road 46 for 3.5 miles to Forest Road 63. Turn right and drive three miles to Forest Road 70. Turn right again and drive one mile to the campground on the left.

**Contact:** Mount Hood National Forest, Clackamas River Ranger District, 503/630-6861, www.fs.usda.gov/mthood.

## 19 EAGLE CREEK

### Scenic rating: 8

near the Columbia Wilderness in Mount Hood National Forest

**Map 9.2, page 488**     **BEST (**

Eagle Creek is the oldest Forest Service Camp in America. Set at 400 feet elevation among old-growth Douglas fir and hemlock, it makes a good base camp for a hiking trip. The Eagle Creek Trail leaves the campground and travels 13 miles to Wahtum Lake, where it intersects with the Pacific Crest Trail. A primitive campground sits at the 7.5-mile point. The upper seven miles of the trail pass through the Hatfield Wilderness.

**Campsites, facilities:** There are 16 sites for tents or RVs up to 20 feet long and one group site for up to 90 people. Picnic tables and fire grills are provided. Drinking water, garbage bins, and flush and vault toilets are available. A camp host is on-site. Boat docks and launching facilities are nearby on the Columbia River. Some facilities are wheelchair accessible. Leashed pets are permitted.

**Reservations, fees:** Reservations are not accepted for single sites, but are required for the Eagle Creek Overlook group site at 877/444-6777 ($10 reservation fee) or www.recreation. gov ($9 reservation fee). Sites are $15 per night, $5 per night per additional vehicle; the group site is $75-125. Open May 1-September 30.

**Directions:** From Portland, drive east on I-84 for 41 miles to Bonneville. Continue east for two miles to the campground.

**Contact:** Columbia River Gorge National Scenic Area, 541/308-1700, www.fs.usda. gov/crgnsa.

## 20 CASCADE LOCKS MARINE PARK

### Scenic rating: 8

in Cascade Locks

**Map 9.2, page 488**　　　　**BEST (**

This public riverfront park covers 23 acres and offers a museum and boat rides. The salmon fishing is excellent here. Stern-wheeler dinner cruises are available. Hiking trails and tennis courts are nearby; the Pacific Crest Trail is within one mile.

**Campsites, facilities:** There are 15 sites for tents or RVs of any length; 10 sites have partial hookups. Picnic tables are provided. Drinking water (May-October), restrooms with flush toilets and showers, a dump station, boat docks, launching facilities, Wi-Fi, book exchange, a picnic area, and a playground are available. A camp host is on-site. Propane gas, gasoline, a store, café, coin laundry, and ice are within one mile. Some facilities are wheelchair accessible. Leashed pets are permitted.

**Reservations, fees:** Reservations are accepted at 509/637-6911. Sites are $15-25 per night. Winter rates available November-April. Some

credit cards are accepted. Open year-round, with limited winter facilities.

**Directions:** From Portland, drive east on I-84 for 44 miles to Cascade Locks. Take Exit 44/ Cascade Locks to Wanapa Street. Turn left and drive 0.5 mile to the sign for the park on the left (well signed). Please note: There is a 12-foot clearance into Marine Park.

**Contact:** Port of Cascade Locks, Cascade Locks Marine Park, 541/374-8619, www. portofcascadelocks.org.

## 21 KOA CASCADE LOCKS

### Scenic rating: 5

near the Columbia River

**Map 9.2, page 488**

This KOA is a good layover spot for RVers touring the Columbia River corridor. The campground offers level, shaded RV sites and grassy tent sites. A pancake breakfast is available on weekends during the summer season. Nearby recreation options include bike trails, hiking trails, and tennis courts. The 200-acre Cascade Locks Marine Park is close by and offers everything from museums to boat trips.

**Campsites, facilities:** There are 33 sites for tents, 78 sites with full or partial hookups for RVs of any length, and 13 cabins and cottages. Most RV sites are pull-through. Picnic tables and fire pits are provided. Restrooms with flush toilets and showers, drinking water, propane gas, a dump station, firewood, a spa, cable TV, Wi-Fi, a recreation hall, convenience store, coin laundry, ice, a playground, bicycle rentals, and a heated seasonal swimming pool are available. A café is within one mile. Some facilities are wheelchair accessible. Leashed pets are permitted.

**Reservations, fees:** Reservations are accepted at 800/562-8698. Sites are $27-42 per night, $5 per person per night for more than two people. Cabins are $45-69 per night; cottages are $55-129 per night. Some credit cards are accepted. Open February-October 15.

**Directions:** From Portland, drive east on I-84 for 44 miles to Cascade Locks and Exit 44. Take that exit to Forest Lane. Turn east on Forest Lane and drive one mile to the campground on the left.

**Contact:** KOA Cascade Locks, 541/374-8668, www.koa.com.

## 22 HERMAN CREEK HORSE CAMP

**Scenic rating: 9**

near the Pacific Crest Trail in Mount Hood National Forest

**Map 9.2, page 488**

This rustic campground sits at 300 feet elevation and is about half a mile from Herman Creek, not far from the Pacific Crest Trail. This area, separated from Washington by the Columbia River, is particularly beautiful. The campsites are spacious, and the many recreation options include biking, boating, fishing, and hiking. Note that new rules regarding stock feed require certified weed-free hay, feed, and crop products on national forest land.

**Campsites, facilities:** There are seven sites for tents or RVs of any length; some sites have stalls. Picnic tables and fire grills are provided. Drinking water, garbage bins, restrooms with flush toilets, and stock-handling facilities, are available. A camp host is on-site. Leashed pets are permitted.

**Reservations, fees:** Reservations are not accepted. Sites are $10 per night, $5 per night per additional vehicle. Open May 1-September 30.

**Directions:** From Portland, drive east on I-84 for 44 miles to Cascade Locks and Exit 44. Take that exit and drive straight ahead (east) onto Wanapa Street and drive back under the highway. Continue 1.5 miles (the road becomes Herman Creek Road) to the campground on the right.

**Contact:** Columbia River Gorge National Scenic Area, 541/308-1700, www.fs.usda.gov/crgnsa.

## 23 WYETH

**Scenic rating: 5**

on Gordon Creek in Mount Hood National Forest

**Map 9.2, page 488**

Wyeth makes a good layover spot for Columbia River corridor cruisers. The camp (100 feet elevation) borders Gordon Creek, near the Columbia River. Recreation options include biking, boating, fishing, and hiking.

**Campsites, facilities:** There are 14 sites for tents or RVs up to 30 feet long and three group sites. Fire grills and picnic tables are provided. A flush toilet is available; call for drinking water availability. A camp host is on-site. Some facilities are wheelchair accessible. Leashed pets are permitted.

**Reservations, fees:** Reservations are not accepted. Sites are $10 per night, $5 per night per additional vehicle, group sites are $15 per night. Open May 1-September 30.

**Directions:** From Portland, drive east on I-84 for 44 miles to Cascade Locks. Continue east on I-84 for seven miles to Wyeth and Exit 51. Turn right and drive 0.25 mile to the campground entrance.

**Contact:** Columbia River Gorge National Scenic Area, 541/308-1700, www.fs.usda.gov/crgnsa.

## 24 VIENTO STATE PARK

**Scenic rating: 8**

along the Columbia River Gorge

**Map 9.2, page 488**

This park along the Columbia River Gorge offers scenic hiking trails and some of the best windsurfing in the Gorge. Just 12 miles to the east, old U.S. 30 skirts the Columbia River, offering a picturesque drive. Viento has a day-use picnic area right next to a babbling creek. Look for weekend interpretive programs during the summer. There are several other day-use state parks along I-84 just west of Viento, including Seneca Fouts, Vinzenz Lausmann, and Wygant. All offer quality hiking trails and scenic views.

**Campsites, facilities:** There are 56 sites with partial hookups for RVs up to 30 feet long (with some up to 40 feet long) and 18 tent sites. Picnic tables and fire grills are provided. Drinking water, garbage bins, restrooms with flush toilets and showers, firewood, and a playground are available. Some facilities are wheelchair accessible. Leashed pets are permitted.

**Reservations, fees:** Reservations are not accepted. RV sites are $16-20 per night, tent sites are $13-17 per night, $5 per night per additional vehicle. Some credit cards are accepted. Open mid-March-October, weather permitting.

**Directions:** From Portland, drive east on I-84 for 56 miles to Exit 56 (eight miles west of Hood River). Take Exit 56 and drive to the park entrance. The park is set on both sides of I-84.

**Contact:** Viento State Park, 541/374-8811 or 800/551-6949, www.oregonstateparks.org.

## 25 TUCKER COUNTY PARK

🛶 🏊 🏕 🚵 🚐 ⛺

Scenic rating: 6

on the Hood River

Map 9.2, page 488

This county park along the banks of the Hood River is just far enough out of the way to be missed by most of the tourist traffic. Many people who choose this county park come for the windsurfing. Other recreation opportunities include rafting and kayaking. Fishing is not allowed at the park.

**Campsites, facilities:** There are 70 sites for tents or RVs and 20 sites with water-only hookups for tents or RVs up to 34 feet long. Picnic tables and fire rings are provided. Drinking water, restrooms with flush toilets and showers, reservable picnic shelter, and a playground are available. A store, café, gasoline, and ice are

within three miles. Some facilities are wheelchair accessible. Leashed pets are permitted.

**Reservations, fees:** Reservations are not accepted. RV sites are $20-25 per night, tent sites are $18 per night, $10 per night per additional tent, and $5 per night per additional vehicle. Open April-October.

**Directions:** From Portland, turn east on I-84 and drive about 65 miles to the town of Hood River and Exit 62. Take the exit and drive east on Cascade Street, continuing to 13th Street (first light). Turn right (south) and drive through and out of town; 13th Street becomes Tucker Road and then Dee Highway (Highway 281). Follow the signs to Parkdale. The park is four miles out of town on the right.

**Contact:** Hood River County Parks, 541/387-6889 or 541/386-4477, www.co.hood-river.or.us.

## 26 MEMALOOSE STATE PARK

🐕 🚵 🚐 ⛺

Scenic rating: 7

in the Columbia River Gorge

Map 9.2, page 488

This park borrows its name from nearby Memaloose Island, which Native Americans used as a sacred burial ground. Situated along the hottest part of the scenic Columbia River Gorge, the campground makes a prime layover spot for campers cruising the Oregon/Washington border. Nature programs and interpretive events are held here. This popular camp receives a good deal of traffic, so plan on arriving early to claim a spot, even if you have a reservation.

**Campsites, facilities:** There are 65 tent sites and 44 sites with full hookups for RVs up to 60 feet long. Picnic tables and fire grills are provided. Drinking water, garbage bins, restrooms with flush toilets and showers, a dump station, playground, and firewood are available. Leashed pets are permitted.

**Reservations, fees:** Reservations are accepted at 800/452-5687 or www.oregonstateparks.

org ($8 reservation fee). RV sites with full hookups are $20-24 per night, tent sites are $15-19 per night, $5 per night per additional vehicle. Some credit cards are accepted. Open mid-March-October.

**Directions:** Memaloose State Park is accessible only to westbound traffic on I-84. From The Dalles, drive west on I-84 for 11 miles to the signed turnoff. (The park is about 75 miles east of Portland.)

If eastbound on I-84, take Exit 76. Drive under the freeway to the I-84 west on-ramp. Once on I-84 west, drive 2.5 miles to the sign for Rest Area/Memaloose State Park. Drive into the rest area and take an immediate right into the campground.

**Contact:** Memaloose State Park, 541/478-3008 or 800/551-6949, www.oregonstate-parks.org.

## 27 WAHTUM LAKE CAMPGROUND

### Scenic rating: 9

east of the Mark O. Hatfield Wilderness on Wahtum Lake in Mount Hood National Forest

Map 9.2, page 488

Located at 3,900 feet elevation, this small but popular campsite is situated amongst old growth Douglas fir trees above a beautiful and pristine alpine lake. Follow a short stair-step trail down to the edge of Wahtum Lake and fish some of the stocked and native rainbow trout. Or continue on another mile or so following the Pacific Crest Trail/Eagle Creek 440 Trail around the perimeter of the lake.

**Campsites, facilities:** There are five sites for tents only. Picnic tables and fire pits are provided. Vault toilets and garbage bins are available. There is no drinking water. Leashed pets are permitted.

**Reservations, fees:** Reservations are not accepted. Sites are $12 per night, $5 extra vehicle fee. Open late May-early September, weather permitting.

**Directions::** From Hood River, take Highway 35 South for about 14 miles and turn right on Woodworth Road. Continue three miles to the intersection with Highway 281. Turn right onto Highway 281 and travel approximately six miles to Dee; turn left on Lost Lake Road. Continue seven miles, then turn right onto Forest Service Road 13. Drive six miles, then turn right onto Forest Service Road 1310 and drive two miles to the campground on the right.

**Contact:** Mount Hood National Forest, Hood River Ranger District, 541/352-6002, www. fs.usda.gov/mthood.

## 28 KINNICKKINNICK

### Scenic rating: 5

on Laurence Lake in Mount Hood National Forest

Map 9.2, page 488

Kinnickkinnick campground sits on a peninsula that juts into Laurence Lake; only non-motorized boats are allowed on the lake. Campsite privacy varies because of the fairly sparse tree cover, and more than half of the sites are a short walk from your vehicle.

**Campsites, facilities:** There are 20 walk-in tent sites. Picnic tables and fire rings with fire grills are provided. There is no drinking water. Vault toilets, garbage bins, and a boat ramp are available. Some facilities are wheelchair accessible. Leashed pets are permitted.

**Reservations, fees:** Reservations are not accepted. Sites are $12 per night, $7 per night per additional vehicle. Open May-September, weather permitting.

**Directions:** From Portland, drive 62 miles west on I-84 to the city of Hood River. Take Exit 64 and drive about 14 miles south on Highway 35 to the town of Mount Hood and Cooper Spur Road. Turn right and drive three miles to Parkdale and Clear Creek Road. Turn left (south) and drive three miles to the Laurence Lake turnoff. Turn right on Forest Road

2840 (Laurence Lake Road) and drive four miles to the campground on the right.

**Contact:** Mount Hood National Forest, Hood River Ranger District, 541/352-6002, www. fs.usda.gov/mthood.

## 29 LOST LAKE

🚶 🚴 🏊 🛶 🚤 🎣 👨 ♿ 🚐 ⛺

**Scenic rating: 9**

on Lost Lake in Mount Hood National Forest

**Map 9.2, page 488**               **BEST (**

Only non-motorized boats are allowed on this clear, 240-acre lake set against the Cascade Range. The campground is nestled in an old-growth forest of cedar, Douglas fir, and hemlock trees at 3,200 feet elevation. Many sites have a lake view, and the campground affords a great view of Mount Hood.

**Campsites, facilities:** There are 125 sites for tents or RVs up to 32 feet long and several group sites. A horse camp with a corral is also available. Picnic tables and fire rings with grills are provided. Drinking water, vault toilets, garbage containers, a dump station, and a covered picnic shelter are available. Cabins, a grocery store, showers, beach picnic areas, a boat launch, and boat rentals are nearby. Some facilities are wheelchair accessible, including a barrier-free boat launch and fishing pier, as well as 3.5 miles of barrier-free trails. Leashed pets are permitted.

**Reservations, fees:** Reservations are not accepted for single sites but are required for the group sites at 541/386-6366. Single sites are $25 per night for up to three tents, $7 per night per additional vehicle; group sites are $40-275 per night and can accommodate up to 50 people. Some credit cards are accepted. Open mid-May-mid-October, weather permitting.

**Directions:** From Portland, drive 62 miles east on I-84 to the city of Hood River. Take Exit 62/Westcliff to Cascade Street. Drive east on Cascade Street to 13th Street. Turn right on 13th Street and drive through Hood River Heights. The road turns into Dee Highway. Continue seven miles to Lost Lake Road/

Forest Road 13. Turn right and drive seven miles to the campground.

**Contact:** Mount Hood National Forest, Hood River Ranger District, 541/352-6002; Lost Lake Resort, 541/386-6366, www.fs.usda.gov/mthood.

## 30 TOLL BRIDGE PARK

🛶 🎣 🚵 ♿ 🚐 ⛺

**Scenic rating: 5**

on the Hood River

**Map 9.2, page 488**

The wild Hood River runs through this campground in a woodsy setting. Fishing for trout is an obvious recreational option; stargazing is another, as there is no light pollution here.

**Campsites, facilities:** There are 21 sites for tents only, 20 sites with full hookups for RVs of any length, 40 sites with partial hookups, and two group sites for up to 50 people. Picnic tables and fire rings are provided. Drinking water, restrooms with flush toilets and showers, a dump station, and a playground are available. Groceries and fishing tackle are available eight miles away in Odell. Some facilities are wheelchair accessible. Leashed pets are permitted.

**Reservations, fees:** Reservations are strongly advised and are accepted via email at reservations@co.hood-river.or.us. RV sites are $20-25 per night, tent sites are $18 per night, $10 per night per additional tent, and $5 per night per additional vehicle; group sites are $75 per night. Open April 1-November 1.

**Directions:** From Portland, take I-84 east for about 65 miles to Exit 64. Take that exit and drive south for X miles to Highway 35. Take Highway 35 south and drive 14.5 miles to Toll Bridge Road. Turn right (west) onto Toll Bridge Road and drive 0.25 mile to the park entrance on the right.

GPS Coordinates: 45.518603567584144, -121.56850576400757

**Contact:** Hood River County Parks, 541/387-6889 or 541/352-5522, www.co.hood-river.or.us.

## 31 KNEBAL SPRINGS

**Scenic rating: 6**

near Knebal Springs in Mount Hood
National Forest

**Map 9.2, page 488**

This spot (4,000 feet elevation) is in a semi-primitive area near Knebal Springs, an ephemeral water source. The Knebal Springs Trail begins at the campground. There is a nice, level family trail available for biking or horseback riding. Another trail from the camp provides access to a network of trails in the area. A U.S. Forest Service map is advised.

**Campsites, facilities:** There are eight sites for tents or RVs up to 22 feet long. Picnic tables and fire grills are provided. There is no drinking water. Vault toilets and horse-loading and -tending facilities are available. Garbage must be packed out. Leashed pets are permitted.

**Reservations, fees:** Reservations are not accepted. Sites are $11 per night, $5 per each additional vehicle. Open mid-May-October, weather permitting.

**Directions:** From Portland, turn east on I-84 and drive about 90 miles to Exit 87. Take Exit 87 and turn south on U.S. 197; drive 13 miles to Dufur and Dufur Valley Road. Turn right on Dufur Valley Road and drive west for 12 miles to Forest Road 44. Continue west on Forest Road 44 for four miles to Forest Road 4430. Turn right and drive four miles to Forest Road 1720. Turn left (southwest) and drive one mile to the campground.

**Contact:** Mount Hood National Forest, Barlow Ranger District, 541/467-2291, www.fs.usda.gov/mthood.

## 32 EIGHTMILE CROSSING

**Scenic rating: 7**

on Eightmile Creek in Mount Hood National
Forest

**Map 9.2, page 488**

This campground sits at an elevation of 4,200 feet along Eightmile Creek. Although pretty and shaded, with sites scattered along the banks of the creek, it gets relatively little camping pressure. From the day-use area, you have access to a nice hiking trail that runs along Eightmile Creek. In addition, a 0.75-mile wheelchair-accessible trail links Eightmile Campground to Lower Crossing Campground. The fishing can be good here, so bring your gear.

**Campsites, facilities:** There are 21 sites for tents or RVs up to 30 feet long. Picnic tables and fire grills are provided. Vault toilets are available. No drinking water is available, and garbage must be packed out. Some facilities are wheelchair accessible. Leashed pets are permitted.

**Reservations, fees:** Reservations are not accepted. Sites are $10 per night, $5 per each additional vehicle. Open June-mid-October, weather permitting.

**Directions:** From Portland, turn east on I-84 and drive about 90 miles to Exit 87. Take Exit 87 and turn south on U.S. 197; drive 13 miles to Dufur and Dufur Valley Road. Turn right on Dufur Valley Road and drive west for 12 miles to Forest Road 44. Continue west on Forest Road 44 for four miles to Forest Road 4430. Turn right and drive 0.5 mile to the campground.

**Contact:** Mount Hood National Forest, Barlow Ranger District, 541/467-2291, www.fs.usda.gov/mthood.

## 33 PEBBLE FORD

### Scenic rating: 6
in Mount Hood National Forest

**Map 9.2, page 488**

This is just a little camping spot by the side of a gravel forest road. Primitive and quiet, it's an alternative to the better-known Eightmile Crossing. There are some quality hiking trails in the area if you're willing to drive two or three miles. The elevation is 4,200 feet.

**Campsites, facilities:** There are three sites for tents or RVs up to 16 feet long. Picnic tables and fire grills are provided. Vault toilets are available. There is no drinking water. Leashed pets are permitted.

**Reservations, fees:** Reservations are not accepted. Sites are $10 per night, $5 per each additional vehicle. Open June-early October, weather permitting.

**Directions:** From Portland, turn east on I-84 and drive about 90 miles to Exit 87. Take Exit 87 and turn south on U.S. 197; drive 13 miles to Dufur and Dufur Valley Road. Turn right on Dufur Valley Road and drive west for 12 miles to Forest Road 44. Continue west on Forest Road 44 for five miles to Forest Road 130. Turn left (south) and drive a short distance to the campground on the left.

**Contact:** Mount Hood National Forest, Barlow Ranger District, 541/467-2291, www.fs.usda.gov/mthood.

## 34 MCNEIL

### Scenic rating: 5
on the Clear Fork of the Sandy River in Mount Hood National Forest

**Map 9.2, page 488**

McNeil campground (2,040 feet elevation) is located in Old Maid Flat, a special geological area along the Clear Fork of the Sandy River. There's a good view of Mount Hood from the campground entrance. Several trails nearby provide access to the wilderness backcountry.

**Campsites, facilities:** There are 34 sites for tents or RVs up to 22 feet long. Picnic tables and vault toilets are provided. There is no drinking water. Leashed pets are permitted.

**Reservations, fees:** Reservations are not accepted. Sites are $15 per night, $8 per night per additional vehicle; $2 per night charge during holidays. Open May-October, weather permitting.

**Directions:** From Portland, drive 40 miles east on U.S. 26 to Zigzag. Turn left on County Road 18/East Lolo Pass Road and drive 4.5 miles to Forest Road 1825. Turn right on Forest Road 1825, drive less than one mile, bear right onto a bridge to stay on Forest Road 1825, and drive 0.25 mile to the campground on the left.

**Contact:** Mount Hood National Forest, Zigzag Ranger District, 503/622-3191, www.fs.usda.gov/mthood.

## 35 RILEY HORSE CAMP

### Scenic rating: 6
near the Clear Fork of the Sandy River in Mount Hood National Forest

**Map 9.2, page 488**

Riley Horse Camp is close to McNeil and offers the same opportunities, except Riley provides stock facilities and is reserved for horse camping only on holidays. Secluded in an area of Douglas fir and lodgepole pine at 2,100 feet elevation, Riley is a popular base camp for horse-packing trips.

**Campsites, facilities:** There are 14 sites for tents or RVs up to 45 feet long. Picnic tables and fire grills are provided. Vault toilets, garbage bins, and firewood are available. There is no drinking water. Corrals and hitching posts for horses are available. Leashed pets are permitted.

**Reservations, fees:** Reservations are accepted for 10 equestrian sites at 877/444-6777 ($10 reservation fee) or www.recreation.gov ($9 reservation fee). Sites are $17-19 per night, $8 per night per additional vehicle; $2 per night charge during holidays. Open May-September, weather permitting.

**Directions:** From Portland, drive 40 miles east on U.S. 26 to Zigzag. Turn left (northeast) on County Road 18/East Lolo Pass Road and drive 4.5 miles to Forest Road 1825. Turn right and drive 0.5 mile to Forest Road 380. Turn right and drive 100 yards to the camp.

**Contact:** Mount Hood National Forest, Zigzag Ranger District, 503/622-3191, www.fs.usda.gov/mthood.

## 36 LOST CREEK

### Scenic rating: 8
on Lost Creek in Mount Hood National Forest

Map 9.2, page 488

This campground near McNeil and Riley has some of the same opportunities. Set in a cool, lush area on a creek at 2,600 feet elevation, it's barrier-free and offers an interpretive nature trail about one mile long, as well as a wheelchair-accessible fishing pier.

**Campsites, facilities:** There are eight sites for tents or RVs up to 40 feet long, including some pull-through sites, five walk-in sites, and two yurts that can accommodate up to six people. Picnic tables and fire grills are provided. Drinking water, garbage service, and vault toilets are available. Some facilities are wheelchair accessible. Leashed pets are permitted.

**Reservations, fees:** Reservations are accepted at 877/444-6777 ($10 reservation fee) or www.recreation.gov ($9 reservation fee). Sites are $19-21 per night, yurts are $38-40 per night, $8 per night per additional vehicle. Open May-late September.

**Directions:** From Portland, drive 40 miles east on U.S. 26 to Zigzag. Turn left (northeast) on County Road 18/East Lolo Pass Road and drive 4.5 miles to Forest Road 1825. Turn right and drive for less than a mile and bear right

at the fork, which keeps you on Forest Road 1825. Continue across the Sandy River Bridge and drive approximately two miles and bear right at the Y junction. The campground is less than a mile past the junction.

**Contact:** Mount Hood National Forest, Zigzag Ranger District, 503/622-3191, www.fs.usda.gov/mthood.

## 37 TOLL GATE

### Scenic rating: 8
on the Zigzag River in Mount Hood National Forest

Map 9.2, page 488                    BEST (

This shady campground along the banks of the Zigzag River near Rhododendron is extremely popular, and finding a site on a summer weekend can be next to impossible. Luckily, you can make a reservation. There are numerous hiking trails in the area. The nearest one leads east for several miles along the river. The campground features a historic Civilian Conservation Corps shelter from the 1930s, which can be used by campers for day use.

**Campsites, facilities:** There are four sites for tents or RVs up to 40 feet long and six sites for tents only. Picnic tables and fire grills are provided. Drinking water, garbage service, firewood, a group picnic area (available by reservation), and vault toilets are available. A camp host is on-site. Leashed pets are permitted.

**Reservations, fees:** Reservations are accepted at 877/444-6777 ($10 reservation fee) or www.recreation.gov ($9 reservation fee). Sites are $19-40 per night, $8 per night per additional vehicle. Open late May-early September, weather permitting.

**Directions:** From Portland, drive east on U.S. 26 for 40 miles to Zigzag. Continue 2.5 miles southeast on U.S. 26 to the campground entrance.

**Contact:** Mount Hood National Forest, Zigzag Ranger District, 503/622-3191, www.fs.usda.gov/mthood.

## 38 GREEN CANYON

### Scenic rating: 8

on the Salmon River in Mount Hood National Forest

**Map 9.2, page 488**

Few out-of-towners know about this winner. But the locals do, and they keep the place hopping in the summer. The camp sits at 1,600 feet elevation along the banks of the Salmon River. A long trail cuts through the area and parallels the river, passing through a magnificent old-growth forest.

**Campsites, facilities:** There are 15 sites for tents or RVs up to 22 feet long. Picnic tables and fire grills are provided. Garbage bins and vault toilets are available. There is no drinking water. A store, café, and ice are within five miles. Leashed pets are permitted.

**Reservations, fees:** Reservations are not accepted. Sites are $20 per night, $8 per night per additional vehicle, $2 additional fee on holidays. Open May-October, weather permitting.

**Directions:** From Portland, drive east on U.S. 26 for 39 miles to Forest Road 2618 (Salmon River Road) near Zigzag. Turn right and drive 4.5 miles to the campground on the right.

**Contact:** Mount Hood National Forest, Zigzag Ranger District, 503/622-3191, www.fs.usda.gov/mthood.

## 39 CAMP CREEK

### Scenic rating: 8

near the Zigzag River in Mount Hood National Forest

**Map 9.2, page 488**

This campground (2,200 feet elevation) sits along Camp Creek, not far from the Zigzag River. It looks similar to Toll Gate, but larger and farther from the road. A hiking trail runs through camp and along the river; another one leads south to Still Creek. This campground, along with Toll Gate to the west, is very popular—you'll probably need a reservation.

**Campsites, facilities:** There are 22 single sites and three double sites for tents or RVs up to 45 feet long. Picnic tables and fire grills are provided. Drinking water, vault toilets, and garbage bins are available. A camp host is on-site. Some facilities are wheelchair accessible. Leashed pets are permitted.

**Reservations, fees:** Reservations are accepted Memorial Day-Labor Day at 877/444-6777 ($10 reservation fee) or www.recreation.gov ($9 reservation fee). Single sites are $18-20 per night, $40 for a double site, and $8 per night per additional vehicle, $2 additional fee on holidays. Open May-September, weather permitting.

**Directions:** From Portland, drive east on U.S. 26 for 40 miles to Zigzag. Continue southeast on U.S. 26 for about four miles to the camp on the right.

**Contact:** Mount Hood National Forest, Zigzag Ranger District, 503/622-3191, www.fs.usda.gov/mthood.

## 40 ALPINE

### Scenic rating: 8

near the Pacific Crest Trail in Mount Hood National Forest

**Map 9.2, page 488**

The small Alpine campground is set on the south slope of Mount Hood at 5,400 feet elevation, one mile from the Timberline Ski Area lodge. If you can bear some traffic noise, you'll be rewarded with big trees, a mountain feel, and year-round skiing and snowboarding less than one mile away. The Pacific Crest Trail is accessible from the Timberline Lodge. It can get quite crowded here on weekends. In the shoulder seasons, come prepared for cold nights.

**Campsites, facilities:** There are 16 sites for tents or RVs up to 16 feet long. Picnic tables and fire grills are provided. Drinking water, a portable toilet, and garbage service are available. Some facilities are wheelchair accessible. Leashed pets are permitted.

**Reservations, fees:** Reservations are not accepted. Sites are $20 per night, $8 per night per additional vehicle, $2 additional fee on holidays. Open mid-July-September, weather permitting.

**Directions:** From Portland, drive east on U.S. 26 for 55 miles to the small town of Government Camp. Continue east for one mile to Timberline Road (Forest Road 173). Turn left and drive 4.5 miles to the campground on the left.

**Contact:** Mount Hood National Forest, Zigzag Ranger District, 503/622-3191, www.fs.usda.gov/mthood.

## 41 NOTTINGHAM

### Scenic rating: 7
near the East Fork of the Hood River

**Map 9.2, page 488**

Nottingham campground, situated at 3,300 feet in elevation on the East Fork of the Hood River, has a variety of shady and sunny spots. The primary tree cover is Douglas fir and ponderosa pine. The Tamanawas Falls Trail (near Sherwood Camp) is three miles away, and the Gumjuwac Trail is 1.5 miles north. Fishing is only fair because of the swift water and lack of pools.

**Campsites, facilities:** There are 23 sites for tents or RVs up to 32 feet long. Picnic tables and fire rings are provided. A portable toilet and garbage bins are available. There is no drinking water. Some facilities are wheelchair accessible. Leashed pets are permitted.

**Reservations, fees:** Reservations are not accepted. Sites are $12 per night, $7 per night per additional vehicle. Open May-October, weather permitting.

**Directions:** From Mount Hood, drive south on Highway 35 for 13 miles to the camp on the right.

**Contact:** Mount Hood National Forest, Hood River Ranger District, 541/352-6002, www.fs.usda.gov/mthood.

## 42 STILL CREEK

### Scenic rating: 6
on Still Creek in Mount Hood National Forest

**Map 9.2, page 488**

This primitive camp, shaded primarily by fir and hemlock, sits along Still Creek where the creek pours off Mount Hood's south slope. Adjacent to Summit Meadows and the site of a pioneer gravesite from the Oregon Trail days, it's a great place for mountain views, sunsets, and wildlife. Anglers should bring along their rods: The fishing in Still Creek can be excellent. The camp sits at 3,600 feet elevation.

**Campsites, facilities:** There are 10 sites for tents or RVs up to 40 feet long and 17 sites for tents only. Picnic tables and fire grills are provided. Vault toilets, drinking water, and garbage service are available. Leashed pets are permitted.

**Reservations, fees:** Reservations are accepted at 877/444-6777 ($10 reservation fee) or www.recreation.gov ($9 reservation fee). Sites are $17-21 per night, $8 per night per additional vehicle. Open mid-June-mid-September, weather permitting.

**Directions:** From Portland, drive 55 miles east on U.S. 26 to Government Camp. Continue east on U.S. 26 for one mile to Forest Road 2650. Turn right and drive south for 500 yards to the campground.

**Contact:** Mount Hood National Forest, Zigzag Ranger District, 503/622-3191, www.fs.usda.gov/mthood.

## 43 GRINDSTONE

### Scenic rating: 7
near Barlow Creek in Mount Hood National Forest

**Map 9.2, page 488**

This tiny campground, located at 3,400 feet elevation in a meadow along Barlow Creek, is a little-known and little-used spot. You won't find much out here but wind, water, and trees—but sometimes that's all you need. High-clearance vehicles are recommended. This camp was a site first used by the pioneers.

**Campsites, facilities:** There are three primitive sites for tents. Picnic tables and fire grills are provided. Vault toilets are available. There is no drinking water, and garbage must be packed out. Leashed pets are permitted.

**Reservations, fees:** Reservations are not accepted. There is no fee for camping. Open May-September, weather permitting.

**Directions:** From Portland, turn east on U.S. 26 and drive 57 miles (just past the town of Government Camp) to the junction with Highway 35. Take that exit, bear right onto Highway 35, and drive 4.5 miles to Forest Road 3530. Turn right and drive two miles to the campground on the right.

**Contact:** Mount Hood National Forest, Hood River Ranger District, 541/352-6002, www.fs.usda.gov/mthood.

## 44 DEVIL'S HALF ACRE MEADOW

### Scenic rating: 8
on Barlow Creek in Mount Hood National Forest

**Map 9.2, page 488**

Note: This camp was closed in 2013 due to bridge construction; it is scheduled to reopen in 2014.

On a site used by the pioneers, this campground is situated a few miles upstream from Grindstone Campground on Barlow Creek. Several hiking trails close to camp, including the Pacific Crest Trail, provide access to small lakes in the area. There are many historic points of interest in the vicinity. High-clearance vehicles are recommended. The camp is at 3,600 feet elevation.

**Campsites, facilities:** There are two sites for tents or RVs up to 16 feet long. Picnic tables and fire grills are provided. Vault toilets are

available. There is no drinking water, and garbage must be packed out. Leashed pets are permitted.

**Reservations, fees:** Reservations are not accepted. There is no fee for camping. Open May-October, weather permitting.

**Directions:** From Portland, drive east on U.S. 26 for 57 miles (just past the town of Government Camp) to the junction with Highway 35. Take that exit, bear right on Highway 35, and drive 4.5 miles to Forest Road 3530. Turn southeast and drive one mile to the campground.

**Contact:** Mount Hood National Forest, Hood River Ranger District, 541/352-6002, www.fs.usda.gov/mthood.

## 45 TRILLIUM LAKE

### Scenic rating: 9
on Trillium Lake in Mount Hood National Forest

**Map 9.2, page 488**       **BEST (**

This campground (3,600 feet elevation) hugs the shores of Trillium Lake, which is about half a mile long and a quarter mile wide. Fishing is good in the evening here, and the nearby boat ramp makes this an ideal camp for anglers. The lake is great for canoes, rafts, and small rowboats. Trillium Lake is an extremely popular vacation destination, so expect plenty of company. Reservations are highly recommended.

**Campsites, facilities:** There are 41 sites for tents or RVs of any length, 21 sites for tents only, and one group site for up to 30 people. Picnic tables and fire grills are provided. Vault toilets and drinking water are available. Boat docks and launching facilities are available on the lake, but no motors are allowed. Some facilities are wheelchair accessible. Leashed pets are permitted.

**Reservations, fees:** Reservations are accepted at 877/444-6777 ($10 reservation fee) or www.recreation.gov ($9 reservation fee). Sites are $19-40 per night, the group site is

$90 per night, $8 per night per additional vehicle. Open late May-late September, weather permitting.

**Directions:** From Portland, drive east on U.S. 26 for 55 miles to the small town of Government Camp. Continue east on U.S. 26 for 1.5 miles to Forest Road 2656. Turn right and drive 1.3 miles to the campground on the right.

**Contact:** Mount Hood National Forest, Zigzag Ranger District, 503/622-3191, www.fs.usda.gov/mthood.

## 46 FROG LAKE

**Scenic rating: 6**

near the Pacific Crest Trail in Mount Hood National Forest

**Map 9.2, page 488**

This classic spot in the Cascade Range is situated on the shore of little Frog Lake (more of a pond than a lake), at an elevation of 3,800 feet and a short distance from the Pacific Crest Trail. Several other trails lead to nearby lakes. Clear Lake, to the south, provides a possible day trip and offers more recreation options.

**Campsites, facilities:** There are 23 sites for tents or RVs up to 35 feet long and nine sites for tents only. Picnic tables and fire rings are provided. Drinking water, vault toilets, garbage bins, and firewood are available. A camp host is on-site. Boat-launching facilities are nearby; no motorized boats are allowed. Some facilities are wheelchair accessible. Leashed pets are permitted.

**Reservations, fees:** Reservations are accepted at 877/444-6777 ($10 reservation fee) or www.recreation.gov ($9 reservation fee). Sites are $20-22 per night, $8 per night per additional vehicle. Open mid-May-mid-September, weather permitting.

**Directions:** From Portland, drive east on U.S. 26 for 57 miles to the junction with Highway 35 (two miles past Government Camp). Take

that exit, bear right onto Highway 35, and drive seven miles to Forest Road 2610. Turn left and drive 0.5 mile to the campground.

**Contact:** Mount Hood National Forest, Hood River Ranger District, 541/352-6002, www.fs.usda.gov/mthood; park phone, 503/622-3191.

## 47 BADGER LAKE

**Scenic rating: 8**

on Badger Lake in Mount Hood National Forest

**Map 9.2, page 488**

This campground (4,400 feet elevation) sits along the shore of Badger Lake. Non-motorized boating is permitted if you can manage to get a boat in here over the rough roads. No trailers are allowed on the campground road. The camp is adjacent to the Badger Creek Wilderness, and numerous trails provide access to the backcountry. Badger Creek Trail heads out of camp, northeast along Badger Creek for several miles.

**Campsites, facilities:** There are four sites for tents only, accessible only by high-clearance vehicles. Picnic tables and fire grills are provided. Vault toilets are available. There is no drinking water, and garbage must be packed out. Leashed pets are permitted.

**Reservations, fees:** Reservations are not accepted. Sites are $11 per night. Wilderness regulations apply. Open June-September, weather permitting.

**Directions:** From Portland, drive east on I-84 for 65 miles to Hood River, Exit 64 and Highway 35. Turn right (south) on Highway 35 and drive 37 miles to Forest Road 48. Turn left and drive 16 miles to Forest Road 4860. Turn left (north) and drive eight miles to Forest Road 140. Bear right and drive four miles to the lake. The last two miles on this primitive road require a high-clearance vehicle.

**Contact:** Mount Hood National Forest, Barlow Ranger District, 541/467-2291, www.fs.usda.gov/mthood.

## 48 BONNEY MEADOW
🏃🎣🐕🚐⛺

### Scenic rating: 9
in Mount Hood National Forest

**Map 9.2, page 488**

This primitive campground is on the east side of the Cascade Range at an elevation of 4,800 feet. As a result, there is little water in the area, and also very few people, so you're liable to have the place all to yourself. Bonney Meadow Trail leaves from the campground and travels 1.5 miles up to a group of small lakes. This trail provides great mountain views.

**Campsites, facilities:** There are six sites for tents or RVs up to 16 feet long. Picnic tables and fire grills are provided. Vault toilets are available. There is no drinking water and garbage must be packed out. Leashed pets are permitted.

**Reservations, fees:** Reservations are not accepted. Sites are $11 per night. Open June-early October, weather permitting.

**Directions:** From Portland, turn east on I-84 and drive 65 miles to the town of Hood River, Exit 64 and Highway 35. Turn right (south) on Highway 35 and drive 37 miles to Forest Road 48. Turn left and drive 14 miles to Forest Road 4890. Turn left and drive four miles north to Forest Road 4891. Turn right and drive a short distance to the campground.

**Contact:** Mount Hood National Forest, Barlow Ranger District, 541/467-2291, www.fs.usda.gov/mthood.

## 49 BONNEY CROSSING
🏃🎣🐕🚐⛺

### Scenic rating: 7
on Badger Creek in Mount Hood National Forest

**Map 9.2, page 488**

Bonney Crossing campground at 2,200 feet elevation along Badger Creek is the trailhead for the Badger Creek Trail, which provides access to the Badger Creek Wilderness. The camp gets fairly light use and is usually very quiet. Fishing is available in the creek and is usually pretty good. Horse campers are welcome here.

**Campsites, facilities:** There are eight sites for tents or RVs up to 16 feet long. Picnic tables and fire grills are provided. Vault toilets are available. There is no drinking water, and garbage must be packed out. Stock facilities include horse corrals. Leashed pets are permitted.

**Reservations, fees:** Reservations are not accepted. Sites are $11 per night, $5 per each additional vehicle. Open mid-April-mid-October, weather permitting.

**Directions:** From The Dalles, drive south on U.S. 197 for 32 miles to Tygh Valley. Take the Tygh Valley exit to Tygh Valley Road. Turn west and drive 0.25 mile to Wamic Market Road (County Road 226). Turn right (west) and drive eight miles to Wamic. Continue through Wamic and drive seven miles to Forest Road 4810. Bear right and drive three miles to Forest Road 4811. Turn right and drive two miles to a junction with Forest Road 2710. Turn right and drive three miles to the campground on the right.

**Contact:** Mount Hood National Forest, Barlow Ranger District, 541/467-2291, www.fs.usda.gov/mthood.

## 50 FOREST CREEK
🏃🎣🐕🚐⛺

### Scenic rating: 6
on Forest Creek in Mount Hood National Forest

**Map 9.2, page 488**

This is a very old camp that borders Forest Creek on the original Barlow Trail, once used by early settlers. Shaded by an old-growth Douglas fir and ponderosa pine forest, you'll camp amid solitude. The elevation here is 3,000 feet. See a U.S. Forest Service map for specific roads and trails.

**Campsites, facilities:** There are eight sites for tents or RVs up to 16 feet long. Picnic tables and fire grills are provided. No drinking water is available. Vault toilets are available.

Garbage must be packed out. Leashed pets are permitted.

**Reservations, fees:** Reservations are not accepted. Sites are $11 per night, $5 per each additional vehicle. Open June-early October, weather permitting.

**Directions:** From Portland, turn east on I-84 and drive 91 miles to The Dalles/Exit 87/ Highway 197. Turn south and drive 31 miles to Tygh Valley and Wamic Market Road. Turn right and drive west for six miles to Forest Road 48. Continue west and drive 12.5 miles southwest to Forest Road 4885. Turn left and drive one mile to Forest Road 3530. Turn left and drive a short distance to the campground.

**Contact:** Mount Hood National Forest, Barlow Ranger District, 541/467-2291, www. fs.usda.gov/mthood.

## 51 ROCK CREEK RESERVOIR

**Scenic rating: 7**

on Rock Creek Reservoir in Mount Hood National Forest

**Map 9.2, page 488**

Fishing is excellent, and the environment is perfect for canoes or rafts at this campground along the shore of Rock Creek Reservoir. Enjoy views of Mount Hood from the day-use area (Northwest Forest Pass required). No hiking trails are in the immediate vicinity, but there are many old forest roads that are ideal for walking or mountain biking. The camp sits at 2,200 feet elevation.

**Campsites, facilities:** There are 28 sites for tents or RVs up to 35 feet long and five sites for tents only. Picnic tables, garbage service, and fire grills are provided. Vault toilets, drinking water, and firewood are available. Water disposal sites are located throughout the campground. There are boat docks nearby, but no motorboats are allowed on the reservoir. Some facilities are wheelchair accessible. Leashed pets are permitted.

**Reservations, fees:** Reservations are accepted

at 877/444-6777 ($10 reservation fee) or www. recreation.gov ($9 reservation fee). Sites are $16-20 per night, $8 per night per additional vehicle. Open late May-early October.

**Directions:** From Portland, turn east on I-84 and drive 91 miles to The Dalles/Exit 87/ Highway 197. Turn south and drive 31 miles to Tygh Valley and Wamic Market Road. Turn right and drive west for six miles to Forest Road 48. Turn west and drive one mile to Forest Road 4820. Turn west and drive a short distance to the campground.

**Contact:** Mount Hood National Forest, Barlow Ranger District, 541/467-2291, www. fs.usda.gov/mthood.

## 52 PINE HOLLOW LAKESIDE RESORT

**Scenic rating: 8**

on Pine Hollow Reservoir

**Map 9.2, page 488**

This resort on the shore of Pine Hollow Reservoir is the best game in town for RV campers, with some shaded lakefront sites and scenic views. Year-round boating, fishing, swimming, and waterskiing are some recreation options here.

**Campsites, facilities:** There are 15 tent sites, 63 sites with partial hookups for RVs of any length, nine cabins, a camp trailer, and a two-bedroom house. Picnic tables and fire pits are provided. Drinking water, restrooms with flush toilets and coin showers, propane gas, a dump station, firewood, a convenience store, café, arcade, volleyball, horseshoe pits, playground, coin laundry, and ice are available. Boat docks, launching facilities, and boat and personal watercraft rentals are on-site. Some facilities are wheelchair accessible. Leashed pets are permitted.

**Reservations, fees:** Reservations are accepted. Tent sites are $20 per night, RV sites are $27 per night, $5 per person per night for more than two people, $5 per night per additional

vehicle, and $5 per pet per night. Some credit cards are accepted. Open mid-March-October.
**Directions:** From Portland, turn east on I-84 and drive 91 miles to The Dalles/Exit 87/ Highway 197. Turn south on Highway 197 and drive 31 miles to Tygh Valley and Wamic Market Road. Turn right (west) and drive four miles to Ross Road. Turn right (north) and drive 3.5 miles to the resort on the right.
**Contact:** Pine Hollow Lakeside Resort, 541/544-2271, www.pinehollowlakeside.com.

## 53 HUNT PARK
🏕🚴🛶🏕♿🚙⛺

**Scenic rating: 6**
near Badger Creek
**Map 9.2, page 488**
This Wasco County campground is set near the confluence of Badger and Tygh Creeks. Hiking trails, marked bike trails, and tennis courts are nearby, and fishing and rafting are available on the Deschutes River.
**Campsites, facilities:** There are 150 tent sites, 141 sites with full or partial hookups for RVs of any length (many are pull-through), and a group site for tents only that can accommodate up to 1,000 people. Picnic tables are provided, and some sites have fire rings. Drinking water, restrooms with flush toilets and coin showers, a dump station, garbage bins, a basketball court, Wi-Fi, and reservable picnic shelters are available. Horse facilities, including stalls and an arena, are also available. A camp host is on-site. A store, café, and ice are within two miles. Some facilities are wheelchair accessible. Leashed pets are permitted.
**Reservations, fees:** Reservations are accepted at 541/483-2288. RV sites are $20 per night, tent sites are $15 per night, $3 per night per additional vehicle. The group site is $7.50 per person per night for up to 100 people, $5 per person per night for larger groups. Open May-October.
**Directions:** From Portland, turn east on I-84 and drive 91 miles to The Dalles/Exit 87/

Highway 197. Turn south on Highway 197 and drive 31 miles to Tygh Valley and Main Street. Turn right on Main Street and drive two blocks to Fairgrounds Road. Turn right and drive one mile to the fairgrounds on the right.
**Contact:** Wasco County, 541/483-2288, co.wasco.or.us.

## 54 HIDEAWAY LAKE
🏕🛶🏊🚣🏕🐕🚙⛺

**Scenic rating: 9**
near the Rock Lakes Basin in Mount Hood National Forest
**Map 9.2, page 488**
This jewel of a spot features a small, deep lake where non-motorized boats are allowed, but they must be carried about 100 yards to the lake. The campsites are separate and scattered around the shore. At the north end of the lake, an 8.5-mile loop trail passes a number of lakes in the Rock Lakes Basin, all of which support populations of rainbow and brook trout. If you don't want to make the whole trip in a day, you can camp overnight at Serene Lake. See a U.S. Forest Service map for information.
**Campsites, facilities:** There are nine sites for tents or small RVs up to 16 feet long. Picnic tables and fire grills are provided. Vault toilets are available. There is no drinking water. Leashed pets are permitted.
**Reservations, fees:** Reservations are not accepted. Sites are $16 per night, $8 per night per additional vehicle. Open mid-June-late September, weather permitting.
**Directions:** From Portland, drive south on U.S. 205 to the junction with Highway 224/ Estacada. Take the exit and turn left onto Highway 224, heading south. Drive approximately 13 miles to Estacada. Continue south on Highway 224 and drive 27 miles to Forest Road 57. Turn left (east) and drive 7.5 miles to Forest Road 58. Turn left (north) and drive three miles to Forest Road 5830. Turn left (northwest) and drive 5.5 miles to the campground on the left.

**Contact:** Mount Hood National Forest, Clackamas River Ranger District, 503/630-6861, www.fs.usda.gov/mthood.

## 55 CLEAR LAKE

### Scenic rating: 4
near the Pacific Crest Trail in Mount Hood National Forest

**Map 9.2, page 488**

This campground is located along the shore of Clear Lake, a spot favored by anglers, swimmers, and windsurfers, but as a reservoir, it is subject to water-level fluctuations. The boating speed limit is 10 mph. This wooded camp features shady sites and is set at 3,600 feet elevation. The camp sometimes gets noisy from the revels of the party set. If you want quiet, this spot is probably not for you. A nearby trail heads north from the lake and provides access to the Pacific Crest Trail and Frog Lake, both good recreation options.

**Campsites, facilities:** There are 16 sites for tents or RVs up to 30 feet long, 12 sites for tents only, and one lookout cabin (available winter only). Picnic tables and fire grills are provided. Drinking water, garbage bins, firewood, and vault toilets are available. Some facilities are wheelchair accessible. Boat-launching facilities are nearby. Leashed pets are permitted.

**Reservations, fees:** Reservations are accepted at 877/444-6777 ($10 reservation fee) or www.recreation.gov ($9 reservation fee). Sites are $19-21 per night, $8 per night per additional vehicle; the lookout cabin is $50 per night. Open mid-May-late September, weather permitting.

**Directions:** From Portland, drive east on U.S. 26 for 57 miles to the junction with Highway 35 (two miles past Government Camp). Bear right (southeast) on U.S. 26 and drive nine miles to Forest Road 2630. Turn right (south) and drive one mile to the campground on the right.

**Contact:** Mount Hood National Forest, Hood River Ranger District, 541/352-6002, www. fs.usda.gov/mthood.

## 56 BARLOW CREEK

### Scenic rating: 7
on Barlow Creek in Mount Hood National Forest

**Map 9.2, page 488**

One of several primitive U.S. Forest Service camps in the immediate vicinity, this campground is set along Barlow Creek at an elevation of 3,100 feet. It is on Old Barlow Road, which was the wagon trail for early settlers in this area. If this campground is full, Barlow Crossing Campground is one mile southeast on Forest Road 3530.

**Campsites, facilities:** There are three sites for tents. Picnic tables and fire grills are provided. Vault toilets are available. There is no drinking water, and garbage must be packed out. Leashed pets are permitted.

**Reservations, fees:** Reservations are not accepted. Sites are $11 per night. Open May-September, weather permitting.

**Directions:** From Portland, drive east on U.S. 26 for 57 miles to the junction with Highway 35 (two miles past Government Camp). Stay on U.S. 26 and continue 12 miles to Forest Road 43. Turn left and drive five miles to Forest Road 3530. Turn left (north) and drive 1.5 miles to the campground on the left.

**Contact:** Mount Hood National Forest, Hood River Ranger District, 541/352-6002, www. fs.usda.gov/mthood.

## 57 WHITE RIVER STATION

### Scenic rating: 9
on the White River in Mount Hood National Forest

**Map 9.2, page 488**

This tiny campground is set along the White River at an elevation of 3,000 feet. It is on Old Barlow Road, an original wagon trail used by early settlers. One of several small, secluded camps in the area, White River Station is quiet and private, but with poor fishing prospects.

**Campsites, facilities:** There are five sites for tents or RVs up to 32 feet long. Picnic tables and fire grills are provided. Vault toilets are available. There is no drinking water, and garbage must be packed out. Leashed pets are permitted.

**Reservations, fees:** Reservations are not accepted. Sites are $11 per night, $5 per night per additional vehicle. Open May-September, weather permitting.

**Directions:** From Portland, drive east on U.S. 26 for 57 miles to the junction with Highway 35 (two miles past Government Camp). Stay on U.S. 26 and continue 12 miles to Forest Road 43. Turn left and drive five miles to Forest Road 3530. Turn right and drive approximately 1.5 miles to the campground on the left. (White River is less than one mile away from Barlow Creek.)

**Contact:** Mount Hood National Forest, Barlow Ranger District, 541/467-2291, www. fs.usda.gov/mthood.

## 58 LAKE HARRIET
🚣🏕🐕♿🚻⛺

### Scenic rating: 5
on Lake Harriet in Mount Hood National Forest

**Map 9.2, page 488**

Formed by a dam on the Oak Grove Fork of the Clackamas River, this little lake is a popular spot during the summer. Rowboats and boats with small motors are permitted, but only non-motorized boats are encouraged. The lake is stocked regularly and can provide good fishing for a variety of trout, including brook, brown, cutthroat, and rainbow. Anglers often stand shoulder to shoulder in summer.

**Campsites, facilities:** There are 11 sites for tents or RVs up to 40 feet long. Picnic tables and fire grills are provided. Drinking water and vault toilets are available. Garbage service is provided in the summer. A fishing pier and boat-launching facilities are on the lake. Some

facilities are wheelchair accessible. Leashed pets are permitted.

**Reservations, fees:** Reservations are accepted at 877/444-6777 ($10 reservation fee) or www. recreation.gov ($9 reservation fee). Sites are $16 per night, $8 per night per additional vehicle. Open year-round, weather permitting, with limited winter services.

**Directions:** From Portland, drive south on U.S. 205 to the junction with Highway 224/ Estacada. Take the exit and turn left onto Highway 224, heading south. Drive approximately 13 miles to Estacada. Continue south on Highway 224 and drive 27 miles to Forest Road 57. Turn east and drive 7.5 miles to Forest Road 4630. Turn left and drive two miles to the campground on the left.

**Contact:** Mount Hood National Forest, Clackamas River Ranger District, 503/630-6861, www.fs.usda.gov/mthood.

## 59 GONE CREEK
🚶🚣🏕🐕🚻⛺

### Scenic rating: 8
on Timothy Lake in Mount Hood National Forest

**Map 9.2, page 488**          **BEST (**

This campground, set along the south shore of Timothy Lake at 3,200 feet elevation, is one of five camps at the lake. Timothy Lake provides good fishing for brook trout, cutthroat trout, kokanee salmon, and rainbow trout. Boats with motors are allowed, but a 10-mph speed limit keeps it quiet. Several trails in the area—including the Pacific Crest Trail—provide access to a number of small mountain lakes.

**Campsites, facilities:** There are 50 sites for tents or RVs up to 45 feet long. Picnic tables and fire grills are provided. Drinking water, garbage service, vault toilets, and firewood are available. A boat ramp is nearby. Leashed pets are permitted.

**Reservations, fees:** Reservations are accepted at 877/444-6777 ($10 reservation fee) or www.

recreation.gov ($9 reservation fee). Sites are $17-18 per night, $8 per night per additional vehicle. Open mid-May-early September, weather permitting.

**Directions:** From Portland, drive on U.S. 26 for 55 miles (just past the town of Government Camp) to the junction with Highway 35. Bear southeast, staying on U.S. 26, and drive 15 miles to Forest Road 42 (Skyline Road). Turn right and drive eight miles to Forest Road 57. Turn right and drive one mile west to the campground on the right.

**Contact:** Mount Hood National Forest, Zigzag Ranger District, 503/622-3191, www.fs.usda.gov/mthood.

## 60 OAK FORK

### Scenic rating: 8

on Timothy Lake in Mount Hood National Forest

**Map 9.2, page 488**

Heavy timber and bear grass surround this forested camp along the south shore of Timothy Lake, where fishing is good for brook trout, cutthroat trout, kokanee salmon, and rainbow trout. Boats with motors are allowed, but a 10-mph speed limit is enforced. Oak Fork is located just east of Hoodview and Gone Creek campgrounds, at an elevation of 3,200 feet. Several area trails—including the Pacific Crest—provide access to various small mountain lakes.

**Campsites, facilities:** There are 47 sites for tents or RVs up to 45 feet long. Picnic tables and fire grills are provided. Drinking water, firewood, and vault toilets are available. A boat ramp and launching facilities are nearby; the speed limit on the lake is 10 mph. Leashed pets are permitted.

**Reservations, fees:** Reservations are accepted at 877/444-6777 ($10 reservation fee) or www.recreation.gov ($9 reservation fee). Sites are $17-18 per night, $8 per night per additional vehicle. Open May-early October, weather permitting.

**Directions:** From Portland, turn east on U.S. 26 and drive 57 miles (just past the town of Government Camp) to the junction with Highway 35. Bear southeast, staying on U.S. 26, and drive 15 miles to Forest Road 42 (Skyline Road). Turn right and drive eight miles to Forest Road 57. Turn right and drive three miles to the camp on the right.

**Contact:** Mount Hood National Forest, Zigzag Ranger District, 503/622-3191, www.fs.usda.gov/mthood.

## 61 PINE POINT

### Scenic rating: 8

on Timothy Lake in Mount Hood National Forest

**Map 9.2, page 488**

One of five camps on Timothy Lake, Pine Point spot sits at an elevation of 3,400 feet on the southwest shore. This camp has lake access and more open vegetation than the other Timothy Lake campgrounds. There's good fishing for brook trout, cutthroat trout, kokanee salmon, and rainbow trout, and a 10-mph speed limit keeps it pleasant for everyone. The trail that leads around the lake and to the Pacific Crest Trail passes along this campground.

**Campsites, facilities:** There are 24 sites for tents or RVs up to 45 feet long, including 13 single sites, six double sites for up to 12 people, and five group sites for up to 18 people each. Picnic tables, garbage service, and fire grills are provided. Drinking water and vault toilets are available. A boat ramp, launching facilities, and fishing pier are nearby; the speed limit on the lake is 10 mph. Leashed pets are permitted.

**Reservations, fees:** Reservations are accepted at 877/444-6777 ($10 reservation fee) or www.recreation.gov ($9 reservation fee). Single sites are $17 per night, $34 per night for a double site, $8 per night per additional vehicle, and group sites are $50 per night. Open late May-mid-September, weather permitting.

**Directions:** From Portland, turn east on U.S. 26 and drive 57 miles (just past the town of Government Camp) to the junction with Highway 35. Bear southeast, staying on U.S. 26, and drive 15 miles to Forest Road 42 (Skyline Road). Turn right and drive eight miles to Forest Road 57. Turn right and drive four miles to the park on the right.

**Contact:** Mount Hood National Forest, Zig-zag Ranger District, 503/622-3191, www.fs.usda.gov/mthood.

## 62 HOODVIEW

### Scenic rating: 9

on Timothy Lake in Mount Hood National Forest

**Map 9.2, page 488**

Here's another camp along the south shore of Timothy Lake; this one is set at 3,200 feet elevation. Timothy Lake provides good fishing for brook trout, cutthroat trout, kokanee salmon, and rainbow trout. Motorized boats are allowed, and the speed limit is 10 mph. A trail out of camp branches south for a few miles and, if followed to the east, eventually leads to the Pacific Crest Trail.

**Campsites, facilities:** There are 43 sites for tents or RVs up to 45 feet long. Picnic tables and fire grills are provided. Vault toilets, drinking water, garbage service, and firewood are available. A boat ramp is nearby. Leashed pets are permitted.

**Reservations, fees:** Reservations are accepted at 877/444-6777 ($10 reservation fee) or www.recreation.gov ($9 reservation fee). Sites are $17-18 per night, $8 per night per additional vehicle. Open mid-May-mid-September, weather permitting.

**Directions:** From Portland, turn east on U.S. 26 and drive 57 miles (just past the town of Government Camp) to the junction with Highway 35. Bear southeast, staying on U.S. 26, and drive 15 miles to Forest Road 42 (Skyline Road). Turn right and drive eight miles

to Forest Road 57. Turn right and drive three miles to the campground on the right.

**Contact:** Mount Hood National Forest, Zig-zag Ranger District, 503/622-3191, www.fs.usda.gov/mthood.

## 63 MEDITATION POINT

### Scenic rating: 9

on Timothy Lake in Mount Hood National Forest

**Map 9.2, page 488**          BEST (

Accessible only by foot or boat, this remote and rustic camp sits at 3,200 feet elevation and offers the most secluded location along Timothy Lake. It's one of two campgrounds on the north shore of the lake, which means you'll get a quieter, less crowded environment, though you'll have to bring your own water. The lake has a 10-mph speed limit for boaters. Timothy Lake Trail makes a 14-mile loop around the lake.

**Campsites, facilities:** There are five boat-in or walk-in tent sites. Picnic tables and fire grills are provided. Vault toilets are available. There is no drinking water, and garbage must be packed out. Boat docks and launching facilities are nearby. Leashed pets are permitted.

**Reservations, fees:** Reservations are not accepted. Access from PGE Day Use Area requires a $5 fee or a Northwest Forest Pass. There is no fee for camping. Open late May-mid-September, weather permitting.

**Directions:** From Portland, drive east on U.S. 26 and drive 57 miles to the junction with Highway 35 (2 miles past Government Camp). Bear right (southeast), staying on U.S. 26, and continue for 15 miles to Forest Road 42/Skyline Road. Turn right and drive eight miles south to Forest Road 57. Turn right and drive five miles, passing Pine Point Campground and crossing the Timothy Lake Dam. Park in the day-use area and hike one mile or take a boat to the north shore of the lake.

**Contact:** Mount Hood National Forest, Zigzag Ranger District, 503/622-3191, www.fs.usda.gov/mthood.

## 64 LITTLE CRATER LAKE

**Scenic rating: 7**

on Clear Creek in Mount Hood National Forest

Map 9.2, page 488

Little Crater campground (3,200 feet elevation) nestles against Crater Creek and scenic Little Crater Lake. This camp is popular with hunters in the fall. Both the drinking water and the lake water are spring fed, and the beautiful turquoise water is numbingly cold. The Pacific Crest Trail is located near camp, providing hiking trail access. Fishing is poor at Little Crater Lake. Little Timothy Lake lies about 10 miles away; note the 10-mph speed limit for boats. Bring your mosquito repellent—you'll need it.

**Campsites, facilities:** There are eight sites for tents or RVs up to 35 feet long and seven sites for tents only. Picnic tables, garbage bins, and fire grills are provided. Vault toilets, firewood, and drinking water are available. Leashed pets are permitted.

**Reservations, fees:** Reservations are accepted at 877/444-6777 ($10 reservation fee) or www.recreation.gov ($9 reservation fee). Sites are $19-21 per night, $8 per night per additional vehicle. Open May-mid-September, weather permitting.

**Directions:** From Portland, drive east on U.S. 26 for 57 miles to the junction with Highway 35 (2 miles past Government Camp). Bear right (southeast), staying on U.S. 26, and drive 15 miles to Forest Road 42 (Skyline Road). Turn right and drive about six miles to Forest Road 58. Turn right and drive about 2.5 miles to the campground on the left.

**Contact:** Mount Hood National Forest, Zigzag Ranger District, 503/622-3191, www.fs.usda.gov/mthood.

## 65 CLEAR CREEK CROSSING

**Scenic rating: 7**

on Clear Creek in Mount Hood National Forest

Map 9.2, page 488

This secluded, little-known spot hugs the banks of Clear Creek at an elevation of 3,600 feet. Clear Creek Trail, a very pretty walk, begins at the campground. Fishing and hiking are two recreation options here.

**Campsites, facilities:** There are seven sites for tents or RVs up to 16 feet long. Picnic tables and fire grills are provided. Vault toilets are available. There is no drinking water, and garbage must be packed out. Leashed pets are permitted.

**Reservations, fees:** Reservations are not accepted. Sites are $10 per night. Open May-September, weather permitting.

**Directions:** From Portland, drive east on U.S. 26 for 55 miles to Government Camp. Continue three miles to a junction and bear right, staying on U.S. 26, and drive south for 12 miles to Highway 216. Turn left (east) on Highway 216 and drive two miles to Forest Road 2130. Turn left (north) on Forest Road 2130 and drive three miles to the campground.

**Contact:** Mount Hood National Forest, Barlow Ranger District, 541/467-2291, www.fs.usda.gov/mthood.

## 66 KEEPS MILL

**Scenic rating: 9**

on Clear Creek in Mount Hood National Forest

Map 9.2, page 488

This small, pretty campground is situated at the confluence of Clear Creek and the White River. No RVs are permitted. The elevation is 2,600 feet. Many hiking trails, some with awesome views of the White River Canyon, crisscross the area, but be warned: These are butt-kicking canyon climbs.

**Campsites, facilities:** There are five sites

for tents only. The road to the campground is not good for trailers. Picnic tables and fire grills are provided. Vault toilets are available. There is no drinking water, and garbage must be packed out. Leashed pets are permitted.

**Reservations, fees:** Reservations are not accepted. Sites are $11 per night. Open May-September, weather permitting.

**Directions:** From Portland, drive east on U.S. 26 for 55 miles to Government Camp. Continue three miles to a junction, turn right on U.S. 26, and drive south for 12 miles to Highway 216. Turn left (east) on Highway 216 and drive three miles to Forest Road 2120. Turn left (north) on Forest Road 2120 and drive three miles to the campground.

**Contact:** Mount Hood National Forest, Barlow Ranger District, 541/467-2291, www.fs.usda.gov/mthood.

## 67 BEAR SPRINGS

### Scenic rating: 6
on Indian Creek in Mount Hood National Forest

**Map 9.2, page 488**

This campground is set along the banks of Indian Creek on the border of the Warm Springs Indian Reservation and features both secluded and open sites set in old-growth forest. The elevation is 3,000 feet.

**Campsites, facilities:** There are 19 single sites and two double sites for tents or RVs up to 32 feet long. Picnic tables and fire grills are provided. Drinking water, garbage bins, vault toilets, and firewood are available. Leashed pets are permitted.

**Reservations, fees:** Reservations are not accepted. Sites are $13 per night and $8 per night for each additional vehicle. Open June-September, weather permitting.

**Directions:** From Portland, drive east on U.S. 26 for 55 miles to Government Camp. Continue three miles to a junction and bear right, staying on U.S. 26, and drive south for 12 miles to Highway 216. Turn left (east) on Highway 216

and drive four miles to Reservation Road. Turn right (east) on Reservation Road and look for the campground on the right.

**Contact:** Mount Hood National Forest, Barlow Ranger District, 541/467-2291, www.fs.usda.gov/mthood.

## 68 MCCUBBINS GULCH

### Scenic rating: 5
in Mount Hood National Forest

**Map 9.2, page 488**

This small, primitive camp sits alongside a small creek at 3,000 feet in elevation and offers decent fishing and off-highway vehicle (OHV) recreation. A 40-mile network of OHV trails runs through the surrounding forest, with access right from camp. So, though out of the way, this camp gets heavy use; claim a spot early in the day. To the south is the Warm Springs Indian Reservation; do not trespass, as large fines are assessed to those prosecuted. Bear Springs provides a nearby camping alternative.

**Campsites, facilities:** There are 15 sites for tents and RVs up to 25 feet long. Picnic tables and fire grills are provided. Vault toilets are available. There is no drinking water, and garbage must be packed out. Leashed pets are permitted.

**Reservations, fees:** Reservations are not accepted. Sites are $11 per night, $8 for each additional vehicle. Open May-September, weather permitting.

**Directions:** From Portland, drive east on U.S. 26 for 55 miles to Government Camp. Continue three miles to a junction and bear right, staying on U.S. 26, and drive south for 12 miles to Highway 216. Turn left (east) on Highway 216 and drive six miles to Forest Road 2110. Take a sharp left and drive 1.5 miles to the campground entrance on the right.

**Contact:** Mount Hood National Forest, Barlow Ranger District, 541/467-2291, www.fs.usda.gov/mthood.

## 69 SHELLROCK CREEK

**Scenic rating: 6**

on Shellrock Creek in Mount Hood
National Forest

**Map 9.2, page 488**

This quiet little campground (2,200 feet elevation) occupies a nice spot on Shellrock Creek and has been used primarily as an overflow area for Lake Harriet campground. Small trout can be caught here, but remember that on the Clackamas River it's catch-and-release only. Obtain a U.S. Forest Service map for details on the backcountry roads and trails.

Note: In 2010, the Forest Service plans some changes to several campgrounds in the Estacada Ranger District.

**Campsites, facilities:** There are eight sites for tents or RVs up to 16 feet long. Picnic tables and fire grills are provided. Vault toilets are available. There is no drinking water and garbage must be packed out. Leashed pets are permitted.

**Reservations, fees:** Reservations are not accepted. Sites are $16 per night, $8 per night per additional vehicle. Open year-round, with limited winter services.

**Directions:** From Portland, drive south on U.S. 205 to the junction with Highway 24. Take the Highway 224/Estacada exit and turn left (south) onto Highway 224. Drive approximately 13 miles to Estacada. Continue south on Highway 224 for 27 miles in national forest (the road becomes Forest Road 46) to Forest Road 57. Turn left (east) and drive 7.5 miles to Forest Road 58. Turn left and drive north one mile to the campground on the left.

**Contact:** Mount Hood National Forest, Clackamas River Ranger District, Estacada Ranger Station, 503/630-6861, www.fs.usda.gov/mthood.

## 70 JOE GRAHAM HORSE CAMP

**Scenic rating: 8**

near Clackamas Lake in Mount Hood
National Forest

**Map 9.2, page 488**

Named for a forest ranger, this campground sits at 3,250 feet elevation among majestic Douglas fir and hemlock, just north of tiny Clackamas Lake. The adjacent wet meadow is home to a wide variety of wildlife. It's one of two campgrounds in the area that allow horses. Timothy Lake (the setting for the Gone Creek, Hoodview, Meditation Point, Oak Fork, and Pine Point camps) provides a nearby alternative to the northwest. The Pacific Crest Trail is just east of camp.

**Campsites, facilities:** There are 14 sites for tents, horse trailers, or RVs up to 45 feet long; 11 have corrals, and two have hitching rails. Picnic tables, hitching posts, garbage service, and fire grills are provided. Drinking water and vault toilets are available. Leashed pets are permitted.

**Reservations, fees:** Reservations are accepted at 877/444-6777 ($10 reservation fee) or www.recreation.gov ($9 reservation fee). Sites are $20 per night, $5 per night per additional vehicle, $2 additional charge during holidays. Open mid-May–mid-October, weather permitting.

**Directions:** From Portland, turn east on U.S. 26 and drive 57 miles (just past the town of Government Camp) to the junction with Highway 35. Bear right, continuing southeast on U.S. 26, and drive 15 miles to Forest Road 42 (Skyline Road). Turn right and drive eight miles to the campground on the left.

**Contact:** Mount Hood National Forest, Zigzag Ranger District, 503/622-3191, www.fs.usda.gov/mthood.

## 71 CLACKAMAS LAKE

🚶 🚣 🚐 🐴 🚙 ⛺

### Scenic rating: 7

near the Clackamas River in Mount Hood
National Forest

**Map 9.2, page 488**

This camp, set at 3,400 feet elevation, is a good
place to go to escape the hordes of people at the
lakeside sites in neighboring camps. The Pacific
Crest Trail passes nearby, and Timothy Lake
requires little more than a one-mile hike from
camp. The Clackamas Lake Historic Ranger
Station, a visitors center built in the early 1900s,
is worth a visit and is still using the old hand
crank-style phones once used in lookout towers and guard stations. This is a popular spot
for campers with horses, although the facilities
could use some updating and repairs.

**Campsites, facilities:** There are 49 sites for
tents or RVs up to 45 feet long. There are also
11 equestrian sites with hitch rails and corrals.
Drinking water, garbage service, fire grills,
and picnic tables are provided. Vault toilets
are available. Boat docks and launching facilities are nearby at Timothy Lake, but only
non-motorized boats are allowed. Leashed pets
are permitted.

**Reservations, fees:** Reservations are accepted
at 877/444-6777 ($10 reservation fee) or www.
recreation.gov ($9 reservation fee). Sites are
$16 per night, $8 per night per additional
vehicle. Open May–mid-September, weather
permitting.

**Directions:** From Portland, turn east on U.S.
26 and drive 57 miles (just past the town of
Government Camp) to the junction with Highway 35. Bear southeast, staying on U.S. 26, and
drive 15 miles to Forest Road 42 (Skyline Road).
Turn right and drive eight miles to Forest Road
57. Continue 500 feet (on Forest Road 42) past
the Clackamas Lake Historic Ranger Station to
Forest Road 4270. Turn left and drive 0.5 mile
to the campground on the left.

**Contact:** Mount Hood National Forest, Zigzag Ranger District, 503/622-3191, www.
fs.usda.gov/mthood.

## 72 DESCHUTES RIVER STATE RECREATION AREA

🚶 🚴 🚣 🚐 🐴 ♿ 🚙 ⛺

### Scenic rating: 7

on the Deschutes River

**Map 9.3, page 489**

This tree-shaded park along the Deschutes
River in the Deschutes Canyon offers bicycling and hiking trails and good steelhead
fishing in season. The river-level Atiyeh Deschutes River Trail is a favorite jaunt for hikers. Reservation-only equestrian trail riding
is available March to June. A small day-use
state park called Heritage Landing, which
has a boat ramp and restroom facilities, is located across the river. The U.S. Army Corps
of Engineers offers a free train ride and tour
of the dam at The Dalles during the summer.
Good rafting is a bonus here. For 25 miles
upstream, the river is mostly inaccessible by
car. Many anglers launch boats here and then
go upstream to steelhead fishing grounds.
Note that boat fishing is not allowed
here; you must wade into the river or fish
from shore.

**Campsites, facilities:** There are 34 sites with
partial hookups for tents or RVs up to 50 feet,
25 primitive sites for tents or self-contained
RVs up to 30 feet, and four group areas for RVs
and tents, which can hold up to 25 people and
five RVs each. Picnic tables and fire grills are
provided, but campfires are prohibited July
1–September 30. Drinking water (seasonal),
garbage bins, and flush toilets are available.
Some facilities are wheelchair accessible.
Leashed pets are permitted.

**Reservations, fees:** Reservations are accepted
at 800/452-5687 or www.oregonstateparks.org
($8 reservation fee). Sites with partial hookups
are $16-20 per night, primitive sites are $5-9
per night, $5 per night per additional vehicle.
Group sites are $51-71 per night. Some credit
cards are accepted. Open year-round, with
limited services November-March.

**Directions:** From Portland, turn east on
I-84 and drive about 90 miles to The Dalles.

Continue east on I-84 for 12 miles to Exit 97/ Deschutes State Recreation Area, turn right, and drive 50 feet to Biggs-Rufus Highway. Turn left and drive about three miles, cross the Deschutes River, and turn right to the campground entrance.

**Contact:** Deschutes River State Recreation Area, 541/739-2322 or 800/452-5687, www.oregonstateparks.org.

## 73 LEPAGE PARK

**Scenic rating: 6**

on the John Day River

**Map 9.3, page 489**

Half of the campsites are adjacent to the John Day River and the other half are on the opposite side of the road at this partially shaded campground. The John Day River feeds into the Columbia just 0.12 mile north of the campground. Rattlesnakes are occasionally seen in the area but are not abundant. Anglers come for the smallmouth bass and catfish during the summer. The day-use area has a swimming beach, lawn, boat launch, and boat docks. There are several other campgrounds nearby.

**Campsites, facilities:** There is a grassy area with 20 walk-in sites for tents and 22 sites with partial hookups for tents or RVs up to 56 feet long; some sites are pull-through. Picnic tables and fire pits are provided. Drinking water, restrooms with flush toilets and showers, and pit toilets are available. A boat ramp, docks, dump station, fish-cleaning station, and garbage containers are also available. Food, gasoline, and coin laundry are available five miles away in the town of Rufus. Some facilities are wheelchair accessible. Leashed pets are permitted.

**Reservations, fees:** Reservations are accepted at 877/444-6777 ($10 reservation fee) or www.recreation.gov ($9 reservation fee). RV sites are $20-22 per night and tent sites are $14-16 per night. Some credit cards are accepted. Open April 1-October 31.

**Directions:** From Portland on I-84, drive east

120 miles (30 miles past The Dalles) to Exit 114, the John Day River Recreation Area. The campground is just off I-84.

**Contact:** Army Corps of Engineers, Portland District, 503/808-5150; LePage Park, 541/739-2713.

## 74 BEAVERTAIL

**Scenic rating: 6**

on the Deschutes River

**Map 9.3, page 489**

This isolated campground is set at an elevation of 2,900 feet along the banks of the Deschutes River, one of the classic steelhead streams in the Pacific Northwest. The camp provides fishing and rafting options. The open landscape affords canyon views. This is my favorite put-in spot for a drift boat for fishing float trips on the Deschutes. I've made the trip from Beavertail to the mouth of the Deschutes, ideal in four days, camping at Bureau of Land Management (BLM) boat-in sites along the river and fly-fishing for steelhead. A boating pass is required to float the river. There are 12 other BLM campgrounds along upper and lower Deschutes River Road. The hardest part is getting used to the freight trains that rumble through the canyon at night.

**Campsites, facilities:** There are 13 sites for tents or RVs up to 30 feet long and two group sites for up to 16 people. Picnic tables, garbage bins, and fire grills are provided. No campfires are allowed June 1-October 15. Drinking water and vault toilets are available. Boat-launching facilities are at the campground. Some facilities are wheelchair accessible. Leashed pets are permitted.

**Reservations, fees:** Reservations are not accepted. Sites are $8-12 per night, $2 per night per additional vehicle, with a 14-day stay limit. Group sites are $25-35 per night. Open year-round.

**Directions:** From Portland, drive east on U.S. 84 to The Dalles and Highway 197. Turn south and drive to Maupin. Continue through Maupin, cross the bridge, and within a mile look for Deschutes River Road on your left. Turn left on Deschutes River Road and drive 21 miles northeast to the campground.

**Contact:** Bureau of Land Management, Prineville District, 541/416-6700, www.blm.gov/or/districts/prineville.

## 75 SHADY COVE

**Scenic rating: 7**

on the Little North Santiam River in Willamette National Forest

**Map 9.4, page 490**

Shady Cove campground is on the Little North Santiam River in the recently designated Opal Creek Scenic Recreation Area. The Little North Santiam Trail runs adjacent to the campground.

**Campsites, facilities:** There are 13 sites for tents or RVs up to 16 feet long. Picnic tables, garbage service (summer only), fire grills, and vault toilets are available. There is no drinking water. Leashed pets are permitted.

**Reservations, fees:** Reservations are not accepted. Single sites are $8 per night, multiple sites are $16 per night, $5 per night per additional vehicle. Open year-round, weather permitting.

**Directions:** From Salem on I-5, take Exit 253 to Highway 22. Turn east and drive 23 miles to Mehama and North Fork Road (Marion County Road). Turn left and drive 17 miles northeast to the fork. Bear right on Forest Road 2207 and continue for two miles to the campground on the right.

**Contact:** Willamette National Forest, Detroit Ranger District, 503/854-3366, www.fs.usda.gov/willamette.

## 76 ELK LAKE

**Scenic rating: 9**

near Bull of the Woods Wilderness

**Map 9.4, page 490**

This remote and primitive campground (3,700 feet elevation) borders the shore of Elk Lake, where boating, fishing, and swimming can be quite good in the summer. Wildflower blooms can be beautiful in the nearby meadows. Several trails in the area provide access to the Bull of the Woods Wilderness (operated by Mount Hood National Forest) and the newly designated Opal Creek Wilderness. The campground also offers beautiful views of Battle Ax Mountain.

**Campsites, facilities:** There are 17 sites for tents only. Pit toilets are available. There is no drinking water, and garbage must be packed out. Primitive boat-launching facilities are available. Leashed pets are permitted.

**Reservations, fees:** Reservations are not accepted. Sites are $10 per night, $5 per each additional vehicle. Open June-October, weather permitting.

**Directions:** From Salem on I-5, take Exit 253, turn east on Highway 22, and drive 52 miles to Detroit. Turn left on Forest Road 46/Breitenbush Road and drive 4.5 miles to Forest Road 4696/Elk Lake Road. Turn left and drive less than one mile to Forest Road 4697. Turn left and drive 9.5 miles to the campground on the left. The road is extremely rough for the last five miles; high-clearance vehicles are recommended.

**Contact:** Willamette National Forest, Detroit Ranger District, 503/854-3366, www.fs.usda.gov/willamette.

## 77 HUMBUG

**Scenic rating: 9**

on the Breitenbush River in Willamette National Forest

**Map 9.4, page 490**

Fishing and hiking are popular at this campground along the banks of the Breitenbush River, about four miles from where it empties into Detroit Lake. The lake offers many other recreation opportunities. The Humbug Flat Trailhead is behind Sites 9 and 10, and a scenic stroll through an old-growth forest follows the Breitenbush River. The rhododendrons put on a spectacular show May-July.

**Campsites, facilities:** There are 21 sites for tents or RVs up to 30 feet long. Picnic tables and fire grills are provided. Garbage service (summer only), drinking water, firewood, and vault toilets are available. Leashed pets are permitted.

**Reservations, fees:** Reservations are not accepted. Sites are $14 per night, $6 per night per additional vehicle. Open year-round, weather permitting, with limited winter facilities.

**Directions:** From Salem on I-5, take Exit 253, turn east on Highway 22, and drive 52 miles to Detroit. Turn left on Forest Road 46/Breitenbush Road and drive five miles northeast to the campground on the right.

**Contact:** Willamette National Forest, Detroit Ranger District, 503/854-3366, www.fs.usda.gov/willamette.

## 78 DETROIT LAKE STATE RECREATION AREA

**Scenic rating: 7**

on Detroit Lake

**Map 9.4, page 490**

This campground is set at 1,600 feet elevation along the shore of Detroit Lake, which is 400 feet deep, 9 miles long, and has more than 32 miles of shoreline. The park offers a fishing dock and a moorage area, and a boat ramp and bathhouse are available nearby at the Mongold Day Use Area. The heavily stocked lake is crowded on the opening day of trout season in late April.

**Campsites, facilities:** There are 178 sites with full or partial hookups for RVs up to 60 feet long, 98 tent sites, and 82 boat slips. Fire grills and picnic tables are provided. Drinking water, restrooms with flush toilets and showers, garbage bins, and firewood are available. Recreation facilities include two playgrounds, swimming areas, horseshoe pits, basketball and volleyball courts, an amphitheater, a gift shop, ice, firewood, and a visitors center. A camp host is on-site. Two boat docks and launching facilities are on-site. Some facilities are wheelchair accessible. Leashed pets are permitted.

**Reservations, fees:** Reservations are accepted at 800/452-5687 or www.oregonstateparks.org ($8 reservation fee). RV sites are $20-24 per night, tent sites are $15-19 per night, $5 per night per additional vehicle. Boating moorage is $10 per night. Some credit cards are accepted. Open year-round.

**Directions:** From Salem, drive east on Highway 22 for 50 miles to the park entrance on the right (located 2 miles west of Detroit).

**Contact:** Detroit Lake State Recreation Area, 503/854-3406 or 503/854-3346, www.oregonstateparks.org.

## 79 PIETY ISLAND BOAT-IN

**Scenic rating: 10**

on Detroit Lake in Willamette National Forest

**Map 9.4, page 490**   **BEST (**

This island gets crowded and has a reputation for sometimes attracting rowdy groups. Other campgrounds along the shore have drinking water. Piety Island Trail climbs 1.5 miles to the top of the island. You'll find great vistas on this island, which sits at 1,600 feet in elevation.

**Campsites, facilities:** This is an island campground with 22 tent sites accessible only by boat. Picnic tables and fire grills are provided. Vault toilets are available. There is no drinking water. Boat docks, launching facilities, and rentals are nearby. Leashed pets are permitted.

**Reservations, fees:** Reservations are not accepted. Single sites are $10 per night; double sites are $20 per night. Open year-round, weather permitting.

**Directions:** From Salem, drive east on Highway 22 for 45 miles to Detroit Lake. Continue east on Highway 22 along the north side of the lake to the boat ramp (three miles west of the town of Detroit). Launch your boat and head southeast to the island in the middle of the lake. The campground is on the east side of the island.

**Contact:** Willamette National Forest, Detroit Ranger District, 503/854-3366, www.fs.usda. gov/willamette.

## 80 SOUTHSHORE

### Scenic rating: 9
on Detroit Lake in Willamette National Forest

Map 9.4, page 490

This popular camp hugs the south shore of Detroit Lake, where fishing, swimming, and waterskiing are some of the recreation options. The Stahlman Point Trailhead is about half a mile from camp. There's a day-use area for picnicking and swimming. The views of the lake and surrounding mountains are outstanding.

**Campsites, facilities:** There are eight walk-in tent sites and 24 sites for tents or RVs up to 30 feet long. Fire grills, garbage service, and picnic tables are provided. Vault toilets, drinking water, and firewood are available. Boat-launching facilities are nearby at a day-use area. Some facilities are wheelchair accessible. Leashed pets are permitted.

**Reservations, fees:** Reservations are not accepted. Sites are $18 for a single site, $36 for double site, and $6 per night per additional vehicle. Open May-late September, with a gate preventing access during the off-season.

**Directions:** From Salem, drive east on Highway 22 for 52 miles to Detroit. Continue southeast on Highway 22 for 2.5 miles to Forest Road 10 (Blowout Road). Turn right and drive four miles to the campground on the right.

**Contact:** Willamette National Forest, Detroit Ranger District, 503/854-3366, www.fs.usda. gov/willamette.

## 81 COVE CREEK

### Scenic rating: 10
on Detroit Lake in Willamette National Forest

Map 9.4, page 490                    BEST (

Cove Creek is a popular campground, and it gets high use in the summer. Situated in a forest, the campground is located on the south side of the lake, about one mile from both Hoover and Southshore campgrounds. Water sports are popular, and both waterskiing and personal watercraft are allowed.

**Campsites, facilities:** There are 63 sites for tents or RVs of any length and one group site for up to 70 people. Picnic tables and fire rings are provided. Drinking water, restrooms with flush toilets and coin showers, garbage bins, firewood, and a boat ramp are available. Some facilities are wheelchair accessible. Leashed pets are permitted.

**Reservations, fees:** Reservations are accepted only for the group site at 877/444-6777 ($10 reservation fee) or www.recreation.gov ($9 reservation fee). Single sites are $20 per night, double sites are $40 per night, $6 per night per additional vehicle. Group sites are $165 per night and require a two-night minimum stay on weekends. Open May-September, with a gate preventing access in the off-season.

**Directions:** From Salem, drive east on Highway 22 for 52 miles to Detroit. Continue southeast on Highway 22 for 2.5 miles to Forest Road 10 (Blowout Road). Turn right and drive three miles to the campground on the right.

**Contact:** Willamette National Forest, Detroit Ranger District, 503/854-3366, www. fs.usda.gov/willamette; park information, 503/854-3251.

## 82 HOOVER

### Scenic rating: 9
on Detroit Lake in Willamette National Forest

Map 9.4, page 490

Hoover campground is located along the

eastern arm of Detroit Lake at an elevation of 1,600 feet, near the mouth of the Santiam River. The camp features a wheelchair-accessible fishing area and interpretive trail; fishing, swimming, and waterskiing are some of the recreation options. You're likely to see osprey fishing during the day, a truly special sight.

**Campsites, facilities:** There are 37 sites for tents or RVs up to 30 feet long. Picnic tables, garbage service, and fire grills are provided. Flush toilets and drinking water are available. Boat docks and launching facilities are nearby. Some facilities are wheelchair accessible. Leashed pets are permitted.

**Reservations, fees:** Reservations are accepted at 877/444-6777 ($10 reservation fee) or www.recreation.gov ($9 reservation fee). Single sites are $18 per night, double sites are $36 per night, $6 per night per additional vehicle. Open mid-May–mid-September; a gate prevents access in the off-season.

**Directions:** From Salem, drive east on Highway 22 for 52 miles to Detroit. Continue southeast on Highway 22 for 2.5 miles to Forest Road 10 (Blowout Road). Turn right and drive one mile to the campground on the right.

**Contact:** Willamette National Forest, Detroit Ranger District, 503/854-3366, www.fs.usda.gov/willamette.

## 83 HOOVER GROUP CAMP

### Scenic rating: 9
on Detroit Lake in Willamette National Forest

Map 9.4, page 490          BEST (

This is a perfect spot for a family reunion or club trip. Detroit Lake offers a myriad of activities, including boating, fishing, hiking, and swimming, just to name a few. The campground has nice, open sites and direct access to the lake.

**Campsites, facilities:** There is one group camp for tents or RVs up to 30 feet long, for up to 70 people and 20 vehicles. Drinking

water, fire rings, and picnic tables are provided. Flush toilets, garbage bins, firewood, and a group picnic shelter are available. Boat docks, launching facilities, and rentals are nearby. Some facilities are wheelchair accessible. Leashed pets are permitted.

**Reservations, fees:** Reservations are accepted at 877/444-6777 ($10 reservation fee) or www.recreation.gov ($9 reservation fee). The site is $165 per night, with a two-night minimum for weekend reservations. Open mid-April–late September; a gate prevents access during the off-season.

**Directions:** From Salem, drive east on Highway 22 for 52 miles to Detroit. Continue southeast on Highway 22 for 2.5 miles to Forest Road 10 (Blowout Road). Turn right and drive 0.5 mile to the campground on the right.

**Contact:** Willamette National Forest, Detroit Ranger District, 503/854-3366, www.fs.usda.gov/willamette; park information, 503/854-3251.

## 84 SUMMIT LAKE

### Scenic rating: 6
on Summit Lake in Mount Hood National Forest

Map 9.5, page 491

This idyllic camp is set in a remote area along the western slopes of the Cascade Range at an elevation of 4,200 feet. On the shore of little Summit Lake, the camp is primitive but a jewel. It's a perfect alternative to the more crowded camps at Timothy Lake, and you have access to all the same recreation options by driving just a short distance north. Non-motorized boats are allowed.

**Campsites, facilities:** There are eight tent sites. Fire grills, garbage service, and picnic tables are provided. Vault toilets are available. There is no drinking water. Leashed pets are permitted.

**Reservations, fees:** Reservations are not accepted. Sites are $15 per night, $8 per each additional vehicle, $2 charge on holidays. Open mid-July-September, weather permitting.

**Directions:** From Portland, turn east on U.S. 26 and drive 57 miles (just past the town of Government Camp) to the junction with Highway 35. Bear southeast, staying on U.S. 26, and drive 15 miles to Forest Road 42 (Skyline Road). Turn right and drive 12 miles south to Forest Road 141 (a dirt road). Turn right and drive west two miles to the campground on the left.

**Contact:** Mount Hood National Forest, Zigzag Ranger District, 503/622-3191, www.fs.usda.gov/mthood.

## 85 CLEATER BEND GROUP CAMP

### Scenic rating: 8

near the Breitenbush River in Willamette National Forest

**Map 9.5, page 491**

Creek views and pretty, shaded sites are the highlights of Cleater Bend, situated on the banks of the Breitenbush River at 2,200 feet elevation. This camp is 0.25 mile from Breitenbush and is a good option if that campground is full. Nearby recreation options include fishing access along the Breitenbush River, the South Breitenbush Gorge National Recreation Trail (three miles away), and Breitenbush Hot Springs (just over a mile away).

**Campsites, facilities:** The site can accommodate a group camp for up to 45 people in tents or RVs up to 28 feet long. Picnic tables and fire grills are provided. Garbage service, drinking water, vault toilets, and firewood are available. Some facilities are wheelchair accessible. Leashed pets are permitted.

**Reservations, fees:** Reservations are accepted at 877/444-6777 ($10 reservation fee) or www.recreation.gov ($9 reservation fee). The site is $110 per night. Open May-September; a gate prevents access during the off-season.

**Directions:** From Salem on I-5, take Exit 253, turn east on Highway 22, and drive 50 miles to Detroit. Turn left on Forest Road 46/Breitenbush Road and drive nine miles to the campground on the right.

**Contact:** Willamette National Forest, Detroit Ranger District, 503/854-3366, www.fs.usda.gov/willamette.

## 86 BREITENBUSH

### Scenic rating: 8

on the Breitenbush River in Willamette National Forest

**Map 9.5, page 491**

There is fishing access at this campground along the Breitenbush River. Nearby recreation options include the South Breitenbush Gorge National Recreation Trail, three miles away, and Breitenbush Hot Springs, just over a mile away. If this campground is crowded, try nearby Cleater Bend.

**Campsites, facilities:** There are 30 sites for tents or RVs up to 24 feet long (longer trailers may be difficult to park and turn). Picnic tables and fire grills are provided. Drinking water, vault toilets, garbage service, and firewood are available. Some facilities are wheelchair accessible. Leashed pets are permitted.

**Reservations, fees:** Reservations are accepted at 877/444-6777 ($10 reservation fee) or www.recreation.gov ($9 reservation fee). Sites are $14 per night for a single site, $28 per night for a double site, and $6 per night per additional vehicle. Open May-September; a gate prevents access during the off-season.

**Directions:** From Salem on I-5, take Exit 253, turn east on Highway 22, and drive 50 miles to Detroit. Turn left (north) on Forest Road 46/Breitenbush Road and drive 10 miles to the campground on the right.

**Contact:** Willamette National Forest, Detroit Ranger District, 503/854-3366, www.fs.usda.gov/willamette.

# 87 LOWER LAKE

**Scenic rating: 7**

near Olallie Lake in Mount Hood National Forest

**Map 9.5, page 491**

This sunny, open campground is set at an elevation of 4,600 feet, about 0.75 mile from Lower Lake, a small but deep lake that's perfect for fishing and swimming. It's also less than a mile from Olallie Lake and near a network of trails that provide access to other nearby lakes. It's advisable to obtain a U.S. Forest Service map that details the backcountry roads and trails.

**Campsites, facilities:** There are eight sites for tents or RVs up to 16 feet long. Picnic tables and fire grills are provided. Vault toilets and garbage service are available. There is no drinking water. Leashed pets are permitted.

**Reservations, fees:** Reservations are not accepted. Sites are $15 per night, $5 per each additional vehicle. Open July-October.

**Directions:** From Portland, drive south on U.S. 205 to the junction with Highway 24. Take the Highway 224/Estacada exit and turn left (south) onto Highway 224. Drive approximately 13 miles to Estacada. Continue south on Highway 224 and drive 27 miles in national forest (the road becomes Forest Road 46). Continue south on Forest Road 46 for 20 miles to Forest Road 4690. Turn left on Forest Road 4690 and drive southeast for 8.2 miles to Forest Road 4220. Turn right (south) and drive about 4.5 miles of rough road to the campground on the right.

**Contact:** Mount Hood National Forest, Clackamas River Ranger District, 503/630-6861, www.fs.usda.gov/mthood.

# 88 CAMP TEN

**Scenic rating: 9**

on Olallie Lake in Mount Hood National Forest

**Map 9.5, page 491**

Here's a camp along the shore of Olallie Lake, a popular area. Camp Ten sits at an elevation of 5,000 feet, on the lake's western shore in the midst of the Olallie Lake Scenic Area, which is home to a number of pristine mountain lakes and a network of hiking trails. (See a U.S. Forest Service map for trail locations.) Boats without motors—including canoes, kayaks, and rafts—are permitted on the lake.

**Campsites, facilities:** There are 10 sites for tents or RVs up to 16 feet long. Picnic tables, garbage service, and fire grills are provided. Vault toilets are available. There is no drinking water. Leashed pets are permitted.

**Reservations, fees:** Reservations are not accepted. Sites are $15 per night. Open July-October, weather permitting.

**Directions:** From Portland, drive south on U.S. 205 to the junction with Highway 24. Take the Highway 224/Estacada exit and turn left (south) onto Highway 224. Drive approximately 13 miles to Estacada. Continue south on Highway 224 and drive 27 miles in national forest (the road becomes Forest Road 46). Continue south on Forest Road 46 for 20 miles to Forest Road 4690. Turn left on Forest Road 4690 and drive southeast for 8.2 miles to Forest Road 4220. Turn right (south) and drive about six miles of rough road to the campground.

**Contact:** Mount Hood National Forest, Clackamas River Ranger District, 503/630-6861, www.fs.usda.gov/mthood.

# 89 PAUL DENNIS

**Scenic rating: 10**

on Olallie Lake in Mount Hood National Forest

**Map 9.5, page 491**          **BEST (**

This campground, set at an elevation of

5,000 feet, borders the north shore of Olallie Lake. From here, you can see the reflection of Mount Jefferson (10,497 feet). Boats with motors are not permitted on the lake. A trail from camp leads to Long Lake (just east of the border of the Warm Springs Indian Reservation), Monon Lake, and Nep-Te-Pa Lake. It's advisable to obtain a U.S. Forest Service map.

**Campsites, facilities:** There are 17 sites for tents or RVs up to 16 feet long (trailers not recommended) and three hike-in tent sites. Picnic tables, garbage service, and fire grills are provided. Pit toilets are available. There is no drinking water. A store and ice are nearby. Leashed pets are permitted.

**Reservations, fees:** Reservations are not accepted. Sites are $15-25 per night. Open July-October, weather permitting.

**Directions:** From Portland, drive south on U.S. 205 to the junction with Highway 24. Take the Highway 224/Estacada exit and turn left (south) onto Highway 224. Drive approximately 13 miles to Estacada. Continue south on Highway 224 and drive 27 miles in national forest (the road becomes Forest Road 46). Continue south on Forest Road 46 for 20 miles to Forest Road 4690. Turn left and drive southeast for 8.2 miles to Forest Road 4220. Turn right (south) and drive 6.2 miles to Forest Road 4220-170. Turn left and drive 0.12 mile to the campground.

**Contact:** Mount Hood National Forest, Clackamas River Ranger District, 503/630-6861, www.fs.usda.gov/mthood.

## 90 PENINSULA

### Scenic rating: 10

on Olallie Lake in Mount Hood National Forest

**Map 9.5, page 491**

Peninsula, the largest of several campgrounds along Olallie Lake, is set at an elevation of 5,000 feet on the south shore. An amphitheater is located near the campground, and rangers present campfire programs during the summer. Non-motorized boats are permitted on the lake, and nearby trails lead to a number of smaller lakes in the area, such as Long Lake, Monon Lake, and Nep-Te-Pa Lake.

**Campsites, facilities:** There are 35 sites for tents or RVs up to 24 feet long, one double site, and six walk-in tent sites. Picnic tables, garbage service, and fire grills are provided. Vault toilets are available. There is no drinking water. Leashed pets are permitted.

**Reservations, fees:** Reservations are not accepted. Sites are $15-25 per night, $6 per night per additional vehicle, and $6 per night for walk-in sites. Open July-October, weather permitting.

**Directions:** From Portland, drive south on U.S. 205 to the junction with Highway 24. Take the Highway 224/Estacada exit and turn left (south) onto Highway 224. Drive approximately 13 miles to Estacada. Continue south on Highway 224 and drive 27 miles in national forest (the road becomes Forest Road 46). Continue south on Forest Road 46 for 20 miles to Forest Road 4690. Turn left and drive southeast for 8.2 miles to Forest Road 4220. Turn right (south) and drive 6.5 miles of rough road to the campground on the left.

**Contact:** Mount Hood National Forest, Clackamas River Ranger District, 503/630-6861, www.fs.usda.gov/mthood.

## 91 OLALLIE MEADOWS

### Scenic rating: 8

near Olallie Lake in Mount Hood National Forest

**Map 9.5, page 491**

Olallie Meadows is set at 4,500 feet elevation along a large and peaceful alpine meadow about three miles from Olallie Lake. Non-motorized boats are allowed on Olallie Lake. The Pacific Crest Trail passes very close to the campground.

**Campsites, facilities:** There are seven sites for

tents or RVs up to 16 feet long. Picnic tables, garbage service, and fire grills are provided. Vault toilets are available. There is no drinking water. Leashed pets are permitted.

**Reservations, fees:** Reservations are not accepted. Sites are $15-25 per night. Open July-October, weather permitting.

**Directions:** From Portland, drive south on U.S. 205 to the junction with Highway 24. Take the Highway 224/Estacada exit and turn left (south) onto Highway 224. Drive approximately 13 miles to Estacada. Continue south on Highway 224 and drive 27 miles in national forest (the road becomes Forest Road 46). Continue south on Forest Road 46 for 20 miles to Forest Road 4690. Turn left and drive southeast for 8.2 miles to Forest Road 4220. Turn right (south) and drive 1.5 miles to the campground on the left.

**Contact:** Mount Hood National Forest, Clackamas River Ranger District, 503/630-6861, www.fs.usda.gov/mthood.

## 92 KAH-NEE-TA RESORT

### Scenic rating: 7
on the Warm Springs Indian Reservation

Map 9.5, page 491

This resort features a stellar-rated, full-concept spa, with the bonus of a nearby casino. It is also the only public camp on the east side of the Warm Springs Indian Reservation; there are no other camps within 30 miles. The Warm Springs River runs nearby. Recreation options in the area include an 18-hole golf course, miniature golf, biking and hiking trails, a riding stable, and tennis courts.

**Campsites, facilities:** There are 51 sites with full hookups for RVs of any length. Some sites are pull-through. A motel, 20 teepees, and a cottage are also available. Some picnic tables are provided. Cable TV, restrooms with flush toilets and coin showers, propane gas, a dump station, seasonal concession stand, coin laundry, ice, a playground, a spa, mineral baths,

and an Olympic-sized, spring-fed swimming pool with a 170- and a 140-foot water slide are available. Some facilities are wheelchair accessible. Leashed pets are permitted, but some areas are restricted.

**Reservations, fees:** Reservations are accepted at 800/554-4786. RV sites are $49 per night for three people, teepees are $69 per night for three people. There is a two-night minimum on weekends, and a three-night minimum on holiday weekends. Some credit cards are accepted. Open year-round.

**Directions:** From Portland, turn east on U.S. 26 and drive about 105 miles to Warm Springs and Agency Hot Springs Road on the left. Turn left and drive 11 miles northeast to Kah-Nee-Ta and the resort on the right.

**Contact:** Kah-Nee-Ta Resort, 541/553-1112, www.kahneeta.com.

## 93 WHISPERING FALLS

### Scenic rating: 10
on the North Santiam River near Detroit Lake in Willamette National Forest

Map 9.5, page 491

This popular campground sits on the banks of the North Santiam River, where you can fish. If the campsites at Detroit Lake are crowded, this camp provides a more secluded option, and it's only about a 10-minute drive from the lake. Ospreys sometimes nest near the campground.

**Campsites, facilities:** There are 16 sites for tents or RVs up to 30 feet long. Picnic tables, garbage service, and fire grills are provided. Drinking water and flush toilets are available. Bring your own firewood. Leashed pets are permitted.

**Reservations, fees:** Reservations are not accepted. Sites are $14 per night, $6 per night per additional vehicle. Open late April-mid-September; a gate prevents access in the off-season.

**Directions:** From Salem, drive east on Highway 22 for 50 miles to Detroit. Continue east on Highway 22 for eight miles to the campground on the right.

**Contact:** Willamette National Forest, Detroit Ranger District, 503/854-3366, www.fs.usda.gov/willamette.

# 94 RIVERSIDE

### Scenic rating: 7

on the North Santiam River in Willamette National Forest

Map 9.5, page 491

This campground is set at an elevation of 2,400 feet along the banks of the North Santiam River, where the fishing can be good. A point of interest, the Marion Forks Fish Hatchery and interpretive site lies just 2.5 miles south. Other day-trip options include the Mount Jefferson Wilderness, directly to the east in Willamette National Forest, and Minto Mountain Trail, three miles east.

**Campsites, facilities:** There are 35 sites for tents or RVs up to 24 feet long and two sites for tents only. Picnic tables and fire grills are provided. Drinking water, vault toilets, and gray water disposal sites are available. Leashed pets are permitted.

**Reservations, fees:** Reservations are accepted for RV sites at 877/444-6777 ($10 reservation fee) or www.recreation.gov ($9 reservation fee). Sites are $14 per night, $6 per night per additional vehicle. Open late May-September; a gate prevents access during the off-season.

**Directions:** From Salem, drive east on Highway 22 for 50 miles to Detroit. Continue southeast on Highway 22 for 14 miles to the campground on the right.

**Contact:** Willamette National Forest, Detroit Ranger District, 503/854-3366, www.fs.usda.gov/willamette.

# 95 MARION FORKS

### Scenic rating: 8

on the Santiam River in Willamette National Forest

Map 9.5, page 491

Situated along Marion Creek at 2,500 feet in elevation, this campground is adjacent to the Marion Forks Fish Hatchery. A U.S. Forest Service guard station and a restaurant are across Highway 22. The area boasts some quality hiking trails; the nearest is Independence Rock Trail, 0.25 mile north of the campground.

**Campsites, facilities:** There are 15 sites for tents or RVs up to 24 feet long. Picnic tables, fire grills, and garbage containers are provided. Vault toilets are available. There is no drinking water. Leashed pets are permitted.

**Reservations, fees:** Reservations are not accepted. Sites are $10 per night, $5 per night per additional vehicle. Open year-round, weather permitting, with no winter services.

**Directions:** From Salem, drive east on Highway 22 for 50 miles to Detroit. Continue southeast on Highway 22 for 16 miles to the campground on the left.

**Contact:** Willamette National Forest, Detroit Ranger District, 503/854-3366, www.fs.usda.gov/willamette.

# 96 BIG MEADOWS
# HORSE CAMP

### Scenic rating: 10

near Mount Jefferson Wilderness in Willamette National Forest

Map 9.5, page 491

Built by the U.S. Forest Service with the support of a horse club, this camp is used heavily by equestrians riding into the Big Meadows area and the adjacent Mount Jefferson Wilderness. There's no local forage, so bring your own weed-free certified hay. If you're not a horse lover, you may want to stick with Riverside or Marion Forks.

**Campsites, facilities:** There are nine sites for tents or RVs up to 36 feet long. Picnic tables, garbage service, fire grills, hitching rack, loading rack, and enclosed four-horse corrals are provided at each site. Drinking water, vault toilets, firewood, and stock water troughs are available. Some facilities are wheelchair accessible. Leashed pets are permitted.

**Reservations, fees:** Reservations are not accepted. Sites are $14 per night, $7 per night per additional vehicle. Open June-October, weather permitting.

**Directions:** From Salem, drive east on Highway 22 for 50 miles to Detroit. Continue southeast on Highway 22 for 27 miles to Big Meadows Road (Forest Road 2267). Turn left and drive one mile to Forest Road 2257. Turn left and drive 0.5 mile to the campground on the left.

**Contact:** Willamette National Forest, Detroit Ranger District, 503/854-3366, www.fs.usda. gov/willamette.

## 97 SHEEP SPRINGS HORSE CAMP

### Scenic rating: 7

near the Mount Jefferson Wilderness in Deschutes National Forest

**Map 9.5, page 491**

This well-shaded equestrian camp with privacy screening between sites is near the trailhead for the Metolius-Windigo Horse Trail, which heads northeast into the Mount Jefferson Wilderness and south to Black Butte. Contact the U.S. Forest Service for details and maps of the backcountry. The camp is set at an elevation of 3,200 feet.

**Campsites, facilities:** There are 11 sites for tents or RVs up to 45 feet long. Fire grills are provided. Drinking water, vault toilets, garbage bins, and corrals and box stalls for horses are available.

**Reservations, fees:** Reservations are accepted until the end of September at 877/444-6777 ($10 reservation fee) or www.recreation.gov ($9 reservation fee). Sites are $12 per night, $8 per night per additional vehicle. Open early May-mid-September, weather permitting.

**Directions:** From Albany, drive east on U.S. 20 for 87 miles to the sign for Jack Lake (located one mile east of Suttle Lake) and Suttle-Sherman Road. Turn left on Forest Road 12 and drive eight miles to Forest Road 1260. Turn left and drive 1.5 miles to Forest Road 1260-200. Turn right and drive 1.5 miles to the campground on the right.

**Contact:** Deschutes National Forest, Sisters Ranger District, 541/549-7700, www.fs.usda. gov/centraloregon.

## 98 JACK CREEK

### Scenic rating: 5

near Mount Jefferson Wilderness in Deschutes National Forest

**Map 9.5, page 491**

A more primitive alternative to the other camps in the area, this campground sits along the banks of Jack Creek in an open setting among ponderosa pine. Sites are large and well shaded and the elevation is 3,100 feet. To protect the bull trout habitat, no fishing is permitted here.

**Campsites, facilities:** There are 20 sites for tents or RVs up to 50 feet long. Some of the larger sites can accommodate up to seven cars and 20 people. Picnic tables and fire grills are provided. Vault toilets and garbage bins are available. There is no drinking water. Leashed pets are permitted.

**Reservations, fees:** Reservations are not accepted. Sites are $12 per night, $6 per night per additional vehicle. Open mid-April-mid-October.

**Directions:** From Albany, drive east on U.S. 20 for 87 miles to the sign for Jack Lake (located one mile east of Suttle Lake) and Suttle-Sherman Road. Turn left on Forest Road 12

and drive five miles to Forest Road 1230. Turn left and drive 0.75 mile to Forest Road 1232. Turn left and drive 0.25 mile to the campground on the left.

**Contact:** Deschutes National Forest, Sisters Ranger District, 541/549-7700, www.fs.usda.gov/centraloregon.

## 99 PELTON
🏊 🎣 🚤 🏕 🚣 ♿ 🚐 ⛺

**Scenic rating: 8**

on Lake Simtustus in Deschutes National Forest

**Map 9.5, page 491**          **BEST (**

This campground claims 0.5 mile of shoreline along the north side of Lake Simtustus. Campsites here are shaded with juniper in an area of rolling hills and sagebrush. One section of the lake is accessible for water skis and personal watercraft. Simtustus is a trophy fishing lake for kokanee and brown, bull, and rainbow trout. Just north of the park is the Pelton Wildlife Overlook, where you can view a variety of waterfowl, such as great blue herons, ducks, geese, and shorebirds, as well as eagles and other raptors. Cove Palisades State Park, about 15 miles south, provides additional recreational opportunities.

**Campsites, facilities:** There are 68 sites, some with partial hookups, for tents or RVs up to 56 feet long, two group sites for up to 12 people, and 13 yomes (canvas cabins). Picnic tables and fire grills are provided. Drinking water, restrooms with flush toilets and showers, garbage service, a restaurant, general store, ice, and fishing supplies are available. Also, a full-service marina with boat rentals, marine fuel, a boat launch, boat dock, fishing pier, moorage, swimming beach, volleyball courts, horseshoe pits, and a playground are available. Some facilities are wheelchair accessible. Leashed pets are permitted, and a dog run area is available.

**Reservations, fees:** Reservations are accepted at 541/325-5292 or www.portlandgeneral.com/parks. Sites are $18-25 per night; the group sites are $50 per night; yomes are $30-60 per night. Some credit cards are accepted. Open late-April-late-September.

**Directions:** From Portland, drive south on U.S. 26 for 108 miles to the town of Warm Springs. Continue south two miles to Pelton Dam Road. Turn right and drive three miles to the campground on the right.

**Contact:** Portland General Electric, 503/464-8515 or 541/475-0516 (store and marina), www.portlandgeneral.com/parks; campground, 541/325-5292.

## 100 PERRY SOUTH
🏊 🎣 🚤 🏕 🚣 ♿ 🚐 ⛺

**Scenic rating: 6**

on Lake Billy Chinook in Deschutes National Forest

**Map 9.5, page 491**

Perry South campground is located near the shore of the Metolius arm of Lake Billy Chinook. The lake borders the Warm Springs Indian Reservation and can get very crowded and noisy, as it attracts powerboat/water-ski enthusiasts. Recreation options include water-skiing and fishing for bass and panfish, and one of Oregon's nicest golf courses is nearby.

**Campsites, facilities:** There are 63 sites for tents or RVs up to 95 feet long. Picnic tables, garbage service, and fire grills are provided. Drinking water, vault toilets, firewood, a fish-cleaning station, boat docks, and launching facilities are available. A camp host is on-site. Some facilities are wheelchair accessible. Leashed pets are permitted.

**Reservations, fees:** Reservations are accepted for some sites at 877/444-6777 ($10 reservation fee) or www.recreation.gov ($9 reservation fee). Sites are $16-18 per night, $8 per night per additional vehicle, $2 additional charge during holidays. Open May-September, weather permitting.

**Directions:** From Bend, drive north on U.S. 97 to Redmond, then continue north for 15 miles to the Culver Highway. Take the Culver

Highway north to Culver, and continue two miles to Gem Lane. Turn left and drive two miles to Frazier Drive. Turn left and drive a short distance to Peck Road. Turn right and drive through Cove Palisades State Park to Jordan Road at the shore of Lake Billy Chinook. Turn left on Jordan Road and drive about 10 miles (over the bridge) to County Road 64. Continue (bearing left) and drive about eight miles to the campground entrance on the left (on the upper end of the Metolius Fork of Lake Billy Chinook).

**Contact:** Deschutes National Forest, Sisters Ranger District, 541/549-7700, www.fs.usda.gov/centraloregon.

## 101 MONTY

**Scenic rating: 5**

on the Metolius River in Deschutes National Forest

**Map 9.5, page 491**

Remote Monty campground is set at 2,000 feet elevation and gets light use. Trout fishing can be good along the banks of the Metolius River, near where it empties into Lake Billy Chinook. The river runs fast through this area so swimming and boating are not advised; however, it is an ideal put-in for kayaks. Warm Springs Indian Reservation is across the river.

**Campsites, facilities:** There are 32 sites for tents or RVs up to 20 feet long. Picnic tables, garbage service, and fire grills are provided. Firewood and pit toilets are available. There is no drinking water. Boat docks and launching facilities are nearby at Perry South. Leashed pets are permitted.

**Reservations, fees:** Reservations are not accepted. Sites are $14 per night, $7 per night per additional vehicle. Open June-mid-September, weather permitting.

**Directions:** From Bend, drive north on U.S. 97 to Redmond and continue north for 15 miles to the Culver Highway. Take

the Culver Highway north to Culver and continue two miles to Gem Lane. Turn left and drive two miles to Frazier Drive. Turn left and drive a short distance to Peck Road. Turn right and drive through Cove Palisades State Park to Jordan Road at the shore of Lake Billy Chinook. Turn left on Jordan Road and drive about 10 miles (over the bridge) to County Road 64. Turn left and drive about 13 miles to the campground entrance (on the Metolius River above the headwaters of Lake Billy Chinook). The last five miles are very rough.

**Contact:** Deschutes National Forest, Sisters Ranger District, 541/549-7700, www.fs.usda.gov/centraloregon.

## 102 COVE PALISADES STATE PARK

**Scenic rating: 7**

on Lake Billy Chinook

**Map 9.5, page 491**

This park is a mile away from the shore of Lake Billy Chinook, where some lakeshore cabins are available. Here in Oregon's high-desert region, summers are warm and sunny with fairly mild but cold winters. Lofty cliffs surround the lake, and about 10 miles of hiking trails crisscross the area. Two popular special events are held here annually: Lake Billy Chinook Day in September and the Eagle Watch in February.

**Campsites, facilities:** There are two campgrounds: Crooked River Campground offers 88 sites with partial hookups for tents or RVs and three deluxe cabins; Deschutes Campground has 91 tent sites, 85 sites with full hookups for RVs up to 60 feet long, and three group tent areas for up to 25 people each. Picnic tables and fire grills are provided. Drinking water, garbage bins, restrooms with flush toilets and showers, a dump station, firewood, a convenience store, amphitheater, horseshoe pit, playground, and ice are available. Boat docks, launching facilities, a marina, boat rentals, fish-cleaning station, and a restaurant are nearby. Some facilities are wheelchair accessible. Leashed pets are permitted, and there is a designated pet exercise area.

**Reservations, fees:** Reservations are accepted at 800/452-5687 or www.oregonstateparks.org ($8 reservation fee). RV sites with full hookups are $21-26 per night, tent sites are $16-20 per night, cabins are $59-80 per night, the group areas are $54-75 per night, $5 per night per additional vehicle. Some credit cards are accepted. Crooked River Campground is open year-round; Deschutes Campground is open May-mid-September.

**Directions:** From Bend, drive north on U.S. 97 for 13 miles to Redmond and continue north for 15 miles to the Culver Highway. Take the Culver Highway north to Culver and continue two miles to Gem Lane. Turn left and drive two miles to Frazier Drive. Turn left and drive a short distance to Peck Road. Turn right and drive to the park entrance.

**Contact:** Cove Palisades State Park, 541/546-3412 or 800/551-6949, www.oregonstateparks.org.

## 103 KOA MADRAS/CULVER

**Scenic rating: 6**

near Lake Billy Chinook

**Map 9.5, page 491**

This KOA has a relaxing atmosphere, with some mountain views. It is set about seven miles from Lake Billy Chinook, a steep-sided reservoir formed where the Crooked River, Deschutes River, Metolius River, and Squaw Creek all merge. Like much of the country east of the Cascades, this is a high-desert area.

**Campsites, facilities:** There are 22 tent sites and 58 sites with full or partial hookups for RVs of any length; most sites are pull-through. There are also six cabins. Drinking water, fire pits, and picnic tables are provided. Restrooms with flush toilets and showers, propane gas, a dump station, firewood, a convenience store, coin laundry, ice, and a playground are available. Recreational activities include a dog run, Pebble Puppies, seasonal heated pool, bicycle rentals, volleyball, horseshoe pits, and tetherball. Boat docks and launching facilities are nearby. Some facilities are wheelchair accessible. Leashed pets are permitted.

**Reservations, fees:** Reservations are accepted at 800/562-1992. Sites are $24-44 per night, $2-5 per person per night for more than two people. Some credit cards are accepted. Open year-round.

**Directions:** From Madras, drive south on U.S. 97 for nine miles to Jericho Lane. Turn left (east) and drive 0.5 mile to the campground on the right.

**Contact:** KOA Madras/Culver, 541/546-3046, www.madras-koa.com.

# NORTHEASTERN OREGON

Even longtime residents often overlook Northeastern Oregon. With its high desert abutting the craggy Blue Mountains, it just doesn't look like the archetypal Oregon. In this corner of the state, you'll find Wallowa-Whitman National Forest and little-known sections of Malheur, Ochoco, and Umatilla National Forests. The Hells Canyon National Recreation Area, Idaho, and the Snake River border this region to the east. Among the highlights are the John Day River and its headwaters, the Strawberry Mountain Wilderness in Malheur National Forest, and various sections of the linked John Day Fossil Beds National Monument. One of the prettiest spots is Wallowa Lake State Park, where 9,000-foot snowcapped mountains surround a pristine lake on three sides. My favorite destinations are the Wallowa Mountains and the Eagle Cap Wilderness, a wildlife paradise.

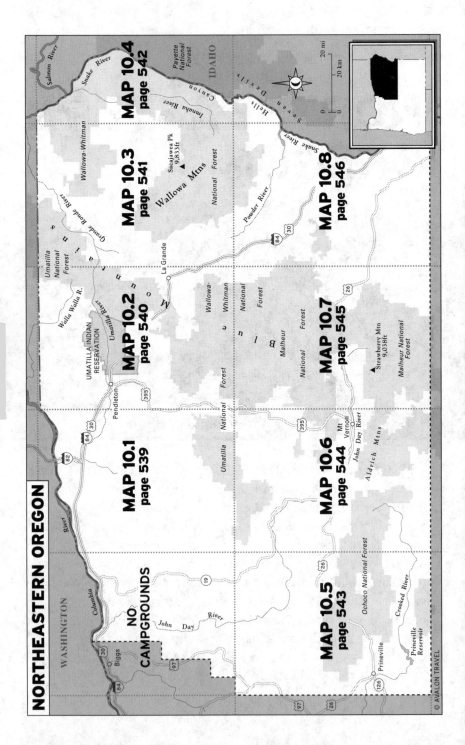

# NORTHEASTERN OREGON

WASHINGTON

IDAHO

**MAP 10.4**
page 542

**MAP 10.3**
page 541

**MAP 10.8**
page 546

**MAP 10.2**
page 540

**MAP 10.7**
page 545

**MAP 10.1**
page 539

**MAP 10.6**
page 544

**MAP 10.5**
page 543

NO CAMPGROUNDS

Salmon River

Snake River

Payette National Forest

Hells Canyon

Seven Devils

Wallowa-Whitman

Imnaha River

Sacajawea Pk 9,833ft

Wallowa Mtns

National Forest

Snake River

Grande Ronde River

Powder River

La Grande

Wallowa-Whitman National Forest

Umatilla National Forest

Walla Walla R.

Umatilla River

UMATILLA INDIAN RESERVATION

Pendleton

Malheur National Forest

Blue Mountains

Strawberry Mtn 9,038ft

Malheur National Forest

Umatilla National Forest

Mt Vernon

John Day River

Aldrich Mtns

Columbia River

Biggs

John Day River

Ochoco National Forest

Crooked River

Prineville Reservoir

Prineville

20 mi

20 km

© AVALON TRAVEL

# Map 10.1

Sites 1-9
Pages 547-550

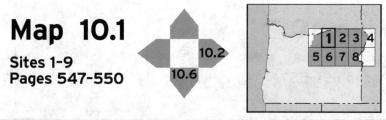

10.2
10.6

| | 1 | 2 | 3 | 4 |
| 5 | 6 | 7 | 8 | |

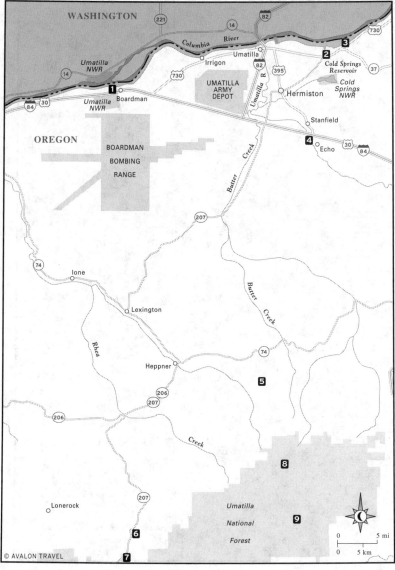

WASHINGTON

Columbia River

221 14 82

730

Umatilla NWR

Irrigon

Umatilla

82

395

**3**

**2** Cold Springs Reservoir

37

14

30

84

Umatilla NWR

Boardman

**1**

Umatilla R

Hermiston

Cold Springs NWR

UMATILLA ARMY DEPOT

Stanfield

OREGON

BOARDMAN BOMBING RANGE

Butter Creek

**4** Echo

30 84

207

74

Ione

Butter Creek

Lexington

Rhea

74

Heppner

**5**

206 207

206

Creek

**8**

Lonerock

207

**9**

Umatilla

**6**

National

**7**

Forest

0 — 5 mi
0 — 5 km

© AVALON TRAVEL

# Map 10.2

**Sites 10-26**
**Pages 551-557**

10.1 10.3
10.7

1 2 3 4
5 6 7 8

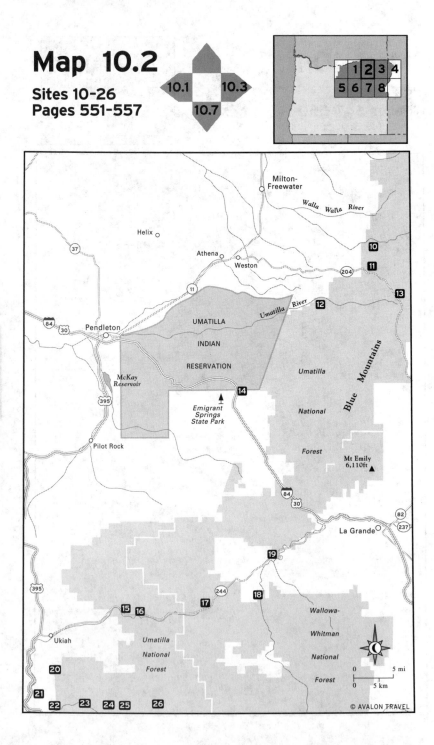

© AVALON TRAVEL

# Map 10.3

## Sites 27-42
## Pages 558-564

10.2  10.4
10.8

1 2 3 4
5 6 7 8

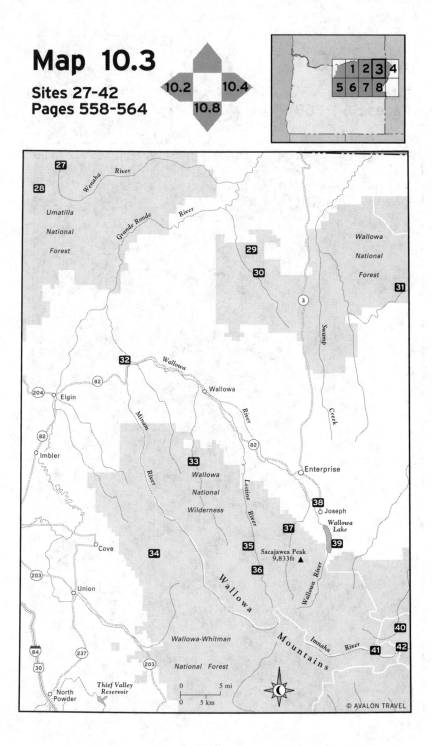

# Map 10.4

**Sites 43-46**
**Pages 564-565**

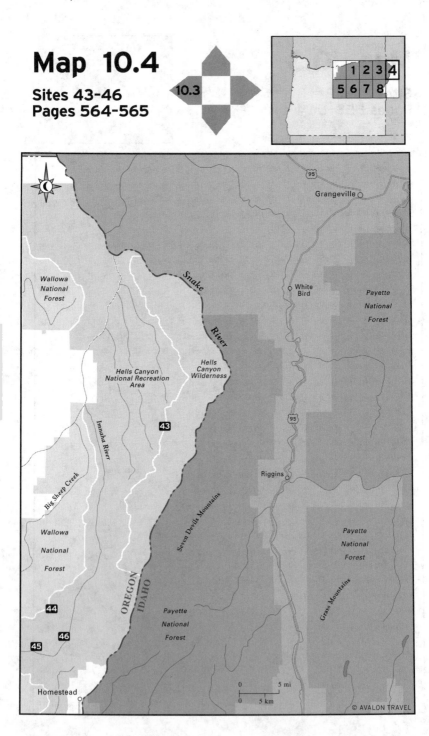

# Map 10.5

**Sites 47-60
Pages 566-571**

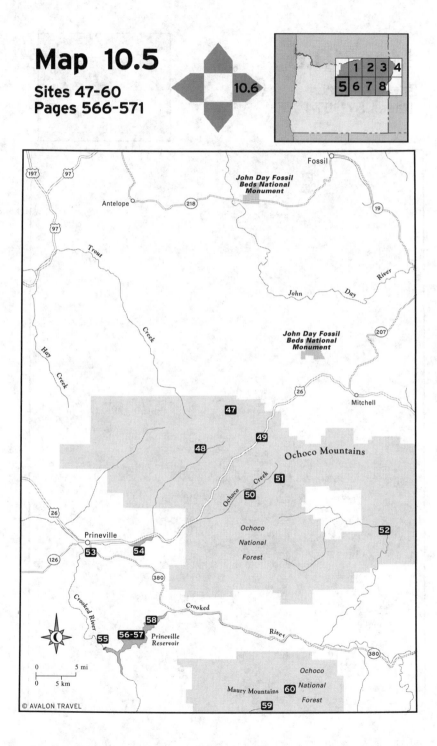

# Map 10.6

**Sites 61-67**
**Pages 571-574**

10.1
10.5  10.7

| 1 | 2 | 3 | 4 |
| 5 | **6** | 7 | 8 |

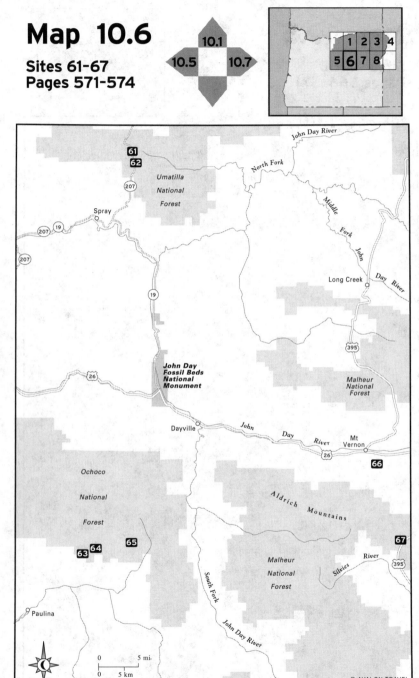

# Map 10.7

**Sites 68-101**
**Pages 574-587**

10.2
10.6   10.8

| 1 | 2 | 3 | 4 |
| 5 | 6 | 7 | 8 |

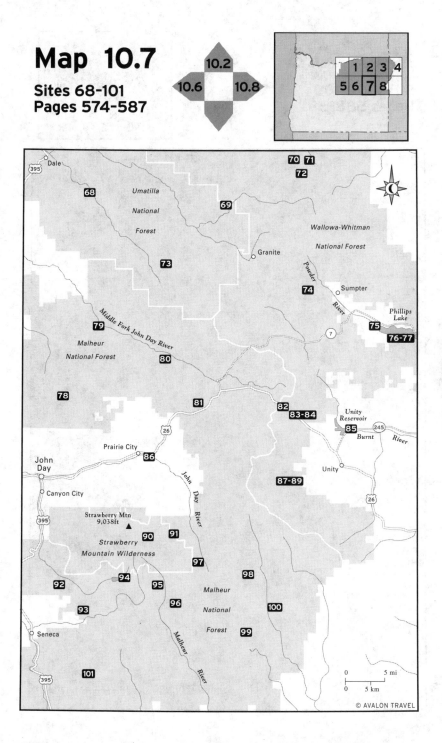

# Map 10.8

**Sites 102-109**
**Pages 588-591**

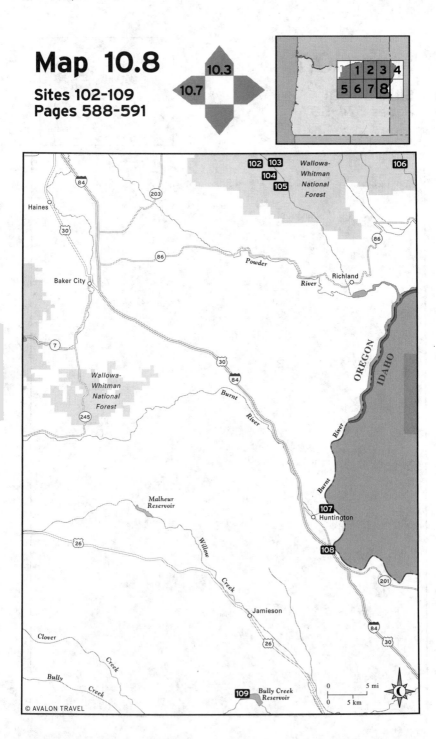

© AVALON TRAVEL

## 1 BOARDMAN MARINA AND RV PARK

### Scenic rating: 7

on the Columbia River

**Map 10.1, page 539**

This public campground is set on the Columbia River among linden, maple, and sycamore trees. Some sites are located along the riverbank. In addition to fishing for bass, crappie, and walleye, nearby recreation options include a marina and golf course (five miles away).

**Campsites, facilities:** There are 63 sites with full hookups for tents or RVs of any length and four sites for tents only; some sites are pull-through. Picnic tables and fire pits are provided. Drinking water, restrooms with flush toilets and showers, a dump station, garbage bins, coin laundry, a day-use area with picnic shelters, a pay phone, Wi-Fi, seasonal firewood and ice for sale, children's playground, and a boat dock, pump-out station, fish-cleaning station, and launch are available. Recreational facilities include a basketball court, softball fields, horseshoe pits, sand volleyball, and a hiking/biking path along the river. A boat marina and grocery store are available within one mile. Some facilities are wheelchair accessible. Leashed pets are permitted.

**Reservations, fees:** Reservations are accepted at 888/481-7217. Tent sites are $15.90 per night; RV sites are $26.50 per night, $5 per night per extra vehicle. Some credit cards are accepted. Open year-round, with limited winter facilities.

**Directions:** From Portland on I-84 eastbound, drive 164 miles to Boardman and Exit 164. Take that exit and turn left (north) on Main Street. Drive 0.25 mile over the railroad bridge, bear left, and continue 0.2 mile to the Y intersection and the park on the right.

**Contact:** Boardman Marina Park, Boardman Park and Recreation District, 541/481-7217 or 888/481-7217, www.boardmanmarinapark.com.

## 2 HAT ROCK CAMPGROUND

### Scenic rating: 7

near the Columbia River

**Map 10.1, page 539**

Hat Rock State Park is a day-use area with a boat launch along the banks of the Columbia River. The campground itself is very pretty, with lots of trees, and offers close access to the river and fishing.

**Campsites, facilities:** There are eight tent sites and 60 sites with full or partial hookups for RVs of any length; some sites are pull-through. Picnic tables and fire pits are provided. Drinking water, restrooms with flush toilets and showers, a dump station, convenience store, café, coin laundry, volleyball and basketball courts, ball field, horseshoe pits, seasonal swimming pool, Wi-Fi, firewood, and ice are available. Boat docks and launching facilities are nearby. Some facilities are wheelchair accessible. Leashed pets are permitted.

**Reservations, fees:** Reservations are accepted at 541/567-4188 or 541/567-0917. Sites are $25-28 per night, $3 per person per night for more than two people. Weekly and monthly rates are available. Some credit cards are accepted. Open year-round.

**Directions:** From Portland, drive east on U.S. 84 for roughly 170 miles past Boardman to the junction of U.S. 84 and U.S. 730. Turn northeast on U.S. 730 and drive 18 miles to the junction with I-82. Continue east on U.S. 730 for seven miles to the state park access road. Turn left (north) and drive 0.5 mile to the park on the left.

**Contact:** Hat Rock Campground, 541/567-4188, www.hatrockcampground.com; Hat Rock Store 541/567-0917.

## 3 SAND STATION RECREATION AREA

**Scenic rating: 5**

on Lake Wallula

**Map 10.1, page 539**

This eight-acre park offers hiking, picnicking, swimming, and fishing for smallmouth bass and steelhead, salmon, and sturgeon in season. It has a shaded day-use area and campsites on the beach.

**Campsites, facilities:** There are five sites (no hookups) for tents or RVs and space for an additional 5-10 tents near the beach. Picnic tables, sun shelters, and fire grills are provided. Vault toilets and a swimming beach are available. There is no drinking water and garbage must be packed out. A grocery store is located within three miles, a boat ramp is about two miles away, and a golf course is nine miles away. Leashed pets are permitted.

**Reservations, fees:** Reservations are not accepted. There is no fee for camping. Open year-round, weather permitting.

**Directions:** In Umatilla, drive north on I Street to U.S. 730/Columbia River Highway. Turn right onto U.S. 730/Columbia River Highway and drive 11 miles to the park entrance on the left.

**Contact:** U.S. Army Corps of Engineers, Walla Walla District, 541/922-2268, www.nww.usace.army.mil.

## 4 FORT HENRIETTA RV PARK

**Scenic rating: 7**

on the Umatilla River

**Map 10.1, page 539**

This park, located in the historic community of Echo, sits along the Umatilla River. It provides a quiet, pleasant layover spot for travelers cruising I-84. The river has some good trout fishing, and a nine-hole public golf course is a short drive away.

**Campsites, facilities:** There are six sites with full hookups (including cable TV) for RVs of any length, two pull-through sites with partial hookups, and an area for dispersed tent camping. Picnic tables are provided. Drinking water, restrooms with flush toilets and showers, and a dump station are available. The camp is within walking distance of two restaurants. Leashed pets are permitted.

**Reservations, fees:** Reservations available at 541/571-3597. Sites are $18-23 per night, $2 per person per night for more than two people. Open year-round.

**Directions:** From Pendleton, drive west on I-84 to Exit 188 and the Echo Highway. Take the exit, turn left (southeast), and drive one mile; cross the railroad tracks and continue 0.5 mile to Dupont Street. Turn right (south) and drive 0.3 mile to Main Street. Turn left (west) and drive one block to the park on the left.

**Contact:** Echo City Hall, 541/571-3597, www.echo-oregon.com.

## 5 CUTSFORTH PARK

**Scenic rating: 8**

on Willow Creek

**Map 10.1, page 539**

Cutsforth is a secluded and private county park set beside a small, wheelchair-accessible pond in a quiet, wooded area. In winter, the park serves as a staging area for snowmobilers, and in spring mushroom hunting is an attraction.

**Campsites, facilities:** There are 54 sites, most with full or partial hookups, for tents or RVs up to 42 feet long, and two cabins. Horse pens and a large building with kitchen facilities are available for rent. Picnic tables and fire rings are provided at most sites. Restrooms with flush toilets, vault toilets, coin showers, a dump station, horseshoe pits, firewood, ice, gazebo, a community building, and a playground are available. Supplies are available in Heppner (22 miles away). Some facilities are wheelchair accessible. Leashed pets are permitted.

**Reservations, fees:** Reservations are accepted ($12 reservation fee) at 541/989-8214 or www.morrowcountyparks.org. Sites with full hookups are $18-21 per night, dry sites are $12 per night, $2 per night per additional vehicle, and $3 per night per horse. Cabins are $45 per night. Weekly and monthly rates are available. Open mid-May-mid-November, weather permitting.

**Directions:** From Pendleton on I-84, drive west for 27 miles to Exit 182 and Highway 207 (Heppner Highway). Turn south and drive 32 miles to Lexington and Highway 74. Turn left (southeast) on Highway 74 (becomes Highway 207) and drive 10 miles to Heppner. Continue south on Highway 207 for 0.5 mile to Willow Creek Road. Turn left on Willow Creek Road and drive 23 miles to the park.

**Contact:** Morrow County Public Works, 541/989-8214, www.morrowcountyparks.org.

# 6 ANSON WRIGHT MEMORIAL PARK

🏃 🚲 🛶 🎣 🐴 👨‍👩‍👧 ♿ 🚐 ⛺

### Scenic rating: 7

on Rock Creek

**Map 10.1, page 539**

Set among wooded hills along a small stream, this county park offers visitors hiking opportunities and prime trout fishing in a stocked, wheelchair-accessible pond. Attractions in the area include Emigrant Springs State Park, Hardman Ghost Town (10 miles away), and the Pendleton Mills. There's also a nearby opal mine, accessible with permission only.

**Campsites, facilities:** There are 52 sites for tents or RVs up to 42 feet long and one cabin. Some sites have full hookups and/or are pull-through. Picnic tables and fire rings are provided. Restrooms with coin showers, a picnic area, dump station, firewood, and a playground are provided. Some facilities are wheelchair accessible. Leashed pets are permitted.

**Reservations, fees:** Reservations are accepted ($12 reservation fee) at 541/989-8214

or www.morrowcountyparks.org. Sites with hookups are $18-21 per night, dry sites are $12 per night, and $2 per night per additional vehicle. Cabins are $45 per night. Weekly and monthly rates are available. Open mid-May-end of October, weather permitting.

**Directions:** From Pendleton, drive west on I-84 for 27 miles to Exit 182 and Highway 207 (Heppner Highway). Turn south and drive 32 miles to Lexington and Highway 74. Turn left (south) on Highway 74 (becomes Highway 20) and drive 10 miles to Heppner. Continue south on Highway 207 for 11 miles to Ruggs and a fork. Bear left at the fork (still Highway 207) and drive 12 miles to the park on the right.

**Contact:** Morrow County Public Works, 541/989-8214, www.morrowcountyparks.org.

# 7 MORROW COUNTY OHV PARK

🛶 🎣 ♿ 🚐 ⛺

### Scenic rating: 5

in Morrow County Park

**Map 10.1, page 539**

This 6,200-acre park is very popular. It is designed primarily for OHV use and has more than 150 miles of trails specifically for off-highway vehicles. There is a day-use area, and the campground itself is wooded.

**Campsites, facilities:** There are 83 sites, some with full or partial hookups, for tents or RVs of any length, five tent-only sites, four group sites for up to 10 people each in an open gravel lot (no trees), and six cabins. Picnic tables and fire rings are provided at some sites. Drinking water, showers, flush toilets, dump station, firewood, coin ATV wash rack, helmet rental, propane, a seasonal restaurant, playground, and a day-use area are available. Some facilities are wheelchair accessible. Leashed pets are permitted.

**Reservations, fees:** Reservations are accepted at 541/989-8214 or www.morrowcountyparks.org ($12 reservation fee). Sites with hookups are $18-21 per night, dry sites are $12 per night, and $2 per night per additional vehicle. Cabins $45. Weekly and monthly rates are available. Cabins are $45-80 per night. Open mid-May-mid-November, weather permitting; call ahead December-February.

**Directions:** From Pendleton, drive west on I-84 for 27 miles to Exit 182 and Highway 207 (Heppner Highway). Turn south and drive 32 miles to Lexington and Highway 74. Turn left (south) on Highway 74 (becomes Highway 20) and drive 10 miles to Heppner. Continue south on Highway 207 for 11 miles to Ruggs and a fork. Bear left at the fork (still Highway 207) and drive 22 miles to the park on the right.

**Contact:** Morrow County Public Works, 541/989-8214, www.morrowcountyparks.org.

# 8 PENLAND LAKE

### Scenic rating: 10

near Penland Lake in the Umatilla National Forest

**Map 10.1, page 539**          **BEST (**

This campground (4,950 feet elevation) has partial tree cover, so there are many open spaces. The lake is small, and electric-motor boats are allowed. The fishing can be good at times, with rainbow trout and bluegill the primary fish species. Hiking and bicycling are popular on the nearby trails. The wildlife viewing can be outstanding; species include bear, deer, and elk, as well as grouse and other birds.

**Campsites, facilities:** There are seven sites for tents and one site for RVs up to 50 feet long. Picnic tables and fire rings are provided. Vault toilets are available. There is no drinking water. Garbage must be packed out. A boat ramp is nearby. Leashed pets are permitted.

**Reservations, fees:** Reservations are not accepted. A fee will be charged starting in 2014. Open May-October, weather permitting. A 14-day stay limit is enforced.

**Directions:** From Heppner, drive south on Highway 207 to Willow Creek Road (Forest

Road 54/County Road 678). Turn left (east) and drive 23 miles to Forest Road 21. Turn right (gravel road) and drive three miles to Forest Road 2103. Turn left and drive two miles to the lake and campground.

**Contact:** Umatilla National Forest, Heppner Ranger District, 541/676-9187, www.fs.usda.gov/umatilla.

# 9 DIVIDE WELL

### Scenic rating: 5

in Umatilla National Forest

**Map 10.1, page 539**

Divide Wells is a primitive campground, but it is busy in the summer, and even occasionally used for reunions. Set at 4,700 feet elevation, it can serve as a good base camp for a hunting trip. Mule deer and Rocky Mountain elk can be spotted in the surrounding ponderosa pine and fir forest. Potamus Point Scenic Overlook, offering a spectacular view of the John Day River drainage, is 11 miles south of the camp on Forest Road 5316 and provides a good opportunity to see bighorn sheep.

**Campsites, facilities:** There are eight sites for tents or RVs up to 20 feet long and three group sites. A vault toilet is provided. There is no drinking water, and garbage must be packed out. Leashed pets are permitted.

**Reservations, fees:** Reservations are not accepted. There is no fee for camping. Open late May-November, weather permitting. A 14-day stay limit is enforced.

**Directions:** From Pendleton, drive south on U.S. 395 for 48 miles to Ukiah and Highway 244. Turn right (the road becomes Forest Road 53) and drive west on Forest Road 53 for about 14 miles to Forest Road 5327. Turn left (south) and drive seven miles to the campground on the right. A U.S. Forest Service map is recommended.

**Contact:** Umatilla National Forest, North Fork John Day Ranger District, 541/427-3231, www.fs.usda.gov/umatilla.

## 10 WOODWARD

### Scenic rating: 7
near Langdon Lake in Umatilla National Forest

**Map 10.2, page 540**

Nestled among the trees at an elevation of 4,950 feet, this popular campground has a view of Langdon Lake (though campers do not have access to the private lake). A flat trail encircles the campground, and there is some privacy screening between the sites.

**Campsites, facilities:** There are 15 sites for tents or RVs up to 28 feet long. Picnic tables, garbage bins, and fire grills are provided. Drinking water and vault toilets are available. Leashed pets are permitted.

**Reservations, fees:** Reservations are not accepted. Sites are $12 per night, $5 per each additional vehicle. Open late June-September, weather permitting. A 14-day stay limit is enforced.

**Directions:** From Pendleton on I-84, turn north on Highway 11 and drive approximately 27 miles to Weston and Highway 204. Turn right (southeast) on Highway 204 and drive 17 miles to the campground on the right (near Langdon Lake).

**Contact:** Umatilla National Forest, Walla Walla Ranger District, 509/522-6290, www. fs.usda.gov/umatilla.

## 11 TARGET MEADOWS

### Scenic rating: 6
near the south fork of the Walla Walla River in Umatilla National Forest

**Map 10.2, page 540**

This quiet campground with shady sites and a sunny meadow is situated at 4,800 feet elevation. The camp is adjacent to the Burnt Cabin Trailhead, which leads to the south fork of the Walla Walla River Trail and an old military site.

**Campsites, facilities:** There are 16 sites for tents or RVs up to 28 feet long and two sites for tents only. Picnic tables and fire grills are provided. Garbage bins, drinking water, and vault toilets are available. Leashed pets are permitted.

**Reservations, fees:** Reservations are not accepted. Sites are $12 per night for up to two vehicles, $5 per each additional vehicle. Open late June-mid-November, weather permitting. A 14-day stay limit is enforced.

**Directions:** From Pendleton, drive north on Highway 11 for 16 miles to Highway 204 near Weston. Turn right (southeast) on Highway 204 and drive 17.5 miles to Forest Road 64. Turn left and drive 0.5 mile to Forest Road 6401. Turn left (north) and drive two miles to Road 6401-050. Turn right (north) and drive 0.5 mile to the camp.

**Contact:** Umatilla National Forest, Walla Walla Ranger District, 509/522-6290, www. fs.usda.gov/umatilla.

## 12 UMATILLA FORKS

### Scenic rating: 3
along the Umatilla River in Umatilla National Forest

**Map 10.2, page 540**

Umatilla Forks campground lies in a canyon between the South and North Forks of the Umatilla River at an elevation of 2,400 feet. Expect warm temperatures in mid- to late summer; tree cover provides some relief. Fishing on the Umatilla River is catch-and-release only, and hiking is possible in the North Fork Umatilla Wilderness.

**Campsites, facilities:** There are eight sites for tents or RVs up to 28 feet long and seven sites for tents only. Picnic tables and fire grills are provided. Drinking water and vault toilets are available. Garbage must be packed out. Leashed pets are permitted.

**Reservations, fees:** Reservations are not accepted. Sites are $10 per night for up to two vehicles, $5 per each additional vehicle. Open

May-October, weather permitting. A 14-day stay limit is enforced.

**Directions:** From Pendleton, drive north on Highway 11 for about 25 miles to Athena and Pambrun Road. Turn right on Pambrun Road and drive five miles to Spring Hollow Road. Turn left on Spring Hollow Road (it becomes Thorn Hollow Road) and drive about 6.5 miles to Bingham Road (River Road). Turn left on Bingham Road (River Road), cross the railroad tracks, and follow signs for about five miles to Gibbon. Cross the railroad tracks at Gibbon and continue on Bingham Road (it becomes Forest Road 32) about 11 miles to the campground on the right.

**Contact:** Umatilla National Forest, Walla Walla Ranger District, 509/522-6290, www. fs.usda.gov/umatilla.

## 13 WOODLAND

### Scenic rating: 4

in Umatilla National Forest

**Map 10.2, page 540**

Primitive Woodland campground is set at 5,200 feet elevation with easy highway access—and related road noise. The camp has both shaded and sunny sites and can be a perfect spot for I-84 cruisers looking for a short detour. During fall, the area is popular with hunters; hikers and mountain bikers will enjoy the area the rest of the year.

**Campsites, facilities:** There are six sites for tents or RVs up to 28 feet long. Picnic tables, fire grills, and vault toilets are provided. There is no drinking water. Garbage must be packed out. Leashed pets are permitted.

**Reservations, fees:** Reservations are not accepted. Sites are $8 per night for up to two vehicles, $5 per each additional vehicle. Open mid-June-mid-November, weather permitting. A 14-day stay limit is enforced.

**Directions:** From Pendleton, drive north on Highway 11 for 16 miles to Highway 204 near Weston. Turn right (southeast) on Highway

204 and drive 23 miles. The campground is just off the highway on the left.

**Contact:** Umatilla National Forest, Walla Walla Ranger District, 509/522-6290, www. fs.usda.gov/umatilla.

## 14 EMIGRANT SPRINGS STATE HERITAGE AREA

### Scenic rating: 7

near the Umatilla Indian Reservation

**Map 10.2, page 540**

Emigrant Springs sits in old-growth forest at the summit of the Blue Mountains. The campground is popular with horse campers and offers wildlife-watching opportunities. The nearby Oregon Trail and Pendleton Woolen Mills provide interesting side-trips.

**Campsites, facilities:** There are 32 sites for tents, 17 sites with full hookups for RVs of any length, a designated horse camp (closed in winter), a group tent site, and seven cabins. Picnic tables, fire grills, and horse corrals are provided. Drinking water, garbage bins, restrooms with flush toilets and showers, firewood, some horse facilities, a reservable community building with kitchen, basketball court, amphitheater, and baseball field are available. Some facilities are wheelchair accessible. Leashed pets are permitted.

**Reservations, fees:** Reservations are accepted at 800/452-5687 or www.reserveamerica.com ($8 reservation fee). Tent sites are $13-17 per night, RV sites are $16-20 per night, cabins are $24-39 per night, equestrian sites are $13-17 per night, and the group site is $51-71 for up to 25 people. Additional vehicles cost $5 per night. Some credit cards are accepted. Open May 1-mid-October, with only the cabins and five campsites open year-round. (Water is off mid-October-mid-April).

**Directions:** From Pendleton, drive southeast on I-84 for 26 miles to Exit 234. Take that exit

to Old Oregon Trail Road (frontage road) and drive 0.5 mile to the park on the right.
**Contact:** Emigrant Springs State Heritage Area, 541/983-2277 or 800/551-6949, www.oregonstateparks.org.

## 15 LANE CREEK

### Scenic rating: 4
on Camas Creek in Umatilla National Forest

**Map 10.2, page 540**

This primitive campground (3,850 feet elevation) borders Camas Creek and Lane Creek, just inside the forest boundary, and provides easy access to all the amenities of town. It's a popular stop for overnighters passing through the area. Some of the sites close to the highway get traffic noise. Highlights in the area include hot springs (privately owned) and good hunting and fishing. A U.S. Forest Service map details the back roads.

**Campsites, facilities:** There are six sites for tents or RVs up to 28 feet long and one group site for up to 25 people. Picnic tables and fire grills are provided. Vault toilets are available. There is no drinking water, and garbage must be packed out. Leashed pets are permitted.

**Reservations, fees:** Reservations are not accepted. Sites are $8 per night for up to two vehicles, $5 per each additional vehicle, and $25 per night for the group site. Open April-November, weather permitting. A 14-day stay limit is enforced.

**Directions:** From Pendleton, drive south on U.S. 395 for 50 miles to Ukiah and Highway 244. Turn east on Highway 244 and drive nine miles to the campground on the left.

**Contact:** Umatilla National Forest, North Fork John Day Ranger District, 541/427-3231, www.fs.usda.gov/umatilla.

## 16 BEAR WALLOW CREEK

### Scenic rating: 5
on Bear Wallow Creek in Umatilla National Forest

**Map 10.2, page 540**

Situated near the confluence of Bear Wallow and Camus Creeks at an elevation of 3,900 feet, Bear Wallow is one of three off Highway 244 (the others are Lane Creek and Frazier). Quiet and primitive, the camp is used primarily in the summer. A 0.5-mile, wheelchair-accessible, interpretive trail meanders next to Bear Wallow Creek, highlighting the steelhead habitat.

**Campsites, facilities:** There are three sites for tents or RVs up to 28 feet long and four sites for smaller RVs or tents. Picnic tables and fire grills are provided. Vault toilets are available. No drinking water is available, and garbage must be packed out. Some facilities are wheelchair accessible. Leashed pets are permitted.

**Reservations, fees:** Reservations are not accepted. Sites are $8 per night for up to two vehicles, $5 per each additional vehicle, and the group site is $25 per night. Open April-November, weather permitting. A 14-day stay limit is enforced.

**Directions:** From Pendleton, drive south on U.S. 395 for 50 miles to Ukiah and Highway 244. Turn east on Highway 244 and drive 10 miles to the camp on the left.

**Contact:** Umatilla National Forest, North Fork John Day Ranger District, 541/427-3231, www.fs.usda.gov/umatilla.

## 17 FRAZIER

### Scenic rating: 5
on Frazier Creek in Umatilla National Forest

**Map 10.2, page 540**

With nearly 130 miles of OHV and motorcycle trails at the Winom-Frazier Off-Highway-Vehicle Complex, this camp is popular in the summer with the OHV crowd. The campground is set at 4,300 feet elevation along the banks of Frazier Creek. It is a popular hunting area in the fall, and some fishing is available in the area. It's advisable to obtain a map of Umatilla National Forest. On weekends, it's not a good spot for the traditional camper looking for quiet and solitude. Lehman Hot Springs, one mile away, provides a side-trip option.

**Campsites, facilities:** There are 15 sites for tents or RVs up to 28 feet long and five group sites. Picnic tables and fire grills are provided. An OHV loading ramp and vault toilets are available. There is no drinking water, and garbage must be packed out. Some facilities are wheelchair accessible. Leashed pets are permitted. A 14-day stay limit is enforced.

**Reservations, fees:** Reservations are not accepted. Sites are $8 per night for up to two vehicles, $5 per each additional vehicle, and group sites are $25 per night. Open April-November, weather permitting.

**Directions:** From Pendleton, drive south on U.S. 395 for 50 miles to Ukiah and Highway 244. Turn left (east) on Highway 244 and drive 18 miles to Forest Road 5226. Turn right (south) and drive 0.5 mile to the campground.

**Contact:** Umatilla National Forest, North Fork John Day Ranger District, 541/427-3231, www.fs.usda.gov/umatilla.

## 18 SPOOL CART

### Scenic rating: 6

on the Grande Ronde River in
Wallowa-Whitman National Forest

**Map 10.2, page 540**

Spool Cart gets its name from the large cable spools that were delivered here by train and then transported to logging sites on a cart. The wooded campground sits at 3,500 feet elevation on the banks of the Grande Ronde River; sites offer privacy. The camp is popular with hunters in the fall, and the gurgling Grande Ronde offers fishing for bull trout.

Hilgard Junction State Park to the north provides numerous recreation options, and the Oregon Interpretive Trail Park at Blue Crossing is nearby.

**Campsites, facilities:** There are 12 sites for tents or RVs up to 22 feet long. Picnic tables and fire grills are provided. Vault toilets are available. There is no drinking water, and garbage must be packed out. Some facilities are wheelchair accessible. Leashed pets are permitted.

**Reservations, fees:** Reservations are not accepted. Sites are $5 per night per vehicle. Open late May-late November.

**Directions:** From Pendleton, drive southeast on U.S. 84 for 42 miles to Highway 244. Turn southwest on Highway 244 and drive 13 miles to Forest Road 51. Turn left (south) and drive five miles to the campground on the right.

**Contact:** Wallowa-Whitman National Forest, LaGrande Ranger District, 541/963-7186, www.fs.usda.gov/ wallowa-whitman.

## 19 BIRD TRACK SPRINGS

### Scenic rating: 7

near the Grande Ronde River in
Wallowa-Whitman National Forest

**Map 10.2, page 540**

Bird Track Springs is located at 3,100 feet elevation and is about a five-minute walk from the Grande Ronde River. The spacious campsites are right off the highway in surrounding woods of primarily ponderosa pine and white fir. The Bird Track Springs Interpretive Trail, across the campground, offers a hiking and bird-watching opportunity.

**Campsites, facilities:** There are 22 sites for tents or RVs up to 22 feet long. Picnic tables and fire rings are provided. Vault toilets are available. There is no drinking water, and garbage must be packed out. A camp host is on-site in the summer. Some facilities are wheelchair accessible. Leashed pets are permitted.

**Reservations, fees:** Reservations are not

accepted. Sites are $5 per night per vehicle. Open mid-May-November, weather permitting.
**Directions:** From Pendleton, drive southeast on U.S. 84 for 42 miles to Highway 244. Turn right (southwest) and drive seven miles to the campground on the left.
**Contact:** Wallowa-Whitman National Forest, LaGrande Ranger District, 541/963-7186, www.fs.usda.gov/wallowa-whitman.

## 20 DRIFT FENCE

### Scenic rating: 5

near Ross Springs in Umatilla National Forest

**Map 10.2, page 540**

Get this: Drift Fence is not marked on the Umatilla National Forest Map. The camp, set at 4,250 feet elevation, is adjacent to Blue Mountain National Forest Scenic Byway. With some elk and deer in the area, hunting is a highlight here. The Bridge Creek Interpretive Trail, three miles northwest of the campground off Forest Road 52, leads to a beautiful view of open meadow with various wildflowers and wildlife. Elk may be seen roaming in the Bridge Creek area.
**Campsites, facilities:** There are six sites for tents or RVs up to 30 feet long and one group site. Picnic tables are provided. A pit toilet is available. There is no drinking water, and garbage must be packed out. Leashed pets are permitted.
**Reservations, fees:** Reservations are not accepted. There is no fee for camping. Open May-November, weather permitting. A 14-day stay limit is enforced.
**Directions:** From Pendleton, drive south on U.S. 395 for 50 miles to Highway 244. Turn east on Highway 244 and drive one mile to Ukiah and Forest Road 52. Turn right (south) on Forest Road 52 and drive eight miles to the campground on the right.
**Contact:** Umatilla National Forest, North Fork John Day Ranger District, 541/427-3231, www.fs.usda.gov/umatilla.

## 21 UKIAH-DALE FOREST STATE SCENIC CORRIDOR

### Scenic rating: 7

near the North Fork of the John Day River

**Map 10.2, page 540**

Fishing is a prime activity at this Camas Creek campground, nestled near the banks of the north fork of the John Day River at an elevation of 3,140 feet. It's a good layover for visitors cruising U.S. 395 looking for a shady spot for the night. Emigrant Springs State Park near Pendleton is a possible side trip.
**Campsites, facilities:** There are 27 sites for tents or self-contained RVs of any length. Picnic tables and fire pits are provided. Drinking water, firewood, and restrooms with flush toilets are available. Leashed pets are permitted.
**Reservations, fees:** Reservations are not accepted. Sites are $5-9 per night, $5 per night per additional vehicle. Open May-mid-October.
**Directions:** From Pendleton, drive south on U.S. 39 for 50 miles to Highway 244 (near Ukiah). Continue south on U.S. 395 for three miles to the park.
**Contact:** Emigrant Springs State Heritage Park, 541/983-2277 or 800/551-6949, www.oregonstateparks.org.

## 22 TOLLBRIDGE

### Scenic rating: 4

on the north fork of the John Day River in Umatilla National Forest

**Map 10.2, page 540**

This small, secluded campground (elevation 3,800 feet) lies at the confluence of Desolation Creek and the north fork of the John Day River and is adjacent to the Bridge Creek Wildlife Area. It can be beautiful or ugly, depending upon which direction you look. It's dusty in the summer, and there's sparse tree cover. Hunting and fishing are two options here, or explore the geological interpretive sign in the camp.

**Campsites, facilities:** There are five sites for tents or RVs up to 26 feet long. Picnic tables and fire grills are provided. A vault toilet is available. There is no drinking water, and garbage must be packed out. Some facilities are wheelchair accessible. Leashed pets are permitted.

**Reservations, fees:** Reservations are not accepted. Sites are $8 per night for up to two vehicles, $5 per each additional vehicle. Open April-November, weather permitting. A 14-day stay limit is enforced.

**Directions:** From Pendleton, drive south on U.S. 395 for 50 miles to the intersection with Highway 244. Continue south on U.S. 395 for 18 miles to Forest Road 55 (1 mile north of Dale). Turn left and drive 0.5 mile southeast to Forest Road 10 and the campground access road. Drive a short distance to the campground.

**Contact:** Umatilla National Forest, North Fork John Day Ranger District, 541/427-3231, www.fs.usda.gov/umatilla.

## 23 GOLD DREDGE CAMP

**Scenic rating: 7**

on the north fork of the John Day River in Umatilla National Forest

**Map 10.2, page 540**

Gold Dredge lies along the banks of the north fork of the John Day River, a federally designated Wild and Scenic River. This camp is an excellent launch point for recreation: swimming, fishing, rafting (spring only), float-tubing, and hunting (fall) are among the many activities. Dredge tailings from old mining activity are visible from the camp. At the end of Forest Road 5506, you can access a trailhead that heads into the adjacent North Fork John Day Wilderness. Special fishing regulations are in effect for the North Fork John Day River; check Oregon fishing regulations before heading out.

Parking is provided at Big Creek Bridge

for the North Fork John Day Wilderness Trailhead and the OHV trail that leads to the Winom-Frazier OHV Complex. Those driving to the end of Forest Road 5506 will need a high-clearance vehicle.

**Campsites, facilities:** There are seven sites for tents or RVs up to 28 feet long. Picnic tables are provided. Vault toilets are available. There is no drinking water, and garbage must be packed out. Some facilities are wheelchair accessible. Leashed pets are permitted.

**Reservations, fees:** Reservations are not accepted. Sites are $8 per night for up to two vehicles, $5 per each additional vehicle. Open May-November, weather permitting. A 14-day stay limit is enforced.

**Directions:** From Pendleton, drive south on U.S. 395 for 62 miles to Forest Road 55 (1 mile north of Dale). Turn left and drive six miles to the crossroads. Continue straight onto Forest Road 5506 and drive 2.5 miles to the campground on the right. Note: The last two miles of road are very rough.

**Contact:** Umatilla National Forest, North Fork John Day Ranger District, 541/427-3231, www.fs.usda.gov/umatilla.

## 24 DRIFTWOOD

**Scenic rating: 6**

on the north fork of the John Day River in Umatilla National Forest

**Map 10.2, page 540**

This tiny campground with ponderosa pine and Douglas fir cover sits on the banks of the north fork of the John Day River at an elevation of 2,500 feet. Recreational opportunities at this remote spot include fishing, float tubing, hunting, rafting, and swimming.

**Campsites, facilities:** There are six sites for tents or RVs up to 28 feet long. Fire grills and picnic tables are provided. A vault toilet is available. No drinking water is available. Garbage must be packed out. Leashed pets are permitted. A 14-day stay limit is enforced.

**Reservations, fees:** Reservations are not accepted. Sites are $8 per night for up to two vehicles, $5 per each additional vehicle. Open April-November, weather permitting.

**Directions:** From Pendleton, drive south on U.S. 395 for 62 miles to Forest Road 55 (1 mile north of Dale; it's easier to find if you know the marker, Texas Bar Road). Turn left and drive six miles to the crossroads. Continue straight ahead onto Forest Road 5506 and drive one mile to the campground on the right. Note: The last two miles of road are very rough.

**Contact:** Umatilla National Forest, North Fork John Day Ranger District, 541/427-3231, www.fs.usda.gov/umatilla.

## 25 ORIENTAL CAMPGROUND
🏃 ⛵ 🐕 ⛺

### Scenic rating: 4
on the north fork of the John Day River in Umatilla National Forest

Map 10.2, page 540

Oriental Creek nestles in a stand of mixed conifer at 3,500 feet elevation along the banks of the north fork of the John Day River. Evidence of old mining activity is visible here. The campground is popular with horse campers, motorcyclists, and off-roaders alike. Hunting and fishing are two possible activities, and nearby trails provide access to the North Fork John Day Wilderness. (No mountain bikes or motorcycles are permitted in the wilderness area.) Be advised that the road into this campground is rough and narrow in places.

**Campsites, facilities:** There are seven primitive tent sites. Pit toilets and picnic tables are available. There is no drinking water, and garbage must be packed out. Leashed pets are permitted.

**Reservations, fees:** Reservations are not accepted. Sites are $8 per night for up to two vehicles, $5 per each additional vehicle. Open April-November, weather permitting. A 14-day stay limit is enforced.

**Directions:** From Pendleton, drive south on U.S. 395 for 62 miles to Forest Road 55 (1 mile north of Dale; it's easier to find if you know the marker, Texas Bar Road). Turn left and drive six miles to the crossroads. Continue straight ahead onto Forest Road 5506 and drive six miles to the campground on the right. This road is rough and not recommended for trailers.

**Contact:** Umatilla National Forest, North Fork John Day Ranger District, 541/427-3231, www.fs.usda.gov/umatilla.

## 26 WINOM CAMPGROUND
🏃 🚴 ⛵ 🐕 🚐 ⛺

### Scenic rating: 2
on Winom Creek in Umatilla National Forest

Map 10.2, page 540

Winom Creek campground is set at 5,000 feet elevation and provides access to the Winom-Frazier Off-Highway-Vehicle Complex, with 130 miles of OHV trails of varying difficulty. The complex was developed in the late 1980s for OHV enthusiasts and has worn in well. The camp is also near the North Fork John Day Wilderness, perfect for hikers. (Check the campground bulletin boards for detailed maps of the terrain.)

**Campsites, facilities:** There are seven sites for tents or RVs up to 28 feet long and three group sites. Picnic tables and fire rings are provided. Vault toilets and an OHV loading ramp are available. There is no drinking water, and garbage must be packed out. Two of the group sites have picnic shelters. Leashed pets are permitted.

**Reservations, fees:** Reservations are not accepted. Sites are $8 per night for up to two vehicles, $5 per each additional vehicle at single sites, $25 per night for group sites. Open May-early November, weather permitting. A 14-day stay limit is enforced.

**Directions:** From Pendleton, drive south on U.S. 395 for 50 miles to Highway 244. Turn east on Highway 244 and drive one mile to Ukiah and Forest Road 52. Turn right (south) on Forest Road 52 and drive 20 miles to Forest Road 440. Turn right and drive one mile to the campground on the right. The last mile of the access road is narrow and steep.

**Contact:** Umatilla National Forest, North Fork John Day Ranger District, 541/427-3231, www.fs.usda.gov/umatilla.

## 27 MOTTET

### Scenic rating: 6
near the south fork of the Walla Walla River in Umatilla National Forest

**Map 10.3, page 541**

Mottet sits perched at 5,200 feet elevation along a ridge top, surrounded by a heavily timbered forest. Far from the beaten path, it's quite primitive and relatively unknown, so you're almost guaranteed privacy. A trailhead across the road leads down to the south fork of the Walla Walla River.

**Campsites, facilities:** There are six sites for tents or RVs up to 22 feet. Picnic tables and fire grills are provided. Spring water and vault toilets are available. Garbage must be packed out. Leashed pets are permitted.

**Reservations, fees:** Reservations are not accepted. Sites are $8 per night for up to two vehicles, $5 per each additional vehicle. Open early July-November, weather permitting. A 14-day stay limit is enforced.

**Directions:** From Pendleton, drive north on Highway 11 for 16 miles to Highway 204 near Weston. Turn right (southeast) on Highway 204 and drive 17.5 miles to Forest Road 64. Turn left and drive about 15 miles to Forest Road 6403. Turn left and drive about two miles to the campground on the left. The road is rough for the last two miles.

**Contact:** Umatilla National Forest, Walla Walla Ranger District, 509/522-6290, www.fs.usda.gov/umatilla.

## 28 JUBILEE LAKE

### Scenic rating: 8
on Jubilee Lake in Umatilla National Forest

**Map 10.3, page 541**   BEST (

Jubilee Lake is the largest and most popular campground in Umatilla National Forest, and it fills up on weekends and holidays. Located along the shore of 90-acre Jubilee Lake (elevation 4,800 feet), this spot offers good fishing, hiking, and swimming. Electric boat motors are permitted on the lake, but gas-powered motors are prohibited. A 2.8-mile trail loops around the lake and provides different levels of accessibility for those in wheelchairs; fishing access is available along the trail.

**Campsites, facilities:** There are 48 sites for tents and RVs up to 28 feet long and five tent-only sites. Picnic tables and fire grills are provided. Drinking water, firewood, picnic areas, and restrooms with flush toilets are available. Boat docks and launching facilities are nearby. Garbage bins are available during the summer. Some facilities are wheelchair accessible. Leashed pets are permitted.

**Reservations, fees:** Reservations are not accepted. Sites are $17 per night for up to two vehicles, $5 per night for each additional vehicle. Open late June-mid-October, weather permitting. A 14-day stay limit is enforced.

**Directions:** From Pendleton, drive north on Highway 11 for 16 miles to Highway 204 near Weston. Turn right (southeast) on Highway 204 and drive 17.5 miles to Forest Road 64. Turn left and drive 12 miles northeast to Forest Road 6400-250. Turn right (south) and drive 0.5 mile to the camp.

**Contact:** Umatilla National Forest, Walla Walla Ranger District, 509/522-6290, www.fs.usda.gov/umatilla.

## 29 DOUGHERTY SPRINGS
🏕 🚐 ⛺

### Scenic rating: 5
near Dougherty Springs in Wallowa-Whitman National Forest

**Map 10.3, page 541**

This wooded, primitive campground (elevation 5,100 feet) adjacent to Dougherty Springs is one in a series of remote camps set near natural springs. The camp is in a grassy open area with sparse Douglas and white fir. Birds, deer, elk, and small mammals can be seen in the area. Hells Canyon National Recreation Area to the east provides many recreation options.

**Campsites, facilities:** There are eight sites for tents only and four sites for tents or RVs up to 22 feet long. Picnic tables and fire rings are provided. Vault toilets are available. There is no drinking water, and garbage must be packed out. Leashed pets are permitted.

**Reservations, fees:** Reservations are not accepted. There is no fee for camping. Open June-October, weather permitting.

**Directions:** From LaGrande, drive northeast on Highway 82 for 64 miles to Enterprise and Highway 3. Turn north on Highway 3 and drive 15 miles to Forest Road 46. Turn right (northeast) and drive 30 miles to the campground on the left.

**Contact:** Hells Canyon National Recreation Area, Wallowa Mountains Visitors Center, 541/426-5546, www.fs.usda.gov/wallowa-whitman.

## 30 COYOTE
🏃 🚴 🏕 🚐 ⛺

### Scenic rating: 4
near Coyote Springs in Wallowa-Whitman National Forest

**Map 10.3, page 541**

Coyote campground is set at 4,800 feet elevation and adjacent to Coyote Springs. This is the largest of the three primitive camps in the vicinity, offering open sites and privacy.

**Campsites, facilities:** There are eight sites for tents or RVs up to 22 feet long and 21 sites for tents only. Picnic tables and fire rings are provided. Vault toilets are available. There is no drinking water, and garbage must be packed out. Leashed pets are permitted.

**Reservations, fees:** Reservations are not accepted. There is no fee for camping. Open May-November, weather permitting.

**Directions:** From LaGrande, drive northeast on Highway 82 for 64 miles to Enterprise and Highway 3. Turn north on Highway 3 and drive 15 miles to Forest Road 46. Turn right (northeast) and drive 25 miles to the campground on the left.

**Contact:** Wallowa-Whitman National Forest, Wallowa Valley Ranger District, Wallowa Mountains Visitors Center, 541/426-5546, www.fs.usda.gov/wallowa-whitman.

## 31 VIGNE
🏃 🚴 🏕 🚐 ⛺

### Scenic rating: 5
on Chesnimnus Creek in Wallowa-Whitman National Forest

**Map 10.3, page 541**

Vigne campground sits at 3,500 feet elevation on the banks of Chesnimnus Creek. The campground has pretty riverside sites shaded by Douglas and white fir. Recreation opportunities include fishing and exploring a few of the many hiking trails in the area.

**Campsites, facilities:** There are six sites for tents or RVs up to 22 feet long. Picnic tables and fire rings are provided. Drinking water and vault toilets are available. Garbage must be packed out. Leashed pets are permitted.

**Reservations, fees:** Reservations are not accepted. Sites are $6 per night. Open May-November, weather permitting.

**Directions:** From LaGrande, drive northeast on Highway 82 for 64 miles to Enterprise and Highway 3. Turn north on Highway 3 and drive 15 miles to Forest Road 46. Turn right (northeast) and drive 10 miles to Forest Road

4625. Turn right (east) and drive 10 miles to the campground. The last 10 miles are pot-holed and rough.

**Contact:** Wallowa-Whitman National Forest, Wallowa Valley Ranger District, Wallowa Mountains Visitors Center, 541/426-5546, www.fs.usda.gov/wallowa-whitman.

## 32 MINAM STATE PARK

### Scenic rating: 7
near the Grande Ronde River

**Map 10.3, page 541**

This small and pretty park is well worth the detour off I-84 necessary to get there. Once you do, you'll be greeted by large pines towering above the sharp valley, cut through by the Wallowa River. Rafting and fishing for steelhead are popular activities, and the area is teeming with wildlife, including bears, cougars, deer, elk, and the occasional Rocky Mountain bighorn sheep downriver.

**Campsites, facilities:** There are 20 primitive sites for tents or self-contained RVs up to 71 feet. Picnic tables and fire grills are provided. Drinking water is available May-mid-October. Garbage bins and vault toilets are available. Raft rentals are available nearby. Leashed pets are permitted.

**Reservations, fees:** Reservations are not accepted. Sites are $5-9 per night, $5 per night for an additional vehicle. Open April-October.

**Directions:** From LaGrande, drive northeast on Highway 82 for 18 miles to Elgin, then continue 14 miles to the park entrance road. Turn left (north) and drive two miles to the park.

**Contact:** Wallowa Lake State Park, 541/432-8855 or 800/551-6949, www.oregonstateparks.org.

## 33 BOUNDARY

### Scenic rating: 6
near the Eagle Cap Wilderness in Wallowa-Whitman National Forest

**Map 10.3, page 541**

This pretty and primitive campground is set 100 yards from the banks of Bear Creek at 3,600 feet elevation and is heavily wooded with Douglas, red, tamarack, and white fir. Recreation options here include hiking, fishing, and horseback riding. Nearby trails provide access to the Eagle Cap Wilderness. This is another in a series of little-known, primitive sites in the area.

**Campsites, facilities:** There are eight primitive tent sites. Picnic tables and fire rings are provided. Vault toilets are available. There is no drinking water, and garbage must be packed out. Leashed pets are permitted.

**Reservations, fees:** Reservations are not accepted. There is no fee for camping. Open mid-June-November, weather permitting.

**Directions:** From LaGrande, drive north on Highway 82 for 46 miles to Wallowa and Forest Road 8250. Turn south and drive eight miles to Forest Road 8250-040. Bear right (south) and drive 0.75 mile to the camp.

**Contact:** Wallowa-Whitman National Forest, Eagle Cap Ranger District, Wallowa Mountains Visitors Center, 541/426-5546, www.fs.usda.gov/wallowa-whitman.

## 34 MOSS SPRINGS

### Scenic rating: 7
near the Eagle Cap Wilderness in Wallowa-Whitman National Forest

**Map 10.3, page 541**

At 6,000 feet elevation, Moss Springs campground is heavily forested with spruce and fir and has good views of the Grande Ronde Valley in some locations. The camp is popular with horse packers, and there is a loading ramp on-site. A trailhead provides access to the Eagle Cap Wilderness, a good jumping-off point for a multi-day backpacking trip. (Obtain a map of Wallowa-Whitman National Forest for detailed trail information.) The Breshears OHV Trail and the Mount Fanny Mountain bike trails are just north of the camp.

**Campsites, facilities:** There are eight sites for tents and RVs up to 16 feet long. Picnic tables and fire grills are provided. No drinking water is provided, but water is available for stock. Horse facilities and vault toilets are available. Garbage must be packed out. Some facilities are wheelchair accessible. Leashed pets are permitted.

**Reservations, fees:** Reservations are not accepted. Sites are $5 per night per vehicle. Open June-mid-October, weather permitting.

**Directions:** From LaGrande, drive east on Highway 237 for 15 miles to Cove and County Road 65 (signed for Moss Springs). Turn right (southeast) and drive 1.5 miles to Forest Road 6220. Turn left (east) and drive eight miles to the camp entrance. Note: The last five miles are on a steep gravel road.

**Contact:** Wallowa-Whitman National Forest, LaGrande Ranger District, 541/963-7186, www.fs.usda.gov/wallowa-whitman.

## 35 SHADY

### Scenic rating: 6

on the Lostine River in Wallowa-Whitman National Forest

**Map 10.3, page 541**

Shady campground sits along the banks of the Lostine River at an elevation of 5,400 feet. The camp has wooded as well as meadow areas. It is close to trails that provide access to the Eagle Cap Wilderness, a beautiful and pristine area that's perfect for an extended backpacking trip. You can sometimes spot mountain sheep in the area.

**Campsites, facilities:** There are 13 sites for tents or RVs up to 16 feet long. Picnic tables

and fire grills are provided. Vault toilets are available. There is no drinking water, and garbage must be packed out. Leashed pets are permitted.

**Reservations, fees:** Reservations are not accepted. Sites are $6 per night. Open mid-June-November, weather permitting.

**Directions:** From LaGrande, turn north on Highway 82 and drive 52 miles to Lostine and Forest Road 8210. Turn right (south) and drive 15 miles to the campground.

**Contact:** Wallowa-Whitman National Forest, Eagle Cap Ranger District, 541/426-5546, www.fs.usda.gov/wallowa-whitman.

## 36 TWO PAN

### Scenic rating: 6

on the Lostine River in Wallowa-Whitman National Forest

**Map 10.3, page 541**

Two Pan lies at the end of a forest road on the banks of the Lostine River. At 5,600 feet elevation, this camp is a prime jumping-off spot for a multi-day wilderness adventure. Adjacent trails provide access to numerous lakes and streams in the Eagle Cap Wilderness. If full, another campground option is Williamson, seven miles north on Forest Road 8210.

**Campsites, facilities:** There are nine sites for tents or RVs up to 16 feet. Picnic tables and fire grills are provided. Vault toilets are available at the trailhead. There is no drinking water, and garbage must be packed out. Leashed pets are permitted.

**Reservations, fees:** Reservations are not accepted. One free Wilderness Visitor Permit per group is required. Registration and self-issued permits are located at each trailhead. There is no fee for camping. Open mid-June-November, weather permitting.

**Directions:** From LaGrande, turn north on Highway 82 and drive 52 miles to Lostine and Forest Road 8210. Turn right (south) and drive 17 miles to the campground.

**Contact:** Wallowa-Whitman National Forest, Eagle Cap Ranger District, Wallowa Mountains Visitors Center, 541/426-5546, www.fs.usda.gov/wallowa-whitman.

## 37 HURRICANE CREEK

### Scenic rating: 5

near the Eagle Cap Wilderness in Wallowa-Whitman National Forest

**Map 10.3, page 541**

Set along Hurricane Creek at an elevation of 5,000 feet, this campground is on the edge of the Eagle Cap Wilderness and provides a good place to begin a backcountry backpacking trip. Sites are wooded, and some sit close to the creek—perfect for fishing. There is no access for medium to large RVs, which gives the camp more of a wilderness environment. Obtaining maps of the area from the ranger district is essential.

**Campsites, facilities:** There are 12 sites for tents only. Picnic tables and fire grills are provided. Vault toilets are available. There is no drinking water, and garbage must be packed out. Leashed pets are permitted.

**Reservations, fees:** Reservations are not accepted. Sites are $6 per night. Open mid-June-November, weather permitting.

**Directions:** From LaGrande, turn north on Highway 82 and drive 62 miles to Enterprise and Hurricane Creek Road. Turn right (south) on Hurricane Creek Road and drive five miles to Hurricane Grange Hall and Forest Road 8205; bear right (off the paved road) and drive two miles to the campground on the left.

**Contact:** Wallowa-Whitman National Forest, Eagle Cap Ranger District, 541/426-5546, www.fs.usda.gov/wallowa-whitman.

## 38 MOUNTAIN VIEW MOTEL AND RV PARK

### Scenic rating: 3

near Wallowa Lake

**Map 10.3, page 541**

Mountain View is centrally located for exploring the greater Wallowa Lake area. Fishing and jet boating are available only a mile away at Wallowa Lake, and nearby recreational facilities include bike paths, a golf course, hiking trails, and a riding stable. The park has a creek with a swimming hole and offers views of the Seven Devils Mountains and of the Eagle Cap Wilderness.

**Campsites, facilities:** There are 30 sites with partial hookups (one pull-through) for RVs up to 39 feet, a grassy area for tents, three cabins, and six motel rooms. Picnic tables and portable fire pits are provided. Restrooms with flush toilets and showers (seasonal), a dump station, Wi-Fi, firewood, and coin laundry are available. Propane gas, a store, and café are within two miles. Some facilities are wheelchair accessible. Leashed pets are permitted with breed restrictions.

**Reservations, fees:** Reservations are accepted. RV sites are $30 per night, tent sites are $20 per night, $2 per person per night for more than two people. Some credit cards are accepted. Open year-round.

**Directions:** From LaGrande, turn north on Highway 82 and drive 62 miles to Enterprise and the junction with Highway 3. Continue north on Highway 82 for four miles to the campground on the right (1.5 miles north of Joseph).

**Contact:** Mountain View Motel and RV Park, 541/432-2982, www.mtviewmotel-rvpark.com.

## 39 WALLOWA LAKE STATE PARK

🏃 🏊 🛶 �" 🎣 🐎 ♿ 🚐 ⛺

**Scenic rating: 8**

on Wallowa Lake

**Map 10.3, page 541**                **BEST (**

Surrounded by snowy peaks, Wallowa Lake is a large lake with plenty of fishing and boating, including waterskiing and parasailing. Recreational activities include canoeing, horseback riding, and hiking. Bumper boats, miniature golf, and an artist community provide other diversions. Other highlights include a pretty one-mile nature trail and trailheads that provide access into the Eagle Cap Wilderness and Hells Canyon gorge. A marina is nearby for boaters and anglers. Picnicking, swimming, and wildlife-viewing are a few of the other activities available to visitors.

**Campsites, facilities:** There are 121 sites with full hookups for RVs of any length, 89 tent sites, three group tent areas for up to 25 people each, and two yurts. Picnic tables and fire rings are provided. Garbage bins, drinking water, restrooms with flush toilets and showers, a dump station, and firewood are available. A store, café, and ice are within one mile. Boat docks, launching facilities, and rentals are nearby. Some facilities are wheelchair accessible. Leashed pets are permitted.

**Reservations, fees:** Reservations are accepted at 800/452-5687 or www.reserveamerica.com ($8 reservation fee). RV sites are $21-25 per night, tent sites are $16-20 per night, hiker/biker sites are $5 per person per night, group areas are $74 per night, yurts are $38 per night, $5 per night per additional vehicle. Some credit cards are accepted. Open year-round, with limited availability in winter (no water).

**Directions:** From LaGrande, turn north on Highway 82 and drive 62 miles to Enterprise and the junction with Highway 3. Continue south on Highway 82 to Joseph. Continue for six miles to the south shore of the lake and the campground.

**Contact:** Wallowa Lake State Park, 541/432-4185, www.oregonstateparks.org.

## 40 LICK CREEK

🏃 🏊 �" ♿ 🚐 ⛺

**Scenic rating: 7**

on Lick Creek in Wallowa-Whitman National Forest

**Map 10.3, page 541**

Located along the banks of Lick Creek in Hells Canyon National Recreation Area, this secluded and pretty campground sits in parklike surroundings at an elevation of 5,400 feet. Interspersed throughout the campground, tall Douglas fir, lodgepole pine, tamarack, and white fir provide a wildlife habitat for the area's birds and small animals.

**Campsites, facilities:** There are seven sites for tents only and five sites for tents or RVs up to 30 feet long. Picnic tables and fire rings are provided. Vault toilets are available. There is no drinking water, and garbage must be packed out. Some facilities are wheelchair accessible. Leashed pets are permitted.

**Reservations, fees:** Reservations are not accepted. Sites are $6 per night. Open mid-June-late November, weather permitting.

**Directions:** From LaGrande, turn north on Highway 82 and drive 64 miles to Enterprise. Continue south on Highway 82 to Joseph and Highway 350. Turn left (east) and drive 7.5 miles to Forest Road 39. Turn right (south) and drive 15 miles to the campground.

**Contact:** Hells Canyon National Recreation Area, Wallowa Mountains Visitors Center, 541/426-5546, www.fs.usda.gov/wallowa-whitman.

## 41 COVERDALE

🏃 🚲 🛶 �" 🚐 ⛺

**Scenic rating: 7**

near the Imnaha River

**Map 10.3, page 541**

Located at 4,300 feet in elevation along the Imnaha River, this campground is in a lushly forested drainage area. Wildflower viewing can be spectacular and fishing can be good. Hiking trails are nearby.

**Campsites, facilities:** There are seven sites for tents only and two sites for tents or RVs up to 24 feet long. Picnic tables and fire rings are provided. Vault toilets are available. There is no drinking water. Garbage must be packed out. Leashed pets are permitted.

**Reservations, fees:** Reservations are not accepted. Sites are $6 per night. Open June-October, weather permitting.

**Directions:** From Joseph, drive east on Highway 350 for eight miles to Wallowa Mountain Loop Road (Forest Road 39). Turn right and drive approximately 38 miles to Forest Road 3960. Turn right and drive four miles to the campground on the left.

**Contact:** Hells Canyon National Recreation Area, Wallowa Mountains Visitors Center, 541/426-5546, www.fs.usda.gov/wallowa-whitman.

# 42 OLLOKOT

### Scenic rating: 5

on the Imnaha River in Wallowa-Whitman National Forest

**Map 10.3, page 541**

This campground sits on the banks of the Imnaha River in Hells Canyon National Recreation Area at an elevation of 4,000 feet. It's named for Chief Joseph's brother, a member of the Nez Perce tribe. For those seeking a little more solitude, this could be the spot.

**Campsites, facilities:** There are 12 sites for tents or RVs up to 30 feet long. Picnic tables and fire rings are provided. Drinking water, vault toilets, and an interpretive display are available. Garbage must be packed out. Some facilities are wheelchair accessible. Leashed pets are permitted.

**Reservations, fees:** Reservations are not accepted. Sites are $8 per night. Open June-late November, weather permitting.

**Directions:** From I-84 at LaGrande, turn

north on Highway 82 and drive 64 miles to Enterprise. Continue six miles south to Joseph and Highway 350. Turn left (east) on Highway 350 and drive eight miles to Forest Road 39. Turn right (south) on Forest Road 39 and drive 30 miles to the campground on the left.

**Contact:** Hells Canyon National Recreation Area, Wallowa Mountains Visitors Center, 541/426-5546, www.fs.usda.gov/wallowa-whitman.

# 43 SADDLE CREEK

### Scenic rating: 8

near the Hells Canyon Wilderness in Wallowa-Whitman National Forest

**Map 10.4, page 542**

Saddle Creek campground is set at 6,800 feet, nestled in on a ridge between two canyons with excellent views of the Seven Devils Mountains. Trees are scarce here because of past wildfires. Nearby trails provide access to Saddle Creek and Hells Canyon National Recreation Area.

**Campsites, facilities:** There are seven sites for tents. Picnic tables and fire rings are provided. Vault toilets are available. There is no drinking water, and garbage must be packed out. Leashed pets are permitted. Some facilities are wheelchair accessible. Note: RVs and trailers are not recommended on the access road.

**Reservations, fees:** Reservations are not accepted. There is no fee for camping. Open July-mid-November, weather permitting.

**Directions:** From LaGrande, turn north on Highway 82 and drive 64 miles to Enterprise. Continue south on Highway 82 and drive six miles to Joseph and Highway 350. Turn left (east) on Highway 350 and drive 30 miles to the small town of Imnaha and Forest Road 4240. Drive straight up the hill on Forest Road 4240 and continue 19 miles (on a gravel road) to the campground.

**Contact:** Hells Canyon National Recreation Area, Wallowa Mountains Visitors Center,

541/426-5546 or 541/426-5522, www.fs.usda.gov/wallowa-whitman.

# 44 BLACKHORSE

**Scenic rating: 7**

on the Imnaha River in Wallowa-Whitman National Forest

## Map 10.4, page 542

This campground along the banks of the Imnaha River in Hells Canyon National Recreation Area is located in a secluded section of Wallowa-Whitman National Forest at an elevation of 4,000 feet.

**Campsites, facilities:** There are 15 single sites and one double site for tents or RVs up to 30 feet long. Picnic tables and fire rings are provided. Vault toilets are available. There is no drinking water, and garbage must be packed out. Some facilities are wheelchair accessible. Leashed pets are permitted.

**Reservations, fees:** Reservations are not accepted. Sites are $8 per night. Open June-late November, weather permitting.

**Directions:** From I-84 at LaGrande, turn north on Highway 82 and drive 64 miles to Enterprise. Continue six miles south to Joseph and Highway 350. Turn left (east) and drive eight miles on Highway 350 to Forest Road 39. Turn right (south) on Forest Road 39 and drive 29 miles to the campground.

**Contact:** Hells Canyon National Recreation Area, Wallowa Mountains Visitors Center, 541/426-5546, www.fs.usda.gov/wallowa-whitman.

# 45 HIDDEN

**Scenic rating: 6**

on the Imnaha River in Wallowa-Whitman National Forest

## Map 10.4, page 542

River views and spacious sites can be found at this campground in a pretty spot along the banks of the Imnaha River in the Hells Canyon National Recreation Area. It's essential to obtain a map of Wallowa-Whitman National Forest that details back roads and hiking trails. If full, Coverdale Campground is an option, just four miles northeast on Forest Road 3960.

**Campsites, facilities:** There are 10 sites for tents or small, self-contained RVs. Picnic tables and fire rings are provided. Vault toilets are available. There is no drinking water, and garbage must be packed out. Some facilities are wheelchair accessible. Leashed pets are permitted.

**Reservations, fees:** Reservations are not accepted. Sites are $6 per night. Open June-late November, weather permitting.

**Directions:** From LaGrande, drive east on Highway 82 for 64 miles to Enterprise. Continue six miles south to Joseph and Highway 350. Turn left (east) and drive eight miles to Wallowa Mountain Loop Road (Forest Road 39). Turn right (south) and drive 30 miles to Forest Road 3960. Turn right (southwest) and drive seven miles to the campground.

**Contact:** Hells Canyon National Recreation Area, Wallowa Mountains Visitors Center, 541/426-5546, www.fs.usda.gov/wallowa-whitman.

# 46 INDIAN CROSSING

**Scenic rating: 6**

on the Imnaha River in Wallowa-Whitman National Forest

## Map 10.4, page 542

Indian Crossing is situated at an elevation of 4,500 feet and is more developed than nearby Hidden Campground. A trailhead for the Eagle Cap Wilderness is near; obtain a U.S. Forest Service map for trail options.

**Campsites, facilities:** There are 14 sites for tents or RVs up to 30 feet long. Picnic tables and fire rings are provided. Drinking water, vault toilets, and horse facilities are available. Garbage must be packed out. Some facilities are wheelchair accessible. Leashed pets are permitted.

**Reservations, fees:** Reservations are not accepted. Sites are $6 per night. Open June-late November, weather permitting.

**Directions:** From LaGrande, turn north on Highway 82 and drive 62 miles to Enterprise. Continue on Highway 82 for six miles to Joseph and Highway 350. Turn left (east) on Highway 350 and drive eight miles to Forest Road 39. Turn right (south) and drive about 30 miles to Forest Road 3960. Turn right and drive 10 miles to the campground at the end of the road.

**Contact:** Hells Canyon National Recreation Area, Wallowa Mountains Visitors Center, 541/426-5546, www.fs.usda.gov/wallowa-whitman.

## 47 WHISTLER

### Scenic rating: 7
in Ochoco National Forest

**Map 10.5, page 543**

Whistler is a trailhead camp for the Wildcat Trail, which heads into the Mill Creek Wilderness. The area is extremely popular with rock hounds, who search for agates, jasper, and thunder eggs. (Digging and collecting are forbidden in wilderness areas, however.) Though primitive, this pretty camp in a conifer forest guarantees quiet and privacy.

**Campsites, facilities:** There are two large open areas for dispersed tent camping. A picnic table and a vault toilet are provided. There is no drinking water, and garbage must be packed out. Horses are welcome. Leashed pets are permitted.

**Reservations, fees:** Reservations are not accepted. There is no fee for camping. Open late May-late October, weather permitting.

**Directions:** From Prineville, drive east on U.S. 26 for about 30 miles to Forest Road 27 (just east of Bandit Spring State Rest Area, near Ochoco Pass). Turn left on Forest Road

27 and drive nine miles to the campground entrance on the left. Note: Trailers are not recommended on this road.

**Contact:** Ochoco National Forest, Lookout Mountain Ranger District, 541/416-6500, www.fs.usda.gov/centraloregon.

## 48 WILDCAT

### Scenic rating: 4
on the east fork of Mill Creek in Ochoco National Forest

**Map 10.5, page 543**

Surrounded by conifer forest, Wildcat campground sits at an elevation of 3,700 feet in a cool canyon. Situated along the east fork of Mill Creek, the quiet camp is near the Twin Pillars Trailhead, which provides access into the Mill Creek Wilderness. No climbing is allowed in the wilderness. Ochoco Lake and Ochoco Lake State Park to the south provide side-trip possibilities.

**Campsites, facilities:** There are 17 sites for tents or RVs up to 30 feet long. Picnic tables and fire grills are provided. Drinking water and vault toilets are available. Garbage must be packed out. Leashed pets are permitted.

**Reservations, fees:** Reservations are not accepted. Sites are $8 per night for one vehicle, $3 per night for each additional vehicle. Open mid-May-late October, weather permitting.

**Directions:** From Prineville, drive east on U.S. 26 for nine miles to Mill Creek Road (Forest Road 33). Turn left on Mill Creek Road and drive about 10 miles to the campground.

**Contact:** Ochoco National Forest, Lookout Mountain Ranger District, 541/416-6500, www.fs.usda.gov/centraloregon.

## 49 OCHOCO DIVIDE

🚶 🚴 🐕 ♿ 🚐 ⛺

### Scenic rating: 5

in Ochoco National Forest

**Map 10.5, page 543**

This quiet campground is set at an elevation of 4,700 feet in a ponderosa pine forest. Hiking is available along a forest road near the camp and at nearby Marks Creek and Bandit Springs. This is a quick jump off U.S. 26; campers tend to set up in the afternoon and leave early in the morning, so you may get the place to yourself.

**Campsites, facilities:** There are 28 sites for tents or RVs up to 30 feet long, with a separate area of walk-in and bike-in sites, and a group site for groups of touring cyclists (up to 35 people). Picnic tables and fire pits are provided. Vault toilets are available. There is no drinking water, and garbage must be packed out. Some facilities are wheelchair accessible. Leashed pets are permitted.

**Reservations, fees:** Reservations are accepted for the group site only at 877/444-6777 ($10 reservation fee) or www.recreation.gov ($9 reservation fee). Sites are $13 per night, plus $6.50 per night for each additional vehicle; hike-in/bike-in sites are $13 per person per night; and the group site is $35 per night. Open late May-mid-October, weather permitting.

**Directions:** From Prineville, drive east on U.S. 26 for 30 miles to the campground at the summit of Ochoco Pass.

**Contact:** Ochoco National Forest, Lookout Mountain Ranger District, 541/416-6500, www.fs.usda.gov/centraloregon.

## 50 OCHOCO CAMPGROUND

🚶 🚴 ⛵ 🐕 ♿ 🚐 ⛺

### Scenic rating: 4

in Ochoco National Forest

**Map 10.5, page 543**

Ochoco Campground sits at an elevation of 4,000 feet along Ochoco Creek amid pine and aspen trees. There's fair fishing for rainbow trout, and hiking is nearby in the Lookout Mountain Recreation Area—that's 15,000 acres without roads. But hey, the truth is: Don't expect privacy and solitude at this campground. The log shelter and picnic area are often reserved for weddings, family reunions, and other group events.

**Campsites, facilities:** There are five sites for tents or RVs up to 24 feet long and one group site. Picnic tables and fire rings are provided. Drinking water, garbage bins, vault toilets, and a picnic shelter (by reservation) are available. Some facilities are wheelchair accessible. Leashed pets are permitted.

**Reservations, fees:** Reservations are only accepted for the group site only at 877/444-6777 ($10 reservation fee) or www.recreation.gov ($9 reservation fee). Sites are $14 per night, the group site is $60-100 per night, $7 per night per each additional vehicle. Open mid-May-October, weather permitting.

**Directions:** From Prineville, drive east on U.S. 26 for 16.5 miles to County Road 23. Turn right on County Road 23 and drive nine miles (County Road 23 becomes Forest Road 42) to the campground, across from the Ochoco Ranger Station.

**Contact:** Ochoco National Forest, Lookout Mountain Ranger District, 541/416-6500, www.fs.usda.gov/centraloregon.

## 51 WALTON LAKE

🚶 🚴 🏊 🚣 🚤 🐕 ♿ 🚐 ⛺

### Scenic rating: 7

on Walton Lake in Ochoco National Forest

**Map 10.5, page 543**

This campground, surrounded by meadows and ponderosa pine, borders the shore of small Walton Lake. Fishing and swimming are popular; the lake is stocked with rainbow trout, and the fishing can range from middle-of-the-road right up to downright excellent. Only non-motorized boats or boats with electric motors are allowed on the lake. Hikers can explore a nearby trail that leads south to Round Mountain.

**Campsites, facilities:** There are 21 sites for tents or RVs up to 28 feet long, six sites for tents only, and two group sites. Picnic tables, garbage bins, and fire grills are provided. Drinking water and vault toilets are available. Boat-launching facilities are nearby (only electric motors are allowed). Some facilities are wheelchair accessible. Leashed pets are permitted.

**Reservations, fees:** Reservations accepted only for the group sites at 877/444-6777 or www.recreation.gov ($9-10 reservation fee). Sites are $13 per night, $6 per each additional vehicle, and group sites are $60-100 per night. Open mid-May-mid-September, weather permitting.

**Directions:** From Prineville, drive east on U.S. 26 for 16.5 miles to County Road 23. Turn right (northeast) and drive nine miles (County Road 23 becomes Forest Road 42) to the Ochoco Ranger Station and Forest Road 22. Turn left and drive north on Forest Road 22 for seven miles to the campground.

**Contact:** Ochoco National Forest, Lookout Mountain Ranger District, 541/416-6500, www.fs.usda.gov/centraloregon.

## 52 DEEP CREEK

### Scenic rating: 5

on the north fork of the Crooked River in Ochoco National Forest

**Map 10.5, page 543**

This small camp on the edge of the high desert (4,200 feet elevation) gets little use, but it's in a nice spot. Located right at the confluence of Deep Creek and the north fork of the Crooked River, the pretty, shady sites allow for river access and fishing.

**Campsites, facilities:** There are six sites for tents or RVs up to 22 feet long. Picnic tables and fire grills are provided. Drinking water and vault toilets are available. Garbage must be packed out. Leashed pets are permitted.

**Reservations, fees:** Reservations are not accepted. Sites are $8 per night for one vehicle,

$3 per each additional vehicle. Open mid-May-mid-October, weather permitting.

**Directions:** From Prineville, drive east on U.S. 26 for 16.5 miles to County Route 23. Turn right (northeast) and drive 8.5 miles (it becomes Forest Road 42). Continue east on Forest Road 42 (paved road) for 23.5 miles to the campground on the right.

**Contact:** Ochoco National Forest, Lookout Mountain Ranger District, 541/416-6500, www.fs.usda.gov/centraloregon.

## 53 CROOK COUNTY RV PARK

### Scenic rating: 6

near the Crooked River

**Map 10.5, page 543**

This five-acre public campground sits in a landscaped, grassy area near the Crooked River, where fly-fishing is popular. The camp is located right next to the Crook County Fairgrounds, which offers seasonal expositions, horse races, and rodeos.

**Campsites, facilities:** There are 81 sites for tents or RVs up to 70 feet long (full hookups); most sites are pull-through. In addition, there are nine tent sites and two log cabins available. Picnic tables are provided. Fire pits are provided at the tent sites. Restrooms with flush toilets and showers, a dump station, cable TV, and Wi-Fi are available. A convenience store, restaurant, ice, gasoline, and propane are available within one mile. Some facilities are wheelchair accessible. Leashed pets are permitted, with restrictions on some breeds.

**Reservations, fees:** Reservations are accepted at 800/609-2599. Tent sites are $11 per night, RV sites are $33-37 per night, $3 per additional person, $5 per night per additional vehicle. Weekly and monthly rates are available. Some discounts available. Some credit cards are accepted. Open year-round.

**Directions:** From Redmond, drive east on Highway 126 for 18 miles to Prineville (Highway 126 becomes 3rd Street) and Main Street.

Turn right on Main Street and drive about 0.5 mile south to the campground on the left, before the fairgrounds.
**Contact:** Crook County RV Park, 541/447-2599, www.ccprd.org.

## 54 OCHOCO LAKE

**Scenic rating: 6**

on Ochoco Lake

**Map 10.5, page 543**

This is one of the nicer camps along U.S. 26 in eastern Oregon. The campground is located on the shore of Ochoco Lake, where boating and fishing are popular pastimes. Some quality hiking trails can be found in the area.
**Campsites, facilities:** There are 21 primitive sites for tents or self-contained RVs up to 50 feet long and a special hiker/biker area. Picnic tables and fire grills are provided. Drinking water, firewood, restrooms with showers and flush toilets, ice, garbage bins, a fish-cleaning station, and boat-launching facilities are available. A camp host is onsite. Some facilities are wheelchair accessible. Leashed pets are permitted.
**Reservations, fees:** Reservations are not accepted. Sites are $16 per night, $5 per person per night for hike-in/bike-in sites, and $7 per night per additional vehicle. Some credit cards are accepted. Open April-October, weather permitting.
**Directions:** From Prineville, drive east on U.S. 26 for seven miles to the park entrance on the right.
**Contact:** Crook County Parks and Recreation, 541/447-1209,

## 55 CHIMNEY ROCK

**Scenic rating: 6**

on the Crooked River

**Map 10.5, page 543**

Chimney Rock Campground is one of eight

Bureau of Land Management (BLM) camps along a six-mile stretch of Highway 27. This well-spaced campground is a favorite for picnicking and wildlife-viewing. The Chimney Rock Trailhead, just across the highway, is the jumping-off point for the 1.7-mile, moderately difficult hike to Chimney Rock. There are numerous scenic overlooks along the trail, and wildlife sightings are common. Crooked River is open to fishing year-round. The elevation here is 3,000 feet.
**Campsites, facilities:** There are 14 sites for tents or RVs of any length and a group site for up to 16 people. Picnic tables and fire rings are provided. Vault toilets, drinking water, and garbage bins are available. Some facilities are wheelchair accessible, including a fishing dock. Leashed pets are permitted.
**Reservations, fees:** Reservations are not accepted. Sites are $8 per night, the group site is $16 per night, $2 per night for an additional vehicle. Open year-round; there is no fee for camping November-March.
**Directions:** In Prineville, drive south on Highway 27 for 16.4 miles to the campground.
**Contact:** Bureau of Land Management, Prineville District, 541/416-6700, www.blm.gov/or/districts/prineville.

## 56 PRINEVILLE RESERVOIR STATE PARK

**Scenic rating: 7**

on Prineville Reservoir

**Map 10.5, page 543**

This state park is set along the shore of Prineville Reservoir, which formed with the damming of the Crooked River. This is one of two campgrounds on the reservoir (the other is Prineville Reservoir Resort). Boating, fishing, swimming, and waterskiing are popular activities here; the nearby boat docks and ramp are a bonus. The reservoir supports rainbow and cutthroat trout, small and largemouth bass, catfish, and crappie; you can even ice fish in the winter.

**Campsites, facilities:** There are 20 sites with partial hookups and 22 sites with full hookups for RVs up to 40 feet long, 23 tent sites, and five deluxe cabins. Picnic tables and fire pits are provided. Drinking water, garbage bins, restrooms with flush toilets and showers, ice, and firewood are available. Boat docks, launching facilities, and moorings that can be reserved are nearby. Some facilities are wheelchair accessible. Leashed pets are permitted.

**Reservations, fees:** Reservations are accepted at 800/452-5687 or www.reserveamerica.com ($8 reservation fee). RV sites are $22-26, tent sites are $16-21 per night, cabins are $60-82 per night, boat moorage is $10, $5 per night per additional vehicle. Some credit cards are accepted. Open year-round.

**Directions:** From Prineville, drive east on U.S. 26 for one mile to Combs Flat Road. Turn right (south) and drive one mile to Juniper Canyon Road. Turn right (south) and drive 18 miles to the campground.

**Contact:** Prineville Reservoir State Park, 541/447-4363 or 800/551-6649, www.oregonstateparks.org.

# 57 PRINEVILLE RESERVOIR RESORT

### Scenic rating: 6

on Prineville Reservoir

Map 10.5, page 543

This resort sits on the shore of Prineville Reservoir in the high desert, a good spot for water sports and fishing. The mostly shaded sites are a combination of dirt and gravel. The camp features easy access to the reservoir and some colorful rock formations to check out.

**Campsites, facilities:** There are 70 sites with partial hookups (including four pull-through sites and 36 waterfront sites) for tents or RVs of any length, seven motel rooms, and one primitive cabin. Picnic tables and fire rings are provided. Drinking water, restrooms with flush toilets and coin showers, propane gas, a dump station, firewood, a convenience store, a café, and ice are available. A full-service marina with boat ramp, boat fuel, boat rentals, fish-cleaning station, and fishing licenses are on-site. Some facilities are wheelchair accessible. Leashed pets are permitted.

**Reservations, fees:** Reservations are accepted at 541/447-7468 ($8 reservation fee). Sites are $24-26 per night, and the cabin is $35 per night for two people, $8 per person per night for 3-4 people. Some credit cards are accepted. Open May-mid-October, weather permitting.

**Directions:** From Prineville, drive east on U.S. 26 for one mile to Combs Flat Road. Turn right (south) and drive one mile to Juniper Canyon Road. Turn right (south) and drive 18 miles to the resort at the end of the road.

**Contact:** Prineville Reservoir Resort, 541/447-7468, www.prinevillereservoirresort.com.

# 58 JASPER POINT STATE PARK

### Scenic rating: 7

on Prineville Reservoir

Map 10.5, page 543

Jasper Point is a quiet alternative to Prineville Reservoir State Park. The park is not as popular as Prineville; although it does fill up on summer weekends, it's used mainly by locals. Although the park is named Jasper Point, the setting is in a cove and the views are not as good as those at Prineville Reservoir State Park. A 1.75-mile trail connects the two campgrounds, and another 0.7-mile trail runs along the shoreline.

**Campsites, facilities:** There are 27 sites with partial hookups for tents or RVs of any length. Picnic tables and fire pits are provided. Drinking water, vault toilets, garbage containers, a day-use area, and a boat launch are available. Leashed pets are permitted.

**Reservations, fees:** Reservations are not accepted. Sites are $26 per night, $5 per night per additional vehicle. Open May-September.

**Directions:** From Prineville, drive east on U.S. 26 for one mile to Combs Flat Road. Turn right (south) and drive one mile to Juniper Canyon Road. Turn right (south) and drive 21 miles to the campground.

**Contact:** Prineville Reservoir State Park, 541/447-4363 or 800/551-6949, www.oregonstateparks.org.

## 59 ANTELOPE FLAT RESERVOIR

### Scenic rating: 6

on Antelope Flat Reservoir in Ochoco National Forest

**Map 10.5, page 543**

This pretty spot is situated along the west shore of Antelope Flat Reservoir amid ponderosa pine and juniper. The campground is on the edge of the high desert at an elevation of 4,600 feet. It features wide sites and easy access to the lake. Trout fishing can sometimes be good in the spring, and boating with motors is permitted. This is also a good lake for canoes.

**Campsites, facilities:** There are 24 sites for tents or RVs up to 30 feet long. Picnic tables and fire grills are provided. Drinking water and vault toilets are available. Garbage must be packed out. Boat-launching facilities are nearby. Leashed pets are permitted.

**Reservations, fees:** Reservations are not accepted. Sites are $8 per night, $3 per night for each additional vehicle. Open early May-late October, weather permitting.

**Directions:** From Prineville, drive southeast on Combs Flat Road (Paulina Highway) for 30 miles to Forest Road 17 (Antelope Reservoir Junction). Turn right on Forest Road 17 and drive about 10 miles to Forest Road 1700-600. Drive 0.25 mile on Forest Road 1700-600 to the campground.

**Contact:** Ochoco National Forest, Lookout Mountain Ranger District, 541/416-6500, www.fs.usda.gov/centraloregon.

## 60 WILEY FLAT

### Scenic rating: 3

on Wiley Creek in Ochoco National Forest

**Map 10.5, page 543**

Wiley Flat campground is set along Wiley Creek in a nice, hidden spot with minimal crowds. It is popular with horseback riders and seasonal hunters. Tower Point Lookout is one mile north of the camp. A map of Ochoco National Forest details nearby access roads.

**Campsites, facilities:** There are five sites for tents or RVs up to 30 feet long. Picnic tables and fire grills are provided. Vault toilets are available. There is no drinking water, and garbage must be packed out. Leashed pets are permitted.

**Reservations, fees:** Reservations are not accepted. There is no fee for camping. Open mid-June-late October, weather permitting.

**Directions:** From Prineville, drive southeast on the Paulina Highway (Combs Flat Road) for 34 miles to Forest Road 16. Turn right (southeast) and drive 10 miles to Forest Road 1600-400. Turn right (west) and drive one mile to the camp.

**Contact:** Ochoco National Forest, Lookout Mountain Ranger District, 541/416-6500, www.fs.usda.gov/centraloregon.

## 61 BULL PRAIRIE LAKE

### Scenic rating: 8

on Bull Prairie Lake in Umatilla National Forest

**Map 10.6, page 544**          **BEST (**

Set on the shore of Bull Prairie Lake, a 28-acre lake at 4,000 feet elevation, this spot attracts little attention from out-of-towners, yet it offers plenty of recreation opportunities, making it an ideal vacation destination. Boating (no motors permitted), fishing for blue gill and trout, hunting, and swimming are some of the attractions here. A hiking trail circles the lake.

**Campsites, facilities:** There are 28 sites for tents or RVs up to 31 feet long and one group site for up to 25 people. Picnic tables and fire grills are provided. Vault toilets are available. Drinking water and garbage bins are available late May-mid-October. Boat docks and a boat ramp are on-site. Some facilities are wheelchair accessible, including the boat ramp. Leashed pets are permitted.

**Reservations, fees:** Reservations are not accepted. Single sites are $14, double sites are $19, the group site is $28, $5 per night for an additional vehicle. Open year-round, weather permitting; there is no fee for camping after the water is turned off in mid-October.

**Directions:** From Heppner, drive south on Highway 207 for roughly 35 miles to the national forest boundary and continue four miles to Forest Road 2039 (paved). Turn left and drive three miles northeast to the campground on the right.

**Contact:** Umatilla National Forest, Heppner Ranger District, 541/676-9187, www.fs.usda. gov/umatilla.

## 62 FAIRVIEW

### Scenic rating: 5
near Bull Prairie Lake in Umatilla National Forest

**Map 10.6, page 544**

This small, rugged campground is located in a remote area at 4,300 feet elevation near Mahogany Butte and adjacent to Fairview Springs. Known by very few people, it's very easy to miss and not even marked on Umatilla National Forest maps. Hunters use it primarily as a base camp. Bull Prairie Lake is only four miles away.

**Campsites, facilities:** There are five sites for tents or RVs up to 16 feet long. Picnic tables and fire grills are provided. Vault toilets are available. Drinking water is available May-October. Garbage must be packed out. Boat docks and launching facilities are nearby at Bull Prairie Lake. Leashed pets are permitted.

**Reservations, fees:** Reservations are not accepted. There is no fee for camping. Open May-October, weather permitting.

**Directions:** From Heppner, drive south on Highway 207 for roughly 35 miles to the national forest boundary. Continue four miles to Forest Road 2039 (the turnoff for Bull Prairie Lake). Continue on Highway 207 for one mile to Forest Road 400 (if you pass through an immediate series of hairpin turns, you have gone too far). Turn west and drive 500 yards to the campground.

**Contact:** Umatilla National Forest, Heppner Ranger District, 541/676-9187, www.fs.usda. gov/umatilla.

## 63 WOLF CREEK

### Scenic rating: 5
on Wolf Creek in Ochoco National Forest

**Map 10.6, page 544**

Wolf Creek and Wolf Creek Industrial Camp, located just across the road, are set along the banks of Wolf Creek, a nice trout stream that runs through Ochoco National Forest. The elevation is 4,000 feet.

**Campsites, facilities:** There are 16 sites for tents or RVs up to 20 feet long. Picnic tables and fire grills are provided. Vault toilets are available. There is no drinking water, and garbage must be packed out. Leashed pets are permitted.

**Reservations, fees:** Reservations are not accepted. Sites are $6 per night, with a 14-day stay limit, and $3 per night for an additional vehicle. Open May-November, weather permitting.

**Directions:** From Prineville, drive southeast on Combs Flat Road (Paulina Highway) for 55 miles to Paulina. Continue east for 3.5 miles to County Road 112. Turn left (north) and drive 6.5 miles to Forest Road 42. Turn left (north) and drive 1.5 miles to the campground on the right.

**Contact:** Ochoco National Forest, Paulina

Ranger District, 541/477-6900, www.fs.usda. gov/centraloregon.

## 64 SUGAR CREEK

**Scenic rating: 6**

on Sugar Creek in Ochoco National Forest

**Map 10.6, page 544**

This small, quiet, and remote campground sits along the banks of Sugar Creek at an elevation of 4,000 feet in a forest of ponderosa pine. A 0.5-mile trail loops along the creek. The camp also offers a covered group shelter in the day-use area and a wheelchair-accessible trail. Bald eagles occasionally nest in the area.

**Campsites, facilities:** There are 17 sites for tents or RVs up to 22 feet long. Picnic tables and fire grills are provided. Drinking water, a picnic shelter, and vault toilets are available. Garbage must be packed out. Some facilities are wheelchair accessible. Leashed pets are permitted.

**Reservations, fees:** Reservations are not accepted. Sites are $8 per night for one vehicle and $3 per night for an additional vehicle. Open May-November with a 14-day stay limit.

**Directions:** From Prineville, drive southeast on Combs Flat Road (Paulina Highway) for 55 miles to Paulina. Continue east and drive 3.5 miles to a fork with County Road 112. Bear left at the fork onto County Road 112 and drive 7.5 miles to Forest Road 58. Bear right on Forest Road 58 and continue for 1.3 miles to the campground on the right.

**Contact:** Ochoco National Forest, Paulina Ranger District, 541/477-6900, www.fs.usda. gov/centraloregon.

## 65 FRAZIER

**Scenic rating: 4**

on Frazier Creek in Ochoco National Forest

**Map 10.6, page 544**

Frazier is a small, remote, and little-used

campground located at an elevation of 4,600 feet. The landscape is open, grassy, and sprinkled with a few large pine trees. Some dirt roads adjacent to the camp are good for mountain biking in summer, and the camp's meadow setting is occasionally the site of family reunions during summer holidays.

**Campsites, facilities:** There are nine sites for tents or RVs up to 22 feet long. Picnic tables and fire grills are provided. Vault toilets are available. There is no drinking water, and garbage must be packed out. Leashed pets are permitted.

**Reservations, fees:** Reservations are not accepted. There is no fee for camping. The stay limit is 14 days. Open May-November, weather permitting.

**Directions:** From Prineville, drive southeast on Combs Flat Road (Paulina Highway) for 55 miles to Paulina. Continue east and drive 3.5 miles to a fork with County Road 112. Bear left at the fork onto County Road 112 and drive 2.5 miles to County Road 135/Puett Road. Turn right (east) and drive 10 miles to Forest Road 58. Turn right and drive six miles to Forest Road 58-500. Turn left and drive two miles (bearing to the left) to the campground.

**Contact:** Ochoco National Forest, Paulina Ranger District, 541/477-6900, www.fs.usda. gov/centraloregon.

## 66 CLYDE HOLLIDAY STATE RECREATION SITE

**Scenic rating: 7**

near the John Day River

**Map 10.6, page 544**

Clyde Holliday campground borders the John Day River, a spawning site for steelhead. Sites are private and shaded with cottonwood trees. Wildlife is prevalent in the area; watch for mule deer and elk near the campsites.

**Campsites, facilities:** There are 31 sites with partial hookups for tents or RVs up to 60 feet long, a hiker/biker tent area, and two tepees.

Picnic tables and fire grills are provided. Drinking water, restrooms with showers and flush toilets, firewood, ice, a dump station, and horseshoe pits are available. Some facilities are wheelchair accessible. Leashed pets are permitted.

**Reservations, fees:** Reservations are not accepted for campsites but are required for the tepees at 541/932-4453 or 800/932-4953. Sites are $17-22 per night, $5 per person per night for hike-in/bike-in sites, $39 per night for tepees, $5 per night for an additional vehicle. Open March-November, weather permitting.

**Directions:** From John Day, drive west on U.S. 26 for six miles to the park on the left.

**Contact:** Clyde Holliday State Recreation Site, 541/932-4453 or 800/551-6949, www.oregonstateparks.org.

## 67 STARR

**Scenic rating: 4**

on Starr Ridge in Malheur National Forest

Map 10.6, page 544

A good layover spot for travelers on U.S. 395, Starr happens to be adjacent to Starr Ridge, a snow play area popular in winter for skiing and sledding. The camp itself doesn't offer much in the way of recreation, but to the northeast is the Strawberry Mountain Wilderness, which has a number of lakes, streams, and trails. The camp sits at an elevation of 5,100 feet.

**Campsites, facilities:** There are eight sites for tents or RVs up to 22 feet long and one group site for 5-20 people. Picnic tables and fire rings are provided. Vault toilets are available. There is no drinking water, and garbage must be packed out. Some facilities are wheelchair accessible. Leashed pets are permitted.

**Reservations, fees:** Reservations are not accepted. Sites are $6 per night, $3 per night for an additional vehicle. Open late May-November, weather permitting.

**Directions:** From John Day, drive south on U.S. 395 for 15 miles to the campground on the right.

**Contact:** Malheur National Forest, Blue Mountain Ranger District, 541/575-3000, www.fs.usda.gov/malheur.

## 68 WELCH CREEK

**Scenic rating: 4**

on Desolation Creek in Umatilla National Forest

Map 10.7, page 545

Welch Creek is a primitive camp set on the banks of Desolation Creek. Road noise and dust may be a problem for some, and there's little privacy among sites. The camp features trail access to the Desolation Area, both for non-motorized and motorized traffic. Hunting and fishing are popular here.

**Campsites, facilities:** There are five sites for tents or RVs up to 30 feet long and one group site. Picnic tables and fire rings are provided. A vault toilet is available. There is no drinking water. Garbage must be packed out. Leashed pets are permitted.

**Reservations, fees:** Reservations are not accepted. Sites are $8 per night for two vehicles, $5 per night for each additional vehicle, and the group site is $25 per night. Open late May-early November, weather permitting. A 14-day stay limit is enforced.

**Directions:** From Pendleton, drive south on U.S. 395 for 62 miles to Forest Road 55 (one mile north of Dale; it's easier to find if you know the marker, Texas Bar Road). Turn left and drive one mile to Forest Road 10. Turn right and drive 13 miles to the campground on the right.

**Contact:** Umatilla National Forest, North Fork John Day Ranger District, 541/427-3231, www.fs.usda.gov/umatilla.

## 69 NORTH FORK JOHN DAY

### Scenic rating: 6
on the north fork of the John Day River in Umatilla National Forest

**Map 10.7, page 545**

Set along the banks of the north fork of the John Day River at an elevation of 5,200 feet, this campground sits in a stand of lodgepole pine at the intersection of Elkhorn and Blue Mountain National Forest Scenic Byways. The campground has a great view of salmon spawning in the river in spring and fall and also makes an ideal launch point for a wilderness backpacking trip. Trails from camp lead into the North Fork John Day Wilderness. A horse-handling area is also available for wilderness users. No mountain bikes or motorcycles are permitted in the wilderness.

**Campsites, facilities:** There are 15 sites for tents or RVs up to 28 feet long, five sites for tents only, and one group site. Picnic tables and fire rings are provided. Vault toilets are available. There is no drinking water. Garbage must be packed out. Some facilities are wheelchair accessible. Leashed pets are permitted.

**Reservations, fees:** Reservations are not accepted. Sites are $8 per night for two vehicles, $5 per night for an additional vehicle, and $25 for the group site. Open June-November, weather permitting. A 14-day stay limit is enforced.

For trailhead use, a Northwest Forest Pass is required ($5 daily fee or $30 annual fee per parked vehicle).

**Directions:** From Pendleton, drive south on U.S. 395 for 50 miles to Highway 244. Turn east on Highway 244 and drive one mile to Ukiah and Forest Road 52. Turn right (south) on Forest Road 52 and drive 36 miles to the campground on the right.

**Contact:** Umatilla National Forest, North Fork John Day Ranger District, 541/427-3231, www.fs.usda.gov/umatilla.

## 70 ANTHONY LAKES

### Scenic rating: 10
on Anthony Lake in Wallowa-Whitman National Forest

**Map 10.7, page 545**　　　　**BEST (**

This campground (7,100 feet elevation) is adjacent to Anthony Lake, where non-motorized boating is permitted. Sites are wooded, providing good screening between them. Alas, mosquitoes are often in particular abundance. Several smaller lakes within two miles by car or trail are ideal for trout fishing from a canoe, float tube, or raft. Sometimes mountain goats can be seen from the Elkhorn Crest Trail, which begins near here. Weekends and holidays the campground tends to fill up.

**Campsites, facilities:** There are 10 sites for tents, 32 sites for RVs up to 22 feet long, and one group site for up to 75 people. (There are also 10 walk-in sites for tents only; follow the lakeshore trail towards the south end of the lake.) Drinking water, fire grills, garbage bins (summer only), and picnic tables are provided. Vault toilets are available. Garbage must be packed out the rest of the year. Boat-launching facilities are nearby. Some facilities are wheelchair accessible. Leashed pets are permitted.

**Reservations, fees:** Reservations are accepted for the group site only at 877/444-6777 ($10 reservation fee) or www.recreation.gov ($9 reservation fee). Sites are $10-14 per night, $5-8 per night per additional vehicle, and $50 per night for the group site. Open June-late September, weather permitting.

**Directions:** From Baker City on I-84, turn north on U.S. 30. Drive north for 10 miles to Haines and County Road 1146 (signed for Anthony Lakes Ski Resort). Turn left on County Road 1146 and drive 20 miles (the road becomes Forest Road 73) to the campground on the left.

**Contact:** Wallowa-Whitman National Forest, Whitman Ranger District, 541/523-6391, www.fs.usda.gov/wallowa-whitman.

## 7 1 GRANDE RONDE LAKE

### Scenic rating: 8

on Grande Ronde Lake in Wallowa-Whitman
National Forest

**Map 10.7, page 545**

Grande Ronde campground sits amid Douglas
and white fir at an elevation of 6,800 feet along
the shore of Grande Ronde Lake. Trout fishing
can be good at this small lake, and mountain
goats are sometimes seen in the area. Several
trails lie to the south, near Anthony Lake.

**Campsites, facilities:** There are eight sites for
tents or RVs up to 16 feet long. Picnic tables
and fire grills are provided. Drinking water
and vault toilets are available. Garbage must
be packed out. Boat launching facilities are
nearby. Some facilities are wheelchair accessible. Leashed pets are permitted.

**Reservations, fees:** Reservations are not accepted. Single sites are $10 per night, double
sites are 18 per night, $5 per night per each
additional vehicle. Open late June-September,
weather permitting.

**Directions:** Drive on I-84 to Baker City and
U.S. 30. From Baker City, drive north on U.S.
30 for 10 miles to Haines and County Road
1146 (signed for Anthony Lakes Ski Resort).
Turn left on County Road 1146 and drive 20
miles (the road becomes Forest Road 73) to
the campground on the right.

**Contact:** Wallowa-Whitman National Forest, Whitman Ranger District, 541/523-6391,
www.fs.usda.gov/wallowa-whitman.

## 7 2 MUD LAKE

### Scenic rating: 7

on Mud Lake in Wallowa-Whitman National
Forest

**Map 10.7, page 545**

Set at an elevation of 7,100 feet, tiny yet pleasant Mud Lake campground is filled with lots
of vegetation and sees relatively little use. The
campground is situated in fir forest on the
shore of small Mud Lake, where the trout fishing can be fairly good. Mud Lake is shallow
and more marshy than muddy. Bring your
mosquito repellent.

**Campsites, facilities:** There are eight sites for
tents or RVs up to 16 feet long and one group
site for up to 60 people. Picnic tables and fire
grills are provided. Drinking water and vault
toilets are available. Garbage must be packed
out. Boat launching facilities are nearby at
Anthony Lake. Leashed pets are permitted.

**Reservations, fees:** Reservations are accepted
for the group site only at 877/444-6777 ($10
reservation fee) or www.recreation.gov ($9
reservation fee). Sites are $8 per night, $4 per
night per additional vehicle, and the group site
is $50 per night. Open June-late September,
weather permitting.

**Directions:** Drive on I-84 to Baker City and
U.S. 30. From Baker City, drive north on U.S.
30 for 10 miles to Haines and County Road
1146 (signed for Anthony Lakes Ski Resort).
Turn left on County Road 1146 and drive 21
miles (the road becomes Forest Road 73) to
the campground on the right.

**Contact:** Wallowa-Whitman National Forest, Whitman Ranger District, 541/523-6391,
www.fs.usda.gov/wallowa-whitman.

## 7 3 OLIVE LAKE

### Scenic rating: 9

on Olive Lake in Umatilla National Forest

**Map 10.7, page 545**

This campground (6,100 feet elevation) is
nestled along the shore of Olive Lake, between two sections of the North Fork John
Day Wilderness. Dammed to hold an increased
volume of water, the glacial lake is a beautiful
tint of blue. Motorized boats are allowed, but
waterskiing is prohibited. Fishing is fair for
kokanee salmon and brook, cutthroat, and
rainbow trout. A 2.5-mile trail circles the lake.
Nearby trails provide access to the wilderness;

motorbikes and mountain bikes are not permitted in the wilderness. Sections of the old wooden pipeline for the historic Fremont Powerhouse can still be seen. The old mining town of Granite is 12 miles east of camp.

**Campsites, facilities:** There are 23 sites for tents or RVs up to 40 feet long, five sites for tents only, and two group sites that can accommodate up to 25 people and five RVs. Picnic tables and fire grills are provided. Vault toilets are available. There is no drinking water, and garbage must be packed out. Two boat docks, launching facilities, and picnic areas are available. A camp host is on-site. Some facilities are wheelchair accessible. Leashed pets are permitted.

**Reservations, fees:** Reservations are not accepted. Sites are $12 per night for up to two vehicles, $5 per night per additional vehicle, and $25 per night for the group camp. Open Memorial Day-November, weather permitting. A 14-day stay limit is enforced.

**Directions:** From Pendleton, drive south on U.S. 395 for 62 miles to Forest Road 55 (1 mile north of Dale). Turn right and drive 0.5 mile to Forest Road 10. Turn right on Forest Road 10 and drive 26 miles to Forest Road 480. Turn right and drive 0.5 mile to the campground.

**Contact:** Umatilla National Forest, North Fork John Day Ranger District, 541/427-3231, www.fs.usda.gov/umatilla.

## 74 MCCULLY FORKS
🏃 🏊 🐕 ♿ ⛺

### Scenic rating: 5
on McCully Creek in Wallowa-Whitman National Forest

**Map 10.7, page 545**

Here's an easy-access campground that's tiny and primitive. Set at 4,600 feet elevation along the banks of McCully Creek, McCully Forks gets moderately heavy use and is often full on weekends. Wedged between highway and mountains, sites are wooded with alder and cottonwood; highway noise can be audible.

**Campsites, facilities:** There are seven sites for tents or small trailers. Picnic tables and fire grills are provided. Vault toilets are available. There is no drinking water, and garbage must be packed out. Some facilities are wheelchair accessible. Leashed pets are permitted.

**Reservations, fees:** Reservations are not accepted. Sites are $6 per night. Open late May-late October, weather permitting.

**Directions:** From Baker City, drive southwest on Highway 7 for 29 miles (bear west at Salisbury) to Sumpter. Continue three miles past Sumpter (the road becomes Forest Road 24) to the campground on the right.

**Contact:** Wallowa-Whitman National Forest, Whitman Ranger District, 541/523-6391, www.fs.usda.gov/wallowa-whitman.

## 75 UNION CREEK
🏃 🚴 🏖 🏊 🏊 🐎 ♿ 🚐 ⛺

### Scenic rating: 8
on Phillips Lake in Wallowa-Whitman National Forest

**Map 10.7, page 545**

Union Creek campground along the north shore of Phillips Lake is easy to reach, yet missed by most I-84 travelers. It's the largest of three camps on the lake and the only one with drinking water. An old narrow-gauge railroad has been restored and runs up the valley from McEwen Depot (six miles from the campground) to Sumpter (10 miles away). Visit Sumpter to see an old dredge.

**Campsites, facilities:** There are 74 sites for tents or RVs up to 32 feet long, two double sites, and two group sites for 20-50 people; some sites have full hookups. Drinking water, garbage bins (summer only), and picnic tables are provided. Flush toilets, a dump station, firewood, and ice are available. There is a seasonal concession stand for packaged goods and fishing tackle. Boat docks and launching facilities are adjacent to the campground. Some facilities are wheelchair accessible. Leashed pets are permitted.

**Reservations, fees:** Reservations are accepted at 877/444-6777 ($10 reservation fee) or www.recreation.gov ($9 reservation fee). Sites are $12-22 per night, double sites are $32 per night (full hookups), the group sites are $60 per night, $6-8 per night per additional vehicle. Open May-September, weather permitting.

**Directions:** From Baker City, drive southwest on Highway 7 for 20 miles to the campground on the left.

**Contact:** Wallowa-Whitman National Forest, Whitman Ranger District, 541/523-6391, www.fs.usda.gov/wallowa-whitman.

## 76 SOUTHWEST SHORE

**Scenic rating: 7**

on Phillips Lake in Wallowa-Whitman National Forest

Map 10.7, page 545

Southwest Shore is one of two primitive campgrounds on Philips Lake, a four-mile-long reservoir created by the Mason Dam on the Powder River. Set at 4,120 feet elevation, the camp borders the south shore of the lake; the boat ramp here is usable only when water is high in the reservoir. An old narrow-gauge railroad runs out of McEwen Depot (six miles from the campground) to Sumpter (10 miles away) for an interesting side-trip.

**Campsites, facilities:** There are 16 sites for tents or RVs up to 24 feet long. Fire grills and vault toilets are available. There is no drinking water, and garbage must be packed out. A boat ramp is adjacent to the campground. Leashed pets are permitted.

**Reservations, fees:** Reservations are not accepted. Sites are $10 per night, $4 per night per additional vehicle. Open May-October, weather permitting.

**Directions:** From Baker City, drive southwest on Highway 7 for 24 miles (just past Phillips Lake) to Hudspeth Lane (County Road 667). Turn left (south) on Hudspeth Lane and drive two miles to Forest Road 2220. Turn left

(southeast) and drive 2.5 miles to the campground on the left.

**Contact:** Wallowa-Whitman National Forest, Whitman Ranger District, 541/523-6391, www.fs.usda.gov/wallowa-whitman.

## 77 MILLERS LANE

**Scenic rating: 7**

on Phillips Lake in Wallowa-Whitman National Forest

Map 10.7, page 545

Millers Lane is one of two primitive camps on Philips Lake (the other is Southwest Shore). Phillips Lake is a long, narrow reservoir (and the largest in the region), and this small campground is situated along the south shore at an elevation of 4,120 feet. The camp is also near an old narrow-gauge railroad that runs out of McEwen Depot.

**Campsites, facilities:** There are eight sites for tents or RVs up to 20 feet long. Picnic tables and fire grills are provided. Vault toilets are available. There is no drinking water, and garbage must be packed out. A boat ramp is at Southwest Shore. Leashed pets are permitted.

**Reservations, fees:** Reservations are not accepted. Sites are $10 per night, $4 per night per additional vehicle. Open May-October, weather permitting.

**Directions:** From Baker City, drive southwest on Highway 7 for 24 miles (just past Phillips Lake) to Hudspeth Lane (County Road 667). Turn left (south) on Hudspeth Lane and drive two miles to Forest Road 2220. Turn left (southeast) and drive 3.5 miles to the campground on the left.

**Contact:** Wallowa-Whitman National Forest, Whitman Ranger District, 541/523-6391, www.fs.usda.gov/wallowa-whitman.

## 78 MAGONE LAKE

**Scenic rating: 8**

on Magone Lake in Malheur National Forest

Map 10.7, page 545

This campground is set along the shore of little Magone Lake at an elevation of 5,500 feet. A 1.8-mile trail rings the lake, and the section extending from the beach area to the campground (about 0.25 mile) is wheelchair accessible. A 0.5-mile trail leads to Magone Slide, an unusual geological formation. Canoeing, fishing, sailing, and swimming are some of the popular activities at this lake. Easy-access bike trails can be found within 0.25 mile of the campground. Just so you know, Magone is pronounced "Ma-Goon." Got it?

**Campsites, facilities:** There are 19 sites for tents or RVs up to 40 feet long (some pull-through), three sites for tents only, and a separate group camp (with picnic shelter) for up to 75 people. Picnic tables and fire grills are provided. Drinking water, flush toilets, a boat ramp, and a beach area are available. A camp host is on-site. Boat docks are nearby. Some facilities, including a fishing pier, are wheelchair accessible. Leashed pets are permitted.

**Reservations, fees:** Reservations are required for the group site and group picnic shelter at 877/444-6777 ($10 reservation fee) or www.recreation.gov ($9 reservation fee). Sites are $13 per night, $60 per night for the group site, $6.50 per night per additional vehicle. Open late May-November, weather permitting.

**Directions:** From John Day, drive east on U.S. 26 for eight miles to County Road 18. Turn north and drive 10 miles to Forest Road 3620. Turn left (west) on Forest Road 3620 and drive 1.5 miles to Forest Road 3618. Turn right (northwest) and drive 1.5 miles to the campground. Note: The road is paved all the way.

**Contact:** Malheur National Forest, Blue Mountain Ranger District, 541/575-3000, www.fs.usda.gov/malheur.

## 79 LOWER CAMP CREEK

**Scenic rating: 5**

in Malheur National Forest

Map 10.7, page 545

Lower Camp Creek is set at 5,026 feet elevation on the edge of a remote national forest. The camp is small and primitive, with a creek nearby, and is often overlooked, so you may have the place to yourself. In fall, a few hunters will often hunker down here and use it as their base camp.

**Campsites, facilities:** There are six sites for tents or RVs up to 40 feet long. Picnic tables, fire rings, and vault toilets are provided. There is no drinking water. Garbage must be packed out. Some facilities are wheelchair accessible. Leashed pets are permitted.

**Reservations, fees:** Reservations are not accepted. Sites are $6 per night for single sites, $3 per night per additional vehicle. Open late May-November, weather permitting.

**Directions:** From John Day, drive east on U.S. 26 for eight miles to County Road 18. Turn north and drive eight miles to Four Corners. Turn right on Forest Road 36 and drive 12 miles to the campground on the left.

**Contact:** Malheur National Forest, Blue Mountain Ranger District, 541/573-4300, www.fs.usda.gov/malheur.

## 80 MIDDLE FORK

**Scenic rating: 6**

on the Middle Fork of the John Day River in Malheur National Forest

Map 10.7, page 545          BEST (

Scattered along the banks of the Middle Fork of the John Day River at 4,100 feet elevation, these rustic campsites are easy to reach off a paved road. Besides wildlife-viewing and berry picking, the main activity at this camp is fishing, so bring along your fly rod and pinch down your barbs for catch-and-release. The John Day is a state scenic waterway.

**Campsites, facilities:** There are nine single sites and one double site for tents or RVs up to 22 feet long. Picnic tables and fire rings are provided. Vault toilets are available. There is no drinking water, and garbage must be packed out. Some facilities are wheelchair accessible. Leashed pets are permitted.

**Reservations, fees:** Reservations are not accepted. Sites are $8 per night, $4 per night per additional vehicle. Open late May-November, weather permitting.

**Directions:** From John Day, drive northeast on U.S. 26 for 28 miles to Highway 7. Turn left (north) and drive one mile to County Road 20. Turn left and drive five miles to the campground on the left.

**Contact:** Malheur National Forest, Blue Mountain Ranger District, 541/575-3000, www.fs.usda.gov/malheur.

## 81 DIXIE

**Scenic rating: 5**

near Dixie Summit in Malheur National Forest

**Map 10.7, page 545**

Perched at Dixie Summit (elevation 5,000 feet), this camp, just off U.S. 26, is close enough to provide easy access to nearby Bridge Creek, where you can toss in a fishing line. Dixie draws overnighters but otherwise gets light use. The Sumpter Valley Railroad interpretive site is one mile west on U.S. 26.

**Campsites, facilities:** There are 11 sites for tents or RVs up to 22 feet long and one group site for 20-50 people. Picnic tables, vault toilets, and fire rings are provided. No drinking water is available and garbage must be packed out. A store, café, gas, and ice are available within nine miles. Some facilities are wheelchair accessible. Leashed pets are permitted.

**Reservations, fees:** Reservations are not accepted. Sites are $8 per night, $4 per night

for an additional vehicle. Open late May-November, weather permitting.

**Directions:** From John Day, drive northeast on U.S. 26 for 24 miles to Forest Road 365. Turn left and drive 0.25 mile to the campground on the left.

**Contact:** Malheur National Forest, Blue Mountain Ranger District, 541/575-3000, www.fs.usda.gov/malheur.

## 82 WETMORE

**Scenic rating: 7**

on the Middle Fork of the Burnt River in Wallowa-Whitman National Forest

**Map 10.7, page 545**

This campground, set at an elevation of 4,320 feet near the Middle Fork of the Burnt River, makes a nice base camp for a fishing or hiking trip. The stream can provide good trout fishing. (Trails are detailed on maps of Wallowa-Whitman National Forest.) An excellent 0.5-mile, wheelchair-accessible trail passes through old-growth forest—watch for bald eagles.

**Campsites, facilities:** There are 10 single sites and one double site for tents or RVs up to 16 feet long. Picnic tables and fire grills are provided. Vault toilets and drinking water (seasonal) are available. Garbage must be packed out. Some facilities are wheelchair accessible. Leashed pets are permitted.

**Reservations, fees:** Reservations are not accepted. Sites are $5 per night, $5 per each additional vehicle. Open mid-May-mid-October, weather permitting.

**Directions:** From John Day, drive east on U.S. 26 for 29 miles to Austin Junction. Continue east on U.S. 26 for 10 miles to the campground on the left.

**Contact:** Wallowa-Whitman National Forest, Whitman Ranger District, 541/523-6391, www.fs.usda.gov/wallowa-whitman.

## 83 OREGON

### Scenic rating: 6
near Austin Junction in Wallowa-Whitman National Forest

**Map 10.7, page 545**

Oregon campground sits at 4,880 feet elevation just off U.S. 26 surrounded by hillside as well as Douglas fir, tamarack, and white fir. It is the staging area for all-terrain vehicle (ATV) enthusiasts, and the popular Blue Mountain OHV Trailhead is here; several trails crisscross the area. Bald eagles nest in the area.

**Campsites, facilities:** There are eight sites for tents or RVs up to 28 feet long. Picnic tables and fire grills are provided. Vault toilets are available. There is no drinking water, and garbage must be packed out. Leashed pets are permitted.

**Reservations, fees:** Reservations are not accepted. Sites are $5 per night, $5 per each additional vehicle. Open mid-May-mid-October, weather permitting.

**Directions:** From John Day, drive east on U.S. 26 for 29 miles to Austin Junction. Continue east for 20 miles to the campground.

**Contact:** Wallowa-Whitman National Forest, Whitman Ranger District, 541/523-6391, www.fs.usda.gov/wallowa-whitman.

## 84 YELLOW PINE

### Scenic rating: 7
near Middle Fork Burnt River

**Map 10.7, page 545**

Yellow Pine is similar to Oregon Campground, but larger; highlights include easy access and good recreation potential. The camp offers a number of hiking trails, including a 0.5-mile-long, wheelchair-accessible trail that connects to the Wetmore Campground. Keep an eye out for bald eagles in this area.

**Campsites, facilities:** There are 21 sites for tents or RVs up to 28 feet long, including one double site and one group site for 20-50 people. Picnic tables and fire grills are provided. Vault toilets and drinking water (seasonal) are available. Garbage must be packed out. Some facilities are wheelchair accessible. Leashed pets are permitted.

**Reservations, fees:** Reservations are not accepted. Sites are $6 per night. Open late mid-May-mid-October, weather permitting.

**Directions:** From John Day, drive east on U.S. 26 for 29 miles to Austin Junction. Continue east for 21 miles to the campground.

**Contact:** Wallowa-Whitman National Forest, Whitman Ranger District, 541/523-6391, www.fs.usda.gov/wallowa-whitman.

## 85 UNITY LAKE STATE RECREATION SITE

### Scenic rating: 7
on Unity Reservoir

**Map 10.7, page 545**

The grassy setting of Unity Lake contrasts nicely with the bordering sagebrush and cheatgrass of the high desert. This camp, set along the east shore of Unity Reservoir, is a popular spot in good weather. Campers can choose from boating, fishing, hiking, picnicking, swimming, or enjoying the scenic views.

**Campsites, facilities:** There are 35 sites with partial hookups for tents or RVs up to 40 feet long, a hiker/biker tent area, and two rustic cabins. Picnic tables, garbage bins, and fire rings are provided. Drinking water, restrooms with flush toilets and showers, a dump station, horseshoe pits, ice and firewood are available. Boat docks and launching facilities are nearby. Some facilities are wheelchair accessible. Leashed pets are permitted.

**Reservations, fees:** Reservations are not accepted for campsites but are required for cabins at 800/452-5687 or www.reserveamerica.com. Sites are $17-22 per night, cabins are $42 per night, $4 per person per night for hike-in/

bike-in sites, and $5 per night for an additional vehicle. Open year-round, weather permitting.
**Directions:** From John Day, drive east on U.S. 26 for 50 miles to Highway 245. Turn left (north) on Highway 245 and drive three miles to the park on the left.
**Contact:** Unity Lake State Recreation Site, 541/446-3470 or 800/452-5687, www.oregonstateparks.org.

## 86 DEPOT PARK

### Scenic rating: 6

on the John Day River

**Map 10.7, page 545**

Depot Park is a more developed alternative to the many U.S. Forest Service campgrounds in the area. This urban park sits on grassy flatlands and provides access to the John Day River, a good trout fishing spot. The camp features a historic rail depot on the premises, as well as a related museum. A nearby attraction, the Strawberry Mountain Wilderness, has prime hiking trails.
**Campsites, facilities:** There are 20 sites for tents or RVs up to 35 feet long (full hookups); some sites are pull-through. There is also a grassy area offering dispersed camping for hikers/bikers and tents. Picnic tables and barbecues are provided. Restrooms with flush toilets and showers, a dump station, playground, and covered picnic area are available. A camp host is on-site seasonally. Some facilities are wheelchair accessible. Leashed pets are permitted.
**Reservations, fees:** Reservations are not accepted. Sites are $16 per night, $6 per night for the hike-in/bike-in sites, $4 per night per additional vehicle. Monthly rates are available. Open May-November, weather permitting.
**Directions:** From John Day, drive east on U.S. 26 for 13 miles to Prairie City and the junction of U.S. 26 and Main Street. Turn right (south) on Main Street and drive 0.5 mile to the park (well signed).

**Contact:** Prairie City Hall, 541/820-3605, www.prairiecityoregon.com.

## 87 ELK CREEK CAMPGROUND

### Scenic rating: 5

in Wallowa-Whitman National Forest

**Map 10.7, page 545**

Elk Creek campground is small, primitive, and remote. It has no designated campsites, but rather an area for dispersed-style tent camping. Its primary use is for OHV riders, with nearby OHV trail access.
**Campsites, facilities:** There is a dispersed camping area that accommodates roughly 10 tents or small RVs. Picnic tables and fire rings are provided. Vault toilets are available. There is no drinking water. Garbage must be packed out. Leashed pets are permitted.
**Reservations, fees:** Reservations are not accepted. Sites are $5 per night. Open mid-May-mid-October, weather permitting.
**Directions:** From John Day, drive east on U.S. 26 for 49 miles to Unity and County Road 600. Turn right on County Road 600 and drive west for six miles (the road becomes Forest Road 6005/South Fork Road). Continue past the forest boundary for three miles to the campground on the right.
**Contact:** Wallowa-Whitman National Forest, Whitman Ranger District, 541/523-6391, www.fs.usda.gov/wallowa-whitman.

## 88 STEVENS CAMPGROUND

### Scenic rating: 5

on the south fork of the Burnt River in Wallowa-Whitman National Forest

**Map 10.7, page 545**

This campground sits at an elevation of 4,480 feet along the banks of the south fork of the Burnt River and provides an alternative to the other small camps along the river. The trout fishing is often good here.

**Campsites, facilities:** There are six single sites and one double site for tents or RVs up to 30 feet. Picnic tables and fire grills are provided. There is no drinking water, and garbage must be packed out. Vault toilets are available. Leashed pets are permitted.

**Reservations, fees:** Reservations are not accepted. Sites are $5 per night, $5 per night per additional vehicle. Open mid-May-mid-October, weather permitting.

**Directions:** From John Day, drive east on U.S. 26 for 49 miles to Unity and County Road 600. Turn right on County Road 600 and drive west for six miles (the road becomes Forest Road 6005/South Fork Road). Continue past the forest boundary for two miles to the campground on the right.

**Contact:** Wallowa-Whitman National Forest, Whitman Ranger District, 541/523-6391, www.fs.usda.gov/wallowa-whitman.

## 89 SOUTH FORK

### Scenic rating: 5

on the south fork of the Burnt River in Wallowa-Whitman National Forest

Map 10.7, page 545

A gem of a spot, South Fork offers drinking water, privacy, and scenery. The campground (4,400 feet elevation) is set on the banks of the south fork of the Burnt River, a nice trout creek with good evening bites for anglers who know how to sneak-fish. An OHV staging area with trail access is across the road from the campground.

**Campsites, facilities:** There are 12 sites for tents or RVs up to 28 feet long and two sites for tents only; most sites are pull-through. Picnic tables and fire grills are provided. There are vault toilets, and drinking water is available seasonally. Garbage must be packed out. Some facilities are wheelchair accessible. Leashed pets are permitted.

**Reservations, fees:** Reservations are not accepted. Sites are $5 per night, $5 per night per additional vehicle. Open mid-May-mid-October, weather permitting.

**Directions:** From John Day, drive east on U.S. 26 for 49 miles to Unity and County Road 600. Turn right on County Road 600 and drive west for six miles (the road becomes Forest Road 6005/South Fork Road). Continue past the forest boundary for one mile to the campground on the left.

**Contact:** Wallowa-Whitman National Forest, Whitman Ranger District, 541/523-6391, www.fs.usda.gov/wallowa-whitman.

## 90 STRAWBERRY

### Scenic rating: 7

on Strawberry Creek in Malheur National Forest

Map 10.7, page 545

At 5,700 feet elevation, this campground hugs the banks of Strawberry Creek. Nearby trails provide access to the Strawberry Mountain Wilderness, Strawberry Lake, and Strawberry Falls. This pretty area features a variety of hiking and hunting options, as well as fishing in Strawberry Creek.

**Campsites, facilities:** There are 10 sites for tents. Picnic tables and fire rings are provided. Drinking water and vault toilets are available. Garbage must be packed out. Some facilities are wheelchair accessible. Leashed pets are permitted.

**Reservations, fees:** Reservations are not accepted. Sites are $8 per night, $4 per night for an additional vehicle. Open late May-November, weather permitting.

**Directions:** From John Day, drive east on U.S. 26 for 13 miles to Prairie City and County Road 62. Turn right (southeast) and drive 0.5 mile to County Road 60. Turn right and drive south on County Road 60 for 8.5 miles (County Road 60 becomes Forest Road 6001). Continue 2.5 miles to the campground on the left.

**Contact:** Malheur National Forest, Prairie City Ranger District, 541/820-3800, www.fs.usda.gov/malheur.

## 91 SLIDE CREEK

### Scenic rating: 5

in Malheur National Forest

**Map 10.7, page 545**

Slide Creek has tiny, overlooked sites known by a handful of backcountry equestrians. It is set at 4,900 feet in Malheur National Forest with a nearby creek to provide water for horses.

**Campsites, facilities:** There are three sites for tents or RVs up to 40 feet long. Picnic tables and fire rings are provided. Vault toilets, corrals, and hitching posts are available. There is no drinking water, and garbage must be packed out. Some facilities are wheelchair accessible. Leashed pets are permitted.

**Reservations, fees:** Reservations are not accepted. There is no fee for camping. Open late May-November, weather permitting.

**Directions:** From John Day, drive east on U.S. 26 for 13 miles to Prairie City and County Road 62. Turn right (southeast) and drive 0.5 mile to County Road 60. Turn right and drive south on County Road 60 for 8.5 miles (County Road 60 becomes Forest Road 6001). Continue on Forest Road 6001 to the campground on the right.

**Contact:** Malheur National Forest, Prairie City Ranger District, 541/820-3800, www.fs.usda.gov/malheur.

## 92 WICKIUP

### Scenic rating: 5

on Wickiup Creek in Malheur National Forest

**Map 10.7, page 545**

This campground sits at an elevation of 4,300 feet along the forks of Wickiup Creek and Canyon Creek at a historic site; many of its original Civilian Conservation Corps structures are still in place. There is limited fishing in the creek. To the north are numerous trails that lead into the Strawberry Mountain Wilderness. Horses are not allowed within the campground except for loading and unloading.

**Campsites, facilities:** There are six sites for tents or RVs up to 22 feet long, including one group site for 5-20 people. Picnic tables and fire rings are provided. A vault toilet is available. There is no drinking water, and garbage must be packed out. Some facilities are wheelchair accessible. Leashed pets are permitted.

**Reservations, fees:** Reservations are not accepted. Sites are $5 per night, $3 per night per additional vehicle. Open late May-November, weather permitting.

**Directions:** From John Day, drive south on U.S. 395 for 10 miles to Forest Road 15. Turn left (southeast) and drive eight miles to the campground on the right.

**Contact:** Malheur National Forest, Blue Mountain Ranger District, 541/575-3000, www.fs.usda.gov/malheur.

## 93 PARISH CABIN

### Scenic rating: 6

on Little Bear Creek in Malheur National Forest

**Map 10.7, page 545**

Parish Cabin campground sits along the banks of Little Bear Creek at an elevation of 4,900 feet. This is a pretty spot that's not heavily used, and the road is paved all the way to the campground. The creek offers limited fishing. The place is popular with groups of families and hunters in season.

**Campsites, facilities:** There are 19 sites for tents or RVs up to 22 feet long and one group site for up to 50 people. Picnic tables and fire rings are provided. Vault toilets are available. Drinking water may be available. Garbage must be packed out. Some facilities are wheelchair accessible. Leashed pets are permitted.

**Reservations, fees:** Reservations are not

accepted. Sites are $8 per night, $4 per night per additional vehicle. Open late May-November, weather permitting.

**Directions:** From John Day, drive south on U.S. 395 for 10 miles to Forest Road 15. Turn left and drive 16 miles southeast to Forest Road 16. Turn right onto Forest Road 16 and drive a short distance to the campground on the right.

**Contact:** Malheur National Forest, Blue Mountain Ranger District, 541/575-3000, www.fs.usda.gov/malheur.

## 94 CANYON MEADOWS

### Scenic rating: 5

on Canyon Meadows Reservoir in Malheur National Forest

**Map 10.7, page 545**

Canyon Meadows campground sits on the shore of Canyon Meadows Reservoir, where non-motorized boating, fishing, hiking, sailing, and swimming are recreation options. However, this reservoir dries up by the Fourth of July because of a leak in the dam. Several hiking trails nearby lead north into the Strawberry Mountain Wilderness.

**Campsites, facilities:** There are five sites for tents or RVs up to 25 feet long. Picnic tables and fire grills are provided. A vault toilet is available. There is no drinking water, and garbage must be packed out. Some facilities are wheelchair accessible. Leashed pets are permitted.

**Reservations, fees:** Reservations are not accepted. There is no fee for camping. Open late May-November, weather permitting.

**Directions:** From John Day, drive south on U.S. 395 for 10 miles to Forest Road 15. Turn left and drive nine miles southeast to Forest Road 1520. Turn left and drive five miles to the campground on the left.

**Contact:** Malheur National Forest, Blue Mountain Ranger District, 541/575-3000, www.fs.usda.gov/malheur.

## 95 MURRAY CAMPGROUND

### Scenic rating: 7

in Malheur National Forest

**Map 10.7, page 545**

Murray Elk Creek is set at an elevation of 5,200 feet with nearby Forest Service roads that provide access to the Strawberry Mountain Wilderness. The camp is used primarily as a layover for those heading into the wilderness to fish or hunt. Note that fishing is restricted to the use of artificial lures with a single, barbless hook.

**Campsites, facilities:** There are five sites for tents or RVs up to 40 feet long. Picnic tables and fire rings are provided. Vault toilets are available. There is no drinking water, and garbage must be packed out. Some facilities are wheelchair accessible. Leashed pets are permitted.

**Reservations, fees:** Reservations are not accepted. Sites are $8 per night, $4 per night for an additional vehicle. Open late May-November, weather permitting.

**Directions:** From John Day, drive east on U.S. 26 for 13 miles to Prairie City and County Road 62. Turn right and drive 24 miles to Forest Road 16. Turn right and follow signs to the campground on the right.

**Contact:** Malheur National Forest, Prairie City Ranger District, 541/820-3800, www.fs.usda.gov/malheur.

## 96 BIG CREEK

### Scenic rating: 6

near the Strawberry Mountain Wilderness in Malheur National Forest

**Map 10.7, page 545**

At 5,100 feet elevation, this campground hugs the banks of Big Creek. Nearby forest roads provide access to the Strawberry Mountain Wilderness. Other recreation options include fishing and mountain biking. Note that fishing is restricted to the use of artificial lures with a single, barbless hook. In the appropriate seasons, bear, coyotes, deer, and elk are hunted here.

**Campsites, facilities:** There are 15 sites for tents or RVs up to 40 feet long. Picnic tables and fire rings are provided. Drinking water and vault toilets are available. Garbage must be packed out. Some facilities are wheelchair accessible. Leashed pets are permitted.

**Reservations, fees:** Reservations are not accepted. Sites are $8 per night, $4 per night for an additional vehicle. Open late May-November, weather permitting.

**Directions:** From John Day, take U.S. 395 south for 10 miles to Forest Road 15. Turn left and on Forest Road 15 drive 16 miles to Forest Road 16. Turn right on Forest Road 16 and drive six miles to Forest Road 815. Turn right and drive 0.5 mile to the campground on the right.

**Contact:** Malheur National Forest, Prairie City Ranger District, 541/820-3800, www. fs.usda.gov/malheur.

# 97 TROUT FARM

### Scenic rating: 6
near Prairie City in Malheur National Forest

**Map 10.7, page 545**

Trout Farm campground (4,900 feet elevation) is situated on the Upper John Day River, which provides good trout fishing with easy access for people who don't wish to travel off paved roads. A picnic shelter is available for family picnics, and a small pond at the campground has a wheelchair-accessible trail.

**Campsites, facilities:** There are six sites for tents or RVs up to 21 feet long. Picnic tables and fire rings are provided. Drinking water and vault toilets are available. Garbage must be packed out. Some facilities are wheelchair accessible. Leashed pets are permitted.

**Reservations, fees:** Reservations are not accepted. Sites are $8 per night, $4 per night per

additional vehicle. Open June-mid-October, weather permitting.

**Directions:** From John Day, drive east on U.S. 26 for 13 miles to Prairie City and Front Street. Turn right on Front Street and drive 0.5 mile to County Road 62. Turn left on County Road 62 and drive 15 miles to the campground entrance on the right.

**Contact:** Malheur National Forest, Prairie City Ranger District, 541/820-3800, www. fs.usda.gov/malheur.

# 98 ELK CREEK

### Scenic rating: 8
on Elk Creek in Malheur National Forest

**Map 10.7, page 545**

This tiny, pretty camp at the confluence of the north and south forks of Elk Creek (elevation 5,000 feet) has lots of hunting and fishing opportunities. The camp gets light use, except during the hunting season. If full, North Fork Malheur is an alternate camp in the area.

**Campsites, facilities:** There are five tent sites. Picnic tables and fire rings are provided. Vault toilets are available. There is no drinking water, and garbage must be packed out. Leashed pets are permitted.

**Reservations, fees:** Reservations are not accepted. There is no fee for camping. Open late May-November, weather permitting.

**Directions:** From John Day, drive east on U.S. 26 for 13 miles to Prairie City and County Road 62. Turn right (southeast) on County Road 62 and drive 8.5 miles to Forest Road 13. Turn left and drive 16 miles to Forest Road 16. Turn right and drive 1.5 miles south to the campground on the right.

**Contact:** Malheur National Forest, Prairie City Ranger District, 541/820-3800, www. fs.usda.gov/malheur.

## 99 CROSSING

### Scenic rating: 5

on Little Crane Creek in Malheur National
Forest

**Map 10.7, page 545**

Quiet, primitive, private, and small: all these
words describe this camp along the banks of
Little Crane Creek at an elevation of 5,500
feet. The creek provides good trout fishing
(only artificial bait and artificial lures are allowed). There are also some nice hiking trails
in the area, the closest one at the north fork
of the Malheur River, about 10 miles away.
This is considered a dispersed camping site so
check current fire restrictions before lighting
a campfire.

**Campsites, facilities:** There are four sites for
tents or RVs up to 20 feet long. Picnic tables
are provided. Vault toilets are available. There
is no drinking water, and garbage must be
packed out. Leashed pets are permitted.

**Reservations, fees:** Reservations are not accepted. There is no fee for camping. Open late
May-November, weather permitting.

**Directions:** From John Day, drive east on U.S.
26 for 13 miles to Prairie City and County
Road 62. Turn right and drive 8.5 miles to
Forest Road 13. Turn left and drive 16 miles
to Forest Road 16. Turn right and drive 5.5
miles south to the campground on the left.

**Contact:** Malheur National Forest, Prairie
City Ranger District, 541/820-3800, www.
fs.usda.gov/malheur.

## 100 NORTH FORK MALHEUR

### Scenic rating: 7

on the north fork of the Malheur River in
Malheur National Forest

**Map 10.7, page 545**

The secluded North Fork Malheur campground sits at an elevation of 4,700 feet along
the banks of the north fork of the Malheur
River, a designated Wild and Scenic River.
Hiking trails and rough dirt roads provide additional access to the river and backcountry
streams. (It's essential to obtain a U.S. Forest Service map.) Good fishing, hunting, and
mountain biking opportunities abound in the
area. Fishing is restricted to the use of artificial
lures with a single, barbless hook.

**Campsites, facilities:** There are five sites for
tents or RVs up to 21 feet long. Picnic tables
and fire rings are provided. Vault toilets are
available. There is no drinking water, and garbage must be packed out. Leashed pets are
permitted.

**Reservations, fees:** Reservations are not accepted. There is no fee for camping. Open late
May-November, weather permitting.

**Directions:** From John Day, drive east on U.S.
26 for 13 miles to Prairie City and County
Road 62. Turn right and drive 8.5 miles to
Forest Road 13. Turn left and drive 16 miles
to Forest Road 16. Turn right and drive two
miles south to a fork with Forest Road 1675.
Take the left fork to Forest Road 1675 and
drive two miles to the camp on the right.

**Contact:** Malheur National Forest, Prairie
City Ranger District, 541/820-3800, www.
fs.usda.gov/malheur.

## 101 ROCK SPRINGS FOREST CAMP

### Scenic rating: 5

at Rock Springs in Malheur National Forest

**Map 10.7, page 545**

If you want to camp in a big forest filled with
the scent of ponderosa pines, Rock Springs
Forest Camp is for you. This primitive camp
has a sprinkling of pretty aspens and several little springs—in fact, it's located right
on Rock Springs, with Cave Spring, House
Creek Spring, and Sunshine Spring within
a few miles. Do not count on the springs for
drinking water, however, without a water filter.
The elevation is 4,800 feet.

**Campsites, facilities:** There are 14 sites for tents or RVs up to 40 feet long. Picnic tables and fire grills are provided. Vault toilets are available. Drinking water is available from a spring (you must filter it first). Garbage must be packed out. Leashed pets are permitted.

**Reservations, fees:** Reservations are not accepted. Sites are $6 per night for first two vehicles, $3 per night for each additional vehicle. Open late May-mid-October, weather permitting.

**Directions:** From Burns, drive north on U.S. 395 for 30 miles to Van-Silvies Highway (County Road 73). Turn right on Van-Silvies Highway (which turns into Forest Road 17) and drive four miles to Forest Road 054. Turn right (south) and drive 0.75 mile to the camp on the left.

**Contact:** Malheur National Forest, Emigrant Creek Ranger District, 541/573-4300, www. fs.usda.gov/malheur.

## 102 WEST EAGLE MEADOW
🏃 🛶 🎣 ♿ 🚐 ⛺

### Scenic rating: 7

near West Eagle Creek in Wallowa-Whitman National Forest

**Map 10.8, page 546**

West Eagle campground sits in a big, open meadow (5,200 feet elevation) about a five-minute walk from West Eagle Creek. The West Eagle Trail starts at the camp, providing access to the Eagle Cap Wilderness and offering a good opportunity to observe wildlife. The adjacent meadow fills with wildflowers in the summer. For campers with horses, there are new stock facilities with water available in a separate, adjacent campground.

**Campsites, facilities:** There are five sites for tents or RVs up to 30 feet long and seven walk-in sites for tents only. The adjacent campground at West Eagle Meadows has six sites for campers with horses. Picnic tables and fire rings are provided. Vault toilets are available. There is no drinking water, and garbage must

be packed out. Stock facilities include corrals and hitching rails. Some facilities are wheelchair accessible. Leashed pets are permitted.

**Reservations, fees:** Reservations are not accepted. Sites are $5 per night per vehicle. Visitors to Eagle Cap Wilderness must obtain a free Wilderness Visitor Permit at the on-site self-service station (one permit per group). Open mid-June-late October, weather permitting.

**Directions:** From Baker City, drive north on I-84 for six miles to Highway 203. Turn east and drive 17 miles to the town of Medical Springs and County Road 71. Turn right (south) and drive two miles to Forest Road 67. Turn left and drive 12 miles to Forest Road 77. Turn left (north) and drive five miles to the camp on the right. Note: Segments of the road are narrow and steep.

**Contact:** Wallowa-Whitman National Forest, LaGrande Ranger District, 541/963-7186, www.fs.usda.gov/wallowa-whitman.

## 103 EAGLE FORKS
🏃 🛶 🎣 ♿ 🚐 ⛺

### Scenic rating: 6

on Eagle Creek in Wallowa-Whitman National Forest

**Map 10.8, page 546**

This campground (3,000 feet elevation) is located at the confluence of Little Eagle Creek and Eagle Creek. A trail follows the creek northwest for several miles, making for a prime day hike, yet the spot attracts few people (except on holiday weekends). It's quite pretty and perfect for a weekend getaway or an extended layover.

**Campsites, facilities:** There are six single sites and two double sites for tents or RVs up to 21 feet long. Picnic tables and fire rings are provided. Drinking water and vault toilets are available. Garbage must be packed out. Some facilities are wheelchair accessible. Leashed pets are permitted.

**Reservations, fees:** Reservations are not

accepted. Sites are $6 per night. Open May-late October, weather permitting.

**Directions:** From Baker City, drive east on Highway 86 for 42 miles to Richland and Newbridge. Turn north on Newbridge (after two miles on paved roads, it becomes Eagle Creek Road); then continue on Forest Road 7735 for seven miles to the campground entrance on the left.

**Contact:** Wallowa-Whitman National Forest, Whitman Ranger District, 541/742-7511, www.fs.usda.gov/wallowa-whitman.

## 104 TWO COLOR

### Scenic rating: 6

on Eagle Creek in Wallowa-Whitman National Forest

**Map 10.8, page 546**

Two Color campground (4,800 feet elevation) sits on the banks of Eagle Creek, about a mile north of Tamarack. Evergreens shade the spacious campsites, and the creek is stocked with rainbow trout. If full, another option for campers is nearby Boulder Park campground, three miles northeast on Forest Road 7755.

**Campsites, facilities:** There are 11 sites for tents or RVs up to 16 feet long. Picnic tables and fire grills are provided. Vault toilets are available. There is no drinking water, and garbage must be packed out. Leashed pets are permitted.

**Reservations, fees:** Reservations are not accepted. There is no fee for camping. Open mid-June-late October, weather permitting.

**Directions:** From Baker City, drive north on I-84 for six miles to Highway 203. Turn east on Highway 203 and drive 17 miles to Medical Springs and County Road 71. Turn right (south) and drive two miles to Forest Road 67. Turn left and drive 12 miles to Forest Road 77. Turn left and drive one mile to Forest Road 7755. Turn right and drive one mile north to the camp.

**Contact:** Wallowa-Whitman National Forest, LaGrande Ranger District, 541/963-7186, www.fs.usda.gov/wallowa-whitman.

## 105 TAMARACK

### Scenic rating: 5

on Eagle Creek in Wallowa-Whitman National Forest

**Map 10.8, page 546**

On the banks of Eagle Creek in a beautiful area with lush vegetation and abundant wildlife sits Tamarack campground at 4,600 feet elevation. This is a good spot for fishing and hiking in a remote setting; a short, accessible trail leads down to two creekside fishing platforms.

**Campsites, facilities:** There are 12 sites for tents or RVs up to 25 feet long. Picnic tables and fire rings are provided. Drinking water and vault toilets are available. Garbage must be packed out. Some facilities are wheelchair accessible. Leashed pets are permitted.

**Reservations, fees:** Reservations are not accepted. Sites are $6 per night. Open June-late October, weather permitting.

**Directions:** From Baker City, drive east on Highway 86 for 42 miles to Richland and Newbridge. Turn north on Newbridge (after two miles on paved roads, it becomes Eagle Creek Road); then continue on Forest Road 7735 for 20 miles to the campground entrance.

**Contact:** Wallowa-Whitman National Forest, Pine Ranger District, 541/742-7511, www.fs.usda.gov/wallowa-whitman.

## 106 FISH LAKE

### Scenic rating: 6

on Fish Lake in Wallowa-Whitman National Forest

**Map 10.8, page 546**

This is a pretty, well-forested camp with comfortable sites along the shore of 20-acre Fish Lake at an elevation of 6,600 feet. Fish Lake makes a good base for a fishing trip; side-trip options include hiking on nearby trails that lead to mountain streams. Bring mosquito repellent.

**Campsites, facilities:** There are 15 sites for tents or RVs up to 20 feet long. Six sites on the upper loop can accommodate longer RVs. Picnic tables and fire rings are provided. Drinking water and vault toilets are available. Garbage must be packed out. Boat-launching facilities (for small boats only) are nearby. Some facilities are wheelchair accessible. Leashed pets are permitted.

**Reservations, fees:** Reservations are not accepted. Sites are $5 per night. Open July-late October, weather permitting.

**Directions:** From Baker City, take I-84 north for four miles to Highway 86. Turn east on Highway 86 and drive 52 miles to Halfway and Main Street. Turn left (north) on Main Street and drive to Fish Lake Road. Turn right on Fish Lake Road, then drive five miles to Forest Road 66. Continue north on Forest Road 66 for 18.5 miles to the campground on the left.

**Contact:** Wallowa-Whitman National Forest, Pine Ranger District, 541/742-7511, www.fs.usda.gov/wallowa-whitman.

## 107 SPRING RECREATION SITE

Scenic rating: 5

on the Snake River

**Map 10.8, page 546**

One of two camps in or near Huntington, this campground hugs the banks of the Brownlee Reservoir. Fishing is popular at this reservoir; it's known for large channel catfish. A more developed alternative, Farewell Bend State Recreation Area offers showers and all the other luxuries a camper could want.

**Campsites, facilities:** There are 35 sites for tents or RVs of any length. Group camping is available. Picnic tables, garbage service, and fire grills are provided. Drinking water (summer only) and vault toilets are available. Boat-launching facilities, a dock, and a fish-cleaning station are on-site. A seasonal camp host is on-site. Some facilities are wheelchair accessible. Leashed pets are permitted.

**Reservations, fees:** Reservations are not accepted. Sites are $5 per night per vehicle, with a 14-day stay limit. Open year-round, weather permitting; there is no fee October 31-April 1.

**Directions:** From Ontario (near the Oregon/Idaho border), drive northwest on I-84 for 28 miles to Huntington and Snake River Road. Turn right (northeast) on Snake River Road and drive three miles (paved road) to the campground.

**Contact:** Bureau of Land Management, Baker City Office, 541/523-1256, www.blm.gov/or.

## 108 FAREWELL BEND STATE RECREATION AREA

Scenic rating: 7

on the Snake River

**Map 10.8, page 546**

Farewell Bend campground offers a green desert experience on the banks of the Snake River's Brownlee Reservoir. Situated along the Oregon Trail, the camp has historic interpretive displays and an evening interpretive program at the amphitheater during the summer. The lake provides good numbers of catfish.

**Campsites, facilities:** There are 101 sites with partial hookups for RVs up to 60 feet long, 30 tent sites, a hiker-biker camp, two cabins, and one group site for up to 50 people. Picnic tables and fire rings are provided. Drinking water, garbage bins, restrooms with flush toilets and showers, a dump station, firewood, ice, a fish-cleaning station, basketball hoops, horseshoe pits, sand volleyball court, and boat-launching facilities are available. Some facilities are wheelchair accessible. Leashed pets are permitted.

**Reservations, fees:** Reservations are accepted at 800/452-5687 or www.reserveamerica.com ($8 reservation fee). Tent sites are $14-18 per night, RV sites are $17-22, $5 per person per night for the hiker/biker camp, $54-76 per night for the group site plus $3 per person per night for more than 50 people, $42 per night for cabins, and $5 per night per extra vehicle. Some credit cards are accepted. Open year-round, with limited winter facilities.

**Directions:** From Ontario (near the Oregon/Idaho border), drive northwest on I-84 for 21 miles to Exit 353. Take that exit and drive one mile to the park.

**Contact:** Farewell Bend State Recreation Area, 541/869-2365 or 800/551-6949, www.oregon-stateparks.org.

## 109 BULLY CREEK PARK

**Scenic rating: 7**

on Bully Creek Reservoir

**Map 10.8, page 546**

Bully Creek reservoir is located in a kind of high desert area with sagebrush and poplar trees for shade. It's beautiful if you like the desert, and the sunsets are worth the trip. People come here to boat, fish (mostly for warm-water fish, such as crappie and large- and smallmouth bass), swim, and water ski, and there is biking on the gravel roads. At 2,300 feet elevation, the primitive setting is home to deer, jackrabbits, squirrels, and many birds. No monthly rentals are permitted here—a big plus for overnighters.

**Campsites, facilities:** There are 40 sites with partial hookups for tents or RVs up to 40 feet in length; one site is pull-through. Picnic tables and fire pits are provided. Drinking water, restrooms with flush toilets and showers, ice, firewood, garbage bins, a dump station, picnic area, and boat ramp and dock are available. A camp host is on-site. A restaurant, café, convenience store, gasoline, propane gas, charcoal, and coin laundry are within nine miles. Some facilities are wheelchair accessible. Leashed pets are permitted.

**Reservations, fees:** Reservations are accepted at 541/473-2969. Sites are $15 per night. Open mid-April-mid-November, weather permitting.

**Directions:** From Ontario (near the Oregon/Idaho border), drive west on U.S. 20/26 for 12 miles to Vale and Graham Boulevard. Turn right (northwest) on Graham Boulevard and drive five miles to Bully Creek Road. Turn right (west) and drive three miles to the park on the left.

**Contact:** Bully Creek Park, 541/473-2969; Malheur County Parks Department, 541/473-5191, www.malheurco.org.

# THE SOUTHERN CASCADES

The Southern Cascades is famous for Crater Lake, but it holds many recreation secrets. Crater Lake's cobalt-blue waters lie within clifflike walls; the lake's Rim Drive is on everybody's to-do list. Beyond the lake, you'll find stellar camping, fishing, and hiking. Neighboring Mount Washington Wilderness and Three Sisters Wilderness in Willamette National Forest are accessible via a beautiful drive on the McKenzie River Highway (Highway 126) east from Eugene. Crane Prairie, Waldo Lake, and Wickiup Reservoir provide boating, camping, and good fishing. The Umpqua and Rogue National Forests offer great water-sport destinations, including Diamond Lake, and the headwaters of the Rogue and North Umpqua Rivers. Upper Klamath Lake and the Klamath Basin are the number one wintering areas in America for bald eagles. Klamath Lake and the Williamson River provide a chance to catch huge but elusive trout.

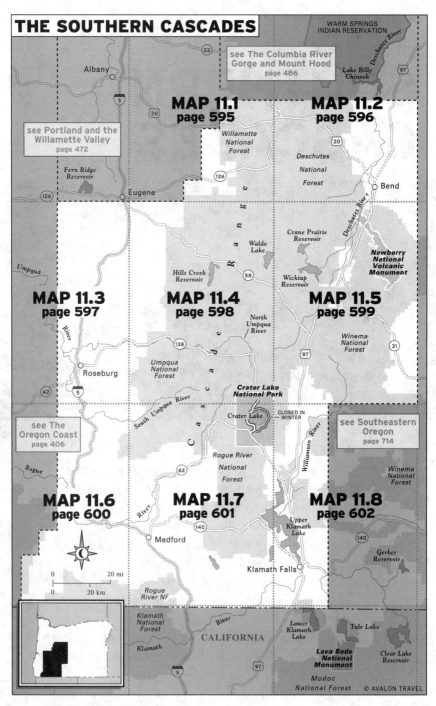

# THE SOUTHERN CASCADES

WARM SPRINGS
INDIAN RESERVATION

Albany

22

see The Columbia River
Gorge and Mount Hood
page 486

Lake Billy
Chinook

97

5

20

**MAP 11.1**
page 595

**MAP 11.2**
page 596

see Portland and the
Willamette Valley
page 472

Willamette
National
Forest

Deschutes

National

Forest

20

126

Fern Ridge
Reservoir

126

Eugene

Bend

Waldo
Lake

Crane Prairie
Reservoir

Deschutes River

Newberry
National
Volcanic
Monument

Umpqua

Hills Creek
Reservoir

58

Wickiup
Reservoir

**MAP 11.3**
page 597

**MAP 11.4**
page 598

**MAP 11.5**
page 599

North
Umpqua
River

Winema
National
Forest

138

River

31

Roseburg

Umpqua
National
Forest

97

42

5

South Umpqua River

Crater Lake
National Park

see Southeastern
Oregon
page 714

see The
Oregon Coast
page 406

Crater Lake

CLOSED IN
WINTER

Rogue

Rogue River
National
Forest

Williamson River

Winema
National
Forest

**MAP 11.6**
page 600

**MAP 11.7**
page 601

**MAP 11.8**
page 602

62

River

140

0          20 mi

0          20 km

Medford

Klamath Falls

Upper
Klamath
Lake

140

Gerber
Reservoir

Rogue
River NF

Klamath
National
Forest

River

Lower
Klamath
Lake

Tule Lake

**CALIFORNIA**

Klamath

Lava Beds
National
Monument

Clear Lake
Reservoir

5

97

Modoc
National Forest

© AVALON TRAVEL

# Map 11.1

## Sites 1-18
## Pages 603-610

11.2

11.4

1 2
3 4 5
6 7 8

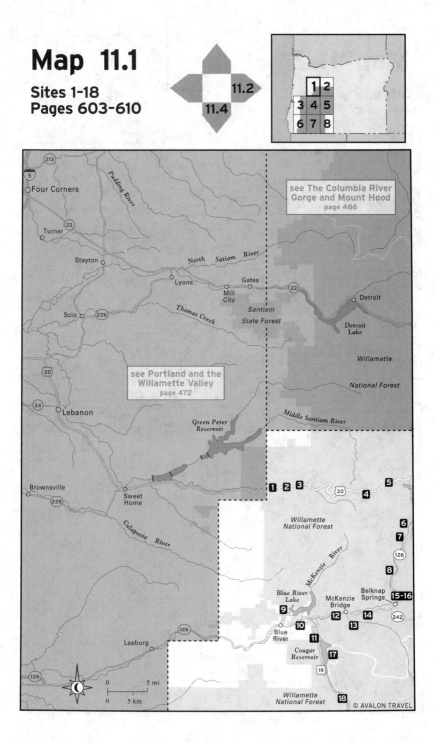

213

5

Four Corners

Pudding River

see The Columbia River
Gorge and Mount Hood
page 486

Turner

22

Stayton

North Satiam River

Lyons

Gates

Mill City

Detroit

22

Detroit Lake

Scio

226

Thomas Creek

Santiam State Forest

Willamette

see Portland and the
Willamette Valley
page 472

National Forest

20

34

Lebanon

Green Peter Reservoir

Middle Santiam River

Brownsville

228

Sweet Home

1 2 3    20    4    5

Willamette
National Forest

6

7

126

Calapooia River

8

Blue River Lake

McKenzie Bridge

Belknap Springs

15-16

9

242

12    14

10

13

Blue River

11

126

Leaburg

Cougar Reservoir

17

19

126

0          5 mi

0          5 km

Willamette
National Forest

18

© AVALON TRAVEL

# Map 11.2

**Sites 19-52**
**Pages 610-623**

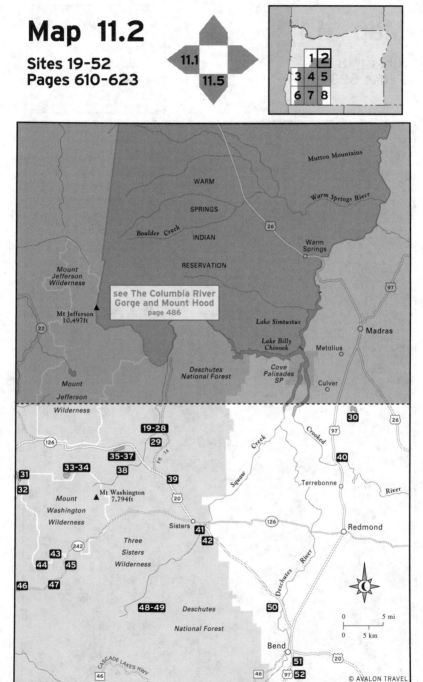

11.1

11.5

1 2
3 4 5
6 7 8

Mutton Mountains

WARM

Warm Springs River

SPRINGS

Boulder Creek

INDIAN

26

Warm Springs

RESERVATION

97

Mount Jefferson Wilderness

see The Columbia River Gorge and Mount Hood page 486

Mt Jefferson 10,497ft

Lake Sintustus

Madras

Lake Billy Chinook

Metolius

22

Deschutes National Forest

Cove Palisades SP

Culver

Mount Jefferson

Wilderness

126

**19-28**

**29**

**30**

97

26

**35-37**

FR 14

Squaw Creek

Crooked

**40**

**33-34**

**38**

**31**

**39**

20

Terrebonne

River

**32**

Mt Washington 7,794ft

Mount Washington Wilderness

126

Three Sisters Wilderness

Sisters

**41**

Redmond

242

**42**

**43**

**44** **45**

Deschutes River

**46** **47**

**48-49**

Deschutes

**50**

National Forest

CASCADE LAKES HWY

Bend

**51**

20

46

46

97 **52**

0     5 mi

0     5 km

© AVALON TRAVEL

# Map 11.3

**Sites 53-61
Pages 624-627**

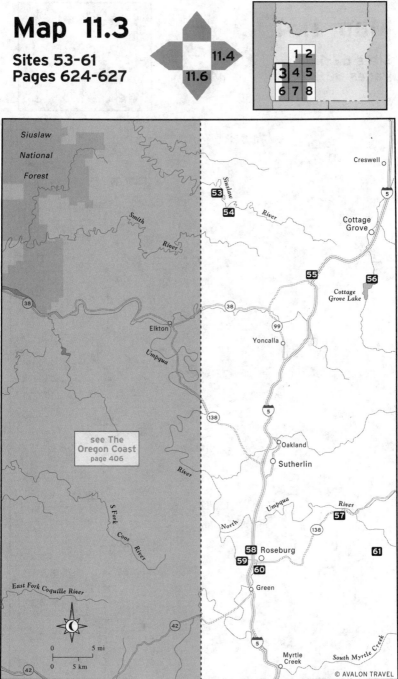

# Map 11.4

## Sites 62-120
## Pages 628-653

11.1
11.3 11.5
11.7

| 1 | 2 |
|---|---|
| 3 | 4 | 5 |
| 6 | 7 | 8 |

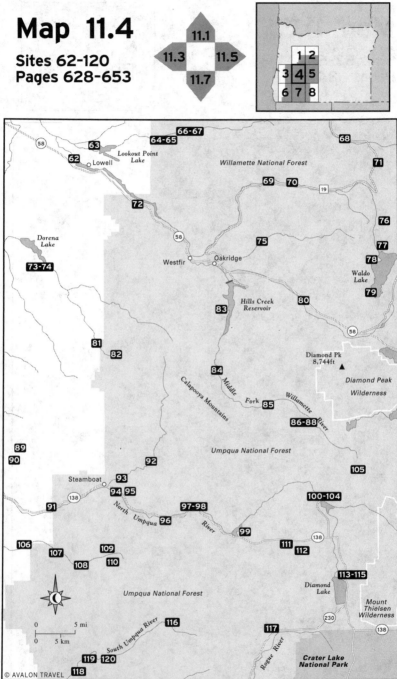

58

63
62 Lowell

64-65  66-67

68

71

Lookout Point Lake

Willamette National Forest

69  70  19

72

76

Dorena Lake

58

75

77

78

73-74

Westfir  Oakridge

Waldo Lake

79

83  Hills Creek Reservoir

80

58

81

Diamond Pk 8,744ft ▲

82

84  Middle

Diamond Peak Wilderness

Calapooya Mountains

Fork  85  Willamette River

86-88

Umpqua National Forest

105

89
90

92

Steamboat  93

100-104

91  138

94  95

97-98

North Umpqua

96

River

99

111  138
112

106

107

109

113-115

108  110

Diamond Lake

Mount Thielsen Wilderness

N

0    5 mi
0    5 km

Umpqua National Forest

116

117

230

138

119  120

South Umpqua River

Rogue River

Crater Lake National Park

© AVALON TRAVEL  118

# Map 11.5

**Sites 121-182**
**Pages 653-677**

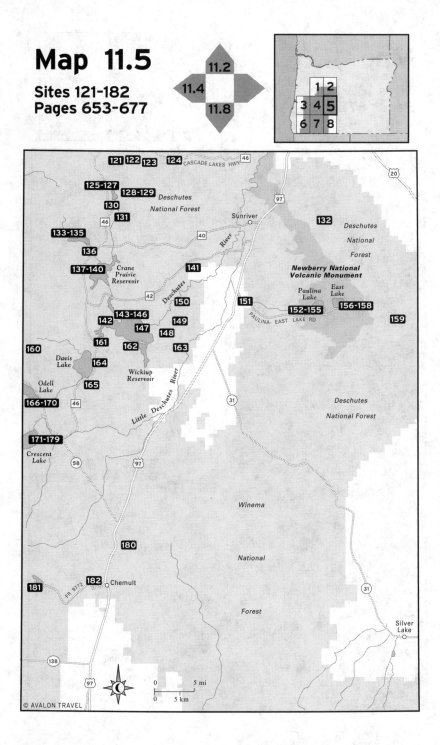

# Map 11.6

**Sites 183-204**
**Pages 678-687**

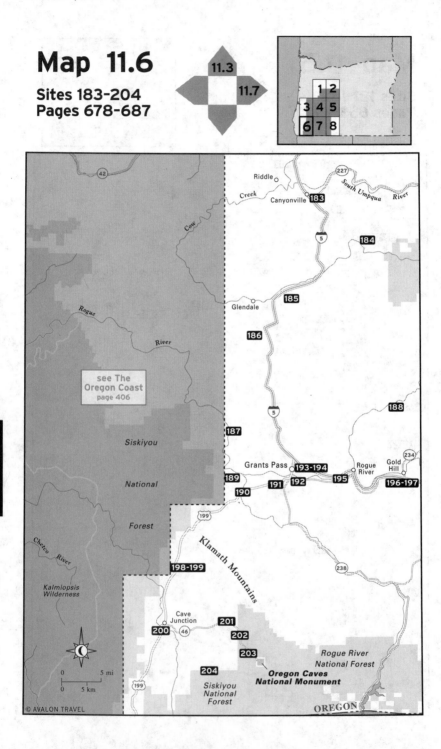

# Map 11.7
## Sites 205-256
## Pages 687-709

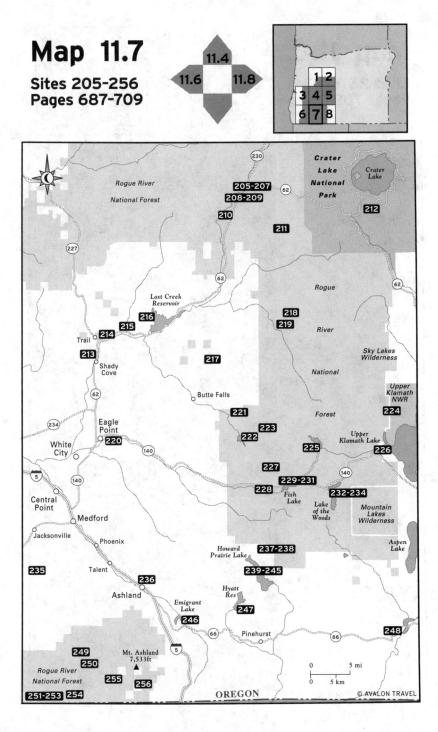

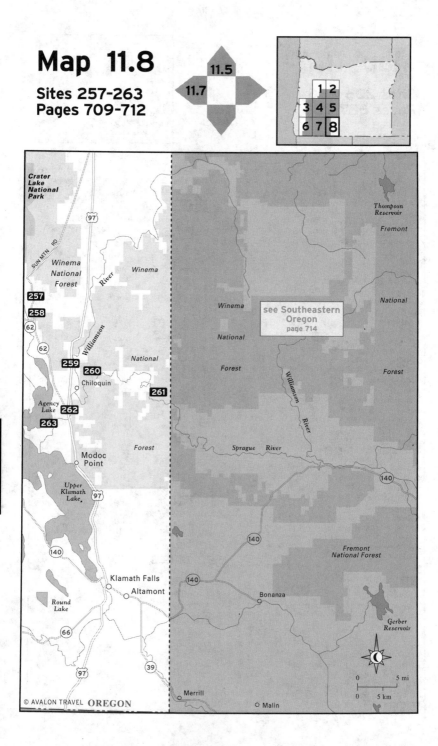

# Map 11.8

## Sites 257-263
## Pages 709-712

11.5
11.7

1 2
3 4 5
6 7 8

Crater Lake National Park

97

SUN MTN RD

Winema National Forest

257

258

62

62

259

260

Chiloquin

261

Agency Lake 262

263

Modoc Point

Upper Klamath Lake

97

140

Round Lake

66

Klamath Falls
Altamont

140

140

97

39

Merrill

© AVALON TRAVEL  OREGON

Winema

River

Williamson

Winema

Winema

National

Forest

National

Forest

see Southeastern Oregon page 714

Williamson River

Sprague    River

140

Bonanza

Thompson Reservoir

Fremont

National

Forest

Fremont National Forest

Gerber Reservoir

Malin

0          5 mi
0          5 km

# 1 TROUT CREEK

**Scenic rating: 8**

on the South Santiam River in Willamette National Forest

**Map 11.1, page 595**

This campground is set along the banks of the South Santiam River at 1,200 feet in elevation, about seven miles east of Cascadia. Fishing and swimming are some of the recreation possibilities here. There is a historic shelter and the remains of stonework from the era of the Civilian Conservation Corps. The Trout Creek Trail, just across the highway, leads into the Menagerie Wilderness. The Long Ranch Elk Viewing Area is immediately west of the campground and, at the Trout Creek Trailhead, you'll also find a short trail leading to an elk-viewing platform. Nearby is the Old Santiam Wagon Road.

**Campsites, facilities:** There are 24 sites for tents or RVs up to 25 feet long, including eight sites that can accommodate RVs up to 32 feet long. Picnic tables, garbage bins, and fire grills are provided. Drinking water and vault toilets are available. Some facilities are wheelchair accessible. Leashed pets are permitted.

**Reservations, fees:** Reservations are accepted at 877/444-6777 ($10 reservation fee) or www.recreation.gov ($9 reservation fee). Sites are $15 per night, $5 per night per additional vehicle. Open May-October, weather permitting.

**Directions:** From Albany, drive east on U.S. 20 for 45 miles (19 miles past Sweet Home) to the campground entrance on the right.

**Contact:** Willamette National Forest, Sweet Home Ranger District, 541/367-5168, www. fs.usda.gov/willamette or www.linnparks.com.

# 2 YUKWAH

**Scenic rating: 7**

on the Santiam River in Willamette National Forest

**Map 11.1, page 595**

Yukwah campground is nestled in a second-growth Douglas fir forest on the banks of the Santiam River. The camp is 0.25 mile east of Trout Creek Campground and offers the same recreation possibilities. The camp features a 0.5-mile, compacted-surface interpretive trail that's barrier-free.

**Campsites, facilities:** There are 20 sites for tents or RVs up to 32 feet long, including a deluxe group site for up to 20 people. Picnic tables, garbage bins, and fire grills are provided. Drinking water, vault toilets, a picnic area, and a fishing platform are available. Some facilities, including the fishing platform, are wheelchair accessible. Leashed pets are permitted.

**Reservations, fees:** Reservations are not accepted. Sites are $15 per night, the deluxe site is $30 per night, $5 per night per additional vehicle. Open early May-late September, weather permitting.

**Directions:** From Albany, drive east on U.S. 20 for 45 miles (19 miles past Sweet Home) to the campground.

**Contact:** Willamette National Forest, Sweet Home Ranger District, 541/367-5168, www. fs.usda.gov/willamette or www.linnparks.com.

# 3 FERNVIEW

**Scenic rating: 7**

on the Santiam River in Willamette National Forest

**Map 11.1, page 595**

This campground is perched high above the confluence of Boulder Creek and the Santiam River, just south of the Menagerie Wilderness. A stepped walkway leads down to the river. Just across U.S. 20 lies the Rooster Rock Trail, which leads to—where else?—Rooster Rock, the site of an old lookout tower. The Old Santiam Wagon Road runs through the back of the campground. The camp is best suited for tent and small RV camping; the sites are small. The elevation is 1,400 feet.

**Campsites, facilities:** There are 11 sites for tents or RVs up to 22 feet long. The entire campground can be reserved as a group site. Picnic tables, garbage bins, and fire grills are provided. Drinking water and vault toilets are available. Some facilities are wheelchair accessible. Leashed pets are permitted.

**Reservations, fees:** Reservations are required for group camping only and can be made at 877/444-6777 ($10 reservation fee) or www.recreation.gov ($9 reservation fee). Single sites are $15 per night, plus $5 per night per additional vehicle; the group campsite is $125 per night. Open May-October, weather permitting.

**Directions:** From Albany drive east on U.S. 20 for 49 miles (23 miles past Sweet Home) to the campground entrance on the right.

**Contact:** Willamette National Forest, Sweet Home Ranger District, 541/367-5168, www.fs.usda.gov/willamette or www.linnparks.com.

## 4 HOUSE ROCK

**Scenic rating: 8**

on the Santiam River in Willamette National Forest

Map 11.1, page 595

House Rock campground is situated at the confluence of Sheep Creek and the South Santiam River. The camp is set in the midst of an old-growth forest and is surrounded by huge, majestic Douglas fir. Trout fishing can be good, particularly during summer evenings. Botany students come here from long distances to see firsthand many uncommon and spectacular specimens of plants. History buffs should explore the short loop trail out of camp, which passes by House Rock, a historic rock shelter

for Native Americans, and continues to the historic Old Santiam Wagon Road.

**Campsites, facilities:** There are 11 sites for tents or RVs up to 22 feet long and five tent-only sites. Picnic tables, garbage bins, and fire grills are provided. Vault toilets and drinking water are available. Some facilities are wheelchair accessible. Leashed pets are permitted.

**Reservations, fees:** Reservations are accepted at 877/444-6777 ($10 reservation fee) or www.recreation.gov ($9 reservation fee). Sites are $15 per night, $5 per night per additional vehicle. Open May-October, weather permitting.

**Directions:** From Albany drive east on U.S. 20 for 52.5 miles (26 miles past Sweet Home) to Latiwi Road (Forest Road 2044). Turn right and drive a short distance to the campground.

**Contact:** Willamette National Forest, Sweet Home Ranger District, 541/367-5168, www.fs.usda.gov/willamette or www.linnparks.com.

## 5 LOST PRAIRIE

**Scenic rating: 7**

on Hackleman Creek in Willamette National Forest

Map 11.1, page 595

Lost Prairie campground hugs the banks of Hackleman Creek at 3,200 feet elevation in an area of Douglas fir and spruce. Three excellent hiking trails can be found within five miles of the camp: Hackleman Old-Growth Grove, Cone Peak, and Iron Mountain. The last two offer spectacular wildflower-viewing in the late spring and early summer. This camp provides an alternative to nearby Fish Lake.

**Campsites, facilities:** There are 10 sites for tents, two of which are suitable for RVs up to 24 feet long, and six walk-in sites for tents only. Picnic tables, garbage bins, and fire grills are provided. Drinking water and vault toilets are available. Some facilities are wheelchair accessible. Leashed pets are permitted.

**Reservations, fees:** Reservations are not accepted. Sites are $15 per night, $5 per night per additional vehicle. Open May-October, weather permitting.

**Directions:** From Albany, drive east on U.S. 20 for 63 miles (approximately 38 miles past Sweet Home) to the camp on the right.

**Contact:** Willamette National Forest, Sweet Home Ranger District, 541/367-5168, www.fs.usda.gov/willamette or www.linnparks.com.

## 6 LAKES END BOAT-IN

### Scenic rating: 9

on Smith Reservoir in Willamette National Forest

**Map 11.1, page 595**

This secluded boat-in campground is set along the shore of the headwaters of Smith Reservoir, a long narrow lake. You'll find no cars and no traffic. The trout fishing in this reservoir can be exceptional; note the 10-mph speed limit. The campground is split into two areas, providing camping opportunities on Smith Creek and on the reservoir. Note: Trees occasionally fall across the river, blocking access; call McKenzie River Ranger District before heading out.

**Campsites, facilities:** There are 17 boat-in tent sites. Picnic tables and fire grills are provided. Pit toilets are available. There is no drinking water, and garbage must be packed out. Boat docks are nearby. Leashed pets are permitted.

**Reservations, fees:** Reservations are not accepted. There is no fee for camping. Open May-September, weather permitting.

**Directions:** From Eugene, drive east on Highway 126 for 47 miles to the town of McKenzie Bridge. Continue on Highway 126 for 13 miles to the signed turnoff for Lakes End at the north end of Trail Bridge Reservoir. Turn left on Forest Road 1477 and drive a short distance; then bear left and continue (past Trail Bridge Campground) for 0.5 mile to Forest Road 730 (Smith Reservoir Road). Continue three miles to the boat launch.

**Contact:** Willamette National Forest, McKenzie River Ranger District, 541/822-3381, www.fs.usda.gov/willamette.

## 7 TRAIL BRIDGE

### Scenic rating: 6

on Trail Bridge Reservoir in Willamette National Forest

**Map 11.1, page 595**

Set along the shore of Trail Bridge Reservoir (2,000 feet elevation), this campground offers boating, fishing, and hiking among its recreation options. From the camp, there is access to the McKenzie River National Recreation Trail. Highway 126 east of McKenzie Bridge is a designated scenic route, providing a pleasant trip to the camp and making Trail Bridge an exceptional spot for car campers. For a good side trip, take the beautiful 40-minute drive east to the little town of Sisters.

**Campsites, facilities:** There are 46 sites, including 19 sites for RVs up to 45 feet long, and a large camping area at Trail Bridge Flats. Picnic tables, garbage service, and fire grills are provided. Drinking water and vault and flush toilets are available. Boat ramps are nearby. Some facilities are wheelchair accessible. Leashed pets are permitted.

**Reservations, fees:** Reservations are not accepted. Sites are $10 per night, $5 per night per additional vehicle. Open late April-September, weather permitting.

**Directions:** From Eugene, drive east on Highway 126 for 47 miles to the town of McKenzie Bridge. Continue on Highway 126 for 13 miles to Forest Road 1477. Turn left on Forest Road 1477 and drive a short distance; then bear left and continue 0.25 mile to the campground on the left.

**Contact:** Willamette National Forest, McKenzie River Ranger District, 541/822-3381, www.fs.usda.gov/willamette.

## 8 OLALLIE

**Scenic rating: 7**

on the McKenzie River in Willamette
National Forest

**Map 11.1, page 595**

Olallie campground sits at an elevation of
2,000 feet along the banks of the McKenzie
River. Boating, fishing, and hiking are among
its recreational opportunities, and fishing for
rainbow trout usually is good. Other bonuses
include easy access from Highway 126. The
campground is two miles southwest of Trail
Bridge Reservoir off Highway 126.

**Campsites, facilities:** There are 16 sites for
tents or RVs up to 35 feet long. Picnic tables
and fire grills are provided. Vault toilets,
drinking water, and garbage service are available. A boat launch is nearby (non-motorized
boats only). Leashed pets are permitted.

**Reservations, fees:** Reservations are accepted
at 877/444-6777 ($10 reservation fee) or www.
recreation.gov ($9 reservation fee). Sites are $16
per night, $6 per night per additional vehicle.
Open late April-October, weather permitting.

**Directions:** From Eugene, drive east on Highway 126 for 47 miles to the town of McKenzie
Bridge. Continue on Highway 126 for 11 miles
to the campground on the left.

**Contact:** Willamette National Forest, McKenzie River Ranger District, 541/822-3381,
www.fs.usda.gov/willamette.

## 9 MONA

**Scenic rating: 8**

near Blue River Reservoir in Willamette
National Forest

**Map 11.1, page 595**

This forested campground (1,360 feet elevation) is set along the shore of Blue River Reservoir, close to where the Blue River joins it.
A boat ramp is located across the river from
the campground (at Lookout Campground);
another boat ramp is situated at the south end
of the reservoir. After launching a boat, campers can ground it near their campsite. Note
that this camp is extremely popular when the
reservoir is full.

**Campsites, facilities:** There are 23 sites for
tents or RVs up to 36 feet long. Picnic tables,
garbage bins, waste-water disposal, and fire
grills are provided. Drinking water and flush
toilets are available. Some facilities are wheelchair accessible. Leashed pets are permitted.

**Reservations, fees:** Reservations are accepted at 877/444-6777 ($10 reservation fee)
or www.recreation.gov ($9 reservation fee).
Single sites are $16 per night, double sites are
$30 per night, $6 per night per additional
vehicle. Open May-mid-September, weather
permitting.

**Directions:** From Eugene, drive east on Highway 126 for 41 miles to Blue River. Continue
east on Highway 126 for three miles to Forest Road 15. Turn left (north) and drive three
miles to the campground on the left.

**Contact:** Willamette National Forest, McKenzie River Ranger District, 541/822-3381,
www.fs.usda.gov/willamette.

## 10 PATIO RV PARK

**Scenic rating: 7**

near the South Fork of the McKenzie River

**Map 11.1, page 595**

This RV park is situated near the banks of the
South Fork of the McKenzie River, not far
from Cougar Lake, which offers opportunities
for fishing, swimming, and waterskiing. Nearby recreation options include a golf course,
hiking trails, and bike paths. The Hoodoo Ski
Area is approximately 30 miles away.

**Campsites, facilities:** There are 60 sites
with full hookups for RVs of any length and a
grassy area for tents. Picnic tables are provided.
Restrooms with flush toilets and showers, a
recreation hall, group kitchen facilities, cable
TV, Wi-Fi, a community fire pit, horseshoe

pits, and a coin laundry are available. A store, gasoline, propane, and a café are within two miles. Some facilities are wheelchair accessible. Leashed pets are permitted.

**Reservations, fees:** Reservations are accepted at 541/822-3596 or via email at reservations@patiorv.com. RV sites are $28-33 per night, tent sites are $20 per night, $2 per person per night for more than two people. Group, weekly, and monthly rates are available. Some credit cards are accepted. Open year-round.

**Directions:** From Eugene, drive east on Highway 126 for 37 miles to the town of Blue River. Continue east on Highway 126 for six miles to McKenzie River Drive. Turn right and drive two miles to the park on the right.

**Contact:** Patio RV Park, 541/822-3596, www.patiorv.com.

## 11 DELTA

### Scenic rating: 8

on the McKenzie River in Willamette National Forest

**Map 11.1, page 595**

This popular campground sits along the banks of the McKenzie River in a spot heavily forested primarily with old-growth Douglas fir. The Delta Old Growth Nature Trail, a 0.5-mile wheelchair-accessible interpretive trail, is adjacent to the campground. The camp also features an amphitheater. Nearby are Blue River and Cougar Reservoirs (seven and five miles away, respectively), both of which offer swimming, trout fishing, and waterskiing.

**Campsites, facilities:** There are 38 sites for tents or RVs up to 36 feet long. Picnic tables, garbage bins, and fire grills are provided. Drinking water, vault toilets, and wastewater disposal are available. Some facilities are wheelchair accessible. Leashed pets are permitted.

**Reservations, fees:** Reservations are accepted at 877/444-6777 ($10 reservation fee) or www.recreation.gov ($9 reservation fee). Single sites

are $16 per night, double sites are $30 per night, and $6 per night per additional vehicle. Open late April-October, weather permitting.

**Directions:** From Eugene, drive east on Highway 126 for 37 miles to the town of Blue River. Continue east on Highway 126 for five miles to Forest Road 19 (Aufderheide Scenic Byway). Turn right (south) and drive 0.25 mile to Forest Road 400. Turn right and drive one mile to the campground.

**Contact:** Willamette National Forest, McKenzie River Ranger District, 541/822-3381, www.fs.usda.gov/willamette.

## 12 MCKENZIE BRIDGE

### Scenic rating: 8

on the McKenzie River in Willamette National Forest

**Map 11.1, page 595**

McKenzie campground is set at 1,400 feet elevation along the banks of the McKenzie River, one mile from the town of McKenzie Bridge. During the summer, this stretch of river provides good evening fly-fishing for trout; only non-motorized boats are permitted on the river.

**Campsites, facilities:** There are 20 sites for tents or RVs up to 40 feet long. Picnic tables, garbage service, and fire rings are provided. Flush toilets and drinking water are available. A grocery store and restaurants are available within one mile. Some facilities are wheelchair accessible. Leashed pets are permitted.

**Reservations, fees:** Reservations are accepted at 877/444-6777 ($10 reservation fee) or www.recreation.gov ($9 reservation fee). Sites are $16 per night, $7 per night per additional vehicle. Open mid-April-late September, weather permitting.

**Directions:** From Eugene, drive east on Highway 126 for 46 miles to the campground entrance on the right (one mile west of the town of McKenzie Bridge).

**Contact:** Willamette National Forest,

McKenzie River Ranger District, 541/822-3381, www.fs.usda.gov/willamette.

## 13 HORSE CREEK GROUP CAMP

**Scenic rating: 9**

on Horse Creek in Willamette National Forest

Map 11.1, page 595

This campground reserved for groups borders Horse Creek near the town of McKenzie Bridge. In spite of the name, no horse camping is permitted. Fishing is catch-and-release only; check current regulations. The camp sits at 1,400 feet elevation.

**Campsites, facilities:** This is a group camp with 60 sites for tents or RVs up to 27 feet long and space for up to 23 vehicles. Picnic tables and fire grills are provided. Vault toilets, drinking water, and garbage service are available. Leashed pets are permitted.

**Reservations, fees:** Reservations are accepted at 877/444-6777 ($10 reservation fee) or www.recreation.gov ($9 reservation fee). Sites are $40 per night for up to 49 people and $60 per night for 50-100 people. Open May-September, weather permitting.

**Directions:** From Eugene, drive east on Highway 126 for 47 miles to the town of McKenzie Bridge and Horse Creek Road. Turn right (south) on Horse Creek Road and drive one mile to the campground on the left.

**Contact:** Willamette National Forest, McKenzie River Ranger District, 541/822-3381, www.fs.usda.gov/willamette.

## 14 PARADISE

**Scenic rating: 9**

on the McKenzie River in Willamette National Forest

Map 11.1, page 595

Paradise campground (1,600 feet elevation), along the banks of the McKenzie River, may be right off the highway, but it offers a rustic, streamside setting with access to the McKenzie River National Recreation Trail. Trout fishing can be good here.

**Campsites, facilities:** There are 33 sites for tents or RVs of any length. Picnic tables, garbage service, and fire rings are provided. Flush and vault toilets, drinking water, a boat ramp, and firewood are available. Some facilities are wheelchair accessible. Leashed pets are permitted.

**Reservations, fees:** Reservations are accepted at 877/444-6777 ($10 reservation fee) or www.recreation.gov ($9 reservation fee). Single sites are $20 per night, double sites are $36 per night, $9 per night per additional vehicle. Open May-September, weather permitting.

**Directions:** From Eugene, drive east on Highway 126 for 47 miles to the town of McKenzie Bridge. Continue east on Highway 126 for 3.5 miles to the campground on the left.

**Contact:** Willamette National Forest, McKenzie River Ranger District, 541/822-3381, www.fs.usda.gov/willamette.

## 15 BELKNAP HOT SPRINGS RESORT

**Scenic rating: 9**

on the McKenzie River

Map 11.1, page 595                BEST (

This beautiful park, with 60 acres of developed and landscaped gardens, has been featured on at least one magazine cover. It's in a wooded, mountainous area on the McKenzie River. Trout fishing can be excellent here. If you're looking for hiking opportunities, the McKenzie River Trail can be accessed from camp. Other hiking opportunities include the Three Sisters and Mount Washington Wilderness Areas, both accessible by driving west of Sisters on Highway 242. Exceptionally scenic and pristine expanses of forest, they are well worth exploring. The Pacific Crest Trail runs north and south through both wilderness areas.

**Campsites, facilities:** There are 47 sites with full or partial hookups for RVs of any length, 25 sites for tents, a lodge with 18 rooms, and seven cabins. Picnic tables and fire pits are provided. Drinking water and restrooms with flush toilets and showers are available. A dump station is one mile away at Camp Yale. Recreational facilities include two hot-spring-fed swimming pools, and a recreation field. Some facilities are wheelchair accessible. Leashed pets are permitted at the campground and in some of the cabins and lodge rooms; pets are not permitted in the other cabins and lodge rooms.

**Reservations, fees:** Reservations are accepted at 541/822-3512 or www.belknaphotsprings. com. Tent sites are $25-30 per night, RV sites are $35 per night, cabins are $130-425, lodge rooms are $100-185, $8-10 per person per night for more than two people, $10-20 one-time pet fee. All fees include access to the hot springs. Some credit cards are accepted. Open year-round.

**Directions:** From Eugene, drive east on Highway 126 for 56 miles to Belknap Springs Road. Turn left and drive 0.5 mile until the road dead-ends at the lodge.

**Contact:** Belknap Hot Springs Resort, 541/822-3512, www.belknaphotsprings.com.

## 16 CAMP YALE

### Scenic rating: 5

on the McKenzie River

**Map 11.1, page 595**

This is the "sister camp" to Belknap Hot Springs, just one mile away, and offers full access to Belknap's pools and gardens. It is surrounded by forest and meadows and offers spectacular views of the Cascade foothills and Frissel Ridge.

**Campsites, facilities:** There are 16 sites with full (110 and 30 amp) hookups for RVs to 65 feet and seven cabins. Picnic tables and fire pits are provided. Drinking water, restrooms with

showers, a coin laundry, and a dump station are available. Some facilities are wheelchair accessible. Leashed pets are permitted.

**Reservations, fees:** Reservations are accepted at 541/822-3512 or www.belknaphotsprings. com. Sites are $25 per night, cabins are $225-325, $8-10 per person per night for more than two people, and a $10-20 one-time pet fee. All fees include access to the hot springs. Some credit cards are accepted. Open year-round.

**Directions:** From Eugene, drive east on Highway 126 for 56 miles to Highway 242. Turn right on Highway 242 and drive 0.5 mile to the campground.

**Contact:** Camp Yale, 541/822-3512, www. belknaphotsprings.com.

## 17 SLIDE CREEK

### Scenic rating: 6

on Cougar Reservoir in Willamette National Forest

**Map 11.1, page 595**

Slide Creek campground sits on a hillside overlooking Cougar Reservoir, which covers about 1,300 acres, has a paved boat landing, and offers opportunities for fishing, swimming, and waterskiing. This pretty lakeside camp at 1,700 feet in elevation is quite popular, so plan to arrive early on weekends. If the camp is full, Cougar Crossing (off Road 19) and Sunnyside (off Road 500) are nearby alternatives.

**Campsites, facilities:** There are eight sites for tents or RVs up to 50 feet long. Picnic tables and fire grills are provided. Drinking water, garbage bins, and vault toilets are available. A boat ramp is also available. Leashed pets are permitted.

**Reservations, fees:** Reservations are accepted at 877/444-6777 ($10 reservation fee) or www.recreation.gov ($9 reservation fee). Single sites are $16 per night, double sites are $30 per night, $8 per night per additional vehicle. Open May-September, weather permitting.

**Directions:** From Eugene, drive east on

Highway 126 for 41 miles to the town of Blue River. Continue east on Highway 126 for five miles to Aufderheide Scenic Byway. Turn right (south) and drive 11 miles (along the west shore of Cougar Reservoir, crossing the reservoir bridge) to Eastside Road (Forest Road 500). Turn left and drive 1.5 miles northeast to the campground set on the southeast shore of the lake.

**Contact:** Willamette National Forest, McKenzie River Ranger District, 541/822-3381, www.fs.usda.gov/willamette.

# 18 FRENCH PETE
🚶 🚴 🏊 🐕 🚐 ⛺

### Scenic rating: 8
on the South Fork of the McKenzie River in Willamette National Forest

**Map 11.1, page 595**

This quiet, wooded campground is set on the banks of the south fork of the McKenzie River and French Pete Creek at 1,800 feet in elevation. Fishing is catch-and-release only. A trail across the road from the campground provides access to the Three Sisters Wilderness (permit required; contact district office). French Pete is only two miles from Cougar Reservoir, and the camp attracts campers wanting to use Cougar Reservoir facilities. Two more primitive camps (Homestead and Frissell Crossing) are located a few miles southeast on the same road.

**Campsites, facilities:** There are 17 sites for tents or RVs up to 40 feet long. Picnic tables, garbage containers, and fire grills are provided. Drinking water, vault toilets, and wastewater disposal are available. Leashed pets are permitted.

**Reservations, fees:** Reservations are not accepted. Sites are $14 per night, $5 per night per additional vehicle. Open May-September, weather permitting.

**Directions:** From Eugene, drive east on Highway 126 for 41 miles to the town of Blue River. Continue east on Highway 126 for five miles to Forest Road 19 (Aufderheide Scenic Byway).

Turn right (south) and drive 12 miles to the campground on the right.

**Contact:** Willamette National Forest, McKenzie River Ranger District, 541/822-3381, www.fs.usda.gov/willamette.

# 19 CAMP SHERMAN
🚶 🏊 🐕 🚐 ⛺

### Scenic rating: 6
on the Metolius River in Deschutes National Forest

**Map 11.2, page 596**

Camp Sherman is set at an elevation of 2,950 feet along the banks of the Metolius River, where you can fish for wild trout. This place is for expert fly anglers seeking a quality fishing experience. Camp Sherman is one of five camps in the immediate area. It's advisable to obtain a map of the Deschutes National Forest that details back roads, streams, and trails.

A personal note: My late pal, John Korb, named his dog Sherman after this camp.

**Campsites, facilities:** There are eight sites for tents or RVs up to 40 feet long and one site for tents only. Picnic tables and fire grills are provided. Drinking water and garbage service is available mid-April-mid-October. Vault toilets and a picnic shelter are available. Leashed pets are permitted.

**Reservations, fees:** Reservations are accepted May through early September at 877/444-6777 ($10 reservation fee) or www.recreation.gov ($9 reservation fee); first-come first-served mid-October through December 31. Sites are $12-30 per night, $8 per night per additional vehicle. Open year-round, weather permitting.

**Directions:** From Albany, drive east on U.S. 20 for 87 miles (near Black Butte) to the sign for Camp Sherman and Forest Road 14. Turn left on Forest Road 14 and drive five miles to Camp Sherman, the store, and Forest Road 900. Turn left on Forest Road 900 and drive 0.5 mile to the campground on the left.

**Contact:** Deschutes National Forest, Sisters

Ranger District, 541/549-7700, www.fs.usda.gov/centraloregon.

## 20 ALLINGHAM

**Scenic rating: 5**

on the Metolius River in Deschutes National Forest

**Map 11.2, page 596**

One of five camps in the immediate area, Allingham sits along the banks of the Metolius River. The river is perfect for trout fishing, and fly anglers will find a quality fishing experience.

**Campsites, facilities:** There are 10 sites for tents or RVs up to 40 feet long. Picnic tables and fire grills are provided. Vault toilets, drinking water, and garbage service are available. A dump station is nearby. Leashed pets are permitted.

**Reservations, fees:** Reservations are not accepted. Sites are $16 per night, $8 per night per additional vehicle. Open May-September, weather permitting.

**Directions:** From Albany, drive east on U.S. 20 for 87 miles (near Black Butte) to the sign for Camp Sherman and Forest Road 14. Turn left on Forest Road 14 and drive five miles to Camp Sherman, the store, and Forest Road 900. Turn left on Forest Road 900 and drive one mile to the campground on the left.

**Contact:** Deschutes National Forest, Sisters Ranger District, 541/549-7700, www.fs.usda.gov/centraloregon.

## 21 HOODOO'S CAMP SHERMAN MOTEL AND RV RESORT

**Scenic rating: 6**

near the Metolius River

**Map 11.2, page 596**

Camp Sherman offers a choice of graveled or grassy sites in a clean, scenic environment. This is a nice spot for bird-watching, fishing, and hiking.

**Campsites, facilities:** There are 15 sites with full or partial hookups for RVs to 45 feet and six motel rooms. Picnic tables and barbecues are provided. Restrooms with flush toilets and showers, a dump station, recreation room, and firewood are available. Propane gas, an additional dump station, a store, café, and ice are within three blocks. Some facilities are wheelchair accessible. Leashed pets are permitted.

**Reservations, fees:** Reservations are accepted. Sites are $26-28 per night, $3 per person per night for more than four people, $7 per additional vehicle (unless towed). Weekly and monthly rates are available. Some credit cards are accepted. Open year-round.

**Directions:** From Albany, drive east on U.S. 20 for 87 miles (near Black Butte) to the sign for Camp Sherman. Turn left (north) on Forest Road 1419 and drive four miles to a stop sign and the resort access road. Turn right and drive 0.25 mile to the park on the right.

**Contact:** Camp Sherman Resort, 541/595-6514, www.campshermanrv.com.

## 22 PINE REST

**Scenic rating: 5**

on the Metolius River in Deschutes National Forest

**Map 11.2, page 596**

Pine Rest campground is set at an elevation of 2,900 feet along the banks of the Metolius River. Fly-fishing and hiking are recreation options.

**Campsites, facilities:** There are eight tent sites. Picnic tables and fire grills are provided. Vault toilets and a picnic shelter are available. There is no drinking water. Garbage service is available in season. Leashed pets are permitted.

**Reservations, fees:** Reservations are not accepted. Sites are $12-16 per night, $6-8 per night per additional vehicle. Open year-round, weather permitting.

**Directions:** From Albany, drive east on U.S. 20 for 87 miles (near Black Butte) to the sign for Camp Sherman and Forest Road 14. Turn left on Forest Road 14 and drive five miles to Camp Sherman, the store, and Forest Road 900. Turn left on Forest Road 900 and drive two miles to the campground on the left.

**Contact:** Deschutes National Forest, Sisters Ranger District, 541/549-7700, www.fs.usda.gov/centraloregon.

# 23 GORGE

### Scenic rating: 5
on the Metolius River in Deschutes National Forest

**Map 11.2, page 596**

Here is another of the camps set along the banks of the Metolius River near Camp Sherman. Gorge campground is located at an elevation of 2,900 feet and is more open, with less vegetation than many of the others. Fly-fishing and hiking trails provide recreation opportunities.

**Campsites, facilities:** There are 18 sites for tents or RVs up to 40 feet long. Picnic tables and fire grills are provided. Vault toilets and garbage service are available. There is no drinking water. Leashed pets are permitted.

**Reservations, fees:** Reservations are not accepted. Sites are $16 per night, $8 per night per additional vehicle. Open May-September, weather permitting.

**Directions:** From Albany, drive east on U.S. 20 for 87 miles (near Black Butte) to the sign for Camp Sherman and Forest Road 14. Turn left on Forest Road 14 and drive five miles to Camp Sherman, the store, and Forest Road 900. Turn left on Forest Road 900 and drive 2.5 miles to the campground on the left.

**Contact:** Deschutes National Forest, Sisters Ranger District, 541/549-7700, www.fs.usda.gov/centraloregon.

# 24 SMILING RIVER

### Scenic rating: 5
on the Metolius River in Deschutes National Forest

**Map 11.2, page 596**

Smiling River sits along the banks of the Metolius River at an elevation of 2,900 feet. Another campground in the popular Camp Sherman area, Smiling River has access to fly-fishing and nearby hiking trails.

**Campsites, facilities:** There are 35 sites for tents or RVs up to 50 feet long. Picnic tables and fire grills are provided. Flush toilets, drinking water, and garbage service are available. Leashed pets are permitted.

**Reservations, fees:** Reservations are accepted at 877/444-6777 ($10 reservation fee) or www.recreation.gov ($9 reservation fee). Sites are $16 per night, $8 per night per additional vehicle. Open May-October, weather permitting.

**Directions:** From Albany, drive east on U.S. 20 for 87 miles (near Black Butte) to the sign for Camp Sherman and Forest Road 14. Turn left on Forest Road 14 and drive five miles to Camp Sherman, the store, and Forest Road 900. Turn left on Forest Road 900 and drive one mile to the campground on the left.

**Contact:** Deschutes National Forest, Sisters Ranger District, 541/549-7700, www.fs.usda.gov/centraloregon.

# 25 ALLEN SPRINGS

### Scenic rating: 7
on the Metolius River in Deschutes National Forest

**Map 11.2, page 596**

Shady Allen Springs campground is nestled in a conifer forest along the banks of the Metolius River, where fishing and hiking can be good. For an interesting side trip, head to the Wizard Falls Fish Hatchery about a mile away.

**Campsites, facilities:** There are 16 sites for

tents or RVs up to 36 feet long. Picnic tables
and fire grills are provided. Vault toilets and
garbage service are available. Water is available
from the river, but must be filtered. A store,
café, and ice are within five miles. Leashed
pets are permitted.
**Reservations, fees:** Reservations are not accepted. Single sites are $12-16 per night, $6-8
per night per additional vehicle. Open April-
October, weather permitting.
**Directions:** From Albany, drive east on U.S.
20 for 87 miles (near Black Butte) to the sign
for Camp Sherman and Forest Road 14. Turn
left on Forest Road 14 and drive about nine
miles to the campground on the left.
**Contact:** Deschutes National Forest, Sisters
Ranger District, 541/549-7700, www.fs.usda.
gov/centraloregon.

## 26 LOWER BRIDGE

**Scenic rating: 6**
on the Metolius River in Deschutes
National Forest

**Map 11.2, page 596**
Lower Bridge campground is set along the
banks of the Metolius River at an elevation of
2,700 feet. The setting is similar to Pioneer
Ford, but with less vegetation. A picnic area
is located across the bridge.
**Campsites, facilities:** There are 12 sites for
tents or RVs up to 30 feet long. Picnic tables
and fire grills are provided. Vault toilets,
drinking water, and garbage service are available. Leashed pets are permitted.
**Reservations, fees:** Reservations are not accepted. Sites are $16 per night, $8 per night
per additional vehicle. Open May-October,
weather permitting.
**Directions:** From Albany, drive east on U.S.
20 for 87 miles (near Black Butte) to the sign
for Camp Sherman and Forest Road 14. Turn
left on Forest Road 14 and drive 12 miles to
the campground on the right.
**Contact:** Deschutes National Forest, Sisters

Ranger District, 541/549-7700, www.fs.usda.
gov/centraloregon.

## 27 PIONEER FORD

**Scenic rating: 7**
on the Metolius River in Deschutes
National Forest

**Map 11.2, page 596**
Quiet and serene Pioneer Ford campground
is set along the banks of the Metolius River
at an elevation of 2,750 feet. The wooded
campground features grassy sites north of the
Camp Sherman area. Hiking and fly-fishing
are activities here.
**Campsites, facilities:** There are 20 sites for
tents or RVs up to 50 feet long. Picnic tables
and fire grills are provided. Drinking water
and garbage service are provided. Vault toilets
are available. Some facilities are wheelchair
accessible. Leashed pets are permitted.
**Reservations, fees:** Reservations are not accepted. Sites are $16 per night, $8 per night
per additional vehicle. Open May-September,
weather permitting.
**Directions:** From Albany, drive east on U.S.
20 for 87 miles (near Black Butte) to the sign
for Camp Sherman and Forest Road 14. Turn
left on Forest Road 14 and drive 11 miles to
the campground on the left.
**Contact:** Deschutes National Forest, Sisters
Ranger District, 541/549-7700, www.fs.usda.
gov/centraloregon.

## 28 COLD SPRINGS RESORT

**Scenic rating: 7**
in Camp Sherman on the Metolius River

**Map 11.2, page 596**
This pretty, wooded RV park on the Metolius
River is world-famous for its fly-fishing and features an acre of riverfront lawn. Bird-watching
is also popular. Recreation options in the area

include boating, swimming, waterskiing, and windsurfing. In addition, nearby facilities include a golf course, hiking and biking trails, a riding stable, and tennis courts. Winter activities vary from alpine and Nordic skiing to sledding, snowmobiling, and winter camping. A private footbridge leads from the resort to Camp Sherman; the towns of Sisters and Bend are nearby (15 miles and 35 miles, respectively).

**Campsites, facilities:** There are 20 sites, some with full hookups, for RVs of any length, eight cottages, and five cabins on the river. Fire pits, picnic tables, and some patios are provided. Restrooms with flush toilets and showers, coin laundry, Wi-Fi, firewood, and a riverfront picnic facility are available. Propane gas, a convenience store, fishing and sport supplies, a café, a post office, and ice are within 0.25 mile. Leashed pets are permitted.

**Reservations, fees:** Reservations are accepted. Sites are $35-40 per night, $5 per person per night for more than two people, and $5 per pet per night. Weekly and monthly rates available. Some credit cards are accepted. Open year-round.

**Directions:** From Albany, drive east on U.S. 20 for 87 miles (near Black Butte) to the sign for Camp Sherman/Metolius River. Turn left (north) on Forest Road 14 and drive 4.5 miles to a stop sign. Turn right (still Forest Road 14) and drive about 300 feet to Cold Springs Resort Lane. Turn right and drive through the forest and the meadow, crossing Cold Springs Creek, to the resort.

**Contact:** Cold Springs Resort, 25615 Cold Springs Resort Lane, Camp Sherman, 541/595-6271 or 541/595-1400, www.cold-springsresort.com.

## 29 RIVERSIDE WALK-IN
🚶 🚲 🛶 🐕 ⛺

### Scenic rating: 7
on the Metolius River in Deschutes National Forest

**Map 11.2, page 596**

Riverside Walk-In is set 100 yards back from the banks of the Metolius River, less than a mile from Metolius Springs at the base of Black Butte. Because this is a tent-only campground, and just far enough off the highway to be missed by most other people, it stays very quiet. You'll find plenty of solitude here. After parking along the road, you must walk to the campsites, carrying any gear in the process.

**Campsites, facilities:** There are 16 tent sites. Picnic tables and fire grills are provided. Vault toilets, garbage service, and drinking water are available. Leashed pets are permitted.

**Reservations, fees:** Reservations are not accepted. Sites are $12 per night, $6 per night per additional vehicle. Open May-September, weather permitting.

**Directions:** From Albany, drive east on U.S. 20 for 87 miles to the sign for Camp Sherman and Forest Road 14. Turn left and drive five miles to Forest Road 800. Turn left and drive a short distance to the campground.

**Contact:** Deschutes National Forest, Sisters Ranger District, 541/549-7700, www.fs.usda.gov/centraloregon.

## 30 HAYSTACK RESERVOIR
🏊 🛶 🛥 🐕 🚐 ⛺

### Scenic rating: 5
on Haystack Reservoir in Crooked River National Grassland

**Map 11.2, page 596**

This campground can be found in the high desert along the shore of Haystack Reservoir, a bright spot in an expansive desert landscape. The camps feature a moderate amount of privacy, as well as views of nearby Mount Jefferson. Haystack Reservoir receives moderate numbers of people who boat, camp, fish, swim, and water ski.

**Campsites, facilities:** There are 24 sites for tents or RVs up to 32 feet long; some sites are pull-through. Picnic tables and fire grills are provided. Vault toilets, drinking water, and covered picnic shelters are available. A store, café, and ice are within five miles. Boat docks and launching facilities are nearby. Leashed pets are permitted.

**Reservations, fees:** Reservations are not accepted. Sites are $13 per night, $6 per night per additional vehicle. Open mid-May-mid-September.

**Directions:** From Madras, drive south on U.S. 97 for nine miles to Jericho Lane. Turn left and drive one mile to County Road 100. Turn right and drive two miles to Forest Road 96. Turn left (north) and drive 0.5 mile to the campground.

**Contact:** Crooked River National Grassland, 541/475-9272 or 541/416-6640, www.fs.usda. gov/centraloregon.

# 31 COLD WATER COVE

### Scenic rating: 10

on Clear Lake in Willamette National Forest

**Map 11.2, page 596**

Cold Water campground sits at 3,000 feet elevation on the south shore of Clear Lake, a spring-fed lake formed by a natural lava dam and the source of the McKenzie River. No motors are permitted on the lake, making it ideal for anglers in rowboats or canoes. The northern section of the McKenzie River National Recreation Trail passes by the camp.

**Campsites, facilities:** There are 35 sites for tents or RVs up to 40 feet long. Picnic tables and fire grills are provided. Vault toilets, drinking water, and garbage service are available. Boat docks, launching facilities, rowboats, a store, a café, and cabin rentals are available nearby at Clear Lake Resort. Some facilities are wheelchair accessible. Leashed pets are permitted.

**Reservations, fees:** Reservations are accepted at 877/444-6777 ($10 reservation fee) or www. recreation.gov ($9 reservation fee). Sites are $18 per night, $34 per night for double sites, $6 per night per additional vehicle. Open mid-May-mid-October, weather permitting.

**Directions:** From Eugene, drive east on

Highway 126 for 47 miles to the town of McKenzie Bridge. Continue on Highway 126 for 14 miles to Forest Road 770. Turn right (east) and drive to the campground.

**Contact:** Willamette National Forest, McKenzie River Ranger District, 541/822-3381, www.fs.usda.gov/willamette.

# 32 ICE CAP CREEK

### Scenic rating: 9

on Carmen Reservoir in Willamette National Forest

**Map 11.2, page 596**

Ice Cap Creek campground is perched at 3,000 feet elevation on a hill above Carmen Reservoir, created by a dam on the McKenzie River. The McKenzie River National Recreation Trail passes by the camp, and Koosah Falls and Sahalie Falls are nearby. Clear Lake, a popular local vacation destination, is two miles away.

**Campsites, facilities:** There are 22 sites for tents or RVs up to 50 feet long; eight sites are walk-in. Picnic tables and fire grills are provided. Vault toilets and garbage service are available. There is no drinking water. Boat-launching facilities and boat rentals are two miles away at Clear Lake Resort. Only non-motorized boats are allowed on Carmen Reservoir. Leashed pets are permitted.

**Reservations, fees:** Reservations are not accepted. Sites are $14 per night, $6 per night per additional vehicle. Open mid-May-September, weather permitting.

**Directions:** From Eugene, drive east on Highway 126 for 47 miles to the town of McKenzie Bridge. Continue east on Highway 126 for 17.3 miles to the campground entrance road on the left. Turn left and drive 200 yards to the campground.

**Contact:** Willamette National Forest, McKenzie River Ranger District, 541/822-3381, www.fs.usda.gov/willamette; Clear Lake Resort 541/967-5030.

## 33 BIG LAKE

Scenic rating: 9

on Big Lake in Willamette National Forest

**Map 11.2, page 596**

This jewel of a spot on the north shore of Big Lake at 4,650 feet elevation offers a host of activities, including fishing, hiking, swimming, and waterskiing. Big Lake has heavy motorized boat use. One of the better hikes is the five-mile wilderness loop trail (Patjens Lakes Trail) that heads out from the south shore of the lake and cuts past a few small lakes before returning. There's a great view of Mount Washington from the lake. The Pacific Crest Trail is only 0.5 mile away.

**Campsites, facilities:** There are 49 sites for tents or RVs up to 35 feet long. Picnic tables and fire grills are provided. Drinking water, vault and flush toilets, and garbage service are available. Boat ramps are nearby. Some facilities are wheelchair accessible. Leashed pets are permitted.

**Reservations, fees:** Reservations are accepted at 877/444-6777 ($10 reservation fee) or www.recreation.gov ($9 reservation fee). Sites are $20 per night, $6 per night per additional vehicle. Open late May-mid-October, weather permitting.

**Directions:** From Eugene, drive east on Highway 126 for 47 miles to the town of McKenzie Bridge. Continue northeast on Highway 126 for 29.5 miles to Big Lake Road (Forest Road 2690). Turn right and drive 4.3 miles to the campground on the left.

**Contact:** Willamette National Forest, McKenzie River Ranger District, 541/822-3381, www.fs.usda.gov/willamette.

## 34 BIG LAKE WEST WALK-IN

Scenic rating: 9

on Big Lake in Willamette National Forest

**Map 11.2, page 596**

This spot, located west of the Big Lake Campground at an elevation of 4,650 feet, has many of the same attractions, but the walk-in sites offer some seclusion and quiet. The Mount Washington Wilderness and Patjens Lake access trails can be reached from here.

**Campsites, facilities:** There are 11 walk-in sites 200 feet from the road. Picnic tables and fire pits are provided. Vault toilets and garbage service are available. Drinking water is available in adjacent Big Lake Campground.

**Reservations, fees:** Reservations are accepted at 877/444-6777 ($10 reservation fee) or www.recreation.gov ($9 reservation fee). Single sites are $20 per night, double sites are $35 per night, $6 per night per additional vehicle. Open late May-early October, weather permitting.

**Directions:** From Eugene, drive east on Highway 126 for 47 miles to the town of McKenzie Bridge. Continue northeast on Highway 126 for 40 miles to Big Lake Road (Forest Road 2690). Turn right and drive four miles to the campground entrance on the left.

**Contact:** Willamette National Forest, McKenzie River Ranger District, 541/822-3381, www.fs.usda.gov/willamette.

## 35 SOUTH SHORE

Scenic rating: 6

on Suttle Lake in Deschutes National Forest

**Map 11.2, page 596**

This campground is at 3,500 feet elevation on the south shore of Suttle Lake, where waterskiing is permitted. A hiking trail winds around the lake and other popular activities include fishing and windsurfing. The camp often fills up on weekends and holidays, so reserve early.

**Campsites, facilities:** There are 38 sites for tents or RVs up to 50 feet long. Picnic tables and fire grills are provided. Vault toilets, drinking water, and garbage service are available. A fish-cleaning station, boat docks, launching facilities, and rentals are nearby. Leashed pets are permitted.

**Reservations, fees:** Reservations are accepted at 877/444-6777 ($10 reservation fee) or www.recreation.gov ($9 reservation fee). Single sites are $16 per night, double sites are $30 per night, $8 per night per additional vehicle. Open May-September, weather permitting.

**Directions:** From Albany, drive east on U.S. 20 to the junction with Highway 126. Continue east on Highway 126 for 12 miles to Forest Road 2070 (Suttle Lake). Turn right and proceed a short distance to the campground.

**Contact:** Deschutes National Forest, Sisters Ranger District, 541/549-7700, www.fs.usda.gov/centraloregon.

## 36 LINK CREEK

**Scenic rating: 6**

on Suttle Lake in Deschutes National Forest

Map 11.2, page 596

Link Creek campground is set at the west end of Suttle Lake at an elevation of 3,450 feet. The high-speed boating area is located on this end of the lake, making it a popular spot with water-skiers. Other activities include fishing, swimming, and windsurfing.

**Campsites, facilities:** There are 30 sites for tents or RVs up to 50 feet long, two double sites, and three yurts with bunk beds, a double-size futon, and a wood stove. Picnic tables and fire grills are provided. Vault toilets, drinking water, and garbage service are available. Boat docks, launching facilities, and rentals are nearby. Leashed pets are permitted.

**Reservations, fees:** Reservations are accepted for the yurts and some sites at 877/444-6777 ($10 reservation fee) or www.recreation.gov ($9 reservation fee). Single sites are $16 per night, double sites are $30 per night, yurts are $40 per night, $8 per night per additional vehicle. Open April-mid-October, weather permitting.

**Directions:** From Albany, drive east on U.S. 20 for 74 miles to the junction of U.S. 20 and Highway 126. Continue east on Highway 126 for 12 miles to Forest Road 2070 (Suttle Lake). Turn right and drive a short distance to the campground.

**Contact:** Deschutes National Forest, Sisters Ranger District, 541/549-7700, www.fs.usda.gov/centraloregon.

## 37 BLUE BAY

**Scenic rating: 7**

on Suttle Lake in Deschutes National Forest

Map 11.2, page 596

Blue Bay campground is situated along the south shore of Suttle Lake at an elevation of 3,450 feet. It's a quieter campground at the low-speed end of the lake, and with more tree cover than South Shore or Link Creek. Recreation activities include fishing, boating, and hiking.

**Campsites, facilities:** There are 21 single sites and three double sites for tents or RVs up to 50 feet long. Picnic tables and fire grills are provided. Vault toilets, drinking water, and garbage service are available. A fish-cleaning station, boat docks, launching facilities, and rentals are nearby. Leashed pets are permitted.

**Reservations, fees:** Reservations are accepted at 877/444-6777 ($10 reservation fee) or www.recreation.gov ($9 reservation fee). Single sites are $16 per night, double sites are $30 per night, $8 per night per additional vehicle. Open May-mid-September, weather permitting.

**Directions:** From Albany, drive east on U.S. 20 for 74 miles to the junction of U.S. 20 and Highway 126. Continue east on Highway 126 for 12 miles to Forest Road 2070 (Suttle Lake). Turn right and drive a short distance to the campground.

**Contact:** Deschutes National Forest, Sisters Ranger District, 541/549-7700, www.fs.usda.gov/centraloregon.

## 38 SCOUT LAKE GROUP

🚶‍ 🚵 🏊 🐕 🚐 ⛺

### Scenic rating: 5

on Scout Lake in Deschutes National Forest

**Map 11.2, page 596**

Scout Lake is a group campground, with a mix of sunny and shady sites, at an elevation of 3,600 feet. The camp lies about 0.5 mile from Suttle Lake and is a good spot for swimming and hiking.

**Campsites, facilities:** There are 10 sites (single, double, and triple) for tents or RVs up to 40 feet long. The entire campground can accommodate up to 100 people. Picnic tables and fire grills are provided. Vault toilets, drinking water, garbage service, a picnic shelter, a volleyball court, and horseshoe pits are available. Leashed pets are permitted in the campground only (not in the day-use area) or in the lake.

**Reservations, fees:** Reservations are accepted at 877/444-6777 ($10 reservation fee) or www.recreation.gov ($9 reservation fee). Single sites are $16 per night, double sites are $30 per night, the triple site is $40 per night, $8 per night per additional vehicle. Open May-September, weather permitting.

**Directions:** From Eugene, drive east on Highway 126 for 74 miles to the junction of U.S. 20 and Highway 126. Continue east on Highway 126 for 12 miles to Forest Road 2070 (Suttle Lake). Turn right and drive to Forest Road 2066. Turn left and drive less than one mile to the campground.

**Contact:** Deschutes National Forest, Sisters Ranger District, 541/549-7700, www.fs.usda. gov/centraloregon.

## 39 BEND/SISTERS GARDEN RV RESORT

🚵 🏊 🎣 🐕 ♿ 🚿 🚐

### Scenic rating: 7

on Branchwater Lake

**Map 11.2, page 596**

This park is located amid wooded mountains outside of Sisters at an elevation of 3,200 feet. Branchwater Lake, a three-acre lake at the campground, offers good trout fishing. (For hiking opportunities, explore the McKenzie River Trail or the Three Sisters and Mount Washington Wilderness Areas (west of Sisters on Highway 242). The Pacific Crest Trail runs north and south through both wilderness areas.

**Campsites, facilities:** There are 96 sites for RVs of any length (full hookups); many sites are pull-through. There are also three cabins and one luxury park model. Picnic tables and fire rings are provided. Drinking water, restrooms with showers, a dump station, coin laundry, barbecue patio, Wi-Fi, video library, dog run, volleyball, badminton, miniature golf, convenience store, ice, RV supplies, and propane gas are available. Recreational facilities include a playground, horseshoes, a spa, and a seasonal heated swimming pool. Some facilities are wheelchair accessible. Leashed pets are permitted.

**Reservations, fees:** Reservations are accepted at 888/503-3588. Sites are $32-48 per night, $2-6 per person per night for more than two people, and $2 per night per additional vehicle. Weekly and monthly rates available. Some credit cards are accepted. Open year-round, weather permitting.

**Directions:** From Eugene, drive east on Highway 126 to its junction with U.S. 20. Turn east on U.S. 20 and drive 26 miles to Sisters. Continue southeast on U.S. 20 for three miles to the park on the right side of the highway.

**Contact:** Bend/Sisters Garden, 541/516-3036 or 888/503-3588, www.bendsistersgardenrv. com.

## 40 CROOKED RIVER RANCH RV PARK

🚵 🏊 🎣 🚐 🐕 ♿ 🚐 ⛺

### Scenic rating: 6

near Smith Rock State Park

**Map 11.2, page 596**     **BEST (**

Crooked River Ranch is a short distance from

Smith Rock State Park, which contains unusual, colorful volcanic formations overlooking the Crooked River Canyon. Spectacular wildlife abounds in this area. Lake Billy Chinook to the north is a good spot for waterskiing and fishing for bass and panfish. The park has a basketball court and a softball field, and seasonal horseback riding is available. Nearby recreation options include fishing, golf, and tennis; one of Oregon's nicest golf courses is nearby.

**Campsites, facilities:** There are 90 sites with full or partial hookups for RVs of any length (some pull-through) and 20 tent sites. Picnic tables are provided. No open fires are allowed; propane is permitted. Restrooms with flush toilets and coin showers, a dump station, cable TV, Wi-Fi, a convenience store, coin laundry, ice, a covered picnic shelter, playground, horseshoe pits, basketball, pickleball, a tennis court, and a seasonal swimming pool are available. A café is nearby. Some facilities are wheelchair accessible. Leashed pets are permitted, with certain restrictions.

**Reservations, fees:** Reservations are accepted at 800/841-0563. RV sites are $40 per night; tent sites are $28 per night, additional tents are $10 per night. Some credit cards are accepted. Open mid-March-October, weather permitting.

**Directions:** From Redmond, drive north on U.S. 97 for six miles to Terrebonne and Lower Bridge Road. Turn left (west) on Lower Bridge Road and drive approximately two miles to 43rd Street. Turn right and drive two miles to a T-intersection with Chinook. Turn left on Chinook and drive approximately 4.5 miles (becomes Clubhouse Road, then Hays Road) to the ranch on the right.

**Contact:** Crooked River Ranch RV Park, 541/923-1441 or 800/841-0563, www.crookedriverranch.com.

## 41 INDIAN FORD

🐕 🚐 ⛺

### Scenic rating: 4

on Indian Ford Creek in Deschutes National Forest

**Map 11.2, page 596**

This campground sits on the banks of Indian Ford Creek at an elevation of 3,250 feet. Used primarily by overnighters on their way to the town of Sisters, the camp is subject to a lot of traffic noise from U.S. 20. The grounds are sprinkled with aspen trees, and great birdwatching opportunities are available.

**Campsites, facilities:** There are 25 sites for tents or RVs up to 50 feet long. Picnic tables, garbage service, and fire grills are provided. Vault toilets are available. There is no drinking water. Leashed pets are permitted.

**Reservations, fees:** Reservations are not accepted. Sites are $12 per night, $6 per night per additional vehicle. Open May-mid-October, weather permitting.

**Directions:** From Albany, drive east on U.S. 20 to the junction with Highway 126. Continue east on Highway 126 and drive 21 miles to the campground on the left.

**Contact:** Deschutes National Forest, Sisters Ranger District, 541/549-7700, www.fs.usda.gov/centraloregon.

## 42 COLD SPRINGS

🐕 🚐 ⛺

### Scenic rating: 7

in Deschutes National Forest

**Map 11.2, page 596**

Wooded Cold Springs campground is set at 3,400 feet elevation at the source of a small seasonal creek. It's just far enough off the main drag to be missed by many campers. Spring and early summer are the times to come for great bird-watching in the area's abundant aspen trees.

**Campsites, facilities:** There are 22 sites for tents or RVs up to 50 feet long. Picnic tables, fire grills, and garbage service are provided. Vault toilets and drinking water are available. Leashed pets are permitted.

**Reservations, fees:** Reservations are not accepted. Sites are $14 per night, $7 per night per additional vehicle. Open May-October, weather permitting.

**Directions:** From Albany, drive east on U.S. 20 to the junction with Highway 126. Continue east on Highway 126 and drive 26 miles to Sisters and Highway 242. Turn right and drive 4.2 miles to the campground on the right.

**Contact:** Deschutes National Forest, Sisters Ranger District, 541/549-7700, www.fs.usda. gov/centraloregon.

## 43 SCOTT LAKE WALK-IN

### Scenic rating: 10
on Scott Lake in Willamette National Forest

**Map 11.2, page 596**     **BEST (**

Scott Lake Walk-In offers hike-in sites just over 0.1 mile from the road. The campground borders Scott Lake at an elevation of 4,680 feet; only non-motorized boats are allowed on the lake. Trails leading out of the camp provide access to several small lakes in the Mount Washington Wilderness, and there are great views of the Three Sisters Mountains. Be forewarned: Mosquitoes are heavy during the spring and early summer.

**Campsites, facilities:** There are 18 walk-in tent sites. Picnic tables and fire rings are provided. Vault toilets are available. There is no drinking water, and garbage must be packed out. Leashed pets are permitted.

**Reservations, fees:** Reservations are not accepted. Sites are $5 per night per vehicle. Open July-October, weather permitting.

**Directions:** From Eugene, drive east on Highway 126 for 54 miles to the junction with Highway 242 (part of the Santiam Scenic Byway). Turn right (east) on Highway 242 and drive 14.5 miles to Forest Road 260. Turn left and drive to the campground.

Note: Highway 242 is spectacularly scenic, but it's also very narrow, winding, and steep; it is not recommended for RVs or trailers. The maximum vehicle length is 35 feet.

**Contact:** Willamette National Forest, McKenzie River Ranger District, 541/822-3381, www.fs.usda.gov/willamette.

## 44 LAVA CAMP LAKE

### Scenic rating: 4
near the Pacific Crest Trail in Deschutes National Forest

**Map 11.2, page 596**

Lava campground sits at an elevation of 5,300 feet among subalpine fir in the McKenzie Pass. It's not far from the Pacific Crest Trail, and a number of other trails provide additional hiking possibilities. Fishing is allowed, but don't expect to catch anything—perhaps that is why this campground gets such light use!

**Campsites, facilities:** There are 10 sites for tents or RVs up to 20 feet long. Picnic tables and fire grills are provided. Vault toilets are available. There is no drinking water and garbage must be packed out. Leashed pets are permitted.

**Reservations, fees:** Reservations are not accepted. There is no fee for camping. Open June-October, weather permitting.

**Directions:** From Eugene, drive east on Highway 126 for 47 miles to the town of McKenzie Bridge. Continue east on Highway 126 for five miles to Highway 242. Turn right (east) and drive 14.6 miles on Highway 242 to the campground entrance on the right. Note: Highway 242 is spectacularly scenic, but also very narrow, winding, and steep. RVs and trailers are strictly held to a 35-foot length limit.

**Contact:** Deschutes National Forest, Sisters Ranger District, 541/549-7700, www.fs.usda. gov/centraloregon.

## 45 WHISPERING PINE HORSE CAMP

### Scenic rating: 5

near the Trout Creek Swamp in Deschutes National Forest

**Map 11.2, page 596**

This wooded campground (elevation 4,400 feet) near Trout Creek Swamp is pretty, isolated, and private. Although generally not crowded, it's set up as a horse camp with corrals and is gaining in popularity; groups of horse users occasionally fill it up. Hikers, beware: You'll be sharing the trails with horses.

**Campsites, facilities:** There are nine primitive sites for tents or RVs up to 30 feet long and 36 individual box stalls. Picnic tables and fire grills are provided. Vault toilets and garbage service are available. There is stock water but no drinking water. Leashed pets are permitted.

**Reservations, fees:** Reservations are not accepted. Sites are $16 per night, $8 per night per additional vehicle. Open May-October, weather permitting.

**Directions:** From Albany, drive east on U.S. 20 to the junction with U.S. 126. Turn east on U.S. 126 and drive for 26 miles to Sisters and Highway 142. Turn right (east) and drive six miles on Highway 242 to Forest Road 1018. Turn left and drive four miles to the campground entrance. Note: Highway 242 is spectacularly scenic, but also very narrow, winding, and steep. RVs and trailers are discouraged (a 35-foot length limit is in effect).

**Contact:** Deschutes National Forest, Sisters Ranger District, 541/549-7700, www.fs.usda. gov/centraloregon.

## 46 LIMBERLOST

### Scenic rating: 9

on Lost Creek in Willamette National Forest

**Map 11.2, page 596**

Limberlost is a secluded campground set at 1,800 feet elevation along Lost Creek, about two miles from where it empties into the McKenzie River. Relatively unknown, the camp gets light use; it makes a good base camp for a trout-fishing trip.

**Campsites, facilities:** There are 12 sites for tents or RVs up to 16 feet long. Picnic tables, garbage service, and fire grills are provided. Vault toilets are available, but there is no drinking water. Some facilities are wheelchair accessible. Leashed pets are permitted.

**Reservations, fees:** Reservations are not accepted. Sites are $12 per night, $6 per night per additional vehicle. Open May-September, weather permitting.

**Directions:** From Eugene, drive east on Highway 126 for 47 miles to the town of McKenzie Bridge. Continue east on Highway 126 for five miles to Highway 242. Turn right (east) and drive 1.5 miles on Highway 242 to the camp. Note: Highway 242 is spectacularly scenic, but also very narrow, winding, and steep. RVs and trailers are discouraged (a 35-foot length limit is in effect). Highway 242 is closed in winter due to snow; check to make sure it's open if you are planning a trip in early or mid-spring.

**Contact:** Willamette National Forest, McKenzie River Ranger District, 541/822-3381, www.fs.usda.gov/willamette.

## 47 ALDER SPRINGS

### Scenic rating: 7

in Willamette National Forest

**Map 11.2, page 596**

Remote Alder Springs campground sits at 3,600 feet elevation in the Willamette Forest. The camp features good hiking possibilities, including access to the Linton Lake Trail, a three-mile hike that leads to Linton Lake... and fishing. The Three Sisters Wilderness is just south of the highway.

**Campsites, facilities:** There are six tent sites. Picnic tables and fire grills are provided. Vault toilets are available. No drinking water is available, and garbage must be packed out. Some facilities are wheelchair accessible. Leashed pets are permitted.

**Reservations, fees:** Reservations are not accepted. There is no fee for camping. Open June-September, weather permitting.

**Directions:** From Eugene, drive east on Highway 126 for 47 miles to the town of McKenzie Bridge. Continue east on Highway 126 for five miles to Highway 242. Turn right (east) and drive 10 miles on Highway 242 to the campground on the left. Note: Highway 242 is spectacularly scenic, but also very narrow, winding, and steep; the road is closed during snow season and is often impassable until late spring. RVs and trailers are discouraged (a 35-foot length limit is in effect).

**Contact:** Willamette National Forest, McKenzie River Ranger District, 541/822-3381, www.fs.usda.gov/willamette.

## 48 DRIFTWOOD

### Scenic rating: 9

on Three Creek Lake in Deschutes National Forest

**Map 11.2, page 596**       BEST (

This wooded campground, at 6,600 feet elevation, is often blocked by snowdrifts until early July. At this high elevation, the views of Tam McArthur Rim are spectacular. Although located on the lakeshore and hidden from outsiders, the area can get very crowded, and the campground is full most weekends from the Fourth of July through Labor Day. Some recreation options include boating (non-motorized only), fishing, hiking, and swimming.

**Campsites, facilities:** There are six sites for tents and RVs up to 40 feet long and 12 sites for tents only. Picnic tables and fire grills are provided. Vault toilets and garbage service are available. There is no drinking water. There is a small store open during the summer months. Leashed pets are permitted.

**Reservations, fees:** Reservations are not accepted. Sites are $14 per night, $7 per night per additional vehicle. Open June-October, weather permitting.

**Directions:** From Eugene, drive east on Highway 126 to its junction with U.S. 20. Turn east and drive 26 miles to Sisters and Forest Road 16. Turn right and drive 16.4 miles to the campground.

**Contact:** Deschutes National Forest, Sisters Ranger District, 541/549-7700, www.fs.usda.gov/centraloregon.

## 49 THREE CREEK LAKE AND THREE CREEK MEADOW HORSE CAMP

### Scenic rating: 8

on Three Creek Lake in Deschutes National Forest

**Map 11.2, page 596**

Three Creek Lake is in a pretty spot at 6,600 feet elevation; this forested campground lies along the south shore of its namesake lake. Boating (non-motorized only), fishing, hiking, swimming and horseback riding are the highlights. The camping area consists of two separate campgrounds; one campground is designed to accommodate campers who need to corral their stock animals. The Three Creek area has a beautiful view of the stretch from Sisters to Bend, as well as the Three Sisters Wilderness above it. Camping in the meadow is prohibited.

**Campsites, facilities:** There are 11 sites for tents or RVs up to 20 feet long, as well as nine equestrian sites with four corrals each, which can accommodate RVs and trailers of any size. Picnic tables and fire grills are provided. Vault toilets and garbage service are available. There is no drinking water. Leashed pets are permitted.

**Reservations, fees:** Reservations are not accepted. Sites are $14 per night, $7 per night per additional vehicle. Open June-October, weather permitting.

**Directions:** From Eugene, drive east on Highway 126 to its junction with Highway 20. Turn east and drive 26 miles to Sisters and Forest Road 16. Turn right and drive 17 miles to the campground.

**Contact:** Deschutes National Forest, Sisters Ranger District, 541/549-7700, www.fs.usda.gov/centraloregon or www.hoodoo.com.

## 50 TUMALO STATE PARK

### Scenic rating: 7
on the Deschutes River

**Map 11.2, page 596**

Tumalo State Park sits along the banks of the Deschutes River, just four miles from Bend. Trout fishing can be good, and bird-watching is popular. The swimming area is generally safe and a good spot for children. Rafting is also an option here. Mount Bachelor is just up the road and provides plenty of winter recreation opportunities.

**Campsites, facilities:** There are 54 sites for tents or self-contained RVs, 23 sites with full hookups for RVs up to 44 feet long, a hiker/bicyclist area, seven yurts, and two group tent areas for up to 25 people each. Drinking water, fire grills, and picnic tables are provided. Restrooms with flush toilets and showers, firewood, and a playground are available. A store, café, and ice are within one mile. Some facilities are wheelchair accessible. Leashed pets are permitted.

**Reservations, fees:** Reservations are accepted at 800/452-5687 or www.reserveamerica.com ($8 reservation fee). RV sites are $22-26 per night, tent sites are $16-21, $5 per person per night for hikers/bikers, $39 per night for yurts, $54-76 per night for the group areas, and $5 per night per additional vehicle. Some credit cards are accepted. Open year-round.

**Directions:** From Bend, drive north on U.S. 97 for two miles to U.S. 20 West. Turn west and drive five miles to Tumalo Junction. Turn left at Tumalo Junction onto Cook Avenue (the

road becomes O. B. Riley), and drive one mile to the campground.

**Contact:** High Desert Management Unit, Oregon State Parks, 541/388-6055 or 800/551-6949, www.oregonstateparks.org.

## 51 SCANDIA RV PARK

### Scenic rating: 5
near the Deschutes River

**Map 11.2, page 596**

This in-town park near the Deschutes River is close to bike paths, a golf course, a stable, and tennis courts.

**Campsites, facilities:** There are 97 sites for tents or RVs of any length (full hookups); some are pull-through sites. Picnic tables are provided. Restrooms with flush toilets and showers, Wi-Fi, cable TV, a picnic area, and a coin laundry are available. Propane gas, a dump station, store, café, and ice are within one mile. Some facilities are wheelchair accessible. Leashed pets are permitted.

**Reservations, fees:** Reservations are recommended. Sites are $38-44 per night, plus $2.20 per person per night for more than four people. Some credit cards are accepted. Open year-round.

**Directions:** In Bend, drive south on Business U.S. 97 (3rd Street) for 0.5 mile to the park entrance on the right.

**Contact:** Scandia RV and Mobile Park, 541/382-6206, www.scandiarv.com.

## 52 CROWN VILLA RV RESORT

### Scenic rating: 6
near Bend

**Map 11.2, page 596**

This RV park offers large and landscaped grassy sites. Nearby recreation options include horseback riding and golf.

**Campsites, facilities:** There are 106 sites with full hookups for RVs of any length; some sites are pull-through. Picnic tables are provided. Restrooms with flush toilets and showers, cable TV, Wi-Fi, clubhouse, spa, a coin laundry, tennis court, pickleball, shuffleboard, horseshoes, a bistro, propane gas, and ice are available. A store and a café are within one mile. Some facilities are wheelchair accessible. Leashed pets are permitted.

**Reservations, fees:** Reservations are accepted at 866/500-5300. Sites are $36-80 per night, $3 per person per night for more than four people. Weekly and monthly rates available. Some credit cards are accepted. Open year-round.

**Directions:** From Bend, drive south on Business U.S. 97 (3rd Street) for two miles to Brosterhous Road. Turn left (east) and drive approximately one mile to a T intersection. Bear right to stay on Brosterhous Road. Continue about one mile to the park on the right.

**Contact:** Crown Villa RV Resort, 541/388-1131, www.crownvillarvresort.com.

## 53 WHITTAKER CREEK

**Scenic rating: 7**

near the Siuslaw River

**Map 11.3, page 597**

Whittaker Creek campground is home to one of the area's premier salmon spawning grounds, where annual runs of chinook, coho salmon, and steelhead can be viewed. Fishing is not allowed in Whitaker Creek. The (Whitaker Creek) Old Growth Ridge Trail, a national recreation trail, is accessible from the campground. This moderately difficult trail ascends 1,000 feet above the Siuslaw River through a stand of old-growth Douglas fir.

**Campsites, facilities:** There are 31 sites for tents or RVs up to 32 feet long. Picnic tables and fire rings are provided. Drinking water, vault toilets, garbage bins, a boat ramp, swimming beach, playground, horseshoe pits, and

picnic shelter are available. A camp host is onsite. Some facilities are wheelchair accessible. Leashed pets are permitted.

**Reservations, fees:** Reservations are not accepted. Sites are $10 per night, $5 per night for each additional vehicle. Open mid-May-September, weather permitting.

**Directions:** From Eugene, drive west on Highway 126 for 33 miles to Siuslaw River Road. Turn left (south) and drive two miles to the first junction. Turn right and drive a short distance across Siuslaw River to the campground on the right.

**Contact:** Bureau of Land Management, Eugene District Office, 541/683-6606 or 888/442-3061, www.blm.gov/or/districts/eugene.

## 54 CLAY CREEK

**Scenic rating: 7**

near the Siuslaw River

**Map 11.3, page 597**

This campground gets a medium amount of use. Sites are situated in a forest of cedar, Douglas fir, and maple trees. Clay Creek Trail, a two-mile loop, takes you to a ridge overlooking the river valley and is well worth the walk. Fishing for trout and crayfish is popular.

**Campsites, facilities:** There are 21 sites for tents or RVs up to 32 feet long. Picnic tables and fire pits are provided. Drinking water, vault toilets, garbage bins, a swimming beach with changing rooms, a softball field, volleyball area, horseshoe pits, and two group picnic shelters with fireplaces are available. There is a camp host. Some facilities are wheelchair accessible. Leashed pets are permitted.

**Reservations, fees:** Reservations are not accepted. Sites are $10 per night, $5 per night for each additional vehicle. Open May-November, weather permitting.

**Directions:** From Eugene, drive west on Highway 126 for 33 miles to Siuslaw River Road. Turn left (south) and drive 16 miles to BLM Road 19-7-2001 (signed for Clay Creek). Turn right and drive a short distance to the campground on the right.

**Contact:** Bureau of Land Management, Eugene District Office, 541/683-6606 or 888/442-3061, www.blm.gov/or/districts/eugene.

## 55 PASS CREEK COUNTY PARK

### Scenic rating: 7

near Cottage Grove

Map 11.3, page 597

Pass Creek provides a decent layover spot for travelers on I-5. Situated in a wooded, hilly area, the camp features many shaded sites, and mountain views give the park scenic value. There is a covered pavilion and gazebo with barbecue grills for get-togethers. A bonus is the fishing pond with bluegill, crappie, and largemouth bass. There are no other campgrounds in the immediate area, so if it's late and you need a place to stay, grab this one.

**Campsites, facilities:** There is a grassy area for tents and 30 sites with full hookups (50 amp) for RVs up to 45 feet long. Picnic tables and fire rings or barbecues are provided. Drinking water, restrooms with flush toilets and showers, a coin laundry, and a playground are available. A store and ice are within one mile. Some facilities are wheelchair accessible. Leashed pets are permitted.

**Reservations, fees:** Reservations are accepted ($10 reservation fee) at 541/957-7001 or www.co.douglas.or.us. Sites are $15-23 per night, $3 per night for an additional vehicle unless towed. Discount available for Douglas County residents. Credit/debit cards are not accepted at the campground but may be used to make reservations. Open year-round.

**Directions:** On I-5, drive to Exit 163 (between Roseburg and Eugene). Take Exit 163 and turn west on Curtin Park Road. Drive west (under the freeway) for a very short distance to the park entrance.

**Contact:** Pass Creek County Park, 541/942-3281, www.co.douglas.or.us.

## 56 PINE MEADOWS

### Scenic rating: 6

on Cottage Grove Reservoir

Map 11.3, page 597

Pine Meadows campground is surrounded by a varied landscape of forest, grassland, and marsh near the banks of Cottage Grove Reservoir. Campsites are within 200 feet of the water. Boating, fishing, swimming, and waterskiing are among the recreation options. It's an easy hop from I-5.

**Campsites, facilities:** There are 92 sites for tents or RVs of any length, with some pull-through sites. There are also 15 primitive sites for tents or small, self-contained RVs. Picnic tables and fire rings are provided. Drinking water, restrooms with flush toilets and showers, a dump station, garbage bins, a children's play area, an amphitheater, and a swimming area are available. A boat dock and launching facilities are nearby. Some facilities are wheelchair accessible. Leashed pets are permitted.

**Reservations, fees:** Reservations are accepted at 877/444-6777 ($10 reservation fee) or www.recreation.gov ($9 reservation fee). Sites are $12-18 per night, $6 per night for an additional vehicle. Primitive campers must have a permit, obtained at the entrance booth. Open mid-May-mid-September.

**Directions:** From Eugene, drive south on I-5 past Cottage Grove to Exit 172. Take that exit to London Road and drive south for 4.5 miles to Reservoir Road. Turn left and drive three miles to the camp entrance on the right.

**Contact:** U.S. Army Corps of Engineers, Recreation Information, Cottage Grove, 541/942-8657 or 541/942-5631, www.nwp.usace.army.mil.

## 57 WHISTLER'S BEND PARK

### Scenic rating: 7

on the North Umpqua River

**Map 11.3, page 597**

This 175-acre county park along the banks of the North Umpqua River is an idyllic spot because it gets little pressure from outsiders, yet it is just a 20-minute drive from I-5. Two boat ramps accommodate boaters, and fishing is a plus. A wildlife reserve provides habitat for deer.

**Campsites, facilities:** There are 23 sites for tents or RVs up to 35 feet long (no hookups) and two yurts. Two group camps are available. Picnic tables and fire rings are provided. Drinking water, restrooms with flush toilets and showers, a playground, disc golf, and launching facilities are available. Some facilities are wheelchair accessible. Leashed pets are permitted.

**Reservations, fees:** Reservations are accepted at 541/957-7001 ($10 reservation fee) or www.co.douglas.or.us. Single sites are $15 per night, $3 per night per additional vehicle, $35 per night for yurts, $50 per night for the group camp for up to 50 people, $100 per night for the group camp for up to 100 people. Discount available for Douglas County residents. Credit/debit cards are not accepted at the campground, but may be used to make reservations. Individual sites are open April-November; group sites and the yurts are open year-round.

**Directions:** From Roseburg, drive east on Highway 138 for 12 miles to Whistler's Bend Park Road (well signed). Turn left and drive two miles to the end of the road and the park entrance.

**Contact:** Whistler's Bend Park, 541/673-4863, www.co.douglas.or.us.

## 58 AMACHER PARK

### Scenic rating: 5

on the Umpqua River

**Map 11.3, page 597**

A wooded Douglas County park set along the banks of the North Umpqua River, Amacher is a prime layover spot for I-5 RV cruisers. This park has one of the few myrtlewood groves in the country. Tent sites are located underneath the freeway next to the railroad tracks; trains come by intermittently. An 18-hole golf course and tennis courts are close by, riding stables are within a 20-minute drive, and Winchester Dam is within 0.25 mile.

**Campsites, facilities:** There are 10 sites for self-contained RVs and 20 sites with full or partial hookups for RVs up to 30 feet long (12-foot height limit). Picnic tables and fire rings are provided. Drinking water, restrooms with flush toilets and showers, a gazebo, and a picnic area are available. Propane gas, a store, café, coin laundry, and ice are within one mile. Boat-launching facilities are available. Some facilities are wheelchair accessible. Leashed pets are permitted.

**Reservations, fees:** Reservations are accepted ($10 reservation fee) at 541/957-7001 or www.co.douglas.or.us. Sites are $15-23 per night, $3 per night per additional vehicle. Credit/debit cards are not accepted at the campground but may be used to make reservations. Open year-round.

**Directions:** From Roseburg, drive five miles north on I-5 to Exit 129. Take that exit and drive south on Old Highway 99 for 0.25 mile to the park on the right (just across Winchester Bridge).

**Contact:** Amacher Park, 541/672-4901; Douglas County, 541/672-4901, www.co.douglas.or.us.

## 59 TWIN RIVERS VACATION PARK

### Scenic rating: 6

near the Umpqua River

**Map 11.3, page 597**

This wooded campground is near the Umpqua River. It features large, shaded pull-through sites and more than 100 kinds of trees on the property. Groups are welcome and clubhouses are available for group use. Nearby recreation options include bike paths, a county park, and a golf course.

**Campsites, facilities:** There are 82 sites with full or partial hookups for RVs of any length; many are pull-through sites. Picnic tables and fire pits are provided. Restrooms with flush toilets and showers, cable TV, propane gas, firewood, a convenience store, a coin laundry, ice, Wi-Fi, clubrooms, and a playground are available. Boat-launching facilities are nearby. Leashed pets are permitted.

**Reservations, fees:** Reservations are accepted. Sites are $22-34 per night, $3 per person per night for more than two people. Some credit cards are accepted. Open year-round.

**Directions:** In Roseburg on I-5, take Exit 125 to Garden Valley Road. Drive west for five miles (over the river) to Old Garden Valley Road. Turn left and drive 1.5 miles to River Forks Road. Turn left and drive a short distance to the park entrance on the left.

**Contact:** Twin Rivers Vacation Park, 541/673-3811, www.twinriversrvpark.com.

## 60 DOUGLAS COUNTY FAIRGROUNDS RV PARK

### Scenic rating: 8

on the South Umpqua River

**Map 11.3, page 597**

This 74-acre county park is very easily accessible off the highway. Nearby Umpqua River, one of Oregon's prettiest rivers, often has good fishing in season. Bike paths, a golf course, and tennis courts are nearby. Horse stalls and a boat ramp are available at the nearby fairgrounds.

**Campsites, facilities:** There are 50 sites with full or partial hookups for tents or RVs of any length. Picnic tables are provided seasonally. Drinking water, restrooms with flush toilets and showers, and a dump station are available. A store, café, coin laundry, and ice are within one mile. Some facilities are wheelchair accessible. Leashed pets are permitted.

**Reservations, fees:** Reservations are not accepted. Sites are $25 per night, with a 14-day stay limit. Tent camping is limited to two nights. Open year-round, except one week in August during the county fair. Phone ahead to confirm current status.

**Directions:** Heading south on I-5 in Roseburg, take Exit 123 and drive south under the freeway to Frear Street. Turn right and enter the park.

**Contact:** Douglas County Fairgrounds & Speedway, 541/957-7010, www.co.douglas.or.us/dcfair.

## 61 CAVITT CREEK FALLS

### Scenic rating: 8

west of Roseburg

**Map 11.3, page 597**

The locals might try to hunt me down for revealing this spot, but here it is. This campground is located near a sensational swimming hole at the base of a 10-foot waterfall on Cavitt Creek. The elevation is 1,040 feet, and an abundant forest of fir, maple, and oak trees surrounds the campground. It is overlooked because it is set on land run by the Bureau of Land Management, not the Park Service or Forest Service. Fishing is closed on Cavitt Creek by the Oregon Department of Fish and Wildlife.

**Campsites, facilities:** There are eight sites for tents or RVs up to 20 feet long (no hookups). Picnic tables, garbage bins, and fire rings are provided. Drinking water and vault toilets are available. A camp host is on-site. Some facilities are wheelchair accessible. Leashed pets are permitted.

**Reservations, fees:** Reservations are not accepted. Sites are $8 per night, $4 per night for an additional vehicle. Open mid-May–mid-October, weather permitting.

**Directions:** From Roseburg, drive east on Highway 138 for 16.5 miles to Little River Road. Turn right (south) on Little River Road and drive 6.7 miles to the covered bridge. Turn right onto Cavitt Creek Road and drive 3.2 miles to Cavitt Creek Falls Recreation Site.

**Contact:** Bureau of Land Management, Roseburg District, 541/440-4930, www.or.blm.gov/or/resources/recreation.

## 62 HOODOO'S DEXTER SHORES RV PARK

🏃 🛶 ⛴ 🐕 ♿ 🚐 ⛺

**Scenic rating: 7**

near Dexter Reservoir

**Map 11.4, page 598**

If you're traveling on I-5, this RV park is well worth the 15-minute drive out of Springfield. It's across the street from Dexter Reservoir, where fishing and boating are permitted year-round. Speedboat races are held at Dexter in the summer. There is seasonal fishing for salmon and steelhead below Dexter dam. The local area is good for bird-watching. Nearby Lookout and Fall Creek Lakes offer sailing, swimming, waterskiing, and windsurfing. Many of the campsites have a lake view.

**Campsites, facilities:** There are 53 sites with full or partial hookups for RVs up to 40 feet long; 12 sites are pull-through. There are also eight tent sites. Picnic tables and fire pits are provided at tent sites; RV sites have tables only. Drinking water, restrooms with flush toilets and showers, a vault toilet, a dump station, cable TV, telephone hookups, Wi-Fi, putting green, a clubhouse, lending library, firewood,

horseshoe pits, and a coin laundry are available. Propane gas, a café, restaurant, and ice are within three miles. Boat docks and launching facilities are nearby. Some facilities are wheelchair accessible. Leashed pets are permitted with size restrictions.

**Reservations, fees:** Reservations are accepted at 866/558-9777. RV sites are $33 per night, tent sites are $22 per night, $3 per person per night for more than four people, and $1 per pet per night. Weekly and monthly rates are available. Some credit cards are accepted. Open year-round.

**Directions:** From south Eugene on I-5, drive to Exit 188A and Highway 58. Take Highway 58 east and drive 11.5 miles to Lost Creek Road. Turn right (south) and drive several hundred feet to Dexter Road. Turn left (in front of the café) and drive east for half a block to the park on the right.

**Contact:** Dexter Shores RV Park, 541/937-3711 or 866/558-9777, www.dextershoresrv.com.

## 63 FALL CREEK STATE RECREATION AREA

🏊 🛶 ⛴ 🐕 ♿ 🚐 ⛺

**Scenic rating: 7**

in Fall Creek State Recreation Area

**Map 11.4, page 598**

There are two campgrounds here: Cascara and the group camp area, Fisherman's Park. Most of these spacious sites have Douglas fir and white fir tree cover. Water recreation is the primary activity here; boating and water skis are allowed. The lake level drops in August, and water temperatures are ideal for summer swimming.

**Campsites, facilities:** There are 39 primitive sites at Cascara Campground for tents or RVs up to 50 feet. Fisherman's Point Campground is a group area that accommodates up to 64 people and 16 RVs of any length. Picnic tables and fire rings are provided. Drinking water, vault toilets, garbage service, and firewood are available. A camp host is on-site. A boat launch, dock, and swimming area are also available. Some facilities are wheelchair accessible. Leashed pets are permitted.

**Reservations, fees:** Reservations are accepted for the RV group area only at 800/452-5687. Sites are $19 per night, $7 per night per additional vehicle. The group RV area is $109 per night for up to 10 RVs, $11 per each additional RV, $7 per night per each additional car. Some credit cards are accepted. Open May 1-September 30.

**Directions:** From south Eugene on I-5, take Exit 188 to Highway 58. Drive 11 miles south to Lowell and Pioneer Street (at the covered bridge). Turn left on Pioneer Street and drive less than 0.25 mile to West Boundary Road. Turn left and drive one block to Lowell Jasper Road. Turn right and drive 1.5 miles to Unity and Place Road. Turn right and drive about one mile to a fork with North Shore Road (Big Fall Creek Road). Bear left onto Big Fall Creek Road and drive about eight miles to the head of Fall Creek Reservoir and Peninsula Road (Forest Road 6250). Turn right and drive 0.5 mile to the campground. The park is approximately 27 miles southeast of Eugene.

**Contact:** Fall Creek State Recreation Area, 541/937-1173 or 800/551-6949, www.oregonstateparks.org.

## 64 DOLLY VARDEN
🏃 🚲 🏊 🎣 🐕 ⛺

### Scenic rating: 6
on Fall Creek in Willamette National Forest

Map 11.4, page 598

This pretty campground is adjacent to Fall Creek and is at the lower trailhead for the scenic, 13.7-mile Fall Creek National Recreation Trail, which follows the creek and varies between 960 and 1,385 feet in elevation. This small campground gets moderate-heavy use. It is set on the inlet stream for Fall Creek Reservoir.

**Campsites, facilities:** There are five sites for tents or RVs up to 30 feet. Picnic tables and fire grills are provided. Vault toilets and garbage service are available. There is no drinking water. Leashed pets are permitted.

**Reservations, fees:** Reservations are not accepted. Sites are $12 per night, $6 per night per additional vehicle. Open May-September, weather permitting.

**Directions:** From south Eugene on I-5, take Exit 188 to Highway 58. Drive 11 miles south to Lowell and Pioneer Street (at the covered bridge). Turn left and drive 0.2 mile to West Boundary Road. Turn left and drive one block to Lowell Jasper Road. Turn right and drive 1.5 miles to Unity and Place Road. Turn right and drive about one mile to a fork with North Shore Road. Bear left onto North Shore Road (Big Fall Creek Road) and drive about 10 miles (the road becomes Forest Road 18) to the campground on the left.

**Contact:** Willamette National Forest, Middle Fork Ranger District, 541/782-2283, www.fs.usda.gov/willamette.

## 65 BIG POOL
🏃 🚲 🏊 🎣 🐕 🚐 ⛺

### Scenic rating: 6
on Fall Creek in Willamette National Forest

Map 11.4, page 598

Big Pool campground is quiet, secluded, and primitive. The camp sits along Fall Creek at about 1,000 feet elevation, and the scenic Fall Creek National Recreation Trail passes the camp on the other side of the creek, providing hiking opportunities. Sites are rather open, with only sparse vegetation between them.

**Campsites, facilities:** There are three tent sites and two sites for tents or RVs up to 24 feet long. Picnic tables, garbage containers, and fire grills are provided. Vault toilets and drinking water are available. Leashed pets are permitted.

**Reservations, fees:** Reservations are not accepted. Sites are $12 per night, $6 per night per additional vehicle. Open late May-September, weather permitting.

**Directions:** From south Eugene on I-5, take Exit 188 to Highway 58. Drive 11 miles south to Lowell and Pioneer Street (at the covered bridge). Turn left and drive 0.2 mile to West Boundary Road. Turn left and drive one block to Lowell Jasper Road. Turn right and drive 1.5 miles to Unity and Place Road. Turn right and drive about one mile to a fork with North Shore Road. Bear left onto North Shore Road (Big Fall Creek Road) and drive about 12 miles (the road becomes Forest Road 18) to the campground on the right.

**Contact:** Willamette National Forest, Middle Fork Ranger District, 541/782-2283, www. fs.usda.gov/willamette.

## 66 BEDROCK
🏃‍♂️ 🚴 🏊 ⛵ 🐕 ♿ 🚐 ⛺

### Scenic rating: 6
on Fall Creek in Willamette National Forest

Map 11.4, page 598

Bedrock lies along the banks of Fall Creek amid Douglas firs and cedars. This is one of the access points for the scenic Fall Creek National Recreation Trail, which in turn offers access to Jones Trail, a six-mile uphill climb. Swimming holes offer relief in summer. This campground suffered damage from the Clark Fire in 2005, but has been rehabilitated and the understory vegetation is returning.

**Campsites, facilities:** There are 18 single sites and one multiple site for tents or RVs up to 36 feet long. Picnic tables and fire grills are provided. Vault toilets and garbage service are available. There is no drinking water. Some facilities are wheelchair accessible. Leashed pets are permitted.

**Reservations, fees:** Reservations are not accepted. Single sites are $14 per night, $22 per night for double sites, and $7 per night per additional vehicle. Open May-mid-September, weather permitting.

**Directions:** From south Eugene on I-5, take Exit 188 to Highway 58. Drive 11 miles south to Lowell and Pioneer Street (at the covered bridge). Turn left and drive 0.2 mile to West Boundary Road.

Turn left and drive one block to Lowell Jasper Road. Turn right and drive 1.5 miles to Unity and Place Road. Turn right and drive about one mile to a fork with North Shore Road. Bear left onto North Shore Road (Big Fall Creek Road) and drive about 14 miles (the road becomes Forest Road 18) to the campground on the left.

**Contact:** Willamette National Forest, Middle Fork Ranger District, 541/782-2283, www. fs.usda.gov/willamette.

## 67 PUMA
🏃‍♂️ 🚴 🏊 ⛵ 🐕 ♿ 🚐 ⛺

### Scenic rating: 6
on Fall Creek in Willamette National Forest

Map 11.4, page 598

Puma campground hugs the banks of Fall Creek at an elevation of 1,100 feet. This is one of four camps in the immediate area, located across from the popular Fall Creek National Recreation Trail. The trail offers hiking opportunities, while Fall Creek provides a nice spot to cool off in summer.

**Campsites, facilities:** There are 11 sites for tents or RVs up to 36 feet long. Picnic tables and fire grills are provided. Vault toilets, drinking water, and garbage bins are available. Some facilities are wheelchair accessible. Leashed pets are permitted.

**Reservations, fees:** Reservations are not accepted. Sites are $14 per night, $6 per night per additional vehicle. Open late May-September, weather permitting.

**Directions:** From I-5 south of Eugene, take Exit 188 to Highway 58. Drive about 11 miles to Lowell. Turn left at Pioneer Street (at the covered bridge), drive 0.2 mile, and turn left on West Boundary Road. Drive one block and turn right at Lowell Jasper Road. Drive 1.5 miles to Place Road and turn right. Drive about one mile to a fork and bear left onto North Shore Road (Big Fall Creek Road). Drive about 16 miles (the road becomes Forest Road 18) to the campground on the left.

**Contact:** Willamette National Forest, Middle

Fork Ranger District, 541/782-2283, www.
fs.usda.gov/willamette.

## 68 FRISSELL CROSSING

### Scenic rating: 8

near the Three Sisters Wilderness in
Willamette National Forest

**Map 11.4, page 598**

If you're looking for solitude, this place should
be heaven to you. Frissell campground (elevation 2,600 feet) sits on the banks of the South
Fork of the McKenzie River, adjacent to a trailhead that provides access to the backcountry of
the Three Sisters Wilderness. Note that Frissell
Crossing is the only camp in the immediate
area that has drinking water.

**Campsites, facilities:** There are 12 sites for
tents or RVs up to 36 feet long. Picnic tables,
garbage bins, and fire grills are provided.
Hand-pumped drinking water and vault toilets are available. Leashed pets are permitted.

**Reservations, fees:** Reservations are not accepted. Single sites are $14 per night, double
sites are $26 per night, $6 per night per additional vehicle. Open mid-May-mid-September,
weather permitting.

**Directions:** From Eugene, drive east on Highway 126 for 37 miles to Blue River. Continue
east on Highway 126 for five miles to Forest
Road 19 (Aufderheide Scenic Byway). Turn
right (south) and drive 21.5 miles to the camp
on the left.

**Contact:** Willamette National Forest, McK-
enzie River Ranger District, 541/822-3381,
www.fs.usda.gov/willamette.

## 69 BLAIR LAKE WALK-IN

### Scenic rating: 6

on Blair Lake in Willamette National Forest

**Map 11.4, page 598**

If you're looking for a pristine, alpine lakeside

setting, you'll find it here. The lake, set at
4,800 feet elevation, is small (only 35 acres)
and shallow (20 feet). It supports a population
of brook and rainbow trout and is stocked in
the summer. The surrounding meadows and
woods are well known for their wide range of
wildflowers and huckleberries.

**Campsites, facilities:** There are seven walk-in
tent sites. Picnic tables and fire rings are provided. Drinking water, a vault toilet, and garbage
bins are available. Some facilities are wheelchair
accessible. Leashed pets are permitted.

**Reservations, fees:** Reservations are not accepted. Sites are $8 per night, $4 per night per
additional vehicle. Open mid-June-October,
weather permitting.

**Directions:** From south Eugene on I-5, take
Exit 188 to Highway 58. Drive 35 miles southeast on Highway 58 to Oakridge. Turn left at
the signal to downtown and Salmon Creek
Road. Turn east and drive nine miles (it becomes Forest Road 24) to Forest Road 1934.
Turn left and drive eight miles to Forest Road
733. Turn right and continue for 1.25 miles to
the campground.

**Contact:** Willamette National Forest, Middle
Fork Ranger Station, 541/782-2283, www.
fs.usda.gov/willamette.

## 70 KIAHANIE

### Scenic rating: 5

on the North Fork of the Willamette River in
Willamette National Forest

**Map 11.4, page 598**

This is one heck of a spot for fly-fishing (and
the only kind of fishing allowed). Kiahanie is
a remote campground that sits at 2,200 feet
elevation along the North Fork of the Willamette River, a designated Wild and Scenic
River. If you want beauty and quiet among
enormous Douglas fir trees, you came to the
right place. An even more remote campground,
Box Canyon Horse Camp, is farther north on
Forest Road 19.

**Campsites, facilities:** There are 19 sites for tents or RVs up to 24 feet long. Picnic tables and fire rings are provided. Drinking water, vault toilets, garbage bins, and a recycling center are available. Some facilities are wheelchair accessible. Leashed pets are permitted.

**Reservations, fees:** Reservations are not accepted. Sites are $10 per night, $5 per night per additional vehicle. Open late May-late October, weather permitting.

**Directions:** From south Eugene on I-5, take Exit 188 to Highway 58. Drive 31 miles southeast on Highway 58 to Westfir. Take the Westfir exit and drive two miles to Westfir and the junction with Aufderheide Scenic Byway (Forest Road 19). Bear left (northeast) and drive 19 miles to the campground.

**Contact:** Willamette National Forest, Middle Fork Ranger Station, 541/782-2283, www. fs.usda.gov/willamette.

# 71 BOX CANYON HORSE CAMP

### Scenic rating: 4

near Chucksney Mountain in Willamette National Forest

**Map 11.4, page 598**

Only 80 miles from Eugene, this secluded campground with sparse tree cover offers wilderness trails, including the Chucksney Mountain Trail, Crossing-Way Trail, and Grasshopper Trail. It's a good base camp for a backpacking trip and is at 3,600 feet in elevation.

**Campsites, facilities:** There are 13 sites for tents or RVs up to 30 feet long that allow horse and rider to camp close together. Picnic tables, fire grills, stock water, and corrals are provided. Vault toilets are available. There is no drinking water, and garbage must be packed out. Leashed pets are permitted.

**Reservations, fees:** Reservations are not accepted. There is no fee for camping. Open June-late October, weather permitting.

**Directions:** From Eugene, drive east on

Highway 126 for 41 miles to Blue River. Continue east on Highway 126 for five miles to Forest Road 19 (Aufderheide Scenic Byway). Turn right (south) and drive 33 miles to the camp on the right.

**Contact:** Willamette National Forest, McKenzie River Ranger District, 541/822-3381, www.fs.usda.gov/willamette.

# 72 BLACK CANYON

### Scenic rating: 7

on the Middle Fork of the Willamette River in Willamette National Forest

**Map 11.4, page 598**

Black Canyon campground is set along the banks of the Middle Fork of the Willamette River, not far above Lookout Point Reservoir, where fishing and boating are available. The elevation is 1,000 feet. The camp is pretty and wooded and has comfortable sites. Within the camp is a one-mile-long nature trail with interpretive signs. You will hear train noise from the other side of the river.

**Campsites, facilities:** There are 70 sites for tents or RVs up to 40 feet long, and one group site is available. Picnic tables, garbage service, and fire grills are provided. Drinking water, vault toilets, and firewood are available. A dump station, café, and coin laundry are within six miles. Launching facilities are nearby at the south end of Lookout Point Reservoir. Some facilities are wheelchair accessible. Leashed pets are permitted.

**Reservations, fees:** Reservations are accepted for 17 sites at 877/444-6777 ($10 reservation fee) or www.recreation.gov ($9 reservation fee). Single sites are $18 per night, double sites are $34 per night, $6 per night per additional vehicle, and $85 for the group site. Open late April-early October, weather permitting.

**Directions:** From south Eugene on I-5, take Exit 188 to Highway 58. Drive southeast on Highway 58 for 27 miles to the camp on the left (six miles west of Oakridge).

**Contact:** Willamette National Forest, Middle Fork Ranger Station, 541/782-2283, www.fs.usda.gov/willamette.

## 73 BAKER BAY COUNTY PARK

🏃‍♂️ 🚴 🏊 🛶 ⛺ 🚤 🐕 ♿ 🚐 ⛺

### Scenic rating: 6

on Dorena Lake

Map 11.4, page 598

Baker Bay is set along the shore of Dorena Lake, where boating, canoeing, fishing, sailing, swimming, and waterskiing are among the recreation options. Row River Trail follows part of the lake for a hike or bike ride, and there are covered bridges in the area. For golf, head to Cottage Grove.

**Campsites, facilities:** There are 48 sites for tents or self-contained RVs up to 40 feet, plus two group sites for up to 35 people each. Picnic tables and fire grills are provided. Drinking water, restrooms with flush toilets and coin showers, firewood, garbage bins, playground, reservable picnic areas, and a dump station are available. A concession stand with ice is in the park, and a store is within five miles. Boat docks, launching, and kayak rentals are nearby, with seasonal onshore facilities for catamarans. Some facilities are wheelchair accessible. Leashed pets are permitted.

**Reservations, fees:** Reservations are accepted at 541/682-2000 or http://ecomm.lanecounty.org/parks ($10 reservation fee). Single sites are $20-22 per night, $7 for an additional vehicle. Group sites are $75 per night. Open April-October.

**Directions:** From Eugene, drive south on I-5 for 22 miles to Cottage Grove and Exit 174 (Dorena Lake exit). Take that exit to Row River Road and drive east for 4.4 miles (the road becomes Shore View Drive). Bear right on Shore View Drive and continue 2.8 miles to the campground entrance on the left.

**Contact:** Baker Bay Park, 541/942-7669, www.co.lane.or.us/parks.

## 74 SCHWARZ PARK

🏃‍♂️ 🚴 🏊 🛶 ⛺ 🚤 🐕 ♿ 🚐 ⛺

### Scenic rating: 7

on Dorena Lake

Map 11.4, page 598

This large campground sits below Dorena Lake on the Row River, where boating, fishing, swimming, and waterskiing are among the recreation options at the lake. Note that chances of rain are high May to mid-June and that there is a posted warning against consumption of fish from Dorena Lake. The Row River Trail, a paved trail for biking, walking, and shoreline access, parallels Dorena Lake's north shoreline and then extends 12 miles.

**Campsites, facilities:** There are 62 single sites and double sites for tents or RVs of any length and six group sites for 15-50 people. Picnic tables and fire rings are provided. Restrooms with flush toilets and showers, drinking water, garbage bins, a playground, and a dump station are available. Boat-launching facilities are on the lake about two miles upstream. Some facilities are wheelchair accessible. Leashed pets are permitted.

**Reservations, fees:** Reservations are accepted at 877/444-6777 ($10 reservation fee) or www.recreation.gov ($9 reservation fee). Sites are $16 per night, double sites are $32 per night, group sites are $140 per night, and an additional vehicle is $6 per night. Open late April-late September.

**Directions:** From Eugene, drive south on I-5 for 22 miles to Cottage Grove and Exit 174. Take that exit to Shoreview Drive and drive one mile to Row River Road. Turn left and drive four miles east to the campground entrance.

**Contact:** U.S. Army Corps of Engineers, Recreation Information, Cottage Grove, 541/942-1418 or 541/942-5631, http://corpslakes.usace.army.mil.

## 75 SALMON CREEK FALLS

🚶 🚵 🏊 🎣 🐕 🚐 ⛺

### Scenic rating: 8

on Salmon Creek in Willamette National Forest

**Map 11.4, page 598**      **BEST (**

This pretty campground sits in a lush, old-growth forest, right along Salmon Creek at 1,500 feet in elevation. The rocky gorge area creates two small but beautiful waterfalls and several deep pools in the clear, blue-green waters. Springtime brings a full range of wildflowers and wild thimbleberries; hazelnuts abound in the summer. This area is a popular recreation spot.

**Campsites, facilities:** There are 14 sites for tents or RVs up to 40 feet long. Picnic tables, garbage bins, and fire grills are provided. Drinking water and vault toilets are available. A store, café, coin laundry, and ice are available within five miles. Leashed pets are permitted.

**Reservations, fees:** Reservations are not accepted. Sites are $14 per night, $6 per night per additional vehicle. Open late April-mid-September, weather permitting.

**Directions:** From south Eugene on I-5, take Exit 188 to Highway 58. Drive southeast on Highway 58 for 35 miles to Oakridge and the signal light for downtown. Turn left on Crestview Street and drive 0.25 mile to 1st Street. Turn right and drive five miles (the road becomes Forest Road 24, then Salmon Creek Road) to the campground entrance on the right.

**Contact:** Willamette National Forest, Middle Fork Ranger District, 541/782-2283, www.fs.usda.gov/willamette.

## 76 SKOOKUM CREEK

🚶 🎣 🐕 ♿ ⛺

### Scenic rating: 7

near the Three Sisters Wilderness in Willamette National Forest

**Map 11.4, page 598**

Skookum Creek, at 4,500 feet elevation, is a popular starting point for backcountry fishing,

hiking, and horseback riding. The Erma Bell Lakes Trail, a portal into the Three Sisters Wilderness, begins here. This trail is maintained for wheelchair accessibility, though it is challenging.

**Campsites, facilities:** There are nine walk-in tent sites. Picnic tables and fire rings are provided. Drinking water, hitching rails, garbage service, and vault toilets are available. Some facilities are wheelchair accessible. Leashed pets are permitted.

**Reservations, fees:** Reservations are not accepted. Sites are $5 per night. Open late May-mid-October, weather permitting.

**Directions:** From Eugene, drive east on Highway 126 for 37 miles to Blue River. Continue east for five miles to Forest Road 19 (Aufderheide Scenic Byway). Turn right and drive 35 miles south to Forest Road 1957. Turn right (south) and drive four miles to the campground.

**Contact:** Willamette National Forest, Middle Fork Ranger Station, 541/782-2283, www.fs.usda.gov/willamette.

## 77 NORTH WALDO

🚶 🚵 🏊 🎣 🚣 🐎 🐕 ♿ 🚐 ⛺

### Scenic rating: 10

on Waldo Lake in Willamette National Forest

**Map 11.4, page 598**      **BEST (**

North Waldo is the most popular of the Waldo Lake campgrounds. Set at an elevation of 5,400 feet, Waldo Lake has the special distinction of being one of the three purest lakes in the world. The boat launch here is deeper than the others on the lake, which makes it more accommodating for large sailboats (gas motors are not allowed on the lake). Amphitheater programs are presented here on weekends late July-Labor Day. North Waldo is also a popular starting point to many wilderness trails and lakes, most notably Rigdon, Torrey, and Wahanna Lakes. The drier environment supports fewer mosquitoes, but they can still be plentiful in season.

**Campsites, facilities:** There are 58 sites for tents or RVs up to 40 feet long. Picnic tables and fire rings are provided. Drinking water, composting toilets, garbage bins, gray-water station, recycling center, swimming area, and amphitheater are available. Boat-launching facilities are available. Restrooms are wheelchair accessible. Leashed pets are permitted.

**Reservations, fees:** Reservations are accepted at 877/444-6777 ($10 reservation fee) or www. recreation.gov ($9 reservation fee). Single sites are $20 per night, double sites $36 per night, $6 per night per additional vehicle. A Northwest Forest Pass ($5 daily fee or $30 annual fee per vehicle) is required at the nearby boat launch and trailheads. Open early June-early October, weather permitting.

**Directions:** From Eugene, drive south on I-5 for four miles to Exit 188 and Highway 58. Turn southeast and drive about 60 miles to Waldo Lake Road (Forest Road 5897). Turn left and drive north on Waldo Lake Road for 14 miles to Forest Road 5898. Turn left and drive about two miles to the campground at the northeast end of Waldo Lake.

**Contact:** Willamette National Forest, Middle Fork Ranger District, 541/782-2283, www. fs.usda.gov/willamette.

## 78 ISLET
🚶 🚵 🏊 🎣 🛥 🐕 🚐 ⛺

### Scenic rating: 10
on Waldo Lake in Willamette National Forest

Map 11.4, page 598

You'll find sandy beaches and an interpretive sign at this campground at the north end of Waldo Lake. The winds blow consistently every afternoon, great for sailing. A picnic table placed strategically on the rock jetty provides a great spot to enjoy a sunset. A one-mile shoreline trail stretches between Islet and North Waldo Campground. Bring your mosquito repellent; June-August you'll need it.

**Campsites, facilities:** There are 55 sites, including four multiple sites, for tents or RVs up to 30 feet long. Picnic tables, garbage bins, a recycling center, and fire rings are provided. Drinking water and composting toilets are available. Boat-launching facilities are available nearby. Leashed pets are permitted.

**Reservations, fees:** Reservations are not accepted. Single sites are $20 per night, double sites are $36 per night, $6 per night per additional vehicle. A Northwest Forest Pass ($5 daily fee or $30 annual fee per parked vehicle) is required at the nearby boat launch and trailheads. Open July-October, weather permitting.

**Directions:** From Eugene, drive south on I-5 for four miles to Exit 188 and Highway 58. Turn southeast and drive about 60 miles to Waldo Lake Road (Forest Road 5897). Turn left and drive north on Waldo Lake Road for 14 miles to Forest Road 5898. Turn left and continue 1.5 miles to the campground at the northeast end of Waldo Lake.

**Contact:** Willamette National Forest, Middle Fork Ranger District, 541/782-2283, www. fs.usda.gov/willamette.

## 79 SHADOW BAY
🚶 🚵 🏊 🎣 🛥 🐕 🚐 ⛺

### Scenic rating: 10
on Waldo Lake in Willamette National Forest

Map 11.4, page 598

Shadow Bay campground, at 5,400 in elevation, is situated on a large bay at the south end of Waldo Lake. It has a considerably wetter environment than either North Waldo or Islet, supporting a more diverse and prolific ground cover—as well as more mosquitoes. The camp receives considerably lighter use than North Waldo. You have access to the Shore Line Trail and then the Waldo Lake Trail from here. Note that gas motors are not permitted on Waldo Lake.

**Campsites, facilities:** There are 92 sites, including several multiple sites, for tents or RVs up to 44 feet long. Picnic tables, garbage bins, a recycling center, and fire grills are provided.

Drinking water and vault and composting toilets are available. A camp host is on-site in season. Boat-launching facilities and a swimming area are nearby. Leashed pets are permitted.

**Reservations, fees:** Reservations are accepted for 57 sites at 877/444-6777 ($10 reservation fee) or www.recreation.gov ($9 reservation fee). Single sites are $20 per night, double sites are $36 per night, $6 per night per additional vehicle. A Northwest Forest Pass ($5 daily fee or $30 annual fee per vehicle) is required at the nearby boat launch and trailheads. Open July-October, weather permitting.

**Directions:** From Eugene, drive south on I-5 for four miles to Exit 188 and Highway 58. Turn southeast and drive about 60 miles to Waldo Lake Road (Forest Road 5897). Turn left on Waldo Lake Road and drive north for 6.5 miles to the Shadow Bay turnoff. Turn left and drive on Forest Road 5896 to the campground at the south end of Waldo Lake.

**Contact:** Willamette National Forest, Middle Fork Ranger District, 541/782-2283, www.fs.usda.gov/willamette.

## 80 BLUE POOL

### Scenic rating: 4
on Salt Creek in Willamette National Forest

**Map 11.4, page 598**

This campground is situated in an old-growth forest alongside Salt Creek at 1,900 feet elevation. The camp features a large picnic area along the creek with picnic tables, a large grassy area, and fire stoves built in the 1930s by the Civilian Conservation Corps. One-half mile east of the campground on Highway 58 is McCredie Hot Springs. This spot is undeveloped, without any facilities. Exercise caution when using the hot springs; they can be very hot.

**Campsites, facilities:** There are 24 sites for tents or RVs up to 36 feet long. Picnic tables, garbage bins, a recycling center, and fire rings are provided. Drinking water, vault and flush toilets, and a gray-water station are available. Leashed pets are permitted.

**Reservations, fees:** Reservations are not accepted. Sites are $16 per night, $6 per night per additional vehicle. Open mid-May-late September, weather permitting.

**Directions:** From Eugene, drive south on I-5 for four miles to Exit 188 and Highway 58. Turn southeast and drive 35 miles to Oakridge. Continue east on Highway 58 for eight miles to the campground on the right.

**Contact:** Willamette National Forest, Middle Fork Ranger District, 541/782-2283, www.fs.usda.gov/willamette.

## 81 SHARPS CREEK

### Scenic rating: 5
on Sharps Creek

**Map 11.4, page 598**

Like nearby Rujada, this camp on the banks of Sharps Creek is just far enough off the beaten path to be missed by most campers. It's quiet, primitive, and remote, and fishing, gold-panning, and swimming are popular activities in the day-use area.

**Campsites, facilities:** There are 11 sites for tents or RVs up to 25 feet long. Picnic tables and fire pits are provided. Drinking water and vault toilets are available. A camp host is here in summer. Some facilities are wheelchair accessible. Leashed pets are permitted.

**Reservations, fees:** Reservations are not accepted. Sites are $12 per night, $5 per night per additional vehicle. Open mid-May-September with a 14-day stay limit, weather permitting.

**Directions:** From Eugene, drive south on I-5 to Cottage Grove and Exit 174. Take that exit and drive east on Row River Road for 18 miles to Sharps Creek Road. Turn right (south) and drive four miles to the campground.

**Contact:** Bureau of Land Management, Eugene District, 541/683-6600 or 888/442-3062, www.blm.gov/or/districts/eugene.

# 82 RUJADA

🚶 🚴 🏊 🛶 🐎 ♿ 🚐 ⛺

### Scenic rating: 7

on Layng Creek in Umpqua National Forest

**Map 11.4, page 598**

Rujada campground is nestled on a river terrace on the banks of Layng Creek, right at the national forest border. The Swordfern Trail follows Layng Creek through a beautiful forest within a lush fern grotto. There is a fair swimming hole near the campground. Those with patience and persistence can fish in the creek. By continuing east on Forest Road 17, you reach a trailhead that leads 0.5 mile to beautiful Spirit Falls, a spectacular 60-foot waterfall. A bit farther east is another easy trail, which leads to Moon Falls, even more awe-inspiring at 125 feet. Another campground option is Cedar Creek, about six miles southeast on Brice Creek Road (County Road 2470).

**Campsites, facilities:** There are 15 sites for tents or RVs up to 22 feet long. Picnic tables, garbage bins, and fire pits are provided. Flush and vault toilets, drinking water, gray-water stations, and a softball field are available. Some facilities are wheelchair accessible. Leashed pets are permitted.

**Reservations, fees:** Reservations are not accepted. Sites are $8 per night, $3 per night per additional vehicle. Open late May-late September, weather permitting.

**Directions:** From Eugene, drive south on I-5 to Cottage Grove and Exit 174. Take that exit and drive east on Row River Road for 19 miles to Layng Creek Road (Forest Road 17). Turn left and drive two miles to the campground on the right.

**Contact:** Umpqua National Forest, Cottage Grove Ranger Station, 541/767-5000, www. fs.usda.gov/umpqua.

# 83 PACKARD CREEK

🚶 🏊 🛶 🚤 🐎 ♿ 🚐 ⛺

### Scenic rating: 6

on Hills Creek Reservoir in Willamette National Forest

**Map 11.4, page 598**

Packard Creek campground is located on a large flat beside Hills Creek Reservoir. This camp is extremely popular with families and fills up on weekends and holidays. The mix of vegetation in the campground unfortunately includes an abundance of poison oak. The speed limit around the swimming area and boat ramp is 5 mph. The elevation is 1,600 feet.

One time at Hills Creek Reservoir my canoe flipped on a cold winter day and I almost drowned after 20 minutes in the icy water. After I'd gone down for the count twice, my brother Bob jumped in, swam out, grabbed the front of the flipped canoe, and towed me to shore. Then, once ashore, he kept me awake, preventing me from lapsing into a coma from hypothermia.

Thanks, Bob.

**Campsites, facilities:** There are 37 sites, including two multiple sites, for tents or RVs up to 40 feet long, and a group area for up to 75 people. Picnic tables and fire rings are provided. Drinking water, vault toilets, garbage bins, a recycling center, and firewood are available. Fishing and boat docks, boat-launching facilities, a roped swimming area, picnic shelter, and an amphitheater are available. Some sites have their own docks. Some facilities are wheelchair accessible. Leashed pets are permitted.

**Reservations, fees:** Reservations are accepted for 13 of the sites at 877/444-6777 ($10 reservation fee) or www.recreation.gov ($9 reservation fee). Single sites are $16 per night, double sites are $30 per night, $6 per night per additional vehicle, $125 for the group site. Open mid-April-mid-September, weather permitting.

**Directions:** From Eugene, drive south on I-5 for four miles to Exit 188 and Highway 58.

Turn southeast and drive 35 miles to Oakridge. Continue east on Highway 58 for two miles to Kitson Springs Road. Turn right and drive 0.5 mile to Forest Road 21. Turn right and continue six miles to the campground on the left.
**Contact:** Willamette National Forest, Middle Fork Ranger Station, 541/782-2283, www.fs.usda.gov/willamette.

## 84 SAND PRAIRIE
🚶 🚴 🏊 🎣 🐕 ♿ 🚗 ⛺

### Scenic rating: 6
on the Willamette River in Willamette National Forest

**Map 11.4, page 598**

Situated at 1,600 feet elevation in a mixed stand of cedar, dogwood, Douglas fir, hazelnut, and western hemlock, this campground provides easy access to the Middle Fork of the Willamette River. An access road leads to the south (upstream) end of the Hills Creek Reservoir. The 27-mile Middle Fork Trail begins at the south end of the campground. Fishing is good here; you can expect to catch large cutthroat trout, rainbow trout, and suckers in the Middle Fork.
**Campsites, facilities:** There are 21 sites for tents or RVs up to 28 feet long. Picnic tables, garbage bins, and fire rings are provided. Vault and flush toilets and a group picnic area are available. There is no drinking water available. A camp host is on-site. A boat launch is nearby on Hills Creek Reservoir. Some facilities are wheelchair accessible. Leashed pets are permitted.
**Reservations, fees:** Reservations are not accepted. Sites are $12 per night, $6 per night per additional vehicle. Open late May-early September, weather permitting.
**Directions:** From Eugene, drive south on I-5 for four miles to Exit 188 and Highway 58. Turn southeast and drive 35 miles to Oakridge. Continue east on Highway 58 for two miles to Kitson Springs Road. Turn right and drive 0.5 mile to Forest Road 21. Turn right and continue 11 miles to the campground on the right.

**Contact:** Willamette National Forest, Middle Fork Ranger Station, 541/782-2283, www.fs.usda.gov/willamette.

## 85 SACANDAGA
🚶 🚴 🎣 🐕 🚗 ⛺

### Scenic rating: 5
on the Willamette River in Willamette National Forest

**Map 11.4, page 598**

Sacandaga campground sits along the middle fork of the Willamette River, where a segment of the historic Oregon Central Military Wagon Road is visible. Two trails from the campground access the Willamette River, and the Middle Fork Trail is in close proximity. Also, a short trail leads to a viewpoint with a bench, great for a short break. This campground gets low use, and the sites are well separated by vegetation. Count on solitude here. The elevation is 2,400 feet.
**Campsites, facilities:** There are 17 sites for tents or RVs up to 24 feet long. Picnic tables and fire rings are provided. Drinking water, vault toilets, and firewood are available. Leashed pets are permitted.
**Reservations, fees:** Reservations are not accepted. Sites are $8 per night, $4 per night per additional vehicle. Open mid-May-mid-November, weather permitting.
**Directions:** From Eugene, drive south on I-5 for four miles to Exit 188 and Highway 58. Turn southeast and drive 35 miles to Oakridge. Continue east on Highway 58 for two miles to Kitson Springs Road. Turn right and drive 0.5 mile to Forest Road 21. Turn right and drive 24 miles to the campground on the right.
**Contact:** Willamette National Forest, Middle Fork Ranger Station, 541/782-2283, www.fs.usda.gov/willamette.

## 86 CAMPERS FLAT

### Scenic rating: 5

on the Willamette River in Willamette
National Forest

**Map 11.4, page 598**

Small, pretty Campers Flat campground sits
adjacent to the Middle Fork Willamette River,
near Deadhorse Creek. Though the camp is right
next to Forest Road 21, you're likely to hear more
river than road. Fishing is a popular activity here,
with good river access. For mountain bikers, the
Young's Rock Trailhead awaits on the other side
of the road. While at camp, be sure to check out
the interpretive sign detailing the history of the
Oregon Central Military Wagon Road.

**Campsites, facilities:** There are five sites for
tents or RVs up to 40 feet long. Picnic tables,
garbage bins, and fire grills are provided. Vault
toilets and firewood are available. Well water
may be available for drinking, but bring your
own just in case. Leashed pets are permitted.

**Reservations, fees:** Reservations are not accepted. Sites are $12 per night, $6 per night per
additional vehicle. Open late May-September.

**Directions:** From Eugene, drive south on I-5
for five miles to Exit 188 and Highway 58.
Turn east and drive 35 miles to the town of
Oakridge. From Oakridge, continue east on
Highway 58 about two miles to Kitson Springs
Road. Turn right and drive 0.5 mile to Forest
Road 21. Turn right and drive 19 miles to the
campground on the right.

**Contact:** Willamette National Forest, Middle
Fork Ranger Station, 541/782-2283, www.
fs.usda.gov/willamette.

## 87 SECRET

### Scenic rating: 5

on the Willamette River in Willamette
National Forest

**Map 11.4, page 598**

This small campground, set on the middle fork

of the Willamette River, gets regular use from
locals in the know. The tree cover is scant,
but there is adequate vegetation to buffer the
campsites from the nearby road noise. Fishing
the Middle Fork Willamette is generally fair.

**Campsites, facilities:** There are six sites for
tents or RVs up to 36 feet long. Picnic tables,
garbage bins, and fire rings are provided. Pit
toilets are available, but there is no drinking
water. Leashed pets are permitted.

**Reservations, fees:** Reservations are not accepted. Sites are $12 per night, $6 per night per
additional vehicle. Open May-late September,
weather permitting.

**Directions:** From Eugene, drive south on I-5
for five miles to Exit 188 and Highway 58.
Turn east and drive 35 miles to the town of
Oakridge. From Oakridge, continue east on
Highway 58 about two miles to Kitson Springs
Road. Turn right and drive 0.5 mile to Forest
Road 21. Turn right and drive 18 miles to the
campground.

**Contact:** Willamette National Forest, Middle
Fork Ranger Station, 541/782-2283, www.
fs.usda.gov/willamette.

## 88 INDIGO SPRINGS

### Scenic rating: 5

near the Willamette River in Willamette
National Forest

**Map 11.4, page 598**

This small, semi-open tent campground sits at
2,800 feet elevation in a stand of old-growth
Douglas fir. A nearby 250-foot walk leads to
the origin of this cold-water spring. A remnant
of the historic Oregon Central Military Wagon
Road passes near the campground, with an
interpretive sign explaining it.

**Campsites, facilities:** There are three sites
for tents. Picnic tables and fire grills are provided. Vault toilets and firewood are available.
There is no drinking water. Leashed pets are
permitted.

**Reservations, fees:** Reservations are not

accepted. There is no fee for camping. Open May-October, weather permitting.

**Directions:** From Eugene, drive south on I-5 for five miles to Exit 188 and Highway 58. Turn east and drive 35 miles to the town of Oakridge. From Oakridge, continue east on Highway 58 about two miles to Kitson Springs Road. Turn right and drive 0.5 mile to Forest Road 21. Turn right and drive 27 miles to the campground on the left.

**Contact:** Willamette National Forest, Middle Fork Ranger Station, 541/782-2283, www.fs.usda.gov/willamette.

## 89 ROCK CREEK

**Scenic rating: 8**

on Rock Creek

**Map 11.4, page 598**

Since I started roaming around the state 20 years ago, this campground on the banks of Rock Creek in a relatively obscure spot has been considerably improved by the Bureau of Land Management (BLM). It's not well known, either, so you're likely to have privacy as a bonus. No fishing is allowed in Rock Creek.

**Campsites, facilities:** There are 17 sites for tents or RVs up to 40 feet long. Picnic tables and fire grills are provided. A camp host is on-site, and vault toilets, drinking water, a reservable pavilion, horseshoe pits, volleyball area, and firewood are available. Some facilities are wheelchair accessible. Leashed pets are permitted but not in the swimming hole.

**Reservations, fees:** Reservations are not accepted. Sites are $10 per night, with a 14-day stay limit, and $4 per night per additional vehicle. Open mid-May-September 30.

**Directions:** From Roseburg, drive east on Highway 138 for 22 miles to Rock Creek Road. Turn right (north) and drive seven miles to the campground on the right.

**Contact:** Bureau of Land Management, Roseburg District, 541/440-4930, www.blm.gov/or/districts/roseburg.

## 90 MILLPOND

**Scenic rating: 8**

on Rock Creek

**Map 11.4, page 598**

Rock Creek flows past Millpond and empties into the North Umpqua River five miles downstream. Just above this confluence is the Rock Creek Fish Hatchery, which is open year-round to visitors, with free access. This campground along the banks of Rock Creek is the first camp you'll see along Rock Creek Road, which accounts for its relative popularity in the area. Like Rock Creek Campground, it's primitive and remote. No fishing is allowed in Rock Creek.

**Campsites, facilities:** There are 12 sites for tents or RVs up to 42 feet long. Picnic tables, garbage service, and fire grills are provided. A camp host is on-site, and flush and vault toilets, drinking water, firewood, a ballfield, horseshoe pits, playground, and reservable pavilion are available. Some facilities are wheelchair accessible. Leashed pets are permitted, but not in the swimming hole.

**Reservations, fees:** Reservations are not accepted. Sites are $10 per night, $4 per night per additional vehicle. Open early May-September 30 with a 14-day stay limit.

**Directions:** From Roseburg, drive east on Highway 138 for 22 miles to Rock Creek Road. Turn right (north) and drive five miles to the campground on the right.

**Contact:** Bureau of Land Management, Roseburg District, 541/440-4930, www.blm.gov/or/districts/roseburg.

## 91 SUSAN CREEK

**Scenic rating: 9**

on the North Umpqua River

**Map 11.4, page 598**     **BEST**

This popular and pretty campground borders the North Umpqua Wild and Scenic River.

This lush setting features plenty of trees and river access. Highlights include two barrier-free trails, one traveling 0.5 mile to the day-use area. From there, a hike of about 0.75 mile leads to the 50-foot Susan Creek Falls. Another 0.4 mile up the trail are the Susan Creek Indian Mounds. These moss-covered rocks are believed to be a spiritual site and are visited by Native Americans in search of guardian spirit visions.

**Campsites, facilities:** There are 30 sites for RVs up to 48 feet long. Picnic tables, garbage service, and fire grills are provided. Restrooms with flush toilets and showers, drinking water, small amphitheater with seasonal interpretive programs, horseshoe pits, and firewood are available, and there is a camp host. Some facilities and trails are wheelchair accessible. Leashed pets are permitted.

**Reservations, fees:** Reservations are not accepted. Sites are $14 per night, with a 14-day stay limit, and $4 per night per additional vehicle. Open mid-April-late October.

**Directions:** From Roseburg, drive east on Highway 138 for 29.5 miles to the campground (turnoff well signed).

**Contact:** Bureau of Land Management, Roseburg District, 541/440-4930, www.blm.gov/or/districts/roseburg.

## 92 STEAMBOAT FALLS

### Scenic rating: 8

on Steamboat Creek in Umpqua National Forest

**Map 11.4, page 598**          **BEST**

This Steamboat Creek campground boasts some excellent scenery. Beautiful Steamboat Falls features a fish ladder that provides passage for steelhead and salmon on their upstream migration. No fishing is permitted in Steamboat Creek. Other nearby camping options are Island and Canton Creek.

**Campsites, facilities:** There are seven sites for tents or RVs up to 24 feet long and three sites

for tents only. Picnic tables, garbage bins, vault toilets, and fire grills are provided. There is no drinking water. Leashed pets are permitted.

**Reservations, fees:** Reservations are not accepted. Sites are $10 per night, $5 per night per additional vehicle. Open year-round, weather permitting.

**Directions:** From Roseburg on I-5, take Exit 120 to Highway 138. Drive east on Highway 138 to Steamboat and Forest Road 38. Turn left on Forest Road 38 (Steamboat Creek Road) and drive six miles to a fork with Forest Road 3810. Turn right and drive one mile on a paved road to the campground.

**Contact:** Umpqua National Forest, North Umpqua Ranger District, 541/496-3532, www.fs.usda.gov/umpqua.

## 93 SCAREDMAN

### Scenic rating: 6

on Canton Creek

**Map 11.4, page 598**

NOTE: This campground was temporarily closed in 2013 for budgetary reasons. Call before planning a trip here.

Scaredman is a small campground along the banks of Canton Creek, virtually unknown to out-of-towners. Set in an old-growth forest, this private and secluded camp offers a chance to swim in the creek. Scaredman gets its name from an old legend that says some early settlers camped here, heard a pack of hungry wolves, and then ran off, scared to death. This is one of the few free camps left in the region. Although fishing is closed on Canton Creek and all Steamboat drainages, the North Umpqua River 3.5 miles downstream offers fly-fishing for steelhead or salmon.

**Campsites, facilities:** There are 10 sites for tents only. Picnic tables, garbage service, and fire grills are provided. Vault toilets and drinking water are available. A camp host is on-site in season. Some facilities are wheelchair accessible. Leashed pets are permitted.

**Reservations, fees:** Reservations are not accepted. There is no fee for camping. The stay limit is 14 days. Open year-round, with limited services November–March.

**Directions:** From Roseburg, drive east on Highway 138 for 40 miles to Steamboat Creek Road. Turn left (north) and drive 0.5 mile to Canton Creek Road. Turn left (north) and drive three miles to the campground.

**Contact:** Bureau of Land Management, Roseburg District, 541/440-4930, www.blm.gov/or/districts/roseburg.

## 94 ISLAND

### Scenic rating: 8

on the Umpqua River in Umpqua National Forest

**Map 11.4, page 598**

The North Umpqua is one of Oregon's most beautiful rivers, and this scenic campground borders its banks at a spot popular for both rafting and steelhead fishing. Note: Only fly-fishing is allowed here. A hiking trail that leads east and west along the river is accessible a short drive to the west.

**Campsites, facilities:** There are seven sites for tents or RVs up to 24 feet long. Picnic tables, garbage bins, gray-water waste sump, and fire grills are provided. There is no drinking water. Some facilities are wheelchair accessible. Leashed pets are permitted.

**Reservations, fees:** Reservations are not accepted. Sites are $10 per night, $5 per night per additional vehicle. Open year-round, weather permitting.

**Directions:** From Roseburg, drive east on Highway 138 for 40 miles (just past Steamboat) to the camp on the right. The campground is along the highway.

**Contact:** Umpqua National Forest, North Umpqua Ranger District, 541/496-3532, www.fs.usda.gov/umpqua.

## 95 CANTON CREEK

### Scenic rating: 8

near the North Umpqua River in Umpqua National Forest

**Map 11.4, page 598**

Set at an elevation of 1,195 feet at the confluence of Canton and Steamboat Creeks, this camp is less than a mile from the North Umpqua River and gets little overnight use—but lots of day swimmers come here in July and August. No fishing is permitted on Steamboat or Canton Creeks because they are spawning areas for steelhead and salmon. Steamboat Falls is six miles north on Forest Road 38.

**Campsites, facilities:** There are five sites for tents or RVs up to 22 feet long. Picnic tables and fire grills are provided. Drinking water, a covered picnic gazebo, and flush toilets are available. Garbage must be packed out. Leashed pets are permitted.

**Reservations, fees:** Reservations are not accepted. Sites are $10 per night, $5 per night per additional vehicle. Open mid-May–mid-October, weather permitting.

**Directions:** From Roseburg, drive east on Highway 138 for 39 miles to Steamboat and Forest Road 38 (Steamboat Creek Road). Turn left and drive 0.25 mile to the campground on the right.

**Contact:** Umpqua National Forest, North Umpqua Ranger District, 541/496-3532, www.fs.usda.gov/umpqua.

## 96 HORSESHOE BEND/ DEER FLAT GROUP

### Scenic rating: 8

on the Umpqua River in Umpqua National Forest

**Map 11.4, page 598**

This campground, set at an elevation of 1,300 feet, is in the middle of a big bend in the North Umpqua River. This spot is a major launching point for white-water rafting. Fly-fishing is popular here and is the only type of fishing allowed.

**Campsites, facilities:** There are 23 sites and two double sites for tents or RVs up to 35 feet long. Deer Flat is a group site for up to 70 people. Picnic tables, fire grills, garbage bins, drinking water, gray-water sump, and flush toilets are provided. A store, gas, and propane are available one mile east. Raft-launching facilities are nearby. Some facilities are wheelchair accessible. Leashed pets are permitted.

**Reservations, fees:** Reservations are accepted for the Deer Flat group site at 877/444-6777 ($10 reservation fee) or www.recreation.gov ($9 reservation fee); reservations are not accepted for single sites. Sites are $15 per night, $5 per night per additional vehicle; the Deer Flat group site is $100 per night. Open mid-May-late September, weather permitting.

**Directions:** From Roseburg on I-5, take Exit 120. Drive east on Highway 138 for 47 miles to Forest Road 4750. Turn right and drive south a short distance to the campground entrance road on the right.

**Contact:** Umpqua National Forest, North Umpqua Ranger District, 541/496-3532, www.fs.usda.gov/umpqua.

## 97 EAGLE ROCK

### Scenic rating: 9
on the North Umpqua River in Umpqua National Forest

**Map 11.4, page 598**

Eagle Rock camp sits next to the North Umpqua River and adjacent to the Boulder Creek Wilderness. It is named after Eagle Rock, which, along with Rattlesnake Rock, towers above the campground. The camp offers outstanding views of these unusual rock formations. It gets moderate use, heavy on weekends. The camp sits at 1,676 feet elevation near Boulder Flat, a major launch point for rafting. Fishing here is restricted to the use of artificial lures with a single barbless hook.

**Campsites, facilities:** There are 25 sites for tents or RVs up to 30 feet long, including two double sites. Picnic tables and fire grills are provided. Vault toilets, garbage bins, and gray-water disposal are available. There is no drinking water. A store, propane, and ice are within five miles. Some facilities are wheelchair accessible. Leashed pets are permitted.

**Reservations, fees:** Reservations are not accepted. Sites are $10 per night, $5 per night per additional vehicle. Open mid-May-October, weather permitting.

**Directions:** From Roseburg, drive east on Highway 138 for 53 miles to the campground on the left.

**Contact:** Umpqua National Forest, North Umpqua Ranger District, 541/496-3532, www.fs.usda.gov/umpqua.

## 98 BOULDER FLAT

### Scenic rating: 8
on the North Umpqua River in Umpqua National Forest

**Map 11.4, page 598**          **BEST (**

Boulder Flat campground is nestled along the banks of the North Umpqua River at the confluence with Boulder Creek. There's good trout fishing here (fly-fishing only) and outstanding scenery. The camp sits at a major launching point for white-water rafting. Across the river from the campground, a trail follows Boulder Creek north for 10.5 miles through the Boulder Creek Wilderness, a climb in elevation from 2,000 to 5,400 feet. It's a good thumper for backpackers. Access to the trail is at Soda Springs Dam, two miles east of the camp. A little over a mile to the east you can see some huge, dramatic pillars of volcanic rock, colored with lichen.

**Campsites, facilities:** There are nine sites for tents or RVs up to 24 feet long. Picnic tables, garbage bins, and fire grills are provided. Vault toilets are available. There is no drinking water. A store, propane, and ice are within five miles. A raft launch is on-site. Some facilities are wheelchair accessible. Leashed pets are permitted.

**Reservations, fees:** Reservations are not accepted. Sites are $8 per night, $4 per night per additional vehicle. Open year-round.

**Directions:** From Roseburg, drive east on Highway 138 for 54 miles to the campground on the left.

**Contact:** Umpqua National Forest, North Umpqua Ranger District, 541/496-3532, www.fs.usda.gov/umpqua.

## 99 TOKETEE LAKE

### Scenic rating: 7
on Toketee Lake in Umpqua National Forest

Map 11.4, page 598

Located just north of Toketee Lake, this campground sits at an elevation of 2,200 feet. The North Umpqua River Trail passes near camp and continues east along the river for many miles. Die-hard hikers can also take the trail west toward the Boulder Creek Wilderness. Toketee Lake, a 97-acre reservoir, offers a good population of brown and rainbow trout and many recreation options. A worthwhile point of interest is Toketee Falls, just west of the lake turnoff. Another is Umpqua Hot Springs, a few miles northeast of the camp. The area sustains a wide variety of wildlife; you might see bald eagles, beavers, a variety of ducks and geese, great blue herons, kingfishers, and otters in fall and winter.

**Campsites, facilities:** There are 33 sites for tents or RVs up to 22 feet long and one group site for up to 50 people. Picnic tables and fire grills are provided. Vault toilets are available, but there is no drinking water or garbage disposal. Boat docks and launching facilities are nearby. Leashed pets are permitted.

**Reservations, fees:** Reservations are not accepted. Sites are $10 per night, $5 per night per additional vehicle, and $25 per night for the group site. Open year-round.

**Directions:** From Roseburg, drive east on Highway 138 for 59 miles to Forest Road 34. Turn left (north) and drive 1.5 miles to the campground on the right.

**Contact:** Umpqua National Forest, Diamond Lake Ranger District, 541/498-2531, www.fs.usda.gov/umpqua.

## 100 EAST LEMOLO

### Scenic rating: 8
on Lemolo Lake in Umpqua National Forest

Map 11.4, page 598

This campground is on the southeastern shore of Lemolo Lake, where boating and fishing are some of the recreation possibilities. Boats with motors and personal watercraft are allowed. The North Umpqua River and its adjacent trail lie just beyond the north shore of the lake. If you hike for two miles northwest of the lake, you can reach spectacular Lemolo Falls. Large German brown trout, a wild, native fish, can be taken on troll and fly. Lemolo Lake also provides fishing for brook trout, kokanee, and a sprinkling of rainbow trout.

**Campsites, facilities:** There are 15 sites for tents or small RVs up to 22 feet long. Picnic tables and fire rings are provided. Vault toilets are available. There is no drinking water and garbage must be packed out. Boat docks, launching facilities, boat rentals, dump station, restaurants, a store, coin laundry, and showers are nearby. Leashed pets are permitted.

**Reservations, fees:** Reservations are not accepted. Sites are $10 per night, $5 per night per additional vehicle. Open mid-May-late October, weather permitting.

**Directions:** From Roseburg, drive east on Highway 138 for 73 miles to Forest Road 2610 (three miles east of Clearwater Falls). Turn left (north) and drive three miles to Forest Road 2614. Turn right and drive two miles to Forest Road 2614-430. Turn left and drive a short distance to the campground at the end of the road.

**Contact:** Umpqua National Forest, Diamond Lake Ranger District, 541/498-2531, www.fs.usda.gov/umpqua.

## 101 POOLE CREEK

### Scenic rating: 8
on Lemolo Lake in Umpqua National Forest

**Map 11.4, page 598**

Poole Creek campground on the western shore of Lemolo Lake isn't far from Lemolo Lake Resort, which is open for recreation year-round. The camp is just south of the mouth of Poole Creek in a lodgepole pine, mountain hemlock, and Shasta red fir forest. This is by far the most popular U.S. Forest Service camp at the lake, especially with water-skiers, who are allowed to ski in designated areas of the lake.

**Campsites, facilities:** There are 60 sites for tents or RVs up to 35 feet long and one group site for up to 60 people. Picnic tables and fire grills are provided. Drinking water and vault toilets are available. A grocery store, a restaurant, boat docks, launching facilities, and rentals are nearby. Leashed pets are permitted.

**Reservations, fees:** Reservations are not accepted for single sites but are required for the group camp at 877/444-6777 or www.recreation.gov ($10 reservation fee). Single sites are $15 per night, double sites are $20 per night, $5 per night per additional vehicle, and $85 per night for the group camp. Open late April-late October, weather permitting.

**Directions:** From Roseburg, drive east on Highway 138 for 73 miles to Forest Road 2610 (Bird's Point Road). Turn left (north) and drive four miles to the signed turnoff for the campground entrance on the right.

**Contact:** Umpqua National Forest, Diamond Lake Ranger District, 541/498-2531, www.fs.usda.gov/umpqua.

## 102 INLET

### Scenic rating: 5
on Lemolo Lake in Umpqua National Forest

**Map 11.4, page 598**

Inlet campground sits on the eastern inlet of Lemolo Lake, hidden in the deep, green, and quiet forest where the North Umpqua River rushes into Lemolo Reservoir. The camp is just across the road from the North Umpqua River Trail, which is routed east into the Oregon Cascades Recreation Area and the Mount Thielsen Wilderness. Lemolo Lake exceeds 100 feet in depth in some spots; boating and fishing for brook trout, kokanee, and rainbow trout are some recreation possibilities. (Boats with motors and personal watercraft are allowed.) Two miles northwest of the lake lies spectacular Lemolo Falls, a good hike.

**Campsites, facilities:** There are 14 sites for tents or RVs up to 22 feet long. Picnic tables and fire grills are provided. Vault toilets are available. There is no drinking water and garbage must be packed out. Boat docks, launching facilities, rentals, a restaurant, groceries, and a gas station are available nearby. Leashed pets are permitted.

**Reservations, fees:** Reservations are not accepted. Sites are $10 per night, $5 per night per additional vehicle. Open mid-May-late October, weather permitting.

**Directions:** From Roseburg, drive east on Highway 138 for 73 miles to Forest Road 2610. Turn left (north) and drive three miles to Forest Road 2614. Turn right (east) and drive three miles to the campground.

**Contact:** Umpqua National Forest, Diamond Lake Ranger District, 541/498-2531, www.fs.usda.gov/umpqua.

## 103 BUNKER HILL

🥾 🚵 🏊 🛶 🚣 🐴 🚐 ⛺

**Scenic rating: 7**

on Crescent Lake in Umpqua National Forest

**Map 11.4, page 598**

Bunker Hill campground, on the northwest shore of Lemolo Reservoir, is in a heavily wooded area of lodgepole pine. Fishing is excellent for kokanee as well as brook, rainbow, and large native brown trout. Nearby hiking trails lead to Lemolo Falls, the North Umpqua River, and the Pacific Crest Trail.

**Campsites, facilities:** There are eight sites for tents or RVs up to 22 feet long. Picnic tables and fire rings are provided. Vault toilets are available. There is no drinking water and garbage must be packed out. A boat ramp, boat rentals, a dump station, a restaurant, coin laundry, and coin showers are available 1.5 miles away at Lemolo Lake Resort. Leashed pets are permitted.

**Reservations, fees:** Reservations are not accepted. Sites are $10 per night, $5 per night per additional vehicle. Open May-October, weather permitting.

**Directions:** From Roseburg, drive east on Highway 138 for 73 miles to Bird's Point Road/Forest Road 2610. Turn left and drive 5.5 miles (crossing the dam) to Forest Road 2612. Turn right and drive to the camp at the north end of the lake.

**Contact:** Umpqua National Forest, Diamond Lake Ranger District, 541/498-2531, www.fs.usda.gov/umpqua; Lemolo Lake Resort 541/643-0750.

## 104 LEMOLO LAKE RV PARK

🥾 🚵 🏊 🛶 🚣 🎣 ♿ 🚐 ⛺

**Scenic rating: 7**

in Umpqua National Forest

**Map 11.4, page 598**

Lemolo Lake is situated high in the Cascade Mountains at just over 4,000 feet elevation. This RV park is set up for folks to bring their own boats and enjoy the lake. Boating, waterskiing, wakeboarding, and Jet Skis are all popular, along, of course, with fishing and swimming, on the lake (40-mph speed limit). Each campground reservation includes free boat launch. There are also miles of hiking trails in the vicinity, plus Crater Lake National Park and Diamond Lake are a quick drive away. In winter, cross-country skiing is popular, and an extensive snowmobile loop runs through the property.

**Campsites, facilities:** There are 28 sites, some with full or partial hookups, for tents or RVs of any length; five cabins and a hotel are also available. Picnic tables and fire rings are provided. Drinking water, flush toilets, coin showers, and coin laundry are available. A restaurant and store are on the premises. A boat launch and boat rentals are available. Some facilities are wheelchair accessible.

**Reservations, fees:** Reservations are accepted at 541/643-0750. RV sites with full hookups are $30 per night, tent sites are $20-25. Open year-round.

**Directions:** From Roseburg, drive east on Highway 138 (Diamond Lake Highway) for about 73 miles to Birds Point Road. Turn left on Birds Point Road and drive five miles to the resort.

**Contact:** Lemolo Lake RV Park, 541/643-0750, www.lemololakeresort.com.

## 105 TIMPANOGAS

🥾 🏊 🛶 🚣 🐴 ♿ 🚐 ⛺

**Scenic rating: 8**

on Timpanogas Lake in Willamette National Forest

**Map 11.4, page 598**

Timpanogas Lake is the headwaters of the Middle Fork Willamette River. This campground, at 5,200 feet elevation, is situated in a stand of grand, noble, and silver fir. Fishing for brook trout and cutthroat is good; only non-motorized boating is permitted. Nearby activities include 23 miles of hiking trails in the Timpanogas Basin trails, with views of the Cowhorn Mountains, Diamond Peak, and Sawtooth. Warning: Time it wrong (July-August) and the mosquitoes will eat you alive if you forget insect repellent.

**Campsites, facilities:** There are 10 sites for tents or RVs up to 24 feet long. Picnic tables, garbage bins, and fire rings are provided. Drinking water, vault toilets, and firewood are available. A primitive boat ramp is nearby, but no boats with motors are allowed. Some facilities are wheelchair accessible. Leashed pets are permitted.

**Reservations, fees:** Reservations are not accepted. Sites are $8 per night, $4 per night per additional vehicle. Open June-October, weather permitting.

**Directions:** From Eugene, drive south on I-5 for five miles to Exit 188 and Highway 58. Turn east and drive 35 miles to the town of Oakridge. Continue east on Highway 58 for two miles to Kitson Springs Road. Turn right and drive 0.5 mile to Forest Road 21. Turn right and drive 32 miles to Forest Road 2154. Turn left and drive about 10 miles to the campground on the left.

**Contact:** Willamette National Forest, Middle Fork Ranger District, 541/782-2283, www.fs.usda.gov/willamette.

## 106 WOLF CREEK
🏃 🏠 ♿ 🚐 ⛺

### Scenic rating: 6
on the Little River in Umpqua National Forest

**Map 11.4, page 598**

This pretty Little River camp is located at the entrance to the national forest, near the Wolf Creek Civilian Conservation Center. It is set at an elevation of 1,100 feet, with easy access to civilization. The campground has abundant wildflowers in the spring. If you want to get deeper into the Cascades, Hemlock Lake and Lake of the Woods are about 21 and 15 miles east, respectively.

**Campsites, facilities:** There are five sites for

tents or RVs up to 30 feet long and three sites for tents only. There is also a group site for up to 150 people. Picnic tables and fire grills are provided. Flush toilets, drinking water, a covered pavilion for groups, garbage bins, horseshoe pits, a softball field, and a volleyball court are available. Note that if the group site is taken, some recreation facilities may not be available to single-site campers. Some facilities are wheelchair accessible. Leashed pets are permitted.

**Reservations, fees:** Reservations are accepted for the group site only at 877/444-6777 ($10 reservation fee) or www.recreation.gov ($9 reservation fee). Sites are $15 per night, $5 per night per additional vehicle, and $110 per night for the group site. Open mid-May-September, weather permitting.

**Directions:** From Roseburg on I-5, take Exit 120. Drive east on Highway 138 for 18 miles to Glide and County Road 17. Turn right (southeast) and drive 12 miles (the road becomes Little River Road) to the campground on the right.

**Contact:** Umpqua National Forest, North Umpqua Ranger District, 541/496-3532, www.fs.usda.gov/umpqua.

## 107 COOLWATER
🏃 🏞 🛶 🐕 🚐 ⛺

### Scenic rating: 6
on the Little River in Umpqua National Forest

**Map 11.4, page 598**

Coolwater campground (1,300 feet elevation) along the banks of the Little River gets moderate use. It features a pretty forest setting with some scenic hiking trails nearby. Overhang Trail is within 0.5 mile of the campground. Fishing and swimming are also options here. Scenic Grotto Falls can be reached by traveling north on Forest Road 2703 (across the road from the camp). Near the falls, you'll find Emile Grove, home of a thicket of old-growth Douglas fir and the huge "Bill Taft Tree," named after the former president.

**Campsites, facilities:** There are seven sites for tents or RVs up to 24 feet long. Picnic tables and fire grills are provided. Drinking water, vault toilets, and garbage disposal are available. Leashed pets are permitted.

**Reservations, fees:** Reservations are not accepted. Sites are $10 per night, $5 per night per additional vehicle. Open year-round, weather permitting.

**Directions:** From Roseburg on I-5, take Exit 120. Drive east on Highway 138 for 18 miles to Glide and County Road 17. Turn right (southeast) and drive 15.5 miles (County Road 17 becomes Little River Road) to the campground on the right.

**Contact:** Umpqua National Forest, North Umpqua Ranger District, 541/496-3532, www.fs.usda.gov/umpqua.

## 108 WHITE CREEK

**Scenic rating: 6**
on the Little River in Umpqua National Forest

Map 11.4, page 598

Hiking and fishing are two of the recreation options at this campground set at the confluence of White Creek and the Little River. There is a sandy beach on shallow Little River, and waterfalls are in the area.

**Campsites, facilities:** There is an open parking area for tents or RVs up to 16 feet long, as well as three walk-in sites and one site near the parking lot. Picnic tables, fire grills, and garbage bins are provided. Drinking water and vault toilets are available. Leashed pets are permitted.

**Reservations, fees:** Reservations are not accepted. Sites are $10 per night, $5 per night per additional vehicle. Open year-round, weather permitting.

**Directions:** From Roseburg on I-5, take Exit 120. Drive east on Highway 138 for 18 miles to Glide and County Road 17. Turn right (southeast) and drive 18 miles (the road becomes Little River Road) to Forest Road 2792 (Red Butte Road). Bear right and drive 0.25 mile to the campground on the left.

**Contact:** Umpqua National Forest, North Umpqua Ranger District, 541/496-3532, www.fs.usda.gov/umpqua.

## 109 LAKE IN THE WOODS

**Scenic rating: 7**
on Lake in the Woods in Umpqua National Forest

Map 11.4, page 598

The shore of little Lake in the Woods is the setting of this camp, which makes a nice home base for several good hikes. One of them leaves the camp and heads south for about three miles to the Hemlock Lake Campground. Two other nearby trails provide short, scenic hikes to either Hemlock Falls or Yakso Falls. The campground sits at 3,200 feet elevation. This is a man-made, four-acre lake, eight feet at its deepest point. Boats without motors are allowed.

**Campsites, facilities:** There are eight sites for tents or RVs up to 35 feet long, one site for tents only, and two double sites. Picnic tables, fire grills, and garbage bins are provided. Drinking water and vault toilets are available. Leashed pets are permitted.

**Reservations, fees:** Reservations are not accepted. Sites are $10 per night, $5 per night per additional vehicle. Open late May-late October, weather permitting.

**Directions:** From Roseburg on I-5, take Exit 120. Drive east on Highway 138 for 18 miles to Glide and County Road 17. Turn right (southeast) and drive 18 miles (the road becomes Little River Road) to Forest Road 27. Continue 11 miles to the campground. The last seven miles are gravel.

**Contact:** Umpqua National Forest, North Umpqua Ranger District, 541/496-3532, www.fs.usda.gov/umpqua.

## 110 HEMLOCK LAKE

### Scenic rating: 8

on Hemlock Lake in Umpqua National Forest

**Map 11.4, page 598**    **BEST (**

This is a little-known jewel of a spot. For starters, it's set along the shore of Hemlock Lake at 4,400 feet elevation. This is a 28-acre, manufactured reservoir that is 33 feet at its deepest point. An eight-mile loop trail called the Yellow Jacket Loop is just south of the campground. Another trail leaves camp and heads north for about three miles to the Lake in the Woods campground. From there, it's just a short hike to either Hemlock Falls or Yakso Falls, both spectacularly scenic.

**Campsites, facilities:** There are nine sites for tents or RVs up to 35 feet long, three sites for tents only, and one double site. Picnic tables, fire grills, and garbage bins are provided. Vault toilets are available, but there is no drinking water. Boat docks and launching facilities are nearby. No motors are allowed on the lake. Leashed pets are permitted.

**Reservations, fees:** Reservations are not accepted. Sites are $10 per night, $5 per night per additional vehicle. Open year-round, weather permitting.

**Directions:** From Roseburg on I-5, take Exit 120. Drive east on Highway 138 for 18 miles to Glide and County Road 17. Turn right (southeast) and drive 32 miles to the campground on the right.

**Contact:** Umpqua National Forest, North Umpqua Ranger District, 541/496-3532, www.fs.usda.gov/umpqua.

## 111 WHITEHORSE FALLS

### Scenic rating: 8

on the Clearwater River in Umpqua National Forest

**Map 11.4, page 598**

Whitehorse Falls campground sits along the Clearwater River, one of the coldest streams in Umpqua National Forest. Even though the camp is adjacent to the highway, the setting is primitive. It is shaded by old-growth Douglas fir and is located at an elevation of 3,790 feet. Pretty Clearwater Falls, a few miles east, makes for a good side trip. Other recreation options include fishing and hiking.

**Campsites, facilities:** There are five sites for tents or RVs up to 25 feet long. Picnic tables and fire grills are provided. Vault toilets are available, but there is no drinking water or garbage service. Leashed pets are permitted.

**Reservations, fees:** Reservations are not accepted. Sites are $10 per night, $5 per night per additional vehicle. Open June-late October, weather permitting.

**Directions:** From Roseburg, drive east on Highway 138 for 66 miles to the campground on the left.

**Contact:** Umpqua National Forest, Diamond Lake Ranger District, 541/498-2531, www.fs.usda.gov/umpqua.

## 112 CLEARWATER FALLS

### Scenic rating: 8

on the Clearwater River in Umpqua National Forest

**Map 11.4, page 598**

The main attraction at this campground along the banks of the Clearwater River is the nearby cascading section of stream called Clearwater Falls. Hiking and fishing opportunities abound. The camp sits at an elevation of 4,100 feet.

**Campsites, facilities:** There are 12 sites for tents or RVs up to 30 feet long. Picnic tables and fire grills are provided. Vault toilets are available. There is no drinking water and garbage must be packed out. Leashed pets are permitted.

**Reservations, fees:** Reservations are not accepted. Sites are $10 per night, $5 per night per additional vehicle. Open mid-May-October, weather permitting.

**Directions:** From Roseburg, drive east on Highway 138 for 70 miles to a signed turn for Clearwater Falls. Turn right and drive to the campground.

**Contact:** Umpqua National Forest, Diamond Lake Ranger District, 541/498-2531, www.fs.usda.gov/umpqua.

## 113 BROKEN ARROW

### Scenic rating: 6

on Diamond Lake in Umpqua National Forest

**Map 11.4, page 598**

Broken Arrow campground sits at 5,190 feet elevation near the south shore of Diamond Lake, the largest natural lake in Umpqua National Forest. Set back from the lake, it is surrounded by lodgepole pine and features views of Mount Bailey and Mount Thielsen. Bicycling, boating, fishing, hiking, and swimming keep visitors busy here. Diamond Lake is adjacent to Crater Lake National Park, Mount Bailey, and the Mount Thielsen Wilderness, all of which offer a variety of recreation opportunities year-round. Diamond Lake is quite popular with anglers because of its good trout trolling, particularly in early summer.

**Campsites, facilities:** There are 130 sites for tents or RVs up to 40 feet long and four group sites which accommodate 40-104 people. Picnic tables, fire grills, and garbage bins are provided. Restrooms with flush toilets and showers, a dump station, and drinking water are available. Boat docks, launching facilities, and rentals are nearby. Some facilities are wheelchair accessible. Leashed pets are permitted.

**Reservations, fees:** Reservations are accepted only for group sites at 877/444-6777 ($10 reservation fee) or www.recreation.gov ($9 reservation fee). Sites are $15-20 per night, $5 per night per additional vehicle, and the group sites are $70-165 per night. Open June-mid-September.

**Directions:** From Roseburg, drive east on Highway 138 for 78.5 miles to Diamond Lake Loop (Forest Road 4795). Turn right (south) and drive four miles (along the east shore) to the campground turnoff road. Turn right and continue one mile to the camp on the left at the southern end of the lake.

**Contact:** Umpqua National Forest, Diamond Lake Ranger District, 541/498-2531, www.fs.usda.gov/umpqua.

## 114 THIELSEN VIEW

### Scenic rating: 7

on Diamond Lake in Umpqua National Forest

**Map 11.4, page 598**

This campground sits along the west shore of Diamond Lake in the shadow of majestic Mount Bailey. There is a beautiful view of Mount Thielsen from here.

Diamond Lake is popular with anglers and for boating, fishing, hiking, and swimming and the 11 miles of bike trails that keep everyone else busy. Nearby Crater Lake National Park, Mount Bailey, and the Mount Thielsen Wilderness offer recreation opportunities year-round.

**Campsites, facilities:** There are 60 sites for tents or RVs up to 30 feet long. Picnic tables, fire grills, and garbage bins are provided. Drinking water, vault toilets, and gray-water waste sumps are available. Boat docks and launching facilities are located adjacent to the campground, and boats can be rented at a resort five miles away. Some facilities are wheelchair accessible. Leashed pets are permitted.

**Reservations, fees:** Reservations are not accepted. Sites are $15-20 per night, $5 per night per additional vehicle. Open mid-May-mid-September, weather permitting.

**Directions:** From Roseburg, drive east on Highway 138 for 78.5 miles to Diamond Lake Loop (Forest Road 4795). Turn right and drive a short distance to the junction with the loop road. Continue on the loop road and drive four miles to the campground on the left.

**Contact:** Umpqua National Forest, Diamond Lake Ranger District, 541/498-2531, www.fs.usda.gov/umpqua.

## 115 DIAMOND LAKE

### Scenic rating: 9
on Diamond Lake in Umpqua National Forest

**Map 11.4, page 598**

Diamond Lake is a true gem of the Cascades, and there's finally hope the trout fishing will return to its once famous status. This extremely popular camp along the east shore of Diamond Lake has all the luxuries: flush toilets, showers, and drinking water. There are campfire programs every Friday and Saturday night in the summer. Jet Skis and other motorized watercraft are not allowed. Bring your mosquito repellent.

**Campsites, facilities:** There are 238 sites for tents or RVs up to 45 feet long. Picnic tables, garbage bins, and fire grills are provided. Restrooms with flush toilets and showers, drinking water, a dump station, and an amphitheater are available. Boat docks, launching facilities, and a fish-cleaning station are available. Boat rentals are nearby. Leashed pets are permitted.

**Reservations, fees:** Reservations are recommended and are accepted at 877/444-6777 ($10 reservation fee) or www.recreation.gov ($9 reservation fee). Sites are $16-27 per night, $5 per night per additional vehicle. Open late April-late October, weather permitting.

**Directions:** From Roseburg, drive east on Highway 138 for 78.5 miles to Diamond Lake Loop (Forest Road 4795). Turn right and drive a short distance to the junction with a loop road. Turn right (south) and drive two miles (along the east shore) to the campground on the right.

**Contact:** Umpqua National Forest, Diamond Lake Ranger District, 541/498-2531, www.fs.usda.gov/umpqua.

## 116 CAMP COMFORT

### Scenic rating: 6
on the South Umpqua River in Umpqua National Forest

**Map 11.4, page 598**

Camp Comfort is located near the upper South Umpqua River, deep in the Umpqua National Forest, at an elevation of 2,000 feet. Large old-growth cedars shade the campsites. No fishing is permitted. South Umpqua Falls (you will pass the access point while driving to this camp) makes a good side trip. Nearby trailheads provide access to Rogue-Umpqua Divide Wilderness (a map of Umpqua National Forest will be helpful in locating them).

**Campsites, facilities:** There are five sites for tents or RVs up to 22 feet long. Picnic tables and fire grills are provided. A vault toilet and garbage bins are available. There is no drinking water. Some facilities are wheelchair accessible. Leashed pets are permitted.

**Reservations, fees:** Reservations are not accepted. Sites are $10 per night, $5 per night per additional vehicle. Open May-October.

**Directions:** At Canyonville on I-5, take Exit 99 to County Road 1. Drive east on County Road 1 for 25 miles to Tiller and County Road 46. Turn left and drive six miles northeast (County Road 46 turns into South Umpqua Road/Forest Road 28). Continue northeast and drive 22 miles to the camp on the right.

**Contact:** Umpqua National Forest, Tiller Ranger District, 541/825-3100, www.fs.usda.gov/umpqua.

## 117 HAMAKER

### Scenic rating: 8
near the Upper Rogue River in Rogue River Siskiyou National Forest

**Map 11.4, page 598**

Set at 4,000 feet elevation near the Upper Rogue River, Hamaker is a beautiful little spot high in a mountain meadow. Wildflowers and wildlife abound in the spring and early summer. One of the least-used camps in the area, it's a prime camp for Crater Lake visitors.

**Campsites, facilities:** There are 10 sites for tents or RVs up to 30 feet long. Picnic tables and fire grills are provided. Drinking water and vault toilets are available. Garbage service must be packed out. Firewood is available for purchase. Leashed pets are permitted.

**Reservations, fees:** Reservations are not accepted. Sites are $14 per night, $7 per night per additional vehicle. Open late May-late October, weather permitting.

**Directions:** From Medford, drive northeast on Highway 62 for 57 miles (just past Union Creek) to Highway 230. Turn left (north) and drive 11 miles to a junction with Forest Road 6530. Continue on Forest Road 6530 for 0.5 mile to Forest Road 6530-900. Turn right and drive 0.5 mile to the campground.

**Contact:** Rogue River-Siskiyou National Forest, Prospect Ranger District, 541/560-3400 or 541/560-3900, www.fs.usda.gov/rogue-siskiyou or www.roguerec.com.

## 118 BOULDER CREEK

### Scenic rating: 4
on the South Umpqua River in Umpqua National Forest

**Map 11.4, page 598**

Set at 1,400 feet elevation, this campground hugs the banks of the South Umpqua River near Boulder Creek. Unfortunately, no fishing is allowed here, but pleasant side trips include the fishing ladder and waterfall at nearby South Umpqua Falls.

**Campsites, facilities:** There are seven sites for tents or RVs up to 22 feet long. Picnic tables, fire grills, and garbage bins are provided. Vault toilets and drinking water are available. Some facilities are wheelchair accessible. Leashed pets are permitted.

**Reservations, fees:** Reservations are not

accepted. Sites are $10 per night, $5 per night per additional vehicle. Open May-October, weather permitting.

**Directions:** At Canyonville on I-5, take Exit 99 to County Road 1. Drive east on County Road 1 for 25 miles to Tiller and County Road 46. Turn left, then drive six miles northeast (County Road 46 turns into South Umpqua Road/Forest Road 28). Continue northeast and drive seven miles to the camp.

**Contact:** Umpqua National Forest, Tiller Ranger District, 541/825-3100, www.fs.usda.gov/umpqua.

## 119 DUMONT CREEK

### Scenic rating: 4
on the South Umpqua River in Umpqua National Forest

**Map 11.4, page 598**

Dumont Creek is set at 1,300 feet elevation along the banks of the South Umpqua River, just above the mouth of Dumont Creek. Quiet, primitive, and remote, it gets moderate to heavy use. A short trail leads to a small beach on the river. No fishing is allowed at this camp, and there is no trailer turnaround here. Boulder Creek, just a few miles east, provides a camping alternative. A good side trip is nearby South Umpqua Falls, a beautiful, wide waterfall featuring a fish ladder and a platform so you can watch the fish struggle upstream.

**Campsites, facilities:** There are three sites for tents. Picnic tables, fire grills, and garbage bins are provided. Vault toilets are available, but there is no drinking water. Some facilities are wheelchair accessible. Leashed pets are permitted.

**Reservations, fees:** Reservations are not accepted. Sites are $10 per night, $5 per night per additional vehicle. Open May-October, weather permitting.

**Directions:** At Canyonville on I-5, take Exit 99 to County Road 1. Drive east on County Road 1 for 25 miles to Tiller and County Road

46. Turn left and drive six miles northeast (County Road 46 turns into South Umpqua Road/Forest Road 28). Continue northeast and drive 5.5 miles to the camp.

**Contact:** Umpqua National Forest, Tiller Ranger District, 541/825-3100, www.fs.usda.gov/umpqua.

## 120 COVER

### Scenic rating: 4
on Jackson Creek in Umpqua National Forest

**Map 11.4, page 598**

If you want quiet, this camp set at 1,700 feet elevation along the banks of Jackson Creek is the right place, since hardly anyone knows about it. Cover gets light use during the summer. During the fall hunting season, however, it is known to fill. If you head east to Forest Road 68 and follow the road south, you'll have access to a major trail into the Rogue-Umpqua Divide Wilderness. Be sure not to miss the world's largest sugar pine tree, a few miles west of camp. No fishing is allowed here.

**Campsites, facilities:** There are seven sites for tents or RVs up to 22 feet long. Picnic tables, fire grills, and garbage bins are provided. Drinking water and vault toilets are available. Some facilities are wheelchair accessible. Leashed pets are permitted.

**Reservations, fees:** Reservations are not accepted. Sites are $10 per night, $5 per night per additional vehicle. Open May-October, weather permitting.

**Directions:** At Canyonville on I-5, take Exit 99 to County Road 1. Drive east on County Road 1 for 25 miles to Tiller and County Road 46. Turn left and drive five miles to Forest Road 29 (Jackson Creek Road). Turn right and drive east for 12 miles to the campground on the right.

**Contact:** Umpqua National Forest, Tiller Ranger District, 541/825-3100, www.fs.usda.gov/umpqua.

## 121 QUINN MEADOW HORSE CAMP

### Scenic rating: 8
near Quinn Creek in Deschutes National Forest

**Map 11.5, page 599**

This scenic campground (elevation 5,100 feet) is open only to horse camping and gets high use. The Elk-Devil's Trail and Wickiup Plains Trail offer access to the Three Sisters Wilderness. There's also a horse route to Devil's Lake via Katsuk Trail.

**Campsites, facilities:** There are 26 sites for tents or RVs up to 40 feet long. Picnic tables and fire rings are provided. Horse corrals, stalls, and a manure-disposal site are available. Drinking water, vault toilets, and garbage bins are also available. Some facilities are wheelchair accessible. Leashed pets are permitted.

**Reservations, fees:** Reservations are accepted at 877/444-6777 ($10 reservation fee) or www.recreation.gov ($9 reservation fee). Two-horse corral sites are $14, four-horse corral sites are $18, $7-9 per night per additional vehicle. Open late June-September, weather permitting.

**Directions:** From Bend, drive southwest on Cascades Lakes Highway (also called Century Drive Highway and County Road 46) for 31.2 miles to the campground entrance on the left.

**Contact:** Deschutes National Forest, Bend-Fort Rock Ranger District, 541/383-4000, www.fs.usda.gov/centraloregon.

## 122 DEVIL'S LAKE WALK-IN

### Scenic rating: 8
on Devil's Lake in Deschutes National Forest

**Map 11.5, page 599**

This walk-in campground borders the shore of a scenic alpine lake with aqua-jade water and fishing access. Devil's Lake, set at 5,500 feet, is a popular rafting and canoeing spot, and several trailheads lead from the lake into the wilderness. No motorized boats are allowed. The Elk-Devil's Trail and Wickiup Plains Trail offer access to the Three Sisters Wilderness. There's also a horse route to Quinn Meadow Horse Camp via Katsuk Trail.

**Campsites, facilities:** There are 11 walk-in sites for tents only. Picnic tables and fire grills are provided. Vault toilets are available. There is no drinking water, and garbage must be packed out. Leashed pets are permitted.

**Reservations, fees:** Reservations are not accepted. There is no fee, but a Northwest Forest Pass ($5 daily fee or $30 annual fee per parked vehicle) is required. Open June-October, weather permitting.

**Directions:** From Bend, drive southwest on Cascades Lakes Highway (Century Drive Highway, which becomes County Road 46) for 28.7 miles to the parking area. Walk 200 yards to the campground.

**Contact:** Deschutes National Forest, Bend-Fort Rock Ranger District, 541/383-4000, www.fs.usda.gov/centraloregon.

## 123 SODA CREEK
🏃 🛶 🚐 🏊 🐴 🚐 ⛺

### Scenic rating: 5
near Sparks Lake in Deschutes National Forest

**Map 11.5, page 599**

This campground, nestled between two meadows in a pastoral setting, is on the road to Sparks Lake. Boating—particularly canoeing—is ideal at Sparks Lake, about a two-mile drive away. Also at the lake, a loop trail hugs the shore; about 0.5 mile of it is paved and barrier-free. Only fly-fishing is permitted. The camp sits at 5,450 feet elevation.

**Campsites, facilities:** There are six sites for tents or RVs up to 30 feet long and one multiple site. Picnic tables and fire grills are provided. Vault toilets are available. There is no drinking water, and garbage must be packed out. Leashed pets are permitted.

**Reservations, fees:** Reservations are not accepted. Single sites are $10 per night, multiple sites are $20 per night, $5 per night per extra vehicle. Open June-October, weather permitting.

**Directions:** From Bend, drive southwest on Cascades Lakes Highway (also called Century Drive Highway and County Road 46) for 26.2 miles to Forest Road 400 (at sign for Sparks Lake). Turn left (east) and drive 25 yards to the campground.

**Contact:** Deschutes National Forest, Bend-Fort Rock Ranger District, 541/383-4000, www.fs.usda.gov/centraloregon.

## 124 TODD LAKE HIKE-IN
🏃 🛶 🚐 🚤 🐴 ⛺

### Scenic rating: 8
near Todd Lake in Deschutes National Forest

**Map 11.5, page 599**

Todd Lake is a trailhead camp, with a trail access point here for hikers and horses to the Three Sisters Wilderness. One of numerous camps in the area that offer a pristine mountain experience yet can be reached by car, small Todd Lake campground sits 0.5 mile from the shore of an alpine lake at 6,200 feet elevation. It's popular for canoeing and offers great views. No bikes or horses are allowed on the trail around the lake.

**Campsites, facilities:** There are three hike-in tent sites. Picnic tables and fire grills are provided. Vault toilets are available. There is no drinking water, and garbage must be packed out. Leashed pets are permitted.

**Reservations, fees:** Reservations are not accepted. There is no fee for camping, but a Northwest Forest Pass ($5 daily fee or $30 annual fee per parked vehicle) is required. Open July-October, weather permitting.

**Directions:** From Bend, drive southwest on Cascades Lakes Highway (also called Century Drive Highway and County Road 46) for 24 miles to Forest Road 370. Turn right (north) and drive 0.5 mile to the parking area. Hike 0.5 mile to the campground.

**Contact:** Deschutes National Forest, Bend-Fort Rock Ranger District, 541/383-4000, www.fs.usda.gov/centraloregon.

## 125 POINT

### Scenic rating: 8
on Elk Lake in Deschutes National Forest

**Map 11.5, page 599**

Point campground is situated along the shore of Elk Lake at an elevation of 4,900 feet. Fishing for kokanee salmon and brook trout can be good; hiking is another option. Swimming and water sports are popular during warm weather.

**Campsites, facilities:** There are eight sites for tents or RVs up to 26 feet long, and one group site. Picnic tables and fire grills are provided. Vault toilets and garbage service are available. Drinking water is usually available. Boat docks and launching facilities are on-site. A store, restaurant, and propane are at Elk Lake Resort, one mile away. Leashed pets are permitted.

**Reservations, fees:** Reservations are not accepted. Sites are $14 per night, $7 per night per additional vehicle; the group site is $26 for up to 15 people and four vehicles. Open late May-late September, weather permitting.

**Directions:** From Bend, drive southwest on Cascades Lakes Highway (Century Drive Highway, which becomes County Road 46) for 34 miles to the campground on the left.

**Contact:** Deschutes National Forest, Bend-Fort Rock Ranger District, 541/383-4000, www.fs.usda.gov/centraloregon.

## 126 ELK LAKE

### Scenic rating: 8
on Elk Lake in Deschutes National Forest

**Map 11.5, page 599**

This campground hugs the shore of Elk Lake at 4,900 feet elevation. It is adjacent to Elk Lake Resort, which has a store, a restaurant, and propane. Elk Lake is popular for windsurfing and sailing.

**Campsites, facilities:** There are 22 sites for tents or RVs up to 30 feet long, but sites are best suited for tents. Picnic tables and fire grills are provided. Vault toilets, drinking water, and garbage service are available. Boat-launching facilities are on-site. Boat rentals can be obtained nearby. Leashed pets are permitted.

**Reservations, fees:** Reservations are not accepted. Sites are $14 per night, $7 per night per additional vehicle. Open mid-May-mid-September, weather permitting.

**Directions:** From Bend, drive southwest on Cascades Lakes Highway (Century Drive Highway, which becomes County Road 46) and drive 33.1 miles to the campground at the north end of Elk Lake.

**Contact:** Deschutes National Forest, Bend-Fort Rock Ranger District, 541/383-4000, www.fs.usda.gov/centraloregon.

## 127 LITTLE FAWN

### Scenic rating: 5
on Elk Lake in Deschutes National Forest

**Map 11.5, page 599**

Choose between sites on the water's edge or nestled in the forest at this campground along the eastern shore of Elk Lake. Afternoon winds are common here, making this a popular spot for sailing and windsurfing. Fishing for kokanee salmon and brook trout can be good; hiking is another option. Swimming and water sports are popular during warm weather. A play area for children can be found at one of the lake's inlets. The camp sits at 4,900 feet elevation, with Little Fawn Group Camp located just beyond Little Fawn campground.

**Campsites, facilities:** There are 20 sites for tents or RVs up to 36 feet long and eight group sites for up to 75 people. Picnic tables and fire grills are provided. Vault toilets, drinking water, and garbage service are available. Boat-launching facilities and rentals are on-site. Leashed pets are permitted.

**Reservations, fees:** Reservations are accepted only for the group site at 877/444-6777 or www.recreation.gov ($10 reservation fee). Sites are $14 per night, $7 per night per additional vehicle, and $75-125 per night for the group sites. Open late May-September, weather permitting.

**Directions:** From Bend, drive southwest on Cascades Lakes Highway (Century Drive Highway, which becomes County Road 46) and drive 35.5 miles to Forest Road 4625. Turn left (east) and drive 1.7 miles to the campground.

**Contact:** Deschutes National Forest, Bend-Fort Rock Ranger District, 541/383-4000, www.fs.usda.gov/centraloregon.

## 128 MALLARD MARSH

**Scenic rating: 8**

on Hosmer Lake in Deschutes National Forest

**Map 11.5, page 599**          **BEST (**

Quiet Mallard Marsh campground is located on the shore of Hosmer Lake, at an elevation of 5,000 feet. The lake is stocked with brook trout and Atlantic salmon and reserved for catch-and-release fly-fishing only. You'll get a pristine, quality fishing experience here. The lake is ideal for canoeing. Only non-motorized boats are allowed.

**Campsites, facilities:** There are 15 sites for tents or RVs up to 26 feet long. Picnic tables, garbage service, and vault toilets are provided. No drinking water is available. Boat-launching facilities are nearby. Leashed pets are permitted.

**Reservations, fees:** Reservations are not accepted. Sites are $10 per night, $5 per night per additional vehicle. Open May-October, weather permitting.

**Directions:** From Bend, drive 35.5 miles southwest on Cascade Lakes Highway

(Highway 46). Turn east onto Forest Road 4625 and drive 1.3 miles toward Hosmer Lake. South Campground will come up on the right side first and then Mallard Marsh.

**Contact:** Deschutes National Forest, Bend-Fort Rock Ranger District, 541/383-4000, www.fs.usda.gov/centraloregon.

## 129 SOUTH

**Scenic rating: 8**

on Hosmer Lake in Deschutes National Forest

**Map 11.5, page 599**

South campground is located along the shore of Hosmer Lake, adjacent to Mallard Marsh, and enjoys the same fishing experience. It's a good option if Mallard Marsh is full.

**Campsites, facilities:** There are 23 sites for tents or RVs up to 20 feet long. Picnic tables, garbage service, and fire grills are provided. Vault toilets and boat-launching facilities are available. There is no drinking water. Leashed pets are permitted.

**Reservations, fees:** Reservations are not accepted. Sites are $10 per night, $5 per night per additional vehicle. Open mid-May-late September, weather permitting.

**Directions:** From Bend, drive southwest on Cascades Lakes Highway (Century Drive Highway, which becomes County Road 46) and drive 35.5 miles to Forest Road 4625. Turn left (east) and drive 1.2 miles to the campground on the right.

**Contact:** Deschutes National Forest, Bend-Fort Rock Ranger District, 541/383-4000, www.fs.usda.gov/centraloregon.

## 130 LAVA LAKE

**Scenic rating: 10**

on Lava Lake in Deschutes National Forest

**Map 11.5, page 599**          **BEST (**

This well-designed campground sits on the

shore of pretty Lava Lake at 4,750 feet elevation. Mount Bachelor and the Three Sisters are in the background, making a classic picture. Boating and fishing are popular here. A bonus is nearby Lava Lake Resort, which has showers, laundry facilities, an RV dump station, store, gasoline, and propane.

**Campsites, facilities:** There are 44 sites for tents or RVs up to 40 feet long. Picnic tables, garbage service, and fire grills are provided. Vault toilets, drinking water, and a fish-cleaning station are available. Boat docks and launching facilities are on-site. Boat rentals are nearby. Some facilities are wheelchair accessible. Leashed pets are permitted.

**Reservations, fees:** Reservations are not accepted. Sites are $14 per night, $7 per night per additional vehicle. Open mid-April-October, weather permitting.

**Directions:** From Bend, drive southwest on Cascades Lakes Highway (Century Drive Highway, which becomes County Road 46) and drive 38.4 miles to Forest Road 4600-500. Turn left (east) and drive one mile to the campground.

**Contact:** Deschutes National Forest, Bend-Fort Rock Ranger District, 541/383-4000, www.fs.usda.gov/centraloregon.

## 131 LITTLE LAVA LAKE

### Scenic rating: 8

on Little Lava Lake in Deschutes National Forest

**Map 11.5, page 599**

Little Lake feeds into the Deschutes River; boating, fishing, hiking, and swimming are some of the recreation options here. Choose from lakeside or riverside sites set at an elevation of 4,750 feet.

**Campsites, facilities:** There are 15 sites for tents or RVs up to 40 feet long and a group site for up to 30 people. Picnic tables and fire grills are provided. Vault toilets, drinking water, and garbage service are available. A

boat launch, docks, and rentals are nearby. There are also launching facilities on-site. Leashed pets are permitted.

**Reservations, fees:** Reservations are accepted at 877/444-6777 ($10 reservation fee) or www.recreation.gov ($9 reservation fee). Single sites are $12 per night, double sites are $22 per night, the group site is $50 per night, $6 per night per additional vehicle. Open early May-late October, weather permitting.

**Directions:** From Bend, drive southwest on Cascades Lakes Highway (Century Drive Highway, which becomes County Road 46) and drive 38.4 miles to Forest Road 4600-500. Turn left (east) and drive 0.7 mile to Forest Road 4600-520. Continue east for 0.4 mile to the campground.

**Contact:** Deschutes National Forest, Bend-Fort Rock Ranger District, 541/383-4000, www.fs.usda.gov/centraloregon.

## 132 SWAMP WELLS HORSE CAMP

### Scenic rating: 3

near the Arnold Ice Caves in Deschutes National Forest

**Map 11.5, page 599**

If you look at the map, this campground may appear to be quite remote, but it's actually in an area less than 30 minutes from Bend. Set at an elevation of 5,450 feet, this camp is a good place for horseback riding, but you don't need a horse to enjoy this spot. Trails heading south re-enter the forested areas. The system of lava tubes at the nearby Arnold Ice Caves is fun to explore; bring a bicycle helmet, a flashlight, and knee pads.

**Campsites, facilities:** There are five primitive sites for tents or RVs up to 16 feet long. Picnic tables and fire grills are provided. There are vault toilets, but no drinking water, and garbage must be packed out. Manure bins are available for horses. Leashed pets are permitted.

**Reservations, fees:** Reservations are not accepted. There is no fee for camping. Open April-late November, weather permitting.

**Directions:** From Bend, drive south on U.S. 97 for four miles to Forest Road 18/China Hat Road. Turn left (southeast) and drive 5.4 miles to Forest Road 1810. Turn right (south) and drive 5.8 miles to Forest Road 1816. Turn left (east) and drive three miles to the campground. The last mile is rough and primitive.

**Contact:** Deschutes National Forest, Bend-Fort Rock Ranger District, 541/383-4000, www.fs.usda.gov/centraloregon.

## 133 WEST CULTUS LAKE
🏃‍♀️ 🏊 🛶 🚤 🐴 ⛺

### Scenic rating: 5
on Cultus Lake in Deschutes National Forest

Map 11.5, page 599

This campground, set at 4,700 feet elevation along the west shore of Cultus Lake, is accessible by boat or trail only. It's about three miles by trail from the parking area to the campground. The lake is a good spot for fishing, swimming, and waterskiing. Trails branch out from the campground and provide access to numerous small backcountry lakes. Drinking water and boat-launching facilities are available at Cultus Lake.

**Campsites, facilities:** There are 12 boat-in or hike-in tent sites. Picnic tables and fire pits are provided. Vault toilets are available. There is no drinking water, and garbage must be packed out. Boat docks are available on-site; boat rentals are at Cultus Lake Resort. Leashed pets are permitted.

**Reservations, fees:** Reservations are not accepted. Sites are $15 per night. A Northwest Forest Pass ($5 daily fee or $30 annual fee per parked vehicle) is required. (The parking fee is waived if you park in the Cultus Lake Boat Launch lot.) Open May-late September, weather permitting.

**Directions:** From Bend, drive southwest on Cascades Lakes Highway (Century Drive Highway, which becomes County Road 46) and drive 46 miles to Forest Road 4635. Turn right (west) and drive two miles to the parking area. Boat or hike in about three miles to the west end of the lake.

**Contact:** Deschutes National Forest, Bend-Fort Rock Ranger District, 541/383-4000, www.fs.usda.gov/centraloregon.

## 134 CULTUS LAKE
🏃‍♀️ 🏊 🛶 🚤 🐴 🚐 ⛺

### Scenic rating: 7
on Cultus Lake in Deschutes National Forest

Map 11.5, page 599

Located along the east shore of Cultus Lake at 4,700 feet elevation, this camp is a popular spot for fishing, hiking, swimming, waterskiing, and windsurfing. The sites fill up early on weekends and holidays.

**Campsites, facilities:** There are 55 sites for tents or RVs up to 36 feet long. Picnic tables and fire grills are provided. Vault toilets, drinking water, and garbage service are available. Boat docks and launching facilities are on-site. Boat rentals are nearby. A restaurant, gasoline, and cabins are available nearby at Cultus Lake Resort. Leashed pets are permitted.

**Reservations, fees:** Reservations are not accepted. Sites are $16 per night, $8 per night per additional vehicle. Open mid-April-late September, weather permitting.

**Directions:** From Bend, drive southwest on Cascades Lakes Highway (Century Drive Highway, which becomes County Road 46) and drive 46 miles to Forest Road 4635. Turn right (west) and drive two miles to the campground.

**Contact:** Deschutes National Forest, Bend-Fort Rock Ranger District, 541/383-4000, www.fs.usda.gov/centraloregon.

## 135 CULTUS CORRAL HORSE CAMP

### Scenic rating: 3
near Cultus Lake in Deschutes National Forest

**Map 11.5, page 599**

Located at 4,450 feet elevation, about one mile from Cultus Lake, this camp sits in a stand of lodgepole pine. Several nearby trails provide access to backcountry lakes. This is a good overflow campground for Quinn Meadow Horse Camp.

**Campsites, facilities:** There are 11 sites for tents or RVs up to 40 feet long. Picnic tables, garbage service, fire grills, and four-horse corrals are provided. Drinking water and vault toilets are available. Leashed pets are permitted.

**Reservations, fees:** Reservations are not accepted. Sites are $14 per night, $7 per night per additional vehicle. Open May-late September, weather permitting.

**Directions:** From Bend, drive southwest on Cascades Lakes Highway (Century Drive Highway, which becomes County Road 46) and drive 46 miles to Forest Road 4635. Turn right (west) and drive one mile to Forest Road 4630. Turn right and drive 0.75 mile to the campground on the right.

**Contact:** Deschutes National Forest, Bend-Fort Rock Ranger District, 541/383-4000, www.fs.usda.gov/centraloregon.

## 136 LITTLE CULTUS LAKE

### Scenic rating: 7
on Little Cultus Lake in Deschutes National Forest

**Map 11.5, page 599**

This campground is set near the shore of Little Cultus Lake at an elevation of 4,800 feet. It's a popular spot for boating (10-mph speed limit), fishing, hiking, and swimming. Nearby trails offer access to numerous backcountry lakes, and the Pacific Crest Trail passes about six miles west of the camp.

**Campsites, facilities:** There are 31 sites for tents or RVs up to 30 feet long. Picnic tables, garbage service, and fire grills are provided. Vault toilets and a boat launch are available. Check to confirm whether drinking water is available. Leashed pets are permitted.

**Reservations, fees:** Reservations are not accepted. Sites are $14 per night, $7 per night per additional vehicle. Open May-September, weather permitting.

**Directions:** From Bend, drive southwest on Cascades Lakes Highway (Century Drive Highway, which becomes County Road 46) and drive 46 miles to Forest Road 4635. Turn right (west) and drive two miles to Forest Road 4630. Turn left (south) and drive 1.7 miles to Forest Road 4636. Turn left (west) and drive one mile to the campground.

**Contact:** Deschutes National Forest, Bend-Fort Rock Ranger District, 541/383-4000, www.fs.usda.gov/centraloregon.

## 137 COW MEADOW

### Scenic rating: 6
on Crane Prairie Reservoir in Deschutes National Forest

**Map 11.5, page 599**

Cow Meadow campground is located near the north end of Crane Prairie Reservoir and near the Deschutes River. It's a pretty spot (elevation is 4,450 feet), great for fly-fishing and bird-watching.

**Campsites, facilities:** There are 18 sites for tents or RVs up to 30 feet long. Picnic tables, garbage service, and fire grills are provided. Vault toilets are available. There is no drinking water. A boat launch for small boats is nearby. Leashed pets are permitted.

**Reservations, fees:** Reservations are not accepted. Sites are $10 per night, $5 per night per additional vehicle. Open May-mid-October, weather permitting.

**Directions:** From Bend, drive southwest on Cascades Lakes Highway (Century Drive Highway, which becomes County Road 46) for 44.7 miles to Forest Road 40. Turn left (east) on Forest Road 40 and drive 0.4 mile to Forest Road 4000-970. Turn right (south) and drive two miles to the campground on the right.

**Contact:** Deschutes National Forest, Bend-Fort Rock Ranger District, 541/383-4000, www.fs.usda.gov/centraloregon.

## 138 CRANE PRAIRIE

### Scenic rating: 6

on Crane Prairie Reservoir in Deschutes National Forest

**Map 11.5, page 599**

This campground along the north shore of Crane Prairie Reservoir is a good spot for anglers and boaters. World-renowned for rainbow trout fishing, the reservoir is also popular for bass fishing. The Forest Service has erected osprey nesting platforms, which allow visitors a good look at these beautiful birds.

**Campsites, facilities:** There are 128 sites for tents or RVs of any length and one group site for up to 90 people. Picnic tables and fire grills are provided. Vault toilets, drinking water, and garbage service are available. Boat docks, launching facilities, and a fish-cleaning station are available on-site. Boat rentals, showers, gas, and a coin laundry are nearby. Some facilities are wheelchair accessible. Leashed pets are permitted.

**Reservations, fees:** Reservations are accepted at 877/444-6777 ($10 reservation fee) or www.recreation.gov ($10 reservation fee). Single sites are $16 per night, multi-sites are $30 per night, the group site is $90-200 per night, $8 per night per additional vehicle. Open April-October, weather permitting.

**Directions:** From Bend, drive south on U.S. 97 for 26.8 miles to Wickiup Junction and County Road 43. Turn right (west) on County Road 43 and drive 11 miles to Forest Road 42. Continue west on Forest Road 42 for 5.4 miles to Forest Road 4270. Turn right (north) and drive 4.2 miles to the campground on the left.

**Contact:** Deschutes National Forest, Bend-Fort Rock Ranger District, 541/383-4000, www.fs.usda.gov/centraloregon.

## 139 QUINN RIVER

### Scenic rating: 5

on Crane Prairie Reservoir in Deschutes National Forest

**Map 11.5, page 599**

Set along the western shore of Crane Prairie Reservoir, this campground is a popular spot for anglers and a great spot for birdwatching. The area is also popular with a wide variety of mammals large and small, so don't leave any food out. A separate, large parking lot is available for boats and trailers. Boat speed is limited to 10 mph. The elevation is 4,450 feet.

**Campsites, facilities:** There are 41 sites for tents or RVs up to 45 feet long. Picnic tables and fire grills are provided. Vault toilets, drinking water, and garbage service are available. Boat-launching facilities are available. Some facilities are wheelchair accessible. Leashed pets are permitted.

**Reservations, fees:** Reservations are not accepted. Sites are $14 per night, $7 per night per additional vehicle. Open late April-September, weather permitting.

**Directions:** From Bend, drive southwest on Cascade Lakes Highway (Century Drive Highway, which becomes County Road 46) for 48 miles to the campground.

**Contact:** Deschutes National Forest, Bend-Fort Rock Ranger District, 541/383-4000, www.fs.usda.gov/centraloregon.

## **140** ROCK CREEK

### Scenic rating: 5

on Crane Prairie Reservoir in Deschutes National Forest

**Map 11.5, page 599**

Rock Creek campground is set along the west shore of Crane Prairie Reservoir at an elevation of 4,450 feet. The setting is similar to Quinn River campground, and provides another good spot for anglers when that camp is full.

**Campsites, facilities:** There are 32 sites for tents or RVs up to 40 feet long, including two multi-sites. Picnic tables, garbage service, and fire grills are provided. Drinking water, a fish-cleaning station, and vault toilets are available. Boat docks and launching facilities are on-site. Leashed pets are permitted.

**Reservations, fees:** Reservations are not accepted. Single sites are $14 per night, multi-sites are $26 per night, $7 per night per additional vehicle. Open April-September, weather permitting.

**Directions:** From Bend, drive southwest on Cascade Lakes Highway (Century Drive Highway, which becomes County Road 46) for 48.8 miles to the campground.

**Contact:** Deschutes National Forest, Bend-Fort Rock Ranger District, 541/383-4000, www.fs.usda.gov/centraloregon.

## **141** FALL RIVER

### Scenic rating: 5

on the Fall River in Deschutes National Forest

**Map 11.5, page 599**

Fall River is beautiful, crystal clear, and cold, and this campground is right on it at an elevation of 4,300 feet. Fishing is restricted to fly-fishing only, and it's wise to check the regulations for other restrictions. The Fall River Trail meanders along the river for 3.5 miles and is open for bicycling.

**Campsites, facilities:** There are 12 sites for tents or RVs up to 40 feet long. Picnic tables, garbage service, and fire grills are provided. Vault toilets are available. There is no drinking water. Leashed pets are permitted.

**Reservations, fees:** Reservations are not accepted. Sites are $10 per night, $5 per night per additional vehicle. Open early May-late October, weather permitting.

**Directions:** From Bend, drive south on U.S. 97 for 17.3 miles to the Vandevert Road exit. Take that exit and turn right on Vandevert Road. Drive 1.5 miles to Forest Road 42. Turn left and drive 12.2 miles to the campground.

**Contact:** Deschutes National Forest, Bend-Fort Rock Ranger District, 541/383-4000, www.fs.usda.gov/centraloregon.

## **142** SHEEP BRIDGE

### Scenic rating: 3

near Wickiup Reservoir in Deschutes National Forest

**Map 11.5, page 599**

This campground is set along the north Deschutes River Channel of Wickiup Reservoir in an open, treeless area that has minimal privacy and is dusty in summer. Dispersed sites here are popular with group campers. The elevation is 4,350 feet.

**Campsites, facilities:** There are 20 sites and three group sites for tents or RVs up to 40 feet long. Picnic tables, garbage service, and fire grills are provided. Drinking water, vault toilets, boat-launching facilities, and a picnic area are available. Leashed pets are permitted.

**Reservations, fees:** Reservations are not accepted for single sites; group sites can be reserved at 877/444-6777 ($10 reservation fee) or www.recreation.gov ($9 reservation fee). Single sites are $12 per night, multiple sites are $22, the group sites are $30, $6 per night per additional vehicle. Open early May-October, weather permitting.

**Directions:** From Bend, drive south on U.S. 97 for 26.8 miles to Wickiup Junction. Turn right (west) on County Road 43 and drive 11 miles to Forest Road 42. Continue 4.6 miles west on Forest Road 42 to Forest Road 4260. Turn left (south) and drive 0.75 mile to the campground on the right.

**Contact:** Deschutes National Forest, Bend-Fort Rock Ranger District, 541/383-4000, www.fs.usda.gov/centraloregon.

## 143 NORTH TWIN LAKE

### Scenic rating: 6

on North Twin Lake in Deschutes National Forest

**Map 11.5, page 599**

Although small and fairly primitive, North Twin Lake has lake access and a pretty setting. The campground is located on the shore of North Twin Lake and is a popular weekend spot for families. Only non-motorized boats are permitted. The elevation is 4,350 feet.

**Campsites, facilities:** There are 20 sites for tents or RVs up to 40 feet long. Picnic tables and fire grills are provided. Vault toilets are available. There is no drinking water. Boat-launching facilities are on-site. There is also an RV dump station ($10 fee). Leashed pets are permitted.

**Reservations, fees:** Reservations are not accepted. Sites are $12 per night, $6 per night per additional vehicle. Open April-October, weather permitting.

**Directions:** From Bend, drive southwest on Cascade Lakes Highway (Century Drive Highway, which becomes County Road 46) for 52 miles and drive past Crane Prairie Reservoir to Forest Road 42. Turn east and drive four miles to Forest Road 4260. Turn right (south) and drive 0.25 mile to the campground.

**Contact:** Deschutes National Forest, Bend-Fort Rock Ranger District, 541/383-4000, www.fs.usda.gov/centraloregon.

## 144 TWIN LAKES RESORT

### Scenic rating: 8

on Twin Lakes

**Map 11.5, page 599**          **BEST (**

Twin Lakes Resort is a popular family vacation destination with a full-service marina and all the amenities, including beach areas. Recreational activities vary from hiking to boating, fishing, and swimming on Wickiup Reservoir. Nearby South Twin Lake is popular with paddleboaters and kayakers; it's stocked with rainbow trout.

**Campsites, facilities:** There are 22 sites with full hookups for RVs of any length. There are also 14 cabins. Picnic tables and fire rings are provided. Restrooms with flush toilets and coin showers, a dump station, coin laundry, convenience store, restaurant, ice, snacks, some RV supplies, propane gas, and gasoline are available. A boat ramp, rentals, and a dock are available; no motors are permitted on South Twin Lake. Some facilities are wheelchair accessible. Leashed pets are permitted.

**Reservations, fees:** Reservations are recommended. Sites are $30 per night, $5 per night per additional vehicle, $10 for RVs with tents. Some credit cards are accepted. Open late April-mid-October, weather permitting.

**Directions:** From Bend, drive south on U.S. 97 for 26.8 miles to Wickiup Junction. Turn right (west) on County Road 43 and drive 11 miles to Forest Road 42. Turn left and continue 4.6 miles west on Forest Road 42 to Forest Road 4260. Turn left (south) and drive two miles to the resort.

**Contact:** Twin Lakes Resort, 541/382-6432, www.twinlakesresort.net.

## 145 SOUTH TWIN LAKE

### Scenic rating: 6

on South Twin Lake in Deschutes
National Forest

**Map 11.5, page 599**

This campground is on the shore of South Twin Lake, a popular spot for boating (non-motorized only), fishing, and swimming. The elevation is 4,350 feet.

**Campsites, facilities:** There are 21 sites for tents or RVs up to 40 feet long. Picnic tables, garbage service, and fire grills are provided. Drinking water, vault and flush toilets, and dump station are available. Boat-launching facilities (small boats only), boat rentals, showers, and laundry facilities are nearby. Some facilities are wheelchair accessible. Leashed pets are permitted.

**Reservations, fees:** Reservations are not accepted. Single sites are $16 per night, multi-sites are $30 per night, $8 per night per additional vehicle. Open April-October, weather permitting.

**Directions:** From Bend, drive south on U.S. 97 for 26.8 miles to Wickiup Junction. Turn right (west) on County Road 43 and drive 11 miles to Forest Road 42. Continue west on Forest Road 42 for 4.6 miles to Forest Road 4260. Turn left (south) and drive two miles to the campground on the left.

**Contact:** Deschutes National Forest, Bend-Fort Rock Ranger District, 541/383-4000, www.fs.usda.gov/centraloregon.

## 146 WEST SOUTH TWIN

### Scenic rating: 4

on South Twin Lake in Deschutes
National Forest

**Map 11.5, page 599**

A major access point to the Wickiup Reservoir, this camp is situated on South Twin Lake adjacent to the reservoir. It's a popular angling spot with very good kokanee salmon fishing. Twin Lakes Resort is adjacent to West South Twin. The elevation is 4,350 feet.

**Campsites, facilities:** There are 24 sites for RVs up to 40 feet long. Picnic tables and fire grills are provided. Drinking water, flush toilets, garbage service, and a dump station ($10 fee) are available. Boat-launching facilities are on-site, and boat rentals, a restaurant, showers, coin laundry, gas, propane, cabins, and a store are nearby. Leashed pets are permitted.

**Reservations, fees:** Reservations are not accepted. Sites are $14 per night, $7 per night per additional vehicle. Open April-mid-October, weather permitting.

**Directions:** From Bend, drive southwest on Cascade Lakes Highway (Century Drive Highway), which becomes County Road 46) for 40 miles (past Crane Prairie Reservoir) to Forest Road 42. Turn left (east) and drive four miles to Forest Road 4260. Turn right (south) and drive 0.25 mile to the campground.

**Contact:** Deschutes National Forest, Bend-Fort Rock Ranger District, 541/383-4000, www.fs.usda.gov/centraloregon.

## 147 GULL POINT

### Scenic rating: 5

on Wickiup Reservoir in Deschutes
National Forest

**Map 11.5, page 599**

Located about two miles from West South Twin Campground, Gull Point is the most popular campground on Wickiup Reservoir. The campground sits in an open ponderosa stand on the north shore of the reservoir. You'll find good fishing for kokanee salmon here—though they are elusive and hard to catch. There are also brown trout in the 15-20 pound range.

**Campsites, facilities:** There are 78 sites for tents or RVs up to 40 feet long and two group sites for up to 30 people each. Picnic tables, garbage service, and fire grills are provided.

Drinking water, a dump station, and flush and vault toilets are available. Boat-launching facilities and fish-cleaning stations are on-site. Coin showers and a small store are nearby. Some facilities are wheelchair accessible. Leashed pets are permitted.

**Reservations, fees:** Reservations are accepted at 877/444-6777 ($10 reservation fee) or www.recreation.gov ($9 reservation fee). Sites are $16 per night, double sites are $30 per night, $8 per night per additional vehicle, and $75 per night for group sites. Open mid-April-October, weather permitting.

**Directions:** From Bend, drive south on U.S. 97 for about 26.8 miles to County Road 43 (three miles north of LaPine). Turn right (west) on County Road 43 and drive 11 miles to Forest Road 42. Turn west on Forest Road 42 and drive 4.6 miles to Forest Road 4260. Turn left (south) and drive three miles to the campground on the right.

**Contact:** Deschutes National Forest, Bend-Fort Rock Ranger District, 541/383-4000, www.fs.usda.gov/centraloregon.

## 148 BULL BEND

### Scenic rating: 5
on the Deschutes River in Deschutes National Forest

**Map 11.5, page 599**

Bull Bend campground is located on the inside of a major bend in the Deschutes River at 4,300 feet elevation. For a mini float trip, start at the upstream end of camp, float around the bend, and then take out at the downstream end of camp. This is a low-use getaway spot.

**Campsites, facilities:** There are 12 sites for tents or RVs up to 40 feet long. Picnic tables, garbage service, fire grills, vault toilets, and boat-launching facilities are available. There is no drinking water. Leashed pets are permitted.

**Reservations, fees:** Reservations are not accepted. Sites are $10 per night, $5 per night

per additional vehicle. Open early May-late September, weather permitting.

**Directions:** From Bend, drive south on U.S. 97 for 26.8 miles to Wickiup Junction. Turn right (west) on County Road 43 and drive eight miles to Forest Road 4370. Turn left (south) and drive 1.5 miles to the campground.

**Contact:** Deschutes National Forest, Bend-Fort Rock Ranger District, 541/383-4000, www.fs.usda.gov/centraloregon.

## 149 PRINGLE FALLS

### Scenic rating: 4
on the Deschutes River in Deschutes National Forest

**Map 11.5, page 599**

This campground fringing the Deschutes River is less than a mile from Pringle Falls. The camp gets light use and is pretty and serene.

**Campsites, facilities:** There are seven sites for tents or RVs up to 30 feet long. Picnic tables, garbage service, and fire grills are provided. Vault toilets are available. There is no drinking water. Leashed pets are permitted.

**Reservations, fees:** Reservations are not accepted. Sites are $10 per night, $5 per night per additional vehicle. Open May-October, weather permitting.

**Directions:** From Bend, drive south on U.S. 97 for 26.8 miles to Wickiup Junction. Turn right (west) on County Road 43 and drive 7.4 miles to Forest Road 4330-500. Turn north (right) and drive one mile to the campground.

**Contact:** Deschutes National Forest, Bend-Fort Rock Ranger District, 541/383-4000, www.fs.usda.gov/centraloregon.

## 150 BIG RIVER

### Scenic rating: 4

on the Deschutes River in Deschutes
National Forest

**Map 11.5, page 599**

Big River is a good spot. Located between the
banks of the Deschutes River and the road, it
has easy access and is popular as an overnight
camp. Fishing, motorized boating, and rafting
are permitted.

**Campsites, facilities:** There are 10 sites for
tents or RVs up to 40 feet long and three group
sites for up to 40 people. Picnic tables, garbage
service, and fire grills are provided. Vault toilets are available. There is no drinking water.
Boat-launching facilities are on-site. Some
facilities are wheelchair accessible. Leashed
pets are permitted.

**Reservations, fees:** Reservations are accepted
for the group sites only at 877/444-6777 ($10
reservation fee) or www.recreation.gov ($9 res-
ervation fee). Sites are $10 per night, $5 per
night per additional vehicle, and the group
sites are $30 per night. Open early May-late
October, weather permitting.

**Directions:** From Bend, drive south on U.S.
97 for 17.3 miles to the Vandevert Road exit.
Take that exit and turn right on Vandevert
Road. Drive 1.5 miles to Forest Road 42. Turn
left and drive 7.9 miles to the campground.

**Contact:** Deschutes National Forest, Bend-
Fort Rock Ranger District, 541/383-4000,
www.fs.usda.gov/centraloregon.

## 151 PRAIRIE

### Scenic rating: 4

on Paulina Creek in Deschutes National Forest

**Map 11.5, page 599**

Here's another good overnight campground
that is quiet and private. Set along the banks
of Paulina Creek, Prairie is located about 0.5
mile from the trailhead for the Peter Skene

Ogden National Recreation Trail. The elevation is 4,300 feet.

**Campsites, facilities:** There are 17 sites for
tents or RVs up to 30 feet long. Picnic tables,
garbage service, and fire grills are provided.
Drinking water, firewood, and vault toilets are
available. Leashed pets are permitted.

**Reservations, fees:** Reservations are not accepted. Sites are $14 per night, $7 per night
per additional vehicle. Open mid-May-late
September, weather permitting.

**Directions:** From Bend, drive south on U.S.
97 for 23.5 miles to County Road 21 (Paulina/
East Lake Road). Turn left (east) and drive 3.1
miles to the campground.

**Contact:** Deschutes National Forest, Bend-
Fort Rock Ranger District, 541/383-4000,
www.fs.usda.gov/centraloregon.

## 152 PAULINA LAKE

### Scenic rating: 8

on Paulina Lake in Deschutes National Forest

**Map 11.5, page 599**

This campground (6,350 feet elevation) is located along the south shore of Paulina Lake
and within the Newberry National Volcanic
Monument. The camp is adjacent to Paulina
Lake Resort. The lake itself sits in a volcanic
crater. Nearby trails provide access to the remains of volcanic activity, including craters
and obsidian flows. My longtime friend, Guy
Carl, caught the state's record brown trout
here, right after I'd written a story about his
unique method of using giant Rapala and
Rebel bass lures for giant browns. The recreation options here include boating, fishing,
hiking, mountain biking, and sailing. The
boat speed limit is 10 mph. Note that food-
raiding bears are common at all the campgrounds in the Newberry Caldera area and
that all food must be kept out of reach. Do
not store food in vehicles.

**Campsites, facilities:** There are 69 sites for
RVs up to 30 feet long. Picnic tables, garbage

service, and fire grills are provided. Drinking water and flush and vault toilets are available. Boat docks, launching facilities, boat rentals, coin showers, coin laundry, a small store, restaurant, cabins, gas, and propane are within five miles. The Newberry RV dump station ($10 fee) is nearby. Some facilities are wheelchair accessible. Leashed pets are permitted.

**Reservations, fees:** Reservations are accepted at 877/444-6777 ($10 reservation fee) or www.recreation.gov ($9 reservation fee). Sites are $16-18 per night, $8 per night per additional vehicle. Open May-late October, weather permitting.

**Directions:** From Bend, drive south on U.S. 97 for 23.5 miles to County Road 21 (Paulina/East Lake Road). Turn left (east) and drive 12.9 miles to the campground on the left.

**Contact:** Deschutes National Forest, Bend-Fort Rock Ranger District, 541/383-4000, www.fs.usda.gov/centraloregon.

## 153 CHIEF PAULINA HORSE CAMP

### Scenic rating: 4
on Paulina Lake in Deschutes National Forest

**Map 11.5, page 599**

Chief Paulina campground sits at an elevation of 6,400 feet, about 0.25 mile from the south shore of Paulina Lake, where fishing is good. Horse trails and a vista point are close by. Horse campers must use only certified weed-seed-free hay.

**Campsites, facilities:** There are 14 sites for tents or RVs up to 40 feet long. Picnic tables and fire grills are provided. A vault toilet, garbage service, and corrals are available. There is no drinking water. Boat docks and rentals and an RV dump station ($10 fee) are nearby. Leashed pets are permitted.

**Reservations, fees:** Reservations are accepted at 877/444-6777 ($10 reservation fee) or www.recreation.gov ($9 reservation fee). Two-horse stall sites are $14 per night, four-horse stall sites

are $18, $7 per night per additional vehicle. Open May-late October, weather permitting.

**Directions:** From Bend, drive south on U.S. 97 for 23.5 miles to County Road 21 (Paulina/East Lake Road). Turn left (east) and drive 14 miles to the campground.

**Contact:** Deschutes National Forest, Bend-Fort Rock Ranger District, 541/383-4000, www.fs.usda.gov/centraloregon.

## 154 LITTLE CRATER

### Scenic rating: 8
near Paulina Lake in Deschutes National Forest

**Map 11.5, page 599**

Little Crater is a very popular campground (6,350 feet elevation) near the east shore of Paulina Lake in Newberry National Volcanic Monument, a caldera. Sites are situated on the scenic lake edge, perfect for fishing, and there are great hiking opportunities in the area. The place fills up most summer weekends.

**Campsites, facilities:** There are 50 sites for tents or RVs up to 40 feet long. Picnic tables and fire grills are provided. Vault toilets, drinking water, and garbage service are available. Boat docks and launching facilities are on-site, and boat rentals are nearby. Some facilities are wheelchair accessible. Leashed pets are permitted.

**Reservations, fees:** Reservations are not accepted. Sites are $16 per night, $8 per night for each additional vehicle. Open early May-late October, weather permitting.

**Directions:** From Bend, drive south on U.S. 97 for 23.5 miles to County Road 21 (Paulina/East Lake Road). Turn left (east) and drive 14.5 miles to Forest Road 2100. Turn left (north) and drive 0.5 mile to the campground on the left.

**Contact:** Deschutes National Forest, 541/383-4000, www.fs.usda.gov/centraloregon.

## 155 NEWBERRY GROUP CAMP

### Scenic rating: 7

west of Roseburg

**Map 11.5, page 599**

Newberry Group has a great location on Paulina Lake and is the only area on Newberry Monument designed exclusively for group camping. The parking area and roads are paved, and the group sites are separated from one another, although group sites B and C can be joined to accommodate large groups. One site accommodates groups of up to 35 people, while the other two accommodate up to 50. The entire campground can be reserved as well.

**Campsites, facilities:** There are three group sites for tents or RVs to 40 feet. Picnic tables and fire rings are provided. Drinking water and vault toilets are available. Leashed pets are permitted.

**Reservations, fees:** Reservations are accepted at 877/444-6777 ($10 reservation fee) or www.recreation.gov ($9 reservation fee). Sites are $60 per night for the smaller camp, $100 per night for the two larger camps. Open June-September, weather permitting.

**Directions:** From Bend, drive south on U.S. 97 for 23.5 miles to County Road 21 (Paulina/East Lake Road). Turn left (east) and drive 1.5 miles to the campground.

**Contact:** Deschutes National Forest, 541/383-4000, www.fs.usda.gov/centraloregon.

## 156 CINDER HILL

### Scenic rating: 7

on East Lake in Deschutes National Forest

**Map 11.5, page 599**

This campground hugs the northeast shore of East Lake at an elevation of 6,400 feet. Located within the Newberry National Volcanic Monument, Cinder Hill makes a good base camp for area activities. Boating, fishing, and hiking are among the recreation options here. Boat speed is limited to 10 mph.

**Campsites, facilities:** There are 55 sites, including pull-through sites, for tents or RVs of any length. Picnic tables and fire grills are provided. Drinking water, flush and vault toilets, and garbage service are available. A camp host is on-site. Boat docks and launching facilities are on-site, and boat rentals, a store, restaurant, coin showers, coin laundry, and cabins are nearby at East Lake Resort. Some facilities are wheelchair accessible. Leashed pets are permitted.

**Reservations, fees:** Reservations are accepted at 877/444-6777 ($10 reservation fee) or www.recreation.gov ($9 reservation fee). Sites are $16 per night, $8 per night per additional vehicle. Open mid-May-September, weather permitting.

**Directions:** From Bend, drive south on U.S. 97 for 23.5 miles to County Road 21 (Paulina/East Lake Road). Turn left (east) and drive 17.6 miles to Forest Road 2100-700. Turn left (north) and drive 0.5 mile to the campground.

**Contact:** Deschutes National Forest, Bend-Fort Rock Ranger District, 541/383-4000, www.fs.usda.gov/centraloregon.

## 157 EAST LAKE

### Scenic rating: 8

on East Lake in Deschutes National Forest

**Map 11.5, page 599**

This campground is set along the south shore of East Lake at an elevation of 6,400 feet. Boating and fishing are popular here, and hiking trails provide access to signs of former volcanic activity in the area. East Lake Campground is similar to Cinder Hill, but smaller. Boat speed is limited to 10 mph.

**Campsites, facilities:** There are 29 sites for tents or RVs up to 40 feet long. Picnic tables and fire grills are provided. Drinking water, flush and vault toilets, and garbage service are available. A camp host is on-site. Boat docks, launching facilities, and rentals are nearby. Some facilities are wheelchair accessible. Leashed pets are permitted.

**Reservations, fees:** Reservations are not accepted. Sites are $16 per night, $8 per night per additional vehicle. Open early May-late October, weather permitting.

**Directions:** From Bend, drive south on U.S. 97 for 23.5 miles to County Road 21 (Paulina/East Lake Road). Turn left (east) and drive 16.6 miles to the campground on the left.

**Contact:** Deschutes National Forest, Bend-Fort Rock Ranger District, 541/383-4000, www.fs.usda.gov/centraloregon.

## 158 EAST LAKE RESORT AND RV PARK

### Scenic rating: 7
on East Lake

**Map 11.5, page 599**

This resort offers shaded sites in a wooded, mountainous setting on the east shore of East Lake. Opportunities for boating, fishing, and swimming abound.

**Campsites, facilities:** There are 40 sites with partial hookups for tents or RVs up to 40 feet long, five sites for tents, and 16 cabins. Some sites are pull-through. Picnic tables and fire pits are provided. Drinking water, restrooms with flush toilets and coin showers, propane gas, firewood, a dump station, convenience store with fishing licenses, café, coin laundry, Wi-Fi, ice, boat-launching facilities, boat rentals, moorage, and a playground are available. Leashed pets are permitted.

**Reservations, fees:** Reservations are accepted. RV sites are $25 per night, tent sites are $20 per night. Monthly rates are available. Some credit cards are accepted. Open mid-May-September, weather permitting.

**Directions:** From Bend, drive south on U.S. 97 for 23.5 miles to County Road 21 (Paulina/East Lake Road). Turn left (east) and drive 18 miles to the park at the end of the road.

**Contact:** East Lake Resort and RV Park, 541/536-2230, www.eastlakeresort.com.

## 159 CHINA HAT

### Scenic rating: 3
in Deschutes National Forest

**Map 11.5, page 599**

Remote China Hat campground is located at 5,100 feet elevation in a rugged, primitive area. There is direct trail access here to the East Fort Rock OHV Trail System. Hunters use China Hat as a base camp in the fall, but in summer it is a base camp for off-road motorcyclists.

**Campsites, facilities:** There are 14 sites for tents or RVs up to 30 feet long. Picnic tables and fire grills are provided. Vault toilets are available. Check to confirm whether drinking water is available. Garbage must be packed out. Leashed pets are permitted.

**Reservations, fees:** Reservations are not accepted. There is no fee for camping. Open April-early November, weather permitting.

**Directions:** From Bend, drive south on U.S. 97 for 29.6 miles to Forest Road 22. Turn left (east) and drive 26.4 miles to Forest Road 18. Turn left (north) and drive 5.9 miles to the campground on the left.

**Contact:** Deschutes National Forest, Bend-Fort Rock Ranger District, 541/383-4000, www.fs.usda.gov/centraloregon.

## 160 GOLD LAKE

### Scenic rating: 8
on Gold Lake in Willamette National Forest

**Map 11.5, page 599**     **BEST (**

Gold Lake campground wins the popularity contest for high use. Although motors are not allowed on this small lake (100 acres and 25 feet deep), rafts and rowboats provide excellent fly-fishing access. A primitive log shelter built in the early 1940s provides a dry picnic area. In the spring and summer, this area abounds with wildflowers and huckleberries. The Gold Lake Bog is another special attraction where one can often see deer, elk, and smaller wildlife.

**Campsites, facilities:** There are 21 sites for tents or RVs up to 24 feet long. Picnic tables, garbage bins, and fire grills are provided. Drinking water, vault toilets, and a grey water station are available. Boat docks and launching facilities are nearby. Some facilities are wheelchair accessible. Leashed pets are permitted.

**Reservations, fees:** Reservations are not accepted. Sites are $18 per night, $6 per night per additional vehicle. Open mid-May-October, weather permitting.

**Directions:** From Eugene, drive south on I-5 for five miles to Exit 188 and Highway 58. Turn east and drive 35 miles to the town of Oakridge. From Oakridge, continue east on Highway 58 for 28 miles to Gold Lake Road (Forest Road 500). Turn left (north) and drive two miles to the campground on the right.

**Contact:** Willamette National Forest, Middle Fork Ranger District, 541/782-2283, www.fs.usda.gov/willamette.

## 161 NORTH DAVIS CREEK

### Scenic rating: 4

on North Davis Creek in Deschutes National Forest

**Map 11.5, page 599**

Set at an elevation of 4,350 feet, this remote, secluded campground is located along a western channel that feeds into Wickiup Reservoir. Fishing for brown and rainbow trout as well as kokanee salmon is good here. In late summer, the reservoir level tends to drop. The camp receives little use and makes a good overflow camp if campsites are filled at Wickiup.

**Campsites, facilities:** There are 14 sites for tents or RVs up to 26 feet long. Picnic tables and fire grills are provided. Vault toilets and garbage service are available. There is no

drinking water. Boat-launching facilities are on-site. Leashed pets are permitted.

**Reservations, fees:** Reservations are not accepted. Sites are $10 per night, $5 per night per additional vehicle. Open April-early September.

**Directions:** From Bend, drive southwest on Cascade Lake Highway (Highway 46/Forest Road 46) for 56.2 miles to the campground on the left.

**Contact:** Deschutes National Forest, Bend-Fort Rock Ranger District, 541/383-4000, www.fs.usda.gov/centraloregon.

## 162 RESERVOIR

### Scenic rating: 4

on Wickiup Reservoir in Deschutes National Forest

**Map 11.5, page 599**

You'll find this campground along the south shore of Wickiup Reservoir, where the kokanee salmon fishing is good. The camp is best in early summer, before the lake level drops. This camp gets little use, so you won't find crowds here. The elevation is 4,350 feet.

**Campsites, facilities:** There are 21 sites for tents or RVs up to 24 feet long. Picnic tables, garbage service, and fire grills are provided. Boat-launching facilities and vault toilets are available, but there is no drinking water. Leashed pets are permitted.

**Reservations, fees:** Reservations are not accepted. Sites are $10 per night, $5 per each additional vehicle. Open April-September, weather permitting.

**Directions:** From Bend, drive southwest on Cascade Lakes Highway (Century Drive Highway), which becomes County Road 46) for 57.8 miles to Forest Road 44. Turn left (east) and drive 1.7 miles to the campground.

**Contact:** Deschutes National Forest, Bend-Fort Rock Ranger District, 541/383-4000, www.fs.usda.gov/centraloregon.

## 163 LAPINE STATE PARK

Scenic rating: 7

on the Deschutes River

**Map 11.5, page 599**

This peaceful and clean campground sits next to the trout-filled Deschutes River (a legendary fly-fishing spot) with many more high-mountain lakes in proximity. The camp is set in a subalpine pine forest populated by eagles or red-tailed hawks. Trails surround the campground; be sure to check out Oregon's "Big Tree." Skiing is a popular wintertime option in the area.

**Campsites, facilities:** There are 125 sites with full or partial hookups for tents or RVs of any length; only 20-amp service is available. There are also 10 cabins; five are rustic, five are deluxe, and two are pet friendly. Picnic tables and fire grills are provided. Drinking water, restrooms with flush toilets and showers, garbage bins, a dump station, a seasonal store, a day-use area with a sandy beach, a meeting hall that can be reserved, ice, and firewood are available. A boat launch is nearby. Some facilities are wheelchair accessible. Leashed pets are permitted.

**Reservations, fees:** Reservations are accepted at 800/452-5687 or online at www.oregonstateparks.org or www.reserveamerica.com ($8 reservation fee). Sites are $17-22 per night, $5 per night per additional vehicle. Rustic cabins are $$42 per night, deluxe cabins are $59-81 per night. Some credit cards are accepted. Open year-round, weather permitting.

**Directions:** From Bend, turn south on U.S. 97 and drive 23 miles to State Recreation Road. Turn right and drive four miles to the park.

**Contact:** LaPine State Park, 541/536-2071 or 800/551-6949, www.oregonstateparks.org.

## 164 LAVA FLOW NORTH

Scenic rating: 8

on Davis Lake in Deschutes National Forest

**Map 11.5, page 599**

North Lava Flow campground is surrounded by old-growth forest along the northeast shore of Davis Lake, a very shallow lake formed by lava flow. The water level fluctuates here, and this campground can sometimes be closed in summer. There's good duck hunting during the fall. Fishing can be decent, but only fly-fishing is allowed. Boat speed is limited to 10 mph.

**Campsites, facilities:** There are six sites for tents or RVs up to 30 feet long. Picnic tables and fire grills are provided. Vault toilets and firewood (which can be gathered from the surrounding area) are available. There is no drinking water, and garbage must be packed out. A primitive boat ramp is nearby. Leashed pets are permitted.

**Reservations, fees:** Reservations are not accepted. There is no fee for camping. Open April-December, weather permitting.

**Directions:** From Eugene, drive south on I-5 for five miles to Exit 188 and Highway 58. Turn east on Highway 58 and drive 86 miles to County Road 61. Turn left and drive three miles to Forest Road 46. Turn left and drive 7.7 miles to Forest Road 850. Turn left and drive 1.8 miles to the campground.

**Contact:** Deschutes National Forest, Crescent Ranger District, 541/433-3200, www.fs.usda.gov/centraloregon.

## 165 EAST DAVIS LAKE

Scenic rating: 7

on Davis Lake in Deschutes National Forest

**Map 11.5, page 599**

This campground sits nestled in the lodgepole pines along the south shore of Davis Lake. There was a large fire here a few years ago, and though it heavily impacted the surrounding vegetation—including the scenic view across the lake—a nice greenbelt along the creek where the sites are located, remains. Recreation options include boating (speed limit 10 mph), fly-fishing, and hiking. Leeches prevent swimming here. Bald eagles and sandhill cranes are frequently seen.

**Campsites, facilities:** There are 17 sites for tents or RVs up to 40 feet long and three double sites. Picnic tables, garbage service, fire grills, drinking water, and vault toilets are provided. Firewood may be gathered from the surrounding area. Primitive boat-launching facilities are available on-site. Some facilities are wheelchair accessible. Leashed pets are permitted.

**Reservations, fees:** Reservations are not accepted. Sites are $12 per night, $6 per night per additional vehicle. Open mid-April-late September, weather permitting.

**Directions:** From Eugene, drive south on I-5 for five miles to Exit 188 and Highway 58. Turn east and drive 73 miles to County Road 61. Turn left (east) and drive three miles to Forest Road 46. Turn left and drive 7.7 miles to Forest Road 850. Turn left and drive 0.25 mile to the campground entrance road on the right.

**Contact:** Deschutes National Forest, Crescent Ranger District, 541/433-3200, www.fs.usda. gov/centraloregon.

## 166 TRAPPER CREEK
🏕️🏊‍♂️🚣‍♂️🛶🐕🚐⛺

### Scenic rating: 8
on Odell Lake in Deschutes National Forest

**Map 11.5, page 599**    **BEST (**

The west end of Odell Lake is the setting for this camp. Boat docks and rentals are available nearby at the Shelter Cove Resort. One of Oregon's prime fisheries for kokanee salmon and mackinaw (lake trout), this lake also has some huge brown trout.

**Campsites, facilities:** There are 18 sites for tents or RVs up to 40 feet long and three group

sites. Picnic tables and fire grills are provided. Drinking water, vault toilets, garbage service, and a boat launch are available. Firewood may be gathered from the surrounding area. A store, coin laundry, and ice are within one mile. Leashed pets are permitted.

**Reservations, fees:** Reservations are accepted at 877/444-6777 ($10 reservation fee) or www.recreation.gov ($9 reservation fee). Sites are $16-18 per night, $8 per night per additional vehicle, group sites are $30-34, $8 per night per additional vehicle. Open mid-May-October, weather permitting.

**Directions:** From Eugene, drive south on I-5 for five miles to Exit 188 and Highway 58. Turn east and drive 61 miles to the turnoff for Odell Lake and Forest Road 5810. Turn right on Forest Road 5810 and drive 1.9 miles to the campground on the left.

**Contact:** Deschutes National Forest, Crescent Ranger District, 541/433-3200, www.fs.usda. gov/centraloregon.

## 167 SHELTER COVE RESORT
🏕️🚴‍♂️🏊‍♂️🛶🚣‍♂️🏠♿🚐⛺

### Scenic rating: 9
on Odell Lake

**Map 11.5, page 599**

Shelter Cove is a private resort along the north shore of Odell Lake, set at the base of the Diamond Peak Wilderness. The area offers opportunities for fishing, hiking, and swimming. The cabins sit right on the lakefront, and a general store and tackle shop are available.

**Campsites, facilities:** There are 72 sites with partial hookups for RVs up to 40 feet long; some sites are pull-through. There are also 13 cabins. Picnic tables and fire rings are provided. Drinking water, restrooms with flush toilets and showers, a dump station, Wi-Fi, an ATM, convenience store, propane, coin laundry, and ice are available. Boat docks, launching facilities, and boat rentals are on-site. Some facilities are wheelchair accessible. Leashed pets are permitted.

**Reservations, fees:** Reservations are recommended at 541/433-2548 or 800/647-2729 (out-of-state only). Sites are $36 per night. Weekly and monthly rates are available. Some credit cards are accepted. Open year-round.

**Directions:** From Eugene, drive south on I-5 for five miles to Exit 188 and Highway 58. Turn east and drive 61 miles to the turnoff for Odell Lake and West Odell Lake Road. Turn right and drive south for 1.8 miles to the resort at the end of the road.

**Contact:** Shelter Cove Resort, 541/433-2548, www.sheltercoveresort.com.

## 168 ODELL CREEK

**Scenic rating: 9**
on Odell Lake in Deschutes National Forest

**Map 11.5, page 599**

You can fish, hike, and swim at this campground (4,800 feet elevation) along the east shore of Odell Lake. A trail from the nearby Crater Buttes trailhead leads southwest into the Diamond Peak Wilderness and provides access to several small lakes in the backcountry. Another trail follows the north shore of the lake. Boat docks, launching facilities, and rentals are available at the Odell Lake Lodge and Resort, adjacent to the campground. Windy afternoons are common here.

**Campsites, facilities:** There are 26 sites for tents or RVs up to 50 feet long. Picnic tables and fire grills are provided. Vault toilets, drinking water, and garbage service are available. Firewood may be gathered from the surrounding area. Some facilities are wheelchair accessible. Leashed pets are permitted.

**Reservations, fees:** Reservations are accepted at 541/433-2540 or at www.odelllakeresort.com. Sites are $14-$18 per night, $5 per night per additional vehicle. Open May-late September, weather permitting.

**Directions:** From Eugene, drive south on I-5 for five miles to Exit 188 and Highway 58. Turn east and drive 68 miles to Odell Lake

and Forest Road 680 (at the east end of the lake). Turn right on Forest Road 680 and drive 400 yards to the campground on the right.

**Contact:** Odell Lake Lodge, 541/433-2540, www.odelllakeresort.com.

## 169 SUNSET COVE

**Scenic rating: 8**
on Odell Lake in Deschutes National Forest

**Map 11.5, page 599**

Sunset Cove campground borders the northeast shore of Odell Lake. Boat docks and rentals are available nearby at Odell Lake Lodge and Resort. Campsites are surrounded by large Douglas fir and some white pine trees. The camp backs up to the highway; expect to hear the noise.

**Campsites, facilities:** There are 20 sites for tents or RVs up to 40 feet long. Picnic tables and fire grills are provided. Drinking water, vault toilets, garbage service, a boat launch and day-use area, and fish-cleaning facilities are available. Firewood may be gathered from the surrounding area. Some facilities are wheelchair accessible. Leashed pets are permitted.

**Reservations, fees:** Reservations are not accepted. Sites are $16 per night, multi-sites are $30 per night, $8 per night per additional vehicle. Open mid-May-mid-October, weather permitting.

**Directions:** From Eugene, drive south on I-5 for five miles to Exit 188 and Highway 58. Turn east and drive 67 miles to the campground on the right.

**Contact:** Deschutes National Forest, Crescent Ranger District, 541/433-3200, www.fs.usda.gov/centraloregon.

## 170 PRINCESS CREEK

### Scenic rating: 9

on Odell Lake in Deschutes National Forest

**Map 11.5, page 599**

This wooded campground is on the northeast shore of Odell Lake, but it backs up to the highway so expect traffic noise. Boat docks and rentals are available nearby at the Shelter Cove Resort. Fishing, hiking, and swimming are popular activities at the lake. A trail from the nearby Crater Buttes trailhead leads southwest into the Diamond Peak Wilderness and provides access to several small lakes in the backcountry.

**Campsites, facilities:** There are 45 sites for tents or RVs up to 30 feet long. Picnic tables and fire grills are provided. Vault toilets, garbage service, and boat-launching facilities are available. There is no drinking water. Firewood may be gathered from the surrounding area. Showers, a store, coin laundry, and ice are within five miles. Leashed pets are permitted.

**Reservations, fees:** Reservations are not accepted. Sites are $14 per night, multi-sites are $26 per night, $7 per night per additional vehicle. Open April-September, weather permitting.

**Directions:** From Eugene, drive south on I-5 for five miles to Exit 188 and Highway 58. Turn east and drive 64 miles to the campground on the right.

**Contact:** Deschutes National Forest, Crescent Ranger District, 541/433-3200, www.fs.usda. gov/centraloregon.

## 171 CONTORTA FLAT

### Scenic rating: 8

on Crescent Lake in Deschutes National Forest

**Map 11.5, page 599**

This campground on Crescent Lake, near the top of Willamette Pass, was named for the particular species of lodgepole pine (*Pinus contorta*) that grows here. It's worth the drive—the last few miles of which are on a gravel road—to discover that you may have this isolated lakeside campground all to yourself. The elevation is 4,850 feet.

**Campsites, facilities:** There are 18 sites for tents or RVs up to 40 feet long. Picnic tables and fire grills are provided. Vault toilets and garbage bins are available. There is no drinking water. Leashed pets are permitted.

**Reservations, fees:** Reservations are not accepted. Sites are $12 per night, $6 per night per additional vehicle. Open June-October, weather permitting.

**Directions:** From Eugene, drive south on I-5 for five miles to Exit 188 and Highway 58. Turn east and drive 69 miles to County Road 60. Turn right (west) and drive 10 miles to the camp on the left.

**Contact:** Deschutes National Forest, Crescent Ranger District, 541/433-3200, www.fs.usda. gov/centraloregon.

## 172 CRESCENT JUNCTION RV PARK

### Scenic rating: 5

on Crescent Lake

**Map 11.5, page 599**

This campground is conveniently located off Highway 58, just two miles from Crescent Lake. Four-wheeling trails are nearby.

**Campsites, facilities:** There are 25 sites with full hookups for tents or RVs of any length. Picnic tables and fire grills are provided. Flush toilets, coin showers, coin laundry, and a recreation room are available. A store is nearby. Some facilities are wheelchair accessible. Leashed pets are permitted.

**Reservations, fees:** Reservations are accepted. Sites are $25-30 per night. Weekly and monthly rates are available. Open year-round.

**Directions:** From Eugene, drive south on I-5 for five miles to Exit 188 and Highway 58. Turn east and drive 69 miles to County Road

60. Turn right (west) and drive a short distance to the camp on the left.

**Contact:** Hoodoo Recreation, Crescent Junction RV Park, 20030 Crescent Lake Highway, Crescent Lake, 541/433-5300, www.crescentjunctionrv.com.

## 173 WINDY GROUP

### Scenic rating: 8

on Crescent Lake in Deschutes National Forest

**Map 11.5, page 599**

Windy Group is located near the beaches on Crescent Lake. The lake warms up more easily than many high-mountain lakes, making swimming and waterskiing two popular options. Mountain biking and hiking are also available.

**Campsites, facilities:** There is one group site for tents or RVs up to 60 feet long and up to 40 people. Picnic tables and fire rings are provided. Vault toilets and garbage bins are available. There is no drinking water. Some facilities are wheelchair accessible. Leashed pets are permitted.

**Reservations, fees:** Reservations are accepted at 877/444-6777 ($10 reservation fee) or www.recreation.gov ($9 reservation fee). The site is $65 per night. Open May-September, weather permitting.

**Directions:** From Eugene, drive south on I-5 for five miles to Exit 188 and Highway 58. Turn east and drive 69 miles to County Road 60. Turn right (west) and drive 7.5 miles to the camp.

**Contact:** Deschutes National Forest, Crescent Ranger District, 541/433-3200, www.fs.usda.gov/centraloregon.

## 174 SIMAX GROUP CAMP

### Scenic rating: 8

on Crescent Lake in Deschutes National Forest

**Map 11.5, page 599**

This camp is set at an elevation of 4,850 feet on Crescent Lake and provides trails to day-use beaches. Fishing is variable year to year and is usually better earlier in the season. A boat launch is available at neighboring Crescent Lake, about two miles away. Nearby Diamond Peak Wilderness (free permit required) provides hiking options.

**Campsites, facilities:** There are three group sites for 30-50 people each and one group site (Site D) with electricity for up to 20 people. Picnic tables, fireplaces, and tent pads (tents must be placed on tent pads) are provided. Drinking water, restrooms with flush toilets and showers, garbage service, and a group shelter are available. Some facilities are wheelchair accessible. Leashed pets are permitted.

**Reservations, fees:** Reservations are accepted at 877/444-6777 ($10 reservation fee) or www.recreation.gov ($9 reservation fee). Site A is $80-100 per night, Sites B and C are $100-120 per night. (Note that Site C is best for RVs.) Site D is $65-75 per night. The group picnic area is $50 per day. Rates may be higher on weekends. Open mid-May-October, weather permitting.

**Directions:** From Eugene, drive south on I-5 for five miles to Exit 188 and Highway 58. Turn east and drive 70 miles to Crescent Lake Highway (Forest Road 60). Turn right and drive two miles to Forest Road 6005. Turn left and drive one mile to the campground on the right.

**Contact:** Deschutes National Forest, Crescent Ranger District, 541/433-3200, www.fs.usda.gov/centraloregon.

## 175 CRESCENT LAKE

### Scenic rating: 8

on Crescent Lake in Deschutes National Forest

**Map 11.5, page 599**

This campground is set along the north shore of Crescent Lake, and it is often windy here in the afternoon. Boat docks, launching facilities, and rentals are available at Crescent

Lake Resort, adjacent to the campground. A trail from camp heads into the Diamond Peak Wilderness (free permit required; available on-site) and also branches north to Odell Lake.

**Campsites, facilities:** There are 47 sites for tents or RVs up to 36 feet long and three yurts. Picnic tables and fire grills are provided. Drinking water, vault toilets, garbage service, and boat-launching facilities are available. Firewood may be gathered from the surrounding area. Leashed pets are permitted.

**Reservations, fees:** Reservations are accepted for yurts only at 877/444-6777 ($10 reservation fee) or www.recreation.gov ($9 reservation fee). Sites are $12-16 per night, $5-8 per night per additional vehicle, yurts are $30-40 per night. Open April-late October, weather permitting.

**Directions:** From Eugene, drive south on I-5 for five miles to Exit 188 and Highway 58. Turn east and drive 70 miles to Crescent Lake Highway (Forest Road 60). Turn right (west) and drive 2.2 miles southwest. Bear right to remain on Forest Road 60, and drive another 0.25 mile to the campground on the left.

**Contact:** Deschutes National Forest, Crescent Ranger District, 541/433-3200, www.fs.usda.gov/centraloregon.

# 176 SPRING

🚶 🚴 ⛵ 🏊 🛶 🎣 🐴 🚙 ⛺

### Scenic rating: 8
on Crescent Lake in Deschutes National Forest

**Map 11.5, page 599**

Spring campground is nestled in a lodgepole pine forest on the southern shore of Crescent Lake. Sites are open, with some on the lake offering Diamond Peak views. Boating, swimming, and waterskiing are popular activities, and the Windy-Oldenburg Trailhead provides access to the Oregon Cascades Recreation Area. The camp is at an elevation of 4,850 feet.

**Campsites, facilities:** There are 56 sites for tents or RVs up to 40 feet long, five sites for tents only, four multi-sites, and 12 sites that

can be reserved as a group site for up to 70 people and 25 vehicles. Picnic tables and fire grills are provided. Drinking water, vault toilets, garbage service, boat-launching facilities, and firewood (may be gathered from the surrounding area) are available. Leashed pets are permitted.

**Reservations, fees:** Reservations are not accepted for single sites. Reservations are accepted for group sites at 877/444-6777 ($10 reservation fee) or www.recreation.gov ($9 reservation fee). Single sites are $16 per night, multiple sites are $30 per night, the group site is $125 per night, $8 per night per additional vehicle. Open May-September, weather permitting.

**Directions:** From Eugene, drive south on I-5 for five miles to Exit 188 and Highway 58. Turn east and drive 70 miles to Crescent Lake Highway (Forest Road 60). Turn right and drive eight miles west to the campground entrance road on the left. Turn left and drive one mile to the campground.

**Contact:** Deschutes National Forest, Crescent Ranger District, 541/433-3200 or 541/338-7869, www.fs.usda.gov/centraloregon.

# 177 CONTORTA POINT GROUP CAMP

🚶 🚴 ⛵ 🏊 🛶 🎣 🐴 🚙 ⛺

### Scenic rating: 8
on Crescent Lake in Deschutes National Forest

**Map 11.5, page 599**

This campground (4,850 feet elevation) sits on the southern shore of Crescent Lake, where boating, swimming, and waterskiing are among the summer pastimes. A number of trails from the nearby Windy-Oldenburg Trailhead provide access to lakes in the Oregon Cascades Recreation Area. Motorized vehicles are restricted to open roads only.

**Campsites, facilities:** There are two group sites for tents or RVs up to 30 feet long that can accommodate up to 40 people each. There is no drinking water. Picnic tables and fire rings are provided. Vault toilets and garbage bins are available. Firewood can be gathered in surrounding forest. Boat docks and launching facilities are three miles away at Spring Campground. Leashed pets are permitted.

**Reservations, fees:** Reservations are accepted at 877/444-6777 ($10 reservation fee) or www.recreation.gov ($9 reservation fee). Sites are $65 per night. Open May-September, weather permitting.

**Directions:** From Eugene, drive south on I-5 for five miles to Exit 188 and Highway 58. Turn east and drive 70 miles to Crescent Lake Highway (Forest Road 60). Turn right and drive 9.9 miles to Forest Road 280. Turn left and drive one mile to the campground.

**Contact:** Deschutes National Forest, Crescent Ranger District, 541/433-3200, www.fs.usda.gov/centraloregon.

## 178 WHITEFISH HORSE CAMP

### Scenic rating: 5

on Whitefish Creek in Deschutes National Forest

**Map 11.5, page 599**

This just might be the best horse camp in the state. Only horse camping is allowed here, and manure removal is required. High lines are not allowed; horses must be kept in stalls. On Whitefish Creek at the west end of Crescent Lake, this campground is set in lodgepole pine and has shaded sites. Although located in a flat area across the road from the lake, the campground has no lake view. Moderately to heavily used, it has access to about 100 miles of trail, leading to Diamond Peak Wilderness, the Metolius-Windigo National Recreation Trail, the Oregon Cascades Recreation Area, and many high mountain lakes. The camp sits at 4,850 feet elevation.

**Campsites, facilities:** There are 19 sites for tents or RVs up to 40 feet long. Picnic tables and fire rings are provided. Drinking water,

garbage bins, vault toilets, horse corrals, and manure disposal site are available. Firewood may be gathered from the surrounding area. Leashed pets are permitted.

**Reservations, fees:** Reservations are accepted at 877/444-6777 ($10 reservation fee) or www.recreation.gov ($9 reservation fee). Sites are $14 per night for two stalls, $18 per night for four stalls, and $7 per night per additional vehicle. Open May-September, weather permitting.

**Directions:** From Eugene, drive south on I-5 for five miles to Exit 188 and Highway 58. Turn east and drive 70 miles to Crescent Lake Highway (Forest Road 60). Turn right (west) and drive 2.2 miles southwest. Stay to the right to remain on Forest Road 60, and drive six miles to the campground on the right.

**Contact:** Deschutes National Forest, Crescent Ranger District, 541/433-3200, www.fs.usda.gov/centraloregon.

## 179 CRESCENT CREEK

### Scenic rating: 7

on Crescent Creek in Deschutes National Forest

**Map 11.5, page 599**

One of the Cascades' classic hidden campgrounds, Crescent Creek camp sits along the banks of its namesake at 4,500 feet elevation. The buzzwords here are pretty, developed, and private. A registered bird-watching area is nearby. Hunters are the primary users of this campground, mainly in the fall. Otherwise, it gets light use. There's some highway noise here, and even if you can't hear it, traffic is visible from some sites.

**Campsites, facilities:** There are nine sites for tents or RVs up to 40 feet long. Picnic tables and fire grills are provided. Vault toilets, drinking water, and garbage service are available. Firewood may be gathered from the surrounding area. Leashed pets are permitted.

**Reservations, fees:** Reservations are not accepted. Single sites are $14 per night, multi-sites are $26 per night, $7 per night per additional vehicle. Open May-late September, weather permitting.

**Directions:** From Eugene, drive south on I-5 for five miles to Exit 188 and Highway 58. Turn east and drive 73 miles to County Road 61. Turn left (east) and drive three miles to the campground on the right.

**Contact:** Deschutes National Forest, Crescent Ranger District, 541/433-3200, www.fs.usda. gov/centraloregon.

## 180 CORRAL SPRINGS FOREST CAMP

### Scenic rating: 4

in Winema National Forest

**Map 11.5, page 599**

This flat campground with no water source is located next to Corral Springs at 4,900 feet elevation. The main attraction is solitude; it's primitive, remote, and quiet. The landscape features stands of lodgepole pine, interspersed by several small meadows.

**Campsites, facilities:** There are six sites for tents or RVs up to 50 feet long. Picnic tables and fire grills are provided. Vault toilets are available. There is no drinking water, and garbage must be packed out. A store, café, coin laundry, and ice are within five miles. Leashed pets are permitted.

**Reservations, fees:** Reservations are not accepted. There is no fee for camping. Open mid-May-late October, weather permitting.

**Directions:** From Eugene, drive southeast on Highway 58 for 86 miles to U.S. 97. Turn south and drive five miles to Forest Road 9774 (2.5 miles north of Chemult). Turn right and drive two miles west to the campground.

**Contact:** Fremont-Winema National Forest, Chemult Ranger District, 541/365-7001, www.fs.usda.gov/fremont-winema.

## 181 DIGIT POINT

### Scenic rating: 7

on Miller Lake in Fremont-Winema National Forest

**Map 11.5, page 599**

This campground is nestled in a lodgepole pine and mountain hemlock forest at 5,600 feet elevation on the shore of Miller Lake, a popular spot for boating, fishing, and swimming. Nearby trails provide access to the Mount Thielsen Wilderness and the Pacific Crest Trail.

**Campsites, facilities:** There are 64 sites for tents or RVs up to 30 feet long. Picnic tables and fire grills are provided. Drinking water, flush toilets, garbage service, and a dump station are available. Boat docks and launching facilities are nearby. Some facilities are wheelchair accessible. Leashed pets are permitted.

**Reservations, fees:** Reservations are not accepted. Sites are $12 per night, $8 per night per additional vehicle. Open Memorial Day-mid-October, weather permitting.

**Directions:** From Eugene, drive southeast on Highway 58 for 86 miles to U.S. 97. Turn south and drive seven miles to Forest Road 9772 (one mile north of Chemult). Turn right and drive 12 miles west to the campground.

**Contact:** Fremont-Winema National Forest, Chemult Ranger District, 541/365-7001, www.fs.usda.gov/fremont-winema.

## 182 WALT HARING SNO-PARK

### Scenic rating: 6

in Fremont-Winema National Forest
near Chemult

**Map 11.5, page 599**

For eons, this has been a tiny, unknown, and free campground used as a staging area for snowmobiling and cross-country skiing in winter. In summer, it has primarily been a picnic site and layover spot. The elevation is 4,700 feet.

**Campsites, facilities:** There are five sites for tents or RVs. Picnic tables and fire rings are provided. Drinking water, vault toilets, and an RV dump station ($5 fee) are available. There is also a nice shelter with a woodstove. Some facilities are wheelchair accessible. Leashed pets are permitted.

**Reservations, fees:** Reservations are not accepted. There is no fee for camping; in winter, a parking permit is required and is available from the Oregon Department of Motor Vehicles. Open year-round.

**Directions:** From Eugene, drive southeast on Highway 58 for 86 miles to U.S. 97. Turn south and drive seven miles to Forest Road 9772 (one mile north of Chemult). Turn right on Forest Road 9772 (Miller Lake Road) and drive 0.5 mile to the campground.

**Contact:** Fremont-Winema National Forest, 541/365-7001, www.fs.usda.gov/fremont-winema; Oregon Department of Motor Vehicles, www.oregon.gov.

## 183 CHARLES V. STANTON PARK
🏊 ⛵ 🚤 🎣 🐕 🚴 ♿ 🚐 ⛺

**Scenic rating: 7**

on the South Umpqua River

**Map 11.6, page 600**

Charles V. Stanton Park, along the banks of the South Umpqua River, is an all-season spot with a nice beach for swimming in the summer and good steelhead fishing in the winter.

**Campsites, facilities:** There are 20 sites for tents or self-contained RVs (no hookups), 20 sites with full hookups for RVs up to 60 feet long, and one group area for up to 13 camping units. Picnic tables and fire rings or barbecues are provided. Drinking water, restrooms with flush toilets and showers, a dump station, pavilion, picnic area, Wi-Fi, and playground are available. Propane gas, a store, café, coin laundry, and ice are within one mile. Some

facilities are wheelchair accessible. Leashed pets are permitted.

**Reservations, fees:** Reservations are accepted ($10 reservation fee) at 541/957-7001 or www.co.douglas.or.us. Sites are $15-23 per night for single sites, the group sites are $70-250 per night. Credit/debit cards are not accepted at the campground, but may be used to make reservations. Open year-round.

**Directions:** Depending on which direction you're heading on I-5, there are two routes to reach this campground. In Canyonville northbound on I-5, take Exit 99 and drive one mile north on the frontage road to the campground on the right. Otherwise: In Canyonville southbound on I-5, take Exit 101. Turn right at the first stop sign, and almost immediately turn right again onto the frontage road. Drive one mile south on the frontage road to the campground on the left.

**Contact:** Charles V. Stanton Park, Douglas County Parks, 541/839-4483, www.co.douglas.or.us/parks.

## 184 CHIEF MIWALETA CAMPGROUND
🚶 🚴 🏊 ⛵ 🚤 🐕 ♿ 🚐 ⛺

**Scenic rating: 7**

on Galesville Reservoir, east of Azalea

**Map 11.6, page 600**

If location is everything, then this camp has got it. Wooded sites are set along the shore of beautiful Gales Reservoir, providing a base camp for a trip filled with fishing, boating, hiking, camping, and picnicking. A pavilion can be reserved in the day-use area.

**Campsites, facilities:** There are 20 sites with full hookups for RVs up to 60 feet long (some pull-through), 13 sites for tents only, and three cabins. Picnic tables and fire rings are provided. Drinking water, vault toilets, a reservable pavilion, a play structure, and a boat ramp are available. Some facilities are wheelchair accessible. Leashed pets are permitted.

**Reservations, fees:** Reservations are accepted

at 541/957-7001 or www.co.douglas.or.us ($10 reservation fee). RV sites with full hookups are $23 per night, $3 per night per additional vehicle, tent sites are $15 per night, and the cabins are $35-50 per night. Discounts available for Douglas County residents. Some credit cards are accepted for reservations only. Open year-round.

**Directions:** From Azalea, take I-5 north about 0.5 mile to Exit 88 east to Upper Cow Creek Road. Merge onto Upper Cow Creek and drive eight miles to the campground on the left. GPS Coordinates: 42.85172, -123.164518

**Contact:** Chief Miwaleta County Campground, 541/837-3302, www.co.douglas.or.us/parks/campgrounds.asp.

## 185 MEADOW WOOD RV PARK

### Scenic rating: 6

in Glendale

**Map 11.6, page 600**

Meadow Wood is a good option for RVers looking for a camping spot along I-5. It features 80 wooded acres and all the amenities. Nearby attractions include a ghost town, gold panning, and Wolf Creek Tavern.

**Campsites, facilities:** There are 25 tent sites and 75 pull-through sites with full or partial hookups for RVs up to 40 feet long. Picnic tables are provided. Drinking water, restrooms with flush toilets and showers, propane gas, a dump station, Wi-Fi, a coin laundry, a playground, and a seasonal heated swimming pool are available. Some facilities are wheelchair accessible. Leashed pets are permitted.

**Reservations, fees:** Reservations are accepted at 800/606-1274. Sites are $14.50-25 per night. Monthly rates are available. Open year-round.

**Directions:** From Grants Pass, drive north on I-5 to Exit 83 (near Glendale) and drive east for 0.25 mile to Autumn Lane. Turn right (south) on Autumn Lane and drive one mile to the park. Alternatively, if you are instead

driving south from Roseburg, drive south on I-5 to Exit 86 (near Glendale). Take that exit and drive over the freeway and turn right onto the frontage road. Continue for three miles to Barton Road. Turn left (east) and drive one mile to Autumn Lane. Turn right (south) on Autumn Lane and drive 0.75 mile to the park.

**Contact:** Meadow Wood RV Park, 541/832-3114 or 800/606-1274.

## 186 WOLF CREEK PARK

### Scenic rating: 6

near the town of Wolf Creek

**Map 11.6, page 600**

This rustic campground is located on Wolf Creek near the historic Wolf Creek Inn. A hiking trail leads to the top of London Peak through old-growth forest. Although close to I-5 and the town of Wolf Creek, this spot gets low to average use.

**Campsites, facilities:** There are 20 sites for tents only, 14 sites for tents or RVs up to 40 feet long (partial hookups), and two group sites for tents that accommodate up to 30 people each. Picnic tables and fire pits are provided. Drinking water, vault toilets, a dump station, softball field, playground, and a picnic shelter are available. A camp host is on-site. Supplies are available nearby. Some facilities are wheelchair accessible. Leashed pets are permitted.

**Reservations, fees:** Reservations are accepted ($8 reservation fee) at 800/452-5687 or www.reserveamerica.com. Sites are $19-22 per night, $5 per night per additional vehicle, the group camps are $32 per night. Open May-early September.

**Directions:** From Grants Pass, drive north on I-5 for approximately 18 miles to exit 76/Wolf Creek. Take that exit to Wolf Creek Road. Turn left and drive 0.5 mile to the town of Wolf Creek and Main Street. Turn left and drive 0.25 mile to the park.

**Contact:** Josephine County Parks, 541/474-5285, www.co.josephine.or.us.

## 187 INDIAN MARY PARK

🚶 🏊 ⛴ 🚤 🐕 🏇 ♿ 🚐 ⛺

**Scenic rating: 9**

on the Rogue River

**Map 11.6, page 600**                    **BEST(**

This park is the crown jewel of the Josephine County parks. Set right on the Rogue River at an elevation of 900-1,000 feet, the park offers disc golf (Frisbee golf), fishing, hiking trails, a picnic shelter, a swimming beach (unsupervised), and volleyball. Rogue River is famous for its rafting, which can be done with a commercial outfit or on your own.

**Campsites, facilities:** There are 34 sites for tents or self-contained RVs (no hookups), 44 sites with full hookups, and 14 sites with partial hookups for tents or RVs of up to 40 feet, a group tent site for up to 20 people, and two yurts. Picnic tables and fire pits are provided. Drinking water, restrooms with flush toilets and coin showers, garbage bins, a dump station, boat ramp, day-use area, a reservable picnic shelter, playground, volleyball court, horseshoe pits, ice, and firewood are available. A camp host is on-site. A store and café are seven miles away, and a coin laundry is 16 miles away. Some facilities are wheelchair accessible. Leashed pets are permitted.

**Reservations, fees:** Reservations are accepted ($8 reservation fee) at 800/452-5687 or www.reserveamerica.com. Sites are $19-22 per night, $5 per night per additional vehicle, the group camp is $32 per night, and yurts are $30 per night. Open year-round.

**Directions:** From Grants Pass, drive north on I-5 for 3.5 miles to Exit 61 (Merlin-Galice Road). Take that exit and drive west on Merlin-Galice Road for 19 miles to Indian Mary Park on the right.

**Contact:** Josephine County Parks, 541/474-5285, www.co.josephine.or.us.

## 188 ELDERBERRY FLAT

🏊 🏇 ♿ ⛺

**Scenic rating: 7**

on West Fork Evans Creek

**Map 11.6, page 600**

This camp is virtually unknown except to the off-highway vehicle (OHV) crowd. On weekends, this is usually not the place to find quiet and serenity. OHV and motorcycle activity is common here. It is located on the banks of Evans Creek, about a 30-minute drive from I-5. Small and primitive, it has access to swimming holes along the creek. No fishing is allowed in the creek.

**Campsites, facilities:** There are 11 sites for tents only. Picnic tables and fire grills are provided. Vault toilets and garbage service are available, but there is no drinking water. Some facilities are wheelchair accessible. Leashed pets are permitted.

**Reservations, fees:** Reservations are not accepted. There is no fee for camping, but there is a 14-day stay limit. Open April 1-October 31.

**Directions:** From Grants Pass, drive south on I-5 for 10 miles to the Rogue River exit. Take that exit, turn right on Depot Street, and drive to Pine Street. Turn left and drive 18 miles (it becomes East Evans Creek Road) to West Fork Evans Creek Road. Turn left and drive nine miles to the campground.

**Contact:** Bureau of Land Management, Medford District, 541/618-2200, www.or.blm.gov/medford.

## 189 GRIFFIN PARK

🚶 🚴 🏊 ⛴ 🚤 🐕 🏇 ♿ 🚐 ⛺

**Scenic rating: 7**

on the Rogue River

**Map 11.6, page 600**

This high-use campground and 16-acre park has grassy sites situated 100-150 yards from the Rogue River. The river current is slow in this area, so it is good for swimming and water play. Fishing and rafting are also popular. Hiking and bicycling are available nearby on Bureau of Land Management property.

**Campsites, facilities:** There are four sites for tents or RVs (no hookups), 15 sites for tents or RVs up to 40 feet long (full hookups), and one yurt. Picnic tables and fire pits are provided. Drinking water, restrooms with flush toilets and showers, a dump station, recreation field, playground, and horseshoe pits are available. A camp host is on-site. A boat ramp, convenience store, swimming area, and playground are within one mile. Some facilities are wheelchair accessible. Leashed pets are permitted.

**Reservations, fees:** Reservations are accepted ($8 reservation fee) at 800/452-5687 or www.reserveamerica.com. Sites are $19-22 per night, $5 per night per additional vehicle; yurts are $30 per night. Open year-round, but with no water November-early April; tent sites are closed mid-October-March 31.

**Directions:** From Grants Pass on I-5, take the U.S. 199 exit. Turn south on U.S. 199 and drive 6.7 miles to Riverbanks Road. Turn right and drive 6.2 miles to Griffin Park Road. Turn right and drive 0.5 mile to the park.

**Contact:** Josephine County Parks, 541/474-5285, www.co.josephine.or.us.

## 190 GRANTS PASS/ REDWOOD HIGHWAY CAMPGROUND
🏃 🚴 🐴 ⛵ 🚐 ⛰️

**Scenic rating: 8**

near Grants Pass

Map 11.6, page 600

This campground along a stream in the hills outside of Grants Pass attracts bird-watchers. It also makes a perfect layover spot for travelers who want to get away from the highway for a while. For an interesting side trip, drive south down scenic U.S. 199 to Cave Junction or Illinois River State Park.

**Campsites, facilities:** There are 40 sites for tents or RVs of any length (some with full hookups); some sites are pull-through. There

are also three cabins. Picnic tables are provided, and tent sites have fire pits. Restrooms with showers, drinking water, a dump station, coin laundry, convenience store, ice, RV supplies, propane gas, and limited Wi-Fi are available. There is also a playground and a recreation field. Leashed pets are permitted with certain restrictions.

**Reservations, fees:** Reservations are accepted and receive a 10 percent discount. RV sites are $29.50-39.50 per night, tent sites are $25 per night, $4 per person per night for more than two people, $3 per night for additional vehicle. Some credit cards are accepted. Open year-round.

**Directions:** In Grants Pass on I-5, take the U.S. 199 exit. Turn southwest on U.S. 199 and drive 14.5 miles to the campground on the right (at Milepost 14.5).

**Contact:** Grants Pass/Redwood Highway Campground, 541/476-6508 or 888/476-6508, www.redwoodhwycampground.com.

## 191 SCHROEDER
🏊 🚣 🚤 🏕️ 🐴 🚶 ♿ 🚐 ⛰️

**Scenic rating: 9**

on the Rogue River

Map 11.6, page 600

Steelhead and salmon fishing, swimming, and boating are among the possibilities at this popular camp along the Rogue River. Just a short jog off the highway, it makes an excellent layover for I-5 travelers. A bonus for RVers is 50-amp service. The park is set close to Hellgate Excursions, which provides jet-boat trips on the Rogue River.

**Campsites, facilities:** There are 22 sites with partial hookups for tents or RVs, 29 sites with full hookups for tents or RVs of any length, and two yurts. Picnic tables and fire pits are provided. Restrooms with flush toilets and coin showers and a picnic shelter that can be reserved are available. Recreational facilities include ballfields, tennis and basketball courts, horseshoe pits, volleyball court, a dog park, picnic area, playground, and boat ramp. A camp host is on-site. Some facilities, including a fishing pier, are wheelchair accessible. Leashed pets are permitted.

**Reservations, fees:** Reservations are accepted ($8 reservation fee) at 800/452-5687 or www.reserveamerica.com. Sites are $19-22 per night, $5 per night per additional vehicle; yurts are $30 per night. Open year-round; tent sites are closed mid-October-March 31.

**Directions:** In Grants Pass on I-5, take Exit 55 to U.S. 199. Drive west on U.S. 199 for 0.7 mile to Redwood Avenue. Turn right and drive 1.5 miles to Willow Lane. Turn right and drive 0.9 mile to Schroeder Lane and the park.

**Contact:** Josephine County Parks, 541/474-5285, www.co.josephine.or.us.

## 192 ROGUE VALLEY OVERNITERS

### Scenic rating: 5

near the Rogue River

**Map 11.6, page 600**

This park is just off the freeway in Grants Pass, the jumping-off point for trips down the Rogue River. The summer heat in this part of Oregon can surprise visitors in late June and early July. This is a nice, comfortable park with shade trees. About half of the sites are taken by monthly renters.

**Campsites, facilities:** There are 43 sites for RVs of any length (full hookups); some are pull-through sites. Picnic tables are provided. Restrooms with flush toilets and showers, Wi-Fi, cable TV, a dump station, meeting room, and coin laundry are available. Propane gas, a store, café, and ice are available within one mile. Leashed pets are permitted.

**Reservations, fees:** Reservations are recommended. Sites are $24.75-33.30 per night, plus $2 per person per night for more than two people. Weekly and monthly rates are available. Open year-round.

**Directions:** In Grants Pass on I-5, take Exit

58 to 6th Street. Drive south on 6th Street for 0.25 mile to the park on the right.

**Contact:** Rogue Valley Overniters, 541/479-2208, www.roguevalleyoverniters.com.

## 193 WHITEHORSE

### Scenic rating: 9

near the Rogue River

**Map 11.6, page 600**

This pleasant county park is set about a quarter mile from the banks of the Rogue River. It is one of several parks in the Grants Pass area that provide opportunities for salmon and steelhead fishing, hiking, and boating. This is a popular bird-watching area. Wildlife Images, a wildlife rehabilitation center, is nearby. Possible side trips include Crater Lake National Park (two hours away), Kerby Museum, and Oregon Caves.

**Campsites, facilities:** There are 34 sites for tents or RVs of any length (no hookups), eight sites for RVs of any length (full hookups), and one yurt. Picnic tables and fire pits are provided. Restrooms with flush toilets and coin showers, a boat ramp, horseshoe pits, volleyball, a picnic shelter, and a playground are available. A camp host is on-site. Some facilities are wheelchair accessible. Leashed pets are permitted.

**Reservations, fees:** Reservations are accepted ($8 reservation fee) at 800/452-5687 or www.reserveamerica.com. Sites are $19-22 per night, $5 per night per additional vehicle, and $30 per night for the yurt. Open seasonally; call before planning a visit.

Reservation note: When making a reservation for this campground, note that ReserveAmerica.com lists it as White Horse, not Whitehorse, and its computer system will not recognize it as one word.

**Directions:** In Grants Pass on I-5, take Exit 58 to 6th Street. Drive south on 6th Street to G Street. Turn right (west) and drive approximately seven miles (the road becomes Upper

River Road, then Lower River Road). The park is on the left at 7600 Lower River Road.

**Contact:** Josephine County Parks, 541/474-5285, www.co.josephine.or.us.

## 194 RIVER PARK RV RESORT

🚶 🚴 🏊 🛶 🦮 🎣 ⛺

**Scenic rating: 6**

on the Rogue River

**Map 11.6, page 600**

This park has a quiet, serene riverfront setting, yet it is close to all the conveniences of a small city. Highlights here include 700 feet of Rogue River frontage for trout fishing and swimming. It's one of several parks in the immediate area.

**Campsites, facilities:** There are two sites for tents only and 47 sites with full hookups for RVs up to 40 feet long. Picnic tables are provided. Cable TV, Wi-Fi, restrooms with flush toilets and showers, a dump station, coin laundry, horseshoe pits, and ice are available. Leashed pets are permitted.

**Reservations, fees:** Reservations are accepted. Sites are $33-40 per night, $2 per person per night for more than two people, and $2 per night for an additional vehicle. Some credit cards are accepted. Open year-round.

**Directions:** In Grants Pass on I-5, take Exit 55 west to Highway 199. Drive west on Highway 199 for two miles to Parkdale. Turn left on Parkdale and drive one block to Highway 99. Turn left on Highway 99 and drive two miles to the park on the left.

**Contact:** River Park RV Resort, 541/479-0046 www.riverparkrvresort.com.

## 195 CHINOOK WINDS RV PARK

🚶 🚴 🏊 🛶 🏕 🦮 ♿ 🎣

**Scenic rating: 6**

on the Rogue River

**Map 11.6, page 600**

This campground along the Rogue River is close to chartered boat trips down the Rogue and a golf course. Fishing and swimming access are available from the campground. (Note: This park was previously known as Circle W RV Park.)

**Campsites, facilities:** There are 25 sites with full or partial hookups for RVs up to 40 feet; some are pull-through sites. Picnic tables are provided. Restrooms with flush toilets and showers, a dump station, Wi-Fi, coin laundry, boat dock, and ice are available. Some facilities are wheelchair accessible. Leashed pets are permitted.

**Reservations, fees:** Reservations are recommended. Sites are $25-40 per night, plus $1.50 per person per night for more than two people. Weekly and monthly rates are available. Cash or check only. Open year-round.

**Directions:** From Grants Pass, drive south on I-5 for 10 miles to Exit 48 at Rogue River. Take that exit west (over the bridge) to Highway 99. Turn right and drive west one mile to the park on the right.

**Contact:** Chinook Winds RV Park, 541/582-1686 or 866/582-1686, www.chinookwindsrv.com.

## 196 VALLEY OF THE ROGUE STATE PARK

🚴 🛶 🏕 🦮 🏕 ♿ 🎣 ⛺

**Scenic rating: 7**

on the Rogue River

**Map 11.6, page 600**

With easy highway access, this popular campground along the banks of the Rogue River often fills to near capacity during the summer. Recreation options include fishing and boating. This spot makes a good base camp for taking in the Rogue Valley and surrounding attractions: Ashland's Shakespeare Festival, the Britt Music Festival, Crater Lake National Park, historic Jacksonville, and Oregon Caves National Monument.

**Campsites, facilities:** There are 147 sites with full or partial hookups for tents or RVs up to

Chapter 11

75 feet long, some with pull-through sites, and 21 sites for tents. There are also three group tent areas for up to 25 people each and six yurts. Picnic tables and fire grills are provided. Restrooms with flush toilets and showers, drinking water, garbage bins, a dump station, firewood, Wi-Fi, coin laundry, a meeting hall, amphitheater, and playgrounds are available. A restaurant is nearby. Boat-launching facilities are nearby. Some facilities are wheelchair accessible. Leashed pets are permitted.

**Reservations, fees:** Reservations are accepted at 800/452-5687 or www.oregonstateparks. org ($8 reservation fee). Tent sites are $19 per night, RV sites are $19-24 per night, $5 per night per extra vehicle. Group areas are $71 per night; yurts are $36 per night. Some credit cards are accepted. Open year-round.

**Directions:** From Grants Pass, drive south on I-5 for 12 miles to Exit 45B/Valley of the Rogue State Park. Take that exit, turn right, and drive a short distance to the park on the right.

**Contact:** Valley of the Rogue State Park, 541/582-1118 or 800/551-6949, www.oregon-stateparks.org.

## 197 KOA GOLD N' ROGUE

🏃 🚲 🏊 🎣 🛶 🐕 🏕 ♿ 🚐 ⛰

### Scenic rating: 6

on the Rogue River

**Map 11.6, page 600**

This campground is set 0.5 mile from the Rogue River, with bike paths, a golf course, and the Oregon Vortex (the house of mystery) in the vicinity. It's one of the many campgrounds between Gold Hill and Grants Pass.

**Campsites, facilities:** There are 55 sites with full hookups, 21 sites with partial hookups for RVs of any length, 12 sites for tents, and four cabins. Some sites are pull-through. Picnic tables are provided, and tent sites have fire rings. Restrooms with flush toilets and showers, Wi-Fi, cable TV, propane gas, a dump station, firewood, a convenience store, coin laundry, ice, horseshoe pits, basketball hoop, a playground, and a seasonal swimming pool are available. A café is within one mile, and boat-launching facilities are within five miles. Some facilities are wheelchair accessible. Leashed pets are permitted.

**Reservations, fees:** Reservations are accepted at 800/562-7608. Sites are $25-38 per night, plus $2 per person per night for more than two people. Some credit cards are accepted. Open year-round.

**Directions:** From Medford, drive north on I-5 for 10 miles to South Gold Hill and Exit 40. Take that exit, turn right, and drive 0.25 mile to Blackwell Road. Turn right (on a paved road) and drive 0.25 mile to the park.

**Contact:** KOA Gold n' Rogue, 541/855-7710, www.koa.com.

## 198 LAKE SELMAC

🏃 🚲 🏊 🎣 🛶 🏕 🐕 🤽 ♿ 🚐 ⛰

### Scenic rating: 9

on Lake Selmac

**Map 11.6, page 600**

Nestled in a wooded, mountainous area, this 300-acre park offers boating, hiking, sailing, swimming, and good trophy bass fishing on beautiful, 160-acre Lake Selmac. Horse trails are also available. There are seasonal hosts and a park ranger on-site.

**Campsites, facilities:** There are 113 sites for tents or RVs up to 40 feet long, some with full or partial hookups, a group area for up to 50 people, and five yurts. There are also six horse camps with corrals. Picnic tables and fire pits are provided. Drinking water, restrooms with flush toilets and coin showers, a dump station, convenience store, picnic area, horseshoe pits, playground, ball fields, two boat ramps, and a dock are available. Some facilities are wheelchair accessible. Leashed pets are permitted.

**Reservations, fees:** Reservations are accepted at 800/452-5687 or www.reserveamerica.com ($8 reservation fee). Sites are $19-22 per night, $5 per night per additional vehicle, horse sites are $19 per night, yurts are $30 per night. The group sites is $32 per night for the first 12 people, $3 per person per night for more than 12 people. Open year-round, with some facility limitations in winter.

**Directions:** In Grants Pass on I-5, take the U.S. 199 exit. Turn south on U.S. 199 and drive for 23 miles to Selma. Continue 0.5 mile to the Lake Selmac exit (Lakeshore Drive). Turn left (east) and drive 2.3 miles to the lake and the campground entrance.

**Contact:** Josephine County Parks, 541/474-5285, www.co.josephine.or.us.

## 199 LAKE SELMAC RESORT

**Scenic rating: 7**

on Lake Selmac

**Map 11.6, page 600**

Named Resort of the Year 2009 by Radio Medford-Grants Pass, this resort borders the shore of Lake Selmac, a 160-acre lake. Fishing is great for largemouth bass (the state record has been set here three times). Bluegill, catfish, crappie, and trout are also catchable here. Fishing derbies are held during the summer. There is a 5-mph speed limit on the lake. Watch for waterfowl, including eagles, geese, ospreys, and swans. A trail circles the lake, and bikers, hikers, and horses are welcome. A disc golf course is 1.5 miles away at the county park, and a golf course is about six miles away. Oregon Caves National Monument, about 30 miles away, makes a good side trip.

**Campsites, facilities:** There are 29 sites with full or partial hookups for tents or RVs of any length; most sites are pull-through. Two cabins and a rental trailer are also available. Picnic tables and fire rings are provided. Drinking water, restrooms with flush toilets and showers, coin laundry, a general store with fishing and hunting licenses, bait and tackle, firewood, ice, Wi-Fi, and a play area with miniature golf, volleyball, tetherball, and horseshoe pits are available. Boat docks and launching facilities

are nearby, and rentals are on-site. Some facilities are wheelchair accessible. Leashed pets are permitted, with breed restrictions.

**Reservations, fees:** Reservations are accepted. Sites are $24-45 per night, $3 per night per additional vehicle, $5 per person per night for more than four. Monthly rates are available. Some credit cards are accepted. Open year-round, with limited winter facilities.

**Directions:** In Grants Pass on I-5, take the U.S. 199 exit. Turn southwest on U.S. 199 and drive 23 miles to Selma and the Lake Selmac exit (Lakeshore Drive). Turn left (east) and drive 2.5 miles to the lake and the resort on the left.

**Contact:** Lake Selmac Resort, 541/597-2277, www.lakeselmacresort.com.

## 200 MOUNTAIN MAN RV PARK

**Scenic rating: 7**

on the Illinois River

**Map 11.6, page 600**

This park on the Illinois River provides good opportunities for swimming and boating (no motors are permitted). And yes, there is a mountain man here who often shows up in costume in the evening when camp groups build a fire. Great Cats World Park, a wildlife park, is 1.5 miles away. Other nearby side trips include Oregon Caves National Monument (21 miles) and Grants Pass (31 miles). Crescent City is 50 miles away. Note that a majority of the campground is taken by monthly rentals, with the remainder available for overnighters. This park was previously known as Town and Country RV Park.

**Campsites, facilities:** There are 51 sites for tents or RVs of any length (full hookups); some sites are pull-through. Picnic tables are provided, and some sites have fire rings. Drinking water, cable TV, restrooms with flush toilets and showers, coin laundry, a community fire ring, ice, horseshoe pits, Wi-Fi, and a clubhouse are available. Leashed pets are permitted.

**Reservations, fees:** Reservations are accepted. Sites are $20-26 per night, plus $4 per person per night for more than two people. Weekly and monthly rates are available. Open year-round.

**Directions:** In Grants Pass on I-5, take the U.S. 199 exit. Go 30 miles west on U.S. 199 (past Cave Junction) to the park on the right.

**Contact:** Mountain Man RV Park, 541/592-2656, www.mountainmanrvpark.com.

## 201 COUNTRY HILLS RESORT

### Scenic rating: 7

near Oregon Caves National Monument

**Map 11.6, page 600**

Lots of sites at this wooded camp border Sucker Creek, a popular spot for swimming. Several wineries are located within two miles. Lake Selmac and Oregon Caves National Monument provide nearby side-trip options.

**Campsites, facilities:** There are 12 sites for tents only and 20 sites with partial or full hookups for RVs of any length; some are pull-through sites. There are also six cabins and a five-unit motel. Picnic tables and fire rings are provided. Restrooms with flush toilets and coin showers, a dump station, Wi-Fi, drinking water, firewood, a convenience store, coin laundry, basketball hoops, volleyball, horseshoe pits, seasonal ice cream parlor, seasonal café, and ice are available. Leashed pets are permitted.

**Reservations, fees:** Reservations are accepted. Sites are $17-28 per night, $3 per night per additional vehicle, $5 per night per pet. Some credit cards are accepted. The campground is open February-November, weather permitting; the resort is open year-round.

**Directions:** In Grants Pass on I-5, take the U.S. 199 exit. Go 28 miles on U.S. 199 to the junction of Cave Junction and Highway 46/Oregon Caves. Turn left on Highway 46 and drive eight miles to the resort on the right.

**Contact:** Country Hills Resort, 541/592-3406, www.countryhillsresort.com.

## 202 GRAYBACK

### Scenic rating: 7

near Oregon Caves National Monument in Rogue River-Siskiyou National Forest

**Map 11.6, page 600**

This wooded campground (2,000 feet elevation) along the banks of Sucker Creek has sites with ample shade. It's a good choice if you're planning to visit Oregon Caves National Monument, about 10 miles away. The camp, set in a grove of old-growth firs, is also a prime place for bird-watching. A 0.5-mile trail cuts through the camp.

**Campsites, facilities:** There are 39 sites for tents and one site with full hookups for RVs up to 42 feet long. Picnic tables, garbage bins, and fire grills are provided. Vault toilets and drinking water are available. Some facilities are wheelchair accessible, including a 0.5-mile trail. Leashed pets are permitted.

**Reservations, fees:** Reservations are not accepted. Sites are $10 per night, $4 per night per vehicle. Open May-September, weather permitting.

**Directions:** In Grants Pass on I-5, take Exit 55 for U.S. 199. Bear southwest on U.S. 199 for 30 miles to Cave Junction and Highway 46. Turn east on Highway 46 and drive 12 miles to the campground on the right.

**Contact:** Rogue River-Siskiyou National Forest, Wild Rivers Ranger District, 541/592-4000, www.fs.usda.gov/rogue-siskiyou.

## 203 CAVE CREEK

### Scenic rating: 7

near Oregon Caves National Monument in Rogue River-Siskiyou National Forest

**Map 11.6, page 600**

No campground is closer to Oregon Caves National Monument than this U.S. Forest Service camp, a mere four miles away. There is even a two-mile trail out of camp that leads directly to the caves. The camp, at an elevation of 2,500 feet, lies in a grove of old-growth timber along the banks of Cave Creek, a small stream with some trout fishing opportunities (catch-and-release only). The sites are shaded, and an abundance of wildlife can be spotted in the area. Hiking opportunities abound.

**Campsites, facilities:** There are 18 sites for tents or RVs up to 16 feet long. Picnic tables and fire rings are provided. Drinking water, garbage bins, and vault toilets are available. Showers are within eight miles. Leashed pets are permitted.

**Reservations, fees:** Reservations are not accepted. Sites are $10 per night, $4 per night per additional vehicle. Open mid-May-mid-September, weather permitting.

**Directions:** In Grants Pass on I-5, take Exit 55 for U.S. 199. Bear southwest on U.S. 199 for 30 miles to Cave Junction and Highway 46. Turn east on Highway 46 and drive 16 miles to the campground on the right.

**Contact:** Rogue River-Siskiyou National Forest, Wild Rivers Ranger District, 541/592-4000, www.fs.usda.gov/rogue-siskiyou.

and fire grills are provided. Vault toilets and firewood are available. There is no drinking water. Garbage must be packed out. Leashed pets are permitted.

**Reservations, fees:** Reservations are accepted for the lookout only at 877/444-6777 ($10 reservation fee) or www.recreation.gov ($9 reservation fee). Sites are $5 per night per vehicle, the lookout is $40 per night. Open June-early October, weather permitting.

**Directions:** From Grants Pass, drive south on U.S. 199 for 30 miles to Cave Junction and Rockydale Road (County Road 5560). Turn left (southeast) on Rockydale Road and drive eight miles to County Road 5828 (also called Waldo Road and Happy Camp Road). Turn southeast and drive 14 miles to Forest Road 4812. Turn left (east) and drive four miles to Forest Road 4812-040. Turn left (south) and drive two miles to the campground. This access road is very narrow and rough. Large RVs are strongly discouraged.

**Contact:** Rogue River-Siskiyou National Forest, Wild Rivers Ranger District, 541/592-4000, www.fs.usda.gov/rogue-siskiyou.

## 204 BOLAN LAKE

🏃🚶 ⛵ 🚃 🏕 🦌 🚙 🛶 ⛺

### Scenic rating: 9

on Bolan Lake in Rogue River-Siskiyou National Forest

**Map 11.6, page 600**    **BEST (**

Very few out-of-towners know about this camp, with pretty, shaded sites along the shore of 15-acre Bolan Lake. The lake is stocked with trout, and the fishing can be good. Only non-motorized boats are allowed. A trail from the lake leads up to a fire lookout and ties into miles of other trails, including the Bolan Lake Trail. This spot is truly a bird-watcher's paradise, with a variety of species to view. The camp is set at 5,500 feet elevation.

**Campsites, facilities:** There are 12 sites for tents or RVs up to 16 feet long. An unfurnished lookout is also available for rent. Picnic tables

## 205 FAREWELL BEND

🏃🚶 ⛵ 🏕 🦌 ♿ 🚙 🛶 ⛺

### Scenic rating: 7

on the Upper Rogue River in Rogue River National Forest

**Map 11.7, page 601**

Extremely popular Farewell Bend campground is set at an elevation of 3,400 feet along the banks of the Upper Rogue River near the Rogue River Gorge. A 0.25-mile barrier-free trail leads from camp to the Rogue Gorge Viewpoint and is definitely worth the trip. The Upper Rogue River Trail passes near camp. This spot attracts a lot of the campers visiting Crater Lake.

**Campsites, facilities:** There are 61 sites for tents or RVs up to 40 feet long. Picnic tables, fire grills, and fire rings are provided. Drinking water, firewood, and flush toilets are available. Some facilities are wheelchair accessible. Leashed pets are permitted.

**Reservations, fees:** Reservations are not accepted. Sites are $18 per night, $9 per night per additional vehicle. Open mid-May-late October, weather permitting.

**Directions:** From Medford, drive northeast on Highway 62 for 57 miles (near Union Creek) to the campground on the left.

**Contact:** Rogue River National Forest, Prospect Ranger District, 541/560-3400, www.fs.usda.gov/rogue-siskiyou; Rogue Recreation, 541/560-3900.

## 206 UNION CREEK
🚶 🛶 🏕️ ♿ 🚐 ⛺

### Scenic rating: 8
near the Upper Rogue River in Rogue River National Forest

**Map 11.7, page 601**

One of the most popular camps in the district, this spot is more developed than the nearby camps of Mill Creek, Natural Bridge, and River Bridge. It sits at 3,200 feet elevation along the banks of Union Creek, where the creek joins the Upper Rogue River. The Upper Rogue River Trail passes near camp. Interpretive programs are offered in the summer, and a convenience store and restaurant are within walking distance.

**Campsites, facilities:** There are 78 sites for tents or RVs up to 30 feet long and three RV sites with full hookups. Picnic tables and fire grills are provided. A restroom with flush toilets, vault toilets, drinking water, and garbage service are available. Firewood is available for purchase. An amphitheater is available for programs. A store and restaurant are within walking distance. Some facilities are wheelchair accessible. Leashed pets are permitted.

**Reservations, fees:** Reservations are not accepted. Sites are $14 per night, $6 per night per additional vehicle; RV sites with full hookups

are $10 per night per additional vehicle. Open mid-May-mid-October, weather permitting.

**Directions:** From Medford, drive northeast on Highway 62 for 56 miles (near Union Creek) to the campground on the left.

**Contact:** Rogue River-Siskiyou National Forest, Prospect Ranger District, 541/560-3400, www.fs.usda.gov/rogue-siskiyou; Rogue Recreation, 541/560-3900.

## 207 NATURAL BRIDGE
🚶 🛶 🏕️ ♿ 🚐 ⛺

### Scenic rating: 8
on the Upper Rogue River Trail in Rogue River-Siskiyou National Forest

**Map 11.7, page 601**  |  **BEST (**

Expect lots of company in midsummer at this popular camp, which sits at an elevation of 3,200 feet, where the Upper Rogue River runs underground. The Upper Rogue River Trail passes by the camp and follows the river for many miles to the Pacific Crest Trail in Crater Lake National Park. There is an interpretive area and a spectacular geological viewpoint adjacent to the camp. A 0.25-mile, barrier-free trail is also available.

**Campsites, facilities:** There are 17 sites for tents or RVs up to 30 feet long. Picnic tables and fire grills are provided. Vault toilets are available. There is no drinking water and garbage must be packed out. Some facilities are wheelchair accessible. Leashed pets are permitted.

**Reservations, fees:** Reservations are not accepted. Sites are $10 per night, $4 per night per additional vehicle. Open May-early November, weather permitting.

**Directions:** From Medford, drive northeast on Highway 62 for 55 miles (near Union Creek) to Forest Road 300. Turn left and drive one mile west to the campground on the right.

**Contact:** Rogue River-Siskiyou National Forest, Prospect Ranger District, 541/560-3400, www.fs.usda.gov/rogue-siskiyou.

## 208 ABBOTT CREEK

### Scenic rating: 8

on Abbott and Woodruff Creeks in Rogue River
National Forest

**Map 11.7, page 601**    **BEST (**

Situated at the confluence of Abbott and
Woodruff Creeks about two miles from the
Upper Rogue River, this camp is a better
choice for visitors with children than some
of the others along the Rogue River. Abbott
Creek is small and tame compared to the roaring Rogue. The elevation here is 3,100 feet.

**Campsites, facilities:** There are 25 sites for
tents or RVs up to 35 feet long, including five
OHV sites. Picnic tables, garbage service, and
fire grills are provided. Drinking water, vault
toilets, and firewood are available. Leashed
pets are permitted.

**Reservations, fees:** Reservations are not accepted. Sites are $12 per night, $6 per night
per additional vehicle. Open mid-May-late
October, weather permitting.

**Directions:** From Medford, drive northeast on
Highway 62 for 50 miles (near Union Creek)
to Forest Road 68. Turn left and drive 3.5
miles west to the campground on the left.

**Contact:** Rogue River-Siskiyou National Forest, Prospect Ranger District, 541/560-3400,
www.fs.usda.gov/rogue-siskiyou; Rogue Recreation, 541/560-3900.

## 209 MILL CREEK

### Scenic rating: 7

near the Upper Rogue River in Rogue
River-Siskiyou National Forest

**Map 11.7, page 601**

This campground (elevation of 2,800 feet)
along the banks of Mill Creek, about two
miles from the Upper Rogue River, features
beautiful, private sites and heavy vegetation.
One in a series of remote, primitive camps

near Highway 62 missed by out-of-towners,
this camp is an excellent choice for tenters.

**Campsites, facilities:** There are 10 sites for
tents. Picnic tables and fire grills are provided.
Vault toilets are available. There is no drinking water and garbage must be packed out.
Leashed pets are permitted.

**Reservations, fees:** Reservations are not accepted. Sites are $8 per night, $4 per night per
additional vehicle. Open early May-November,
weather permitting.

**Directions:** From Medford, drive north on
Highway 62 for 46 miles (near Union Creek)
to Forest Road 6200-030. Turn right (southeast) and drive one mile to the campground
on the left.

**Contact:** Rogue River-Siskiyou National Forest, Prospect Ranger District, 541/560-3400,
www.fs.usda.gov/rogue-siskiyou; Rogue Recreation, 541/560-3900.

## 210 RIVER BRIDGE

### Scenic rating: 7

on the Upper Rogue River in Rogue River
National Forest

**Map 11.7, page 601**

River Bridge campground, situated at 2,900
feet elevation along the banks of the Upper
Rogue River, is particularly scenic, with secluded sites and river views. This is a calmer
part of the Wild and Scenic Upper Rogue
River, but swimming and rafting are not
recommended. The Upper Rogue River Trail
passes by the camp and follows the river for
many miles to the Pacific Crest Trail in Crater
Lake National Park.

**Campsites, facilities:** There are eleven sites
for tents or RVs up to 25 feet long. Picnic tables and fireplaces are provided. Vault toilets
are available, but there is no drinking water.
Leashed pets are permitted.

**Reservations, fees:** Reservations are not accepted. Sites are $8 per night, $4 per night per

additional vehicle. Open early May-November, weather permitting.

**Directions:** From Medford, drive northeast on Highway 62 (Crater Lake Highway) for 42 miles (before reaching Union Creek) to Forest Road 6210. Turn left and drive one mile to the campground on the right.

**Contact:** Rogue River-Siskiyou National Forest, Prospect Ranger District, 541/560-3400, www.fs.usda.gov/rogue-siskiyou.

## 211 HUCKLEBERRY MOUNTAIN

### Scenic rating: 6

near Crater Lake National Park in Rogue River-Siskiyou National Forest

**Map 11.7, page 601**

Here's a hideaway for Crater Lake visitors. The camp is located at the site of an old 1930s Civilian Conservation Corps camp, and an OHV trail runs through and next to the campground. Set at an elevation of 5,400 feet, this spot, about 15 miles from the entrance to Crater Lake National Park, really does get overlooked by highway travelers, so you have a good shot at privacy. About 10 miles of rough roads keep traffic down most of the time.

**Campsites, facilities:** There are 25 sites for tents or RVs up to 16 feet long. Picnic tables and fireplaces are provided. Vault toilets are available. There is no drinking water and garbage must be packed out. Leashed pets are permitted.

**Reservations, fees:** Reservations are not accepted. There is no fee for camping. Open June-late October, weather permitting.

**Directions:** From Medford, drive north on Highway 62 for 50 miles (near Union Creek) to Forest Road 60. Turn right and drive 12 miles to the campground.

**Contact:** Rogue River-Siskiyou National Forest, Prospect Ranger District, 541/560-3400, www.fs.usda.gov/rogue-siskiyou.

## 212 MAZAMA

### Scenic rating: 6

near the Pacific Crest Trail in Crater Lake National Park

**Map 11.7, page 601**

One of two campgrounds at Crater Lake—the other being Lost Creek, which remained closed at time of publication—this camp sits at 6,000 feet elevation and is known for cold nights, even in late June and early September. (I once got caught in a snowstorm here at the opening in mid-June.) The Pacific Crest Trail passes through the park, but the only trail access down to Crater Lake is at Cleetwood Cove. Seasonal boat tours and junior ranger programs are available. Note that winter access to the park is from the west only on Highway 62 to Rim Village.

**Campsites, facilities:** There are 213 sites for tents or RVs up to 50 feet long; some have partial hookups. Picnic tables and fire rings are provided. Drinking water, restrooms with flush toilets and coin showers, bear-proof food lockers, garbage bins, a dump station, coin laundry, gasoline, mini-mart, restaurant, gift shop, firewood, and ice are available. Some facilities are wheelchair accessible. Leashed pets are permitted in the campground and on paved roads only.

**Reservations, fees:** Reservations are recommended at 888/774-2728 or www.craterlake-lodges.com. RV sites are $29-35 per night, tent sites are $21 per night, $3.50 per person per night for more than two people. There is a $10 park entrance fee per vehicle. Some credit cards are accepted. Open early June-September, weather permitting.

**Directions:** From I-5 at Medford, turn east on Highway 62 and drive 72 miles into Crater Lake National Park and to Annie Springs junction. Turn left and drive a short distance to the national park entrance kiosk. Just beyond the kiosk, turn right to the campground and Mazama store entrance.

**Contact:** Crater Lake National Park, 541/594-3000, www.nps.gov/crla.

## 213 FLY CASTERS RV PARK

### Scenic rating: 6

on the Rogue River

**Map 11.7, page 601**

This spot along the banks of the Rogue River is a good base camp for RVers who want to fish or hike. The county park, located across the river in Shady Cove, offers picnic facilities and a boat ramp. Lost Creek Lake is about a 15-minute drive northeast. Note that about half of the sites are taken by long-term rentals.

**Campsites, facilities:** There are 41 sites with full hookups for RVs of any length; two are pull-through sites. Five mobile homes are also available. Picnic tables are provided and a loaner fire pit is available. Restrooms with flush toilets and showers, satellite TV, Wi-Fi, a clubhouse, barbecue area, horseshoe pits, and coin laundry are available. A store, café, and ice are within one mile. Boat-launching facilities are nearby. Some facilities are wheelchair accessible. Leashed pets are permitted.

**Reservations, fees:** Reservations are recommended. Sites are $33-44 per night. Some credit cards are accepted. Weekly and monthly rates are available. Open year-round.

**Directions:** From Medford, drive northeast on Highway 62 for 21 miles to the park on the left.

**Contact:** Fly Casters RV Park, 541/878-2749, www.flycastersrv.com.

## 214 BEAR MOUNTAIN RV PARK

### Scenic rating: 7

on the Rogue River

**Map 11.7, page 601**

This campground is set in an open, grassy area on the Rogue River about six miles from Lost Creek Lake, where boat ramps and picnic areas are available for day use. The campsites are spacious and shaded.

**Campsites, facilities:** There is a grassy area for tent sites and 37 sites with full or partial hookups for RVs of any length. Picnic tables are provided. Drinking water, restrooms with flush toilets and showers, coin laundry, ice, and a playground are available. A store and café are within one mile. Boat docks and launching facilities are nearby. Leashed pets are permitted.

**Reservations, fees:** Reservations are accepted at 541/878-2400. Sites are $20-26 per night, plus $2 per person per night for more than two adults. Cash or check only; credit cards are not accepted. Open year-round.

**Directions:** From Medford, drive northeast on Highway 62 to the junction with Highway 227. Continue east on Highway 62 for 2.5 more miles to the park on the left.

**Contact:** Bear Mountain RV Park, 541/878-2400.

## 215 ROGUE ELK CAMPGROUND

### Scenic rating: 8

on the Rogue River east of the city of Trail

**Map 11.7, page 601**

Right on the Rogue River at an elevation of 1,476 feet, the park has creek swimming (unsupervised), a Douglas fir forest, fishing, hiking trails, rafting, and wildlife on 33 acres of space with 0.75 mile of river frontage. The forest is very beautiful here. Lost Creek Lake on Highway 62 makes a good side trip.

**Campsites, facilities:** There are 38 sites for tents or RVs of up to 25 feet long; some have partial hookups. Picnic tables and fire pits are provided. Drinking water, restrooms with flush toilets and coin showers, garbage bins, a dump station, boat ramp, and playground are available. A café, mini-mart, ice, coin laundry, and firewood are available within three miles. Some facilities are wheelchair accessible. Leashed pets are permitted.

**Reservations, fees:** Reservations are accepted

($8-10 reservation fee). Sites are $20-24 per night, $6 per night per additional vehicle. Open mid-March-mid-October.

**Directions:** From Medford, take Exit 30 for the Crater Lake Highway (Highway 62) and drive northeast on Highway 62 for 29 miles to the park entrance on the right.

**Contact:** Jackson County Parks, 27766 Highway 62, Trail 97541, 541/774-8183, www.jacksoncountyparks.com.

## 216 JOSEPH H. STEWART STATE RECREATION AREA

🚶 🚴 ⛴ 🎣 🚤 🐕 🎪 ♿ 🚐 ⛺

**Scenic rating: 7**

on Lost Creek Reservoir

**Map 11.7, page 601**

This state park is on the shore of Lost Creek Reservoir, about 40 miles from Crater Lake National Park, and is home to 11 miles of hiking and biking trails, a lake with a beach, boat rentals, and a marina. Grassy sites are spacious and sprinkled with conifers. The Cole River Hatchery is available for tours.

Note: At time of publication, a blue-green algae health advisory was in effect.

**Campsites, facilities:** There are 151 sites with partial hookups for tents or self-contained RVs, including some sites for RVs of any length, and 50 sites with water for tents or self-contained RVs. There are also two group areas for tents and RVs for up to 50 people each. Picnic tables and fire grills are provided. Restrooms with flush toilets and showers, garbage bins, drinking water, a dump station, firewood, and a playground with volleyball and horseshoes are available. Boat rentals, launching facilities, a swimming area, and a picnic area that can be reserved are nearby. Some facilities are wheelchair accessible. Leashed pets are permitted.

**Reservations, fees:** Reservations are at 800/452-5687 or www.oregonstateparks.org ($8 reservation fee). Sites are $13-20 per night, $5 per night per additional vehicle. Group sites are $51-71 per night for up to 25 people and one RV, $3 per person per night for more than 25 people; up to four additional RVs are permitted for $10 each. Some credit cards are accepted. Open March 1-October 31, weather permitting.

**Directions:** From Medford, drive northeast on Highway 62 for 34 miles to the Lost Creek Reservoir and the campground on the left.

**Contact:** Joseph H. Stewart State Recreation Area, 541/560-3334 or 800/551-6949, www.oregonstateparks.org.

## 217 WHISKEY SPRINGS

🚶 🚴 ⛴ 🎣 🐕 ♿ 🚐 ⛺

**Scenic rating: 9**

near Butte Falls in Rogue River National Forest

**Map 11.7, page 601**

This campground at Whiskey Springs, near Fourbit Ford Campground, is one of the larger, more developed backwoods U.S. Forest Service camps in the area. A one-mile, wheelchair-accessible nature trail passes nearby. You can see beaver dams and woodpeckers here. The camp is set at 3,200 feet elevation.

**Campsites, facilities:** There are 34 sites for tents or RVs up to 30 feet long. Picnic tables, garbage service, and fire grills are provided. Drinking water and vault toilets are available. Some facilities are wheelchair accessible. Leashed pets are permitted.

**Reservations, fees:** Reservations are not accepted. Sites are $14 per night, $7 per night per additional vehicle. Open mid-May-September, weather permitting.

**Directions:** From Medford, drive northeast on Highway 62 for 14 miles to the Butte Falls Highway. Turn right and drive east for 16 miles to the town of Butte Falls. Continue southeast on Butte Falls Highway for nine miles to Forest Road 3065. Turn left on Forest Road 3065 and drive 300 yards to the campground on the left.

**Contact:** Rogue River-Siskiyou National Forest, Butte Falls Ranger District, 541/865-2700, www.fs.usda.gov/rogue-siskiyou.

## 218 IMNAHA

**Scenic rating: 7**

near the Sky Lakes Wilderness in Rogue River-Siskiyou National Forest

**Map 11.7, page 601**

Located along Imnaha Creek at an elevation of 3,800 feet, this campground makes a good base camp for a wilderness trip. Trailheads at the ends of the nearby forest roads lead east into the Sky Lakes Wilderness; there are also two shorter interpretive trails.

**Campsites, facilities:** There are four sites for tents or RVs up to 30 feet long. A cabin is also available. Picnic tables and fire grills are provided. Vault toilets, drinking water, and garbage service are available. Leashed pets are permitted.

**Reservations, fees:** Reservations are accepted only for the cabin at 877/444-6777 ($10 reservation fee) or www.recreation.gov ($9 reservation fee). Sites are $10 per night, $5 per night per additional vehicle, and $40 per night for the cabin. Open mid-May-October, weather permitting.

**Directions:** From Medford, drive northeast on Highway 62 for about 35 miles to Prospect and Mill Creek Drive. Turn right and drive one mile to County Road 992/Butte Falls Prospect Highway. Turn right and drive 2.5 miles to Forest Road 37. Turn left and drive 10 miles east to the campground.

**Contact:** Rogue River-Siskiyou National Forest, Butte Falls Ranger Station, 541/865-2700, www.fs.usda.gov/rogue-siskiyou.

## 219 SOUTH FORK

**Scenic rating: 7**

on the South Rogue River in Rogue River-Siskiyou National Forest

**Map 11.7, page 601**

South Fork campground is set at an elevation of 4,000 feet along the South Rogue River. To the east, trails at the ends of the nearby forest roads provide access to the Sky Lakes Wilderness. The Southfork Trail, across the road from the campground, has a good biking trail in one direction and a hiking trail in the other. A map of Rogue River-Siskiyou National Forest details all back roads, trails, and waters.

**Campsites, facilities:** There are two sites for tents and four sites for tents or RVs up to 16 feet long. Picnic tables, drinking water, garbage service, and fire grills are provided. Vault toilets are available. Leashed pets are permitted.

**Reservations, fees:** Reservations are not accepted. Sites are $10 per night, $5 per night per additional vehicle. Open early June-mid-November, weather permitting.

**Directions:** From Medford, drive northeast on Highway 62 for 14 miles to Butte Falls Highway. Turn right and drive 16 miles east to the town of Butte Falls. Continue one mile past Butte Falls to County Road 992 (Butte Falls Prospect Highway) and drive nine miles to Forest Road 34. Turn right and drive 8.5 miles to the campground on the right.

**Contact:** Rogue River-Siskiyou National Forest, Butte Falls Ranger station, 541/865-2700, www.fs.usda.gov/rogue-siskiyou.

## 220 MEDFORD OAKS RV PARK

**Scenic rating: 6**

near Eagle Point

**Map 11.7, page 601**

This park is in a quiet, rural setting among the trees. Just a short hop off I-5, it's an excellent choice for travelers heading to or from California. The campground is located along the shore of a pond that provides good catch-and-release fishing (barbless hooks only). Most sites are filled with monthly renters.

**Campsites, facilities:** There are 55 sites with full or partial hookups for RVs of any length and six sites for tents; most sites are pull-through. There are also three cabins.

Restrooms with flush toilets and coin showers, a dump station, Wi-Fi, coin laundry, limited groceries, ice, and RV supplies are available. Recreational facilities include a seasonal, heated swimming pool, movies, horseshoe pits, table tennis, a recreation field for baseball, basketball, football, and volleyball, and a playground. Leashed pets are allowed with certain restrictions.

**Reservations, fees:** Reservations are recommended. RV sites are $30-35 per night, tent sites are $20 per night, $3 per person per night for more than four people. Group rates are available. Some credit cards are accepted. Open year-round.

**Directions:** From Medford, drive northeast on Highway 62 for five miles to Exit 30 and Highway 140. Turn east on Highway 140 and drive 6.8 miles to the park on the left.

**Contact:** Medford Oaks RV Park, 541/826-5103, www.medfordoaks.com.

## 221 FOURBIT FORD

**Scenic rating: 6**

on Fourbit Creek in Rogue River National Forest

**Map 11.7, page 601**

Fourbit Ford campground, situated at an elevation of 3,200 feet along Fourbit Creek, is one in a series of hidden spots tucked away near County Road 821.

**Campsites, facilities:** There are seven sites for tents or trailers up to 16 feet long. Picnic tables and fire grills are provided. Vault toilets, drinking water, and garbage service are available. Leashed pets are permitted.

**Reservations, fees:** Reservations are not accepted. Sites are $12 per night, $6 per extra vehicle per night. Open mid-May-late September, weather permitting.

**Directions:** From Medford, drive northeast on Highway 62 for 14 miles to Butte Falls Highway. Turn right and drive 16 miles east to the town of Butte Falls and County Road

821. Turn left and drive nine miles southeast to Forest Road 3065. Turn left and drive one mile to the campground on the left.

**Contact:** Rogue River National Forest, Butte Falls Ranger District, 541/865-2700, www.fs.usda.gov/rogue-siskiyou.

## 222 WILLOW LAKE RESORT

**Scenic rating: 9**

on Willow Lake

**Map 11.7, page 601**

This campground sits on the shore of Willow Lake. Located at the base of Mount McLoughlin at an elevation of 3,200 feet, it encompasses 927 wooded acres. The lake has fishing opportunities for bass, crappie, and trout. A hiking trail starts near camp. Waterskiing is allowed at the lake.

**Campsites, facilities:** There are 32 sites for tents or RVs (no hookups), 31 sites for tents or RVs (full or partial hookups), and a group area with 11 sites that can accommodate up to 150 people. There are also four cabins and two yurts. Picnic tables and fire rings are provided. Restrooms with flush toilets and coin showers, a dump station, and firewood are available. A store, boat ramp, and boat rentals are onsite. Some facilities are wheelchair accessible. Leashed pets are permitted.

**Reservations, fees:** Reservations are accepted ($8-10 reservation fee) for groups, yurts, and cabins only at 541/774-8183. Sites are $20-30 per night, yurts are $35 per night, cabins are $125 per night, $6 per night per additional vehicle. The group area is $175 per night. Open mid-April-October.

**Directions:** From Medford, drive northeast on Highway 62 for 15 miles to Butte Falls Highway. Turn east and drive 25 miles to Willow Lake Road. Turn right (south) and drive two miles to the campground.

**Contact:** Jackson County Parks, 541/774-8183, www.jacksoncountyparks.com.

## 223 PARKER MEADOWS

### Scenic rating: 7

on Parker Meadow in Rogue River
National Forest

**Map 11.7, page 601**

Fantastic views of nearby Mount McLoughlin are among the highlights of this rustic camp set at 5,000 feet elevation in a beautiful meadow. Trailheads at the ends of the forest roads lead into the Sky Lakes Wilderness. Parker Meadows is a nice spot, and lots of privacy between sites. Except during hunting season in the fall, this camp does not get much use.

**Campsites, facilities:** There are eight sites for tents or RVs up to 16 feet long. Picnic tables and fire grills are provided. Drinking water and vault toilets are available.

**Reservations, fees:** Reservations are not accepted. There is no fee for camping. Open mid-June-late October, weather permitting.

**Directions:** From Medford, drive northeast on Highway 62 for 14 miles to Butte Falls Highway. Turn right and drive 16 miles east to the town of Butte Falls and County Road 821. Turn left and drive 10 miles southeast to Forest Road 37. Turn left and drive 11 miles to the campground on the left.

**Contact:** Rogue River-Siskiyou National Forest, Butte Falls Ranger District, 541/865-2700, www.fs.usda.gov/rogue-siskiyou.

## 224 ODESSA

### Scenic rating: 4

near Klamath Lake in Fremont-Winema
National Forest

**Map 11.7, page 601**

This campground (4,100 feet elevation) borders Odessa Creek, near the shore of Upper Klamath Lake. The lake is the main attraction, with fishing the main activity. The lake can provide excellent fishing for rainbow trout on both flies and Rapalas. Boating is also popular.

Campsites sit among scattered mixed conifers and native brush.

**Campsites, facilities:** There are five tent sites. Picnic tables, garbage bins, and fire grills are provided. Vault toilets are available, but there is no drinking water. Leashed pets are permitted.

**Reservations, fees:** Reservations are not accepted. There is no fee for camping. Open year-round, weather permitting.

**Directions:** From Klamath Falls, drive west on Highway 140 about 18 miles to Forest Road 3639. Turn right (northeast) and drive one mile to the campground.

**Contact:** Fremont-Winema National Forests, Klamath Ranger District, 541/885-3400, www.fs.usda.gov/fremont-winema.

## 225 FOURMILE LAKE

### Scenic rating: 8

at Fourmile Lake in Fremont-Winema
National Forest

**Map 11.7, page 601**

This beautiful spot is the only camp on the shore of Fourmile Lake. Several nearby trails provide access to the Sky Lakes Wilderness. The Pacific Crest Trail passes about two miles from camp. Primitive and with lots of solitude, it attracts a calm and quiet crowd. Afternoon winds can be a problem, and in the evening, if the wind isn't blowing, the mosquitoes often arrive. Although this campground is near the foot of Mount McLoughlin (9,495 feet), there is no view of the mountain from here. Go to the east side of the lake for a good view.

**Campsites, facilities:** There are 28 sites for tents or RVs up to 22 feet long and one double site. Picnic tables, garbage bins, and fire grills are provided. Drinking water and vault toilets are available. Some facilities are wheelchair accessible. Leashed pets are permitted.

**Reservations, fees:** Reservations are not accepted. Single sites are $17 per night, the double site is $34 per night, $5 per night per additional vehicle. Open June-late September, weather permitting.

**Directions:** From Medford, drive northeast on Highway 62 for five miles to Exit 30 and Highway 140. Turn east on Highway 140 and drive approximately 40 miles to Forest Road 3661. Turn left (north) and drive six miles to the campground.

**Contact:** Fremont-Winema National Forests, Klamath Ranger District, 541/885-3400, www.fs.usda.gov/fremont-winema.

## 226 ROCKY POINT RESORT

### Scenic rating: 7

on Upper Klamath Lake

**Map 11.7, page 601**

Rocky Point Resort, at the Upper Klamath Wildlife Refuge, boasts 10 miles of canoe trails, along with opportunities for motorized boating and fishing. Ponderosa pines and Douglas firs create a quite picturesque setting for stellar sunsets and a peaceful retreat.

**Campsites, facilities:** There are 25 sites with partial or full hookups for RVs to 40 feet, five sites for tents, four cabins, and five motel rooms. Some sites are pull-through. Picnic tables and fire rings are provided. Restrooms with flush toilets and showers, drinking water, a convenience store, firewood, coin laundry, ice, fishing licenses, and a marina with boat gas, boat launch, and boat and canoe rentals are available. A restaurant and lounge overlook the lake. Some facilities are wheelchair accessible, including a fishing dock. Leashed pets are permitted.

**Reservations, fees:** Reservations are accepted. RV sites are $28-30 per night, tent sites are $22 per night, $3-4 per person per night for more than two people, $3 per pet per night, and $5 per night per additional vehicle. Weekly and monthly rates are available. Some credit cards are accepted. Open April 1-November 1.

**Directions:** From Klamath Falls, drive

northeast on Highway 140 for 25 miles to Rocky Point Road. Turn right and drive three miles to the resort on the right.

**Contact:** Rocky Point Resort, 541/356-2287, www.rockypointoregon.com.

## 227 WILLOW PRAIRIE HORSE CAMP

### Scenic rating: 7

near Fish Lake in Rogue River-Siskiyou National Forest

**Map 11.7, page 601**

There are two campgrounds here, including one for equestrian campers. This spot is located near the origin of the west branch of Willow Creek and next to a beaver swamp and several large ponds that attract deer, ducks, elk, geese, and sandhill cranes. A number of riding trails pass nearby. A map of Rogue River National Forest details the back roads and can help you get here. Fish Lake is four miles south.

**Campsites, facilities:** There are 10 sites for tents or RVs up to 16 feet long, one primitive cabin with cots, and 10 equestrian sites. Picnic tables and fire grills are provided. Drinking water, vault toilets, and garbage service are available. The equestrian camp has 10 sites for tents or small RVs, two stock water troughs, and horse corrals. A store, café, ice, boat docks, launching facilities, and rentals are nearby. A camp host is on-site. Leashed pets are permitted.

**Reservations, fees:** Reservations are accepted only for the horse camp and cabin at 877/444-6777 ($10 reservation fee) or www.recreation.gov ($9 reservation fee). Sites are $10 per night, $5 per night per additional vehicle. The cabin is $15 per night. Open late May-late October, weather permitting.

**Directions:** From Medford, drive northeast on Highway 62 for five miles to Exit 30 and Highway 140. Turn east on Highway 140 and drive 31.5 miles to Forest Road 37. Turn left and drive north 1.5 miles to Forest Road 3738. Turn left and drive one mile west to Forest Road 3735. Turn left and drive 100 yards to the campground. For the equestrian camp, continue for 0.25 mile to the campground entrance.

**Contact:** Rogue River-Siskiyou National Forest, High Cascades Ranger District, 541/560-3400, www.fs.usda.gov/rogue-siskiyou.

## 228 NORTH FORK

### Scenic rating: 7
near Fish Lake in Rogue River-Siskiyou National Forest

**Map 11.7, page 601**

Here is a small, pretty campground with easy access from the highway and proximity to Fish Lake. Situated on the north fork of Little Butte Creek at an elevation of 4,500 feet, it's fairly popular, so grab your spot early. Excellent fly-fishing can be found along the Fish Lake Trail, which leads directly out of camp.

**Campsites, facilities:** There are nine sites for tents or RVs up to 24 feet long. Picnic tables and fire grills are provided. Vault toilets and drinking water are available. Garbage must be packed out. A camp host is on-site. Boat docks, launching facilities, and rentals are nearby. Some facilities are wheelchair accessible. Leashed pets are permitted.

**Reservations, fees:** Reservations are not accepted. Sites are $10 per night, $4 per night per additional vehicle. Open May-mid-November, weather permitting.

**Directions:** From Medford, drive northeast on Highway 62 for five miles to Exit 30 and Highway 140. Turn east on Highway 140 and drive 31.5 miles to Forest Road 37. Turn right (south) and drive 0.5 mile to the campground.

**Contact:** Rogue River-Siskiyou National Forest, High Cascades Ranger District, 541/560-3400, www.fs.usda.gov/rogue-siskiyou.

## 229 FISH LAKE

### Scenic rating: 8
on Fish Lake in Rogue River-Siskiyou National Forest

**Map 11.7, page 601**

Bicycling, boating, fishing, and hiking are among the recreation options at this campground on the north shore of Fish Lake. Easy, one-mile access to the Pacific Crest Trail is also available. If this campground is full, Doe Point and Fish Lake Resort are nearby.

**Campsites, facilities:** There are 19 sites for tents or RVs up to 40 feet long and two walk-in tent sites. Picnic tables, fire grills, and garbage bins are provided. Drinking water, flush toilets, a picnic shelter that can be reserved, a store, café, firewood, and ice are available. A camp host is on-site. Boat docks, launching facilities, boat rentals, coin laundry, dump station, and coin showers are nearby. Some facilities are wheelchair accessible. Leashed pets are permitted.

**Reservations, fees:** Reservations are accepted only for the picnic shelter at 541/560-3900. Sites are $18 per night, $9 per night per additional vehicle. Open mid-May-mid-October, weather permitting.

**Directions:** From Medford, drive northeast on Highway 62 for five miles to Exit 30 and Highway 140. Turn east on Highway 140 and drive 30 miles to the campground on the right.

**Contact:** Rogue River-Siskiyou National Forest, Siskiyou Mountains District, 541/899-3800, www.fs.usda.gov/rogue-siskiyou; Rogue Recreation, 541/560-3900.

## 230 DOE POINT

### Scenic rating: 8
on Fish Lake in Rogue River-Siskiyou National Forest

**Map 11.7, page 601**

This campground (at 4,600 feet elevation) sits

along the north shore of Fish Lake, nearly adjacent to Fish Lake Campground. Doe Point is slightly preferable because of its dense vegetation, offering shaded, quiet, well-screened sites. Privacy, rare at many campgrounds, can be found here. Recreation options include biking, boating, fishing, and hiking, plus an easy, one-mile access trail to the Pacific Crest Trail.

**Campsites, facilities:** There are 24 sites for tents or RVs up to 30 feet long and five walk-in sites for tents. Picnic tables and fire grills are provided. Drinking water, garbage service, flush toilets, a store, café, firewood, and ice are available. Boat docks, launching facilities, boat rentals, showers, and a dump station are nearby. Some facilities are wheelchair accessible. Leashed pets are permitted.

**Reservations, fees:** Reservations are not accepted. Sites are $18 per night, $9 per night per additional vehicle. Open mid-May-late September, weather permitting.

**Directions:** From Medford, drive northeast on Highway 62 for five miles to Exit 30 and Highway 140. Turn east on Highway 140 and drive 30 miles to the campground on the right.

**Contact:** Rogue River-Siskiyou National Forest, High Cascades District, 541/560-3400, www.fs.usda.gov/rogue-siskiyou; Rogue Recreation, 541/560-3900.

## 231 FISH LAKE RESORT

**Scenic rating: 7**

on Fish Lake

**Map 11.7, page 601**

This resort along Fish Lake is privately operated under permit by the U.S. Forest Service and offers a resort-type feel, catering primarily to families. This is the largest and most developed of the three camps at Fish Lake. Bicycling, boating, fishing, and hiking are some of the activities here. Cozy cabins are available for rent. Boat speed on the lake is limited to 10 mph.

**Campsites, facilities:** There are 12 sites for

tents, 45 sites with full hookups for RVs up to 40 feet long, and 11 cabins. Some sites are pull-through. Picnic tables and fire rings are provided. Drinking water, restrooms with flush toilets and coin showers, propane gas, dump station, recreation hall, convenience store, café, coin laundry, ice, garbage bins, boat docks, boat rentals, and launching facilities are available. Some facilities are wheelchair accessible. Leashed pets are permitted, with breed restrictions.

**Reservations, fees:** Reservations are accepted at 541/949-8500 or www.fishlakeresort.net. Tent sites are $20-30 per night, and RV sites are $38 per night, $3 per person per night for more than four people, $3 per extra vehicle per night. Weekly, monthly, and group rates are available. Some credit cards are accepted. Open year-round, weather permitting, with limited winter facilities.

**Directions:** From Medford, take I-5 to Exit 30 and go to Highway 140. Turn east on Highway 140 and drive 30 miles to Fish Lake Road. Turn right (south) and drive 0.5 mile to the resort on the left.

**Contact:** Fish Lake Resort, 541/949-8500, www.fishlakeresort.net.

## 232 LAKE OF THE WOODS RESORT

**Scenic rating: 9**

on Lake of the Woods

**Map 11.7, page 601**   **BEST**

On beautiful Lake of the Woods, this resort offers fishing (four kinds of trout, catfish, and bass) and boating in a secluded forest setting. It's on one of the most beautiful lakes in the Cascade Mountains, surrounded by tall pine trees. A family-oriented campground, it has all the amenities. In the winter, snowmobiling and cross-country skiing are popular. Attractions in the area include the Mountain Lakes Wilderness and the Pacific Crest Trail.

**Campsites, facilities:** There are 22 sites with

full or partial hookups for tents or RVs up to 35 feet long and 32 cabins. Picnic tables and fire rings are provided. Restrooms with showers, a dump station, coin laundry, seasonal convenience store, ice, snacks, a restaurant, lounge, barbecue area, gasoline, and propane gas are available. There is also a boat ramp, dock, marina, and boat rentals. Some facilities are wheelchair accessible. Leashed pets are permitted.

**Reservations, fees:** Reservations are accepted at 866/201-4194 or www.lakeofthewoodsresort.com. Sites are $40-50 per night, $5 per night per additional vehicle, and $1 per pet per night. Monthly and winter rates are available. Some credit cards are accepted. Open spring-fall, weather permitting; call for winter availability.

**Directions:** In Medford on I-5, take Exit 14 to Highway 62. Go six miles on Highway 62 to Highway 140/Lake of the Woods. Drive 59.6 miles on Lake of the Woods Road to the resort on the left.

**Contact:** Lake of the Woods Resort, 541/949-8300, www.lakeofthewoodsresort.com.

## 233 ASPEN POINT

### Scenic rating: 8

on Lake of the Woods in Winema
National Forest

**Map 11.7, page 601** **BEST (**

This campground (at 5,000 feet elevation) is near the north shore of Lake of the Woods, adjacent to Lake of the Woods Resort. It's heavily timbered with old-growth fir and has a great view of Mount McLoughlin (9,495 feet). A hiking trail just north of camp leads north for several miles, meandering around Fourmile Lake and extending into the Sky Lakes Wilderness. Other trails nearby head into the Mountain Lakes Wilderness. Boating, fishing, swimming, and waterskiing are among the activities here. Note that of the 39 campsites, 20 are available by reservation; the rest are first-come, first-served.

**Campsites, facilities:** There are 18 single sites and two double sites for tents or RVs up to 55 feet long. Picnic tables, garbage bins, and fire grills are provided. Drinking water, a dump station, and flush toilets are available. Boat docks, launching facilities, and rentals are nearby. Some facilities are wheelchair accessible. Leashed pets are permitted.

**Reservations, fees:** Reservations are accepted at 877/444-6777 ($10 reservation fee) or www.recreation.gov ($9 reservation fee). Single sites are $17 per night, double sites are $34 per night, $5 per night per each additional vehicle. A group site is available for $90-95 per night. Open late May-early September, weather permitting.

**Directions:** In Ashland on I-5, take Exit 14 to Highway 66. Drive east for less than a mile to Dead Indian Memorial Road. Turn left (east) and drive 40 miles to Lake of the Woods. Continue along the east shore to the campground turnoff on the left.

**Contact:** Fremont-Winema National Forests, Klamath Ranger District, 541/885-3400, www.fs.usda.gov/fremont-winema.

## 234 SUNSET

### Scenic rating: 8

near Lake of the Woods in Winema
National Forest

**Map 11.7, page 601**

Sunset campground, near the eastern shore of Lake of the Woods, is fully developed and offers a myriad of recreation options. It's particularly popular for both fishing and boating. The elevation is 5,000 feet.

**Campsites, facilities:** There are 64 sites for tents or RVs up to 50 feet long. Picnic tables, garbage bins, and fire grills are provided. Drinking water and flush toilets are available. Boat docks, launching facilities, and rentals are nearby. Some facilities are wheelchair accessible. Leashed pets are permitted.

**Reservations, fees:** Reservations are accepted

for some sites at 877/444-6777 ($10 reservation fee) or www.recreation.gov ($9 reservation fee). Sites are $17 per night, $5 per night per additional vehicle. Open late May-early September.
**Directions:** In Ashland on I-5, take Exit 14 to Highway 66. Drive east for less than a mile to Dead Indian Memorial Road. Turn left (east) and drive 40 miles to Lake of the Woods. Continue along the east shore to Forest Road 3738. Turn left (west) and drive 0.5 mile to the camp.
**Contact:** Fremont-Winema National Forests, Klamath Ranger District, 541/885-3400, www.fs.usda.gov/fremont-winema.

## 235 CANTRALL-BUCKLEY PARK & GROUP CAMP

### Scenic rating: 8

on the Applegate River

**Map 11.7, page 601**

This county park outside of Medford offers pleasant, shady sites in a wooded setting. Encompassing 88 acres of land, the camp has 1.75 miles of frontage along the Applegate River, which has good trout fishing.

**Campsites, facilities:** There are 30 sites for tents or self-contained RVs up to 25 feet long and one group area for up to 100 people. Picnic tables and fire pits are provided. Drinking water, restrooms with flush toilets and coin showers, and a reservable picnic area are available. Recreational facilities include horseshoes, a playground, and a recreation field. Some facilities are wheelchair accessible. Leashed pets are permitted.

**Reservations, fees:** Reservations are accepted only for the group site at 541/774-8183. Sites are $16 per night; the group site is $65 for the first night and $50 each night thereafter. Some credit cards are accepted with reservations only. Open mid-April-mid-October.

**Directions:** In Medford on I-5, take the Jacksonville exit to the Jacksonville Highway. Drive west on the Jacksonville Highway (Highway 238) for seven miles to Jacksonville. Bear left

on Highway 238 and drive to Hamilton Road. Turn left (south) on Hamilton Road and drive approximately 0.4 mile to Cantrall Road. Turn right on Cantrall and drive approximately 0.5 mile to the campground.
**Contact:** Jackson County Parks, 154 Cantrall Road, Ruch 97530, 541/774-8183, www.jacksoncountyparks.com.

## 236 GLENYAN CAMPGROUND OF ASHLAND

### Scenic rating: 7

near Emigrant Lake

**Map 11.7, page 601**

This campground, located within seven miles of Ashland and less than one mile from Emigrant Lake, offers shady sites. Recreation options in the area include a golf course and tennis courts. It's an easy jump from I-5 at Ashland.

**Campsites, facilities:** There are 22 tent sites and 46 sites with full or partial hookups for tents or RVs of any length. Picnic tables and fire rings are provided. Drinking water, restrooms with flush toilets and showers, propane gas, a dump station, Wi-Fi, firewood, a recreation hall, seasonal convenience store, coin laundry, ice, a playground, horseshoe pits, and a seasonal heated swimming pool are available. Some facilities are wheelchair accessible. Leashed pets are permitted.

**Reservations, fees:** Reservations are accepted at 877/453-6926 or www.glenyancampground. com. RV sites are $33-36 per night, tent sites are $23.50-25.50, plus $2.50 per person per night for more than five people. Weekly and monthly rates are available. Some credit cards are accepted. Open year-round.

**Directions:** From Ashland, drive east on Highway 66 for 3.5 miles to the campground on the right.
**Contact:** Glenyan Campground of Ashland, 541/488-1785, www.glenyancampground. com.

# 237 DALEY CREEK

🏃🛶🏕️♿🚐⛺

### Scenic rating: 6

on Daley Creek in Rogue River-Siskiyou National Forest

**Map 11.7, page 601**

Daley Creek campground is a primitive alternative to some of the more developed spots in the area. Situated at 4,500 feet elevation, the camp borders the banks of Daley Creek near the confluence of Beaver Dam and Daley Creek. Sites are scattered among old-growth Douglas and white fir, and the Beaver Dam Trail heads right out of camp, running along the creek. Fishing can be decent downstream from here.

**Campsites, facilities:** There are six sites for tents or RVs up to 18 feet long. Picnic tables and fire grills are provided. There is no drinking water, and garbage must be packed out. Some facilities are wheelchair accessible. Leashed pets are permitted.

**Reservations, fees:** Reservations are not accepted. There is no fee for camping. Open early May-mid-November, weather permitting.

**Directions:** In Ashland on I-5, take Exit 14 to Highway 66. Drive east for less than a mile to Dead Indian Memorial Road. Turn left (east) and drive 22 miles to Forest Road 37. Turn left (north) and drive 1.5 miles to the campground.

**Contact:** Rogue River-Siskiyou National Forest, High Cascades Ranger District, 541/560-3400, www.fs.usda.gov/rogue-siskiyou.

# 238 BEAVER DAM

🏃🛶🐎🚐⛺

### Scenic rating: 5

on Beaver Dam Creek in Rogue River National Forest

**Map 11.7, page 601**

This campground sits at an elevation of 4,500 feet along Beaver Dam Creek. Look for beaver dams. There's not much screening between sites, but it's a pretty, rustic, and quiet spot, with unusual vegetation along the creek for botany fans. The trailhead for the Beaver Dam Trail is also here. The camp is adjacent to Daley Creek Campground.

**Campsites, facilities:** There are four sites for tents or RVs up to 16 feet long. Picnic tables and fire grills are provided. Vault toilets are available. There is no drinking water and garbage must be packed out. Leashed pets permitted.

**Reservations, fees:** Reservations are not accepted. There is no fee for camping. Open early May-early November, weather permitting.

**Directions:** In Medford on I-5, take Exit 14 to Highway 66. Drive east for less than a mile to Dead Indian Memorial Road. Turn left (east) and drive 22 miles to Forest Road 37. Turn left (north) and drive 1.5 miles to the campground.

**Contact:** Rogue River Siskiyou National Forest, Ashland Ranger District, 541/552-2900, www.fs.usda.gov/rogue-siskiyou.

# 239 HOWARD PRAIRIE RESORT

🏃🚴🏊🛶🚤🏕️🐎🚐⛺

### Scenic rating: 7

on Howard Prairie Lake

**Map 11.7, page 601**

This wooded campground is located along the shore of Howard Prairie Lake, where boating, fishing, hiking, and swimming are among the recreation options. This is one of the largest campgrounds in over 100 miles and is Jackson County's most popular park.

**Campsites, facilities:** There are 251 sites with full or partial hookups for tents or RVs of any length and one furnished cabin. Some sites are pull-through. Picnic tables and fire rings are provided. Restrooms with flush toilets and showers, propane gas, a dump station, firewood, 24-hour security, a convenience store, café, coin laundry, boat docks, boat rentals, moorage, and launching facilities are available. Leashed pets are permitted.

**Reservations, fees:** Reservations are not accepted. Sites are $20-29 per night, plus $5 per person per night for more than two people. Some credit cards are accepted. Open mid-April-October.

**Directions:** In Ashland on I-5, take Exit 14 to Highway 66 and drive for less than a mile to Dead Indian Memorial Road. Turn left and drive 17 miles to Hyatt Prairie Road. Turn right and drive 3.5 miles to the resort.

**Contact:** Howard Prairie Lake Recreational Area, Jackson County Parks, 3249 Hyatt Prairie Road, 541/774-8183, www.jacksoncountyparks.com.

## 240 APSERKAHA

### Scenic rating: 5

on Howard Prairie Lake

**Map 11.7, page 601**

This park's 66 acres offer almost half a mile of lake frontage. Secluded lake access is a big feature at Apserkaha, along with breathtaking scenery.

**Campsites, facilities:** There are nine sites with partial hookups for RVs up to 65 feet long and 12 rustic sleeping cabins. The entire park may be reserved for group camping. Picnic tables and fire pits are provided. Drinking water, vault toilets, covered dining shelter, group campfire rings, and a swimming beach are available. Showers and an enclosed commercial kitchen are available to group reservations only. Some facilities are wheelchair accessible. Leashed pets are permitted.

**Reservations, fees:** Reservations are accepted. RV sites are $24 per night, sleeping cabins are $30, group camping is $350-450 for 50-120 people. Some credit cards are accepted. Open mid-April-October, weather permitting.

**Directions:** In Ashland on I-5, take Exit 14 to Highway 66. Drive east for 0.25 mile to Dead Indian Memorial Road. Turn left and drive 17 miles to Hyatt Prairie Road. Turn right on Howard Prairie Road and drive five miles to Dam Road. Turn left and drive 2.5 miles to Apserkaha.

**Contact:** Howard Prairie Lake Recreational Area, Jackson County Parks, 541/774-8183, www.jacksoncountyparks.com.

## 241 LILY GLEN

### Scenic rating: 6

near Howard Prairie Lake

**Map 11.7, page 601**

Set along the shore of Howard Prairie Lake, this horse camp is a secluded, primitive getaway. Trout fishing is available. Tubb Springs Wayside State Park and the nearby Rogue River National Forest are possible side trips. There is also nearby access to the Pacific Crest Trail. The elevation is 4,500 feet.

**Campsites, facilities:** There are 12 sites for tents or self-contained RVs and two group sites for up to 75 people. Picnic tables and fire rings are provided. Drinking water, vault toilets, and corrals are available. Some facilities are wheelchair accessible. Leashed pets are permitted.

**Reservations, fees:** Reservations are accepted for group sites at 541/774-8183 but are not accepted for family sites. Sites are $18 per night, $6 per night per additional vehicle, $1 per pet per night, and $2 per horse per night for more than two horses; group sites are $75-150 per night. Some credit cards are accepted for reservations. Open mid-April-October, weather permitting.

**Directions:** In Ashland on I-5, take Exit 14 to Highway 66. Drive east for less than a mile to Dead Indian Memorial Road. Turn left (east) and drive 21 miles to the campground on the right.

**Contact:** Howard Prairie Lake Recreational Area, Jackson County Parks, 541/774-8183, www.jacksoncountyparks.com.

## 242 GRIZZLY

### Scenic rating: 7

near Howard Prairie Lake

**Map 11.7, page 601**

One of a series of seven county campgrounds

at Howard Prairie Lake, Grizzly features well-spaced campsites amid a forest and lake setting. The lake level is known to fluctuate; in low-water years, this camp is sometimes shut down. It gets moderate use. The elevation is 4,550 feet.

**Campsites, facilities:** There are 21 sites for tents or RVs (no hookups). Picnic tables and fire rings are provided. Drinking water, vault toilets, garbage bins, and a boat ramp are available. A store, café, laundry facilities, and boat rentals are available within two miles. Some facilities are wheelchair accessible. Leashed pets are permitted.

**Reservations, fees:** Reservations are not accepted. Sites are $18 per night, $6 per night per additional vehicle, and $1 per pet per night. Open mid-April-mid-September, weather permitting.

**Directions:** In Ashland on I-5, take Exit 14 to Highway 66. Drive east for less than a mile to Dead Indian Memorial Road. Turn left (east) and drive 17 miles to Howard Prairie Road. Turn right (south) and drive eight miles to Howard Prairie Dam Road. Turn left (east) and drive 0.25 mile to the campground.

**Contact:** Howard Prairie Lake Recreational Area, Jackson County Parks, 541/774-8183, www.jacksoncountyparks.com.

## 243 WILLOW POINT

**Scenic rating: 7**

near Howard Prairie Lake

**Map 11.7, page 601**

Willow Point is similar to Grizzly (see listing in this chapter), offering flat tent sites in an area well covered by trees. The lake is stocked with about 100,000 trout annually.

**Campsites, facilities:** There are 41 sites for tents or self-contained RVs. Picnic tables and fire rings are provided. Drinking water, vault toilets, garbage bins, fish-cleaning station, and a boat ramp are available. A store, café, laundry facilities, and boat rentals are available within

four miles. Some facilities are wheelchair accessible. Leashed pets are permitted.

**Reservations, fees:** Reservations are accepted at 541/774-8183 or www.jacksoncountyparks.com ($8-10 reservation fee). Sites are $18 per night, $6 per night per additional vehicle, $1 per pet per night. Open mid-April-October.

**Directions:** In Ashland on I-5, take Exit 14 to Highway 66. Drive east for less than a mile to Dead Indian Memorial Road. Turn left (east) and drive 17 miles to Howard Prairie Road. Turn right (south) and drive three miles to the reservoir.

**Contact:** Howard Prairie Lake Recreational Area, Jackson County Parks, 541/774-8183, www.jacksoncountyparks.com.

## 244 KLUM LANDING

**Scenic rating: 7**

near Howard Prairie Lake

**Map 11.7, page 601**

Klum Landing is one of seven county campgrounds on Howard Prairie Lake. A bonus at this one is that coin-operated showers are available.

**Campsites, facilities:** There are 30 sites for tents or self-contained RVs at Klum Landing, Picnic tables and fire rings are provided. Drinking water, garbage bins, and restrooms with flush toilets and coin showers, firewood, and boat-launching facilities are available. Some facilities are wheelchair accessible.

A boat ramp is nearby. A store, café, laundry facilities, and boat rentals are available at Howard Prairie Lake Resort. Leashed pets are permitted.

**Reservations, fees:** Reservations are not accepted for Klum Landing. Sites are $20 per night, $6 per night per additional vehicle, and $1 per pet per night. Reservations are accepted for Sugar Pine Group at 541/774-8183. The group camp is $150-200 per night. Open mid-April-mid-September.

**Directions:** In Ashland on I-5, take Exit 14

to Highway 66. Drive east for less than a mile to Dead Indian Memorial Road. Turn left (east) and drive 17 miles to Howard Prairie Road. Turn right (south) and drive eight miles to Howard Prairie Dam Road. Turn left (east) and drive 1.0 mile to reach Klum Landing.

**Contact:** Jackson County Parks, 541/774-8183, www.jacksoncountyparks.com.

## 245 SUGAR PINE GROUP

**Scenic rating: 7**

near Howard Prairie Lake

**Map 11.7, page 601**

Sugar Pine Group Camp offers a more primitive group camping experience than the other Jackson County campgrounds in this area.

**Campsites, facilities:** There is one group site for tents or self-contained RVs that can accommodate up to 100 people. Vault toilets, a group fire ring, and horseshoe pits are available. A boat ramp is nearby. A store, café, laundry facilities, and boat rentals are available at Howard Prairie Lake Resort. Some facilities are wheelchair accessible. Leashed pets are permitted.

**Reservations, fees:** Reservations are accepted at 541/774-8183. The site is $150-200 per night. Open mid-April-mid-September.

**Directions:** In Ashland on I-5, take Exit 14 to Highway 66. Drive east for less than a mile to Dead Indian Memorial Road. Turn left (east) and drive 17 miles to Howard Prairie Road. Turn right (south) and drive eight miles to Howard Prairie Dam Road. Turn left (east) and drive 0.25 mile to Sugar Pine Group Camp on the right.

**Contact:** Jackson County Parks, 541/774-8183, www.jacksoncountyparks.com.

## 246 EMIGRANT LAKE CAMPGROUND

**Scenic rating: 8**

on Emigrant Lake

**Map 11.7, page 601**

This camp is nestled among the trees above Emigrant Lake, a well-known recreational area. Activities at this park include boating, fishing, hiking, swimming, and waterskiing. There are also two 280-foot water slides. The park has its own swimming cove (unsupervised). Side-trip possibilities include exploring nearby Mount Ashland, where a ski area operates in the winter, as well as visiting Ashland's world-renowned Shakespeare Festival, the Britt Music Festival, and historic Jacksonville.

**Campsites, facilities:** There are two campgrounds: Point RV Park and Oak Slope Campground. Point RV Park has 32 sites with full hookups for RVs to 45 feet. Oak Slope has 42 sites for tents. There is also a group camp area for up to 100 people. Restrooms with flush toilets, coin showers, a dump station, snacks in summer, firewood, and a barbecue are available. A group picnic and day-use area that can be reserved are also available. Recreational facilities include horseshoe pits, volleyball, a swim cove, a waterslide, and a playground. Two boat ramps are available. Laundry and food are within six miles. Some facilities are wheelchair accessible. Leashed pets are permitted in designated areas only.

**Reservations, fees:** Reservations are accepted at 541/774-8183 or www.jacksoncountyparks.com ($8-10 reservation fee). Tent sites are $20 per night, RV sites with full hookups are $30 per night, $6 per night per additional vehicle. The group site is $125-175 per night. Some credit cards are accepted for reservations. Point RV Park is open year-round; Oak Slope is open April 1-mid-October, weather permitting.

**Directions:** From Ashland, drive east on Highway 66 for five miles to the campground on the left.

**Contact:** Jackson County Parks, 5505 Highway 66, 541/774-8183, www.jacksoncountyparks.com.

## 247 HYATT LAKE

### Scenic rating: 8

on Hyatt Lake

Map 11.7, page 601

Hyatt Lake campground is situated on the south end of Hyatt Reservoir, which has six miles of shoreline. Fishing is good for brook and rainbow trout and smallmouth bass. The boat speed limit here is 10 mph. The Pacific Crest Trail runs next to the campground. Another campground option is Wildcat, about two miles north, with 12 sites.

**Campsites, facilities:** There are 47 sites for tents or RVs up to 40 feet long (no hookups), five equestrian sites, seven walk-in tent sites, and one group site for up to 50 people. Picnic tables and fire grills are provided. Drinking water, restrooms with flush toilets and showers, garbage service, dump station, fish-cleaning station, group kitchen, day-use area, softball fields, volleyball, a playground, horseshoe pits, firewood, docks, and two boat ramps are available. Some facilities are wheelchair accessible. Leashed pets are permitted.

**Reservations, fees:** Reservations are accepted only for the group camp or horse camp at 541/482-2031 or 541/618-2306. Sites are $12-15 per night, $3 per night per additional vehicle, with a 14-day stay limit. Equestrian sites are $10 per night; the group site is $95 per night. Sites at nearby primitive Wildcat Campground are $7 per night. Pacific Crest Trail hikers pay $2 per person per night for camping. Open late April-October, weather permitting.

**Directions:** From Ashland, drive east on Highway 66 for 17 miles to East Hyatt Lake Road. Turn north and drive three miles to the campground entrance on the left. Latitude: 42.170430 / Longitude: -122.463300.

**Contact:** Bureau of Land Management, Ashland Resource Area, 541/618-2200, www.blm.gov/or/districts/medford.

## 248 TOPSY

### Scenic rating: 7

on the Upper Klamath River

Map 11.7, page 601

This campground is on Boyle Reservoir near the Upper Klamath River, a good spot for trout fishing. Swimming is not recommended because of the murky water. This is a top river for rafters (experts only, or non-experts with professional, licensed guides). There are Class IV and V rapids about four miles southwest at Caldera, Hells Corner, and Satan's Gate. I flipped at Caldera and ended up swimming for it, finally getting out at an eddy. Luckily, I was wearing a dry suit and the best life jacket available, perfect fitting, which saved my butt.

**Campsites, facilities:** There are 13 sites for RVs up to 32 feet long. Picnic tables and fire grills are provided. Drinking water, vault toilets, garbage service, and a dump station are available. Boat-launching facilities are on-site. A camp host is on-site in season. Some facilities are wheelchair accessible. Leashed pets are permitted.

**Reservations, fees:** Reservations are not accepted. Sites are $7 per night, $4 per night per additional vehicle, with a 14-day stay limit. Open mid-May-mid-September, weather permitting.

**Directions:** From Klamath Falls, drive west on Highway 66 for 20 miles to Topsy Road. Turn south on Topsy Road and drive 1.5 miles to the campground on the right.

**Contact:** Bureau of Land Management, Klamath Falls Resource Area, 541/883-6916, www.blm.gov/or/districts/lakeview.

## 249 JACKSON

Scenic rating: 7

on the Applegate River in Rogue
River-Siskiyou National Forest

**Map 11.7, page 601**

Jackson campground is nestled in an old mining area at 1,700 feet elevation. Situated between the Applegate River and the road, under a canopy of ponderosa pine, it features a swimming hole and good trout fishing. An interpretive trail is across the road from the campground. Mine tailings can be seen from the camp. Trailers and large RVs are not allowed.

**Campsites, facilities:** There are eight sites for tents only and one group site. Picnic tables and fire rings are provided. Drinking water, garbage service, and flush toilets are available. Some facilities are wheelchair accessible. Leashed pets are permitted.

**Reservations, fees:** Reservations are not accepted. Sites are $15 per night, the group site is $30 per night, $5 per night per additional vehicle. Open year-round, weather permitting, with limited services in winter.

**Directions:** In Medford on I-5, take the Jacksonville exit to the Jacksonville Highway. Drive west on the Jacksonville Highway (Highway 238) for seven miles to Jacksonville. Bear left on Highway 238 and drive eight miles to the town of Ruch and Upper Applegate Road (County Road 10). Turn left and drive 10 miles to the campground on the right.

**Contact:** Rogue River-Siskiyou National Forest, Siskiyou Mountains District, 541/899-3800, www.fs.usda.gov/rogue-siskiyou; concessionaire, 541/899-9220.

## 250 BEAVER SULPHUR GROUP

Scenic rating: 7

on Beaver Creek in Rogue River-Siskiyou
National Forest

**Map 11.7, page 601**

This group camp is well hidden along the banks of Beaver Creek. It is set at an elevation of 2,100 feet and situated in an area with mixed tree cover, including tall Douglas fir, live oak, and maple. The camp is about nine miles from Applegate Reservoir, features attractive shaded sites, and offers easy access to the creek.

**Campsites, facilities:** There is one group site for up to 50 people. Picnic tables and fire grills are provided. Vault toilets and garbage bins (summer only) are available. There is no drinking water. Some facilities are wheelchair accessible. Leashed pets are permitted.

**Reservations, fees:** Reservations are accepted at 877/444-6777 ($10 reservation fee) or www.recreation.gov ($9 reservation fee). The site is $50 per night. Open May-mid-September, weather permitting.

**Directions:** In Medford on I-5, take the Jacksonville exit to the Jacksonville Highway. Drive west on the Jacksonville Highway (Highway 238) for seven miles to Jacksonville. Bear left on Highway 238 and drive eight miles to the town of Ruch and Upper Applegate Road (County Road 10). Turn left (south) and drive 9.5 miles to Forest Road 20. Continue three miles to the campground on the right.

**Contact:** Rogue River–Siskiyou National Forest, Siskiyou Mountains District, 541/899-3800, www.fs.usda.gov/rogue-siskiyou.

## 251 HART-TISH PARK WALK-IN

### Scenic rating: 7

on Applegate Lake, Rogue River National Forest

**Map 11.7, page 601**

This concessionaire-managed campground on Applegate Lake has shaded sites and a great view of the lake. Bald eagles and ospreys nest in the area, and it's a treat to watch them fish. A boat launch with boat and kayak rentals is available nearby. The walk-in campsites are only 200 yards from the parking area.

**Campsites, facilities:** There are seven walk-in tent sites and eight lakeside sites in the parking lot for RVs up to 45 feet long. Picnic tables and fire pits are provided. Drinking water, flush toilets, and garbage bins are provided. Firewood is available at a small on-site store. A day-use area is nearby. Some facilities are wheelchair accessible. Leashed pets are permitted.

**Reservations, fees:** Reservations are accepted at 877/444-6777 or www.reserveamerica.com ($9 reservation fee). Sites are $15 per night, $5 per night per additional vehicle. Open mid-April-September, weather permitting.

**Directions:** In Medford on I-5, take the Jacksonville exit to the Jacksonville Highway. Drive west on the Jacksonville Highway (Highway 238) for seven miles to Jacksonville. Bear left on Highway 238 and drive eight miles to the town of Ruch and Upper Applegate Road (County Road 10). Turn left (south) and drive 15.5 miles to the campground on the left.

**Contact:** Rogue River-Siskiyou National Forest, Siskiyou Mountains District, 541/899-3800, www.fs.usda.gov/rogue-siskiyou; concessionaire, 541/899-9220.

## 252 WATKINS

### Scenic rating: 6

on Applegate Reservoir in Rogue River National Forest

**Map 11.7, page 601**

Set on the southwest shore of Applegate Reservoir, this pretty campground is small and quite primitive—like Carberry Walk-In and French Gulch—and offers the same recreation options. Few campers know about this spot, so it usually doesn't fill up quickly. There are good views of the lake and the surrounding Siskiyou Mountains. The Seattle Bar day-use area at the lake is approximately two miles away. The elevation is 2,000 feet.

**Campsites, facilities:** There are 14 walk-in sites for tents only and one group site for 20-50 people. Picnic tables and fire grills are provided. Vault toilets are available. There is no drinking water and garbage must be packed out. A general store, boat docks, and launching facilities are within two miles. Leashed pets are permitted.

**Reservations, fees:** Reservations are not accepted. Sites are $15 per night, $5 per night per additional vehicle. Open year-round, weather permitting.

**Directions:** In Medford on I-5, take the Jacksonville exit to the Jacksonville Highway. Drive west on the Jacksonville Highway (Highway 238) for seven miles to Jacksonville. Bear left on Highway 238 and drive eight miles to the town of Ruch and Upper Applegate Road (County Road 10). Turn left (south) and drive 17 miles to the campground.

**Contact:** Rogue River-Siskiyou National Forest, Siskiyou Mountains District, 541/899-3800, www.fs.usda.gov/rogue-siskiyou; concessionaire, 541/899-9220.

## 253 CARBERRY WALK-IN

🚶 🚴 🏊 🛶 🛥️ 🏕️ ♿ 🚐 ⛺

### Scenic rating: 5

near Applegate Reservoir in Rogue River-Siskiyou National Forest

**Map 11.7, page 601**

You'll find recreational opportunities aplenty, including boating, fishing, hiking, mountain biking, and swimming, at this campground on Cougar Creek near the southwest shore of Applegate Reservoir. Dense forest covers the campsites, providing much-needed shade. This camp is similar to Watkins Walk-in.

**Campsites, facilities:** There are 10 walk-in sites for tents and three spaces in the parking lot for RVs up to 25 feet long. Picnic tables and fire grills are provided. Vault toilets are available. There is no drinking water. A general store, firewood, boat docks, and launching facilities are within two miles. Some facilities are wheelchair accessible. Leashed pets are permitted.

**Reservations, fees:** Reservations are not accepted. Sites are $15 per night, $5 per night per additional vehicle. Open late May-early September, weather permitting.

**Directions:** In Medford on I-5, take the Jacksonville exit to the Jacksonville Highway. Drive west on the Jacksonville Highway (Highway 238) for seven miles to Jacksonville. Bear left on Highway 238 and drive eight miles to the town of Ruch and Upper Applegate Road (County Road 10). Turn left (south) and drive 18 miles to the campground parking area. A short walk is required.

**Contact:** Rogue River-Siskiyou National Forest, Siskiyou Mountains District, 541/899-3800, www.fs.usda.gov/rogue-siskiyou; concessionaire, 541/899-9220.

## 254 SQUAW LAKE HIKE-IN

🚶 🚴 🏊 🛶 🛥️ 🏕️ ♿ ⛺

### Scenic rating: 10

on Squaw Lake in Rogue River-Siskiyou National Forest

**Map 11.7, page 601**          **BEST (**

"Paradise Found" should be the name of this campground. The setting on the shore of spectacular Squaw Lake is more intimate than that of larger Applegate Reservoir to the west. Numerous trails crisscross the camp and the area attracts the canoe and kayak crowd. This spot has a mix of developed and primitive sites and it's also more popular. In fact, it's the only campground in the district that requires reservations, so be sure to reserve ahead for a space. Campers with disabilities are welcome, but should make arrangements in advance with the local U.S. Forest Service office. The elevation is 3,000 feet.

**Campsites, facilities:** There are 17 walk-in sites for tents and two family group sites that can accommodate up to 10 people each. Picnic tables and fire grills are provided. Vault toilets are available. Drinking water is available at one end of the camp during the summer only. Garbage must be packed out. Leashed pets are permitted.

**Reservations, fees:** Reservations are accepted at 877/444-6777 or www.reserveamerica.com ($9 reservation fee). Sites are $10 per night, group sites are $20 per night. Open mid-May-mid-September, weather permitting.

**Directions:** In Medford on I-5, take the Jacksonville exit to the Jacksonville Highway. Drive west on the Jacksonville Highway (Highway 238) for seven miles to Jacksonville. Bear left on Highway 238 and drive eight miles to the town of Ruch and Upper Applegate Road (County Road 10). Turn left (south) and drive 15 miles to Forest Road 1075. Continue eight miles to Squaw Lake and the trailhead. Hike is from 150 feet to one mile to the campsites.

**Contact:** Rogue River-Siskiyou National Forest, Siskiyou Mountains District, 541/899-3800, www.fs.usda.gov/rogue-siskiyou.

## 255 WRANGLE

### Scenic rating: 10

near the Pacific Crest Trail in Rogue River-Siskiyou National Forest

**Map 11.7, page 601**

This campground is located at the headwaters of Glade Creek in the Siskiyou Mountains at an elevation of 6,400 feet. The Pacific Crest Trail passes near camp. Dutchman Peak Lookout, built in the late 1920s and featured in the National Historic Register, is within five miles. This lovely campground, in a beautiful, high-country setting, boasts huge Shasta red firs and views of the Siskiyou Mountains. Wrangle is along the Scenic Siskiyou Loop driving tour.

**Campsites, facilities:** There are five sites for tents. Picnic tables and fire grills are provided. Vault toilets, a pole shelter, and a community kitchen are available. There is no drinking water, and garbage must be packed out. Leashed pets are permitted.

**Reservations, fees:** Reservations are not accepted. There is no fee for camping. Open early July-late October, weather permitting.

**Directions:** In Ashland on I-5, take the Jacksonville exit. Drive east on the Jacksonville Highway to Jacksonville and Highway 238. Bear left on Highway 238 and drive eight miles to the town of Ruch and County Road 10 (Upper Applegate Road). Turn left and drive 9.5 miles to Forest Road 20. Turn left and drive 21 miles to Forest Road 2030. Continue one mile on Forest Road 2030 to the campground.

**Contact:** Rogue River-Siskiyou National Forest, Siskiyou Mountains District, 541/899-3800, www.fs.usda.gov/rogue-siskiyou.

## 256 MOUNT ASHLAND

### Scenic rating: 8

on the Pacific Crest Trail in Klamath National Forest

**Map 11.7, page 601**          **BEST (**

Set at 6,600 feet elevation along the Pacific Crest Trail, this beautiful camp is heavily wooded and has abundant wildlife. On a clear day, enjoy great lookouts from nearby Siskiyou Peak, particularly to the south, where California's 14,162-foot Mount Shasta is an awesome sight. Mount Ashland Ski Resort is one mile east of the campground and has mountain bike trails. Remember, this is bear country, so keep your food secured.

**Campsites, facilities:** There are nine sites for tents or RVs up to 28 feet long, with extremely limited space for RVs. Picnic tables and fire grills are provided. Vault toilets are available. There is no water. Garbage must be packed out. Leashed pets are permitted.

**Reservations, fees:** Reservations are not accepted. There is no fee for camping, but donations are accepted. Open May-late October, weather permitting.

**Directions:** From Ashland, drive south on I-5 for 12 miles to Mount Ashland Ski Park Road (County Road 993). Turn west and drive 10 miles (the road becomes Forest Road 20) to the campground.

**Contact:** Klamath National Forest, Happy Camp/Oak Knoll Ranger District, 530/493-2243, www.fs.usda.gov/klamath.

## 257 JACKSON F. KIMBALL STATE PARK

### Scenic rating: 7

on the Wood River

**Map 11.8, page 602**

This primitive state campground at the headwaters of the Wood River is another nice spot just far enough off the main drag to remain a secret. A trail from camp leads to a nearby spring. Fishing from canoe is good on the Wood River.

**Campsites, facilities:** There are 10 primitive sites for tents or self-contained RVs up to 45 feet long. Picnic tables, fire grills, and garbage bins are provided. Vault toilets are available. There is no drinking water. Leashed pets are permitted.

**Reservations, fees:** Reservations are not accepted. Sites are $5-10 per night, $5 per night per additional vehicle. Open year-round, weather permitting.

**Directions:** From Klamath Falls, drive north on U.S. 97 for 21 miles to Highway 62. Turn left (northwest) on Highway 62 and drive 10 miles to Highway 232/Sun Pass Road (near Fort Klamath). Turn right (north) and drive three miles to the campground.

**Contact:** Jackson F. Kimball is managed by Collier Memorial State Park, 541/783-2471 or 800/551-6949, www.oregonstateparks.org.

## 258 CRATER LAKE RESORT

**Scenic rating: 6**

on the Wood River

**Map 11.8, page 602**

The campground at Crater Lake Resort is dotted with huge pine trees on the banks of the beautiful, crystal-clear Fort Creek. It's located just outside Fort Klamath, the site of numerous military campaigns against the Modoc people in the late 1800s.

**Campsites, facilities:** There are 14 sites with full or partial hookups for RVs of any length, five sites for tents, and 11 cabins. Picnic tables and fire rings are provided. Drinking water, restrooms with flush toilets and showers, Wi-Fi, a recreation hall, playground, store, ice, and a coin laundry are available. Propane gas and a café are within 12 miles. Leashed pets are permitted.

**Reservations, fees:** Reservations are accepted. RV sites are $30 per night, $5 per person

per night for more than two people, and $5 per pet per night. Tent sites are $10 per person per night. Some credit cards are accepted. Open mid-April-mid-October.

**Directions:** From Klamath Falls, drive north on U.S. 97 for 21 miles to Highway 62. Bear left on Highway 62 and drive 12.5 miles north to the resort (just before reaching Fort Klamath).

**Contact:** Crater Lake Resort, 541/381-2349, www.craterlakeresort.com.

## 259 COLLIER MEMORIAL STATE PARK

**Scenic rating: 7**

on the Williamson River

**Map 11.8, page 602**

This campground sits at the confluence of Spring Creek and the Williamson River, both of which are superior trout streams. An area for equestrian campers is situated at a trailhead for horses. A nature trail is also available. The park features a pioneer village and a logging museum. Movies about old-time logging and other activities are shown on weekend nights during the summer.

**Campsites, facilities:** There are 50 sites for tents or RVs of any length (full hookups), 18 sites for tents or self-contained RVs up to 50 feet (no hookups), and an area for up to four groups of equestrian campers. Some sites are pull-through. Picnic tables, fire grills, and garbage bins are provided. Drinking water, restrooms with flush toilets and showers, a dump station, firewood, coin laundry, playground, and day-use hitching area are available. Some facilities are wheelchair accessible. Leashed pets are permitted.

**Reservations, fees:** Reservations are accepted at 800/452-5687 or www.reserveamerica.com ($8 reservation fee). Tent sites are $14-22 per night, RV sites are $17-22 per night, $5 per night per additional vehicle. The equestrian area is $14-19 per night. Some credit cards are accepted. Open year-round, weather permitting.

**Directions:** From Klamath Falls, drive north on U.S. 97 for 28 miles to the park (well signed).

**Contact:** Collier Memorial State Park, 800/551-6949 or 541/783-2471, www.oregonstateparks.org.

## 260 WILLIAMSON

**Scenic rating: 6**

near Collier Memorial State Park in Winema National Forest

**Map 11.8, page 602**

Another great little spot is discovered, this one at 4,200 feet elevation, with excellent trout fishing along the banks of the Williamson River, a world-famous fly-fishing river. Mosquitoes are numerous in spring and early summer, which can drive people away. A map of Winema National Forest details the back roads and trails. Collier Memorial State Park provides a nearby side-trip option.

**Campsites, facilities:** There are 20 sites for tents or RVs up to 30 feet long. Picnic tables, garbage bins, and fire grills are provided. Drinking water and vault toilets are available. A restaurant is within five miles. Some facilities are wheelchair accessible. Leashed pets are permitted.

**Reservations, fees:** Reservations are not accepted. Sites are $10 per night, $2 per night per additional vehicle. There is no fee in winter. Open late April-late November, weather permitting.

**Directions:** From Klamath Falls, drive north on U.S. 97 for 30 miles to Chiloquin. Continue north on U.S. 97 for 5.5 miles to Forest Road 9730. Turn right (northeast) and drive one mile to the campground.

**Contact:** Fremont-Winema National Forests, Chiloquin Ranger District, 541/883-6714, www.fs.usda.gov/fremont-winema.

## 261 POTTER'S PARK

**Scenic rating: 6**

on the Sprague River

**Map 11.8, page 602**

This park on a bluff overlooking the Sprague River is in a wooded setting and bordered by the Winema National Forest. Canoeing and rafting are options here. For the most part, the area east of Klamath Lake doesn't get much attention.

**Campsites, facilities:** There are 17 tent sites and 22 sites with full hookups for RVs of any length. Drinking water, picnic tables, and fire pits are provided. Restrooms with flush toilets and (seasonal) showers, a convenience store, coin laundry (seasonal), pay telephone, and ice are available. Some facilities are wheelchair accessible. Leashed pets are permitted.

**Reservations, fees:** Reservations are accepted. Sites are $15-20 per night, plus $5 per person per night for more than two adults. Monthly rates are available for RV sites. Open year-round, with limited winter facilities.

**Directions:** From Klamath Falls, drive north on U.S. 97 for 27 miles to Chiloquin and Sprague River Highway. Turn right (east) on Sprague River Highway and drive 12 miles to the park on the right.

**Contact:** Potter's Park, 541/783-2253.

## 262 WALT'S RV PARK

**Scenic rating: 7**

on the Williamson River

**Map 11.8, page 602**

This heavily treed campground, across the highway from the Williamson River near Collier Memorial State Park, is one of three camps in the immediate area. The Williamson River has excellent trout fishing. For those looking for a more remote setting, head east to Potter's Park.

**Campsites, facilities:** There are 20 sites for

tents and 14 sites with full or partial hookups for RVs of any length; some are pull-through sites. Picnic tables and fire pits are provided. Drinking water, restrooms with flush toilets and showers, firewood, and ice are available. A café is within 0.25 mile and there is a grocery and a hardware store in Chiloquin. Some facilities are wheelchair accessible. Leashed pets are permitted with breed restrictions.

**Reservations, fees:** Reservations are accepted. RV sites are $22-25 per night, tent sites are $15.50 per night, $4 per person per night for more than three people, and $1 per night for air-conditioning. Open year-round, weather permitting.

**Directions:** From Klamath Falls, drive north on U.S. 97 for 24 miles to Chiloquin Junction. Continue north for 0.25 mile to the campground (adjacent to the Chiloquin Ranger Station) on the left.

**Contact:** Walt's RV Park, 541/783-2537, www.waltsrvpark.com.

## 263 AGENCY LAKE RESORT

**Scenic rating: 5**

on Agency Lake

**Map 11.8, page 602**

This campground sits along Agency Lake in an open, grassy area with some shaded sites. The resort has more than 700 feet of lakefront property, offering world-class trout fishing. Look across the lake and watch the sun set on the Cascades. Note that some sites are filled with monthly renters.

**Campsites, facilities:** There are 15 sites for tents, 25 sites with full or partial hookups for tents or RVs of any length, and three cabins. Picnic tables are provided. Drinking water, restrooms with flush toilets and showers, a general store (with hunting and fishing licenses), ice, boat docks, and launching facilities are available. Leashed pets are permitted.

**Reservations, fees:** Reservations are accepted. RV sites are $15-25 per night, tent sites are $13-15 per night. Some credit cards are accepted. Open year-round, weather permitting.

**Directions:** From Klamath Falls, drive north on U.S. 97 for 17 miles to Modoc Point Road. Turn left and drive about 10 miles to the resort on the left.

**Contact:** Agency Lake Resort, 541/783-2489, www.agencylakeresort.net.

# SOUTHEASTERN OREGON

© LINDSAY DOUGLAS/123RF.COM

Some people think that southeastern Oregon is one big chunk of nothing. This high-desert region is dry and foreboding, with many miles between campgrounds. However, it is so undervisited that you'll often have vast areas to yourself. Highlights include the Newberry National Volcanic Monument, with East and Paulina Lakes set within its craters, trailhead camps with access to Gearhart Mountain Wilderness in Fremont National Forest, and camps at Steens Mountain Recreation Lands. Some of the most remote drive-to campgrounds in Oregon are in underused Ochoco and Malheur National Forests. The Owyhee River watershed is like a miniature Grand Canyon, with steep, orange walls and the river cutting a circuitous route through the desert. I have paddled a canoe through most of it—from remote stretches below the Jarbridge Mountains in Nevada through Idaho and into Oregon.

# SOUTHEASTERN OREGON

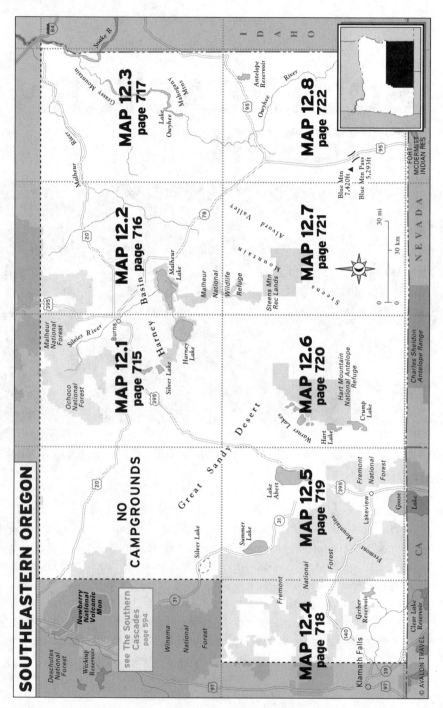

MAP 12.1 page 715

MAP 12.2 page 716

MAP 12.3 page 717

MAP 12.4 page 718

MAP 12.5 page 719

MAP 12.6 page 720

MAP 12.7 page 721

MAP 12.8 page 722

NO CAMPGROUNDS

see The Southern Cascades page 594

IDAHO

NEVADA

CALIFORNIA

FORT McDERMITT INDIAN RES

Snake R

Grassy Mountain

Malheur River

Lake Owyhee

Mahogany Mtns

Antelope Reservoir

Owyhee River

Malheur River

Malheur Lake

Malheur National Wildlife Refuge

Harney Basin

Silvies River

Burns

Harney Lake

Silver Lake

Ochoco National Forest

Malheur National Forest

Alvord Valley

Steens Mountain

Steens Mtn Rec Lands

Blue Mtn 7,420ft ▲
Blue Mtn Pass 5,293ft

Great Sandy Desert

Warner Lakes

Hart Lake

Crump Lake

Hart Mountain National Antelope Refuge

Charles Sheldon Antelope Range

Lake Abert

Summer Lake

Silver Lake

Fremont National Forest

Fremont Mountains

Lakeview

Fremont National Forest

Goose Lake

Newberry National Volcanic Mon

Deschutes National Forest

Wickiup Reservoir

Winema National Forest

Gerber Reservoir

Klamath Falls

Clear Lake Reservoir

30 mi

30 km

0

0

© AVALON TRAVEL

# Map 12.1

**Sites 1-5**
**Pages 723-724**

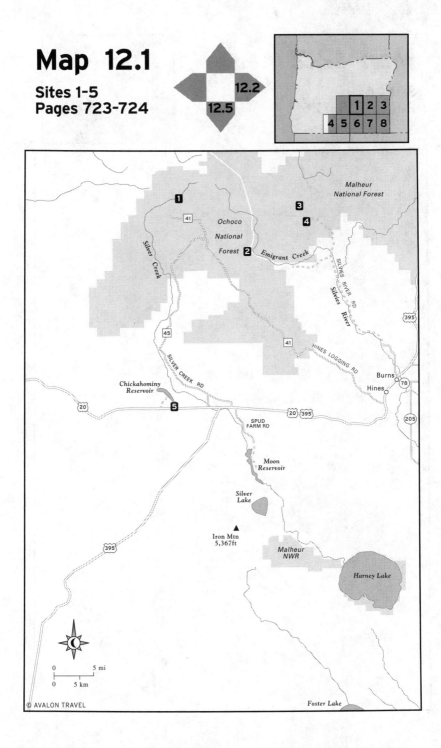

# Map 12.2

**Sites 6-9**
**Pages 725-726**

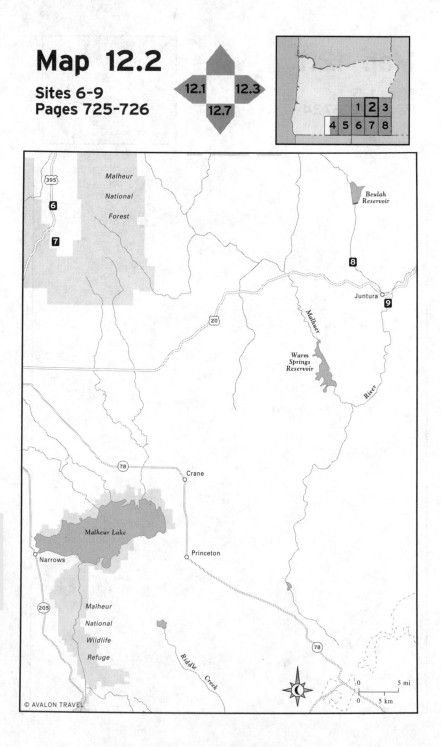

12.1 12.3
12.7

1 2 3
4 5 6 7 8

395
6
7

Malheur
National
Forest

Beulah
Reservoir

8

Juntura ○ 9

20

Malheur

Warm
Springs
Reservoir

River

78 Crane ○

Malheur Lake

Narrows ○

○ Princeton

205

Malheur
National
Wildlife
Refuge

78

Riddle
Creek

0          5 mi
0        5 km

© AVALON TRAVEL

# Map 12.3

**Sites 10-13**
**Pages 726-727**

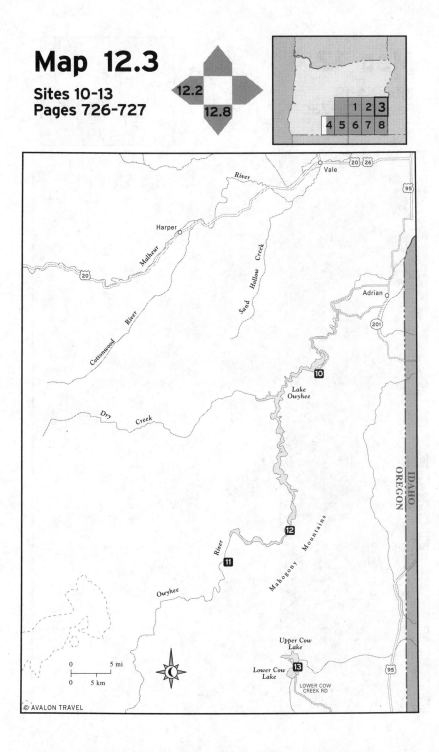

# Map 12.4

## Sites 14-19
## Pages 728-730

12.5

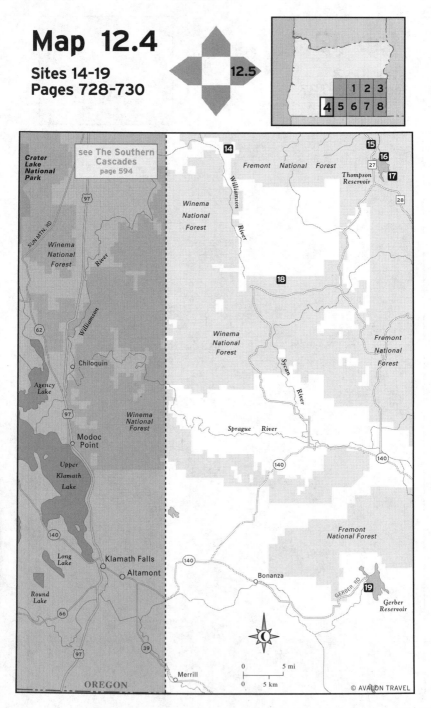

see The Southern Cascades page 594

Crater Lake National Park

Winema National Forest

Fremont National Forest

Thompson Reservoir

Williamson River

Winema National Forest

River

Williamson

Chiloquin

Agency Lake

Winema National Forest

Modoc Point

Upper Klamath Lake

Winema National Forest

Sycan River

Sprague River

Fremont National Forest

Fremont National Forest

Long Lake

Klamath Falls

Altamont

Round Lake

Bonanza

GERBER RD

Gerber Reservoir

Merrill

OREGON

0    5 mi
0    5 km

© AVALON TRAVEL

# Map 12.5

## Sites 20-36
## Pages 731-737

12.4      12.6

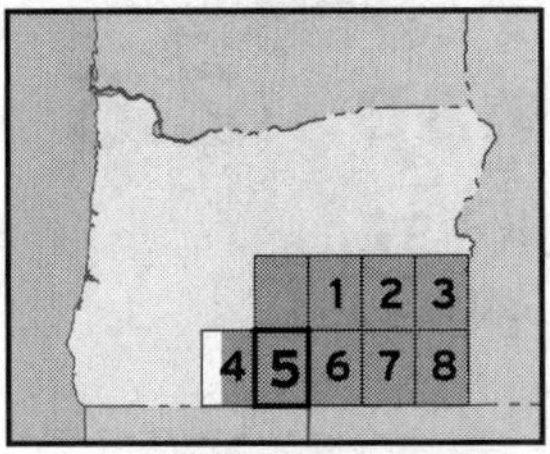

| | | | 1 | 2 | 3 |
|---|---|---|---|---|---|
| 4 | 5 | 6 | 7 | 8 |

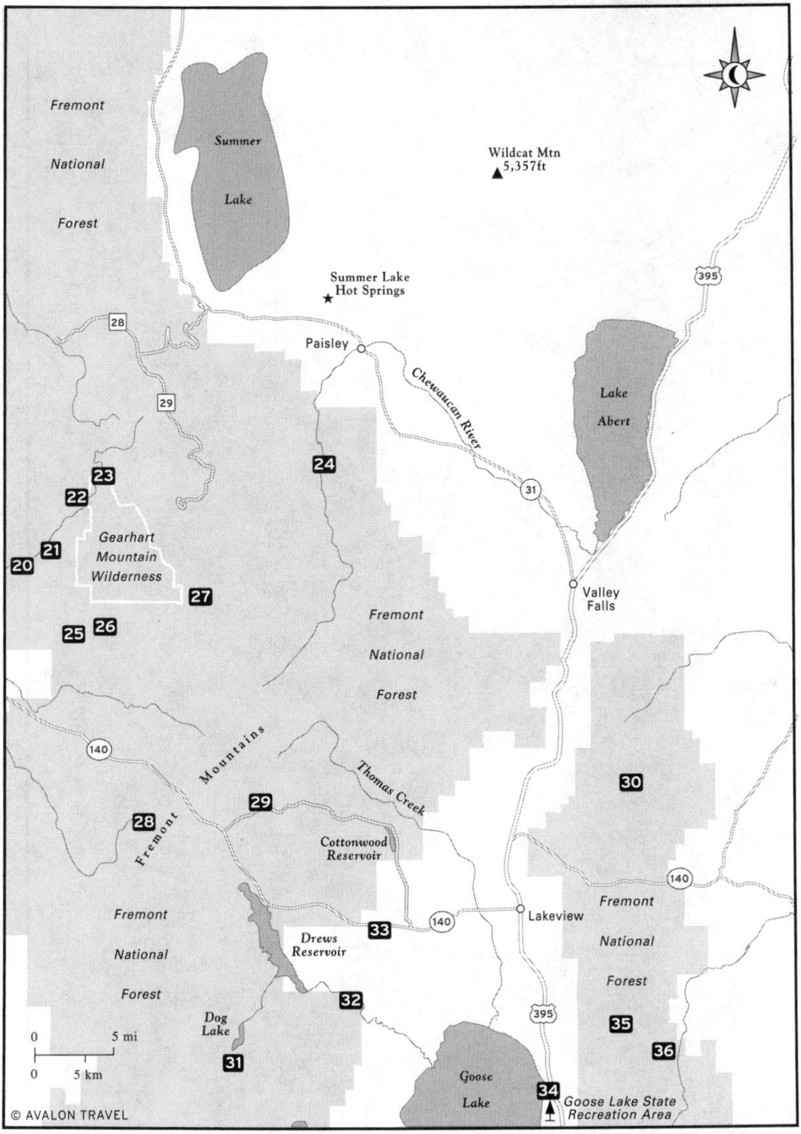

Fremont

National

Forest

Summer

Lake

Wildcat Mtn
▲ 5,357ft

Summer Lake
★ Hot Springs

28

Paisley

*Chewaucan River*

29

24

31

Lake
Abert

23

22

21

20

Gearhart
Mountain
Wilderness

27

Valley
Falls

25  26

Fremont

National

Forest

140

*Mountains*

Thomas Creek

30

29

28

Cottonwood
Reservoir

*Fremont*

140

Fremont

National

Forest

33

140

Lakeview

Fremont

National

Forest

Drews
Reservoir

32

35

Dog
Lake

395

36

0        5 mi

0      5 km

31

Goose
Lake

34  ⬕ Goose Lake State
Recreation Area

© AVALON TRAVEL

# Map 12.6

**Site 37**
**Page 738**

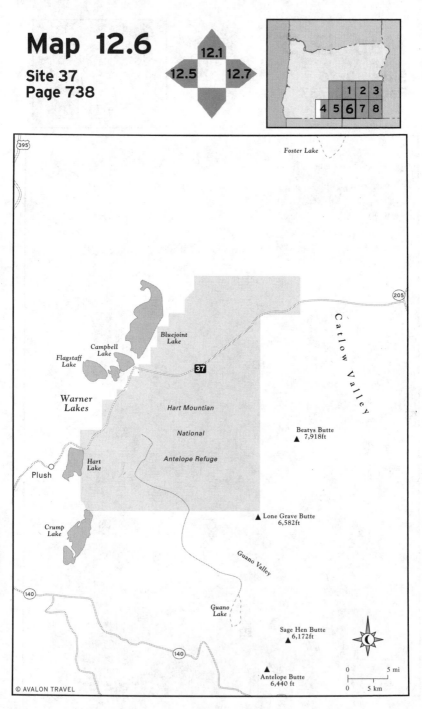

12.1
12.5   12.7

1 2 3
4 5 6 7 8

395

Foster Lake

205

Catlow Valley

Bluejoint Lake

Campbell Lake

Flagstaff Lake

Warner Lakes

37

Hart Mountain

National

Antelope Refuge

▲ Beatys Butte
7,918ft

Hart Lake

Plush

▲ Lone Grave Butte
6,582ft

Crump Lake

Guano Valley

Guano Lake

Sage Hen Butte
▲ 6,172ft

0          5 mi

▲ Antelope Butte
6,440 ft

0      5 km

© AVALON TRAVEL

# Map 12.7

### Sites 38-44
### Pages 738-741

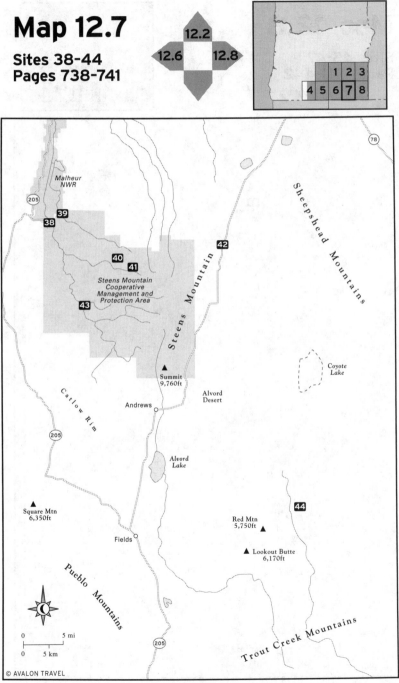

12.2
12.6   12.8

1 2 3
4 5 6 7 8

Malheur
NWR

205

39
38

40
41

Steens Mountain
Cooperative
Management and
Protection Area

43

Steens Mountain

42

Sheepshead Mountains

78

Coyote
Lake

▲
Summit
9,760ft

Andrews ○

Alvord
Desert

Catlow Rim

205

Alvord
Lake

▲
Square Mtn
6,350ft

Red Mtn
5,750ft ▲

44

Fields ○

▲ Lookout Butte
6,170ft

Pueblo Mountains

0        5 mi
0        5 km

205

Trout Creek Mountains

© AVALON TRAVEL

# Map 12.8

**Sites 45-47**
**Pages 741-442**

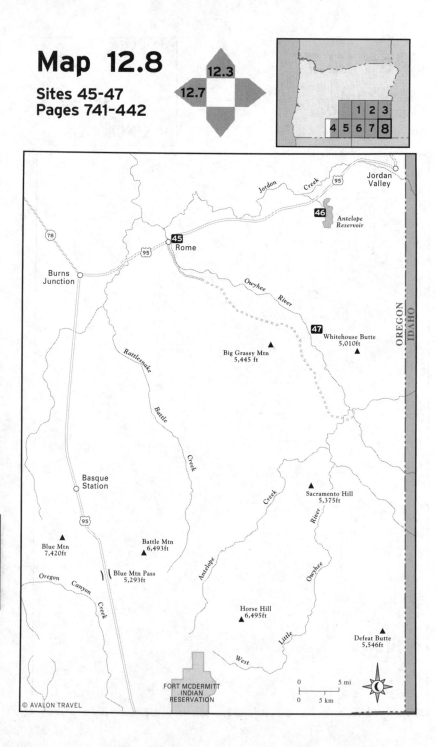

# 1 DELINTMENT LAKE

**Scenic rating: 7**

on Delintment Lake in Malheur National Forest

Map 12.1, page 715

This very pretty, forested camp skirts the shore of Delintment Lake. Originally a beaver pond, the lake was gradually developed to its current size of 62 acres. It is now pretty and blue and is stocked with trout, providing good bank and boat fishing. Note that electric motors only are allowed on the lake. Insider's note: Rainbow trout here average 12-18 inches.

**Campsites, facilities:** There are 29 sites for tents or RVs up to 30 feet long and six walk-in tent-only sites. Picnic tables and fire grills are provided. Drinking water, vault toilets, garbage service, a group picnic area, and boat-launching facilities are available. Some facilities are wheelchair accessible. Leashed pets are permitted.

**Reservations, fees:** Reservations are not accepted. Sites are $10 per night, $5 per night for an additional vehicle. Open May-October, weather permitting.

**Directions:** From Burns, drive southwest on U.S. 20 for three miles to County Road 127. Turn right (northwest) and drive 11 miles to Forest Road 41. Turn left on Forest Road 41 and drive about 26.5 miles (staying on Forest Road 41 at all junctions, paved all the way) to the campground at the lake.

**Contact:** Malheur National Forest, Emigrant Creek Ranger District, 541/573-4300, www.fs.usda.gov/malheur.

# 2 EMIGRANT

**Scenic rating: 4**

near Emigrant Creek in
Malheur National Forest

Map 12.1, page 715

One of two camps in the immediate area, Emigrant is set at an elevation of 5,200 feet in Malheur National Forest, in a meadow near Emigrant Creek. You'll get peace and quiet here, because this spot is usually not crowded. There's good fly-fishing in the spring and early summer, and several nearby backcountry dirt roads are fun for mountain biking. Falls camp, two miles away, is busier but has drinking water.

**Campsites, facilities:** There are seven sites for tents or RVs up to 28 feet long. Picnic tables and fire grills are provided. Vault toilets and garbage service are available. There is no drinking water (but drinking water is available nearby at Falls campground). Some facilities are wheelchair accessible. Leashed pets are permitted.

**Reservations, fees:** Reservations are not accepted. Sites are $8 per night, $4 per night for an additional vehicle. Open May-October, weather permitting.

**Directions:** From Burns, drive southwest on U.S. 20 for three miles to County Road 127. Turn right (northwest) and drive 25 miles (passing Forest Road 41 on the left) to Forest Road 43 and the junction for Allison Guard Station, Delintment Lake, and Paulina. Turn left on Forest Road 43 and drive 9.75 miles to Forest Road 4340-050. Turn left and drive on Forest Road 4340-050 to the campground.

**Contact:** Malheur National Forest, Emigrant Creek Ranger District, 541/573-4300, www.fs.usda.gov/malheur.

# 3 YELLOWJACKET

**Scenic rating: 8**

on Yellowjacket Lake in
Malheur National Forest

Map 12.1, page 715

This quiet and crowd-free campground is set at an elevation of 4,800 feet in the ponderosa pines along the shore of Yellowjacket Lake. Fishing for rainbow trout can be very good in the summer; boats without motors are allowed.

**Campsites, facilities:** There are 20 sites for

tents or RVs up to 22 feet long and a group camping area. Picnic tables are provided. Drinking water, vault toilets, and garbage service are available. A boat launch is nearby. Leashed pets are permitted.

**Reservations, fees:** Reservations are not accepted. Sites are $10 per night, $5 per night for an additional vehicle. Open late May-October, weather permitting.

**Directions:** From Burns, drive southwest on U.S. 20 for three miles to County Road 127. Turn right (northwest) and drive 32 miles to Forest Road 47. Turn right and drive three miles to Forest Road 3745. Turn right and drive one mile to the campground on the right.

**Contact:** Malheur National Forest, Emigrant Creek Ranger District, 541/573-4300, www. fs.usda.gov/malheur.

## 4 FALLS

### Scenic rating: 5

near Emigrant Creek in Malheur National Forest

**Map 12.1, page 715**

Falls camp is set in a beautiful meadow next to Emigrant Creek and is surrounded by ponderosa pine forests. This is a great place to see wildflowers in the early summer. A short trail leads to a small waterfall on the creek, which gives the camp its name. Fly-fishing and mountain biking are good here, as well as at nearby Emigrant, located two miles down the road. The elevation is 5,200 feet.

**Campsites, facilities:** There are six sites for tents or RVs up to 28 feet long. Picnic tables and fire grills are provided. Drinking water, vault toilets, and garbage service are available. Some facilities are wheelchair accessible. Leashed pets are permitted.

**Reservations, fees:** Reservations are not accepted. Sites are $8 per night, $4 per night for an additional vehicle, except for towed vehicles. Open May-October, weather permitting.

**Directions:** From Burns, drive southwest on

U.S. 20 for three miles to County Road 127. Turn right (northwest) and drive 25 miles (passing Forest Road 41 on the left) to Forest Road 43 and the junction for Allison Guard Station, Delintment Lake, and Paulina. Turn left on Forest Road 43 and drive eight miles to the campground on the left.

**Contact:** Malheur National Forest, Emigrant Creek Ranger District, 541/573-4300, www. fs.usda.gov/malheur.

## 5 CHICKAHOMINY RESERVOIR

### Scenic rating: 4

on Chickahominy Reservoir

**Map 12.1, page 715**

While a good spot for group camping, this camp is located in the high desert with no shade. Weather conditions can be extreme, so come prepared to tie everything down when the wind blows (a common occurrence). The camp is used primarily as an overnight stop for travelers driving through the area. Boats with motors are allowed on the reservoir. There is an access road on the northwest side of the reservoir for day use. The nearest services are five miles east (via U.S. 20) in Riley.

**Campsites, facilities:** There are 28 sites for tents or RVs up to 35 feet long. Picnic tables, garbage bins, and fire grills are provided. Drinking water (summer only, subject to fluctuations), vault toilets, a fish-cleaning station, and a boat launch are available. Some facilities are wheelchair accessible. Leashed pets are permitted.

**Reservations, fees:** Reservations are not accepted. Sites are $8 per night per vehicle, with a stay limit of 14 days. Open year-round, with limited winter facilities.

**Directions:** From Burns, drive west on U.S. 20 for 30 miles to the campground on the right.

**Contact:** Bureau of Land Management, Burns District, 541/573-4400, www.blm.gov/or/ districts/burns.

## 6 JOAQUIN MILLER HORSE CAMP
🏃 🚴 🐎 🚙 🏕

### Scenic rating: 5
in Malheur National Forest

**Map 12.2, page 716**

Set among mature ponderosa pines and adjacent to a meadow, campsites here are spread out, and there's a fair amount of privacy at this camp. It does receive some highway noise, though. Lots of old logging roads are available for biking, horseback riding, and walking. The camp gets low use, and while it caters to horse campers, all are welcome. Campers with horses are strongly advised to arrive early, before the weekend, to claim the campsites nearest to the corrals.

**Campsites, facilities:** There are 18 sites for tents or RVs up to 28 feet long. Picnic tables and fire rings are provided. Drinking water (supplied by a solar-powered water system), vault toilets, and garbage service are available. Stock facilities include four corrals and two hitching rails. Some facilities are wheelchair accessible. Leashed pets are permitted.

**Reservations, fees:** Reservations are not accepted. Sites are $8 per night, $4 per night per additional vehicle. Open mid-May-November, weather permitting.

**Directions:** From Burns, drive north on U.S. 395 for 19 miles to the campground on the left (this turnoff is easy to miss; watch for a very small green sign on the right that says Joaquin Miller Horse Camp).

**Contact:** Malheur National Forest, Emigrant Creek Ranger District, 541/573-4300, www.fs.usda.gov/malheur.

## 7 IDLEWILD
🏃 🚴 ⛷ 🐎 ♿ 🚙 🏕

### Scenic rating: 8
in Devine Canyon in Malheur National Forest

**Map 12.2, page 716**

This campground sits at an elevation of 5,300 feet in Devine Canyon, a designated winter Sno-Park that's popular with locals for snowmobiling and cross-country skiing. Several hiking and biking trailheads start here, including the Divine Summit Interpretive Loop Trail and the Idlewild Loop Trail. Since it provides easy access and a pretty setting, it's also a popular spot for visitors traveling up U.S. 395 and in need of a stopover. Bird-watching for white-headed woodpeckers and goshawks is popular. Expect to hear some highway noise. But the ponderosa pine forest and area trails are so beautiful that this area can feel divine, even if Devine Canyon and neighboring Devine Ridge were named back in the good old days when nobody worried about spelling.

**Campsites, facilities:** There are 19 single sites for tents and RVs up to 28 feet long, three double sites, and one group site for 20-50 people. Picnic tables and fire grills are provided. Drinking water, vault toilets, picnic areas, and garbage service are available. A group shelter can be reserved. Some facilities are wheelchair accessible. Leashed pets are permitted.

**Reservations, fees:** Reservations are accepted for the group shelter only at 877/444-6777 ($10 reservation fee) or www.recreation.gov ($9 reservation fee). Sites are $10 per night, $5 per night for an additional vehicle, except for towed vehicles. Open late May-mid-October, weather permitting.

**Directions:** From Burns, drive north on U.S. 395 for 17 miles to the campground on the right.

**Contact:** Malheur National Forest, Emigrant Creek Ranger District, 541/573-4300, www.fs.usda.gov/malheur.

## 8 CHUKAR PARK
🏊 🐎 🚙 🏕

### Scenic rating: 7
on the north fork of the Malheur River

**Map 12.2, page 716**

Chukar Park campground hugs the banks of the north fork of the Malheur River. The general area provides habitat for chukar, an upland game bird species. Hunting can be good in season during the fall but requires much hiking in rugged terrain. Trout fishing is also popular here. Bureau of Land Management (BLM) asks that visitors please respect the surrounding private property.

**Campsites, facilities:** There are 18 sites for tents or RVs up to 28 feet long. Picnic tables, fire rings, and garbage service are provided. Drinking water (May-October only) and vault toilets are available. Firewood is not available. Some facilities are wheelchair accessible. Leashed pets are permitted.

**Reservations, fees:** Reservations are not accepted. Sites are $5 per night per vehicle, with a 14-day stay limit. Open year-round, with limited winter facilities.

**Directions:** From Burns, drive north on U.S. 395 for three miles to U.S. 20. Take U.S. 20 east and drive 55 miles to Juntura and Beulah Reservoir Road. Turn northwest and drive six miles to the campground.

**Contact:** Bureau of Land Management, Vale District, 541/473-3144, www.blm.gov/or/districts/vale.

## 9 OASIS CAFÉ, MOTEL & RV PARK

**Scenic rating: 6**

in Juntura

**Map 12.2, page 716**

One of the only camps in the area, this well-maintained RV park is close to Chukar Park. The general area provides habitat for chukar, an upland game bird species. Hunting during the fall and trout fishing are recreation opportunities here.

**Campsites, facilities:** There are 22 sites with full hookups for RVs of any length, two cabins, and seven motel rooms. Some sites are pull-through. Picnic tables are provided. Restrooms with flush toilets and showers, a café, and ice are available. Leashed pets are permitted.

**Reservations, fees:** Reservations are not accepted. Sites are $22 per night and $6 per night per pet. Some credit cards are accepted. Open year-round.

**Directions:** From Burns, drive north on U.S. 395 for three miles to U.S. 20. Turn east and drive 55 miles to Juntura (a very small town). The park is on the left along U.S. 20.

**Contact:** Oasis Café, Motel & RV Park, 5838 U.S. 20, 541/277-3605.

## 10 LAKE OWYHEE STATE PARK

**Scenic rating: 7**

on Owyhee Lake

**Map 12.3, page 717**

There are two campgrounds here: McCormack and Indian Creek, which are located 1.5 miles apart. This state park is situated along the shore of 53-mile-long Owyhee Lake, a good lake for waterskiing in the day and fishing for warm-water species in the morning and evening. Owyhee is famous for its superb bass fishing; the place even has floating restrooms. Other highlights include views of unusual geological formations and huge rock pinnacles. Bighorn sheep, coyotes, golden eagles, mountain lions, mule deer, pronghorn antelope, and wild horses live in the area.

**Campsites, facilities:** McCormack has 31 sites with partial hookups for tents and RVs of any length, eight tent sites, and two tepees. Indian Creek has 26 sites with partial hookups for tents or RVs up to 50 feet long and nine tent sites. Drinking water, picnic tables, and fire grills are provided. Vault toilets, garbage bins, firewood, a dump station, and a picnic area are available. Restrooms with flush toilets and showers are available at McCormack. Boat launches are at Indian Creek, Gordon Gulch day-use, and near the dam. Fuel and ice are available at the park. Marine fuel is available at Indian Creek. Some facilities are wheelchair accessible. Leashed pets are permitted.

**Reservations, fees:** Reservations are accepted

at 800/452-5687 or www.reserveamerica.com ($8 reservation fee). RV sites are $16-20 per night, tent sites are $13-17 per night, tepees are $36 per night, $5 for the hiker/biker site at Indian Creek, and $5 per night for an additional vehicle. Some credit cards are accepted. Open year-round.

**Directions:** From Ontario (near the Oregon/Idaho border), drive south on U.S. 20/26 for six miles to the Nyssa exit. Turn south and drive eight miles to Nyssa and Highway 201. Turn left (southeast) on Highway 201 and drive eight miles to Owyhee. Turn east and drive about 20 miles to road's end and the entrance to the park, approximately 33 miles from Nyssa.

**Contact:** Lake Owyhee State Park, 541/339-2331 or 800/551-6949, www.oregonstateparks.org.

## 11 COW LAKES

### Scenic rating: 6

near Cow Lakes

Map 12.3, page 717

Cow Lakes is a little-used campground adjacent to an old lava flow. The lake is shallow and murky, which makes fishing popular here. The campsites are open and treeless, and the road is rutted and rough in places.

**Campsites, facilities:** There are 10 sites for tents or very small RVs. Picnic tables and fire rings are provided. A vault toilet and a primitive boat ramp are available. No drinking water or firewood is available, and garbage must be packed out. Leashed pets are permitted.

**Reservations, fees:** Reservations are not accepted. There is no fee for camping. Open year-round, weather permitting.

**Directions:** From Burns Junction, drive east on U.S. 95 for 30 miles to Danner Loop Road. Turn left (north) and drive 14 miles (past Danner) to Cow Lakes and the campground.

**Contact:** Bureau of Land Management, Vale District, 541/473-3144, www.blm.gov or/districts/vale.

## 12 SLOCUM CREEK

### Scenic rating: 6

on Owyhee Lake

Map 12.3, page 717

This campground sits on the eastern shore of Owyhee Lake, about 20 miles from the Oregon/Idaho border. Hiking, warm-water fishing, and waterskiing are among the recreation options in this high-desert area. Lake Owyhee State Park provides the other developed recreation destination on the lake.

**Campsites, facilities:** There are 12 sites for tents or RVs up to 20 feet long. Picnic tables are provided. Vault toilets and garbage service are available. There is no drinking water onsite but can be found a half-mile away. Firewood is not available. Boat-launching facilities (for boats less than 17 feet long) are available onsite. Some facilities are wheelchair accessible. Leashed pets are permitted.

**Reservations, fees:** Reservations are not accepted. There is no fee for camping. Open early March-mid-November.

**Directions:** From U.S. 95 where it crosses the Idaho/Oregon border, drive north for five miles to McBride Creek Road. Turn west and drive 10 miles to Leslie Gulch Road. Turn left (west) and drive 15 miles to the campground.

**Contact:** Bureau of Land Management, Vale District, 541/473-3144, www.blm.gov.

## 13 BIRCH CREEK HISTORIC RANCH

### Scenic rating: 9

near the Owyhee River

Map 12.3, page 717

This is one of the most remote campgrounds in Oregon. When I stayed here, it was known as "Hole in the Ground." The official name, Birch Creek Ranch, is the collective name for two ranches founded about 100 years ago. The remote setting is an oasis in the arid, scenic

Owyhee River Canyon, its green fields contrasting strongly with the sun-drenched cream-and chocolate-colored formations and the red and black volcanic rocks that soar up from the edges of its narrow meadows. This section of the Owyhee River holds Class III, IV, and V+ rapids. Hiking options include the Jordan Crater, a 4,000-year-old caldera offering domes, kipukas, lava tubes, trenches, and more. The Owyhee Canyon rim looks like a miniature Grand Canyon. This camp/ranch's stone walls, water wheel, and barn contribute to its inclusion on the National Register of Historic Places. I canoed nearly the entire length of the Owhyee, from the headwaters below the Jarbridge Mountains in Nevada, through Idaho and into Oregon.

**Campsites, facilities:** There are five sites for tents or small RVs. Picnic tables and fire rings are provided. A vault toilet is available. There is no drinking water, but water can be found within 0.25-mile. Garbage must be packed out. There is access to the Owyhee River by self-registration for non-motorized boats only. Some facilities are wheelchair accessible. Leashed pets are permitted.

**Reservations, fees:** Reservations are not accepted. There is no fee for camping. Open mid-March-mid-October, weather permitting.

**Directions:** From Jordan Valley, take U.S. 95 north for 10 miles to Cow Creek Road at the Jordan Craters sign. Turn left (west) on Cow Creek Road and follow BLM Owyhee River access signs 28 miles to campground. High-clearance 4WD vehicles recommended. Road may be impassable when wet.

**Contact:** Bureau of Land Management, Vale District, 541/473-3144, www.blm.gov or/districts/vale.

# 14 JACKSON CREEK
🏃 🚴 🛶 ❄ 🐕 🚐 ⛺

### Scenic rating: 8
on Jackson Creek in Winema National Forest

**Map 12.4, page 718**　　　**BEST (**

Jackson Creek is a remote campground in a beautiful stand of old-growth ponderosa pine at an elevation of 4,600 feet. Horseback riding and mountain biking are popular. Wildlife-viewing can be outstanding some years. Note that there are many mosquitoes in spring and early summer, so bring repellent. The campground borders private land so watch for forest boundary signs to avoid trespassing.

**Campsites, facilities:** There are 12 sites for tents or RVs up to 25 feet long. Picnic tables and fire grills are provided. Vault toilets are available. There is no drinking water. Garbage must be packed out. Leashed pets are permitted.

**Reservations, fees:** Reservations are not accepted. There is no fee for camping. Open year-round, weather permitting.

**Directions:** From Chemult and Highway 97, drive south for 25 miles to Silver Lake Road (County Road 676). Turn left (northeast) and drive 22 miles to Forest Road 49. Turn right (southeast) and drive five miles to the camp.

**Contact:** Fremont-Winema National Forests, Chemult Ranger District, 541/365-7001, www.fs.usda.gov/fremont-winema.

# 15 SILVER CREEK MARSH
🏃 🛶 🐕 ⛺

### Scenic rating: 4
near Silver Creek in Fremont National Forest

**Map 12.4, page 718**

A trailhead and terminus for segments of the National Recreational Trail are located at this small, quiet, and primitive camp that gets little attention. It's a short walk to the creek, a popular fishing spot, and the camp is also close to a wildlife area boundary.

**Campsites, facilities:** There are 14 sites for tents or RVs up to 50 feet long. Picnic tables and fire grills are provided. Drinking water, vault toilets, garbage bins, and hitching rails and corrals for horses are available. Note that drinking water and garbage service availability is uncertain. Firewood is available nearby. Leashed pets are permitted.

**Reservations, fees:** Reservations are not accepted. Sites are $6 per night, $2 per night per additional vehicle. There is a 14-day stay limit. Open May-mid-November, weather permitting.

**Directions:** From Bend, drive south on U.S. 97 for 32 miles to Highway 31. Turn southeast on Highway 31 and drive 48 miles to County Road 4-11 (one mile west of the town of Silver Lake). Turn right and drive six miles (the road becomes Forest Road 27). Continue south for five miles to the campground entrance road on the left.

**Contact:** Fremont-Winema National Forests, Silver Lake Ranger District, 541/576-2107, www.fs.usda.gov/fremont-winema.

## 16 THOMPSON RESERVOIR

**Scenic rating: 3**

on Thompson Reservoir in Fremont National Forest

**Map 12.4, page 718**

Located on the north shore of Thompson Reservoir among black-bark ponderosa pines the height of telephone poles, this simple and pretty camp features shaded sites close to the water. The area is popular for fishing and boating. Water in the reservoir fluctuates and sometimes nearly dries up altogether in late summer.

**Campsites, facilities:** There are 19 sites for tents or RVs up to 22 feet long, plus a separate group camping area. Picnic tables and fire grills are provided. Drinking water, garbage bins, and vault toilets are available. Boat-launching facilities are nearby. Leashed pets are permitted.

**Reservations, fees:** Reservations are not accepted. Sites are $6 per night, $2 per night per additional vehicle. Open May-mid-November, weather permitting.

**Directions:** From Bend, drive south on U.S. 97 for 32 miles to Highway 31. Turn southeast on Highway 31 and drive 48 miles to County

Road 4-11 (one mile west of the town of Silver Lake). Turn right and drive six miles (the road becomes Forest Road 27) and continue south for nine miles to the campground entrance road. Turn left and drive one mile to the camp.

**Contact:** Fremont-Winema National Forests, Silver Lake Ranger District, 541/576-2107, www.fs.usda.gov/fremont-winema.

## 17 EAST BAY

**Scenic rating: 3**

on Thompson Reservoir in Fremont National Forest

**Map 12.4, page 718**

This campground on the east shore of Thompson Reservoir has paved roads, but it's still a long way from home, so be sure to bring all of your supplies with you. A day-use area is adjacent to the camp. Nearby Silver Creek Marsh Campground provides an even more primitive setting along a stream.

**Campsites, facilities:** There are 17 sites for tents or RVs up to 50 feet long and one double site. Picnic tables and fire grills are provided. Drinking water, garbage bins, vault toilets, and a fishing pier are available. Boat-launching facilities are nearby. Some facilities are wheelchair accessible. Leashed pets are permitted.

**Reservations, fees:** Reservations are not accepted. Sites are $10 per night, $4 per night per extra vehicle. Open May-mid-November, weather permitting.

**Directions:** From Bend, drive south on U.S. 97 for 32 miles to Highway 31. Turn southeast on Highway 31 and drive 49 miles to Silver Lake. Continue east a short distance on Highway 31 to Forest Road 28. Turn right on Forest Road 28 and drive 13 miles to Forest Road 014. Turn right on Forest Road 014 and drive two miles to the campground.

**Contact:** Fremont-Winema National Forests, Silver Lake Ranger District, 541/576-2107, www.fs.usda.gov/fremont-winema.

## 18 HEAD OF THE RIVER

### Scenic rating: 8

on the Williamson River in Winema National Forest

**Map 12.4, page 718**

Almost nobody knows about this small, extremely remote spot on the edge of a meadow in the lodgepole and ponderosa pines, though hunters use it in the fall. The only camp for miles around, it's set at 4,500 feet elevation along the Williamson River headwaters, where you can actually see the beginning of the river bubbling up from underground springs.

**Campsites, facilities:** There are five sites for tents or RVs up to 30 feet long. Picnic tables, garbage bins, and fire pits are provided. A vault toilet is available. There is no drinking water. Leashed pets are permitted.

**Reservations, fees:** Reservations are not accepted. There is no fee for camping. Open Memorial Day weekend-late November, weather permitting.

**Directions:** From Klamath Falls, drive north on U.S. 97 for 30 miles to Chiloquin and Sprague River Highway. Turn right (east) on Sprague River Highway and drive five miles to Williamson River Road. Turn left (northeast) and drive 20 miles to Forest Road 4648. Turn left (north) on Forest Road 4648 and drive 0.5 mile to the campground.

**Contact:** Fremont-Winema National Forests, Klamath Ranger District, 541/885-3400, www.fs.usda.gov/fremont-winema.

## 19 GERBER NORTH, SOUTH, AND HORSE CAMP

### Scenic rating: 6

on Gerber Reservoir

**Map 12.4, page 718**

This camp can be found at an elevation of 4,800 feet alongside the west shore of Gerber Reservoir. Off the beaten path, Gerber attracts mainly locals. Recreation options include boating (10-mph speed limit), fishing, and hiking. Swimming is not popular here because the water is murky with algae.

**Campsites, facilities:** There are 50 sites for tents or RVs up to 30 feet long at Gerber North and Gerber South. Gerber Horse Camp has seven equestrian sites about 0.25-mile above Gerber North. Some dispersed primitive sites are also available; these have no garbage service. Picnic tables and fire grills are provided at the three developed campgrounds. Drinking water, a dump station, vault toilets, two boat ramps with docks, and two fish-cleaning stations are available at Gerber North and Gerber South. Drinking water, a dump station, vault toilets, and corrals are available at Gerber Horse Camp. Garbage service, restroom maintenance and a camp host are available in summer only. Some facilities are wheelchair accessible. Leashed pets are permitted.

**Reservations, fees:** Reservations are not accepted. Sites are $7 per night, $4 per night for an additional vehicle. There is no fee for camping at the primitive sites. Open year-round, weather permitting. Drinking water and garbage service are only available May-mid-September.

**Directions:** From Klamath Falls, drive east on Highway 140 for 16 miles to Dairy and Highway 70. Turn right (south) on Highway 70 and drive seven miles to Bonanza and East Langell Valley Road. Turn left (east) on East Langell Valley Road and drive 11 miles to Gerber Road. Turn left on Gerber Road and drive eight miles to the campground on the right.

**Contact:** Bureau of Land Management, Klamath Falls Resource Area, 541/883-6916, www.blm.gov/or/districts/lakeview.

## 20 LEE THOMAS

**Scenic rating: 6**

near the north fork of the Sprague River in
Fremont National Forest

**Map 12.5, page 719**

Lee Thomas is located near the trailhead that
provides access to the Dead Horse Rim Trail.
Nestled along the north fork of the Sprague
River in the interior of Fremont National Forest, this small, cozy camp is a genuine hideaway, with all the necessities provided. It is
set in a meadow at an elevation of 6,306 feet
and, like Sandhill Crossing Campground (two
miles downstream), it's popular with anglers
and hunters in the fall.

**Campsites, facilities:** There are eight sites for
tents or RVs up to 16 feet long. Picnic tables
and fire grills are provided. Drinking water
and vault toilets are available. Garbage must
be packed out. Some facilities are wheelchair
accessible. Leashed pets are permitted.

**Reservations, fees:** Reservations are not accepted. There is no fee for camping. Open
June-late October, weather permitting.

**Directions:** From Lakeview, drive north on
U.S. 395 for 23 miles to Highway 31. Turn
northwest and drive 22 miles to Paisley.
Continue on Highway 31 for 0.5 mile to Mill
Street. Turn west on Mill Street and drive
20 miles (the road becomes Forest Road 33)
and continue to the T intersection with Forest Road 28. Turn right on Forest Road 28
and drive 0.5 mile to Forest Road 3411. Turn
right and drive one mile to the campground
on the right.

**Contact:** Fremont-Winema National Forests,
Paisley Ranger District, 541/943-3114, www.
fs.usda.gov.

## 21 SANDHILL CROSSING

**Scenic rating: 6**

on the north fork of the Sprague River in
Fremont National Forest

**Map 12.5, page 719**

If you're looking for a combination of beauty
and solitude, you've found it. This camp
(6,306 feet elevation) sits on the banks of
the designated Wild and Scenic North Fork
Sprague River, where fishing is superior. Although a low-use camp, it is popular with anglers and hunters in the fall. A nearby trailhead
leads into the Gearheart Wilderness.

**Campsites, facilities:** There are five sites for
tents or RVs up to 25 feet long. Picnic tables
and fire grills are provided. Vault toilets and
drinking water are available. Garbage must
be packed out. Some facilities are wheelchair
accessible. Leashed pets are permitted.

**Reservations, fees:** Reservations are not accepted. There is no fee for camping. Open
June-October, weather permitting.

**Directions:** From Lakeview, drive north on U.S.
395 for 23 miles to Highway 31. Turn northwest
and drive 22 miles to Paisley. Continue on Highway 31 for 0.5 mile to Mill Street. Turn west on
Mill Street and drive 20 miles (the road becomes
Forest Road 33); continue to the T intersection
with Forest Road 28. Turn right and drive 11
miles to Forest Road 3411. Turn left and drive
eight miles to the campground on the left.

**Contact:** Fremont-Winema National Forests,
Paisley Ranger District, 541/943-3114, www.
fs.usda.gov/fremont-winema.

## 22 DEAD HORSE LAKE

**Scenic rating: 9**

on Dead Horse Lake in Fremont National
Forest

**Map 12.5, page 719**

The shore of Dead Horse Lake is home to this
camp sitting at 7,372 feet elevation; it generally

fills up on most weekends and holidays. A hiking trail winds around the perimeter of the lake, hooking up with other trails along the way. One original Civilian Conservation Corps canoe, a relic of the 1930s, remains in the lake. No gas motors are permitted on the lake, and a 5-mph speed limit is in effect. Nearby Fremont National Forest provides good side trips.

**Campsites, facilities:** There are 14 sites for tents or RVs up to 25 feet long and a separate group area for up to 40 people. Picnic tables and fire grills are provided. Drinking water and vault toilets are available, but garbage must be packed out. A boat launch and day-use area are nearby. Leashed pets are permitted.

**Reservations, fees:** Reservations are not accepted. Sites are $6 per night, $2 per night per additional vehicle. Open July-October, weather permitting.

**Directions:** From Lakeview, drive north on U.S. 395 for 23 miles to Highway 31. Turn northwest and drive 22 miles to Paisley. Continue on Highway 31 for 0.5 mile to Mill Street. Turn west on Mill Street and drive 20 miles (the road becomes Forest Road 033); continue to the T intersection with Forest Road 28. Turn right and drive 11 miles (watch for the turn to Campbell-Dead Horse Lakes) to Forest Road 033. Turn left and drive three miles (gravel road) to the campground.

**Contact:** Fremont-Winema National Forests, Paisley Ranger District, 541/943-3114, www.fs.usda.gov/fremont-winema.

## 23 CAMPBELL LAKE
🏃 🏊 ⛴ 🛶 🦌 🚐 ⛺

### Scenic rating: 9
on Campbell Lake in Fremont National Forest

**Map 12.5, page 719**      **BEST (**

This campground on the pebbled shore of Campbell Lake is located near Dead Horse Lake Campground. These high-elevation, crystal-clear lakes were formed during the glacier period, evidence of which can be found

on the nearby Lakes Trail system. Both camps are very busy, filling up most weekends in July and August. No gas motors are permitted on Campbell Lake, and a 5-mph speed limit is in effect. A U.S. Forest Service map details the back roads.

**Campsites, facilities:** There are 18 sites for tents or RVs up to 25 feet long. Picnic tables and fire grills are provided. Drinking water and vault toilets are available. Garbage must be packed out. A boat launch and day-use area are adjacent to the camp. Boats with electric motors are permitted, but gas motors are prohibited. Leashed pets are permitted.

**Reservations, fees:** Reservations are not accepted. Sites are $6 per night, $2 per night per additional vehicle. Open July-late October, weather permitting.

**Directions:** From Lakeview, drive north on U.S. 395 for 23 miles to Highway 31. Turn northwest and drive 22 miles to Paisley. Continue on Highway 31 for 0.5 mile to Mill Street. Turn west on Mill Street and drive 20 miles (the road becomes Forest Road 33) and continue to the T intersection with Forest Road 28. Turn right and drive eight miles to Forest Road 033. Turn left and drive two miles to the campground.

**Contact:** Fremont-Winema National Forests, Paisley Ranger District, 541/943-3114, www.fs.usda.gov/fremont-winema.

## 24 MARSTER SPRING
🏃 🏊 🦌 🚐 ⛺

### Scenic rating: 6
on the Chewaucan River in Fremont National Forest

**Map 12.5, page 719**

The largest of several popular camps in this river corridor, Marster Spring sits right on the banks of the Chewaucan River at an elevation of 4,845 feet. This pretty campground is set among ponderosa pine trees in a good fishing area, yet is close to the town of Paisley. The Fremont National Recreation Trail is accessible at the Chewaucan Crossing Trailhead, 0.25 mile to the south.

**Campsites, facilities:** There are 10 sites for tents or RVs up to 22 feet long. Picnic tables and fire grills are provided. Drinking water and vault toilets are available. Leashed pets are permitted.

**Reservations, fees:** Reservations are not accepted. Sites are $6 per night, $2 per night per additional vehicle. Open May-October, weather permitting.

**Directions:** From Lakeview, drive north on U.S. 395 for 23 miles to Highway 31. Turn northwest and drive 22 miles to Paisley. Continue on Highway 31 for 0.5 mile to Mill Street. Turn west on Mill Street and drive 7.5 miles (the road becomes Forest Road 33) to the campground on the left.

**Contact:** Fremont-Winema National Forests, Paisley Ranger District, 541/943-3114, www.fs.usda.gov/fremont-winema.

## 25 CORRAL CREEK

### Scenic rating: 4
near the Gearhart Mountain Wilderness in Fremont National Forest

**Map 12.5, page 719**

Set along Corral Creek, this camp is adjacent to a trailhead that provides access into the Gearhart Mountain Wilderness, making it a prime base camp for a backpacking trip. Access is also available from camp to the Palisade Rocks, a worthwhile side trip. Another option is Quartz Mountain Sno-Park, which is 14 miles east of the campground. The elevation is 6,000 feet.

**Campsites, facilities:** There are six sites for tents or RVs up to 22 feet long. Picnic tables and fire grills are provided. Vault toilets are available. There is no drinking water, and garbage must be packed out. Stock facilities include hitching posts, stalls, and corrals. Some facilities are wheelchair accessible. Leashed pets are permitted.

**Reservations, fees:** Reservations are not accepted. There is no fee for camping. Open mid-May-late October, weather permitting.

**Directions:** From Klamath Falls, drive east on Highway 140 for 53 miles to the town of Bly. Continue east on Highway 140 for one mile to Campbell Road. Turn left and drive 0.5 mile to Forest Road 34. Turn right and drive 15 miles to Forest Road 012. Turn right and drive to the campground.

**Contact:** Fremont-Winema National Forests, Bly Ranger District, 541/353-2700, www.fs.usda.gov/fremont-winema.

## 26 DAIRY POINT

### Scenic rating: 6
on Dairy Creek in Fremont National Forest

**Map 12.5, page 719**

This campground, elevation 5,200 feet, is situated next to the Dairy Creek Bridge in a stand of ponderosa pine and white fir at the edge of a large and open meadow. The setting is beautiful and peaceful, with a towering backdrop of mountains. In the spring, wildflowers are a sight to behold; bird-watching can also be excellent this time of year. Fishing and inner tubing are popular activities at Dairy Creek. Warning: This campground is suitable for large groups and is often full on holidays and most weekends.

**Campsites, facilities:** There are four sites for tents or self-contained RVs up to 25 feet long. Picnic tables and fire grills are provided. A vault toilet and drinking water are available. Garbage must be packed out. Leashed pets are permitted.

**Reservations, fees:** Reservations are not accepted. There is no fee for camping. Open mid-May-October, weather permitting.

**Directions:** From Lakeview, drive north on U.S. 395 for 23 miles to Highway 31. Turn northwest and drive 22 miles to Paisley. Continue on Highway 31 for 0.5 mile to Mill Street. Turn west on Mill Street and drive 20

miles (the road becomes Forest Road 33); continue to the T intersection with Forest Road 28. Turn left and drive two miles (crossing the Dairy Creek Bridge) to Forest Road 3428. Turn left and drive to the campground (just past the intersection on the left).
**Contact:** Fremont-Winema National Forests, Paisley Ranger District, 541/943-3114, www.fs.usda.gov/fremont-winema.

## 27 HAPPY CAMP

### Scenic rating: 6
on Dairy Creek in Fremont National Forest
**Map 12.5, page 719**

Here's a pleasant spot with open sites along Dairy Creek, though only one site is close to the water. The camp features some old 1930s Civilian Conservation Corps shelters, preserved in their original state. Fishing is available for rainbow trout, though the creek is no longer stocked. The camp sits at 5,289 feet elevation.

**Campsites, facilities:** There are nine sites for tents or RVs up to 16 feet long. Picnic tables and fire grills are provided. Vault toilets, picnic shelters, and horseshoe pits are available. There is no drinking water (drinking water is available 1.5 miles west on Forest Road 047 at Clear Spring). Garbage must be packed out. Leashed pets are permitted.

**Reservations, fees:** Reservations are not accepted. There is no fee for camping. Open mid-May-late October, weather permitting.

**Directions:** From Lakeview, drive north on U.S. 395 for 23 miles to Highway 31. Turn northwest and drive 22 miles to Paisley. Continue on Highway 31 for 0.5 mile to Mill Street. Turn west on Mill Street and drive 20 miles (the road becomes Forest Road 33); continue to the T intersection with Forest Road 28. Turn left and drive two miles (just before Dairy Creek) to Forest Road 047. Turn right and drive two miles to the campground on the left.

**Contact:** Fremont-Winema National Forests, Paisley Ranger District, 541/943-3114, www.fs.usda.gov/fremont-winema.

## 28 LOFTON RESERVOIR

### Scenic rating: 6
on Lofton Reservoir in Fremont National Forest
**Map 12.5, page 719**

This remote campground sits on the shore of Lofton Reservoir, a small lake that can provide the best trout fishing in this region. Other nearby lakes are accessible by forest roads. This area marks the beginning of the Great Basin, a high-desert area that extends to Idaho. A large fire burned much of the surrounding forest about 20 years ago, making this campground an oasis of sorts.

**Campsites, facilities:** There are 22 sites for tents or RVs up to 25 feet long and four double sites. Picnic tables and fire grills are provided. Vault toilets are available. There is no drinking water and garbage must be packed out. Boat docks and launching facilities are nearby. A camp host is on-site. Some facilities are wheelchair accessible. Leashed pets are permitted.

**Reservations, fees:** Reservations are not accepted. Sites are $6 per night, $2 per night per additional vehicle. Open mid-May-late October, weather permitting.

**Directions:** From Klamath Falls, drive east on Highway 140 for 54 miles to Bly. Continue east on Highway 140 for 13 miles to Forest Road 3715. Turn right and drive seven miles to Forest Road 013. Turn left on Forest Road 013 and drive one mile to the campground.

**Contact:** Fremont-Winema National Forests, Bly Ranger District, 541/353-2700, www.fs.usda.gov/fremont-winema.

## 29 COTTONWOOD COMPLEX CAMPGROUND

🏃 🚲 🛶 ⛓ 🐕 🚐 ⛺

### Scenic rating: 6

on Cottonwood Meadow Lake in Fremont National Forest

**Map 12.5, page 719**

Cottonwood Recreation Area, along the upper shore of Cottonwood Meadow Lake, is one of the better spots in the vicinity for fishing and hiking. The camp is set at an elevation of 6,130 feet in a forested setting with aspen and many huge ponderosa pines. Boats with electric motors are allowed on the lake, but gas motors are prohibited. Three hiking trails wind around the lake, and facilities for horses include hitching posts, feeders, water, and corrals.

**Campsites, facilities:** There are 25 sites for tents or RVs up to 35 feet long and nine tent sites. Picnic tables and fire grills are provided. Drinking water and vault toilets are available, but garbage must be packed out. A camp host is on-site. Boat docks are nearby. No gasoline motors are allowed on the lake. The boating speed limit is 5 mph. Leashed pets are permitted.

**Reservations, fees:** Reservations are not accepted. Sites are $6 per night, $2 per night per additional vehicle. Open early June-mid-October, weather permitting.

**Directions:** From Lakeview, drive west on Highway 140 for 21 miles to Forest Road 3870. Turn right and drive about eight miles to the campground.

**Contact:** Fremont-Winema National Forests, Lakeview Ranger District, 541/947-6300, www.fs.usda.gov/fremont-winema.

## 30 MUD CREEK

🏃 🛶 🐕 🚐 ⛺

### Scenic rating: 4

on Mud Creek in Fremont National Forest

**Map 12.5, page 719**

Remote and quiet, this camp sits at 6,600 feet elevation in an isolated stand of lodgepole pines along the banks of Mud Creek. Fishing in Mud Creek is fairly good, and Drake Peak (8,405 feet elevation) is nearby. There are no other camps in the immediate vicinity.

**Campsites, facilities:** There are seven sites for tents or RVs up to 16 feet long. Picnic tables and fire grills are provided. Drinking water and vault toilets are available. Garbage must be packed out. Leashed pets are permitted.

**Reservations, fees:** Reservations are not accepted. There is no fee for camping. Open June-mid-October, weather permitting.

**Directions:** From Lakeview, drive five miles north on U.S. 395 to Highway 140. Turn right on Highway 140 and drive eight miles to Forest Road 3615. Turn left and drive seven miles to the campground.

**Contact:** Fremont-Winema National Forests, Lakeview Ranger District, 541/947-6300, www.fs.usda.gov/fremont-winema.

## 31 DOG LAKE

🛶 ⛓ 🐕 🚐 ⛺

### Scenic rating: 5

on Dog Lake in Fremont National Forest

**Map 12.5, page 719**          **BEST (**

This campground is located on the west shore of Dog Lake at an elevation of 5,100 feet. Native Americans named the lake for its resemblance in shape to the hind leg of a dog. The lake provides a popular fishery for bass, crappie, and perch. Boats with motors are permitted, though speeds are limited to 5 mph. Prospects for seeing waterfowl and eagles are good.

**Campsites, facilities:** There are 12 sites for tents or RVs up to 40 feet long and four double sites. Picnic tables and fire grills are provided. Vault toilets are available. There is no drinking water. Garbage must be packed out. A boat launch is nearby. Leashed pets are permitted.

**Reservations, fees:** Reservations are not accepted. Sites are $6 per night, $2 per night per additional vehicle. Open mid-April-mid-October, weather permitting.

**Directions:** From Lakeview, drive west on Highway 140 for seven miles to County Road 1-13. Turn left on County Road 1-13 and drive four miles to County Road 1-11D (Dog Lake Road). Turn right and drive four miles (the road becomes Forest Road 4017) into national forest. Continue on Forest Road 4017 for 12 miles (two miles past Drew Reservoir) to Dog Lake and the campground entrance on the left.

**Contact:** Fremont-Winema National Forests, Lakeview Ranger District, 541/947-3334, www.fs.usda.gov/fremont-winema.

## **32** DREWS CREEK

### Scenic rating: 9

near Lakeview in Fremont National Forest

Map 12.5, page 719                    BEST (

This exceptionally beautiful campground is set along Drews Creek at 4,900 feet elevation. Gorgeous wild roses grow near the creek, and several unmarked trails lead to nearby hills where campers can enjoy scenic views. A great spot for a family trip, Drews Creek features horseshoe pits, an area for baseball, and a large group barbecue, making it equally popular with group campers. Fishing is available in nearby Dog Lake, which also provides facilities for boating. Waterskiing is another option at Drews Reservoir, two miles to the west.

**Campsites, facilities:** There are three sites for tents or RVs up to 25 feet long and two group sites for 20-50 people. Picnic tables, fire grills, vault toilets, and drinking water are provided. Garbage must be packed out. Leashed pets are permitted.

**Reservations, fees:** Reservations are not accepted. There is no fee for camping. Open early mid-May-mid-October, weather permitting.

**Directions:** From Lakeview, drive west on Highway 140 for 10 miles to County Road 1-13. Turn left and drive four miles to County Road 1-11D. Turn right and drive six miles (the road will become Forest Road 4017) to the bridge that provides access to the campground.

**Contact:** Fremont-Winema National Forests, Lakeview Ranger District, 541/947-3334, www.fs.usda.gov/fremont-winema.

## **33** JUNIPERS RESERVOIR RV RESORT

### Scenic rating: 6

on Junipers Reservoir

Map 12.5, page 719

This resort on an 8,000-acre cattle ranch is situated in a designated Oregon Wildlife Viewing Area, and campers may catch glimpses of seldom-seen species. Many nature-walking trails meander through the park, and guests can also take driving tours. Fishing for catfish and trout can be good and, because it is a private lake, no fishing license is required. The summer climate is mild and pleasant. Antelope and elk can be spotted in this area.

**Campsites, facilities:** There is a grassy area for tents and 40 pull-through sites with full or partial hookups (some 50 amp) for RVs of any length; a 20-foot camping trailer is also available. Group camping, with group rates, is available. Picnic tables are provided. Weather permitting, small campfires are allowed in the meadow. Drinking water, restrooms with showers, a dump station, Wi-Fi, coin laundry, community fire pit, and ice are available. Recreational facilities include a recreation hall, a volleyball court, and horseshoe pits. Some of the facilities are wheelchair accessible. Leashed pets are permitted.

**Reservations, fees:** Reservations are recommended. Tent sites are $20 per night, and RV sites are $30-35 per night; weekly and monthly rates are available. Open May 1-mid-October.

**Directions:** From Lakeview, drive west on Highway 140 for 10 miles to the resort (at Milepost 86.5) on the right.

**Contact:** Junipers Reservoir RV Resort, 541/947-2050, www.junipersrv.com.

## 34 GOOSE LAKE STATE PARK

**Scenic rating: 7**

on Goose Lake

**Map 12.5, page 719**

This park is situated on the east shore of un-usual Goose Lake, which lies half in Oregon and half in California. The fishing at the lake is poor, but better fishing is available in nearby streams. Waterfowl from the Pacific flyway frequent this out-of-the-way spot, as do many other species of birds and wildlife, like the mule deer that frequent the shaded campground. Note that only 15- and 20-amp service is available for RVs.

**Campsites, facilities:** There are 48 sites with partial hookups (water and electricity) for tents or RVs up to 50 feet long. Picnic tables, fire grills, garbage bins, and drinking water are provided. A camp host is on-site. Restrooms with flush toilets and showers, a dump station, ice, and firewood are available. Leashed pets are permitted.

**Reservations, fees:** Reservations are not accepted. Sites are $16-20 per night, $5 per night for an additional vehicle. Open mid-April-mid-October.

**Directions:** From Lakeview, drive south on U.S. 395 for 14 miles to the California border and Stateline Road. Turn right (west) and drive one mile to the campground.

**Contact:** Goose Lake State Park, 541/947-3111 or 800/551-6949, www.oregonstateparks.org.

## 35 WILLOW CREEK

**Scenic rating: 4**

near Willow Creek in Fremont National Forest

**Map 12.5, page 719**

This campground (at 5,800 feet elevation) is situated in a canyon among tall pines and quaking aspen not far from the banks of Willow Creek. Campsites are private, and some are located along the creek. Watch for wildflowers blooming in the spring. A hiking trail offers access to the Crane Mountain Trail, and a nearby dirt road heads north to Burnt Creek.

**Campsites, facilities:** There are eight sites for tents or RVs up to 22 feet long. Picnic tables and fire grills are provided. There is no drinking water, and garbage must be packed out. Vault toilets are available. Leashed pets are permitted.

**Reservations, fees:** Reservations are not accepted. There is no fee for camping. Open June-mid-October, weather permitting.

**Directions:** From Lakeview, drive five miles north on U.S. 395 to Highway 140. Turn right (east) on Highway 140 and drive seven miles to Forest Road 3915. Turn right and drive nine miles to Forest Road 4011. Turn right and drive one mile to the campground on the right.

**Contact:** Fremont-Winema National Forests, Lakeview Ranger District, 541/947-3334, www.fs.usda.gov.

## 36 DEEP CREEK

**Scenic rating: 8**

on Deep Creek in Fremont National Forest

**Map 12.5, page 719**

Shaded by huge ponderosa pines and cottonwoods and nestled on the banks of Deep Creek, this pretty, little-used campground is the place if you're after privacy. Deep Creek is a good fishing stream. Magnificent spring wildflowers are a highlight here. The camp sits at an elevation of 5,600 feet.

**Campsites, facilities:** There are five sites for tents or RVs up to 22 feet long. Picnic tables and fire grills are provided. Vault toilets are available. There is no drinking water, and garbage must be packed out. Leashed pets are permitted.

**Reservations, fees:** Reservations are not accepted. There is no fee for camping. Open June-mid-October, weather permitting.

**Directions:** From Lakeview, drive five miles

north on U.S. 395 to Highway 140. Turn right (east) on Highway 140 and drive six miles to Forest Road 3915. Turn right on Forest Road 3915 and drive 14 miles to Deep Creek and the campground entrance road on the right (Forest Road 4015). Turn right and drive one mile to the campground on the right.

**Contact:** Fremont-Winema National Forests, Lakeview Ranger District, 541/947-3334, www.fs.usda.gov/fremont-winema.

## 37 HART MOUNTAIN NATIONAL ANTELOPE REFUGE

🚶 🚵 〰 🎣 🐕 ♿ 🚐 ⛺

### Scenic rating: 6

near Adel

**Map 12.6, page 720**

The U.S. Fish and Wildlife Service operates very few areas with campgrounds—Hart Mountain is one of them. This unusual refuge features canyons and hot springs in a high-desert area. There are three primitive campgrounds: Hot Springs Campground, Post Meadows Horse Camp, and Camp Hart Mountain (CCC Camp). Hot Springs gets the highest use in the summer. Some of Oregon's largest antelope herds roam this large area, and the campground is popular with hunters in the fall.

**Campsites, facilities:** Hot Springs Campground has 25 primitive sites for tents or RVs up to 20 feet long. Post Meadows Horse Camp has six primitive sites with corrals, hitching posts, and stock water (100 yards away) available; pellet (or certified weed-free) feed is required for horses. Camp Hart Mountain has eight primitive tent sites. Some sites have fire rings. Pit toilets are provided, and there is a seasonal camp host. There is no drinking water except at Camp Hart Mountain or at headquarters, which you pass on the way in. Firewood is not available. Garbage must be packed out. Supplies are available in the town of Plush. Some facilities are wheelchair accessible. Leashed pets are permitted.

**Reservations, fees:** Reservations are not accepted. There is no fee for camping, but there is a 14-day stay limit. Open year-round, weather permitting.

**Directions:** From Lakeview, drive north on U.S. 395 for five miles to Highway 140. Turn east on Highway 140 and drive 16 miles to the Plush-Hart Mountain Cutoff. Turn left (signed for Hart Antelope Refuge) and drive north for 43 miles (first paved, then gravel) to the refuge headquarters. Continue 0.5 miles to CCC Campground, four miles to Hot Springs Campground (the road is often impassable in the winter). For the Post Meadows Horse Camp, follow the above directions to the refuge headquarters. At headquarters, turn onto Blue Sky Road and drive 10 miles to the camp.

**Contact:** Hart Mountain National Antelope Refuge, 541/947-3315 or 541/947-2731, www.fws.gov/refuges.

## 38 STEENS MOUNTAIN RESORT

🚶 🚵 🛶 🎣 🐕 ♿ 🚐 ⛺

### Scenic rating: 9

on the Blitzen River

**Map 12.7, page 721**

The self-proclaimed "gateway to Steens Mountain," this resort is bordered by the Malheur National Wildlife Refuge on three sides, and it has great views. The mile-high mountain and surrounding gorges make an excellent photo opportunity. Hiking and hunting are other possibilities in the area. Fishing is available on the Blitzen River, with easy access from the camp.

**Campsites, facilities:** There are 14 tent sites, 37 pull-through sites with full hookups (30 or 50 amps), and 39 sites with partial hookups for tents or RVs of any length, plus eight cabins and one rental home. Picnic tables and fire pits are provided. Drinking water, restrooms with showers, a dump station, coin laundry, limited groceries and fishing supplies, and ice are available. Some facilities are wheelchair accessible. Leashed pets are permitted.

**Reservations, fees:** Reservations are accepted at 800/542-3765 or www.steensmountainresort.com. Tent sites are $15 per night, RV sites are $25-30 per night, $5 per person per night for more than two people. Some credit cards are accepted. Open year-round.
**Directions:** From Burns, drive east on Highway 78 for two miles to Highway 205. Turn right (south) on Highway 205 and drive 59 miles to Frenchglen and Steens Mountain Road. Turn left (east) and drive three miles to the resort on the right.
**Contact:** Steens Mountain Resort, 541/493-2415, www.steensmountainresort.com.

## 39 PAGE SPRINGS

### Scenic rating: 7

near Malheur National Wildlife Refuge

Map 12.7, page 721

Page Springs campground lies adjacent to the Malheur National Wildlife Refuge at an elevation of 4,200 feet. Sites are shaded by juniper and cottonwood, with some near the Donner und Blitzen River. Activities include hiking on the area trails, bird-watching, fishing, hunting, and sightseeing. The Frenchglen Hotel (three miles away) is administered by the state parks department and offers overnight accommodations and meals.
**Campsites, facilities:** There are 31 sites for tents or RVs up to 35 feet long. Picnic tables and fire rings are provided. Drinking water, vault toilets, a day-use area with a shelter, garbage bins, and a seasonal camp host are available. Some facilities are wheelchair accessible. Leashed pets are permitted.
**Reservations, fees:** Reservations are not accepted. Sites are $8 per vehicle per night, with a 14-day stay limit. Open year-round.
**Directions:** From Burns, drive east on Highway 78 for two miles to Highway 205. Turn south on Highway 205 and drive 60 miles to Frenchglen and Steens Mountain Loop Road. Turn left (east) and drive three miles to the campground.

**Contact:** Bureau of Land Management, Burns District, 541/573-4400, www.blm.gov/or/districts/burns.

## 40 FISH LAKE

### Scenic rating: 8

on Fish Lake

Map 12.7, page 721

The shore of Fish Lake is the setting for this primitive but pretty camp. Set among the aspens at 7,400 feet elevation, it can make an excellent weekend-getaway spot for sightseeing. Trout fishing is an option, made easier by the boat ramp near camp.
**Campsites, facilities:** There are 23 sites for tents or RVs up to 20 feet long. Picnic tables and fire grills are provided. Drinking water, garbage bins, and vault toilets are available. Boat-launching facilities are onsite (non-motorized boats only). Leashed pets are permitted.
**Reservations, fees:** Reservations are not accepted. Sites are $8 per vehicle per night, with a 14-day stay limit. Open July 1-mid-November, weather permitting.
**Directions:** From Burns, drive east on Highway 78 for two miles to Highway 205. Turn south on Highway 205 and drive 60 miles to Frenchglen and Steens Mountain Loop Road. Turn left (east) and drive 17 miles to the campground.
**Contact:** Bureau of Land Management, Burns District, 541/573-4400, www.blm.gov/or/districts/burns.

## 41 JACKMAN PARK

### Scenic rating: 8

near Fish Lake

Map 12.7, page 721

One of four camps in the area, Jackman Park sits at 7,800 feet elevation in the eastern Oregon desert. This scenic campground, with its aspen and willow trees, is known as one of the best places to view the golden aspen leaves on Steens Mountain in the fall. Fish Lake is 2.5 miles away. Note that trailers and RVs are not recommended in the campground.

**Campsites, facilities:** There are six sites for tents only. Picnic tables and fire rings are provided. Drinking water and vault toilets are available. Leashed pets are permitted.

**Reservations, fees:** Reservations are not accepted. Sites are $6 per vehicle per night, with a 14-day stay limit. Open July 1-mid-November, weather permitting.

**Directions:** From Burns, drive east on Highway 78 for two miles to Highway 205. Turn south on Highway 205 and drive 60 miles to Frenchglen and Steens Mountain Loop Road. Turn left (east) and drive 22 miles to the campground.

**Contact:** Bureau of Land Management, Burns District, 541/573-4400, www.blm.gov/or/districts/burns.

## 42 MANN LAKE

### Scenic rating: 8

on Mann Lake

**Map 12.7, page 721**

Mann Lake sits at the base of Steens Mountain. This scenic, high-desert camp is mainly used as a fishing camp—fishing can be very good for cutthroat trout. Wintertime ice fishing, rock-hounding, and wildlife-viewing are also popular. Sites are open, with sagebrush and no trees. There is a small boat ramp and a 10-horsepower limit on motors. Weather can be extreme. Nearby Alvord Desert is also an attraction.

Note: Please respect private property on parcels of land next to the lake.

**Campsites, facilities:** There are dispersed sites for tents or RVs of up to 35 feet long on each side of the lake. Vault toilets and a boat ramp are available. No drinking water is available. Garbage must be packed out. Leashed pets are permitted.

**Reservations, fees:** Reservations are not accepted. There is no fee for camping. A 14-day stay limit is enforced. Open year-round.

**Directions:** From Burns, drive southeast on Highway 78 for 65 miles to East Steens Road. Turn right (south) and drive 22 miles to the campground at Mann Lake.

**Contact:** Bureau of Land Management, Burns District, 541/573-4400, www.blm.gov/or/districts/burns.

## 43 SOUTH STEENS FAMILY AND EQUESTRIAN

### Scenic rating: 6

near Steens Mountain Wilderness

**Map 12.7, page 721**

This campground hugs the edge of the Steens Mountain Wilderness. The area features deep, glacier-carved gorges, volcanic uplifts, stunning scenery, and a rare chance to see elk and bighorn sheep. Redband trout fishing is nearby at Donner und Blitzen Wild and Scenic River and its tributaries, a designated reserve. Trails are accessible from the campground.

**Campsites, facilities:** There are 36 sites for tents or RVs up to 25 feet long at the family camp; there are 15 sites designated for horse campers at the equestrian camp. Picnic tables and fire grills are provided. Drinking water and vault toilets are available. Corrals and hitching posts are available at the equestrian campground. Leashed pets are permitted.

**Reservations, fees:** Reservations are not accepted. Sites are $6 per vehicle per night. There is a 14-day stay limit. Open May-November, weather permitting.

**Directions:** From Burns, drive east on Highway 78 for two miles to Highway 205. Turn south on Highway 205 and drive 60 miles to Frenchglen. Continue south on Highway 205 for 10 miles to Steens South Loop Road. Turn left (east) and drive 18 miles to the campground on the right.

**Contact:** Bureau of Land Management, Burns District, 541/573-4400, www.blm.gov/or/districts/burns.

## 44 WILLOW CREEK HOT SPRINGS

🏃 🎿 ♨ 🐕 🚐 ⛺

**Scenic rating: 7**

near Whitehorse Butte

**Map 12.7, page 721**

A very small campground with no privacy, Willow Creek features campsites about 100 feet from the hot springs, which consist of two connected, smaller pools. This campground can be difficult to find, and only the adventurous should attempt this trip. Despite being out of the way, it still attracts travelers from far and wide. The surrounding scenery features rocky hills, not a flat expanse.

**Campsites, facilities:** There are four sites for tents or small RVs. Picnic tables and fire rings are provided. A vault toilet is available. Drinking water and firewood are not available, and garbage must be packed out. Leashed pets are permitted.

**Reservations, fees:** Reservations are not accepted. There is no fee for camping. Open year-round, weather permitting.

**Directions:** From Burns, drive southeast on Highway 78 for 105 miles to Burns Junction and U.S. 95. Turn right (south) on U.S. 95 and drive 20 miles to Whitehorse Road. Turn right (southwest) and drive 21 miles (passing Whitehorse Ranch); continue for 2.5 miles to a fork (look for the telephone pole). Bear left and drive two miles to the campground.

**Contact:** Bureau of Land Management, Vale District, 541/473-3144, www.blm.gov/or/districts/vale.

## 45 ROME LAUNCH

🚣 🛶 🚐 🎣 🏕 🚐 ⛺

**Scenic rating: 6**

on the Owyhee River

**Map 12.8, page 722**

Rome Launch campground is used mainly by folks rafting the Owyhee River and overnighters passing through. A few cottonwood trees and sagebrush dot the camp, with some sites adjacent to the Owyhee River. Rome Launch is also good for wildlife-viewing; mountain lions and bobcats have been spotted, and there are some farms and ranches in the area. This is a popular spot to fish for trout and catfish.

The Owyhee Canyon is quite dramatic, like a miniature Grand Canyon. I have canoed most of the Owyhee from the headwaters in Nevada below the Jarbidge Mountains all the way through Idaho and into Oregon, and I would rate this river as one of the top canoeing destinations in North America. Note: No motorized boats are allowed on the river.

**Campsites, facilities:** There are five sites for tents or small RVs. Picnic tables and fire rings are provided. Drinking water, vault toilets, and a boat launch are available. No firewood is available. Garbage must be packed out. Some facilities are wheelchair accessible. Leashed pets are permitted.

**Reservations, fees:** Reservations are not accepted. There is no fee for camping. Open March-November, weather permitting.

**Directions:** From Burns Junction, drive east on U.S. 95 for 15 miles to Jordan Valley and the signed turnoff for the Owyhee River and BLM-Rome boat launch. Turn south and drive 0.25 mile to the campground.

**Contact:** Bureau of Land Management, Vale District, 541/473-3144, www.blm.gov/or/districts/vale.

## 46 ANTELOPE RESERVOIR

🎣 🚐 🐕 🚐 ⛺

**Scenic rating: 3**

on the Antelope Reservoir

**Map 12.8, page 722**

This campground gets little use, except during hunting season. An open area on a slope above the reservoir, the camp has no tree cover—be prepared for extreme weather. Water levels fluctuate at shallow Antelope Reservoir and it can dry up.

**Campsites, facilities:** There are four sites for

tents or small RVs. Picnic tables and fire rings are provided. Vault toilets and primitive boat access are available. No drinking water is available, and garbage must be packed out. Some facilities are wheelchair accessible. Leashed pets are permitted.

**Reservations, fees:** Reservations are not accepted. There is no fee for camping. Open year-round, weather permitting.

**Directions:** From Burns Junction, drive east on U.S. 95 for 36 miles to the signed turnoff for Antelope Reservoir. Turn south and drive one mile to the campground on the left.

**Contact:** Bureau of Land Management, Vale District, 541/473-3144, www.blm.gov/or/districts/vale.

## 47 THREE FORKS

**Scenic rating: 9**

near the Owyhee River

**Map 12.8, page 722**

This remote camp is set along the east bank of the Owyhee River, where several warm streams snake through tall grass to the river.

The area offers fishing for brown trout in the river and day hiking to secluded springs and a waterfall pool in the upper Owyhee Canyon (swimwear optional). Clusters of 95°F springs are located on both sides of the river, and the rugged Owyhee Canyon forms a magnificent backdrop. To the west are a number of wild horse herds. (The BLM recreation map has the general locations of the herds.)

**Campsites, facilities:** There are four sites for tents or small RVs. Picnic tables and fire rings are provided. Vault toilets are available. There is no drinking water, and garbage must be packed out. There is access to the Owyhee River by permit for non-motorized boats only. Leashed pets are permitted.

**Reservations, fees:** Reservations are not accepted. There is no fee for camping. Open year-round, weather permitting.

**Directions:** On U.S. 95 (15 miles southwest of Jordan Valley), turn south on Three Forks Road and drive 35 miles to the campground. High-clearance vehicles recommended. Road may be impassable when wet.

**Contact:** Bureau of Land Management, Vale District, 541/473-3144, www.blm.gov/or/districts/vale.

# RESOURCES

# NATIONAL FORESTS

The U.S. Forest Service provides many secluded camps and allows camping anywhere except where it is specifically prohibited. If you ever want to clear the cobwebs from your head and get away from it all, this is the way to go.

Many Forest Service campgrounds are remote and have no drinking water. You usually don't need to check in or make reservations, and sometimes there is no fee. At many Forest Service campgrounds that provide drinking water, the camping fee is often only a few dollars, with payment made on the honor system. Because most of these camps are in mountain areas, they are subject to winter closure due to snow or mud.

Dogs are permitted in national forests with no extra charge. Always carry documentation of current vaccinations.

## Northwest Forest Pass

A Northwest Forest Pass is required for certain activities in some national forests. The pass is required for parking at participating trailheads, non-developed camping areas, boat launches, picnic areas, and visitors centers.

Daily passes cost $5 per vehicle; annual passes are $30 per vehicle. Combined recreation passes for Washington and Oregon are also available. You can buy Northwest Forest Passes at national forest offices and dozens of retail outlets and online vendors. Holders of Golden Age and Golden Access (not Golden Eagle) cards can buy the Northwest Forest Pass at a 50 percent discount at national forest offices only, or at retail outlets for the retail price. Major credit cards are accepted at most retail and online outlets and at some Forest Service offices.

More information about the Northwest Forest Pass program, including a listing of retail and online vendors, can be obtained at 503/808-6008 or www.fs.usda.gov/main/r6/passes-permits.

An Interagency Pass is available for $80 annually in lieu of a Northwest Forest Pass. The Interagency Pass is honored nationwide at all Forest Service, National Park Service, Bureau of Land Management, Bureau of Reclamation, and U.S. Fish and Wildlife Service sites charging entrance or standard amenity fees. Valid for 12 months from the month of purchase, the America the Beautiful Pass is available at most national forest or grassland offices or online at http://store.usgs.gov.

## National Forest Reservations

Some of the more popular camps and most of the group camps are on a reservation system. Reservations can be made up to 240 days in advance and up to 360 days in advance for groups. To reserve a site, call 877/444-6777 or visit www.recreation.gov. The reservation fee is usually $10 for a campsite in a national forest, but group site reservation fees are higher. Major credit cards are accepted. Holders of Golden Age or Golden Access passports receive a 50 percent discount on campground fees, except for group sites.

## National Forest Maps

National Forest maps are among the best you can get for the price. They detail all backcountry streams, lakes, hiking trails, and logging roads for access. They cost $9<\#208>12 or more and can be obtained in person at Forest Service offices or by contacting:

**U.S. Forest Service**
National Forest Store
P.O. Box 8268
Missoula, MT 59807
406/329-3024
www.fs.usda.gov/recreation/nationalforeststore

## Forest Service Information

Forest Service personnel are most helpful for obtaining camping or hiking trail information. Unless you are buying a map or Adventure Pass, it is advisable to phone in advance to get the best service.

For further information on individual national forests, contact the following offices:

## U.S. Forest Service
Pacific Northwest Region 6
333 SW 1st Avenue
Portland, OR 97204-3440
503/808-2468
www.fs.usda.gov
or
P.O. Box 3623
Portland, OR 97208-3623

## WASHINGTON
### Colville National Forest
765 South Main St.
Colville, WA 99114
509/684-7000
www.fs.usda.gov/colville

### Gifford Pinchot National Forest
10600 NE 51st Cir.
Vancouver, WA 98682
360/891-5000
www.fs.fed.us/giffordpinchot

### Mount Baker-Snoqualmie National Forest
2930 Wetmore Ave.
Everett, WA 98201
425/783-6000 or 800/627-0062
www.fs.usda.gov/mbs

### Okanogan-Wenatchee National Forest
215 Melody Ln.
Wenatchee, WA 98801
509/664-9200
www.fs.usda.gov/okawen

### Olympic National Forest
1835 Black Lake Blvd. SW
Olympia, WA 98512-5623
360/956-2402
www.fs.usda.gov/olympic

### Umatilla National Forest
Pomeroy Ranger District
71 West Main St.

Pomeroy, WA 99347
509/843-1891
www.fs.usda.gov/umatilla

Walla Walla Ranger District
1415 West Rose St.
Walla Walla, WA 99362
509/522-6290

## OREGON
### Deschutes National Forest
1001 SW Emkay Drive
Bend, OR 97702
541/383-5300
www.fs.usda.gov/centraloregon

### Fremont-Winema National Forests
HC 10 Box 337
1301 South G Street
Lakeview, OR 97630
541/947-2151
www.fs.usda.gov/fremont-winema

### Malheur National Forest
P.O. Box 909
431 Patterson Bridge Road
John Day, OR 97845
541/575-3000
www.fs.usda.gov/malheur

### Mount Hood National Forest
16400 Champion Way
Sandy, OR 97055
503/668-1700
www.fs.usda.gov/mthood

### Ochoco National Forest
3160 NE 3rd Street
Prineville, OR 97754
541/416-6500
www.fs.usda.gov/centraloregon

### Rogue River-Siskiyou National Forest
3040 Biddle Road
Medford, OR 97504
541/618-2200
www.fs.usda.gov/rogue-siskiyou

**Siuslaw National Forest**
P.O. Box 1148
4077 SW Research Way
Corvallis, OR 97339
541/750-7000
www.fs.usda.gov/siuslaw

**Umatilla National Forest**
2517 SW Hailey Avenue
Pendleton, OR 97801
541/278-3716
www.fs.usda.gov/umatilla

**Umpqua National Forest**
2900 NW Stewart Parkway
Roseburg, OR 97471
541/672-6601
www.fs.usda.gov/umpqua

**Wallowa-Whitman National Forest**
P.O. Box 907
1550 Dewey Avenue
Baker City, OR 97814
541/523-6391
www.fs.usda.gov/wallowa-whitman

**Willamette National Forest**
3106 Pierce Parkway, Ste. D
Springfield, OR 97477
541/225-6300
www.fs.usda.gov/willamette

## NATIONAL PARKS AND RECREATION AREAS

The national parks and recreational areas are natural wonders, varying from the spectacular Mount St. Helens National Volcanic Monument to the breathtaking Crater Lake National Park. Reservations are available at some of the campgrounds at these parks and recreation areas. Various discounts are available for holders of Golden Age and Golden Access passports, including a 50 percent reduction of camping fees (group camps not included).

For information about each of the national parks, contact the parks directly:

## Washington

**Lake Roosevelt National Recreation Area**
1008 Crest Dr.
Coulee Dam, WA 99116-1259
or
1368 South Kettle Park Rd.
Kettle Falls, WA 99141
509/633-9441
www.nps.gov/laro

**Mount Rainier National Park**
55210 238th Ave. East
Ashford, WA 98304
360/569-2211
www.nps.gov/mora

**Mount St. Helens National Volcanic Monument**
42218 NE Yale Bridge Rd.
Amboy, WA 98601
360/449-7800
www.fs.usda.gov/mountsthelens

Mount St. Helens Visitor Center
360/274-0962

**North Cascades National Park**
810 State Route 20
Sedro-Woolley, WA 98284-1239
Visitor Information 360/854-7200
Wilderness Information 360/854-7245
www.nps.gov/noca

**Olympic National Park**
600 East Park Avenue
Port Angeles, WA 98362-6798
360/565-3130 or 800/833-6388
www.nps.gov/olym

## Oregon

**Columbia River Gorge National Scenic Area**
902 Wasco Avenue, Suite 200
Hood River, OR 97031
541/308-1700
www.fs.usda.gov/crgnsa

**Crater Lake National Park**
P.O. Box 7
Crater Lake, OR 97604
541/594-3100
www.nps.gov/crla

**Crooked River National Grassland**
813 SW Highway 97
Madras, OR 97741
541/475-9272
www.fs.usda.gov/centraloregon

**Hells Canyon National Recreation Area**
Wallowa Mountains Visitor Center
88401 Highway 82
Enterprise, OR 97828
541/426-5546
www.fs.usda.gov/wallowa-whitman

**Oregon Dunes National Recreation Area**
855 Highway Avenue
Reedsport, OR 97467
541/271-6000
www.fs.usda.gov/siuslaw

# STATE PARKS

The state parks system provides many popular camping spots. Reservations are often a necessity during the summer. The camps include drive-in numbered sites, tent spaces, and picnic tables, with showers and bathrooms provided nearby. Although some parks are well known, there are still some little-known gems in the state parks system where campers can find seclusion, even in the summer.

Many of the state park campgrounds are on a reservation system, and campsites can be booked up to nine months in advance at these parks.

## Washington

Reservations for Washington state parks can be made at 888/CAMP-OUT (888/226-7688) or at www.parks.wa.gov. The reservation number is open 7am-8pm (Pacific Standard Time) every day of the year except Christmas Day and New Year's Day, with shortened hours on Christmas Eve and New Year's Eve. Major credit cards are accepted for reservations, and credit cards are accepted at some of the parks during the summer. A $6.50 reservation fee is charged for a campsite reservation made online, $8.50 for one made by phone. The reservation fee for group sites is $25. Discounts are available for pass holders of Disability, Senior Citizen Limited Income, Off-Season Senior Citizen, and Disabled Veteran Lifetime.

**Washington State Parks and Recreation Commission**
7150 Cleanwater Ln.
P.O. Box 42650
Olympia, WA 98504-2650
360/902-8844
www.parks.wa.gov

## Oregon

Reservations for Oregon state parks can be made through Reserve America at 800/452-5687 or online at www.reserveamerica.com. A nonrefundable reservation fee of $8 and the first night's fee will be required as a deposit, charged to a MasterCard or Visa credit card (debit cards linked to MasterCard or Visa also accepted).

**Oregon Parks and Recreation Department: State Parks**
725 Summer St. NE, Ste. C
Salem, OR 97301
800/551-6949
www.oregon.gov/OPRD/PARKS/index.aspx

# STATE FORESTS
**Oregon Department of Forestry**
2600 State Street
Salem, OR 97310
503/945-7200
www.oregon.gov/ODF

**Tillamook State Forest**
**Forest Grove District**
801 Gales Creek Road
Forest Grove, OR 97116-1199

503/357-2191
www.oregon.gov/ODF/pages/field/fg/aboutus.
aspx

**Tillamook State Forest**
**Tillamook District**
5005 3rd Street
Tillamook, OR 97141-2999
503/842-2545
www.oregon.gov/ODF/pages/field/tillamook/
abouttillamook.aspx

# DEPARTMENT OF NATURAL RESOURCES

The Department of Natural Resources manages more than five million acres of public land in Washington. All of it is managed under the concept of "multiple use," designed to provide the greatest number of recreational opportunities while still protecting natural resources.

The campgrounds in these areas are among the most primitive, remote, and least known of the camps listed in this book. The campsites are usually free, and campers are asked to remove all litter and trash from the area, leaving only footprints behind. Due to budget cutbacks, some of these campgrounds have been closed in recent years; expect more closures in the future.

In addition to maps of the area it manages, the Department of Natural Resources also has Washington public lands maps, U.S. Geological Survey maps, and U.S. Army Corps of Engineers maps. For information, contact the Department of Natural Resources at its state or regional addresses:

**State of Washington**
**Department of Natural Resources**
1111 Washington St. SE
P.O. Box 47000
Olympia, WA 98504-7000
360/902-1000
www.dnr.wa.gov

**Northeast Region**
225 South Silke Rd.

P.O. Box 190
Colville, WA 99114-0190
509/684-7474

**Northwest Region**
919 North Township St.
Sedro Woolley, WA 98284-9384
360/856-3500

**Olympic Region**
411 Tillicum Ln.
Forks, WA 98331-9271
360/374-2800

**Pacific Cascade Region**
601 Bond Rd.
P.O. Box 280
Castle Rock, WA 98611-0280
360/577-2025

**Southeast Region**
713 Bowers Rd.
Ellensburg, WA 98926-9301
509/925-8510

**South Puget Sound Region**
950 Farman Ave. North
Enumclaw, WA 98022-9282
360/825-1631

# U.S. ARMY CORPS OF ENGINEERS

Some of the family camps and most of the group camps operated by the U.S. Army Corps of Engineers are on a reservation system. Reservations can be made up to 240 days in advance for family camps and up to 360 days in advance for groups. To reserve a site, call 877/444-6777 or visit www.recreation. gov. The reservation fee is usually $10 for a campsite, but group site reservation fees are higher. Major credit cards are accepted. Holders of Golden Age or Golden Access passports receive a 50 percent discount on campground fees, except for group sites.

**Walla Walla District**
201 North 3rd Ave.
Walla Walla, WA 99362-1876
509/527-7020
www.nww.usace.army.mil

**Portland District**
333 SW 1st Ave
Portland, OR 97204
503/808-4510
www.nwp.usace.army.mil
or
P.O. Box 2946
Portland, OR 97208-2946

# BUREAU OF LAND MANAGEMENT (BLM)

Most BLM campgrounds are primitive and in remote areas. Often, there is no fee charged for camping. Holders of Golden Age or Golden Access passports receive a 50 percent discount at BLM campgrounds with fees (group camps excluded).

**Oregon Office**
333 SW 1st Avenue
Portland, OR 97204
503/808-6008
www.blm.gov/or
or
P.O. Box 2965
Portland, OR 97208-2946
503/808-4510

**Burns District**
28910 Highway 20 West
Hines, OR 97738
541/573-4400
www.blm.gov/or/districts/burns

**Coos Bay District**
1300 Airport Lane
North Bend, OR 97459
541/756-0100
www.blm.gov/or/districts/coosbay

**Eugene District**
3106 Pierce Parkway, Ste. E
Springfield, OR 97477
541/683-6600
www.blm.gov/or/districts/eugene
or
P.O. Box 10226
Eugene, OR 97440

**Lakeview District**
1301 South G Street
Lakeview, OR 97630
541/947-2177
www.blm.gov/or/districts/lakeview

**Medford District**
3040 Biddle Road
Medford, OR 97504
541/618-2200
www.blm.gov/or/districts/medford

**Prineville District**
3050 NE 3rd Street
Prineville, OR 97754
541/416-6700
www.blm.gov/or/districts/prineville

**Roseburg District**
777 NW Garden Valley Boulevard
Roseburg, OR 97471
541/440-4930
www.blm.gov/or/districts/roseburg

**Salem District**
1717 Fabry Road SE
Salem, OR 97306
503/375-5646
www.blm.gov/or/districts/salem

**Vale District**
100 Oregon Street
Vale, OR 97918
541/473-3144
www.blm.gov/or/districts/vale

# OTHER VALUABLE RESOURCES

## WASHINGTON
**Tacoma Power**
P.O. Box 11007
Tacoma, WA 98411
Fishing and Recreation Hotline
888/502-8690
www.mytpu.org/tacomapower/parks-rec

**U.S. Geological Survey**
345 Middlefield Rd.
Menlo Park, CA 94025
650/853-8300 or 888/ASK-USGS
(888/275-8747)
www.usgs.gov

**Washington Department of Fish and Wildlife**
600 Capitol Way North
Olympia, WA 98501-1091
360/902-2200
www.wdfw.wa.gov

**Washington State Department of Transportation**
Washington State Highway Information
800/695-ROAD (800/695-7623)

**Greater Seattle Area Information**
206/DOT-HIWY (206/368-4499)
www.wsdot.wa.gov

## OREGON
**Oregon Department of Fish and Wildlife**
3406 Cherry Avenue
Salem, OR 97303
503/947-6000
www.dfw.state.or.us

**Oregon State Department of Transportation**
888/275-6368
www.oregon.gov/ODOT

**U.S. Geological Survey**
345 Middlefield Rd.
Menlo Park, CA 94025
650/853-8300 or 888/ASK-USGS
(888/275-8747)
www.usgs.gov

# Index

# Acknowledgments

The following state and federal resource experts provided critical information and galley reviews regarding changes in reservations, fees, directions, and recreational opportunities. We are extremely grateful for their timely help and expert advice.

## U.S. Forest Service

Nan Berger, Colville National Forest, Newport Ranger District

Eric McQua, Colville National Forest, Republic Ranger District

Wendy Zoodsman, Colville National Forest, Sullivan Lake Ranger District

Carmen Nielsen, Colville National Forest, Three Rivers Ranger District

Cheryl Mack, Gifford Pinchot National Forest

Amber Malandry, Gifford Pinchot National Forest, Cowlitz Ranger District

Julie Knutson and Byron Carlisle, Gifford Pinchot National Forest, Mount Adams Ranger District

Diane Tharp, Gifford Pinchot National Forest, Mount St. Helens National Volcanic Monument

Shayla Hooper, Mt. Baker/Snoqualmie National Forest, Darrington Ranger District

Ann Dunphy, Mt. Baker/Snoqualmie National Forest, Mt. Baker Ranger District

Pam Young, Mt. Baker/Snoqualmie National Forest, Skykomish Ranger District

Carol Bow, Okanogan and Wenatchee National Forests

Linda Belcher, Christina Perez, Rena Rex, Kelly Underwood, Okanogan and Wenatchee National Forests, Chelan Ranger District

Kim Larned, Okanogan and Wenatchee National Forests, Cle Elum Ranger District

Monte Bowe, Okanogan and Wenatchee National Forests, Entiat Ranger District

Terri Halstead, Okanogan and Wenatchee National Forests, Lake Wenatchee Ranger District

Mary Anderson, Okanogan and Wenatchee National Forests, Leavenworth Ranger District

Kathy Corrigan, Okanogan and Wenatchee National Forests, Methow Valley Ranger District

Kevin Hill, Mike Rowan, Okanogan and Wenatchee National Forests, Naches Ranger District

Joseph Cox, Okanogan and Wenatchee National Forests, Tonasket Ranger District

Mary Spear, Olympic National Forest

Debbie Schreuer, Olympic National Forest, Hood Canal Ranger District

Molly Erickson, Mary O'Neil, Olympic National Forest, Pacific Ranger District

Ruth Forcier, Umatilla National Forest, Pomeroy Ranger District

Jan Nelson-Dean, Deschutes National Forest

Amy Tinderholt, Deschutes National Forest, Bend-Fort Rock Ranger District

Bob Hennings, Deschutes National Forest, Sisters Ranger District

Clark Higgler, Erica Hupp, Heidi Ratliff, Jeremy Sugden, Vicky Zacharias, Fremont-Winema National Forests

Larry Hills, Fremont-Winema National Forests, Bly and Lakeview Ranger Districts

Tim Stack, Fremont-Winema National Forests, Silver Lake Ranger District

Phil McNeil, Klamath National Forest, Happy Camp/Oak Knoll Ranger District

Shawna Clark, Melissa Walker, Malheur National Forest

Chris Bentley, Rachel Drake, Delva Nelson, Jenny Wade, Mount Hood National Forest

Katherine Martin, Ochoco National Forest, Paulina Ranger District

Pam Carr, Virginia Gibbons, Rogue-Siskiyou National Forest

Melonie Smeltz, Rogue-Siskiyou National Forest, Butte Ranger District

Teresa Miller, Jackie Ringulet, Rogue-Siskiyou National Forest, Gold Beach Ranger District

Nancy Wallace, Rogue-Siskiyou National Forest, Powers Ranger District

Nancy Schwieger, Siskiyou National Forest, Gold Beach Ranger District

David Wickwire, Siskiyou National Forest, Galice Ranger Districts

Marcus Elder, Siuslaw National Forest

Briana Guenther, George Vogel, Siuslaw National Forest, Hebo Ranger District

Zack Hayes, Siuslaw National Forest, Waldport Ranger District

Kathy Rankin, Umatilla National Forest, Heppner Ranger District

Janelle Lacey, Umatilla National Forest, North Fork John Day Ranger District

Jeff Bloom, Umatilla National Forest, Walla Walla Ranger District

Dennis Scott, Umpqua National Forest, North Umpqua Ranger District

Mariance Spence, Wallowa-Whitman National Forest

Mike Montgomery, Wallowa-Whitman National Forest, LaGrande Ranger District

Yvonne Santiago, Wallowa-Whitman National Forest, Wallowa Valley Ranger District/Eagle Cap Ranger District/Hells Canyon National Recreation Area

Annie Moore, Wallowa-Whitman National Forest, Whitman Ranger District

Linda Watson, Willamette National Forest, Chilla Ranger District

Angela Stagg, Willamette National Forest, Clackamas Ranger District

Ellaine Burnett, Jeff Lunsford, Willamette National Forest, Detroit Ranger District

Shelly Parsons, Willamette National Forest, Hood River Ranger District

Jennifer McDonald, Willamette National Forest, McKenzie Ranger District

Holly Cotton, Willamette National Forest, Middle Fork Ranger District

Isabel Shackelford, Willamette National Forest, Sweet Home Ranger District

## National Parks and Recreation Areas

Lorie Carstensen, Lake Roosevelt National Recreation Area

Mindy Garvin, Daniel Keebler, Mare Staton, Mount Rainier National Park

Aaron Pouliot, North Cascades National Park

Benjamin Komar, Josh McLean, Kirran Peart, Olympic National Park

Diana Camcho, Columbia River Gorge National Scenic Area

Vicky Mugnai, Jacob Rhone, Oregon Dunes National Recreation Area

## State Parks

Katie Brieoff, Linda Burnett, Angela Harper, Virginia Painter, Washington State Parks

Morris Shook, Alta Lake State Park

Breeanne Jordan, Beacon Rock State Park

Kathy Stermolle, Belfair State Park

Nancy Wallwork, Brooks Memorial State Park

Dolores Delk, Camano Island State Park

Tracy Zuern, Cape Disappointment State Park

Fritz Osborne, Columbia Hills State Park

Ryan Layton, Conconully State Park

Don Robertson, Curlew Lake State Park

John Wennes, Daroga State Park

Douglas Hinton, Dosewallips State Park

Peggy Russell, Fay Bainbridge State Park

Shaun Bristol, Fields Spring State Park

Brett Bayne, Fort Casey State Park

Lori Bond, Fort Flagler State Park

Susan Thomas, Fort Worden State Park

James Mitchell, Ginkgo-Wanapum State Park

Candace Rodda, Grayland Beach State Park

Reuben Stuart, Ike Kinswa State Park

Roy Salisbury, Illahee State Park

Chris Patterson, Jarrell Cove and Hope Island State Parks

Kristie Cronin, Joemma Beach State Park

Karlene Herron, Kanaskat-Palmer State Park

Vern Matzen, Kitsap Memorial State Park

Matthew Smith, Kopachuck State Park

Carina Silva, Lake Chelan State Park

Teri Milbert, Lake Easton State Park

Brian Hageman, Lake Sylvia State Park

Gary Lentz, Lewis and Clark Trail State Park
Roy Torgerson, Manchester State Park
Kim Shupe, Maryhill State Park
Jim Schmidt, Ocean City State Park
Marlene Jeffries, Osoyoos Veterans Memorial
Park
Daniel Cox, Pacific Beach State Park
Cynthia Brown, Potholes State Park
Becky Meyer, Potlatch State Park
Dave Rush, Rainbow Falls State Park
Lori Cobb, Riverside State Park
William Hoppe, San Juan Marine Area
Brad Muir, Seaquest State Park
Arnold Hampton, Schafer State Park
Teresa McCullough, Sequim State Park
Patty Anderson, South Whidbey State Park
Tina O'Brian, Spencer Spit State Park
Stacy Czebotar, Twanoh State Park
Dennis Mills, Twenty-Five Mile Creek State
Park
Tyler Vanderpool, Twin Harbors State Park
Matt Morrison, Wenatchee Confluence State
Park
Bryce Erickson, Yakima Sportsman State Park
Chris Havel, Sheri Miller, Renee Okerman,
Oregon State Parks
Allison Mangini, Beverly Beach State Park
Paul Wayne, Cape Blanco State Park
Mary Nulty, Carl G. Washburne State Park
Linda Brege, Deschutes State Recreation Area
Debi Hill, Fort Stevens State Park
Larry Moniz, Goose Lake State Park
Cathi Dunn, Harris Beach Management Unit
Rick Duda, Milo McIver State Park
Ami Ericdon, Nehalam Bay State Park
Linda Taylor, South Beach State Park
Janet Sobezak, Sunset Bay State Park
Sandy Anderson, Umpqua Lighthouse State
Park

## Department of Natural Resources

Brett Walker, Northeast Region
Jim Cahill, Stan Kurowski, Candace Johnson
and Christ Thompsen, Northwest Region
Cathryn Baker, Olympic Region

Nick Cronquist, Brian Poehlein, Pacific
Cascade Region
Erin Kreutz, Mike Williams, Southeast Region
Nancy Barker, Karen Robertson, Jesse Sims,
South Puget Sound Region

## U.S. Army Corps of Engineers

Kathy Johnston, Central Ferry Park
Wayne O'Neal, Chief Timothy Park
Jesus Navarro, Walla Walla District

## Bureau of Land Management

Dennis Byrd, Ashland Resource Area
Kevin McCoy, Brett Paige, Baker City Office
Trish Lindemann, Medford District
Greg Currie, Prineville District
Greg Morgan, Roseburg District
Traci Meredith, Salem District
Deb Drake, Tillamook District
David Draheim, Vale District

## Other

Cathy Mether, Mike Miller, City of Auburn
Tracey Paddock, City of Chehalis
Lori Peña, Clallam County
Blanca Anderson, City of Entiat
Rhonda Dow, Shawn DuFault, Kaly Harward,
HooDoo Recreation
Randy Juette, Naches Valley Chamber of
Commerce
Hank Nydam, City of Oak Harbor
Ron Curran, Pend Oreille County Public
Works
Erin Grasseth, Port of Wahkiakum No. 2
Jackie Boplin, Quinault Nation
Kyle Peninger, Skagit County
Marcie Allen, Linda McCrea, Joe Miller,
Snohomish County
Jeanne Blackburn, Wenberg County Park
Janel Goebel, Terry Jeffries, Ernie Miller,
Whitman County Parks and Recreation
Gale Bridges, Tisa Pelletier, Trish Stanfield,
Tacoma Power
Clara Johnson, Crook County Parks and
Recreation
Kathy Hammons, Douglas County Parks
JoAnn Woelfle, Lane County Parks

Kristi Mosier, Lane County, Richardson Park
Christie Harris, Linn County Parks
Peggy Murphy, Lost Lake Resort
Jill Hammond, Jackson County Parks
Alisha Howard, Josephine County Parks

Bill Doran, Metro Regional Parks and Green Spaces
Kirsti Cason, Morrow County Parks
Lynn Studley, Portland General Electric
Ken Hill, Port of Siuslaw

# www.moon.com

DESTINATIONS | ACTIVITIES | BLOGS | MAPS | BOOKS

**MOON.COM** is ready to help plan your next trip! Filled with fresh trip ideas and strategies, author interviews, informative travel blogs, a detailed map library, and descriptions of all the Moon guidebooks, Moon.com is all you need to get out and explore the world—or even places in your own backyard. While at Moon.com, sign up for our monthly e-newsletter for updates on new releases, travel tips, and expert advice from our on-the-go Moon authors. As always, when you travel with Moon, expect an experience that is uncommon and truly unique.

MOON IS ON FACEBOOK—BECOME A FAN!
JOIN THE MOON PHOTO GROUP ON FLICKR

**MOON PACIFIC NORTHWEST CAMPING**
Avalon Travel
a member of the Perseus Books Group
1700 Fourth Street
Berkeley, CA 94710, USA
www.moon.com

Editor and Series Manager: Sabrina Young
Research Editors: Kathie Morgan, Donna Sager
Copy Editor: Kim Runciman
Production and Graphics Coordinator:
    Domini Dragoone
Cover Designer: Domini Dragoone
Map Editor: Mike Morgenfeld
Cartographers: Brian Shotwell

ISBN-13: 978-1-61238-773-4
ISSN: 1078-9588

Printing History
1st Edition – 1998
11th Edition – June 2014
5 4 3 2

Text © 2014 by Tom Stienstra.
Maps © 2014 by Avalon Travel.
All rights reserved.

Front cover photo: the Alpine Lakes Wilderness,
    © Danita Delimont/Getty Images

Title page photo: Liberty Bell Mountain in the
Okanogan National Forest, © Mike Norton/123RF
Table of contents photos: pg. 4, Puget Sound
water bird © Mark Payne/123rf.com; pg.
5, looking up in Olympic National Park ©
Ablestock Premium/123rf.com
Back cover photo: © Al Valeiro / Getty Images

Printed in Canada by Friesens

## Keeping Current

We are committed to making this book the most accurate and enjoyable camping guide to
the region. You can rest assured that every campground in this book has been carefully
reviewed in an effort to keep this book as up-to-date as possible. However, by the time you
read this book, some of the fees listed herein may have changed and campgrounds may
have closed unexpectedly.

If you have a favorite gem you'd like to see included in the next edition, or see anything
that needs updating, clarification, or correction, please drop us a line. Send your comments
via email to feedback@moon.com, or use the address above.